eGrade Plus

for *Financial Accounting: A User Perspective*, Fourth Canadian Edition

Check with your instructor to find out if you have access to eGrade Plus!

Study More Effectively with a Multimedia Text

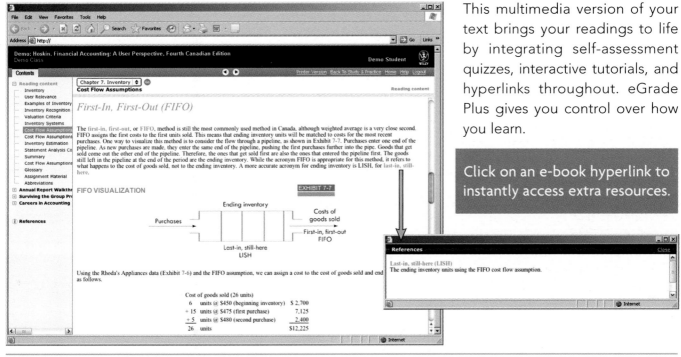

This multimedia version of your text brings your readings to life by integrating self-assessment quizzes, interactive tutorials, and hyperlinks throughout. eGrade Plus gives you control over how you learn.

Click on an e-book hyperlink to instantly access extra resources.

Preparing for a test has never been easier! eGrade Plus brings all of your course materials together and takes the stress out of organizing your study aids. A streamlined study routine saves you time and lets you focus on learning.

Grasp key concepts by exploring the various interactive tools in Study & Practice.

John Wiley & Sons Canada, Ltd.

Complete and Submit Assignments Online Efficiently

Your homework questions contain links to the relevant section of the multimedia text, so you know exactly where to go to get help solving each problem. In addition, use the Assignment area of eGrade Plus to monitor all of your assignments and their due dates.

Your instructor can assign homework online for automatic grading and you can keep up-to-date on your assignments with your assignment list.

Keep Track of Your Progress

Your personal Gradebook lets you review your answers and results from past assignments as well as any feedback your instructor may have for you.

Keep track of your progress and review your completed questions at any time.

Financial Accounting
A USER PERSPECTIVE
FOURTH CANADIAN EDITION

Robert E. Hoskin
UNIVERSITY OF CONNECTICUT

Maureen R. Fizzell
SIMON FRASER UNIVERSITY

Donald C. Cherry
DALHOUSIE UNIVERSITY

JOHN WILEY & SONS CANADA, LTD.

Library and Archives Canada Cataloguing in Publication

Hoskin, Robert E., 1949-
      Financial accounting : a user perspective / Robert E. Hoskin, Maureen R. Fizzell, Don C. Cherry. -- 4th Canadian ed.

Includes index.
ISBN 10: 0-470-83445-5
ISBN 13: 978-0-470–83445-9

      1. Accounting. I. Fizzell, Maureen II. Cherry, Don C. III. Title.

HF5635.H68 2005   657'.044
C2005-900790-7

Production Credits
Publisher: John Horne
Editorial Manager: Karen Staudinger
Publishing Services Director: Karen Bryan
Developmental Editor: Zoë Craig
Senior Marketing Manager: Isabelle Moreau
New Media Editor: Elsa Passera
Associate Editor: Gail Brown
Editorial Assistant: Lindsay Humphreys
Cover Illustration: Anson Liaw
Cover and Interior Design: Interrobang Graphic Design, Inc.
Printing and Binding: Tri-Graphic Printing Limited

Printed and bound in Canada
10 9 8 7 6 5 4 3 2 1

John Wiley & Sons Canada, Ltd.
6045 Freemont Blvd.
Mississauga, Ontario L5R 4J3
Visit our website at: www.wiley.ca

To my family.
— MRF

To my mother,
for her great gift of always
looking at the bright side of things.
— DCC

About the Authors

Maureen R. Fizzell

Maureen R. Fizzell, B.Ed, B.Comm., M.Sc., CMA, FCMA has been teaching at the university level for 21 years, nine years at the University of Saskatchewan and 12 years at Simon Fraser University, where she is now Associate Dean of the Faculty of Business Administration. In 2003 she was named a CMA/SFU Business Academic Fellow, and in 2004 she was awarded the FCMA designation. Over her university career, she has taught financial accounting from the introductory to the advanced level.

Maureen is an active CMA member who is currently serving on the B.C. Board of Directors. She served on the CMA Canada National Board of Examiners from 2000 to 2004 and on the B.C. Board of Directors from 1997 to 1999. As well, she has been a member of the Saskatchewan Provincial Council, critiqued exams and acted as liaison between university students and the Society. During her 21 years, she received numerous teaching awards. Some of them are: Most Effective Professor in the Classroom Award at the University of Saskatchewan in 1990, TD Canada Trust Distinguished Teaching Award in 1996, and membership on the Teaching Honour Roll in 1997 at Simon Fraser University.

Donald C. Cherry

Donald C. (Don) Cherry, B.Comm., MBA, CMA has been teaching accounting for over 30 years. He began his teaching career at Seneca College in 1974, before moving to Dalhousie University in 1978. He has taught both financial and managerial accounting, from the introductory undergraduate level to advanced graduate classes, and has won numerous Professor of the Year awards from both Commerce and MBA students.

In addition to teaching, Don has also been, at various times, Director of Dalhousie's Commerce Program, Associate Director of the School of Business, Associate Director of the Lester B. Pearson International Institute, Director of the Centre for Development Projects, and Director of the Centre for International Business Studies. The latter roles reflect his long-standing interest in economic development and social justice issues and his involvement in international development programs. Over the years, Don has been involved in management education activities in over on dozen countries.

Don has published articles in *CA Magazine*, *CMA Magazine*, and *Cost and Management*, as well as in the proceedings of various accounting conferences, and he has authored a number of case studies dealing with financial management issues. He has also been an active member of the Society of Management Accountants, in which he served on its Financial Accounting Curriculum Committee. In addition, Don has chaired the national Syllabus Committee, and served on the Board of Examiners, as well as on the Provincial Council for Nova Scotia. At the local level, he has served on the Board of Directors and as Treasurer for community organizations providing social services to low-income families and youth in conflict with the law.

Preface

Background

Financial Accounting: A User Perspective sets out to teach students about accounting information and how it affects decision-making by complementing the fundamental procedural aspects of accounting with discussions about who uses accounting information and what decisions they make from it. This unique balance has been widely appreciated through three editions of the text and is just as relevant today as when it was first published in Canada in 1997. What has changed is the means available to students in order to enhance their learning experience. The third edition of Hoskin introduced an exciting new CD that contained a wealth of interactive resources. The fourth edition takes things even further, as the text forms the centre of an exciting learning environment with a unique set of technology tools.

Financial Accounting Balanced with Technology

We have created a complete suite of tools to introduce students to the world of financial accounting. Cognizant of the fact that every school has different wants and needs, Wiley provides you with a variety of technology resources, giving you flexibility to incorporate some or all of these tools into your class—you create the balance that is right for you and your students.

eGRADE PLUS

Technology offers many opportunities to enrich the learning experience for both students and instructors. This edition of the text is available with eGrade Plus—an exciting online homework and quiz assessment system intrinsically linked with a multimedia version of the textbook.

In the Study & Practice area, the interactive textbook encourages students to complete their readings by bringing the content to life. Embedded in its pages are self-assessment exercises, animated tutorials, as well as helpful study and analytical tools to build confidence and understanding. Students have their own personal Gradebook, which allows them to monitor their progress and encourages them to stay on track.

Instructors can prepare and manage their lectures with ease using the unique Prepare & Present tool. It allows them to upload any digital file and combine this material with the Wiley-provided resources. PowerPoint slides, Instructor Supplements, and any of the interactive resources found in the multimedia section are available to create customized presentations.

Assigning homework and quizzes is simple in the Assignment area. Instructors can select questions from the programmed end-of-chapter material provided by Wiley, or they have the option of creating questions from scratch. With many Wiley questions programmed algorithmically, each student can work the same problem with a different set of numbers, providing instructors with an endless bank of assessment questions.

The Course Administration function in eGrade Plus allow instructors to easily communicate with students and manage the class roster. The Gradebook displays a list of all student scores and progress on assignments, and it allows instructors to view detailed information regarding individual student submissions.

EXPANDED COMPANION WEBSITE

Based on user feedback, the student resources have been enhanced and expanded in this edition and they are all available FREE on the text's companion website. Five Animated Tutorials help bring key concepts to life, and the updated Ethics in Accounting section provides detailed discussion of ethical issues as they relate to the financial reporting environment. Revised Study Tools, including Self-Assessment Quizzes and Demonstration Problems, aid students in preparing and practising for tests. The Analyst Tools section encourages students to develop analytical skills through analysis of real accounting data. The Financial Statement Analysis Primer, Technology Tools, and other resources guide them through the processes.

CLASSROOM RESPONSE SYSTEM

Another addition to the Hoskin technology package is Classroom Response System content. Wiley provides Financial Accounting questions adapted to be used with a CRS. These networks have proven effective in teaching and can fulfill a variety of functions. Because these systems recognize the individual ID of each student response unit, they can be used to take attendance and administer pop quizzes, as well as manage student grades. They also provide an excellent method for stimulating classroom discussion.

The Evolution of a Textbook

While *Financial Accounting: A User Perspective* has been used successfully for many years, small refinements continue to take place. Following is an outline of some of the key pedagogical and content changes in this edition:

PEDAGOGICAL CHANGES

- "Helpful Hints" boxes have been added throughout the text, giving students tips to help them avoid common difficulties.

- Colour-coding has been introduced in the section dealing with closing entries, to differentiate them from others and make the postings easier to follow.

- Solutions to the Summary Problems have been expanded to include fuller explanations of the answers.

- More "thinking points" have been added to the quantitative problems. These are additional requirements asking students to comment upon or interpret the results, so that they make the connection between the quantitative and the analytical.

- Throughout the book, changes have been made to make the text more "reader friendly" (i.e., shorter paragraphs; more concise wording; more illustrations;

more links with underlying concepts) and more variety has been introduced in the assignment material. This is especially true in the first few chapters, where students often struggle with what seems to be a whole new language.

CONTENT CHANGES

- There has been a significant revision of Chapters 2 and 3, covering the accounting cycle, to include more links between procedures and underlying principles or concepts.

- An appendix has been added to Chapter 3 dealing with Comprehensive Income—a new feature in Canadian financial statements. This complex new area is presented briefly and simply, to make it appropriate for introductory students.

- Performance Measurement has been moved from the beginning to the end of Chapter 4, where students will have a better understanding of its importance and the factors affecting it.

- Accounting for Investments has been totally rewritten to reflect new Canadian requirements. Again, this complex new area is presented briefly and simply, so as to be appropriate for introductory students.

- Coverage of the aging of accounts receivable method of estimating bad debts is now provided on the Companion Website, allowing instructors to cover this as well as the percentage of credit sales method presented in the text.

- An appendix has been added to Chapter 7 dealing with cost flows under the Perpetual Inventory System. This will allow instructors the flexibility to teach both the Periodic and Perpetual systems, or just one of them.

- The discussion of Future Income Taxes in Chapters 8 and 9 has been revised to make it more easily understandable to introductory students.

- An explanation of Income Trusts has been added to the discussion of types of business organizations. With the growth of income trusts, students are likely to come across them at some point in their careers and therefore should have a general understanding of how they are different from a corporation.

- Ratios related to cash flows have been added to Chapter 12, for a more comprehensive view of Financial Statement Analysis.

- Coverage of internal control, auditor independence, and earnings management has been expanded—either in the text itself or as a supplement available through the website.

TEXT ORGANIZATION

In order to focus on the understanding and use of financial statements and to emphasize the importance of topics such as decision-making, cash flows, and ratio analysis, this text is organized in a unique manner.

Chapter 1 lays the conceptual groundwork for the mechanics of the accounting system, and guides students through the annual report of Le Château Inc. The section on the users of financial statements has been revised so that students have a better understanding of who the people are, what kind of decisions they make, and how the financial statements can provide that information. Students learn basic accounting terminology and are introduced to the three major financial statements: income statement, balance sheet, and cash flow statement. This chapter also presents background material on the standard-setting process and the conceptual framework underlying accounting.

Chapters 2 and 3 build on the basics from Chapter 1, providing the traditional presentation of the accounting system using the basic accounting equation, followed by a full explanation of the double entry accounting system and the accounting cycle. The early introduction of the cash flow statement enables students to appreciate the differences between the income statement and cash flow statement that are crucial to understanding accrual basis financial statements.

Chapter 4 caps the coverage of the income statement with a discussion of revenue recognition criteria and methods. This topic is often not emphasized in introductory texts. However, the authors recognize that the revenue recognition policies established by a company have a major impact on its reported operating results. It is, therefore, important for students to have a good understanding of these accounting policy choices early in the course.

Chapter 5 reflects the importance of the cash flow statement in at least two ways: it covers the interpretation as well as the construction of the statement, and the coverage occurs earlier than in most other introductory texts. Because this topic is a difficult one for many students, the chapter explains the linkage of the cash flow statement to the operating policies of the company (accounts receivable, inventory, and accounts payable policies), which helps students to interpret the information in the operating section of the cash flow statement. By the end of Chapter 5, students will have a basic understanding of the three major financial statements. However, the authors realize that, because of the complexity of the cash flow statement, some instructors prefer to teach this topic later in the course. The chapter has therefore been designed so that it can be taught after Chapter 11 instead of after Chapter 4.

Chapters 6 through 11 discuss the major asset, liability, and equity accounts that students will see in published financial statements. In each of these chapters, students are alerted to the important aspects of these items so that they can better interpret financial accounting information. The chapter material and the assignment materials provide numerous examples of disclosures from the financial statements of real companies.

Financial statement analysis issues are discussed in all chapters and are summarized and extended in Chapter 12. Financial ratios associated with the topics under discussion are introduced in each chapter. Thus, from their first exposure to accounting, students are given tools that they can use to analyze financial statements. By the time they reach Chapter 12, where all the ratios are summarized and extended, they have worked with all the ratios. Chapter 12 gives them an opportunity to pull the analysis together and work with the total corporate entity. In some cases, this takes the coverage slightly beyond what is usual in introductory texts.

Because real corporations are complex, and generally prepare consolidated financial statements, an appendix that covers long-term investments in other corporations and the consolidation process is included. Recognizing that consolidation procedures are complicated and beyond the usual scope of an introductory text, this discussion is kept very simple. In keeping with the user orientation, the financial statement impacts of the consolidation policies are considered.

Hallmark Features of This Book

The text's user orientation aims to prepare students for their future in business, no matter what their area of concentration, and has been successfully followed at universities across Canada. In addition to the content and organizational features described above, a variety of proven pedagogical features that support this approach continue to be present.

THE USE OF FINANCIAL STATEMENTS

Virtually all introductory accounting students, both graduate and undergraduate, will become users of accounting information, while only a few will become preparers. The user perspective featured in this text focuses on the understanding and use of corporate financial statements as a primary source for accounting information. Over the years, instructors across the country have found this approach to be a very effective way of preparing students to work with accounting information. As well, it provides a solid foundation for students who continue on in accounting.

Integral to this approach is the extensive use of real financial statement data. Throughout the text, you will find excerpts from the annual reports of actual corporations, reprinted exactly as they originally appeared. The annual report of Le Château Inc. is presented in its entirety, along with a variety of excerpts from over 55 Canadian and international corporations. An icon in the margin identifies material from the annual reports of these companies. In addition, the annual report of Sun-Rype Products Limited and a database of over 50 other Canadian companies are available on the Companion Website. Each chapter also provides a unique set of problems in the "Reading and Interpreting Published Financial Statements" section, which requires students to analyze and interpret actual corporate financial statement disclosures.

USER RELEVANCE

Another key feature that complements the use of real financial statements is the User Relevance section, found at the start of each chapter from Chapter 2 onward. It describes why the content of the chapter is important to users of accounting information as they make business decisions. It prepares the students to view the material from a user perspective as they read. Also, throughout the chapter there are now frequent references to what users will see on financial statements and how that information is relevant to decision-making. At the end of each chapter there is a set of problems called "User Perspective Problems" that require students to consider issues and concepts from the perspective of different users.

AN INTERNATIONAL PERSPECTIVE: REPORTS FROM OTHER COUNTRIES

International issues are integrated into the text in several ways. Where appropriate, international differences in accounting practices are discussed in the main body of the text. Additional international material is set off from the main body, in boxed-in areas that often feature "NAFTA Facts." Actual foreign financial statements are included in some of the boxed-in areas and in some of the assignment materials.

ETHICS IN ACCOUNTING

Ethical issues are raised in most chapters by special boxed-in sections. These exhibits are designed to raise the reader's consciousness on ethical issues, and to provide a source of in-class discussion topics. The focus of these boxes is what students need to think about in order to act responsibly. This feature is complemented by additional material on ethical issues in accounting provided on the Companion Website.

CRITICAL THINKING & COMMUNICATION

While many of the problems in the "Reading and Interpreting Published Financial Statements" sections are challenging problems, special critical thinking problems and cases have been included at the end of most chapters. These problems require students to critically analyze issues. They can be used as the basis for student papers, class discussion, or debates, providing opportunities for students to polish their written and oral communication skills. Additional help with their writing skills is available on the Companion Website.

IN-TEXT STUDENT AIDS

In addition to the Helpful Hints described previously, each chapter includes the following sections: summary problems, synonyms & abbreviations, glossary, and assignment materials.

Summary Problems   The summary problem at the end of each chapter is designed to illustrate the main points in the chapter. Many of these problems elaborate on topics discussed in the chapter and provide an example for students in order to aid them when tackling the assignment materials. Additional demonstration problems are available on the Companion Website.

Synonyms & Abbreviations   This section contains terms used in the chapter and their common synonyms, as well as any common abbreviations that are used in the chapter.

Glossary   There is a glossary at the end of each chapter that defines the key terms introduced in the chapter. Key terms are boldfaced in red the first time they are used in a chapter. A searchable glossary is also available on the Companion Website.

Assignment Materials   The end-of-chapter materials are divided into seven parts: Assessing Your Recall, Applying Your Knowledge, User Perspective Problems, Reading and Interpreting Published Financial Statements, Beyond the Book, Cases, and Critical Thinking Questions.

- The *Assessing Your Recall* section is designed to assess the understanding of basic terms and concepts introduced in the chapter.

- The *Applying Your Knowledge* section asks students to apply the concepts and procedures discussed in the chapter in a hypothetical situation. These problems are most like those found in traditional texts, and will often reinforce the technical side of accounting.

- The *User Perspective Problems* let students assume the role of a particular user and consider and discuss chapter topics from that perspective.

- The *Reading and Interpreting Published Financial Statements* section is unique to this book and contains problems that make use of actual corporate financial statement disclosures. The problems typically involve some type of analysis and interpretation of financial statement data.

- The *Beyond the Book* section provides an opportunity for instructors to have students do individual or group research. Students are asked to find financial information about a company of their choice and to answer questions about topics introduced in each chapter. The Beyond the Book section in Chapter 1 gives several library and Internet sources of corporate financial statements that students can use throughout the course.

- The *Cases* are hypothetical scenarios in which students are asked to identify problems, evaluate situations, and make recommendations. The required part of the cases often asks for a written report. Additional cases can be found on the Companion Website.

- The *Critical Thinking Questions* often take students beyond the structured data in the chapter by asking them to consider controversial areas associated with one or more of the chapter's topics.

Acknowledgements

We would like to thank Robert Hoskin, who developed the original concept for this book and who put so much thought and energy into its construction.

We would also like to acknowledge the many reviewers who provided very valuable comments on our plans for the fourth edition and on our writing as we progressed through the chapters. We have tried to incorporate as many of your suggestions as possible. Your comments were especially valuable when we incorporated some of the new complex accounting requirements. We needed to describe them in ways that were simple and yet reasonably comprehensive, and you helped us accomplish that.

Reviewers were:

Teresa Anderson   University of Ottawa
Ron Baker   University of Regina
Christopher Burnley   Malaspina University College
Mariann Glynn   Ryerson University
Valorie Leonard   Laurentian University
Ralph McPherson   College of New Caledonia
Jean Pai   University of Manitoba
David Scallen   Wilfrid Laurier University
Paul Thompson   Wilfrid Laurier University
Daniel Thornton   Queen's University

We are very grateful to everyone at John Wiley and Sons Canada, Limited. John Horne and Karen Staudinger got us going on the fourth edition and found us a great developmental editor, Zoë Craig, who worked tirelessly to keep us on schedule and to organize the resources needed to complete the comprehensive package of materials for this edition. We also want to thank the many people who worked behind the scenes producing materials that make this book unique: Alison Arnot, who researched and wrote the real-company stories that open each chapter, and found and summarized many of the numerous news articles that bring the real business world into this book; Laurel Hyatt, the copyeditor who made the important grammatical decisions; Maureen Moyes, who proofread all of the pages; Ian Farmer, who checked all of the solutions; and Edwin Durbin, who produced the index. We also want to thank Isabelle Moreau, who has developed creative ways of marketing this edition of the text. Last, but by no means least, sincere thanks go to all of the university/college representatives for all their energy and enthusiasm in promoting the merits of the book to instructors.

There are several people who worked on supplemental material for the text that also deserve a special thank you: Anne Macdonald, who wrote some of the additional problems; Ron Baker, who prepared the Solutions Manual; and Julia Scott, who prepared the Test Bank and Instructor's Manual.

We also want to thank Rosalind Woolfrey, who was of great assistance in assembling various materials for this edition and proofreading much of the final product.

We would also like to thank the companies who granted us permission to reproduce their financial statements, especially Le Chateau Inc. and Sun-Rype Products Ltd.

Concluding Remarks

We hope that both students and instructors will find the material contained in this book useful as they attempt to understand the complex and fascinating world of corporate financial reporting. We have tried to be very careful in the editing of this book and the associated Solutions Manual and Instructors' Manual, to minimize the number of errors. Any remaining errors are, of course, ours and we look forward to hearing from you concerning any that you find or any suggestions that you would like to make, so that we can continue to make improvements.

Maureen Fizzell   Don Cherry
Simon Fraser University   Dalhousie University

January 2005

Brief Table of Contents

Table of Contents

Trust in Numbers

Ben Voss of Saskatoon seemed primed for business success from the start. He established his own engineering consulting business, BDI Inc., before graduating with an engineering degree from the University of Saskatchewan in 1999. Now, he's the President and CEO of Clear-Green Environmental Inc., which recycles farm waste into renewable energy.

The company takes manure from large agricultural operations and treats it to the point that just water is left. Energy is manufactured from the methane produced during this process, while the purified chemicals extracted are sold to the fertilizer industry. "Because manure is about 95% water, we are able to purify the water and minimize or eliminate any effects on the environment," Mr. Voss explains.

Officially launched in September 2000, Clear-Green has used $2 million in equity and debt financing from private investors and a Calgary-based venture capital fund to develop its first plant in Saskatoon, and there are plans to build 10 more plants across Canada in the next five years. Its annual sales for the 2003 fiscal year were less than $0.5 million, but projections for 2004 are for $1.5 to $2 million, and the company is expected to continue to grow at this pace.

Mr. Voss attributes his business success to careful planning and attention to the company's accounting information. "BDI provided the infrastructure and paid the bills in order to develop Clear-Green Environmental," the young entrepreneur says. From the start, Mr. Voss sought help from experts to plan his business. "We had to use some accounting consultants to help us develop an accounting model that we could use to forecast all of our sales and expenses," he says.

An oil and gas company was the model followed in planning and running Clear-Green. "We're not selling equipment; we're providing more of a service," Mr. Voss says. Any money earned will be invested in the development of another plant, which, when up and running, will have minimal operating costs since it is essentially automated. "The more plants we build, the

more money we can make, and the more the economies of scale can be applied," he adds.

Mr. Voss and his three management partners, Chris Nimegeers, Amber New, and Clayton Sparks, have no accounting education, and, despite the careful planning, they have learned a few lessons along the way. "When you're starting a company without any track record, you have to use your best guess in forecasting your working capital requirement," Mr. Voss says. "We learned a lot about what are the critical expenses and what aren't, and where to have your priority list of expenditures."

The management team's ability to secure the trust of investors and clients has allowed it to grow, Mr. Voss says. For example, Clear-Green has a strong relationship with SaskPower. "When you have a very large corporation that buys into your business from the angle of being your customer, it sends signals throughout the industry," he says.

In addition to strong management, accounting is of huge importance to business success, Mr. Voss adds. "You can't bring in investors without good accounting records... They want to see the projections and they want to see historical financial statements. Unless that stuff makes sense, you have no chance of gaining their trust... A true measure of your trust is your numbers."

chapter 1

Overview of Corporate Financial Reporting

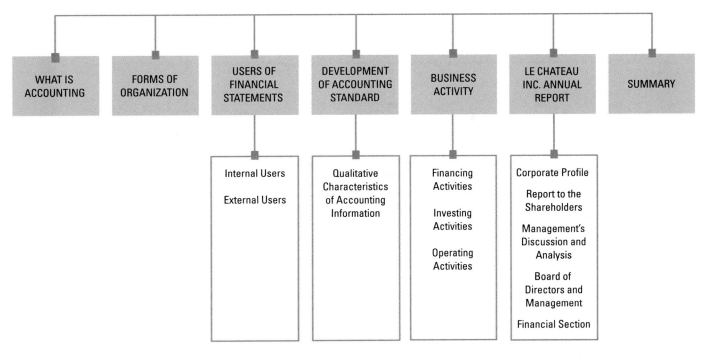

WHAT IS ACCOUNTING	FORMS OF ORGANIZATION	USERS OF FINANCIAL STATEMENTS	DEVELOPMENT OF ACCOUNTING STANDARD	BUSINESS ACTIVITY	LE CHATEAU INC. ANNUAL REPORT	SUMMARY
		Internal Users External Users	Qualitative Characteristics of Accounting Information	Financing Activities Investing Activities Operating Activities	Corporate Profile Report to the Shareholders Management's Discussion and Analysis Board of Directors and Management Financial Section	

LEARNING OBJECTIVES

After studying this chapter, you should be able to:

1. Define accounting and understand its relationship to economic decision-making.
2. Understand what an annual report is and what it contains.
3. Describe the major forms of organization in which accounting is used.
4. Identify several users of financial statements and begin to understand how they use accounting information.
5. Know what the term generally accepted accounting principles (GAAP) means.
6. Identify the qualitative characteristics of accounting information.
7. Describe the three fundamental business activities.
8. Identify the major financial statements and describe their major components.
9. Begin to understand the role of ethics in financial accounting.

The opening story tells how accounting and business success work hand in hand. Whether you are performing day-to-day operations, borrowing money for start-up or expansion, planning a new avenue of operations, deciding to purchase or lease, etc., you need to have information that will enable you to make the most advantageous decisions. One of the most important sources of that information is the accounting system. Mr. Voss had no accounting knowledge when he began **Clear-Green Environmental Inc.** but he recognized the importance of having good accounting information in order to make his company successful. He sought help from accounting experts to develop an accounting information system that would capture information he needed for decision-making and that could forecast revenues and expenses for future operations. Accounting systems represent the backbone of businesses.

WHAT IS A BUSINESS?

This book describes the role of accounting within a business setting. It is, therefore, important to start with an understanding of a business entity. The goal of a business is to earn a profit for its owners. A business usually sells goods or services and/or invests in other businesses. Its owners can be one single individual or thousands of people. A local business in your area may be owned by a few individuals whereas a large company such as **Canadian Tire** likely has thousands of investors (**owners**). Accounting is present in all these entities.

WHAT IS ACCOUNTING?

LEARNING OBJECTIVE 1

Define accounting and understand its relationship to economic decision-making.

Accounting is an information system in which the underlying economic conditions of organizations and, indeed, individuals, are recorded, summarized, reported, and understood. Accounting can be as simple as balancing your personal cheque book or as complex as recording and reporting on the economic condition of a multinational corporation such as **Microsoft** or a government such as the federal Government of Canada. All these entities need to know economic information in order to continue to operate efficiently and effectively. Accounting is the system that provides vital financial information. It provides the very framework around which people and organizations make decisions. It is therefore important that you, as a future user, have at least a basic understanding of what accounting is (and is not), what it is trying to accomplish, and how it goes about doing so.

LEARNING OBJECTIVE 2

Understand what an annual report is and what it contains.

The focus of this book is on the accounting information produced by profit-oriented organizations, although we will occasionally refer to not-for-profit organizations or governments. We will concentrate mainly on the **financial statements**, which are the reports from the management of companies to their owners summarizing how the company performed during a particular period. The financial statements are the final set of documents produced at the end of an accounting period. They are included in a larger **annual report** that is the main method management uses to report the results of the company's activities during the year. The annual report is sent to all owners, but many other parties that have an interest in the company (for example, lenders, analysts, and credit-rating agencies) use it as well. Many companies have created websites and include their most recent financial statements as part of the information users can access.

The primary goal of this book is to help you become an intelligent user of accounting information by enhancing your ability to read and understand corporate financial statements. You may become a manager, accountant, banker, or financial analyst, and even if you don't, you probably will become an investor in the shares or bonds of a company at some point in your career. Whatever your business role, you will make decisions about companies, such as whether or not to invest in their shares, lend them money, or sell them goods or services on credit. In making these decisions, it will be important for you to understand the information that is presented in corporate financial statements. You must know not only what each piece of information tells you about the company, but also what it doesn't tell you. You should also recognize that some important information is not contained in the financial statements, yet is useful in certain decision-making contexts.

We have written this book for a broad readership, understanding that many of you will play multiple roles as owners (shareholders), creditors, and managers of companies. We have assumed that you know little or nothing about accounting. We have not assumed that you are training to be an accountant, although that may be your objective. Therefore, this book does not emphasize accounting procedures. Instead, the underlying concepts of accounting and the analysis of financial statements are emphasized. However, a knowledgeable understanding of the end result of the accounting process is probably not possible without an overall view of how the accounting system works. For this reason, the first few chapters present the mechanics of the accounting system. Subsequent chapters are devoted to more detailed accounting issues and concepts, and to analyzing financial statements.

Throughout the book, information from real companies is used to illustrate the topic at hand. In addition to numerous examples of financial statement information from a variety of companies, the complete annual report of **Le Château Inc.** for 2004 is included in Appendix A at the end of the book. Le Château sells clothing to women and men aged 15 to 35+. Recently it opened a new division, JUNIOR GIRL, that sells to girls 8 to 14. A second complete annual report, that of **Sun-Rype Products Ltd.** for 2003, has been included on the text companion website, which is located at www.wiley.com/canada/hoskin. Sun-Rype Products Ltd. manufactures fruit juice products. The inclusion of two complete annual reports, one for a retailer (Le Château) and one for a manufacturing company (Sun-Rype Products), will provide you with more reference material. Many references will be made to the Le Château (LC) report and the Sun-Rype Products (SRP) report throughout the text. Page numbers from these annual reports will be preceded by LC- or SRP- ; that is, page 10 from an annual report will be referred to as LC-10 or SRP-10. At the end of each chapter, additional problems, labelled Beyond the Book, require that you find a company of your own choosing or one suggested by your instructor. At most colleges and universities, annual reports of other companies may be accessed through electronic means. Reports are also currently available on the Internet through the SEDAR filings. Your instructor may provide you with information about how to access this information on your campus, or you can contact your librarian.

**Sun-Rype Products
Ltd. Annual Report**

accounting in the news

WHERE HAS ALL THE PAPER GONE?

Recent surveys have indicated that companies are producing fewer paper copies of their annual reports. In the past, companies would spend thousands of dollars creating an attractive annual report that was used as a communication tool to showcase their company. Companies still produce annual reports. They are required by securities regulators to produce quarterly and annual reports for their shareholders; however, they are not required to produce a paper product. With the increased use by investors of the Internet, more companies are now including their financial statement information on their website. Some companies may still want to produce a report that showcases their company but that report might not have the financial statements in it any more.

Source: "End of the Annual Report," by Michael McCullough, Business BC, *The Vancouver Sun*, August 28, 2003, p. D1.

Because different companies use slightly different terminology to refer to items in their financial statements, it is sometimes confusing to read them. To assist you in interpreting these financial statements, lists of abbreviations and synonyms are provided at the end of most chapters. A glossary that briefly defines or explains the terms used is also provided at the end of each chapter.

AN INTERNATIONAL PERSPECTIVE

Reports from Other Countries

Because we live in a global environment, another goal of this book is to expose you to financial statement requirements in countries other than Canada. Integrated into the discussion of most chapters are examples of how accounting standards in other countries might differ from those in Canada. These sections are set off from the main text, as is this paragraph, so that you can easily identify discussions of international standards rather than Canadian ones. Some of these international boxes are used to highlight accounting principles used in the United States and Mexico, which we have labelled "NAFTA FACTS."

FORMS OF ORGANIZATION

LEARNING OBJECTIVE 3

Describe the major forms of organization in which accounting is used.

Financial information captured by the accounting system is used in many different types of organization: profit-seeking entities such as corporations; governing organizations such as federal, provincial, and municipal governments; service entities such as hospitals and academic institutions; and not-for-profit entities such as charities and clubs. Although these entities have different objectives, they all need information that tells their users whether they are financially sound, meeting their goals, and likely to remain viable in the future. Within the accounting system, financial statements attempt to capture financial information about an **entity** and present it to users so that they can make informed decisions. Because these entities have different objectives, the underlying accounting approaches associated with them may be different. To try to capture all the variations adequately would make this book too complicated. We are, therefore, concentrating on the profit-seeking entities, although we will occasionally add information about the other types of entity.

Many different types or forms of organization conduct business in Canada. Although the accounting issues discussed in this book apply to some degree to all these forms of organization, attention is directed primarily toward the accounting issues facing corporations. Almost every large business in Canada is a corporation. Other forms of business include sole proprietorships, partnerships, limited partnerships, joint ventures, and Crown corporations. These forms of organization are discussed in more detail in Chapter 11.

In all business organizations, the owners make some type of initial investment in the business entity in the form of cash or property. In sole proprietorships and partnerships, this ownership interest is referred to as the owners' or partners' capital. In a corporation, owners make similar investments in the company but their ownership interest is referred to as **shareholders' equity** and is represented by documents known as shares. A share is simply a document that represents a small part of ownership in the corporation. The owners therefore are referred to as **shareholders**. One advantage of the corporate form of business is that the shares can be easily transferred to another investor, allowing one investor to sell and another to buy ownership in a given company, usually without significantly affecting the company itself. It is not as easy to transfer ownership in a sole proprietorship or a partnership. Corporations whose shares are held by a small number of individuals are sometimes referred to as **privately held corporations**. The shares in these corporations do not trade on the public stock exchanges, which makes the transfer of ownership more difficult. Corporations whose shares are held by a larger number of individuals or entities and trade on a public stock exchange (such as the Toronto Stock Exchange) are referred to as **publicly traded corporations**. Some portion of their ownership often changes hands on a daily basis.

Except in some small corporations, shareholders typically do not become involved in the day-to-day operation of the business. Because of the large number of shareholders and their lack of involvement in day-to-day activities, the shareholders typically elect a **board of directors** to represent them. The board of directors then hires (and fires) individuals known as senior management to manage the day-to-day operations. These senior managers, along with the managers they hire, are collectively referred to as **management**. To keep shareholders informed of the performance of their investment in the company, management reports periodically to the shareholders. This periodic information is sent to shareholders on a quarterly basis (every three months) in a quarterly report. The fourth-quarter report is combined with the prior three quarters to produce financial statements that cover the entire fiscal year. These annual financial statements are included in the company's annual report. It is these annual statements that we will be studying.

USERS OF FINANCIAL STATEMENTS

Accounting is primarily concerned with the communication of financial information to users. Accountants must first identify what information should be communicated to users, then must ensure that the company's accounting system will accurately collect

Describe the major forms of organization in which accounting is used.

and record this information so that the desired communication is possible. Because businesses are involved in many thousands of transactions each year, accountants must summarize this information in a format that is understandable, and therefore useful, to users. Accountants are very concerned that the information they provide is both reliable and relevant to users.

Although annual reports and corporate financial statements are prepared by managers primarily for shareholders, other users of financial data who are both external and internal to the company also analyze them. The various users do not have the same goals with respect to the information that they need. As mentioned previously, in the future you will probably be a user of financial information. What kind of user is still unclear. It is important, therefore, at this stage that you understand who the typical users of financial information are and what they want to know. At the end of each chapter there is a series of questions entitled User Perspective Problems that describe situations for you to consider from different user perspectives. Exhibit 1-1 lists some of these users.

EXHIBIT 1-1

USERS OF FINANCIAL STATEMENT INFORMATION

Internal users:
Management
Board of directors
External users:
Shareholders
Potential investors
Creditors (for example, bankers and suppliers)
Regulators (for example, a stock exchange)
Taxing authorities
Other corporations, including competitors
Security analysts
Credit-rating agencies
Labour unions
Journalists

Internal Users

MANAGEMENT AND THE BOARD OF DIRECTORS

Professional Profiles

Management and the board of directors, as primary internal users, make use of accounting data to make many decisions such as pricing products, expanding operations, deciding whether to buy or lease equipment, and controlling costs. Because of their position inside the company, managers have access to many sources of financial information beyond what is included in the financial statements that external users see. Their uses of these additional accounting data are important, but are generally covered in books devoted to **managerial accounting** or **cost accounting** and will not be discussed in this text. Our primary focus will be on the value of accounting data to external users. **Financial accounting** courses are oriented primarily to the study of the accounting data provided to outside users through the use of financial statements. In most business programs, both a financial and a managerial accounting course are required to expose students to both types of accounting information.

External Users

The information disclosed in financial statements is sensitive to external users' needs because management, who prepares the statements, wants to communicate information to shareholders, creditors, and others about the company's financial status. Management can, therefore, disclose almost any information it considers important for an understanding of the company, subject to some limitations set by various regulatory bodies.

SHAREHOLDERS AND POTENTIAL INVESTORS

Shareholders and potential investors need information that will enable them to assess how well management has been running the company. They want to make decisions about buying more shares or selling some or all of the shares they already own. They will be analyzing the current share prices (as reflected on the stock exchange) and comparing them with the original price that was paid for the shares. Are they now worth more or less? They will also be comparing the share price with the company's underlying value, as reflected in the financial statements and in other sources of information they have about the company. They also want to decide if the people currently sitting on the board of directors are adequately overseeing the management team they have selected. Is the company heading in the right direction? Is it making decisions that result in increased value to the shareholders? Information in the financial statements will contribute to those decisions. Other sources of information for these users include press releases, websites, business newspapers and magazines, and experts such as stockbrokers and financial advisors. Because shareholders are concerned with the company as a whole, they probably have the broadest need for information of all the external users.

CREDITORS

Creditors usually come from three major groups. The first group includes those who sell goods or services to the company and are willing to wait a short period of time for payment. Examples of these users are suppliers, employees, and government (with respect to payroll deductions). These users focus on the short-term cash level in the company because they want to be paid. The second group consists of financial institutions, such as banks, that have loaned money to the company. The loans can either be short-term or extend over several years. Like the people in the first group, they are also interested in the company's cash level, but they often need to assess the cash flow further into the future, so their need for information is broader. They want not only the principal of the debt repaid, but also an interest charge paid. The third group is made up of investors who have purchased long-term debt instruments such as corporate bonds from the company. Similar to banks, these users have both a long-term and a short-term interest in the cash level. These creditor groups use the financial statements as a source of information that enables them to assess the company's future cash flows. They will make their lending or investing decisions and establish interest levels based on their assessment of the risk of non-collection.

REGULATORS

The regulators who are interested in the financial statements are numerous. For example, the government establishes regulations for how a business becomes incorporated and for its conduct after incorporation. It is, therefore, interested in ensuring that the company follows those regulations. The stock exchanges on which shares are traded establish regulations about the timing and format of information that must be conveyed to it and to investors. If companies do not comply with those regulations they could be de-listed (their shares can no longer trade on the stock exchange), which greatly affects their ability to raise capital. Environmental groups, as well, monitor the activities of companies to ensure that they meet environmental standards.

TAXING AUTHORITIES

The federal **taxing authority** in Canada, Parliament, has established the Canada Revenue Agency (CRA) as its collection agency. Parliament establishes the rules for how taxable income should be measured. The tax rules use accounting financial statements extensively in the assessment of the amount of tax to be paid by businesses, but there are several areas in which they vary. Later in this text we will describe some of those variations and explain their impact on the financial statements.

OTHER USERS

Additional users of financial statement information include other companies, security analysts, credit-rating agencies, labour unions, and journalists. Other companies may want information about the performance of a company if they enter into cooperative agreements or contracts with that company. If it is a direct competitor, the company may want information that will enable it to assess the strength and future plans of the competitor. Security analysts and credit-rating agencies use the financial statements to provide information about the strengths and weaknesses of companies to people who want to invest. Labour unions need to understand the company's financial health in order to negotiate labour issues with management. Journalists are often given press releases from companies where financial information such as expected earnings are disclosed. They may want to refer to the actual financial statements when they are released to validate the information that was provided and to supplement the original information.

All these users, with their various needs, use the same set of financial statements. It is therefore important that the financial statements provide information to the widest possible group of users. As you would guess, however, there are many pieces of information particular users may want but cannot find in the financial statements. They must therefore develop alternate sources of information.

DEVELOPMENT OF ACCOUNTING STANDARDS

LEARNING OBJECTIVE 5

Know what Generally Accepted Accounting Principles (GAAP) are.

When management begins the task of measuring, collecting, recording, and reporting financial information for users, it needs some guidelines to follow so that users can read and understand the financial statements. If there were no guidelines, each company would develop its own information reporting system and it would be very difficult for users to evaluate the statements and to compare them with other companies as they attempt to make knowledgeable decisions. Each country has developed guidelines for this purpose.

In Canada, the **Accounting Standards Board (AcSB)** of the Canadian Institute of Chartered Accountants (CICA) sets accounting recommendations and guidelines, which are published in the *CICA Handbook*. These accounting recommendations and guidelines have the force of law as they are recognized in both federal and provincial statutes that regulate business corporations. In the United States, the **Financial Accounting Standards Board (FASB)** sets accounting standards for American corporations.

The set of accounting recommendations and guidelines that corporations use is referred to as generally accepted accounting principles, or **GAAP** (usually pronounced as "gap"). Many different methods of deriving these principles have been used over time. Deductive methods have been used that start with some generally accepted definitions (of assets, liabilities, and income, for instance) and concepts, and then logically derive accounting methods and other accounting principles from them. These methods are similar to the process mathematicians use in the development of mathematical theory. The problem with this approach has been the difficulty in achieving a consensus on the underlying definitions and concepts. Inductive approaches have also been used. These approaches generally take into consideration the methods in current practice and attempt to develop (induce) general principles from these methods. Current standard setting under the CICA combines both an inductive and a deductive approach. On the deductive side, the CICA has developed a set of underlying objectives and concepts called financial statement concepts, or the **conceptual framework**. This framework has then been used deductively to justify new accounting standards and to revise old ones. On the inductive side, the conceptual framework and the new accounting standards have all been established by a political process of reaching consensus among the various users of financial information.

AN INTERNATIONAL PERSPECTIVE

Reports from Other Countries

The development of accounting standards has, in general, been a country-specific process. Each country has developed its own standards, which reflect its political, social, and economic environment. However, with the development of world markets for both products and financial capital, there has been an increasing need for better understanding among countries with regard to financial reporting. Over the years, numerous organizations have attempted to set international accounting standards. There are currently several groups involved in the process of trying to formulate international accounting standards. Predominant among them is the **International Accounting Standards Board (IASB)**. The IASB is an independent, private-sector body that is funded by donations from accounting organizations around the world and from the **International Federation of Accountants (IFAC)**. By the end of March 2004, the IASB had issued 41 **International Accounting Standards (IASs)** and five **International Financial Reporting Standards (IFRSs)**. The IFRSs were previously known as International Accounting Standards (IASs).

The IASB has developed relationships with the primary standard-setting bodies in numerous countries, including the CICA in Canada, in order to promote the development of international accounting standards. The IASB encourages countries to change their accounting standards so that they more closely resemble the international standards. Through its deliberations about new standards and the revisions of old standards, the AcSB has attempted to realign Canadian standards more closely with the IASB and with the FASB in the United States.

As a future user of accounting information, it is important that you understand the concepts that underlie financial accounting. The conceptual framework in which these concepts lie is used to develop accounting guidelines from which financial statements are prepared so that external users can find information on which they can base decisions about the entity. The financial statements should describe what the entity owns, to whom it has obligations, and what is left over after the obligations are satisfied. They should also show how cash flowed in and out of the entity. The final purpose of financial statements should be to describe the results of the entity's operations.

LEARNING OBJECTIVE 6

Identify the qualitative characteristics of accounting information.

Qualitative Characteristics of Accounting Information

Accounting data should possess four essential characteristics. Exhibit 1-2 provides a hierarchy of these characteristics.

EXHIBIT 1-2

CHARACTERISTICS OF ACCOUNTING INFORMATION

Understandability
Relevance
      Predictive value and feedback value
      Timeliness
Reliability
      Representational faithfulness
      Verifiability
      Neutrality
      Conservatism
Comparability

Understandability, the first qualitative characteristic, simply means that the information must be understandable to the user. For example, if you see an item called "Current portion of long-term debt" listed on a financial statement, you should understand that this means that over the next year, the amount listed for this item will be paid in cash to the group that loaned the money to the company. If preparers of the financial statements were not interested in understandability, they would show the amount of long-term debt in total without pulling out the amount that has to be paid back in the next year. Then, users would not be able to assess the company's probable cash outflow in the coming year. The underlying assumptions behind this qualitative characteristic are that the users are reasonably well informed about accounting terminology and procedures and that they have a reasonable understanding of the business environment. It is unlikely that you have such a background, which means that initially you will find the financial statements difficult to understand.

Relevance refers to whether the information is capable of making a difference in a decision. If you were told that you had an exam next week, that would be relevant to you. It would affect what you planned to do with your time during the next week. However, if you were told that it was snowing at the North Pole, you would probably not find that relevant. It is not always easy for management to know what information will be relevant to users. In some cases, there are accounting guidelines that direct management to disclose certain information. For example, the market value (current selling price) of a short-term investment is likely a relevant piece of information to a user. If the investment is short-term, it means that the company intends to sell it in the near future. Knowing what its market value is enables the user to estimate the potential cash inflow from its sale. Management is required to disclose this information.

Relevant information may have three kinds of value: predictive value, feedback value, and timeliness. **Predictive value** means that the information is useful in predicting future results such as income or cash flow and, therefore, should be helpful to users who make decisions that depend on predictions of future events. Predictive value is based on an underlying assumption that the past is a good predictor of the future. The example in the previous paragraph has potential predictive value in that the market value of the investment may be a good predictor of future cash inflows. **Feedback value** is information that allows users to assess the outcomes of previous decisions, providing them with feedback on decisions made in the past. This can be helpful as users learn from their past successes and failures. Following the investment example, if the user saw financial statements following the sale of the investment, the user could determine whether the investment sold for the market value previously disclosed. If it did, the user would be confident that relying on the market value was a reasonable decision. If the investment sold for less or more, the user might decide that the market value was one piece of information, but that other sources of information are needed to make a better prediction of future cash inflows. Finally, **timeliness** is important because old information quickly loses its relevance to users. If the information is not timely, it may lose its ability to make a difference in a decision. For example, if you were interested in investing in a company, one of the things you would want to see would be its financial statements. Companies produce financial statements for the public every three months (quarterly) and annually. If you request information from a company, this is what you will receive. If it is June and the most recent financial statements you can get are dated March 31, is this timely information? With the rapid changes in the business environment that are evident around us, timeliness will become even more important in decision-making. It may be that, in the future, companies will publish monthly financial statements in order to satisfy users' demand for timely information.

accounting in the news

On February 6, 2001, **Cisco Systems Inc.** surprised the business world when it announced its second quarter results, complete with financial statements, for the quarter ending January 31, 2001. Most companies take about three weeks to produce the previous quarter's results. Providing information within one week enabled users to make decisions based on actual results rather than speculation. How was Cisco able to report so fast? Its accounting system uses the Internet and it enables near-real-time financial reporting. It continued this fast reporting by announcing on

May 8, 2001, its third quarter results and on August 7, 2001, its fourth quarter and annual results for the period ended July 28, 2001.

Although Cisco Systems Inc. continues to be the market leader for early reporting of its financial results, most companies continue to take about three weeks to get their information to the market.

Source: "Speed Matters. Cisco Systems pocketed $86 million last year thanks partly to virtual-close financial reporting," by Desirée de Myer, *Smart Business*, May 2001; also news releases by Cisco Systems on February 6, 2001, May 8, 2001, and August 7, 2001.

Reliability of information rests on four fundamental characteristics: representational faithfulness, verifiability, neutrality, and conservatism.

Representational faithfulness means that the information faithfully represents the attribute, characteristic, or economic event that it purports to represent. It requires that we look for the underlying substance of the transactions when we are deciding how to account for them. For example, suppose the accounting system produces a dollar total for sales that is supposed to represent all sales made during a single year. This amount should include all sales made in that year and exclude all sales made in any other year. If it does, the information has representational faithfulness.

Verifiability means that independent measurers using the same measurement methods should agree on the appropriate value. Determining the cost of an item based on evidence such as invoices and cancelled cheques possesses a high degree of verifiability. Determining the market value of a piece of real estate involves a much lower degree of verifiability because it is based solely on opinions.

Neutrality means that the information is not calculated or presented in a way that would bias users toward making certain desired decisions and not making other, undesired decisions. For example, an inflated estimate of the value of inventory on hand is biased and not neutral. On the other hand, recording inventory at what you paid for it is neutral.

Conservatism means that, if estimates must be made in financial statements, they should err on the side of understating rather than overstating net assets and net income. For example, if a company bought a piece of land for $50,000, it would be on its records at $50,000. If there was a downturn in the economy and the land's market value dropped to $40,000, the company would be required to reduce the land on the records to $40,000 and recognize a loss in the value of the land. This writedown is necessary even though the company has no intention of selling the land in the near future. The writedown illustrates conservatism. If, instead of declining to $40,000, the land's market value increased to $100,000, no change would be made in the company's records unless the company actually sold the land for $100,000. This also represents conservatism. Note that conservatism may conflict with neutrality. If conflict occurs, conservatism overrides neutrality.

Comparability generally refers to the ability of information produced by different companies, particularly within a given industry, to be compared. A high degree of comparability allows for better comparisons across companies and potentially better decisions. Within Canadian GAAP, however, there are no guidelines that require all companies in an industry to use the same accounting methods. Because different methods will produce different financial statement amounts, it is important for users to understand what methods are available to companies and how the various methods will affect the accounting numbers. Comparability also refers to comparing the financial statements of the same company over more than one time period. Information derived from comparing results from one period to another is enhanced with the consistent application of accounting methods by a given company over time. Much of the predictive value of accounting information depends on the long-term data trends. If different methods are used to produce that information over time, the information's predictive value is diminished.

Finally, there are two overriding constraints that affect the information provided by management: the benefit vs. cost constraint, and the materiality criterion. The **benefit vs. cost constraint** states simply that the value of benefits expected to be received from information should exceed the cost of producing it. The value of benefits received from information, however, is very difficult to measure. This can lead to problems because the company bears the cost of producing the information, yet the benefits are perceived mainly by outside users. For example, a company could consider publishing financial statements every week instead of every three months. To publish the financial statements every week would be very costly in terms of hours required to produce the financial statements and ensure their accuracy. If there was perceived to be very little benefit from weekly financial statements, the company would not provide them because the cost would exceed the benefit.

Materiality is a pervasive concept that affects many aspects of the production of information. It is generally thought of as the minimum amount that can significantly affect decisions made by users. For example, when a company purchases a building, the amount spent is usually substantial. Because the building will be used for several years, it is appropriate to spread that cost over several years, which affects the company's profitability. The effect on profitability over a period of years may affect an investor's decision to buy shares. On the other hand, if the company purchases a pencil sharpener, the cost is so small that it will not affect an investor's decision.

Materiality is used by the company's external auditors in their annual audit of the financial statements. Auditors are independent third parties that the shareholders hire to review the financial statements presented by management. They provide a professional opinion as to whether the financial statements fairly present the results of the company's operations. In their tests of the financial statements, auditors will ignore discrepancies below a certain dollar level because the explanation of the discrepancy would not significantly change their opinion about the financial statements. More is said about the work of auditors later in the chapter.

Both the materiality concept and the benefit vs. cost constraint are kept in mind as the CICA adopts and implements new accounting guidelines and as accountants apply those guidelines.

These qualitative characteristics and constraints help form the underlying basis on which accounting recommendations and guidelines are established. As we discuss these in the book, referring back to these characteristics and constraints should help you understand and remember the recommendations and guidelines being used.

accounting in the news
FULL DISCLOSURE?

When it released its 2003 third-quarter financial results, **Maax Inc.**, a Quebec-based manufacturer of bathroom products and accessories, forgot a cardinal rule: don't surprise analysts and investors. It was known that the company was trying to find a buyer and had plans to internalize its management, replacing its external management contract with individual employment contracts. However, investors and analysts did not know the company would pay a $4.2-million kill fee—essentially 13 cents a share—to end the contract with the external manager, **Gestion Camada Inc.** Maax entered into the management contract with Gestion Camada in 2001. Under the contract, for the year ending February 28, 2003, Maax had paid Gestion a base of $1.177 million (adjusted yearly in line with inflation) plus a variable amount set at 4.3% of earnings before taxes and bonuses.

Source: Barry Critchley, *Financial Post*, January 21, 2004.

BUSINESS ACTIVITIES

LEARNING OBJECTIVE 7

Describe the three fundamental business activities.

To understand the information in financial statements, it is useful to think about the fundamental types of activities that all businesses engage in and report on. The basic activities of businesses are **financing**, **investing**, and **operating**.

Financing Activities

Financing refers to the activity of obtaining **funds** (cash) that can be used to buy major assets such as the buildings and equipment used by virtually every business. This activity is necessary, of course, to start the business, but it is also a continuing activity as the business grows and expands its operations. Funds are obtained from two primary sources outside the company: **creditors** and **investors**. Creditors expect to be repaid on a timely basis and very often charge the business, in the form of interest, for the use of their money, goods, or services. The amount to be repaid is generally a fixed amount. Examples of creditors are banks that offer both short-term and long-term loans, and suppliers who are willing to provide goods and services today with the expectation of being paid for those products later. Investors, on the other hand, invest in the company in the hope that their investment will generate a profit. They earn profits either by receiving **dividends** (payments of funds from the company to the shareholders) or by selling their shares to another investor. Of course, investors may experience either a gain (receive more than the initial amount paid for the shares) or a loss (receive less than the initial amount paid for the shares) when the sale occurs.

A primary internal source of new funds to the company is the profit generated by the business that is not paid out to shareholders in the form of dividends. These profits are called **retained earnings**. If the company is not profitable, or if all profits are distributed to shareholders in the form of dividends, the only way the company can expand is to either get more funds from investors (existing shareholders or new investors), or borrow more from creditors. How much to borrow from creditors and how much to obtain from investors are important decisions that the company's management must make. Those decisions can determine whether a company grows, goes bankrupt, or is bought by some other company. Examples of financing activities follow.

TYPICAL FINANCING ACTIVITIES

Borrowing money
Repaying loans
Issuing shares
Repurchasing shares
Paying dividends on shares

Investing Activities

Once the company obtains funds, it must invest those funds to accomplish its purposes. It must acquire things that will enable it to carry on activities for which it was created. Most companies make both long-term and short-term investments. Most short-term investments (such as the purchase of raw materials and inventories) are related to the day-to-day operations of the business, and are therefore considered operating activities. Some short-term investments, such as the investment in the shares of other companies (called marketable securities) and most long-term investments are considered investing activities. A long-term investment in property, plant, and equipment to produce goods and services for sale is a typical investing activity. Long-term investments in the shares of other companies would also be considered an investing activity. Examples of investing activities follow.

TYPICAL INVESTING ACTIVITIES

Purchase of property, plant, and equipment
Sale of property, plant, and equipment
Purchase of the shares of other companies
Sale of the shares of other companies

Operating Activities

Operating activities are those activities associated with developing, producing, marketing, and selling the company's products and/or services. While financing and investing activities are necessary to conduct operations, they tend to occur on a more sporadic basis than the activities thought of as operating activities. The day-to-day continuing activities are generally classified as operations. Examples of operating activities follow.

TYPICAL OPERATING ACTIVITIES

Sales to customers
Collections of amounts owed by customers
Purchases of inventory
Payments of amounts owed to suppliers
Payments of expenses such as wages, rent, and interest
Payments of taxes owed to the government

Financial statements provide information about a company's operating, financing, and investing activities. By the end of this book, you should be able to interpret financial statements as they relate to these activities. To start you on the journey to becoming a successful user of financial statement information, we have included for you, in Appendix A at the back of the book, the annual report of a Canadian corporation, Le Château Inc. A survey of the various types of information contained in the Le Château annual report follows.

LE CHÂTEAU INC. ANNUAL REPORT

Annual Report Walkthrough

The 2004 annual report for Le Château constitutes Appendix A at the back of the book. Le Château's fiscal year runs from February 1 to January 31 of the following year. The annual report at the end of the book is labelled as the 2003 annual report by the company but its financial statements show you the financial information for 2004 and 2003. We are, therefore, going to refer to this as the 2004 annual report (fiscal year January 26, 2003, to January 31, 2004). As mentioned earlier, references to its page numbers are prefixed by LC-. Le Château's annual report will probably appear very complex, particularly if you have never before been exposed to accounting. The fact is, however, that Le Château is a fairly uncomplicated company. We selected its annual report because it is a good example of annual reporting, illustrates almost all the reporting issues discussed in this book, and offers a challenge to you to understand a modern company. The pain you may experience in trying to understand Le Château's financial information will be rewarded by the gain in your understanding of real, complex business organizations.

A survey of the various types of information contained in Le Château's annual report follows.

Corporate Profile

The annual report starts with a short section describing the company's business activities during the year. Le Château sells clothing, footwear, and accessories to consumers through 161 specialty stores located throughout Canada and 4 stores located in the New York City area. Its headquarters are in Montreal, Quebec.

When you evaluate a company for the first time, it is extremely important to know what kind of businesses it is in so that you can assess its risk level. You may be deciding whether to invest in the company or whether to lend it money. The decision will be heavily influenced by the risk being taken. An investment in an oil exploration company, for instance, would have a much greater risk than an investment in a grocery store chain. When you read the financial statements, you must weigh the financial results against the investment's level of risk. Le Château sells clothing and, therefore, must ensure that the products it sells are the products that people want to buy. The clothing industry is constantly changing and companies like Le Château need to stay on the leading edge of fashion in order to be successful. On the inside of the front cover of its annual report, Le Château has a chart in which it lists the number of stores it has in various provinces across Canada. This section enables you to determine how extensive its operations are. A third of its stores (54) are located in Ontario, the province with the highest population. By having a third of its stores in a highly populated area, it is increasing the probability that it will be profitable (assuming, of course, that it is selling merchandise that people want to buy). This information will be a component in your risk assessment of the company.

Message to Shareholders

The message to shareholders appears on page LC-3. The report is written by the Chairman of the Board and Chief Executive Officer, Herschel H. Segal, and the Vice-Chairman of the Board, Jane Silverstone. The Chairman and Vice-Chairman have the opportunity to give a global view of where the company has been, what it accomplished during the year, and where it is going in the future. You can see that they have highlighted their report with information about the continued growth in sales, the improvement in the quality and design of their products, their advances in the planning, buying, and production processes, their plans to further improve profitability, and their appreciation of the people who have made the business a success.

Management's Discussion and Analysis

Many companies use this report (page LC-5 to LC-11) to make more extensive, detailed comments on the company and its operating results. This report provides an opportunity for senior management to discuss the company's performance with shareholders. Often the information is presented from the perspective of the various divisions of the company. Le Château has information about sales in the various divisions of the business and the various regions in which it has stores on page LC-6. On pages LC-7 to LC-9, the discussion and analysis focuses on the financial aspects of the business including expenses, earnings, liquidity and capital resources, financial position, dividends, accounting standards implemented in 2003, recently issued accounting standards, and critical accounting estimates.

On page LC-10, there is a discussion of the risks and uncertainties facing the company. The focus of this section is on the competitive and economic environment, leases, and foreign exchange. Earlier we mentioned that because Le Château was in the clothing business, it needed to stay on the leading edge of the fashion world. This section tells you how it expects to do that.

Page LC-10 includes a quarterly summary of operations for the last year. Page LC-1 has a five-year summary that highlights for the user the changes that have occurred in Le Château over an extended period of time. Such a summary is often included in the Management's Discussion and Analysis section and allows a user to identify possible trends that may continue into the future. Some companies include this summary in the notes to the financial statements.

Page LC-11 includes sections on the company's outlook and forward-looking statements. This section of the annual report is one of the few places in the document where you will find prospective (forward-looking) information. As you will discover shortly, most of the information presented in the annual report is retrospective (based on past events). If your interest is in the future of the company, management's discussion and analysis is a good place to get management's opinion about the company's future directions and prospects. The report should be read sceptically, however, since much of what is said reflects top management's opinion.

In such a report, there is an inherent bias toward presenting results to the shareholders in the best possible light.

Board of Directors and Management

Somewhere in every annual report there is a list of the company's board of directors. The directors often hold positions in other companies as well. These directors are elected by shareholders to serve as their representatives, and as such they provide advice and counsel to company management. They also have broad powers to vote on issues relevant to shareholders (e.g., the declaration of dividends), and to hire and fire management. A listing of the senior management of the company is also often included in the report; for Le Château, the list of the board of directors and senior officers can be found inside the back cover (LC-28).

Financial Section

The remainder of the annual report contains all the financial information about the company's performance and status (LC-13 through LC-27). In general, this section contains the following major components.

COMPONENTS OF THE FINANCIAL SECTION

Statement of management's responsibility
Auditors' report
Financial statements:
Income statement
Balance sheet
Statement of retained earnings
Cash flow statement
Notes to the financial statements
Statement on corporate governance

Each of these components is discussed at some length in the sections that follow. Virtually all the disclosure contained in this section of the annual report is in compliance with either the recommendations in the *CICA Handbook* or the Ontario Securities Commission (OSC), although management would probably disclose most of this information voluntarily to shareholders in the absence of requirements by the CICA or the OSC.

There are three major statements that appear in all sets of financial statements. They are the **income statement**, the **balance sheet**, and the **cash flow statement**. In addition to these, a company will often include a statement of retained earnings. In this chapter, only the income statement, balance sheet, and cash flow statement will be discussed. The statement of retained earnings will be discussed later in the book.

INCOME STATEMENT   The income statement is also known as the **statement of earnings**. This statement describes the results of the operating activities of the current period. The results of those activities add up to the **net income** amount or "bottom line." In companies, net income is defined as revenues (money or resources flowing into the company as a result of sale transactions) less expenses (money or resources flowing out of the company in order to generate sale transactions). This is different from the concept of income used in preparing individual income tax returns. Income to individuals, for tax purposes, is generally the gross amount of money earned by the individual (salary) with very few deductions allowed. Individuals cannot, for example, deduct the cost of groceries or clothing. In a business, the rules are such that almost all expenditures qualify as expenses in the determination of earnings.

There may be a delay in recognizing some expenditures as expenses. Because items such as machinery contribute to the generation of revenues over several years, we normally recognize as an expense a portion of the original cost of the machine each period over its life. This expense is called amortization. Eventually, the entire expenditure will be expensed in the determination of net income.

Refer to the Consolidated Statements of Earnings of Le Château in Exhibit 1-3. The statement covers a period of time as indicated at the top of the statement where it reads, Year Ended January 31, 2004 [with comparative figures for the year ended January 25, 2003]. The revenues and expenses are the amounts recognized during each of the years ended January 31, 2004, and January 25, 2003. The activities reported in this statement are primarily the operating activities of the company. The statement is a report of the company's operating performance during the year and measures the inflow of revenues and the outflow of expenses from the shareholders' point of view. For this reason, it is sometimes called a flow statement. Another way of putting it is that the earnings statement captures the net change in the shareholders' wealth, as measured in the accounting records, across a designated time period. In this case, that time period is one year.

LEARNING OBJECTIVE 8

Identify the major financial statements and describe their major components.

CONSOLIDATED STATEMENT OF EARNINGS OF LE CHÂTEAU INC.

EXHIBIT 1-3

CONSOLIDATED STATEMENTS OF EARNINGS
Year ended January 31, 2004
[With comparative figures for the year ended January 25, 2003]
[In thousands of dollars, except share data]

	2004 $	2003 $
Sales	226,766	217,660
Cost of sales and expenses		
Cost of sales, buying and occupancy	140,537	140,705
Selling, general and administrative	60,511	57,012
Interest on long-term debt	339	350
Depreciation and amortization	7,745	6,937
Write-off of fixed assets	511	281
	209,643	205,285
Earnings before income taxes	17,123	12,375
Provision for income taxes [note 9]	6,475	4,813
Net earnings	10,648	7,562
Net earnings per share [note 10]		
Basic	2.07	1.52
Diluted	1.98	1.45
Weighted average number of shares outstanding	5,133,949	4,979,581

See accompanying notes

As you will note in the statement, there is one revenue category called Sales that represents the inflow of resources from the sale of inventory in its various stores. Depending on a company's operating activities, you might also find revenue from performing services or earning interest. The level of detail provided in a company's income statement depends on the usefulness of the disclosure. Since Le Château is involved only in the sale of apparel, the statement can be quite simple.

Another related reason for the breakdown into different types of revenues is that shareholders (and other users of financial statements) want to forecast the company's future performance. The amounts that are reported in the financial statements are largely historical in nature. For example, the values reported for the company's assets (the things the company owns) are generally based on what the company originally paid for them, not on what they are currently worth on the market. These historical numbers may be useful to forecast the future. Because of the differences in the nature of various aspects of a company, the growth rates of the different types of revenues and expenses may differ greatly. If the reader of the financial statements is not provided with any detail about the breakdown in revenues and expenses, it will be very difficult to forecast them accurately.

Costs and expenses are also listed under various categories, including cost of sales (or cost of goods sold or cost of merchandise sold) and operating expenses. These cost and expense categories are also provided to explain to the shareholders, in more detail, the company's performance. Le Château's income statement has a couple of interesting expenses that likely require further explanation. "Depreciation and amortization" represents the allocation of the original cost of a long-lived asset such as a building. Le Château owns buildings, furniture and equipment, and automobiles that it uses to sell its inventory and, thereby, generate revenue. The cost of using the items, the depreciation or amortization, is included every year as an expense. "Write-off of fixed assets" represents a loss that occurred when the company got rid of some of the long-lived assets that it was no longer using. The last expense, "Provision for income taxes," is listed as a separate expense because its amount depends on both the revenues and expenses reported. Taxes are calculated on the amount by which revenues exceed expenses.

At the bottom of the income statement is an **earnings per share** disclosure. Basic earnings per share is the company's net income divided by the average number of common shares that are outstanding during the year. Shareholders find this calculation useful since it puts the performance of their investment in the company into perspective. In other words, a shareholder who holds, say, 1,000 shares of Le Château can determine his or her share of the earnings during the period. In 2004, Le Château earned $2.07 per share. Therefore, that investor's share of the earnings for 2004 would be $2,070.

Le Château also has a fully diluted earnings per share amount that indicates that the company has either convertible debt, stock options, or preferred shares that can be converted into voting shares (Note 10, page LC-25, states that there are stock options outstanding). If they were exercised, the earnings per share would drop to $1.98 per share. In other words, when the additional shares are issued there will be a negative effect on the earnings per share.

Le Château is a straightforward company, with most of its operations concentrated in retail sales in various locations across Canada and a few stores in the United States. Unlike other retail clothing stores, Le Château designs and manufactures approximately 45% of the goods that it sells. It is the parent company and it runs the stores in Canada and controls its manufacturing operations while its subsidiary company runs the stores in the United States. Subsidiary companies are separate business entities, but when Le Château prepares its annual financial statements, it prepares **consolidated financial statements**. These consolidated financial statements are the combination of all the elements of the subsidiary's financial statements with the elements of the parent's financial statements. More detail concerning consolidated financial statements is contained in Appendix B at the end of the book. When businesses expand, they will often establish other companies or buy shares in other companies. This enables them to expand operations and diversify the risk.

When the subsidiary companies are in a business that is fairly similar to the parent company's business, consolidated financial statements provide much more useful information because they cover the entire group of companies that are under common ownership and work together as an economic unit. Le Château's subsidiary is like this. However, when the business of a subsidiary is very different from that of the parent company, the combined set of financial statements may not be easy to interpret because of the complexity of the combined companies. In Canada, parent companies must prepare consolidated financial statements unless there is some impediment that prevents the earnings of the subsidiary from flowing to the parent.

Reviewing the income statement for Le Château, you can see that the net earnings (net income) for 2004 were $10,648 thousand. You will notice that the net earnings have increased from the $7,562 thousand of the previous year. Companies provide the previous year's results along with the current year's so that users can better evaluate the current year. They will often round amounts to the nearest $100, $1,000, or in the case of very large companies, $1,000,000. The units in which the numbers are expressed must be stated somewhere on the statement. Usually, they can be found in parentheses at the top of the statement. Le Château tells you that its numbers are in thousands of dollars. This brings up an issue that was discussed earlier in the section on the development of accounting standards: materiality. If an auditor were to find a $2,000 mistake when trying to verify how fairly the statements presented the earnings of a company, how much difference would it make assuming the company rounded its amounts to the nearest $1,000? The answer is, it would not make much difference in the overall analysis of the company's financial status. On the other hand, a $2,000 mistake in the tax reporting of an individual's earnings would certainly get the attention of the Canada Revenue Agency. How material an item is often depends, in part, on the size of the entity being considered.

Below is a list of some of the more common items you can expect to see on an income statement.

COMMON INCOME STATEMENT ITEMS

Sales Revenues	The total amount of sales of goods and/or services for the period.
Other Income	Various types of revenues or income to the company other than sales.
Cost of Goods Sold	The cost of the units of inventory that were sold during the period.
Selling, General, and Administrative Expense	The total amount of other expenses (e.g., salaries, rent) of the company during the period that do not fit into any other category.
Amortization Expense	The allocation of part of the cost of long-lived items such as equipment.
Interest Expense	The amount of interest incurred on the company's debt during the period.
Income Tax Expense (Provision for Taxes)	The taxes levied on the company's profits during the period.

BALANCE SHEET The consolidated balance sheet for Le Château Inc. is displayed in Exhibit 1-4. It is also known as the statement of financial position. Financial position suggests that this statement represents the company's financial status at a particular point in time. In fact, at the top of the statement, the words January 31, 2004 and January 25, 2003 appear, indicating that the amounts in the statement are those that existed on January 31, 2004, and January 25, 2003, respectively. These dates may also be thought of as the beginning and end points of the current accounting period. In the transition from one accounting period to the next, the

EXHIBIT 1-4 **LE CHÂTEAU INC. 2003 ANNUAL REPORT**

CONSOLIDATED BALANCE SHEETS

As at January 31, 2004

[With comparative figures as at January 25, 2003]
[In thousands of dollars]

	2004 $	2003 $
ASSETS [note 2]		
Current		
Cash and cash equivalents [note 15]	22,067	15,040
Accounts receivable and prepaid expenses	1,394	1,169
Inventories [note 3]	26,075	25,482
Loan to director [note 4]	566	—
Total current assets	50,102	41,691
Loan to director [note 4]	—	566
Fixed assets [note 5]	44,444	38,262
	94,546	80,519
LIABILITIES AND SHAREHOLDERS' EQUITY		
Current		
Accounts payable and accrued liabilities [note 11]	20,148	17,609
Dividend payable	525	503
Income taxes payable	2,003	2,877
Current portion of capital lease obligations [note 6]	1,525	776
Current portion of long-term debt [note 7]	914	1,483
Total current liabilities	25,115	23,248
Capital lease obligations [note 6]	3,728	212
Long-term debt [note 7]	852	1,766
Future income taxes [note 9]	1,758	1,888
Deferred lease inducements	1,931	1,913
Total liabilities	33,384	29,027
Shareholders' equity		
Capital stock [note 8]	14,774	13,680
Retained earnings	46,388	37,812
Total shareholders' equity	61,162	51,492
	94,546	80,519

Commitments [note 11]

See accompanying notes

On behalf of the Board:

Herschel H. Segal
Director

Jane Silverstone, B.A.LLL
Director

ending balances of one accounting period become the beginning balances of the next accounting period. This statement has been described by various authors as a snapshot of the company's financial position at a particular point in time.

So what makes up the company's financial position? Individuals, if asked about their own financial position, would probably start by listing what they own such as a car, a computer, or a house, and then listing what they owe to others, such as bank loans and credit card balances. What is owned less what is owed would be a measure of their net worth (wealth or equity) at a particular point in time. A company lists exactly the same types of things in its balance sheet. In Le Château's statement, there are two major categories: assets, and liabilities and shareholders' equity.

Assets When asked for a simple definition of an asset, many people reply that it is something of value that the company either owns or has the right to use. In fact, the accounting definition of an asset is very similar. In this book, assets will be those things that meet the following criteria: (1) they have probable future value that can be measured; (2) the company can control the benefit from the future value through ownership or rights to use the assets; and (3) the event that gave the company the ownership of or right to them has already happened. The word "future" has been added to "value" since the company would not want to list things that had value in the past, but do not have value in the future. "Probable" has been added because businesses exist in an uncertain world and an asset's value is subject to change. One of the risks of ownership of an asset, in fact, is that its value may change over time.

CHARACTERISTICS OF AN ASSET

1. Something that has probable future value that can be measured.
2. The company can control the benefit from the future value through ownership or rights to use the assets.
3. The event that gave the company the ownership or right has already occurred.

The assets that Le Château lists in its balance sheet include cash and cash equivalents, accounts receivable and prepaid expenses, inventories, loan to director (in the Current section and in the long-term section), and fixed assets. The "cash equivalents" are usually very short-term investments that can be converted into cash very quickly. The "note to director" indicates that a director owes money to the company. Some of the loan will be paid back within the next year (the current part) and the rest will be paid sometime beyond the next year. For more information about the note, look up Note 4 on page LC-19. A full discussion of how each of these assets meets the criteria of ownership and probable future value is left to later chapters. As an example, however, ownership of inventory by the company is evidenced either by possession of the inventory or by legal documentation. It has future value because the company can later sell the inventory and receive cash in the amount of the selling price. The presence of the inventory or the underlying documents of the purchase indicates that the event that gave ownership to the company has already happened.

The total assets of Le Château as at January 31, 2004, were $94,546 thousand. Following is a list of assets normally found in a balance sheet.

COMMON BALANCE SHEET ASSETS

Cash	The amount of currency that the company has, including amounts in bank accounts.
Short-Term (Temporary) Investments	Short-term investments in securities of other companies, such as treasury bills, shares, and bonds.
Accounts Receivable	Amounts owed to the company that result from credit sales to customers.
Inventory	Goods held for resale to customers.
Prepaid Expenses	Expenses related to items that have been paid for but have not yet been used. An example is insurance that is paid in advance.
Capital Assets	Investments in land, buildings, and intangibles that the company uses over the long term. Fixed assets are investments in land, buildings, and equipment. Intangibles are investments in assets such as patents, trademarks, and goodwill.

Le Château prepares a **classified balance sheet**. A classified balance sheet is one in which the assets and liabilities are classified as **current** and **noncurrent**. For assets, "current" means that the asset will be turned into cash or be consumed (used up) in the next year or operating cycle. The **operating cycle** of a company refers to the time period between the initial investment of cash in products or services and the return of cash from the sale of the product or service.

Assets such as cash, accounts receivable, and inventories are classified as current, and assets such as capital assets (fixed assets in the case of Le Château) are classified as noncurrent. Assets and liabilities are listed on the balance sheet in liquidity order. **Liquidity** refers to how quickly the company can turn the asset into cash or will use the cash to settle an outstanding liability. Noncurrent assets are the least liquid because they will be used over a long period of time and will not be quickly turned into cash. Accounts receivable, on the other hand, are amounts owed to the company by its customers who bought goods or services on credit. Normally, these will be collected quickly. Therefore, accounts receivable are fairly liquid. In the case of Le Château, its accounts receivable are from credit card sales. It will be collecting the credit card amounts from companies such as VISA or MasterCard within a few days. Inventories are less liquid than receivables since they must be sold first, which often results in an account receivable. Cash is then received when the account receivable is collected.

An **unclassified balance sheet** is, then, a balance sheet in which current assets or liabilities are not distinguished from noncurrent assets or liabilities. Even in an unclassified balance sheet, however, assets and liabilities are still listed primarily in the order of their liquidity. For instance, the cash, receivables and prepaid expenses, inventories, loan to director, and fixed assets will have the same order as in the Le Château report even if they are not specifically identified as current or noncurrent.

Liabilities A simple definition of liabilities might be amounts that the company owes to others. The accounting definition of liabilities encompasses this concept and, consistent with the earlier definition of assets, will be used to refer to items that require a probable future sacrifice of resources. In most cases, the resource is cash, but a company could satisfy a liability with services or goods. For example, a warranty liability could be satisfied with a new part or with the services of a repairperson.

Le Château, in its classified balance sheet (refer to Exhibit 1-4), lists among its liabilities accounts payable and accrued liabilities, dividend payable, income taxes payable, current portion of capital lease obligations, current portion of long-term debt, capital lease obligations, long-term debt, future income tax, and deferred lease inducements. Note that Le Château labels the current liabilities as such, and then lists the long-term liabilities in a separate section in its balance sheet. Current liabilities are those that will require the use of current assets or will be replaced by another current liability in the next year or operating cycle. The following list includes some of the more common liabilities found in financial statements.

COMMON BALANCE SHEET LIABILITIES

Bank Indebtedness	Amounts owed to the bank on short-term credit.
Accounts Payable	Amounts owed to suppliers from the purchase of goods on credit.
Notes Payable	Amounts owed to a creditor (bank or supplier) that are represented by a formal agreement called a note (sometimes called a promissory note). Notes payable often have an interest component whereas accounts payable usually do not.
Dividends Payable	Amounts owed to shareholders for dividends that are declared by the board of directors.
Accrued Liabilities	Amounts owed to others based on expenses that have been incurred by the company but are not yet due, such as interest expense and warranty expense.
Income Taxes Payable	Amounts owed to taxing authorities.
Long-Term Debt	Amounts owed to creditors over periods longer than one year.
Future Income Tax Liabilities	Amounts representing probable future taxes the company will have to pay (sometimes called deferred taxes).

Shareholders' Equity The last major category in the balance sheet is the section called equity. It is frequently referred to as shareholders' equity. In Le Château's section on shareholders' equity, note the listings for capital stock and retained earnings. This section captures the value of the shareholders' interest in the company as measured by the accounting recommendations and guidelines. Note that the total assets equal the total liabilities plus the equity. Both are listed as $94,546 thousand by Le Château on January 31, 2004. This relationship is described by the basic accounting equation.

BASIC ACCOUNTING EQUATION

Assets = Liabilities + Shareholders' Equity

This equation gives meaning to the description of this statement as the balance sheet. If the equation is rearranged, you can see that shareholders' equity is equal to assets minus liabilities.

BASIC ACCOUNTING EQUATION (REARRANGED)

Shareholders' Equity = Assets − Liabilities
(Net Assets)

To state this relationship another way, shareholders' equity is the difference between what the investors own and what the company owes to others, as measured in the **accounting records**. Because of this relationship, shareholders' equity is sometimes referred to as the net assets of the company ("net" refers to the assets' net value less the liabilities) or the net book value of the company. It is the equivalent to an individual's personal net wealth. The shareholders' wealth as measured by the accounting statements is a residual concept. The shareholders can claim the assets that are left over after paying all the liabilities.

You should note that the shares' market value is another measure of the shareholders' wealth in the company. By **market value**, we mean the price at which the shares trade in the stock market. This value could be very different from the book value of shareholders' equity because accounting records are not necessarily based on market values.

We can look at the proportion of liabilities and shareholders' equity on the balance sheet to better understand the financing strategy used by the company. For Le Château, total liabilities are $33,384 thousand and total shareholders' equity is $61,162 thousand, for a total of $94,546 thousand. The proportion of liabilities is 36% ($33,384 ÷ $94,546), which is less than half the total financing. This means that Le Château uses more shareholders' equity than debt to finance activities in the company. Specifically, it derives 65% of its financing from shareholders' equity.

Shareholders' equity is generally made up of two accounts: **share capital** and retained earnings. The first, share capital (Le Château uses the term **capital stock**), is used to record the amount that the investors originally paid (invested) for the shares that the company issued. The second account, retained earnings, is used to keep track of the company's earnings less any amounts that are paid from the company to the shareholders in the form of dividends. Dividends will be paid to shareholders only when approved by a vote of the board of directors. The change in a company's retained earnings during a given period can be explained by the net income less the dividends declared, as follows.

CHANGE IN RETAINED EARNINGS

Change in Retained Earnings = Net Income − Dividends

Other accounts can appear in this section. During the early part of this book, these other accounts will be ignored in order to concentrate on share capital and retained earnings. The other accounts will be discussed in later sections of the book. Following is a list of some of the more common account titles that appear in the shareholders' equity section.

COMMON BALANCE SHEET
SHAREHOLDERS' EQUITY ACCOUNTS

Share Capital	Represents the shares that have been issued by the company and is usually stated at an amount equal to what was originally paid by investors for the shares. This can be referred to as capital stock. Shares can be of different types, with different rights and privileges attached to each.
Retained Earnings	The company's earnings (as measured on the Income Statement) that have been kept (retained) and not paid out in the form of dividends.

CASH FLOW STATEMENT The cash flow statement, sometimes called the **statement of cash flows** or the **statement of changes in financial position**, is a flow statement that is, in some ways, similar to the income statement. Le Château's consolidated statement of cash flows is included in Exhibit 1-5. It measures inflows and outflows of cash during a specific period of time. Note how the words at the top of the statement indicate that the statement is for the years ended January 31, 2004, and January 25, 2003, which is the same terminology used on the income statement. The difference is that instead of measuring the increase and decrease in shareholders' wealth, this statement measures the increase and decrease in cash and highly liquid assets and liabilities called "cash equivalents." Remember that a liquid item is one that can be converted very quickly to cash. Since cash is very important to the company's operations, this statement is vital to any user's evaluation of a business.

The cash flow statement has three sections that report the sources and uses of cash and cash equivalents for the three business activities described earlier: operating, financing, and investing.

SUBSECTIONS OF THE CASH FLOW STATEMENT

Cash from operating activities

Cash from financing activities

Cash from investing activities

In order to evaluate a company's liquidity position, users need to evaluate where cash is coming from and where it is being spent. Le Château generated a positive cash flow of $19,158 thousand from its operating activities in 2004.

Operating activities include all inflows and outflows of cash related to the company's sale of goods and services. The starting point in this section is net income (net earnings), which is a summary of the income from operating activities from the income statement. There are adjustments to this number because the recognition of revenues and expenses (as will be seen in future chapters) does not necessarily coincide with the receipt and payment of cash. For instance, sales could be either cash sales or sales on account (i.e., customers can pay at a later date,

EXHIBIT 1-5 **LE CHÂTEAU INC. 2003 ANNUAL REPORT**

CONSOLIDATED STATEMENTS OF CASH FLOWS

Year ended January 31, 2004

[With comparative figures for the year ended January 25, 2003]
[In thousands of dollars]

	2004 $	2003 $
OPERATING ACTIVITIES		
Net earnings	**10,648**	7,562
Adjustments to determine net cash from operating activities		
Depreciation and amortization	**7,745**	6,937
Write-off of fixed assets	**511**	281
Amortization of deferred lease inducements	**(463)**	(393)
Future income taxes	**(130)**	116
	18,311	14,503
Net change in non-cash working capital items related to operations [note 13]	**847**	1,526
Cash flows from operating activities	**19,158**	16,029
FINANCING ACTIVITIES		
Repayment of loan to director	**—**	120
Proceeds of capital leases	**5,620**	—
Repayment of capital lease obligations	**(1,355)**	(1,537)
Proceeds of long-term debt	**—**	2,500
Repayment of long-term debt	**(1,483)**	(1,210)
Deferred lease inducements	**481**	82
Issue of capital stock	**1,094**	235
Dividends paid	**(2,050)**	(1,990)
Cash flows from financing activities	**2,307**	(1,800)
INVESTING ACTIVITIES		
Additions to fixed assets	**(14,438)**	(9,019)
Cash flows from investing activities	**(14,438)**	(9,019)
Increase in cash and cash equivalents	**7,027**	5,210
Cash and cash equivalents, beginning of year	**15,040**	9,830
Cash and cash equivalents, end of year	**22,067**	15,040
Supplementary information:		
Interest paid during the year	**339**	350
Income taxes paid during the year, net	**7,473**	3,555

See accompanying notes

resulting in an accounts receivable rather than cash). Expenses may also be paid later if the company is given credit by its suppliers (this would result in an account payable). Because operating activities are the backbone of the company, a positive cash flow from operations is essential to its health. Le Château's liquidity position improved from the previous year, when its cash flow from operations was $16,029 thousand.

The positive cash flow of $2,307 thousand from **financing activities** indicates that Le Château brought in more cash from outside sources than it used; the proceeds from capital leases ($5,620 thousand) and the issuing of shares ($1,094 thousand) exceeded the repayment of lease obligations ($1,355 thousand), the repayment of long-term debt ($1,483 thousand), and the payment of dividends ($2,050 thousand). Financing activities, as you will recall, are those transactions that either generate new funds from investors or return funds to investors. Investors can be either shareholders or lenders, and the typical activities in this category are the issuance and repurchase of shares and the issuance and repayment of debt.

Investing activities generally involve the purchase and sale of long-term assets such as property, plant, and equipment, and investments in other companies. One of these activities can be seen from the disclosure by Le Château. The negative cash flow of $14,438 thousand from investing activities results solely from the investment in new fixed assets during the year. In the future, the company will use these assets for operating activities. It is important to note that Le Château did not need to go to outside sources to pay for its investment in fixed assets. It generated sufficient cash from its operating activities to pay for them. If the current year is an indicator of future results, the future operating activities will generate a positive cash flow and the company's investment in new fixed assets will have been a worthwhile investment. These amounts in 2004 indicate that Le Château is doing quite well with respect to cash flow.

The preparation and interpretation of the cash flow statement is discussed in greater detail in Chapter 5. Until you study the statement in more detail, confine your study of this statement to understanding what its three sections are measuring.

SUMMARY OF FINANCIAL STATEMENTS

Income Statement
- Measures the operating performance of a company over a period of time.

Balance Sheet
- Measures the resources controlled by a company (assets) and the claims on those resources (liability and equity holders) at a given point in time.

Cash Flow Statement
- Measures the change in cash flow through operating, financing, and investing activities over a period of time.

NOTES TO THE FINANCIAL STATEMENTS   You may have noticed that various items in the financial statements direct the reader to specific notes. In such notes to the financial statements (LC-17 to LC-27), management has a chance to provide more detail about the referenced items. For example, on Le Château's income statement, the income taxes item includes a reference to Note 9. Note 9 goes into greater detail about taxes owed, future income taxes, and tax rates. Financial statements are thus kept simple and uncluttered by including additional explanations in notes rather than on the financial statements themselves. A full discussion of notes will be left to succeeding chapters, but some attention should be paid to the note that discusses the Accounting Policies. It is usually the first note, as it is in Le Château's financial statements. Within GAAP there are choices and judgements to be made by management. This note describes the choices that were made by this particular company. The auditors, of course, review these choices for conformity with GAAP.

As you progress through the book, you will learn that the choices made by management have important implications for the interpretation of the statements.

As an example, note how on page LC-17, Le Château's raw materials and work-in-process inventories (those it uses to make the garments it sells) are valued at the lower of specific cost and net realizable value, whereas its finished goods inventory (the finished garments that it sells) are valued using the retail inventory method. These are acceptable methods under GAAP for valuing inventory, but there are other alternatives that are also acceptable. Valuing the inventory under these methods will produce a different balance in the inventory account on the balance sheet, and a different net income on the income statement, from that produced by a similar company using an alternative method. Comparing two companies that use two different methods would pose difficulties. To aid users in comparing various companies, management must disclose the major accounting policies in this note.

SEGMENTED INFORMATION   Information about various segments of the company is provided as a part of the notes to the financial statements. This is a requirement for any company that has more than one significant segment. A segment represents a business activity. Le Château has only one operating segment: the retail of apparel. However, it made sales outside of Canada, which means that it has to report the percentage of those sales (see page LC-26). This information is important to users because it helps to explain the kinds of risks an investor takes when buying Le Château's shares. Segments can differ significantly with regard to risk and are affected in different ways by economic factors such as commodity prices, inflation, exchange rates, and interest rates. It is important to know the relative amounts invested in these segments if an overall assessment of the company's risk is to be made. Because companies produce consolidated financial statements that provide aggregate information, it would be difficult to assess segment risks without this additional information.

LEARNING OBJECTIVE 9

Begin to understand the role of ethics in financial accounting.

**Ethics in
Accounting**

ethics in accounting

The management of a company, through the direction given to it by the board of directors, has both a moral and a legal obligation to safeguard the investment shareholders have entrusted to it. To ensure that management fulfills this stewardship function with regard to company resources, shareholders typically provide some incentives for and controls over management. You have probably heard about stock option plans and bonuses given to top management. These additional compensation arrangements are often tied to the company's financial performance and provide incentives for management to make decisions that are in the best interests of the shareholders.

Sometimes bonus compensation is given in years when the financial performance is down. When this occurs, shareholders and others often question the ethics of the decision. For example, in November 2003, **Air Canada** announced a compensation package for its CEO and its chief reconstruction officer that totalled $21 million in shares over four years. At the time, Air Canada was under bankruptcy protection and had already negotiated deals with its employees to accept lower wages and with its creditors to accept less than what was owed to them.

Source: "Air Canada executives pay causes turbulence," by Allan Swift, *Financial Post*, November 17, 2003, p. FP5.

STATEMENT OF MANAGEMENT'S RESPONSIBILITY   This section contains a statement by management that it is responsible for the contents of the annual report. In addition, it discusses the steps management has taken to ensure the safe-keeping of the company's assets and to assure the shareholders that management is operating in an ethical and responsible way. Review Exhibit 1-6, Le Château's statement of management's responsibility, to see what a typical statement contains.

LE CHÂTEAU INC. 2003 ANNUAL REPORT

EXHIBIT 1-6

CONSOLIDATED FINANCIAL STATEMENTS

MANAGEMENT'S RESPONSIBILITY
For Financial Information

The accompanying consolidated financial statements of Le Château Inc. and all the information in this annual report are the responsibility of management.

The financial statements have been prepared by management in accordance with Canadian generally accepted accounting principles. When alternative accounting methods exist, management has chosen those it deems most appropriate in the circumstances. Financial statements are not precise since they include certain amounts based on estimates and judgement. Management has determined such amounts on a reasonable basis in order to ensure that the financial statements are presented fairly, in all material respects. Management has prepared the financial information presented elsewhere in the Annual Report and has ensured that it is consistent with that in the financial statements.

The Company maintains systems of internal accounting and administrative controls of high quality, consistent with reasonable cost. Such systems are designed to provide reasonable assurance that the financial information is relevant, reliable and accurate and the Company's assets are appropriately accounted for and adequately safeguarded.

The Board of Directors is responsible for ensuring that management fulfills its responsibilities for financial reporting and is ultimately responsible for reviewing and approving the financial statements. The Board carries out this responsibility principally through the Audit Committee which consists of three outside directors appointed by the Board. The Committee meets quarterly with management as well as with the independent external auditors to discuss internal controls over the financial reporting process, auditing matters and financial reporting issues. The Committee reviews the consolidated financial statements and the external auditors' report thereon and reports its findings to the Board for consideration when the Board approves the financial statements for issuance to the Company's share-holders. The Committee also considers, for review by the Board and approval by the shareholders, the engagement or re-appointment of the external auditors. The external auditors have full and free access to the Audit Committee.

On behalf of the shareholders, the financial statements have been audited by Ernst & Young LLP, the external auditors, in accordance with Canadian generally accepted auditing standards.

Herschel H. Segal
Chairman of the Board and
Chief Executive Officer

Emilia Di Raddo, CA
President and Secretary

AUDITORS' REPORT
To the Shareholders of Le Château Inc.

We have audited the consolidated balance sheets of Le Château Inc., as at January 31, 2004 and January 25, 2003 and the consolidated statements of retained earnings, earnings and cash flows for the years then ended. These financial statements are the responsibility of the Company's management. Our responsibility is to express an opinion on these financial statements based on our audits.

We conducted our audits in accordance with Canadian generally accepted auditing standards. Those standards require that we plan and perform an audit to obtain reasonable assurance whether the financial statements are free of material misstatement. An audit includes examining, on a test basis, evidence supporting the amounts and disclosures in the financial statements. An audit also includes assessing the accounting principles used and significant estimates made by management, as well as evaluating the overall financial statement presentation.

In our opinion, these consolidated financial statements present fairly, in all material respects, the financial position of the Company as at January 31, 2004 and January 25, 2003 and the results of its operations and its cash flows for the years then ended in accordance with Canadian generally accepted accounting principles.

Ernst & Young LLP

Montreal, Canada
March 25, 2004

Chartered Accountants

INDEPENDENT AUDITORS' REPORT   It is important to remember that the financial statements are prepared by the company's management. They are reporting on the results of their management of activities. Because shareholders do not participate in the day-to-day activities of the company, it is impossible for them to evaluate the validity of the financial statements. To provide them with an external evaluation of the financial statements, the shareholders hire independent auditors to provide an opinion about the fairness of the presentation and the conformity to accounting guidelines. **Auditors** are professionally trained accountants who add credibility to the financial statements by expressing their professional opinion as to whether the financial statements fairly present the company's results. The auditors review the financial statements, visit the company to verify various procedures and confirm the reasonableness of financial numbers, and investigate any discrepancies that may arise in the process of their investigation. Because they are independent from the company and are knowledgeable about the requirements of GAAP, they can provide assurance to the shareholders that GAAP has been followed in the preparation of the statements.

Companies such as Le Château are not audited by one person alone, but by a firm of auditors. Auditors apply a set of procedures to test the financial statements to determine if they comply with generally accepted accounting principles and to assess the fairness of the presentation. Audit reports are often expressed in a standard format of three paragraphs. The first paragraph states which financial statements have been audited, that the financial statements are the responsibility of management, and that the auditors' responsibility is to express an opinion about the financial statements. The second paragraph explains how the auditors conducted the audit using generally accepted auditing standards. The third paragraph is the auditors' opinion about the financial statements. The audit report of Le Château (Exhibit 1-6) follows this format. A standard format like this is called an **unqualified opinion**. It means that the financial statements present fairly, in all material respects, the financial position, results of operations, and cash flows of the entity in conformity with generally accepted accounting principles.

In Canada the unqualified or **clean opinion** is the most commonly seen audit opinion. Companies prefer to have a clean opinion attached to their financial statements. If the auditors are considering an opinion other than an unqualified one, management is informed about the reason(s) for the opinion prior to the issuance of the financial statements. Management then has an opportunity to change the financial statements to resolve the problem(s) the auditors have detected. If the issue is controversial, there may be some negotiation between management and the auditors as to how best to resolve the problem. If no resolution is reached and management decides to issue the statements as originally prepared, a **qualified** or **adverse opinion** will be included with the statements. This rarely happens in practice because the problems are usually resolved prior to statement issuance. As the article below indicates, sometimes the auditors withdraw from an audit if they do not think they can find enough information to verify the amounts on the financial statements.

In any set of financial statements, the auditors' report should be read because it can alert the reader to major problems the company may be experiencing. In other words, it can provide a red flag. Readers must then investigate further to make their own assessments of the extent of the problems the company is facing. Also, it is important to recognize that there may be significant problems that the auditors did not identify with their tests or that are beyond the responsibility of the auditors.

accounting in the news

AUDITORS RESIGN BEFORE CERTIFYING STATEMENTS

In relatively rare cases, a company is not able to provide audited financial statements. In January 2001, **Ernst & Young LLP** resigned as auditors to **CINAR Corporation** after the company indicated that "its management will not be able, until at least the completion of fiscal 2001, to make the necessary representations regarding the accuracy of the Company's financial statements." The financial statements for the years ended November 30, 1999 and 2000 had not been audited. Throughout 2001, the company produced unaudited financial statements for its shareholders. In November 2001, it announced that new auditors had been hired.

Source: News Releases from CINAR Corporation by L. Sansregret, VP Investor Relations and Public Affairs, January 26, 2001, and November 26, 2001.

An unqualified opinion means that the financial statements are a fair representation of the company's financial position. It is up to the user to determine what the financial position is by reading the statements carefully.

The Changing Face of the Large Public Accounting Firms

Most large companies are audited by large accounting firms because of the size and expertise needed on the audit team. Until the late 1980s, the eight largest accounting firms were known as the Big Eight. The Big Eight audited virtually all the large companies in Canada and, as international firms themselves, many companies in other parts of the world. In the late 1980s, two mergers among the Big Eight resulted in what became known as the Big Six. In 1998 a merger between two of the Big Six, **Price Waterhouse** and **Coopers & Lybrand**, was finalized to form **PricewaterhouseCoopers**, the largest public accounting firm in Canada. This created the Big Five. In 2001, however, in the United States, **Enron**, which was audited by one of the Big Five, **Arthur Andersen**, went bankrupt. In the subsequent investigation, it was determined that the auditors had shredded Enron documents; Andersen was thus charged with obstruction of justice and found guilty. Andersen no longer carries an accounting practitioner licence in the United States. The remaining Big Four firms are, in alphabetical order, **Deloitte & Touche**, **Ernst & Young**, **KPMG**, and PricewaterhouseCoopers. There are also several large and medium-sized national accounting firms that perform audits in Canada.

In Canada, there are three professional accounting organizations that establish the professional standards followed by accountants. The members of the Canadian Institute of Chartered Accountants are called Chartered Accountants (CAs), CMA Canada is the organization of the Certified Management Accountants (CMAs), and the Certified General Accountants Association of Canada establishes the standards for the Certified General Accountants (CGAs). These professional accountants perform audits, supervise and perform accounting functions inside organizations, and provide decision-making functions inside and outside organizations. Canada is one of the few countries in the world that has more than one professional accounting body. In the past, there have been attempts to combine the three bodies into one, but so far these attempts have been unsuccessful. At the time of the writing of this book, the Canadian Institute of Chartered Accountants and CMA Canada were discussing a merger.

What do professional accountants do? Accountants, whether they are in public practice (i.e., work in an accounting firm) or in industry, government, or education, provide their clients and employers with information and advice so that they can make effective, informed decisions. They are often strategic advisors who are part of a company's management team. Much of the day-to-day recording of transactions and events is not performed by accountants, although some of them may have some supervisory role over those who do perform this function. Today, most financial information is collected in computer systems that enable the rapid summarization of the data into financial statements and other reports. Computer systems enable managers to access financial information as often as they want. With up-to-the-minute data, financial statements can be updated in real time.

Ethics in Accounting

ethics in accounting

Auditors are hired by the shareholders to review the financial statements presented to the shareholders by the company's management. The auditors, as they conduct their review, must maintain their independence from the company's management team. In order to ensure their independence and encourage ethical behaviour, the professional accounting organizations have developed codes of professional conduct. The codes state the responsibilities of professional accountants to the public, clients, and colleagues. For example, accountants normally cannot audit companies in which they own shares. In addition, the codes describe the scope and nature of the services provided by auditors. Each professional accounting organization has also developed a peer review process to monitor its members in the performance of audit work.

SUMMARY

In this chapter, we discussed what a business is, what accounting is, and what financial statements are. We looked at the activities in which companies engage. We discussed the various users of financial accounting information and provided an overview of the types of information that they would need. We included a brief introduction to the development of accounting standards that underlie accounting recommendations and guidelines so that you can begin to understand the basic concepts that govern how we collect and report financial information.

The majority of the chapter was used to provide a detailed explanation of the various components of an annual report, using Le Château Inc. as an example. In the annual report, you discovered the information components of three major financial statements: the income statement, balance sheet, and cash flow statement. Subsequent chapters will build on this framework. In Chapters 2 through 5, the mechanics of preparing these statements and more information about their decision-making value are discussed. Details of individual asset, liability, and shareholders' equity accounts are discussed in Chapters 6 through 11. Chapter 12 considers financial statement analysis to provide some tools to interpret and link the major financial statements. Throughout the book we will be introducing ratios as they pertain to the chapter topic under discussion. In Chapter 1, we introduced the ratio of liabilities to the total of liabilities plus shareholders' equity. This ratio tells you to what extent the company is using debt and equity to finance its activities. To provide some understanding of complex business organizations and the major accounting issues related to mergers, acquisitions, and consolidated financial statements, Appendix B goes into these issues.

Additional Demonstration Problems

SUMMARY PROBLEM

The major financial statements of **Petro-Canada** from its 2003 annual report are included in Exhibit 1-7.

EXHIBIT 1-7
PART A

PETRO CANADA 2003 ANNUAL REPORT

Consolidated Statement of Earnings

For the years ended December 31,	2003	2002	2001
REVENUE			
Operating	**$ 12 209**	$ 9 917	$ 8 582
Investment and other income *(Note 4)*	**12**	–	154
	12 221	9 917	8 736
EXPENSES			
Crude oil and product purchases	**5 098**	4 556	4 687
Operating, marketing and general *(Note 5)*	**2 407**	2 036	1 670
Exploration *(Note 14)*	**271**	301	245
Depreciation, depletion and amortization *(Notes 5 and 14)*	**1 539**	957	568
Foreign currency translation *(Note 6)*	**(251)**	52	102
Interest	**182**	187	135
	9 246	8 089	7 407
EARNINGS BEFORE INCOME TAXES	**2 975**	1 828	1 329
PROVISION FOR INCOME TAXES *(Note 7)*			
Current	**1 247**	959	528
Future	**59**	(105)	(45)
	1 306	854	483
NET EARNINGS	**$ 1 669**	$ 974	$ 846
EARNINGS PER SHARE *(dollars) (Note 8)*			
Basic	**$ 6.30**	$ 3.71	$ 3.19
Diluted	**$ 6.23**	$ 3.67	$ 3.16

1. Find the following amounts in the statements:
    a. Total revenues in 2003
    b. Total operating costs (from crude oil and product purchases through to depreciation, depletion, and amortization) in 2003
    c. Interest expense in 2003
    d. Income tax expense (current and future) in 2003
    e. Net income (earnings) in 2003
    f. Inventories at the end of 2003

EXHIBIT 1-7
PART B

PETRO CANADA 2003 ANNUAL REPORT

Consolidated Statement of Cash Flows

For the years ended December 31.	2003	2002	2001
OPERATING ACTIVITIES			
Net earnings	$ 1 669	$ 974	$ 846
Items not affecting cash flow (Note 9)	1 432	1 001	597
Exploration expenses (Note 14)	271	301	245
Cash flow	3 372	2 276	1 688
(Increase) decrease in non-cash working capital			
related to operating activities and other (Note 10)	(164)	(226)	55
Cash flow from operating activities	3 208	2 050	1 743
INVESTING ACTIVITIES			
Expenditures on property, plant and			
equipment and exploration (Note 14)	(2 315)	(1 861)	(1 681)
Proceeds from sales of assets	165	26	127
Increase in deferred charges and other assets, net	(147)	(72)	(10)
Decrease (increase) in non-cash working capital related to			
investing activities (Note 10)	94	(16)	96
Acquisition of oil and gas operations of			
Veba Oil & Gas GmbH (Note 11)	–	(2 234)	–
	(2 203)	(4 157)	(1 468)
FINANCING ACTIVITIES			
Proceeds from issue of long-term debt	804	2 100	–
Reduction of long-term debt	(1 352)	(465)	(475)
Proceeds from issue of common shares	50	30	34
Dividends on common shares	(106)	(105)	(106)
Purchase of common shares (Note 18)	–	–	(362)
	(604)	1 560	(909)
INCREASE (DECREASE) IN CASH AND CASH EQUIVALENTS	401	(547)	(634)
CASH AND CASH EQUIVALENTS AT BEGINNING OF YEAR	234	781	1 415
CASH AND CASH EQUIVALENTS AT END OF YEAR (Note 12)	$ 635	$ 234	$ 781

    g. Accounts payable and accrued liabilities at the beginning of 2003

    h. Shareholders' equity at the end of 2003

    i. Future income taxes at the beginning of 2003

    j. Cash provided from operating activities in 2003

    k. Cash payments, net of disposals (sales), to acquire capital assets in 2003

    l. Dividends paid in 2003

    m. Cash proceeds from issuing new shares in 2003

    n. Cash provided from (used for) investing activities in 2003

2. Does Petro-Canada finance its business primarily with debt or with shareholders' equity? Support your answer with appropriate data.

3. List the two largest sources of cash and the two largest uses of cash in 2003. (Consider operating activities to be a single source or use of cash.)

4. Does Petro-Canada use a classified balance sheet? Explain.

PETRO CANADA 2003 ANNUAL REPORT

EXHIBIT 1-7
PART C

Consolidated Balance Sheet

As at December 31,	2003	2002
ASSETS		
CURRENT ASSETS		
Cash and cash equivalents *(Note 12)*	$ 635	$ 234
Accounts receivable	1 503	1 596
Inventories *(Note 13)*	551	585
Prepaid expenses	16	19
	2 705	2 434
PROPERTY, PLANT AND EQUIPMENT, NET *(Note 14)*	10 759	10 084
GOODWILL *(Note 11)*	810	709
DEFERRED CHARGES AND OTHER ASSETS *(Note 15)*	316	212
	$ 14 590	$ 13 439
LIABILITIES AND SHAREHOLDERS' EQUITY		
CURRENT LIABILITIES		
Accounts payable and accrued liabilities	$ 1 822	$ 1 901
Income taxes payable	300	263
Current portion of long-term debt *(Note 16)*	6	356
	2 128	2 520
LONG-TERM DEBT *(Note 16)*	2 223	2 701
DEFERRED CREDITS AND OTHER LIABILITIES *(Note 17)*	688	621
FUTURE INCOME TAXES *(Note 7)*	1 830	1 821
COMMITMENTS AND CONTINGENT LIABILITIES *(Note 22)*		
SHAREHOLDERS' EQUITY *(Note 18)*	7 721	5 776
	$ 14 590	$ 13 439

Approved on behalf of the Board

R. A. Brenneman
Director

B. F. MacNeill
Director

SUGGESTED SOLUTION TO SUMMARY PROBLEM

All answers are in millions of dollars unless otherwise stated.

1. The following answers are found on the financial statements included in Exhibit 1-7:
   a. Total revenues in 2003: $12,221 million
   b. Operating costs in 2003: $10,315 million ($6,098 + $2,407 + $271 + $1,539)
   c. Interest expense in 2003: $182 million
   d. Income tax expense in 2003: $1,306 million ($1,247 + $59)
   e. Net income (earnings) in 2003: $1,669 million
   f. Inventories at the end of 2003: $551 million
   g. Accounts payable and accrued liabilities at the beginning of 2003: $1,901 million
      (the end of 2002 is the same as the beginning of 2003)

    h. Shareholders' equity at the end of 2003: $7,721 million

    i. Future income taxes at the beginning of 2003: $1,821 million

    j. Cash provided from operating activities in 2003: $3,208 million

    k. Cash payments, net of disposals (sales), to acquire capital assets in 2003: ($2,150 million) (expenditures on property, plant, and equipment and exploration less Proceeds from sales of assets, under the investing activities). Putting the amount in parentheses indicates that it is a negative number.

    l. Dividends paid in 2003: ($106 million) (listed under the financing activities on the Statement of Cash Flows)

    m. Cash proceeds from issuing new shares in 2003: $50 million

    n. Cash provided from investing activities in 2003: ($2,203 million)

2. Petro-Canada uses marginally more shareholders' equity than liabilities to finance its business. You can see this when you compare the total liabilities with the total liabilities plus shareholders' equity (on the balance sheet) as shown below.

Total liabilities (12/31/03): $6,869 million

Total shareholders' equity (12/31/03): $7,721 million

Total liabilities and shareholders' equity: $14,590 million

Total liabilities are, therefore, 47% ($6,869 ÷ $14,590) of the total sources of financing for Petro-Canada.

3. The two largest sources of cash are proceeds from the operating activities, $3,208 million, and proceeds from the issuance of debt, $804 million. The two largest uses are the expenditures on property, plant, and equipment and exploration ($1,861 million), and the reduction of long-term debt ($1,352 million).

4. Petro-Canada does use a classified balance sheet. It has labelled a section for current assets and current liabilities but not for the noncurrent assets and liabilities. It has included the noncurrent assets and liabilities in bold type after the total of the current assets and liabilities. It has not, however, given you a total for the non-current assets or liabilities.

ABBREVIATIONS USED

AcSB	Accounting Standards Board	IAS	International Accounting Standards
CA	Chartered Accountant		
CGA	Certified General Accountant	IASB	International Accounting Standards Board
CICA	Canadian Institute of Chartered Accountants	IFAC	International Federation of Accountants
CMA	Certified Management Accountant	IFRS	International Financial Reporting Standards
CRA	Canada Revenue Agency		
FASB	Financial Accounting Standards Board	OSC	Ontario Securities Commission
GAAP	Generally accepted accounting principles		

SYNONYMS

Balance sheet equation/Accounting equation

Books/Accounting records/Accounting information system

Capital assets/Property, plant, and equipment/Plant assets/Fixed assets

Cash Flow Statement/Statement of Changes in Financial Position/Statement of Cash Flows

Common shares/Share capital/Capital stock

Earnings Statement/Statement of Earnings/Income Statement/Profit and Loss Statement/Statement of Operations

Equity/Owners' equity/Shareholders' equity

Liabilities/Debt/Obligations

Managerial accounting/Cost accounting

Net income/Profit/Net earnings

Retained earnings/Earnings retained in the business/Earnings reinvested in the business

GLOSSARY

Accounting records   The accounting system (usually computerized) in which financial transactions are recorded and stored.

Accounting Standards Board (AcSB)   The CICA committee that sets accounting standards in Canada.

Adverse opinion   Synonym for qualified opinion.

Amortization   The expense taken each period based on the use of a noncurrent asset, such as equipment. Amortization is the process that uses a systematic and rational method to allocate the cost of a noncurrent asset to each of the years of its useful life.

Annual report   An annual document prepared and published by a corporation in which it reports on its business activities during the year. The report includes the corporation's annual financial statements.

Assets   Elements of the balance sheet that have probable future benefits that can be measured, are owned or controlled by the company, and are the result of a past transaction.

Auditor   A professionally trained accountant who examines a company's accounting records and financial statements to determine whether they fairly present the company's financial position and operating results in accordance with GAAP.

Balance sheet   A financial statement showing a company's asset, liability, and shareholders' equity account balances at a specific point in time.

Basic accounting equation   The equation that describes the relationship between assets, liabilities, and shareholders' equity. It is as follows: Assets = Liabilities + Shareholders' Equity.

Benefit vs. cost constraint   A constraint that states that the cost of implementing a new accounting standard should be less than the benefits that will be derived.

Board of directors   The governing body of a company elected by the shareholders to represent their ownership interests.

Books   The accounting records of a company. Usually this term refers to the records reported to shareholders rather than to any other body, such as the tax authority.

Capital stock   Synonym for share capital.

Cash flow statement   A financial statement that shows the cash flows of a company during the accounting period, categorized into operating, investing, and financing activities.

Classified balance sheet   A balance sheet in which the assets and liabilities are listed in liquidity order and are categorized into current and noncurrent sections.

Clean opinion   Synonym for unqualified opinion.

Common shares   The shares issued by a company to its owners. Shares represent the ownership interest in a company.

Comparability   A quality of accounting information that improves the ability of financial statement readers to compare different sets of financial statements.

Conceptual framework   The framework set out in the *CICA Handbook* to guide the AcSB as it sets new accounting standards.

Conservatism   A quality of accounting information stating that when estimates are made in financial statements, they should err on the side of understating rather than overstating net assets and net income.

Consolidated financial statements   Financial statements that represent the combined financial results of a parent company and its subsidiaries.

Cost accounting   A branch of accounting that studies how cost information is used internally within the company.

Creditors Individuals or entities that are owed something by the company.

Current asset/liability For assets, current means that the asset will be turned into cash or consumed in the next year or operating cycle of a company. For liabilities, current means that the liability will require the use of cash or the rendering of a service, or will be replaced by another current liability, within the next year or operating cycle of the company.

Dividends Payments made to shareholders that represent a return on their investment in a company. Dividends are paid only after they are declared by the board of directors.

Earnings Synonym for net income.

Earnings per share A ratio calculated by dividing the earnings for the period by the average number of shares outstanding during the period.

Entity The business reported by the financial statements, usually a company.

Equity A term sometimes used to describe the sum of liabilities and shareholders' equity; sometimes also used to refer simply to the shareholders' equity section, which can lead to some confusion in the use of this term.

Expenses The resources used in the production of revenues by a company, representing decreases in the shareholders' wealth.

Feedback value A quality of accounting information that gives it relevance to decision-makers. The information provides feedback on previous decisions.

Financial accounting The study of the accounting concepts and principles used to prepare financial statements for external users.

Financial Accounting Standards Board (FASB) The regulatory body that sets accounting standards in the United States.

Financial statements Reports from the management of the companies to their owners summarizing how the company performed during a particular period. Specific financial statements are the balance sheet, the income statement and the statement of cash flows.

Financing activities Activities of a company in which funds are raised to support the other activities of the company. The two major ways to raise funds are to issue new shares or borrow money.

Flow statement A statement that describes certain types of company inflows and outflows. The cash flow statement and the income statement are both examples of this type of statement.

Funds Resources, usually money, that the company obtains and uses to purchase assets or conduct operations.

GAAP Generally accepted accounting principles. The set of accounting recommendations and guidelines that corporations use in measuring, recording, and reporting for financial accounting information.

Income statement A financial statement that measures the results of a company's operating activities over a period of time, in terms of profitability.

Investing activities Company activities involved in long-term investments, primarily investments in property, plant, and equipment, and in the shares of other companies.

Investors Individuals or entities that acquire shares of a company as an investment.

Liability An element of the balance sheet characterized by a probable future sacrifice of a company's resources.

Liquidity The length of time required to turn assets into cash.

Management The individuals responsible for running or managing the company.

Managerial accounting The study of the preparation and uses of accounting information by a company's management.

Market value The amount that the item would generate if it were sold.

Materiality A concept used to indicate items that will affect decision-making. In auditing, it means those items that are large enough to have a significant effect on the evaluation of a company's financial results.

Net income The profits generated by a company during a specified time period. Net income is determined by subtracting expenses from a company's revenues.

Neutrality A quality of accounting information indicating that the methods or principles applied should not depend on a company's self-interest being measured but be unbiased with regard to the potential outcomes for the company.

Noncurrent asset/liability Assets or liabilities whose lives extend beyond one year or operating cycle.

Operating activities A company's activities that involve the sale of goods and services to customers.

Operating cycle The time period between the initial investment of cash in products or services and the return of cash from the sale of the products or services.

Owners Synonym for shareholders.

Predictive value A quality of accounting information that makes the information relevant to decision-makers. Its relevance stems from its ability to predict the future.

Privately held corporation   A company whose shares are held by a few individuals and do not trade in a public stock market.

Publicly traded corporation   A company whose shares are traded in a public stock market.

Qualified opinion   An audit opinion that expresses some exception to the fair presentation of the financial results.

Relevance   A quality of accounting information indicating that the information should have an impact on the user's decisions.

Reliability   A quality of accounting information indicating that the information can be depended on with respect to verifiability, representational faithfulness, neutrality, and conservatism.

Representational faithfulness   A quality of accounting information indicating that the information should accurately represent the attribute or characteristic that it purports to represent.

Retained earnings   Earnings that are kept within the company and not paid out to shareholders in the form of dividends.

Revenues   Inflows of resources to the company that result from the sale of goods and/or services.

Share capital   The shares issued by a company to its owners. Shares represent the ownership interest in the company.

Shareholders   The individuals or entities that own shares in a company.

Shareholders' equity   The section of the balance sheet that represents the shareholders' wealth; equivalent to the assets less the liabilities.

Statement of cash flows   Synonym for cash flow statement.

Statement of changes in financial position   Synonym for cash flow statement.

Statement of earnings   Synonym for income statement.

Statement of financial position   Synonym for balance sheet.

Taxing authority   An agency that assesses and collects taxes from a company.

Timeliness   A quality of accounting information indicating that information must be current in order to be relevant to decision-makers.

Unclassified balance sheet   A balance sheet that does not classify assets and liabilities into current and noncurrent categories.

Understandability   A qualitative characteristic that states that accounting information should be prepared with sufficient information and in a format that enables users to comprehend the contents.

Unqualified opinion   An audit opinion that states that the financial statements present fairly the company's financial position and operating results in conformity with GAAP.

Verifiability   The characteristic of accounting information that states that independent measurers, using the same methods, would agree on the calculated amount for an item.

Working capital   The difference between the current assets and the current liabilities.

Assignment Material

Assessing Your Recall

1-1   Explain the difference between a public corporation and a private corporation.

1-2   Identify at least three major users of corporate financial statements, and briefly state how they might use the information from the statements.

1-3   Discuss the meaning of generally accepted accounting principles, and describe the organizations that establish these principles.

Self-Assessment Quiz

1-4   List and briefly describe the major qualitative characteristics that accounting information should possess, according to the CICA conceptual framework.

1-5   Describe and illustrate the three major types of activities in which all companies engage.

1-6   Describe and illustrate the three major categories of items that appear in a typical balance sheet.

1-7 Describe the purpose of the three main financial statements that are contained in all annual reports.

1-8 Explain the purpose behind the notes to the financial statements.

1-9 What is the purpose of the auditors' opinion, and what types of opinion can they render?

1-10 Describe the impact of the use of computers on the collection and reporting of financial information.

Applying Your Knowledge

1-11 (Importance of accounting)

In the opening story to this chapter, Ben Voss stressed the importance of forecasting Clear-Green Environmental Inc.'s working capital requirement.

> *Required:*
> a. What is working capital?
>
> b. Why do you think it is particularly important for a new business to monitor its working capital?

1-12 (Identification of financing, investing, and operating transactions)

For a company like Air Canada, provide two examples of transactions that you would classify as each of financing, investing, and operating.

1-13 (Identification of financing, investing, and operating transactions)

For a company like **West Fraser Timber Co. Ltd.** (a paper and forest products company), provide two examples of transactions that you would classify as financing, investing, and operating.

1-14 (Application of qualitative characteristics)

The BMAC Company purchased land many years ago for $100,000 as a potential site for a new building. No building was ever constructed. A comparable lot near the site was recently sold for $350,000.

> *Required:*
> a. At what value should BMAC carry the land on its balance sheet? Support your answer with consideration for the conservatism, relevance, and reliability of the information that would result.
>
> b. If BMAC wanted to borrow money from a bank, what information about the land would the bank want to know? Explain your answer.
>
> c. What information about the land would potential investors in BMAC want to know? Explain your answer.

1-15 (Application of qualitative characteristics)

Provide an example of how the characteristics of relevance and reliability may be in conflict when valuing an asset on the balance sheet. Which characteristic do you think is most important? Why?

1-16 (Application of qualitative characteristics)

Matrix Technologies designs and installs computer software for businesses. Recently, it learned that one of its major customers, representing 20% of annual sales, is in financial difficulty and is unlikely to be ordering for some time. Matrix is about to issue its quarterly report to shareholders.

> *Required:*
> Do you think the information about the customer should be disclosed in the quarterly report? Support your answer by referring to the qualitative characteristics described in this chapter.

1-17 **(Comparison of the income statement and the cash flow statement)**
Compare and contrast the statement of income and the statement of cash flows with regard to their purpose. Outline how they are similar.

1-18 **(Comparison of the income statement and balance sheet accounts)**
On what financial statement would you expect to find wages expense, and what does it represent? On what financial statement would you expect to find wages payable, and what does it represent? What is the connection between these two accounts?

1-19 **(Identifying items on financial statements)**
Use the following abbreviations to respond to this question.

CA   Current assets
NCA Noncurrent assets
CL   Current liabilities
NCL Noncurrent liabilities
SC   Share capital
RE   Retained earnings
IS   Income statement item
SCF Statement of cash flows item

> *Required:*
> Classify the following items according to where the item would appear in the financial statements:
>
> a. Accounts receivable
>
> b. Taxes payable
>
> c. Interest expense
>
> d. Inventory
>
> e. Short-term investment in the shares of another company
>
> f. Sales to customers
>
> g. Manufacturing equipment
>
> h. Common shares
>
> i. Cash
>
> j. Mortgage payable (debt due in 10 years)

1-20 **(Identifying items on financial statements)**
Use the following abbreviations to respond to this question.

CA   Current assets
NCA Noncurrent assets
CL   Current liabilities
NCL Noncurrent liabilities
SC   Share capital
RE   Retained earnings
IS   Income statement item
SCF Statement of cash flows item

> *Required:*
> Classify the following items according to where the item would appear in the financial statements:
>
> a. Dividends payable
>
> b. Selling expenses

    c. Purchase of manufacturing equipment

    d. Amounts owed to suppliers

    e. Amounts owed by customers to the company

    f. Short-term bank loan (debt due in six months)

    g. Cash proceeds from sale of a building

    h. Net income for the year

    i. Dividend declared to shareholders

    j. Cost to the company of inventory sold to customers this year

1-21   **(Identifying items on financial statements)**

Use the following abbreviations to respond to this question.

CA   Current assets
NCA Noncurrent assets
CL   Current liabilities
NCL Noncurrent liabilities
SC   Share capital
RE   Retained earnings
IS   Income statement item
SCF Statement of cash flows item

    Required:
    Classify the following items according to where the item would appear in the financial statements:

    a. Intangible assets

    b. Interest revenue

    c. Cash collections from amounts owed by customers on account

    d. Cost of developing a new advertising campaign

    e. Earnings over the years that have not been paid to shareholders as dividends

    f. Revenue from provision of services to customers

    g. Rent payable

    h. Increase in bank loan (additional borrowings)

    i. Office supplies used this year

    j. An investment in the shares of another corporation (the intent of the investment is not to sell it in the near future)

1-22   **(Classifying items on the cash flow statement)**

Use the following abbreviations to respond to this question.

OA   Operating activities item
FA   Financing activities item
IA   Investing activities item

    Required:
    Classify each of the following transactions according to whether they are operating, financing, or investing activities:

    a. Cash paid to suppliers

    b. Cash collected from customers

    c. Payment of dividends

    d. Purchase of a truck for use in deliveries

    e. Purchase of inventory

    f. Purchase of shares of another company

    g. Sale of manufacturing equipment

    h. Issuance of shares

1-23   **(Classifying items on the cash flow statement)**
Use the following abbreviations to respond to this question.

OA   Operating activities item
FA   Financing activities item
IA   Investing activities item

Required:
Classify each of the following transactions according to whether they are operating, financing, or investing activities:

    a. Repurchase of a corporation's own shares

    b. Net income

    c. Payment of employee wages

    d. Acquisition of a long-term bank loan

    e. Amortization of the factory building

    f. Repayment of a bank loan

    g. Purchase of land

    h. Payment of dividends

1-24   **(Identifying items on the balance sheet and income statement)**
Indicate whether each of the following items will be reported in the balance sheet (BS), income statement (IS), or both the balance sheet and the income statement (B). If you believe an item would not appear on either the balance sheet or the income statement (for example, it might appear only on the cash flow statement), you should answer neither (N).

    a. Cash

    b. Accounts receivable

    c. Prepaid rent

    d. Interest revenue

    e. Sales of goods and services

    f. Dividends paid to shareholders

    g. Rent expense

    h. Sales anticipated next period

    i. Payment made to reduce the principal amount of a bank loan

    j. Common shares issued this year

1-25   **(Identifying items on the balance sheet and income statement)**
Indicate whether each of the following items will be reported in the balance sheet (BS), income statement (IS), or both the balance sheet and the income statement (B). If you believe an item would not appear on either the balance sheet or the income statement (for example it might appear only on the cash flow statement), you should answer neither (N).

a. Revenue earned from selling inventory

b. Wages expense

c. Retained earnings

d. Inventory

e. Cost to the company of inventory sold to customers

f. Bank loan payable

g. Purchase of computer system, for use in head office

h. Amortization of computer system used in head office

i. Securing a new short-term bank loan

j. Common shares

1-26 **(Relationship of balance sheet and income statement)**
In question 1-24 or 1-25 did you identify any items that appeared on both the balance sheet and income statement? Would you expect to? Explain, by describing the nature of each financial statement.

1-27 **(Determine missing balance sheet amounts)**
Calculate the missing balance sheet amounts in each of the following independent situations.

	A	B	C	D
Current assets	?	$ 300,000	$ 80,000	$ 810,000
Noncurrent assets	620,000	?	240,000	?
Total assets	?	770,000	?	1,200,000
Current liabilities	150,000	120,000	100,000	360,000
Noncurrent liabilities	?	320,000	?	270,000
Shareholders' equity	275,000	?	160,000	?
Total liabilities and shareholders' equity	800,000	?	?	?

1-28 **(Determine missing balance sheet amounts)**
Calculate the missing balance sheet amounts in each of the following independent situations.

	A	B	C	D
Current assets	$ 740,000	?	$80,000	$150,000
Noncurrent assets	?	150,000	?	850,000
Total assets	2,100,000	?	290,000	?
Current liabilities	650,000	120,000	30,000	200,000
Noncurrent liabilities	1,100,000	?	100,000	?
Shareholders' equity	?	350,000	?	500,000
Total liabilities and shareholders' equity	?	700,000	?	?

1-29 **(Determine missing retained earnings amounts)**
The change in retained earnings from the beginning of the year to the end of the year is caused by net income minus dividends. Calculate the missing amounts in the reconciliation of retained earnings in each of the following independent situations.

	A	B	C	D
Retained earnings				
Dec. 31, Year 1	$80,000	$220,000	?	$940,000
Net income	20,000	?	650,000	160,000

	A	B	C	D
Dividends declared and paid	10,000	25,000	150,000	?
Retained earnings Dec. 31, Year 2	?	310,000	2,300,000	1,050,000

1-30   (Prepare a simple income statement)

Susan Reed operates a bookstore called Buy the Book. During the month of July, the following things occurred: she paid $1,800 for rent; spent $210 on the telephone system and $180 on electricity and water; she took in $19,780 from selling books; the cost of the books sold was $9,125; she paid her employees $4,300 in wages and paid an additional $420 for the month to cover her employees' participation in a dental plan.

> *Required:*
>
> a. Prepare an income statement to determine how much Buy the Book earned in July.
>
> b. Are there any other costs that you think might have been incurred in July that are not listed?

1-31   (Prepare a simple income statement)

Klaus Schuss runs a ski school in the Rocky Mountains. His busiest months are December through March. For the month of February, he recorded the following items: he paid $5,420 for employee wages; spent $1,350 on insurance; spent $820 on advertising; people paid him $8,100 for ski lessons in February and paid him another $3,200 to rent ski equipment during the lessons; amortization on ski equipment was $750; office costs (rent, telephone, supplies used) totalled $1,610.

> *Required:*
>
> a. Prepare an income statement for Klaus Schuss to determine how much he earned in February.
>
> b. Are there any other costs that you think Klaus Schuss might have incurred in February that were not listed?

1-32   (Prepare a simple balance sheet)

Problem 1-30 introduced Susan Reed and her bookstore. At the end of July, the following items were in her records.

Inventory of books	$12,300
Wages owed to employees	320
Amounts owing to book publishers	1,240
Bank loan owed to the bank	4,500
Cash held in a chequing account	1,810
Cost of display shelving in the bookstore	5,200
Prepaid rent for August	1,800
Common shares	5,000
Retained earnings	10,050

> *Required:*
>
> a. Identify each of the items in her records as an asset, liability, or shareholders' equity item.
>
> b. Prepare a balance sheet for the end of July.
>
> c. Susan Reed does not have accounts receivable in her records. Suggest an explanation for why it is unlikely that she will have an account called accounts receivable. Under what business circumstances would it be necessary for her to have such an account?

1-33   **(Prepare a simple balance sheet)**

Problem 1-31 introduced Klaus Schuss and his ski school. At the end of February, the following items were in his records.

Bank loan owed to the bank	$ 2,500
Prepaid insurance for March	1,350
Cash in bank accounts	4,150
Common shares	6,000
Cost of ski equipment available for rent during lessons	17,400
Retained earnings	11,930
Amounts prepaid by customers for March lessons	2,470

Required:

a. Identify each of the items in his records as an asset, liability, or shareholders' equity item.

b. Prepare a balance sheet for the end of February.

c. Does Klaus Schuss have any inventory? Explain.

d. Klaus Schuss does not have accounts receivable in his records. Explain why it is unlikely that he will have an account called accounts receivable. Under what business circumstances would it be necessary for him to have such an account?

1-34   **(Identification of assets and liabilities)**

For each of the following companies, list at least two types of assets and one type of liability that you would expect to find on its balance sheet (try to include at least one item for each company that is unique to its business).

a. **Danier Leather Inc.** This company designs and sells leather clothing.

b. **Maple Leaf Foods Inc.** This company is a food processor.

c. **Noranda Inc.** This company is a mining company and a leading producer of copper and nickel.

d. **Royal Bank** This is a major commercial bank.

e. **Westjet Airlines Ltd.** This is an airline company.

f. **Winpak Ltd.** This company is involved in manufacturing packaging materials that are used to package perishable foods, beverages, and pharmaceuticals.

g. **Ballard Power Systems Inc.** This company is involved in the development and commercialization of fuel cells and related power generation systems.

1-35   **(Identification of income statement items)**

For each of the companies listed in Problem 1-34, list at least two line items that you would expect to find on its income statement (try to include at least one item for each company that is unique to its business).

1-36   **(Identification of statement of cash flow items)**

For each of the companies listed in Problem 1-34, list at least two line items that you would expect to find on its statement of cash flows (try to include at least one item for each company that is unique to its business).

User Perspective Problems

1-37   **(Use of accounting information)**

You are a junior accountant in a transportation company. Your company transports people (buses travelling between cities in eastern Canada) and goods (trucks used for the transportation of merchandise across Canada). The company has to replace its buses and trucks on a regular basis. The controller (the person in charge of the overall accounting system) needs information about whether it would be more advantageous for the company to lease the vehicles rather than buy them. She has asked you to do some research on the issue.

> ***Required:***
> A lease is a long- or short-term contract with a dealer that sells and leases vehicles. The company doing the leasing (the lessee) usually pays a monthly fee that includes an interest charge. At the end of the lease term, the company can either return the vehicle to the dealer or pay an additional amount to the dealer to buy the vehicle. What kind of information about leasing and the company's financial situation do you think the controller would need before a decision could be made about leasing the vehicles?

1-38   **(Use of accounting information)**

Using the information provided in Problem 1-37, assume the controller wants you to do the background work for a buy decision instead of a leasing one. What kind of information about the purchase and the company's financial situation do you think the controller would need before a decision could be made about buying the vehicles?

1-39   **(Use of accounting information)**

You are the accounting manager for a Canadian company that has just been acquired by a German company. Helmut Schmidt, the CEO of the German company, has just paid you a visit and is puzzled as to why Canadian companies use different information when reporting to the Canada Revenue Agency and their shareholders. In Germany, the same set of information is sent to both parties.

> ***Required:***
> Draft a memo explaining to Mr. Schmidt why the two users accept different information. In answering this question, consider the reporting objectives of the two users.

1-40   **(Information for decision-making)**

Suppose that the CICA proposed that inventory be accounted for at its current market price (what you could sell it for) rather than its historical cost. Provide an argument that supports or opposes this change on the basis of relevance and reliability.

1-41   **(Information for decision-making)**

Suppose that the CICA proposed that equipment used in manufacturing a company's product be accounted for at its current market price (what the equipment could be sold for) rather than amortized historical cost (original cost minus accumulated amortization). Provide an argument that supports or opposes this change on the basis of relevance and reliability.

1-42   **(Information for decision-making)**

How does the preparation of a classified balance sheet assist the user of the financial statement in predicting a company's future cash flows? What qualitative characteristic(s) is/are illustrated?

1-43   **(Information for decision-making)**

Suppose that you started your own company that assembles and sells laptop computers. You do not manufacture any of the parts yourself. The computers are sold through orders received over the Internet and through mail orders.

> ***Required:***
> Make a list of the information that you think would be relevant to running this business. When you are through, discuss how you would reliably measure the information that you want to keep track of.

1-44   **(Information for decision-making)**

Suppose that you own and operate your own private company. You need to raise money to expand your operation and you approach a bank for a loan. The bank loan officer has asked for financial statements prepared according to GAAP.

Required:

a. Why would the loan officer make such a request?

b. Assuming that your statements were prepared according to GAAP, how could you convince the loan officer that this was so?

c. What items on your financial statements would be of the most interest to the loan officer?

1-45 (Value of auditors)

In order for a company's shares to be listed (traded) on a Canadian stock exchange, the company's annual financial statements must be audited by an independent auditor. Why is an audit important to shareholders? And why is independence of the auditor necessary?

1-46 (Raising new capital)

Suppose that your best friend wants to start a new business providing website construction services to customers. Your friend has some savings to start the business but not enough to buy all the equipment that she thinks she needs. She has asked you for some advice about how to raise additional funds.

Required:

Give her at least two alternatives and provide the pros and cons for each alternative.

1-47 (Value of future-oriented information)

From time to time there have been calls from the user community for management to disclose its own forecasts of future expectations, such as net income.

Required:

a. As an external user of the financial statements, discuss the relevance and reliability of this type of information.

b. Why might management be reluctant to disclose future-oriented information?

1-48 (Distribution of a dividend to shareholders)

The board of directors of a public company is having its monthly meeting. One of the items on the agenda is the possible distribution of a cash dividend to shareholders. If the board decides to issue a cash dividend, its decision obliges the company to issue cash to shareholders based on the number of shares each shareholder owns.

Required:

Before making its decision, what kinds of information about the company should the board consider? Think of the items on the financial statements that you saw in this chapter.

Reading and Interpreting Published Financial Statements

Financial Statement Analysis Assignments

Base your answers to Problems 49–54 on the financial statements for **Le Château Inc.** in Appendix A at the end of the book. In the questions below, the year 2004 refers to Le Château Inc.'s fiscal year, which ends January 31, 2004, and the year 2003 refers to the prior fiscal year ending January 25, 2003.

1-49 (Find dividends declared)

Determine the amount of dividends that Le Château declared in 2004. On which financial statement(s) did you find this information?

1-50 (Verify basic accounting equation)

Verify that total assets equal total liabilities and shareholders' equity for Le Château Inc. at January 31, 2004.

1-51 **(Find financial statement balances)**

Find the following amounts in the statements of Le Château Inc.:

   a. Revenues from the sale of merchandise in 2004

   b. Cost of merchandise sold, buying, and occupancy in 2004

   c. Interest expense in 2004

   d. Income tax expense in 2004

   e. Net earnings in 2003

   f. Inventories at the end of 2003

   g. Accounts payable and accrued liabilities at the beginning of 2004

   h. Retained earnings at the end of 2004

   i. Long-term debt at the beginning of 2004 (include the current portion of long-term debt)

   j. Cash flows generated from operating activities in 2004

   k. Cash payments to acquire fixed assets in 2004

   l. Cash proceeds from the issuance of new capital stock in 2004

   m. Cash flows generated from (used for) financing activities in 2003

   n. Cash payments to reduce long-term debt in 2004

1-52 **(Identify sources and uses of cash)**

List the two largest sources of cash and the two largest uses of cash in 2004. (Consider operations to be a single source or use of cash.)

1-53 **(Net income versus cash from operations)**

Suggest two reasons why net earnings were $10,648,000 in 2004, yet cash flows generated from operations were $19,158,000.

1-54 **(Comparison of change in sales with change in net income)**

During 2004, total sales revenue was approximately $9 million higher than in 2003. However, net earnings in 2004 was only $3 million higher than 2003. By examining the statement of earnings, suggest some explanations as to where the additional sales revenue went.

   Base your answers to Problems 55–62 on the 2003 financial statements for **Winpak Ltd.** in Exhibit 1-8. This Canadian company manufactures high-quality packaging materials used for the protection of perishable foods, beverages, and pharmaceuticals.

1-55 **(Find dividends declared)**

Determine the amount of dividends that Winpak declared in 2003. On which financial statement did you find this information? Determine the amount of dividends that Winpak paid in 2003. On which financial statement did you find this information?

1-56 **(Verify basic accounting equation)**

Verify that total assets equal total liabilities and shareholders' equity for Winpak in 2003.

1-57 **(Calculation of current assets and current liabilities)**

Winpak prepared a classified balance sheet. Calculate the difference between the current assets and current liabilities at the end of 2003 and at the end of 2002. These amounts are referred to as working capital. Has the company's working capital improved in 2003? Explain.

EXHIBIT 1-8
PART A

WINPAK LTD. 2003 ANNUAL REPORT

CONSOLIDATED STATEMENTS OF EARNINGS AND RETAINED EARNINGS

Years ended December 31, 2003 and 2002
(thousands of CDN dollars, except per share amounts)

	2003	2002
Sales	513,286	491,067
Costs and Expenses		
Manufacturing and operating	414,458	383,576
Depreciation and amortization (note 5)	24,659	22,267
Research and technical	10,702	9,295
Pre-production	787	985
Earnings from operations	62,680	74,944
Interest (note 9)	3,595	5,168
Earnings before income taxes and minority interest	59,085	69,776
Provision for income taxes (note 10)	21,809	24,477
Minority interest	2,465	2,019
Net earnings	34,811	43,280
Retained earnings, beginning of year	173,938	133,908
Net earnings	34,811	43,280
Dividends declared	(3,900)	(3,250)
Retained earnings, end of year	204,849	173,938
Basic and fully diluted earnings per share	5.36	6.66
Average number of shares outstanding (000's)	6,500	6,500

See accompanying notes to consolidated financial statements.

WINPAK LTD. 2003 ANNUAL REPORT

EXHIBIT 1-8
PART B

CONSOLIDATED BALANCE SHEETS

December 31, 2003 and 2002
(thousands of CDN dollars)

	2003	2002
Assets		
Current assets:		
Cash	2,398	2,585
Accounts receivable	58,839	61,879
Inventories	72,793	69,654
Future income taxes (note 10)	2,992	4,087
Prepaid expenses	2,311	2,819
	139,333	141,024
Property, plant and equipment (note 6)	210,852	211,734
Other assets (note 7)	11,303	13,048
Intangible assets (note 8)	18,297	25,470
Goodwill (note 8)	20,216	22,593
	400,001	413,869
Liabilities and Shareholders' Equity		
Current liabilities:		
Accounts payable and accrued liabilities	29,716	45,831
Long-term debt (note 9)	70,200	88,480
Deferred credits	8,731	8,593
Future income taxes (note 10)	31,933	27,081
Postretirement benefits (note 11)	1,162	3,352
	141,742	173,337
Minority interest	13,068	13,137
Shareholders' equity:		
Share capital (note 12)	44,669	44,669
Retained earnings	204,849	173,938
Cumulative currency translation adjustments	(4,327)	8,788
	245,191	227,395
	400,001	413,869

See accompanying notes to consolidated financial statements.

On behalf of the Board:

_____ Director

_____ Director

EXHIBIT 1-8
PART C

WINPAK LTD. 2003 ANNUAL REPORT

CONSOLIDATED STATEMENTS OF CASH FLOWS

Years ended December 31, 2003 and 2002
(thousands of CDN dollars)

	2003	2002
Cash provided by (used in):		
Operating activities:		
Net earnings	34,811	43,280
Items not involving cash:		
Depreciation and amortization	24,659	22,267
Pension plan and postretirement benefits	2,144	2,098
Future income taxes	6,275	4,317
Minority interest	2,465	2,019
Other	(384)	282
Cash flow from operating activities before change in working capital	69,970	74,263
Change in working capital:		
Accounts receivable	(1,051)	1,265
Inventories	(8,813)	2,413
Prepaid expenses	254	(525)
Accounts payable and accrued liabilities	(12,559)	(356)
Pension plan and postretirement benefits payments	(2,572)	(352)
	45,229	76,708
Investing activities:		
Acquisition of property, plant and equipment	(38,616)	(20,548)
Business acquisition (note 4)	-	(41,246)
	(38,616)	(61,794)
Financing activities:		
Proceeds from long-term debt	-	40,560
Repayments of long-term debt	(2,900)	(65,125)
Dividends paid	(3,900)	(2,925)
	(6,800)	(27,490)
Decrease in cash	(187)	(12,576)
Cash, beginning of year	2,585	15,161
Cash, end of year	2,398	2,585
Supplemental disclosure of cash flow information:		
Cash paid during the year for:		
Interest expense	4,253	5,799
Income tax expense	24,596	17,654

See accompanying notes to consolidated financial statements.

1-58 **(Find financial statement balances)**

Find the following amounts in the statements of Winpak:

    a. Sales revenues in 2003

    b. Manufacturing and operating expenses in 2003

    c. Interest expense in 2002

    d. Income tax expense in 2003

    e. Net earnings (income) in 2002

    f. Intangible assets at the end of 2003

    g. Accounts receivable at the beginning of 2003

    h. Retained earnings at the end of 2002

    i. Property, plant, and equipment at the end of 2003

    j. Cash produced from operating activities in 2003

    k. Cash payments to acquire property and equipment in 2002

    l. Cash used for the repayment of long-term debt in 2003

    m. Cash produced or used for financing activities in 2003

1-59 **(Determine financing strategy)**

Did Winpak finance the company's assets mainly from creditors (total liabilities) or from shareholders (shareholders' equity) in 2003? Support your answer with appropriate calculations.

1-60 **(Identify sources and uses of cash)**

List the two largest sources of cash and the two largest uses of cash in 2003 (if possible).(Consider cash generated from operating activities to be a single source or use of cash.)

1-61 **(Net income versus cash from operations)**

Suggest some reasons why net earnings were $34,811 thousand in 2003, yet cash generated from operating activities was $45,229 thousand.

1-62 **(Firm valuation)**

Winpak is a publicly traded company, listed on the Toronto Stock Exchange. The price of Winpak's common shares ranged between approximately $94 and $121 per share during the fourth quarter of 2003. Assume the price at December 31, 2003, was $100 per share. There were 6,500,000 common shares outstanding at that date. Calculate the total market value of the common shares of Winpak at the end of 2003. Compare this with the value of shareholders' equity at the end of 2003, as represented in the balance sheet. If these numbers are different, offer an explanation for this discrepancy.

    Base your answers to Problems 63–69 on the 2004 financial statements of Mosaid Technologies Incorporated, which are in Exhibit 1-9. Mosaid Technologies, an Ontario corporation, designs memory chips and supplies engineering test systems around the world. In the questions below, the year 2004 refers to Mosaid Technologies' fiscal year, which ends April 23, 2004, and the year 2003 refers to the prior fiscal year ending April 25, 2003.

1-63 **(Fiscal year end)**

When is the business year end for Mosaid Technologies?

1-64 **(Find financial statement balances)**

Find the following amounts in the statements of Mosaid Technologies:

EXHIBIT 1-9
PART A

MOSAID TECHNOLOGIES INC. 2004 ANNUAL REPORT

MOSAID TECHNOLOGIES INCORPORATED *(Incorporated under the Ontario Business Corporations Act)*

CONSOLIDATED BALANCE SHEETS

(In thousands)

As at	April 23, 2004	April 25, 2003
Current Assets		
Cash and cash equivalents	$ 9,021	$ 4,144
Short-term marketable securities (Note 2)	29,140	38,167
Accounts receivable	6,020	7,635
Inventories (Note 3)	3,201	3,517
Prepaid expenses	292	802
	47,674	54,265
Capital Assets (Note 4)	9,108	13,402
Long-Term Investments (Note 5)	670	2,032
Future Income Taxes (Note 11)	12,025	12,708
	$ 69,477	$ 82,407
Current Liabilities		
Accounts payable and accrued liabilities	$ 7,466	$ 12,461
Deferred revenue	1,265	659
Mortgage payable (Note 6)	207	191
	8,938	13,311
Mortgage Payable (Note 6)	4,815	5,022
	13,753	18,333
Contingency (Note 17)		
Shareholders' Equity		
Share capital (Note 7)	84,556	84,268
Contributed surplus	108	165
Deficit	(28,940)	(20,359)
	55,724	64,074
	$ 69,477	$ 82,407

See accompanying Notes to the Consolidated Financial Statements.

Thomas I. Csathy
Director

John B. Millard
Director

MOSAID TECHNOLOGIES INC. 2004 ANNUAL REPORT

EXHIBIT 1-9
PART B

CONSOLIDATED STATEMENTS OF OPERATIONS AND DEFICIT

(In thousands, except per share amounts)

Year ended	April 23, 2004	April 25, 2003
Revenues		
Operations	$ 28,417	$ 36,874
Interest	979	1,107
	29,396	37,981
Expenses		
Labour and materials	5,912	7,793
Research and development (Note 9)	6,218	8,877
Selling and marketing	11,951	9,177
General and administration	4,984	6,932
Bad debts (recovery)	–	(70)
Restructuring (Note 10)	(288)	3,378
	28,777	36,087
Income from operations	619	1,894
Write-down of long-term investment (Note 5)	(580)	(518)
Loss on disposal of long-term investment (Note 5)	(157)	(426)
(Loss) income before income tax expense and discontinued operations	(118)	950
Income tax expense (Note 11)	798	1,357
Loss before discontinued operations	(916)	(407)
Discontinued operations (net of tax) (Note 12)	(7,665)	(19,490)
Net Loss	(8,581)	(19,897)
Deficit, beginning of year	(20,359)	(462)
Deficit, end of year	$ (28,940)	$ (20,359)
Loss per share (Note 13)		
Basic – before discontinued operations	$ (0.09)	$ (0.04)
Diluted – before discontinued operations	$ (0.09)	$ (0.04)
Basic – net loss	$ (0.83)	$ (1.94)
Diluted – net loss	$ (0.83)	$ (1.94)
Weighted average number of shares		
Basic	10,300,763	10,238,808
Diluted	10,300,763	10,238,808

See accompanying Notes to the Consolidated Financial Statements.

MOSAID TECHNOLOGIES INC. 2004 ANNUAL REPORT

CONSOLIDATED STATEMENTS OF CASH FLOWS

(In thousands)

Year ended	April 23, 2004	April 25, 2003
Operating		
Net loss	$ (8,581)	$ (19,897)
Items not affecting cash		
Amortization	2,972	5,692
Loss on disposal of capital assets	7	369
Future income taxes	683	(2,384)
Write-down of long-term investment	580	518
Loss on disposal of long-term investment	162	426
Non-cash restructuring	2,266	2,015
	(1,911)	(13,261)
Change in non-cash working capital items (Note 14)	(1,966)	1,371
	(3,877)	(11,890)
Investing		
Acquisition of capital assets – net	(933)	(2,310)
Acquisition of short-term marketable securities	(42,168)	(64,060)
Proceeds on maturity/disposal of short-term marketable securities	51,195	69,949
Proceeds on disposal of long-term investment	620	3,221
	8,714	6,800
Financing		
Repayment of mortgage	(191)	(178)
Repurchase of shares	(267)	(359)
Issue of common shares	498	397
	40	(140)
Net cash inflow (outflow)	4,877	(5,230)
Cash and cash equivalents, beginning of year	4,144	9,374
Cash and cash equivalents, end of year	$ 9,021	$ 4,144

See accompanying Notes to the Consolidated Financial Statements.

a. Revenues from operations in 2004

b. Research and development in 2004

c. Interest revenue in 2003

d. Income tax expense in 2004

e. Net income (loss) in 2004

f. Inventories at the end of 2004

g. Accounts payable and accrued liabilities at the beginning of 2004

h. Retained earnings at the end of 2004 (a negative retained earnings balance is known as a deficit)

i. Mortgage payable at the end of 2004 (current and long-term)

j. Cash produced from operating activities in 2004

k. Cash payments to acquire short-term marketable securities in 2004

l. Cash used to repay the mortgage in 2004

m. Cash proceeds from new share issuances in 2004

n. Cash produced or used for investing activities in 2004

1-65   (Determine financing strategy)
Did Mosaid Technologies Inc. finance its business primarily from creditors (total liabilities) or from shareholders (shareholders' equity) in 2004? Support your answer with appropriate calculations.

1-66   (Identify sources and uses of cash)
List the two largest sources of cash and the two largest uses of cash in 2004. (Consider operations to be a single source or use of cash.)

1-67   (Declaration of dividends)
Did Mosaid Technologies Inc. declare and pay a dividend in 2004? Explain. On which financial statement(s) did you look for your answer?

1-68   (Change in short-term marketable securities)
The short-term marketable securities decreased on the balance sheet from $38,167 thousand in 2003 to $29,140 thousand in 2004. Using information from the cash flow statement, explain the net change in this account.

1-69   (Determine financing strategy)
Total assets of Mosaid Technologies Inc. at April 25, 2003, and April 23, 2004, were $82,407 thousand and $69,477 thousand, respectively. Total shareholders' equity at these dates was $64,074 thousand and $55,724 thousand, respectively. Calculate the ratio of debt to total assets for each of the years 2003 and 2004. Explain the change from 2003 to 2004.

Base your answers to Problems 70–75 on the 2003 financial statements of **Norske Skog Canada Limited**, which are included in Exhibit 1-10. Norske Skog Canada Limited is one of North America's leading producers of paper, and operates the largest paper recycling facility in Western Canada.

1-70   (Fiscal year end)
When is Norske Skog's fiscal year end?

1-71   (Find financial statement balances)
Find the following amounts in the statements of Norske Skog:

a. Net sales in 2003

b. Cost of sales in 2003

c. Depreciation and amortization in 2002

EXHIBIT 1-10
PART A

NORSKE SKOG CANADA LTD. 2003 ANNUAL REPORT

Consolidated Balance Sheets

In millions of Canadian dollars	As at December 31	
	2003	2002
Assets		
Current assets		
Accounts receivable	$ 253.5	$ 277.3
Inventories (note 3)	235.9	242.7
Prepaid expenses	6.6	9.2
	496.0	529.2
Fixed assets (note 4)	2,290.2	2,326.6
Other assets (note 5)	30.0	37.7
	$ 2,816.2	$ 2,893.5
Liabilities		
Current liabilities		
Accounts payable and accrued liabilities (note 6)	$ 244.2	$ 288.8
Long-term debt (note 7)	845.8	886.2
Other long-term obligations (note 8)	272.7	188.3
Future income taxes (note 9)	363.3	397.0
Deferred credits (note 10)	21.0	8.5
	1,747.0	1,768.8
Shareholders' Equity		
Share capital (note 11)	913.6	884.6
Retained earnings	155.6	240.1
	1,069.2	1,124.7
	$ 2,816.2	$ 2,893.5

Commitments, Guarantees and Indemnities (notes 18 and 19)
Contingency (note 20)

See accompanying Notes to Consolidated Financial Statements

Approved by the Board:

Russell J. Horner
Director

William P. Rosenfeld
Director

NORSKE SKOG CANADA LTD. 2003 ANNUAL REPORT

Consolidated Statements of Earnings

In millions of Canadian dollars, except where otherwise stated	Years ended December 31	
	2003	2002
Gross sales	**$ 1,820.5**	$ 1,704.0
Distribution costs	**229.3**	221.7
Net sales	**1,591.2**	1,482.3
Operating expenses		
Cost of sales	**1,458.2**	1,360.4
Selling, general and administrative	**54.7**	65.3
Depreciation and amortization	**189.9**	178.5
	1,702.8	1,604.2
Operating earnings (loss)	**(111.6)**	(121.9)
Foreign exchange gain on translation of long-term debt	**58.2**	12.3
Write-down of fixed assets (note 4)	**(14.2)**	–
Other expense, net (note 13)	**(3.9)**	(13.3)
Interest expense, net	**(75.0)**	(76.2)
Earnings (loss) before income taxes	**(146.5)**	(199.1)
Income tax recovery (note 9)	**(62.0)**	(75.8)
Net earnings (loss)	**$ (84.5)**	$ (123.3)
Basic and diluted earnings (loss) per share (in dollars) (note 12)	**$ (0.41)**	$ (0.64)

Consolidated Statements of Retained Earnings

In millions of Canadian dollars	Years ended December 31	
	2003	2002
Balance, beginning of year	**$ 240.1**	$ 363.4
Net earnings (loss)	**(84.5)**	(123.3)
Balance, end of year	**$ 155.6**	$ 240.1

See accompanying Notes to Consolidated Financial Statements.

EXHIBIT 1-10
PART C

NORSKE SKOG CANADA LTD. 2003 ANNUAL REPORT

Consolidated Statements of Cash Flows

In millions of Canadian dollars	Years ended December 31	
	2003	2002
	$	$
Cash provided by (used for):		
Operations		
Net earnings (loss)	(84.5)	(123.3)
Items not requiring (providing) cash		
Depreciation and amortization	189.9	178.5
Future income taxes	(67.9)	(91.5)
Increase in other long-term obligations	17.5	19.8
Foreign exchange gain on translation of long-term debt	(58.2)	(12.3)
Write-down of fixed assets (note 4)	14.2	–
Write-off of deferred financing costs	–	15.8
Other	6.2	(3.3)
	17.2	(16.3)
Changes in non-cash working capital		
Accounts receivable	40.4	30.4
Inventories	10.2	(13.0)
Prepaid expenses	2.6	(4.9)
Accounts payable and accrued liabilities	(47.9)	9.0
	5.3	21.5
Cash provided (used) by operations	22.5	5.2
Investing		
Acquisition of paper recycling business (note 2)	(32.1)	–
Additions to fixed assets	(81.4)	(82.2)
Proceeds from sale of marketable securities	–	39.2
Proceeds from sale of fixed assets	0.4	1.5
Proceeds from termination of interest rate swaps (note 8)	15.9	3.4
Decrease (increase) in other assets	1.1	(4.4)
	(96.1)	(42.5)
Financing		
Issue of common shares, net of share issue costs (note 11)	(0.1)	208.1
Increase (decrease) in revolving loan (note 7)	(105.7)	119.1
Issue of long-term debt	212.7	–
Repayment of long-term debt	–	(386.7)
Deferred financing costs	(5.6)	–
Decrease in other long-term obligations	(27.7)	(8.0)
	73.6	(67.5)
Cash, decrease during year [1]	–	(104.8)
Cash, beginning of year [1]	–	104.8
Cash, end of year [1]	$ –	$ –
Supplemental information:		
Income taxes paid	$ 7.1	$ 12.8
Net interest paid	80.2	78.3
Common shares issued for acquisition of paper recycling business (note 2)	29.1	–

1 Cash includes cash and short-term investments.

See accompanying Notes to Consolidated Financial Statements.

    d. Income tax recovery in 2003

    e. Net earnings (loss) in 2003

    f. Inventory at the beginning of 2003

    g. Accounts receivable at the end of 2002

    h. Retained earnings at the end of 2003

    i. Total long-term liabilities at the end of 2003

    j. Cash flows from operating activities in 2003

    k. Cash payments to acquire fixed assets in 2002

    l. Dividends paid in 2003 (if any)

    m.Cash produced or used for investing activities in 2003

1-72   **(Determine financing strategy)**
Did Norske Skog finance its business primarily from creditors (total liabilities) or from share-holders (shareholders' equity) in 2003? Support your answer with appropriate calculations.

1-73   **(Identify sources and uses of cash)**
List the two largest sources of cash and the two largest uses of cash in 2003. (Consider operating activities to be a single source or use of cash.)

1-74   **(Cash balance and working capital)**
Norske Skog is not holding any cash on its balance sheet at the end of either 2002 or 2003. Calculate working capital (current assets − current liabilities) at the end of both years. How do you think the company continues to operate despite having no cash at year end?

1-75   **(Net earnings versus cash balance changes)**
The company has reported net losses in both 2002 and 2003, of $123.3 million and $84.5 million respectively. Based on a review of the cash flow statement, can you suggest reasons why Norske Skog has been able to continue to operate?

      Base your answers to Problems 1-76–79 on the 2003 financial statements of **DaimlerChrysler AG** presented in Exhibit 1-11. DaimlerChrysler is a German company that produces its financial statements using U.S. GAAP. In 2003, DaimlerChrysler presented two monetary amounts on each of its financial statements, U.S. dollars and Euros.

1-76   **(Fiscal year end)**
When is DaimlerChrysler's fiscal year end?

1-77   **(Find financial statement balances)**
Find the following amounts in the consolidated statements of DaimlerChrysler (express your answers in Euros):

    a. Revenues in 2003

    b. Cost of sales in 2003

    c. Financial income (expense) in 2003

    d. Research and development in 2002

    e. Net income in 2003

    f. Inventories at the end of 2003

    g. Accounts payable (trade liabilities) at the end of 2003

    h. Retained earnings at the end of 2003

    i. Capital stock at the beginning of 2003

    j. Property, plant, and equipment at the end of 2002

    k. Cash and cash equivalents at the end of 2003

    l. Total current assets at the end of 2003

EXHIBIT 1-11
PART A

DAIMLERCHRYSLER 2003 ANNUAL REPORT

Consolidated Balance Sheets

Consolidated Statements of Income (Loss)

(in millions, except per share amounts)	Note	2003 (Note 1) $	2003 €	Year ended December 31, 2002 €	2001 €
Revenues	34.	171,870	136,437	147,368	150,386
Cost of sales	5.	(138,474)	(109,926)	(119,624)	(126,247)
Gross margin		33,396	26,511	27,744	24,139
Selling, administrative and other expenses	5.	(22,388)	(17,772)	(18,166)	(18,235)
Research and development		(7,018)	(5,571)	(5,942)	(5,848)
Other income (therein gain on issuance of related company stock of €24 in 2003)	6.	899	713	777	1,201
Turnaround plan expenses – Chrysler Group	7.	(591)	(469)	(694)	(3,064)
Income (expense) before financial income		4,298	3,412	3,719	(1,807)
Impairment of investment in EADS		(2,469)	(1,960)	–	–
Other financial income (expense), net (therein gain on issuance of associated company stock of €747 in 2001)		(1,078)	(856)	2,206	153
Financial income (expense), net	8.	(3,547)	(2,816)	2,206	153
Income (loss) before income taxes		751	596	5,925	(1,654)
Income tax benefit (expense)	9.	(1,234)	(979)	(1,115)	849
Minority interests		(44)	(35)	(15)	42
Income (loss) from continuing operations		(527)	(418)	4,795	(763)
Income from discontinued operations, net of taxes	10.	18	14	82	101
Income on disposal of discontinued operations, net of taxes	10.	1,111	882	–	–
Cumulative effects of changes in accounting principles: transition adjustments resulting from adoption of FIN 46R and SFAS 142, net of taxes	11.	(38)	(30)	(159)	–
Net income (loss)		564	448	4,718	(662)
Earnings (loss) per share	35.				
Basic earnings (loss) per share					
Income (loss) from continuing operations		(0.52)	(0.41)	4.76	(0.76)
Income from discontinued operations		0.01	0.01	0.08	0.10
Income on disposal of discontinued operations		1.10	0.87	–	–
Cumulative effects of changes in accounting principles		(0.04)	(0.03)	(0.16)	–
Net income (loss)		0.55	0.44	4.68	(0.66)
Diluted earnings (loss) per share					
Income (loss) from continuing operations		(0.52)	(0.41)	4.74	(0.76)
Income from discontinued operations		0.01	0.01	0.08	0.10
Income on disposal of discontinued operations		1.10	0.87	–	–
Cumulative effects of changes in accounting principles		(0.04)	(0.03)	(0.15)	–
Net income (loss)		0.55	0.44	4.67	(0.66)

DAIMLERCHRYSLER 2003 ANNUAL REPORT

Consolidated Statements of Loss

EXHIBIT 1-11
PART B

Consolidated Balance Sheets

(in millions)	Note	2003 (Note 1) $	Consolidated At December 31, 2003 €	Consolidated At December 31, 2002 €	Industrial Business [1] At December 31, 2003 €	Industrial Business [1] At December 31, 2002 €	Financial Services [1] At December 31, 2003 €	Financial Services [1] At December 31, 2002 €
Assets								
Goodwill	12.	2,288	1,816	2,071	1,757	2,009	59	62
Other intangible assets	13.	3,551	2,819	2,855	2,731	2,755	88	100
Property, plant and equipment, net	14.	41,466	32,917	36,269	32,761	36,111	156	158
Investments and long-term financial assets	20.	11,020	8,748	9,291	8,416	8,922	332	369
Equipment on operating leases, net	15.	30,717	24,385	28,243	2,890	3,313	21,495	24,930
Fixed assets		89,042	70,685	78,729	48,555	53,110	22,130	25,619
Inventories	16.	18,830	14,948	15,642	13,560	13,965	1,388	1,677
Trade receivables	17.	7,660	6,081	6,297	5,851	6,005	230	292
Receivables from financial services	18.	66,308	52,638	52,088	–	10	52,638	52,078
Other receivables	19.	19,964	15,848	17,573	11,129	11,159	4,719	6,414
Securities	20.	4,117	3,268	3,293	2,801	2,911	467	382
Cash and cash equivalents	21.	13,878	11,017	9,130	9,719	8,191	1,298	939
Non-fixed assets		130,757	103,800	104,023	43,060	42,241	60,740	61,782
Deferred taxes	9.	3,386	2,688	3,613	2,527	3,496	161	117
Prepaid expenses	22.	1,379	1,095	962	1,002	866	93	96
Total assets (thereof short-term 2003: €65,051; 2002: €65,100)		224,564	178,268	187,327	95,144	99,713	83,124	87,614
Liabilities and stockholders' equity								
Capital stock		3,317	2,633	2,633				
Additional paid-in capital		9,971	7,915	7,819				
Retained earnings		36,638	29,085	30,156				
Accumulated other comprehensive income		(6,490)	(5,152)	(5,604)				
Treasury stock		–	–	–				
Stockholders' equity	23.	43,436	34,481	35,004	26,361	26,384	8,120	8,620
Minority interests		592	470	432	454	414	16	18
Accrued liabilities	25.	49,345	39,172	43,622	38,439	42,619	733	1,003
Financial liabilities	26.	95,347	75,690	79,283	11,779	12,372	63,911	66,911
Trade liabilities	27.	14,591	11,583	12,171	11,359	11,935	224	236
Other liabilities	28.	11,091	8,805	8,843	6,030	6,152	2,775	2,691
Liabilities		121,029	96,078	100,297	29,168	30,459	66,910	69,838
Deferred taxes	9.	3,447	2,736	2,312	(3,377)	(4,425)	6,113	6,737
Deferred income	29.	6,715	5,331	5,660	4,099	4,262	1,232	1,398
Total liabilities (thereof short-term 2003: €70,542; 2002: €72,673)		181,128	143,787	152,323	68,783	73,329	75,004	78,994
Total liabilities and stockholders' equity		224,564	178,268	187,327	95,144	99,713	83,124	87,614

1 Additional information about the Industrial Business and Financial Services is not required under U.S. GAAP and is unaudited.

1-78 **(Determine financing strategy)**
Did DaimlerChrysler finance its business primarily from creditors (total liabilities) or from shareholders (shareholders' equity) in 2003? Support your answer with appropriate calculations.

1-79 **(Format of balance sheet)**
The balance sheet of DaimlerChrysler is organized differently from the Canadian balance sheets that you have seen in this chapter. Describe the areas where there are major differences. (Notice that Deferred Taxes are listed under both the assets and the liabilities and shareholders' equity sections of the balance sheet. The asset represents taxes recoverable in the future from the government.)

Beyond the Book

The Beyond the Book problems are designed to give you the opportunity to find and use company information found outside this book.

1-80 **(Using the library and other sources to find company information)**
Familiarize yourself with the resources that are available at your university to acquire information about corporations. Most universities have some type of electronic database that contains financial statement information. The following is a short list of resources that may be available.

LEXIS/NEXIS Database This is an incredibly large database that contains all sorts of news and financial information about companies. It contains information about Canadian, U.S., and international companies. The financial information is in full text form.

Carlson On-line Service A directory site with Canadian investment information. Research any company traded on a Canadian exchange for links to other sites that have reliable and up-to-date information on that company.

Compact/Disclosure Canada Contains descriptive and financial data for more than 8,500 public, private, and Canadian government owned (Crown) corporations. Provides more than 60 financial items including assets, liabilities, sales, profits, number of employees, and selected ratios.

CD-Disclosure This database contains full-text financial footnote information for thousands of companies, but does not contain full text of the major financial statements.

EDGAR Filings The EDGAR filings are electronic forms of the SEC filings that are included in the Lexis/Nexis database but are also accessible through the Internet at www.sec.gov/edgar.shtml.

ABI Inform (UMI, Inc.) This database contains full-text information from numerous business periodicals.

You can also surf the web for sites that list information about companies. The SEDAR website (www.sedar.com) contains most securities-related information required by the Canadian securities regulatory authorities and is probably your best source for financial statements of Canadian companies on the Internet.

1-81 **(Find information about a new company)**
For a company of your choosing, answer the following questions.

    a. What are the products (or product lines) and/or services that your company sells? Please be as specific as possible.

    b. Who are the customers of your company?

    c. In what markets, domestic and global, does your company sell its products and/or services?

    d. Who are the major competitors of your company?

    e. What are the major inputs your company needs to produce its product? Who are the suppliers of these inputs?

    f. Are any of the items listed in the questions above changing substantially? Use a two-year time span as a window to address this question.

To answer these questions, it will be useful to collect a series of articles concerning your company over the most recent two-year period. Try to find at least five reasonably sized articles. Use these as references to write a two- to three-page background paper about your company. If your company has a website (most companies do), it will probably have news releases accessible there.

1-82   **(Find information about a new company)**
Go to the Accounting Perspectives website and find the annual report of **Sun-Rype Products Ltd.** for 2003. Answer the following questions.

Sun-Rype Annual Report

    a. What are the major sections included in the annual report?

    b. What are the three most important points made in the letter to the shareholders?

    c. What are the titles of the major financial statements included in the report?

    d. What are the company's total assets, total liabilities, and total shareholders' equity? What percentage of the company's total assets is financed through liabilities?

    e. Is the balance sheet classified or nonclassified? If classified, what are the major categories used?

    f. What were the net sales in the most recent year? Is this up or down from the previous year? (Answer in both dollar and percentage amounts.)

    g. What is the net income and earnings per share in the most recent year? Is this up or down from the previous year? (Answer in both dollar and percentage amounts.)

    h. What is the net cash provided (used) by operating, financing, and investing activities for the most recent year?

    i. What is the last day of the company's fiscal year?

    j. Who are the independent auditors and what type of opinion did they give the company?

1-83   **(Find information about a new company)**
For a Canadian company of your choosing, find its most recent annual report and answer the following questions.

    a. What are the major sections included in your annual report?

    b. What are the three most important points made in the letter to the shareholders?

    c. What are the titles of the major financial statements included in the report?

    d. What are the company's total assets, total liabilities, and total shareholders' equity? What percentage of the company's total assets is financed through liabilities?

    e. Is the balance sheet classified or nonclassified? If classified, what are the major categories used?

    f. What were the net sales in the most recent year? Is this up or down from the previous year? (Answer in both dollar and percentage amounts.)

g. What is the net income and earnings per share in the most recent year? Is this up or down from the previous year? (Answer in both dollar and percentage amounts.)

h. What is the net cash provided (used) by operating, financing, and investing activities for the most recent year?

i. What is the last day of your company's fiscal year?

j. Who are the independent auditors and what type of opinion did they give the company?

Cases

Case Primer

1-84 Weible Inc.

Weible Inc. is a small manufacturing company located in northern Canada. The company prepares its financial statements on an annual basis. Weible is currently owned privately by the members of the Weible family. They have very little debt and the main purpose in preparing the financial statements has been to assist in the preparation of annual tax returns. Consequently, the financial statements have never been audited.

You are an accountant employed by a local accounting firm and Weible Inc. has been your client for several years. Karen Weible, president of the company, has recently approached you to advise you of a large investment Weible Inc. is planning to undertake. To complete this project, the company will have to make significant investments in property and equipment. Additionally, more than 100 employees will have to be hired. To raise capital for this project, she would like to sell shares to outside investors and is also looking for financing from a local bank.

Karen Weible has approached you because she is interested in knowing how the planned changes will affect the preparation of Weible Inc.'s financial statements. Specifically, she wants information about who may be using the company's financial statements and whether the cost of having the financial statements prepared will change dramatically.

Required:

Prepare a memo to Karen Weible addressing her concerns.

1-85 Rust Consulting

Heather Rust is the owner-operator of a small consulting business. She has recently taken a brief accounting seminar and was introduced to the idea of the qualitative characteristics of accounting information. She is having some difficulty understanding the concept of materiality. Her question to you is: "How can certain accounting rules apply in some situations and not in others? Doesn't this lead to inconsistent financial reporting?"

Required:

Using the concepts discussed in the text, draft a brief reply to Heather Rust's question.

Critical Thinking Question

1-86 (The role of the Auditor General of Canada)

Peter Diekmeyer (*Management*, November 2001) comments on the appointment of Sheila Fraser, CA, as the first woman Auditor General of Canada.

1. Briefly describe the responsibilities of the Auditor General of Canada. To whom and on what does she report?

2. Explain why it is critically important to have an Auditor General.

3. In the article it states that government accounting is different than private sector accounting. Using the example given in the article, describe one aspect of how they are different.

A Recipe for Success—Starting Up a Business

Ever since high school, Chris Emery and Larry Finnson knew they wanted to go into business together. Sure enough, one day Mr. Emery's grandmother came up with an irresistible recipe for a vanilla fudge treat, and Krave's Candy Co. was born. In 1996, with $20,000 scraped together from family and friends, the two Winnipeg entrepreneurs set up some old kettle cookers in a tiny industrial space and started churning out 80-lb. batches of the sweets, which they called Clodhoppers.

In its first year of operation, Krave's sold its product mostly through local retailers and craft fairs, recording $59,000 in sales. Today, Chris & Larry's Clodhoppers are found in stores across Canada—including Wal-Mart, Zellers, Safeway, The Bay, and Shoppers Drug Mart—and sales for 2003–04 are projected to exceed $10 million.

The company experienced rapid growth in the Canadian market in 2003, so in order to meet demand, it expanded its production and warehousing facilities, doubling its space with an additional 20,200 square feet. Staff has also doubled, to 30 full-time employees.

While their company has enjoyed remarkable success, Mr. Emery and Mr. Finnson, neither of whom had any prior business experience, have learned a lot along the way. "At the beginning, we just thought we'd fire up a manufacturing plant and start making millions of pounds of candy and be rich within two years," said Mr. Finnson. "It didn't work out that way. It's been step by step for everything, from manufacturing to money."

As Mr. Emery recalls, during the company's start-up period, the pair ran into unanticipated expenses. "First, we needed a computer, then there was the development of the packaging and artwork, plus we had to hire people to help us make the candy," he says. "Before we knew it, the money was pretty much spent." Meanwhile, as their sales continued to climb, the two had to find more cash to finance their expansion, including much-needed upgrades to their production equipment: the large mixers, cooling tunnels, and other devices used in the manufacturing process.

Krave's recently purchased two additional form-and-fill machines to weigh and package the candy. To ensure adequate cash flow, the company financed the purchases, negotiating favourable term loan rates with its bank on the basis of its strong financials. Currently, Mr. Emery and Mr. Finnson keep their financing balanced among several sources, including a venture capitalist, a traditional bank, and the Business Development Bank of Canada, from which the company secured a $100,000 loan in 1999.

As the business has become more sophisticated, so too has its accounting function. Controller Brenda Scott joined the company on a part-time basis in 1997, moving to full time in 2000, and two accounts receivable and accounts payable positions have been added since. "Our use of technology grows continually, as we find more efficient ways of handling the growing amount of data," Ms. Scott says. These data include information on production planning, warehouse management, product tracing, shipment scheduling, budgeting, and sales commissions. Ms. Scott uses pivot tables in Excel to manipulate the data for analysis, and a Sharepoint server to access important company information at any time from anywhere.

"The most important thing is to know your numbers," Mr. Finnson says, "and how your business works from A to Z."

chapter **2**

Business Transaction Analysis and Financial Statement Effects

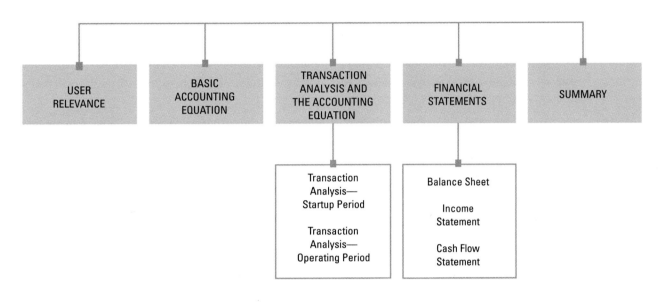

LEARNING OBJECTIVES

After studying this chapter, you should be able to:

1. Understand the basic accounting equation.

2. Analyze simple transactions and describe their effect on the basic accounting equation.

3. Describe the difference between accrual-basis accounting and cash-basis accounting.

4. Describe how inventory is accounted for when it is purchased and when it is sold.

5. Identify operating activities and describe their impact on retained earnings.

6. Describe the revenue recognition and expense matching process.

7. Prepare a balance sheet, income statement, and cash flow statement after a series of transactions.

8. Calculate three profitability ratios.

9. Begin to analyze the information on a cash flow statement.

Chris Emery and Larry Finnson started **Krave's Candy** as a small company and grew the business through hard work and effective marketing. They started with a product that they thought customers would want, and have proven that they were right. They are in their ninth year and well on the way to being a successful business.

What did Mr. Emery and Mr. Finnson do that made Krave's a success, when many new businesses do not survive the first few years? First, they had a product that people liked. Second, they worked hard at producing and distributing it. They had to make sure that the quality of the product remained consistent, as they moved to producing it in larger batches. They also had to get the product to consumers. They chose to go to craft fairs and to convince local retailers to carry their product. As the name "Clodhoppers" became known, they were able to convince multi-outlet retailers such as The Bay, Zellers, and Shoppers Drug Mart to carry their product. This was the start of their real growth.

However, along with growth comes a need for additional funding. It is financing that often causes young companies their greatest problems, and Krave's was no exception. Within a short time, the founders had exhausted their original investment of $20,000; however, by that time, they convinced a bank that they were an acceptable credit risk. Today, they are using multiple sources of funds (including a venture capitalist, as discussed in the accounting in the news item below). Investors are convinced that they have a good product, that the company is well managed, and that there is growth potential.

Behind all of its success and through all of its decisions, Krave's had to rely on its accounting information. Sometimes as young companies grow, the owners lose track of the numbers, especially if the growth is rapid. Mr. Emery and Mr. Finnson did not make that mistake. They knew that they had to keep track of all aspects of their business, and that the accounting numbers were the tool that would enable them to do this. Therefore, as the company expanded its manufacturing and marketing operations, it also increased its accounting staff. In addition, it used computer technology to analyze its financial data efficiently and effectively.

The way Mr. Emery and Mr. Finnson started their business is typical of the way many small businesses begin: their original sources of funding are from personal savings, family, and friends. Financial institutions are often reluctant to take a chance on new companies until they see some indicators of success. The following story illustrates this. It is about high-tech start-ups, but it applies to most new small businesses.

accounting in the news

VENTURE CAPITAL

Fledgling companies often need to prove themselves before they can secure financing from traditional sources such as banks. Outside of "angel investors" or "love money" from family and friends, venture capital has provided these start-up companies with large amounts of capital.

Once the centre for venture capital investment in Canada, Ottawa has seen this money source diminish to a trickle, in comparison with past levels. According to the Ottawa Centre for Research and Innovation, local firms received a total of $287 million in venture capital in 2003, less than half of the $680 million invested in 2002. The amount that year was itself a drastic decline from levels in previous years. Area companies attracted almost $922 million in 2001, while a record $1.3 billion poured into companies in 2000.

Source: "2003 a weak year for local VC investment," *Ottawa Business Journal*, Jan. 16, 2004; "Ottawa pull weakens for startup cash," by Jill Vardy, National Post, Jan. 26, 2002

USER RELEVANCE

If accounting information is to be useful, it must (among other things) be understandable and relevant. In order for users like Mr. Emery and Mr. Finnson to understand the information that is provided on financial statements, they must have some knowledge of the accounting system: what items are identified, measured, and recorded; how those items are recorded; and how financial statements are generated from the recorded data. Without that knowledge, they will have difficulty understanding the importance (relevance) of the numbers and may not be able to make the best decisions.

The accounting system measures, records, and aggregates the effects on the company of numerous economic events. To interpret the information in financial statements, you must be able to understand the process by which accounting information is obtained, and the guidelines by which it is classified and aggregated for financial statements. Only then can you use accounting information sensibly to make decisions. Chapter 1 provided an overview of the types of information that are presented in financial statements. This chapter and the next explain how accountants collect, classify, and aggregate that information.

BASIC ACCOUNTING EQUATION

There are several possible approaches to understanding the accounting systems that companies use. The approach taken in this chapter is to focus on the balance sheet, which will demonstrate how a typical set of transactions would be reflected in the financial records, and also how the three major financial statements would be prepared using the transaction information. We will use the basic accounting equation discussed in Chapter 1, which is the basis of all accounting systems.

LEARNING OBJECTIVE 1

Understand the basic accounting equation.

BASIC ACCOUNTING EQUATION

Assets = Liabilities + Shareholders' Equity

When transactions are recorded in the accounting system, the equality of this equation must always be maintained. The balance sheet provides readers with information about this equality at the beginning and at the end of the current accounting period (usually by showing amounts from the previous year in the outside column, and amounts from the current year in the inside column). A statement with the amounts for two years is called a comparative statement (see Le Château's balance sheet in Appendix A at the end of the book).

The users of financial information typically want to know more than just the balance sheet amounts. They usually want to know more about how the company's financial position changed from the beginning to the end of the year. An income statement and a cash flow statement are both useful for this. In the remainder of this chapter, the balance sheet equation will be used to record a set of typical transactions for a hypothetical company, and an income statement and a cash flow statement will be constructed from this information.

In Chapter 1, we explained that share capital (one of the components of shareholders' equity) increases when the owners make investments in the company and are issued shares. We also showed you that retained earnings (the other main component of shareholders' equity) increases when the company earns **net income** (revenues minus expenses), and decreases when the company declares a dividend (a payment of income back to the owners).

To help you understand the links between the financial statements and how the various items are affected by transactions, we will include the following notations beside the amounts that affect retained earnings: R for revenue, E for expense, and D for dividend. Similarly, to help you understand the cash flows, we will designate the amounts that affect cash as follows: O for operating, F for financing, and I for investing.

TRANSACTION ANALYSIS AND THE ACCOUNTING EQUATION

LEARNING OBJECTIVE 2

Analyze simple transactions and describe their effect on the basic accounting equation.

The basic accounting equation can now be used to illustrate the functioning of the accounting system and the preparation of financial statements. We will use typical transactions of a retail sales company to demonstrate the analysis and recording of transactions in the accounting system.

Assume that the Demo Retail Company Ltd. is formed as a corporation in December 2005 with the issuance of common shares for $7,500.[1] Before the end of December, Demo uses $4,500 of the cash received from the investors to buy equipment. It also buys $2,500 of inventory on account. (On account means that Demo has been extended credit by its suppliers and will be required to pay for the inventory at some later date. Typical terms for this type of credit require payment within 30 days.)

Transaction Analysis—Start-up Period

On December 31, 2005, just prior to commencing operations, Demo would like to prepare financial statements. Because Demo has not yet begun its normal operation of selling goods to customers, it has not yet earned any income. Therefore, it has no need for an income statement. It could, however, prepare a cash flow statement and a

---

[1] The amounts used in this and most other examples are stated in small, round numbers for ease of presentation. If you want to think of them in more realistic terms, you could multiply all numbers by a factor such as one thousand.

balance sheet. The cash flow statement for December would simply show the $7,500 cash inflow from the issuance of shares (a financing activity), the $4,500 outflow to buy equipment (an investing activity), and the ending balance of cash ($3,000). To prepare the balance sheet, we would use the basic accounting equation developed earlier.

Balance sheet preparation begins with an analysis of the transactions. In December 2005, there were three transactions to record. They are as follows:[2]

A. $7,500 issuance of common shares for cash.

B. $4,500 purchase of equipment for cash.

C. $2,500 purchase of inventory on account.

Each of these transactions is analyzed in the following subsections.

TRANSACTION A

Demo issued common shares for $7,500.

ANALYSIS   The company shareholders have contributed $7,500 to the company in exchange for ownership rights. The cash received by the company increased its cash asset, and the ownership interest is represented by an increase in common shares. The entry can be summarized as follows.

> ### ANALYSIS OF TRANSACTION A
>
> Assets (Cash) increased by $7,500
> Shareholders' Equity (Common Shares) increased by $7,500

The effects of this transaction can be summarized as follows.

> ### EFFECTS OF TRANSACTION A ON THE BALANCE SHEET
>
> | Assets | = | Liabilities | + | Shareholders' Equity |
> |---|---|---|---|---|
> | Cash + Inventory + Equipment | = | Accounts Payable + | | Common Shares + Retained Earnings |
> | +7,500 F | = | | | +7,500 |

Note that the entries maintain the balance in the basic accounting equation. Also note that the cash transaction has been designated with an F, indicating that this is a financing-type cash flow.

TRANSACTION B

Demo purchased equipment for $4,500.

ANALYSIS   Because the purchase of equipment required an outflow of cash, cash decreased. The equipment purchased is generally regarded as a long-term asset because the company will use it over several future periods. The asset will be used up or consumed over those future periods, and the annual amount that is consumed or used will be shown as an amortization expense. The expensing of part of this amount is shown later, in the transactions for January. By the end of December, however, none of the asset has been used up or consumed and the full amount should be reported as an asset.

---

[2] We will designate these transactions with letters to distinguish them from the numbered transactions in January, which are discussed later in this chapter.

The entry can be summarized as follows.

ANALYSIS OF TRANSACTION B

Assets (Cash) decreased by $4,500

Assets (Equipment) increased by $4,500

The effects of this transaction can be summarized as follows.

EFFECTS OF TRANSACTION B ON THE BALANCE SHEET

Assets	=	Liabilities	+	Shareholders' Equity

Cash + Inventory + Equipment	= Accounts Payable + Common Shares + Retained Earnings
−4,500 I + 4,500	

Note that the cash outflow has been designated with an I, indicating that it is an investing cash flow, and that the equilibrium of the basic accounting equation has been maintained.

LEARNING OBJECTIVE 3

Describe the difference between accrual-basis accounting and cash-basis accounting.

GAAP   The treatment of this transaction under GAAP is based on an assumption of **accrual-basis** accounting. Under accrual accounting, costs (such as the cost of the equipment) are only represented as decreases in the shareholders' wealth (expenses) when the item is consumed. In this transaction, therefore, the view under GAAP is that one asset, cash, has simply been exchanged for another asset, equipment, and there has not (yet) been any expense or change in the shareholders' wealth.

Accrual-basis accounting is different from **cash-basis** accounting, in which costs are represented as decreases in shareholders' wealth (expenses) when the cash is paid. In the cash-basis system, therefore, this transaction would result in an expense that would be reported on the income statement. However, cash-basis accounting is not GAAP. GAAP requires accrual-basis accounting. This is discussed in more detail later in this chapter.

TRANSACTION C

Demo purchased $2,500 of inventory on account.

ANALYSIS   The substance of this transaction is that Demo has received an asset (inventory) from its supplier and in exchange has given the supplier a promise to pay for the inventory at a later date. The promise to pay represents an obligation of the company and is therefore recorded as a liability. This type of liability is usually referred to as an **account payable.** The entry can be summarized as follows.

ANALYSIS OF TRANSACTION C

Assets (Inventory) increased by $2,500

Liabilities (Accounts Payable) increased by $2,500

Note that the inventory is recorded at the amount the company has to pay for it (its cost), not its resale (retail) value.

The effects of this transaction can be summarized as follows.

EFFECTS OF TRANSACTION C ON THE BALANCE SHEET

Assets	=	Liabilities	+	Shareholders' Equity
Cash + Inventory + Equipment	=	Accounts Payable	+	Common Shares + Retained Earnings
+ 2,500		= +2,500		

GAAP   As with Transaction B, this transaction involves the purchase of an asset, but this time no cash changes hands immediately. The inventory will be held until it is sold, and GAAP requires that the inventory be recorded at its cost and shown as an asset until it is sold. The cost is, therefore, recorded as an asset until the company relinquishes title to it. There is no immediate income statement impact from this transaction. It will only affect the income statement later, in the period in which the inventory is sold. Note that the transaction also has no impact on the cash flow statement in December, since no cash changed hands. Cash flow will be affected when the company pays the supplier.

The effects of all three of these transactions have been recorded in the balance sheet equation that appears in Exhibit 2-1. Note that the beginning balances in all the accounts are zero because this is a new company.

DEMO RETAIL COMPANY LTD.

EXHIBIT 2-1

BASIC ACCOUNTING EQUATION
(Amounts in Dollars)

	Assets				=	Liabilities	+	Shareholders' Equity	
	Cash	+ Inventory	+	Equipment	= Accounts Payable	+	Common Shares	+	Retained Earnings
Balances	0 +	0	+	0	= 0	+	0	+	0
Transaction #									
A	+7,500 F				=		+7,500		
B	−4,500 I			+4,500	=				
C		+2,500			= +2,500				
Balances	3,000 +	2,500	+	4,500	= 2,500	+	7,500	+	0

At the bottom of Exhibit 2-1, you can see the net result of transactions A, B, and C. These figures represent the balance sheet at the end of December 2005. The balance sheet could be formally represented as shown below. Note that the total assets of Demo equal the sum of the liabilities and shareholders' equity, as they should, to satisfy the basic accounting equation.

DEMO RETAIL COMPANY LTD.
Balance Sheet
As at December 31, 2005

Assets		**Liabilities**	
Cash	$ 3,000	Accounts payable	$ 2,500
Inventory	2,500		
Equipment	4,500	**Shareholders' equity**	
		Common shares	7,500
Total assets	$10,000	Total liabilities and shareholders' equity	$10,000

Note that because the retained earnings has a zero balance, it was not included in the balance sheet.

Now that you have seen how a few simple transactions are analyzed and reported on the financial statements, we are going to continue with the example. Assume that during January the following events occurred that affect Demo's account balances.

1. During January, 2006, Demo sold some inventory (purchased in December) to customers, on account,[3] for $2,500.[4]

2. The cost of the items removed from inventory for sales in January was $1,800.

3. Purchases of new inventory in January totalled $2,100. All these purchases were made on account.

4. During the month, Demo received $2,200 from customers as payments on their accounts.

5. Demo made payments of $2,700 on its accounts payable during January.

6. Demo paid $360 in cash on January 1 for an insurance policy to cover its inventory and equipment.

7. The above insurance policy covers the period from January 1 through June 30, 2006.*

8. Demo's accountant determined that the equipment should be amortized by $150 for January.*

9. On the first day of January, Demo purchased land for $15,000 as a site for a future retail outlet. In order to pay for the land, Demo raised money by borrowing $10,000 from the bank and issuing new shares for $5,000.

10. The interest rate charged on the loan from the bank in Transaction 9 was 6%, to be paid every three months.*

11. Dividends in the amount of $250 were declared and paid in January.

* As discussed later in this chapter, such items relate to adjustments (which would normally be recorded as at the end of the accounting period) rather than regular transactions.

Transaction Analysis—Operating Period

For each of the events or transactions that affect the company, the accountant must analyze the economic substance of the transaction in order to decide what accounts are affected and by how much. We call this **transaction analysis**. We have already done this for Transactions A, B, and C, which occurred in December. It is at this stage of the accounting process that the accountant's training and knowledge are most needed. Not only must the economic substance of the transaction be analyzed, but the accountant must know the accounting guidelines that apply to the transaction.

---

[3] The term "on account" in a sales transaction means that the company is granting the customer credit. The customer will then pay for the goods at some later date, based on the agreement with the seller about the terms.

[4] The dollar amounts here are aggregate totals of all units that were sold during the month. Information about individual units would likely be recorded daily, and would be of use to the sales or marketing manager, but we are interested in the aggregate effect of sales in this example.

For each of the January transactions, the economic substance will be analyzed, GAAP for the transaction will be discussed, and an appropriate accounting entry will be proposed.

The transaction will be entered into the accounting system (the basic accounting equation). Exhibit 2-6, at the end of this section, shows how all the January transactions affect the basic accounting equation. You may want to try to construct your own exhibit as you work through the transactions.

TRANSACTION 1

Demo sold some of its inventory to customers, on account, for $2,500.

ANALYSIS   The substance of a sale transaction is that the company has exchanged an asset that it possesses for an asset that the customer possesses. The asset given up by the company may be an item of inventory, if the company is a retailer or a manufacturer, or it may be some type of expertise or service if the company is a service provider. In this case, Demo is a retailer and the asset given up is inventory. The asset received in exchange from the customer is generally cash, but other possibilities exist. For example, when a new car is purchased, the buyer's old car is often traded in as part of the deal. Also, the customer may exchange a promise to pay later. This is typically called a sale on account, and it results in the company receiving the right to receive payment, usually called an account receivable, in exchange for the inventory. An account receivable is an account that will be received by the company (when it is paid by the customer) in the future. It becomes a receivable on the day the inventory is sold, even though the amount is not due to be received until later. This transaction is called a credit sale or a sale on account.

Because this is an exchange, there are two parts of the transaction to consider: the inflow of the asset received in the exchange and the outflow of the asset given up. The inflow increases assets (accounts receivable) and increases the wealth of the shareholders (retained earnings). The outflow decreases assets (inventory) owned by the company and decreases the wealth of the shareholders (retained earnings). If the inflow is worth more than the outflow in the exchange, the company has generated a profit from the sale transaction. If the inflow is less than the outflow, a loss results. The increases and decreases in shareholders' wealth in this transaction are typically called sales revenue (inflow) and cost of goods sold (outflow), respectively.

Because the analysis shown in Exhibit 2-6 focuses only on the balance sheet, the effects of both the sales revenue and the cost of goods sold will be shown as affecting the retained earnings portion of the shareholders' equity. Remember that net income (revenue minus expenses) increases retained earnings. It should, therefore, be logical that revenues increase retained earnings and expenses decrease retained earnings. This approach of showing revenues and expenses as increases or decreases in retained earnings is a temporary shortcut we are going to use to introduce you to transactions.

The question remaining in the analysis is how to value the inflow and the outflow. Based on the information in Transaction 1, the total selling price of the goods sold was $2,500. Therefore, sales revenue (retained earnings) and accounts receivable both increase by $2,500. There is no information given in Transaction 1 regarding the cost of goods sold; this is covered in Transaction 2. It may seem odd to analyze and record these two simultaneous events separately.

Nonetheless, it is necessary because the transactions occur at two different value levels: retail and cost. For example, in a department store, when a clerk rings up a sale, a record is made of the sales revenue amount and of the increase in cash (or accounts receivable in the case of a sale on account). The salesperson does not know, and is not responsible for, the cost of the item sold. The cost is determined separately, as described under Transaction 2.

To summarize:

ANALYSIS OF TRANSACTION 1

Assets (Accounts Receivable) increased by $2,500
Shareholders' Equity (Retained Earnings) increased by $2,500

GAAP The timing of the recognition of revenues and expenses is an important decision that management must make in preparing financial statements. There is an underlying conflict between reporting income information in a timely manner and being assured that the information is reliable.

To take two extreme positions, it might be argued at one extreme that a company should record a sale when a customer signs a contract for the future delivery of the product. At the other extreme, it might be argued that the company should wait until cash is collected before recording a sale.

- In the first case, the company is counting on delivering the product and ultimately collecting the cash from the sale. These are both uncertain events and, if they do not materialize, shareholders may be misled by the income statement into thinking the company is doing better than it really is.

- In the second case, by delaying recognition of the sale until the cash is collected (assuming that it isn't collected when the goods change hands), the uncertainty will be resolved, but the income statement will not provide shareholders with a very good measure of the company's business activity during the period prior to collection of the cash. Sales that had been made but are in the process of collection would not appear on the income statement.

LEARNING OBJECTIVE 6

Describe the revenue recognition and matching criteria.

The two extremes just discussed have evolved over time into two bases on which accountants generally prepare financial statements: the accrual basis and the cash basis. The accrual basis attempts to measure performance (i.e., revenues and expenses) in the period in which the performance takes place rather than when the cash is collected. When the accrual basis is used, **revenue recognition criteria** are considered to determine if performance has been achieved (i.e., the earning process has been substantially completed). These criteria are discussed in detail in Chapter 4. In brief, the criteria state that revenue can be recognized as earned when

- the company has performed the majority of the things it has to do associated with the sale (e.g., completed the work, transferred the inventory to the buyer, etc.),

- the amount that has been earned is known, and

- there is reasonable assurance that the amount will be collected.

You can see from these criteria that when a customer signs a contract, as described in the previous paragraph, revenue would not be recognized because the first criterion, that of completion of the work, was not fulfilled. The company must still deliver the product, which is a major part of the earning process. Once the product is delivered, however, revenue could be recognized even if cash was not received at that point, provided the other two criteria were met. The criteria provide shareholders with assurance that the amounts stated as revenues and expenses are reasonable, and that there is a high probability that the revenues and expenses recorded will ultimately result in similar cash flows. The accrual basis is used by most businesses and will be used throughout this book.

When the cash basis is used, events are recorded only when their cash effects occur. For example, sales revenue is recorded only when cash is received from the customer, and the cost of goods sold is recorded only when the cash is paid out for inventory. You can see that on this basis you could record expenses for inventory earlier than you record the revenue for selling it. Or, if the company purchased its inventory on account (to be paid for later), you could record the cash from the sale before you record the expense for the inventory. In either case, if the financial statements were prepared between the dates the cash was collected for the sale and the cash was paid for the inventory, you would have the revenue recorded in one period and its associated expense in another. The mistiming of recording activities such as these would result in the income statement not showing the company's performance clearly. Because of the potentially misleading information produced by the cash basis, it is not used very often. It is, however, still used by some farmers, fishers, and professional service companies to account for their businesses. In the past, most not-for-profit organizations used the cash basis, but today most of them have switched to the accrual basis.

In a business such as Demo, the revenue recognition criteria are generally met when the product is transferred to the customer. Therefore, in the preceding analysis, the result of Transaction 1 is to recognize revenues (increase retained earnings). Demo should not wait until the cash is collected (see Transaction 4). On a cash basis, of course, Demo would not recognize revenue as a result of Transaction 1.

Another equally important aspect of accrual-basis accounting is the **matching concept**. This concept requires that all costs associated with generating sales revenue should be matched on the income statement with the revenue earned. That is, the cost of goods sold related to this revenue should be recognized in the same period as the sales revenue. See the analysis of Transaction 2 for the recording of the cost of goods sold.

Refer to the following summary for the proper recording of Transaction 1 in the basic accounting equation. Note that the equation is balanced after the entry is made. Note also that the entry to the retained earnings account has been designated with an R, indicating that this is a revenue item that will be reported on the income statement for the accounting period.

EFFECTS OF TRANSACTION 1 ON THE BALANCE SHEET

| Assets | = | Liabilities | + Shareholders' Equity |

Cash +	Accounts Receivable +	Inventory +	Prepaid Insurance +	Land +	Equipment =	Accounts Payable +	Interest Payable +	Bank Loan +	Common Shares +	Retained Earnings
	+2,500				=					+2,500 R

Note that this transaction has no effect on cash. The cash effects of the sale of goods will be felt by the company only in the period in which the receivable is collected. This will lead to a difference between the cash received from operations and the net income for the period.

TRANSACTION 2

The cost of goods removed from inventory for sales in January totalled $1,800.

ANALYSIS As explained in the analysis of Transaction 1, there are two parts to a sale transaction. Transaction 1 included information about the revenue side of the transaction. Here in Transaction 2, the costs that are to be matched with the revenue are given.

The effect of the outflow of the inventory is to decrease both the inventory asset and the shareholders' equity by the cost of the inventory that has been transferred to customers. The decrease in shareholders' wealth (retained earnings) by the cost of goods sold is one of the many expenses that the company shows on its income statement.

To summarize:

> **ANALYSIS OF TRANSACTION 2**
>
> Assets (Inventory) decreased by $1,800
> Shareholders' Equity (Retained Earnings) decreased by $1,800

GAAP As explained earlier, in the analysis of Transaction 1, when the revenues from the sale are recognized, the matching concept requires that the expenses associated with that revenue be recognized as well. Under accrual-basis accounting, the cost of the inventory is held in an asset account until it is sold; when it is sold, it is transferred to an expense account. This illustrates a very important concept in accrual accounting, so further elaboration may be warranted.

Under accrual-basis accounting, a **cost** can be classified as either an asset or an expense, depending on its nature.

- If the cost represents something that still has value to the company, and will be of economic benefit to it in the future, then it is classified as an **asset** and reported on the balance sheet.

- If the cost represents something that has already given up its value to the company, and will not be of further benefit to it in the future, then it is classified as an expense and reported on the income statement.

Many costs are initially classified as assets but eventually must be reclassified as expenses.

For example, while Demo Company held the inventory, its cost was recorded as an asset (inventory); but when the inventory is sold, its cost ceases to be an asset and must be transferred to an expense account (cost of goods sold). For a retailer such as Demo, the cost of the inventory is simply the wholesale price that Demo paid to acquire it.

Typically, the cost of goods sold is determined at the end of the period by physically counting the number of units still available in inventory and then attaching unit costs to those units. Knowing the cost of the inventory that is still unsold at the end of the period (ending inventory) and the cost of the inventory at the beginning of the accounting period (beginning inventory), as well as the purchases during the period, the company can calculate the cost of the goods that were sold as follows.

COST OF GOODS SOLD CALCULATION

Beginning inventory
+   *Goods purchased* during the period

=   *Goods available for sale* during the period
−   *Ending Inventory*

=   *Goods Sold* during the period

Note that all the above amounts would be recorded at their *cost.*

The determination of the cost of the ending inventory and goods sold is discussed in greater depth in Chapter 7.

The entry for Transaction 2 is summarized as follows.

EFFECTS OF TRANSACTION 2 ON THE BALANCE SHEET

Assets						=	Liabilities			+ Shareholders' Equity	
Cash +	Accounts Receivable +	Prepaid Inventory + Insurance +		Land +	Equipment	=	Accounts Payable +	Interest Payable +	Bank Loan +	Common Shares +	Retained Earnings
		−1,800				=					−1,800E

Note that the entry to the retained earnings account has been designated with an E, indicating that this is an expense that will be reported in the income statement for this accounting period. Also note that this transaction has no effect on cash. The cash flow effects of inventory occur when payment for the inventory is made. This leads to a difference between the cash from operations and the net income for the period.

TRANSACTION 3

Purchases of new inventory in January totalled $2,100. All these purchases were made on account.

ANALYSIS   The purchase of inventory has the effect of increasing the inventory asset. Because the inventory is bought on account, Demo has given the seller a promise to pay at some time in the future. Demo should record an increase in accounts payable to indicate its liability to the supplier. The term "account payable" means an account that will be paid in the future. It becomes a payable on the day the inventory is purchased, even though payment is not due until later. (Note that on the seller's books, this transaction results in a corresponding account receivable.)

To summarize:

EFFECTS OF TRANSACTION 3

Assets (Inventory) increased by $2,100
Liabilities (Accounts Payable) increased by $2,100

GAAP   The valuation principle for inventory under GAAP is that it be recorded at its acquisition cost (i.e., the price paid to obtain it). When inventory is purchased on account, it is valued at the amount of the liability incurred in the transaction; that is, the value of the account payable. Accounts payable are liabilities that are generally settled in a short amount of time (30 to 60 days) and are valued at the gross amount owed. There is generally no interest on accounts payable even though they are loans from the seller.

Occasionally, inventory is purchased on longer-term credit, which results in a formal loan document called a **note payable**. In the case of a note payable, interest is usually explicitly recognized. The interest would be recorded as an expense and as either an outflow of cash, if it is paid, or as a new liability on its own (interest payable), if the interest is going to be paid in the future. The accounting for interest is explained further in Transaction 9.

The entry for Transaction 3 is summarized as follows.

EFFECTS OF TRANSACTION 3 ON THE BALANCE SHEET

		Assets				=	Liabilities			+ Shareholders' Equity	
	Accounts		Prepaid				Accounts	Interest	Bank	Common	Retained
Cash +	Receivable +	Inventory +	Insurance +	Land +	Equipment =		Payable +	Payable +	Loan +	Shares +	Earnings
		+2,100					= +2,100				

Note that this transaction had no effect on cash. The cash effects of purchasing inventory will occur when the account payable is paid. Also note that it had no effect on shareholders' wealth (retained earnings). Income will be affected only when the inventory is sold.

TRANSACTION 4

During the month, Demo received $2,200 from customers as payments on their accounts.

ANALYSIS The receipt of cash from customers means that cash increases. Because the customer no longer owes this amount to the company, the value of the accounts receivable decreases by the amount of the payment. The entry can be summarized as follows.

ANALYSIS OF TRANSACTION 4

Assets (Cash) increased by $2,200

Assets (Accounts Receivable) decreased by $2,200

GAAP Accounts receivable are generally short-term loans from the seller to the buyer and do not typically result in the recognition of interest. The amount of the receivable is stated at the selling price to the buyer. If this were a **note receivable** that explicitly included interest, the cash received would be more than the selling price, and the excess amount above the selling price would represent interest revenue.

The effects of this transaction can be summarized as follows.

EFFECTS OF TRANSACTION 4 ON THE BALANCE SHEET

		Assets				=	Liabilities			+ Shareholders' Equity	
	Accounts		Prepaid				Accounts	Interest	Bank	Common	Retained
Cash +	Receivable +	Inventory +	Insurance +	Land +	Equipment =		Payable +	Payable +	Loan +	Shares +	Earnings
+2,200	O −2,200					=					

Note that the cash entry has been designated with an O, indicating that this is an operating cash flow.

It is very important to note that this transaction does not affect shareholders' wealth (retained earnings). The income effect related to accounts receivable was recorded earlier, when the original sale occurred. Since the revenue has already been recognized, when the sale was made, there is no revenue at this point; one asset (accounts receivable) is simply being replaced by another asset (cash).

TRANSACTION 5

Demo made payments of $2,700 on its accounts payable.

ANALYSIS   Cash payments result in a decrease in the asset: cash. In this case, because the payment is on account, there is a corresponding decrease in the liability: accounts payable.

To summarize:

ANALYSIS OF TRANSACTION 5

Assets (Cash) decreased by $2,700

Liabilities (Accounts Payable) decreased by $2,700

GAAP   Note that there is no interest involved in this case. When longer-term loans are involved, the payment would have to be divided between the amount that represents interest and the amount that represents repayment of the original amount of the loan.

The effects of this transaction on the accounting equation can be summarized as follows.

EFFECTS OF TRANSACTION 5 ON THE BALANCE SHEET

			Assets			=	Liabilities			+	Shareholders' Equity	
			Prepaid				Accounts	Interest	Bank	Common	Retained	
Cash +	Receivable +	Inventory +	Insurance +	Land +	Equipment	=	Payable +	Payable +	Loan +	Shares +	Earnings	
−2,700 O							= −2,700					

The cash outflow will be reported in the operating section of the cash flow statement.

Note that shareholders' equity (retained earnings) is not affected by this transaction. The income effects of inventory are shown in the period in which the inventory is sold (when the cost of the inventory is transferred to an expense account, cost of goods sold). This could occur either before or after the payment of cash.

TRANSACTIONS 6 AND 7

Demo paid $360 in cash on January 1 for an insurance policy to cover its inventory and equipment. The policy covers the period from January 1 to June 30, 2006.

ANALYSIS   This transaction is an example of a **prepaid expense**. The cost of the insurance coverage is paid in advance of the coverage period. At the date of the payment (January 1 in this case) the cost of the policy should be shown as an asset, since it has not been used up yet. Another way to think about this as an asset is to consider what would happen if you cancelled the policy immediately after it was paid. Except for any cancellation and/or processing fees, you should be entitled to get your money back because the insurance company has not provided any coverage yet. Only as time passes is the coverage consumed. In this example, the amount of the coverage that is consumed in January is one month's worth, or $60; we simply spread the coverage out evenly over the six-month period. Therefore, by the end of January, $60 of the insurance should be treated as an expense to represent the month that has passed, and the rest ($300) should be treated as an asset representing the coverage to which the company is still entitled as of the end of January.

Exhibit 2-2 displays a timeline that illustrates the effects of a prepaid expense and the timing issue involved. (Note that the proportions illustrated in this exhibit are not specific to the insurance example for Demo.) Part of the cost results in an expense being recognized on the income statement in the current period, and the remaining portion represents an asset carried forward on the balance sheet into the following period.

| EXHIBIT 2-2 | **PREPAID EXPENSES: General Model** |

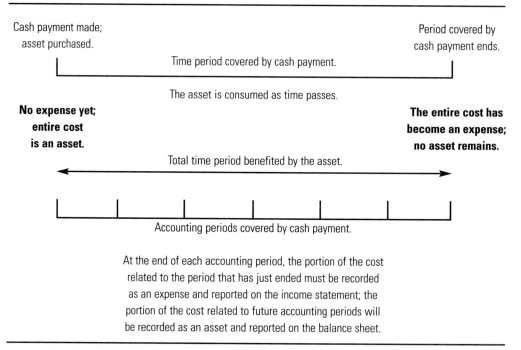

At the end of each accounting period, the portion of the cost related to the period that has just ended must be recorded as an expense and reported on the income statement; the portion of the cost related to future accounting periods will be recorded as an asset and reported on the balance sheet.

Exhibit 2-3 illustrates how the general concepts related to prepaid expenses are applied to the specific case of the insurance policy purchased by Demo Company.

PREPAID EXPENSES: Insurance Example EXHIBIT 2-3

January 1, 2005:
$360 payment made;
insurance purchased.

June 30, 2005:
Period covered by
insurance policy ends.

Six-month period covered by insurance policy.

The insurance policy expires as time passes.

**No expense yet;
entire cost is an asset
(prepaid insurance).**

**Entire cost has become
insurance expense;
no asset remains.**

If financial statements are prepared on a monthly basis, six
separate accounting periods are covered by the insurance policy.

At the end of each month, the portion of the cost related to that
period (one-sixth of $360, or $60) is recorded as insurance
expense and reported on the income statement; the portion of
the cost related to future accounting periods is recorded as
prepaid insurance (an asset) and reported on the balance sheet.

	January	February	March	April	May	June

On the Income Statement:

Insurance expense for the month:	$60	$60	$60	$60	$60	$60

On the Balance Sheet:

Prepaid insurance at end of the month:	$300	$240	$180	$120	$60	$0

There are several ways that a company might record this insurance transaction. One way would be to record the initial cash outflow of $360 on January 1 as a decrease in cash and an increase in a prepaid expense account (Transaction 6). Then, on January 31, the company would have to record a decrease in the prepaid expense (asset) account and a decrease in retained earnings for the $60 portion of the cost that has expired and become an expense (Transaction 7). This set of effects is shown below.

ANALYSIS OF TRANSACTION 6

Assets (Prepaid Insurance) increased by $360
Assets (Cash) decreased by $360

ANALYSIS OF TRANSACTION 7

Shareholders' Equity (Retained Earnings) decreased by $60
Assets (Prepaid Insurance) decreased by $60

The net result of the above would be to record a decrease in cash of $360, a decrease in retained earnings of $60, and an increase in prepaid insurance of $300. Therefore, another way to record this transaction would be to make one three-part entry reflecting this net result. For our purposes, we will use the first approach in recording the transaction, but recognize that different companies might use different methods.

GAAP The handling of the prepaid expense as part expense and part asset is dictated by the accrual basis of accounting and the principle of matching expenses with revenues in the proper accounting period.

The effects of the insurance transactions can be summarized as follows.

EFFECTS OF TRANSACTIONS 6 AND 7 ON THE BALANCE SHEET

	Assets					=	Liabilities			+	Shareholders' Equity	
	Accounts		Prepaid				Accounts	Interest	Bank	Common		Retained
Cash +	Receivable +	Inventory +	Insurance +	Land +	Equipment =		Payable +	Payable +	Loan +	Shares +		Earnings
−360 O			+360			=						
			−60			=						−60 E

Note that these transactions decrease cash by $360, which represents an operating cash flow, and decrease income by $60 in January.

TRANSACTION 8

Demo's accountant determined that the equipment should be amortized by $150 for January.

ANALYSIS Whenever an expenditure is made by a company to acquire an asset, there are three general questions to ask regarding the nature of the transaction:

1. Has an asset been created?

2. If so, what is the value of the asset?

3. How does the asset get used up over time, and when does it cease to exist?

To address the first question, the criteria for an asset must be evaluated. Does the item have probable future value, and does the company own it or have the right to use it? If the answer to both of these questions is yes, an asset exists and should be recorded. When Demo originally purchased its equipment, the answers to both recognition criteria questions were yes. Demo owned the equipment, and the equipment had future value (because it was to be used to sell products and thus generate revenues). The equipment, therefore, qualified as an asset.

The answer to the second question is that, under GAAP, the equipment is valued at its acquisition cost (sometimes called historical cost). In this example, the $4,500 value of the equipment at December 31, 2005 represents its historical cost.

The third question is a little more difficult to answer. For an asset such as inventory, the answer is relatively simple: the asset ceases to exist when it is sold and the company gives up title to it. The inventory stays on the balance sheet as an asset until it is sold, and then its cost appears as an expense (cost of goods sold) on the income statement. For equipment, the answer is more complicated. The equipment is used up as time passes and the equipment is used. Equipment has a useful life that can be estimated. For example, it may be expected to last for five years, at which time it will be sold, discarded, or traded in for a new piece of equipment.

Because the asset is used up over time, some of the cost of the asset should be shown as an expense in each period in which it is used. Another reason to show some of the cost as an expense each period is that the expense of using the equipment must be matched (the matching concept) with the revenues generated from the use of the equipment. The amount shown as an expense in any period is called the **amortization** (sometimes known as **depreciation**) of the asset.

How much should be shown as amortization expense in any particular period is a function of how much of the asset's value gets used up during that period of time. Consequently, there are numerous ways to calculate how much amortization should be taken in a given period; these are discussed in detail in Chapter 8. The most common method used is **straight-line amortization**, which assumes that an asset is used evenly throughout its life and that the same amount of amortization should be charged to expense in every accounting period. The formula for calculating straight-line amortization is:

$$\text{Straight-Line Amortization} = \frac{\text{Original Cost} - \text{Estimated Residual Value}}{\text{Estimated Useful Life}}$$

Note that two estimates are required to perform this calculation. First, the **useful life** of the asset must be estimated. This could be expressed in years or months, depending on the length of the accounting period. In the Demo example, this would be months. The second estimate is **residual value.** This is an estimate of what the asset will be worth at the end of its useful life. The quantity in the numerator of the calculation is sometimes called the **amortizable value** (or **depreciable cost**) of the asset because it is the amount that should be amortized over the asset's useful life.

In the case of Demo Retail Company Ltd., if it is assumed that the equipment would have an estimated useful life of two years (24 months), and a residual value at the end of two years of $900, the monthly amortization would then be calculated as:

$$\text{Straight-Line Amortization} = \frac{\$4,500 - \$900}{24 \text{ months}}$$
$$= \$150/\text{month}$$

At the end of each month, Demo should reduce the value of the equipment by $150 and show a $150 expense on the income statement (amortization expense). To summarize:

ANALYSIS OF TRANSACTION 8

Assets (Equipment) decreased by $150
Shareholders' Equity (Retained Earnings) decreased by $150

In our example, it is assumed that the share issuance and bank borrowing are separate from the purchase of the land. The transaction is, therefore, a monetary exchange, even though there is no net effect on cash.

The effects of this transaction can be summarized as follows.

EFFECTS OF TRANSACTION 9 ON THE BALANCE SHEET

	Assets					=	Liabilities			+ Shareholders' Equity	
Cash +	Accounts Receivable +	Inventory +	Prepaid Insurance +	Land +	Equipment =		Accounts Payable +	Interest Payable +	Bank Loan +	Common Shares +	Retained Earnings
+5,000 F						=				+5,000	
+10,000 F						=			+10,000		
−15,000 I				+15,000		=					

Note that these transactions do not affect income (retained earnings), and the effects on cash are offsetting. As we will explain in Chapter 5, this particular transaction would be treated as a noncash transaction and, as such, would not be reported in the cash flow statement. (It would, however, be disclosed in the notes to the financial statements.) Nevertheless, in this chapter we will treat the components of this transaction as separate items and report them all in the cash flow statement.

TRANSACTION 10

The interest rate charged on the loan from the bank in Transaction 9 is 6% and is paid quarterly (at the end of every three months).

ANALYSIS Interest is the amount charged by lenders for the use of their money. From the borrower's point of view, interest is an expense and therefore results in a decrease in the shareholders' wealth during the period in which it is incurred. By the end of January, the $10,000 loan has been outstanding for one month and, therefore, one month's interest expense should be recognized. Since the interest has not been paid yet (and will not be paid until the end of March), Demo will have to recognize a liability for its obligation to pay the interest at the end of the quarter. This is an example of an **accrued expense**: a cost that has been incurred but not yet been paid.

As illustrated in Exhibit 2-4, accrued expenses are those that are recognized on the income statement in the period in which they are incurred, which is prior to the period in which they are paid in cash. A related liability will therefore appear on the balance sheet. Note that the proportions illustrated in this exhibit are not representative of the interest example for Demo.

ACCRUED EXPENSES: General Model

EXHIBIT 2-4

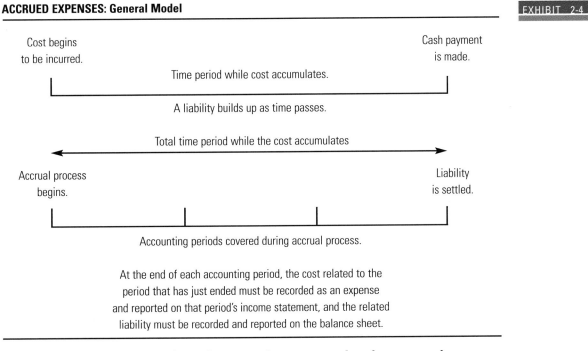

Cost begins
to be incurred.

Cash payment
is made.

Time period while cost accumulates.

A liability builds up as time passes.

Total time period while the cost accumulates

Accrual process
begins.

Liability
is settled.

Accounting periods covered during accrual process.

At the end of each accounting period, the cost related to the
period that has just ended must be recorded as an expense
and reported on that period's income statement, and the related
liability must be recorded and reported on the balance sheet.

Exhibit 2-5 illustrates how the general concepts related to accrued expenses
are applied to the specific case of the interest on Demo Company's loan.

EXHIBIT 2-5

ACCRUED EXPENSES: Interest Example

January 1, 2006:
$10,000 borrowed;
interest begins to be incurred.

March 31, 2006:
Quarterly interest
payment is made.

Three-month period covered by quarterly interest payment.

Interest expense and interest payable accrue as time passes.

If financial statements are prepared on a monthly basis, three separate
accounting periods are covered by each quarterly interest payment.

At the end of each month, the cost related to that period ($10,000 $\times$ 6%
$\times$ 1/12, or $50) is recorded as interest expense and reported on the
income statement. At the same time, a liability for the amount to be
paid in the future is recorded and reported on the balance sheet.

January	February	March

On the Income Statement:

Interest expense for the month:	$50	$50	$50

On the Balance Sheet:

Interest payable end of the month:	$50	$100	$150	before the payment is made;
			$0	after the payment is made.

To calculate the amount of interest expense each period, you multiply the amount of the loan (known as the principal) by the interest rate and then by the fraction of the year that has passed (since the interest rate is always expressed as a yearly rate). In Demo's case, the amount of interest incurred in January is $50 [$10,000 × 6% × 1/12]. Shareholders' equity (retained earnings) should therefore decrease by $50, to recognize the interest expense, and liabilities (interest payable) should increase by $50, to recognize the obligation to pay the interest when it is due at the end of the quarter.

To summarize:

ANALYSIS OF TRANSACTION 10

Shareholders' Equity (Retained Earnings) decreased by $50

Liabilities (Interest Payable) increased by $50

GAAP Accrual-basis accounting requires that expenses be recognized in the period in which they are incurred, rather than the period in which they are paid. Accrued expenses, therefore, typically result in a liability that appears on the balance sheet at the end of the period, representing the amount of expenses that have been accrued by that date that will be paid in a subsequent period.

This transaction can be summarized as follows.

EFFECTS OF TRANSACTION 10 ON THE BALANCE SHEET

		Assets				=	Liabilities			+Shareholders' Equity	
Cash +	Accounts Receivable +	Inventory +	Prepaid Insurance +	Land +	Equipment =		Accounts Payable +	Interest Payable +	Bank Loan +	Common Shares +	Retained Earnings

---

Note that this transaction affects income (retained earnings) but it does not affect cash. Because the interest is paid quarterly, the effect on cash will occur at the end of the quarter.

TRANSACTION 11

Dividends in the amount of $250 were declared and paid in January.

ANALYSIS Dividends are payments to the shareholders of the company, as authorized by the company's board of directors. They are a return to the shareholders of part of the accumulated earnings of the company. They are not expenses of doing business, because they are not incurred for the purpose of generating revenues.

The effect of declaring dividends is to reduce the shareholders' equity (retained earnings) and either to increase the liabilities (dividends payable), if the dividends have not yet been paid, or to decrease the assets (cash), if they have been paid.

ANALYSIS OF TRANSACTION 11

Assets (Cash) decreased by $250

Shareholders' Equity (Retained Earnings) decreased by $250

GAAP Dividends are declared by a vote of a company's board of directors. At the date of declaration, they become a legal liability of the company. As just illustrated, the accounting records should show a decrease in retained earnings (usually through an account called the **dividends declared** account).

The dividends declared account affects retained earnings. It explains part of the change in the retained earnings account from the beginning of the period to the end of the period. Many companies prepare a statement of retained earnings, which shows the dividends declared during the period. It is very important, however, to note that dividends are not an expense and do not appear on the income statement. They will appear on a cash flow statement when they are paid.

There is generally a delay between the date the dividends are declared and the date they are paid, and therefore a liability (dividends payable) arises; the cash effects are not recognized until the payment date. In the case of Demo, however, the dividends are declared and paid in the same accounting period, so that the dividends payable account is ignored.

This transaction can be summarized as follows.

EFFECTS OF TRANSACTION 11 ON THE BALANCE SHEET

Assets	=	Liabilities	+ Shareholders' Equity
Cash + Accounts Receivable + Inventory + Prepaid Insurance + Land + Equipment	=	Accounts Payable + Interest Payable + Bank Loan	+ Common Shares + Retained Earnings

Note that dividends are not part of income, but they do appear on the cash flow statement (as a financing activity) because they affect cash.

This completes the analysis of the 11 transactions of the Demo Retail Company Ltd. Exhibit 2-6 shows the effects of all these transactions on the basic accounting equation, and the resulting account balances at the end of January.

BASIC ACCOUNTING EQUATION: Showing the Effects of Transactions in January 2006   EXHIBIT 2-6

	Cash +	Accounts Receivable +	Inventory +	Prepaid Insurance +	Land +	Equipment =	Accounts Payable +	Interest Payable +	Bank Loan +	Common Shares +	Retained Earnings
Beginning balances	3,000 +	0 +	2,500 +	0 +	0 +	4,500 =	2,500 +	0 +	0 +	7,500 +	0
Transactions						=					
1		+2,500				=					+2,500 R
2			−1,800			=					−1,800 E
3			+2,100			=	+2,100				
4	+2,200 0	−2,200				=					
5	−2,700 0					=	−2,700				
6	−360 0			+360		=					
7				−60		=					−60 E
8						=		150			−150 E
9a	+5,000 F					=				+5,000	
9b	+10,000 F					=			+10,000		
9c	−15,000 I				+15,000	=					
10						=		+50			−50 E
11	−250 F					=					−250 D
Ending balances	1,890 +	300 +	2,800 +	300 +	15,000 +	4,350 =	1,900 +	50 +	10,000 +	12,500 +	190
Totals						24,640	=	24,640			

This provides all the information needed to prepare Demo's financial statements.

FINANCIAL STATEMENTS

Balance Sheet

LEARNING OBJECTIVE 7

Prepare a balance sheet, income statement, and cash flow statement after a series of transactions.

Using the beginning and ending balances from Exhibit 2-6, the balance sheet for Demo could be constructed as follows.

DEMO RETAIL COMPANY LTD.
Balance Sheet

	January 31, 2006	December 31, 2005
Current Assets		
Cash	$ 1,890	$ 3,000
Accounts receivable	300	0
Inventory	2,800	2,500
Prepaid insurance	300	0
Total current assets	5,290	5,500
Land	15,000	0
Equipment	4,350	4,500
Total assets	$24,640	$10,000
Current Liabilities		
Accounts payable	$ 1,900	$ 2,500
Interest payable	50	0
Total current liabilities	1,950	2,500
Bank loan	10,000	0
Total liabilities	11,950	2,500
Shareholders' Equity		
Common shares	12,500	7,500
Retained earnings	190	0
Total shareholders' equity	12,690	7,500
Total liabilities and shareholders' equity	$ 24,640	$10,000

This is a *classified* balance sheet, in which current assets and liabilities are distinguished from noncurrent. It is also a *comparative* balance sheet, in which the amounts for both the beginning and the end of the accounting period (in this case, the month of January) are shown. Note that the beginning balances for January 2006 are the same as the ending balances from December 2005.

Income Statement

The income statement can be constructed from the information on the transactions recorded in the retained earnings account in Exhibit 2-6 (refer to Chapter 1 for a description of the income statement). Each of the items identified as either R (for revenue) or E (for expense) in the retained earnings column of Exhibit 2-6 is reported on the income statement. Note that the dividend amount does not belong on the income statement, because it is not an expense used to derive net income. Rather, it is a payment of a portion of the income to the shareholders.

The income statement would be constructed as follows. (Since this is Demo's first month of operations, we cannot show comparative figures in this case.)

DEMO RETAIL COMPANY LTD.
Income Statement
For the month ended January 31, 2006

Sales revenues	$ 2,500
Less: Cost of goods sold	(1,800)
Gross profit	700
Amortization expense	(150)
Insurance expense	(60)
Interest expense	(50)
Net income	$ 440

Note that the combination of the net income earned and the dividends declared during the period accounts for the change in retained earnings, shown on the balance sheet, as follows.

Beginning balance of retained earnings (December 31, 2005)	$ 0
Add: Net income	440
Deduct: Dividends declared	(250)
Ending balance of retained earnings (January 31, 2006)	$190

The income statement shows that Demo operated profitably during the month of January, earning a net income of $440. By itself, however, a net income of $440 tells users very little about a company. To understand the profitability of a company more fully, users will often use ratio analysis, a technique you will see used frequently throughout this text.

A ratio divides one financial statement amount by another financial statement amount. This allows users to understand how some amounts are related to other amounts. As you have seen from the financial statements illustrated so far, there are many numbers from which meaningful relationships can be derived. Ratios allow users to compare companies that are of different sizes, or to compare the same company over time. Ratio analysis can be used to assess profitability, the effectiveness of management, and the company's ability to meet debt obligations. As we introduce new topics to you, we will be showing you ratios that can help users understand and evaluate a set of financial statements. A complete discussion of these ratios can be found in Chapter 12.

We are going to start by using the Demo example to examine *profitability ratios*. Profitability ratios are usually constructed by comparing some measure of the company's profit (net income) with the amount invested, or by comparing it with the company's revenues. We will calculate three such measures.

PROFITABILITY RATIOS

The **profit margin ratio** is calculated by dividing the company's profit by the revenues that produced that profit. For Demo, this ratio is 17.6% (net income/sales revenues = $440/$2,500). This indicates that Demo earned, as profit, 17.6% of the revenue amount. Stated another way, of the $2,500 in sales revenues generated by the company, Demo retained 17.6% and increased the company's wealth by this amount.

LEARNING OBJECTIVE 8

Calculate three profitability ratios.

The **return on assets** is another measure of profitability. It is calculated by dividing the company's profit by the average total assets invested in the company.

Total assets is a balance sheet amount that is determined at a point in time. Thus, to get a measure of the balance over the year, we use the average. The average assets can be calculated using the information in the balance sheet. For Demo, the average is $17,320 [($10,000 + $24,640)/2]. In January 2006, the return on assets was 2.5% (net income/average total assets = $440/$17,320). Remember that a company invests in assets so that it can use them to generate profits. Demo's return of 2.5% means that for each $100.00 invested in assets, Demo earned $2.50 of profit during its first month of operations.

The third measure of performance is the **return on equity**. This measure compares the return (profit) with the amount invested by the shareholders (average total shareholders' equity). The return on equity for January is 4.4% (net income/average shareholders' equity = $440/$10,095). The average total shareholders' equity (based upon the sum of the common shares and retained earnings accounts) is calculated as [$7,500 + $12,690]/2 = $10,095. This measure shows that Demo's shareholders have earned a 4.4% return on their investment in one month.

These ratios must be interpreted either within the context of the company's past performance or in comparison with other companies in the same industry. More will be said about these ratios and their interpretation in Chapter 12.

Cash Flow Statement

A cash flow statement can now be constructed from the information in the cash column in Exhibit 2-6. The cash flow statement explains the changes in cash flow by detailing the changes in operating, financing, and investing activities (refer to Chapter 1). Remember that we marked all the cash transactions in the exhibit with an O, I, or F to make the preparation of this statement easier.

DEMO RETAIL COMPANY, LTD.
Cash Flow Statement
For the Month Ended January 31, 2006

Cash from operating activities:		
Cash receipts from customers	$2,200	
Cash disbursement to suppliers	(2,700)	
Cash disbursement for insurance	(360)	
Cash flow from operating activities		$ (860)
Cash from investing activities:		
Purchase of land		(15,000)
Cash from financing activities:		
Proceeds from issuance of common shares	5,000	
Proceeds from bank loan	10,000	
Dividends paid	(250)	
Cash flow from financing activities		14,750
Decrease in cash during the month		$(1,110)
Cash balance on December 31, 2005		3,000
Cash balance on January 31, 2006		$ 1,890

Note that the final figures shown above are what appear on the balance sheet for cash.

You might have noticed that the operating section of Demo's cash flow statement appears somewhat different from that of Sun-Rype Products, shown in Chapter 1. The reason is that GAAP allows for this section to be prepared using a direct or an indirect method. The direct method has been used here, whereas Sun-Rype used the indirect method. The explanation for this difference is presented in Chapter 5.

The important part of the cash flow analysis is interpreting what the cash flow statement shows about the health of the company. Subsequent chapters discuss many of the detailed analyses that can be done with the data in the cash flow statement. For now, there are two basic questions that can serve as a start for the analysis of this statement.

LEARNING OBJECTIVE 9

Begin to analyze the information on a cash flow statement.

1. Is the cash from operating activities sufficient to sustain, in the long run, other company activities? A company can be healthy in the long run only when it produces a reasonable amount of cash from operations. Cash can be obtained from financing activities (issuance of new debt or shares) and from investment activities (the sale of investments or capital assets), but these sources cannot sustain the company forever because there are limits to the company's access to them.

2. Of the sources and uses of cash, which ones are related to items or activities that will continue from period to period, and which are sporadic or noncontinuing? A large source or use of cash in one period may not have long-run implications if it does not continue in the future. To address this question, the historical trend in the cash flow statement data must be considered.

The cash flow statement for Canada Bread Company Limited is shown in Exhibit 2-7 (in thousands of dollars). Note that operating activities generated a positive amount of cash in each of the two years presented, but that the amount decreased over those two years.

To assess whether the cash flow from operations is adequate to meet Canada Bread's needs, we can begin by looking at the company's use of cash for maintaining and expanding the business. The statement of cash flows shows that, in 2003, Canada Bread's investing activities used cash of $72,853.

The cash generated by operating activities and financing activities is used to cover these requirements. In Canada Bread's case, its operating activities generated cash of $66,374, which covered 91% of its investing requirements ($66,374 ÷ $72,853 = 0.91). As a result, the company had to generate only a small amount of cash from financing activities.

Within the company's financing activities, it is important to note whether the long-term financing is in the form of debt (which involves legal obligations for payments) or equity (which does not). Canada Bread's cash flow statement shows that there was a net decrease in long-term debt and an increase in share capital during 2003. As a result of having decreased its debt and increased its equity financing during the year, the company has lowered its level of risk.

Year-to-year comparisons can also be very informative. For example, looking at Canada Bread's financing activities reveals that:

EXHIBIT 2-7

CANADA BREAD COMPANY LIMITED 2003 ANNUAL REPORT

Consolidated Statements of Cash Flows

As at December 31
(in thousands of Canadian dollars)

		2003		2002
CASH PROVIDED BY (USED IN)				
Operating activities				
Net earnings	$	35,633	$	38,697
Add (deduct) items not affecting cash:				
Depreciation		39,529		28,506
Minority interest		—		57
Future income taxes		(3,010)		108
Other		196		(295)
Change in non-cash operating working capital		(5,974)		25,112
		66,374		92,185
Financing activities				
Dividends paid		(5,860)		(5,140)
Increase in long-term debt		79,609		333,456
Decrease in long-term debt		(174,131)		(98,676)
Increase in share capital (Note 8)		106,000		—
		5,618		229,640
Investing activities				
Purchase of intangible assets		(1,279)		—
Additions to property and equipment		(63,792)		(20,678)
Proceeds from sale of property and equipment		1,146		817
Purchase of net assets of businesses, net of cash acquired (Note 15)		(8,928)		(288,910)
		(72,853)		(308,771)
Increase (decrease) in cash and cash equivalents		(861)		13,054
Cash and cash equivalents (bank indebtedness), beginning of year		12,389		(665)
Cash and cash equivalents, end of year	$	11,528	$	12,389
Supplemental cash flow information:				
Net interest paid	$	10,384	$	3,722
Net income taxes paid		23,235		18,464

See accompanying Notes to Consolidated Financial Statements.

- During 2002, there was a very large net increase in long-term debt ($333,456 − $98,676 = $234,780) and no increase in share capital.

- During 2003, there was a significant net decrease in long-term debt ($174,131 − $79,609 = $94,522) and a substantial increase in share capital ($106,000)

The twoyear pattern shows that while Canada Bread increased its use of debt financing in 2002, during 2003 it replaced some of its debt with equity financing. As indicated above, this type of change in a company's capital structure has the effect of reducing its financial risk.[5]

    Returning to the analysis of Demo Retail Company, even though the company was profitable, based on the net income of $440 shown on income statement, the analysis of cash flow indicates a negative cash flow from operations of $860 and an overall decrease in cash of $1,110. Considering the starting balance in cash of $3,000, it is clear that Demo could operate for a few months at this rate and still have some cash remaining. It cannot, however, continue to operate indefinitely with a negative cash flow (i.e., net cash outflow). If it continued to consume cash at this rate, the company would run out of cash in the very near future. This should raise questions about why Demo has this cash drain, even though it appears to be profitable.

    When we look at the three types of activities, the biggest concern is the negative cash flow from operations. Analyzing why Demo is having difficulty generating cash from operations is beyond the scope of this chapter, but Demo's problem represents an important issue that will be addressed in various sections of this book, most thoroughly in Chapter 5. In fact, problems related to cash flows are key reasons why new businesses fail in their first year. For now, it is important to understand that, while the income statement provides important information about the changes in the shareholders' wealth, it does not reveal everything that is important to know about the company. The cash flow statement can provide additional useful information about the company's operations that is not adequately captured by the income statement.

SUMMARY

This chapter has introduced the accounting system, using the basic accounting equation. A basic set of transactions was examined in detail and the effect of the transactions on the basic accounting equation was demonstrated. A retail company served as the example in this explanation, but the same procedures would be used in any for-profit organization. By analyzing the effects of the transactions on the basic accounting equation, the three basic financial statements were developed.

    The additional explanations that accompanied the financial statements build on the information provided in Chapter 1. In the next chapter, we will use the same example to expand on the operation of the accounting system in a more formal way.

Additional Demonstration Problems

SUMMARY PROBLEM

You should carefully work through the following problem and then check your work against the suggested solution that is provided, as it will reinforce and extend what you have learned in this chapter.

---

[5] A cautionary note should be stated here: a complete analysis of Canada Bread's financial position is not possible without a review of all the financial statements and related footnotes.

EXHIBIT 2-8

The balance sheet of Sample Retail Company Ltd. is shown in Exhibit 2-8.

SAMPLE RETAIL COMPANY LTD.
Balance Sheet
December 31, 2005

Cash	$ 4,500
Accounts receivable	500
Inventory	7,500
Prepaid rent	1,300
Total current assets	13,800
Equipment	9,200
Total assets	$23,000
Accounts payable	$ 5,400
Accrued salaries payable	400
Income tax payable	360
Total current liabilities	6,160
Bank loan	1,800
Total liabilities	7,960
Common shares	3,600
Retained earnings	11,440
Total shareholders' equity	15,040
Total liabilities and shareholders' equity	$23,000

The following transactions occurred during 2006.

1. Goods with an aggregate selling price of $80,000 were sold, all on account.

2. A review of accounts receivable showed that $750 remained uncollected as at December 31, 2006.

3. Salaries totalling $20,500 were earned by employees. Cash payments for salaries totalled $20,375.

4. Purchases of inventory, all on account, totalled $39,700.

5. Payments on accounts payable totalled $37,300.

6. A count of inventory at December 31, 2006 revealed that $9,700 remained unsold in ending inventory.

7. Rent for each month is prepaid on the last day of the preceding month. Monthly payments during 2006 were $1,300 per month from January 31 through November 30, and $1,500 on December 31 (because the rent was increasing for 2007).

8. Interest on the bank loan accrues at 9% and is paid at the end of each month. On December 31, 2006, $200 of the principal of the loan was repaid.

9. Amortization expense on the equipment totalled $2,000.

10. New equipment was purchased for $4,500 in cash.

11. The tax rate is 40% for 2006. Taxes of $1,650 were paid during 2006.

12. Dividends of $500 were declared and paid.

Required:

a. Analyze the effect of the transactions above, using the basic accounting equation.

b. Prepare an income statement, balance sheet, and cash flow statement.

SUGGESTED SOLUTION TO SUMMARY PROBLEM

The basic accounting equation analysis is shown in Exhibit 2-9. The entries are numbered to correspond with the transaction numbers in the problem. Financial statements are shown in Exhibits 2-10, 2-11, and 2-12.

The following explanations are provided for selected transactions.

Transaction 2. It is important to note that the $750 given in the problem is the ending balance in accounts receivable. As an account balance, it does not represent the amount of any individual transaction; rather, it is the net result of all the transactions that affected the account up to that point.

The cash receipts from customers can be determined by using the $750 ending balance, together with the other information about accounts receivable (i.e., the beginning balance and the sales on account) given in Transaction 1, as follows: $500 + 80,000 = 80,500; $80,500 − 750 = 79,750.

Transaction 3. Salaries earned by employees during the period should be shown as expenses. Salaries paid during the period reflect the payment of salaries from the previous period (i.e., the beginning balance in the accrued salaries payable account) as well as partial payment of salaries for the current period. The ending balance in the salaries payable account reflects the salaries that were earned during the current period but have not yet been paid.

Transaction 6. Note again that the amount given is the ending balance in an account, rather than a transaction.

The physical count of unsold inventory provides the ending balance in the inventory account. The cost of goods sold is then determined by considering the beginning balance, the purchases of inventory, and the ending balance, as follows: $7,500 + 39,700 = 47,200; $47,200 − 9,700 = 37,500. (Refer to the explanation given for Transaction 2 for Demo Retail if you want to review the calculation of cost of goods sold.)

Transaction 7. The beginning balance in prepaid rent is the payment made on December 31 of the prior year that covered rent expense in January 2006. This, along with 11 months of payments during 2006, constitutes the rent expense for the year of $15,600 (i.e., the rent expense is the cost for one full year: 12 × $1,300). The final payment of $1,500 on December 31, 2006 applies to the first month in 2007 and is, therefore, the ending balance in the prepaid rent (an asset) account.

Transaction 8. Because the interest expense is paid at the end of each month, there is no accrued liability to be shown at the end of the period. The cash payments for interest, in this case, are the same as the expense. The expense is calculated by multiplying the principal ($1,800) times the interest rate (9%) times one year. Remember that interest rates are expressed as an annual rate.

Transaction 11. To determine the tax expense for the period, income before taxes must first be determined. The income before taxes is $4,238, found by subtracting the expenses from the revenues (all of which are listed in the retained earnings column in Exhibit 2-9). The tax expense is then calculated by taking 40% of this number, resulting in $1,695 for the year (40% × $4,238 = $1,695).

EXHIBIT 2-9 **BASIC ACCOUNTING EQUATION: Sample Retail Company Ltd.**

	Assets					=	Liabilities			+	Shareholders' Equity	
	Cash +	A/R +	Inventory +	Prepaid Rent +	Equip. =		A/P +	Accrued Salaries +	Tax Payable +	Bank Loan +	Common Shares +	Retained Earnings
Beginning balances	4,500 +	500 +	7,500 +	1,300 +	9,200 =		5,400 +	400 +	360 +	1,800 +	3,600 +	11,440
Transactions												
1		+80,000										+80,000 R
2	+79,750 O	−79,750										
3a								+20,500				−20,500 E
3b	−20,375 O							−20,375				
4			+39,700				+39,700					
5	−37,300 O						−37,300					
6			−37,500									−37,500 E
7a	−15,800 O			+15,800								
7b				−15,600								−15,600 E
8a	−162 O											−162 E
8b	−200 F									−200		
9					−2,000							−2,000 E
10	−4,500 I				+4,500							
11a									+1,695			−1,695 E
11b	−1,650 O								−1,650			
12	−500 F											−500 D
Ending balances	3,763 +	750 +	9,700 +	1,500 +	11,700 =		7,800 +	525 +	405 +	1,600 +	3,600 +	13,483

The beginning balance in the taxes payable account was tax owing from the previous year that was paid in 2006. The ending balance in the taxes payable account will be paid in 2007.

EXHIBIT 2-10

SAMPLE RETAIL COMPANY LTD.
Income Statement
For the year ended December 31, 2006

Revenues		$80,000
Expenses:		
Cost of goods sold	$37,500	
Salary expense	20,500	
Rent expense	15,600	
Amortization expense	2,000	
Interest expense	162	
Total expenses		75,762
Income before taxes		4,238
Tax expense		1,695
Net income		$ 2,543

EXHIBIT 2-11

SAMPLE RETAIL COMPANY LTD.
Balance Sheet
As at December 31

	2006	2005
Assets		
Current assets		
Cash	$ 3,763	$ 4,500
Accounts receivable	750	500
Inventory	9,700	7,500
Prepaid rent	1,500	1,300
Total current assets	15,713	13,800
Equipment	11,700	9,200
Total assets	$27,413	$23,000
Liabilities		
Current liabilities		
Accounts payable	$ 7,800	$ 5,400
Accrued salaries	525	400
Taxes payable	405	360
Total current liabilities	8,730	6,160
Bank loan	1,600	1,800
Total liabilities	10,330	7,960
Shareholders' equity		
Common shares	3,600	3,600
Retained earnings	13,483	11,440
Total shareholders' equity	17,083	15,040
Total liabilities and shareholders' equity	$27,413	$23,000

Note that the ending balance in retained earnings equals the beginning balance plus the net income minus the dividends (i.e., $11,440 + 2,543 – 500 = $13,483).

EXHIBIT 2-12

SAMPLE RETAIL COMPANY LTD.
Cash Flow Statement
For the year ended December 31, 2006

Cash from operating activities:		
Cash receipts from customers	$79,750	
Cash disbursements to suppliers	(37,300)	
Cash disbursements for salaries	(20,375)	
Cash disbursements for rent	(15,800)	
Cash disbursements for interest	(162)	
Cash disbursements for taxes	(1,650)	
Cash flow from operating activities		$ 4,463
Cash from investing activities:		
Purchase of new equipment		(4,500)
Cash from financing activities:		
Repayment of bank loan	(200)	
Dividends paid	(500)	
Cash flow from financing activities		(700)
Decrease in cash		($737)
Beginning balance of cash		4,500
Ending balance of cash		$3,763

A final note regarding the cash flow statement: under GAAP, companies report interest and tax payments as operating items, even though you could think of interest as a part of financing activities and tax payments as being spread over all types of activities. When the amounts paid for interest and income taxes are not listed separately in the operating section or in the notes, companies need to disclose these items and they usually do so at the bottom of the cash flow statement. (Refer to Exhibit 2-7 for an illustration of this.) In our example, all interest and tax amounts are shown in the operating section of Exhibit 2-12, so no further disclosure is necessary.

ABBREVIATIONS USED

A/P	Accounts payable
A/R	Accounts receivable
CS	Common shares
Equip.	Equipment
GAAP	Generally Accepted Accounting Principles
Inv.	Inventory
RE	Retained earnings
SE	Shareholders' equity

SYNONYMS

Amortization/Depreciation
Profit/Income/Earnings

GLOSSARY

Accounts payable   The liabilities that result when the company buys inventory or supplies on credit. They represent a future obligation.

Accounts receivable   The assets that result when a customer buys goods or services on credit. They represent the right to receive cash from the customer.

Accrual basis   The accounting basis used by almost all companies, which recognizes revenues and expenses in the period in which they are earned or incurred and not necessarily in the period in which the cash inflow or outflow occurs.

Accrued expense   An expense that has been incurred and recognized in the financial statements but has not yet been paid for.

Amortization   The expense taken each period based on the use of a noncurrent asset, such as plant or equipment. Amortization is a process that uses a systematic and rational method to allocate the cost of a noncurrent asset to each of the years of its useful life. Amortization is sometimes referred to as depreciation.

Amortizable cost or value   The portion of the cost of a noncurrent asset that is to be amortized over its useful life. The amortization value is equal to the original cost of the asset less its estimated residual value.

Cash basis   The accounting basis used by some entities in which revenues and expenses are recognized when the cash inflows or outflows occur.

Cost of goods sold   The expense that is recorded to reflect the value of the inventory sold during the period.

Credit sale   A business transaction in which one party (the seller) provides goods or services to another party (the buyer) in exchange for the buyer's promise to pay cash at at later date. This is also referred to as a *sale on account*, as it results in an account receivable on the seller's books.

Depreciable cost or value   A synonym for amortizable cost or value.

Depreciation   A synonym for amortization.

Dividends declared   A distribution of assets (usually cash) to the shareholders of a company. The Board of Directors of the company votes to formally declare the distribution, at which point it becomes a legal obligation of the company. The distribution of cash occurs at a date specified at the time of declaration.

Fair market value   The value of an asset or liability based on the price that could be obtained from, or paid to, an independent third party in an arm's-length transaction.

Loss A reduction in shareholders' equity resulting from a transaction in which the value of the resources flowing into the company is less than the resources flowing out. For example, a loss occurs if an item is sold for less than its cost. The opposite of *gain* or *profit*.

Historical cost A valuation method that values assets at the price paid to obtain those assets.

Matching concept A concept in accounting that requires all expenses related to the production of revenues to be recorded during the same time period as the revenues. The expenses are said to be matched with the revenues, on the income statement.

Net income The difference between the revenues and the expenses recognized during the period.

Nonmonetary exchange An exchange of goods or services in which the assets or liabilities exchanged are not cash.

Note payable A formal document representing the amount owed by a company. There is usually interest on this type of debt.

Note receivable An amount due from a customer who bought goods or services on credit and gave a written promise to pay, as evidence of their obligation. Similar to an *account receivable*, except that the note constitutes legal documentation that the seller has the right to receive payment in the future. The note usually specifies the amount, due date, and interest rate.

Prepaid expense A current asset representing a past expenditure whose benefits are expected to be consumed in the next accounting period. A prepaid expense represents a past cash outflow for which the company will receive future economic benefits. Sometimes referred to as a *deferred expense*.

Profit A synonym for net income.

Profit margin ratio A ratio that compares the profit (net income) during an accounting period with the related revenues.

Residual value The estimated value of an asset at the end of its useful life. The estimate is made when the asset is purchased.

Return on assets A ratio that compares the net income for the period with the investment in assets.

Return on equity A ratio that compares the net income for the period with the investment shareholders have made in the company.

Revenue recognition criteria Criteria established within GAAP that stipulate when revenues should be recognized in the financial statements.

Sale on account A sale in which the seller receives a promise from the buyer to pay at a later date.

Sales revenue The amount of sales recognized during the accounting period, based on the revenue recognition criteria.

Straight-line amortization A method of calculating amortization in which the amount of expense for each period is found by dividing an asset's amortizable value by its estimated useful life.

Transaction An exchange of resources with an outside entity or an internal event that affects the balance in individual asset, liability, or shareholders' equity accounts.

Transaction analysis The process by which the accountant decides what accounts are affected, and by how much, by an economic transaction or event.

Useful life The estimated period of time over which a capital asset (such as equipment) is expected to be used.

ASSIGNMENT MATERIAL

Assessing Your Recall

2-1 Describe how the basic accounting equation is used when transactions are recorded in the accounting system.

2-2 Discuss why dividends do not appear on the income statement but do appear on the cash flow statement.

2-3 What advantages and disadvantages are there in using the cash basis of accounting rather than the accrual basis?

2-4 Identify the three major sections in the cash flow statement and briefly describe the nature of the transactions that appear in each section.

2-5 Respond to each of the following statements with a true or false answer.

Self-Assessment Quiz

a. Revenues increase shareholders' equity.

b. Cash receipts from customers increase accounts receivable.

c. Dividends declared decrease cash immediately.

d. The cash basis recognizes expenses when they are incurred.

e. In the cash basis of accounting, there is no such thing as a prepaid rent account.

f. Dividends are an expense of doing business and should appear on the income statement.

g. On the accrual basis, interest should be recognized only when it is paid.

h. Interest paid on bank loans is reported in the operating section of the cash flow statement.

2-6 Briefly describe how a company typically calculates the cost of goods sold.

2-7 What are revenue recognition criteria and how does the matching concept relate to these criteria?

2-8 Explain how a prepaid expense (such as rent) gets handled under accrual-basis accounting.

2-9 Explain how an accrued expense (such as interest) gets handled under accrual-basis accounting.

2-10 Suppose that a company has an accounting policy that recognizes warranty expense only when warranty service is provided. Discuss whether this meets the matching concept under accrual-basis accounting, and suggest other ways that this might be handled.

2-11 Explain what amortization is, and how it is calculated using the straight-line method.

Applying Your Knowledge

2-12 (Aspects of a successful business)
Using the information in the opening vignette about **Krave's Candy Company**, describe the aspects of the business that are indicators of growth and success. Identify any areas of the operation where you think Mr. Emery and Mr. Finnson will have to be vigilant so that they continue to be a successful enterprise.

2-13 (Cash basis versus accrual basis)
Given the following transactions, what income would be reported on the cash basis and on the accrual basis?

• Credit sales to customers totalled $36,000.

• Cash sales totalled $105,000.

• Cash collections on account from customers totalled $34,000.

• Cost of goods sold during the period was $79,000.

• Payments made to suppliers of inventory totalled $75,500.

• Wages of $23,000 were paid during the year; wages of $900 remained unpaid at year end; there were no wages unpaid at the beginning of the year.

• Half-way through the year, insurance premiums on a two-year policy were paid in the amount of $960.

2-14 (Cash basis versus accrual basis)
Given the following transactions, what income would be reported on the cash basis and on the accrual basis?

- Inventory costing $65,000 was purchased on account.

- Inventory costing $61,000 was sold for $106,000. Eighty percent of the sales were for cash.

- Cash collected from customers who bought inventory on account totalled $19,000.

- Rent of $1,000 was paid on the last day of each month. The rent was to cover the following month. The rent for the first month of the year was paid on the last day of the previous year.

- Office supplies costing $6,800 were purchased for cash. At the end of the year, $400 of the office supplies were still unused.

- Wages of $18,000 were paid during the year; wages of $200 remained unpaid at year end; and wages of $300 were unpaid at the end of the previous year.

2-15 (Nature of retained earnings)
Explain why you agree or disagree with the following statement: Retained earnings are like money in the bank: you can always use them to pay your bills if you get into cash flow trouble.

2-16 (Income statement and cash flow statement)
Compare and contrast the income statement and the cash flow statement with regard to their purpose. Outline how they are similar, and briefly describe their relationship to the balance sheet.

2-17 (Transaction analysis)
For each of the transactions below, indicate which accounts are affected and whether they increase or decrease.

   a. Issue common shares for cash.

   b. Buy equipment from a supplier on credit (short-term).

   c. Buy inventory from a supplier partly with cash and partly on account.

   d. Sell a unit of inventory to a customer on account.

   e. Receive a payment from a customer on his or her account.

   f. Borrow money from the bank.

   g. Declare a dividend (to be paid later).

   h. Pay a dividend (that was previously declared).

   i. Recognize wages earned by employees (to be paid later).

   j. Buy office supplies using cash.

2-18 (Transaction analysis and the basic accounting equation)
For each of the following transactions, give the effect on the basic accounting equation.

   a. Issuance of shares for cash.

   b. Payment of a liability.

   c. Purchase of land for cash.

   d. Purchase of equipment on credit.

   e. Payment of cash to shareholders reflecting a distribution of income.

   f. Receipt of a loan from the bank.

g. Payment of interest on a bank loan.

h. Purchase of inventory on credit.

i . Payment of insurance to cover one year.

j . Payment to a delivery company for the delivery of goods to a customer.

2-19 (Transaction analysis)

For each of the following transactions, indicate how income and cash flow are affected (increase, decrease, no effect) and by how much.

a. Issue common shares for $60,000.

b. Sell, on account, a unit of inventory for $450 that cost $250. The unit was already in inventory prior to its sale.

c. Purchase equipment for $1,200 cash.

d. Amortize plant and equipment by $500.

e. Purchase a unit of inventory, on account, for $300.

f . Make a payment on accounts payable for $950.

g. Receive a payment from a customer for $100 for inventory previously sold on account.

h. Declare (but do not pay yet) a dividend for $2,000.

i . Pay a $2,000 dividend that had been declared earlier.

2-20 (Transaction analysis and the basic accounting equation)

Show how each of the following transactions affects the basic accounting equation.

a. Buy land for $50,000 in cash.

b. Declare a dividend of $9,000.

c. Issue common shares for $150,000.

d. Buy inventory costing $35,000 on account.

e. Sell inventory costing $32,500 to customers, on account, for $52,000.

f . Borrow $15,000 from the bank.

g. Receive a payment from a customer for $300 representing a down payment on a unit of inventory that must be ordered.

h. Amortize equipment by $1,200.

i . Make a payment of $200 to the electric company for power used during the current period.

2-21 (Transaction analysis and the basic accounting equation)

Show how each of the following transactions affects the basic accounting equation, and identify those that have an immediate impact on the income statement and/or the cash flow statement.

a. Bought supplies for $15,000 on account. The inventory is to be used in the repair of vehicles. The company repairs and services vehicles.

b. Completed the repair and service of several vehicles and received $25,000 in cash. In the repair of the vehicles, $8,000 of the supplies inventory was used.

c. The owners invested a further $25,000 in the business, and shares were issued to them in exchange.

d. Some of the inventory that was used in the repair of the vehicles carried two-year warranties. The company estimates that $500 in free replacements will be necessary in the future, under the terms of the warranties. Hint: This is a possible future cost to the company. If the sale is recognized in the current period, all associated expenses should be matched to that revenue in the same period.

e. Paid $14,000 to suppliers of the inventory.

f. Received the utility bills (electricity, water, telephone), which totalled $650. Paid all but one bill for $100, which will be paid next month.

g. Borrowed $50,000 from the bank. It is intended that the money be used to purchase a new hoist.

h. Bought a hoist for $48,000, using cash that had been borrowed from the bank.

i. Paid the wages of the employees, $7,000.

2-22 **(Transaction analysis and the basic accounting equation)**
For each of the following transactions, indicate how each immediately affects the basic accounting equation, and what other effects there will be in the future as a result of the transaction.

a. Purchase equipment for cash.

b. Borrow money from the bank.

c. Purchase inventory on account.

d. Pay rent in advance for a warehouse.

e. Pay for an insurance policy on an office building.

f. Sell inventory to customers for cash.

g. Sign warranty agreements with customers that cover products that were sold to them. (See 2-21 d. for more information about this type of transaction.)

h. Buy a patent for a new production process.

2-23 **(Transaction analysis and the basic accounting equation)**
Indicate the effects of the following transactions on the basic accounting equation. The company's fiscal year end is December 31.

a. Borrowed $12,500 from the bank on January 1, 2006.

b. Paid interest on the bank loan described in transaction a. on December 31, 2006. The interest rate is 8%.

c. Bought equipment on January 1, 2006 for $8,000 cash.

d. Recorded the amortization for the equipment as at December 31, 2006 using the straight-line method. The equipment has an estimated useful life of six years and an estimated residual value of $800.

e. Purchases of inventory on account during 2006 totalled $24,700.

f. Sales for the period totalled $35,500, of which $7,500 were on account.

g. The cost of the products sold from inventory during the year was $21,600.

h. Payments to suppliers totalled $22,900 during 2006.

i. Collections on account from customers totalled $6,800.

j. Employees earned wages of $6,400 during 2006 (recorded as Wages Payable).

k. All employee wages were paid by year end except the wages for the last week in December, which totalled $150.

l. Dividends were declared and paid in the amount of $400.

2-24 **(Transaction analysis and the basic accounting equation)**
Indicate the effects of the following transactions on the basic accounting equation. The fiscal year end of the company (which has been operating for several years) is December 31.

a. Paid an insurance premium of $600 on July 1 that provides coverage for the 12-month period starting July 1.

b. Purchased $31,350 of inventory on account.

c. Recorded sales for the period totalling $60,000, of which $25,000 were cash sales.

d. Paid cash to suppliers totalling $35,000 (including some for the previous year).

e. Collected cash on customer accounts totalling $37,000 (including some from the previous year).

f. Signed a contract to purchase a piece of equipment that cost $1,200, and put a down payment of $100 on the purchase.

g. Declared dividends of $1,500.

h. Paid dividends of $1,150.

i. Recognized the amount of insurance expense that had been used from July 1 through December 31.

j. Recorded amortization of $3,300 on the capital assets.

k. Determined that the cost of the inventory (including some from the previous year) that had been sold during the year was $37,000.

2-25 **(Basic accounting equation evaluation)**
Ballentine Company Ltd. has assets of $100,000, liabilities of $40,000, and shareholders' equity of $60,000. Using the basic accounting equation, answer each of the following independent questions.

a. At what amount will shareholders' equity be stated if Ballentine pays off $6,000 of liabilities with cash?

b. At what amount will assets be stated if total liabilities increase by $5,000 and shareholders' equity remains constant?

c. At what amount will assets be stated if total liabilities decrease by $3,000 and shareholders' equity increases by $2,000?

d. What would be the impact on the accounting equation for Ballentine if the shareholders received $4,000 in cash as a dividend?

e. At what amount will liabilities be stated if total assets increase by $3,000 and shareholders' equity remains constant?

2-26 **(Preparation of an income statement)**
Sara's Bakery had the following account balances at the end of December 2006.

Wage expense	$22,000
Sales	95,000
Cash	26,000
Cost of goods sold	52,000
Accounts payable	6,000
Rent expense	9,000
Common shares	60,000
Accounts receivable	8,000
Retained earnings	23,000

Required:

a. Prepare an income statement for the year ended December 31, 2006, following the format given in the chapter.

b. You did not need to use all the items listed. For every item that you did not use, explain why you did not use it.

2-27 **(Preparation of an income statement)**

The Wizard's Corner, a company that sells adventure games, figures, cards, and clothing, had the following account balances at the end of June 2006.

Wage expense	$ 35,000
Sales	160,000
Accounts receivable	14,000
Rent expense	12,000
Cost of goods sold	100,000
Common shares	30,000
Advertising expense	6,000
Dividends declared	3,000
Accounts payable	10,000

Required:

a. Prepare an income statement for the year ended June 30, 2006 following the format given in the chapter.

b. You did not need to use all the items listed. For every item that you did not use, explain why you did not use it.

2-28 **(Preparation of an income statement)**

The Garment Tree Ltd. sells sports clothing. At the end of December 2006, it had the following account balances.

Miscellaneous expense	$ 5,000
Wages expense	32,000
Wages payable	500
Cost of goods sold	52,000
Accounts payable	6,000
Sales	120,000
Accounts receivable	9,000
Rent expense	10,000
Inventory	18,000
Advertising expense	5,000
Cash	4,000
Dividends declared	1,000

Required:

a. Prepare an income statement for the year ended December 31, 2006 following the format given in the chapter.

b. You did not need to use all the items listed. For every item that you did not use, explain why you did not use it.

2-29 **(Preparation of a balance sheet)**

The Tree Top Restaurant Ltd., a restaurant chain that has several restaurants in cities across Canada, had the following account balances at December 31, 2006.

Accounts payable	$ 80,000
Prepaid insurance	10,000
Common shares	200,000
Cash	63,000
Land	120,000
Inventory	44,000
Furniture and equipment	70,000
Retained earnings	65,000
Wages payable	12,000
Accounts receivable	100,000
Bank loan (due in five years)	250,000
Buildings	200,000

Required:

Prepare a classified balance sheet for Tree Top Restaurant Ltd. for December 31, 2006. Follow the examples in the chapter (such as in Exhibit 2-11).

2-30 (Preparation of a balance sheet)

At the end of its first year of operations, Minute Print Company had the following account balances at December 31, 2006.

Wages payable	2,500
Equipment	$230,000
Sales	488,000
Loan payable (due in three years)	30,000
Wages expense	62,000
Supplies on hand	18,000
Cash	34,000
Supplies used	204,000
Retained earnings	?
Prepaid rent	2,000
Interest charges	2,500
Amortization expense	30,000
Dividends declared	3,000
Accounts payable	8,000
Common shares	100,000
Rent expense	24,000
Accounts receivable	10,000
Other expenses	9,000

Required:

a. Identify the income statement accounts and calculate net income for the year.

b. Subtract the dividends declared from the net income you calculated in part a. to find the amount of retained earnings at December 31, 2006.

c. Prepare a classified balance sheet for December 31, 2006 following the format given in the chapter. Use the amount calculated in part b. for retained earnings.

2-31 (Preparation of a balance sheet)

Little Tots Ltd. sells children's clothing. At the end of December 2006 (its first year of operations), it had the following account balances.

Interest on bank loan	$ 100
Cash	3,000
Wages payable	500
Display counters	4,000
Wages expense	15,000
Prepaid rent	150
Cost of goods sold	32,000
Sales	55,750
Rent expense	3,600
Bank loan (due in two years)	1,800
Advertising expense	800
Accounts payable	2,000
Electricity expense	200
Dividends declared	1,200
Amortization expense	500
Common shares	9,000
Telephone expense	100
Inventory	8,000
Other expenses	400
Retained earnings	?

Required:

a. Prepare a calculation to determine the amount of retained earnings.

b. Use what you need to prepare a classified balance sheet, following the format given in the chapter (such as in Exhibit 2-11).

2-32 **(Transaction analysis and financial statement preparation)**
The T. Singh Company started business on January 1, 2006. Listed below are the transactions that occurred during 2006.

Required:

a. Use the basic accounting equation to analyze the transactions for 2006.

b. Prepare a balance sheet, an income statement, and a cash flow statement for 2006.

Transactions:

1. On January 1 the company issued 10,000 common shares for $175,000.

2. On January 2 the company borrowed $125,000 from the bank.

3. On January 3 the company purchased (for cash) land and a building costing $200,000. The building was recently appraised at $140,000. Hint: because the building will be amortized in the future and the land will not, you must record the land and building in separate accounts.

4. Inventory costing $100,000 was purchased on account.

5. An investment was made in Calhoun Company Ltd. shares in the amount of $75,000.

6. Sales to customers totalled $190,000. Of these, $30,000 were cash sales.

7. Collections on accounts receivable totalled $135,000.

8. Payments to suppliers totalled $92,000.

9. Salaries paid to employees totalled $44,000. There were no unpaid salaries at year end.

10. A physical count of unsold inventory at year end revealed inventory with a cost of $10,000 was still on hand.

11. The building was estimated to have a useful life of 20 years and a residual value of $20,000. The company uses straight-line amortization.

12. The interest on the bank loan is recognized each month and is paid in the succeeding month; that is, January's interest is recognized in January and paid in February. The interest rate is 8%.

13. The investment in Calhoun Company paid dividends of $5,000, all of which had been received by year end. The receipt of dividends from an investment is treated as investment income, a revenue.

14. Dividends of $15,000 were declared on December 15, 2006, and were scheduled to be paid on January 10, 2007.

2-33 **(Transaction analysis and financial statement presentation)**
The Hughes Tool Company started business on October 1, 2005. Its fiscal year runs through to September 30 the following year. Following are the transactions that occurred during fiscal 2006 (the year starting October 1, 2005 and ending September 30, 2006).

Required:

a. Use the basic accounting equation to analyze the transactions for fiscal 2006.

b. Prepare an income statement, a balance sheet, and a cash flow statement for fiscal 2006.

c. Comment on the results of the first year's operations.

Transactions:

1. On October 1, 2005, J. Hughes contributed $120,000 to start the business. Hughes is the only owner. She received 10,000 shares.

2. On October 1, Hughes Tools borrowed $300,000 from a venture capitalist (a lender who specializes in start-up companies). The interest rate on the loan is 12%.

3. On October 1, Hughes Tools rented a building. The rental agreement was a two-year contract that called for quarterly rental payments (every three months) of $20,000, payable in advance on December 31, March 31, June 30, and September 30. The first payment was made on October 1, 2005, and covers the period from October 1 to December 31.

4. On October 2, Hughes Tools purchased equipment costing $240,000 cash.

5. On October 3, Hughes purchased initial inventory with a cash payment of $100,000.

6. Sales during the year totalled $800,000, of which $720,000 were credit sales.

7. Collections from customers on account totalled $640,000.

8. Additional purchases of inventory during the year totalled $550,000, all on account.

9. Payments to suppliers totalled $500,000.

10. Inventory on hand at year end amounted to $115,000.

11. The company declared and paid a dividend of $40,000 to J. Hughes.

12. Interest on the loan from the venture capitalist was paid at year end (September 30, 2006), as well as $20,000 of the principal.

13. Other selling and administrative expenses totalled $90,000 for the year. Of these, $10,000 were unpaid as at year end.

14. The equipment purchased on October 2 had an estimated useful life of seven years and a residual value of $30,000. Amortization for the year was recorded.

15. The income tax rate is 30%. Hughes made payments during the year equal to three-quarters of the ultimate tax bill, and the rest is accrued at year end.

2-34 (**Transaction analysis and financial statement preparation**)
The A.J. Smith Company started business on January 1, 2006. Following are the transactions that occurred during 2006.

Required:

a. Use the basic accounting equation to analyze the transactions for 2006.

b. Prepare a balance sheet, an income statement, and a cash flow statement for fiscal 2006.

c. Comment on the results of the company's first year of operations.

Transactions:

1. On January 1, the company issued 25,000 common shares at $15 per share.

2. On January 1, 2006, the company purchased land and buildings from another company in exchange for $50,000 in cash and 25,000 common shares. The land's value is approximately one-fifth of the total value of the transaction. Hint: You need to determine a value for the common shares using the information you were given in Transaction 1, and the land and building should be recorded in separate accounts.

3. The buildings purchased in Transaction 2 are amortized using the straight-line method, with an estimated useful life of 30 years and an estimated residual value of $40,000.

4. On March 31, the company rented out a portion of its building to Fantek Company. Fantek is required to make quarterly payments of $5,000. The payments are due on March 31, June 30, September 30, and December 31 of each year, with the first payment on March 31, 2006. All scheduled payments were made during 2006.

5. Equipment worth $100,000 was purchased on July 1, in exchange for $50,000 in cash and a one-year, 10% note with a principal amount of $50,000. The interest was unpaid on December 31, 2006.

6. The equipment is amortized using the straight-line method, with an estimated useful life of 10 years and an estimated residual value of $0. Because the equipment was purchased on July 1, only a half year of amortization is recognized in 2006.

7. During the year, inventory costing $200,000 was purchased, all on account.

8. Sales during the year were $225,000, of which credit sales were $175,000.

9. The inventory sold during the year had a cost of $160,000.

10. Payments to suppliers during the year totalled $175,000.

11. At the end of the year, accounts receivable had a balance of $10,000.

12. Operating expenses amounted to $30,000, all paid in cash.

13. The company pays taxes at a rate of 30%. During the year, $3,000 was paid to the Canada Revenue Agency.

14. Dividends of $4,000 were declared during the year, and $1,000 remained unpaid at year end.

2-35 **(Preparation of cash flow statement)**
Following are descriptions of line items that should appear on a cash flow statement for Gordon Company. Organize these items into a formal cash flow statement and comment, to the extent that you can, on the health of the company.

Cash receipts from customers	$5,000
Purchase of equipment	$12,000
Proceeds from the issuance of shares	$20,000
Investment in WestJet Airline shares	$3,000
Cash disbursements to suppliers	$3,400
Cash payments to employees for salaries	$1,900
Proceeds from the sale of equipment	$6,000
Dividends paid	$2,500
Repayment of bank loan	$8,000
Cash payments for other expenses	$800

2-36 **(Transaction analysis)**
Many transactions take place between two independent entities. How you record a particular transaction depends on whose perspective you take.

> ***Required:***
>
> For each of the following transactions, comment on how it would affect the basic accounting equation from each of the perspectives given.
>
> a. Purchase of inventory from a supplier (buyer's and seller's perspectives)
>
> b. Loan from the bank (borrower's and bank's perspectives)
>
> c. Deposit by customer on the purchase of a unit of inventory to be delivered at a later time (supplier's and customer's perspectives)
>
> d. Company A invests in shares of Company B and obtains the shares directly from Company B (Company A's and Company B's perspectives)
>
> e. Company A invests in shares of Company B and obtains the shares by buying them on the Toronto Stock Exchange; that is, they had previously been issued by Company B and now trade in the stock market (Company A's and Company B's perspectives)
>
> f. Prepayment of insurance premiums (client's and insurance company's perspectives)

User Perspective Problems

2-37 **(Areas of risk in a new company)**
Assume that you are a commercial loan officer at a bank. The two owners of Krave's Candy Company (see the opening story) come to the bank for a loan shortly before the last of their initial $20,000 is gone. Draft a list of items that you would want to know about the company's operations before you decide whether to loan them any money.

2-38 **(Accrual versus cash basis with respect to manipulation of earnings)**
Under the accrual basis of accounting, revenues are recognized when the revenue recognition criteria are met and expenses are then matched with the revenues under the matching concept. Discuss the opportunities that management has to manipulate income reported to shareholders under the accrual basis as compared with the cash basis.

2-39   (Revenue recognition)

Suppose that your company sells appliances to customers under instalment contracts that require them to pay for the appliance over three years using monthly payments. Two potential methods of revenue recognition would be to either recognize the full purchase price at the time of the sale or to defer recognition of the revenue until you receive the cash from the payments. Discuss the incentives that management might have to choose one method of revenue recognition over the other, from both a tax perspective and the perspective of reporting income to shareholders.

2-40   (Cash basis of accounting)

Under the cash basis of accounting, the purchase of a new piece of equipment for cash would be treated as an expense during the accounting period in which it was purchased.

> a. From the perspective of a company shareholder, how would this treatment affect your assessment of the company's income and the value of the remaining assets on the balance sheet?
>
> b. From the perspective of a buyer of the company (someone who wanted to purchase all the outstanding company shares), how would this treatment affect your assessment of the value of the company as a potential acquisition?

2-41   (Warranty expense and tax implications)

Under accrual-basis accounting, warranty expenses are typically estimated at the time of the sale and accrued. If you were allowed to determine tax law, would you allow companies to deduct warranty expenses at the time of the sale, or would you make the companies wait until they have actually provided the warranty service? Why?

2-42   (Calculation of the value of a company)

One of the shareholders of The Really Sinful Cookie Shop is considering selling her 25% ownership, and wishes to determine her equity in the cookie shop using good accounting principles. The shareholders know the following transactions have occurred since the shop started operations at the beginning of the year.

> 1. $35,000 was borrowed from the bank to help get the business started and $10,000 was repaid by year end. In addition, the shareholders contributed $15,000 to get the business started.
>
> 2. Ingredients costing $40,000 were purchased during the year, and 80% were used in goods baked during the year. All but $6,000 of the ingredients were paid for by the end of the year.
>
> 3. Cookie ovens were rented during the year for $13,000. At year end, an option to purchase the ovens was exercised and $37,000 was paid to acquire ownership.
>
> 4. Wages of $20,000 were earned by employees during the year; all were paid to the employees except income taxes of $3,000, which had been withheld from their paycheques and will be forwarded to the Canada Revenue Agency early next year.
>
> 5. After collecting $86,000 from the sale of goods (which was the full sales amount), the cash balance at the end of the year was $25,000, and net income of $21,000 was reported.

Required:

> a. Show calculations to prove that the ending cash balance was $25,000 and the net income was $21,000.
>
> b. List each of the bakery's assets and liabilities at the end of the year.
>
> c. Calculate the amount of shareholders' equity at year end. (Hint: There are two ways to calculate this.)

EXHIBIT 2-13
PART A **ENERFLEX SYSTEMS LTD. 2003 ANNUAL REPORT**

consolidated balance sheets

	December 31	
(Thousands)	**2003**	2002
Assets		
Current assets		
Cash	**$ 6,741**	$ 5,027
Accounts receivable	**120,432**	89,327
Inventory (Note 3)	**71,162**	81,241
Income taxes receivable	**–**	5,905
Assets held for sale (Note 6)	**–**	4,591
Future income taxes (Note 13)	**4,065**	9,470
Total current assets	**202,400**	195,561
Rental equipment (Note 4)	**71,810**	68,092
Property, plant and equipment (Note 5)	**65,032**	70,309
Future income taxes (Note 13)	**2,748**	1,907
Intangible assets	**3,231**	2,815
Goodwill	**112,453**	112,527
	$ 457,674	$ 451,211
Liabilities and Shareholders' Equity		
Current liabilities		
Operating bank loans (Note 7)	**$ 27,627**	$ 45,254
Accounts payable and accrued liabilities	**70,163**	62,112
Income taxes payable	**4,683**	-
Future income taxes (Note 13)	**–**	2,235
Current portion of long-term debt (Note 7)	**17,097**	17,250
Total current liabilities	**119,570**	126,851
Long-term debt (Note 7)	**51,289**	51,750
Future income taxes (Note 13)	**12,272**	11,708
	183,131	190,309
Guarantees, commitments and contingencies (Note 12)		
Shareholders' equity		
Share capital (Note 8)	**176,928**	176,589
Cumulative translation adjustment	**1,501**	595
Retained earnings	**96,114**	83,718
	274,543	260,902
	$ 457,674	$ 451,211

See accompanying Notes to the Consolidated Financial Statements.

On behalf of the Board:

(signed)   (signed)

ENERFLEX SYSTEMS LTD. 2003 ANNUAL REPORT

EXHIBIT 2-13
PART B

consolidated statements of income

(Thousands, except share amounts)	Year ended December 31	
	2003	2002
Revenue (Note 1)	**$ 515,528**	$ 326,706
Cost of goods sold	**411,569**	256,929
Gross margin	**103,959**	69,777
Selling, general and administrative expenses	**72,499**	53,348
Foreign currency (gains) losses	**(1,985)**	2
Gain on sale of assets	**(3,059)**	(1,492)
Income before interest and taxes	**36,504**	17,919
Interest	**5,280**	3,641
Income before income taxes	**31,224**	14,278
Income taxes (Note 13)	**10,841**	5,046
Net income	**$ 20,383**	$ 9,232
Net income per common share – basic (Note 9)	**$ 0.92**	$ 0.51
– diluted	**$ 0.91**	$ 0.51
Weighted average number of common shares	**22,212,700**	18,166,000

consolidated statements of retained earnings

(Thousands)	Year ended December 31	
	2003	2002
Retained earnings, beginning of year	**$ 83,718**	$ 83,089
Adjustment to retained earnings (Note 1)	**900**	–
Net income	**20,383**	9,232
Common shares purchased for cancellation	**–**	(1,181)
Stock options purchased	**–**	(20)
Dividends	**(8,887)**	(7,402)
Retained earnings, end of year	**$ 96,114**	$ 83,718

See accompanying Notes to the Consolidated Financial Statements.

EXHIBIT 2-13
PART C **ENERFLEX SYSTEMS LTD. 2003 ANNUAL REPORT**

consolidated statements of cash flows

	Year ended December 31	
(Thousands)	**2003**	2002
Operating Activities		
Net income	**$ 20,383**	$ 9,232
Depreciation and amortization	**14,680**	12,054
Future income taxes	**2,877**	2,868
Gain on sale of assets	**(3,059)**	(1,492)
	34,881	22,662
Changes in non-cash working capital	**(823)**	13,642
	34,058	36,304
Investing Activities		
Acquisition of EnSource Energy Services Inc. (Note 2)	**–**	(3,029)
Acquisition of assets of VR Systems, Inc.	**–**	(4,061)
Adjustment of Landré Ruhaak acquisition	**–**	(97)
Purchase of:		
Rental equipment	**(23,682)**	(17,711)
Property, plant and equipment	**(6,310)**	(3,325)
Proceeds on disposal of:		
Rental equipment	**19,943**	9,219
Property, plant and equipment	**3,538**	1,116
	(6,511)	(17,888)
Changes in non-cash working capital	**952**	815
	(5,559)	(17,073)
Financing Activities		
Decrease in operating bank loans	**(17,627)**	(16,244)
Increase in (repayment of) long-term debt	**(1,647)**	9,940
Stock options exercised	**339**	153
Common shares purchased for cancellation	**–**	(1,352)
Stock options purchased	**–**	(31)
Dividends	**(8,887)**	(7,402)
	(27,822)	(14,936)
Changes in non-cash working capital and other	**1,037**	732
	(26,785)	(14,204)
Increase in cash	**1,714**	5,027
Cash, beginning of year	**5,027**	–
Cash, end of year	**$ 6,741**	$ 5,027
Supplemental disclosure of cash flow information		
Interest paid	**$ 5,354**	$ 3,472
Interest received	**$ 321**	$ 322
Income taxes paid	**$ 5,080**	$ 15,094
Income taxes received	**$ 6,953**	$ 16

See accompanying Notes to the Consolidated Financial Statements.

d. Prepare a simple balance sheet for the bakery at year end.

e. If a shareholder sells her 25% interest in the bakery, what does the foregoing tell you regarding how much she should expect to get for it?

Reading and Interpreting Published Financial Statements

Financial Statement Analysis Assignments

2-43 **(Determination of items from a Canadian company's financial statements)**
Base your answers to the following questions on the 2003 financial statements of **Enerflex Systems Ltd.** that you will find in Exhibit 2-13.

a. Determine the amount of cash dividends **declared** during fiscal 2003. Where did you find this information?

b. Determine the amount of dividends **paid** during fiscal 2003. Where did you find this information?

c. Assuming that all revenue was on account, determine the amount of cash collected from customers in 2003.

d. Assuming that the only transactions that flow through the accounts payable and accrued liabilities are purchases of inventory, determine the cash payments made to suppliers in 2003.

e. Under current liabilities on the balance sheet there is an item called Current portion of long-term debt. What does this represent, and why is this information important to users?

f. What was the cash generated from operating activities in 2003? Did it increase or decrease from the previous year?

2-44 **(Determination of items from a Canadian company's financial statements)**
Base your answers to the following questions on the financial statements of Le Château Inc. in Appendix A at the end of the book.

a. Notice from the balance sheets that Le Château's fixed assets (property, plant, and equipment) increased from $38,262 to $44,444 (thousands) during the year ended January 31, 2004. Examine the statements of earnings and cash flows, and prepare a reconciliation that explains how this change occurred.

b. Determine the amount of dividends declared during the year ended January 31, 2004.

c. Look at the statements of cash flows. By how much have the company's cash and cash equivalents increased during the two-year period? Express your answer in terms of both a dollar amount and a percentage.

d. Calculate the following ratios for each of the two years presented. Use total assets and shareholders' equity for each year in the ratios, rather than average total assets and average shareholders' equity.

1. profit margin ratio

2. return on assets

3. return on equity

e. Comment on Le Château's profitability during the year ended January 31, 2004 in comparison with the preceding year.

EXHIBIT 2-14 PART A — SLEEMAN BREWERIES LTD. 2003 ANNUAL REPORT

SLEEMAN BREWERIES LTD.
Consolidated Balance Sheets
(in thousands of dollars)

	December 27, 2003	December 28, 2002
ASSETS		
CURRENT		
Accounts receivable-Trade	$30,322	$25,454
-Other (Note 4)	7,556	3,910
Income taxes recoverable	-	190
Inventories (Note 5)	31,054	22,843
Prepaid expenses	5,379	1,677
	74,311	54,074
NOTE RECEIVABLE (Note 4)	2,166	3,072
PROPERTY, PLANT AND EQUIPMENT (Note 6)	74,691	70,120
LONG-TERM INVESTMENT AND EXECUTIVE LOANS (Note 7)	6,337	7,586
INTANGIBLE ASSETS (Note 8)	86,443	86,581
	$243,948	$221,433
LIABILITIES		
CURRENT		
Bank indebtedness (Note 9)	555	10,461
Accounts payable and accrued liabilities	40,492	28,847
Income taxes payable	2,284	-
Current portion of long-term debt (Note 10)	13,374	9,672
	56,705	48,980
LONG-TERM DEBT (Note 10)	71,916	73,950
FUTURE INCOME TAXES (Note 11)	11,527	8,306
	140,148	131,236
SHAREHOLDERS' EQUITY		
SHARE CAPITAL (Note 12)	45,075	43,753
CONTRIBUTED SURPLUS	28	-
RETAINED EARNINGS	58,697	46,444
	103,800	90,197
	$243,948	$221,433

APPROVED BY THE BOARD

Pierre Des Marais II, Director

Ken Hallat, Director

EXHIBIT 2-14
PART B

SLEEMAN BREWERIES LTD.
Consolidated Statements of Earnings and Retained Earnings
(in thousands of dollars except per share amounts)

	Fiscal Year Ended	
	December 27, 2003	December 28, 2002
NET REVENUE	$185,036	$157,053
COST OF GOODS SOLD	96,703	79,059
GROSS MARGIN	88,333	77,994
GAIN ON SALE OF AGENCY AGREEMENT	-	3,595
GAIN ON SETTLEMENT OF OBLIGATION (NOTE 3)	591	-
SELLING, GENERAL AND ADMINISTRATIVE	55,523	51,659
EARNINGS BEFORE THE UNDERNOTED	33,401	29,930
DEPRECIATION AND AMORTIZATION	6,301	5,402
INTEREST EXPENSE-NET	6,097	6,017
EARNINGS BEFORE INCOME TAXES	21,003	18,511
INCOME TAXES (NOTE 11)	8,750	6,190
NET EARNINGS	12,253	12,321
RETAINED EARNINGS, BEGINNING OF YEAR	46,444	34,123
RETAINED EARNINGS, END OF YEAR	$58,697	$46,444
EARNINGS PER SHARE (NOTE 14)		
BASIC	$ 0.77	$ 0.79
DILUTED	$ 0.76	$ 0.77

EXHIBIT 2-14
PART C
SLEEMAN BREWERIES LTD. 2003 ANNUAL REPORT

SLEEMAN BREWERIES LTD.
Consolidated Statements of Cash Flows
(in thousands of dollars except per share amounts)

	Fiscal Year Ended	
	December 27, 2003	December 28, 2002
NET INFLOW (OUTFLOW) OF CASH RELATED TO THE FOLLOWING ACTIVITIES:		
OPERATING		
Net earnings	**$12,253**	$12,321
Items not affecting cash		
Depreciation and amortization	**6,301**	5,402
Future income taxes	**3,221**	2,000
Gain on sale of agency agreement	**-**	(3,595)
Gain on settlement of obligation (Note 3)	**(591)**	-
Non cash interest charges in income	**(90)**	(69)
Stock-based compensation expense	**28**	-
Loss (gain)on disposal of equipment	**4**	(388)
	$21,126	$15,671
Changes in non-cash operating working capital items (Note 15)	**(7,533)**	(2,277)
	13,593	13,394
INVESTING		
Business acquisitions	**-**	(52)
Proceeds from sale of agency agreement	**980**	351
Additions to property, plant and equipment	**(8,652)**	(6,986)
Additions to intangible assets	**(2,105)**	(7,975)
Proceeds from executive loans	**249**	504
Proceeds from disposal of equipment	**19**	839
	(9,509)	(13,319)
FINANCING		
Net decrease in bank operating loans	**(9,906)**	(5,602)
Stock options exercised	**1,322**	2,288
Long-term debt - proceeds	**90,000**	11,161
Long-term debt - principal repayments	**(85,500)**	(7,922)
	(4,084)	(75)
NET CASH FLOW AND CASH BALANCE, END OF YEAR	**$ -**	$ -
Supplemental disclosures of cash flows:		
Interest paid	**$6,121**	$6,028
Income taxes paid, net of cash refunds of $885 (2002 -$221)	**$3,332**	$7,158

WESTJET AIRLINES LTD. 2003 ANNUAL REPORT

EXHIBIT 2-15
PART A

Consolidated Balance Sheets

Years ended December 31, 2003 and 2002
(Stated in Thousands of Dollars)

	2003	2002
Assets		
Current assets:		
Cash and cash equivalents	$ 241,384	$ 100,410
Accounts receivable	11,781	20,532
Prepaid expenses and deposits	19,928	19,759
Inventory	3,764	2,314
	276,857	143,015
Property and equipment (note 2)	1,140,226	605,124
Other long-term assets (note 3)	59,775	36,066
	$ 1,476,858	$ 784,205
Liabilities and Shareholders' Equity		
Current liabilities:		
Accounts payable and accrued liabilities	$ 82,822	$ 67,008
Income taxes payable	9,820	7,982
Advance ticket sales	58,086	44,195
Non-refundable guest credits	21,718	15,915
Current portion of long-term debt (note 4)	59,334	32,674
Current portion of obligations under capital lease (note 5)	6,297	7,290
	238,077	175,064
Long-term debt (note 4)	589,531	198,996
Obligations under capital lease (note 5)	7,015	16,352
Future income tax (note 7)	61,423	38,037
	896,046	428,449
Shareholders' equity:		
Share capital (note 6)	376,081	211,564
Retained earnings	204,731	144,192
	580,812	355,756
Commitments and contingencies (notes 5 and 8)		
	$ 1,476,858	$ 784,205

See accompanying notes to consolidated financial statements.

On behalf of the Board:

Clive Beddoe, Director

Wilmot Matthews, Director

EXHIBIT 2-15
PART B

WESTJET AIRLINES LTD. 2003 ANNUAL REPORT

Consolidated Statements of Earnings and Retained Earnings

Years ended December 31, 2003 and 2002
(Stated in Thousands of Dollars, Except Per Share Data)

	2003	2002
Revenues:		
Guest revenues	$ 794,450	$ 643,174
Charter and other	65,146	36,822
	859,596	679,996
Expenses:		
Aircraft fuel	155,756	111,737
Airport operations	116,135	88,586
Flight operations and navigational charges	104,955	75,759
Maintenance	75,718	81,973
Amortization	63,208	52,637
Sales and marketing	57,871	44,707
General and administration	46,105	39,791
Aircraft leasing	44,179	35,822
Inflight	38,077	27,284
Reservations	22,213	20,106
Employee profit share (note 8(b))	15,855	15,233
	740,072	593,635
Earnings from operations	119,524	86,361
Non-operating income (expense):		
Interest income	4,003	3,078
Interest expense	(24,915)	(7,038)
Gain (loss) on foreign exchange	(1,848)	346
Gain on disposal of property and equipment	631	97
	(22,129)	(3,517)
Earnings before income taxes	97,395	82,844
Income taxes (note 7):		
Current	11,264	12,626
Future	25,592	18,438
	36,856	31,064
Net earnings	60,539	51,780
Retained earnings, beginning of year	144,192	92,412
Retained earnings, end of year	$ 204,731	$ 144,192
Earnings per share (note 6(d)):		
Basic	$ 0.79	$ 0.70
Diluted	$ 0.77	$ 0.69

See accompanying notes to consolidated financial statements.

WESTJET AIRLINES LTD. 2003 ANNUAL REPORT

EXHIBIT 2-15
PART C

Consolidated Statements of Cash Flows

Years ended December 31, 2003 and 2002
(Stated in Thousands of Dollars)

	2003	2002
Cash provided by (used in):		
Operations:		
Net earnings	$ 60,539	$ 51,780
Items not involving cash:		
Amortization	63,208	52,637
Gain on disposal of property and equipment	(631)	(97)
Issued from treasury stock	3,063	–
Future income tax	25,592	18,438
	151,771	122,758
Decrease in non-cash working capital	40,646	38,866
	192,417	161,624
Financing:		
Increase in long-term debt	466,353	190,366
Repayment of long-term debt	(49,158)	(8,471)
Issuance of common shares	165,545	84,634
Share issuance costs	(6,297)	(3,672)
Increase in other long-term assets	(25,101)	(32,257)
Decrease in obligations under capital lease	(6,498)	(6,088)
	544,844	224,512
Investments:		
Aircraft additions	(564,130)	(320,871)
Other property and equipment additions	(34,249)	(24,031)
Other property and equipment disposals	2,092	234
	(596,287)	(344,668)
Increase in cash	140,974	41,468
Cash, beginning of year	100,410	58,942
Cash, end of year	$ 241,384	$ 100,410

Cash is defined as cash and cash equivalents.

See accompanying notes to consolidated financial statements.

**Sun-Rype Ltd.
Annual
Report**

2-45 **(Determination of items from a Canadian company's financial statements)**
Base your answers to the following questions on the 2003 financial statements of **Sun-Rype Ltd.** on the text companion website.

a. Assuming that all sales were on account, determine the amount of cash collected from customers in 2003.

b. Assuming that the only transactions that flow through the accounts payable and accrued liabilities are purchases of inventory, determine the cash payments made to suppliers in 2003.

c. Calculate the following ratios for 2003:

1. profit margin ratio

2. return on assets

3. return on equity

d. Comment on Sun-Rype's profitability during 2003.

e. Did Sun-Rype declare dividends during fiscal 2003? Explain your answer.

2-46 **(Determination of items from a Canadian company's financial statements)**
Base your answers to the following questions on the 2003 financial statements of **Sleeman Breweries Ltd.** in Exhibit 2-14.

a. Determine the amount of dividends (if any) declared during fiscal 2003.

b. Assuming that all sales were on account, determine the amount of cash collected from customers in 2003.

c. Assuming that the only transactions that flow through the accounts payable and accrued liabilities are purchases of inventory, determine the cash payments made to suppliers in 2003.

d. Calculate the following ratios for 2003:

1. profit margin ratio

2. return on assets

3. return on equity

e. Consider the company's cash position. Did its situation regarding cash improve or worsen over the two-year period?

2-47 **(Determination of items from a Canadian company's financial statements)**
Base your answers to the following questions on the financial statements for **WestJet Airlines Ltd.** in Exhibit 2-15.

a. Refer to the consolidated statements and compare the net income in each of the last two years with the cash flow from operations in the last two years. Note the amounts involved.

b. In general, why are there differences between cash flows from operations and net income?

c. Explain briefly how amortization and future income tax can result in cash flow from operations being higher than net income.

d. Comment on WestJet's ability to pay for its cash needs over the last two years using its cash from operations. Do you think that the company is in a favourable cash flow position? Support your answer.

MCDONALD'S CORPORATION 2003 ANNUAL REPORT

EXHIBIT 2-16
PART A

CONSOLIDATED STATEMENT OF INCOME

IN MILLIONS, EXCEPT PER SHARE DATA	Years ended December 31, **2003**	2002	2001
REVENUES			
Sales by Company-operated restaurants	**$12,795.4**	$11,499.6	$11,040.7
Revenues from franchised and affiliated restaurants	**4,345.1**	3,906.1	3,829.3
Total revenues	**17,140.5**	15,405.7	14,870.0
OPERATING COSTS AND EXPENSES			
Company-operated restaurant expenses			
Food & paper	**4,314.8**	3,917.4	3,802.1
Payroll & employee benefits	**3,411.4**	3,078.2	2,901.2
Occupancy & other operating expenses	**3,279.8**	2,911.0	2,750.4
Franchised restaurants–occupancy expenses	**937.7**	840.1	800.2
Selling, general & administrative expenses	**1,833.0**	1,712.8	1,661.7
Other operating expense, net	**531.6**	833.3	257.4
Total operating costs and expenses	**14,308.3**	13,292.8	12,173.0
Operating income	**2,832.2**	2,112.9	2,697.0
Interest expense–net of capitalized interest of $7.8, $14.3 and $15.2	**388.0**	374.1	452.4
McDonald's Japan IPO gain			(137.1)
Nonoperating expense, net	**97.8**	76.7	52.0
Income before provision for income taxes and cumulative effect of accounting changes	**2,346.4**	1,662.1	2,329.7
Provision for income taxes	**838.2**	670.0	693.1
Income before cumulative effect of accounting changes	**1,508.2**	992.1	1,636.6
Cumulative effect of accounting changes, net of tax benefits of $9.4 and $17.6	**(36.8)**	(98.6)	
Net income	**$ 1,471.4**	$ 893.5	$ 1,636.6
Per common share–basic:			
Income before cumulative effect of accounting changes	**$ 1.19**	$ .78	$ 1.27
Cumulative effect of accounting changes	**(.03)**	(.08)	
Net income	**$ 1.16**	$ .70	$ 1.27
Per common share–diluted:			
Income before cumulative effect of accounting changes	**$ 1.18**	$ .77	$ 1.25
Cumulative effect of accounting changes	**(.03)**	(.07)	
Net income	**$ 1.15**	$ .70	$ 1.25
Dividends per common share	**$ .40**	$ .24	$ .23
Weighted-average shares outstanding–basic	**1,269.8**	1,273.1	1,289.7
Weighted-average shares outstanding–diluted	**1,276.5**	1,281.5	1,309.3

See notes to consolidated financial statements.

EXHIBIT 2-16
PART B

MCDONALD'S CORPORATION 2003 ANNUAL REPORT

CONSOLIDATED BALANCE SHEET

IN MILLIONS, EXCEPT PER SHARE DATA	December 31, **2003**	2002
ASSETS		
Current assets		
Cash and equivalents	$ **492.8**	$ 330.4
Accounts and notes receivable	**734.5**	855.3
Inventories, at cost, not in excess of market	**129.4**	111.7
Prepaid expenses and other current assets	**528.7**	418.0
Total current assets	**1,885.4**	1,715.4
Other assets		
Investments in and advances to affiliates	**1,089.6**	1,037.7
Goodwill, net	**1,665.1**	1,558.5
Miscellaneous	**960.3**	1,075.5
Total other assets	**3,715.0**	3,671.7
Property and equipment		
Property and equipment, at cost	**28,740.2**	26,218.6
Accumulated depreciation and amortization	**(8,815.5)**	(7,635.2)
Net property and equipment	**19,924.7**	18,583.4
Total assets	**$25,525.1**	$23,970.5
LIABILITIES AND SHAREHOLDERS' EQUITY		
Current liabilities		
Accounts payable	$ **577.4**	$ 635.8
Income taxes	**71.5**	16.3
Other taxes	**222.0**	191.8
Accrued interest	**193.1**	199.4
Accrued restructuring and restaurant closing costs	**115.7**	328.5
Accrued payroll and other liabilities	**918.1**	774.7
Current maturities of long-term debt	**388.0**	275.8
Total current liabilities	**2,485.8**	2,422.3
Long-term debt	**9,342.5**	9,703.6
Other long-term liabilities and minority interests	**699.8**	560.0
Deferred income taxes	**1,015.1**	1,003.7
Shareholders' equity		
Preferred stock, no par value; authorized–165.0 million shares; issued–none		
Common stock, $.01 par value; authorized–3.5 billion shares;		
issued–1,660.6 million shares	**16.6**	16.6
Additional paid-in capital	**1,837.5**	1,747.3
Unearned ESOP compensation	**(90.5)**	(98.4)
Retained earnings	**20,172.3**	19,204.4
Accumulated other comprehensive income (loss)	**(635.5)**	(1,601.3)
Common stock in treasury, at cost; 398.7 and 392.4 million shares	**(9,318.5)**	(8,987.7)
Total shareholders' equity	**11,981.9**	10,280.9
Total liabilities and shareholders' equity	**$25,525.1**	$23,970.5

See notes to consolidated financial statements.

Used with permission of McDonald's Corporation.

MCDONALD'S CORPORATION 2003 ANNUAL REPORT

EXHIBIT 2-16
PART C

CONSOLIDATED STATEMENT OF CASH FLOWS

IN MILLIONS	Years ended December 31, **2003**	2002	2001
Operating activities			
Net income	**$ 1,471.4**	$ 893.5	$ 1,636.6
Adjustments to reconcile to cash provided by operations			
Cumulative effect of accounting changes	**36.8**	98.6	
Depreciation and amortization	**1,148.2**	1,050.8	1,086.3
Deferred income taxes	**181.4**	(44.6)	(87.6)
Changes in working capital items			
Accounts receivable	**64.0**	1.6	(104.7)
Inventories, prepaid expenses and other current assets	**(30.2)**	(38.1)	(62.9)
Accounts payable	**(77.6)**	(11.2)	10.2
Taxes and other accrued liabilities	**(147.2)**	448.0	270.4
Other (including noncash portion of special items)	**622.0**	491.5	(60.0)
Cash provided by operations	**3,268.8**	2,890.1	2,688.3
Investing activities			
Property and equipment expenditures	**(1,307.4)**	(2,003.8)	(1,906.2)
Purchases of restaurant businesses	**(375.8)**	(548.4)	(331.6)
Sales of restaurant businesses and property	**390.6**	369.5	375.9
Other	**(77.0)**	(283.9)	(206.3)
Cash used for investing activities	**(1,369.6)**	(2,466.6)	(2,068.2)
Financing activities			
Net short-term repayments	**(533.5)**	(606.8)	(248.0)
Long-term financing issuances	**398.1**	1,502.6	1,694.7
Long-term financing repayments	**(756.2)**	(750.3)	(919.4)
Treasury stock purchases	**(391.0)**	(670.2)	(1,068.1)
Common stock dividends	**(503.5)**	(297.4)	(287.7)
Other	**49.3**	310.9	204.8
Cash used for financing activities	**(1,736.8)**	(511.2)	(623.7)
Cash and equivalents increase (decrease)	**162.4**	(87.7)	(3.6)
Cash and equivalents at beginning of year	**330.4**	418.1	421.7
Cash and equivalents at end of year	**$ 492.8**	$ 330.4	$ 418.1
Supplemental cash flow disclosures			
Interest paid	**$ 426.9**	$ 359.7	$ 446.9
Income taxes paid	**608.5**	572.2	773.8

See notes to consolidated financial statements.

2-48 **(Determination of items from a Canadian company's financial statements)**
Base your answers to the following questions on the financial statements of WestJet
Airlines Ltd. in Exhibit 2-15.

a. Determine the value of new shares issued during 2003.

b. Determine the amount of dividends paid during fiscal 2003.

c. Taking into consideration that some of WestJet's revenues were on account, determine the amount of cash collected from customers during 2003.

d. A company such as WestJet has an extensive investment in noncurrent property and equipment (capital assets). From 2002 to 2003, these assets on the balance sheet changed from $605,124 thousand to $1,140,226 thousand, an increase of $535,102 thousand. Using the three financial statements, find as many items as you can that will help explain this change. There is not enough information in the financial statements to totally explain the change, so do not be concerned if you cannot explain everything.

e. Calculate the following ratios for 2003:

1. profit margin ratio (use total revenues)

2. return on assets

3. return on equity

2-49 **(Determination of items from an international company's financial statements)**
Base your answers to the following questions on the 2003 financial statements of
McDonald's Corporation, a global company headquartered in the United States, in Exhibit
2-16.

a. Refer to the cash flow statement and compare the net income in each of the last three years with the cash flow from operations in the last three years. Note the amounts involved.

b. Using the cash flow statement, list the four largest items that McDonald's used to reconcile the accrual-based net income to cash from operations.

c. Calculate the following ratios for 2003:

1. return on assets

2. return on equity

d. From the financial statements, discuss how important inventory is in relation to other assets on the company's balance sheet. Knowing what McDonald's does, explain why the inventory amount is reasonable.

Beyond the Book

2-50 **(Find items from a Canadian company's financial statements)**
Find the annual report of a Canadian company in the retailing business. Answer the following questions.

a. From the financial statements, discuss how important inventory is in relation to other assets on the company's balance sheet.

b. How does the company finance its business?

c. Read through the management discussion of operations and determine if there is any information there that is not included in the financial statements. If you were a shareholder, would you want to know the extra information? Why or why not?

d. How many directors does the company have? What positions do they hold? Are any of them directors of other companies?

e. Who are the independent auditors? Was the company given an unqualified opinion by the auditors?

2-51 (Research about a Canadian company)

For the company you selected to answer Problem 50, find at least three articles in the financial press that discuss the nature of the markets for this company and the forecast of what the future may be for this sector of the economy. If the company has a website, you may find recent articles about the company posted there. Write a one-page summary of your findings.

Cases

2-52 Shirley's Snack Shop

Shirley Sherry incorporated Shirley's Snack Shop on May 1, 2006 by investing $3,000 in cash. She thinks she has had fairly successful operations since opening the business. However, it is now December 31 and Shirley has no idea how to calculate her income or determine her financial position. The following is a summary of the other events affecting the business during its first eight months of operations.

Case Primer

On May 2, Shirley acquired a licence from the municipality at a cost of $120. The licence allows her to operate the snack shop for a period of one year.

On May 3, she borrowed $10,000 from the bank and used most of it to buy equipment costing $9,600 for her shop. The interest rate on the loan is 12%, and the interest is to be paid annually (i.e., each May). The entire principal amount is repayable at the end of three years. Shirley estimates that the equipment will last 10 years, after which time it will be scrapped. At December 31, 2006, she estimates that the equipment could have been sold for $9,500.

At the beginning of September, Shirley realized that she should have liability insurance, and purchased a one-year policy effective immediately. The premium paid was $900.

Her business is located in a small shop near the university campus, for which the rent is $900 per month. Nine months of rent have been paid thus far.

Shirley paid herself a salary of $1,000 a month, and a part-time assistant earned wages of $300 each month. However, she has not yet paid her assistant his wages for the month of December.

Shirley's purchases of food supplies, on account, cost a total of $22,400. All but $4,500 of this has been used, and she still owes the supplier $4,000. Of the food supplies that have been used, most went into snacks that were sold to customers; however, Shirley ate some of them herself, as on-the-job meals. She estimates that the snacks she consumed had cost approximately $200 when purchased from the supplier, and would have been priced to sell to her customers for approximately $400.

According to her bank records, Shirley received $42,250 from her customers and deposited this in the bank during the period. However, a customer still owes her $500 for snacks provided for a company party held shortly before the end of the year. The balance in her bank account at December 31 is $8,030.

Required:

a. Provide Shirley with an income statement showing the results for the eight-month period ended December 31, and a balance sheet as at December 31, 2006.

b. Comment on the snack shop's performance during its first eight months of operations, and its financial standing as of December 31, 2006.

2-53 Saskco Chicken Products

Saskco Chicken Products is a new company established by four entrepreneurs from Moose Jaw. They intend to purchase live chickens, process them, and sell them as frozen pieces and whole chickens. They initially anticipate hiring three workers to process the chickens. The four owners will work in the business and have the following titles: President (oversees the whole operation, including finance and accounting), VP Marketing, VP Operations (in charge of the processing operations), and VP Procurement (in charge of purchasing chickens from farmers). The President of Saskco Chicken Products has hired you for three months to help the company set up its accounting system. In anticipation of establishing a computerized accounting package, develop a list of account titles that you think this company will need to start operations. For each account title, write a brief one-line explanation of its inclusion in the list of accounts.

2-54 Daisy Dry Cleaning

Daisy Dry Cleaning is in the process of preparing its annual financial statements. The owner of the business is not an accountant, but likes to prepare the financial statements himself. Most of the business transactions are straightforward and can be easily recorded; however, the owner is having trouble determining how to account for three events that occurred in 2006.

1. On January 1, Daisy Dry Cleaning paid $3,600 for a three-year insurance policy. The owner has expensed the entire amount in the current year.

2. On October 31, the company paid a dividend of $10,000. The owner has recorded this payment as dividend expense.

3. On December 1, the company borrowed $20,000 from a bank. Since it does not have to be repaid until four years later, the owner does not think the loan should be recorded as a payable at this time.

Required:

It is now December 31, 2006, and the owner is getting ready to prepare Daisy's financial statements. Advise him as to how the above transactions should be recorded.

2-55 Grill and Associates

Grill and Associates has prepared the following financial ratios based on the company's 2006 and 2005 financial statements. Briefly explain each ratio and comment on the company's performance.

	2004	2003	INDUSTRY AVERAGE
Profit Margin Ratio	18%	16%	18%–20%
Return on Assets	9%	7%	8%–10%
Return on Equity	12%	10%	10%–12%

Critical Thinking Question

2-56 (Comparison of financing strategies)

Using the statements of cash flows for **Sierra Wireless Inc.** in Exhibit 2-17 and **Intrawest Corporation** in Exhibit 2-18, compare the methods used by the two companies to finance their activities during 2003. (Caution: Notice that Sierra Wireless presents its financial statements with the most recent year in the right-hand column, while Intrawest follows the more common practice of showing the most recent year in the left-most column.) What are the future implications of the methods of financing used? By referring to the statements, explain why the companies need outside financing.

SIERRA WIRELESS, INC. 2003 ANNUAL REPORT

EXHIBIT 2-17

S I E R R A   W I R E L E S S ,   I N C .

Consolidated Statements of Cash Flows

(Expressed in thousands of United States dollars)
(Prepared in accordance with Canadian GAAP)

Year ended December 31	2001	2002	2003
Cash flows from operating activities:			
Net earnings (loss)	$ (24,769)	$ (41,913)	$ 2,255
Adjustments to reconcile net earnings (loss) to net cash provided by operating activities			
Amortization	7,161	7,038	5,669
Non-cash restructuring and other charges	–	28,593	895
Loss on disposal	–	597	2
Deferred income taxes	(15)	3,754	–
Accrued warrants	671	481	386
Changes in operating assets and liabilities			
Accounts receivable	12,084	(3,361)	(5,360)
Inventories	(13,031)	2,517	5,878
Prepaid expenses	59	159	(1,087)
Accounts payable	(6,945)	(1,339)	225
Accrued liabilities	3,420	(463)	5,296
Deferred revenue and credits	300	(753)	101
Net cash provided by (used in) operating activities	(21,065)	(4,690)	14,260
Cash flows from investing activities:			
Business acquisitions (note 3)	–	–	33
Proceeds on disposal	–	338	4
Purchase of fixed assets	(10,523)	(2,219)	(1,972)
Increase in intangible assets	(3,328)	(1,431)	(4,077)
Increase in other assets	(143)	–	–
Purchase of long-term investments	–	–	(24,639)
Purchase of short-term investments	(69,411)	(14,662)	(25,103)
Proceeds on maturity of short-term investments	109,676	46,541	10,492
Net cash provided by (used in) investing activities	26,271	28,567	(45,262)
Cash flows from financing activities:			
Issue of common shares, net of share issue costs	499	374	68,623
Increase in long-term liabilities	255	–	–
Repayment of long-term liabilities	(766)	(1,495)	(2,104)
Net cash provided by (used in) financing activities	(12)	(1,121)	66,519
Net increase in cash and cash equivalents	5,194	22,756	35,517
Cash and cash equivalents, beginning of year	6,891	12,085	34,841
Cash and cash equivalents, end of year	$ 12,085	$ 34,841	$ 70,358

See supplementary cash flow information (note 17)
See accompanying notes to consolidated financial statements.

EXHIBIT 2-18

INTRAWEST CORP. 2003 ANNUAL REPORT

Consolidated Statements of Cash Flows

For the years ended June 30, 2003 and 2002
(In thousands of United States dollars)

	2003	2002
CASH PROVIDED BY (USED IN):		
OPERATIONS:		
Income from continuing operations	**$ 34,754**	$ 58,602
Items not affecting cash:		
Depreciation and amortization	67,516	65,434
Future income taxes	(3,914)	(2,873)
Income from equity accounted investment	—	(3,901)
(Gain) loss on asset disposals, net of write-offs	858	(323)
Write-down of technology assets	12,270	—
Non-controlling interest	11,274	11,675
Funds from continuing operations	**122,758**	128,614
Recovery of costs through real estate sales	437,690	402,700
Acquisition and development of properties held for sale	(601,524)	(565,863)
Increase in amounts receivable, net	(12,109)	(8,936)
Changes in non-cash operating working capital (note 21)	26,590	49,191
Cash provided by (used in) continuing operating activities	**(26,595)**	5,706
Cash provided by discontinued operations	**140**	3,898
	(26,455)	9,604
FINANCING:		
Proceeds from bank and other borrowings	599,112	351,259
Repayments on bank and other borrowings	(469,235)	(304,933)
Issue of common shares for cash, net of issuance costs	4,782	53,037
Redemption and repurchase of non-resort preferred shares (note 12(a))	(6,697)	(358)
Dividends paid	(5,051)	(4,737)
Distributions to non-controlling interests	(6,923)	(6,534)
	115,988	87,734
INVESTMENTS:		
Expenditures on:		
Revenue-producing properties	—	(2,353)
Ski and resort operations assets	(64,546)	(91,490)
Other assets	(11,778)	(8,463)
Business acquisitions (note 3)	(2,849)	(8,876)
Proceeds from asset disposals	39,783	4,103
	(39,390)	(107,079)
Increase (decrease) in cash and cash equivalents	50,143	(9,741)
Cash and cash equivalents, beginning of year	76,689	86,430
Cash and cash equivalents, end of year	**$ 126,832**	$ 76,689

Supplementary information (note 21)
See accompanying notes to consolidated financial statements.

From Quill Pens to Computers

In the 1840s, when the maple sugar operation on this picturesque spot in Lanark County, Ontario (some 60 km west of Ottawa) first went into business, accounting records were kept with quill pens dipped in ink, debits on the left and credits on the right of the pages of a handmade book. Today, bookkeeper Jean LeClaire enters all the accounts for Fulton's Pancake House and Sugar Bush using the Accpac *Simply Accounting* computer program.

But really, not much has changed. Four generations later, the sugar bush remains in the same family, and its accounting records still follow essentially the same principles, although they are now kept electronically. In fact, many of the accounts in the general ledger would look familiar to the farm's first owners: income from sale of syrup and food, expenses for containers, equipment repairs, payroll, advertising, and so on. The business still makes most of its $300,000 of revenue each year from direct sales. "We sell our syrup only from the store here, or by mail order," Ms. LeClaire says.

Of course, those early books probably didn't include huge evaporators (which cut down the boiling time of sap into syrup using a reverse osmosis process) among the capital assets. Nor did they include a system for tracking GST! But they had to be flexible enough to account for the vagaries of Canadian weather—a nineteenth-century page might well have included, just as Ms. LeClaire's electronic records for 1998 did, a special account for "ice storm expenses."

Essentially, even the simplest and most old-fashioned of accounting systems had the same aim as the most up-to-date electronic one does today: to provide its users with the information they need to make sound decisions. For owners Shirley and George Deugo, these decisions have included diversifying their operations by adding a restaurant, craft sales, international group tours, and, most recently, corporate team-building retreats on an outdoor challenge course, and dogsledding in winter.

By carefully tracking each of these activities, the Deugos have been able to adapt their efforts as needed. "When the high-tech sector in Ottawa suffered a downturn, that affected our challenge course. But it wasn't a problem because our farm tours were doing well. Then September 11 hit, and many international groups cancelled," says Ms. Deugo.

Fulton's marketing efforts are now split 50/50 between the team-building programs, run by the Deugos' daughter Lorraine Downey, and the Pancake House and Sugar Bush. LeClaire keeps two separate accounts for the two different facets of the business. "We have a separate account for the team-building income," LeClaire says, "to compare expenses against revenue."

While recent events have reduced the number of visitors to less than the usual 40,000 each year, the numbers are picking up again, Ms. LeClaire says. The website, launched in 1998, has generated increased business through mail orders, reservations, and interest in the team-building programs. Now, the company even sends e-mail newsletters to regular customers.

With luck, diversity, and careful accounting, this family operation hopes it will continue to serve many thousands of visitors for another four generations.

chapter 3

Processing Data through the Accounting System

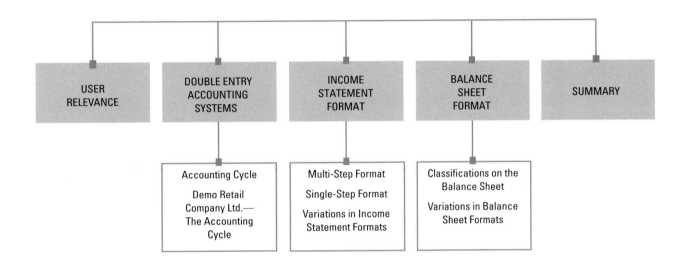

USER RELEVANCE	DOUBLE ENTRY ACCOUNTING SYSTEMS	INCOME STATEMENT FORMAT	BALANCE SHEET FORMAT	SUMMARY

DOUBLE ENTRY ACCOUNTING SYSTEMS	INCOME STATEMENT FORMAT	BALANCE SHEET FORMAT
Accounting Cycle Demo Retail Company Ltd.— The Accounting Cycle	Multi-Step Format Single-Step Format Variations in Income Statement Formats	Classifications on the Balance Sheet Variations in Balance Sheet Formats

LEARNING OBJECTIVES

After studying this chapter, you should be able to:

1. Understand the relationship of debits and credits in the recording of transactions.

2. Explain the difference between permanent and temporary accounts.

3. Identify the steps in the accounting cycle.

4. Analyze transactions and record them in journal format.

5. Post transactions to T accounts and prepare a trial balance.

6. Understand the necessity of adjusting entries and determine how they should be recorded.

7. Describe why closing entries are necessary.

8. Understand the difference between a single-step income statement and a multi-step one.

9. Calculate a gross margin percentage.

10. Describe the criteria for unusual or infrequent items, discontinued operations, and extraordinary items.

11. Understand the criteria for listing items on a balance sheet.

As you read in the opening story about Fulton's Pancake House and Sugar Bush, the accounting records kept by Ms. Deugo and her family have evolved from keeping accounts in a handmade book to keeping them in a computer accounting program. The system of double entry accounting that we are going to show you in this chapter can be traced back to the late fifteenth century. Although the mode of keeping the records has changed, from pen and paper to computers, the underlying system has not.

Now that you understand the basic accounting equation and can work through the analysis of some transactions, we are going to take you one step deeper into the practical side of accounting. We are going to show you how to get the amounts into the records in a way that will enable you to easily extract information that you need and summarize it into financial statements and reports. The computer accounting system used by Ms. Deugo enables her to pull out information daily, because of the program's automated functions.

When you were working through the problems in Chapter 2, you were using columnar tables to record the effects of transactions on the basic accounting equation. You could probably see that if you had to handle dozens of accounts and transactions, this type of framework would become awkward to manage. Since real companies typically have hundreds of accounts and thousands of transactions, recording, summarizing, and reporting information about their economic activities requires something more elaborate than columnar tables.

USER RELEVANCE

Why is it important for users to have a more in-depth understanding of how accounting data are collected, stored, and reported? A business owner, such as Ms. Deugo, should understand how the various business activities will be reflected in financial statements, especially if the owner intends to use the financial results to make decisions. This is especially important for a business that has diversified operations, such as syrup production and sales, a restaurant, craft sales, international group tours, corporate team-building retreats, and dogsledding.

A financial analyst, who advises others on buying or selling shares, should also have in-depth knowledge of how the accounting system works. An analyst needs to understand what the numbers on financial statements mean, how they are determined, and how relevant they are in understanding a company's overall profitability. Creditors, such as loan officers, need an in-depth understanding so that they can assess whether future cash flows will be adequate to meet the lending obligations already in place and any future ones being contemplated by the company. They need to understand what types of transactions affect which financial statement amounts.

Users should also be aware that decisions should not be made on single amounts or ratios. Rather, decision-makers should review the total results, because changes in one area of the financial statements will often have implications for other areas, which could affect the conclusions drawn.

DOUBLE ENTRY ACCOUNTING SYSTEMS

The recording of transactions in a spreadsheet reflecting the basic accounting equation is sufficient if the entity has only a few transactions to record. We call this type of system a **synoptic journal**. It is used, for example, by community clubs that only need to maintain information about dues collected and activities undertaken. However, the plus and minus system used in spreadsheets becomes confusing and somewhat cumbersome when large numbers of accounts and transactions are considered. To overcome this confusion, accountants have developed an alternative system to record transactions, known as a **double entry accounting system**.

We will demonstrate the double entry accounting system by using a device known as a **T account**. To translate from the equation system to the T account system, imagine replacing the equality sign in the basic accounting equation with a big T, as follows.

Replace the basic accounting equation:

$$\text{Assets} \quad = \quad \text{Liabilities} + \text{Shareholders' Equity}$$

With a T account:

Assets	Liabilities + Shareholders' Equity

Note that assets appear on the left side of the T account, and liabilities and shareholders' equity appear on the right side. The equality expressed in the basic accounting equation must still be maintained in the T account system. This means that the totals from the left side of the T accounts must equal the totals from the right side of the T accounts.

The left side of the account is known as the **debit** side, and the right side as the **credit** side. The words "debit" and "credit" have no meaning in accounting other than left and right. Do not try to attach any other meaning to these terms, as this will likely lead you astray in your thinking about the accounts. The balance in the accounting system can now be expressed in terms of debits and credits, rather than in terms of the left and right side of the basic accounting equation. The balance sheet equality requires that debits equal credits. (The abbreviations for debit and credit are Dr. and Cr., respectively.)

LEARNING OBJECTIVE 1

Understand the relationship of debits and credits in the recording of transactions.

GENERAL FORM OF A T ACCOUNT

EXHIBIT 3-1

Name of account

Debit side	Credit side

EXAMPLES OF INDIVIDUAL T ACCOUNTS

Cash (A)		Inventory (A)		Accounts Payable (L)		Common Shares (SE)	
Bal. xx		Bal. xx			Bal. xx		Bal. xx

By recording Assets on the left side of their accounts, and Liabilities and Shareholders' Equity on the right-hand side of their accounts, we can maintain the basic accounting equation (Assets = Liabilities + Shareholders' Equity) by ensuring that the sum of all the debits in the accounts equals the sum of all the credits. Thus, provided that Debits = Credits, the accounting system will be "balanced."

The T account concept also carries over into the accounting for specific asset, liability, and shareholders' equity accounts. Each asset, liability, and shareholders' equity item has its own T account. Regardless of the type of account (Asset, Liability, or Shareholders' Equity), debits are always on the left side and credits are always on the right. However, for Asset accounts the balances are debits, while for Liability and Shareholders' Equity accounts the balances are credits. In this way, by ensuring that the total debits equal the total credits, the accounting system ensures that Assets = Liabilities + Shareholders' Equity.

In Exhibit 3-1, note that there are letters following the account names. These letters will be used throughout this book to designate the type of account. At this point, there are only three designations to worry about: A represents an asset account, L a liability account, and SE a shareholders' equity account. We will periodically add other designations as we proceed through the book. These letters will be a helpful reminder of the nature of the account with which you are dealing.

Remember that assets have balances on the debit side of the individual T accounts, whereas liabilities and shareholders' equity accounts have credit balances. In Exhibit 3-2, the beginning balances for Demo Retail Company Ltd. (from Exhibit 2-1) have been entered into a set of T accounts. Beside each balance, you will see the notation "Bal.", which is used to identify a balance in the account (representing the net result of all previous entries in the account) rather than a new entry (representing an individual transaction). Also, note that the sum of the debit balances ($10,000) equals the sum of the credit balances ($10,000), which means that the system is balanced.

EXHIBIT 3-2 | **DEMO RETAIL COMPANY LTD.**

T Accounts

Because assets have debit balances, increases in asset accounts should be entered on the debit side of the account. It logically follows that decreases in assets should be entered on the credit side. For liabilities and shareholders' equity, the reverse is true: increases are entered on the credit side of the account, and decreases are entered on the debit side.

Exhibit 3-3 lists the appropriate entries for asset, liability, and shareholders' equity accounts. This summarizes what are often referred to as the rules of debit and credit. If these "rules" are new to you, the easiest way to remember them is to focus on how increases are recorded for each type of account. Logically, then, decreases are recorded on the opposite side of the account, and (since there will be more increases than decreases) positive balances are recorded on the same side as the increases.

ENTRIES TO T ACCOUNTS

EXHIBIT 3-3

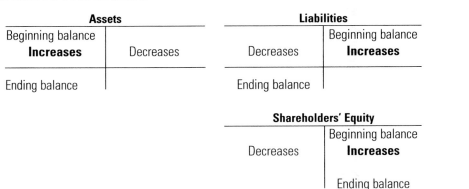

One way to think about the accounts and debits and credits is to imagine that the accounting system is a large warehouse that is balanced on a central point (like the equal sign between the two parts of the basic accounting equation). Inside the warehouse, the company has boxes stacked on either side, which maintain the balance. The boxes themselves are weightless, which means that you do not need the same number of boxes on each side. The weight is added when something is put in a box. Each box represents an account. When the company needs to keep track of information about a specific financial item, it creates a new box and labels it so that everyone knows what is in that box. For example, there would be a box labelled Cash on one side of the warehouse and another box labelled Common Shares on the other side. As financial activities are recorded, things are added to or removed from the appropriate boxes. Therefore, in order to preserve the balance, if you add something to an asset box on one side of the warehouse, you would need to either take something out of a different asset box that is on the same side or go to the other side of the warehouse and add something to one of the boxes there (a liability or a shareholders' equity box). Debiting and crediting accounts is like putting things into boxes and taking things out. If the box is on the left side of the warehouse, it is an asset box. Each time you add something to the box, you debit it; each time you take something out of the box, you credit it. If the box is on the right side of the warehouse (liabilities and shareholders' equity boxes), the opposite is true. Each time you put something into a liability or shareholders' equity box, you credit it; each time you take something out, you debit it. If you are careful to ensure that the debits are balanced with credits, your warehouse will not tilt to one side. Periodically you can check all the boxes, record what is in each one, and prepare a balance sheet.

The accounts shown in Exhibits 3-2 and 3-3 are all balance sheet accounts. They have balances that carry over from one period to the next. (Recall that a balance sheet shows what the entity has at that point in time, to be carried forward to future periods.) Therefore, balance sheet accounts are sometimes called **permanent accounts**.

LEARNING OBJECTIVE 2

Explain the difference between permanent and temporary accounts.

One of the permanent accounts is the retained earnings account. You learned in Chapter 1 that the change in the retained earnings account during a given period is the increase or decrease due to the net income or loss (the net of the revenues and expenses for the period) and the decrease due to the dividends declared. In order to keep track of the individual revenue and expense amounts, as well as the dividends declared during the period, the retained earnings account can be subdivided into several separate accounts. These separate accounts are called **temporary accounts** because they are used temporarily, during the accounting period, to keep track of revenues, expenses, and dividends. The balances in these accounts ultimately affect the retained earnings account.

Exhibit 3-4 shows the subdivision of the retained earnings account into the temporary revenue, expense, and dividends declared accounts.

EXHIBIT 3-4   **RETAINED EARNINGS: REVENUES, EXPENSES AND DIVIDENDS ACCOUNTS**

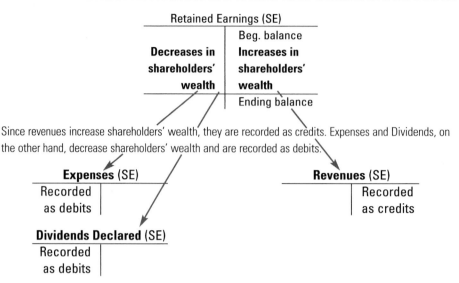

Several things should be noted concerning the revenue, expense, and dividends declared accounts. First, notice that the beginning balance in each of these accounts is zero. Because these accounts are used to keep track of revenues, expenses, and dividends declared during the period, their beginning balances must be zero so that the last period's data are not combined with those of the current period. At the end of the period, the balance in each of the temporary revenue and expense accounts will be used to help prepare the income statement, but then must be transferred into the permanent retained earnings account, along with the dividends, to produce the final ending balance in the retained earnings account.

In this way, the retained earnings account keeps track of the cumulative amounts of revenues and expenses less dividends, and the temporary accounts keep track of only the current year amounts. In other words, using our warehouse example, the contents of the revenue, expense, and dividends declared boxes are all dumped into the retained earnings box. A revenue box with a credit balance will add to the retained earnings box, which also has a credit balance. An expense or dividends declared box with a debit balance will reduce the contents of the retained earnings box.

Note further that while revenues, expenses, and dividends declared are all shareholders' equity accounts, increases and decreases are handled differently. For revenues, credits represent increases, and debits represent decreases. For expenses and dividends declared, the opposite is true: debits represent increases, and credits represent decreases.

The logic of this is directly connected to the eventual effect on shareholders' wealth: **revenues increase shareholders' equity and thus are shown as credits, while expenses decrease it and so are shown as debits.** Therefore, by the end of a given accounting period (prior to transferring the balances to the retained earnings account), revenues have credit balances, expenses have debit balances, and the dividends declared account has a debit balance.

The debit balances in the expense and dividends declared accounts are probably best understood if we remember that they both represent decreases in the shareholders' equity. Because shareholders' equity is represented by a credit balance, the decreases therein must be represented by debit balances. Further, because these are temporary accounts and their balances will be transferred to retained earnings, the debit balances will not persist in the permanent accounts; they will be offset by the credit balance revenue accounts.

It is possible to have a debit balance in the retained earnings account, if expenses have exceeded revenues (i.e., the company has suffered losses). For example, if you look at the balance sheets of **Ballard Power Systems Inc.** in Exhibit 3-5 you will see that its retained earnings amounts in 2003 and 2002 were deficits (debit balances). Most companies do not have deficit positions (i.e., negative balances) in their retained earnings. However, it is not unusual for a company such as Ballard to have a deficit. The company is in the process of developing new fuel cell technology; it will be several years before it has perfected the technology to the stage where it can commercialize it and begin to generate revenue. In the meantime, it will be incurring losses.

BALLARD POWER SYSTEMS INC. 2003 ANNUAL REPORT

Consolidated Balance Sheets

December 31	(restated-note 1(p))	
(Expressed in thousands of U.S. dollars)	2003	2002
ASSETS		
Current assets:		
Cash and cash equivalents	$ 278,099	$ 237,233
Short-term investments	49,013	139,637
Accounts receivable (notes 4 and 15)	22,648	28,123
Inventories (note 5)	26,284	26,134
Prepaid expenses and other current assets	2,420	2,219
	378,464	433,346
Property, plant and equipment (note 6)	85,685	98,720
Intangible assets (note 7)	133,362	156,024
Goodwill (note 2)	220,308	200,639
Investments (note 8)	13,841	26,546
Other long-term assets	3,175	3,349
	$ 834,835	$ 918,624
LIABILITIES AND SHAREHOLDERS' EQUITY		
Current liabilities:		
Accounts payable and accrued liabilities (notes 9 and 15)	$ 42,946	$ 46,749
Deferred revenue	3,890	4,492
Accrued warranty liabilities	32,936	25,637
	79,772	76,878
Long-term liabilities (note 10)	13,360	12,894
Minority interest	—	4,726
	93,132	94,498
Shareholders' equity:		
Share capital (note 12)	1,227,079	1,187,127
Contributed surplus (notes 12(c) and (i))	2,717	—
Accumulated deficit	(487,857)	(362,765)
Cumulative translation adjustment	(236)	(236)
	741,703	824,126
	$ 834,835	$ 918,624

Commitments, guarantees and contingencies (notes 12(j) and 13)
See accompanying notes to consolidated financial statements.
Approved on behalf of the Board:

"Douglas Whitehead"   "Ian Bourne"
Director   Director

Identify the steps in the accounting cycle.

Accounting Cycle Tutorial

Accounting Cycle

We are now ready to look at the whole system by which transactions are measured, recorded, and communicated to users in the form of financial statements. This system is called the **accounting cycle**.

Envision for a moment a company that has just been formed and whose managers need to set up an accounting system. What is the first thing they need to decide? One of the first decisions they must make is what information they need to run the business. What information is important for them to make decisions? What information do outside users need to know about the company? What does GAAP require? Accounting systems are information systems, so managers should decide at the outset what information they want and need to operate the business. Although companies may be in the same industry, each company will develop its own unique information system.

As we proceed through a discussion of the accounting cycle, we are going to demonstrate each stage using the transactions of Demo Retail Company Ltd. from Chapter 2.

CHART OF ACCOUNTS

The types of accounting information to be recorded in the accounting system (represented by the accounts to be used) are generally summarized in a **chart of accounts**. Exhibit 3-6 lists the chart of accounts for Demo Retail Company Ltd. The chart of accounts should be viewed as dynamic, rather than something that can never be changed. As the business changes, there may be a need for different types of accounts. For example, suppose that the company originally was unwilling to provide credit to its customers. There would be no need for an accounts receivable account at that time, because the company was strictly a cash business. Later, if the company decided to allow customers to buy on credit, it would need to add an accounts receivable account to the chart of accounts. A key point to note is that the design of the chart of accounts can facilitate additional information or be a handicap, depending upon how carefully it is developed.

EXHIBIT 3-6

DEMO RETAIL COMPANY LTD.

Chart of Accounts

Permanent Accounts	**Temporary Accounts**
Assets	Income Statement Accounts
Cash	Sales Revenues
Accounts Receivable (A/R)	Cost of Goods Sold
Inventory (Inv.)	Amortization Expense
Prepaid Insurance	Insurance Expense
Land	Interest Expense
Equipment	Dividends Declared
Liabilities	
Accounts Payable (A/P)	
Interest Payable	
Bank Loan	
Shareholders' Equity	
Common Shares	
Retained Earnings (RE)	

In an actual system, each account in the chart of accounts would be identified by a number that would facilitate the sequencing of the accounts and the recording of transactions within a computer system. In this book, accounts will be designated by their names and not by account numbers. An account can be given any name that makes sense and is descriptive of its purpose. Commonly used terms for each type of account will be discussed throughout the book. Several of these names, such as accounts receivable, inventory, accounts payable, and retained earnings, have already been mentioned. Going back to our warehouse example, putting a name on an account is like putting a label on one of the boxes. In order to find a box (or an account) so that you can put something into it or take something out, you need to know what is written on the label.

The chart of accounts is the starting point for the company's accounting cycle. The complete cycle is illustrated in Exhibit 3-7. Each of the steps in the cycle is discussed in the following subsections.

EXHIBIT 3-6
CONTINUED

THE ACCOUNTING CYCLE

EXHIBIT 3-7

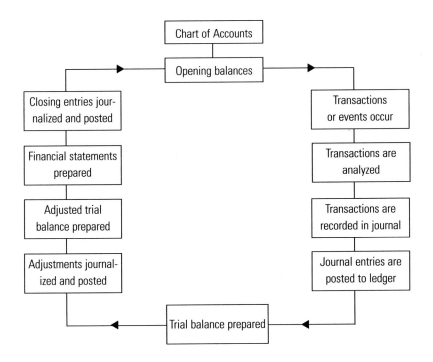

OPENING BALANCES After the chart of accounts has been established and the company commences business, the accountant needs to record in the accounting system the results of the various transactions that affect the company. The system could be as simple as a notebook with sheets of paper representing the accounts and entries made by hand, or it could be as sophisticated as an on-line system in which entries are made via computers. For the purpose of this book, a manual system will be used, but the same entries apply to any accounting system, no matter how simple or how sophisticated. Before a company begins, all the account balances are zero. In subsequent accounting periods, the beginning balances will be the balances carried forward from the end of the last accounting cycle. Demo's opening balances at the beginning of 2006 (brought forward from the end of 2005, in Exhibit 2-1) are shown in Exhibit 3-8.

EXHIBIT 3-8

DEMO RETAIL COMPANY LTD.

T Accounts: Beginning Balances

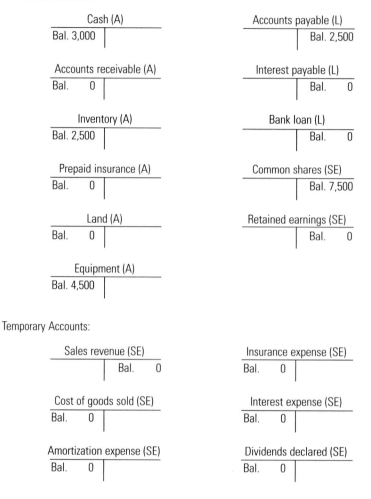

Permanent Accounts:

Cash (A)			Accounts payable (L)	
Bal. 3,000				Bal. 2,500

Accounts receivable (A)			Interest payable (L)	
Bal. 0				Bal. 0

Inventory (A)			Bank loan (L)	
Bal. 2,500				Bal. 0

Prepaid insurance (A)			Common shares (SE)	
Bal. 0				Bal. 7,500

Land (A)			Retained earnings (SE)	
Bal. 0				Bal. 0

Equipment (A)	
Bal. 4,500	

Temporary Accounts:

Sales revenue (SE)			Insurance expense (SE)	
	Bal. 0		Bal. 0	

Cost of goods sold (SE)			Interest expense (SE)	
Bal. 0			Bal. 0	

Amortization expense (SE)			Dividends declared (SE)	
Bal. 0			Bal. 0	

Note that a T account is shown for each account listed in the Chart of Accounts (Exhibit 3-6). Also note that the temporary accounts for revenues, expenses, and dividends declared have been segregated from the permanent accounts, and all the temporary accounts have zero balances.

TRANSACTIONS OR EVENTS The next step in the cycle is to recognize when some event or transaction has occurred that affects company assets, liabilities, and/or shareholders' equity. The transaction or event is usually evidenced by some sort of signal such as a source document: a piece of documentation received or created by the company. Examples of source documents would be invoices, cheques, cash register tapes, bank deposit slips, or purchase order forms. Usually, the first transaction signalled would be the receipt of cash from the shareholders and the issuance of common shares. This first transaction provides the first inflow of cash, which can then be used to buy the assets that are necessary to operate the business.

TRANSACTION ANALYSIS After a signal has been received that a transaction or event has occurred, the accountant must analyze the transaction or event to decide what accounts have been affected and by how much. This phase of the process is called transaction analysis, which we did in Chapter 2 when we analyzed the effect of various transactions on the basic accounting equation. For routine transactions, such as the purchase and sale of goods, the transaction needs to be analyzed only once. After that, each subsequent sale or purchase transaction is the same and can be entered into the accounting system without further analysis. Unique and unusual transactions require further transaction analysis, and generally require the services of a professional accountant who understands the use of appropriate (GAAP) accounting methods. For routine transactions, an accountant is probably not needed, and an accounting clerk could record the transactions in the accounting system.

LEARNING OBJECTIVE 4

Analyze transactions and record them in journal format.

TRANSACTION JOURNAL ENTRIES After the accountant has decided how to account for the transaction, an entry must be made in the system. The initial entry is usually made in what is known as the journal. The journal is a chronological listing of all the events that are recorded in the accounting system. The entry made to the journal is called a journal entry. The journal could be as simple as a piece of paper on which is recorded a chronological list of the transactions that have occurred. The transactions are dated and often assigned a transaction number. The journal entry then consists of the date, the transaction number, the accounts affected (and their account numbers), and a listing of the appropriate debits and credits.

Exhibit 3-9 demonstrates what a journal entry might look like for the first two transactions for Demo Retail Company Ltd. in January. For simplicity, we have assumed that all transactions in January took place on January 31.

By convention, in a journal entry, the debit entries are listed first and credit entries second. Credit entries are also indented from the debit entries. Note that each complete journal entry maintains the balance in the system; that is, debits equal credits. A proper journal entry must always maintain this balance. (Accounting software generally contains internal subroutines that check for balanced journal entries and alert the user to any problems before he or she can proceed.) An explanation is included with each transaction so that the circumstances of the transaction are available for future reference.

DEMO RETAIL COMPANY LTD.

EXHIBIT 3-9

Journal Entries

Transaction	Date	Account name	Debit	Credit
1	Jan. 31	Accounts receivable (A)	2,500	
		Sales revenue (SE)		2,500
		Sold inventory on account		
2	Jan. 31	Cost of goods sold (SE)	1,800	
		Inventory (A)		1,800
		Recorded cost of inventory sold		

Note that in Transaction 1 there is a debit to Accounts receivable. Accounts receivable is an asset account and a debit to it will increase it. Sales revenue is a shareholders' equity account. Because shareholders' equity accounts normally have credit balances, a credit to this account will increase it. The increase in these two accounts is appropriate, because Demo has a new asset (customers owe it $2,500) and shareholders' wealth has increased by the sale price of the goods sold.

Consider Transaction 2 and see if you can follow the same kind of logic to explain why a debit to Cost of goods sold and a credit to Inventory are appropriate. After you have done so, check your thinking against the following explanation.

- The cost of goods sold is an expense account, which (like any expense) decreases shareholders' equity; decreases in shareholders' equity are recorded as debits.

- The inventory is an asset account that is being decreased; decreases in assets are recorded as credits.

LEARNING OBJECTIVE 5

Post transactions to T accounts and prepare a trial balance.

POSTING TO THE LEDGER Once the journal entries are recorded, the information needed to run the business would be entered in the accounting system (in the journal) but it would not be very accessible. If, for example, the manager wanted to know the balance in the cash account, the accountant would have to take the beginning balance in cash and add or subtract all the journal entries that affected cash. If a company has recorded hundreds of journal entries, this could take a long time. To make the individual account information more accessible in a logical and deliberate way, in the next step in the accounting cycle the journal entries are posted to the ledger.

The ledger is a system (in a very simple case, a set of notebook pages) in which each account is listed separately on an individual page. In our warehouse analogy, each account would have its own box. In a computerized system, each account would be represented by a separate computer file accessible by the account number. Posting is the process of transferring the information from the journal entry to the ledger accounts.

Each account in the ledger represents a separate, specific T account. The ledger account would include the name and number of the account, its beginning balance, and then a listing of all the postings that affected the account during the period. Each listing would include the transaction number reference, the date, and the appropriate debit or credit. The transaction number reference would allow a user to go backward in the system to determine the source of each amount in the account.

Exhibit 3-10 shows four ledger T accounts and the posting of the first two January transactions for Demo Retail Company Ltd. To illustrate how the posting process results in the information from the journal (in Exhibit 3-9) being transferred to the accounts in the ledger (in Exhibit 3-10), the related portions have been colour-coded.

EXHIBIT 3-10 **DEMO RETAIL COMPANY LTD.**

Posting to the Ledger

Accounts receivable (A)		Sales revenue (SE)	
Balance 0		Balance 0	
Jan. 31 #1 2,500		Jan. 31 #1 2,500	

Inventory (A)		Cost of goods sold (SE)	
Balance 2,500		Balance 0	
	Jan. 31 #2 1,800	Jan. 31 #2 1,800	

The posting to the ledger can take place monthly, weekly, daily, or at any frequency desired. The timing of the postings is determined to some extent by the management's (or the shareholders') need for up-to-date information. If managers need to know the balance in a particular account, say inventory, on a daily basis, then the postings should be done at least daily. If management needs to know the amount of inventory on an hourly basis, then the posting has to be done more frequently. Many computer systems account for transactions in what is called real time, which means that accounts are updated instantaneously. Once the data entry person has completed the journal entry, the system automatically posts the information to the designated accounts. Other computer systems collect journal entries in batches and post them all at one time. In general, managers like to have information sooner rather than later and, as the cost of computer technology continues to decrease, there has been a proliferation of real-time systems in the corporate world. Remember the news story in Chapter 1 about how fast Cisco Systems gets its financial statements out at the end of the quarter. It uses a real-time system to record its transactions.

At this point, it is important to note that a system consisting only of journal entries would make it difficult to determine the balances in the accounts. On the other hand, a system of only ledger accounts, without the original journal entries, would make it difficult to understand the sources of amounts in the accounts. We need both journal entries and ledger accounts in order to collect information in a way that makes it readily accessible and as complete as possible.

Finally, note that, since each journal entry must have equal debits and credits, if the journal entries are posted properly, the ledger system will balance (i.e., debits will equal credits).

TRIAL BALANCE   While most errors should be detected at the journal entry and posting phases of the accounting cycle, some errors may persist. As stated earlier, most computerized systems will not post a journal entry unless the debits equal the credits. This type of system catches many errors at the input stage. In a manual system, errors may not be detected at the journal entry stage. Moreover, even if the debits equal the credits at the journal entry stage, it is possible for the amounts to be posted incorrectly to the accounts. One device for detecting errors is to produce a **trial balance**. The trial balance is a listing of all the account balances in the general ledger at a specific point in time. To use our warehouse example, we would look into each box and make a list of what we find. A check can then be done to ensure that the total of the debit balances equals the total of the credit balances. If these are not equal, a mistake has been made at some point during the process, which must be found and corrected.

The trial balance assists in detecting balance errors, but it does not, in general, allow detection of errors in which the correct amount was debited or credited, but to the wrong account. Errors such as these can be detected by examining the accounts and their balances for reasonableness. However, if one minor entry was made to a wrong account, it may not be detected in this phase. The trial balance process will also be unable to detect the complete omission of an entire journal entry, as the totals on the trial balance will nonetheless be equal to each other.

Exhibit 3-11 illustrates the format of a trial balance, using the accounts from the Demo Retail Company Ltd. example.

EXHIBIT 3-11

FORMAT OF A
TRIAL BALANCE

Account	Debit balances	Credit balances
Cash	$ xxxx	
Accounts receivable	xxx	
Inventory	xxxx	
Prepaid insurance	xxx	
Land	xxxxx	
Equipment	xxxx	
Accounts payable		$ xxxx
Interest payable		xx
Bank loan		xxxxx
Common shares		xxxxx
Retained earnings		xxxx
Sales revenues		xxxx
Cost of goods sold	xxxx	
Amortization expense	xxx	
Insurance expense	xx	
Interest expense	xx	
Dividends declared	xxx	
Totals	$ xxxxx	$ xxxxx

Note that a trial balance is prepared before the revenues, expenses, and dividends declared are put into retained earnings. Therefore, the revenue, expense, and dividends declared accounts will still have amounts in them. More importantly, the retained earnings account will still show its beginning balance for the period.

Note, as well, the order in which the accounts are listed on the trial balance. They are in the order in which they will appear on the balance sheet and income statement. Accounts will be kept in the ledger in this order so that it is easier to prepare financial statements. If account numbers are assigned to the accounts, as they will be in a computerized system, a set of account numbers will be assigned to a section of the financial statement, say the current assets section of the balance sheet, and all the accounts given those numbers will be readily identifiable as current assets. When the computer system prepares a balance sheet, it will list the current assets in the current asset section of the balance sheet in numerical order according to the account number they were assigned. For example, many companies using four-digit account numbers will assign numbers between 1000 and 1999 to current assets only.

LEARNING OBJECTIVE 6

Understand the necessity of adjusting entries and determine how they should be recorded.

ADJUSTING ENTRIES If an error is detected in the trial balance phase, it must be corrected. A journal entry to correct an error is one type of **adjusting entry** that is made at the end of the accounting period. A second type of adjusting entry is made for transactions or events that were not recognized and recorded during the period. Examples of adjustments that must be made at the end of the accounting period are the recognition that a portion of the prepaid insurance has expired, the amortization of the capital assets, the recognition of interest that is owed on loans, and the recognition that wages are owed to some employees. Care must be taken to ensure that all events and transactions related to the period have been accounted for, so that the financial statements will be as accurate as possible. The adjusting entry phase of the accounting cycle ensures that all the appropriate revenues and expenses have been recorded and reported for the period. Accountants in most business-es have a set of this second type of adjusting entry that they typically make at the end of every period.

Adjusting entries are journalized and posted in the same way as other accounting entries. In our Demo example, the transactions that would be dealt with as adjusting entries are the expiration of a portion of the insurance policy during January, the amortization of the equipment for the month, and the recording of the interest owed on the bank loan.

Notice that the types of items that need to be adjusted are generally time-related: the expiration of prepaid expenses, the amortization of capital assets, and the accrual of interest all occur daily. However, recording them daily would be impractical. Therefore, they are typically updated only at the end of the accounting period, through adjusting entries.

Under GAAP, companies take care to measure their revenues so that all the revenues earned in a period are recorded and reported in that period. Also, the expenses incurred to generate those revenues are identified, recorded, and report-ed (matched). The final adjustments to the revenues and expenses are achieved through the adjusting entries. Although profit-oriented companies adhere to these requirements, governments have been slower to move to accrual accounting, as the following report illustrates.

accounting in the news

Accrual-based Accounting in the Federal Government

In its 2003 budget, the federal government announced its adoption of full accrual accounting, replacing the modified accrual standard it had been using since the mid-1980s. Responding to recommendations from the Auditor General, the govern-ment has moved to accrual accounting in order to provide more comprehensive and up-to-date financial information.

With full accrual accounting, the value of government buildings will appear on its balance sheet for the first time, as will liabilities for cleaning up contamination on its properties. In addition, government decisions causing an increase (or decrease) in liabilities for environmental clean-ups, potential liabilities related to Aboriginal claims, and post-employment and retirement benefits for federal employ-ees will be recorded as expenses in the year in which they arise. Under the modified accrual system that was previously used, the full costs of some of these decisions would not show up on the financial statements until the resulting cash payments were made, years later.

Since full accrual accounting recognizes the value of the government's physical assets, departments should develop better policies for maintaining those assets and make better decisions about whether to buy, lease, or sell buildings and equipment. Also, the cost of owning and operating capital equipment will be shown more accurate-ly, providing a clearer picture of the cost of government programs and services.

"The Budget in Brief 2003," the Department of Finance Canada, 2003.

ethics in accounting

Ethics in Accounting

> Many adjusting entries require estimates and judgements by management, which provide opportunities to manipulate both balance sheet values and income amounts.
>
> For example, suppose that you, as a staff accountant, are asked to postpone the write-off of some old plant and equipment. The equipment is currently idle, and it is clear to you that it will never be used again. You therefore think that it should be written off immediately. However, the write-off would need to be recognized as a loss (like an expense on the income statement, reducing the income) and would, therefore, have a significant negative impact on the company's income for the period. Management has asked you to postpone the write-off, because the company has applied for a large loan from the bank and the loss from the write-off would have a negative impact on the bank's assessment of the company. What should you do?
>
> As you consider your response to this or any ethical question, it is sometimes helpful to think about who will be affected by your decision (including yourself), and how they will be helped or hurt by your decision. Particularly, think of who the users or potential users of the financial statements are. This should help you structure your understanding of the situation and make an ethical decision in the context of these effects.

ADJUSTED TRIAL BALANCE After all the adjusting entries have been recorded and posted, an **adjusted trial balance** is prepared. This is done to ensure that the total debits still equal the total credits, and that any imbalance is corrected before financial statements are prepared.

FINANCIAL STATEMENTS After the adjusted trial balance has been prepared and any necessary corrections have been made, the financial statements for the period can be prepared. Note that, at this point, the temporary accounts still have balances in them. No entries have been made directly to the retained earnings account. The income statement can, therefore, be prepared from the information in the temporary accounts. Note also that the dividends declared account is not a part of the income statement. Dividends are not an expense of doing business; they are a return to shareholders of part of the income earned by the company. Also note that the retained earnings account has the same balance as it did at the beginning of the period.

The balance sheet can be prepared from the balances in the permanent accounts with the one exception of retained earnings, which does not, at this point, include the effects of revenues, expenses, and dividends. However, once the income statement has been prepared, the updated balance for the retained earnings account can be easily calculated, as follows: Beginning balance + Net income − Dividends declared = Ending balance. The latter amount is what will appear on the balance sheet.

The cash flow statement could be prepared, in a simple case such as this, from the information in the ledger account for cash. The preparation of the cash flow statement in more complex cases is discussed in greater detail in Chapter 5.

LEARNING OBJECTIVE 7

Describe why closing entries are necessary.

CLOSING ENTRIES After the income statement is prepared, the balances in the temporary accounts must be transferred to the retained earnings account (a permanent account). This will reset the balance in each temporary account to zero, to start the next accounting cycle. The entries that accomplish this are called **closing entries**. Closing entries will be distinguished from other entries in the examples in this book by lettering them (using A, B, C, etc.) rather than numbering them.

Sometimes companies use a single temporary account to accumulate all the income statement accounts. This account is usually called an **income summary account**. The balances from all the individual revenue and expense accounts are closed to this summary account. The balance in the income summary account is then closed to retained earnings. This will be demonstrated for the Demo Retail Company Ltd. in the next few pages. Because the dividends declared account is not an income statement account, it would be closed directly to retained earnings and would not affect the income summary account.

Exhibit 3-12 illustrates the closing process. In this example, the company's revenues are $100 and its expenses are $60, resulting in a net income of $40 for the period. The beginning balance of retained earnings is $500, and dividends declared during the period are $10. After the net income is added to the retained earnings and the dividends are deducted, the ending balance of retained earnings is $530.

CLOSING THE TEMPORARY ACCOUNTS

EXHIBIT 3-12

Step 1: Close the Revenue accounts and transfer their balances to the Income Summary account, by debiting the Revenues (to bring their balances to zero) and crediting the Income Summary.

Revenues				Income Summary	
	Balance	100			
Closing entry 100	———		⟶	Closing entry	100
	Balance	0			

This would be done for each individual Revenue account.

Step 2: Close the Expense accounts and transfer their balances to the Income Summary account, by crediting the Expenses (to bring their balances to zero) and debiting the Income Summary.

Expenses				Income Summary	
Balance	60			Closing entry	100
		Closing entry 60 ⟶	Closing entry 60		
Balance	0			Balance	40

This would be done for each individual Expense account.

Note that the balance in the Income Summary account is now equal to the Revenues minus the Expenses, which is the amount of Net Income for the period. (If the expenses are larger than the revenues, there will be a Net Loss for the period and the balance in the Income Summary account will be on the debit side.)

Step 3: Close the Income Summary account and transfer its balance to the Retained Earnings account, by debiting the Income Summary (to bring its balance to zero) and crediting Retained Earnings.

Income Summary				Retained Earnings	
	Balance	40		Balance	500
Closing entry 40	———		⟶	Closing entry	40
	Balance	0			

Step 4: Close the Dividends Declared account and transfer its balance to the Retained Earnings account, by crediting Dividends Declared (to bring its balance to zero) and debiting Retained Earnings.

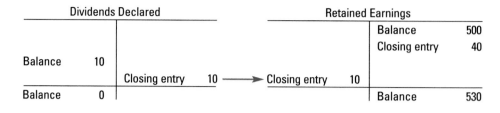

Note that the ending balance in the Retained Earnings account is now equal to the beginning balance plus the Net Income for the period minus the Dividends Declared during the period. Thus, the ending amount in this account is the updated Retained Earnings figure, which appears on the Balance Sheet.

(If there is a Net Loss for the period, it will appear on the debit side of the Retained Earnings account and be deducted in calculating the ending balance.)

Note that the closing entries accomplish two important goals.

- The balances in the temporary accounts are all brought to zero (ready to begin the next period).

- The balance in the retained earnings account is updated to reflect the income earned and the dividends declared during the period just ended.

In a computerized system, the accounting program would perform the closing process automatically when instructed to do so. Since the closing entries are the final step in the accounting cycle, you should make sure that you have finished all the adjusting entries and the financial statements before you instruct the program to close the books for the period.

ACCOUNTING CYCLE FREQUENCY   One final issue with regard to the accounting cycle is: how often should the cycle be completed? That is, how long should an accounting period be? Another way to put it is: how often should financial statements be prepared? The answer is that financial statements should be prepared as often as necessary to provide timely information to management and shareholders. Since this preparation is not without cost, especially in a manual system, a balance must be struck between the benefits of having up-to-date information and the cost of preparing the statements. In some businesses, the need for up-to-date information is great, in which case daily or weekly reports may be necessary. In other businesses, monthly statements are probably sufficient. For companies whose shares are traded on a public stock exchange, there is a requirement to file financial statements quarterly, as well as annually. Regardless of what time period is selected, the procedures described above are appropriate.

The frequency with which financial statements are prepared is sometimes expressed in terms of how often a company closes its books. If it closes its books monthly, the company's accounting cycle is one month long, and the temporary accounts are reset monthly. In such cases, adjusting entries (such as those for amortization, interest, and wages) are also made once a month. In a computerized system, the accounts are not reset monthly. Instead, the system produces an income statement just for the month. The system can isolate all the transactions that were recorded for the month and then prepare an income statement recording only the appropriate transactions. The ease and frequency with which financial statements can be prepared in a computerized system helps reduce the preparation costs significantly.

Demo Retail Company Ltd.— The Accounting Cycle

Return now to Demo Retail Company Ltd. We are going to demonstrate the various stages of the accounting cycle by using the same transactions for January that we used in Chapter 2. The beginning balances in the accounts (the balances that carried over from the end of December 2005) were displayed in Exhibit 3-8.

We now want to show you the rest of the transactions for Demo. The transactions from January 2006 are listed here again for your convenience. They are described in detail in Chapter 2.

1. During January, Demo sold some inventory (purchased in December) to customers, on account, for $2,500.

2. The cost of the items removed from inventory for sales in January was $1,800.

3. Purchases of new inventory in January totalled $2,100. All these purchases were made on account.

4. During the month, Demo received $2,200 from customers as payments on their accounts.

5. Demo made payments of $2,700 on its accounts payable during January.

6. Demo paid $360 in cash on January 1 for an insurance policy to cover its inventory and equipment.

7. On the first day of January, Demo purchased land for $15,000 as a site for a future retail outlet. To pay for the land, Demo raised money by borrowing $10,000 from the bank and issuing new shares for $5,000.

8. Dividends in the amount of $250 were declared and paid in January.

9. The above insurance policy covers the period from January 1 through June 30, 2006.

10. Demo's accountant determined that the equipment should be amortized by $150 for January.

11. The interest rate charged on the loan from the bank in Transaction 7 was 6%, to be paid every three months.

Note that the transactions have been organized differently from the way they were listed in Chapter 2. The insurance expense for January, the amortization of the equipment, and the interest transaction have been moved to the end of the list, because adjustments for items such as these are made at the end of the period. These three entries are the **adjusting entries** and will be recorded and posted separately, in the adjusting entry phase of the accounting cycle.

Exhibit 3-13 shows the first eight transactions for Demo during January, in journal entry form.

EXHIBIT 3-13 **DEMO RETAIL COMPANY LTD.**

Journal Entries for Transactions in January 2006

1.	Accounts receivable (A)	2,500	
	Sales revenue (SE)		2,500
	Sold inventory on account		
2.	Cost of goods sold (SE)	1,800	
	Inventory (A)		1,800
	Recorded cost of inventory sold		
3.	Inventory (A)	2,100	
	Accounts payable (L)		2,100
	Bought inventory on account		
4.	Cash (A)	2,200	
	Accounts receivable (A)		2,200
	Collected on accounts receivable		
5.	Accounts payable (L)	2,700	
	Cash (A)		2,700
	Paid amounts owed on accounts payable		
6.	Prepaid insurance (A)	360	
	Cash (A)		360
	Purchased six-month insurance policy		
7a.	Cash (A)	5,000	
	Common shares (SE)		5,000
	Issued common shares		
7b.	Cash (A)	10,000	
	Bank loan (L)		10,000
	Borrowed from bank		
7c.	Land (A)	15,000	
	Cash (A)		15,000
	Purchased land		
8.	Dividends declared (SE)	250	
	Cash (A)		250
	Declared and paid dividends		

In Exhibit 3-14, all these journal entries have been posted to the ledger T accounts. Notice how the transactions have been numbered so that it is easy to determine which entries are associated with one another. The title of Exhibit 3-13 indicates that the accounts are in the trial balance phase, which means that the adjusting entries have not been recorded and posted and the temporary accounts have not been closed to retained earnings. The term given to calculating the balance in an account is **footing the account**.

DEMO RETAIL COMPANY LTD.
T Accounts after Posting of Transactions

EXHIBIT 3-14

Permanent Accounts:

Cash (A)			
Bal. 3,000			
(4) 2,200	2,700	(5)	
(7a) 5,000	360	(6a)	
(7b) 10,000	15,000	(7c)	
	250	(8)	
Bal. 1,890			

Accounts payable (L)			
	2,500	Bal.	
(5) 2,700	2,100	(3)	
	1,900	Bal.	

Accounts receivable (A)			
Bal. 0			
(1) 2,500	2,200	(4)	
Bal. 300			

Interest payable (L)	
	0 Bal.

Inventory (A)			
Bal. 2,500			
(3) 2,100	1,800	(2)	
Bal. 2,800			

Bank loan (L)	
	0 Bal.
	10,000 (7b)
	10,000 Bal.

Prepaid insurance (A)	
Bal. 0	
(6) 360	
Bal. 360	

Common shares (SE)	
	7,500 Bal.
	5,000 (7a)
	12,500 Bal.

Land (A)	
Bal. 0	
(7c) 15,000	
Bal. 15,000	

Retained earnings (SE)	
	0 Bal.

Equipment (A)	
Bal. 4,500	

Temporary Accounts:

Sales revenue (SE)	
	0 Bal.
	2,500 (1)
	2,500 Bal.

Insurance expense (SE)	
Bal. 0	

Cost of goods sold (SE)	
Bal. 0	
(2) 1,800	
Bal. 1,800	

Interest expense (SE)	
Bal. 0	

Amortization expense (SE)	
Bal. 0	

Dividends declared (SE)	
Bal. 0	
(8) 250	
Bal. 250	

After the month's transactions have been posted, a trial balance is prepared to ensure that debits equal credits. Exhibit 3-15 shows the trial balance before the adjusting entries.

EXHIBIT 3-15 **DEMO RETAIL COMPANY LTD.**

Trial Balance (before adjustments)
January 31, 2006

Account	Debit	Credit
Cash	$ 1,890	
Accounts receivable	300	
Inventory	2,800	
Prepaid insurance	360	
Land	15,000	
Equipment	4,500	
Accounts payable		$ 1,900
Interest payable		0
Bank loan		10,000
Common shares		12,500
Retained earnings		0
Sales revenues		2,500
Cost of goods sold	1,800	
Amortization expense	0	
Insurance expense	0	
Interest expense	0	
Dividends declared	250	
Totals	$26,900	$26,900

Note that the accounts that have zero balances need not be listed on the trial balance.

The accountant would then move to the next stage of the accounting cycle and record the adjusting entries. For Demo, those entries record the use of insurance for one month, the amortization of the equipment, and the interest for January. Exhibit 3-16 shows the adjusting entries for January.

EXHIBIT 3-16 **DEMO RETAIL COMPANY LTD.**

Adjusting Entries in the Journal

9.	Insurance expense (SE)	60	
	Prepaid insurance (A)		60
	Recorded the use of insurance for January		
10.	Amortization expense (SE)	150	
	Accumulated amortization (XA)		150
	Recorded the amortization of the equipment for January		
11.	Interest expense (SE)	50	
	Interest payable (L)		50
	Recorded the interest owed on the bank loan for January		

Note that in Transaction 10, a new account, Accumulated amortization, has been introduced. Its account type, XA, is also different. In the detailed explanation of this transaction in Chapter 2, we told you that rather than reduce a capital asset account balance directly, as the asset value is used up, we instead record the portion of the asset's cost that has expired (i.e., has been transferred to expense) in an account called **accumulated amortization**. This is a **contra asset account**, which is why we have labelled it XA. A contra asset account has a balance opposite to an asset account; therefore, it has a credit balance. Over the life of the equipment, this account will grow by the amount of amortization recorded each period. A contra asset account is shown on the balance sheet, contra to the asset account to which it is associated. On the balance sheet you would see:

Equipment	$4,500	
Less: accumulated amortization	150	$4,350

HELPFUL HINT

Notice that an adjusting entry always involves both Balance Sheet and Income Statement accounts. That is, one half of the entry (either the debit or the credit) will involve an asset or liability account, while the other half of the entry will involve a revenue or expense account.

From now on, we will always use an accumulated amortization account when we are amortizing capital assets.

Exhibit 3-17 shows the accounts after the adjusting entries have been posted. Note that the posted adjusting entries are in bold type.

DEMO RETAIL COMPANY LTD.
T Accounts after Posting of Adjusting Entries

EXHIBIT 3-17

Permanent Accounts:

Cash (A)

Bal.	3,000		
(4)	2,200	2,700	(5)
(7a)	5,000	360	(6a)
(7b)	10,000	15,000	(7c)
		250	(8)
Bal.	1,890		

Accounts receivable (A)

Bal.	0		
(1)	2,500	2,200	(4)
Bal.	300		

Inventory (A)

Bal.	2,500		
(3)	2,100	1,800	(2)
Bal.	2,800		

Prepaid insurance (A)

Bal.	0		
(6)	360	60	(11)
Bal.	300		

Land (A)

Bal.	0	
(7c)	15,000	
Bal.	15,000	

Accounts payable (L)

		2,500	Bal.
(5)	2,700	2,100	(3)
		1,900	Bal.

Interest payable (L)

	0	Bal.
	50	(10)
	50	Bal.

Bank loan (L)

	0	Bal.
	10,000	(7b)
	10,000	Bal.

Common shares (SE)

	7,500	Bal.
	5,000	(7a)
	12,500	Bal.

Retained earnings (SE)

	0	Bal.

Equipment (A)

Bal. 4,500

Accumulated amortization (XA)

		0	Bal.
		150	(9)
		150	Bal.

Temporary Accounts:

Sales revenue (SE)

0	Bal.		
		2,500	(1)
		2,500	Bal.

Insurance expense (SE)

Bal.	0	
(11)	60	
Bal.	60	

Cost of goods sold (SE)

Bal.	0	
(2)	1,800	
Bal.	1,800	

Interest expense (SE)

Bal.	0	
(10)	50	
Bal.	50	

Amortization expense (SE)

Bal.	0	
(9)	150	
Bal.	150	

Dividends declared (SE)

Bal.	0	
(8)	250	
Bal.	250	

Exhibit 3-18 shows the Adjusted Trial Balance after the adjusting entries have been posted.

EXHIBIT 3-18 **DEMO RETAIL COMPANY LTD.**

Adjusted Trial Balance
January 31, 2006

Account	Debit	Credit
Cash	$ 1,890	
Accounts receivable	300	
Inventory	2,800	
Prepaid insurance	300	
Land	15,000	
Equipment	4,500	
Accumulated amortization		$ 150
Accounts payable		1,900
Interest payable		50
Bank loan		10,000
Common shares		12,500
Sales revenues		2,500
Cost of goods sold	1,800	
Amortization expense	150	
Insurance expense	60	
Interest expense	50	
Dividends declared	250	
Totals	$27,100	$27,100

Note that the balance of accumulated amortization, the contra asset account, is listed in the credit column.

At this stage in the accounting cycle, the financial statements would be prepared, using the amounts shown in the adjusted trial balance. The income statement, balance sheet, and cash flow statement for Demo Retail Company Ltd. for this accounting period were shown in Chapter 2. Because of the introduction of the new account, accumulated amortization, the balance sheet would now be slightly different. See the explanation on page 165 about how this change affects the statement.

The income statement and balance sheet can be prepared directly from the balances in Exhibit 3-18. The cash flow statement can be prepared using the transactions listed in the cash account in Exhibit 3-17.

Exhibit 3-19 shows one additional statement that many companies prepare, a statement of retained earnings. Note that dividends are shown on this statement. The statement of retained earnings provides a link between the net income shown on the income statement and the retained earnings shown on the balance sheet.

DEMO RETAIL COMPANY LTD.

EXHIBIT 3-19

Statement of Retained Earnings
For the month ended January 31, 2006

Retained earnings, January 1	$0
Add: Net income for the month of January	440
	440
Deduct: Dividends declared during January	250
Retained earnings, January 31	$190

Note that, like the income statement and the cash flow statement, the statement of retained earnings covers a period of time (in this case, the month of January 2006), rather than a single date like the balance sheet.

The format and order of presentation of the line items on the income statement and balance sheet are addressed in more detail later in this chapter. The format of the cash flow statement is discussed in more detail in Chapter 5.

The temporary accounts now need to be closed. Exhibit 3-20 shows the closing entries to transfer the balances from the temporary accounts to the permanent account, retained earnings. In addition, T accounts for the revenues, expenses, and dividends accounts (i.e., the temporary accounts) and the retained earnings account have been carried forward to Exhibit 3-20 from Exhibit 3-17. Note that these entries have been lettered to distinguish them from the regular entries for the period. An income summary account has been used to collect all the revenue and expense balances, before closing the net amount ($440) to the retained earnings account. The dividends declared account has been closed directly to retained earnings. For easy reference, the journal entries have been colour-coded to match the related postings in the T accounts.

EXHIBIT 3-20

DEMO RETAIL COMPANY LTD.

Closing Journal Entries at January 31, 2006
and Posting of Closing Entries to the Accounts

Journal Entries:

A.	Sales revenue (SE)	2,500	
	Income summary (SE)		2,500
B.	Income summary (SE)	1,800	
	Cost of goods sold (SE)		1,800
C.	Income summary (SE)	150	
	Amortization expense (SE)		150
D.	Income summary (SE)	60	
	Insurance expense (SE)		60
E.	Income summary (SE)	50	
	Interest expense (SE)		50
F.	Income summary (SE)	440	
	Retained earnings (SE)		440
G.	Retained earnings (SE)	250	
	Dividends declared (SE)		250

Temporary Accounts:

Sales revenue (SE)

		0	Bal.
		2,500	(1)
		2,500	Bal.
(A)	2,500		
		0	Bal.

Cost of goods sold (SE)

Bal.	0		
(2)	1,800		
Bal.	1,800		
		1,800	(B)
Bal.	0		

Amortization expense (SE)

Bal.	0		
(9)	150		
Bal.	150		
		150	(C)
Bal.	0		

Income summary (SE)

		0	Bal.
		2,500	(A)
(B)	1,800		
(C)	150		
(D)	60		
(E)	50		
		440	Bal.
(F)	440		
		0	Bal.

Insurance expense (SE)			
Bal.	0		
(11)	60		
Bal.	60		
		60	(D)
Bal.	0		

Interest expense (SE)			
Bal.	0		
(10)	50		
Bal.	50		
		50	(E)
Bal.	0		

Dividends declared (SE)			
Bal.	0		
(8)	250		
Bal.	250		
		250	(G)

Permanent Account:

Retained earnings (SE)			
		0	Bal.
		440	(F)
(G)	250		
		190	Bal.

Note that in Exhibit 3-20, each of the revenue and expense accounts has been closed individually. Remember that you must name the accounts in the journal entries so that you can post the amounts to the right accounts and reduce the temporary account balances to zero. Although we used four separate journal entries to close all the expense accounts, we could have used one, as follows.

Income summary (SE)	2,060	
Cost of goods sold (SE)		1,800
Amortization expense (SE)		150
Insurance expense (SE)		60
Interest expense (SE)		50

This typical journal entry, referred to as a **compound entry**, demonstrates that journal entries can involve more than two accounts. Even though there are four credits, to four different accounts, debits still equal credits.

To conclude our discussion of how the temporary accounts are closed at the end of each period, the process can be summarized as consisting of the following four journal entries:

1. transfer the balance(s) in the Revenue accounts(s) into the Income Summary.

2. transfer the balances in the Expense accounts into the Income Summary.

3. transfer the balance in the Income Summary account into the Retained Earnings.

4. transfer the balance in the Dividends Declared account into the Retained Earnings.

At this stage, the company could prepare a post-closing trial balance. This trial balance would only include the permanent accounts, because all the temporary accounts now have zero balances. This is the final check on the system to ensure that the debits and credits are equal, before transactions for the next period are entered into the system.

Now that you have a better idea about the source of the numbers on the financial statements, we are going to have a more detailed look at the income statement and balance sheet. Up to this point, we have kept the preparation of the two statements as simple as possible. Now that you know more about how the numbers are collected, you are ready to expand your knowledge regarding the format of the financial statements.

INCOME STATEMENT FORMAT

One of the most fundamental objectives of financial reporting is to ensure that financial statements provide information that is useful to the users. To be useful, information should help current and potential investors, creditors, and other users assess the amount, timing, and certainty of prospective net cash flows to the enterprise.

As you learned in Chapter 1, the income statement's purpose is to provide information about the company's performance. The income statement summarizes all revenues and expenses to show the net income. The information provided is primarily historical. The revenues are the historical amounts received or receivable from the sale of goods and services, and the expenses are based on the amounts actually paid or payable in the future for the goods and services used to produce the revenues. Some of the expenses may represent very old costs, such as the amortization of very old assets such as buildings.

For the income statement to provide information about future cash flows, the connection between the amounts presented in the income statement and those future cash flows must be understood. Accrual-basis accounting requires that revenues and expenses be recorded at amounts that are ultimately expected to be received or paid in cash. For example, to estimate the actual amount of cash that will be collected from sales, the company estimates the amount of sales that will not be collected (bad debts) and deducts that amount from the sales. On the expense side, estimates are made for some expenses where amounts are not yet paid, such as tax expense. In both cases, the figures reflect management's estimates about future cash flows. Thus, the income statement provides information to readers about management's assessment of the ultimate cash flows that will result from the period's operations. This means that the income statement, prepared according to GAAP on an accrual basis, actually provides more information about future cash flows than an income statement prepared on a cash basis, which only reflects the cash flows that have already occurred.

A second aspect of providing information about future cash flows is the income statement's forecasting ability. If the trends in revenues and expenses over several time periods are examined, the revenues and expenses that will occur in the future may be predicted (assuming that earning trends in the past continue into the future). An understanding of the relationship of revenues and expenses to future cash flows will allow a reasonable prediction of the amount of cash flows that will result in future periods.

The ability to predict future revenues and expenses depends on the type of item being considered, the industry in which the company operates, and the company's history. If the business is in a fairly stable product line, the sales revenues and cost of goods sold figures may be reasonably predictable. New businesses and new products, however, can make this type of forecasting much more difficult. Some other types of items are not as predictable. Sales of plant and equipment, for example, tend to be more sporadic than normal sales of goods or services. Some items may occur only once and cannot, therefore, be projected into the future. For example, the closing of a plant or the sale of a business unit is an event that has income statement implications in the current period, but will likely not be repeated in the future.

To enable readers of the income statement to make the best estimates or projections of future results, the continuing items should be separated from any non-continuing items. For this reason, the format of the income statement is designed to highlight these differences.

In general terms, there are two approaches to presenting information on an income statement: the multi-step format and the single-step format. We will illustrate and discuss the multi-step format first.

Exhibit 3-21 provides an overview of the major sections of a typical income statement presented in **multi-step format**. The major components are discussed in the subsections following the exhibit.

LEARNING OBJECTIVE 8

Understand the difference between a single-step income statement and a multi-step one.

EXHIBIT 3-21

MULTI-STEP INCOME STATEMENT FORMAT

Income from normal operations:			
Sales or service revenues	$XXX		
Cost of goods or services sold	(XXX)		
Gross margin	XXX		
Other operating revenues	XXX		
Other operating expenses (e.g., selling expenses,			
general and administrative expenses)	(XXX)		
Income from normal operations		$XXX	
Income from non-operating sources:			
Interest revenue and expense	$XXX		
Other non-operating revenues and expenses	XXX		
Gains (losses) on sales of capital assets or investments	XXX		
Income from non-operating sources		XXX	
Gains (losses) from unusual or infrequent events		XXX	
Income before taxes, discontinued operations and extraordinary items			$XXX
Corporate income taxes			(XXX)
Income before discontinued operations and extraordinary items			
(frequently referred to as Income from continuing operations)			$XXX
Gains (losses) from discontinued operations (net of tax)			XXX
Income before extraordinary items			$XXX
Gains (losses) from extraordinary items (net of tax)			XXX
Net income			$XXX

Income from Normal Operations

This section provides information about the revenues and expenses resulting from selling goods and services to customers. The operations reported are those that represent the company's normal operating activities that are expected to continue in the future. Separate sections later in the income statement contain the items that are not part of regular activities, and the results of any operations that management has decided to discontinue.

LEARNING OBJECTIVE 9

Calculate a gross margin percentage.

A distinguishing feature of many multi-step income statements is that the statement starts with sales less the cost of the goods sold (or cost of sales), to arrive at a **gross profit** or **gross margin** amount. If a company's major source of revenues is selling goods, it must make enough profit or margin from sales of its goods to cover all the other costs of operating the business. By examining the gross margin, users can assess the profitability of the company's products. You can also calculate a gross margin percentage, which is the gross margin divided by the sales. You can then use this percentage to evaluate a company's performance over time (by noting whether this percentage has been increasing, decreasing, or remaining stable), and to compare it with other companies in the same industry. The gross margin can therefore be a very informative and useful figure.

Following this, other normal operating revenues (if any) will be added and all the normal operating expenses will be deducted, to show the amount of income that was generated from normal business operations that the company will be continuing in the future. For predictive purposes, this is usually a key figure on the income statement.

Income from Non-Operating Sources

This section of the income statement reports the results of transactions that do not involve the normal sale of goods and services. The typical types of items found here are interest income and expense, gains or losses on disposals of capital assets such as property, plant, and equipment, and other events or transactions that are not considered part of the company's core business operations. GAAP guidelines do not strictly specify what should be included in each section of a multi-step income statement.

LEARNING OBJECTIVE 10

Describe the criteria for unusual or infrequent items, discontinued operations, and extraordinary items.

Income from Unusual or Infrequent Events

Sometimes unusual or infrequent events occur that the company wants to segregate from the rest of its results, so that the reader of the income statement can better understand the nature of the events and assess their continuing or non-continuing status. These types of items can be reported either with the other non-operating items, discussed above, or in a section by themselves.

Corporate Income Taxes

At the end of the income statement sections that have been discussed so far, there is a line item for corporate income **tax expense**, which is calculated on the net of all the items listed above. Sometimes the term *provision for income taxes* is used instead of income tax expense. Taxes are calculated based on the aggregate income to this point, and are not listed separately for each operating and non-operating item.

The tax expense listed on a company's income statement may not be the actual taxes that are currently owed to the Canada Revenue Agency. The rules used to calculate the taxes owed to the government are specified in the *Income Tax Act*. Although many of these rules parallel the accounting guidelines, there are some tax regulations that differ significantly from GAAP. When the amount of income tax expense for the period differs from the amount of tax that must be paid in the current period, the difference is shown as **future income tax**. This means that additional taxes will be paid in future years, as some of the revenues and expenses that were recognized currently, under accounting principles, become taxable in the future, based on the rules in the *Income Tax Act*. More will be said about these dual income tax calculations in future chapters.

Two additional items may appear after the calculation of income tax expense: **discontinued operations** and **extraordinary items** (although extraordinary items are very rarely found in Canada). Because of their unusual or unique nature, these items appear below all the other items on the income statement, including the income tax. This enables readers to focus on the income before discontinued operations and extraordinary items (frequently called *income from continuing operations*) as a key figure for predictive purposes. For this reason, discontinued operations and extraordinary items are sometimes referred to as "below the line" items.

Because they appear after the calculation of income taxes, the tax effects of discontinued operations and extraordinary items must be reported along with the items themselves. The company must pay taxes on these items, just as it does on the items in the upper part of the income statement; so discontinued operations and extraordinary items are reported on what is known as a net of tax basis. This means that the tax effect of each such item is netted against the before-tax number to produce a net, after-tax number. If, for example, discontinued operations result in a gain of $1,000 before taxes and the tax on this is $400, the net-of-tax amount would be a $600 gain (i.e., the $1,000 gain minus the $400 tax expense related to it). Losses from discontinued operations and extraordinary items are handled in the same manner. For example, if discontinued operations result in a loss of $1,000 before taxes and save the company $400 in taxes (due to the deductibility of the loss), the net-of-tax amount would be a $600 loss (i.e., the $1,000 loss minus the $400 tax saving arising from it). In this manner, the taxes related to these below-the-line items are not included in the line item called income tax expense; rather, they are deducted directly from the discontinued operations and extraordinary items.

Discontinued Operations

Discontinued operations are significant segments of the company that management has decided to eliminate. There are specific criteria for deciding what constitute discontinued operations; however, the basic idea is that this category involves dispositions where the business unit or segment can be clearly distinguished, both operationally and for financial reporting purposes, from the rest of the enterprise.

Once management has discontinued a company segment or a separately identifiable portion of its business, there are two types of results that must be reported in the discontinued operations section of the income statement.

- The income from operating the business segment that has been discontinued must be reported separately from other (continuing) income. In prior periods, income from this segment was included with the company's regular operations. However, once the company has exited from this portion of its operations, it is important to show users the income effect of discontinuing this business segment.

- The gain or loss on the closure and/or disposal of the discontinued business segment must also be reported in the discontinued operations section of the income statement.

Extraordinary Items

Although extraordinary items are rarely found in income statements, they are interesting. To be classified as extraordinary, items must be unusual, infrequent, and not resulting from management decisions. Such items are segregated on the income statement, because they are not useful for assessing management's performance or predicting future results.

A recent example of an extraordinary item was a company that reported a gain when the provincial government expropriated some of its property in order to construct a road. The amount paid to the company as compensation was more than the land's carrying value in the company's accounting system; the resulting gain was classified as extraordinary because it was unusual, infrequent, and did not result from a management decision.

Because management may have an incentive to try to place all its "bad news" events in the category of "extraordinary items," the above criteria (i.e., unusual, infrequent, and not resulting from management decisions) were developed to severely restrict what can be classified as extraordinary. Extraordinary items sometimes arise as a result of natural causes, such as earthquakes or floods. However, such events cannot always be classified as extraordinary. For example, if you had business operations in Saskatoon and the South Saskatchewan River overflowed its banks, any losses you incurred would likely be classified as extraordinary because that section of the river rarely floods, and management could not control or anticipate this event. If, however, your business was in the Red River Valley south of Winnipeg, damage from a flood would probably not be considered extraordinary. Although it is beyond management's control, the Red River often floods in this area, causing extensive damage; therefore, such losses are not unusual or infrequent.

Extraordinary items are shown separately because they are beyond the company's control and are not expected to recur in the future. It is important to segregate them because they may have a material effect on net income, and users need to know that the company's income is not likely to be affected by these items again in the near future. Users should, therefore, put more weight on the income before any extraordinary items than they put on the final net income figure.

AN INTERNATIONAL PERSPECTIVE

Reports from Other Countries

In the United States, there are only two criteria necessary for an item to be classified as extraordinary. It must be both unusual and infrequent. One would assume that losses directly associated with the events of September 11, 2001 would meet the criteria set out under GAAP. However, in a surprise move on October 2, 2001, the Emerging Issues Task Force (EITF) directed the accounting community not to treat them as extraordinary. Their reasoning was that although the events were both unusual and infrequent, if companies treated them as extraordinary then the full impact of the losses, which could have many facets, would be shown as only one number on the financial statements. The EITF thought that users would need more information than could be gained from a one-line item. They also thought that in many instances it would be very difficult to separate direct effects of September 11 from indirect effects in a consistent way. They therefore directed the accounting community not to treat such losses as extraordinary.

Source: "US EITF decides against extraordinary treatment for terrorist attack costs," by FASB, www.fasb.org, October 1, 2001.

An alternative to the income statement's multi-step format of the income statement illustrated thus far is the single-step format. This approach to presenting data in the income statement is illustrated in Exhibit 3-22.

SINGLE-STEP INCOME STATEMENT FORMAT

EXHIBIT 3-22

Revenues and gains:			
Sales or service revenues	$XXX		
Other operating revenues	XXX		
Interest revenue	XXX		
Other non-operating revenues	XXX		
Gains on sales of capital assets or investments	XXX		
Gains from unusual or infrequent events	XXX		
Total revenues and gains		$XXX	
Expenses and losses:			
Operating expenses (e.g., cost of goods or services sold, selling expenses,			
general and administrative expenses)	$XXX		
Interest expense	XXX		
Other non-operating expenses	XXX		
Losses on sales of capital assets or investments	XXX		
Losses from unusual or infrequent events	XXX		
Corporate income taxes	XXX		
Total expenses and losses		XXX	
Income before discontinued operations and extraordinary items			
(frequently referred to as Income from continuing operations)			$XXX
Gains (losses) from discontinued operations (net of tax)			XXX
Income before extraordinary items			$XXX
Gains (losses) from extraordinary items (net of tax)			XXX
Net income			$XXX

Note that this method of presenting the income statement contains the same data as the multi-step format shown earlier; the differences relate to how the data are organized within the statement. Although there are many variations in practice, the general idea of the single-step format of the income statement is that all the revenues and gains (other than any related to discontinued operations or extraordinary items) are listed together. Then, all the expenses and losses (other than any related to discontinued operations or extraordinary items) are listed. As a result, there are fewer subsections and subtotals in a single-step income statement than in one prepared according to the multi-step format.

To ensure that you grasp the difference between the multi-step and single-step approaches to the income statement, take a few minutes to compare Exhibits 3-21 and 3-22, and notice that although the same line items appear in each income statement format, they are organized quite differently. You should also note that, regardless of whether you use the multi-step or single-step format, discontinued operations and extraordinary items have to be segregated in the bottom portion of the income statement and shown on a net-of-tax basis.

Variations in Income Statement Formats

It should be noted that Exhibits 3-21 and 3-22 illustrate "pure" forms of multi-step and single-step income statements. In actual practice, companies often use hybrid forms of these approaches, using elements of both the multi-step and single-step formats in their income statements. The income statement for **WestJet Airlines**, which is shown in Exhibit 2-15 on page 131, provides a good example of a hybrid form of presentation that includes elements of both the multi-step and single-step formats.

It should also be noted that published financial statements are often very condensed, with several different items combined and presented as a line item. A consequence of this practice is that information on individual revenues and expenses is often unavailable. In particular, many companies do not disclose their cost of goods sold. Instead, they combine the cost of goods sold amount with other operating expenses and deduct the combined figure as a single amount. (An example of this can be seen in **Le Château's** income statement, in Appendix A. Le Château combines its cost of sales, buying, and occupancy expenses into a single line item.) The usual reason for doing this is that, for competitive reasons, companies do not wish to reveal their cost of goods sold. Unfortunately, when the cost of goods sold is not disclosed it is not possible to calculate a gross margin figure, and as a result the income statement is less informative and useful to readers.

Examples of Actual Income Statements

Exhibit 3-23, which shows the consolidated statements of income for **Enerflex Systems Ltd.**, provides an actual example of the multi-step income statement format. Notice that these income statements begin with revenue minus cost of goods sold, to give a subtotal called *gross margin*, representing the profit that was earned on the company's sales. Then, the company's operating expenses (i.e., its selling, general, and administrative expenses) and gains or losses related to its operations (i.e., from foreign currency transactions and disposal of assets) are shown, resulting in a subtotal for the income from operations, or *income before interest and taxes*. Interest (which is considered a financing expense, rather than an operating expense) is then deducted, to give a subtotal for *income before income taxes*. Finally, the income taxes are deducted, to give the *net income* for the year.

consolidated statements of income

	Year ended December 31	
(Thousands, except share amounts)	**2003**	2002
Revenue (Note 1)	**$ 515,528**	$ 326,706
Cost of goods sold	**411,569**	256,929
Gross margin	**103,959**	69,777
Selling, general and administrative expenses	**72,499**	53,348
Foreign currency (gains) losses	**(1,985)**	2
Gain on sale of assets	**(3,059)**	(1,492)
Income before interest and taxes	**36,504**	17,919
Interest	**5,280**	3,641
Income before income taxes	**31,224**	14,278
Income taxes (Note 13)	**10,841**	5,046
Net income	**$ 20,383**	$ 9,232
Net income per common share – basic (Note 9)	**$ 0.92**	$ 0.51
– diluted	**$ 0.91**	$ 0.51
Weighted average number of common shares	**22,212,700**	18,166,000

In Exhibit 3-24, the statements of operations for **Purcell Energy Ltd.** provide an example of an actual income statement prepared using the single-step format. Notice that all the company's revenues (from its core oil and gas sales plus interest and other sources) are listed together, totalling $38,787,097 for the year ended December 31, 2003. Then all its expenses (except corporate taxes) are listed, totalling $35,220,192, resulting in income before tax expense of $3,566,905 during 2003. After corporate taxes totalling $1,870,722 (of which $1,383,094 does not need to be paid at this time but will likely have to be paid in the future), Purcell Energy shows a net income for the year of $1,696,183.

Examples of unusual and infrequent items can be found in the statement of consolidated income for **Canadian Pacific Railway**, shown in Exhibit 3-25. It lists three such items: a special charge (i.e., a loss) related to labour restructuring and asset impairment; a loss arising from the transfer of assets to an outsourcing firm; and spin-off related, incentive compensation, and unusual charges. Although these items are related to the company's operations, and thus are part of its operating income, they are listed separately from the company's operating expenses because they are not typical of its regular operations.

EXHIBIT 3-24
PURCELL ENERGY LTD. 2003 ANNUAL REPORT
Example of a Single-Step Income Statement

*Consolidated Statements of
Operations and Retained Earnings*

For the years ended December 31	2003	2002
		(Restated Note 2)
Revenue		
Revenues (Note 12)	$ 38,603,278	$ 26,568,116
Interest and other income	183,819	108,442
	38,787,097	26,676,558
Expenses		
Production	10,893,675	7,879,766
Depletion, depreciation and amortization	17,066,733	12,399,453
Amortization of deferred financing costs	167,608	17,260
General and administrative, net	3,211,778	2,194,677
Interest	2,809,434	1,441,263
Accretion of asset retirement obligation (Note 9)	560,756	369,866
Stock-based compensation (Note 2 (b))	510,208	–
	35,220,192	24,302,285
Income before corporate taxes	3,566,905	2,374,273
Corporate taxes (Note 11)		
Capital and large corporation taxes	487,628	466,151
Future income taxes	1,383,094	926,060
	1,870,722	1,392,211
Net income for the year	1,696,183	982,062
Retained earnings, beginning of year		
As previously reported	4,299,434	4,463,475
Retroactive adjustment for changes in accounting policies (Note 2)	(410,900)	(303,351)
As restated	3,888,534	4,160,124
Purchase price of common shares repurchased in excess of book value (Note 10)	(1,622,098)	(1,253,652)
Retained earnings, end of year	$ 3,962,619	$ 3,888,534
Earnings per common share - basic	$ 0.049	$ 0.037
- diluted	$ 0.049	$ 0.036

The accompanying notes are an integral part of these consolidated financial statements.

CANADIAN PACIFIC RAILWAY 2003 ANNUAL REPORT
Example of Unusual or Infrequent Items

EXHIBIT 3-25

statement of consolidated income

Year ended December 31 (in millions, except per share data)	2003	2002	2001
Revenues			
Freight	$3,479.3	$3,471.9	$3,496.7
Other	181.4	193.7	201.9
	3,660.7	3,665.6	3,698.6
Operating expenses			
Compensation and benefits	1,152.6	1,131.1	1,122.1
Fuel	393.3	357.5	403.0
Materials	176.8	165.7	180.9
Equipment rents	238.2	255.0	272.1
Depreciation and amortization	381.5	348.4	334.4
Purchases services and other	577.7	551.4	545.1
	2,9201	2,809.1	2,857.6
Operating income, before the following:	740.6	856.5	841.0
Labour restructuring and asset impairment (Note 4)	228.5	–	–
Loss on transfer of assets to outsourcing firm (Note 4)	28.9	–	–
Incentive compensation and unusual charges (Note 18)	–	–	24.5
Operating income	483.2	856.5	816.5
Other charges (Note 5)	33.5	21.8	26.4
Foreign exchange (gain) loss on long-term debt	(209.5)	(13.4)	58.2
Bridge financing fees related to spin-off (Note 18)	–	–	17.2
Interest expense (Note 6)	218.7	242.2	209.6
Income tax expense (Note 7)	41.8	109.9	132.6
Net income	$ 398.7	$ 496.0	$ 372.5
Basic earnings per share (Note 8)	$ 2.51	$ 3.13	$ 2.35
Diluted earnings per share (Note 8)	$ 2.51	$ 3.11	$ 2.34

The disclosure of discontinued operations is illustrated for **Aliant Inc.** in Exhibit 3-26. During 2003, Aliant discontinued the Emerging Business and Remote Communications segments of its operations. The details of the income from discontinued operations ($111,342,000 in 2003 and $25,879,000 in 2002) are disclosed in a note accompanying the financial statements. Note 2 reveals all the revenues, expenses, gains, losses, and income taxes related to this segment of the company's business, which have been segregated from the rest of its operations and reported separately as discontinued operations.

EXHIBIT 3-26

ALIANT INC. 2003 ANNUAL REPORT
Example of Disclosure of Discontinued Operations

CONSOLIDATED STATEMENTS OF INCOME

For the years ended December 31

(thousands of dollars except per share amounts)	2003	2002
		(note 2)
Operating revenues (note 13)	2,069,389	2,046,474
Expenses		
Cost of operating revenues	310,718	361,487
Operating expenses	929,320	849,099
Depreciation and amortization	390,597	385,604
Restructuring charge (note 9)	14,550	—
	1,645,185	1,596,190
Operating income	424,204	450,284
Other income (expenses) (note 14)		
Writedown of goodwill	—	(50,000)
Other income (expenses)	(8,203)	159
	(8,203)	(49,841)
Interest charges		
Interest on long-term debt	81,038	87,991
Other interest expense	2,067	2,302
	83,105	90,293
Income before underlisted items	332,896	310,150
Income taxes (note 4)	137,574	157,250
Income before non-controlling interest	195,322	152,900
Non-controlling interest	453	1,203
Net income from continuing operations	194,869	151,697
Net income from discontinued operations (note 2)	111,342	25,879
Net income	306,211	177,576
Earnings per common share (note 15)		
Basic from continuing operations	1.35	1.02
Basic from discontinued operations	0.81	0.19
Basic	2.16	1.21
Diluted from continuing operations	1.35	1.02
Diluted from discontinued operations	0.81	0.19
Diluted	2.16	1.21

See accompanying notes to the consolidated financial statements

2 DISCONTINUED OPERATIONS

For the years ended December 31

(thousands of dollars)	2003	2002
Operating revenues	546,806	583,879
Operating expenses	479,158	533,693
Other income (expenses)	(21,958)	3,310
Gain on foreign exchange	—	23,944
Gain on disposal	121,131	—
Interest on long-term debt	19,689	36,171
Income tax (recovery)	23,050	(8,349)
Non-controlling interest	12,740	23,739
Net income from discontinued operations	111,342	25,879

Earnings Per Share

GAAP stipulates that the **earnings per share** figures be reported, either in the income statement itself or in a note to the financial statements. The earnings per share figures express the amount of income earned during the period to the number of common shares held by the owners. Although this can be a complex calculation in some situations, in many cases it is a simple calculation that consists of dividing the company income by the number of common shares outstanding during the period. If the number of common shares outstanding changed during the year, a weighted average number must be used.

Look at the disclosure of earnings per share in Exhibit 3-23 for Enerflex Systems. The *basic earnings per share* figure is 92 cents for 2003, vs. 51 cents for 2002. Another earnings per share figure is also reported, called *diluted earnings per share*. The diluted earnings per share figure is usually lower than the basic earnings per share; for Enerflex, it is 91 cents for 2003. The inclusion of the diluted earnings per share figure is a signal to users that the company has some financial instruments (e.g., convertible debt or shares) or some obligations such as stock options given to its employees that could result in more common shares being issued. Remember that earnings per share is calculated by dividing the income by the number of shares outstanding. Therefore, if more shares are issued, the amount earned per share could decline. The diluted earnings per share tells current shareholders what the earnings per share would have been reduced to, if new shares had been issued as a result of existing financial instruments and obligations. These issues are discussed in more detail in Chapter 12.

An example of additional earnings per share figures can be found for Aliant Inc. in Exhibit 3-26. Because it discontinued some operations in 2003, Aliant had to report earnings per share figures for income from continuing operations, as well as for net income. The amounts were $1.35 per share based upon income from continuing operations, and $2.16 per share based upon net income. The disclosure of these two earnings per share figures enables users to better assess the earnings impact of the decision to discontinue the operations ($0.81 per share). When companies have either discontinued operations or extraordinary items, they must show users the earnings per share amounts for both before and after such items.

AN INTERNATIONAL PERSPECTIVE

NAFTA Facts

The criteria used in other countries to identify extraordinary items are different from those used in Canada. As noted in the previous International Perspectives box, transactions or events that are both unusual and infrequent are classified as extraordinary in the United States. Note that they do not have the third condition, of no management influence. Mexico's criteria for classifying an item as extraordinary are the same as in the United States: the transaction must be both unusual and infrequent. When evaluating an income statement from any of these three countries, you should know by which criteria an extraordinary item was classified.

If the company has different lines of business that can be clearly separated, or operations in several geographic areas, additional information regarding the performance and profitability of the various business units and operations in different geographic areas can usually be found in the notes to the financial statements (under a section called Segmented Information).

BALANCE SHEET FORMAT

LEARNING OBJECTIVE 11

Understand the criteria for listing items on a balance sheet.

The format of the balance sheet is less varied than that of the income statement. There are always separate sections for assets, liabilities, and shareholders' equity. A commonly used format presents assets on the left side of the page, and liabilities and shareholders' equity on the right side. Alternatively, assets may be presented in the upper portion of the page, with liabilities and shareholders' equity in the lower portion. Under either method of presentation, the assets and liabilities sections are usually subdivided into short-term and long-term items, so as to present a *classified balance sheet*.

Within both the *current assets* and *current liabilities* sections, the individual items are generally listed in the order of their **liquidity**. In the case of assets, liquidity refers to the ability to convert the assets into cash. For liabilities, liquidity refers to how quickly the liabilities will require the use of cash. Current assets and current liabilities are generally listed from most liquid to least liquid.

Within the *noncurrent assets* section, the assets are usually listed in order of permanency, with the assets that will last the longest being listed first. Thus, within the *capital assets* or *property, plant, and equipment* group, the assets will typically be listed as land, buildings, and then machinery, vehicles, etc., because of the length of time they will be useful to the company.

In the *noncurrent liabilities* section, the items are often listed in order of their duration or the length of time before they become due. However, there is no fixed guideline. The noncurrent liabilities can be listed in whatever order the company thinks is most informative.

Some companies choose not to follow the balance sheet format described above. For example, **Rogers Communications Inc.** in its 2003 balance sheet does not start with current assets, but instead begins with property, plant, and equipment; goodwill and other intangibles; and investments. Cash and accounts receivable are somewhere in the middle of the assets section. This format is quite commonly seen in Europe. Among the liabilities, long-term debt is listed before accounts payable and accrued liabilities. Another difference in European practice is that the liabilities and shareholders' equity sections would typically be reversed; this part of the balance sheet starts with the shareholders' equity and then moves to liabilities.

The balance sheet of **DaimlerChrysler**, a German/U.S. transportation products manufacturer (shown in Exhibit 1-11, on page 66), illustrates a fairly typical European balance sheet. In it, the assets section starts with intangible assets and ends with cash. This is the opposite of what you would normally see in Canada. Also, two of the assets (deferred taxes and prepaid expenses) have been separated from the others and shown at the end of the assets section. The liabilities and shareholders' equity section of the balance sheet starts with the capital stock and ends with the current liabilities. Again, this is the opposite of what you would usually see in Canada. Also, two of the items (deferred taxes and deferred income) have been separated from the others and shown at the end of the liabilities section.

What we have talked about here are general practices, or conventions, in format. These conventions are not universal and, as the case of Rogers Communications illustrates, not all companies in Canada follow the Canadian conventions.

SUMMARY

This chapter adds to your understanding of the procedures underlying how financial information is collected, recorded, and summarized. You now understand debits and credits, journal entries, ledger accounts, posting, trial balances, adjusting entries, and closing entries. This structure, whether in a manual system or a computerized one, is the same. In a computerized system, the computer takes over many of the mechanical tasks such as posting, closing, and preparing trial balances and financial statements. People are still required to formulate and input the actual journal entries.

After the in-depth discussion of the accounting cycle, we built on your previous understanding of the income statement and balance sheet. We showed you some of the complexities of the income statement, such as operating income, non-operating income, unusual items, income taxes, discontinued operations, and extraordinary items. As we move through the text, you will have some of these items explained more fully. For now, an awareness of the general nature of these items is sufficient. With the balance sheet, we elaborated on its format, talking about the conventional way of preparing the statement and then showing you some other formats used in Canada and in Europe.

By now, you should be starting to be more familiar with accounting language and procedures. As you work through the problems at the end of this chapter, remember that the more effort you put in here, the easier the course will become later.

SUMMARY PROBLEM 1

Use the data from Sample Retail Company Ltd. from the summary problem in Chapter 2.

Additional Demonstration Problems

Required:

a. Record the effects of the transactions in the form of journal entries, number the entries made, and post them to T accounts.

b. Journalize and post the closing entries. (Close the temporary income statement accounts first to an income summary account and then to retained earnings, and close the temporary dividends account to retained earnings.)

SUMMARY PROBLEM 2

The balance sheet of Template Company Ltd. as at December 31, 2005 is given in Exhibit 3-27.

Required:

a. Prepare T accounts for Template Company Ltd., and enter the opening balances from the December 31, 2005 balance sheet. Using the transactions outlined below, prepare journal entries for the transactions for 2006. Open new accounts as you need them. Post the journal entries to the T accounts. Identify the transactions that represent adjusting entries.

b. Prepare a classified balance sheet (showing amounts at the beginning and end of the year) and a single-step income statement for Template Company Ltd. for 2006.

c. Prepare journal entries for the closing entries and post them to the T accounts.

EXHIBIT 3-27 **TEMPLATE COMPANY LTD.**

Balance Sheet
December 31, 2005

Assets

Current Assets

Cash			$ 45,000
Accounts receivable			39,500
Inventory			43,000
Prepaid rent			15,000
Total current assets			142,500

Capital Assets

Building and equipment	$350,000		
Less: Accumulated amortization	100,000		
		250,000	
Office furniture	76,000		
Less: Accumulated amortization	16,000		
		60,000	310,000
Total Assets			$452,500

Liabilities

Current Liabilities

Accounts payable		$ 33,000
Wages payable		9,000
Taxes payable		6,000
Total current liabilities		48,000

Noncurrent Liabilities

Notes payable		8,000
Long-term debt		75,000
Total noncurrent liabilities		83,000
Total Liabilities		131,000

Shareholders' Equity

Common shares	$185,000	
Retained earnings	136,500	
Total Shareholders' Equity		321,500
Total Liabilities and Shareholders' Equity		$452,500

Transactions for 2006:

1. Sales for the year totalled $760,000, all of which were on account.

2. A review of accounts receivable at the end of 2006 showed a balance of $35,000.

3. Amortization of $19,600 was incurred, 80% of which was related to the building and equipment, and the remainder to office furniture.

4. Purchases of new equipment totalled $40,700, all paid in cash.

5. Rent is paid for leased equipment. Payments are made quarterly, in advance, on March 31, June 30, September 30, and December 31. Two payments of $15,000 each were made through the end of June. Rent increased to $16,500 per quarter, starting with the September 30 payment.

6. Employees earned wages of $150,000 during the year. As at December 31, 2006, $11,000 was owed to employees.

7. Purchases of inventory, all on account, amounted to $431,000. (This is the only item that affects accounts payable).

8. The company owed inventory suppliers $36,000 as at December 31, 2006.

9. A count of ending inventories revealed $57,000 in ending inventory.

10. The note payable carries a 9% interest rate, and interest is due semi-annually on June 30 and December 31. On June 30, 2006, the company paid off $6,000 of the principal, as well as the accrued interest. The rest of the principal is not due until June 30, 2007.

11. Long-term debt at December 31, 2005, carried an interest rate of 10%, with interest payments due annually on December 31. On January 1, 2006, the company paid off $25,000 of the principal of this long-term debt. On September 30, 2006, the company issued $27,000 of additional long-term debt at an interest rate of 8% with interest payment terms identical to the existing borrowings.

12. Other selling and administrative expenses of $45,000 were paid in cash.

13. The company's net income is taxed at 30% and, as at December 31, 2006, $4,273 was owed to the Canada Revenue Agency.

14. The company declared $5,000 in dividends each quarter during 2006; dividends were payable on April 15, 2006, July 15, 2006, October 15, 2006, and January 15, 2007.

SUGGESTED SOLUTION TO SUMMARY PROBLEM 1

Exhibits 3-28 and 3-29 show the solution to the Sample Retail Company Ltd. problem.

SAMPLE RETAIL COMPANY LTD.

EXHIBIT 3-28

Journal Entries for Transactions and Adjustments

1.	Accounts receivable (A)	80,000	
	Revenue (SE)		80,000
	Sold inventory on account		
2.	Cash (A)	79,750	
	Accounts receivable (A)		79,750
	Collected accounts receivable		
3a.	Salary expense (SE)	20,500	
	Accrued salaries payable (L)		20,500
	Salaries owed to employees		
3b.	Accrued salaries payable (L)	20,375	
	Cash (A)		20,375
	Paid salaries		

4.	Inventory (A)	39,700	
	Accounts payable (L)		39,700
	Purchased inventory on account		

5.	Accounts payable (L)	37,300	
	Cash (A)		37,300
	Paid accounts payable		

6.	Cost of goods sold (SE)	37,500	
	Inventory (A)		37,500
	Recorded inventory sold		

7a.	Prepaid rent (A)	15,800	
	Cash (A)		15,800
	Paid monthly rent		

7b.	Rent expense (SE)	15,600	
	Prepaid rent (A)		15,600
	Recorded rent used during month		

8a.	Interest expense (SE)	162	
	Cash (A)		162
	Paid interest owed on loan		

8b.	Bank loan (L)	200	
	Cash (A)		200
	Paid part of principal on loan		

9.	Amortization expense (SE)	2,000	
	Accumulated amortization (XA)		2,000
	Amortization of equipment		

10.	Equipment (A)	4,500	
	Cash (A)		4,500
	Bought new equipment		

11a.	Tax expense (SE)	1,695	
	Tax payable (L)		1,695
	Income tax owed		

11b.	Tax payable (L)	1,650	
	Cash (A)		1,650
	Paid income tax		

12.	Dividends declared (SE)	500	
	Cash (A)		500
	Declared and paid dividends		

Closing Entries

| A. | Revenue (SE) | 80,000 | |
| | Income summary (SE) | | 80,000 |

B. Income summary (SE)   77,457

      Cost of goods sold (SE)   37,500
      Salary expense (SE)   20,500
      Rent expense (SE)   15,600
      Amortization expense (SE)   2,000
      Interest expense (SE)   162
      Tax expense (SE)   1,695

C. Income summary (SE)   2,543

      Retained earnings (SE)   2,543

D. Retained earnings (SE)   500

      Dividends declared (SE)   500

SAMPLE RETAIL COMPANY LTD.

EXHIBIT 3-29

T Accounts

The amounts shown in bold face are the opening balances, brought forward from December 31, 2005. Postings for the transactions and adjustments (part a. of the problem) are shown in black; postings for the closing entries (part b. of the problem) are shown in green.

Cash (A)

	4,500		
2	79,750	20,375	3b
		37,300	5
		15,800	7a
		162	8a
		200	8b
		4,500	10
		1,650	11b
		500	12
	3,763		

Accounts Payable (L)

		5,400	
5	37,300	39,700	4
		7,800	

Accrued Salaries (L)

		400	
3b	20,375	20,500	3a
		525	

Accounts Receivable (A)

	500		
1	80,000	79,750	2
	750		

Taxes Payable (L)

		360	
11b	1,650	1,695	11a
		405	

Inventory (A)

	7,500		
4	39,700	37,500	6
	9,700		

Bank Loan (L)

		1,800	
8b	200		
		1,600	

Prepaid Rent (A)

	1,300		
7a	15,800	15,600	7b
	1,500		

Common Shares (SE)

		3,600	
		3,600	

Equipment (A)	
9,200	
10 4,500	
13,700	

Retained Earnings (SE)	
	11,440
D 500	2,543 C
	13,483

Accumulated Amort. – Equip. (XA)	
	0
	2,000 9
	2,000

Temporary accounts:

Revenue (SE)	
	0
	80,000 1
A 80,000	
	0

Cost of Goods Sold (SE)	
0	
6 37,500	
	37,500 B
0	

Salary Expense (SE)	
0	
3a 20,500	
	20,500 B
0	

Amortization Expense (SE)	
0	
9 2,000	
	2,000 B
0	

Rent Expense (SE)	
0	
7b 15,600	
	15,600 B
0	

Interest Expense (SE)	
0	
8a 162	
	162 B
0	

Income Tax Expense (SE)	
0	
11a 1,695	
	1,695 B
0	

Income Summary (SE)	
	0
B 77,457	
	80,000 A
	2,543
C 2,543	
	0

Dividends Declared (SE)	
	0
12 500	
	500 D
0	

SUGGESTED SOLUTION TO SUMMARY PROBLEM 2

Required

a. The journal entries are shown in Exhibit 3-30. The T accounts for Template Company Ltd. are shown in Exhibit 3-31. The December 31, 2005 balances are shown in bold, and the posted transactions from 2006 are numbered. Additional explanations for some of the transactions are given below.

Transaction 2 The information given is the ending balance in the account. The cash collections are calculated based on the beginning and ending balances in the account and the debit for sales on account, as follows.

Beginning balance of A/R	$ 39,500
Sales on account (new A/R)	760,000
Total A/R to be collected	799,500
Less: Ending balance of A/R	35,000
Payments received on account	$764,500

Note that, after the journal entries for Transactions 1 and 2 are posted to the T accounts, the ending balance in the A/R account will be the specified $35,000.

Transaction 3 The amortization for the period is split between the building and equipment and the office furniture account. Both of these could use the same amortization expense account (or they could be recorded in separate expense accounts), but accumulated amortization must be recorded in the appropriate contra asset accounts, in order to be reported on the balance sheet.

Transaction 5

a. The total cash payments during the period total $63,000 [(2 × $15,000) + (2 × $16,500)]. At the time these payments are made, they constitute an asset, prepaid rent.

b. The beginning balance in the prepaid rent account on December 31, 2005, of $15,000 represents the payment made on December 31, 2005, covering the rent for the first quarter of 2006. The first two payments in 2006 (of $15,000 each, on March 31 and June 30) cover quarters two and three. The third payment of $16,500 on September 30 covers the fourth quarter. Therefore, the rent expense during 2006 should be the sum of these amounts, or $61,500 [(3 3 $15,000) 1 $16,500]. The last payment of $16,500 on December 31, 2006, applies to the first quarter of 2007 and should be the ending balance in the prepaid rent account (after posting entry 5b).

Note that, after the journal entries for Transaction 5 are posted to the T accounts, the ending balance in the prepaid rent account will be the specified $16,500.

Also note that various combinations of entries could be made to record these events. Any journal entries that result in the correct balances in the accounts are acceptable.

Transaction 6 The amount of wages earned by employees ($150,000) and the ending balance in the wages payable account ($11,000) given in the problem allow the calculation of the amount that was paid for wages during 2006, as follows.

Beginning balance of W/P	$ 9,000
Wages earned (new W/P)	150,000
Total wages to be paid	159,000
Less: Ending balance of W/P	11,000
Wage payments made during period	$148,000

Note that, after the journal entries for Transaction 6 are posted to the T accounts, the ending balance in the wages payable account will be the specified $11,000.

Again, note that various combinations of entries could be made to record these events; any journal entries that result in the correct balances in the accounts are acceptable.

Transaction 8 The same procedure can be used as in Transaction 6, as follows.

Beginning balance of A/P	$ 33,000
Additional purchases on account	431,000
Total A/P to be paid	464,000
Less: Ending balance of A/P	36,000
Payments made during the period	$428,000

Note that, after the journal entries for Transaction 8 are posted to the T accounts, the ending balance in accounts payable will be the specified $36,000.

Transaction 9 The beginning and ending balances in inventory and the amount of inventory purchased are used to determine the cost of goods sold, as follows.

Beginning inventory	$ 43,000
Purchases of additional inventory	431,000
Total goods available for sale	474,000
Less: Ending inventory	57,000
Cost of goods sold	$417,000

Transaction 10 The interest is paid for the first six months on the initial balance of $8,000. For the last six months of the year, the interest is calculated on the new balance in the account, $2,000. The total interest for the year can be calculated according to the following schedule.

$8,000 × 9% × 6/12 =	$360
$2,000 × 9% × 6/12 =	90
Interest expense	$450

Transaction 11 The interest incurred during the year on the initial long-term debt is calculated on the new balance of $50,000, after the principal was reduced by $25,000 on January 1, 2006. The interest on the new debt that was taken out on September 30, 2006, is calculated only on the last three months of the year. The total interest is calculated as follows.

$50,000 × 10% × 12/12 =	$5,000
$27,000 × 8% × 3/12 =	540
Interest expense	$5,540

Transaction 13 Taxes are calculated on the income before taxes, which is $60,910 in 2006 (see the income statement in Exhibit 3-32). The tax expense is $18,273 (30% × $60,910). The ending balance in the taxes payable account is then used to calculate how much Template paid in taxes in 2006, as follows.

Beginning balance of T/P	$ 6,000
Tax expense for the period (new T/P)	18,273
Total tax to be paid	24,273
Less: Ending balance of T/P	4,273
Tax payments made during the period	$20,000

Transaction 14 Because the last dividend declared in 2006 is still payable as at December 31, a new account, dividends payable, will appear on the balance sheet. The first three dividends are paid in cash.

EXHIBIT 3-30 **TEMPLATE COMPANY LTD.**

Journal Entries for 2006

1.	Accounts receivable (A)	760,000	
	Sales revenue (SE)		760,000
	Sold inventory on account		

2.	Cash (A)	764,500	
	Accounts receivable (A)		764,500
	Collected accounts receivable		
3.	Amortization expense (SE)	19,600	
	Accumulated amortization—		
	building and equipment (XA)		15,680
	Accumulated amortization—		
	office furniture (XA)		3,920
	Amortized capital assets		
4.	Building and equipment (A)	40,700	
	Cash (A)		40,700
	Purchased new equipment		
5a.	Prepaid rent (A)	63,000	
	Cash (A)		63,000
	Paid rent in quarterly instalments		
5b.	Rent expense (SE)	61,500	
	Prepaid rent (A)		61,500
	Recorded rent expired for the year		
6a.	Wage expense (SE)	150,000	
	Wages payable (L)		150,000
	Recorded wages owed to employees		
6b.	Wages payable (L)	148,000	
	Cash (A)		148,000
	Paid wages to employees		
7.	Inventory (A)	431,000	
	Accounts payable (L)		431,000
	Bought inventory on account		
8.	Accounts payable (L)	428,000	
	Cash (A)		428,000
	Paid suppliers		
9.	Cost of goods sold (SE)	417,000	
	Inventory (A)		417,000
	Recorded cost of inventory sold		
10a.	Notes payable (L)	6,000	
	Interest expense (SE)	360	
	Cash (A)		6,360
	Paid part of principal of notes payable,		
	plus interest for January 1–June 30		

10b.	Interest expense (SE)	90	
	Cash (A)		90
	Paid interest on notes payable		
	for July 1–December 31		
11a.	Long-term debt (L)	25,000	
	Cash (A)		25,000
	Paid part of principal of long-term debt		
11b.	Cash (A)	27,000	
	Long-term debt (L)		27,000
	Borrowed additional funds		
11c.	Interest expense (SE)	5,540	
	Cash (A)		5,540
	Paid interest on the long-term debt		
12.	Selling and administrative expenses (SE)	45,000	
	Cash (A)		45,000
	Paid selling and administrative expenses		
13a.	Income tax expense (SE)	18,273	
	Taxes payable (L)		18,273
	Recorded income taxes owed for the year		
13b.	Taxes payable (L)	20,000	
	Cash (A)		20,000
	Paid income taxes		
14a.	Dividends declared (SE)	20,000	
	Dividends payable (L)		20,000
	Recorded dividends declared (4 3 $5,000)		
14b.	Dividends payable (L)	15,000	
	Cash (A)		15,000
	Paid dividends (3 3 $5,000)		

Transactions 3, 5b, and 13a would be adjusting entries.

TEMPLATE COMPANY LTD.

EXHIBIT 3-31

T Accounts with Posted Balances
The amounts shown in bold face are the opening balances, brought forward from December 31, 2005.

		Cash (A)		
	45,000			
2	764,500	40,700	4	
11b	27,000	63,000	5a	
		148,000	6b	
		428,000	8	
		6,360	10a	
		90	10b	
		25,000	11a	
		5,540	11c	
		45,000	12	
		20,000	13b	
		15,000	14b	
	39,810			

		Accounts Payable (L)		
		33,000		
8	428,000	431,000	7	
		36,000		

		Wages Payable (L)		
		9,000		
6b	148,000	150,000	6a	
		11,000		

		Accounts Receivable (A)		
	39,500			
1	760,000	764,500	2	
	35,000			

		Taxes Payable (L)		
		6,000		
13b	20,000	18,273	13a	
		4,273		

		Inventory (A)		
	43,000			
7	431,000	417,000	9	
	57,000			

		Dividends Payable (L)		
		0		
14b	15,000	20,000	14a	
		5,000		

		Prepaid Rent (A)		
	15,000			
5a	63,000	61,500	5b	
	16,500			

		Notes Payable (L)		
		8,000		
10a	6,000			
		2,000		

		Building and Equipment (A)		
	350,000			
4	40,700			
	390,700			

		Long-term Debt (L)		
		75,000		
11a	25,000	27,000	11b	
		77,000		

	Accumulated Amort. – B & E (XA)		
	100,000		
	15,680	3	
	115,680		

	Common Shares (SE)		
	185,000		
	185,000		

Office Furniture (A)			Retained Earnings (SE)		
76,000				**136,500**	
		D	20,000	42,637	C
76,000				159,137	

Accumulated Am.–O.F. (XA)		
	16,000	
	3,920	3
	19,920	3

Temporary accounts:

Sales Revenue (SE)			Cost of Goods Sold (SE)		
	0			**0**	
	760,000	1	9	417,000	
A	760,000			417,000	B
	0			0	

Wage Expense (SE)			Amortization Expense (SE)		
	0			**0**	
6a	150,000		3	19,600	
	150,000	B		19,600	B
	0			0	

Rent Expense (SE)			Interest Expense (SE)		
	0			**0**	
5b	61,500		10a	360	
	61,500	B	10b	90	
	0		11c	5,540	5,990	B
				0	

Selling & Admin. Expense (SE)			Income Tax Expense (SE)		
	0			**0**	
12	45,000		13a	18,273	
	45,000	B		18,273	B
	0			0	

Income Summary (SE)			Dividends Declared (SE)		
	0			**0**	
B	717,363	760,000	A	14a	20,000
	42,637			20,000	D
C	42,637			0	
	0				

Required:

b. The financial statements for Template Company Ltd. are included in Exhibit 3-32.

TEMPLATE COMPANY LTD.

EXHIBIT 3-32

Financial Statements

Template Company Ltd.
Income Statement
For the year ended December 31, 2006

Sales revenue		$760,000
Less operating expenses:		
Cost of goods sold	$417,000	
Wage expense	150,000	
Amortization expense	19,600	
Rent expense	61,500	
Interest expense	5,990	
Selling and administrative expense	45,000	
Total operating expenses		699,090
Income before income tax		60,910
Income tax expense		18,273
Net income		$ 42,637

Template Company Ltd.
Balance Sheet
December 31, 2006 and 2005

		2006		2005
Assets				
Current Assets				
Cash		$ 39,810		$ 45,000
Accounts receivable		35,000		39,500
Inventory		57,000		43,000
Prepaid rent		16,500		15,000
Total current assets		148,310		142,500
Capital Assets				
Building and equipment	$390,700		$350,000	
Less: Accumulated amortization	115,680		100,000	
	275,020		250,000	
Office furniture	76,000		76,000	
Less: Accumulated amortization	19,920		16,000	
	56,080		60,000	
Total capital assets		331,100		310,000
Total Assets		$479,410		$452,500
Liabilities				
Current Liabilities				
Accounts payable		$ 36,000		$ 33,000
Wages payable		11,000		9,000
Taxes payable		4,273		6,000
Dividends payable		5,000		—

Notes payable	2,000		—	
Total current liabilities		58,273		48,000
Noncurrent Liabilities				
Notes payable	—		8,000	
Long-term debt	77,000		75,000	
Total noncurrent liabilities		77,000		83,000
Total Liabilities		135,273		131,000
Shareholders' Equity				
Common shares	$185,000		$185,000	
Retained earnings	159,137		136,500	
Total Shareholders' Equity		344,137		321,500
Total Liabilities and Shareholders' Equity		$479,410		$452,500

Notice that notes payable was a noncurrent liability in 2005, but it is classified as a current liability in 2006. The reason for the different treatment is that the last $2,000 portion of the notes payable is due in 2007, which means that it is now current. The current portion of any long-term debt should be classified as a current liability.

Required

c. The closing entries are shown in Exhibit 3-33. These are labelled with letters instead of numbers, and they have been posted to the T accounts in Exhibit 3-32. For easy reference, the closing entries have been colour-coded.

Note that after posting the closing entries, all the revenue and expense accounts and the dividends declared account have zero balances. They are now ready for transactions in 2007. Also, the retained earnings account has been updated to reflect the cumulative amount as of the end of 2006.

EXHIBIT 3-33   **TEMPLATE COMPANY LTD.**

Closing Entries

A	Sales revenue (SE)	760,000	
	Income summary (SE)		760,000
B	Income summary (SE)	717,363	
	Cost of goods sold (SE)		417,000
	Amortization expense (SE)		19,600
	Wage expense (SE)		150,000
	Rent expense (SE)		61,500
	Interest expense (SE)		5,990
	Selling and administrative (SE)		45,000
	Income tax (SE)		18,273
C	Income summary (SE)	42,637	
	Retained earnings (SE)		42,637
D	Retained earnings (SE)	20,000	
	Dividends declared (SE)		20,000

ABBREVIATIONS USED

A	Asset		L	Liability
A/P	Accounts payable		PP&E	Property, plant, and equipment
A/R	Accounts receivable		S&A	Selling and administrative
GAAP	Generally accepted accounting principles		SE	Shareholders' equity
XA	Contra asset account			

SYNONYMS

Gross margin/Gross profit
Tax expense/Provision for taxes/Tax provision

GLOSSARY

Accounting cycle   The sequence of steps that occurs in the recording of transactions and events in the accounting system.

Accrued expense   An expense that has been incurred and recognized in the financial statements but has not yet been paid for.

Accumulated amortization   The total amount of amortization that has been taken on an asset to a particular point in time.

Adjusted trial balance   A listing of the account balances after adjusting entries have been made but before the closing entries have been made.

Adjusting entry   An entry made at the end of the period to record an event or transaction that has not been recorded during the current accounting period. Events or transactions that are not signalled in any other way are recorded through adjusting entries.

Chart of accounts   A listing of the names of the accounts used in the accounting system.

Closing the books   The process by which a company makes closing entries to complete one accounting period and set the balances in the temporary accounts to start the next period. The temporary accounts are closed into the retained earnings account.

Closing entries   Entries made at the end of the accounting period to transfer the balances from the temporary income statement and dividend accounts to the retained earnings account.

Compound entry   A journal entry with more than two parts(i.e., multiple debits and/or multiple credits). Of course, as with any journal entry, the total amount debited must equal the total amount credited.

Contra asset account   An account used to record reductions in a related asset account. An example is accumulated amortization.

Credit   A reference to the right side of an account, or an entry made to the right side of an account.

Debit   A reference to the left side of an account, or an entry made to the left side of an account.

Discontinued operations   Business operations that are being phased out and will, therefore, not continue in the future. Reported separately, on the income statement.

Double entry accounting system   An accounting system that maintains the equality of the balance sheet equation. Each entry requires that equal amounts of debits and credits be made.

Earnings per share   A calculation in which earnings are divided by the average number of common shares outstanding during the period.

Extraordinary items   A gain or loss appearing on the income statement that meets three criteria: (1) it is unusual, (2) it is infrequent, and (3) it is not caused primarily by a decision made by someone inside the company. Reported separately, on the income statement.

Footing the account   Calculating the balance in a T account.

Future income tax   An asset or liability representing tax on the difference between the accounting balance of assets/liabilities at a given point in time and the tax balance of the same assets/liabilities at the same time. These differences arise when the company uses one method for accounting purposes and a different method for tax purposes.

Gross margin Sales minus cost of goods sold.

Gross profit Synonym for gross margin.

Income summary account An account used to summarize all the temporary income statement accounts, prior to their being closed to retained earnings.

Journal A place where transactions and events are originally recorded in the accounting system.

Journal entry An entry made in a journal, to record a transaction or event.

Ledger A place where transactions and events are summarized in accounts. Entries are recorded in the ledger by a process known as posting.

Liquidity A quality of an asset that describes how quickly it can be converted into cash.

Multi-step income statement An income statement in which revenues and expenses from different types of operations are shown in separate sections of the statement.

Permanent accounts Accounts whose balances carry over from one period to the next. All balance sheet accounts are permanent accounts.

Posting the accounts A synonym for posting to the ledger.

Posting to the ledger The process of transferring the information recorded in a journal entry to the ledger accounts.

Provision for taxes A synonym for tax expense.

Single-step income statement An income statement in which all revenues are listed in one section and all expenses, except income taxes, in a second section.

Statement of comprehensive income See appendix.

Synoptic journal A journal in which transactions are recorded in a spreadsheet format. Each account is assigned its own column, and amounts are added or subtracted inside the columns.

T account A device used to represent a ledger account.

Tax expense The expense for income taxes calculated on the accounting income (revenues minus expenses).

Temporary accounts Accounts used to keep track of information temporarily during an accounting period. Balances in these accounts are eventually transferred to a permanent account, at the end of the period, using closing entries.

Transaction analysis The process by which the accountant decides what accounts are affected, and by how much, by an economic transaction or event.

Trial balance A listing of all the ledger account balances.

ASSIGNMENT MATERIAL

Self Assessment Quiz

Assessing Your Recall

3-1 Why is it important for users of financial information to have an understanding of how transactions are recorded, summarized, and reported?

3-2 In the adjusted trial balance phase of the accounting cycle, the retained earnings account has its beginning-of-period balance, whereas the rest of the permanent accounts have their proper end-of-period balances. Explain why.

3-3 Respond to each of the following statements with a true or false answer.

   a. Credits increase asset accounts.

   b. Revenues are credit entries to shareholders' equity.

   c. Cash receipts from customers are debited to accounts receivable.

   d. Dividends declared decrease cash on the date of declaration.

   e. The cash basis recognizes expenses when they are incurred.

   f. There is no such thing as a prepaid rent account on the cash basis.

g. Dividends are an expense of doing business and should appear on the income statement.

3-4 Indicate whether each of the following accounts normally has a debit or a credit balance.

a. Accounts Receivable

b. Accounts Payable

c. Sales Revenue

d. Dividends Declared

e. Dividends Payable

f. Amortization Expense

g. Rent Expense

h. Prepaid Rent

i. Retained Earnings

j. Investment in Shares of X Company

3-5 Indicate whether each of the following accounts normally has a debit or credit balance.

a. Wage Expense

b. Cash

c. Cost of Goods Sold

d. Interest Revenue

e. Equipment

f. Long-term Debt

g. Common Shares

h. Accumulated Amortization—Equipment

i. Inventory

j. Wages Payable

3-6 Draw a diagram of the accounting cycle and briefly describe each step.

3-7 Expense accounts have debit balances, and debit entries increase these accounts. Reconcile this statement with the normal effects of entries on shareholders' equity accounts and the resulting balances.

3-8 Discuss why one company might close its books monthly and another might close them weekly.

3-9 Identify and briefly describe the major sections of a multi-step income statement.

3-10 Describe the standard format of the balance sheet.

3-11 Explain the meaning of the terms "current" and "noncurrent" as they apply to the balance sheet.

3-12 Explain the meaning of the term "liquidity."

3-13 What two types of disclosures are made in the income statement with regard to discontinued operations?

3-14 What is an extraordinary item and why is it disclosed separately on the income statement?

Applying Your Knowledge

3-15 **(Effect of transactions on balance sheet accounts)**

Ann and Greg Fenway run a small art gallery and custom framing business. Using the basic balance sheet accounts of assets, liabilities, and shareholders' equity, explain how each of these would be affected by the following transactions and activities.

    a. Pictures are purchased by the gallery for cash.

    b. Framing materials are purchased on credit.

    c. A loan from the bank is repaid, with interest.

    d. A picture is sold for cash at a profit.

    e. A plaster statue falls from a shelf and is broken and discarded.

    f. A receivable is collected on a major framing project completed last month for a local law office.

    g. Payment is made for the framing materials previously purchased.

3-16 **(Effect of transactions on balance sheet accounts)**

Gagnon's Autobody Ltd. repairs and paints automobiles after vehicular accidents. Using the basic balance sheet accounts of assets, liabilities, and shareholders' equity, explain how each of these would be affected by the following transactions and activities.

    a. Gagnon's Autobody purchases new spray painting equipment. The supplier gives the company 60 days to pay.

    b. The company pays for one year's worth of liability insurance.

    c. The company pays its employees for work done during a two-week period.

    d. A car is repaired and repainted. The customer pays the deductible required by her insurance and the remainder of the bill is sent to her insurance company.

    e. Supplies such as paint, putty, etc. are acquired on credit.

    f. Cash is collected from the customer's insurance company.

    g. The company pays for the new spray painting equipment at the end of the 60 days.

3-17 **(Debit and credit balance identification)**

For each of the following accounts, indicate whether the account would normally have a debit or a credit balance.

    a. Cash

    b. Accounts Payable

    c. Common Shares

    d. Sales Revenue

    e. Inventory

    f. Cost of Goods Sold

    g. Wage Expense

h. Long-term Debt

3-18 **(Debit and credit balance identification)**

For each of the following accounts, indicate whether the account would normally have a debit or a credit balance.

a. Accounts Receivable

b. Retained Earnings

c. Accumulated Amortization

d. Interest Revenue

e. Prepaid Insurance

f. Amortization Expense

g. Bank Loan

h. Salaries Payable

3-19 **(Construction of journal entries)**

For each of the following transactions, construct journal entries.

a. Inventory costing $3,100 is purchased on account.

b. Inventory costing $1,800 is sold on account for $2,700. (Two journal entries are required.)

c. Accounts receivable of $2,000 are collected.

d. The company borrows $12,000 from a bank.

e. The company issues common shares for $20,000.

f. New equipment costing $7,500 is purchased with cash.

g. Miscellaneous expenses of $400 are paid.

h. A vehicle costing $20,000 is purchased. $5,000 is paid in cash and a note payable is signed for the remainder, with interest at 8% per year.

3-20 **(Construction of journal entries)**

For each of the following transactions, construct journal entries.

a. Wages totalling $6,300 were earned by employees and paid to them.

b. A payment of $3,000 was made on accounts payable.

c. The company made a payment of $2,000 on its bank loan, $150 of which was an interest payment.

d. The company sold inventory for $13,300. Cash was collected immediately for the sale. The inventory cost the company $7,900. (Two journal entries are required.)

e. Land costing $23,000 was purchased. The company paid $3,000 in cash and the remainder was financed with a mortgage.

f. The company paid $2,500 for the monthly rent on its leased premises.

g. Office supplies costing $1,400 were purchased on account.

h. Office supplies costing $500 were consumed.

3-21 **(Journalize, post, and prepare a trial balance)**

Sweet Dreams Chocolatiers Ltd. began operations on January 1, 2006. During 2006 the following transactions occurred.

1. Issued common shares for cash, $200,000.

2. Purchased inventory on credit, $460,000.

3. Sold inventory on credit for $650,000. The original cost of the inventory that was sold was $380,000.

4. Collected $580,000 from customers.

5. Paid $440,000 to the suppliers for inventory previously purchased on account.

6. Paid the rent for the year of $24,000.

7. Paid other expenses, $20,000.

8. Bought a delivery vehicle for cash, $36,000.

9. Recorded $2,000 of amortization related to the vehicle.

10. Declared and paid dividends of $8,000.

Required:

a. Prepare journal entries to record each of the above transactions.

b. Create T accounts and post the journal entries to the T accounts.

c. Prepare a December 31, 2006, trial balance.

3-22 **(Journalize, post, and prepare a trial balance)**

Sparkling Clean Dry Cleaners Inc. began operations on January 1, 2006. During 2006 the following transactions occurred.

1. Issued common shares for cash, $150,000.

2. Purchased equipment to use in the operations. The company paid cash of $76,000 for the equipment.

3. Purchased supplies on account for $7,500.

4. Used $6,000 of the supplies for the cleaning process.

5. Collected $124,300 from customers for dry cleaning.

6. Paid $23,500 for utilities including telephone, electricity, and water.

7. Paid $48,500 for wages to employees.

8. Amortized the equipment by $950 for the year.

9. Borrowed $10,000 from the bank at 8% interest.

10. Paid interest charges of $400 on the bank loan (the loan was taken out on July 1, 2006).

Required:

a. Prepare journal entries to record each of the above transactions.

b. Create T accounts and post the journal entries to the T accounts.

c. Prepare a December 31, 2006, trial balance.

3-23 **(Journalize, post, and prepare a trial balance)**

The Riders Shop Ltd. repairs motorcycles. It has two major sources of revenue, one from the sale of repair parts (parts are sold for twice their cost) and the other from the performance of repair service. The company began operations in March 2006 with the following chart of accounts.

Cash

Accounts receivable

Parts inventory

Shop supplies on hand

Prepaid insurance

Equipment

Accumulated amortization—equipment

Accounts payable

Advances from customers

Common shares

Retained earnings

Sale of parts

Service revenue

Cost of parts sold

Wage expense

Rent expense

Other expenses

During March the following transactions occurred.

March 1 Issued common shares for $100,000.

2 Paid the March rent, $2,100.

5 Purchased spare parts from a supplier on credit for $24,000.

7 Purchased shop supplies for cash, $11,100.

9 Billed a customer $310 for parts and $220 for labour in repairing a motorcycle.

11 Purchased additional motorcycle parts from a supplier, paying $750 cash.

12 Paid the supplier for the spare parts purchased on March 5.

15 Charged a customer $190 for parts and $350 for labour for repairing a motorcycle. The customer paid in cash.

15 Paid the wages for the first two weeks totalling $900.

16 Signed an agreement with Cruising Wheels Ltd., a local used motorcycle dealer, to perform maintenance repairs on all its used motorcycles to make them ready for sale. The dealer agreed to pay $750 per month for the work. All parts used will be extra. The contract started on March 16, when the dealer paid the first month's $750.

20 Purchased a one-year fire insurance policy for cash for $540. The policy comes into effect on April 1.

22 Repaired several motorcycles, charging $846 for parts and $1,400 for labour. The customers paid in cash.

25 Billed Cruising Wheels Ltd. $510 for parts used in repairing some motorcycles.

28 The customer whose work was completed on March 9 paid the amount owed.

31 Paid wages for the last half of March, $925.

Required:

a. Prepare the journal entries to record the above transactions, and any adjustments that may be needed as of March 31.

b. Set up T accounts, organizing them in the order in which they will appear on the financial statements. (Refer to the Chart of Accounts.) Post the journal entries to the T accounts.

c. Prepare an adjusted trial balance for March 31.

d. From the adjusted trial balance, prepare an income statement and balance sheet for the month of March.

3-24   (Journalize, post, and prepare a trial balance and closing entries)

Refer to Problem 2-32 in Chapter 2, Singh Company.

1. Prepare journal entries for each of the transactions and adjustments listed in the problem.

2. Prepare the necessary T accounts and post the transactions and adjustments to them.

3. Prepare an adjusted trial balance.

4. Prepare the closing entries and post them to the T accounts.

3-25   (Journalize, post, and prepare a trial balance and closing entries)

Refer to Problem 2-33 in Chapter 2, Hughes Tool Company.

1. Prepare journal entries for each of the transactions and adjustments listed in the problem.

2. Prepare the necessary T accounts and post the journal entries to them.

3. Prepare an adjusted trial balance.

4. Prepare the closing entries and post them to the T accounts.

3-26   (Journalize, post, and prepare a trial balance and closing entries)

Refer to Problem 2-34 in Chapter 2, A.J. Smith Company.

1. Prepare journal entries for each of the transactions and adjustments listed in the problem.

2. Prepare the necessary T accounts and post the transactions and adjustments to them.

3. Prepare an adjusted trial balance.

4. Prepare the closing entries and post them to the T accounts.

3-27 (Income statement determination)

Jake Redding owns and operates a tire and auto repair shop named Jake's Jack'em and Fix em Shop. During the current month the following activities occurred.

1. The shop charged $8,300 for repair work completed. All but one of his customers had paid and collected their vehicles. The one customer who had not paid owed Jake $250. Jake still has the car parked in the shop's parking lot and he intends to keep it until the customer pays the bill. The $250 is included in the $8,300.

2. The total cost of parts used in repair work during the month was $2,700. Jake usually pays for the parts with cash, except for items such as fan belts and oil, which he orders in bulk from a supplier on 30 days' credit. At the end of the month, he still owes $450 to his supplier.

3. Jake earned $40 in interest on the company's bank account during the month.

4. Jake paid $600 monthly rent on the repair shop. He pays on the first day of each month.

5. On the 10th of the month, Jake paid the previous month's utility bills of $250. At the end of the month, he received this month's utility bills totalling $198, which he intends to pay on the 10th of next month.

6. Jake paid his friend David $350 for helping him in the repair shop.

7. Other expenses related to operating the repair shop for the month totalled $990. All of these have been paid, plus $210 that was owed from the previous month.

Required:

Using the concepts discussed so far in the text, determine the amounts that would properly be reported in the income statement for Jake's shop this month. If an item is excluded, explain why.

3-28 (Income statement determination)

Janice Wylkie owns a cycle and ski store named Jan's Outdoor Blast. Besides equipment, she sells clothing and other accessories. During the month of June, the following activities occurred.

1. The business earned $32,600 from the sale of bicycles, clothing, and accessories. Half of this business was for cash and the other half was paid for with credit cards. The money for the credit card sales had been collected from the credit card company, less a 3% charge.

2. The merchandise that was sold originally cost $19,430.

3. Jan purchased new merchandise on credit for $21,800.

4. By month end, Jan had paid $18,000 to the suppliers of the new merchandise.

5. The telephone, electricity, and water for the month came to $480. At the end of the month, one of these bills, for $120, had not yet been paid.

6. At the end of May, Jan had a 9% loan for $5,000 outstanding with the bank. On the last day of June, Jan paid the interest that was owed on the loan and also paid $200 on the principal of the loan.

7. On the last day of June, a customer ordered a $1,200 bicycle. Jan did not have it in stock; it will be delivered in July.

Required:

Using the concepts discussed so far in the text, determine the amounts that would properly be reported in the June income statement for Jan's shop. If an item is excluded, explain why.

3-29   (Determination of expenses using matching)

For each of the following independent cases, indicate how much of the cost should be recognized as expense in the months of September and October, applying the matching concept.

1. Employees work Monday through Friday and are paid on Monday for the previous week's work. September 30 falls on a Wednesday. The total payroll for the week September 28 to October 2 (paid on October 5) is $8,000.

2. A new lease for the business premises goes into effect on October 1 and increases the rent from $900 to $1,000. Rent for the next month is always prepaid on the last day of the current month.

3. The company borrowed $7,000 on September 1. The loan is to be repaid on the last day of October, along with $90 interest.

4. The company purchased several large barrels of lubricant for $2,100 on September 1. The lubricant is to be used in the company's operations and is expected to last for three months.

3-30   (Journalize, post, prepare an income statement and balance sheet, and prepare closing entries)

On December 31, 2005, Clean and White Linen Supplies Ltd. had the following account balances.

Cash	$210,000
Accounts receivable	85,000
Uniforms for sale	20,000
Supplies on hand	12,000
Investment	100,000
Equipment	340,000
Accumulated amortization	80,000
Accounts payable	40,000
Wages payable	9,000
Long-term bank loan, 8%	150,000
Common shares	300,000
Retained earnings	188,000

During 2006 the following transactions occurred.

1. On January 1, paid $3,300 for a three-year fire insurance policy.

2. During the year, purchased additional uniforms on credit for $120,000.

3. Sold uniforms for $160,000 on account. The inventory that was sold originally cost $95,000.

4. Performed cleaning for customers for a total of $520,000. One-quarter of the customers paid in cash and the remainder received their cleaning services on account.

5. Paid $130,000 to suppliers, to settle some of the accounts payable.

6. Received $580,000 from customers in settlement of amounts owed to the company.

7. Paid $15,000 for advertising during the year.

8. Paid the interest on the bank loan for the year, and paid $30,000 on the principal at the end of 2009.

9. Received a $4,000 dividend from the investment.

10. Paid $24,000 for utilities for the year.

11. Paid dividends of $20,000 at the end of the year.

12. Paid $102,000 for wages over the year. In December, the company still owed $8,500 to the employees for the last 10 days of work in December.

13. Amortized the equipment for the year. The company had bought its equipment at the beginning of 2004, and it was expected to last for eight years and have a residual value of $20,000.

Required:

a. Prepare the journal entries to record the above items. Be sure to include the adjusting entry for the expiration of the insurance.

b. Create T accounts. Enter the beginning balances from 2005 and post the 2006 transactions and adjustments.

c. Prepare an adjusted trial balance.

d. Prepare an income statement and a balance sheet for 2006.

e. Prepare the closing entries and post them to the T accounts.

3-31   (Journalize, post, prepare an income statement and balance sheet, and prepare closing entries)

On the Go Pizza had the following account balances at December 31, 2005.

Cash	$50,000
Accounts receivable	5,000
Supplies inventory	15,000
Prepaid rent	36,000
Equipment	60,000
Delivery vehicles	80,000
Wages payable	4,000
Common shares	200,000
Retained earnings	42,000

During 2006, the following transactions occurred.

1. Sales of pizzas for cash, $480,000. Sales of pizzas on account, $50,000.

2. Purchase of ingredients for the pizzas and other supplies (supplies inventory), $220,000. All these items were paid for.

3. Supplies inventory valued at $215,000 was used.

4. The company paid $75,000 in wages.

5. $52,000 was paid for other expenses.

6. $52,000 was collected on the accounts receivable.

7. A dividend of $10,000 was declared and paid.

Information for adjusting entries:

8. Wages owed to employees at the end of the year were $2,000.

9. By the end of 2006, half of the prepaid rent had been used.

10. The equipment had a useful life of eight years, with no residual value at the end of the eight years.

11. The delivery vehicles had a useful life of five years with a residual value of $5,000 at the end of the five years.

Required:

a. Prepare journal entries for Transactions 1 through 7. Create new accounts as necessary.

b. Create T accounts. Enter the beginning balances from 2005 and post the 2006 transactions.

c. Prepare a trial balance.

d. Prepare journal entries for adjustments 8 through 11. Post these journal entries and prepare an adjusted trial balance.

e. Prepare an income statement and a balance sheet for 2006.

f. Prepare the closing entries and post them to the T accounts.

3-32   (Journal entries, trial balances, and closing entries)

Evergreen Retail Company had the following transactions. The company's fiscal year end is December 31.

1. Borrowed $6,500 from the bank on January 1, 2006.

2. Bought equipment on January 1, 2006 for $12,000.

3. Purchases of inventory on account during 2006 totalled $24,600.

4. Sales for the period totalled $34,500, of which $19,300 were on account. The cost of the products sold was $19,900.

5. Bought office supplies for $500 cash.

6. Collections from customers on account totalled $17,700.

7. Payments to suppliers for the inventory totalled $18,800.

8. Employees were paid $6,300 during the year.

9. Dividends were declared in the amount of $2,500, but have not yet been paid.

10. Paid the interest on the bank loan on December 31, 2006. The interest rate was 9%.

Information for adjusting entries:

> 11. The equipment purchased on January 1 has an estimated useful life of five years and an estimated residual value at the end of five years of $1,000.
>
> 12. Office supplies costing $150 were still on hand at the end of the year.
>
> 13. Wages in the amount of $400 were owed to employees at the end of the year. They will be paid early in 2007.

> ***Required:***

> a. Prepare journal entries for Transactions 1 through 10.
>
> b. Create T accounts and post the 2006 transactions.
>
> c. Prepare a trial balance.
>
> d. Prepare journal entries for adjustments 11 to 13. Post these journal entries and prepare an adjusted trial balance.
>
> e. Prepare the closing entries and post them to the T accounts.

3-33   (Journal entries, trial balances, and closing entries)

Genesis Sportswear Ltd. is a wholesale company that buys sports clothing from manufacturers and sells it to various retail stores. It had the following transactions during its first period of operations. The company's fiscal year end is December 31.

> 1. Issued common shares for $40,000.
>
> 2. Paid an insurance premium of $1,200 on April 1 that provides coverage for the 12-month period starting April 1.
>
> 3. Purchased $48,500 of clothing on account.
>
> 4. Paid $26,900 in wages to employees.
>
> 5. Sales recorded for the period totalled $85,000, all on credit.
>
> 6. Cash collections on customer accounts totalled $76,000.
>
> 7. Inventory costing $41,800 was sold.
>
> 8. Payments to suppliers for clothing purchased totalled $37,100.
>
> 9. Purchased some new equipment that cost $11,000; paid cash.
>
> 10. Dividends of $1,300 were declared but not yet paid.

Adjusting entries (you may need to use information recorded in the first 10 transactions):

> 11. Recognize the amount of insurance expense that was incurred during the period.
>
> 12. Record amortization of $1,500 on the equipment.

Required:

> a. Prepare journal entries to record Transactions 1 through 10.
>
> b. Create T accounts and post the transactions to them.
>
> c. Prepare a trial balance.
>
> d. Prepare journal entries for items 11 and 12, post these adjustments, and calculate the new balances in the affected accounts.
>
> e. Prepare the closing entries and post them to the T accounts.

3-34 **(Adjusting entries)**

The trial balance for Snowcrest Ltd. for December 31, 2006, is presented below.

	Debit	Credit
Cash	$ 11,000	
Inventory	24,000	
Advances to salespersons (Prepaid commissions)	1,000	
Prepaid rent	0	
Office supplies	2,000	
Equipment	20,000	
Accumulated amortization—equipment		$ 4,000
Deposits from customers (Revenue received in advance)		0
Common shares		40,000
Retained earnings		9,000
Sales revenue		220,000
Cost of goods sold	130,000	
Salespersons' commissions	35,000	
Office salaries	25,000	
Rent expense	6,500	
Miscellaneous expenses	15,000	
Dividends declared	3,500	
Totals	$273,000	$273,000

Adjusting entries:

1. The sales figure includes deposits from customers of $2,000 for goods to be delivered in the future.

2. Half of the advances to salespersons have been earned by them, by December 31.

3. Office salaries owed at year end but not paid are $600.

4. The rent expense figure includes $500 paid in advance for 2007.

5. A count of the office supplies revealed that $500 was still on hand at year end.

6. Amortization on the equipment for 2006 was $1,000.

7. Income tax for the year should be calculated using a tax rate of 25%. (Hint: After you finish the other adjusting entries, you will have to determine income before income tax so that you have a basis on which to calculate the 25%.)

Required:

Prepare the adjusting entries.

3-35   (Adjusting entries)

The trial balance for Cozy Fireplaces Inc. for December 31, 2006, is presented below.

	Debit	Credit
Cash	$ 109,000	
Accounts receivable	25,000	
Inventory	95,000	
Office supplies	7,500	
Prepaid rent	3,000	
Land	80,000	
Building	140,000	
Accumulated amortization—building		$ 20,000
Accounts payable		18,400
Deposits from customers (Revenue received in advance)		12,400
Bank loan, 8%, long-term		40,000
Common shares		150,000
Retained earnings		6,700
Sales		850,000
Cost of goods sold	480,000	
Salaries and wages	95,000	
Rent expense	43,000	
Miscellaneous expenses	15,000	
Dividends declared	5,000	
Totals	$1,097,500	$1,097,500

Adjusting entries:

1. The deposits from customers had been made for future deliveries. As at December 31, one-third of these goods had been delivered.

2. The bank loan was taken out on March 1, 2006. The first payment of interest is due on March 1, 2007.

3. Salaries and wages owed at year end but not paid are $2,200.

4. Rent is paid in advance on the last day of the month. The $3,000 in prepaid rent represents the monthly rent for January 1, 2006. At the end of January 2006, $3,000 was paid for the February rent and was debited directly to rent expense. All payments during the year were treated the same way. The rent for July to December increased to $4,000. (Hint: Rent expense of $43,000 includes five months at $3,000 and seven months at $4,000.)

5. A count of the office supplies revealed that $500 was still on hand at year end.

6. The building is being amortized over 20 years with a residual value of $20,000.

7. Income tax for the year should be calculated using a tax rate of 30%. (Hint: After you finish the other adjusting entries, you will have to determine income before income tax so that you have a basis on which to calculate the 30%.)

Required:

Prepare the adjusting entries.

3-36 (Determine income statement and balance sheet values)

The Gawdy Graphics Group was organized as a company on July 1, 2006, by Gil Gobber. At the end of the first six months of operations, before any adjustments had been made, the trial balance contained the following accounts.

	Debit	Credit
Cash	$ 8,600	
Accounts Receivable	13,000	
Equipment	48,000	
Accounts Payable		$11,000
Notes Payable		18,000
Capital Stock (Common Shares)		22,000
Graphic Fees Revenue		55,500
Consulting Fees Revenue		7,600
Insurance Expense	2,100	
Salaries Expense	33,000	
Supplies Expense	3,300	
Advertising Expense	1,700	
Rent Expense	2,500	
Utilities Expense	1,900	
	$114,100	$114,100

Analysis reveals the following additional data.

1. At December 31, there were $1,200 of supplies on hand.

2. The note payable was issued on September 1, 2006. It is a 10%, nine-month note.

3. The balance in Insurance Expense is the premium on a one-year policy that began October 1, 2006.

4. At December 31, $2,600 of the amount recorded in Consulting Fees Revenue had not yet been earned.

5. Graphic fees earned but unbilled at December 31 total $6,000.

6. Amortization is $4,200 per year.

Required:

Calculate the amounts that should appear (after adjustments) on the December 31, 2006 financial statements for each of the following items.

  a. On the Income Statement for supplies

  b. On the Balance Sheet related to interest

  c. On the Balance Sheet related to insurance

  d. On the Income Statement for consulting fees

  e. On the Balance Sheet for receivables

  f. On the Balance Sheet as the equipment's net book value of the equipment

3-37   (Prepare income statement)

Prepare an income statement, in proper form, from the following information concerning the results of Biggs & Company Ltd. (a company located in a part of Nova Scotia where earthquakes are not common but windstorms are) for the year ended December 31, 2006. The income tax rate is 40%.

Cost of goods sold	$125,000
Dividends declared	3,500
Dividend revenue	500
Gain on expropriation of land	6,000
Gain on sale of land	2,200
Interest expense	5,000
Loss due to earthquake damage	4,500
Loss from windstorm damage	5,300
Loss on discontinued operations	32,000
Operating expenses	45,000
Sales revenue	195,000

3-38   (Prepare balance sheet)

Prepare a classified balance sheet for Novasco Manufacturing Corporation as at December 31, 2006, based upon the following adjusted trial balance data at that date. Ignore income taxes.

	Debit	Credit
Accounts receivable	$ 107,000	
Administration and general expenses	55,000	
Cash	30,000	
Cost of goods sold	450,000	
Dividends declared	35,000	
Finished goods inventory	160,000	
Interest expense	25,000	
Loss on sale of equipment	1,900	
Prepaid insurance	3,000	

Property, plant, and equipment	280,000	
Raw materials inventory	55,000	
Selling expenses	95,500	
Short-term (temporary) investments	85,000	
Work-in-process inventory	95,000	
Accounts payable		$ 75,000
Accrued salaries payable		28,000
Accumulated amortization		65,000
Common shares		150,000
Dividends payable		7,000
Interest revenue		10,000
Long-term debt		250,000
Retained earnings		117,400
Sales revenues		650,000
Short-term borrowings		125,000
	$1,477,400	$1,477,400

User Perspective Problems

3-39 (The year-end closing process)

The accounting system closing process takes some time at the end of the accounting period in order to check for errors, make adjusting entries, and prepare the financial statements. In recent years, there has been a real push to speed up this end-of-period process for most companies. Discuss the incentives that companies might have to make this a faster process.

3-40 (Correction of errors and omissions revealed during the audit)

During the auditing process at year end, the auditing firm may find errors and omissions in the recording of transactions and will then ask management to make adjusting entries to correct these errors. In light of the purpose of the audit opinion (see discussion in Chapter 1), discuss plausible arguments that management might give to try to convince the auditor to waive making these suggested adjustments.

3-41 (Understanding financial statement information)

Recently, a financial advisor was asked if his firm had recommended the purchase of Enron shares to its clients. (In 2001, Enron declared bankruptcy, to the surprise of many investors, and questions were raised about the company's accounting practices and the credibility of the firm that performed the audit.) The financial advisor said that his firm had not advised any clients to buy Enron because the company was just too complex and, therefore, it was too difficult to read and understand the financial statements. He would not advise any clients to buy shares in a company in which it was not possible to analyze the financial information.

Your knowledge of financial statements is still very limited; even fairly simple financial statements are probably still overwhelming. Nevertheless, based on your limited knowledge, comment on the policy established by this financial advisor's firm. What are the advantages of following such a policy? Are there any disadvantages that you can think of?

3-42   (Revision of income statement amounts)

Leadfoot Al decided to retire from stock car racing and invest all his winnings in a fish farm. He had majored in genetics in college and experimented with many different species of fish before coming up with a catfish that had the texture and taste of ocean trout. Moreover, contacts from his previous profession made it possible for him to acquire feed for his unique form of fish at very low prices. After operating for two years, Al decided to explore expansion possibilities. He talked with his banker about getting a loan and presented an income statement for the past year, based strictly on cash flows, as follows.

Cash collected from sale of Al's Gourmet Fish		$520,000
Less: Feed purchases	$470,000	
Purchase of new fish tank	40,000	
Wages paid	70,000	580,000
Operating loss		(60,000)
Plus: Sale of land		110,000
Net income		$ 50,000

From discussions with Al, the banker learned the following.

- $120,000 of the cash collected from the sale of fish in the current period was for shipments delivered prior to the start of the year. All the sales this year were paid for prior to year end.

- The feed can be stored indefinitely, and about 40% of this year's purchases remain on hand at year end.

- Two fish tanks were purchased the previous year at a total cost of $80,000. These tanks, along with the one purchased at the beginning of this year, were used all year. Each tank is expected to last five years.

- The land that was sold for $110,000 had been purchased two years earlier for $65,000.

   Required:

   Provide Al and his banker with responses to the following.

   a. Why is the matching concept important in this case?

   b. What amount of revenue from the sale of merchandise should be included this period?

   c. What amount of expense for fish food should be reported this period? How should the remainder of the food purchased be reported?

   d. Should some amount for the fish tanks be included in calculating income for the current period? How much?

   e. The land was sold for more than its original purchase price. This difference is called a gain and is usually included on the income statement. What is the amount of the gain on the sale of the land that should be included in income this period?

   f. Should Al stay in the fish business or go back to auto racing? What factors other than the income calculations would be relevant to evaluating the potential future for Al's fish farm?

3-43   **(Multi-step income statement)**

Northland Enterprises sells and services snowmobiles and recreational equipment, and has reported the following revenues and expenses in 2006.

Equipment sales	$6,300,000
Cost of parts and equipment sold	4,200,000
Wages and salaries	1,000,000
Sales of replacement parts	900,000
Revenue from labour charges for repair work	700,000
Income tax expense	730,000
Shipping and delivery costs	490,000
Property taxes	100,000
Interest expense on mortgage payable	90,000
Interest income on investments	40,000

Required:

a. Prepare a 2006 multi-step income statement for Northland Enterprises.

b. In 2005, Northland reported net income of $1,050,000 and earned an 18% return on total revenue (net income divided by revenue). The goal for 2006 was to earn income in excess of $1,150,000 and earn a 20% return on total revenue. What amounts were reported? Did Northland attain its goals in 2006?

c. In setting its goals for net income and return on sales for future periods, what types of factors should Northland take into consideration?

Reading and Interpreting Published Financial Statements

Financial Statement Analysis Assignments

3-44   **(Income statement and balance sheet items)**

Finning International Inc. sells, rents, finances, and provides customer support services for Caterpillar and complementary equipment on three continents around the world. Refer to its 2003 income statement and balance sheet, in Exhibit 3-34, and answer the following questions.

a. Has Finning International used a single-step or a multi-step income statement? What aspects of the statement influenced your answer?

b. Explain why Finning International has two earnings per share amounts for each year.

c. Finning International had over a $1 billion dollars in assets subject to amortization or depreciation (i.e., rental equipment, buildings, and other equipment) at the end of 2003. However, there is no separate disclosure of amortization or depreciation expense on the income statement. Explain why you do not see these expenses on the income statement.

d. At the end of 2003, what percentage of Finning International's total assets was invested in inventory? What kind of inventory does Finning International have?

FINNING INTERNATIONAL INC. 2003 ANNUAL REPORT

EXHIBIT 3-34
PART A

CONSOLIDATED FINANCIAL STATEMENTS

CONSOLIDATED BALANCE SHEETS AS AT DECEMBER 31

(C$ thousands)

	2003	2002
ASSETS		
Current assets		
Cash and short-term investments	$ 66,385	$ 34,626
Accounts receivable	481,397	465,601
Inventories		
On-hand equipment	438,715	402,316
Parts and supplies	270,984	248,093
Other assets	98,379	107,352
Future income taxes (Note 2)	35,133	15,698
Current portion of instalment notes receivable	25,944	13,926
Total current assets	1,416,937	1,287,612
Finance assets		
Instalment notes receivable	7,145	13,410
Equipment leased to customers (Note 3)	97,925	197,115
Total finance assets	105,070	210,525
Rental equipment (Note 4)	1,046,130	897,891
Land, buildings and equipment (Note 5)	287,778	257,200
Future income taxes (Note 2)	39,344	35,863
Goodwill (Note 7)	393,109	379,866
Intangible assets (Note 7)	9,692	2,300
Other assets (Note 11)	130,550	91,290
	$ 3,428,610	$ 3,162,547
LIABILITIES		
Current liabilities		
Short-term debt (Note 9)	$ 104,910	$ 258,140
Accounts payable and accruals	848,888	868,069
Income tax payable	8,884	39,068
Future income taxes (Note 2)	5,711	8,186
Current portion of long-term debt (Note 9)	235,243	42,324
Total current liabilities	1,203,636	1,215,787
Long-term debt (Note 9)	748,181	514,051
Future income taxes (Note 2)	93,212	77,349
Total liabilities	2,045,029	1,807,187
Commitments and Contingencies (Notes 21 and 22)		
NON-CONTROLLING INTERESTS (Note 10)	425,000	425,000
SHAREHOLDERS' EQUITY		
Share capital (Note 12)	248,939	233,450
Retained earnings	775,113	699,741
Cumulative currency translation adjustments (Note 13)	(65,471)	(2,831)
Total shareholders' equity	958,581	930,360
	$ 3,428,610	$ 3,162,547

Approved by the Directors:

D.W.G. Whitehead, Director

C.A. Pinette, Director

EXHIBIT 3-34
PART B

FINNING INTERNATIONAL INC. 2003 ANNUAL REPORT

CONSOLIDATED FINANCIAL STATEMENTS

CONSOLIDATED STATEMENTS OF INCOME AND RETAINED EARNINGS FOR THE YEARS ENDED DECEMBER 31

(C$ thousands except per share amounts)

	2003	2002
Revenue		
New mobile equipment	$ 966,042	$ 825,301
New power & energy systems	262,352	192,036
Used equipment	363,549	329,661
Equipment rental	821,315	744,506
Operating leases	65,925	87,610
Customer support services	1,109,571	1,019,184
Finance and other	4,541	9,188
Total revenue	3,593,295	3,207,486
Cost of sales	2,555,682	2,247,760
Gross profit	1,037,613	959,726
Selling, general and administrative expenses	778,138	687,523
Other expenses (income) (Note 14)	4,307	(5,580)
Earnings before interest, income taxes and non-controlling interests	255,168	277,783
Finance cost and interest on other indebtedness (Notes 9 and 17)	76,868	79,828
Income before provision for income taxes and non-controlling interests	178,300	197,955
Provision for income taxes (Note 2)	26,648	47,730
Non-controlling interests (Note 10)	19,701	17,972
Net income	$ 131,951	$ 132,253
Retained earnings, beginning of year	$ 699,741	$ 590,588
Net income	131,951	132,253
Dividends on common shares	(27,816)	(23,100)
Premium on common share repurchase (Note 12)	(28,763)	–
Retained earnings, end of year	$ 775,113	$ 699,741
Earnings per share (Note 15)		
Basic	$ 1.71	$ 1.72
Diluted	$ 1.68	$ 1.68
Weighted average number of shares outstanding	77,326,253	76,954,609

NOTES TO CONSOLIDATED FINANCIAL STATEMENTS

(e) Inventories

Inventories are stated at the lower of cost and net realizable value. Cost is determined on a specific item basis for on-hand equipment. For approximately two-thirds of parts and supplies, cost is determined on a first-in, first-out basis. An average cost basis is used for the remainder.

BRAMPTON BRICK LTD. 2003 ANNUAL REPORT

Consolidated Balance Sheets

As at December 31, 2003 and 2002 (in thousands of dollars)	2003	2002
Assets		
Current assets		
Cash and cash equivalents	$ 356	$ 5,073
Accounts receivable	10,036	10,638
Inventories	12,987	11,066
Income taxes recoverable	1,229	–
Other current assets (note 14)	1,447	2,202
Future tax asset (note 10)	–	145
	26,055	29,124
Property, plant and equipment, at cost (note 3)	160,862	154,007
Less: Accumulated amortization	(51,513)	(45,181)
	109,349	108,826
Other assets		
Goodwill	27,663	30,229
Investment in Richvale York Block Inc. (note 4)	8,278	8,027
Investment in Futureway Communications Inc. (note 5)	2,000	2,000
Property held for sale	1,600	1,600
Other	150	150
	39,691	42,006
	$ 175,095	$ 179,956
Liabilities		
Current liabilities		
Bank operating advances (note 6)	$ 1,810	$ 1,280
Accounts payable and accrued liabilities	12,234	12,370
Income taxes payable	327	5,241
Long-term debt, current portion (notes 6 and 7)	2,163	1,975
Deferred gain on sale of land (note 14)	–	670
	16,534	21,536
Long-term debt, less current portion (notes 6 and 7)	17,646	33,953
Non-controlling interests	18,157	19,537
Future income taxes (note 10)	11,214	8,647
	63,551	83,673
Shareholders' Equity		
Capital stock (note 8)	33,113	32,973
Contributed surplus (note 8)	77	45
Retained earnings	80,938	62,934
Cumulative translation adjustment	(2,584)	331
	111,544	96,283
	$ 175,095	$ 179,956

The accompanying notes are an integral part of these consolidated financial statements.

Approved by the Board of Directors

EXHIBIT 3-35
PART B

BRAMPTON BRICK LTD. 2003 ANNUAL REPORT

Consolidated Statements of Income and Retained Earnings

For the years ended December 31, 2003 and 2002
(in thousands of dollars, except per share amounts)

	2003	2002
Net sales	$ 102,679	$ 93,518
Cost of sales, selling, general and administrative expenses	64,576	54,946
Amortization	10,066	8,071
	74,642	63,017
Operating income before the undernoted items	28,037	30,501
Other income (expense)		
Interest on long-term debt	(1,585)	(1,699)
Other interest expense	(191)	(80)
Equity income from Richvale York Block Inc.	251	550
Foreign exchange gain	47	53
Other income (expense)	(247)	228
	(1,725)	(948)
Income before gain on sale of land	26,312	29,553
Gain on sale of land (note 14)	719	1,950
Income before income taxes and non-controlling interests	27,031	31,503
Provision for income taxes (note 10)		
Current	6,155	7,998
Future	2,735	1,818
	8,890	9,816
Income before non-controlling interests	18,141	21,687
Non-controlling interests	137	888
Net income for the year	18,004	20,799
Retained earnings – Beginning of year	62,934	42,214
Premiums paid on repurchase of capital stock	–	(79)
Retained earnings – End of year	$ 80,938	$ 62,934
Net income per Class A and B share (note 9)		
Basic	$ 1.66	$ 1.93
Diluted	$ 1.65	$ 1.91

The accompanying notes are an integral part of these consolidated financial statements.

3-45   (Income statement items)

Use the financial statements for **Le Château Inc.** in Appendix A at the end of the book to answer the following questions.

    a. Explain whether Le Château Inc. prepares a single-step or multi-step income statement.

    b. Le Château lists its earnings per share as "Basic" and "Fully diluted." Briefly explain what these two terms mean.

    c. Identify the two largest assets in Le Château's balance sheet. Why is it reasonable that these two assets would be the largest?

3-46   (Income statement and balance sheet items)

Refer to the 2003 financial statements of **Brampton Brick Limited**, in Exhibit 3-35, and answer the following questions.

    a. Has Brampton Brick used a single-step or a multi-step income statement? What aspects of the statement influenced your answer?

    b. You will notice that Brampton Brick combines cost of sales with selling, general, and administrative expenses on its income statement. Is it possible to determine a meaningful gross profit? If not, why would the company present its expenses in this manner?

    c. Does Brampton Brick prepare a classified balance sheet? What aspects of the statement influenced your answer?

    d. Identify the items on the balance sheet that appear to be noncurrent liabilities.

3-47   (Income statement items)

Use the 2003 statement of operations for **Intrawest Corporation**, in Exhibit 3-36, to answer the following questions.

    a. Has Intrawest Corporation used a single-step or a multi-step income statement? What aspects of the statement influenced your answer?

    b. You will notice that Intrawest's first three revenues have three corresponding expenses listed by the same name. For each of these revenues, calculate the gross profit rate [(revenue − expense) ÷ revenue] for 2003 and 2002. Has the gross profit rate increased, decreased, or stayed the same over the two years?

    c. Intrawest has reported losses from discontinued operations. Briefly explain what kind of activity results in an amount for discontinued operations. Why is this item reported at the end of the income statement?

    d. Intrawest's income statement does not specify whether its losses from discontinued operations are shown net of tax. Are they? Explain your reasoning.

    e. Intrawest has reported four earnings per share amounts for each year. Explain why each of those earnings per share amounts may be important to users.

3-48   (Income statement items)

Use the statements of earnings and retained earnings of **Sleeman Breweries Ltd.**, in Exhibit 3-37, to answer the following questions.

    a. Has Sleeman Breweries used a single-step or a multi-step income statement? What aspects of the statement influenced your answer?

    b. Calculate Sleeman's gross profit or margin percentage (gross margin divided by net revenue) for 2002 and 2003. Has the gross margin percentage increased or decreased?

EXHIBIT 3-36

INTRAWEST CORPORATION 2003 ANNUAL REPORT

Consolidated Statements of Operations

For the years ended June 30, 2003 and 2002
(In thousands of United States dollars, except per share amounts)

	2003	2002
REVENUE:		
Ski and resort operations	$ 571,527	$ 485,142
Real estate sales	512,695	487,775
Rental properties	—	8,038
Interest and other income	2,417	1,115
Income from equity accounted investment	—	3,901
	1,086,639	985,971
EXPENSES:		
Ski and resort operations	454,861	377,801
Real estate costs	437,690	402,700
Rental properties	—	4,963
Interest (note 16)	47,142	43,072
Depreciation and amortization	67,516	65,434
Corporate general and administrative	14,889	12,175
Write-down of technology assets (note 8(b))	12,270	—
	1,034,368	906,145
Income before undernoted	52,271	79,826
Provision for income taxes (note 13)	6,243	9,549
Income before non-controlling interest and discontinued operations	46,028	70,277
Non-controlling interest	11,274	11,675
Income from continuing operations	34,754	58,602
Results of discontinued operations (note 4)	(578)	(122)
Net income	$ 34,176	$ 58,480
INCOME FROM CONTINUING OPERATIONS PER COMMON SHARE:		
Basic	$ 0.73	$ 1.33
Diluted	0.73	1.31
NET INCOME PER COMMON SHARE:		
Basic	0.73	1.33
Diluted	0.73	1.31

See accompanying notes to consolidated financial statements.

SLEEMAN BREWERIES LTD. 2003 ANNUAL REPORT

EXHIBIT 3-37

SLEEMAN BREWERIES LTD.
Consolidated Statements of Earnings and Retained Earnings
(in thousands of dollars except per share amounts)

	Fiscal Year Ended	
	December 27, **2003**	December 28, 2002
NET REVENUE	**$185,036**	$157,053
COST OF GOODS SOLD	**96,703**	79,059
GROSS MARGIN	**88,333**	77,994
GAIN ON SALE OF AGENCY AGREEMENT	**-**	3,595
GAIN ON SETTLEMENT OF OBLIGATION (NOTE 3)	**591**	-
SELLING, GENERAL AND ADMINISTRATIVE	**55,523**	51,659
EARNINGS BEFORE THE UNDERNOTED	**33,401**	29,930
DEPRECIATION AND AMORTIZATION	**6,301**	5,402
INTEREST EXPENSE-NET	**6,097**	6,017
EARNINGS BEFORE INCOME TAXES	**21,003**	18,511
INCOME TAXES (NOTE 11)	**8,750**	6,190
NET EARNINGS	**12,253**	12,321
RETAINED EARNINGS, BEGINNING OF YEAR	**46,444**	34,123
RETAINED EARNINGS, END OF YEAR	**$58,697**	$46,444
EARNINGS PER SHARE (NOTE 14)		
BASIC	**$ 0.77**	$ 0.79
DILUTED	**$ 0.76**	$ 0.77

c. Sleeman lists its earnings per share as "Basic" and "Diluted." Briefly explain the difference between these two terms.

Beyond the Book

3-49 (Financial statement disclosures)

Find the annual report of a Canadian company that is listed on a Canadian stock exchange. Answer the following questions.

a. From the financial statements, discuss how important inventory is in relation to other assets on the company's balance sheet. Also address how important capital assets are to the company.

b. How does the company primarily finance its business (debt or equity)?

c. Does the company prepare a single-step or multi-step income statement? How do you know?

d. Does the company have any unusual items, discontinued operations, or extraordinary items? If so, search through the information provided with the financial statements and explain why these items were classified in the manner they were.

e. Has the company prepared a classified balance sheet? Using the items in the balance sheet, explain what liquidity is and how it is used in preparing the balance sheet.

f. How many directors does the company have? How old are they and what percentage of the board is female?

3-50 (Finding additional information about a company)

For the company you selected in Problem 3-49, find at least three articles in the financial press that discuss the nature of the markets for this company and the forecast of what the future may be for this sector of the economy. Write a one-page summary of your findings.

Cases

Case Primer

3-51 Downunder Company

You have been retained by the Downunder Company to straighten out the company's accounting records. It seems that the company's trusted accountant for the past 25 years, Icabod Cranium, has just run off to the Bahamas. Unfortunately, in his rush, he seems to have misplaced the company's books. Now the bank is asking for the latest financial statements so it can determine whether or not to renew the company's loan. Luckily, you manage to find a listing of accounts and balances Cranium left on the back of a travel brochure.

Cash on hand (in third desk drawer)	$ 120
Amounts receivable from customers	24,200
Sales to customers	71,500
Loan balance owed to Last National Bank	15,000
Amount invested by owners (for shares)	18,000
Wages owed to employees (not yet paid)	1,200
Cash in bank account	780
Wages expense	7,500

Interest income	500
Equipment (original cost)	51,500
Cost of inventory sold to customers	40,000
Inventory still on shelves	8,900
Amounts payable to suppliers	14,000
Miscellaneous expenses	10,000

Required:

a. Based on the information available, prepare an income statement for the year 2006 and a balance sheet as at December 31, 2006.

b. Identify several additional pieces of information that are needed in order to be able to prepare more complete and accurate financial statements.

3-52   Exploits Corporation

Exploits Corporation, a manufacturing facility located in Grand Falls, Newfoundland, had the following three events occur during the current year.

1. The company incurred damages of $200,000 resulting from a nearby river flooding. Since the river has not flooded in the past 50 years, Exploits carried no flood insurance and was therefore required to pay all the repair costs itself.

2. Two years ago the company purchased land in a local neighbourhood for $50,000. The property value has fallen dramatically, due to general economic decline in the area, and management has therefore decided to write down the value of the land to $25,000.

3. One of the company's major customers unexpectedly declared bankruptcy, which resulted in $100,000 of accounts receivable becoming worthless. Exploits had never experienced a loss like this before.

The management of Exploits Corporation is currently preparing its financial statements and would like to report these three events as extraordinary items. Discuss whether or not the company can record each of these events as extraordinary.

3-53   Peeble's Hardware

In January 2006, Mark Peeble, the owner of Peeble's Hardware, decided to expand the business by buying out a local lumberyard. To finance the purchase, Mark will have to obtain financing from a local bank. As support for the loan application, the bank has asked Mark to provide financial statements for the year ended December 31, 2005. Mark is very busy managing the store and has not made time to review the store's financial operations over the last year.

When the bookkeeper provides Mark with the hastily prepared financial statements, Mark is pleasantly surprised to learn that the hardware store has had a significant increase in net income over the past year. He comments, "With financial results like these, we should have no trouble obtaining the bank loan."

In January 2006, the following transactions occurred.

1. Salaries of $20,000 were paid on January 2. A review of the time cards shows that the salaries relate to work performed in the last two weeks of December 2005.

2. On January 3, 2006, Mark repaid a $100,000 loan. The loan, a one-year, 10% term loan, was repaid in full including interest. No interest expense was recorded in 2005.

3. Goods that had originally cost $9,000 and had been sold in December of 2005 for $12,300 were returned by the customer on January 4, 2006. Accompanying the goods was a letter that stated, "As we agreed on December 30, these goods are not what we had ordered and are therefore being returned for full credit."

4. Peeble's received a bill for utilities on January 5, 2006, for $700. The bill was for the period ending December 31, 2005. The bill was recorded as an account payable in January 2006.

Mark is concerned that some of these transactions may affect the ability of Peeble's to obtain the necessary bank financing, and has instructed the bookkeeper not to make any adjustments to the 2005 statements for these amounts.

Required:

1. Calculate the overall effect of these transactions on Peeble's reported net income for 2005.

2. How should Mark proceed, given this information?

3. Does the bank have any responsibility to ensure that it is being provided with accurate financial information? Explain briefly.

APPENDIX

Comprehensive Income

The Accounting Standards Board has recently introduced changes to Canadian GAAP requiring companies to report *comprehensive income*, as well as net income, in their financial statements. Comprehensive income is defined as the total change in the shareholders' equity (or net assets) of the enterprise from non-owner sources. That is, it includes all the changes in shareholders' equity during a period except investments by owners or distributions to owners.

Related changes in Canadian GAAP will require some gains and losses (such as certain exchange gains/losses arising from the translation of foreign currencies, and gains/losses arising from changes in the fair values of certain types of financial investments or hedging instruments) to be excluded from net income but included in comprehensive income. Some of the concepts and procedures related to this issue are very complex. At this introductory level, you should focus on the basic concept that companies will be required to present certain gains and losses outside net income, in a category referred to as *other comprehensive income*. These items may be presented immediately below net income on the income statement, or in a separate statement that begins with net income; in either case, the end result will be a total representing comprehensive income.

The concept of comprehensive income is based upon an all-inclusive approach to income measurement. This means that all transactions affecting the net change in shareholders' equity during a period are to be included when determining income, except contributions (or investments) by the owners and distributions (or dividends) to them. Previously, Canadian GAAP took an approach to income determination that was close to all-inclusive, in that items such as discontinued operations and extraordinary items—although not related to normal operations of the business, and therefore probably of little value for assessing past performance and/or predicting future results—have nevertheless been included in when calculating income. However, there were a few items that were charged or credited directly to retained earnings.[1] These items are covered in intermediate and advanced accounting courses. All you need to know at this stage is that all changes in shareholders' equity during a period except investments by owners or distributions to owners will be included in comprehensive income.

---

[1] Items that were previously included directly in shareholders' equity but will now be considered part of other comprehensive income include gains and losses on certain foreign exchange translations, appraisal increase credits, and gains and losses on certain hedging instruments.

Companies will be required to present comprehensive income and its components in a financial statement displayed with the same prominence as the rest of the financial statements. This statement must show net income, each component of comprehensive income (on a net-of-tax basis), and the total comprehensive income. **Note that net income, as traditionally defined, is a component of comprehensive income**, with other comprehensive income making up the comprehensive income in total.

For example, a **statement of comprehensive income** might appear as follows.

	2007	2006
Net income	$150	$120
Other components of comprehensive income, net of tax:		
Unrealized gains (losses) on certain types of foreign currency translations	20	(10)
Unrealized gains (losses) on certain types of financial investments	(30)	20
Gains (losses) on certain types of derivatives transactions	(10)	30
Other comprehensive income	(20)	40
Comprehensive income	$130	$160

No specific format or terminology has been prescribed by the Accounting Standards Board for such statements, but there is a requirement that net income be shown as a component of comprehensive income.

Note that the presentation of the tax effects of the items included in other comprehensive income is similar to the presentation for discontinued operations and extraordinary items, which are also presented net of their related tax effects.

On the balance sheet, *accumulated other comprehensive income* would be shown, along with (but separate from) retained earnings. Again, no specific format has been prescribed, except that each component of other comprehensive income that is presented separately above should also be displayed in the equity section of the balance sheet. An example is presented below.

	2007	2006
Shareholders' equity		
Share capital	$3,000	$2,000
Retained earnings	800	700
Accumulated other comprehensive income:		
Unrealized gains (losses) on certain types of foreign currency translations	70	50
Unrealized gains (losses) on certain types of financial investments	(100)	(70)
Gains (losses) on certain types of derivatives transactions	50	60
	20	40
Total shareholders' equity	$3,820	$2,740

The above statements have been greatly simplified, for illustrative purposes. However, they show everything that you need to know at this stage in your study of accounting.

Charting a Course—
When to Recognize Revenue

"An adventurous and realistic look at the world and how people travel through it," is what *Outpost* magazine offers readers through real-life stories of journeys off the beaten track. Since its March 1996 launch, the Toronto-based publication has grown from a quarterly to six issues per year and seen its circulation climb to over 28,000.

What does it take to keep a magazine running smoothly? With little prior experience in publishing, founding partners Chris Frey, Kisha Ferguson, and Matt Robinson have learned it pays to have a revenue recognition policy that makes sense.

"Like most magazines, advertising is our principal source of revenue," explains Mr. Frey. "We always bill on a per-issue basis, even with long-term contracts. If we were to take payment too far in advance, that would create a liability if anything ever happened and we had to stop printing." Because the company only triggers a new set of invoices every eight weeks, it depends on those revenues to tide it over that two-month period. Still, because *Outpost's* advertisers can take up to 45 days or more to pay, the magazine has little control over when the money actually comes in. Meanwhile, it has to pay all its principal suppliers—the printer, landlord, and contributors.

With subscriptions, it makes more sense to count the entire subscription sale as revenue right away. "Although it's on our revenue sheets, we have to make sure that somewhere on the books we indicate the liability—in other words, how much of the subscription remains unfulfilled," says Mr. Frey. "Since subscriptions can begin and end with any issue, keeping track of things for each individual subscriber can be complicated for a small company like ours." As for newsstand sales, the company typically receives payment from distributors six months after an issue has gone out, based on the number of copies left over.

Outpost's subscriber base and newsstand sales have remained constant despite recent

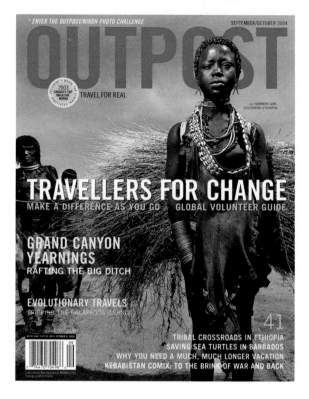

world events that have affected the travel industry. "We've had September 11, SARS, the wars in Afghanistan and Iraq—all of which to some measure have affected travel," Mr. Frey says. "I would characterize us as holding steady in spite of other external circumstances that affect our industry."

In addition to advertising and circulation, *Outpost* records some revenue from other ventures such as its website, consumer shows, and radio spots. In 2002, it sponsored a speaking tour for Ian Wright, host of the travel show *Pilot Guides*, which airs on the Outdoor Life Network. It also launched a redesigned website in October 2003. Whenever there's a bit of extra cash on hand, Mr. Frey and his partners try to invest in circulation promotions. "Because we're a small business, we like to keep focused on the core product," he says. "Growing the circulation of the magazine is our number one focus."

Revenue Recognition

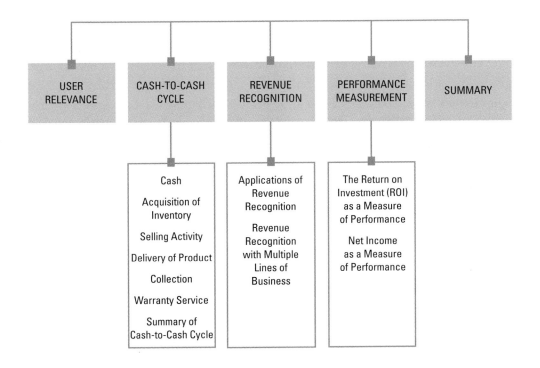

| USER RELEVANCE | CASH-TO-CASH CYCLE | REVENUE RECOGNITION | PERFORMANCE MEASUREMENT | SUMMARY |

CASH-TO-CASH CYCLE

Cash

Acquisition of Inventory

Selling Activity

Delivery of Product

Collection

Warranty Service

Summary of Cash-to-Cash Cycle

REVENUE RECOGNITION

Applications of Revenue Recognition

Revenue Recognition with Multiple Lines of Business

PERFORMANCE MEASUREMENT

The Return on Investment (ROI) as a Measure of Performance

Net Income as a Measure of Performance

LEARNING OBJECTIVES

After studying this chapter, you should be able to:

1. Describe the cash-to-cash cycle of a retail company.

2. Explain the relationship between performance and revenue recognition.

3. List and explain the criteria for revenue recognition.

4. Describe various applications of the revenue recognition criteria.

5. Calculate amounts to be recognized under the completed contract method and the percentage of completion method.

6. Explain the impact various revenue recognition methods have on earnings recognition.

7. Describe how return on investment can give you one measure of performance.

8. Calculate the return on investment under some basic scenarios.

The opening story describes a company that publishes an adventure magazine called *Outpost*. The magazine publishing industry is very competitive. Among other things, it is difficult to find a focus that will attract readers year after year. *Outpost* has managed to do this despite the downturn in the travel market over the last three years.

From an accounting perspective, this company provides an opportunity to look at a variety of revenue models. It has three distinct forms of revenue: first, advertising revenue. *Outpost* has contracts from advertisers for ads in future issues of its magazine. When should it recognize this revenue? When it signs the agreement with the advertiser? When it puts the advertisement in the magazine? When it gets paid for the advertisement? It has chosen to send an invoice to the advertiser and recognize the revenue as each issue is published. This delays the recognition of revenue until the invoice is sent. The receipt of cash from the advertiser follows the revenue recognition. The second form of revenue is from individual subscribers. These people pay in advance. Subscriptions are of varying length and start at different times during the year. *Outpost* recognizes this revenue when it receives the subscription request and the money. However, it also recognizes that not all this revenue should be included in an accounting period if the company must provide additional issues to the subscriber in the following periods. This means that it is initially recognizing the total amount paid by the subscriber as revenue, but then it later backs out some of the revenue and records it as a liability to be recognized as revenue later when it sends the remaining issues. The third form of revenue is from sales of magazines to distributors who supply retailers who sell individual copies. In this case, the company does not even know how much revenue it has earned until about six months after it sends the magazines to the distributors. It receives revenue from the number of issues sold and gets the unsold issues back from the distributors. This means that the revenue recognition is delayed until the cash is received, which is much later than when the magazines were issued. *Outpost* has little choice here as to when to recognize this revenue. It must wait until it knows how much has been earned. In this chapter, we are going to provide you with some guidelines that companies can use when making decisions about when to recognize revenue.

In Chapters 1 through 3, the basic financial statements of a company were discussed. Two of those statements, the income statement and the cash flow statement, measure the company's performance across some time period. In this chapter, the accounting concepts and guidelines for the recognition of income are discussed and some of the problems inherent in performance measurement are considered. Chapter 5 discusses the cash flow statement and the measurement of performance using cash flows in more detail.

USER RELEVANCE

Why is knowledge about the **recognition** of revenue important to users? First, the revenue amount often represents the largest single amount on the financial statements. Total revenues need to be large enough to cover all the expenses. When users see that total revenues are greater than total expenses (the company has a positive net income), they take this as a signal that the company is viable, that it has the ability to take advantage of opportunities, and that it is growing. Companies can and do sometimes experience losses. This is a signal that all is not well with the company. When losses occur, it is important for users to evaluate both the size and cause of the loss. They need to observe the company over time to see how serious the problems are.

When evaluating revenue information, users also want to assess the quality of the earnings. All earnings must, at some time, translate into cash. Cash is essential to a company's ultimate survival. We determine the quality of earnings by comparing the cash flow from operations (cash flow statement) with the net income. If these two amounts are moving together (both up or both down) and if the cash flow is greater than the net income, we consider the earnings to be of high quality. If the two amounts do not move together and if the cash flow is less than the net income, we consider the earnings to be of low quality.

The second reason users need to be aware of a company's revenue recognition policies is that revenues earned by companies are not all the same, as we have illustrated in our opening story. Sometimes cash is received at the time the revenue is recognized; sometimes it precedes it or comes after it. A company can have different revenue recognition policies associated with different types of revenue. Users need to be aware of the company's revenue recognition policies so that they can make judgements about the validity of the revenue amount being reported. Sometimes investors are surprised by the revenue source. Look at the following article.

accounting in the news

High-Priced Accessories

A bizarre dynamic has developed in the consumer technology sector: high-tech companies now view their original product lines as loss-leaders, with the real profits coming from the peripherals and accessories these products require. Take for example, ink-jet printers, for which the replacement ink cartridges sell for $50 to $60 each, half the price of the printers themselves. Ink-jet manufacturer Lexmark, with $4.4 billion (U.S.) in sales in 2002, predicts it will generate slightly more revenue from its printer supplies than from printers in 2004. For its part, Hewlett-Packard's ink division generated profits of $2.2 billion (U.S.), a 35% margin and 68% of the company's profits. A 2002 study predicted that the worldwide market for "micro-electromechanical systems," such as ink jet cartridges, will leap from $11 billion (U.S.) to more than $26 billion (U.S.) by 2007.

Source: "The beast must be fed," by John Lorinc, *Report on Business* magazine, February 2004.

As you will see later in this chapter, there are guidelines under GAAP for revenue recognition. Those guidelines can be applied in various ways. Even within the same industry, companies may choose to recognize the same type of revenue in a different manner. As a user, it is therefore very important to understand the implications on the financial statements of various revenue recognition policies and also to read the disclosures about revenue recognition that accompany the financial statements so that you can evaluate a company's performance.

Before we look at the revenue recognition policies in detail, it is important to understand how cash typically flows through a company. As you saw in the opening story, cash and revenue sometimes coincide and sometimes do not.

CASH-TO-CASH CYCLE

LEARNING OBJECTIVE 1

Describe the cash-to-cash cycle of a retail company.

As we have seen, corporate managers engage in three general types of activities: financing, investing, and operating. Let us focus for a moment on operating activities (the ones that generate revenue).

Operating activities include all the normal, day-to-day activities of every business that almost always involve cash, These activities include the normal buying and selling of goods and/or services for the purpose of earning profits. The typical business operation involves an outflow of cash that is followed by an inflow of cash, a process commonly called the **cash-to-cash cycle**. Exhibit 4-1 shows the cash-to-cash cycle of a typical retail company. Each phase in the cash-to-cash cycle is discussed in the following subsections.

EXHIBIT 4-1   **CASH-TO-CASH CYCLE OF RETAIL COMPANY**

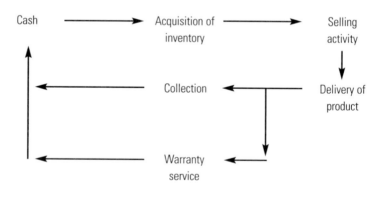

Cash

The initial amount of cash in a company comes from the original investment by shareholders and from any loans that the company may have taken out to provide the initial financing. To simplify matters, you might think of the company as being totally financed by shareholders; that is, there are no loans.

Acquisition of Inventory

Before the company acquires the inventory needed to sell to customers or to provide its services, it must first undertake the investing activities of acquiring property, plant, and equipment. Next, labour is hired and the first shipments of inventory are purchased (or contracts are signed to acquire them). Note that in a retail company, the costs involved in this initial phase may be larger than those of a service-oriented company. If you visualize even a small retail store, the amount of inventory that must be purchased to initially fill the shelves can be substantial.

Selling Activity

The selling phase includes all those activities designed to promote and sell the product. These may include pricing the product, advertising the product, hiring and managing a sales force, establishing retail sales outlets, contracting with agencies, signing supply agreements, and attending trade shows, among other activities. The end results of this phase are sales contracts between the buyer and seller. These may be verbal agreements or formal written documents. For most retail outlets selling to customers, the agreement occurs when the goods are paid for in the sales outlet (the store). Some outlets, however, sell to other businesses or to large enterprises such as hospitals or schools. For these sales, it is more likely that a formal contract is drawn up specifying prices, times of delivery, and methods of payment.

Delivery of Product

Once a sales contract has been agreed upon, the product must be delivered to the customer. Depending on the type of product, this may be instantaneous (as in a grocery store), or it may take time (as with a car dealership). Some sales contracts require periodic deliveries of inventory (as with fresh produce to a restaurant).

Collection

Upon delivery of the product, collection of the sales price in cash may be immediate, as in a shoe store, or it could take place at some later date, resulting in an amount owing at the time of delivery, which is called an **account receivable**. Payment at a later date is the same as the seller making a loan to the buyer and accepting the risk that the buyer will not pay (this is called credit risk). The loan to the buyer may carry explicit interest charges, but usually no interest is charged if payment is made within a specified short period of time (typically 30 to 60 days). If the buyer does not pay within the specified time, the seller may try to obtain the product back (repossession) or may try other methods to collect on the account, such as turning it over to a collection agency.

Other events could also occur that would affect the collection of cash. The goods may be returned for various reasons, resulting in no cash collection. The goods may be damaged in shipment, and the buyer may ask for a price adjustment (generally called a **price allowance**). There may also be an incentive built in to encourage prompt payment of cash, such as a **cash discount**, which means that less than the full amount will be accepted as full payment. For example, a seller may offer a 2% price discount if the account is paid within 10 days instead of the usual 30 days. These terms are sometimes stated as 2/10 net 30, which means that a 2% discount is offered if payment is made within 10 days; otherwise, the total amount is due at the end of 30 days.

In the opening story, you read about customers paying for a magazine subscription in advance. In this instance the company has the cash before using cash to generate magazines. Collecting cash is not a concern but creating the magazine issues to satisfy the obligation to the customers is.

Warranty Service

Some goods carry a written or implied guarantee of quality. Automobiles, for example, are warranted for a certain number of years or for a certain number of kilometres. During this period, the seller is responsible, to some extent, for product replacement or repair. Because the provision of warranty work often involves additional outlays of cash for employees' time and for the purchase of repair parts, warranty service affects the ultimate amount of cash that is available at the end of the cycle.

Summary of the Cash-to-Cash Cycle

The net amount left in cash after this cycle is completed is then available to purchase more goods and services in the next cycle. If the cash inflows are less than the cash outflows, the amount of cash available is reduced, and the company may be unable to begin a new cycle without getting additional cash from outside the company in the form of equity or debt. To the extent that cash inflows exceed cash outflows, the company can expand its volume of activity, add another type of productive activity, or return some of the extra cash to shareholders in the form of dividends.

Note that the order of the phases in the cash-to-cash cycle may be different from one company to the next. For example, a transportation contractor such as **Bombardier** may do most of its selling activity early in the cycle to obtain contracts to deliver products at a future date, with much of the acquisition of raw materials and production taking place after the contract is signed. Also, in some companies, the separate phases may take place simultaneously. At **Safeway**, for example, the delivery of groceries to the customer and the collection of cash take place at the same time.

REVENUE RECOGNITION

LEARNING OBJECTIVE 2

Explain the relationship between performance and revenue recognition.

Managers do not want to wait until the end of the cash-to-cash cycle to assess the performance of their company, because they must make day-to-day decisions that will ultimately affect the final cash outcome. If they wait until the end, they may not be able to make appropriate adjustments. For example, if the first few items sold result in significant uncollected accounts or require significant warranty service, they might want to rethink their policies on granting credit and providing warranties. If the cost of warranty service is too high, they might also want to purchase a better quality of inventory so that the products last longer. Furthermore, the cash-to-cash cycle is a continual process that is constantly beginning and ending for different transactions. There is no specific point in time at which all the cash-to-cash transactions reach an end.

To measure operating performance as accurately as possible, accountants divide normal operating activities into two groups, called revenues and expenses. **Revenues** are the inflows of cash or other assets from the business's normal operating activities, which usually involve the sale of goods or provision of services. **Expenses** are the costs incurred to earn revenues. The difference between revenues and expenses, called **net income**, is one of the key measurements of performance. The expression "in the red" is related to net income. In the past, if a company had a negative net income (expenses > revenues), the net loss figure was actually written in red ink. The expression came to mean that a company had experienced a loss. Similarly, but less commonly used, the expression "in the black" meant that you had a positive net income.

Some companies make profits by charging higher prices, others by controlling costs. Note the following article.

accounting in the news
Bare-Boned Flights

Cutting costs can increase profits, but how far can the cost cutting go? European discount airline Ryanair has taken the low-cost, no-frills flight to new heights. It offers no assigned seats, no free food or drinks, and no help with connecting flights. It flies to secondary airports, has strict baggage weight limits, issues most tickets over the Internet, and doesn't use enclosed ramps to take customers from the terminal to the airplane. The airline also plans to dispense with window blinds, reclining seats, Velcro anchored headrest covers and the seat pockets where safety notices and magazines are stored. The required safety notices will be stitched into the back of the seat. The budget airline is also switching to leather upholstery, which lasts longer and is easier to clean, and may also charge for checked-in luggage. Removing these "non-essential" extras from new Boeing 737s will save hundreds of thousands of dollars per plane in purchase costs, which the airline plans to pass on to customers, says the airline's spokesperson Paul Fitzsimmons. Customers, paying as little as 10 pounds [roughly $22 Cdn] a flight, aren't likely to miss these amenities because the lengths of Ryanair's flights range from one to two-and-a-half hours.

Source: "Low flight: How frill-free can an airline go?" by Thomas Wagner, *The Associated Press*, *The Ottawa Citizen*, March 13, 2004.

The need for timely information to make decisions argues for recognizing revenue as early as possible in the cash-to-cash cycle. The earlier in the cycle revenue is recognized, however, the greater the number of estimates needed to measure the net performance. For example, if the company chooses to recognize revenue at the time the product is delivered to customers (a common practice for many businesses), it will have to make estimates regarding the collectibility of the receivables, the possibility of the customer returning the goods, and the costs of warranty service. To measure the return (profitability) on the sale of a product accurately, these items should be considered; otherwise, the company may be overestimating the return on the sales of its products. To produce the most accurate measurement of net operating performance, all costs incurred to earn revenues are matched to the revenues they helped earn. In accrual accounting, this is called the **matching principle** (refer to Chapter 2). The matching principle requires that all costs incurred or to be incurred (in the past, present, or future) to produce the revenue must be recognized in the same period as the revenue is recognized.

The question of when to recognize revenue is quite straightforward for some industries (e.g., clothing retailers). Revenue is recognized when the customer buys the goods in the store. Normally customers pay cash or use a debit or credit card, which means that the collection of cash for the sale is not an issue. There are no warranty costs to consider, but items are sometimes returned. Returns are often handled by giving the customer another article of clothing, if one is available, or the value of the returned clothing as a credit to buy a different article. Some retailers may return the original cash paid. Clothing stores also usually put a time frame on returns (typically customers have two weeks to return merchandise), which means the issue of returns is a known quantity very quickly. For other industries, the decision is not as clearly defined. For a manufacturing company such as Bombardier, contracts are signed, merchandise such as a railway car is manufactured, the merchandise is delivered, money is collected from the customer (usually some time after delivery), and warranty services are provided on the merchandise sold. When should such a company recognize revenue: when the contract is signed, when the goods are delivered, when the cash is collected, or when the warranty period expires and all obligations with respect to the sale have been satisfied?

The earlier in the cash-to-cash cycle the company chooses to recognize revenues, the less reliable the company's estimate of the effects of future events. In return, however, the company receives more timely information. To reduce the uncertainty inherent in estimating future events, the company would need to recognize revenues later in the cash-to-cash cycle when those estimates are more reliable, but the information would be less useful for making management decisions. The decision about when to recognize revenue is a very important one for managers, because it has a major impact on net income. Knowing about the revenue recognition policy is also important for users so that they can assess the reliability of the information and the quality of the earnings.

There is obviously a conflict between the desire to measure performance on a timely basis (early in the cycle) and the ability to measure performance reliably (late in the cycle). **Revenue recognition criteria** have been developed within GAAP to resolve this conflict, and to produce a measure of performance that is intended to balance the need for timely information with the need for reliable information. The issue is further complicated when the company is involved in two or more lines of business in which the cash-to-cash cycles may differ. A revenue recognition policy must be developed for each line and they may not be the same.

AN INTERNATIONAL PERSPECTIVE

Reports from Other Countries

In countries other than Canada, income recognition may be based on different attributes. For instance, in Mexico, Argentina, Brazil, and the Netherlands, income is determined on a current-cost basis; that is, net income reflects adjustments of the inventory and property, plant, and equipment to a constant currency dependent on the country. The following excerpt from the annual report of **Grupo Bimbo, S.A.** (a Mexican company that produces, distributes, and markets breads, cakes, cookies, candy, chocolates, snacks, and processed foods) illustrates the income recognition principles.

The Company restates the financial statements of the Mexican entities and foreign subsidiaries in terms of the purchasing power of the Mexican peso at the date of the latest balance sheet, thereby recognizing the effects of inflation. Consequently, the financial statements presented for the prior year have also been restated based on the same purchasing power, while their figures differ from those originally present, which are shown in pesos of purchasing power at the close of that year. Consequently the figures in the accompanying financial statements are therefore comparable as they are expressed in constant pesos.

Source: Grupo Bimbo, S.A. Note 3.b. of the 2003 financial statements.

There are three specific factors considered before a revenue item can be recognized. The first factor is whether the revenue has been **earned**. Revenue is considered to have been earned when the company has substantially completed what it must do to be entitled to the benefits of the revenue. This is sometimes referred to as the earnings process being substantially complete. In general, this would mean that the company has completed most of what it agreed to do and there are very few costs yet to be incurred in the cash-to-cash cycle, or that the remaining costs are subject to reasonable estimation, or both. Another way to consider this factor is to determine if all the risks and rewards of the goods or services have been transferred to the buyer. If they have, there can be very little left for the seller to do.

The second factor to consider is whether it is possible to measure how much has been earned. This is often a straightforward matter. When goods or services are sold for cash or an agreed selling price, the **measurement** issue is easy to determine. Sometimes, however, goods or services are sold in exchange for other products, services, or assets (other than accounts receivable). Now the measurement problem is more difficult. The accountant must examine the value of the goods or services sold and compare them with the value of the products, services, or assets received. In deciding which of these values to use, the accountant will look for the most reliable amount—the amount that can be most objectively determined.

The third factor is that there must be reasonable assurance that the amounts earned can be *realized*, or collected, from the buyer. If cash is tendered at the time of sale, this third factor is automatically satisfied. If, however, the goods or services are sold on credit, the seller must be reasonably assured that the amount owing will be collected. Companies will rarely sell goods or services on credit without a credit check on the buyer. This is to provide assurance of the probable future collection of the accounts receivable. Even with this assurance, it is possible that some customers will not pay the amounts owed. Because of this possibility, companies that recognize credit sales as revenue must, in the same period, recognize an expense that measures the probable uncollectibility of the accounts receivable. This is to keep the revenues from being overstated. We call this expense "bad debt expense." More will be said about this expense in Chapter 6.

REVENUE RECOGNITION CRITERIA

1. The revenue has been earned. (The company has completed substantially everything it has to do with respect to the sale.)

2. The amount earned can be measured.

3. There is reasonable assurance of collectibility of the amount earned.

LEARNING OBJECTIVE 3

List and explain the criteria for revenue recognition.

In conclusion, if revenues have been earned, the amounts earned can be measured, and there is reasonable assurance that they will be collected, they should be recognized in the financial statements. These conditions are usually met at the time of delivery of the product to the customer, so this is the point at which many companies recognize their revenues. The following sections discuss various applications of revenue recognition, including at the point of sale to the customer as well as at other points on the cash-to-cash cycle.

Applications of Revenue Recognition

The revenue recognition criteria can be met at different points on the cash-to-cash cycle. Therefore, the point at which different companies recognize revenues varies, as you observed in the opening story about *Outpost* magazine. Several different applications that you will see in practice are discussed in the following subsections.

REVENUE RECOGNITION AT THE TIME OF SALE

The most common point at which revenues are recognized is the time of sale and/or shipment of goods to the customer. Once the goods have been taken by or shipped to the customer, the company has usually completed everything it has to do with respect to the transaction. The title to the goods has been transferred and the revenue has been earned. The first criterion has been met. At the time of sale, the amount that is earned is known. Often the customer will pay cash, which is easy to measure. If the company sells the goods on credit, the amount owed is still fairly easy to determine, which means the second criterion is met. Lastly, the company will have to be reasonably assured of collection of the account receivable before revenue can be recognized. Most companies will not sell on credit if they have doubts about the future collectibility of the amount. An estimate of potential uncollectibility must be made and an allowance for uncollectible accounts established, with respect to the second and third criteria.

Outpost magazine recognizes two of its revenues at the time of sale. The time of sale occurs when an issue is completed and sent to subscribers and distributors. At this point, it has completed the earning process on that issue. It recognizes the revenue from individual subscribers and the revenue from advertisers on a per-issue basis. Prior to releasing an issue, the company knows how much it has earned because subscribers have paid in advance and advertisers have signed a contract that specifies how much will be paid for advertisements in each issue. The only unknown at the point of sale is whether the advertisers will pay when they receive the bill from the magazine. The company would need to estimate the likelihood of uncollectibility of its advertising revenue.

In annual reports, most companies state their revenue recognition policy as part of the first footnote, which includes a summary of the company's significant accounting policies. For example, in its 2003 financial statements, **Cangene Corporation** states its revenue recognition policy in Note 1 to the financial statements.

CANGENE CORPORATION (2003)
REVENUE RECOGNITION

The Corporation recognizes revenue from product sales, net of trade discounts and allowances, upon shipment when all significant obligations have been satisfied and collection is reasonably assured.

The Corporation has an agreement with a distributor that provides exclusive rights to market and distribute the Corporation's WinRho® SDF product in the United States until March 2005. The Corporation's share of the revenue from sales of Win Rho® SDF by the distributor is recognized by the Corporation upon shipment by the distributor from its warehouse to the customer.

Revenue under contract-manufacturing agreements is for commercial manufacturing and development services. Revenue is recognized when goods are shipped or services are provided in accordance with the terms of the related agreements.

Revenue from research contracts is recognized when the related costs are incurred, except for revenue received in respect of equipment used for research, which is recorded as deferred income and amortized over the life of the related asset.

This is a very detailed statement from Cangene. Because it creates and distributes pharmaceutical products, there are often agreements made with distributors to help the corporation sell its products in other countries. Under these agreements it only earns a percentage of the revenue. Note as well the timing of the recognition—when the product is shipped from the distributor's warehouse. Remember the matching concept. For research contracts, Cangene recognizes revenue when it incurs the costs associated with those revenues. Like *Outpost*, Cangene has different types of revenue and must establish different revenue recognition policies.

If a company's revenue is very homogeneous, it will only need a simple statement about revenue recognition. **Scott Paper Limited**, in Note 2 to its 2003 financial statements, states: "Revenue is recognized at the time the goods are shipped, and is net of discounts, rebates and allowances." Scott Paper manufactures and sells paper products. It has a single source of revenue that does not require lengthy disclosure.

Sometimes when you read a description of a company's revenue recognition policy, you will see reference to the term "F.O.B." F.O.B. means "free on board" and is a legal term used to describe the point at which title to the goods passes. It is used by companies like Scott Paper Limited that deliver goods to customers. If the goods are shipped F.O.B. shipping point, the title passes after the goods leave the seller's loading dock (the shipping point). If they were shipped F.O.B. destination, the goods would remain the property of the seller until they reached their destination: the buyer's receiving dock. The way the goods are shipped will affect the point at which revenue can be recognized. The point at which title to the goods passes is a clear indication that the seller has earned the revenue. Prior to that point, the seller is still responsible for the goods.

To illustrate revenue recognition at the time of sale, assume that Hawke Company sells 1,000 units of its product during 2006 at $30 per unit. Assume further that the costs of these units totalled $22,000 and that, at the time of sale, Hawke estimated they would cost the company an additional $500 in warranty expenses in the future. Ignoring all other operating expenses, the income statement for Hawke for 2006 would appear as in Exhibit 4-2.

EXHIBIT 4-2 **REVENUE RECOGNITION AT TIME OF SALE**

HAWKE COMPANY
Income Statement
For the period ended December 31, 2006

Revenues	$30,000
Cost of goods sold	22,000
Gross profit	8,000
Warranty expense	500
Net income	$ 7,500

Note that although Hawke Company may not have incurred any actual warranty expenses yet, it recognizes an expense equal to its estimate of what the future warranty costs might be. Recognizing the warranty expense is appropriate because the future warranty costs are directly related to the revenue. Therefore, if the company wants to recognize the revenue before it knows the actual warranty cost, it must estimate what those costs might be so that the income is not overstated. At the same time as it recognizes the warranty expense, it recognizes a liability for these future costs. When actual costs are incurred, the liability is reduced and no further expense is recognized.

In some cases, a company might receive a deposit for a product to be delivered in the future. Because it is unlikely that the revenue recognition criteria would be met by this transaction (until the product is delivered, the company has not earned the revenue), the revenue from this order would not be recorded until the goods are delivered (title passes). The deposit is therefore recorded as *revenue received in advance, deferred revenue, or unearned revenue* (a liability account that represents an obligation either to deliver the goods or to return the deposit). For example, if Hawke Company received a $500 deposit on an order, it would make the following entry.

Cash (A)	500	
Unearned revenue (L)		500

When the goods are delivered, the liability to provide the product is satisfied (the company has completed what it had to do with respect to the sale), and the deposit can then be recognized as a revenue item with the following entry.

Unearned revenue (L)	500	
Sales revenue (SE)		500

Businesses that require deposits or advance payments on products or services may disclose this in their footnote on revenue recognition. Note that liabilities are created for the obligation to provide the service or product in the future. Typical disclosures for this type of situation are shown here for WestJet Airlines Ltd. (2003).

WESTJET AIRLINES LTD. (2003)

1. Significant Accounting Policies

c) Revenue recognition:

Guest revenue is recognized when air transportation is provided. Tickets sold but not yet used are included in the balance sheet as advance ticket sales under current liabilities.

Users should be aware of one other aspect of revenue recognition: sales returns. In many retail stores, customers are allowed to return merchandise. Usually a time is specified, such as 10 days or one month. When goods are returned, the company either returns the amount paid or provides the customers with a credit that allows them to buy new merchandise. Technically, the company should take into consideration the cost of possible returns when it recognizes revenue, otherwise its income may be overstated. In reality, the time period in which returns are allowed is usually short, which means that the income is not materially misstated if the returns are recorded when they happen. For companies that sell to other companies (business-to-business sales), the amount of returns can be substantial. For example, in the bookselling business, publishers often accept back from booksellers the books that have not been sold. This can result in a substantial amount of returns, depending on how well a book has sold. If such companies want to recognize revenue when they ship books to a bookseller, they must estimate the probable extent of the returns and recognize that amount when the revenue is recognized. The issue of returns has been particularly problematic for companies that sell through the Internet. Note the following example.

accounting in the news

SHOP ON-LINE/RETURN IN-STORE

Many retailers that have on-line shopping give the customer the option of returning goods to the retail outlet. This sale feature has created several problems for the retailers because most of them are not prepared for in-store returns. In many instances, the on-line receipt the customer has lacks important pieces of information such as tax, credit card, and order number information. Many retailers require that a manager override the system in order to facilitate the return. This is time consuming and irritating for customers. At issue may be salespeople who are trained to sell and not to deal with returns.

Source: "Many Unhappy Returns," by Robyn Greenspan, *CyberAtlas*, Sept. 4, 2003.

REVENUE RECOGNITION AT THE TIME OF CONTRACT SIGNING

Even though the point of sale—or more correctly, the point at which title to the product is transferred to the buyer from the seller—is the most common method used to recognize revenues, several situations exist that require exceptions to this application of revenue recognition. Over the years, certain types of transactions have caused concern among investors and accountants because of the revenue recognition practices employed. Two of those were in the areas of franchising and retail land sales. Both of these industries initially recognized revenues at the date of contract signing. In the case of franchisors, this contract was the initial franchise agreement. In the case of retail land sale companies, it was the land sale agreement. The problem was that, in both cases, a considerable amount of uncertainty existed with regard to future costs on the seller's part subsequent to contract signing, and to the collectibility of the receivables from buyers. Questions were raised as to whether any of the revenue recognition criteria were being met.

The uncertainty stemmed from industry practices. Franchisors (such as **Wendy's**) typically agree to provide a significant amount of service, such as assistance in locating and designing the franchise facility and in training the staff, subsequent to the signing of a franchise agreement and prior to the opening of the business. Therefore, at the time of contract signing, is the earning process complete? In addition, the initial franchise fee is typically paid in instalments, which raises questions about the future collectibility.

Retail land sale companies often sell land before it is developed and therefore have yet to incur the development costs. This means that the seller has not completed all the things that must be done; the earning process is not substantially complete. There is also the problem of matching the future development costs to the revenues. Remember that if you want to recognize revenue before all the costs associated with the sale are incurred (note the warranty example), you must be able to estimate those future costs so that they can be recognized at the same time as the revenue (according to the matching principle). Sales contracts typically require low down payments and sometimes include below-market interest rates to entice buyers to sign contracts. These conditions make it relatively easy for a buyer to back out of the transaction before all the cash is collected, thereby negating the sale.

Given that the earning process was rarely complete, and there were uncertainties with regard to future costs and the collectibility of the receivables, revenue for franchisors and retail land sale companies is now recognized at the time of contract signing only if certain minimum criteria are met. These criteria require first, that there be only minimal costs yet to be incurred (this means that the seller has completed substantially all the things that have to be done to conclude the sale), and second, that the receivables created in the transaction have a reasonable chance of being collected. These industries have special accounting guidelines because of the special nature of the activities surrounding revenue recognition. The following excerpts from the financial statements of **Comac Food Group Inc.** and **Intrawest Corporation** typify the revenue recognition policies of franchisors and land sale companies.

COMAC FOOD GROUP INC. (2003)

Franchise revenue

Income from the sale of franchised stores is recognized when the franchise commences store operations. Revenue received for franchised store locations not open at year end is recorded as deferred revenue and included in long term liabilities.

Franchise royalties are based on a percentage of gross sales as reported by the franchisees. These revenues are recognized on an accrual basis as they are earned.

Revenue from sales by Company owned and operated stores is recognized when products are purchased by customers.

INTRAWEST CORPORATION (2003)

Revenue recognition

(ii) Revenue from the sale of properties is recorded when title to the completed unit is conveyed to the purchaser, the purchaser becomes entitled to occupancy and the purchaser has made a payment that is appropriate in the circumstances.

REVENUE RECOGNITION AT THE TIME OF PRODUCTION

Revenue recognition at the time of production is common in two industries: mining and long-term construction. If the product's market value and sale are both fairly certain at the time of production, as in certain mining operations, then the inventories produced can be valued at their net realizable value (selling price) and the resulting revenues can be recognized immediately. The reason for this practice is that the critical event in the revenue earning process for the mine is not the ore's sale, but its production. If the market for the ore is well-established with fairly stable prices, the sale is assured as soon as the ore is produced. By recording the revenues as soon as possible, these companies have more timely information for making decisions.

An example of this revenue recognition method is **Bema Gold Corporation**, which operates gold and silver mines.

BEMA GOLD CORPORATION (2003)

Revenue Recognition

Revenue is recorded at the estimated net realizable value when title has passed.

Adjustments to these amounts are made after final prices, weights, and assays are established. Silver revenues are recorded as a cost recovery. The Company may fix the price it will receive for part or all of its production by entering into forward or option contracts.

Note that for Bema Gold Corporation, the earning process is complete when title to the gold has passed. At this point the sale's final amount is certain but it can still change as a result of final prices, weights, and assays (the determination of ore weight, measure and quality). Although the exact amount earned may not be known, Bema Gold can reasonably estimate the amount and adjusts future revenues for any differences that occur. If it uses forward or option contracts, the amount earned is known for certain. A forward or option contract stipulates the amount that will be received for the gold in the future.

The second type of industry that recognizes revenue at the time of production is one where the production period is long, such as in the long-term construction industry. In the long-term construction industry, two methods of recognizing revenue are generally accepted: the **completed contract method**, and the **percentage of completion method**. The completed contract method defers the recognition of revenue until the contract is completed. It is generally used for projects that are completed in a reasonably short time. Longer-term projects are generally accounted for using the percentage of completion method, which recognizes a portion of a project's revenues and expenses during the construction period based on the percentage of completion. The

LEARNING OBJECTIVE 5

Calculate amounts to be recognized under the completed contract method and the percentage of completion method.

basis for determining the percentage completed is usually the costs incurred relative to the estimated total costs.

As an example, suppose that Solid Construction Company agrees to construct a building for $300 million that will take three years to build, and the company expects to incur costs of $75 million, $105 million, and $30 million in years 1, 2, and 3, respectively. The total expected costs are $210 million and, therefore, the profit on the project is expected to be $90 million. If all goes according to plan, Solid Construction would recognize the revenues and expenses (and related profits) shown in Exhibit 4-3 during the three years with the percentage of completion method.

EXHIBIT 4-3   **REVENUE RECOGNITION WITH THE PERCENTAGE OF COMPLETION METHOD**

(Amounts in millions)

Year	Degree of Completion			Revenue Recognized			Expenses Recognized	Profit
1	$75 ÷ $210	=	36%	36% × 300 =	$ 108		$ 75	$33
2	$105 ÷ $210	=	50%	50% × 300 =	$ 150		105	45
3	$30 ÷ $210	=	14%	14% × 300 =	$ 42		30	12
			100%		$ 300		$210	$90

The formulae to arrive at these amounts are as follows.

$$\frac{\text{Expenses for this period}}{\text{Total cost of project}} = \text{Percentage completed}$$

$$\text{Percentage completed} \times \text{Total revenue} = \text{Revenue to be recognized this period}$$

How well does the percentage of completion method apply the revenue recognition criteria? The first criterion is that the amount has been earned (or the work the company agreed to do has been performed). Instead of waiting until all the contract work has been completed (which can take several years), this method allows the company to measure how much work has been completed so far and then recognize as revenue the same percentage of the total contract price. The expenses for the period and the percentage of revenue earned are recognized each period, which provides information to users sooner. The second criterion is that you can measure how much you have earned. We do that using the formulae given above. The third criterion is that there is a reasonable probability of collection. For many long-term construction contracts, the buyer is billed periodically through the construction process. The periodic billing and collection provide the seller with the ability to estimate collectibility. Because the revenue recognition criteria have been satisfied, the percentage of completion method is preferable to waiting until the contract work is complete.

If Solid Construction had used the completed contract method, all the revenues and expenses would have been deferred and recognized at the time of completion. That is, the entire $300 million in revenue, $210 million in expenses, and $90 million in profit would have been recognized in year 3.

The disclosure below for **Bombardier Inc.** illustrates the percentage of completion method of revenue recognition.

BOMBARDIER INC. (2004)

Revenue recognition

Revenues from the sale of commercial aircraft and narrow-body business aircraft (Bombardier* Learjet*), fractional interests in business aircraft and other products and services are recognized upon delivery of products or when the services are rendered.

Wide-body business aircraft (Bombardier* Challenger* 300, Bombardier Challenger 604 and Bombardier* Global Express*) contracts are segmented between green aircraft (i.e. before interiors and optional avionics are installed) and completion of interiors. Revenues are recognized based on green aircraft deliveries when certain conditions are met, and upon final acceptance of interiors and optional avionics by customers.

Revenues from long-term contracts consisting of designing, engineering and manufacturing products, including major refurbishments, are recognized using the percentage-of-completion method of accounting... The degree of completion is generally determined by comparing the costs incurred to the total costs anticipated for the entire contract, excluding costs that are not representative of the measure of performance.

Revenues from long-term service contracts are recognized based on service performance over the term of the contract for service contracts entered into on or after December 17, 2003. Service contracts entered into prior to December 17, 2003, are accounted for using the percentage-of-completion method of accounting.

Estimated revenues from long-term contracts include revenues from charge orders and claims when it is probable that they will result in additional revenues in an amount that can be reliably estimated.

Knowing how the percentage of completion method works and that it satisfies the revenue recognition criteria, under what circumstances would it be appropriate to use the completed contract method? Some contracts take less than a year to complete. For such contracts, it might be just as informative for users to wait until the entire contract is finished. If the contract took longer than a year, the company would choose to use the completed contract method if one or more of the revenue recognition criteria were not met. It may not be possible to measure how much of the project is completed, which would make it difficult to measure the revenue earned. There could also be a question about the future collectibility on the contract, although it is doubtful if a company would continue to work on a project if it was concerned about the future payment for its work.

With either the percentage of completion method or the completed contract method, if an overall loss is projected on the project, GAAP requires that the loss be recognized as soon as it can be estimated. For example, if it turned out that, at the end of year 2, the total estimated costs to complete the Solid Construction contract were $315 million ($180 million in year 2, and $60 million in year 3, plus the $75 million already incurred in year 1, instead of the original $210 million), an overall loss of $15 million would be indicated for the contract. At the end of year 2, Solid Construction would have to recognize a loss of $48 million. This loss would offset the $33 million profit reported in year 1 and would result in a net loss at this point of $15 million on the contract. If the actual costs equalled the new estimated costs in year 3, no additional profit or loss would be recorded in year 3, as the overall loss on the contract would already have been recognized.

The recognition of the estimated loss in the preceding example is partially a result of the conservative nature of accounting. Conservatism requires that losses generally be recognized as soon as they can be estimated, but profits are seldom recognized until they are realized.

REVENUE RECOGNITION AT THE TIME OF COLLECTION

Except for cash sales, revenue recognition criteria are almost always met prior to the collection of cash. Therefore, for reporting purposes, the collectibility of cash rarely delays the recognition of revenue. Magazines such as *Outpost* have one of those rare circumstances. When *Outpost* sends magazines to a distributor for sale on newsstands, it does not know how much it has earned until it receives the money from the distributor some six months later. It has no choice but to delay the recognition of revenue.

There are other circumstances under which the collection of receivables is so uncertain that GAAP would require that revenue recognition be postponed until cash is actually collected. Some companies allow their customers to pay for their merchandise through instalments over an extended period of time. Many companies that sell merchandise this way have learned about the probability of collecting all the amounts owed by their customers. These companies will recognize revenue at the time of the original sale and recognize the probability of uncollectibility at the same time. However, there are rare situations where it is not possible to estimate the probability of collection. In these rare cases, the **instalment method** can be used. This method delays the recognition of revenue until the actual cash is received.

In an instalment type of sale, the buyer agrees to pay for the goods or service over time, sometimes over many months or years. The seller sets the payments that the buyer makes so that all costs incurred can be recovered, a profit is made on the sale, and suitable interest is charged for the loan the seller is making to the buyer. Therefore, the payments received by the seller can be viewed as covering three things: cost recovery, interest, and profits.

The instalment method can be illustrated with a simple example. Assume that the Sunshine Land Company sells a home site for $100,000 that has a cost of $70,000. Further, assume that the buyer has agreed to make three instalment payments over the next three years of $40,000, $40,000, and $40,000, for a total of $120,000. The excess of the payments over the selling price, $20,000, represents interest. Assume that Sunshine decides to recognize interest evenly over the three years, or $6,667 per year. (This is not generally done, but it will simplify matters for the purposes of this example.) Exhibit 4-4 shows the amount of income that will be recognized with the instalment method.

EXHIBIT 4-4 | **REVENUE RECOGNITION WITH THE INSTALMENT METHOD**

Profit % $= (\$100,000 - \$70,000) \div \$100,000 = 30\%$

Gross profit $=$ Payments applied to principal $\times$ profit %

$\qquad\quad = $ (Cash received $-$ interest) $\times$ profit %

Year	Gross Profits	Interest
1	($40,000 − $6,667) × 30% = $10,000	$ 6,667
2	($40,000 − $6,667) × 30% = $10,000	6,667
3	($40,000 − $6,666) × 30% = $10,000	6,666
Total	$30,000	$20,000

In year 1, an Account Receivable of $100,000 would be recognized along with a Deferred Gross Profit of $30,000. The complete journal entry at the time of sale would be as follows.

Accounts receivable (A)	100,000	
Land (A)		70,000
Deferred gross Profit (L)		30,000

The Deferred Gross Profit would be included with the liabilities and represent profit that will be recognized in the future. When the first payment of $40,000 is received, the following journal entry would result.

Cash (A)	40,000	
Deferred gross profit (L)	10,000	
Accounts receivable (A)		33,333
Realized gross profit on sale of land (SE)		10,000
Interest revenue (SE)		6,667

In subsequent years, as payments are received, the accounts receivable and the deferred gross profit will continue to be reduced and realized gross profit will be recognized.

Although we have shown you some of the accounting behind the instalment method, we do not expect that you will be required to learn the details behind the method, for two reasons. First, it is quite complicated and more appropriately handled in an intermediate accounting course. For an introductory course, it is only important that you understand a little about the method so that you will understand how revenue is recognized in a company that is using the instalment method. Second, this method is not used very often in Canada. If you think about companies where the instalment method might be used, such as **Sears Canada**, which allows customers to use their credit cards and pay over time, you would probably be surprised to learn that Sears does not use this method. Remember that this method is only used if there is a question about the potential collectibility of the amount owed. Sears has been using credit card sales for a long time and has developed reliable methods to estimate uncollectibility. If it can estimate potential uncollectibility, it can recognize both the revenue and potential uncollectibility at the point of sale. Therefore, the instalment method becomes unnecessary.

Revenue Recognition with Multiple Lines of Business

In businesses that have multiple lines of business or that sell products in either standard or customized models, the revenue recognition criteria may be met at different points for different products. The disclosures for **CHC Helicopter Company** illustrate this point.

CHC HELICOPTER COMPANY (2003)

Revenue Recognition

Revenues from helicopter operations are recognized based on the terms of customer contracts that generally provide for revenue on the basis of hours flown at contract rates or fixed monthly charges or a combination of both.

Training revenue is recognized based on the terms of customer contracts that generally provide for revenue on the basis of training hours provided.

Revenue from engine and component repair and overhaul and composites manufacturing operations is recognized on the percentage of completion basis and is measured on the basis of the sales value of the actual costs incurred and work performed. Customers are invoiced in advance for repair and overhaul services performed under "power by the hour" ("PBH") contracts. Typically, a portion of this revenue is recognized on a monthly basis to reflect ongoing services provided with the balance recognized when the major repair and overhaul activities are completed. Any loss on repair and overhaul and composites manufacturing contracts is recognized into earnings immediately when known.

ethics in accounting

Ethics in Accounting

Pressures to show profit or growth in revenues, or both, can create ethical dilemmas for managers and accountants. Some of these pressures are self-imposed, particularly if the manager's compensation is tied to reported profits or revenues. Other pressures may be externally imposed by someone more senior in the organization or by the shareholders. Suppose, for example, that you are the accountant of a company division and that the division manager has asked you to make an adjusting entry for the period to recognize a large order. Revenue in your company is usually recorded when the goods are shipped, not when the order is placed. The manager has indicated that this order will bump the division over its sales target for the year and that the bonuses of several managers in the division will be significantly affected. She has also said that the company is about to issue more common shares and that the company would like to show improved results from last year to get the most favourable price for the shares that will be issued. What should you do? Identify the individuals who will be helped and hurt by your decision, in order to help you determine what to do.

The choice of a revenue recognition policy is one of the critical policy decisions a company makes. Current and future profitability measures will be affected by when revenue is recognized. Companies must choose a revenue recognition policy that is appropriate for their revenue streams and must tell users what that policy is so that they can make informed decisions.

AN INTERNATIONAL PERSPECTIVE

Reports from Other Countries

In the United States, the revenue recognition policy established by the FASB requires that revenue should be recognized when it is realized or realizable and when it is earned. Other standards have additional requirements that must be met. In light of conflicting requirements, the FASB is currently revisiting the revenue recognition criteria.

PERFORMANCE MEASUREMENT

Now that you have a good idea about revenue recognition criteria and the various ways that revenue can be recognized, let's use that information to have a closer look at how we can measure performance. After making an investment, investors generally want to know how well their investment is performing. To put this in a simple context, suppose an investment is made in a savings account at a bank. The money is put in the bank so that it can earn something and it is safe. Periodically, information is received from the bank that details any new deposits or withdrawals and any interest earned on the savings. The interest earned can then be compared with the balance in the account to indicate the investment's performance. The comparison of the interest earned to the balance in the account is called a ratio. Ratios can help us assess performance.

LEARNING OBJECTIVE 7

Describe how return on investment can give you one measure of performance.

The Return on Investment (ROI) Ratio as a Measure of Performance

A common measure of performance used in business is a ratio called the **return on investment (ROI)**, which is generally calculated as follows (in Chapter 12 we will discuss several other ratios that also calculate returns).

$$ROI = \frac{Return}{Average\ investment}$$

In the case of the bank account, the numerator is the interest earned during the period, and the denominator is the average amount invested over the period. By averaging the denominator, additional deposits or withdrawals made during the period are taken into account. A simple average of the beginning balance and the ending balance in the investment is often used; however, more sophisticated averaging methods may be more appropriate. Suppose the average investment in a bank account was $1,000, and the return was $50. The ROI from the investment would be:

LEARNING OBJECTIVE 8

Calculate the return on investment under some basic scenarios.

$$ROI = \frac{\$50}{\$1,000} = 5\%$$

Based on this return, two questions might be asked: (1) is this a good return on investment? and (2) how confident is the investor that this really is the return? To answer Question 1, the return on this investment should be compared with the returns that could have been earned on alternative investments, or with the returns that similar investors are earning. If the next best alternative would have returned only 4%, the bank account was a good investment. If, however, similar investors are earning 6.5% for investments of similar risk, it would seem that the best investment was not made.

To answer Question 2, the investors must assure themselves that their $1,000 investment plus their $50 return is really worth $1,050 today. Ultimately, the only way to be sure that the investment is worth $1,050 is to sell the investment; that is, to withdraw the $1,050 from the bank. If the investors do not sell the investment, there is still some chance that the bank will not have the money to repay them; the bank might, for example, file for bankruptcy. In the late 1980s and early 1990s, this was not an

HELPFUL HINT

Risk is the potential that you will not earn the interest that you are expecting and/or that you will not be able to get your initial investment back when you want it. Both of these aspects of risk depend on the investment's financial health and viability.

inconceivable event, as several small Canadian banks went out of business. In banks insured by the Canada Deposit Insurance Corporation (CDIC), small accounts (those up to $60,000) are insured so that, even in the event of a bank collapse, the investor would still be repaid by the CDIC. A bank account of this type is about the safest investment you can make. An uninsured account would not give you the same comfort level with regard to the possible failure of the banking institution.

Now suppose that instead of investing in a savings account, an investment is made in a house. Assume that the house is bought for investment purposes for $200,000. The buyer is hoping the property value will rise. Assume also that there are no further cash outlays or inflows during the year from this investment. To assess the return on the investment, the investment's value at the end of the period must be determined. This value could be estimated by getting the house appraised by a real estate agent, or by comparing the house with the selling prices of similar houses in the area that have recently sold. In either case, the value will be an estimate. Confidence in these estimates will surely be lower than the confidence in the return earned from the investment in the savings account at the bank. In fact, the only certain way to determine the return on the house would be to sell it. If the investor does not want to sell the property, however, the only alternative would be to use an estimate of the selling price to measure performance. If the investor estimates the selling price to be $225,000, the ROI will be:

$$\text{ROI} = \frac{\$225,000 - \$200,000}{\$200,000} = 12.5\%$$

Measuring the performance of a business is much like estimating the return on the investment in a house. The business makes investments in capital assets (property, plant, and equipment), inventory, accounts receivable, and other assets, and periodically measures the performance of these investments. However, it does not want to sell its investment in these assets at the end of every accounting period simply to determine the proper ROI. It must, therefore, estimate any changes in the value of its assets and liabilities that may have occurred during the accounting period, and report these as net income. We then use that net income amount to calculate two more specific kinds of ROI that you will see in greater detail later in the book. The first is a return on assets (ROA). This ratio measures the amount of income earned per $1 of assets. It attempts to provide the user with information about how effectively the assets are being used to generate income. A second ratio is the return on equity (ROE). This ratio measures the amount of income earned per $1 invested in the company's shares. It provides users with information about the amount of return being earned by shareholders. They can compare this ROE with investments of other types and risks to determine if investing in this company is still a good idea.

Some of the changes in value (returns) are easy to measure, such as the interest earned on a savings account. Other changes, such as the change in the value of property, plant, and equipment, are not as easily measured, as the example concerning the investment in a house demonstrates. Because accounting data should be reliable as well as relevant (as we discussed in Chapter 1), accountants have established concepts and guidelines for recognizing the changes in value of assets and liabilities to ensure that the measure of performance most commonly used (net income) reliably measures the effects of the transactions that took place during the period.

Net Income as a Measure of Performance

The income statement attempts to measure the return to the shareholders on their investment in the company; that is, it measures changes in shareholders' wealth in the company. The accounting value of this shareholders' wealth is measured by the value of shareholders' equity accounts. Remember that these accounts include both common shares and retained earnings.

Shareholders' equity accounts are typically affected by three general types of transactions: shareholder investment activities, the declaration of dividends, and transactions that result in profits or losses. Shareholders may invest more money in the company by buying, for example, new shares when they are issued. This does not directly affect their return on the investment, but does affect the amount of investment they have in the company. Second, shareholders may receive a dividend (via a vote by the board of directors) that reduces their wealth in the company by reducing the company's total assets. This also does not directly affect the return on investment, but again affects the amount of the investment. Finally, those transactions that result in profits or losses will affect shareholders' wealth through their effects on retained earnings. It is this last set of transactions and their impact on value that are measured by the income statement.

Because the company does not want to sell its investments each period to determine its performance, the net income amount is used as part of several ratios that inform users about how their investment is doing. Now that you have a better idea of the various ways that revenue can be determined, you can better assess the underlying strength of the net income amount. You also understand the value of reading the notes to the financial statements to learn about the company's revenue recognition policy.

SUMMARY

In this chapter, we first discussed the importance of revenue to a company's overall health, which led into an explanation of why we have established revenue recognition criteria. We then explained the cash-to-cash cycle and its importance in understanding a company's performance. Tying in with the cash-to-cash cycle are the concepts underlying the recognition of revenue. We looked at revenue at the time of sale, at contract signing, at the time of production, and at the time of collection. These concepts were explored to improve your understanding of net income as a measure of performance for a business. Companies use different revenue recognition criteria according to the type of revenue they are generating. When assessing a company's performance, it is important to understand the type of revenue it is generating and the revenue recognition policy it has established. If you know these two things, you will be better able to understand its cash-to-cash cycle. We then concluded the chapter with a brief look at some measures of performance, or returns on investment. These measures enable users to better assess how their investments are doing. While net income is a useful measure of performance, it is not the only measure in which users of financial statements should be interested. In the next chapter, the cash flow statement is considered. We had a brief look at this statement in Chapter 1. Now we will explore it in more detail. The construction of the statement itself, as well as the interpretation of the information contained therein, will be discussed. The implications regarding the health of the company above and beyond matters shown on the income statement will also be discussed.

SUMMARY PROBLEMS

Additional Demonstration Problems

1. Jonathan, Anthony, and Kendra operate a bicycle shop, The Silver Spoke. They sell assembled bicycles and bicycle accessories. They have a shop in the back where Kendra repairs bicycles. Occasionally they are given a contract to assemble 20 to 50 bicycles for a major retailer. Customers use either cash or credit cards when buying bicycles or bicycle accessories. For minor repairs, the customer pays at the completion of the repairs. For major repairs, The Silver Spoke asks for a down payment equal to 25% of the repair's estimated cost. The remaining 75% is paid when the work is complete. When the company assembles bicycles for another retailer, it bills the other retailer at the completion of the work. The company normally receives payment within 30 days of the bill submission.

Required:

Using the revenue recognition criteria, recommend when The Silver Spoke should recognize revenue for each of its various revenue-generating activities.

2. Suppose that Guenther Construction Ltd. is in the construction business and enters into a contract with a customer to construct a building. The contract price is $10 million, and the building's estimated cost is $6 million. The construction is estimated to take three years to complete.

Required:

Prepare a schedule of the revenues and expenses that would be recognized in income in each of the three years with each of the following methods.

a. Recognition of income at contract signing

b. Percentage of completion method, assuming the following schedule of estimated costs.

Year	Amount
1	$3,000,000
2	$1,800,000
3	$1,200,000

c. Completed contract method

SUGGESTED SOLUTIONS TO SUMMARY PROBLEMS

1. **Sales of bicycles and bicycle accessories**: the company should recognize revenue at the time of the sale. At this time, the customer leaves with the merchandise (title transfers); therefore, the company has completed what it has to do, the amount that has been earned is measurable, and it has been collected either in cash or through a credit card.

Minor repairs: the company should recognize revenue when the work is completed. Similar to the situation with the sale of bicycles, the company has completed the work, the amount owed has been measured, and the customer has already paid.

Major repairs: the company should recognize revenue when the work is completed. When the customer makes the 25% down payment, the work has not yet been completed. As well, the total amount owed is still unknown. Therefore, two of the criteria have not been met. The company should record the down payment as unearned revenue. When the repairs are done, the company will have completed the work (therefore earned the revenue), the total amount owed is known, and the customer pays for the work with cash or a credit card. At this time, all three criteria have been met.

Assembly contract: the company should recognize revenue when the assembly work is complete. At the time of the contract signing, although the company knows how much it will receive and is confident that it will receive that amount, it has not assembled any bicycles. Because a substantial amount of work is yet to be done, the company has not earned the revenue. When the work is complete, the amount it has earned is known and it is reasonable to assume that it will collect the amount owed. At this time, the revenue recognition criteria have been met and revenue should be recognized.

2. a. Recognizing revenue at the time of contract signing would probably not be allowed under GAAP because of the contract's extended construction period. If it were allowed, all the profit, $4 million, would be recognized in the first year and none in later years.

b. Percentage of completion method (answers in thousands)

Year	Degree of Completion			Revenue Recognized			Expenses Recognized	Profit
1	$3,000 ÷ $6,000 =	50%		50% × $10,000 =	$ 5,000		$3,000	$2,000
2	$1,800 ÷ $6,000 =	30%		30% × $10,000 =	$ 3,000		1,800	1,200
3	$1,200 ÷ $6,000 =	20%		20% × $10,000 =	$ 2,000		1,200	800
		100%			$10,000		$6,000	$4,000

c. Completed contract method (answers in thousands)

Year	Revenue	Expense	Profit
1	0	0	0
2	0	0	0
3	$10,000	$6,000	$4,000
	$10,000	$6,000	$4,000

ABBREVIATIONS USED

FASB Financial Accounting Standards Board
GAAP Generally accepted accounting principles
ROA Return on assets

ROE Return on equity
ROI Return on investment

GLOSSARY

Account receivable An amount owing as a result of the sale of a product or service.

Cash discount A reduction in the amount that has to be paid on an account payable or receivable if payment is made within a specified time limit.

Cash-to-cash cycle A company's operating cycle: its operating activities from the initial outlays of cash to buy a product or to provide a service, to the replacement of cash through collections from customers.

Completed contract method A method of revenue recognition used in the construction industry in which the revenues from a contract are recognized only when the contract is completed.

Cost The value of whatever is given up to acquire an item.

Earned A term used to indicate that the company has completed its earnings process sufficiently to allow the recognition of the revenues from the sale.

Expenses   The costs incurred to earn revenues.

Instalment method   A method of revenue recognition based on cash collections in which each payment received is viewed as part profit and part recovery of costs. A fraction of each payment received is recorded as profit.

Matching principle   A concept that requires all expenses related to the production of revenues to be recorded during the same time period as the revenues. The expenses are said to be matched with the revenues.

Measurement   The process of determining an appropriate amount or value for some attribute of the item being measured.

Net income   The difference between revenues and expenses.

Operating activities   Those activities involving the cash effects of the normal operations of a business, such as the buying and selling of goods and services.

Percentage of completion method   A method of revenue recognition used in the construction industry in which a percentage of the profits that are expected to be realized from a given project is recognized in a given period, based on the percentage of the project's completion. The percentage completed is typically measured as the fraction of costs incurred to date relative to the total estimated costs to complete the project.

Price allowance   An adjustment made to the selling price of a good or service to satisfy a customer, typically for some defect in the good or service provided.

Recognition   Recording an event in the accounting system and/or reporting an item in a financial statement, including both the description and the amount.

Return on investment (ROI)   A measure of an investment's performance, calculated as the ratio of the return from the investment to the average amount invested.

Revenues   The inflows of cash or other assets from the normal operating activities of a business, which mainly involve the sale of goods or provision of services.

Revenue recognition criteria   Criteria developed in GAAP that specify the conditions under which revenue should be recognized.

ASSIGNMENT MATERIAL

Assessing Your Recall

Self-Assessment Quiz

4-1   Diagram a typical cash-to-cash cycle of a retail company and briefly explain the cycle's various components.

4-2   List the three major revenue recognition criteria that exist under GAAP.

4-3   Explain the meaning of revenue being earned.

4-4   Explain the difference between the percentage of completion method and the completed contract method.

4-5   Describe how the instalment method is implemented and explain why it is rarely used in practice.

4-6   Explain the meaning of the matching principle.

4-7   Describe the accounting treatment for a deposit made by a customer for the future delivery of inventory. Using the revenue recognition criteria, explain the rationale for this treatment.

4-8   Explain how ROI measures performance.

Applying Your Knowledge

4-9   (Revenue recognition criteria)

In the opening story to this chapter, the owner of *Outpost* magazine explained how the company recognized revenue. Using the revenue recognition criteria described in this chapter, explain the appropriateness of the revenue policy the company has adopted for revenue from advertisers and revenue from subscribers.

4-10   (Revenue recognition and the income statement)

Tanya Simpson and Brad Woo started a website development company. They purchased two new computers for $2,100 each and determined that they would probably last three years and then would have a residual value of $250 each. During the year they developed 45 websites and received a total of $62,500 from customers for website development. At year end, they had five websites in various stages of completion. They had received $600 each in advance for these sites and this amount was included in the $62,500 they had received during the year. During the year they spent $18,250 for various things such as printing, disks, computer programs, and office supplies. They also spent $8,300 for Internet connections, telephone and fax services, and other utilities.

> *Required:*
>
> Prepare as much of the income statement for Simpson and Woo as you can, showing the proper amount of sales and any other amounts that should be included. Show all calculations. Do you have a cost of goods sold? Why or why not? What other expenses do you think they would probably have?

4-11   (Revenue recognition and the income statement)

The Warm as Toast Company installs furnaces and fireplaces in homes and businesses. Each furnace and fireplace carries a four-year warranty. During 2006, the company had sales of $950,000. Customers paid half of the sales price when they arranged the installation of a furnace or fireplace and paid the other half after it was installed. At year end, $52,000 of the sales amount represented amounts paid for furnaces or fireplaces that were not yet installed and the second half of the payment had not been received yet. The cost associated with the sales was $460,000 for the furnaces and fireplaces that had been installed that year. An additional cost of $210,000 was incurred for the labour associated with the installation. The accountant estimated that total future warranty costs associated with the installed items would likely be $50,000 over the next five years.

> *Required:*
>
> Prepare as much of the income statement for Warm as Toast Company for 2006 as you can, showing the proper amount of sales, cost of goods sold, gross profit, and any other amounts that can be included. Show all calculations. What other expenses do you think the company would probably have?

4-12   (Revenue recognition on long-term contract)

Smith Brothers Construction Company signs a three-year contract to construct a bridge for $40 million. The expected costs for each year are (in millions):

Year 1	$9.5
Year 2	$7.5
Year 3	$7.0
Total	$24.0

The bridge is completed in Year 3.

> *Required:*
>
> Calculate for each year the total revenue, expense, and profit using each of the following methods.
>
> a. The percentage of completion method

b. The completed contract method

4-13 (Revenue recognition on layaway sale)

Unique Jewellery Store bought jewellery from local jewellery designers and sold the items for cash, by credit card, or on a layaway plan. Because each piece of jewellery was unique, the company was able to sell it for a markup of 200%. This means that if the company bought a piece of jewellery from the designer for $200, it could sell that piece for $600. ($400 profit ÷ $200 cost equals 200% markup.) Because the jewellery was expensive, the company provided a layaway plan for customers who did not have enough immediate cash to buy the jewellery. Under the layaway plan, the company would keep the piece of jewellery in a safe place until it was fully paid for. The usual payment plan involved four monthly payments of one quarter of the purchase price plus $8. The additional $8 was to cover storage and handling costs. When the last payment was made, the piece of jewellery was transferred to the customer.

Required:

Using the revenue recognition criteria described in this chapter, explain how the company should account for the four monthly payments made by the customer. Assume that the additional $8 paid monthly is not refundable to the customer if s/he does not make all four payments. Under the revenue recognition you are recommending, explain when the jewellery's original cost would be recognized as an expense.

4-14 (Revenue recognition on instalment sale)

Kraft's Discount Furniture began operations in 2006. It bought furniture from discount furniture suppliers and companies going out of business. It sold the furniture for cash, by credit card, or on instalment. Because Kraft's was a new business, it could not estimate the potential customers who would default on their payments. It, therefore, chose to use the instalment method to account for these sales. A customer bought a bedroom suite for $900 on instalment. Kraft's had originally paid $530 to a supplier for the bedroom suite. The terms of the sale were that the customer would make 12 monthly instalments of $79.96. The payments are made at the end of each month. Part of that monthly payment represented interest at 1% per month.

Required:

a. Calculate the accounts receivable, interest revenue, and profit at the end of each of the first three months assuming that the profit is recognized each month when the payment is received.

b. What options are open to Kraft's if the customer stops making payments after the fourth month?

4-15 (Revenue recognition on instalment sale)

Imperial Company purchases a factory from Superior Manufacturing Company for $1.5 million. The cost of the factory in Superior's records is $975,000. The agreement terms are that yearly payments of $705,000, $505,000, $455,000, and $255,000 will be made over the next four years. Each of these payments includes an interest payment of $105,000 per year.

Required:

a. Under what conditions would it be reasonable for Superior to recognize all the profit on the sale in the first year?

b. Under what conditions would it be important to delay recognition until the actual cash payments are received?

c. Calculate the accounts receivable, interest revenue, and profit at the end of each of the four years assuming all the profit is recognized in the first year.

4-16   (Revenue recognition on long-term contract)

Northumberland Ferries arranged for Maritime Shipbuilders to build three new ferries for its Nova Scotia to Prince Edward Island run. Northumberland agreed to pay $12 million for the ferries ($4 million each). The contract was signed on June 30, 2005, with a delivery date of September 30, 2007. Northumberland agreed to pay the $12 million as follows.

$3 million at the signing of the contract

$5 million on December 31, 2006

$4 million on September 30, 2007 (at completion)

The following costs were incurred by Maritime Shipbuilders (in millions).

2005	$2.0
2006	3.9
2007	3.2
Total	$9.1

Required:

a. Calculate the revenue, expense, and profit (ignoring interest) that Maritime Shipbuilders should report for each of the three years using each of the following methods.

   1. Percentage of completion method

   2. Completed contract method

b. Which method do you think should be employed by Maritime Shipbuilders to show the company's performance under the contract? Why?

4-17   (Revenue recognition on long-term contract)

Concord Construction Inc. agreed to build a new science building on the Northern University campus. Both parties signed the contract on October 31, 2005, for $60 million, which is to be paid as follows.

$5 million at the signing of the contract

$15 million on December 31, 2005

$30 million on December 31, 2006

$10 million at completion, on August 15, 2007

The following costs were incurred by Concord Construction (in millions).

2005	$9.2
2006	20.4
2007	16.4
Total	$46.0

Required:

a. Calculate the revenue, expense, and profit (ignoring interest) that Concord Construction should report for each of the three years using each of the following methods.

   1. Percentage of completion method

2. Completed contract method

b. Which method do you think should be employed by Concord Construction to show the company's performance under the contract? Why?

4-18 (Revenue recognition on long-term contract)

Computronics Company received a contract on March 3, 2005, to set up a central information system for a college. The contract price was $1 million, which was to be paid as follows.

$200,000 at the signing of the contract

$60,000 on July 1, 2005

$50,000 on December 31, 2005

$50,000 on March 25, 2006

$100,000 on August 25, 2006

$150,000 on December 31, 2006

$390,000 on June 30, 2007

The system was completed on June 30, 2007.

Estimated and actual costs were:

$140,000	for the four months ending June 30, 2005
210,000	for the six months ending December 31, 2005
240,500	for the six months ending June 30, 2006
90,000	for the six months ending December 31, 2006
69,500	for the six months ending June 30, 2007
Total $750,000	

Required:

a. Calculate the revenue, expense, and profit that Computronics should report for each six-month period ending June 30 and December 31 using each of the following methods.

1. Percentage of completion method

2. Completed contract method

b. Which method should Computronics Company use? Why?

4-19 (Revenue recognition on long-term contract)

Laroque Construction Inc. takes on both short- and long-term contracts. For short-term contracts (nine months or less), it uses the completed contract method and for long-term contracts (over nine months), it uses the percentage of completion method. It recently agreed to do two contracts. On June 30, 2006, the company agreed to a six-month contract to replace the brick on the outside of an apartment building. The contract was for $450,000 and the company expected to incur costs of $325,000. The contract was completed by December 20, 2006, and had actual costs of $340,000.

The second contract was for the construction of a new apartment complex for $3,675,000. The contract was signed on August 1, 2006, and was expected to be finished September 30, 2007. The expected costs for the contract are as follows.

Year	Cost
2006	$ 920,750
2007	1,750,500
Total	$2,671,250

Laroque Construction closes its books every December 31.

Required:

a. For each of the two contracts, determine the revenue, expense, and profit/loss as at December 31, 2006.

b. Explain why the accounting methods chosen for the two types of contracts is appropriate for Laroque Construction.

4-20   (Revenue recognition on long-term contract)

On June 21, 2005, Solid Concrete Company signed a contract with Reliance Power Incorporated to construct a dam over a river in Manitoba. The contract price was $35 million, and it was estimated that the project would cost Solid Concrete $22.5 million to complete over a three-year period. On June 21, 2005, Reliance paid Solid Concrete $1 million as a default deposit. In the event that Reliance backed out of the contract, Solid Concrete could keep this deposit. Otherwise, the default deposit would apply as the final payment on the contract (assume, for accounting purposes, that this is treated as a deposit until contract completion). The other contractual payments are as follows.

Date	Amount
October 15, 2005	$11,900,000
April 15, 2006	5,100,000
December 15, 2006	6,800,000
March 15, 2007	6,630,000
August 10, 2007	3,570,000
Total	$34,000,000

Estimated construction costs were as follows.

Year	Amount
2005	$10,125,000
2006	7,875,000
2007	4,500,000
Total	$22,500,000

The contract was completed on September 30, 2007. Solid Concrete closes its books on December 31 each year.

Required:

Calculate the revenue, expense, and profit to be recognized in each year using each of the following methods.

a. The percentage of completion method

b. The completed contract method

4-21 **(Revenue recognition decision)**

Jocelyn Black started a catering service in February 2006. She started by catering small functions in homes and businesses. By June she was providing food for weddings and graduations for up to 500 people. She hired three people who helped cook and serve at the larger functions. For functions of under 20 people, she took the order, prepared the food, and delivered it. She was paid when the food was delivered. For functions of more than 20 people, she took the order and requested a 20% deposit from the customer. The remaining 80% was required at the end of the function. For each function, Jocelyn kept a record of who placed the order, the quantity and type of food ordered, the cost of the materials used to prepare the food, the time spent by the hired people to cook and serve the food, the deposit received, and the final cheque. So far, she has not had trouble with customers failing to pay or of cheques not being good, but she knows that, as she expands the business, such things could happen.

> *Required:*
>
> It is the beginning of December and Jocelyn Black would like to have some financial statements prepared by December 31. She has asked you to help set up her records and to provide her with some accounting advice. As one small part of that, advise her about how she should account for the revenue she earns from the small and the large jobs. At what stage should she recognize revenue? Support your answer using the revenue recognition criteria.

4-22 **(Revenue recognition decision)**

Tom Gilles had seen many signs during the previous summers advertising house painters. Between his third and fourth year of university, he decided that he would start a painting business so that he could earn enough money to pay his tuition in the fall. He had talked with a fellow student who had run a business like this in the previous summer and knew what the rates were that he could charge. He made the following decisions: when he had a customer sign a contract for the inside or outside painting of a house, he would ask for a 20% down payment. The remainder of the contract price would be required when the job was completed. He made a deal with a local paint supplier for a discount on paint and other supplies. He assumed that most of the brushes and other paint supplies would be worth very little by the end of the summer. Other supplies, such as ladders, he would sell at the end of the summer. If he needed a piece of equipment to do a job that he would likely not need again, he would rent it. His parents provided him with $500 in start-up money that needed to be repaid to them when he closed his business.

> *Required:*
>
> a. Describe Tom's cash-to-cash cycle.
>
> b. What revenue recognition options are open to him? Which one would you recommend and why?
>
> c. Using your recommended revenue recognition policy, how would Tom account for all the costs for his various painting contracts?
>
> d. How should he account for the original $500 that he received from his parents?

4-23 **(Revenue recognition decision)**

Sonya's Christmas Tree Company began operations on April 1, 2004. She bought a parcel of land on which she intended to grow Christmas trees. The normal growth time for a Christmas tree is approximately six years, so she divided her land into six plots. In 2004 she planted the first plot with trees and watered, cultivated, and fertilized her trees all summer. In 2005 she planted her second plot with trees and watered, cultivated, and fertilized both planted plots. She continued with her plantings and cultivation every year through 2009, when she planted the last plot. On November 1, 2009, she harvested the first plot of trees that she had planted in 2004. In 2010 she replanted the first plot.

> ***Required:***
>
> a. Describe Sonya's cash-to-cash cycle.
>
> b. What revenue recognition options are open to her? Which one would you recommend and why?
>
> c. Using your recommended revenue recognition policy, how would Sonya account for all her costs for growing the trees?

4-24   (Revenue recognition decision)

Sparkling Cleaners operated six outlets in the city. At each outlet, customers could drop off clothes to be either dry cleaned or laundered. Such clothes were normally ready for pick up within one to three days. Customers used cash, debit, or credit to pay for the clothes when they were picked up. Sparkling Cleaners had a central facility at which the clothing was cleaned. The company also did large contracts with hospitals and hotels. Under these contracts, laundry was picked up daily, cleaned, and returned the following day. Under the contract, the customer was sent a weekly invoice for the laundry cleaned that week. The invoice was due before the next invoice was sent out. If payment had not been received by the time that next invoice needed to be sent, the previous invoice amount was added to the new invoice.

> ***Required:***
>
> a. Describe Sparkling Cleaners' cash-to-cash cycle. To do this, you will need to determine the types of expenditures that the company will likely incur in the operations of its business as well as outline when cash is given to the company in return for the services it provides.
>
> b. What revenue recognition options are open to the company with respect to its two types of customer? Which one would you recommend for each type of customer and why?

4-25   (Revenue recognition decision)

After graduating with a degree in computer systems and design, Terry Park set up a business to design and produce computer games for use in arcades. Terry hired two other designers because of the anticipated volume of business. One designer, Kim, is paid an hourly wage. The second, Sandy, is paid 50% of the revenue received by Terry on the games designed or redesigned by Sandy. Terry rents an office where they all work and provides all the necessary equipment, supplies, and other items. Terry is not paid a wage but keeps all the profits earned.

Terry quickly realized there were two kinds of business: speculative design and custom design. For the speculative designs, Terry or one of the designers would think of a new game and design, program, and test it. Terry would then try to sell it to a distribution company, for either a fixed price or a percentage (which ranges from 10% to 25%) of the total revenues earned by the games. To date, Terry has sold three of the four games produced. Terry is currently negotiating the sale of the fourth game.

For the custom design business, Terry would receive an order from a distribution company for either the design of a new game or the redesign of an existing game (which occurs frequently because games have a useful life of only six months as players quickly get bored with them). Terry negotiates either a fixed fee payable upon completion, or an hourly rate based on the estimated length of time it should take to redesign the game. Terry sets the hourly rate based on the project's perceived difficulty, but the rate is always at least triple the amount paid to Kim. For the hourly rate contracts, Terry submits monthly invoices showing the number of hours worked on the project.

Required:

a. Describe Terry's cash-to-cash cycle.

b. What revenue recognition options are open to Terry? Which one(s) would you recommend and why?

c. Using your recommended revenue recognition policy, how would you account for all the costs incurred by Terry?

d. What recommendations would you make to Terry about the running of this business?

4-26 (Calculate the ROI)

Calculate the ROI for the following independent investments.

a. Maria Chevas bought a GIC (guaranteed investment certificate) on June 1 for $3,000. The certificate reached maturity on December 1 (it was a six-month certificate). On December 1, she cashed in the certificate and received her original $3,000 back plus $37 in interest.

b. On January 2, Jim Wilson bought 10 shares of a pharmaceutical company for $12.00 a share. At year end, he received a dividend of $0.30 per share. At that time, the shares were trading for $12.50 per share.

c. Susan Blanchard bought a 25% interest in an outdoor adventure partnership for $15,000. During the year, the partnership earned net income of $50,000.

d. The Free-flow Plumbing Company had $250,000 in net assets (shareholders' equity) at the beginning of the year, and $280,000 at the end. During the year it earned net income of $60,000.

e. Anastasia Kostovia bought a condo for $125,000 in Ottawa. One year later, a real estate agent suggested that she could sell the condo for $130,000.

4-27 (Calculate the ROI)

Calculate the ROI for the following independent investments.

a. The Bainbridge family bought a home in Calgary for $180,000. Two years later, a real estate agent told them that they could probably sell their home for $210,000.

b. The Melrose Motor Company bought an investment in a supply company for $110,000. During the year it received dividends equal to $4,000.

c. Jack Valaas bought 5,000 shares in his sister's retail company for $20,000. The company earned net income of $72,000, which resulted in earnings per share of $3.75.

d. Margot Chan bought 10 shares in Transit Airlines for $6.60 per share. One year later she had not received a dividend but the shares were selling at $8.10 per share.

e. The Down Rite Dirty Disposal Company had $1,340,000 in assets at the beginning of the year, and $1,150,000 at the end. During the year it earned net income of $120,000.

User Perspective Problems

4-28 (Revenue recognition and earnings)

Financial analysts frequently refer to the quality of a company's earnings. By quality, they mean that the earnings are showing growth and that they are good predictors of future earnings. Discuss how the quality of two companies' earnings might differ depending on the revenue recognition method used.

4-29 (Changing revenue policy to affect earnings)

Suppose that a company is currently private (its shares do not trade on a public stock exchange) but it is thinking of going public (issuing shares on a public stock exchange). Discuss the incentives that the company might have to misstate its income statement via its revenue recognition policies. If a company decided to change its revenue recognition policy so that its earnings would be enhanced, would the investors realize what it was doing? Where would a new investor look for information about the changes?

4-30 (Short-term borrowing)

Suppose that a company would like to increase a short-term loan outstanding that it has with a local financial institution. The institution currently requires monthly payments on the loan. Would the financial institution be interested in receiving periodic financial statements from the company? Why? If it did receive financial statements, what items would it find of particular interest?

4-31 (Revenue policy and management performance measurement)

Suppose that you are the sales manager of a company with an incentive plan that provides a bonus based on meeting a certain sales target. Explain how meeting your sales target is affected by the company's revenue recognition policies.

4-32 (Revenue policy and sales targets)

Suppose that you are the vice-president in charge of marketing and sales in a large company. You want to boost sales, so you have developed an incentive plan that will provide a bonus to the salespeople based on the revenue they generate. At what point would you recommend that the company count a sale: when the salesperson generates a purchase order, when the company ships the goods, or when the company receives payment for the goods? Explain.

4-33 (Revenue policy for accounting and tax purposes)

The guidelines for revenue recognition for accounting are not always the same as the rules for revenue recognition for tax purposes. Describe some incentives a company might have for setting its revenue recognition policy for accounting. Describe some incentives that the government might have for setting the rules for revenue recognition for tax purposes.

4-34 (Revenue policy and return policies)

In the toy manufacturing industry, it is common to allow customers (retail stores) to return unsold toys within a specified period of time. Suppose that a toy manufacturer's year end is December 31 and that the majority of its products are shipped to customers during the last quarter of the year in anticipation of the holiday season. Is it appropriate for the company to recognize revenue upon shipment of the product? Support your answer, making reference to revenue recognition criteria.

4-35 (Revenue policy and modes of shipping goods)

Suppose that an exporter in Vancouver sells goods to a customer in Australia. The goods are shipped by cargo vessel. For goods that are in transit at year end, what recognition should the Vancouver exporter make in its financial statements? Support your answer based on revenue recognition criteria.

4-36 (Revenue recognition for apartment rentals)

Suppose that you are the owner of a car dealership that sells and leases cars. When customers lease a vehicle, they are required to sign a three- or five-year lease. A lease is a contract whereby the customer agrees to make monthly payments for the duration of the lease. There are penalties if the customer decides to return the vehicle before the end of the lease. During the lease, the customer is required to keep the vehicle in good condition with respect to mechanical operations and appearance. When the customer returns the vehicle at the end of the lease, it is inspected for damage. The customer is often expected to pay for mechanical work or repainting that is required. Using revenue recognition criteria, explain when you would recognize the revenue from the monthly lease payments. Knowing that the customers pay a penalty if they return the vehicle early and that they pay for any damages at the end of the lease term, how does that affect your decision?

4-37 (Advertising revenue recognition)

Suppose the sports channel on television sells $10 million in advertising slots to be aired during the games that it broadcasts during the World Cup. Suppose also that these slots are contracted out during the month of October with a down payment of $2 million. The ads will be aired in June and July of the following year. If the sports channel's fiscal year end is December 31, how should it recognize this revenue in its financial statements?

4-38 (Revenue recognition for gift certificates)

Suppose that **The GAP** (a clothing retailer) sells gift certificates for merchandise. During the Christmas holiday period, suppose that it issues $500,000 in gift certificates. If the company's fiscal year end is December 31, how should it recognize the issuance of these gift certificates in its financial statements at year end? Explain your answer in relation to the revenue recognition criteria.

4-39 (Revenue recognition on software sales)

Suppose that the Solution Software Company produces inventory tracking software that it sells to retail companies such as **Canadian Tire**. The software keeps track of what inventory is on hand and where it is located. It automatically adjusts the information when items are sold and alerts the company when new inventory needs to be ordered. The software package sells for $100,000 and the company agrees to customize it to the buyer's operations, which can take several months. If the fiscal year end is September 30 and the company sells 10 units in August, how should it recognize these sales in the financial statements at year end? Use the revenue recognition criteria to support your answer.

4-40 (Revenue and expenses associated with obsolete inventory)

Suppose that you are the auditor of Nichol's Department Store and during your audit of the company's inventory you observe a significant amount of inventory that appears to be extremely old. How would you recommend that the company deal with this inventory, and how will it affect the revenues and expenses recognized during the period? Explain the incentives that management might have for keeping the inventory in its warehouse.

Reading and Interpreting Published Financial Statements

Financial Statement Analysis Assignments

4-41 (Revenue recognition for multiple products)

Brampton Brick Limited's main area of operation is in the manufacture of clay and concrete bricks that it sells for residential and industrial construction. It has expanded its operations into truck transportation services and the disposal of biomedical and pharmaceutical wastes.

Required:

Using the revenue recognition criteria, describe how you think Brampton Brick should recognize revenue for its brick sales, its trucking operations, and its medical waste disposal. You might find it useful to know more about the company by going to its website at www.bramptonbrick.com.

4-42   (Catalogue production, revenue recognition, and matching)

Eddie Bauer, Inc. sells clothing and other items from retail stores, through catalogue mailings, and over the Internet. The cost of catalogue production and mailing is fairly substantial for a company such as Eddie Bauer. In that these costs occur before any revenue can be generated from the sale of items from the catalogue, discuss how they could be recorded in the accounting system so that they can be matched with the revenue that is eventually generated.

4-43   (Application of revenue recognition criteria)

Refer to the statement of financial position (balance sheet) of **Air Canada** in Exhibit 4-5. You will notice that at the top of the statement it says, "Under Creditor Protection as of April 1, 2003." This means that in 2003, Air Canada faced severe financial difficulties. It needed time to restructure its organization, search for new investors, and bring its costs under control. The organizations to whom Air Canada owed money could not force it to sell its assets while it was under creditor protection. Despite being under creditor protection, the financial statements still tell us interesting things about Air Canada. In the notes to the financial statements, Air Canada states its Air Transportation Revenue policy.

Airline passenger and cargo advance sales are deferred and included in current liabilities. Passenger and cargo revenues are recognized when the transportation is provided. The Corporation has formed alliances with other airlines encompassing loyalty program participation, code sharing and coordination of services including reservations, baggage handling and flight schedules. Revenues are allocated based upon formulas specified in the agreements and are recognized as transportation is provided.

The Corporation performs regular evaluations on the liability which may result in adjustments being recognized as revenue. Due to the complex pricing structures; the complex nature of interline and other commercial agreements used throughout the industry; historical experience over a period of many years; and other factors including refunds, exchanges and unused tickets, certain relatively small amounts are recognized as revenue based on estimates. Events and circumstances may result in actual results different from estimates, however these differences have historically not been material.

> ### Required:
>
> a. Referring to the balance sheet in Exhibit 4-5, what is the value of the transportation that Air Canada is committed to provide at year end in 2003 and 2002?
>
> b. Referring to the revenue recognition criteria, explain why Air Canada's revenue recognition policy is appropriate.
>
> c. Air Canada has a frequent flyer program where customers earn travel miles that can be exchanged at a later date for trips. Suggest how you think Air Canada should account for these free trips.

4-44   (Application of revenue recognition criteria)

According to Note 2 to its 2003 financial statements, the revenue policy used by **IPSCO**, a steel manufacturer, is as follows.

Revenue Recognition

Sales and related costs are recognized upon transfer of ownership which coincides with shipment of products to customers or specific terms included in customer contracts.

> ### Required:
>
> a. Describe IPSCO's revenue recognition policy and explain how it satisfies the revenue recognition criteria.
>
> b. Explain why you think it has specified "shipment of products."

EXHIBIT 4-5   AIR CANADA 2003 ANNUAL REPORT

AIR CANADA
Consolidated Statement of Financial Position

(Under Creditor Protection as of April 1, 2003 - note 1)
(in millions - Canadian dollars)

December 31		2003		2002
ASSETS				
Current				
Cash and cash equivalents	$	670	$	558
Restricted cash (note 2)		157		63
Accounts receivable		502		697
Spare parts, materials and supplies		211		358
Prepaid expenses		171		86
		1 711		1 762
Property and equipment (note 3)		1 771		2 288
Deferred charges (note 4)		2 332		1 781
Goodwill		510		510
Other assets (note 5)		586		1 071
	$	6 910	$	7 412
LIABILITIES				
Liabilities not subject to compromise				
Current				
Accounts payable and accrued liabilities	$	1 700	$	1 713
Advance ticket sales		529		506
Current portion of long-term debt and capital lease obligations (note 9)		173		373
		2 402		2 592
Long-term and subordinated perpetual debt and capital lease obligations (note 9)		332		4 314
Future income taxes (note 17)		11		28
Other long-term liabilities (note 13)		1 643		1 405
Deferred credits (note 14)		1 364		1 361
		5 752		9 700
Liabilities subject to compromise (note 10)		5 313		-
		11 065		9 700
Commitments (note 18) and Contingencies, Guarantees and Indemnities (note 21) and Going Concern (note 1)				
SHAREHOLDERS' EQUITY				
Share capital and other equity (note 15)		967		977
Contributed surplus		25		15
Deficit		(5 147)		(3 280)
		(4 155)		(2 288)
	$	6 910	$	7 412

The accompanying notes are an integral part of the consolidated financial statements

4-45 **(Application of revenue recognition criteria)**

The revenue recognition policy of **Imperial Metals Corporation**, a mining company, from Note 1 to its 2003 financial statements, is as follows.

> Estimated mineral revenue, based upon prevailing metal prices, is recorded in the financial statements when title to the concentrate transfers to the customer. The estimated revenue is subject to adjustment upon final settlement, which is usually four to five months after the date of shipment.
>
> These adjustments reflect changes in metal prices, changes in currency rates, and changes in quantities arising from final weight and assay calculations.

Required:

a. Explain why this revenue recognition conforms to GAAP. Include consideration of the treatment of estimated revenues and settlement adjustments (adjustments caused by changes in metal prices, changes in currency rates, and changes in quantities arising from final weight and assay calculations).

b. What alternative revenue recognition policies and recording could Imperial Metals use that would also conform with GAAP?

4-46 **(Application of revenue recognition criteria)**

The revenue recognition policies used by **Canadian Pacific Railway Limited**, a transportation provider, according to Note 2 to its 2003 financial statements, is as follows.

> Railway freight revenues are recognized based on the percentage of completed service method. Other revenue is recognized as service is performed or contractual obligations are met.

Required:

Explain how you think the percentage of completed service method would work for a railway transportation provider. Why do you think Canadian Pacific Railway chose this method for its freight revenues rather than waiting until all the service was provided? You might find it useful to know more about the company by going to its website at www.cpr.ca/english.

4-47 **(Revenue recognition decision-making)**

There are companies today that provide additional funds to retired individuals. They offer reverse mortgages. A reverse mortgage is a loan against the person's home that requires no repayment for as long as the person lives in the home. The person still owns the home and must pay for property taxes, insurance, and upkeep. However, when the person stops living in the home, the loan comes due. The person receives the loan either as an immediate cash advance, as a creditline account, as monthly cash payments, or as a combination of the other options. The amount that must be paid back cannot be higher than the equity in the home, which means that the company cannot seek additional funds from the owner or the owner's heirs. The company runs the risk of the person staying in the home a long time and/or of the equity in the home not growing as quickly as anticipated.

Required:

a. If you were a manager in a company offering reverse mortgages, how would you decide how much money you should loan to a homeowner?

b. Having decided on the amount, how would you recognize revenue over the life of this agreement?

c. Given your revenue recognition method outlined in b), how would you treat the payments made to the homeowner and the various expenses incurred in administering the agreement?

d. Are there any ethical dilemmas that the managers of such a company might face in contracting reverse mortgages?

Beyond the Book

4-48 (Revenue recognition policies used)

Using an electronic database, select a company in the oil and gas industry. Using the information on its financial statements and in the notes to the financial statements, answer the following questions.

    a. Describe the types of revenue generated by the company.

    b. Describe the policies used by the company for revenue recognition for its various revenues. Using the revenue recognition criteria, explain how the policies selected are suitable for the revenues generated.

4-49 (Change in revenue recognition criteria)

Using an electronic database, search for a company that has changed its revenue recognition methods during the last three years.

    a. Describe the method that company used before the change as well as the new method.

    b. Does the company give a reason for the change? If so, describe the reason; if not, speculate on why the change occurred.

    c. How significant an effect did the change have on the company's financial statements? As in investor, how would you view this change?

    d. Did the auditor agree with the change? Do you agree? Why or why not?

Cases

4-50 Quebec Supercheese Company (QSC)

Case Primer

Quebec Supercheese Company (QSC) produces many varieties of cheese that are sold in every province in Canada, mainly through large grocery stores and specialty cheese shops. The cheese is produced at its factory in Montreal and shipped across Canada using commercial refrigerated trucks that pick up the cheese at the factory loading dock. All cheese is shipped F.O.B. shipping point, meaning that the purchasers pay for the trucking and assume responsibility for the cheese as soon as the trucks pick it up at the factory. In accordance with generally accepted accounting principles, QSC recognizes the sale as soon as the trucks load the cheese, as the purchasers have title and responsibility for the cheese at this point.

    QSC is not happy with these arrangements because it has received many complaints from purchasers about spoilage. Even though the purchasers and their truckers have full responsibility for this spoilage, many disputes have occurred because the truckers insist the cheese is spoiled when they pick it up. QSC is considering setting up its own fleet of trucks to deliver its cheese across Canada. It estimates the additional freight costs can be regained through the higher prices it would charge for including shipping in the price (F.O.B. destination).

    If the company makes the deliveries, the title to the cheese will not transfer until the cheese is delivered. QSC's president was not happy when she learned that sales would be recognized and recorded only upon delivery to the customer, since she knew that an average of five days' sales are in transit at all times because of the distances involved. One day's sales total approximately $100,000 on average. The effect of this change would be an apparent drop in sales of $500,000 and a $50,000 decrease in net income in the year of the change.

> **Required:**
>
> a. Advise the president about revenue recognition guidelines.
>
> b. Do you see a solution to the problem of changing the shipping method while avoiding the resulting effect on the income statement?

4-51   Windsor Contracting Ltd.

Windsor Contracting Ltd. uses the completed contract method to record revenue. In the past the company has focused on performing small renovation and home improvement jobs that typically lasted from two weeks to three months. The company has a very good reputation for quality work and fair pricing. Due in large part to its strong reputation, the company has begun to expand its operations to encompass larger contracts, some of which may take up to two years to complete. Dan Fielding, the president, is thrilled with the company's success but is a little concerned about accepting these larger contracts. He contacts you, John Philpot, a local accountant, to obtain some advice concerning the accounting for these larger long-term contracts.

Dan Fielding says, "John, I'm concerned about accepting these long-term contracts. If I cannot recognize any of the revenue associated with these jobs until they are completed, my income statement is going to look very poor for the years in which the contracts are in progress but not completed. I will need financing to undertake these large jobs and the bank needs a yearly income statement to support my line of credit. What do you suggest?"

> **Required:**
>
> Write a memo to Dan Fielding as John Philpot addressing his concerns. Your memo should focus on a discussion of the percentage of completion method of accounting for revenue recognition and how this method would meet the needs of Windsor Contracting. The memo should also include a discussion of any estimates that Windsor will have to make to apply this method of revenue recognition.

4-52   (Revenue recognition decision-making)

John Young and Sandra Grill are both CEOs of very successful businesses. John Young runs a plant that manufactures lawnmowers and sells them wholesale to a variety of hardware stores in Western Canada. Sandra Grill, on the other hand, is a speculator and her company mines gold in various provinces across Canada. Both companies are very successful and recognize significant amounts of revenue annually.

At a recent charity golf tournament, the two ended up on the same team and began discussing their companies' performance in the last quarter.

Grill: "Our company had exceptional performance over the past quarter due to a large gold strike in central Newfoundland. We have been able to mine several thousand ounces of gold and now have significant reserves. It has really helped our bottom line being able to record so much revenue in this quarter."

Young: "Did I hear you right? You are able to record revenue when the gold is produced? My accountant told me that our company couldn't record revenue until we have actually sold our inventory. I am going have a long talk with my accountant this week and demand that we get to record sales at the time of production as well!"

> **Required:**
>
> Discuss why there is a difference between the ways in which these two companies recognize revenue. Is John Young's accountant correct in requiring that inventory be sold before recognizing revenue? If so, then why can the mining company record revenue as soon as the gold is produced?

4-53   **Furniture Land Inc.**

Furniture Land Inc. is a producer and retailer of custom designed and built high-end furniture. The company only produces to special order and requires a one-third down payment before any work begins. The customer is then required to pay one-third at the time of delivery and the balance is to be paid within 30 days following delivery.

It is now February 1, 2006, and Furniture Land has just accepted $3,000 as a down payment from H. Gooding, a wealthy stockbroker. As per the contract, Furniture Land is to deliver the custom furniture to Gooding's residence by June 15, 2006. Gooding is an excellent customer and has always abided by the contract terms in the past. If Furniture Land cannot make the delivery by June 15, the contract terms state that Gooding has the option of cancelling the sale and receiving a full reimbursement of any down payment.

> *Required:*
>
> As Furniture Land's accountant, describe what revenue recognition policy the company should be using. Prepare all journal entries related to the sale in a manner that supports the revenue recognition policy selected.

Critical Thinking Questions

4-54   **(Inclusion of items in revenue)**

The statement of operations and the revenue recognition note from **Big Rock Brewery Income Trust** for the nine months ended December 31, 2003, are shown in Exhibit 4-6. Big Rock Brewery Income Trust changed its year end from March 31 to December 31.

> *Required:*
>
> a. Explain what "Government taxes and commissions" are.
>
> b. Argue why they should (or should not) be included in the revenues of Big Rock Brewery.

4-55   **(Revenue recognition decision-making)**

An article by Mahendra Gujarathi ("Bridging the GAP in GAAP: A Case Study of Accounting for Frequent Flyer Plans," Accounting Horizons, September 1991) examines accounting for frequent flyer plans offered by airlines.

> *Required:*
>
> a. Briefly summarize the three methods proposed to account for frequent flyer plans. Describe how, and examine why, the revenue recognition alternatives are linked to liability recognition.
>
> b. Do you agree with the recommendations made by the author?

4-56   **(Revenue recognition decision-making)**

Alliance Atlantis Communications Inc. is a fully integrated supplier of entertainment products to the television and motion picture production industries. One thing it produces is television series that it sells to TV networks. Often these series involve the development of an idea and production of a pilot show. This is followed by attempts to market the show to television stations. If the series is sold, weekly shows are produced for later airing by participating stations.

> *Required:*
>
> Discuss the revenue generation process of this kind of television series, emphasizing the critical points in the revenue recognition process and pointing out the similarities and differences between the revenue process for Alliance Atlantis and for a company manufacturing television sets.

BIG ROCK BREWERY 2003 ANNUAL REPORT
Consolidated Statements of Operations and Undistributed Income

Big Rock Brewery Income Trust

	Nine months ended December 31, 2003 $	Year ended March 31, 2003 $
Revenue		
Sales	36,875,008	39,330,418
Government taxes and commissions	(8,371,168)	(8,867,408)
	28,503,840	30,463,010
Cost of sales	10,298,575	11,728,022
Gross profit	18,205,265	18,734,988
Expenses		
Selling	8,155,972	9,573,047
General and administrative	3,095,802	3,201,955
Reorganization costs [note 2]	—	909,909
Interest on long-term debt	190,727	257,273
Interest on short-term debt	58,175	22,930
Amortization	1,257,190	1,729,510
	12,757,866	15,694,624
Income before income taxes	5,447,399	3,040,364
Income tax expense [note 10]	891,543	747,367
Net income for period	4,555,856	2,292,997
Undistributed income/retained earnings, beginning of period	10,058,529	8,652,143
Cash distributions declared	(3,004,004)	(886,611)
Undistributed income, end of period	11,610,381	10,058,529
Net income per unit		
Basic	0.82	0.43
Diluted	0.81	0.42

See accompanying notes

Revenue Recognition
Revenue is recognized upon shipment of product at the gross sales price charged to the purchaser. Invoices for sales to Canadian customers are submitted to the respective provincial liquor control boards who pay Big Rock after deducting liquor control board commissions. Excise taxes, which are assessed on production, and liquor control board commissions, which are assessed on sales, are recorded as reductions to gross sales prices.

Maintaining a Healthy Cash Flow

The Wellness Institute at Winnipeg's Seven Oaks General Hospital is Canada's first and only medical fitness facility. Owned and operated by the hospital, the institute provides various services to promote health and prevent illness. "We're different from a commercial facility because everyone undergoes a health risk assessment and receives an individual exercise prescription," says Executive Director Carrie Solmundson.

The 7,430-square-metre, state-of-the-art facility is also not-for-profit, meaning it has to keep close attention to its accounting, particularly its cash flow.

The number one priority, says Ms. Solmundson, is to ensure that the institute is constantly offering members a clean facility, good customer service, and the best equipment. This means investing any extra cash back into equipment maintenance and facility improvements.

The Wellness Institute receives its $5 million in annual income from membership fees, which comprise approximately half the total revenues, and other fees for services, such as the sports injury clinic, rehabilitation services, massage therapy, children's health and fitness programs, and food services. Its 5,700 members pay monthly dues ranging from $31 to $44, as well as an enrolment fee of $89. Program participants or their private insurance providers pay separately for special services, such as massage therapy or cardiac rehabilitation, though members do get a discount.

One of the lessons learned in managing cash flow from these various income sources is the importance of setting aside funds to continually reinvest in the building, Ms. Solmundson says. "One of the reasons people join this facility is because of the quality of the facility itself."

When setting the institute's budget, Ms. Solmundson creates two reserve funds: one restricted and one unrestricted. Any building and equipment replacements are covered by the restricted reserve fund. Each piece of equipment is assessed to determine its real life cycle, rather than its book life cycle, and decisions to improve the equipment are based on these assessments. Facilities improvements, such as new equipment,

lockers, or an expanded parking lot, are funded by the unrestricted reserve fund. Each cost consideration goes through a return on investment analysis before the decision to spend the funds is made.

For example, the $546,000 cash left in the 2003 budget was divided into the restricted and unrestricted reserve funds. Two-thirds was set aside to replace building and equipment items, including treadmills, stair climbers, bikes, carpeting, and computers, while a third will be used for improvements (new capital), such as more computer terminals and software for electronic health risk assessments, new weight machines, equipment for the expanded Pilates program, and a new sound system for the pool area.

But ensuring there is enough cash to maintain and enhance access to services, like the institute's successful smoking cessation program, is a challenge. A huge strategic issue for the institute is to secure government funding or health promotion and disease prevention services, says Ms. Solmundson. The institute receives no government funding, and Medicare covers only sports medicine. "Prevention isn't insured, which then makes you to some extent a middle-class facility," Ms. Solmundson says. Although the institute does some outreach, as a non-profit organization, it has limited ability to provide services to those who can't afford to pay.

Cash Flow Statement

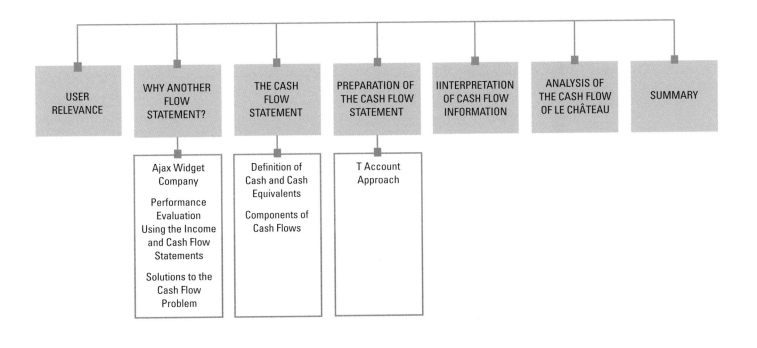

After studying this chapter, you should be able to:

1. Understand the importance of cash to a company's financial health.

2. Describe the relationship between the cash flow statement and the income statement in assessing management performance.

3. Describe the cash-to-cash cycle for a retail company through a discussion of the lead/lag relationship.

4. Identify some solutions to cash flow problems.

5. Identify the three major activities disclosed in the cash flow statement and describe the components of each activity.

6. Prepare a cash flow statement from a company's balance sheets and income statement.

7. Provide a basic analysis of a company's financial health using a cash flow statement.

Every organization, whether a profit-oriented business or a not-for-profit health promotion institute like the one described in the opening story, needs to manage its cash flow. The health of the organization depends on its ability to predict when cash is coming in and when it needs to be spent. For a not-for-profit organization like the Wellness Institute, cash prediction and management is a fine balancing act. Most not-for-profit organizations have a fixed access to funds from either granting agencies or donations. The Wellness Institute receives half its funding from membership fees and the other half from charging for services such as rehabilitation services. If it experiences a cash shortage, it can't just sell more items or provide more services. When not-for-profit organizations provide services, they may or may not get paid for them. The Wellness Institute does charge for its services but its ability to add more is limited by its facility and the number of staff it has to provide the service. Not-for-profits can't issue shares and often cannot borrow money. This greatly limits their choices and makes management of cash essential to their survival.

There is an interesting component to the Wellness Institute's decision-making. In Chapter 4 we talked about using the ROI ratio to measure the return received on investments of various kinds. The Wellness Institute uses ROI measures to make decisions about each new cost investment for the facility. Cash is a scarce commodity and, therefore, the institute tries to ensure that it gets the best return for each dollar spent.

Profit-oriented companies have similar concerns with respect to cash. They need to know how cash is flowing in and out. If a company has difficulty paying its debts on time, it soon loses its credit rating, and suppliers and lenders will be reluctant to continue to sell goods on credit or loan money to it. These actions will affect its ability to grow and could contribute to an eventual slide into bankruptcy. In 2003, Air Canada ran into just this kind of difficulty. In April 2003, it applied for and was granted creditor protection. If companies are unable to pay their liabilities when they fall due, creditors can seek legal action to force them to sell assets to raise the necessary cash to settle the debt. Creditor protection provides breathing space for the company to restructure its operations: cut costs, refinance its debt (extend the debt period or reduce the interest rate), and find new financial backers who are willing to provide an inflow of cash. During this time creditors cannot take any legal action against the company.

In Chapter 4, the basic concepts underlying the recognition of revenue were discussed from the company shareholders' point of view. Although this is an important perspective, other measures of performance that affect the company's overall health are not adequately captured by the income statement. Because the income statement is based on accrual accounting, the flows represented on the income statement do not necessarily correspond to the company cash flows. Since the company cannot operate without cash, it is important to understand its cash-generating performance during the period. Knowing the importance of cash flow, outside users need some way to assess an organization's future cash position. For example, creditors use cash flow information to assess the company's ability to pay periodic interest and the principal of debt as it comes due. This chapter discusses the second major measure of performance: the cash flows that are summarized in the statement called the **cash flow statement**. The cash flow statement is quite simple in intent, but a bit more difficult to prepare and understand properly. Because of this difficulty, you may find that your instructor has chosen to leave this chapter until later in the course.

USER RELEVANCE

Some users consider the cash flow statement the most important statement in determining a company's future prospects. Remember the three basic activities of a business that were described in Chapter 1.

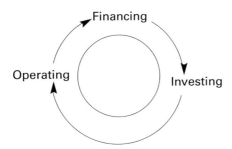

Users will look at these activities on the cash flow statement to assess a company's financial health. They will examine the statement to see whether the operations—the lifeblood of any company—are generating a positive **cash flow**. These are the activities for which the company was first established and upon which it will grow or decline. A positive cash flow indicates that more cash is flowing into the company than is flowing out as a result of operations. That cash may be used for other activities such as purchase of new assets, payment of debt, or payment of dividends to shareholders. A negative cash flow indicates that more cash flowed out of the company than flowed in as a result of operations. This means that external sources of cash may have to be found such as new debt or the issuance of additional shares.

Users need to examine the items under financing to determine what decisions the company made in the last year with respect to debt and equity. Did it incur more debt, pay some debt off, issue dividends, issue new shares? This information enables users to estimate the company's reliance on debt and equity in the future.

Under investing, users can see what decisions the company has made with respect to the buying and selling of long-term assets as well as long-term investments in other companies. This information enables users to assess the company's plans with respect to the timing and replacement of assets that it needs to continue its operations.

Many users still consider the income statement the most important statement, but they will examine it with the cash flow statement to try to understand and analyze a company. As a future user of financial information, it is important for you to know what to look for on the cash flow statement and to understand what the amounts in the various categories in the statement mean. For this reason, we are going to show you how the statement is developed and also talk about how you should analyze it.

WHY ANOTHER FLOW STATEMENT?

LEARNING OBJECTIVE 1

Understand the importance of cash to a company's financial health.

The income statement was the first flow statement we examined. The need for another flow statement is probably best conveyed by the use of a hypothetical example, the Ajax Widget Company. The assumptions for the example are listed in the boxes below.

Ajax Widget Company

PRODUCT LINE

The Ajax Widget Company sells widgets. A widget* is a hypothetical product for this example.

*Widget is also the trade name for a paint scraper produced by the Gillette Company.

SUPPLIER CREDIT

Widgets cost Ajax $4 apiece. Since Ajax's suppliers do not allow it to purchase the widgets on credit, all inventory must be paid in cash when it is ordered.

SALES/CUSTOMER CREDIT

The widgets currently sell for $5 apiece. Ajax allows its customers up to 30 days to pay for the widgets they buy. For the purpose of this example, it is assumed that all customers pay Ajax on the 30th day after a sale. Ajax is a relatively new company and has been experiencing fairly rapid growth in sales. Exhibit 5-1 shows this growth during the first three months of 2006. Ajax expects that sales will continue to grow at the rate of 600 units per month for at least the next year.

INVENTORY POLICY

Ajax's supply of widgets is such that it cannot get them from the supplier instantly. Therefore, it must maintain a certain level of inventory so that units are available when a customer comes to buy one. Ajax's policy is to maintain inventory at the end of the period equal to 50% of the current month's sales. The relationship can be seen in the data in Exhibit 5-1, which lists the sales in units for each month and the ending inventory.

EXHIBIT 5-1 **AJAX WIDGET COMPANY**

Sales/Inventory Data

	January	February	March
Beginning inventory	250	500	800
New inventory purchases	1,250	1,900	2,500
Goods available for sale	1,500	2,400	3,300
Sales	1,000	1,600	2,200
Ending inventory	500	800	1,100

Performance Evaluation Using the Income and Cash Flow Statements

LEARNING OBJECTIVE 2

Describe the relationship between the cash flow statement and the income statement in assessing management performance.

As we have discussed earlier in the text, Ajax's performance can be measured by constructing an income statement. Assuming that the revenues are recognized at the time of sale and that no expenses are incurred other than inventory costs, Exhibit 5-2 shows the income statement for each of the first three months of 2006.

AJAX WIDGET COMPANY

EXHIBIT 5-2

Income Statement

	January	February	March
Revenues	$5,000	$8,000	$11,000
Cost of goods sold	(4,000)	(6,400)	(8,800)
Net income	$1,000	$1,600	$ 2,200

As you can see in Exhibit 5-2, net income is growing at a predictable rate: the shareholders and managers should certainly be happy with this growth. Assuming that sales continue to increase at a rate of 600 units per month, this growth in income should continue. In the long run, the investment in Ajax should be profitable.

Exhibit 5-3 provides some information about Ajax's balance sheet. The trends in cash, accounts receivable, and inventory shown in Exhibit 5-3 reflect rapid business growth. Accounts receivable reflects an increased level of sales, as does inventory, because ending inventory is a function of sales. The disturbing trend in Exhibit 5-3 is, of course, the decline in the amount of cash on hand for Ajax. To understand the decline in cash, Ajax's cash-to-cash cycle must be considered. Exhibit 5-4 shows the cycle for Ajax.

AJAX WIDGET COMPANY

EXHIBIT 5-3

Partial Balance Sheet

	Dec. 31	Jan. 31	Feb. 28	Mar. 31
Cash	$8,000	$5,500	$2,900	$ 900
Accounts receivable	2,500	5,000	8,000	11,000
Inventory	1,000	2,000	3,200	4,400

AJAX WIDGET COMPANY

EXHIBIT 5-4

Cash-to-Cash Cycle

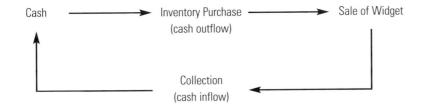

LEARNING OBJECTIVE 3

Describe the cash-to-cash cycle for a retail company through a discussion of the lead/lag relationship.

The cash-to-cash cycle illustrates the **lead/lag relationship** between the cash paid out to buy inventory and the cash coming in from collections of accounts receivable. The lag between inventory purchase and sale varies depending on which units are involved. Some units are bought and sold in the same month. Other units are bought in one month, remain in ending inventory, and are sold in the following month. This creates a one-month lag between the outflow of cash for inventory purchases and the sale of those widgets that are carried over in ending inventory. Therefore, considering both units purchased and units sold in the same period, as well as those that end up in ending inventory, the average lag between purchase and sale is somewhat less than a month. Once a widget is sold, the lag between sale and collection is one month because the collection policy is to allow customers 30 days to pay. Consequently, the total lag between cash outflow and cash inflow is somewhere between one and two months.

Because the income statement measures performance over a particular period in the cash-to-cash cycle, it ignores all the timing differences between revenues and expenses recognized and the related cash flows. Therefore, the income statement is not very useful in tracking cash flows. The income statement will continue to be positive as long as sales are increasing for Ajax and the cost of inventory remains below the selling price. The growth in sales, however, forces Ajax to buy more and more units each month. It is possible that the inventory costs paid in cash in a given month could exceed the cash collections from the previous month's sales. It is evident from the decline in the cash balance in Exhibit 5-3 that this has happened during the first three months of 2006. Thus, even though net income is increasing each month, the company's cash position is declining. Because Ajax cannot operate without enough cash, it would make sense to prepare a separate statement in addition to the income statement to measure the company's performance on a cash basis. Hence the need for a cash flow statement.

The cash flow statement cannot replace the income statement; each provides useful information. The income statement summarizes the profitability of the company's operations, while the cash flow statement summarizes the cash flows. To analyze the operations of any company properly, you must consider both profits and cash flows. In the long run, the total profits and net cash flows will be very similar, but they may be quite different for any single year or even over a period of several years.

To understand the usefulness of the information provided by the cash flow statement, think of managing cash as one of the basic duties of the company's management, who must ensure that sufficient cash is maintained on hand both to generate profits now and to invest in assets that will produce profits in the future. Simply producing profits now is not sufficient to ensure the company's long-term survival. Without enough cash to make investments in revenue-producing assets, the company's long-term viability may be in doubt.

EXHIBIT 5-5

AJAX WIDGET COMPANY

Cash Flow Statement

	January	February	March
Receipts (collections)	$2,500	$5,000	$ 8,000
Payments (inventory costs)	(5,000)	(7,600)	(10,000)
Net cash flow	($2,500)	($2,600)	($ 2,000)

Exhibit 5-5 shows Ajax's cash flow statement for the first three months in 2006. As can be seen from Exhibit 5-5, the Ajax Widget Company's cash flow has been negative in that period. The receipts in the cash flow statement are the collections from the previous month's sales, and the payments are the inventory purchase costs for the month. The inventory costs can be calculated by taking the units purchased in Exhibit 5-1 and multiplying them by the unit cost of $4.

The cash flow statement paints a very different picture of Ajax's performance during the first quarter of 2006 than does the income statement. Cash flow is obviously a problem. Because Ajax has only $900 left in its cash account, the question it faces is whether cash will run out in April and, if so, how it will be able to buy more inventory so that it can continue doing business. In order to decide whether the problem will persist, Ajax should prepare a forecast for the next several months. In practice, companies prepare these forecasts for 12-, 24-, and even 36-month periods. This provides them with the information needed to manage their cash flows. Assuming continued growth in sales of 600 units a month and no change in the collection, inventory, and payment policies of the Ajax Widget Company, Exhibit 5-6 illustrates the forecast for the months of April to June.

AJAX WIDGET COMPANY

EXHIBIT 5-6

Net Income, Cash Flow, and Cash Balance Forecast

	April	May	June
Revenues	$ 14,000	$ 17,000	$ 20,000
Cost of goods sold	(11,200)	(13,600)	(16,000)
Net income	$ 2,800	$ 3,400	$ 4,000
Receipts (collections)	$ 11,000	$ 14,000	$ 17,000
Payments (inventory costs)	(12,400)	(14,800)	(17,200)
Net cash flow	$ (1,400)	$ (800)	$ (200)
End of month cash balance	$ (500)	$ (1,300)	$ (1,500)

As can be seen from Exhibit 5-6, income continues to grow by $600 each month, reflecting the growth in sales of 600 units times the net profit margin of $1 per unit. The cash flow statement indicates that net cash flow will be negative for the next three months, but the trend is that net cash flow is improving and it looks as though it will be positive by July. The ending cash balance is projected to be negative for the next three months and will take longer to return to a positive cash balance. This is a problem because Ajax cannot operate with a negative cash balance. Operating with a negative cash balance is feasible only if the bank permits a company to overdraw its bank accounts; that is, if it allows more cash to be withdrawn than was deposited. A negative cash balance is really a loan from the bank. Companies will often make arrangements with the bank for circumstances like this. The loan arrangement is called a **line of credit**. The bank will set a maximum limit on how much can be borrowed in this way and will also establish the repayment schedule if the line of credit is used.

The problem is perhaps best portrayed by Exhibit 5-7, which graphs the situation with regard to net income, cash flow, and cash balance for the entire year 2006. Note the cash balance line, which drops below zero in April and returns to a positive balance in September. In reality, the company cannot have a negative cash balance without making special arrangements with its bank, and something must be done to prevent the problem from continuing for too long. Nevertheless, the graph clearly shows the magnitude and duration of Ajax's cash flow problem.

GRAPH OF CASH FLOW PROBLEM

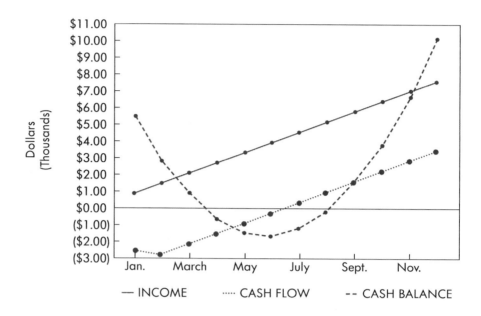

Cash flow problems such as the one just described may appear to be extreme and, indeed, we developed it so that you could easily see that Ajax had a cash flow problem. The following report about Les Boutiques San Francisco illustrates how cash flow problems can affect a real company.

accounting in the news

TRIMMING DOWN FOR EXTRA CASH

A company in financial trouble will offload some of its investments and assets in an attempt to free up all-important cash. Les Boutiques San Francisco did just that, drastically downsizing its 20,250-square-metre flagship Les Ailes de la Mode department store in downtown Montreal and selling 54 smaller stores. After experiencing huge losses at the downtown Les Ailes and taking a $38 million writedown, the retailer sought creditor protection in December 2003. San Francisco's restructuring plan included focusing on two core businesses: the four Les Ailes de la Mode stores in Montreal and Quebec City and 60 Bikini Village/San Francisco Maillots swimwear stores in Eastern Canada. It sold 33 of the 36 stores operating under the San Francisco banner to Groupe Marie Claire for $3.2 million. The downtown Montreal Les Ailes store was to be reduced to 6,750 square metres, the same size as the company's three other Les Ailes stores. The company also planned to sell its head office building, moving its administration to one of the department stores. Annual cost savings were estimated at $8.5 million.

Source: "Quebec retail chain downsizing flagship; 54 stores to be sold," by Robin Gibbens, *National Post*, January 15, 2004; "Boutique San Francisco stores and name sold to Groupe Marie Claire," *The Canadian Press*, January 26, 2004.

Les Boutiques San Francisco is attempting to recover from its cash flow problems by selling assets and reducing its overall operation to a more manageable, and hopefully, profitable size. Is this an option that Ajax should consider to address its cash flow problem? There are many ways it can do this. It has not been operating very long and there are promising signs on the horizon. Before we consider some options for Ajax, you might want to take a few moments to think about how you would solve Ajax's cash flow problem.

Solutions to the Cash Flow Problem

LEARNING OBJECTIVE 4

Identify some solutions to cash flow problems.

The cash flow difficulties that Ajax is experiencing are typical of many new companies. These problems have three fundamental causes: high growth rates in sales, significant lead/lag relationships in cash inflows and outflows, and undercapitalization. The use of the term "**capitalization**" in this situation refers to how much cash the company has to start with. Start-up companies generally experience rapid growth of sales. This increase in sales requires them to buy or produce more and more inventory as well as to expand their storage or operating capacity. Buying more inventory and expanding capacity both require cash.

Compounding the growth problem is the presence of significant lead/lag relationships between the company's cash inflows and outflows. If there were no lead/lag relationship, then, as long as the product could be sold for more than it cost to produce or buy, there would be no cash flow problem. Most companies, however, do have some significant lead/lag relationships in their cash flows, which are magnified in periods of high growth.

Finally, start-up companies tend to be undercapitalized; that is, they do not have a large pool of cash to start with. When the large cash needs appear, imposed by rapid growth and the lead/lag relationships, the company has no cash reserves to get it through prolonged periods of cash outflows. Start-up companies (as well as other companies in rapid growth phases) will experience cash flow problems at some point. In Ajax's case, the problems create a crisis during the month of April. Solutions to the three causes of Ajax's cash flow problems are discussed in the following subsections.

Growth   One way to solve Ajax's problem is to slow down the sales growth rate. Exhibit 5-8 shows graphically what happens when the rate of growth in sales is 500 units per month rather than 600. All other facts and assumptions are considered unchanged. You can see from the graph that this solves the cash flow problem because the cash balance line does not dip below zero in any month. Cash flows are still negative in some early months, but the balance in cash is sufficient to absorb these cash outflows. Limiting growth may not be the proper response in this case because it may be detrimental to the company in the long run. Limiting growth is likely to divert customers to competitors, and those customers may develop loyalties to those competitors and reduce the company's long-run potential in terms of developing a strong customer base.

CASH FLOW WITH A SLOWER GROWTH STRATEGY

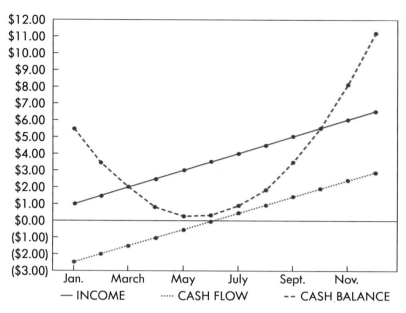

Capitalization A second way to solve the cash problem is to address the undercapital-ization problem; that is, to start with more cash. This larger amount of cash may be obtained in numerous ways. Two typical ways are to issue additional shares (equity) in the company and to borrow the cash (debt). If Ajax issues new shares, the cash flow projections will have to be adjusted to incorporate the additional cash inflow from the issuance and any subsequent outflows for dividends. If money is borrowed, the cash flow projections will have to be adjusted for the initial inflow from the borrowing as well as for the subsequent payments of principal and interest that will occur in the future. Exhibit 5-9 shows what will happen if an additional $2,000 is obtained at the beginning of January from the issuance of shares. For simplicity, it is assumed that there are no dividends. Note, again, that this solves the cash flow problem.

CASH FLOW WITH AN INCREASED CAPITALIZATION STRATEGY

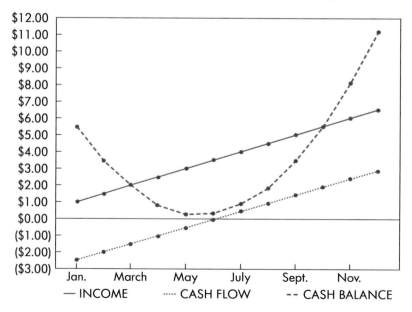

This solution of increased capitalization is not without its own problems. The first is that if shares are issued, the current Ajax shareholders will be giving up control of some portion of their investment in the company, and they may not want to do that. It may also be difficult to find additional investors willing to take the risk of buying company shares. Second, if Ajax attempts to borrow the additional capital, it may not be able to convince a lender that it is worthy of a loan. Lenders are typically very sceptical of new ventures.

Lead/Lag Relationships   The third way to solve Ajax's cash flow problem is to change the lead/lag relationships between the cash inflows and outflows. There are numerous ways to do this. One is to change Ajax's accounts receivable, accounts payable, or inventory policies. Collecting on accounts receivable sooner or selling for cash or via credit card, paying accounts payable later, or reducing the amount of inventory on hand would all reduce the difference between the cash outflow and inflow in a given month. Exhibit 5-10, for example, shows what will happen if the accounts receivable policy is changed to require customers to pay within three weeks rather than one month.

CASH FLOW WITH A CHANGE IN THE LEAD/LAG RELATIONSHIP   EXHIBIT 5-10

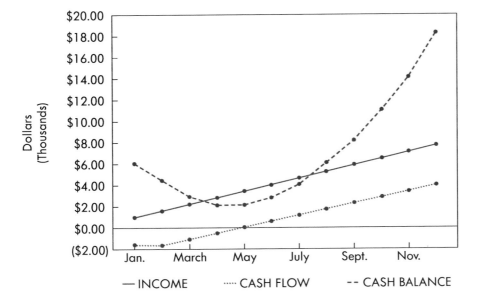

This change would be enough to solve the cash flow problem, assuming everything else remains the same. Of course, everything else may not stay the same. If Ajax institutes this change, it is likely that some customers will no longer do business with it if they can get better payment terms from a competitor. Thus the rate of growth in sales may be affected. Ajax, therefore, may need to make changes in some other assumptions before it can realistically conclude that this will solve its problem. In this case, however, you know from Exhibit 5-8 that slowing the rate of growth will actually help solve the cash flow problem.

In our example, Ajax must pay cash for the inventory that it buys from its supplier. A supplier may be reluctant initially to sell inventory to a new company on credit. The company has no track record on which the supplier can gauge its creditworthiness. Once Ajax has proved to the supplier that it can pay cash for increasing amounts of inventory, the supplier may be willing to grant 30-day credit terms. Establishing this creditworthiness takes time, however, and does not solve Ajax's initial cash flow problem.

Besides changing Ajax's receivables, payables, and inventory policies, there are other ways to affect the lead/lag relationship. Changing either the price or cost of a widget would affect the amounts in the lead/lag relationship and could therefore solve the problem. Remember, however, that changes in these items may also affect other assumptions, such as sales growth.

Intrawest Corp. is a real estate developer. Companies like Intrawest usually have significant lead/lag relationships in that it often takes a considerable length of time to complete a development project and, although units in the development may be sold early in the process, the cash does not begin to flow back to the developer until the project is complete and customers take possession. How is Intrawest dealing with this cash flow situation?

accounting in the news
INTRAWEST'S SLIPPERY SLOPE

Vancouver-based Intrawest Corp. has been growing at a heroic pace. The ski resort developer has an 11% share in the North American market, up from less than 8% in 1999. Development and expansion is taking place on 10 mountains, and there are plans for six more developments in Europe and North America. And now the company's flagship property, Whistler Blackcomb, will host the 2010 Winter Olympics, benefiting from a $460 million upgrade to the Sea-to-Sky highway from Vancouver and the construction of new facilities.

Despite financial reports showing $900 million in EBITDA profit (earnings before interest, taxes, depreciation, and amortization) since 1999, Intrawest has been cash flow negative, outspending its revenue by some $604 million over the last five years, according to Toronto-based Veritas Investment Research. The company has been able to show yearly profits only by capitalizing development costs, delaying the point at which spending has to be accounted for on its income statement. This has resulted in more than $1.1 billion in debt.

In February 2003, the company announced a plan to offload the cost of future resort development to third-party financiers. Intrawest says this arrangement will free up $250 million in cash in fiscal 2004 and reduce overall debt by $300 million, to $825 million.

Source: "Subject: Intrawest Corp., Case Study," by Mark Anderson, *National Post Business Magazine*, January 1, 2004.

To summarize, it is clear that a cash flow statement provides additional information that is not captured by the income statement and balance sheet alone. For a shareholder, manager, or other financial statement user, it is important to understand the relationship between the company's income, its cash-to-cash cycle, and its cash flow statement. Also, understanding how receivables, payables, and inventory policies affect the company's cash flows is extremely important in evaluating its performance. We discuss in greater detail later in the chapter how users interpret cash flow information.

We now turn to the components of cash flow; then we explain the preparation of a cash flow statement. Finally, we explain how the cash flow statement can be used to assess a company's financial health.

THE CASH FLOW STATEMENT

A Short History of the Cash Flow Statement

In 1985, the cash flow statement, then called the statement of changes in financial position, became a true cash flow statement. Prior to 1985, companies could prepare a cash flow statement or a statement of **working capital** flows. Working capital is current assets minus current liabilities. In 1985, companies no longer had a choice; they had to show the changes in cash flows. It was in 1985 that companies were first asked to show the changes in the cash flows through the three activities: operating, financing, and investing.

In 1998, some changes were introduced to the statement. First, the title "cash flow statement" replaced "statement of changes in financial position." As well, the articulation of what to include in operating, financing, and investing activities was more clearly defined. The cash flow statements from real companies and the discussions in this chapter follow the new guidelines.

Definition of Cash and Cash Equivalents

As we have seen above, proper management of cash is one of the critical tasks that managers of all organizations must achieve. Having too little cash on hand results in not being able to pay liabilities and expenses. If this continues, bankruptcy will result. Having too much cash on hand is also not efficient. Cash held in chequing accounts typically earns little or no interest. It is much better to invest excess cash in some kind of temporary investment that will earn interest. Thus, the proper management of cash involves managing cash, short-term borrowings, and temporary investments.

Therefore, in considering cash flows that are to be summarized in the cash flow statement, rather than restricting our consideration to just cash, we must consider the broader concept of cash and cash equivalents, sometimes called the **cash position**. We use the term **cash equivalents** to include the short-term, highly liquid investments that are readily convertible into known amounts of cash. They also must be close enough to maturity that there is little risk of changes in their value due to changes in interest rates. The time frame suggested is three months or less. Items that commonly meet these criteria are Government of Canada treasury bills and demand loans of other companies. A demand loan is payable on demand, which means that it is very liquid. Cash equivalents also include short-term borrowings that companies use to cover their cash shortages for short periods of time, such as lines of credit. However, a normal short-term bank loan would not be called a cash equivalent. Rather, it would be a financing activity.

Components of Cash Flows

LEARNING OBJECTIVE 5

Identify the three major activities disclosed in the cash flow statement and describe the components of each activity.

In discussing the components of cash flows, we are going back to Chapter 1, where we discussed the three components of managing any business. First, you must find sufficient long-term financing from investments by shareholders or long-term borrowings to provide sufficient capitalization for the business. Next you must invest these funds in assets that you will use to produce revenues and profits. Finally, you must operate the business, carrying on the revenue-generating activities for which the company was established.

The basic format of the cash flow statement summarizes all the cash flows into these three groups of activities. The cash flow statement for **Le Château Inc.** for the year ended January 31, 2004, and January 25, 2003, is included in Appendix A at the end of the book and included here as Exhibit 5-11 to facilitate discussion of the cash flow statement. We will use it as an example. Note that the cash flow statement is divided into the three activities: Operating Activities, with a net cash inflow of $19,158 thousand for 2004; Financing Activities, with a net cash inflow of $2,307 thousand for 2004; and Investing Activities, with a net cash outflow of $14,438 thousand for 2004. The net cash inflow for 2004 is $7,027 thousand. The final section of the cash flow statement shows how this net cash inflow, when added to the cash position at the beginning of the year of $15,040 thousand, results in a cash position of $22,067 thousand at year end. Le Château defines its cash equivalents as "restricted to investments that are readily convertible into a known amount of cash, that are subject to minimal risk of changes in value and which have a maturity of three months or less at acquisition" (Note 1, in the notes to the financial statements). At the bottom of the cash flow statement, Le Château includes supplementary information about interest paid during the year ($339 thousand) and income taxes paid during the year ($7,473 thousand). These two additional disclosures enable users to better understand the impact of these two items on cash flow. In summary, the cash flow statement summarizes all the cash flows for 2004 that resulted in the increase in cash position during the year.

FINANCING ACTIVITIES

Financing activities are the activities involved in obtaining resources from shareholders and from lenders, and repaying those shareholders and lenders. Transactions classified as financing typically involve balance sheet accounts associated with equity capital and with short- and long-term borrowing. Typical cash inflows would come from issuing shares, bonds, mortgages, notes, and other borrowings. Outflows include dividends paid to shareholders, repurchase of shares, and repayment of the principal of any debt obligation.

A special word is needed about interest and dividends. A company pays interest to lenders in exchange for the use of their money. Shareholders are repaid with dividends. Interest expense is associated with a debt, which is a financing activity, but because interest is used in the determination of net income, interest payments are included in the operating section. Dividends, on the other hand, are not used in the determination of net income. They are therefore included in the financing section. Some analysts (particularly bank lenders) would prefer, in their own analyses, to show the interest outflow in the financing section. They can accomplish this quite easily by simply moving the interest from the operating section to the financing section. This can readily be done because companies are required to disclose the

LE CHÂTEAU INC. 2003 ANNUAL REPORT

EXHIBIT 5-11

CONSOLIDATED STATEMENTS OF CASH FLOWS

Year ended January 31, 2004
[With comparative figures for the year ended January 25, 2003]
[In thousands of dollars]

	2004 $	2003 $
OPERATING ACTIVITIES		
Net earnings	**10,648**	7,562
Adjustments to determine net cash from operating activities		
Depreciation and amortization	**7,745**	6,937
Write-off of fixed assets	**511**	281
Amortization of deferred lease inducements	**(463)**	(393)
Future income taxes	**(130)**	116
	18,311	14,503
Net change in non-cash working capital items related to operations *[note 13]*	**847**	1,526
Cash flows from operating activities	**19,158**	16,029
FINANCING ACTIVITIES		
Repayment of loan to director	**—**	120
Proceeds of capital leases	**5,620**	—
Repayment of capital lease obligations	**(1,355)**	(1,537)
Proceeds of long-term debt	**—**	2,500
Repayment of long-term debt	**(1,483)**	(1,210)
Deferred lease inducements	**481**	82
Issue of capital stock	**1,094**	235
Dividends paid	**(2,050)**	(1,990)
Cash flows from financing activities	**2,307**	(1,800)
INVESTING ACTIVITIES		
Additions to fixed assets	**(14,438)**	(9,019)
Cash flows from investing activities	**(14,438)**	(9,019)
Increase in cash and cash equivalents	**7,027**	5,210
Cash and cash equivalents, beginning of year	**15,040**	9,830
Cash and cash equivalents, end of year	**22,067**	15,040
Supplementary information:		
Interest paid during the year	**339**	350
Income taxes paid during the year, net	**7,473**	3,555

See accompanying notes

amount of cash used for interest expense. Le Château included it as supplementary information at the bottom of the cash flow statement.

In the cash flow statement of Le Château, the items included in 2004 in the financing activities section are fairly typical.

Proceeds of capital leases: inflow of $5,620 thousand; repayment of capital lease obligations: outflow of $1,355 thousand; repayment of long-term debt: outflow of $1,483 thousand; deferred lease inducement: inflow of $481 thousand; issue of capital stock: inflow of $1,094 thousand; and dividends paid: outflow of $2,050 thousand.

Le Château used both the debt and the issuance of shares as ways of raising additional cash in both 2004 and 2003. It has also been paying off substantial amounts of its long-term debt each year. In both 2004 and 2003, it paid dividends of $2,050 thousand and $1,990 thousand respectively. This is a sign of stability in a company. Investors who are interested in an annual dividend as a form of income would look for a company such as Le Château, which generates a positive cash flow and pays a regular dividend.

AN INTERNATIONAL PERSPECTIVE

Reports from Other Countries

The categorization of cash flows under Canadian GAAP is somewhat different from that in other countries. In the UK, for instance, cash flows are categorized under seven standard headings:

>Operating activities
>Returns on investments and servicing of finance
>Taxation
>Capital expenditures and financial investment
>Acquisition and disposals
>Equity dividends paid
>Management of liquid resources
>Financing

Cash is defined as "cash in hand and deposits repayable on demand at any qualifying institution less overdrafts from any qualifying institution repayable on demand."

Source: Financial Reporting Standards (FRS) 1: Cash Flow Statements, revised 1996.

INVESTING ACTIVITIES

Transactions classified as **investing activities** typically involve balance sheet accounts classified as long-term assets. Typical transactions in this section would be investments in property, plant, and equipment and its subsequent sale or disposal, as well as investments in long-term marketable securities. The purchase or sale of any short-term investments that are not classified as cash equivalents would also be included in the investing section. In Le Château's cash flow statement, there is only one item.

Additions to fixed assets: an outflow of $14,438 thousand.

Note that Le Château had an outflow of cash for investment activities in 2004 and 2003. This is typical of companies. Usually, as companies are going through the normal process of replacing long-lived assets, they spend more for the new assets than they get for selling the old ones. This usually results in a net cash outflow for investing activities.

Before moving on to operating activities, we want to give you some more information about the acquisition of capital assets and investments. The amounts you see reported on the cash flow statement for the acquisition of capital assets and investments represent the amount of cash equivalents that was used by the company in the acquisition. For example, assume a company purchased a piece of land with a building for $500,000. The company paid 25% down ($125,000) and assumed a long-term mortgage for the balance ($375,000). The cash flow statement would only show the acquisition cash outflow of $125,000 under investing activities. Neither the remaining $375,000 of the acquisition cost nor the $375,000 representing the new mortgage would appear on the cash flow statement because cash did not flow in or out for the $375,000. Because the information about the new debt and a portion of the information about the new acquisition do not appear on the cash flow statement, users need to be very vigilant about examining the assets and liabilities on the balance sheet and reading the notes to the financial statements to find information like this that is not specifically reported on one of the financial statements.

OPERATING ACTIVITIES

Operating activities include all other cash transactions not covered by financing or investing activities. The operating section typically includes the cash flows that result directly from the sale of goods and services to customers. Transactions classified as operating activities typically involve balance sheet accounts classified as current assets and current liabilities. The major cash inflow is from the collection of revenues from customers. The major cash outflow is from payments to suppliers (for inventory, materials, labour, etc.). As mentioned earlier in the Financing Activities section in this chapter, interest payments are also included in this section of the cash flow statement. One other cash flow worth noting in the operating section is related to taxes. Even though taxes are affected by all three types of activity, the net results of taxes are reported in the operating section of the cash flow statement.

A complete record of the gross amount of cash coming into the company from operating activities would show the total amount of cash received from revenues and collections from customers as inflows, and the total amount of cash paid out to suppliers for expenses and accounts payable as outflows. This approach, called the **direct approach**, is theoretically very informative, and its use is encouraged by the *CICA Handbook*. However, it is rarely used in Canada in the cash flow statement. When we prepared the cash flow statement for Demo Retail Company Ltd. in Chapter 2, we used the direct approach. The method normally used in published cash flow statements is the **indirect approach**. Le Château uses the indirect approach. Note that these two approaches differ only in the format and content of the Operating Activities section. The Investing and Financing Activities sections are the same for both approaches.

The indirect approach does not report the full gross cash flows from operating activities; instead, it shows only the net cash flows. Using the indirect approach, the operating section starts with reported net income and then shows adjustments to net income to arrive at the net cash flows from operations. The adjustments are in two groups. The first group includes items from the income statement that do not involve cash flows. In the Le Château cash flow statement, note that the net income is adjusted by the items listed under the heading "Adjustments to determine net cash from operating activities." The items in this group are depreciation and amortization, write-off of fixed assets, amortization of deferred lease inducements, and future income taxes. Depreciation and amortization do not involve a cash payment the way other expenses such as wages do. These expenses merely involve recognizing the use of a long-term asset. The cash outflow related to that asset occurred when the asset was purchased, which probably happened several years ago and was initially reported in the Investing Section of the cash flow statement as an outflow of cash. As a result of recognizing depreciation and amortization, the net income figure has been reduced by the amount of the expense that does not represent a current cash outflow. Note the journal entries in the following example.

When the asset was purchased:

Equipment (A)	10,000	
Cash (A)		10,000

As the asset is used to generate revenue:

Amortization expense (SE)	1,000	
Accumulated amortization (XA)		1,000

There was an outflow when the asset was purchased, but each time it is amortized there is no cash effect. The depreciation and amortization expenses are thus added back to net income to determine the actual net cash flows from operating activities for the year. The adding back of future income taxes is similar in nature. On the income statement, the income tax expense represents the amount of tax that will likely have to be paid on the revenues less expenses that are recognized in the current period. All of those income taxes may not be owed to the Canada Revenue Agency (CRA) in the current year, because the CRA rules about recognition are not always the same as those in accounting. Income tax expense that is deducted to arrive at net income is the amount owed for this year (which is probably paid, and thus is a cash outflow) plus the amount that will be owed in future years (the future income taxes). To arrive at the net cash flow from operating activities, it is necessary to add the future income taxes to the net income amount because they do not represent a cash outflow yet. For now, we are going to leave aside explaining the write-off of fixed assets.

The second group involves adjustments for various current assets and liabilities to convert revenue and expense amounts included on the income statement to their cash values. Adjustments in the second group are needed because all revenues and expenses do not result in immediate cash flows. For example, if accounts receivable increases, this means that not all the revenues have been collected in cash; some will be collected later. Thus Le Château's cash flow statement shows an adjustment for net change in non-cash working capital items related to operations of $847 thousand. Remember that working capital is current assets minus current liabilities. If we look at Note 13 referred to on the cash flow statement, the 2004 changes in the following current assets and liabilities are identified (in thousands).

Accounts receivable and prepaid expenses	$ (225)
Inventories	(593)
Accounts payable and accrued liabilities	2,539
Income taxes payable	(874)
	$ 847

On Le Château's balance sheet in Appendix A at the end of the book, the accounts receivable and prepaid expenses amount has increased from $1,169 thousand in 2003 to $1,394 thousand in 2004, an increase of $225 thousand. The maximum amount of cash that could have been collected from the sales activity would have been the accounts receivable that was there at the beginning of the year plus all the sales from the current year. If there are accounts receivable at the end of the year, some of that maximum amount has not been collected yet. In the case of Le Château, $225 thousand less than the sales amount reported on the income statement was collected during the year. More accounts receivable are owed at the end of the year than were owed at the beginning of the year. The cash flow is represented by the following formula.

Beginning A/R + Sales − Ending A/R = Cash Flow from Sales

When the amounts from Le Château's financial statements are slotted into this formula, the following emerges.

$1,169 thousand + $226,766 thousand − $1,394 thousand = $226,541 thousand

The cash flow from sales is $225 thousand less than the sales amount ($226,541 thousand − $226,766 thousand). To summarize, when there is an increase in accounts receivable over the year, the sales figure that is included in the income statement does not represent the amount of cash flow from sales. It is too large. Thus an increase in accounts receivable is deducted from the net income amount in order to determine the cash flow from operations.

Changes in other current assets and liabilities included in this second group follow similar reasoning. An increase in non-cash current assets reflects a decrease in the amount of cash inflow from operating activities. A decrease in non-cash current assets reflects an increase in the amount of cash inflow or a net cash inflow from operating activities. An increase in current liabilities such as accounts payable means that less cash was used to pay down the liabilities than is reflected in the expenses on the income statement. This, therefore, represents a saving or cash inflow adjustment. A decrease in current liabilities indicates that more cash was used to pay the expenses during the year than is reflected in the expenses on the income statement. This is a cash outflow and is the same as a decrease in cash from operations. The following chart should help you learn whether to add or subtract the change in the current assets and liabilities.

	Change in the Current Account	
	Increase	Decrease
Current Assets	Subtract	Add
Current Liability	Add	Subtract

Referring to Note 13 from Le Château's financial statements, the accounts receivable and prepaid expenses, inventories, and income taxes payable are negative. This means that the accounts receivable and prepaid expenses and inventories increased, and the income taxes payable decreased. The accounts payable and accrued liabilities are positive. This means that they increased. You can verify this by calculating the changes in these accounts on the balance sheet in Appendix A at the end of the book.

AN INTERNATIONAL PERSPECTIVE

Reports from Other Countries

NAFTA Facts

United States   A cash flow statement is required and can be prepared using either the direct or indirect approach. As in Canada, the indirect approach is used most often. Cash flows are segregated into operating, investing, and financing activities. The disclosure requirements in the United States are very similar to those required in Canada under the 1998 changes.

Mexico   The statement of changes in financial position is typically presented as a cash flow statement. Mexican GAAP requires that the financial statements be adjusted for the effect of inflation. A portion of inflation adjustment is typically shown in the operating section, and another portion due to adjustments to the company's debt balances is shown in the financing section.

PREPARATION OF THE CASH FLOW STATEMENT

LEARNING OBJECTIVE 6

Prepare a cash flow statement from a company's balance sheets and income statement.

To illustrate the preparation of a cash flow statement, a new hypothetical example will be used. Exhibit 5-12 shows the balance sheet for Huskies Industries Ltd. for the year ended December 31, 2006. Exhibit 5-13 shows the income statement for Huskies Industries for the same period.

EXHIBIT 5-12   **HUSKIES INDUSTRIES LTD.**

Balance Sheet

	Dec. 31, 2006	Dec. 31, 2005
Cash	$ 6,050	$ 19,500
Accounts receivable	10,000	20,000
Inventory	40,000	30,000
Prepaid rent	600	500
Total current assets	56,650	70,000
Property, plant, and equipment	159,000	100,000
Accumulated amortization	(69,200)	(50,000)
Net capital assets	89,800	50,000
Total assets	$146,450	$120,000
Accounts payable	$ 11,000	$ 6,000
Notes payable	200	100
Accrued salaries	400	300
Dividends payable	470	300
Total current liabilities	12,070	6,700
Bonds payable	46,000	40,000
Total liabilities	58,070	46,700
Common shares	29,000	25,000
Retained earnings	59,380	48,300
Total shareholders' equity	88,380	73,300
Total liabilities and shareholders' equity	$146,450	$120,000

HUSKIES INDUSTRIES LTD.

EXHIBIT 5-13

Income Statement
For the year ended December 31, 2006

Sales revenue		$130,000
Cost of goods sold		80,000
Gross profit margin		50,000
Rent expense	$ 7,100	
Miscellaneous cash expenses	600	
Amortization	20,000	
Salaries expense	9,600	
Total expenses		37,300
Income from operations		12,700
Gain on sale of property, plant, and equipment		300
Income before income tax		13,000
Income tax		520
Net income		$ 12,480

In addition to the balance sheet and income statement, the following information applies to the transactions of Huskies Industries Ltd. for 2006.

1. Huskies Industries is a retailer and, as such, all amounts added to its inventory reflect purchases at wholesale prices. All inventory is purchased on credit from suppliers.

2. Huskies Industries sells its products to customers on credit. There are no cash sales.

3. During the year, Huskies Industries sold (for $500 in cash) equipment that had an original cost of $1,000 and a book value of $200, thus recording a gain on sale of $300.

4. Huskies Industries borrowed an additional $8,000 by issuing bonds in 2006.

5. Notes payable were used during 2006 for short-term financing.

T Account Approach

Our objective is to construct a cash flow statement from the information given above, which is typical of most companies, although simplified for illustrative purposes. We want to determine all the cash flows that would have occurred to produce the balances shown above. Several methods can be used to determine the underlying cash flows, but all of them require, at a minimum, a balance sheet showing balances at the beginning and end of the year, plus an income statement for the current year. Some additional information may be required.

Two common methods to determine the underlying cash flows are a set of T accounts or a work sheet. The T account approach will be used here, but remember that a work sheet could also be used for the same task. Also, we will show the preparation of a cash flow statement using only the indirect approach, as virtually all published cash flow statements use this format. For completeness, we have included the T account preparation of the cash flow statement using the direct approach on the text companion website.

**Cash Flow
Statement:
Direct Approach**

Exhibit 5-14 shows the set-up of the T account approach. Note that a large T account has been included for cash because the objective of this exercise is to reconstruct all the transactions that affected cash in this account. All the accounts from the balance sheet are listed, including their beginning and ending balances. The objective is to reconstruct the transactions that occurred during 2006 and to include as much detail as possible regarding the nature of the cash transactions. Within the cash account, the transactions are categorized into the three basic activities discussed above: operating, financing, and investing activities. Note that as we start to reconstruct the transactions, we are working outside the formal company records. The transactions that we are reconstructing already occurred during the year and were recorded in the accounting system as isolated transactions. We are trying to determine what the aggregate of those transactions is and how they are related to cash.

EXHIBIT 5-14

HUSKIES INDUSTRIES LTD.

Cash Flow T Accounts

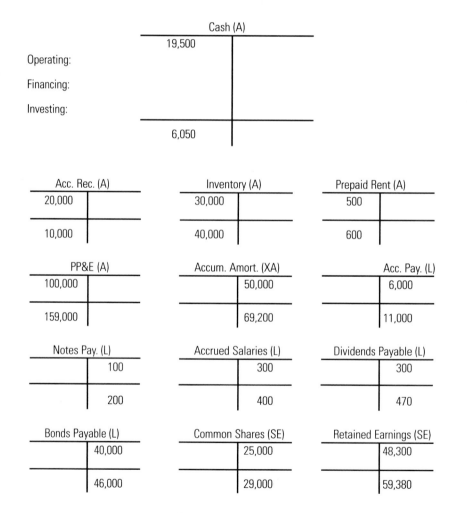

In Exhibit 5-15, the analysis for the cash flow statement has been reconstructed for 2002. The entries in the T accounts have been given transaction numbers and each is discussed in its section.

HUSKIES INDUSTRIES LTD.

EXHIBIT 5-15

Cash Flow T Accounts

Cash (A)

		19,500			
Operating:					
Net income	(1)	12,480	10,000	(3)	Increase in inventory
Decrease in A/R	(2)	10,000	100	(4)	Increase in ppd. rent
Increase in A/P	(5)	5,000	300	(8)	Gain on sale of equip.
Incr. in acc. sal.	(6)	100			
Amortization	(7)	20,000			
Financing:					
Proceeds from note	(10)	100	2,000	(12)	Prepay. of bond
Proceeds from bond	(11)	8,000	1,230	(15)	Pay. of dividends
Issue of shares	(13)	4,000			
Investing:					
Sale of equip.	(8)	500	60,000	(9)	Purchase of PP&E
		6,050			

Acc. Rec. (A)

20,000	
	10,000 (2)
10,000	

Inventory (A)

30,000	
(3) 10,000	
40,000	

Prepaid Rent (A)

500	
(4) 100	
600	

PP&E (A)

100,000	
(9) 60,000	1,000 (8)
159,000	

Accum. Amort. (XA)

	50,000
(8) 800	20,000 (7)
	69,200

Acc. Pay. (L)

	6,000
	5,000 (5)
	11,000

Notes Pay. (L)

	100
	100 (10)
	200

Accrued Salaries (L)

	300
	100 (6)
	400

Dividends Payable (L)

	300
(15) 1,230	1,400 (14)
	470

Bonds Payable (L)

	40,000
(12) 2,000	8,000 (11)
	46,000

Common Shares (SE)

	25,000
	4,000 (13)
	29,000

Retained Earnings (SE)

	48,300
(14) 1,400	12,480 (1)
	59,380

In the indirect approach, the operating activities section is constructed by starting with net income and then reconciling it to its net cash flow equivalent. In this approach, net income is initially assumed to increase cash by the amount of the net income (or decrease cash by the amount of a net loss). As we have already discussed, this is not strictly true because many of the items in income do not represent cash flows. For example, as we discussed on pages 289 and 290, amortization has no effect on cash. The remaining entries in the operating section, except for the gain on the sale of equipment, use the current asset and liability accounts to adjust all the items that comprise the net income to the amount of the cash flows that actually occurred.

In using the T account method, it is very convenient to reconstruct the summary journal entries that would have been recorded for each account to determine the resulting net cash flows. These reconstructed journal entries are not essential, but they are a convenient method of determining what happened. Remember that they are only intended for us to understand what occurred; they are not recorded in the accounting system. For example, the cash impact of net income on cash is as follows.

(1) The entry is:

Cash (Operating) (A)	12,480	
Retained Earnings (SE)		12,480

When all the net income is assumed to increase cash, one of the adjustments that must be made results from the assumption that all the revenues included in net income are collected in cash. The change in the balance of accounts receivable shows the net effect of the difference between the sales revenue recorded during the period and the cash collected from customers.

In the case of Huskies Industries, the accounts receivable balance decreased during the year, which means that there were more collections (credit entries to the accounts receivable account) than sales (debit entries to the accounts receivable account). This, in turn, means that Huskies collected more cash than its sales figure shows. The adjustment to the cash account, therefore, shows an increase in cash over that represented by the revenues included in net income. In effect, this adjustment adds $10,000 to the revenues shown of $130,000 and is included in net income to produce a net figure of $140,000 in cash received from customers as follows.

Sales revenues	$130,000
Decrease in accounts receivable	10,000
Cash collections from sales	$140,000

The net or summary entry to represent this adjustment is as follows.

(2) The entry is:

Cash (Operating) (A)	10,000	
Accounts receivable (A)		10,000

A second assumption that requires an adjustment is that the cost of goods sold reduced cash during the period by the same amount. There are two reasons why this may be incorrect. The first is that the goods sold, represented by the amounts shown in cost of goods sold, may have come from the beginning inventory (i.e., purchases that were made last year) and may not have required an outflow of cash this year (assuming the accounts payable associated with the inventory purchased were paid last year). The change in the balance of inventory provides information about this potential adjustment.

A second reason would be the assumption that purchases of inventory during the period resulted in accounts payable, assuming all purchases are bought on credit.

Therefore, if these accounts were not paid as at year end, the expenses reported would not yet have resulted in cash outflows. The effects of both these factors can be corrected by adjusting the net income number by the net change in the inventory balance and the net change in the accounts payable balance. The effect of these two entries is to adjust the cost of goods sold amount included in the net income ($80,000) to its cash equivalent of cash paid to suppliers ($85,000) as follows.

Cost of goods sold as reported (assumed cash outflow)	($80,000)
Increase in inventory (requiring extra cash outflow)	(10,000)
Increase in accounts payable (meaning less cash paid out)	5,000
Actual cash paid to suppliers	($85,000)

The entries to represent these adjustments are as follows.

(3) and (5) The entries are:
Inventory (A)	10,000	
Cash (Operating) (A)		10,000
Cash (Operating) (A)	5,000	
Accounts payable (L)		5,000

Two other expenses on the income statement have corresponding current assets or liabilities: rent expense (prepaid rent) and salaries expense (accrued salaries). Since there is prepaid rent on the balance sheet, Huskies evidently prepays its rent. The increase in the prepaid rent ($100) indicates that more cash was paid out than is reflected in the rent expense. The entry to represent this adjustment is as follows.

(4) The entry is:
Prepaid rent (A)	100	
Cash (Operating) (A)		100

The salaries expense account has a related liability account, accrued salaries. The increase in accrued salaries ($100) means that Huskies reduced the outflow of cash by owing more to employees at the end of the year than it owed at the beginning. The salaries expense on the income statement is $100 larger than the actual cash outflow for salaries. The entry to represent this adjustment is as follows.

(6) The entry is:
Cash (Operating) (A)	100	
Accrued salaries (L)		100

A third type of adjustment results from the assumption that all other expenses represent cash outflows. Amortization expense is not a cash expense. Amortization is merely a recognition that part of the long-term assets are used up each year, but no cash flows are associated with amortization expense. The associated cash flow occurred years before when the assets were purchased. Therefore, because amortization expense is included in calculating net income and results in a decrease in net income, its effect must be removed by adding it back to net income to show the net income figure that would have resulted if we had not included amortization expense.

One caveat at this point: because this adjustment is on the debit side of the cash account, it looks as though amortization is a source of cash. This is not true.

Cash collections from customers are the source of cash from operations. It is only because the indirect method is attempting to correct the misstatements made by assuming that all net income increases cash that this item appears as if it were a source of cash. Many analysts approximate the cash from a company's operations by adding amortization to its net income. This is a quick and reasonably close approximation to cash received from operations. However, this method ignores the adjustments due to the other accounts that are shown in Exhibit 5-15.

The entry to adjust for amortization is as follows.

(7) The entry is:

Cash (Operating) (A)	20,000	
Accumulated amortization (XA)		20,000

The last adjustment in the operating section adjusts the net income number for the gain from the sale of the equipment. The $300 gain shown in income assumes that $300 was received in cash. However, point 3 from the additional information, provided at the outset of the example, indicated that $500 cash was received on the disposal of the equipment. Thus the effect on cash is $500, not $300. Therefore, making the assumption that the $300 increase in the net income figure represents the cash inflow is not correct.

The *original* entry to record the sale was as follows.

Cash (A)	500	
Accumulated amortization (XA)	800	
PP&E (A)		1,000
Gain on sale of equipment (SE)		300

The second problem is that, even if this were the right amount, it would be reported in the wrong section of the cash flow statement. Companies invest in property, plant, and equipment, so cash flows resulting from disposals of property, plant, and equipment are also investing (or, more properly, disinvesting) activities. These are not operating cash flows. The entry to correct for these two misstatements requires two adjustments. It adjusts the amount of cash that actually was received, and it corrects the activity that was affected. The entry to represent these two items is as follows.

(8) The entry is:

Cash (Investing) (A)	500	
Accumulated amortization (XA)	800	
Cash (Operating) (A)		300
PP&E (A)		1,000

Remember when we were discussing Le Château's cash flow statement earlier? In the operating activities section, it had included a write-off of fixed assets as part of its adjustments for non-cash items included in net earnings. The write-off means that the carrying value of the fixed assets in the system was higher than the value of the expected future recoveries from the use of the assets. The company therefore reduced the value of the assets in the accounting system. No cash was involved although it was reported on the income statement as a loss, which reduced the net income. Because no cash was involved, it would be added back to the net income amount under operating activities but it would not be included at all in the investing activities.

The remaining items adjust for the cash flows that resulted from the financing and investing activities. To determine the cash flows for financing and investing activities, look for changes in long-term assets, financing liabilities (both short- and long-term), and shareholders' equity accounts. The amount of the purchases of new property, plant, and equipment can be determined by considering the beginning and ending balances in the property, plant, and equipment summary account and the credit entry made to this account in entry (8). Note that to reach the ending balance of $159,000 an additional debit of $60,000 is needed. We assume that additional assets were purchased for cash. This cash outflow is shown in the investing section. The entry is represented as follows.

(9) The entry is:

PP&E (A)	60,000	
Cash (Investing) (A)		60,000

The other accounts that still have changes that remain to be explained at this point are the notes payable, dividends payable, bonds payable, common shares, and retained earnings accounts. Using the extra information provided, an analysis is now made of each of these accounts.

The entry for notes payable is a net entry. It is net because not enough information is given to determine how many new notes were issued for cash or how many were retired (paid off by paying cash). All that is known is the net change in the notes payable account. The net change indicates that more notes were issued during this period than were retired because the balance in the account increased. This net effect is then shown as increasing the notes payable account. The net cash inflow appears in the financing section. The entry is represented as follows.

(10) The entry is:

Cash (Financing) (A)	100	
Notes payable (L)		100

Entry (11) for the bonds payable is similar to that in (10) except that, in this case, the additional information indicated that there was $8,000 in new long-term borrowings this year. Therefore, there would be a new credit of $8,000 to this account. However, the balance in this account only increased by $6,000. It can, therefore, be inferred that $2,000 worth of bonds were paid off during the year. The entries are represented as follows.

(11) The entry is:

Cash (Financing) (A)	8,000	
Bonds payable (L)		8,000

(12) The entry is:

Bonds payable (L)	2,000	
Cash (Financing) (A)		2,000

In the common shares account, credits represent a new issuance of shares, and debits represent a repurchase of shares. Again, because there is no explicit information that there were new issuances or repurchases, you can only infer the net effect. The net effect is that the account increased, indicating that more shares were issued than were repurchased. The entry is represented as follows.

(13) The entry is:

Cash (Financing)(A)	4,000	
Common shares (SE)		4,000

Because all the income statement transactions have now been explained, we can turn our attention to the retained earnings account to determine if the entire change in this account has been explained. The account needs an additional debit of $1,400 to explain the change in the balance. The logical assumption about this debit is that it represents the dividends declared during the period. The entry is represented as follows.

(14) The entry is:

Retained earnings (SE)	1,400	
Dividends payable (L)		1,400

When dividends are declared, they become legally payable, but there may be a lag between the time they are declared and the time they are paid. Therefore, the credit side of entry (14) is to a dividend payable account. The cash entry for dividends takes into consideration the change in the balance of the dividends payable account. The balance in the dividends payable account probably reflects the last quarter's dividend, which has yet to be paid. The entry is represented as follows.

(15) The entry is:

Dividends payable (L)	1,230	
Cash (Financing) (A)		1,230

Entry (15) completes the cash flow analysis. All the net changes in the balance sheet accounts have been explained. The cash account now contains all the information necessary to produce a cash flow statement. The net cash flows from the three types of activities, as taken from the Cash T account, are as follows.

HUSKIES INDUSTRIES LTD.

Cash Flow Statement
For the Year Ended December 31, 2006

Operating activities		
Net income	$ 12,480	
Add (deduct) items not representing cash flows:		
Amortization	20,000	
Gain on Disposal	(300)	
Adjustments for the effect of changes in non-cash working capital items:		
Decrease in Accounts Receivable	10,000	
Increase in Inventory	(10,000)	
Increase in Prepaid Rent	(100)	
Increase in Accounts Payable	5,000	
Increase in Salaries Payable	100	
Cash from operating activities		$ 37,180

Financing activities		
Issue of Notes Payable	$ 100	
Issue of Common Shares	4,000	
Issue of Bonds Payable	8,000	
Payment of Bonds Payable	(2,000)	
Payment of Dividends	(1,230)	
Cash from financing activities		8,870
Investing activities		
Purchase of Property, Plant, and Equipment	($60,000)	
Sale of Property, Plant, and Equipment	500	
Cash used for investing activities		(59,500)
Decrease in Cash		(13,450)
Cash—beginning of the year		19,500
Cash—end of the year		$ 6,050
Supplementary information:		
Cash used for income taxes		$520

The information from the Cash T accounts was used to prepare a proper cash flow statement. The totals of the cash flows from the three types of activities, a net cash outflow of $13,450 ($37,180 + $8,870 − $59,500 = ($13,450)), must be the same as the net change in cash for the year, a $13,450 reduction ($19,500 − $6,050 = $13,450), which it is. Although the cash flow statement is technically finished with the Decrease in Cash amount, most companies will add the two lines to the statement about the beginning and ending balances in cash so that users can more easily verify the change in cash. As well, they often add the supplementary information about the amount of cash used for interest and income taxes. We had no information about interest but were able to include information about the income taxes. In our example, we had cash but no cash equivalents. Many companies have cash equivalents added (or subtracted if they happen to be liabilities) to the cash to arrive at a change in cash and cash equivalents. Such companies must inform users as to which accounts are used for cash equivalents.

HELPFUL HINT

Remember that debits in the cash account represent sources or inflows of cash, and credits represent uses or outflows of cash. The formal cash flow statement shows the operating, investing, and financing activities separately.

INTERPRETATION OF CASH FLOW INFORMATION

Once the cash flow statement has been prepared, users will want to interpret what the statement tells them about the company. While many users will be interested in what has happened to cash in the current period, they are likely to be more interested in predicting the company's future cash flows. A bank loan officer, for example, wants to be sure that, if money is loaned to the company, the company will be able to pay it back. A stock analyst, on the other hand, will want to know what the cash flows will be over a long period of time to ensure an adequate return on the investment in shares. Users interested in the company's future will try to decide which cash flows will continue in the future and which will not.

LEARNING OBJECTIVE 7

Provide a basic analysis of a company's financial health using a cash flow statement.

In addition to deciding which cash flows are likely to continue, users will want to make sure that cash from continuing operations is sufficient over the long run to pay for the continuing investing and financing activities. There is a limit to the cash inflows that can be achieved from investing and financing activities. Investing inflows are limited by the kinds of returns that can be earned from investments in long-term assets and the level of investment by the company. The financing inflows are limited by the willingness of lenders and investors to invest their money in the company. At some level of debt, the company becomes so risky that no lender will agree to lend more. Because the inflows from investing and financing are limited, the company, if it is to remain in business, must generate sufficient cash inflow from operating activities to pay the interest and dividends on the financing activities and to continue investing at appropriate levels in property, plant, and equipment and other long-term assets.

Huskies Industries, as an example, generated $37,180 from operations. Assuming that these are continuing operations (as opposed to discontinued operations) and that Huskies is in a fairly stable industry, you would expect this amount of cash flow to continue into the future. One way to evaluate this is to look at the trend in cash flow from operations over the last five years to see how stable this figure is. The next question to address is whether this flow is sufficient to cover the continuing cash needs of Huskies.

If you look at the uses of cash in the investing and financing sections, you will see that Huskies spent $60,000 to buy new equipment, $1,230 to pay dividends, and $2,000 to pay off debt. It is likely that purchasing new property, plant, and equipment will be a continuing need because buildings and equipment wear out over time. But does the company buy $60,000 in property, plant, and equipment every year, or is this year's purchase larger (or smaller) than usual? If Huskies buys $60,000 every year, you could quickly conclude that the cash from operations will not be sufficient in the long run to pay for this one need, not to mention other needs. If, however, Huskies has this large need only once every three years and if, in the other two years, the purchases are, say, $15,000, then the average amount of property, plant, and equipment purchased is $30,000 per year [($60,000 + 15,000 + 15,000) ÷ 3 = $30,000]. Cash flow from operations would be sufficient to pay for this need, with $10,000 left over to pay for other needs. Again, this can be learned by looking at the trend in property, plant, and equipment spending over the last five years to determine the average spending pattern.

Once started, the payment of dividends is generally a continuing need. Companies are reluctant to stop or reduce the payment of dividends because such action sends a negative signal to the market about their future profitability. The amount of dividends paid, of course, is affected by the number of shares outstanding. If there was an additional issuance of shares in a given year, some growth in the total amount of dividend payments would be expected. Huskies is, in fact, in this position. New shares were issued in 2006, and this could mean more dividends paid in future years.

The repayment of debt is another generally continuing item, but it is not dependent on cash from operations. Most companies carry a certain amount of debt. The level of debt is sometimes measured by comparing the dollar amount of debt on the balance sheet with the total amount of debt plus shareholders' equity. This measure is called a **debt/equity ratio**.

$$\text{Debt/Equity ratio} = \frac{\text{Debt}}{\text{Debt} + \text{Shareholders' Equity}}$$

For Huskies, this ratio at year end was $58,070 ÷ $146,450 = 39.7%. This measure indicates that 39.7% of Huskies' total financing is in the form of debt. As will be discussed in Chapter 12, there is a theoretical optimal level of debt that will maximize the return to shareholders. Most companies try to maintain this optimal level of debt. Therefore, if some debt must be paid off in a given year (which would lower the debt/equity ratio), it is generally replaced by a new borrowing (which would bring the debt/equity ratio back to its original value). This process of replacing old debt with new debt is sometimes called the rollover of debt. In the cash flow statement, this type of transaction would show up as both an inflow of cash and an outflow of cash in the financing section. If the financing activities involve short-term debt like the note payable used by Huskies, it is acceptable to show the net cash flow rather than the inflows and outflows separately.

With regard to debt, Huskies did pay off some long-term debt but at the same time borrowed additional long-term debt, increasing the long-term borrowings by $6,000. It may be that Huskies saw an opportunity to acquire long-term debt at acceptable interest rates. Huskies also took out some additional short-term borrowings to finance the company. Recognize that this short-term debt will probably require a cash payoff in a relatively short period of time, whereas the long-term borrowing will require cash payments over a longer period. If the company has some short-term cash inflow shortages, short-term debt can be a difficult problem. As the reader of the financial statements, you should have some understanding of how soon a company's debt comes due because this will affect its need for cash. In the notes to the financial statements, companies usually describe their borrowings quite extensively, including information about interest rates and due dates.

In addition to the borrowing, Huskies generated cash from two other sources: the sale of equipment and the issuance of common shares. Neither of these is considered a continuing source of cash. In addition, the inflow of cash from the sale of the equipment is very small.

In summary, Huskies required $63,230 in cash to pay for the purchase of property, plant, and equipment, dividends, and the repayment of debt. It generated a total of $49,780 from operations, issuance of notes payable, issuance of common shares, and the sale of property, plant, and equipment. This produced a shortfall of $13,450 for the period, which was covered by the beginning cash balance. Cash declined during this period from $19,500 to $6,050. If all the items in the cash flow statement were continuing items, Huskies could continue to operate for only part of another year before it ran out of cash. Nothing definitive can be said about Huskies' cash flow health because not enough historical data are available. You can say that, if all items are continuing, Huskies will be in trouble next year. If, on the other hand, the purchase of property, plant, and equipment does not continue at its present level, then Huskies may be in reasonable shape.

Cash from operations can also be examined further to determine whether there are any problems in the company's operations. This analysis is easily done using the indirect format of the cash flow statement, where net income is reconciled to cash from operations. For Huskies Industries, the operating section shows that the two reasons for the increase in cash from operations during this period were that accounts receivable decreased and accounts payable increased. This gives some information about the management of the company's receivables and payables, which are critical in determining the lead/lag relationship in the cash-to-cash cycle. In general, these two accounts would be expected to move in unison. When business is growing, the company usually generates more receivables and more payables. When business contracts, both these accounts decrease. In the case of Huskies, they are moving in opposite directions with accounts receivable decreasing and accounts payable increasing. This should raise a red flag, leading the reader of the statement to question why these amounts are moving in opposite directions. It could mean that there is a problem in the management of receivables or payables, especially the accounts payable.

Another concern regarding cash from operating activities is that Huskies increased inventories during the period, causing cash from operations to decline. If a business was expanding, you would expect a larger inventory. But increased sales normally mean that a larger amount of accounts receivable should also be present, which was not the case. Again, this raises a red flag, which should prompt the user to ask why inventory has increased so much. It is possible that Huskies is stockpiling inventory in anticipation of a strike by employees, or it may be that its product is not selling and it has not adjusted inventory purchases sufficiently. This situation may lead to obsolete inventory that cannot be sold.

ANALYSIS OF THE CASH FLOW OF LE CHÂTEAU

Refer to Exhibit 5-11 to find the cash flow statement for Le Château Inc. First of all, Le Château uses the indirect approach for the operating section. Note that the two adjustments to net income in 2004 are the non-cash items included in net earnings (depreciation and amortization, write-off of fixed assets, amortization of deferred lease inducements, and future income taxes) and the changes in the non-cash working capital items related to operations (the current assets and liabilities). The second of these groups is produced as a summary amount; in order to get more information about the individual components, you will have to examine the notes to the financial statements. Also note that Le Château produces a substantial amount of cash from operations ($19,158 thousand in 2004) and that the amount has increased from the prior year when it was $16,029 thousand. The two biggest uses of cash in 2004 are the purchases of fixed assets ($14,438 thousand), and the dividends ($2,050 thousand). The trend over the last two years in these items indicates that they are both continuing items, although in 2003 less cash was used than in 2004. To understand more fully the impact of these two items, the user would need to examine the balance sheet and the accompanying notes.

First, let's look more closely at the cash flows associated with borrowings. To understand the net effects of borrowing, examine the information about debt included in Note 7.

(in thousands)	January 31, 2003	January 25, 2004
Loan repaid in the year	$	$ 446
6.97% Specific Security Agreement II, maturing July 15, 2004	178	524
6.35% Specific Security Agreement III, maturing February 27, 2006	1,588	2,279
	1,766	3,249
Less current portion	914	1,766
	$ 852	$ 1,766

Le Château does not appear to rely very heavily on long-term debt financing. As of January 31, 2004, Le Château has only two debt instruments outstanding. One is due within six months and the second is due in two years. In the next year more than half the total debt will be paid off. Some companies roll over their debt (using new debt issues to pay off debt that is due). Le Château does not appear to be doing this. It generates more than enough cash from operations to cover these debt repayments. Because of its ability to pay back its debt in a timely manner, Le Château would probably have an excellent credit rating.

Returning to the overall analysis, the cash flow from operations in 2004 ($19,158 thousand) was sufficient to cover the continuing needs for the repayment of debt (including the repayment of capital lease obligations) and the purchases of capital (fixed) assets. The proceeds of capital leases ($5,620 thousand) and the issuance of capital stock ($1,094 thousand) enabled the company to finish the year with a positive inflow of cash of $7,027 thousand. Le Château seems to perform quite well when it comes to cash generation. It also appears that, based on the past trend, this will continue into the future.

S U M M A R Y

This chapter opened with a discussion about the importance to organizations of effective cash management. We showed you how a company can be earning profits yet, at the same time, have serious cash flow problems. We outlined the information that users can obtain from the cash flows that are summarized in the cash flow statement. Remember that for a business to be successful, both cash flows and profits must be generated. We also went through the cash flow statement, describing its three essential components and the kinds of activity that are included in each section. We then described the procedure for preparing a cash flow statement. This statement is more complex than the balance sheet and the income statement: you need to analyze both those statements and seek out additional information before you can organize all the data that you need to prepare the cash flow statement. With the income statement and balance sheet, you mostly copy balances from accounts to the right place on the statement. Little analysis is required.

The concepts in the last part of this chapter are more important than the actual preparation of the statement. It outlined for you how the cash flow statement could be used in assessing a company's future cash flow. Remember that it is important to see a positive cash flow from operations. The operations are the lifeblood of the company; it is through them that the company will live or die.

The next chapters provide details of the items that appear in the balance sheet to give you a better understanding of the source of the amounts that appear in the financial statements.

SUMMARY PROBLEMS

1. The 2006 balance sheet and income statement of Hayes Industries, Inc. are provided in Exhibit 5-16. Hayes Industries manufactures and distributes a broad range of clothing and provides related services to retailers. Using these statements, construct the cash flow statement for Hayes for the year ended May 31, 2006. Use T accounts and the indirect approach. The following additional information and assumptions are also provided (all numbers are in thousands unless otherwise indicated).

Additional Demonstration Problems

a. Dividends declared in fiscal 2006 totalled $6,594.

b. Amortization totalled $7,805 in 2006.

c. Purchases of new property, plant, and equipment totalled $14,790 in 2006.

d. Property, plant, and equipment sold in 2006 produced a gain of $1,169.

e. All changes in the shareholders' equity accounts other than earnings and dividends are due to the issuance of new common shares.

f. Treat the issuance and repayment of long-term debt on a net basis.

g. Within the accrued liabilities on the balance sheet, $463 (2006) and $521 (2005) represent the interest payable.

EXHIBIT 5-16

HAYES INDUSTRIES, INC.

Balance Sheet

($ in thousands)

	May 31, 2006	May 31, 2005
Assets		
Current Assets:		
Cash and equivalents	$ 2,225	$ 3,227
Accounts receivable	83,962	75,165
Inventories	169,978	114,465
Prepaid expenses	13,023	12,402
Other Assets	1,190	1,471
Total Current Assets	270,378	206,730
Property, plant, and equipment	110,343	102,870
Less: Accumulated amortization	(71,693)	(69,653)
Total Assets	$ 309,028	$ 239,947
Liabilities and Shareholders' Equity		
Current Liabilities:		
Notes payable	$ 43,500	$ 19,500
Accounts payable	54,331	45,023
Accrued salaries	8,235	11,687
Other accrued expenses	13,039	12,977
Income taxes	4,732	5,352
Dividends payable	1,739	1,555
Total Current Liabilities	125,576	96,094
Long-term debt	50,873	16,118
Total Liabilities	176,449	112,212
Shareholders' Equity		
Common shares	15,714	14,791
Retained earnings	116,865	112,944
Total Shareholders' Equity	132,579	127,735
Total Liabilities and Shareholders' Equity	$ 309,028	$ 239,947

INCOME STATEMENT

Consolidated Statements of Earnings

($ in thousands except per share amounts)

Year Ended	May 31, 2006	May 31, 2005
Net Sales	$ 656,987	$624,568
Costs and Expenses:		
Cost of goods sold	543,624	498,790
Selling, general, and administrative	91,601	91,209
Interest	4,136	2,297
	639,361	592,296
Earnings Before Income Taxes	17,626	32,272
Income Taxes	7,051	13,071
Net Earnings	$ 10,575	$ 19,201
Net Earnings Per Common Share	$ 1.22	$ 2.23

2. Based on the answer to Question 1 and the previous two years' cash flow statements for Hayes Industries shown in Exhibit 5-17, answer the following questions.

    a. Discuss the company's ability to meet its needs for cash over the last three years. Comment on the continuing nature of the major items that have appeared over the last three years.

    b. Explain why so much cash was generated from operations in 2006.

HAYES INDUSTRIES, INC.

EXHIBIT 5-17

Cash Flow Statements

($ in thousands)

Year Ended	May 31, 2005	May 31, 2004
Operating Activities:		
Net earnings	$ 19,201	$ 14,786
Adjustments to reconcile net earnings to net cash provided by operating activities:		
Amortization	7,041	6,457
(Gain) loss on sale of property, plant, and equipment	488	(211)
Changes in working capital:		
(Increase) decrease in:		
Receivables	(7,072)	(935)
Inventories	(11,872)	(19,687)
Prepaid expenses	(704)	(1,851)
(Decrease) increase in:		
Accounts payable	10,121	(3,734)
Accrued salaries and other current expenses	2,428	1,078
Income taxes payable	–	(402)
Other noncurrent assets	52	(513)
Net cash provided by operations	19,683	(5,012)

Investing Activities:		
Purchase of property, plant, and equipment	(9,395)	(8,050)
Proceeds from sale of property, plant, and equipment	414	1,824
Net cash used in investing activities	(8,981)	(6,226)
Financing Activities:		
Short-term borrowings	1,000	18,500
Dividends on common shares	(5,956)	(5,486)
Payments on long-term debt	(4,913)	(14,733)
Addition to long-term debt	–	10,000
Purchase and retirement of common shares	(1,885)	(2,449)
Net cash used in financing activities	(11,754)	5,832
Net Change in Cash	(1,052)	(5,406)
Cash at Beginning of Period	4,279	9,685
Cash at End of Period	$ 3,227	$ 4,279

SUGGESTED SOLUTIONS TO SUMMARY PROBLEMS

1. T Accounts:

Cash (A)

		3,227			
Operations:					
Net income	(1)	10,575	8,797	(2)	Incr. in A/R
Increase in A/P	(5)	9,308	55,513	(3)	Incr. in inventories
Incr. other acc. exp.	(7)	62	621	(4)	Incr. in ppd. exp.
Decr. in other assets	(9)	281	3,452	(6)	Decr. in accrued sal.
Amortization	(10)	7,805	620	(8)	Decr. in inc. taxes
			1,169	(12)	Gain on sale of PP&E
Investing:					
Proceeds from sale of PP&E	(12)	2,721	14,790	(11)	Purchase of PP&E
Financing:					
Issuance of notes pay.	(13)	24,000	6,470	(15)	Dividends
Iss. of long-term debt	(16)	34,755			
Iss. of shares	(17)	923			
		2,225			

Accounts Receivable (A)		
	75,165	
(2)	8,797	
	83,962	

Inventories (A)		
	114,465	
(3)	55,513	
	169,978	

Prepaid Expenses (A)		
	12,402	
(4)	621	
	13,023	

PP&E (A)				
	102,870			
(11)	14,790	7,317	(12)	
	110,343			

Accum. Amort. (XA)			
		69,653	
(12)	5,765	7,805	(10)
		71,693	

Other Assets (A)			
1,471			
		281	(8)
1,190			

Notes Payable (L)			
		19,500	
		24,000	(13)
		43,500	

Accounts Payable (L)			
		45,023	
		9,308	(5)
		54,331	

Accrued Salaries (L)			
		11,687	
(6)	3,452		
		8,235	

Other Accrued Expenses (L)			
		12,977	
		62	(7)
		13,039	

Taxes Payable (L)			
		5,352	
(8)	620		
		4,732	

Dividends Payable (L)			
		1,555	
(15)	6,470	6,654	(14)
		1,739	

Long-term Debt (L)			
		16,118	
		34,755	(16)
		50,873	

Common Shares (SE)			
		14,791	
		923	(17)
		15,714	

Retained Earnings (SE)			
		112,944	
(14)	6,654	10,575	(1)
		116,865	

Explanations of selected transactions:

Transaction 10. The debit entry to the cash account is the amortization of property, plant, and equipment, which is a non-cash expense and, therefore, must be added back. The reconstruction entry is:

Cash (Operating) (A)	7,805	
Accumulated amortization (XA)		7,805

Transaction 12. The sale of property, plant, and equipment resulted in a gain of $1,169. The cost (in the PP&E account) and the accumulated amortization associated with this sale are determined by balancing these two accounts in the T accounts. The reconstruction entry that results is as follows.

Cash (Investing) (A)	2,721	
Accumulated amortization (XA)	5,765	
Property, plant, and equipment (A)		7,317
Cash (Operating) (A)		1,169

Transactions 14 and 15. Determining the amount of dividends that were actually paid during 2006 involves first determining the amount of dividends declared. If you balance the retained earnings account, it is obvious that an additional debit of $6,654 is needed. This debit represents the dividends declared. The reconstruction entry to record this is as follows.

Retained earnings (SE)	6,654	
Dividends payable (L)		6,654

With the additional entry to the dividends payable account, it is now possible to determine the amount of dividends actually paid during the year by balancing the account. An additional debit of $6,470 is required to reach the end balance of $1,739. The reconstruction entry to record this is as follows.

Dividends payable (L)	6,470	
Cash (Financing) (A)		6,470

HAYES INDUSTRIES, INC.

Cash Flow Statement
For the Year Ended May 31, 2006

Operating activities		
Net income	$ 10,575	
Adjustments to reconcile net earnings to cash provided by operating activities:		
Amortization	7,805	
Gain on sale of equipment	(1,169)	
Effect from changes in working capital:		
Increase in accounts receivable	(8,797)	
Increase in inventory	(55,513)	
Increase in prepaid expenses	(621)	
Increase in accounts payable	9,308	
Decrease in accrued salaries	(3,452)	
Increase in other accrued expenses	62	
Decrease in income taxes	(620)	
Decrease in other assets	281	
Cash provided by operations		($42,141)
Investing		
Sale of property, plant, and equipment	2,721	
Purchase of property, plant, and equipment	(14,790)	
Cash provided by investing		(12,069)
Financing		
Issuance of notes payable	24,000	
Issuance of long-term debt	34,755	
Issuance of shares	923	
Payment of dividends	(6,470)	
Cash provided by financing		53,208
Decrease in cash		(1,002)
Beginning cash balance		3,227
Ending cash balance		$ 2,225
Supplementary information:		
Interest paid during the year*		$4,194
Income taxes paid during the year*		$7,671

*Interest paid is calculated as $521 + $4,136 − $463 = $4,194
*Income taxes paid is calculated as $5,352 + $7,051 − $4,732 = $7,671

2. a. The two major continuing needs for cash over the last three years have been the purchase of property, plant, and equipment and the payment of dividends. The combination of these two items has averaged $16,715 over the last three years. Only in 2005 did Hayes produce enough cash from operations to cover these needs. In both 2004 and 2006, Hayes had to use cash in its operations (there was a negative amount), with a significant amount used in 2006.

   In 2004, Hayes also used a significant amount of cash to retire long-term debt and buy back shares. Since operations did not provide cash in that year, short-term borrowings were used to meet Hayes' cash needs. Hayes also drew down its cash balance significantly in 2004 to pay for its cash needs. In 2005, Hayes continued to retire long-term debt and buy back shares. In that year, however, there was some extra cash left over from operations after paying for property, plant, and equipment and dividends.

   Additional cash was raised from short-term borrowings again, such that Hayes ended the year in about the same cash position as at the beginning of the year. In 2006, cash from operations was significantly negative and the expenditures for property, plant, and equipment and dividends were the largest in the three-year period shown on the cash flow statements. Hayes primarily paid for these items by issuing more debt, with more than half of the issuance being long-term and the rest short-term. A look at the balance sheet indicates that long-term debt increased approximately four-fold in 2006. Short-term debt more than doubled. This has significant implications for 2007, as this debt carries with it additional interest expense that will appear in the income statement that year.

   b. In analyzing the operating section of Hayes' cash flow statements, it is clear that the biggest negative adjustment over the last three years has been the change in inventories. These changes represent increases in inventories. In 2006, inventories increased $55,513 or almost 49% over the levels in 2005 ($114,465). There is clearly a problem here as sales have not increased this dramatically, only increasing $32,419 or 5.2% in 2006. Receivables have also increased fairly dramatically, by $8,797 or 11.7% in 2006. As an offset to the increase in receivables, accounts payable have also increased by $9,308 or 20.7% in 2006. While this helps the company's cash flow, it may also indicate that the company is having trouble paying its bills and is slowing down payment on its accounts. The biggest concern is the increase in the level of inventory; you would want to investigate why inventories have grown this much.

GLOSSARY

Capitalization The amount of resources contributed to the company by shareholders and debtholders. The term "capitalization" is used in several ways in accounting. Besides the definition given above, it can also mean the recording of an asset or the deferring of a cost.

Cash equivalents Current assets and liabilities that are very liquid and readily convertible into cash or that may require the short-term use of cash. Examples are short-term investments and bank overdrafts or lines of credit.

Cash flow The net change in cash that occurs from the beginning of an accounting period to the end of the period.

Cash flow statement A financial statement that shows the cash flows of the company during the accounting period, categorized into operating, investing, and financing activities.

Cash position The amount of cash and cash equivalents.

Debt/equity ratio The ratio calculated by dividing total liabilities by the sum of total liabilities and shareholders' equity. It indicates whether the company relies more heavily on debt or equity for financing.

Direct approach   A method of calculating the cash from a company's operations in which the direct gross cash receipts from revenues and payments used for expenses are shown.

Financing activities   Company activities that are directed to obtaining resources from investors or debtholders. The return of resources to shareholders and debtholders is also considered part of these activities.

Indirect approach   A method of calculating a company's cash from operations in which the net income number is adjusted for all non-cash revenues or expenses to convert it from an accrual basis to its cash-basis equivalent.

Investing activities   Company activities that are directed to investing its resources over extended periods of time in long-term assets.

Lead/lag relationship   The relationships between the recognition of revenues and expenses for income statement purposes and the recognition of their cash flow effects.

Line of credit   An arrangement with a financing institution that allows a company to overdraw its accounts. The overdrawn amounts become a loan that must be repaid.

Operating activities   Company activities that are directed to selling goods and services to customers.

Working Capital   Current assets minus current liabilities

ASSIGNMENT MATERIAL

Assessing Your Recall

Self-Assessment Quiz

5-1   Discuss why it is important for companies to prepare a cash flow statement in addition to an income statement.

5-2   Discuss how a company's receivables, inventory, and payables policies affect cash flows relative to the income produced in a given period.

5-3   What is meant by a lead/lag relationship in terms of the cash flow statement?

5-4   For a company with a cash flow problem, list at least three potential reasons for the problem and suggest a possible solution for each.

5-5   Describe the three major categories of activities that are shown on the cash flow statement.

5-6   Discuss the major difference between the direct approach and the indirect approach for constructing the operating section of a cash flow statement.

5-7   Explain why it is important with respect to a company's financial health to have a positive cash flow from operations.

5-8   "Amortization is a source of cash." Explain your reasons for agreeing or disagreeing with this statement.

5-9   In what section of the cash flow statement (operating, financing, or investing) would each of the following items appear?

　　a. Purchase of new property, plant, and equipment

　　b. Proceeds from a bank loan

　　c. Collections from customers

　　d. Dividends to shareholders

　　e. Proceeds from the sale of marketable securities

　　f. Retirement of debt

    g. Changes in accounts receivable

    h. Net income

    i. Gain or loss on the sale of property, plant, and equipment

5-10 Indicate whether each of the following items should be classified as an operating, investing, or financing activity on the cash flow statement. If an item does not belong on the statement indicate why.

    a. Payment of cash dividends on common shares

    b. Sale of a warehouse

    c. Interest payments on an outstanding long-term bank loan

    d. Purchase of a company's own common shares on the stock market

    e. Acquisition of land

    f. Obtaining cash through a long-term bank loan

    g. Purchase of an investment in another company by buying some of its shares

    h. Collection of an accounts receivable

    i. Declaration of dividends on common shares

    j. Purchase of operating equipment

5-11 Explain why the total cash flows from investing are often negative.

5-12 When analyzing the cash flow statement, explain why it is important to compare the current year's amounts with prior years.

Applying Your Knowledge

5-13 **(Identification of sources and uses of cash)**

In the chapter's opening story, Carrie Solmundson, Executive Director of the **Wellness Institute** in Winnipeg's Seven Oaks General Hospital, described the importance of cash to the institute's viability.

> *Required:*
>
>   a. Identify three possible sources of cash and three possible uses of cash for the Wellness Institute.
>
>   b. Ms. Solmundson described the establishment of two funds, one restricted and one unrestricted. Briefly describe what you think a restricted fund and an unrestricted fund are. How do the establishment of these funds better enable the institute to manage its cash?
>
>   c. With respect to the acquisition of cash, describe how a not-for-profit organization is different from a profit-oriented organization.

5-14 **(Cash flow and sales growth)**

Explain why a high sales growth rate can create significant cash flow problems for a company.

5-15 **(Cash flow and capital assets)**

Explain how the timing of the cash flows relates to the purchase, use, and ultimate sale of property, plant, and equipment.

5-16 **(Cash flow and interest)**

Discuss the classification of interest cash flows in the cash flow statement and whether you think this is appropriate.

5-17 **(Effect of transactions on cash flows)**

Classify each of the following transactions as increasing, decreasing, or having no effect on cash flows.

a. Purchasing inventory on account

b. Paying wages owed to employees

c. Buying a new building by making a down payment and taking out a mortgage for the balance of the amount owed

d. Receiving interest that is owed from a customer

e. Purchasing office supplies and writing a cheque to cover the amount

f. Selling inventory to a customer on account

g. Making a monthly payment on a bank loan that included interest and principal repayment

h. Declaring and paying a dividend to shareholders

i. Issuing new shares

j. Amortizing capital assets

5-18 **(Effect of transactions on cash flows)**

Classify each of the following transactions as increasing, decreasing, or having no effect on cash flows.

a. Paying for inventory purchased earlier on account

b. Paying the monthly interest owed on a bank loan

c. Buying new equipment for cash

d. Selling merchandise to a customer who used a debit card to pay for the purchase

e. Buying the company's own shares on the stock market

f. Selling surplus equipment at a gain

g. Paying CRA the income taxes owed for the year

h. Accruing the wages owed to employees at the end of the month. The cheques will be issued the first Friday of the next month.

i. Prepaying rent that is owed for the month

j. Sold (issued) bonds to investors. The bonds are 10-year bonds paying 6.5% interest.

5-19 **(Effect of transactions on cash flows)**

For each of the following items: (1) identify the accounts affected and give the amounts by which they would be increased or decreased; (2) state the amount of any cash flow and whether cash is increased or decreased; and (3) identify how each item would be reported in the cash flow statement.

a. Two years ago a licence was purchased for $50,000. The licence is amortized over four years at a rate of $12,500 per year.

b. A capital asset is sold for $90,000. The asset originally cost $165,000 and the accumulated amortization is $95,000.

c. A capital asset is purchased for $250,000. A cash payment of $50,000 is made and the remainder is paid with a long-term note of $200,000.

d. Annual interest of 7% is paid on bonds that were issued for $1 million.

e. Income tax expense for the year is $95,000. The tax payment during the year was $80,000. The remainder will be paid next year.

5-20   (Effect of transactions on cash flows)

For each of the following items: (1) identify the accounts affected and give the amounts by which they would be increased or decreased; (2) state the amount of any cash flow and whether cash is increased or decreased; and (3) identify how each item would be reported in the cash flow statement.

a. During the year, a company made a payment on its debt of $20,000; $6,000 of the $20,000 was for the interest owed on the debt.

b. A new vehicle costing $26,000 is purchased. The company paid $5,000 as a down payment and the remaining $21,000 was financed through a loan.

c. A tract of land is sold for $75,000, which is $16,000 more than its original cost.

d. A company declared and paid a dividend of $35,000 to shareholders.

e. Inventory costing $327,000 was purchased on account.

5-21   (Effect of transactions on cash flows)

For each of the transactions listed below:

a. Indicate the effect on balance sheet categories by using the following format:

Trans. No.	Cash	Other Current Assets	Noncurrent Assets	Current Liabilities	Noncurrent Liabilities	Shareholders' Equity

b. For the transactions affecting cash shown below, state whether they relate to an operating, investing, or financing activity.

Transactions:

1. Cash paid on accounts payable, $290,000

2. Paid rent during the year, $36,000; the last payment of $3,000 was for the first month of the next year

3. Borrowed $60,000 from the bank; amount is due in two years

4. Cost of goods sold, $300,000

5. Issued new shares for $120,000 cash

6. Paid wages to employees, $27,000

7. Equipment having a book value (cost minus accumulated amortization) of $4,100 sold for $4,900 cash

8. Bought inventory on credit, $305,000

9. Declared and paid dividends, $6,300

10. Purchased a new machine for cash, $17,000

11. Income taxes accrued and paid, $11,300

12. Sold inventory on credit, $510,000

13. Bought office supplies for cash, $5,000; at year end, $3,500 of the supplies had been used

14. At year end, $900 was owed to the employees

15. Paid for advertising, $1,100

16. Interest of $2,100 was paid on the amount borrowed

17. Cash collected on accounts receivable, $480,000

18. Amortization expense on equipment, $2,500

5-22 **(Effect of transactions on cash flows)**

For each transaction listed below:

a. Indicate the effect on balance sheet categories by using the following format:

Trans. No.	Cash	Other Current Assets	Noncurrent Assets	Current Liabilities	Noncurrent Liabilities	Shareholders' Equity

b For the transactions affecting cash, state whether they relate to an operating, investing, or financing activity.

Transactions:

1. 5,000 common shares were issued at $30 per share.

2. Equipment worth $110,000 was purchased for $70,000 in cash and the balance in common shares.

3. Rent payment of $2,000 was received in advance.

4. Sales contracts for $150,000 were signed, and a $37,500 deposit was received in cash.

5. Merchandise inventory costing $210,000 was purchased on account.

6. Goods costing $10,000 were found defective and returned to suppliers. These goods had been purchased on account.

7. Sales were $450,000, of which $90,000 was on account.

8. Cash was paid to suppliers on account in the amount of $215,000.

9. Equipment recorded at $10,000 was destroyed by fire. The insurance company paid $9,000 for the loss.

10. The company purchased 100 shares of Allied Company at $9 per share for short-term investment purposes.

11. The company purchased 50,000 shares of Zider Company at $4 per share in an effort to buy a controlling interest in Zider (a supplier).

12. Interest expense for the year amounted to $2,500 and was paid in cash.

13. One of the sales contracts in Transaction 4 was cancelled; $10,000 of the deposit was returned and the rest was forfeited.

14. A bank loan for $100,000 was taken out and is due in five years.

15. Equipment with a cost of $30,000 was sold for $35,000. The buyer agreed to pay $20,000 in the future and signed a note receivable that required interest payments.

16. During the year, warranty services costing $5,500 were provided to customers. A provision for warranty services was provided earlier in a separate transaction.

17. Amortization for the year totalled $20,000.

18. Dividends of $7,000 were declared, and $5,000 remained unpaid at year end.

19. Patents on a new manufacturing process were purchased for $15,000.

20. Research and development expenses amounted to $45,000 and were charged to expense as incurred.

5-23 (Cash flow from operations)

Calculate the cash flow from operations in each of the following cases.

	I	II	III
Sales revenues	$355,000	$575,000	$935,000
Cost of goods sold	210,000	320,000	620,000
Selling and admin. expenses	65,000	95,500	105,500
Amortization expense	6,500	18,000	28,000
Income tax expense	18,000	35,000	45,000
Dividends paid	7,000	5,000	25,000
Increase/(Decrease) in:			
Accounts receivable	(2,500)	(5,000)	8,500
Inventories	4,000	8,000	(14,000)
Prepaid expenses	1,000	2,500	(2,400)
Accounts payable	(3,500)	6,500	(4,200)
Wages payable	2,500	(1,500)	3,500
Interest payable	1,500	1,200	(6,500)

5-24 (Cash flow from operations)

Calculate the cash flow from operations in each of the following cases.

	I	II	III
Sales revenues	$410,000	$735,000	$940,000
Cost of goods sold	225,000	410,000	575,000
Amortization expense	40,000	70,000	90,000
Interest expense	15,000	20,000	35,000
Gain (loss) on sale of equipment	9,000	(15,000)	14,000
Dividends paid	–	15,000	12,000
Increase/(Decrease) in:			
Building and equipment	225,000	(100,000)	150,000
Common shares	50,000	75,000	120,000
Bonds payable	20,000	(50,000)	60,000
Interest payable	5,000	8,000	(5,000)
Accounts payable	8,000	(12,000)	(8,000)
Accounts receivable	(15,000)	16,000	(15,000)
Interest payable	20,000	25,000	(30,000)

5-25 **(Preparation of cash flow statement)**

Financial statement data for Comfort Shoes Company for 2006 are as follows.

COMFORT SHOES COMPANY
Comparative Balance Sheets

	Dec. 31, 2006	Dec. 31, 2005
Assets		
Cash	$ 121,000	$ 94,000
Accounts receivable	22,000	26,000
Inventory	135,000	90,000
Prepaid expenses	40,000	42,000
Total current assets	318,000	252,000
Capital assets	420,000	370,000
Accumulated amortization	(168,000)	(129,000)
Total noncurrent assets	252,000	241,000
Total assets	$570,000	$ 493,000
Liabilities and shareholders' equity		
Accounts payable	$ 32,000	$ 35,000
Wages payable	6,000	5,000
Interest payable	3,000	2,000
Total current liabilities	41,000	42,000
Mortgage payable	100,000	60,000
Total liabilities	141,000	102,000
Common shares	200,000	200,000
Retained earnings	229,000	191,000
Total liabilities and shareholders' equity	$ 570,000	$ 493,000

COMFORT SHOES COMPANY
Income Statement

For the Year Ended December 31, 2006

Sales		$ 972,000
Expenses		
Cost of goods sold	$ 550,000	
Wage expense	95,000	
Utilities expense	160,000	
Amortization expense	69,000	
Interest expense	6,000	
Gain on sale of capital assets	(5,000)	
Total expenses		875,000
Net income		$ 97,000

1. Some capital assets originally costing $40,000 were sold for $15,000.

2. A new capital asset was purchased for $90,000. It was financed with cash and a $50,000 mortgage.

3. Dividends declared and paid during the year were $59,000.

Required:

Prepare a cash flow statement for Comfort Shoes Company for the year ended December 31, 2006, supported by a set of T accounts.

5-26   **(Preparation of cash flow statement)**

Financial statement data for First Moving Company for 2006 are as follows.

FIRST MOVING COMPANY
Comparative Balance Sheets

	Dec. 31, 2006	Dec. 31, 2005
Assets		
Cash	$ 88,600	$ 49,100
Accounts receivable	85,000	59,400
Prepaid insurance	70,000	60,000
Total current assets	243,600	168,500
Property, equipment, and vehicles	360,000	305,000
Accumulated amortization	(110,400)	(105,900)
Total noncurrent assets	249,600	199,100
Total assets	$493,200	$ 367,600
Liabilities and shareholders' equity		
Accounts payable	$ 21,500	$ 18,600
Wages payable	3,000	4,000
Total current liabilities	24,500	22,600
Bank loan	50,000	60,000
Total liabilities	74,500	82,600
Common shares	200,000	200,000
Retained earnings	218,700	85,000
Total liabilities and shareholders' equity	$ 493,200	$ 367,600

FIRST MOVING COMPANY
Income Statement
For the Year Ended December 31, 2006

Moving revenue		$ 450,000
Expenses		
Vehicle maintenance	$ 102,400	
Wage expense	134,000	
Amortization expense	59,500	
Interest expense	5,400	
Gain on sale of vehicles	(5,000)	
Total expenses		296,300
Net income		$ 153,700

Additional information:

1. Vehicles originally costing $65,000 were sold for $15,000.

2. Dividends declared and paid during the year were $20,000.

Required:

Prepare a cash flow statement for First Moving Company for the year ended December 31, 2006, supported by a set of T accounts.

5-27 **(Preparation of financial statements)**

Financial statement data for Cool Air Ltd. are as follows.

COOL AIR LTD.
Balance sheet
December 31, 2006

Assets

Cash	$ 31,000
Accounts receivable	20,000
Notes receivable	10,000
Inventories	41,000
Total current assets	102,000
Property, plant, and equipment	320,000
Accumulated amortization	(71,000)
Total noncurrent assets	249,000
Total assets	$351,000

Liabilities and shareholders' equity

Accounts payable	$ 10,000
Salaries payable	30,000
Interest payable	6,000
Total current liabilities	46,000
Bonds payable	100,000
Total liabilities	146,000
Common shares	200,000
Retained earnings	5,000
Total liabilities and shareholders' equity	$351,000

COOL AIR LTD.
Trial Balance for the Year Ended December 31, 2007

	Debits	Credits
Cash	$ 5,800	
Accounts receivable	25,000	
Prepaid rent	12,000	
Inventories	37,800	
Property, plant, and equipment	320,000	
Accumulated amortization		$ 91,000
Accounts payable		27,600
Interest payable		18,000
Salaries payable		12,000
Bonds payable		20,000
Common shares		200,000
Retained earnings		5,000
Sales		700,000
Cost of goods sold	551,000	
Amortization expense	20,000	
Rent expense	24,000	
Interest expense	30,000	
Salaries expense	48,000	
Totals	$1,073,600	$1,073,600

Required:

a. Prepare an income statement and a reconciliation of retained earnings for the year ended December 31, 2007.

b. Prepare a balance sheet as at December 31, 2007.

c. Prepare a cash flow statement for the year ended December 31, 2007.

5-28 **(Preparation of cash flow statement)**

Financial statement data for Gibbons Electronics Company for 2006 are as follows.

GIBBONS ELECTRONICS COMPANY
Comparative Balance Sheets

	Dec. 31, 2006	Dec. 31, 2005
Assets		
Cash	$ 285,000	$ 335,000
Accounts receivable	350,000	400,000
Inventory	290,000	240,000
Prepaid insurance	55,000	35,000
Total current assets	980,000	1,010,000
Property, equipment, and vehicles	650,000	590,000
Accumulated amortization	(165,000)	(130,000)
Total noncurrent assets	485,000	460,000
Total assets	$1,465,000	$1,470,000
Liabilities and shareholders' equity		
Accounts payable	$ 60,000	$ 50,000
Wages payable	15,000	20,000
Unearned revenue	50,000	35,000
Income taxes payable	55,000	35,000
Total current liabilities	180,000	140,000
Bond payable	490,000	575,000
Total liablities	670,000	715,000
Common shares	365,000	285,000
Retained earnings	$ 430,000	$ 470,000
Total liabilities and shareholder's equity	$ 1,465,000	$ 1,470,000

GIBBONS ELECTRONICS COMPANY
Income statement
For the Year Ended December 31, 2006

Revenue		$3,855,000
Expenses		
Cost of goods sold	$1,905,000	
Wage expense	335,000	
Amortization expense	95,000	
Interest expense	150,000	
Income taxes	345,000	
Administration expense	525,000	
Gain on sale of vehicles	(10,000)	
Total expenses		3,345,000
Net income		$510,000

Additional information:

1. Property, plant, and equipment originally costing $90,000 was sold for $40,000.

2. New equipment costing $150,000 was purchased during the year.

3. New shares were issued for $80,000 during the year.

4. Dividends declared and paid during the year were $550,000.

Required:

Prepare a cash flow statement for Gibbons Electronic Company for the year ended December 31, 2006, supported by a set of T accounts. Include the supplementary information about the interest paid and the income taxes paid.

5-29 **(Preparation of cash flow statement)**

Athabasca Company reported the following abbreviated balance sheet and income statement for 2006.

ATHABASCA COMPANY
Income Statement
For the Year Ended December 31, 2006

Sales		$450,000
Cost of goods sold		240,000
Gross profit		210,000
Other expenses:		
Supplies expense	$ 15,000	
Amortization expense	35,000	
Wages and salaries	110,000	
Interest expense	24,000	184,000
		26,000
Other income		21,000
Net income		$ 47,000

ATHABASCA COMPANY
Balance Sheets

	2006	2005
Cash	$ 80,000	$ 70,000
Accounts receivable	120,000	140,000
Inventory	320,000	280,000
Buildings and equipment (net)	440,000	420,000
Total Assets	$960,000	$910,000
Accounts payable	$ 90,000	$ 80,000
Wages and salaries payable	20,000	15,000
Bonds payable	350,000	400,000
Common shares	200,000	150,000
Retained earnings	300,000	265,000
Total Liabilities and Shareholders' Equity	$960,000	$910,000

Required:

a. Prepare a cash flow statement for Athabasca Company for the year ended December 31, 2006.

b. Did the working capital change by the same amount as cash generated by operations? Should these two be the same? Explain.

5-30   **(Preparation of cash flow statement)**

The balance sheets for Johnson Company as at the beginning and end of 2006 are as follows.

JOHNSON COMPANY
Balance Sheets

	Dec. 31, 2006	Dec. 31, 2005
Assets		
Current assets		
Cash	$ 50,000	$ 58,000
Accounts receivable	81,000	95,000
Inventories	92,000	72,000
Prepaid expenses	30,000	40,000
Total current assets	253,000	265,000
Property, plant, and equipment	775,000	750,000
Accumulated amortization	(325,000)	(300,000)
Total noncurrent assets	450,000	450,000
Total assets	$ 703,000	$715,000
Liabilities and shareholders' equity		
Current liabilities		
Accounts payable	$ 33,000	$110,000
Wages payable	20,000	40,000
Total current liabilities	53,000	150,000
Bonds payable	125,000	100,000
Total liabilities	178,000	250,000
Shareholder's equity		
Common shares	300,000	275,000
Retained earnings	225,000	190,000
Total shareholder's equity	525,000	465,000
Total liabilities and shareholder's equity	$ 703,000	$715,000

Additional information:

1. No dividends were declared or paid.

2. No property, plant, or equipment was sold.

3. No long-term debt was repaid.

4. Net income was $35,000, including $25,000 of amortization expense.

Required:

Prepare a cash flow statement for the year ended December 31, 2006.

5-31 **(Preparation of cash flow statement)**

Comparative balance sheets of Janxen Jeans Company for 2006 and 2005 are as follows.

JANXEN JEANS COMPANY
Comparative Balance Sheets

	Dec. 31, 2006	Dec. 31, 2005
Assets		
Current assets		
Cash	$ 200,000	$ 188,000
Accounts receivable	120,000	133,000
Notes receivable	70,000	61,000
Inventories	439,000	326,000
Total current assets	829,000	708,000
Noncurrent assets		
Land	525,000	500,000
Machinery	483,000	238,000
Accumulated amortization	(143,000)	(97,500)
Total noncurrent assets	865,000	640,500
Total assets	$1,694,000	$1,348,500
Liabilities and shareholders' equity		
Current liabilities		
Accounts payable	$ 145,000	$ 158,000
Interest payable	17,500	10,000
Total current liabilities	162,500	168,000
Long-term debt	350,000	200,000
Total liabilities	512,500	368,000
Shareholders' equity		
Common shares	650,000	550,000
Retained earnings	531,500	430,500
Total shareholders' equity	1,181,500	980,500
Total liabilities and shareholders' equity	$ 1,694,000	$1,348,500

Additional information:

1. Net income is $145,000 and includes amortization expenses of $95,500.

2. Dividends declared and paid during the year were $44,000.

3. A machine costing $70,000 was sold at its book value (cost minus accumulated amortization) of $20,000.

4. No repayment of long-term debt occurred in 2006.

Required:

Prepare a cash flow statement for the year ended December 31, 2006.

5-32 **(Preparation of cash flow statement)**

Comparative balance sheets (2006 and 2005) and the income statement (2006) of Standard Card Company are as follows.

STANDARD CARD COMPANY
Comparative Balance Sheets

	Dec. 31, 2006	Dec. 31, 2005
Assets		
Current assets		
Cash	$ 173,000	$120,000
Accounts receivable	60,000	65,000
Inventories	210,000	110,000
Prepaid insurance	14,000	24,000
Total current assets	457,000	319,000
Noncurrent assets		
Equipment	275,000	350,000
Accumulated amortization	(67,000)	(75,000)
Total noncurrent assets	208,000	275,000
Total assets	$ 665,000	$ 594,000
Liabilities and shareholders' equity		
Current liabilities		
Accounts payable	$ 55,000	$ 48,000
Wages payable	31,000	35,000
Interest payable	5,000	4,000
Unearned revenue	13,000	18,000
Total current liabilities	104,000	105,000
Long-term debt	150,000	150,000
Total liabilities	254,000	255,000
Shareholders' equity		
Common shares	200,000	135,000
Retained earnings	211,000	204,000
Total shareholders' equity	411,000	339,000
Total liabilities and shareholders' equity	$ 665,000	$ 594,000

STANDARD CARD COMPANY
Income Statement
For the Year Ended December 31, 2006

Sales		$ 160,000
Expenses		
Cost of goods sold	$ 100,000	
Insurance expense	10,000	
Interest expense	11,000	
Amortization expense	12,000	
Gain on sale of equipment	(10,000)	
Total expenses		123,000
Net income		$ 37,000

Additional information:

1. Dividends declared and paid during the year were $30,000.

2. A machine costing $100,000 was sold when its accumulated amortization was $20,000.

Required:

Prepare a cash flow statement for the year ended December 31, 2006.

5-33 **(Determine cash collected from customers and paid to suppliers)**

Southbend Company had sales of $735,600 for the year. The company reported accounts receivable of $55,000 at the end of last year and $58,900 at the end of this year. Southbend's cost of goods sold this year was $440,000. In last year's balance sheet, Southbend reported inventory of $62,000 and accounts payable of $32,400. In this year's balance sheet, Southbend reported inventory of $59,700 and accounts payable of $28,200.

Required:

a. How much cash did Southbend collect from customers during the year?

b. How much cash did Southbend pay to suppliers for inventory during the year?

5-34 **(Determine cash collected from customers and paid to suppliers)**

Practical Things Company had sales of $310,000 for the year. The company reported accounts receivable of $42,000 at the end of last year and $11,000 at the end of this year. Practical Things' cost of goods sold this year was $240,000. In last year's balance sheet, Practical Things reported inventory of $32,000 and accounts payable of $37,000. In this year's balance sheet, Practical Things reported inventory of $43,000 and accounts payable of $33,000.

Required:

a. How much cash did Practical Things collect from customers during the year?

b. How much cash did Practical Things pay to suppliers for inventory during the year?

5-35 **(Preparation of cash flow statement)**

Steeler and James Company had a $54,000 cash balance at the beginning of 2006. The company reported net income of $112,000 for 2006. Included in the company's income statement were amortization expense of $62,000, interest expense of $29,000, and income tax expense of $44,000. The following also occurred during 2006.

1. Accounts receivable increased by $22,000.

2. Inventory decreased by $6,000.

3. Prepaid rent decreased by $6,000.

4. Accounts payable decreased by $34,000.

5. Wages payable increased by $22,000.

6. Interest payable decreased by $7,000.

7. Unearned revenue increased by $18,000.

8. New equipment was purchased for $122,000.

9. Steeler and James declared and paid cash dividends of $31,000 during 2006.

Required:

To help the management of Steeler and James Company better understand its sources and uses of cash, do the following.

a. Calculate the cash generated from operations.

b. Calculate the cash flow related to investing activities.

c. Calculate the cash flow related to financing activities.

d. Prepare a cash flow statement for Steeler and James for 2006 in good form.

5-36 **(Preparation of cash flow statement)**

Downsview Company had a $261,800 cash balance at the beginning of 2006. The company reported net income of $388,900 for 2006. Included in the company's income statement were amortization expense of $67,000, interest expense of $31,600, and income tax expense of $102,000. The following also occurred during 2006.

1. Accounts receivable increased by $13,000.

2. Inventory decreased by $7,000.

3. Accounts payable increased by $3,500.

4. Wages payable decreased by $1,300.

5. Income taxes payable increased by $3,100.

6. The patent account increased by $27,400. One patent was purchased during the year for $31,200.

7. The plant and equipment account increased by $465,000. One piece of equipment was sold during the year for $22,000. It had originally cost $51,000 and had a $17,000 book value at the time of the sale.

8. Downsview declared and paid cash dividends of $52,000 during 2006.

9. The company repurchased some of its common shares during the year for $44,000.

10. The company issued $100,000 of bonds during the year.

Required:

To help the management of Downsview Company better understand its sources and uses of cash, do the following.

a. Calculate the cash generated from operations.

b. Calculate the cash flow related to investing activities.

c. Calculate the cash flow related to financing activities.

d. Prepare a cash flow statement for Downsview for 2006 in good form.

5-37 **(Interpretation of cash flow statement)**

The following are the comparative cash flow statements for Yellow Spruce Incorporated.

YELLOW SPRUCE INCORPORATED
Comparative Cash Flow Statements
($ millions)

	2006	2005	2004
Operating activities			
Net income	57	86	98
Add back:			
Amortization	82	75	65
Loss (gain) on sale of investment	1	-0-	(11)
Effect from changes in working capital items:			
Receivables	(38)	20	(39)
Inventories	(21)	(17)	(21)
Prepaid expenses	4	23	(9)
Accounts payable	(7)	(12)	35
Cash from operations	78	175	118

Investing activities			
Acquisition of noncurrent assets	(54)	(61)	(52)
Acquisitions of investments	(123)	(151)	(172)
Proceeds from sale of noncurrent assets	16	11	27
Cash used for investing	(161)	(201)	(197)
Financing activities			
Issue in long-term debt	213	156	332
Repayment of long-term debt	(131)	(72)	(93)
Issuance of common shares	2	2	7
Repurchase of common shares	-0-	(38)	(84)
Dividends paid	(16)	(14)	(15)
Cash flow from financing	68	34	147
Net increase (decrease) in cash	(15)	8	68
Cash position at beginning of year	109	101	33
Cash position at end of year	94	109	101

Required:

a. Discuss the company's ability to meet its needs for cash over the last three years. Comment on the continuing nature of the major items that have appeared over the last three years.

b. Comment on Yellow Spruce's accounts receivable, accounts payable, and inventory policies.

c. How did Yellow Spruce finance its repayment of long-term debt and acquisition of noncurrent assets in 2006?

User Perspective Problems

5-38　(Cash flows from operations)

In this chapter, we have emphasized the importance of carefully analyzing the operating section of the cash flow statement. In fact, this section is the first one listed on the statement. From a user perspective, explain why this section is so important for an understanding of a company's financial health.

5-39　(Cash flow statement and lending decisions)

From the perspective of a bank loan officer, discuss why the cash flow statement may or may not be more important than the income statement in your analysis of a company that is applying for a loan.

5-40　(Cash flow statement and investing decisions)

From the perspective of a stock analyst, discuss why the cash flow statement may or may not be more important than the income statement in the analysis of a company for which you must make a recommendation.

5-41　(Cash flow and compensation plans)

If you were a CEO (Chief Executive Officer) of a company and wanted to use a management compensation plan to motivate your top management, would you want to base your performance targets on cash flows from operations or net income? Discuss the pros and cons of using these two measures of performance.

5-42　(Format of the cash flow statement from lending perspective)

As a lender, discuss whether you would be satisfied with the current method of classifying cash flows into only three categories. In particular, comment on the classification of interest cash flows and whether you think placing them under operating activities is appropriate.

5-43 (Accrual and cash flow accounting)

Loan officer Han Blackford once commented that cash flow analysis has risen in importance due to a "trend over the past 20 years toward capitalization and deferring more and more expenses. Although the practice may match expenses and revenues more closely, it has also made it harder to find the available cash in a company and easier for lenders to wind up with a loss." He further noted that recessions draw attend to the need for better warning signals of the sort that cash flow analysis could provide.

Required:

a. Why would the process of capitalization match expenses and revenues more closely, yet make it harder to find the cash available in a company?

b. Discuss the difference between earning power and solvency, why both are essential for a successful business, and how current financial accounting statements provide measures of each.

c. Explain why a wave of bankruptcies would draw attention to cash flow analysis.

5-44 (Cash flow analysis)

Jacques Rousseau is considering investing in Health Life Ltd., a pharmaceutical company. He read in the paper that this company is doing cancer research and is close to a breakthrough in developing a new drug that will be effective against bone cancer. The author of the article said that this was a good time to buy because, once the breakthrough happens, the share price is going to grow very rapidly. Jacques decided to look at the company's most recent financial statements. On the balance sheet, he saw that the company had a significant amount of cash and short-term investments. It had some assets listed as capital assets under capital leases, which he interpreted to mean that the company leased its buildings and equipment rather than buying them. When he looked at the income statement, he saw that there was no revenue. The largest expense was for research and development. The company had a loss last year and this year the total retained earnings on the balance sheet was in a deficit position. He thought that this made sense because the company had yet to make its first medical breakthrough. The company had very little debt, but its common shares totalled approximately $35 million. When he looked at the notes, he saw that there were about 7 million shares issued. In fact, one million of those shares were issued in the current year.

Required:

Help Jacques with his decision by answering the following questions.

a. Do you think that investing in this company would be risky? Explain.

b. Does the fact that Health Life is holding a large amount of cash and short-term investments mean that management is doing a good job? Explain in detail.

c. Is it possible for Jacques to make a rough estimate as to how much longer the cash/short-term investments will last, assuming that the company does not get its breakthrough? What information would help him make this estimate?

d. Based on the number of shares that have been issued and the amount that is recorded in common shares, it is obvious that many investors have concluded that this is a good investment. Think carefully and then list three or four advantages and disadvantages to buying shares in Health Life right now.

5-45 (Cash flow analysis)

The 2006 financial statements of Green Company include the cash flow statement reproduced below.

GREEN COMPANY
Cash Flow Statement
For the year ended December 31, 2006

Operating:		
Net income	$ 544,000	
Adjustments to convert to cash:		
Amortization	230,000	
Gain on sale of operating assets	(14,000)	
Change in current assets other than cash	(120,000)	
Change in current liabilities	80,000	
Cash provided by operations		$720,000
Investing:		
Purchase of operating assets	(1,200,000)	
Sale of operating assets	400,000	
Cash used for investing		(800,000)
Financing:		
Issuance of common shares	1,000,000	
Retirement of bonds	(1,300,000)	
Dividends paid	(250,000)	
Cash used by financing		(550,000)
Decrease in cash		($630,000)

Required:

a. Did Green Company increase or decrease its current assets other than cash in 2006? Is this change consistent with an increase or a decrease in sales during the period? Explain.

b. Has Green Company become more or less risky during 2006 from an investor's point of view? Explain.

c. Does Green Company appear to be expanding or contracting its operations? How can you tell? What other financial statement information might you examine to determine whether Green is expanding?

d. Does Green appear to be able to maintain its productive capacity without additional financing? Explain.

5-46   **(Operating section analysis)**

The operating section of Johann Manufacturing Company's cash flow statement is shown below.

JOHANN MANUFACTURING COMPANY
Cash Flow Statement
For the year ended December 31, 2006

Cash flows from operations:		
Net income		$632,000
Adjustments to convert to cash:		
Amortization	$110,000	
Loss on sale of investments	50,000	160,000
Change in current non-cash items:		
Accounts receivable	(80,000)	
Inventory	20,000	
Prepaid expenses	(15,000)	
Accounts payable	75,000	
Income tax payable	(4,000)	(4,000)
Cash provided by operations		788,000
Cash balance, January 1		566,000
Cash balance, December 31		$1,354,000

Required:

Using this information, answer the following questions. If a question cannot be answered from the information given, indicate why.

1. Have accounts receivable increased or decreased this year?

2. Does the company appear to be more or less inclined to prepay expenses than in the past? Does this help or hurt its cash position? Explain.

3. Has inventory increased or decreased this year? Explain how this affects cash.

4. Compared with last year, does the company seem to be relying more or less heavily on trade credit to finance its activities?

5. Has amortization expense increased from last year?

6. If you were a potential creditor of Johann, do you see any warning signs in the cash flow statement that you would want to investigate further before lending the company money? Explain.

7. Johann has $2 million of bonds maturing on January 12, 2007. It does not have a bond sinking fund (cash fund used to repay the bond debt) established to pay off the bonds. Do you think Johann will be able to meet its obligation to pay off the bonds without additional long-term financing? Explain.

Reading and Interpreting
Published Financial Statements

5-47 (Analysis of cash flow statement)

Exhibit 5-18 shows the consolidated statements of cash flows for **Purcell Energy Ltd.** at December 31, 2003 and 2002 and Note 16. There have been some dramatic changes in Purcell's cash position since the end of 2002.

Financial Statement Analysis Assignments

Required:

a. Prepare a list of all the sources of cash and the percentage of cash coming from each. Use cash from operating activities as one source.

b. Prepare a list of all the uses of cash and the percentage going to each.

c. Describe the changes in each of the current non-cash assets and liabilities.

d. Comment on the change in cash position and sources and uses of cash during the year, including an explanation of the major changes that occurred from the previous year.

5-48 (Analysis of cash flow statement)

Exhibit 5-19 shows the consolidated statements of cash flows for **CCL Industries Inc.** at December 31, 2003 and 2002. CCL Industries uses cash and short-term investments for its definition of cash and cash equivalents.

Required:

a. Prepare a list of all the sources of cash and the percentage of cash coming from each. Use cash provided by operating activities as one source.

b. Prepare a list of all the uses of cash and the percentage going to each.

c. Comment on the change in cash position and sources and uses of cash during the year and explain the major changes that occurred from the previous year.

d. CCL does not include any details about the items that make up the "Net change in non-cash working capital." Where would you look to find information about these items?

EXHIBIT 5-18
PART A

PURCELL ENERGY LTD. 2003 ANNUAL REPORT

Consolidated Statements of Cash Flows

For the years ended December 31	**2003**	2002
		(Restated Note 2)
Cash flows from operating activities		
Net income for the year	$ 1,696,183	$ 982,062
Adjust for non-cash items:		
Depletion, depreciation and amortization	17,066,733	12,399,453
Accretion of asset retirement obligation (Note 9)	560,756	369,866
Stock-based compensation	510,208	–
Future income taxes	1,383,094	926,060
Cash flow from operations	21,216,974	14,677,441
Net change in non-cash working capital balances (Note 16)	(1,855,989)	2,831,922
	19,360,985	17,509,363
Cash flows from financing activities		
Payments from (to) Liard Resources Ltd.	419,976	(407,768)
Decrease (increase) in deferred financing costs	166,779	(396,977)
Increase in debenture	–	5,000,000
Issue of common shares, net of related expenses	26,410,677	6,091,578
Repurchase of common shares	(3,683,436)	(3,013,588)
Issue of warrants, net of related expenses	2,914,125	–
Repayment of capital leases	–	(5,462)
Increase (decrease) in utilization of bank credit facilities	(1,906,565)	10,702,581
	24,321,556	17,970,364
Cash flows from investing activities		
Net change in non-cash working capital balances (Note 16)	(3,082,805)	488,979
Decrease (increase) in loan receivable	210,880	(736,488)
Purchase of BelAir Energy Corporation (net of cash acquired)	(6,382,769)	–
Site restoration costs incurred	(43,435)	–
Purchases of property, plant and equipment	(32,701,889)	(38,357,216)
Proceeds on disposition of property, plant and equipment	28,729	3,124,735
	(41,971,289)	(35,479,990)
Increase (decrease) in cash	1,711,252	(263)
Cash, beginning of year	300	563
Cash, end of year	$ 1,711,552	$ 300

The accompanying notes are an integral part of these consolidated financial statements.

PURCELL ENERGY LTD. 2003 ANNUAL REPORT

EXHIBIT 5-18
PART B

16. Supplemental Disclosure of Cash Flow Information

(a) Net change in non-cash working capital:

Operating activities		2003		2002
Accounts receivable	$	1,181,931	$	(2,776,540)
Prepaid expenses and deposits		140,510		(159,073)
Inventory		304,782		(294,301)
Deferred pension asset		(238,082)		(387,821)
Accounts payable and accrued liabilities		(2,961,848)		6,166,172
Corporate taxes payable		(283,282)		283,485
	$	(1,855,989)	$	2,831,922

Investing activities		2003		2002
Accounts receivable	$	(3,061,923)	$	(646,043)
Accounts payable and accrued liabilities		(20,882)		1,135,022
	$	(3,082,805)	$	488,979

(b) Additional information:

Interest and taxes paid

		2003		2002
Interest paid	$	2,764,065	$	1,438,571
Corporate taxes paid	$	770,910	$	182,666

5-49   (Analysis of cash flow statement)

Exhibit 5-20 shows the consolidated statements of cash flows for **Bema Gold Corporation** (a mining exploration company) at December 31, 2003, 2002, and 2001.

> *Required:*

a. Considering only the information presented in the statements of cash flows, describe the apparent operations and cash management policies of Bema Gold over these three years.

b. In 2003, Bema Gold had a net loss. However, it had a positive cash flow from operating activities. Explain how this occurred.

c. Assume you are considering investing in shares of Bema Gold. What additional information would you require before you could make your decision?

5-50   (Analysis of cash flow statement)

Exhibit 5-21 shows the consolidated statements of cash flows for **Algoma Central Corporation** (a shipping and real estate company) at December 31, 2003 and 2002.

> *Required:*

> a. Discuss the company's ability to meet its need for cash over the last two years. Comment on the continuing nature of the major items that have appeared over these years.

EXHIBIT 5-19 **CCL INDUSTRIES 2003 ANNUAL REPORT**

Consolidated Statements of Cash Flows

Years ended December 31, 2003 and 2002 *(in thousands of dollars)*

	2003	2002
Cash provided by (used for)		
Operating activities		
Net earnings	$ 53,033	$ 21,819
Items not requiring cash:		
Depreciation and amortization	67,385	75,785
Stock options granted	6	–
Future income taxes	7,994	4,675
Unusual items	4,245	36,878
	132,663	139,157
Net change in non-cash working capital	(3,169)	32,894
Cash provided by operating activities	129,494	172,051
Financing activities		
Proceeds of long-term debt	–	6,195
Retirement of long-term debt	(13,849)	(16,053)
Decrease in bank advances	(1,679)	(12,659)
Issue of shares	2,707	3,753
Repurchase of shares	(20,729)	(20,483)
Settlement of exercised stock options	–	(1,343)
Dividends	(11,494)	(11,441)
Cash used for financing activities	(45,044)	(52,031)
Investing activities		
Additions to capital assets	(112,247)	(71,443)
Proceeds on disposals	77,168	17,726
Business acquisitions	(104,443)	(18,249)
Other	(2,439)	(4,858)
Cash used for investing activities	(141,961)	(76,824)
Effect of exchange rates on cash	(16,783)	8
Increase (decrease) in cash	(74,294)	43,204
Cash and cash equivalents at beginning of year	156,095	112,891
Cash and cash equivalents at end of year	$ 81,801	$ 156,095

BEMA GOLD CORPORATION 2003 ANNUAL REPORT

CONSOLIDATED STATEMENTS OF CASH FLOWS

for the years ended December 31
(in thousands of United States dollars)

EXHIBIT 5-20

	2003	2002	2001
Operating activities			
Loss for the year	$(30,576)	$(3,257)	$(11,218)
Non-cash charges (credits)			
Depreciation and depletion	17,909	12,476	5,905
Amortization of deferred financing costs	1,707	2,836	2,231
Equity in losses of associated companies	94	424	100
Derivative instruments	10,565	942	(1,696)
Investment losses (gains)	45	(1,957)	(554)
Write-off of mineral property	720	–	–
Write-down of inventory	342	–	2,248
Foreign exchange	548	96	(1)
Stock-based compensation	3,147	–	–
Future income tax expense	1,255	–	–
Other	743	1,529	459
Changes in non-cash working capital *(Note 15)*	1,629	(2,760)	2,388
	8,128	10,329	(138)
Financing activities			
Common shares issued, net of issue costs *(Note 9)*	58,714	35,872	4,609
Subsidiary shares issued *(Note 5)*	–	1,540	–
Julietta project loans and overrun facility	–	–	21,200
Julietta project loan repayments	(11,167)	(5,583)	–
Petrex project loan repayments	(8,000)	–	–
Refugio loans repayments	–	(6,000)	(8,000)
Deferred financing costs	–	–	(1,840)
Other	(450)	(1,345)	(303)
	39,097	24,484	15,666
Investing activities			
Petrex Mines	(7,593)	–	–
Julietta Mine	(3,813)	(2,519)	–
Refugio exploration and development	(2,981)	(446)	(111)
Julietta development and construction	–	(2,435)	(20,064)
Kupol exploration and development	(35,920)	(8,684)	–
Acquisition, exploration and development	(6,275)	(2,145)	(1,082)
Arbitration settlement *(Note 6)*	–	5,512	–
Acquisition of EAGC, net cash acquired *(Note 4)*	6,742	–	–
Sale/ (purchase) of EAGC special warrants *(Note 4)*	16,935	(10,000)	–
Proceeds from the sale of notes receivable	–	–	3,300
Other	(977)	(1,475)	3,336
	(33,882)	(22,192)	(14,621)
Effect of exchange rate changes on cash and cash equivalents	772	(96)	1
Increase in cash and cash equivalents	14,115	12,525	908
Cash and cash equivalents, beginning of year	16,658	4,133	3,225
Cash and cash equivalents, end of year	$30,773	$16,658	$4,133

Supplementary cash flow information *(Note 15)*

EXHIBIT 5-21 **ALGOMA CENTRAL CORPORATION 2003 ANNUAL REPORT**

Years ended December 31, 2003 and 2002 (In thousands of dollars)

Consolidated Statements of Cash Flows

	2003	2002
NET INFLOW (OUTFLOW) OF CASH RELATED TO THE FOLLOWING ACTIVITIES:		
OPERATING		
Income from continuing operations	$ 11,602	$ 23,120
Items not affecting cash		
Amortization	24,965	27,508
Future income taxes	(58)	(5,660)
Other	165	(2,188)
	36,674	42,780
Net change in non-cash operating working capital *(Note 11)*	(10,876)	(5,026)
	25,798	37,754
INVESTING		
Restricted cash	8,541	(5,490)
Additions to capital assets	(22,263)	(12,592)
Proceeds from sale of capital assets	207	365
Long-term receivables	4,270	(565)
Other	(973)	(338)
	(10,218)	(18,620)
FINANCING		
Proceeds from issue of long-term debt	38,500	-
Repayment of long-term debt	(41,267)	(3,802)
Dividends paid	(3,797)	(3,795)
	(6,564)	(7,597)
LOSS ON CASH HELD IN FOREIGN CURRENCY	(903)	(4)
TOTAL CASH INCREASE FOR YEAR FROM CONTINUING OPERATIONS	8,113	11,533
CASH FROM DISCONTINUED OPERATIONS *(Note 2)*	2,059	254
CASH POSITION, BEGINNING OF YEAR	52,141	40,354
CASH POSITION, END OF YEAR	$ 62,313	$ 52,141

ACETEX CORPORATION 2003 ANNUAL REPORT

EXHIBIT 5-22

ACETEX CORPORATION

Consolidated Statements of Cash Flows

(Expressed in thousands of United States dollars)

Years ended December 31, 2003, 2002 and 2001

	2003	2002	2001
Cash provided by (used for):			
Operations:			
Net earnings (loss)	$ (18,977)	$ (12,923)	$ (1,644)
Charges and credits to income not involving cash:			
Amortization	23,091	16,248	14,854
Loss on debt refinancing	–	–	6,352
Pension expense (recovery)	(375)	(36)	499
Amortization of deferred financing costs	898	971	890
Distributions received from equity			
investee in excess of income	(256)	(29)	328
Unrealized foreign exchange loss	3,347	–	–
Other	3,655	1,011	–
Changes in non-cash operating working capital:			
Accounts receivable	1,633	8,318	2,234
Inventory	4,584	1,174	(3,046)
Prepaid expenses and other	(283)	(1,116)	2,421
Accounts payable and accrued liabilities	(3,305)	4,175	(10,337)
	14,012	17,793	15,839
Investments:			
Acquisition of AT Plastics	(9,129)	–	–
Purchase of property, plant, and equipment	(6,954)	(12,893)	(2,920)
Other	(217)	(246)	(1,101)
	(16,300)	(13,139)	(4,021)
Financing:			
Increase in share capital	125	449	505
Proceeds from issuance of long-term debt	82,125	–	190,000
Repayment of long-term debt	(90,496)	–	(180,000)
Financing costs incurred	(3,427)	–	(11,867)
Increase (decrease) in pension obligation	(81)	589	(61)
Repurchase of common shares	(597)	(2,305)	–
	(12,351)	(1,267)	(1,423)
Foreign exchange gain (loss) on cash and cash			
equivalents held in foreign currencies	6,652	6,898	(2,365)
Increase (decrease) in cash and cash equivalents	(7,987)	10,285	8,030
Cash and cash equivalents, beginning of year	61,890	51,605	43,575
Cash and cash equivalents, end of year	$ 53,903	$ 61,890	$ 51,605
Supplementary information:	$ 21,511	$ 20,318	$ 17,550
Interest paid	425	150	1,838
Issuance of equity instruments on acquisition of business (note 3)	40,759	–	–

See accompanying notes to consolidated financial statements.

b. Which items would require more investigation or further explanation, or both, to help you understand the company's financial health?

c. Explain why, although the amount of net income declined by approximately half in 2003, the difference in cash from operations declined by less than half.

5-51 **(Analysis of cash flow statement)**

Exhibit 5-22 shows the consolidated statements of cash flows for **Acetex Corporation** for the years ended December 31, 2003, 2002, and 2001.

Required:

a. Discuss the company's ability to meet its needs for cash over the last three years. Comment on the continuing nature of the major items that have appeared over these years.

b. Which items would require more investigation or further explanation, or both, to help you understand the company's financial health?

c. Discuss why there was a positive cash flow from operations during 2003 although the company experienced a net loss for 2003.

d. In this chapter, we talked about the inclusion of supplementary information about the amount of cash paid for interest and income tax. Note at the bottom of the Acetex cash flow statement that both the interest and the income taxes paid during the year are disclosed and that there is a third item: issuance of equity instruments on acquisition of business. To whom do you think the company is aiming this information and why do you think it was included? Explain.

5-52 **(Analysis of cash flow statement)**

Exhibit 5-23 shows the consolidated statements of cash flows for **The Forzani Group** for the years ended February 1, 2004 and February 2, 2003.

Required:

a. Discuss the company's ability to meet its needs for cash over the last two years. Comment on the continuing nature of the major items that have appeared over these years.

b. Which items would require more investigation or further explanation, or both, to help you understand the company's financial health?

c. In 2004, The Forzani Group's net income declined slightly from 2003. However, the amount of cash generated from operating activities increased dramatically. Provide an explanation as to what happened during the year to produce this result.

5-53 **(Analysis of cash flow statement)**

Sun-Rype Products Ltd. Annual Report

Go to the text companion website and find the cash flow statements for **Sun-Rype Products Ltd.** for the years 2003 and 2002.

Required:

a. Discuss the company's ability to meet its needs for cash over the last two years. Comment on the continuing nature of the major items that have appeared over these years.

b. Which items would require more investigation or further explanation, or both, to help you understand the company's financial health?

THE FORZANI GROUP LTD. 2003 ANNUAL REPORT

THE FORZANI GROUP LTD.

Consolidated Statements of Cash Flows

(in thousands)

(audited)

	For the 52 weeks ended February 1, 2004	For the 53 weeks ended February 2, 2003 (Note 3)
Cash provided by (used in) operating activities		
Net earnings	$ 28,019	$ 29,985
Items not involving cash		
Amortization	31,183	29,624
Amortization of deferred finance charges	430	571
Amortization of deferred lease inducements	(8,092)	(8,767)
Stock-based compensation	2,342	546
Gain on sale of investment	-	(1,445)
Future income tax expense (recovery)	374	(2,201)
	54,256	48,313
Changes in non-cash elements of working capital (Note 8)	10,989	(27,300)
	65,245	21,013
Cash provided by (used in) financing activities		
Proceeds from issuance of share capital	4,014	40,416
Increase (decrease) of long-term debt	2,595	(13,786)
(Decrease) in revolving credit facility	(4,204)	(12,890)
Proceeds from deferred lease inducements	8,795	14,395
	11,200	28,135
Cash provided by (used in) investing activities		
Addition of capital assets	(48,394)	(50,085)
Net change in other assets	(5,727)	(1,000)
Sale of investment	-	1,690
Disposal of capital assets	468	276
	(53,653)	(49,119)
Increase in cash	22,792	29
Net cash position, opening	523	494
Net cash position, closing	$ 23,315	$ 523

Supplementary cash flow information (Note 8)

c. In this chapter, we talked about the inclusion of supplementary information about interest and income taxes paid during the year. Note at the bottom of Sun-Rype's cash flow statement that both of these items are disclosed. To whom do you think it is aiming this information? Explain.

Beyond the Book

5-54   (Analysis of cash flow statement)

For a company of your own choosing, answer the following questions related to its cash flow statement.

a. Summarize the results for cash from operating, investing, and financing activities over the last two years.

b. Explain any significant changes from last year to this year in the items listed in part a).

c. What were the four most significant uses of cash (from the investing and financing sections)?

d. What were the four most significant sources of cash, including operations?

e. How is the company financing its investing activities, through operating or financing activities, or both? Support your answer with numbers.

Cases

5-55   Atlantic Service Company

Case Primer

Atlantic Service Company was established five years ago to provide services to the home construction industry. It has been very successful, with assets, sales, and profits increasing each year. However, Atlantic is experiencing serious cash shortages and is in danger of going into bankruptcy because it cannot pay its suppliers and already has a very substantial overdraft at its bank. The president has asked you to analyze the cash flow statement for the years ended December 31, 2006 and 2005, in Exhibit 5-24, to explain what appears to be causing the cash shortage, and to recommend a plan to save the company from bankruptcy.

EXHIBIT 5-24

ATLANTIC SERVICE COMPANY

Cash Flow Statement

For the years ended December 31, 2006 and 2005

	2006	2005
Operations:		
Net income	$150,000	$135,000
Adjustments to convert to cash:		
Amortization	25,000	20,000
Changes in non-cash working capital:		
Increase in accounts receivable	(35,000)	(30,000)
Increase in inventory	(30,000)	(25,000)
Increase in accounts payable	55,000	45,000
	165,000	145,000
Financing:		
Increase in one-year bank loan	50,000	30,000
Dividends paid	(15,000)	(10,000)
	35,000	20,000

Investing:

Purchase of equipment	(300,000)	(250,000)
Net cash used in the year	(100,000)	(85,000)
Cash position, beginning of the year	(130,000)	(45,000)
Cash position, end of the year	($230,000)	($130,000)

5-56 Robertson Furniture Ltd.

Kayla Moss has just received a small inheritance from her grandparents' estate. She would like to invest the money and is currently reviewing several investment opportunities. A friend has brought her the financial statements of Robertson Furniture Ltd., a great company she found on the Internet. Kayla has reviewed the financial statements of Robertson Furniture and is ready to invest in this company. Before she invests, Kayla comes to you for some financial advice because she knows you have just finished an accounting course and may be able to give her some insight into the financial statements. She is very certain that this company will be a profitable investment because the balance sheet indicates that the company has cash balances of over $300,000. She has copied Robertson's statement of cash flow so that you can see how much cash the company is able to generate each year.

ROBERTSON FURNITURE LTD.

EXHIBIT 5-25

Cash Flow Statement
For the Year Ended December 31, 2006

	2006	2005
Operations activities		
Net income (loss)	$ (5,000)	$ 1,000
Add back items not representing cash flows:		
Amortization	20,000	50,000
Loss on disposal	2,000	1,000
Adjustment for working capital items:		
Increase in accounts receivable	(40,000)	(36,000)
Increase in inventories	(56,000)	(42,000)
Decrease in prepaid insurance	8,000	2,000
Increase in accounts payable	45,000	28,000
Cash from operating activities	(26,000)	4,000
Financing activities		
Issue of bonds payable	100,000	-
Issue of common shares	50,000	50,000
Payment of dividends	(1,000)	(20,000)
Cash from financing activities	149,000	30,000
Investing activities		
Sale of property, plant, and equipment	70,500	22,400
Sale of investments	50,000	20,000
Cash from investing activities	120,500	42,400
Increase in cash	243,500	76,400
Cash—beginning of the year	84,950	8,550
Cash—end of the year	$ 328,450	$ 84,950

Required:

a. Comment on Robertson Furniture's cash flow statement, keeping in mind Kayla's opinion that the company must be a good investment given the amount of cash shown on the balance sheet.

b. Based on the results in the cash flow statement, outline several questions that Kayla should investigate before investing her inheritance in this company.

5-57   **Vassar Inc.**

The 2006 comparative income statement and balance sheet of Vassar Inc. have just been distributed at a meeting of the company's board of directors.

While discussing the business's year-end results, the board raises concerns over the year-end cash balance. The directors cannot understand why the cash balance is so low given the increase in profitability over the past year. As the chief financial officer, the board is looking to you for answers to their questions.

Required:

a. Using the indirect method, prepare a cash flow statement for the year ended December 31, 2006. In addition to the balance sheet and income statement presented below, you gather the following information (amounts in thousands).

- In 2005, the company sold capital assets for $2,500. These assets had originally cost $4000 and had a net book value of $2,750. While no capital assets were sold in 2006, equipment costing $165 was purchased for use in the company's manufacturing facilities.

- Vassar paid dividends of $1,000 in 2006.

- The company sold no other long-term assets or investments.

- Vassar issued no common shares or long-term debt in 2006, but did issue bonds worth $10,000 in 2005.

b. Using all the information available to you, prepare an answer to the questions raised by the board explaining why the cash balance is low when the company is experiencing record profits.

EXHIBIT 5-26   **VASSAR INC.**

Balance Sheet
At December 31, 2006
(in thousands)

	2006	2005
Assets		
Cash	$ 89	$ 398
Accounts receivable	1,580	1,578
Inventory	9,852	8,750
Total current assets	11,521	10,726
Capital assets	10,917	10,752
Less: accumulated amortization	(862)	(745)
Total assets	$ 21,576	$ 20,733
Liabilities and Shareholders' Equity		
Accounts payable	$ 1,450	$ 1,276
Salaries payable	85	66
Interest payable	22	36
Total current liabilities	1,557	1,378
Bonds payable	10,000	10,000
Total liabilities	11,557	11,378
Common shares	8,000	8,000
Retained earnings	2,019	1,355
Total shareholders' equity	10,019	9,355
Total liabilities and shareholders' equity	$ 21,576	$ 20,733

VASSAR INC.
Income Statement
For the Year Ended December 31, 2006
(in thousands)

	2006	2005
Sales revenue	$ 70,595	$ 56,238
Cost of goods sold	46,120	36,555
Gross profit	24,475	19,683
Salaries expense	10,586	9,265
Administrative expense	8,850	7,952
Rent and maintenance expense	1,620	1,541
Amortization	117	121
Insurance expense	52	66
Advertising expense	76	43
Income from operations	3,174	695
Other income (expenses)		
Gain on sale of capital assets	—	250
Interest expense	(1,000)	(375)
Income before income tax	2,174	570
Income tax	510	139
Net income	$ 1,664	$ 431

5-58 Ridlow Shipping

Jim Shea is an accountant at Powers, Barnes, and King, an accounting firm based in Halifax, Nova Scotia. The firm specializes in dealing with small business clients and, while most clients are very successful businesspeople, many have limited accounting knowledge. Owen Ridlow is the sole owner of Ridlow Shipping and he recently called Jim with some questions about the financial statements prepared for the year ended December 31, 2006.

Owen: "Jim, I am wondering why I have to pay you guys to prepare a cash flow statement. I understand the importance of the balance sheet and the income statement, but since I always know how much cash I have in the bank and I reconcile my accounts regularly, why do I need a cash flow statement? I feel that paying to have this statement prepared is an unnecessary expense."

Required:

Do you feel that Owen is justified in his comments? Outline several points that Jim should raise in his discussions with Owen to justify the need for a cash flow statement. The cash flow statement for Ridlow Shipping has been provided to assist you in preparing your answer.

EXHIBIT 5-27

RIDLOW SHIPPING LTD.
Cash Flow Statement
For the Year Ended December 31, 2006

	2006	2005
Operating activities		
Net income	$ 206,450	$ 254,560
Add back items not representing cash flows:		
Amortization	40,000	50,000
Loss on disposal	2,000	6,000
Adjustment for working capital items:		
Decrease (increase) in accounts receivable	(40,000)	16,000
Increase in inventories	(5,000)	(2,000)
Decrease in prepaid rent	500	200
Increase (decrease) in accounts payable	45,000	(28,000)
Cash from operating activities	248,950	296,760

Financing activities		
Payment of bonds	(100,000)	-
Issue of common shares	50,000	-
Payment of dividends	(75,000)	(75,000)
Cash from financing activities	(125,000)	(75,000)
Investing activities		
Sale of investments	50,000	20,000
Purchase of capital assets	(215,000)	(197,000)
Cash from investing activities	(165,000)	(177,000)
Increase in cash	(41,050)	44,760
Cash—beginning of the year	53,310	8,550
Cash—end of the year	$ 12,260	$ 53,310

5-59   Jones Printing

Ben Jones would like to expand his printing business to include a new computerized colour printing system. To finance the equipment, Ben has applied for a loan from a government venture capital agency. The agency requires a complete set of financial statements before it can approve any loan application and has employees assigned to each applicant to assist them in preparing the necessary financial statements.

You have been assigned to assist Ben and he has provided you with a basic income statement and balance sheet for his business. You explain to Ben that a complete set of financial statements includes a cash flow statement and that one will have to be prepared for his business before the loan application can be processed. Ben does not understand the purpose of the cash flow statement and what types of information he will have to gather in order to prepare it.

Required:

Prepare a brief memo to Ben Jones outlining the purpose and structure of the cash flow statement and any additional information beyond the income statement and balance sheet that he will have to provide to assist you in preparing a cash flow statement for his business.

Critical Thinking Question

5-60   (Universality of the definition of cash and cash equivalents)

As discussed in this chapter, the cash flow statement provides users of financial information with another flow measure of a company's performance. However, several issues have been raised in both academic and practitioner-oriented research relative to the meaning, usefulness, and calculation of cash flows. For example, Wallace and Collier ("The Cash in Cash Flow Statements: A Multi-Country Comparison," *Accounting Horizons*, December 1991) describe how various countries, including Canada, have issued standards regarding the presentation of cash flows but have failed to define the term "cash" either consistently or adequately. The changes made in 1998 in Canada with respect to the cash flow statement define cash as cash on hand and demand deposits and cash equivalents as short-term, highly liquid investments that are readily convertible to known amounts of cash and which are subject to an insignificant risk of changes in value (*CICA Handbook*, Sec. 1540.06). It goes on to define short-term as three months or less, and to restrict investments to non-equity ones. It also includes bank overdrafts, which are payable on demand, in the cash equivalents.

Required:

Look up the Wallace and Collier article in your library, briefly summarize the authors' arguments, and discuss the potential problems associated with the lack of a uniform definition of cash both for companies that have only domestic operations and for those that have both domestic and foreign operations. Discuss whether the new Canadian requirements address their arguments or whether they are still deficient.

Santa's Village, in Ontario's beautiful Muskoka region, offers tourists a variety of attractions, including Rudolph's Roller Coaster, the Christmas Ball Ferris Wheel, and Santa's Summer Sleigh River Boat Cruise. Visitors to the theme park can also get wet at the Splashzone, feed deer at Santa's farm, or see Santa himself in his summer home. Adjacent to Santa's Village is Sportsland, which includes go-carts, minigolf, batting cages, laser tag, and an arcade.

This busy tourist operation deals with a large amount of money—in the neighbourhood of $45,000 to $50,000 in cash alone on any given day, says finance manager Laura Pepper. With this kind of cash flow, strict control procedures must be in place. All the cash at Santa's Village is kept in a "cash vault," a secured concrete room where three staff members distribute and receive cash through an opening in a Plexiglas window. "They're responsible for balancing and controlling the cash that's coming in, as well as the floats that go out in the morning," says Ms. Pepper.

Approximately 35 cashiers work at various locations throughout the park: at the front gate, gift shop, food kiosks, and Sportsland, to name a few. In the morning, each cashier counts and signs out a pre-determined float, the amount of which varies depending on where the cashier is working. Throughout the day, supervisors collect excess cash as needed and take it to the vault. Any money taken from the cash registers is recorded; the cashiers keep a copy of the "cash overflow" for their records.

At the end of the day, the cashiers bring all the cash, as well as credit card and Interac transaction records, to the "cash out area" near the vault. After removing the float, they add up all their revenue, including any overflows, and fill out a daily cash register report. Meanwhile, their manager collects the cash register's Z-report, which lists all the transactions that took place that day. A vault staff member then compares the two reports.

If there is a discrepancy of more than $5, the cashier's supervisor is called in to help find

the problem. "Usually they can find the difference," Ms. Pepper says, indicating it is often a matter of voided bills that weren't taken off the register, or a roll of quarters that was counted as nickels.

Once the cash is taken into the vault, the bills and coins are sorted and recounted, the total again compared with the Z-reports. The vault staff then does a "coin changeover," exchanging all the coins for larger bills from the vault's money. The day's revenue is then deposited in the bank each evening.

Ms. Pepper goes on-line to the bank every day to ensure that the previous night's cash deposit is in the company's account, although she has to wait a few days for the processing of credit card or Interac transactions. Monthly bank reconciliation, however, is not an option in the seasonal tourist trade. Since Santa's Village is open for only 95 days (daily from mid-June to Labour Day, then on weekends through September), its managers need balanced financial statements biweekly. "The cut-off is every other Saturday night, and we provide them complete financial statements by the following Tuesday," Ms. Pepper says. There's no rest for the finance staff who control the cash at Santa's summer home.

chapter 6

Cash, Temporary Investments, and Accounts and Notes Receivable

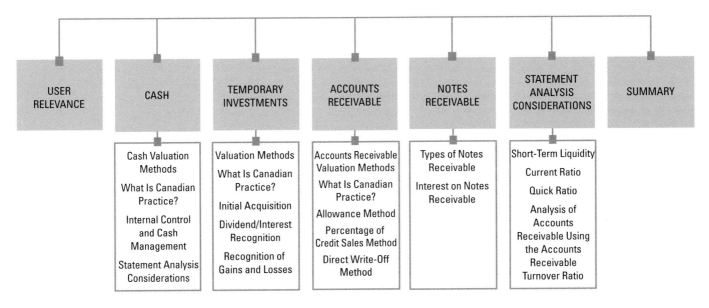

After studying this chapter, you should be able to:

1. Discuss the main control issues related to cash.

2. Recognize the importance of cash to the success of a business.

3. Prepare a simple bank reconciliation.

4. Identify the criteria for classifying an investment as temporary.

5. Explain why temporary investments are recorded market using valuation.

6. Prepare the journal entries associated with the acquisition, holding, and selling of temporary investments.

7. Explain why estimating the potential uncollectibility of accounts receivable is required.

8. Identify two methods for recognizing uncollectibility, and describe the circumstances under which each is appropriate.

9. Describe the main types of notes receivable and explain the circumstances under which they are used.

10. Calculate interest associated with notes receivable and prepare the necessary journal entries.

11. Calculate the current ratio, the quick ratio, and the accounts receivable turnover ratio.

12. Explain how the current ratio, the quick ratio, and the accounts receivable turnover ratio help users to understand short-term liquidity issues.

Our opening story talks about handling and controlling large amounts of cash, which is one of the topics in this chapter. Cash is obviously a very important asset for any organization, and a business like Santa's Village needs to have a well-designed system for processing its cash receipts, in order to ensure that they are dealt with securely and recorded properly. Such a system is usually referred to as *internal control.*

Many of the features of a good system of internal control are mentioned in the description of the operations at Santa's Village. These include measures such as having independent counts of the cash receipts, reconciliations of the cash receipts with the register tapes, daily bank deposits, and biweekly reconciliations of the accounting records for cash with the statements produced by the company's bank. These and other elements of systems for controlling and accounting for cash will be discussed further in this chapter.

USER RELEVANCE

The three major topics discussed in this chapter—cash, temporary investments, and accounts and notes receivable—represent the most liquid of a company's assets. It is mainly from these items that the company is going to meet its immediate, short-term obligations. Users need to be aware of what these items are when they see them on financial statements. For example, cash seems to be very straightforward, but in reality it constitutes a series of things ranging from physical money to amounts in bank accounts to cheques and money orders. The temporary investments are an indication to the user that the company is managing its cash. It is taking cash that it does not need immediately and investing it, so that rather than lying idle, it is earning revenue. When the cash is needed, these investments will be sold. Accounts receivable are usually collected within 30 days. However, as a user you need to be aware of potential uncollectibility and of any agreements that allow the customer more than the usual period of time to pay.

Having these items on the financial statements enables users who are interested in the company's short-term ability to meet its obligations to evaluate its capacity to do so. A deeper understanding of these items will improve your ability to assess a company's short-term vulnerability.

The assets discussed in this chapter have the unique property that all are either cash or will become cash very soon. In accounting terms, we often call them **monetary** assets because their value is fixed in current monetary terms. Obviously, they are very important to every business since, as we learned in Chapter 5, sufficient cash must be available at all times to pay for purchases and other obligations as they become due.

In this chapter, the accounting methods and principles that apply to cash, temporary investments, and accounts and notes receivable are considered. In each account category, we discuss recognition criteria, valuation methods, income statement implications, financial statement analysis considerations, and other issues that are important to understanding that account category. The complexities of financial statement analysis associated with this group of accounts are discussed in this chapter, and each subsequent chapter, in a section entitled "Statement Analysis Considerations."

CASH

In Chapter 1, we discussed the criteria that are used to decide whether, for accounting purposes, something is an asset. Assets are identified as items that: (1) have probable future value that can be measured, (2) the company owns or has the right to use, and (3) arose from a past event. In this chapter, we will use these criteria to decide whether and how we will categorize cash, temporary investments, and accounts and notes receivable as assets.

Cash meets the probable future value criterion. It derives its value from its ability to be exchanged for goods and services in the future, which is also called its **purchasing power**. Cash serves as the medium of exchange in every economy, but it relies on the individuals who use it to have faith in the economy. If there is a loss of confidence about its exchangeability in the future, the currency loses its value. For example, Argentina recently experienced difficulty making its international borrowing repayments. Up until early 2002, the country's currency, the peso, was tied one-to-one with the U.S. dollar. In an attempt to get greater control of its economy, Argentina unpegged its currency from the U.S. dollar. People in Argentina immediately became concerned that the peso would lose value, and attempted to withdraw their money from banks so that they could invest it in assets that would not lose value. A full run on the banks could have precipitated a complete collapse of the Argentine economy. To stop this happening, the country has on several occasions frozen bank accounts, preventing depositors from withdrawing their money. By the end of April 2002, the Argentine peso had dropped to half its former value.

Cash also meets the ownership/right-to-use criterion. Ownership of cash is generally evidenced by possession: currency, cheques, money orders, etc. in safes, and money deposited in banks. Currency (bills and coins) is difficult to differentiate, except by using serial numbers on bills. It is therefore a very difficult asset to control. To deal with this problem, companies make extensive use of banks, and more and more cash transactions are conducted electronically using credit or debit cards, thus eliminating the physical handling of cash. This makes the control of cash much easier and the processing of transactions much more efficient. All companies must establish effective internal control procedures to govern how they handle and control their cash. Auditors review the internal control systems established by a company and design special audit procedures to test whether these controls adequately safeguard the handling and recording of cash.

The third criterion, the occurrence of a past event that transferred the cash to the company, is also met. Cash flowing in or out of a company is a signal that a transaction has occurred. If cash is present, a past event must have occurred.

Cash Valuation Methods

Knowing that cash meets the recognition criterion, the next problem is how to record the cash in the accounting system. For this account and for all other accounts discussed in this text, a number of possible valuation methods will be discussed. Some of these methods are not allowed under Canadian GAAP but are allowed in other countries. The purpose of discussing the range of possible methods is to lay out, conceptually, the possibilities that serve as the basis for current practice. A separate section is devoted to Canadian GAAP requirements. In some

LEARNING OBJECTIVE 1

Discuss the main control issues related to cash.

cases, the methods used under Canadian GAAP are a combination of the various possible valuation methods discussed here.

One possible method of valuing cash is to record it at its face value. This means that as long as cash is held, its value is assumed not to change. If we had $100 in cash, the cash would be valued at $100. If that same $100 was present several weeks later, it would still be valued at $100. Its face value does not change.

Even though the face value of the $100 does not change, its ability to be converted into goods and services—called its purchasing power—may change. Purchasing power is affected by inflation and deflation. During periods of inflation, cash sustains a loss in purchasing power because of its relative loss in terms of exchangeability for goods and services. If prices have risen, the $100 can buy fewer goods and services than it could before. In the example we are using here, the attribute of face value does not change, but the attribute of purchasing power does. If, however, the attribute of purchasing power is used to value cash, then a gain or loss would have to be recognized for the change in purchasing power during the accounting period. Consequently, the choice of which attribute of cash to measure is critical to how it is represented on the balance sheet and how it affects the income statement.

accounting in the news

From Burgernomics to Lattenomics

The Economist magazine put a new spin on its annual Big Mac index, the much-anticipated survey of a currency's purchasing power, by testing whether a Starbucks tall latte (served in 32 countries) would result in the same conclusions as the Big Mac index. The index is based on the concept of *purchasing power parity*, which predicts that the exchange rate should adjust to equalize the prices of the same goods and services across countries.

The survey determined what exchange rates would make the cost of buying a latte in the United States the same as buying one in other countries. The rates were then compared with actual exchange rates, providing a measure of how under- or overvalued the currencies were. Coincidentally, at $2.80, the tall latte's average price in the United States was the same as a Big Mac's.

For most Western currencies, the latte index provided basically the same information as the Big Mac index. The euro was about 30% overvalued against the dollar, based on the average latte price of €2.93 ($3.70). The cost of the Starbucks coffee in the United Kingdom indicated that the pound sterling was 17% overvalued. By both the Big Mac and the latte measures, the Swiss franc was the world's most overvalued currency, while the Canadian, Australian, and New Zealand dollars remained undervalued against the U.S. dollar.

In Asia, the two measures differed. In Japan, the yen was 12% undervalued according to the burger index, but 13% overvalued based on the price of lattes. Similarly, the Chinese yuan was 56% undervalued according to the Big Mac, but on par with the U.S. dollar according to the Starbucks index. The pricing differences likely reflect differences in the extent of market competition for the two products.

Source: "Burgers or beans?" *The Economist*, January 15, 2004; "The Big Mac index," *The Economist*, January 15, 2004.

What Is Canadian Practice?

Recognize the importance of cash to the success of a business.

In Canada, there is an underlying assumption, referred to as the **unit-of-measure assumption**, which specifies that the results of business activities should be measured in terms of a **monetary unit** (e.g., the Canadian dollar). This precludes measuring activities in terms of purchasing power; cash is, therefore, measured at its face value rather than by any other method.

While the unit-of-measure assumption requires that Canadian currency be measured at face value, this is not the case for foreign currency. Suppose, for example, that a company does business with a German customer and that the agreement with the customer is denominated in euros (the currency used by most European countries). This means that the customer is required to pay in euros rather than Canadian dollars. The company will receive euros and may hold a certain amount of euro currency at the beginning and the end of the accounting period. Because this asset is measured in a different monetary unit than the rest of the company's assets, a conversion will have to be made from euros to Canadian dollars.

In Canada, the conversion of euros into dollars is done using the exchange rate that exists on the date of the balance sheet. For example, suppose the exchange rate is 1 euro = 1.65 Canadian dollars at the beginning of the year and 1 euro = 1.60 Canadian dollars at the end of the year. Further, suppose that the company holds 1,000 euros at the beginning and the end of the year. Exhibit 6-1 shows how the euro would be valued on the balance sheet. You can see that, while there is no gain or loss during the year in terms of euros (the face value does not change), there is a loss in terms of dollars. This loss will appear on the income statement and will be called a foreign currency translation loss.

FOREIGN CURRENCY VALUATION

EXHIBIT 6-1

Date	Amount of Foreign Currency	Amount of Exchange Rate	Cdn. Currency
Jan. 1	1,000 euros	1 euro = $1.65	$1,650
Dec. 31	1,000 euros	1 euro = $1.60	$1,600
Loss	0 euros		$50

Exchange rates are determined in the foreign currency markets. Reasons for changes in the exchange rates of currencies are difficult to pinpoint precisely but, in theory, one major cause is differential inflation rates in the two countries (the economic theory that describes this is called the purchasing power parity theory). Individuals who hold currencies in countries with high inflation rates lose more purchasing power than those in countries with low inflation rates. Exchange rates adjust to compensate for these differences in purchasing power. In effect, GAAP recognizes the changes in purchasing power of foreign currency by allowing the dollar value of the foreign currencies to rise and fall with the exchange rates.

One final note with regard to purchasing power. In the mid- to late 1970s and in the early 1980s, Canada experienced high rates of inflation (by Canadian standards). Accounting regulators became concerned with the problem that income, as measured by GAAP, did not take into consideration the changes in the purchasing power of assets and liabilities. In 1982, the Canadian Institute of Chartered Accountants (CICA) adopted guidelines that required companies to present supplementary information regarding the effects of changing price levels on their financial results. These requirements were dropped in 1992, when inflation was down to more normal levels. Therefore, in

Canada, there is currently no systematic reporting of the effects of inflation or changing prices on companies' financial results. However, in many countries where inflation rates are high, financial statements must be prepared in ways that recognize the loss in purchasing power of their currencies over time.

AN INTERNATIONAL PERSPECTIVE

NAFTA Facts

United States   Inflation levels have been very low in the United States. As a result, its financial statements are based primarily on historical costs, as in Canada. The U.S. currently does not require any inflation adjustments.

Mexico   In the past, Mexico has had periods of high inflation. In 1983, for example, its consumer price index increased by 101.9%. By 1993, however, its inflation rate was reduced to 9.8%, and by 2003 it was down to 2.9%.

Even though its inflation raes have been much lower recently than in the past, financial statements in Mexico are adjusted for changes in the general price level. Inventory, fixed assets, and their related expenses may, alternatively, be adjusted to reflect current replacement costs.

Internal Control and Cash Management

Despite the issues discussed so far, accounting for cash is relatively straightforward: you simply report how much cash the company owns. By cash, we mean currency, cheques, money orders, and amounts in bank accounts that can be used with very short notice.

The main issues with cash are the control of cash to ensure that it is not lost or stolen, and the management of cash balances. Proper control of cash includes policies such as ensuring that all cash is deposited into bank accounts daily (or even more frequently), using secure safes and tills to hold cash until it is deposited, writing cheques instead of using cash to pay expenses, and keeping as little cash on hand as possible. Control of cash is one part of a company's **internal control system**.

Management is responsible for safeguarding all the company assets. To accomplish this, policies and procedures are established to help protect and manage assets such as cash, inventory, supplies, and equipment. Besides the features mentioned above, an effective control system should include the following.

1. **Physical measures** aimed at protecting the assets from theft or vandalism. Management needs to protect the assets by ensuring that premises are secure through the use of locks and/or alarms. In the case of cash, this means depositing cash in the bank regularly and keeping cash that is on the premises securely stored in tills and safes.

2. **Separation of duties**. Employees have the opportunity to defraud a company if, for example, they are in charge of purchasing assets, inspecting them on arrival to ensure that what was ordered has been received, and recording the receipt of the assets in the accounting system. To reduce this opportunity for

fraud, management should ensure that one person is not responsible for all these activities. When one person is responsible for verifying the work of another, dishonest behaviour requires collusion, which is more difficult to plan and execute. With respect to cash, separation of duties means that one person receives cash, another is authorized to write cheques, and a third records the receipt or payment of cash in the accounting records. In a small company, separation of duties may be more difficult to achieve, because of the limited number of employees. In this case, management itself must periodically verify the work of employees.

3. **An effective record-keeping system**. Management establishes an accounting system such that all transactions are recorded on a timely basis, only authorized personnel record transactions, and all personnel authorized to record transactions have the appropriate training, to ensure that errors are minimized.

You may think that this concern about internal control is excessive. However, Canadian companies lose millions of dollars annually due to fraud perpetrated by their employees.

accounting in the news

A Company's New Chapter

The financial and organizational woes of Cinar Corp. came to a close in 2004 with the completion of a takeover led by Michael Hirsh, the founder of Toronto animation house Nelvana Ltd.

Cinar, creator of the popular children's television shows *Arthur* and *Caillou*, demonstrated major weaknesses in internal control of its money when it disclosed in March 2000 that $122 million (U.S.) had been invested in Bahamian hedge funds without authorization from the board. The company was also accused of tax-credit fraud by using federal Canadian-content subsidies to pay American scriptwriters. Trading of the company's stock was halted in April 2000, and founders Micheline Charest and Ronald Weinberg were fired from management and the board, and fined $1 million each as part of a settlement with the Quebec Securities Commission.

The trading ban was temporarily lifted in January 2004 to allow the takeover bid to go through. With the takeover, the president and the board were replaced. The new owners plan to expand the company and to take it private.

Source: "Cinar Corp. president and board to step down after takeover closes," *The Canadian Press*, January 22, 2004.

One control procedure used by virtually every company is the **bank reconciliation**, which ensures that any difference between the accounting records and the bank records are identified and explained.

Every bank account has a corresponding general ledger account in the company's accounting system. The company's records and the bank's records ultimately reflect the same transactions, such as cash deposits and cheques written, but the transactions may be recorded at different times. For example, a company writes, records, and mails a cheque on November 1; the payee receives it on November 7 and deposits it in its bank account on November 8. The payee's bank then forwards the cheque to the company's bank, which withdraws the money from the company's account on November 9. Because the transaction takes several days to complete, the cheque will be outstanding from the time the company records it on November 1 until the bank shows it as a withdrawal from the company's account on November 9. While the cheque is outstanding, the two accounts (the general ledger and the bank's records) will be different. As illustrated below, there can also be other reasons for differences between the company's cash records and the bank's records. The bank reconciliation is the process used to account for all such differences.

The following information about Gelardi Company illustrates a bank reconciliation.

- The balance in Gelardi's cash account on March 31 was $9,763.42.

- The balance in Gelardi's bank account on March 31 was $9,043.92.

- The accountant reviewed the bank statement and the transactions in the cash account, and discovered the following.

  - Cheque #8889 for $462.89 and #8891 for $65.78 were still outstanding (they had been mailed to suppliers, but they had not yet been processed by the bank).

  - The last deposit of the month, for $1,035.62, was made as a night deposit and the bank did not record it in Gelardi's bank account until April 2.

  - The bank had included a bank charge of $25.75 for March, but the accountant had not yet recorded it in the company's books.

  - The bank had returned a cheque from one of Gelardi's customers marked NSF (not sufficient funds). This was a cheque for $186.80 that a customer had given the company in payment for some merchandise. Gelardi had accepted the cheque, recorded it as an increase to the cash account, and deposited it in its bank account. The bank increased the balance in Gelardi's account to reflect this deposit. However, when Gelardi's bank presented the cheque to the customer's bank for payment, it was informed that the customer did not have enough money in his bank account to cover the cheque. Consequently, Gelardi's bank returned the cheque to Gelardi and removed the amount from the bank account.

Using this information, the accountant would prepare a bank reconciliation such as the following.

BANK RECONCILIATION
FOR THE MONTH OF MARCH

Balance per bank statement		$ 9,043.92
Add: Outstanding deposit		1,035.62
		10,079.54
Deduct: Outstanding cheques		
#8889	$ 462.89	
#8891	65.78	528.67
Adjusted bank balance		$ 9,550.87
Balance per cash account		$ 9,763.42
Deduct: Bank charges	$ 25.75	
NSF cheque	186.80	212.55
Adjusted cash balance		$ 9,550.87

The accountant now knows that all the differences between the company's records and the bank's records with respect to cash have been identified and explained, and also that the appropriate cash balance is $9,550.87. After the bank reconciliation is complete, the accountant needs to make a journal entry to adjust the cash account so that it reflects the information that was just received from the bank, as shown in the reconciliation. The entry would be:

Bank charges expense (SE)	25.75	
Accounts receivable (A)	186.80	
Cash (A)		212.55

After posting, the balance in the cash account would be the correct amount: $9,550.87.

Bank reconciliations are an important control procedure. They ensure that all transactions affecting the bank account have been properly recorded, so the company knows that no transactions have been missed or recorded incorrectly. They are normally made every month for every bank account as soon as the bank statement is received. The bank reconciliation procedure consists of reconciling the balance recorded by the company with the balance recorded by the bank. The main reconciling items are outstanding cheques, outstanding deposits, bank service charges that have been deducted from the bank account but not recorded by the company, errors in recording items, and any other item that affects cash and is recorded by either the company or the bank, but not yet both.

Bear in mind that appropriate separation of duties is essential for effective internal control. Consequently, it is important to ensure that the person who reconciles the bank account is not the person who is responsible for either the bank account or the accounting records. This will ensure that any error or discrepancy will be found and properly corrected. It also ensures that an individual is not given the opportunity to take cash and then change the books to cover the theft.

The other issue associated with cash is cash management. Proper cash management requires that sufficient cash be maintained in readily accessible bank accounts to pay expenses, while at the same time excess amounts of cash not be kept. Cash is a non-earning asset; that is, it is not earning a return (except, perhaps, a small amount of interest). The company will want to keep as much of its cash invested in income-earning assets as possible. (Income-earning assets include short-term investments, which are discussed later in this chapter.) A company's cash management policies are critical to the effective management of its cash position, and to the maximization of total earnings. Advanced cash management techniques are not discussed in this book, but are very important to company shareholders and management.

Statement Analysis Considerations

Sometimes a company's cash is restricted with regard to withdrawal from the bank because of a feature known as **compensating balances**. These are minimum balances that must be maintained in the bank account to avoid significant service charges or, in some cases, to satisfy restrictive loan covenants (which are clauses in loan agreements that are designed to reduce the risk to the lender). A company might also restrict a portion of its cash for a specific use. In such cases, the restricted cash should be segregated from other amounts of cash. Other than these, and those discussed in conjunction with the understanding of the cash flow statement in Chapter 5, there are no special considerations with regard to cash for financial statement analysis.

Ethics in Accounting

ethics in accounting

Because of the easy portability of money and difficulty of identifying its rightful owner, the handling of cash in a business can be an ethical challenge for managers and employees. Strict controls must be placed on who handles cash, and how they handle it. The set of controls put in place by a business to manage its cash (or any other asset or liability) is referred to as the *internal control system*.

Although protecting the company's assets from misappropriation may be a major concern, controls are needed for broader objectives as well. A good system of internal control can provide assurance regarding three general categories: the effectiveness and efficiency of the company's operations, the reliability of its financial statements and management reporting, and compliance with applicable laws, regulations, and company policies.

Suppose, for example, that you own a parking lot and have hired employees to collect fees from people who park in the lot. What operating procedures do you think would be necessary to ensure that you receive all the cash that the employees collect? What characteristics would you look for in the employees you hire to do this job?

Ethical questions arise with respect to management's attitude toward its employees. Should management assume that all employees are basically dishonest, and will steal if they think they can get away with it? Or should management simply establish controls to ensure that employees are not given any opportunity to steal? In considering such questions and determining what internal control measures to establish, management must also consider the motivational impact on the employees. The dilemma is that employees generally have a more positive attitude and better motivation toward their jobs when they feel that they are trusted.

TEMPORARY INVESTMENTS

LEARNING OBJECTIVE 4

Identify the criteria for classifying an investment as temporary.

As discussed in the last section, managing cash is an important part of managing a company. One of its aspects is the company's need to minimize its cash balance, given that current or chequing accounts normally earn no returns. One way to convert cash into an earning asset is to invest it in temporary (short-term) **marketable securities**. These are financial assets that are publicly traded or otherwise easily converted back to cash and represent either a debt interest (treasury bills, bonds, or guaranteed investment certificates) or an equity interest (shares) in another entity. The investor's usual intention in acquiring them is simply to hold them as income-generating alternatives to cash; they will be sold when the cash is needed for other purposes. The more active the trading in the security, the easier it is to convert back into cash when the cash is needed. The ability to turn an investment back into cash quickly is known as *liquidity* and is an important aspect of managing the company's cash position.

Securities that are not marketable or otherwise easily liquidated would likely not qualify as current assets, because they might not be easily converted into cash within a year; they would probably be classified as noncurrent investments. The discussion in this section is restricted to temporary investments that are held as current assets.

The probable future value associated with temporary investments comes from two sources. One source is the periodic payments that these securities produce while they are being held. If the security is a debt security, these payments are interest. When a debt security has a maturity date of three months or less, it is often classified as a cash equivalent because it will quickly become a known amount of cash. Periodic payments received from equity securities are dividends. Because equity securities do not have a maturity date, and their values are subject to fluctuations, they are never classified as cash equivalents.

The second source of value associated with temporary investments is the value of the securities when they are sold in the future. If the intention is to hold these securities for a short term (less than one year), the current market value or resale price is very relevant and important. If the intention is to hold them for the long term, the current market value may be less relevant and important. Securities held for the long term do not appear under the heading of temporary investments in the balance sheet; they are reported in a separate section for long-term investments.

The uncertainty, or risk, associated with the future value of temporary investments relates to both the periodic payments and the ultimate sales value. For example, the issuers of debt may default on the interest payments. This not only causes uncertainty with regard to the periodic payments, but it also reduces the value of a security in terms of its final price. If a company cannot make interest payments, it is unlikely that it will be able to pay back the principal when the debt matures. With regard to equity securities, there is no guarantee that dividends will continue at present levels, nor is there any guarantee of the ultimate sales value. The company may grow, increasing the future selling price of its shares, or it may fail, rendering the equity shares worthless.

The uncertainty with regard to a security's future cash flows is sometimes evidenced by the volatility of its price in the securities markets. You are probably well aware of the volatility of the markets for equity securities (shares). For example, during the one-year period from July 1, 2003 to July 1, 2004, the shares of Rogers Communications Inc. varied from a low of $18.46 to a high of $27.60. The variability in price is partially due to the highly competitive telecommunications market in which this company operates. However, share prices fluctuate for many reasons. For example, the terrorist acts of September 11, 2001, in the United States sent most share prices tumbling as investor confidence was seriously shaken. Some companies' shares recovered quickly, while others have not yet reached pre-September 11 levels.

Volatility has also been present in recent years in the markets for debt securities (bond markets). The degree of uncertainty depends on the type of security and the financial health of the issuing entity. Debt securities, for example, may be viewed as quite safe if they are issued by the government. At the other extreme are corporate bonds issued by very highly leveraged companies (highly leveraged means total liabilities greatly exceed total shareholders' equity). These bonds are sometimes called "junk bonds." Junk bonds pay very high interest rates to compensate for the high risk of their principal not being repaid. Equity securities offer a similar spectrum of risk.

The ownership criterion for these assets is relatively straightforward. For some securities, pieces of paper representing ownership (share certificates and bonds) can be held by the owner. In many cases, however, no certificates are issued and ownership is evidenced by entries in records maintained by an outside party (such as an investment dealer or a trust company).

Valuation Methods

One method that could be used to value temporary investments is to record them at their original acquisition cost, or **historical cost**. With this method, changes in an investment's market value have no effect on the balance sheet or income statement until the investment is actually sold. When the investment is sold, the difference between its original cost and its final market value is recognized and is termed a

realized gain or loss. In addition, income is recognized with this method as periodic payments are received in the form of dividends or interest revenue.

A second method would be to value temporary investments at their **market value.** In its pure form, this method means that changes in the market value of the investments would cause changes in the carrying values on the balance sheet and corresponding gains or losses on the income statement. The changes in market values while the investments are held are called **unrealized gains or losses.** When an investment is sold, the final change in value is considered a realized gain or loss. In addition, the periodic receipts of interest and dividends are recognized as income.

A third method for valuing temporary investments is the **lower of cost and market (LCM)** method. This is a hybrid of the two methods discussed above, historical cost and market value. The lower of cost and market method uses historical cost (i.e., the amount paid for the securities when they were purchased), except in situations where the market value is less than the cost, in which case the market value is used. Note that this combination of the above methods is intended to report a conservative figure. Under the LCM method, temporary investments are shown at their cost unless their market value has declined to below cost, in which case the investments' value on the balance sheet is reduced to their market value and an unrealized loss is recognized on the income statement. No gains (resulting from market values higher than cost) are recognized, until the investment is sold. This one-sided rule with regard to market values was adopted based on the conservatism principle in accounting that states, in essence, that losses should be recognized as soon as they can be estimated, but that gains should not be recognized until they are realized.

What Is Canadian Practice?

LEARNING OBJECTIVE 5

Explain why temporary investments are recorded using market valuation.

Traditionally, the method of accounting for temporary investments in Canada has been the lower of cost and market (LCM) method. However, for fiscal years commencing on or after October 1, 2006, most short-term investments will be reported at **fair (market) value.**

This change recognizes the fact that temporary investments are generally held in place of cash, so the intention is to value them at the amount of cash that could be received from selling them. This will provide information that is more relevant to readers of the financial statements. The new standard also recognizes that the market values of such investments are usually easily determinable, objective, and verifiable. Thus, the market value information will also be reliable.

AN INTERNATIONAL PERSPECTIVE

Reports from Other Countries

In the United States, all short-term marketable securities are carried at their market values. American accountants used the lower of cost and market method until 1994, but then they switched to market values. In 2003, the AcSB in Canada announced that it planned to make changes in the accounting for financial instruments, and to recommend that standards be harmonized with those in the United States. The end result is that, for fiscal years commencing after September 30, 2006, under Canadian GAAP most temporary investments will be carried at their fair (market) value, thus eliminating the need for the LCM approach.

The specific requirements of the new Canadian standards are quite complex, and the details will be left to intermediate or advanced accounting courses. However, following is a simplified overview of the new approach to investments or **financial instruments**.

Four types of financial instruments are identified, which are referred to as:

1. Held for trading

2. Available for sale

3. Held to maturity

4. Loans and receivables

Each of these four categories is accounted for differently, as follows.

1. *Held-for-trading investments* are valued at market, with gains and losses included in net income.

2. *Available-for-sale investments* are valued at market,[1] with gains and losses included in other comprehensive income[2] until disposition, and then transferred to net income.

3. *Held-to-maturity investments* are valued at amortized cost, using the effective interest method.[3]

4. *Investments in loans and receivables* are valued using the effective interest method.[3]

However, the new standard permits companies to designate any security as "held for trading," and account for it accordingly, if they wish. The Accounting Standards Board therefore seems to be encouraging companies to report temporary investments on the balance sheet at their fair market values, and to report any resulting gains and losses directly in net income. Most companies with temporary investments will probably opt to do so, since this will be the simplest approach and the differences in results, for short-term investments, are not likely to be material. Therefore, **for simplicity we will treat all temporary investments in this manner: temporary investments will be reported on the balance sheet at their fair market values, and any resulting gains or losses will be reported on the income statement as part of net income**.

Proper accounting for financial instruments or investments presents several other issues that must be resolved. The first is one of classification. When a company invests in a security, or financial instrument, it must first decide whether to classify the investment as a current or noncurrent asset. The classification is generally based on the intention of management and on the marketability of the asset. If management intends to hold the security for less than one year, and if it is readily marketable, it will be classified as a current asset. Otherwise, it will be classified as noncurrent, in which case the account will be called a long-term investment rather than a temporary or short-term investment. Long-term investments are subject to different rules for valuation, which are discussed in Appendix B at the back of the book.

Another issue that is important in accounting for investments arises with respect to equity securities. Most equity securities are shares that entitle the owner to vote for the board of directors, which has direct authority over management.

HELPFUL HINT:

Here's a brief summary of what you should know about the valuation of short-term investments. Although there are a number of different categories for investments and each has specific requirements regarding how they are to be accounted for. At the introductory level, it is sufficient to know that short-term investments will generally be valued at their current market values on each balance sheet date, rather than at cost or LCM. When gains or losses arise on these investments because of changes in their values, these gains or losses will generally be reported directly in net income.

---

[1] If reliable market values are not available, they are valued at cost.

[2] Comprehensive income is discussed in the Appendix to Chapter 3.

[3] The effective interest method is discussed in Chapter 10.

When a company invests in shares of another company, the buyer will have some voting power, based on the number of shares it owns. The larger the proportion of shares owned by the buyer, the more influence or control it can exercise over the other company. For short-term investments, there is usually no intention on the part of the buying company to exercise influence or control. In fact, the number of shares usually purchased as a short-term investment (a relatively small number) does not allow a buying company to exercise much influence or control. With long-term investments in shares, however, there may be some intention to exercise influence or control over the other company. In some cases, for example, the acquiring company will buy 100% of the outstanding shares of another company. In this case, the acquiring company exercises absolute control over the acquired company. The accounting for an investment in which a company exercises significant influence or control (i.e., a "strategic investment") is different from that in which the company has little or no influence (i.e., a "passive investment"). The accounting for investments in which there exists significant influence or control is discussed in Appendix B. In this chapter, only passive short-term investments in securities are considered.

The data in Exhibit 6-2 for Clifford Company will be used to illustrate the application of the market value method to short-term investments, and other aspects of accounting for them. Assume that Clifford's year end is December 31, and that it prepares financial statements on a quarterly basis. You will notice that Clifford buys three securities during the first quarter (the first three months in the year). The exhibit then tracks the portfolio's performance during the year, valuing each security each quarter until it is sold. Dividend and interest payments received over the year are also included.

EXHIBIT 6-2

CLIFFORD COMPANY

Temporary Investment Data

Security	Type	Quarter Acquired	Acquisition Cost	Quarter Sold	Selling Price
HTB Corp.	Bonds	1	$10,000	3	$12,000
ATS Inc.	Shares	1	$20,000	4	$18,000
LFS Ltd.	Shares	1	$30,000	-	NA

	Values as at the End of							
	Quarter 1		Quarter 2		Quarter 3		Quarter 4	
Security	Cost	Market	Cost	Market	Cost	Market	Cost	Market
HTB Corp.	$10,000	$11,000	$10,000	$13,000	NA	NA	NA	NA
ATS Inc.	20,000	17,000	20,000	21,000	$20,000	$17,000	NA	NA
LFS Ltd.	30,000	29,000	30,000	28,000	30,000	29,000	$30,000	$28,500
Portfolio	$60,000	$57,000	$60,000	$62,000	$50,000	$46,000	$30,000	$28,500

Dividends/Interest Received

Quarter	Amount
1	$1,200
2	$1,200
3	$ 500
4	$ 500

Initial Acquisition

If Clifford Company makes many such investments, the details of each would probably be recorded in its own **subsidiary account**. The Temporary investments account would then be a **control account** that holds the sum of all the subsidiary accounts (see below).

LEARNING OBJECTIVE 6

Prepare the journal entries associated with the acquisition, holding, and selling of temporary investments.

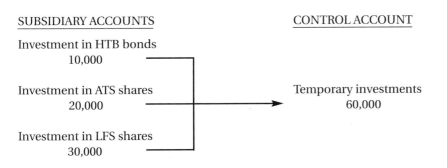

It is the control account that is reported in the financial statements. Transactions are recorded in the subsidiary accounts, which are then used to update the control account. To illustrate, the following entry would record the acquisition of the temporary investments during the first quarter of the year.

Investment in HTB bonds (A)	10,000	
Investment in ATS shares (A)	20,000	
Investment in LFS shares (A)	30,000	
Cash (A)		60,000

In order to simplify the illustration that follows, we will use a single Temporary investments account, rather than separate accounts for the investments in HTB, ATS, and LFS. Under this approach, the entry to record the purchase of the investments would be as follows.

Temporary investments (A)	60,000	
Cash (A)		60,000

Dividend and Interest Recognition

Dividend and interest income is recognized each period as it is earned. In the case of Clifford Company, we will assume that all dividend and interest income is received in cash. However, recognize that the interest could be accrued and result in interest receivable rather than cash, and dividends could have been declared but not paid, which would result in dividends receivable. In Exhibit 6-2, the dividends and interest from all three investments have been aggregated into one amount. The entry to record these dividends in Quarter 1 would be as follows.

Cash (A)	1,200	
Dividend/interest revenue (SE)		1,200
(an income statement account)		

Recognition of Gains and Losses

The fair (market) value method requires that, at any financial statement date, the company must determine the aggregate market value of its portfolio of temporary investments. Note in Exhibit 6-2 that, on the balance sheet at the end of Quarter 1 (March 31), the portfolio should be carried at $57,000 because this is the market value. The writedown from the cost of $60,000 would result in an unrealized loss of $3,000, which would appear in the income statement.

The entry to record the reduction in the carrying value of the temporary investments and the unrealized loss would be:

Unrealized loss on temporary investments (SE)	3,000	
Temporary investments (A)		3,000

The preceding debit entry reduces the current period's net income, because unrealized losses are shown on the income statement. The balance in the temporary investments account is now $57,000.

In Quarter 2, Clifford again recognizes dividend/interest revenue. This would be recorded exactly as it was in Quarter 1. At the end of Quarter 2 (June 30), the company applies the market valuation rule again. Note from Exhibit 6-2 that the portfolio's market value has increased from $57,000 to $62,000. (In fact, it has gone up above the original cost of the securities; however, the original cost is no longer relevant.) This means that Clifford can record a $5,000 unrealized gain, to bring the portfolio up from the previous $57,000 to its current market value of $62,000. The entry to record the increase in the value of the securities would be as follows.

Temporary investments (A)	5,000	
Unrealized gain on temporary investments (SE)		5,000

In Quarter 3, the company recognizes dividend/interest revenue of $500, recorded as follows.

Cash (A)	500	
Dividend/interest revenue (SE)		500

Clifford sells the HTMS bonds for $12,000 during Quarter 3. Since, as shown in Exhibit 6-2, these securities (since the end of Quarter 2) were being carried at their market value of $13,000, the sale results in a realized loss of $1,000. This would be recorded as follows.

Cash (A)	12,000	
Loss on sale of temporary investments (SE)	1,000	
Temporary investments (A)		13,000

At the end of Quarter 3 (September 30), the company applies the market valuation rule again. Note from Exhibit 6-2 that the combined market value of the two remaining securities in the portfolio has decreased from $49,000 (i.e., $21,000 + 28,000) at the end of Quarter 2 to $46,000 at the end of Quarter 3. This means that Clifford must record a $3,000 unrealized loss, to bring the portfolio's value down to its current market value. The entry to record the decrease in the value of the securities would be as follows.

Unrealized loss on temporary investments (SE)	3,000	
Temporary investments (A)		3,000

Finally, in Quarter 4 the company again recognizes dividend/interest revenue of $500, which would be recorded exactly as it was in Quarter 3.

Clifford also sells the ATS shares during Quarter 4, for $18,000. Since, as shown in Exhibit 6-2, these securities (since the end of Quarter 3) were being carried at their market value of $17,000, the sale results in a realized gain of $1,000. This would be recorded as follows.

Cash (A)	18,000	
Gain on sale of temporary investments (SE)		1,000
Temporary investments (A)		17,000

At the end of Quarter 4 (December 31), the company applies the market valuation rule again. Note from Exhibit 6-2 that the market value of the one remaining security in the portfolio has decreased from $29,000 at the end of Quarter 3 to $28,500 at the end of Quarter 4. This means that Clifford must record a $500 unrealized loss, to bring the portfolio's value down to its current market value. The entry to record the decrease in the value of the securities would be as follows.

Unrealized loss on temporary investments (SE)	500	
Temporary investments (A)		500

The effects on the income statement and balance sheet of applying the market valuation rule, as well as the other events that affected marketable securities during the year, are summarized in Exhibit 6-3.

CLIFFORD COMPANY

EXHIBIT 6-3

Partial Income Statement

For the quarter ended	Mar. 31	June 30	Sept. 30	Dec. 31
Unrealized gain (loss) on temporary investments	($3,000)	$5,000	($3,000)	($ 500)
Realized gain (loss) on sale of temporary investments	–	–	(1,000)	1,000
Dividend/interest revenue	1,200	1,200	500	500
Overall effect of temporary investments on net income	($1,800)	$6,200	($3,500)	$1,000

Partial Balance Sheet

As of	Mar. 31	June 30	Sept. 30	Dec. 31
Temporary investments (at fair market value)	$57,000	$62,000	$46,000	$28,500

Refer to the third quarter, when Clifford sold the investment in HTMS bonds for $12,000. Bonds have a face amount or maturity value (in this case $10,000) that the purchaser will receive when the bonds mature. The fact that Clifford sold the bonds for $12,000 indicates that they had not reached maturity yet. If they had, Clifford would have only received $10,000. Between the date of issue and the date of maturity, it is possible that the value of the bonds will be either higher or lower than their face value (depending upon competing interest rates and other economic factors).

The disclosure of the effects of transactions involving temporary investments in a typical set of financial statements tends to be somewhat limited, because of the insignificant nature of these transactions relative to the company's other transactions. Many companies will simply list a line item for temporary investments on the balance sheet, stating that the securities are carried at their market value. No details may be provided concerning the amount of dividend or interest revenue earned during the period, or the amount of realized and unrealized gains and losses that have been recognized. When the amounts are significant, however, a note to the financial statements generally provides the details.

Long-Term Investments

Accounting issues related to noncurrent investments are different from those for short-term investments, and are discussed in Appendix B at the end of the book.

ACCOUNTS RECEIVABLE

Accounts receivable are amounts owed by customers from normal business transactions of selling goods and services on credit. The ownership criterion for accounts receivable is evidenced either by a formal contractual agreement or by some other less formal documentation, such as a sales invoice. The sale itself represents the past event that gave rise to the accounts receivable. The probable future value criterion would be met by the fact that a receivable is the right to receive payment at some future date. The value of the cash that is to be received in the future is affected by the same uncertainties that we described in the earlier section on cash. In addition to those uncertainties, there is also the uncertainty that the customer will pay the cash as agreed. A default by the customer would be called a **bad debt**. This makes the valuation of accounts receivable less certain than the valuation of cash. Other uncertainties with accounts receivable are that the customer might return the goods for credit, the customer might request a price adjustment if the goods are damaged in shipment, or the customer might pay less than what is listed on the bill if a discount is allowed for prompt payment. All these factors can affect the uncertainty of collecting accounts receivable and complicate the determination of the appropriate valuation amount.

Accounts Receivable Valuation Methods

An account receivable is a right to receive to pay a certain amount at some point in the future. A simple way to value the receivable is to add up the gross payments called for in the agreement. This *gross payments method* ignores the effects of bad debts (customers who do not pay), returns, and so forth, as well as the effects of the *time value of money*.

A second method for valuing an account receivable is to take into consideration the time value of the gross payments to be received. The time value of money is the concept that a dollar received in the future is worth less than a dollar received today. The reasoning here is that an investor can invest the dollar received today and have more than a dollar in the future. Therefore, if the company has a receivable for $100 to be received a month from now, it is worth less than $100 today. Using the terminology of the time value of money, we would want to calculate the *present value* of the receivable's future cash flows. We would *discount* the future cash flows, using an appropriate interest rate, to arrive at this present value. See the text companion website for a full discussion of the calculation of present values.

A third method is to take into consideration the possibility that the receivable may not be paid. This could result from a default by the customer or the return of the goods. Partial payment might also result if the customer pays early, taking advantage of a cash discount, or if the customer demands a price reduction (because, for example, the goods were not exactly as ordered or were received in damaged condition). Incorporating these events into the valuation would mean reducing the receivable. This alternative can be used in conjunction with either the first (gross payments) or the second (present value) method of valuing the receivable.

Time Value of Money

Finally, a valuation method based on the market value of the accounts receivable might also be considered. Accounts receivable can be sold to other parties, who then collect from the customer. The process of selling accounts receivable is referred to as **factoring**. If a ready market is available in which to sell a receivable, a market price can be used as a value for the receivable.

What Is Canadian Practice?

Most Canadian companies show receivables at the gross payments amount less appropriate allowances for bad debts, returns, and so forth. Ideally, the use of present values would be more appropriate, but there is a materiality consideration. If there is little difference between the present values and the gross payments, such as occurs with receivables expected to be paid in a relatively short period of time, the gross payments can be used. The use of present values adds some complications to the accounting for receivables and, unless the use of present values makes a significant difference, it is probably not worth the effort. For most companies, the time between sale and collection is relatively short (30 to 60 days). Unless interest rates are extremely high, the differences between the present values and the gross payments for these types of receivables are relatively small. This is why most companies account for their receivables at gross amounts rather than using present values.

Bad Debt Tutorial

Allowances for returns, bad debts, etc., are necessary because the company must be careful not to overstate the value of its assets or its income from sales to customers. For example, consider a company that sells $10,000 worth of goods during the accounting period, all on account. The entry to record this transaction is:

Accounts receivable (A)	10,000	
Sales revenue (SE)		10,000

If the company anticipates that it will collect the entire $10,000, the preceding entry would appropriately state the effects of the transaction on assets and revenues.

However, if the company anticipates that some customers will not pay, this entry overstates the receivables as well as the shareholders' wealth.

The likelihood that a customer will default on payments depends on the customer's creditworthiness. A company can improve its chances of receiving payments by performing a credit check on its customers before it grants them credit. The company must balance its desire to sell its product to the customer against the likelihood that the customer will pay. Too strict a credit policy means that many customers will be denied credit and may, therefore, purchase their goods from other suppliers. Too loose a credit policy, and the company may lose more money from bad debts than it makes from good sales. The company should do a cost/benefit analysis to decide what its credit policy should be.

The company must also stay aware of the changes in the industry in which it operates and changes in the economy in general. Changes in interest rates, inflation, or the global economy can quickly affect a customer's credit status. The following article summary illustrates how a changing economy can affect a company's ability to collect its accounts receivable.

accounting in the news

BAD DEBTS IN THE BANKING SECTOR

Banks always face exposure to bad debts because the major services they offer are loans to businesses and individuals. Each reporting period, banks review their outstanding loans and establish an appropriate loan-loss provision.

Early in the summer of 2001, the Toronto-Dominion Bank, one of the major lenders to the telecom sector which was suffering from severe excess capacity, increased its loan-loss provision by $140 million, bringing its total provision to $620 million. Each time the loan-loss provision is adjusted, it affects the profits earned in that period.

Sometimes, when banks determine that the probability of collecting on some of their loans is low, they sell their loans in the distress-loans market. This market for business loans is similar to collection agencies for individual loans. Whoever buys the loans understands that the chance of collection is low. To counter this risk, the purchaser buys the loans at amounts considerably below their carrying value. In this way, if they collect, they make money. If they don't, they do not lose a lot. From the banks' perspective, they at least recover something where otherwise they might not recover anything.

Source: "Bad debts expected to erode banks' profits," by Paula Arab, Canadian Press, page B4, globeandmail.com, August 20, 2001.

In addition to a policy on bad debts, other policies can affect the amounts collected. One of these is the company's returns policy. Can customers return goods, and under what circumstances? Again, the policy's strictness or looseness will have an effect on whether customers will buy goods from the company. In 2002, a large Canadian publishing and distribution company, **General Publishing**, filed for bankruptcy protection while it attempted to restructure its organization. One main cause of its financial difficulty was the demands placed on it by the mega bookstore company **Chapters Inc.** Chapters had extended its payment terms to 250 days from its former 90 days. Often, instead of making its payment in 250 days, Chapters returned unsold books to settle its debt. The long delay in receiving payment, coupled with the fact that General Publishing had to pay its own suppliers in 90 days, drained the company of cash and pushed it into financial difficulty. Here is a situation where customer returns affected not only the company's revenue picture but its cash flow as well.

A second policy that should be considered is one concerning cash discounts for early payment. If the company decides to offer a cash discount to encourage prompt payment, the amount of cash that will be collected from the receivables will depend on the number of customers who pay early and therefore get the discount. The number of customers who pay early will depend on the attractiveness of the discount. Both of these policies require some adjustment to the amounts recorded in accounts receivable, as well as in the sales revenue account.

The accounting methods for anticipated bad debts or doubtful (sometimes referred to as uncollectible) accounts are illustrated in the next section. Recognize that similar methods could be used to account for the other adjustments to accounts receivable, such as cash discounts and sales returns. For a complete description of the accounting for discounts and returns, refer to an intermediate accounting text.

Accounting for doubtful accounts requires adjusting the value of the accounts receivable on the balance sheet, as well as recognizing the related bad debt expense in the income statement. Some smaller businesses use the **direct write-off method**, but most medium and large companies use what is called the **allowance method** to recognize doubtful accounts.

Allowance Method

Let us review two key points already discussed earlier in the text. First, the matching concept requires that when a company recognizes revenue from a sale, it must also recognize all expenses relating to that sale. Second, bad debts are technically not expenses; they are reductions in revenues. Nevertheless, they are usually recorded as expenses, and must be recognized at the same time as the related revenues are recognized. Because, at the point of sale, the company does not know which customers will end up as bad debts, it must estimate what dollar amount of sales will ultimately be uncollectible. These estimates are usually based on the company's past experience with its customers. New businesses usually have little basis for initial estimates, and so must use some other method of making estimates.

Consider the example accompanying the preceding journal entry. Assume that the company estimates that, of the $10,000 in sales, $325 will ultimately prove to be uncollectible. (One method used to arrive at this estimate is discussed later in the chapter.) As the company is not able to identify the customers who will not pay, the $325 cannot directly reduce specific accounts receivable. Therefore, the following entry records this amount in an account that is contra to the accounts receivable account. This contra account, which is usually called the *allowance for doubtful accounts*, reduces the aggregate amount of accounts receivable by the anticipated effects of **uncollectible accounts**. The journal entry would be as follows.

Bad debt expense (SE)	325	
Allowance for doubtful accounts (XA)		325

LEARNING OBJECTIVE 7

Explain why estimating the potential uncollectibility of accounts receivable is required.

This would be an adjusting entry, made at the end of the accounting period. The allowance for doubtful accounts has a credit balance because its purpose is to show that the debit balance amount in the accounts receivable will not be fully collected. In effect, it reduces the accounts receivable total to the net amount of cash that the company actually expects to receive. The allowance account is contra to accounts receivable and is grouped with that current asset on the balance sheet, as follows.

Accounts receivable (gross)	$10,000
Less: Allowance for doubtful accounts	325
Net accounts receivable	$ 9,675

Note that this entry has the effect of reducing the net carrying value of the accounts receivable (the accounts receivable balance less the balance in the allowance account) by $325, from $10,000 to $9,675. Accounts receivable is now stated at the amount the company ultimately expects to collect in cash. At the same time, the bad debts expense reduces net income by the same amount.

The actual **write-off** of an account receivable, under the allowance method, occurs at a later date, determined by the company's write-off policy. The company's decision that the account is uncollectible is usually based on a bad debt policy. For example, the policy may state that accounts will be written off as uncollectible if they have been outstanding for more than 120 days. This policy is based on the company's experience with collecting from its customers, and usually means that the probability of collecting the account after 120 days is so small that it is not worth pursuing. Assume that we are using this policy for the company in our example; that is, accounts that have not been collected within 120 days are written off. Assume that nonpayments result in $300 of actual write-offs. With the allowance method, this means that we have now specifically identified customer accounts that are bad, which we were unable to identify at the time we recognized the bad debt expense. Because we recognized the expense when the estimate was made, no further expense should be recognized when the accounts are written off. We should simply remove the specific accounts from accounts receivable and remove an equivalent amount from the allowance account (because that portion of the allowance account is no longer necessary). The entry is:

Allowance for doubtful accounts (XA)	300	
Accounts receivable (A)		300

What happens if one of the accounts that we have written off is later paid by the customer? This is called a **recovery**. Under the allowance method, recoveries are accounted for by *reinstating the account receivable*. This is accomplished by reversing the write-off entry and then showing the normal cash collection entry. For example, the following two entries would be made if an account worth $50 was recovered after having been written off.

Accounts receivable (A)	50	
Allowance for doubtful accounts (XA		50
Cash (A)	50	
Accounts receivable (A)		50

Note that one net entry (debiting cash and crediting the allowance for doubtful accounts) could be made to accomplish the recording of this transaction; however, if no entry is made to the accounts receivable account, the customer's account will always be shown in the records as having been a bad debt. Therefore, it is preferable to make the two entries illustrated above.

Assume that this was the first year of this company's operations and that the company had collected $8,500 from its customers by year end. Exhibit 6-4 illustrates the entries and balances in the accounts receivable and the allowance for doubtful accounts.

ALLOWANCE METHOD FOR DOUBTFUL ACCOUNTS

EXHIBIT 6-4

Accounts Receivable			
Beginning Balance	0		
Credit sales	10,000	8,500	Cash collections
		300	**Write-offs**
Reinstatement	**50**		
		50	Cash collection
Ending Balance	1,200		

Sales Revenue	
	10,000

Allowance for Doubtful Accounts			
		0	Beginning balance
		325	Estimated bad debts
Write-offs	**300**		
		50	**Reinstatement**
		75	Ending balance

Bad Debts Expense	
325	

The ending balance in the accounts receivable account ($1,200) represents those accounts that have not been collected as at the end of the accounting period. In our example, the maximum amount of time any of these accounts can have been outstanding is 120 days; any account beyond that time is written off. The ending balance in the allowance for doubtful accounts should be the remaining allowance that applies to the ending balance in accounts receivable. In other words, the company expects that, of the remaining $1,200 in accounts receivable, $75 will prove to be uncollectible.

In most financial statements, the allowance account is netted against the accounts receivable account to produce a single line item on the balance sheet. In the example above, this would be $1,125. Few companies provide details of the amount of the allowance, either by showing the balance in the allowance for doubtful accounts or by including information about it in the notes to the financial statements.

One final point to consider about the accounting for doubtful accounts is the method used to estimate the dollar amounts that are doubtful. A method that is commonly used is called the **percentage of credit sales method**. This method will be described below. Another method that is used is called the aging of accounts receivable method. This method is discussed and illustrated on the text companion website.

HELPFUL HINT:

The allowance for doubtful accounts is a contra asset, and therefore a permanent account whose balance is cumulative and carried forward from one period to another. On the other hand, bad debts expense (like all expenses) is a temporary account, and therefore begins each period with a zero balance.

LEARNING OBJECTIVE 8

Identify two methods for recognizing uncollectibility, and describe the circumstances under which each is appropriate.

Percentage of Credit Sales Method

The percentage of credit sales method is based on the assumption that the amount of bad debt expense is a function of the total sales made on credit. The bad debt expense for the period is estimated by multiplying the credit sales during the period by an appropriate percentage. The percentage is usually determined based on the company's collection history. In the example above, the $325 of bad debt expense that was used could have been the result of using 3.25% of credit sales as an estimate of the bad debts (3.25% of the $10,000 in credit sales would have resulted in the estimated bad debt expense of $325).

In a new company, the percentage may be determined initially by considering the bad debt experience of other companies in the same industry. In an existing company, historical data are generally used to estimate this percentage, as adjusted for present and anticipated future economic conditions. For example, during an economic downturn, bad debt percentages often rise.

The estimate of the percentage that will be uncollectible must be adjusted from time to time to reflect the company's recent credit experience. If the company is experiencing more write-offs than were estimated, the percentage should be increased. Companies typically do not go back to prior periods to adjust this percentage, but adjust it on a prospective basis. Therefore, an overestimate or an underestimate in one period will be adjusted in the following period. The percentage can be affected by the types of customers that the company has, a change in credit policy, and general economic conditions, such as economic downturns and changes in unemployment.

Note that with the percentage of credit sales method, the ending balance in the allowance for doubtful accounts results from simply totalling the entries to the account. The percentage relationship between the ending balance in the allowance account and the accounts receivable account has nothing directly to do with the percentage used to estimate bad debt expense. In the example, the ratio of the ending balance in the allowance account to the accounts receivable account is 6.25% ($75 ÷ $1,200). This is considerably higher than the 3.25% bad debts that the company estimated as its percentage of sales. This is not necessarily inconsistent, however, as a higher percentage of the accounts receivable that are left at the end of the period may be doubtful. For example, many of them may be approaching the 120-day limit, which means that the probability of not collecting them is becoming greater.

AN INTERNATIONAL PERSPECTIVE

Reports from Other Countries

The estimation of uncollectible accounts is accomplished in some countries (for example, France and Germany) by considering the circumstances of individual accounts rather than by estimating an overall percentage rate such as with the percentage of credit sales method. This method is similar to the aging of accounts receivable, which is often used in Canada and by some companies in Japan.

Direct Write-Off Method

The direct write-off method is often used by small companies. It recognizes the loss from the uncollectible account in the period in which the company decides the account is, in fact, uncollectible. Assume that we are using the same policy as with the allowance method; that is, that accounts are written off after 120 days. In our example, $300 worth of accounts receivable were identified as being more than 120 days overdue, and therefore should be written off. With the direct write-off method, the entry to record this is:

| Bad debt expense (SE) | 300 | |
| Accounts receivable (specific accounts) (A) | | 300 |

Note that no allowance for doubtful accounts is used with the direct write-off method, and the debit to the bad debt expense account reduces net income in the period in which the uncollectible accounts receivable are written off.

The credit entries to the accounts receivable account refer to specific customer accounts; the company has identified exactly who has not paid. For example, the $300 might be in two specific accounts, a $180 account from Joe Lee and a $120 account from Mary Smith. The accounts receivable balance is generally supported by what is called a subsidiary ledger (similar to the subsidiary ledger used with temporary investments) in which separate receivable accounts are maintained for each customer. This entry would cause reductions in the accounts of both Joe Lee and Mary Smith.

The direct write-off method is a simple way to account for bad debts. The company makes every reasonable effort to collect the account, and when it finally decides that an account is uncollectible, it records the preceding entry to remove it from the accounting system. The problem with this method is that it violates the matching concept discussed in Chapter 4. As you will recall, the matching concept states that all the expenses related to the production of revenue should be matched with the revenue, i.e., recognized in the same period in which the revenue is recognized. The direct write-off method could result in the revenue being recognized in one accounting period, and the associated bad debt expense recorded in a subsequent period. If bad debts are not significant, then this mismatching will not be material and can be ignored. If bad debts are significant, however, this mismatching can distort the measurement of performance enough that most accountants would find this method unacceptable. The appropriate method to use when bad debts are significant is the allowance method that was discussed earlier.

Finally, note that bad debt expense is somewhat different from other expenses. It is more like a reduction in a revenue account, in the sense that it represents revenue the company will never receive. In recognition of this, a few companies report it as a direct reduction of the sales revenue amount on the income statement. The majority of companies, however, show bad debts as an operating expense and not as a reduction of revenues.

> **HELPFUL HINT:**
>
> There are two main methods for dealing with bad debts: the direct write-off method and the allowance method. If the allowance method is used (as it should be, whenever bad debts are significant), then there are two alternative approaches that can be used to estimate the amount of bad debts: the aging of accounts receivable method and the percentage of credit sales method.

NOTES RECEIVABLE

Types of Notes Receivable

Notes receivable are very similar to accounts receivable in their fundamental characteristics. Therefore, we will not discuss the recognition criteria and valuation methods; they are the same as for accounts receivable. The difference between an account receivable and a note receivable is that the note receivable is evidenced by a more formal agreement referred to as a **promissory note**. A promissory note is a written contract between two parties, the maker and the payee. The maker promises to pay specific amounts, either upon demand by the payee or at a definite date in the future.

Interest may be shown explicitly as a part of the note, or it may be implicit in the contractual payments. When interest is explicit, it is typically calculated by multiplying the explicit interest rate times the face value of the note times the time factor. The presumption here is that the face value is the amount that has been

> **LEARNING OBJECTIVE 9**
>
> *Describe the main types of notes receivable and explain the circumstances under which they are used.*

borrowed via the note. A note in which the interest is implicit specifies the amount to be paid at maturity (the face value), which will be larger than the initial amount borrowed. The interest is the difference between the amount borrowed and the face value. These are sometimes called *discounted notes.*

The maturity of notes is generally longer than for accounts receivable, but if the maturity date is within a year the notes are considered current assets. Long-term notes receivable are classified in the noncurrent assets section, along with long-term investments.

Notes are most commonly arranged with banks or other financial institutions. These financial institutions may require that the maker of the note put up some type of **collateral** for the note. Collateral is some asset that the payee has the right to receive if the maker defaults on the note. As an example, think of an individual who purchases a car with a loan from a bank or finance company. The bank would use the car as collateral for the loan. If the person defaults on the loan, the bank or finance company can reclaim the car and sell it to satisfy the outstanding debt.

A note secured by collateral is called a **secured note**. The collateral may be some type of real property, such as real estate, or personal property, such as equipment or inventory. Depending on the creditworthiness of the maker, a payee may agree to issue an unsecured note, which means no collateral is specified.

Companies will sometimes agree to issue a note to a customer if the customer cannot pay an account receivable within the normal payment period. If the customer wants a longer period of time to pay, the company may agree to this arrangement provided the customer signs a promissory note and pays interest on the outstanding debt covered by the note. Extending credit beyond the normal credit terms without demanding interest is not effective cash management.

Interest on Notes Receivable

LEARNING OBJECTIVE 10

Calculate interest associated with notes receivable and prepare the necessary journal entries.

Time Value of Money

As stated earlier, interest on notes receivable can be either implied or explicit. A note with implied interest might state: the maker of the note agrees to pay $1,050 at maturity in exchange for $1,000 today. The maker is borrowing $1,000 and, as the maturity payment is $1,050, the difference ($50) is interest. A note with explicit interest might state: the maker agrees to pay the principal amount of $1,000 at maturity plus interest at a rate of 10% [always stated as an annual rate unless otherwise indicated] in exchange for $1,000 today. The dollar amount of interest in this case depends on how long the period is between now and maturity.

Short-term notes receivable generally require that interest payments be calculated using **simple interest** calculations. Long-term notes, on the other hand, generally use **compound interest** calculations. Compound interest calculations are discussed in the Time Value of Money section on the text companion website. Simple interest calculations are demonstrated in the following equation.

Interest charges are calculated based on the amount borrowed, the interest rate, and the amount of time that has passed. The formula is:

Simple Interest Formula:

Interest = Principal × Interest Rate × Time

The principal is the amount borrowed, the interest rate is specified in the note and is stated as a yearly amount, and the time is the period that has elapsed, stated as a fraction of a year. The time that has elapsed is generally measured in days. While the actual number of days can be used, many companies simplify the calculation by treating each month as 30 days and, therefore, treating 360 days as being equivalent to one year. This simplifying convention is used in the calculations that follow.

To illustrate the calculation of interest and the accounting for notes, assume the following.

1. On November 30, Bierstaker Company agrees to accept a $1,000 note from Wilkicki Company to satisfy an outstanding account receivable. (This could happen if Wilkicki is having trouble meeting its payments or temporarily has some more pressing needs for its cash.) The note has a maturity of two months (60 days) and an interest rate of 12%.

2. Bierstaker's fiscal year end is December 31, and Wilkicki does not pay the note until maturity.

On November 30, Bierstaker makes the following entry.

Notes receivable (A)	1,000	
Accounts receivable (A)		1,000

To record receipt of a note in settlement of an account receivable.

Bierstaker's entry reflects receipt of the note from Wilkicki and the reduction in its accounts receivable.

On December 31, one month after receiving the note, Bierstaker must make adjusting entries and close its books. This means that it must record the accrual of interest on the note from Wilkicki. The interest through December 31 is calculated as follows.

$$\text{Interest} = \text{Principal} \times \text{Interest Rate} \times \text{Time}$$
$$= \$1,000 \times 12\% \times \frac{30}{360}$$
$$= \$10$$

The entry to record the interest on December 31 is:

Interest receivable (A)	10	
Interest revenue (SE)		10

To accrue interest for the month of December.

At the end of January, Bierstaker will receive payment from Wilkicki of $1,020. Bierstaker will have to record the accrual of interest for the month of January and the receipt of cash. The calculation of interest is the same as the earlier one, because another month has passed. Two entries are shown on January 31. The first records the accrual of the interest, and the second records the cash receipt. (One combined entry could have been made.)

The entries to record the interest on January 31 are:

Interest receivable (A)	10	
Interest revenue (SE)		10

To accrue interest for the month of January.

Cash (A)	1,020	
Notes receivable (A)		1,000
Interest receivable (A)		20

To record receipt of the principal of the note plus interest for two months.

In order to receive cash for a note without waiting until its maturity date, a note may be sold to another party. This is the same as factoring accounts receivable. The note may be sold with or without **recourse**, meaning that if the maker does not pay the note at maturity, the third party that bought the note will or will not have the right to collect the amount owed from the original payee. Further information about the accounting for the factoring of notes receivable will be given in intermediate accounting courses.

Relatively few short-term notes receivable appear on balance sheets, because they are not very common and their amounts are usually relatively small. Normally, in external financial statements, notes receivable are grouped with accounts receivable.

STATEMENT ANALYSIS CONSIDERATIONS

Short-Term Liquidity

LEARNING OBJECTIVE 11

Calculate the current ratio, the quick ratio, and the accounts receivable turnover ratio.

As discussed in Chapter 1, liquidity refers to the company's ability to convert assets into cash to pay liabilities. An important part of the analysis of short-term liquidity comes from considering the short-term monetary assets on the balance sheet. There are at least two ratios that provide quantitative measures of short-term liquidity: the current ratio and the quick ratio.

CURRENT RATIO

The **current ratio** is measured by comparing the current assets to the current liabilities. It is calculated as:

$$\text{Current Ratio} = \frac{\text{Current Assets}}{\text{Current Liabilities}}$$

LEARNING OBJECTIVE 12

Explain how the current ratio, the quick ratio, and the accounts receivable turnover ratio help users to understand short-term liquidity issues.

Remember that current assets are those that are going to be converted into cash in the next year or operating cycle, and that current liabilities are going to require the use of cash in the next year or operating cycle. As such, this ratio should normally be greater than 1; otherwise, it is difficult to see how the company will remain solvent in the next year. The rule of thumb for this ratio is that, in order to provide a reasonable margin of safety for most businesses, the ratio should be approximately 2 or greater. However, the size of this ratio depends on the type of business and the types of assets and liabilities that are considered current.

Refer to the balance sheet of **Sun-Rype Products Ltd.** in Exhibit 6-5. The current ratio for Sun-Rype at the end of 2003 was just above 2, calculated as follows.

CURRENT RATIO — SUN-RYPE PRODUCTS

$$\text{Current Ratio} = \frac{\$32,829}{\$16,083} = 2.04$$

This represents an improvement in Sun-Rype's current ratio during 2003. At the end of the preceding year it was significantly lower, at 1.73 ($24,758 ÷ $14,308).

SUN-RYPE PRODUCTS LTD. 2003 ANNUAL REPORT

 EXHIBIT 6-5 PART A

Sun-Rype Products Ltd.

Balance Sheets
As at December 31 (in thousands of dollars)

	2003	2002
Assets		
Current assets		
Cash	$ 8,595	$ 1,894
Accounts receivable (note 2)	10,259	10,183
Income taxes receivable	-	1,388
Inventories (note 3)	13,271	10,520
Prepaid expenses	416	372
Future income tax benefit (note 11)	288	401
	32,829	24,758
Property, plant and equipment (note 4)	23,120	23,941
Deferred expenses	53	65
	$ 56,002	$ 48,764
Liabilities and Shareholders' Equity		
Current liabilities		
Promissory note (note 6)	$ 675	$ 675
Accounts payable and accrued liabilities	14,257	13,603
Income taxes payable	647	-
Current portion of long-term obligations (note 7)	504	30
	16,083	14,308
Long-term obligations (note 7)	153	389
Future income taxes (note 11)	1,486	1,016
	17,722	15,713
Shareholders' equity		
Share capital and contributed surplus (note 8)	18,797	18,688
Retained earnings	19,483	14,363
	38,280	33,051
	$ 56,002	$ 48,764

Commitments and guarantees (note 13)

APPROVED BY THE BOARD OF DIRECTORS

D. Selman, Director

J. **Alfonso**, Director

See accompanying notes to these financial statements.

EXHIBIT 6-5
PART B

SUN-RYPE PRODUCTS LTD. 2003 ANNUAL REPORT

Sun-Rype Products Ltd.

Statements of Earnings and Retained Earnings

For the years ended December 31 (in thousands of dollars except per share amounts)

	2003	2002
Net sales	$ 111,248	$ 104,071
Cost of sales	71,925	67,528
Gross profit	39,323	36,543
Selling, general & administrative expenses	27,501	26,547
Amortization	3,209	2,446
Interest expense (note 9)	99	89
Loss on capital dispositions	223	7
	31,032	29,089
Earnings before income taxes	8,291	7,454
Income taxes (note 11)	3,171	2,581
Net earnings	5,120	4,873
Retained earnings, beginning of year	14,363	9,490
Retained earnings, end of year	$ 19,483	$ 14,363
Earnings per share (note 14)		
Basic	$ 0.48	$ 0.46
Diluted	0.48	0.45

See accompanying notes to these financial statements.

One caveat: the current ratio is sometimes subject to manipulation by a company at year end. This ratio may not, therefore, be a very reliable measure of liquidity. For example: remember the two criteria for classifying a marketable security as a current asset? It must be possible to sell the security and management must intend to sell it within the next year. Management could declare that it intended to sell a long-term investment within the next year and thus reclassify it as short-term. This change in intent would have the effect of increasing the current ratio. Here is another example. Consider a company that has $100 in current assets and $50 in current liabilities just before the end of a given year. Its current ratio would be 2 ($100 ÷ $50). Suppose that $30 of the $100 is in cash and the rest is in inventory. Suppose further that the company uses all its $30 in cash to pay off $30 worth of current liabilities at year end. The current ratio becomes 3.5 ($70 ÷ $20), and the company looks more liquid. Notice, however, that the company is actually less liquid; in fact, it is very illiquid in the short term because it has no cash, and must sell its inventory and wait until it collects on those sales before it will have any cash to pay its bills. In this case, the current ratio is deceptive. Therefore, a second short-term liquidity ratio, the "quick ratio," is used to help provide more information on the company's liquidity.

QUICK RATIO

As illustrated in the above example, one problem with the current ratio is that some assets in the current section may be much less liquid than others. For example, inventory is less liquid than accounts receivable, which is less liquid than cash. In some industries, inventory is very illiquid because of the long period of time that it may have to be held before sale. Consider, for example, the holding period in the manufacture of 12-year-old Scotch whisky. The current ratio in such cases will not adequately measure the company's short-term liquidity. Therefore, the **quick ratio** is also used to assess short-term liquidity. It differs from the current ratio in that inventories, and often prepaid expenses, are omitted from the numerator, because they could not (in most cases) be converted into cash quickly. It is calculated as:

$$\text{Quick Ratio} = \frac{\text{Current Assets} - \text{Inventory} - \text{Prepaid Expenses}}{\text{Current Liabilities}}$$

The rule of thumb for this ratio is that it should be approximately 1 or more. Again, the actual value depends somewhat on the type of industry. For Sun-Rype Products (refer to the balance sheet in Exhibit 6-5), the ratio at the end of 2003 was as follows.

QUICK RATIO — SUN-RYPE PRODUCTS

$$\text{Quick Ratio} = \frac{\$32,829 - 13,271 - 416 - 288}{\$16,083} = 1.17$$

Note that we have subtracted the amount of the "Future income tax benefit" (along with the inventory and prepaid expenses) from the total current assets in the above calculation. We have done so because it was listed at the end of the current assets section on Sun-Rype's balance sheet, which implies that it is not very liquid. Remember that the current assets are listed in the order of their liquidity. Therefore, it is logical that any current assets listed after the inventory should be subtracted when determining the quick ratio.

As shown in the above calculation, Sun-Rype's quick ratio for 2003 was slightly above 1. At the end of the preceding year it was somewhat lower, at 0.94 ([$24,758 − 10,520 − 372 − 401] ÷ $14,308). Thus, Sun-Rype's quick ratio (like its current ratio) improved during 2003.

Analysis of Accounts Receivable Using the Accounts Receivable Turnover Ratio

A company's cash flows are critical to its profitability and even to its survival. Because most companies receive a significant amount of operating cash from the collection of their accounts receivable, the analysis of a company's short-term liquidity should consider its success in collecting its accounts receivable. One common ratio used to assess the management of accounts receivable is the **accounts receivable turnover ratio**. This is calculated by dividing the credit sales for the period by the average accounts receivable, as follows.

$$\text{Accounts Receivable Turnover Ratio} = \frac{\text{Credit Sales}}{\text{Average Accounts Receivable}}$$

Calculating this ratio from financial statement data usually requires you to assume that all the sales are credit sales. If the analyst has more detailed information about the composition of sales, then some adjustment can be made in the numerator to include only credit sales. In addition, information in the financial statements may indicate that not all receivables are from customers. Therefore, a more sophisticated calculation might include only customer receivables in the denominator, as only these relate to the credit sales figure in the numerator.

As an example, consider the information provided in Exhibit 6-5 from the financial statements of Sun-Rype Products Ltd. A quick review of this information shows that Sun-Rype's accounts receivable were slightly higher at the end of 2003 in comparison to 2002. This should not be a surprise, however, because the sales were higher in 2003. The calculation below shows how this growth affected Sun-Rype's collection rate for 2003.

ACCOUNTS RECEIVABLE TURNOVER — SUN-RYPE PRODUCTS

$$\text{Receivables turnover rate} = \frac{\$111,248}{(\$10,259 + 10,183) \div 2} = \frac{\$111,248}{\$10,221} = 10.88$$

In this context, turnover means how often the accounts receivable are "turned over," or how often they are collected in full and replaced by new accounts. Thus, the turnover analysis above shows that Sun-Rype's accounts were collected and replaced by new receivables approximately 11 times during the year.

Another way to analyze the performance of accounts receivable collection is to calculate the number of days required to collect the average account. This analysis assumes that the sales are spread evenly over a 365-day year. The calculation divides the number of days in the year (365) by the accounts receivable turnover rate. Using this calculation, Sun-Rype's average collection period for accounts receivable was 33.5 days (365 ÷ 10.88) in 2003. It would be very useful to compare this with the company's normal credit terms. If its normal credit terms are 30 days, then you would expect that the number of days to collect receivables would be 30 days or fewer. Companies usually do not disclose their credit policy time frames or terms. Bear in mind, however, that Sun-Rype does not sell products directly to end customers; rather, it sells to retailers, which then sell to consumers. The credit terms for business-to-business sales are often longer than 30 days. Remember the earlier reference to General Publishing Co.? That company gave its business customers 90 days to pay. Sun-Rype's average collection period of between 33 and 34 days in 2003 is probably very reasonable, and an indication of good receivables management.

One way to check the reasonableness of the ratio would be to compare it with a competitor's.

It would also be very informative to compare the above ratios for Sun-Rype in 2003 with the results for the preceding year. However, we don't know the amount of accounts receivable at the end of 2001, which is needed in order to calculate the average balance outstanding during 2002. (In order to get around this frequently encountered problem, analysts often base their calculations on end-of-year balances, even though average balances are preferable.)

In doing these analyses, several complicating factors should be considered. For example, some receivables such as financing receivables do not correspond directly to the sales revenues produced during the period. These financing receivables may reflect loans made by the company to its customers. These loans do not immediately generate an equivalent amount of revenue, the way sales of goods or services do. Revenue from financing receivables is earned over time, as the loans accrue interest. Therefore, an accounts receivable turnover based on these receivables would have little meaning.

Finally, trends over time should be considered. For example, when analyzing a company, you may find that the amounts written off over the last several years have been increasing. Whether this is good or bad, though, depends on how the accounts receivable balance has changed over the same period of time. To address this question, a ratio such as the amount written off to the balance in the receivables could be calculated. If this ratio is increasing over the last several years, it may represent some relative degradation in the quality of the receivables. If this were to continue, this would not be good news for the company.

Another way to address the same issue would be to compare the ratio of the ending balance in the allowance for doubtful accounts with the ending balance in the accounts receivable (before deducting the allowance). An increase in this ratio over time would indicate that a higher percentage of the ending accounts receivable was considered uncollectible. This, too, would be a negative indication.

SUMMARY

In this chapter, we have discussed four major types of current assets that are either cash, or about to become cash. We discussed how each could be valued and what the current Canadian practice is with respect to valuation. For cash, we spent some time outlining the importance of internal controls. For temporary investments, we described how these are reported at their fair market values at the end of each period. We discussed the measuring and recording of potential bad debts associated with accounts receivable. The discussion of notes receivable included a section on how to account for the interest that is earned on notes.

The discussion of these four types of current assets was completed with the introduction of three ratios: the current ratio, the quick ratio, and the accounts receivable turnover ratio, which can be used to assess a company's short-term liquidity.

The next chapter considers the last major component of current assets: inventory. Because of the complexities associated with inventory accounting, an entire chapter is devoted to this discussion.

SUMMARY PROBLEM 1

Exhibit 6-6 provides information about the transactions involving short-term investments for LABBÉ LTÉE.

EXHIBIT 6-6 **LABBÉ LTÉE.**

Additional Demonstration Problems

Security	Quarter Acquired	Acquisition Cost	Quarter Sold	Selling Price
Alpha Co.	1	$20,000	–	–
Beta Co.	1	$35,000	4	$29,000
Gamma Co.	1	$15,000	2	$19,000

Security	Cost	Market Values as at the End of			
		Quarter 1	Quarter 2	Quarter 3	Quarter 4
Alpha	$20,000	$21,000	$22,000	$17,000	$15,000
Beta	35,000	32,000	36,000	37,000	–
Gamma	15,000	14,000	–	–	–
Portfolio	$70,000	$67,000	$58,000	$54,000	$15,000

Dividends Received	
Quarter	Amount
1	$650
2	$525
3	$550
4	$150

All dividends are received in cash during the quarter.

Assuming that LABBÉ prepares financial statements on a quarterly basis, construct the journal entries that it would make each quarter to record the above events (do not bother making closing entries).

SUMMARY PROBLEM 2

The Gujarathi Company sells goods on credit to its customers. During 2006, Gujarathi sold $150,000 worth of goods on credit and collected $125,000 from its customers. The company started the period with a balance of $15,000 in accounts receivable and a balance in the allowance for doubtful accounts of $450. During 2006, Gujarathi wrote off $2,725 of accounts receivable. Gujarathi estimates that 2% of the sales amount will ultimately be uncollectible.

 a. Calculate the amount of bad debt expense that should be recorded for 2006.

 b. Show all journal entries that would be made during the year that would affect accounts receivable and the related allowance account.

 c. What amount(s) would be reported on the balance sheet at the end of 2006 regarding accounts receivable?

SUMMARY PROBLEM 3

Using the balance sheet and income statement of **Danier Leather Inc.** in Exhibit 6-7, calculate the current ratio, the quick ratio, and the accounts receivable turnover rate and average collection period for 2003. Write a brief interpretation of the ratios.

DANIER LEATHER 2003 ANNUAL REPORT

CONSOLIDATED BALANCE SHEETS

(THOUSANDS OF DOLLARS)

EXHIBIT 6-7
PART A

	June 28, 2003	June 29, 2002
ASSETS		
Current Assets		
Cash	$ 7,254	$ 3,777
Accounts receivable	600	484
Income taxes recoverable	83	-
Inventories (Note 2)	37,029	38,662
Prepaid expenses	889	603
Future income tax asset (Note 8)	1,044	628
	46,899	44,154
Other Assets		
Capital assets (Note 3)	34,246	31,199
Goodwill (Note 4)	342	342
	$ 81,487	$ 75,695
LIABILITIES		
Current Liabilities		
Accounts payable and accrued liabilities	$ 10,559	$ 10,472
Income taxes payable	-	80
	10,559	10,552
Deferred lease inducements	2,238	1,837
Future income tax liability (Note 8)	696	784
	13,493	13,173
SHAREHOLDERS' EQUITY		
Share capital (Note 6)	23,995	23,917
Retained earnings	43,999	38,605
	67,994	62,522
	$ 81,487	$ 75,695

Approved by the Board

Edwin F. Hawken, Director   *Jeffrey Wortsman*, Director

PART B

DANIER LEATHER 2003 ANNUAL REPORT

CONSOLIDATED STATEMENTS OF EARNINGS

(THOUSANDS OF DOLLARS, EXCEPT PER SHARE AMOUNTS)

	For the Years Ended	
	June 28, 2003	June 29, 2002
Revenue	$ 175,487	$ 179,977
Cost of sales (Note 7)	88,788	92,098
Gross profit	86,699	87,879
Selling, general and administrative expenses (Note 7)	77,390	69,264
Earnings before interest and income taxes	9,309	18,615
Interest expense – net	66	461
Earnings before income taxes	9,243	18,154
Provision for income taxes (Note 8)		
Current	4,353	7,314
Future	(504)	115
	3,849	7,429
Net earnings	$ 5,394	$ 10,725
Net earnings per share (Notes 1(k) & 6 (c))		
Basic	$0.78	$1.57
Diluted	$0.76	$1.53

SUGGESTED SOLUTION TO SUMMARY PROBLEM 1

The journal entries that LABBÉ LTÉE. would make each quarter are as follows.

Quarter 1

Acquisition entry:

Temporary investments (A)	70,000	
Cash (A)		70,000

Dividend revenue:

Cash (A)	650	
Dividend revenue (SE)		650

Realized gain or loss on sale of investments:
 No investments were sold this quarter.

Unrealized gain or loss on securities held:

Unrealized loss on temporary investments (SE)	3,000	
Temporary investments (A)		3,000

To record decrease in market value from $70,000 to $67,000.

Quarter 2

> <u>Acquisition entry:</u>
> No investments were acquired this quarter.
>
> <u>Dividend revenue:</u>
> Cash (A)   525
>   Dividend revenue (SE)   525
>
> <u>Realized gain or loss on sale of investments:</u>
> Cash (A)   19,000
>   Gain on sale of temporary investment (SE)   5,000
>   Temporary investments (A)   14,000
>
> <u>Unrealized gain or loss securities held:</u>
> Temporary investments (A)   5,000
>   Unrealized gain on temporary investments (SE)   5,000
>
> To record increase in market value from $53,000 ($21,000 + 32,000) to $58,000.

Quarter 3

> <u>Acquisition entry:</u>
> No investments were acquired this quarter.
>
> <u>Dividend revenue:</u>
> Cash (A)   550
>   Dividend revenue (SE)   550
>
> <u>Realized gain or loss on sale of investments:</u>
> No investments were sold this quarter.
>
> <u>Unrealized gain or loss on securities held:</u>
> Unrealized loss on temporary investments (SE)   4,000
>   Temporary investments (A)   4,000
>
> To record decrease in market value from $58,000 to $54,000.

Quarter 4

> <u>Acquisition entry:</u>
> No investments were acquired this quarter.
>
> <u>Dividend revenue:</u>
> Cash (A)   150
>   Dividend revenue (SE)   150
>
> <u>Realized gain or loss on sale of investments:</u>
> Cash (A)   29,000
> Loss on sale of temporary investment (SE)   8,000
>   Temporary investments (A)   37,000
>
> <u>Unrealized gain or loss securities held:</u>
> Unrealized loss on temporary investments (SE)   2,000
>   Temporary investments   2,000
>
> To record decrease in market value from $17,000 to $15,000.

SUGGESTED SOLUTION TO SUMMARY PROBLEM 2

a. Bad debts expense equals 2% of credit sales
   .02 × $150,000 = $3,000

b. The following journal entries would be made during the year by Gujarathi Company.

Credit sales:

Accounts receivable (A)	150,000	
Sales revenue (SE)		150,000

Collections from customers:

Cash (A)	125,000	
Accounts receivable (A)		125,000

Write-off of bad debts:

Allowance for doubtful accounts (XA)	2,725	
Accounts receivable (A)		2,725

Recording of annual bad debt expense:

Bad debt expense (SE)	3,000	
Allowance for doubtful accounts (XA)		3,000

c. The balance sheet at the end of 2006 would show the following.

Accounts receivable	$37,275*	
Less: Allowance for doubtful accounts	725**	
Net carrying value of accounts receivable		$36,550

or

Accounts receivable (net of allowance for doubtful accounts)	$36,550

* Beginning balance $15,000 + 150,000 − 125,000 − 2,725

** Beginning balance $450 − 2,725 + 3,000

SUGGESTED SOLUTION TO SUMMARY PROBLEM 3

Current ratio:

$$\frac{\$46,899}{\$10,559} = 4.44$$

Quick ratio:

$$\frac{\$46,899 - 37,029 - 889 - 1,044 \ (\text{or} \ \$7,254 + 600 + 83)}{\$10,559} = 0.75$$

Accounts receivable turnover ratio:

$$\frac{\$175,487}{(\$600 + 484) \div 2} = 324 \ \text{times}$$

Average collection period for accounts receivable:

$$365 \ \text{days} \div 324 \ = 1.13 \ \text{days}$$

Interpretation:

The current ratio is far above the "rule of thumb" minimum level of 2. It indicates that Danier Leather has more than four times as many current assets as liabilities. However, the quick ratio falls below the "rule of thumb" level of at least 1. The reason that it is so low is that 83% ([$37,029 + 889 + 1,044] ÷ $46,899) of the current assets are held in the form of inventory or other assets that are not very liquid. The inventory alone accounts for 79% of the total current assets. However, the inventory level is lower than the previous year, and the company has been operating without running into financial difficulty. It should be borne in mind that Danier Leather is a retailer, which means that inventory generates cash daily. The company probably relies on this cash inflow from sales to facilitate the payment of its current obligations.

The accounts receivable turnover rate, at 324 times per year, looks incredibly good. It indicates that the accounts receivable are collected, on average, every 1.13 days. This is extremely fast, indicating that the ratio may be distorted. To calculate the ratio we used the total revenue amount. We did not have the credit sales amount available. Danier Leather probably sells the majority of its merchandise for cash or by credit card. Since credit card sales are effectively cash sales (minus the fees charged by the bank and/or credit card company), this means that the majority of Danier's revenue is probably in the form of cash sales. Because it is not possible to determine the credit sales amount, we cannot calculate a more accurate ratio and we should not put too much weight on the accounts receivable turnover rate or the average collection period.

GLOSSARY

Accounts receivable   Assets of a seller that represent the promise by a buyer to pay the seller at some date in the future.

Accounts receivable turnover ratio   A ratio that divides the total credit sales (if known) by the average accounts receivable. It indicates how many times during the year the accounts receivable balance is collected in total.

Allowance method   A method used to value accounts receivable by estimating the amount of accounts receivable that will not be collected in the future. Bad debts expense is thereby recognized in the period of the sale.

Bad debt   An account receivable that cannot be collected.

Bank reconciliation   The procedure used to reconcile a company's record of its bank account balance to the record provided by the bank.

Collateral   An asset that is pledged as security for a debt. If the borrower defaults on the debt, the lender receives title to the asset, which can then be sold to cover the amount owed to the lender.

Compensating balances   Minimum balances that must be maintained in a bank account to avoid significant service charges or, in some cases, to satisfy restrictive loan covenants.

Compound interest   Interest calculated by adding the interest earned in one period to the balance in the account and multiplying the total by the interest rate. The interest earned in one period then earns interest itself in the next period.

Control account   An account that contains the overall amounts related to a particular item in the financial statements, the details of which are recorded in subsidiary accounts. For example, the control account for Accounts Receivable would contain the total balance for all the company's receivables, while a set of subsidiary accounts for Accounts Receivable would contain the balances for each of the individual customers. The balance in the control account should equal the sum of all the balances in the related subsidiary accounts.

Current ratio   A ratio calculated by dividing the total current assets by the total current liabilities.

Direct write-off method   A method of recognizing bad debts. Bad debt expense is recognized under this method at the time the account receivable is written off. No estimates of future write-offs are made, and no allowance for doubtful accounts is used.

Factoring   The process of selling accounts receivable to a third party to generate immediate cash.

Fair (market) value   The economic value of an item as determined in a transaction between independent parties. The amount for which the item could be bought or sold in an open marketplace. Often referred to as simply "market value".

Financial instruments   A term that encompasses financial assets, financial liabilities, and certain equity items.

Historical cost   A valuation attribute or method that values assets at the price paid to obtain those assets.

Internal control system The set of policies and procedures that are established by an enterprise to safeguard its assets and ensure the integrity of its accounting system.

Lower of cost and market (LCM) A valuation method that reports an asset's value at the lower of its historical cost and its current market value.

Marketable securities Shares or debt securities that actively trade in a market.

Market value The economic value of an item as determined in a transaction between independent parties. The amount for which the item could be bought or sold in an open marketplace. Often referred to as simply "fair value".

Monetary An attribute of an asset or liability that indicates that the asset or liability represents a fixed number of monetary units.

Monetary unit The nominal units used to measure assets and liabilities. The monetary unit used is usually the local currency unit (such as the Canadian dollar).

Note receivable An asset that represents the right of the holder of the note to receive a fixed set of cash payments in the future.

Percentage of credit sales method A method of estimating the bad debt expense by using a percentage of the credit sales for the period.

Promissory note A document in which the issuer of the note agrees to pay fixed amounts to the holder of the note at some point in the future.

Purchasing power An attribute of an asset that measures its ability to be exchanged for goods and services.

Quick ratio A ratio calculated by dividing the most liquid current assets (cash, temporary investments, accounts receivable) by the total current liabilities.

Realized gain/loss A gain or loss that is the result of a completed transaction, such as the sale of an asset. (In general, it means that cash or an agreement to pay cash has been received in exchange.)

Recourse A provision in agreements to sell receivables in which the buyer of the receivables has the right to return them to the seller if the buyer cannot collect the receivables.

Recovery (of accounts receivable) The reinstatement and collection of an account receivable that was previously written off.

Secured note A note receivable secured by collateral.

Securities Financial instruments, usually shares or debt, that may be publicly traded.

Simple interest Interest that is calculated by multiplying the interest rate in the agreement by the principal involved. Interest earned in one period does not earn interest in a subsequent period.

Subsidiary account An account that contains detailed amounts related to a particular item in the financial statements, for which the totals are recorded in a control account. For example, a set of subsidiary accounts for Accounts Receivable would contain the balances due from each of the individual customers, while the control account for Accounts Receivable would contain the total balance for all the company's receivables. The sum of all the balances in the subsidiary accounts should equal the balance in the related control account.

Uncollectible accounts Accounts receivable that are deemed to be bad debts. The point at which they are deemed uncollectible is generally established by company policy.

Unit-of-measure assumption An assumption made under GAAP that all transactions should be measured using a common unit (in our case, the Canadian dollar).

Unrealized gain/loss A gain or loss recognized in the financial statements that has not resulted in the receipt of cash or the right to receive cash, but represents a change in value of an asset prior to its sale.

Write-off The process by which an account receivable is removed from a company's books when it is deemed uncollectible.

ASSIGNMENT MATERIAL

Self-Assessment Quiz

Assessing Your Recall

6-1 Briefly describe how cash, temporary investments, accounts receivable, and notes receivable meet the criteria of probable future value and ownership to qualify as assets.

6-2 Explain what the unit-of-measure assumption means in accounting.

Managing a Growing Inventory

When Veseys Seeds first began operations in 1939, orders were filled using a spoon and kitchen scale, and inventory was tracked on the backs of little cards. Sixty-five years later, the York, Prince Edward Island, mail order company processes more than 100,000 customer orders each year, shipping to gardeners across Canada and the United States. Today, using state-of-the-art inventory and bookkeeping software, it has a perpetual inventory system that is automatically updated with each transaction.

Over the years, Veseys' inventory has grown to include hundreds of different vegetable, flower, and herb seeds, as well as a wide range of bulbs, gardening accessories, and tools. Since seeds—which Veseys purchases in bulk and packages on site—are sold in five different packet sizes, the company has to keep track of thousands of individual items sold through its six printed catalogues, a retail outlet, and its website, which now brings in about 29% of total sales.

"Our entire inventory is stored in a database, so to create a purchase order, we simply type in a vendor name and item number, and the current price and ordering information pops up," explains John Barrett, Sales and Marketing Director at Veseys. "When the product arrives, our receiver records the shipment against the original purchase order. As a result, at any given time, our customer sales staff can tell whether an item is available or not, or if it's back-ordered."

Because Veseys uses a just-in-time system—it buys seeds in large quantities but packages them in increments—an item may occasionally show up as unavailable when in fact it is currently in packaging and will be on the shelf by the end of the day. "When that happens, our staff does an override and the sale goes through," says Mr. Barrett. "We control our own destiny when it comes to creating the inventory, unlike other companies that are dependent on outside suppliers. This way, basically, nothing is ever out of stock."

But the just-in-time system has posed a challenge for tracking web-based orders. Veseys' website isn't fully integrated with the system. Although orders from the website are automatically entered, they are reviewed and processed by staff each day. "If we let the website run by itself, at 3 a.m. when somebody orders something from Phoenix and the computer tells them we're out of stock on an item, that person ends up not ordering it," explains Mr. Barrett. "With our system, we'll make sure they get that item."

In addition to tracking inventory, the system produces reports such as sales by week or by category. It can even show the number of items and dollar revenue per item on any page of Veseys' catalogues. "By comparing those figures with what we've bought so far, I can come up with a pretty good estimate of what we're going to need," Mr. Barrett says. "In the end, it will tell me whether I've bought too much or too little based on my projections. Due to the nature of our business, we can't have any surplus. Our product is alive, and it has to be sold and planted within a certain period of time or it's finished."

6-16 **(Temporary investments)**

The following transactions relate to the Abbe Investment Company for 2005 and 2006. Abbe closes its books on December 31 each year.

Transactions:

2005

June 30	Abbe purchased 5,000 common shares of Signal Corp. at $12.50 per share. It also paid fees to its stockbroker of $0.15 per share.
September 1	Signal Corp. declared a dividend of $0.90 per share to be paid on September 20.
September 25	Abbe received the dividend cheque from Signal Corp.
December 31	The market value of Signal Corp.'s common shares was $13.95 per share.

2006

January 16	Abbe sold the common shares of Signal Corp. at $14.25 per share. Brokerage fees were $0.15 per share.

Required:

a. Prepare journal entries to record all the preceding transactions in the books of Abbe Investment Company, assuming the shares purchased are considered temporary investments. Note that we have not discussed fees to stockbrokers, or brokerage fees. In answering this question, use your knowledge of accounting principles to determine a logical method for recording them.

b. What amount of temporary investments would appear in Abbe's balance sheet at December 31, 2005?

c. How much gain or loss would be reported with respect to these investments in 2005? In 2006?

6-17 **(Temporary investments)**

The Corona Company holds a portfolio of temporary investments. The portfolio's acquisition costs and aggregate market values are as follows.

Three Months Ended	Acquisition Cost of Securities Purchased During the Quarter	Aggregate Market Value of Securities Held at the End of the Quarter
March 31	$450,000	$410,000
June 30	50,000	480,000
September 30	20,000	510,000
December 31	20,000	530,000

Required:

a. What amount of temporary investments would appear in Corona's balance sheets at the end of each quarter?

b. Give the necessary journal entries for each quarter.

6-18 **(Temporary investments)**

Upper Company purchased 500 shares each of Jack, Queen, and King companies on July 1, at a cost of $52, $18, and $40 per share, respectively. On December 31 the market values of the shares were $58, $16, and $38, respectively. Upper Company considers the shares temporary investments.

Required:

a. At what amount will the investments be reported in the December 31 balance sheet of Upper Company?

b. What other balance sheet or income statement account will be affected by the accounting treatment of these securities? What will the effect be?

6-19   (Dividends earned on temporary investments)

During the period July 1 – December 31, Upper Company received dividends of $4, $2, and $3 per share, respectively, from the common shares of Jack, Queen, and King companies acquired in Problem 6-18.

Required:

a. What amount will it report for dividend revenue for the period?

b. If Upper Company has a goal of earning a 12% annual return (before tax) on its temporary investments, has it accomplished its goal this period?

6-20   (Temporary investments)

The following information relates to the temporary investments held by Anders Corp. as current assets.

Security	Acquisition Date	Acquisition Cost	Date Sold	Selling Price	Market Value Dec. 31 2004	2005	2006
Alpha	Apr. 13/2004	$ 70,000	NA	NA	$68,000	$72,000	$69,000
Beta	Aug 24/2004	45,000	May 27/2005	52,000	48,000	NA	NA
Delta	Jan. 8/2005	35,000	NA	NA	NA	38,000	41,000
Omega	Jan. 3/2006	95,000	June 30/2006	98,000	NA	NA	NA

The Anders Corp. closes its books on December 31 each year.

Required:

a. Prepare journal entries relating to these temporary investments for each year.

b. Show how the information regarding marketable securities would be presented on the income statement and balance sheet for each year.

6-21   (Accounts receivable and uncollectible accounts)

Dundee Company started business on January 1 of the current year. The company made credit sales of $760,000 during the year and received payments of $680,000 to the end of the year. It also wrote off as uncollectible $12,000 of its receivables when it learned that the customer who owed the $12,000 had filed for bankruptcy. Other than the entry to write off the $12,000, Dundee Company has made no entries related to bad debt expense for the period. The industry average for bad debt expense for companies similar to Dundee is 3% of credit sales. Dundee uses the allowance method of accounting for bad debts and adopts the industry percentage in estimating bad debt expense.

Required:

a. What should be the balance reported in the allowance for doubtful accounts at December 31?

b. What accounts receivable balance would be reported in the balance sheet at December 31?

c. Evaluate the reasonableness of the balance in the allowance for doubtful accounts at December 31.

6-22 (**Accounts receivable and uncollectible accounts**)

Supreme Equipment Sales Company had a balance in its accounts receivable account at December 31, 2005, of $120,000 and a $4,000 balance in its allowance for doubtful accounts. During 2006, the company sold equipment on credit in the amount of $820,000. Total cash collections during 2006 were $780,000. The company also determined that $6,000 of accounts would not be collectible, and it wrote them off. At the end of 2006, management determined that it should increase its allowance percentage to 1% of credit sales, from the previous year's 0.5%, because of an economic slowdown and the amount of accounts receivable that proved to be uncollectible during the year.

> *Required:*
>
> a. Prepare the necessary journal entries for recording all the 2006 transactions, including the adjustment for bad debts expense at year end.
>
> b. Show the accounts receivable section of the balance sheet at December 31, 2006.

6-23 (**Accounts receivable and uncollectible accounts**)

The Global Sales Company's accounts receivable show the following balances at October 31, before adjustment: accounts receivable, $1,838,000; allowance for doubtful accounts, $8,000 (credit balance). Total sales for the year then ended were $26,300,000. Global Sales estimates that 1.5% of its sales on credit will prove to be uncollectible. Of the total sales, 25% are cash sales and 75% are made on credit.

> *Required:*
>
> a. Prepare the necessary journal entry to record the bad debt expense for the year.
>
> b. Show the accounts receivable section of the balance sheet at October 31.
>
> c. What amount of bad debt expense would appear in the income statement for the year ended October 31?

6-24 (**Accounts receivable and uncollectible accounts**)

Belkou Company began operations on January 1, 2005. Its first year's sales were $1,100,000, which were 70% on credit. On December 31, 2005, the accounts receivable had a debit balance of $75,000. The management estimated that 0.5% of all credit sales would probably be uncollectible. The company wrote off accounts worth $2,800 at year end.

At the end of 2006, the balances in selected accounts were: accounts receivable, $86,000; allowance for doubtful accounts, $4,200 (debit balance); sales, $1,540,000 (70% on credit). The bad debt expense for 2006 had not been determined or recorded.

After reviewing the write-off of accounts receivable during 2006, the company decided that the estimate of uncollectibility should be increased from 0.5% to 0.75%.

> *Required:*
>
> a. Give the journal entry to record the bad debt expense for 2006.
>
> b. Prepare a T account for the allowance for doubtful accounts, and enter into the account all the transactions that have affected it since the company started operations.
>
> c. What is the net amount of accounts receivable at the end of 2006?

6-25 (**Note receivable with interest calculations**)

On March 1 the Moon Company determined that it would not be able to pay the account receivable that was owed to Gamma Company. Moon was confident that it would have the necessary cash near the end of the year. It therefore signed a 10-month, 9% note for the $10,000 that was owed. The interest that is owed on this note will be paid when the note matures (is due). On August 31, the Gamma Company closed its books for the year.

Required:

a. Prepare all the journal entries that would be made by Gamma Company associated with this note up to the end of August 31.

b. Prepare the journal entry to record the receipt from Moon of the amount owed to Gamma on December 31.

6-26 (Note receivable with interest calculations)

On June 1, 2005, Active Networks sold a computer networking system to Finn Motors for $36,000. Finn Motors signed a note receivable with interest at 11%, agreeing to pay the $36,000 in eight months. Active Networks' year end is December 31.

Required:

a. Prepare all the necessary journal entries associated with this note, including the year-end entries and the receipt of payment from Finn Motors on February 1, 2006.

b. What items would be included on the balance sheet and income statement of Active Networks on December 31, with respect to this note?

6-27 (Note receivable with interest calculations)

Kristi Scudeler bought a laptop computer priced at $2,270 (including tax) on May 1 from a store called The Computer Tutor. She didn't have all the money right then, but she was confident that she would have enough by the end of the summer. Therefore, she made a down payment of $570 and signed a four-month note promising to pay the balance of $1,700 plus interest at 12%.

Required:

a. Calculate how much interest will be earned by The Computer Tutor on this note.

b. Do you think that the 12% charged by The Computer Tutor is reasonable or unreasonable? Explain. What factors would a supplier such as The Computer Tutor consider when it determines how much interest to charge?

6-28 (Current and quick ratios)

The following amounts were reported by Liquid Company in its most recent balance sheet.

Cash	$ 40,000
Accounts receivable	130,000
Short-term investments	18,000
Inventory	390,000
Prepaid insurance	35,000
Accounts payable	85,000
Wages payable	37,000
Income tax payable	45,000
Sales tax payable	10,000
Short-term notes payable	115,000

Required:

a. Calculate the current ratio and the quick ratio for Liquid Company.

b. Based on a review of other companies in the industry, the management of Liquid Company thinks it should maintain a current ratio of 2 or more, and a quick ratio of 1 or more. The ratios at the end of the prior year were 1.8 and 1.2, respective-

ly. How successful has the company been in achieving the desired results in this period?

c. How could the company improve its current position? What risks, if any, are associated with the strategy you have suggested?

6-29 (Liquidity decisions)

The following balance sheet accounts and amounts were included in the balance sheet of Wanhill Processors Ltd.

Equipment and vehicles	$205,000
Bank loan (long-term)	250,000
Prepaid expenses	2,000
Accumulated amortization	88,000
Taxes payable	14,000
Inventory	255,000
Wages payable	26,000
Accounts receivable	25,000
Unearned revenue	48,000
Retained earnings	60,000
Trademarks (capital assets)	45,000
Common shares	30,000
Cash	39,000
Accounts payable	55,000

Required:

a. Prepare a classified balance sheet in good form.

b. At the beginning of the period, Wanhill reported total current assets of $300,000 and current liabilities of $260,000. Calculate the current ratios for Wanhill at the beginning and end of the period. Has the current ratio improved or declined during the period?

c. Calculate the amount of Wanhill's working capital (current assets minus current liabilities) at the beginning and end of the period.

d. Have Wanhill's working capital position and its overall liquidity improved or declined during the period?

e. How might Wanhill evaluate whether or not its overall liquidity is adequate?

6-30 (Cash flow analysis)

The balance sheet and the income statement of the Smythe Company for the year 2006 (in thousands of dollars) are given on the following page. In addition to these statements, the following information is available.

1. There were no sales of property, plant, and equipment during 2006.

2. No dividends were declared or paid during 2006.

3. Temporary investments that were carried at $75 at the end of 2005 were sold for $100 during 2006.

4. Temporary investments costing $175 were acquired during 2006.

SMYTHE COMPANY
Balance Sheet
At December 31

	2006	2005
Assets		
Cash	$ 540	$ 500
Accounts receivable	900	850
Allowance for doubtful accounts	(15)	(10)
Temporary investments	500	450
Inventory	1,800	1,350
Property, plant, and equipment	8,000	5,800
Accumulated amortization	(2,800)	(1,800)
Total assets	$ 8,925	$ 7,140
Liabilities and Shareholders' Equity		
Accounts payable	$ 1,700	$ 1,550
Common shares	3,000	3,000
Retained earnings	4,225	2,590
Total liabilities and shareholders' equity	$ 8,925	$ 7,140

SMYTHE COMPANY
Income Statement
For the year ended December 31, 2006

Revenues		$12,000
Cost of goods sold		6,500
Gross profit		5,500
Expenses:		
Bad debt expense	$ 150	
Amortization	1,000	
Other operating expenses	2,000	3,150
Operating income		2,350
Unrealized loss on valuation of temporary investments		(50)
Realized gain on sale of temporary investments		25
Income before taxes		2,325
Income taxes		690
Net income		$ 1,635

Required:

Prepare a statement to show why cash increased from $500 to $540 (thousand).

User Perspective Problems

6-31 (Internal control and the audit process)

You are the auditor of a medium-sized business (revenues of $10 million). Before you begin the audit, you review the company's internal control system. Why is this preliminary step necessary? What are you hoping to learn? If you had reviewed the internal control system last year before the audit, is it necessary to do it again this year? Explain.

6-32   (Estimation of uncollectibility of accounts receivable)

Suppose that there is a stock option plan at the SeeSaw Company that rewards managers for achieving a certain level of reported net income. What incentives might management have to influence the estimation of uncollectibility of accounts receivable?

6-33   (Market value of temporary investments and decision-making)

As a loan officer at a bank, why would you be interested in the market value of a company's temporary investments? Would you want them recorded at their market value or would you be satisfied with just the disclosure of the market valuation? Explain your reasoning.

6-34   (Market value of temporary investments and decision-making)

As a shareholder, why would you be interested in the market value of a company's temporary investments? Would you also want to know their cost?

6-35   (Impact of a negative cash balance)

You are a shareholder of a large retail company. When you received the annual report, you noticed that the company did not have any cash recorded on the balance sheet. Instead, there was an entry in the current liabilities called Bank overdraft. What do you think happened to the cash? Should you be concerned? What ratio analysis could you do that might help you understand the seriousness of this situation?

6-36   (Bank reconciliation and decision-making)

As a company manager, explain why a bank reconciliation is important to your management of cash.

6-37   (Accounts receivable and uncollectibility)

Ontario Company is involved in the manufacture and sale of high-quality racing and mountain bicycles. At the end of 2005, Ontario's balance sheet reported total accounts receivable of $350,000 and an allowance for doubtful accounts of $28,000. During 2006, the following events occurred.

1. Credit sales in the amount of $1,300,000 were made.

2. Collections of $1,250,000 were received.

3. Customers with total debts of $36,000 to Ontario were declared bankrupt and those accounts receivable were written off.

4. Ontario recorded bad debt expense for 2006 as 3% of credit sales.

As the Director of Finance for Ontario, you have been asked by a member of the executive committee to:

a. Analyze the above activities by giving the journal entries to be recorded by Ontario for each of the transactions.

b. Illustrate Ontario's balance sheet disclosure of accounts receivable at December 31, 2006.

c. Evaluate the adequacy of Ontario's allowance for doubtful accounts at December 31, 2006.

6-38   (Accounts receivable and uncollectible accounts)

Lowrate Communications is involved in the telephone/cellular phone industry. The following selected information is taken from the financial statements of Lowrate (in thousands of dollars).

	2006	2005	2004
Accounts receivable (net)	$ 1,469.8	$ 1,230.6	$ 1,044.8
Allowance for doubtful accounts	128.9	121.9	118.0
Accounts written off	305.4	267.6	296.8
Bad debt expense	312.4	271.5	267.0
Sales	12,661.8	11,367.8	10,420.0

Required:

Based on the information from Lowrate's financial statements, answer the following questions.

a. What percentage of total accounts receivable is considered uncollectible in each of the three years presented?

b. What percentage of sales is bad debt expense in each of the three years presented?

c. Did Lowrate's collection of accounts receivable improve over the three-year period?

d. The cloning of cellular phones is currently a serious problem. Cloning involves copying access/billing codes from cellular phones belonging to others. Cellular phone companies typically absorb charges for unauthorized calls on cellular phones, amounts involving many thousands of dollars. If cloning continues to be a problem as the cellular business grows, how would this affect the financial statements of a company like Lowrate?

Reading and Interpreting
Published Financial Statements

6-39   (Cash and short-term investments)

**Financial
Statement
Analysis
Assignments**

Air Canada reported cash and cash equivalents balances of $670 million at December 31, 2003, and $558 million at the end of 2002. The notes accompanying its financial statements revealed that these amounts included short-term investments of $458 million at December 31, 2003, and $343 million at the end of 2002. The notes also state that the company's policy is to include any short-term investments that may be liquidated promptly and have maturities of less than 90 days in cash and cash equivalents.

Air Canada also reported *restricted cash* balances of $157 million at December 31, 2003, and $63 million at the end of 2002, under current assets. The notes accompanying its financial statements revealed that these amounts represented funds held in trust by Air Canada Vacations in accordance with regulatory requirements governing advance ticket sales, recorded under current liabilities, for certain related travel activities.

Required:

a. Explain why some of Air Canada's short-term investments are reported as part of its cash and cash equivalents. What can you infer from this about the company's cash management practices?

b. Explain in your own words why some of Air Canada's cash is classified as restricted. What effect would this have on the company's cash management practices?

6-40   (Accounts receivable, uncollectible accounts, and ratio analysis)

Cara Operations Limited reported the following selected amounts (stated in thousands of dollars) in its financial statements for the years ended March 30, 2003, and March 31, 2002.

	2003	2002
from Cara's Consolidated Statements of Earnings		
Gross revenues	$1,133,202	$1,036,749
Provision for Air Canada (note 4)	$15,362	--
from Cara's Consolidated Balance Sheets		
Accounts receivable* (note 4)	$51,280	$68,793
*net of provision for bad debts		

Note 4 accompanying Cara's financial statements is reproduced in Exhibit 6-8.

CARA OPERATIONS LIMITED 2003 ANNUAL REPORT

 EXHIBIT 6-8

4 PROVISION FOR AIR CANADA

Air Canada filed for creditor protection under the Companies' Creditors Arrangement Act ("CCAA") on April 1, 2003 and obtained a Court Order. In addition, it subsequently filed a petition under Section 304 of the United States Bankruptcy Code. Based on those events, the ensuing court proceedings and other related events subsequent to April 1, 2003, management, in its judgment, expensed a provision totaling $15.4 million representing all amounts owed by Air Canada to the Corporation. As required under the Court Order, Cara is required to continue to provide services to Air Canada during the restructuring period. The Court Order also states that suppliers will be paid for services provided after April 1 on the same terms and conditions as before the filing. Air Canada, the largest customer of the Corporation's Airport Services Division, represented 13.7% (2002 – 14.5%) of the Corporation's total gross revenue and 8.8% (2002 – 9.7%) of total system sales.

Required:

    a. Discuss the significance of what is disclosed on Cara's financial statements and in Note 4 in terms of how it would affect the analysis and interpretation of its financial ratios for the years ended March 31, 2002, and March 30, 2003.

    b. In terms of its effect on a reader's expectations regarding Cara's future performance, what is the significance of the information disclosed in Note 4?

6-41 (Cash and short-term investments)

In the 2003 balance sheet of **MOSAID Technologies Incorporated**, the first two current assets listed are *cash and cash equivalents* and *short-term marketable securities*. Why are the short-term marketable securities not included in cash equivalents? Is it possible that there are other short-term investments included in the cash equivalents? If so, what can you infer about them?

6-42 (Current ratio, quick ratio, and accounts receivable turnover ratio)

Refer to the balance sheets and statements of operations for MOSAID Technologies Incorporated, which are presented in Exhibit 6-9.

    Required:

    a. Calculate the following ratios for both 2003 and 2002.

        1. The current ratio.

        2. The quick ratio.

        3. The accounts receivable turnover ratio. Use the balances of accounts receivable at each year end, rather than average balances, and use the revenues from operations rather than total revenues.

EXHIBIT 6-9
PART A

MOSAID TECHNOLOGIES INCORPORATED 2003 ANNUAL REPORT

Consolidated Balance Sheets

(in thousands)

As at	April 25, 2003	April 26, 2002
Current Assets		
Cash and cash equivalents	$ 4,144	$ 9,374
Short-term marketable securities (Note 2)	38,167	44,056
Accounts receivable	7,635	5,019
Inventories (Note 3)	3,517	4,531
Prepaid expenses	802	997
	54,265	63,977
Capital Assets (Note 4)	13,402	19,073
Long-Term Investments (Note 5)	2,032	6,197
Future Income Taxes (Note 11)	12,708	10,324
	$ 82,407	$ 99,571
Current Liabilities		
Accounts payable and accrued liabilities	$ 12,399	$ 9,572
Deferred revenue	659	675
Obligation under capital lease	29	-
Mortgage payable (Note 6)	191	177
	13,278	10,424
Obligation Under Capital Lease	33	-
Mortgage Payable (Note 6)	5,022	5,214
	18,333	15,638
Contingency (Note 16)		
Shareholders' Equity		
Share capital (Note 7)	84,268	84,395
Contributed surplus	165	-
Deficit	(20,359)	(462)
	64,074	83,933
	$ 82,407	$ 99,571

See accompanying Notes to the Consolidated Financial Statements.

Thomas I. Csathy
Director

John B. Millard
Director

MOSAID TECHNOLOGIES INCORPORATED 2003 ANNUAL REPORT

EXHIBIT 6-9
PART B

Consolidated Statements of Operations and Deficit

(in thousands, except per share amounts)

Year ended	April 25, 2003	April 26, 2002
Revenues		
Operations	$ 37,067	$ 50,153
Interest	1,108	1,708
	38,175	51,861
Expenses		
Labour and materials	7,827	9,734
Research and development (Note 9)	23,987	28,139
Selling and marketing	10,685	13,811
General and administration	6,918	8,590
Bad debt	(165)	88
Restructuring (Note 10)	6,519	11,005
	55,771	71,367
Loss from operations	(17,596)	(19,506)
Write-down of long-term investment (Note 5)	(518)	(700)
Loss on disposal of long-term investment (Note 5)	(426)	-
Loss before income taxes	(18,540)	(20,206)
Income tax expense (Note 11)	1,357	4,480
Net loss	(19,897)	(24,686)
(Deficit) retained earnings, beginning of year	(462)	24,552
Premium on redemption of common shares	-	(328)
Deficit, end of year	$ (20,359)	$ (462)
Loss per share (Note 12)		
Basic	$ (1.94)	$ (2.45)
Diluted	$ (1.94)	$ (2.45)
Weighted average number of shares		
Basic	10,238,808	10,086,543
Diluted	10,238,808	10,086,543

See accompanying Notes to the Consolidated Financial Statements.

b. Comment on the ratio results and any significant trends.

6-43 **(Analysis of accounts receivable)**

The following appeared in the 2003 financial statements of **Domtar Inc.** (in millions of Canadian dollars).

	2003	2002
on the earnings statement:		
Net sales	$4,777	$5,490
on the balance sheet:		
Receivables (net of allowances for doubtful accounts of $18 in 2003 and $24 in 2002)	$197	$304

Required:

a. What percentages of Domtar's accounts receivable were considered uncollectible in 2003 and 2002?

b. Calculate Domtar's accounts receivable turnover rates for 2003 and 2002, using the ending balances of the receivables for each year rather than the average receivables. Convert the turnover rates into the average number of days required to collect the accounts receivable.

c. Domtar's notes reveal that it frequently enters into agreements to sell some of its accounts receivable on a limited recourse basis. Why would a company want to sell its accounts receivable? What does it mean to sell them on a "limited recourse" basis?

6-44 **(Accounts receivable, uncollectible accounts, and the receivables turnover ratio)**

Suncor Energy Inc. reported total revenues of $6,306 million for 2003, $5,032 million for 2002, and $4,294 million for 2001, and net accounts receivable balances of $505 million at the end of 2003, $403 million at the end of 2002, and $306 million at the end of 2001. The notes that accompanied its financial statements revealed that the allowance for doubtful accounts for those years was $4 million, $3 million, and $3 million, respectively.

Required:

a. What percentage of Suncor's accounts receivable was considered uncollectible in each of these three years?

b. Although Suncor's sales increased significantly between 2001 and 2002, its allowance for doubtful accounts stayed the same. Suggest some possible explanations for this.

c. Calculate the accounts receivable turnover rate for 2002 and 2003, using the average balances of the receivables. Convert the turnover rates into the number of days required to collect the receivables. What do you observe?

d. For 2003, reconstruct the journal entries to record Suncor's transactions relating to sales and collections of accounts receivable, assuming that all its sales were on account.

Beyond the Book

6-45 **(Accounts receivable and related allowances)**

The Thomson Corporation is a global leader in the information services industry, including publishing and printing. The following amounts (in millions of U.S. dollars) were reported in its financial statements for the years ended December 31.

	2003	2002
Revenues	$7,606	$7,444
Accounts receivable, net of allowances of $345 million (2002: $369 million)	$1,521	$1,489

Required:

a. For each year, express the allowances (1) as a percentage of the revenues and (2) as a percentage of the accounts receivable. Do these percentages seem rather high?

b. Note 9 accompanying Thomson's 2003 financial statements provided additional information regarding its accounts receivable allowances. Refer to this note, and determine what these allowances cover. Do the percentages that you calculated in part a. now seem more reasonable? (Hint: You can easily access Thomson's financial statements though either the company's website or the SEDAR website.)

6-46 **(Examination of corporate financial statements)**

Refer to the financial statements of a large retail company such as the **Hudson's Bay Company**, a large resource industry company such as **Weyerhaeuser Company Ltd.**, and a large bank such as the **Royal Bank Financial Group**. Prepare a short report in which you outline your findings from the following.

a. Do an analysis of the cash and other financial asset balances held by each company. Be sure to review the balance sheet accounts and all related notes.

b. Make a list comparing the companies' operating characteristics that might affect the amount of financial assets they would have on hand. For example, which of the three businesses would likely have the most dependable and predictable cash inflows and outflows? Which company would realize most of its profits from holding financial assets?

c. Look at the cash flow statements to determine the major sources of cash inflows and outflows during the past year. Did the companies borrow money during the year? Did they issue shares? What types of investments did they make?

6-47 **(Examination of a company's financial statements)**

Choose a company as directed by your instructor and answer the following questions.

a. Prepare an analysis of the cash (and cash equivalents, if applicable), temporary investments or marketable securities, gross accounts receivable, and the allowance for doubtful accounts, by listing the beginning and ending balances in these accounts and calculating the net change, in both dollar and percentage terms, for the most recent year.

b. If any of the accounts in part a. has changed more than 10%, suggest an explanation for this change.

c. If the company has any temporary investments or marketable securities, determine if there were any gains or losses recognized during the year, and describe where they were reported in the financial statements.

d. Calculate the following ratios for the most recent two years.

　1. Bad debt expense divided by net sales

　2. Allowance for doubtful accounts divided by gross accounts receivable

　3. Accounts receivable turnover (how many times and days)

Comment on both the reasonableness of these ratios and any significant changes in them.

Cases

Case Primer

6-48 Sanjay Supplies Limited

Sanjay Supplies Limited is concerned about its ability to pay its debts. Analyze the information provided below and explain why Sanjay is experiencing problems with its cash balance. What could Sanjay do to reduce these problems?

SANJAY SUPPLIES LIMITED
Selected Financial Information (in thousands)

Years ended March 31	2004	2005	2006
Sales on credit	$12,700	$14,100	$17,100
Cash	310	50	10
Temporary investments (cashable on demand)	25	——	——
Accounts receivable	1,180	1,510	1,980
Inventories	940	1,250	1,470
Short-term bank loans (payable on demand)	——	240	760
Accounts payable	610	390	440
Other short-term liabilities	80	80	80

6-49 Versa Tools Inc.

Versa Tools Inc. is a small tool and die manufacturing shop located in southwestern Ontario. The company's main shareholder, Arthur Henderson, is becoming increasingly concerned over the safety and security of the company assets and, in particular, cash. In the past, Arthur or his wife, Jeannine, have handled all cash transactions. However, with increasing production and the possibility of expanding into a plastics division, Arthur realizes that he will be unable to continue with this hands-on approach.

Currently, there is only one person in the accounting department who is responsible for recording all cash receipts and disbursements and for depositing all cash. Because this person is so busy, cash is generally only deposited in the bank once a week. All cash collected is locked in a desk drawer in the main office.

The accounting clerk has no formal accounting education. In fact, she is a graduate of a local art school and is working at Versa to earn enough money to move to Toronto and begin a career as a graphic artist. She often notes the cash receipts on slips of paper until she has time to enter them into the computer system several days later.

Finally, Arthur has not been preparing bank reconciliations. When asked about the bank reconciliations, Arthur replied, "I'm so busy running the business that I don't have time to check every item on the bank statement each month."

Required:

Prepare a memo to Arthur outlining basic cash controls that should be put into place at Versa Tools Inc. to ensure the protection and management of cash balances.

6-50 Beltway International

Beltway International is an import-export company. Due to the nature of the business, the company often has significant amounts of cash on hand. Some of this cash has been invested in other companies as a means of achieving vertical integration. These investments are intended to be held for many years. At other times, Beltway's management invests extra cash in temporary investments. Management believes that it is better to have excess cash earning some return rather than just sitting in a bank account.

At December 31, 2005, Beltway's year-end date, the company had the following temporary investments.

Investment	Cost	Market Value at December 31, 2005
Equity investment in the Royal Bank. These shares were purchased to be held for the short term.	Purchased 20,000 shares at $48.00 per share	$52.00 per share
Equity investment in Fishery Products International. Purchased as a short-term investment.	Purchased 4,000 shares at $8.30 per share	$ 9.40 per share

Beltway's CEO has recently approached you, the corporate controller, with some exciting news. The company plans to sell a significant bond issue in 2006 to provide funding for a large expansion into Eastern European markets. The CEO wants the income statement for 2006 to be as strong as possible, and therefore tells you to record all the investments at their cost in the balance sheet on December 31, 2005, so that the increase in value will be reflected as a large gain when they are sold in 2006.

The CEO says he knows that assets are usually recorded at their cost, and that accountants tend to be conservative. Accordingly, he doesn't think there would be a problem in showing the investments at their cost at the end of 2005, and waiting until they are sold in 2006 to report any gain on them.

Required:

Is the CEO correct? With reference to accounting principles, prepare a response to the CEO's position. Your response should include an outline of the proper accounting treatment for temporary investments, and a brief explanation of the reasoning behind it.

6-51 Heritage Mill Works

Heritage Mill Works sells finished lumber and mouldings to a variety of housing contractors. Given the nature of the business, most of its sales are on credit and careful management of credit and bad debts is a critical success factor for this business. The normal credit period is 60 days.

The company owners place significant emphasis on the operating results as they appear on the income statement. They believe that accurate net income is the best indicator of the success of a business. The owners are currently looking at revising their credit-granting policies in light of a number of large write-offs that were made in the past year.

Karen Starkly is the accounts receivable clerk for the business and has been asked by the controller to prepare an estimate of bad debt expense for the company, to be used in preparing the annual financial statements. The company had sales of $1,490,000 during the year, of which 90% were on credit. Historically, the percentage of bad debts has varied from 2% to 4% of credit sales. Bad debts are usually higher in times of economic downturns. Karen notes that business has been strong this year for the entire industry, since interest rate reductions have led to a boom in new housing starts.

The balance in the accounts receivable at December 31 is $330,000. During the year, the company wrote off $53,800 of accounts receivable as uncollectible.

Required:

a. Provide the controller with an estimate of bad debts expense. Be prepared to justify your recommendation to the controller.

b. Discuss the trade-offs that must be considered when selecting a credit policy. What steps could this company take to reduce the risk of not collecting its accounts receivable in the future?

6-52   Braditch Global Manufacturing

Braditch Global Manufacturing produces a variety of products for the airline industry. It is the world's largest manufacturer of luggage carts and carriers, and sells to both large and small airlines. Each airline will purchase anywhere from 50 to 200 carts at a given time, which leads to Braditch's carrying large balances in its accounts receivable.

With recent problems in the airline industry, Braditch's board of directors is becoming concerned over the collectibility of many of its larger receivables, some of which have been outstanding for several months. They are considering requesting that these customers convert their accounts receivable into 6-month, 10% notes receivable. As well, the board would like more of the company's larger sales to be negotiated using notes receivable in the future.

Required:

Explain the difference between an account receivable and a note receivable. Discuss the benefits and risks associated with the proposed change in receivables policy, so that the board can make a well-informed decision.

Critical Thinking Questions

6-53   (Short-term investments, accounts receivable, and doubtful accounts)

The balance sheets and statements of cash flows for **Sierra Wireless, Inc.** at December 31, 2003, are shown in Exhibit 6-10.

Required:

a. Using the information in the balance sheets and statements of cash flows for Sierra Wireless, determine the changes that occurred in its short-term investments during 2003 and reconstruct the journal entries that would have been made relating to them. (Notice that Sierra Wireless puts the most recent year's amounts in the outside column instead of the inside column.)

b. Is the balance in accounts receivable at the end of 2003 significantly higher or lower than it was at the end of 2002? Is the balance in its allowance for doubtful accounts significantly higher or lower at the end of 2003, compared with the end of 2002? What possible explanations can you suggest for the change in the relationship between the company's accounts receivable and its allowance for doubtful accounts during 2003?

6-54   (Accounts receivable disclosures)

In its 2003 financial statements, **Cangene Corporation**, a pharmaceutical company, included the following note about its accounts receivable.

3. ACCOUNTS RECEIVABLE

As of July 31, 2003, accounts receivable include approximately $11.8 million (2002: $1.5 million) due from a major customer and $4.2 million (2002: $2.4 million) due from **Apotex Inc.**, a company under common control.

Cangene's accounts receivable balances were approximately $25.5 million as of July 31, 2003, and $13.0 million as of July 31, 2002.

Required:

Provide reasons why it is important for companies to provide this type of disclosure about the components of their accounts receivable balances.

SIERRA WIRELESS, INC. 2003 ANNUAL REPORT

EXHIBIT 6-10
PART A

SIERRA WIRELESS, INC.

Consolidated Balance Sheets

(Expressed in thousands of United States dollars)
(Prepared in accordance with Canadian GAAP)

December 31,	2002	2003
Assets		
Current assets:		
Cash and cash equivalents	$ 34,841	$ 70,358
Short-term investments	—	14,760
Accounts receivable, net of allowance for doubtful accounts of $2,230 (2002 — $3,068)	13,865	21,566
Inventories (note 6)	6,673	1,511
Prepaid expenses	864	2,223
	56,243	110,418
Long-term investments	—	24,639
Capital assets (note 7)	7,198	5,985
Intangible assets (note 8)	6,907	14,620
Goodwill (note 8)	—	19,706
Future income taxes (note 13)	500	500
Other	241	—
	$ 71,089	$ 175,868
Liabilities and Shareholders' Equity		
Current liabilities:		
Accounts payable	$ 3,017	$ 5,966
Accrued liabilities	12,431	22,221
Deferred revenue and credits	297	399
Current portion of long-term liabilities (note 9)	2,803	1,328
Current portion of obligations under capital lease (note 10)	831	141
	19,379	30,055
Long-term liabilities (note 9)	2,896	2,266
Obligations under capital lease (note 10)	60	—
Shareholders' equity:		
Share capital (note 11)		
Authorized		
Unlimited number of common and preference shares with no par value		
Common shares, 24,822,071 (2002 – 16,345,396)		
issued and outstanding	121,824	212,824
Warrants	—	1,538
Deficit	(72,586)	(70,331)
Cumulative translation adjustments	(484)	(484)
	48,754	143,547
	$ 71,089	$ 175,868

Commitments and contingencies (note 16)

See accompanying notes to consolidated financial statements.

DAVID B. SUTCLIFFE   S. JANE ROWE
Director   Director

EXHIBIT 6-10
PART B

SIERRA WIRELESS, INC. 2003 ANNUAL REPORT

S I E R R A W I R E L E S S , I N C .

Consolidated Statements of Cash Flows

(Expressed in thousands of United States dollars)
(Prepared in accordance with Canadian GAAP)

Years ended December 31,	2001	2002	2003
Cash flows from operating activities:			
Net earnings (loss)	$ (24,769)	$ (41,913)	$ 2,255
Adjustments to reconcile net earnings (loss) to net cash provided by operating activities			
Amortization	7,161	7,038	5,669
Non-cash restructuring and other charges	—	28,593	895
Loss on disposal	—	597	2
Deferred income taxes	(15)	3,754	—
Accrued warrants	671	481	386
Changes in operating assets and liabilities			
Accounts receivable	12,084	(3,361)	(5,360)
Inventories	(13,031)	2,517	5,878
Prepaid expenses	59	159	(1,087)
Accounts payable	(6,945)	(1,339)	225
Accrued liabilities	3,420	(463)	5,296
Deferred revenue and credits	300	(753)	101
Net cash provided by (used in) operating activities	(21,065)	(4,690)	14,260
Cash flows from investing activities:			
Business acquisitions (note 3)	—	—	33
Proceeds on disposal	—	338	4
Purchase of fixed assets	(10,523)	(2,219)	(1,972)
Increase in intangible assets	(3,328)	(1,431)	(4,077)
Increase in other assets	(143)	—	—
Purchase of long-term investments	—	—	(24,639)
Purchase of short-term investments	(69,411)	(14,662)	(25,103)
Proceeds on maturity of short-term investments	109,676	46,541	10,492
Net cash provided by (used in) investing activities	26,271	28,567	(45,262)
Cash flows from financing activities:			
Issue of common shares, net of share issue costs	499	374	68,623
Increase in long-term liabilities	255	—	—
Repayment of long-term liabilities	(766)	(1,495)	(2,104)
Net cash provided by (used in) financing activities	(12)	(1,121)	66,519
Net increase in cash and cash equivalents	5,194	22,756	35,517
Cash and cash equivalents, beginning of year	6,891	12,085	34,841
Cash and cash equivalents, end of year	$ 12,085	$ 34,841	$ 70,358

See supplementary cash flow information (note 17)

See accompanying notes to consolidated financial statements.

6-55 (**Assessing internal control procedures**)

The MegaMax Theatre is located in the MetroMall and employs six cashiers. Two of them work from 1:00 to 6:00 pm, and the other four from 6:00 to 11:00 pm. The cashiers receive payments from customers and operate machines that eject serially-numbered tickets. Some customers use debit or credit cards, but most payments are in the form of cash.

The rolls of admission tickets are inserted and locked into the machines by the theatre manager at the beginning of each cashier's shift.

The cashiers' booths are located just inside the entrance to the lobby of the theatre. After purchasing their tickets, customers take them to a doorperson stationed at the entrance of the theatre, about ten metres from the cashiers' booths. The doorperson tears each ticket in half and drops the ticket stub into a locked box. The other half of the ticket is returned to the customer.

At the end of each cashier's shift, the theatre manager removes the ticket rolls from each cashier's machine, counts the cash and then totals it with the debit card and credit card transactions. Each cash count sheet is initialed by the cashier involved. The cash receipts from the first shift are stored in a safe located in the manager's office until the end of the day.

At the end of the day, the manager deposits the cash receipts from both shifts in a bank night deposit vault located in the mall. In addition, the theatre manager sends copies of the cash count sheets and the deposit slip to the company controller to be verified, and to the accounting department to be recorded.

Finally, the manager compares the total amount received by each of the cashiers to the number of tickets they issued, and makes a note of any discrepancies. These are discussed with the cashiers involved before their next shift.

Required

a. Outline the main internal control considerations related to cash receipts, and briefly discuss their application to the cash receipts procedures followed by MegaMax Theatre.

b. Are there any weaknesses in the current internal control system that could enable a cashier and/or doorperson to misappropriate cash?

6-56 **(Assessing internal control procedures)**

Superior Supply Company's system of internal control over cash disbursements includes the following features:

1. All cheques are prenumbered and produced using a special printer. Blank forms for the cheque printer are stored in a safe in the controller's office. The combination to the safe is known only by the controller and the assistant controller.

2. Before a cheque can be issued, the related invoice must be approved by both the Purchasing Department and the Receiving Department.

3. All cheques must be signed by either the controller or the assistant controller. They have agreed, however, that any cheques over $5,000 are to be signed by the controller. Before signing a cheque, the signer is expected to compare the amount of the cheque with the amount on the invoice.

4. After signing a cheque, the signer stamps the invoice PAID and notes the date, the cheque number, and the amount of the cheque on it. The paid invoice is then sent to the Accounting Department to be recorded and filed.

5. Each month, a member of the accounting staff assembles the data required to reconcile the bank statement with the balance in the company's cash account in the ledger. The chief accountant then prepares the bank reconciliation and reviews it with the controller.

Required

a. Outline the main internal control considerations related to cash disbursements, and briefly discuss how they apply to the cash disbursements procedures followed by Superior Supply Company.

b. What suggestions can you make for improvements in Superior's system of internal control over cash disbursements?

chapter 7

Inventory

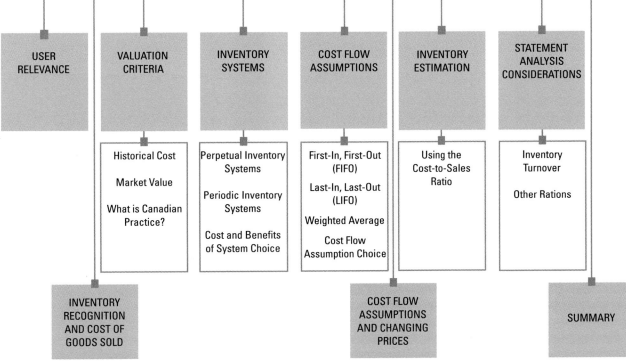

LEARNING OBJECTIVES

After studying this chapter, you should be able to:

1. Discuss the importance of inventory to a company's overall success.

2. Describe the valuation criteria used for inventory in Canada.

3. Describe how the lower of cost and market rule is applied to inventory.

4. Explain the difference between the perpetual inventory system and the periodic inventory system.

5. Discuss some criteria used by companies when choosing an inventory system.

6. Describe the three cost flow assumptions and calculate cost of goods sold and ending inventory under each.

7. Explain the shortcomings of LIFO and why it is rarely used in Canada.

8. Describe the impact of inflation on each of the cost flow assumptions.

9. Estimate a value for ending inventory using the cost-to-sales ratio method.

10. Calculate the inventory turnover ratio and explain how it can be interpreted by users.

Purchasing, stocking, and selling inventory is a complicated process. Veseys Seeds is particularly vulnerable because its products have a short shelf life. Management must have enough seeds in stock to fill orders as they come in because customers want to get the seeds planted and growing. They are not willing to wait. There are many other seed companies and if Veseys does not have the seeds that customers want, they may go elsewhere. At the same time, management must not overstock. Any seeds that are not sold will have to be discarded. Keeping the inventory at just the right level requires Veseys to generate up-to-date information about past sales, current demand, and current inventory levels. Veseys uses a perpetual inventory system (which keeps track of each sale and purchase of inventory as it happens), which gives managers information about current inventory levels, enabling them to place orders with suppliers on a daily basis. Veseys' management of inventory is further complicated by its three modes of sales: store outlet, catalogues, and Internet. All customer personnel must have access to the same information and must update that information with each sale so that the next person had the most current information possible. Management of inventory is a complicated process, but is essential to the efficient sale of goods.

Inventory is any item purchased by a company for resale to customers or to be used in the manufacture of items to be sold to customers. For any retailer or manufacturer that sells goods to customers, inventory is generally its most important asset. The company's success or failure depends upon buying or making inventory with a unit cost lower than its selling price. It also depends upon buying or making the inventory that people want to buy. Management must be very careful to buy or make the right items, at the right cost, and in the right quantities so that sufficient profit can be made on their sales to cover all the other necessary business expenditures.

Visualize, for a moment, a music store that sells CDs, tapes, and movies. Imagine the complications that can arise with inventory: the store must select from its supplier the music and movies that people want to buy in quantities that will ensure it does not run out of stock of an item (called a **stockout**) and force buyers to go elsewhere—where they may buy more than just the item that was out of stock. It must make sure that it does not have too many items in inventory because it increases storage and handling costs and there is the risk of obsolescence. It must also make sure that it sets prices that are competitive but, at the same time, high enough to provide sufficient profit for the company. The store must also provide safeguards so that people cannot steal the inventory. Complicating this activity even further are the variety and volume of items typically sold by any one company.

USER RELEVANCE

LEARNING OBJECTIVE 1

Discuss the importance of inventory to a company's overall success.

When you think about inventory, you probably think about items you have purchased recently in stores. Inventory includes not only those items, but much more. To a property developer, inventory is land and buildings; to a forest products company, it is logs, lumber, and pulp; to a recycler, it is old newspapers, plastic bottles, and aluminum cans. Exhibit 7-1 includes two other examples of inventory.

EXAMPLES OF INVENTORY

Suncor Energy Inc. is an integrated oil and gas company operating in the tar sands in Northern Alberta. Exhibit 7-1a shows Note 15 from its 2003 annual report, which describes its inventory.

Comac Food Group Inc. owns and holds franchise interests in a chain of retail bakery cafés, coffee shops, and restaurants in Canada. Exhibit 7-1b shows Note 4 from its 2003 annual report, which lists its inventory items. Note how the value of the stores held for resale has declined from the previous year.

SUNCOR ENERGY INC. 2003 ANNUAL REPORT
Excerpt from the Notes to the Statements

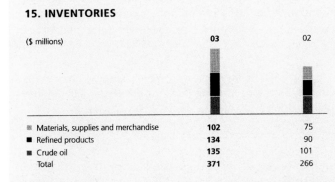

15. INVENTORIES

($ millions)	03	02
Materials, supplies and merchandise	102	75
Refined products	134	90
Crude oil	135	101
Total	371	266

As at December 31, 2003, the replacement cost of crude oil and refined product inventories, valued using the LIFO cost method, exceeded their carrying value by $48 million (2002 – $84 million).

COMAC FOOD GROUP INC. 2003 ANNUAL REPORT
Excerpt from the Notes to the Statements

4. Inventories
Inventories are comprised of the following:
in dollars

	2003	2002
Stores held for sale	$ 20,000	$ 26,000
Ingredients, uniforms and selling supplies	45,000	32,000
	$ 65,000	$ 58,000

Investment in inventory can be substantial, so companies manage inventory levels carefully to maximize their return and minimize their costs. For example, the following articles about Wal-Mart explain some of its strategies for inventory management.

accounting in the news
WIRELESS INVENTORY TRACKING

At the Retail Systems Show in Chicago in June 2003, Wal-Mart announced that its suppliers needed to start using electronic tags on all of the goods that they ship to Wal-Mart. By January 2005, Wal-Mart wants them to include a computer chip on each pallet of goods. The computer chip has a tiny antenna that enables Wal-Mart to track its location. Wal-Mart believes that this makes its transportation system more effective and less prone to errors.

This technology (RFID, or radio frequency identification detection) does have some problems. There is the possibility of radio interference, which could cause errors in the accurate reading of the chip's information.

Wal-Mart has 160 inventory distribution centres that act as the clearinghouse for its 3,000 stores. Its suppliers must make deliveries to its distribution centres within a short window of the time the order is placed. Suppliers that cannot provide the inventory that quickly may be fined by Wal-Mart. It buys in volume from its suppliers, which enables it to demand lower per unit prices. This efficient inventory system means there are few stockouts and its inventory is priced lower than many other retail stores.

Source: "The Retail Revolution," by John Schofield, *Maclean's*, March 1, 1999, pp. 34–36; "Wal-Mart Endorsement Puts Wireless Inventory Tracking Pedal to the Medal," by Antone Gonsalves, InternetWeek.com, June 12, 2003 (9:00 AM).

For companies whose major source of revenue is the sale of inventory, managing the inventory inflows and outflows can mean the difference between success and failure. As a user of financial information, you should make yourself aware of the types of inventory that a company sells. You should also determine the margin (sales minus cost of goods sold) that the company earns in the current year and over the last several years. Has the company been earning enough margin to cover the rest of its costs? Has that margin been increasing, decreasing, or staying constant?

A variety of accounting methods for estimating the total cost of inventory have been developed and are acceptable under GAAP. This makes the accounting for inventory a fairly complicated process. As a user, you need to be aware of what those methods are and how each method affects the margin and the net income. Because companies are required to disclose their inventory costing method(s), once you know the method you can make some assumptions about how it is affecting income. The basics of inventory accounting are covered in this chapter so that you will have a reasonable understanding of how inventory is measured, recorded, and reported. You can then use this information to make informed evaluations of companies.

INVENTORY RECOGNITION AND COST OF GOODS SOLD

Does inventory meet the criteria for being an asset? The probable future value associated with inventory is measured by the company's ability to sell it in the future and to use the proceeds to buy other goods and services. Since inventory has not yet been sold, the collection of cash from its sale is even more uncertain than collecting accounts receivable. Inventory involves all the uncertainties associated with the collection of accounts receivable, as well as two others that are unique to this asset: finding buyers and obsolescence/spoilage. If a sufficient number of buyers cannot be found at the initial price set for the product or service, the price may have to change in order to attract buyers. A second uncertainty is obsolescence and spoilage. Computer hardware, for instance, is at considerable risk of becoming obsolete. Spoilage, on the other hand, is a major factor for food inventories.

Ownership of inventories is evidenced by possession and by legal title. Usually ownership of low-priced inventories is evidenced by possession because it is impractical to keep track of legal title to such items. It is very much like cash in terms of management. Adequate controls must be maintained so that the inventory is not lost or stolen. Ownership of high-priced inventories may also be evidenced by possession, but there are generally legal documents that also prove ownership. The ownership of automobiles, for instance, is evidenced by registration of serial numbers.

The fact that the company possesses inventory indicates that a past transaction occurred. Inventory, therefore, meets the recognition criteria for an asset, and should be recorded as such in the company's accounting system. The amount that is placed in the system then depends on the valuation or measurement criteria that are applied. Cost of goods sold represents the expense side of the inventory asset. Once inventory is sold, it is no longer an asset. Its cost is reported on the income statement as cost of goods sold and is matched against the revenue that its sale generated. Determining what that cost is can be problematic. Much of the discussion in this chapter will centre on establishing an appropriate cost for the inventory and for the cost of goods sold.

VALUATION CRITERIA

The valuation method allowed under GAAP is a combination of several valuation approaches. GAAP generally specifies cost, but it recognizes that the cost figure used should not differ materially from more recent costs. If it does, the company can use one of a number of methods to recognize a decline in inventory value. Before GAAP is discussed in detail, however, we need to examine these different approaches to valuation.

LEARNING OBJECTIVE 2

Describe the valuation criteria used for inventory in Canada.

Historical Cost

One possible valuation method is to carry inventory at its historical cost. According to this method, inventory is recorded at its cost on the date it was acquired. In the purest application of this method, no recognition is made of changes in the inventory's market value while it is held. Income is recognized only when the inventory is sold. At that time, a profit or loss is recorded.

Market Value

A second possible valuation method is to carry inventory at its market value. To apply this method, the term "**market**" must be more clearly defined. Inventory really has two markets. The first is the market in which the company buys its products.

In the case of a retailer, this is called the **wholesale market**. For a manufacturing company, there is no one market in which the company buys its inventory because numerous costs are incurred when constructing the product. If the market price can be found in the market where the inventory is bought (the wholesale market), the term **replacement cost** is used. Replacement cost refers to what it would cost the company to replace the product today. The market in which these products are acquired is called the **input market** or the **entry market**, since this is the market from which the products enter the company.

Another measure of market value might be obtained from the market in which the company sells its products. This is called the **retail market**. The company, of course, hopes prices in the retail market are higher than those in the wholesale market so that it can earn a profit. The markets in which companies sell their products are sometimes referred to as **output markets** or **exit markets**. In accounting terminology, the exit price is sometimes referred to as the **net realizable value (NRV)**, which is the net amount that can be realized from the sale of the product in question. Net realizable value is not the same as selling price. The net part of NRV refers to the company's need to net some costs against the selling prices. For example, there are generally some selling costs that must be incurred to sell a product. Net realizable value is then the selling price less the costs necessary to sell the item. In a manufacturing company, some inventory is not ready for sale (work in process). Net realizable value, in this case, is the selling price less the selling costs as well as the costs necessary to complete the item. There is one final issue with regard to the definition of market. The markets referred to in the preceding paragraphs are assumed to be the normal markets in which the company does normal business. There are also markets for goods that must be sold quickly (such as in a fire sale) or in abnormally large or small quantities. The prices in these markets do not reflect the value of inventory in its normal use and should not be used in valuing inventory of a going concern (a company that will continue to operate in the foreseeable future). These markets may be important in valuing inventory, however, if the company is in bankruptcy or going out of business. Under these distress conditions, normal accounting procedures would not be appropriate because the conditions violate the **going-concern assumption** that underlies GAAP financial accounting.

REPLACEMENT COST

If a company uses a pure replacement cost valuation system, inventory is carried at its replacement cost. At acquisition, replacement cost is the same as historical cost. As the company holds the inventory, however, unrealized increases and decreases in value are recognized as the inventory's replacement cost changes. The balance sheet reflects the inventory's replacement cost at the end of each period, and the income statement shows the unrealized profits and losses. At the time of sale, the only additional profit or loss that is recognized is the difference between the replacement cost at the date of sale and the selling price. This difference is called a realized profit or loss.

NET REALIZABLE VALUE

A pure net realizable value system records inventory at its net realizable value. At the date of acquisition, this means that a profit or loss is recorded equal to the difference between the historical cost and the net realizable value. While the inventory is held, this system requires that changes in net realizable value be recognized as unrealized profits or losses. At the time of ultimate sale, no profit is recognized because the item has already been recorded at its net realizable value.

What Is Canadian Practice?

The application of historical cost is used extensively in Canada. When the use of cost results in a figure that is materially different from recent cost figures, companies should apply a lower of cost and market (LCM) rule at the end of the period. Market, as defined here, is most commonly either replacement cost or net realizable value. If market value is used, there is an impact on the inventory amount on the balance sheet and a loss is reflected on the income statement. In Canada, most companies describe their inventories as being valued at the lower of cost and market. In order to understand the implications for inventory, we will first discuss what should be included in the cost of inventory, and then consider how to apply the LCM rule.

ACQUISITION COSTS

The value assigned to inventory should contain all **laid-down costs**. For a retailer, laid-down costs include the invoice price as well as any customs, tariff, and excise duties in addition to freight and cartage costs. As a practical matter, it is often difficult to assign the specific dollar amount of freight and cartage to a specific item of inventory. Imagine, for example, that a major grocery store received a new shipment of inventory that contained everything from cereal boxes to heads of lettuce. It would be totally impractical to assign freight costs to a single head of lettuce. Therefore, many companies do not assign these costs to inventory, but treat them instead as period costs in the period in which they are incurred. The shipping costs, often called **transportation in** or **freight in**, may be assigned to inventory, but are more commonly treated as period costs in the cost of goods sold calculation. The calculation of cost of goods sold was first introduced in Chapter 2. With the inclusion of transportation costs, the calculation becomes:

$$
\begin{array}{ll}
& \text{Beginning inventory} \\
+ & \text{Purchases} \\
+ & \text{Transportation in} \\
= & \text{Goods available for sale} \\
- & \text{Ending inventory} \\
= & \text{Cost of goods sold}
\end{array}
$$

For a manufacturing company the inventory costs are more complicated. Typically, a manufacturing company buys materials that it intends to use to make new products. These materials are called raw materials and their cost is kept in a raw materials inventory account. The cost assigned to this account includes the cost of the materials plus any transportation costs. The company takes the raw materials and begins to make its new products. The process of manufacturing involves additional costs such as workers' labour costs, the costs of the machines and buildings, and the cost of utilities to run the manufacturing facilities. The labour costs associated with manufacturing are referred to as direct labour and all of the other more indirect costs are referred to as overhead. A typical product includes raw materials, direct labour, and overhead.

A company uses three inventory accounts in the manufacturing process: the raw materials inventory account, a work-in-process account, and a finished goods account. The work-in-process account collects all of the costs (raw materials, direct labour, and overhead) that are incurred as the product is being made. Once the product is complete, the full cost of making the product is transferred from the work-in-process account to the finished goods account. Products that are sold are deducted from the finished goods account. Exhibit 7-2 diagrams how the costs flow through the three inventory accounts to cost of goods sold.

EXHIBIT 7-2

MANUFACTURING COST FLOWS

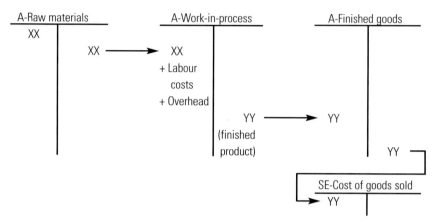

Exhibit 7-3 includes the inventory disclosure of a manufacturing company, **Cangene Corporation**.

Cangene Corporation is a biopharmaceutical company that develops, manufactures, and markets specialty plasma products. It is also involved in developing genetic solutions to certain diseases. Its 2003 inventory disclosure is included below.

EXHIBIT 7-3

CANGENE CORPORATION 2003 ANNUAL REPORT

Excerpted from the Notes to the Statements

3. INVENTORIES

in thousands of Cdn dollars	2003	2002
Raw materials	$ 8,467	$ 5,706
Work in process	6,797	11,219
Finished goods	3,558	3,973
	$ 18,822	$20,898

Lower of Cost and Market

LEARNING OBJECTIVE 3

Describe how the lower of cost and market rule is applied to inventory.

Because inventory is crucial to the success of companies in the retail and manufacturing business, users are very interested in its value. When inventory is listed as a current asset on the balance sheet, users assume that it will be sold in the subsequent period for at least its stated value, but more optimistically, at a profit. During an accounting period, economic circumstances may arise that negatively affect the inventory's value. At the end of every accounting period, most companies compare the cost of the inventory with its market value and apply the LCM rule. Companies can use either the direct method or the allowance method. Under the direct method, the ending inventory is reduced to the lower market value, which causes the cost of goods sold amount to rise in the income statement. In the subsequent year, the lower market value becomes part of the cost of goods sold when it becomes beginning inventory. Under the allowance method, the inventory account remains at the original cost and an allowance account is used to hold the decline in value. The allowance account, which is shown contra to the inventory on the balance sheet, is usually adjusted each year to reflect the inventory's changing value. LCM can be applied to individual items, to pools of similar items, or to the inventory as a whole. It is generally impractical to apply it on an individual item basis, so companies will use either pools of similar items or the total inventory.

AN INTERNATIONAL PERSPECTIVE

Reports from other Countries

In Canada, the LCM rule is usually applied on a total inventory basis because companies are required to use this method for tax purposes. It is more efficient to apply the same method for both purposes.

In the United States, the LCM rule is more commonly applied on an individual item basis because the U.S. tax department requires the application on an individual basis.

Under the direct method, the unrealized losses that result from the application of the LCM rule are often hidden in the cost of goods sold expense. Remember that the cost of goods sold calculation is:

	Cost of Beginning inventory
+	Purchases
+	Transportation in
=	Goods available for sale
−	Ending inventory
=	Cost of goods sold

If the inventory's market value is lower than the calculated cost amount, ending inventory is assigned the lower value. If the ending inventory value goes down, the cost of goods sold expense goes up, thereby incorporating the loss. Under this method, users will not know how large the loss was.

Under the allowance method, a separate loss account is created to hold the amount of the loss. It is usually called Loss Due to Market Decline of Inventory. This loss account could be listed separately on the income statement but is more frequently summarized with other expenses, which are listed after Cost of Goods Sold. Similar to the direct method, the amount of the loss is frequently not disclosed as an individual item in the income statement. Companies would probably disclose the loss in inventory value as a separate item on the income statement if it was a material amount. They could also discuss it in a note to the financial statements.

To determine the appropriate market value to use in applying the LCM rule, we need to go back to the previous discussion about market value. In Canada, companies usually define market as net realizable value, net realizable value less a normal profit margin, or replacement cost. The most common is net realizable value. This makes sense, because if the selling price has dropped below the cost, the company may experience a loss next period when the inventory is sold. Because the decline in value occurred in the current period, we reduce the value of the inventory in the current period. Then when it is sold in the next period, it will sell at no profit if the selling price does not change. The option of net realizable value less a normal profit margin reduces the inventory value even more in the current period, so that when it is sold in the next period it will sell at a profit. This option is not used very often, but it is available to companies under GAAP. When replacement cost is used, it is often with inventory that is used to manufacture items (raw materials) rather than with inventory that is held for resale.

Exhibit 7-4 includes the inventory disclosure for **Finning International Inc.**, which distributes and services heavy equipment and related products. Note that it uses net realizable value as well as specific identification, first-in, first-out, and average cost in its inventory disclosure. More will be said about these other cost bases later in the chapter.

EXHIBIT 7-4

FINNING INTERNATIONAL INC. 2003 ANNUAL REPORT

Excerpted from the Notes to the Statements
Inventories
Inventories are stated at the lower of cost and net realizable value. Cost is determined on a specific item basis for on-hand equipment. For approximately two-thirds of parts and supplies, cost is determined on a first-in, first-out basis. An average cost basis is used for the remainder.

AN INTERNATIONAL PERSPECTIVE

Reports from other Countries

Most countries require the application of a lower of cost and market rule. Some countries, such as the United States, refer to it as the lower of cost or market rule. The application of this rule, however, can vary across countries. The market value used in the rule is interpreted to mean replacement cost in a few countries (Italy and Japan, for example), whereas in many more countries it is interpreted as net realizable value (France, Germany, and the United Kingdom, for example). The **International Accounting Standards Board (IASB)** defines market value as net realizable value. Very few countries allow the flexibility that is available under Canadian GAAP. The United States uses all three values for market when it requires that, regardless of how high the replacement costs are, the company cannot carry the inventory at a value higher than net realizable value (called a ceiling value). In addition, the carrying value cannot be lower than net realizable value less a profit margin (called a floor value). Another difference is that the United States is somewhat alone in viewing the writedown of inventory as permanent. Most other countries, including Canada, either require or permit the recovery of value back to original cost if the market recovers.

INVENTORY SYSTEMS

Now that we have discussed the valuation of inventory in a general way, we need to look at various systems companies have developed to manage the volume and variety of inventory that they purchase and subsequently sell. Keeping track of inventory units and their associated costs is essential to managing the company profitably. Information concerning the units sold and those in inventory is necessary for intelligent decisions about pricing, production, and reordering. An inventory system is needed to keep track of this information. As you saw in our opening story, computerized inventory systems are easing the task of inventory management.

At least two types of information about inventory are needed. The first relates to the number of units sold during a period and the number that remain. This information is needed to establish a value for cost of goods sold, to trigger the reordering of inventory, or to set the level of production for the current period. It may also be necessary to fill sales orders. The second type of information is data about the cost of goods sold during the period and the cost of those that remain. This information is needed to prepare the financial statements, to evaluate performance, and to make pricing decisions.

Some inventory systems keep track of units of inventory but not their cost; others keep track of both units of inventory and cost. Systems that keep track of units but not costs are referred to as physical inventory systems. Major grocery chains, for example, have their cash registers connected to computers that record the sale of each item of inventory when the item is scanned for its bar code. The computerized inventory system is programmed to trigger new orders when the number of items remaining drops to a predetermined level. Unless the computer program is very sophisticated, it will not identify the purchase cost of the item sold.

Systems that keep track of the number of units and the costs associated with units of inventory are referred to as cost inventory systems. A cost inventory system can most easily be implemented when the inventory items are uniquely identifiable. For example, a car dealership records the unique characteristics of each vehicle that it buys for resale. When a vehicle is sold, it is relatively easy to record the sale of that specific vehicle and to record its original cost to the dealer. A grocery store, on the other hand, would not be able to determine the original cost of a can of peas because it would have no way of identifying the case from which the can was sold. The bar code on the can tells the computer simply that it is a can of a particular brand of peas. With the increasing sophistication of computer technology, more businesses will be able to convert to cost inventory systems and manage their inventories in more detail.

In any inventory system, it is important for you to understand how inventory flows through it. To illustrate these flows, consider the inventory T account in Exhibit 7-5. The company starts the period with a certain amount of beginning inventory that, in a physical inventory system, is the number of units and, in a cost inventory system, is the number of units multiplied by the cost of those units. These amounts are known from the end of the last period. The number of units purchased during the period and the cost of those purchases are known from the invoices for the period (in the case of a manufacturer, the debits are for direct materials, labour, and overhead, all of which are known during the period). What is unknown is the cost of goods sold (the number of units sold in a physical system) and the cost (number) of units left in ending inventory. The sum of the cost of the beginning inventory and that of purchases is known as the cost of **goods available for sale**. The problem is deciding how to divide the total cost between the cost of goods sold and the cost of those that remain in ending inventory. Whatever inventory system is implemented, it must be able to allocate cost of the goods available for sale between the cost of goods sold and ending inventory.

EXHIBIT 7-5

INVENTORY INFORMATION

	Inventory (A)		
Beginning balance	KNOWN		
Purchases	KNOWN	?????	Cost of goods sold
Ending balance	?????		

The type of inventory system used depends on the type and size of inventory involved and the cost of implementing the system. We will discuss two general types of inventory systems: perpetual and periodic systems.

Perpetual Inventory Systems

LEARNING OBJECTIVE 4

Explain the difference between the perpetual inventory system and the periodic inventory system.

Perpetual inventory systems may be either physical inventory systems or cost inventory systems. They keep track of units or their associated costs, or both, on a continuous basis. Veseys Seeds uses a perpetual system. This means that as soon as a unit is sold, it (or its cost) is immediately removed from the inventory account. In terms of the T account in Exhibit 7-5, a credit is made to the account at the time of sale. The ending balance in the account can be calculated at any time to provide information about what is left in the account. In this type of system, the ending inventory balance and the cost of goods sold account are always up to date in terms of units and/or costs. Therefore, the information provided by this type of system is the most timely for decision purposes.

Up-to-date information, which is useful in any business, is crucial to some businesses, such as car dealerships. In the automobile business, the sales personnel must know what stock is still available for sale so that a car is not sold twice. Because selling prices are negotiated and the costs of different cars may vary dramatically, the cost of a specific car must be known at the time of sale to earn an appropriate profit margin. The dealer's profitability depends on up-to-date information. Fortunately, the cost of keeping track of this information on a perpetual basis is not very high because the number of units of inventory is relatively small and each vehicle can be uniquely identified.

Contrast this with the decisions faced by the owner of a hardware store. Prices are not negotiated at the time of sale but rather each item is pre-priced and customers pay the stated price. Therefore, knowing the cost of each unit on a per-sale basis is not as important. The amount of inventory must be known in order to reorder stock, but reordering is probably not done daily. The cost of keeping track of each inventory item on a perpetual basis would be fairly substantial because the hardware store deals with numerous items in relatively large quantities. Consider, for example, using the perpetual system to keep track of all the types of nuts and bolts the store sells. The cost of implementing a perpetual system in this case would probably outweigh the benefits of having up-to-date information. Therefore, the hardware store would no doubt develop a periodic inventory system.

Periodic Inventory Systems

In a **periodic inventory system,** there is no entry to record the reduction in inventory at the time of sale. This may be because a perpetual inventory tracking system is too expensive to maintain, or because the cost of the item sold may not be known at the time of sale. In a retail store, for example, clerks know an item's retail price because it is written on the sales tag, but they probably do not know the cost of the item to the store. To determine the amount sold and the amount left in inventory, the company must periodically stop business and physically count the units that are left, and then assign costs to them. The cost of goods sold is then determined by subtracting the ending inventory value established by the count from the sum of the beginning inventory value and the purchases made during the period. This process assumes that all items included in the cost of goods sold were indeed sold, which may not always be the case. If items were stolen or misplaced, they would not be on the shelves or in the warehouse when the inventory was counted, and the company would assume they had been sold. With a periodic inventory system, the company does not have up-to-date information during the period regarding the level of inventory or the cost of goods sold. It therefore needs to develop other methods to determine reorder points.

The counting and costing of ending inventory can be an expensive process, particularly for companies with large amounts of inventory. The company must close during the counting process and perhaps even turn away business. It must also pay individuals to do the counting. Because of the cost, it generally makes sense to count inventory only once a year. For internal control purposes, some companies count key items of inventory more frequently than once a year and often prepare financial statements more frequently than once a year. Accountants have therefore developed estimation methods that are used to establish inventory values for these interim reports.

A company may use a perpetual system to keep track of the physical units (remember the use of bar codes in the grocery store) but, because of the difficulty in determining unit costs, may use a periodic system to assign costs to units. This type of mixed system provides up-to-date information regarding the number of units available to aid in reordering or production decisions. It does not provide up-to-date cost information. This may be perfectly acceptable to management if up-to-date unit information is more important than cost information.

Costs and Benefits of System Choice

One of the key factors in the choice of inventory systems is the cost of maintaining the system. The perpetual system provides better, more current information than the periodic system, but does so at a higher cost. However, as the cost of computer technology continues to decline, the implementation of perpetual systems has become a real possibility for companies that formerly would not have considered it. For example, the introduction of the bar code scanner in the grocery business has allowed stores to keep track of units of inventory on a perpetual basis. Furthermore, with the introduction of **electronic data interchange (EDI)**, some retailers use this information to automatically reorder inventory directly from the wholesaler or manufacturer. An EDI system links the seller's inventory system computers with the computers in the supplier's inventory system. When the seller's inventory drops to a pre-specified level, a new order is automatically generated that tells the supplier to send a new shipment of inventory.

With a perpetual system, managers can make better business decisions. From the system, they know what items are selling and how many items they still have. They can more accurately determine what items to reorder and when that new order should be placed. In a periodic system, managers must develop other techniques to determine the information that the perpetual system provides. For example, they might have a card placed near the bottom of a stack of merchandise. When the merchandise is sold and the card is visible, it is a signal that more must be ordered. This is a very

LEARNING OBJECTIVE 5

Discuss some criteria used by companies when choosing an inventory system.

crude system that depends on the card not being removed and on someone noticing it when it becomes visible. Managers also use estimation methods in the periodic system to provide them with the information they need.

One advantage of the perpetual basis that we have not yet discussed is the identification of **inventory shrinkage**. Shrinkage refers to losses of inventory due to theft, damage, and spoilage. Periodic systems are incapable of identifying shrinkage because shrinkage appears as part of the cost of goods sold when the ending inventory value is subtracted from the beginning inventory plus purchases. A perpetual system can identify shrinkage because the system tells the company what the ending inventory should be. The company can then do a count to see what is actually left in its physical inventory. The difference is the shrinkage. Physically counting the inventory is necessary under both systems and the fact that shrinkage can be identified under the perpetual system is a bonus. Companies with perpetual systems may, however, stagger the counting of inventories so that not all inventories are counted at the same time. The closest that a periodic system can come to the perpetual system in identifying shrinkage is to use estimation methods. A company may be able to estimate how much inventory should be on hand. When it counts the inventory, it can then compare it with the estimated amount and get a crude measure of shrinkage.

accounting in the news
INVENTORY SHRINKAGE

In 2002, Ernst & Young conducted a survey of 55 of the largest and most successful U.S. retailers. It found that retailers lose approximately $46 billion annually due to inventory shrinkage mostly caused by employee theft. Other causes of inventory shrinkage that were identified by the survey were shoplifting, administrative and paperwork errors, and vendor errors/issues. The survey also looked at the effectiveness of various programs and tools that companies were using to combat shrinkage. One of the survey's outcomes was the development of a four-step action plan for controlling inventory shrinkage.

Source: "Ernst & Young Study Estimates Retailers Lose $46 Billion Annually to Inventory Shrinkage; Employee Theft is the Biggest Problem," Business Wire, May 13, 2003.

The cost of an inventory system must be balanced against the benefits of the information it provides. The main benefit of the perpetual system is its timely information. When inventory information is needed on a timely basis for pricing, reordering, or other important decisions, the benefits of the perpetual system must be carefully considered even though the system is likely to be more expensive.

COST FLOW ASSUMPTIONS

In order to determine the cost of goods sold and the cost of ending inventory, the cost of specific units must somehow be linked to the actual physical units that either were sold (cost of goods sold) or remain in ending inventory. For some businesses, this is not difficult because the physical units are unique and records are kept that specifically identify the unit and its cost. Under these circumstances, the company can match the physical units with their costs using the specific identification method. Finning International Inc. (Exhibit 7-4) would be able to identify the cost of its on-hand equipment in its inventory. Each piece of equipment would have its own invoice price and registration number and, therefore, be unique.

In some businesses, the ability to specifically identify costs of individual physical units is not feasible. Consider a shoe retailer that buys multiple styles, sizes, and colours of shoes in a single order. If the retailer never ordered the same shoe again, it would be possible to determine the cost of a specific pair of shoes. However, once a second order is placed and arrives at the store, it is no longer possible to identify whether a specific pair of shoes came from the first order or from the second unless the retailer took the time to mark the second purchase to distinguish it from the first. It is unlikely that retailers would incur the additional cost of specifically identifying each new order. Therefore, in businesses in which specific identification is not feasible, a logical assumption is generally made about how costs flow through the company.

POSSIBLE COST-FLOW ASSUMPTIONS

1. The first item purchased is the first item sold (FIFO).
2. The last item purchased is the first item sold (LIFO).
3. The cost of the items is determined using an average of the cost of the items purchased.

As we get into the various cost flow possibilities, we are going to describe the cost flow assumptions related to a periodic inventory system only. The reason for restricting the choice to just the periodic system is that we want to concentrate on showing you the methods and their financial statement implications, rather than working through six methods (three under each system). If you are interested in seeing the cost assumptions under the perpetual system, we have included a description of them in the Appendix at the end of this chapter. Under the perpetual system, LIFO and the average method will produce slightly different inventory cost amounts. FIFO will produce the same amounts under both the periodic and perpetual systems.

ethics in accounting

Determining the ending balance in inventory is crucial not only for determining the balance sheet value for inventory, but also for establishing the cost of goods sold for the income statement. Any overstatement of ending inventory will result in an understatement of cost of goods sold and, therefore, an overstatement of income. There are many situations that put pressure on managers and employees to show higher net income, such as budget targets and bonus plans. There may also be incentives to overstate ending inventory if it is to serve as collateral for loans. Auditors are also interested in validation of ending inventory values and typically are required under audit guidelines to be present at the physical count of ending inventory to make sure inventory counts are accurate and values are appropriately determined.

Note as we go through the following assumptions that we are discussing *cost flows*, not *physical flows*. We will be suggesting logical assumptions for cost flows that may be entirely opposite to the way inventory physically flows through the company.

LEARNING OBJECTIVE 6

Describe the three cost flow assumptions and calculate cost of goods sold and ending inventory under each.

Inventory Cost Flow Tutorial

Ethics in Accounting

To illustrate these assumptions, we will use the data in Exhibit 7-6 for Rhoda's Appliances, Inc.

Three cost flow assumptions—first-in, first-out (FIFO), last-in, first-out (LIFO), and weighted average—constitute three logical ways of assigning costs to units sold or remaining in inventory. FIFO assumes that the first unit purchased is also the first unit sold, hence first-in, first-out. LIFO assumes, however, that the last unit purchased is the first unit sold, hence last-in, first-out. Weighted average assigns an average cost to both cost of goods sold and ending inventory. Let's look at each of these approaches in more detail.

EXHIBIT 7-6

RHODA'S APPLIANCES, INC.

Inventory of Refrigerators

Date		Units	Unit cost	Total
January 1	Beginning inventory	6	$450	$ 2,700
January 10	Purchase #1	15	475	7,125
January 20	Purchase #2	12	480	5,760
Goods available for sale		33		$15,585

Sale record				
		Units	Unit price	Total
January 15	Sale #1	16	$725	$11,600
January 25	Sale #2	10	750	7,500
		26		$19,100

Rhoda's Appliances starts the period with six refrigerators in inventory. Note that the beginning inventory cost is $2,700 and that the unit cost is $450. Only in the very first period of operations are the beginning values in inventory the same under all three assumptions. Because different cost flow assumptions assign costs to units in different ways, in subsequent periods each assumption will result in different per-unit amounts being assigned to ending inventory, which in turn becomes beginning inventory for the next period. Each of these cost flow assumptions are discussed in the following subsections. Refer to Exhibit 7-6 as each method is discussed.

First-In, First-Out (FIFO)

The **first-in, first-out**, or **FIFO**, method is still the most commonly used method in Canada, although weighted average is a very close second. FIFO assigns the first costs to the first units sold. This means that ending inventory units will be matched to costs for the most recent purchases. One way to visualize this method is to consider the flow through a pipeline, as shown in Exhibit 7-7. Purchases enter one end of the pipeline. As new purchases are made, they enter the same end of the pipeline, pushing the first purchases further into the pipe. Goods that get sold come out the other end of the pipeline. Therefore, the ones that get sold first are also the ones that entered the pipeline first. The goods still left in the pipeline at the end of the period are the ending inventory. While the acronym FIFO is appropriate for this method, it refers to what happens to the cost of goods sold, not to the ending inventory. A more accurate acronym for ending inventory is LISH, for **last-in, still-here**.

FIFO VISUALIZATION

EXHIBIT 7-7

Using the Rhoda's Appliances data (Exhibit 7-6) and the FIFO assumption, we can assign a cost to the cost of goods sold and ending inventory as follows.

Cost of goods sold (26 units)

6	units @ $450 (beginning inventory)		$ 2,700
+ 15	units @ $475 (first purchase)		7,125
+ 5	units @ $480 (second purchase)		2,400
26	units		$12,225

Ending inventory (7 units)

7	units @ $480 (second purchase)		$ 3,360

Note how the sum of units in cost of goods sold and ending inventory (26 + 7) equals the 33 units in goods available for sale. The sum of the dollar amounts ($12,225 + $3,360) equals the dollar amount of the goods available for sale, $15,585. If the dollar amount of ending inventory were to increase, the dollar amount of the cost of goods sold would have to decrease because the sum of the two must add up to the dollar amount of the goods available for sale. Any errors in counting ending inventory or assigning costs will have an immediate impact on the cost of goods sold and, therefore, net income.

FIFO describes fairly accurately the physical flow of goods in most businesses. For example, in grocery stores new items are put behind old items on the shelf so that old items are sold first. If the grocery store did not rotate inventory in this way, some items would sit on the shelf for months, risking spoilage.

Under GAAP, the matching of costs to physical units does not depend on the physical flow of goods. GAAP attempts to provide the best measure of periodic net income, which is not necessarily achieved by choosing a cost flow assumption that matches the physical flow of the goods. Under FIFO, the costs assigned to the cost of goods sold are the costs from beginning inventory and from earlier purchases. The costs assigned to ending inventory are the most recent purchase costs.

Last-In, First-Out (LIFO)

The **last-in, first-out** or **LIFO** method is used very infrequently in Canada. It assigns the last costs (i.e., the costs of the most recent purchases) to the first units sold. This means that ending inventory is assigned the costs associated with the first purchases (or beginning inventory). The LIFO method is visualized in Exhibit 7-8. Imagine inventory as something stored in a bin. New purchases are added to the bin from the top, adding new layers of inventory to what is already in the bin (beginning inventory). Goods sold are taken from the top layer of the bin. The costs associated with these units are, therefore, the costs associated with the most recent purchases. Ending inventory, on the other hand, is associated with the cost of the layers at the date each was purchased. The bottom layers could have been purchased in a much earlier period. The acronym used to refer to ending inventory is **FISH**, for **first-in, still-here**.

EXHIBIT 7-8 **LIFO VISUALIZATION**

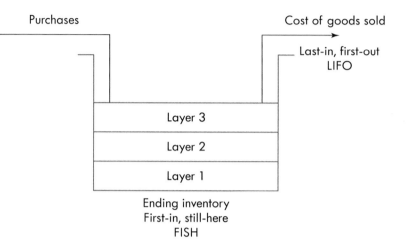

Using Rhoda's Appliances (Exhibit 7-6) and the LIFO assumption, let us now assign a cost to the cost of goods sold and ending inventory.

Cost of goods sold (26 units)

12	units @ $480 (second purchase)	$5,760
14	units @ $475 (first purchase)	6,650
26	units	$12,410

Ending inventory (7 units)

1	units @ $475 (first purchase)	$475
6	units @ $450 (beginning inventory)	2,700
7	units	$3,175

Note again how the sum of the units in cost of goods sold and ending inventory (26 + 7) equals the 33 units in goods available for sale. The sum of the dollar amounts ($12,410 + $3,175) equals the dollar amount of the goods available for sale, $15,585. Note also that the dollar amount of ending inventory is lower than it is under FIFO and that, therefore, the dollar amount of the cost of goods sold is higher. The unit cost of inventory has been rising through January, and because the cost of goods sold is assigned costs from the most recent purchases, it receives higher unit costs than under FIFO.

The main problem with LIFO is the cost assigned to ending inventory. In Rhoda's Appliances, the cost was the $450 from beginning inventory and the $475 from the first purchase. When purchases are made in February, LIFO will assign those new purchase costs to the cost of goods sold, and again assign the $450 and $475 to ending inventory. Several years from now, the unit cost assigned to ending inventory could still be the $450 and $475. These old costs will not show the inventory on the balance sheet at a very realistic value. In fact, if they were left unadjusted, the inventory costs could be substantially below market value. Recognizing this problem with LIFO, accountants have developed several techniques to adjust the inventory amount to a more realistic value while still assigning the most recent costs to the cost of goods sold. The discussion of these methods is, however, beyond the scope of an introductory textbook.

Remember that the diagram in Exhibit 7-8 is concerned with the flow of costs, not the physical flow of inventory. Not many inventories actually follow a LIFO physical flow, although there are a few examples: using steel plates from the top of a pile, taking coal from the top of a pile, or selling nails from a keg of nails. This, however, does not prevent companies from using the LIFO cost assumption to assign costs. LIFO represents a systematic, logical way of assigning costs. In fact, the cost of goods sold on the income statement includes the most recent costs and is, therefore, a good match to the revenue of the period.

LIFO and FIFO represent the two extremes of cost assumptions. LIFO will produce the highest cost of goods sold and, therefore, the lowest net income when unit costs are rising. This might be of interest to a manager who wants to discourage shareholders from requesting cash dividends. FIFO, on the other hand, will produce the lowest cost of goods sold and, therefore, the highest net income under the same conditions. This might be of interest to a manager who wants to attract new investors. Because these two assumptions produce dramatically different financial results during times of changing prices, it is important for users of financial statements to know which method is being used and to understand the managerial objectives that might underlie the selection of that method.

Of the three methods we have examined thus far (specific identification, FIFO, and LIFO), LIFO is used the least often in Canada for several reasons. First, it produces the lowest net income when costs are rising. Second, the value of inventory on the balance sheet quickly becomes unrealistic. Third, the Canada Revenue Agency does not accept it as a method for determining inventory costs for tax purposes, probably because it produces the lowest net income and would therefore produce the lowest taxable income.

We now turn our attention to the fourth and final potential cost flow assumption: the weighted average method.

Weighted Average

The **weighted average** method, the second most commonly used method in Canada, calculates an average cost for all the units available for sale in a given period and assigns that average cost to both the units that are sold during the period, and those that remain in ending inventory. Exhibit 7-9 provides a visualization of this method. Imagine inventory as a liquid stored in a tank, such as gasoline at a service station. Purchases of new gasoline are dumped into the tank and mixed with beginning inventory and previous purchases. Inventory that is sold is therefore a mixture of beginning inventory and recent purchases.

EXHIBIT 7-9

WEIGHTED AVERAGE VISUALIZATION

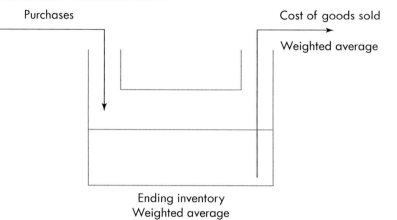

Ending inventory
Weighted average

HELPFUL HINT

When using the weighted average method, calculate the unit cost to a minimum of three decimal places and use the calculated unit cost to determine either the ending inventory or the cost of goods sold. Determine the other amount by subtracting your calculated amount from the value of goods available for sale.

In Rhoda's Appliances, the average cost is calculated by taking the total cost of the goods available for sale ($15,585) and dividing it by the number of refrigerators available (33) to produce an average cost of $472.273 per unit. This unit cost is then assigned to all the units in ending inventory (7 × $472.273 = $3,305.91), and to the 26 units sold (26 × $472.273 = $12,279.10). Note that when the ending inventory of $3,305.91 is added to the cost of goods sold of $12,279.10, the total is $15,585.01, a one-cent difference in the total value of goods available for sale. This error occurred because we had to round the unit cost.

Note that the weighted average method produces results on the income statement and balance sheet that lie somewhere between those of LIFO and FIFO. Because it produces a lower pre-tax income than FIFO when prices are rising, many companies in Canada choose it for tax purposes. They like the higher net income produced by FIFO for reporting purposes and so will maintain two sets of inventory records. This is acceptable practice. The recent increase in the use of the weighted average method for reporting purposes is an indication that companies are choosing to maintain only one set of inventory records.

Cost Flow Assumption Choice

All three of the cost flow assumptions we have discussed are in accordance with GAAP. Given free choice, which method should Rhoda's Appliances use to represent the operating results for the period? This depends on the fundamental objectives of management. Examine Exhibit 7-10 to see the different financial statement effects of each of the three assumptions.

EXHIBIT 7-10   **FINANCIAL STATEMENT RESULTS**

	FIFO	Weighted Average	LIFO
		Cost flow assumption	
Sales revenue	$19,100	$19,100	$19,100
Cost of goods sold	12,225	12,279	12,410
Gross profit	$6,875	$6,821	$6,690
Balance sheet			
Inventory	$3,360	$3,306	$3,175

COST FLOW ASSUMPTIONS AND CHANGING PRICES

LEARNING OBJECTIVE 8

Describe the impact of inflation on each of the cost flow assumptions.

As the Rhoda's Appliances example illustrates, the use of LIFO during periods of rising prices generally produces the lowest net income, whereas the use of FIFO produces the highest net income. The reverse would be true during periods of deflation, although the use of the lower of cost and market rule would tend to modify this. In Canada, there have been virtually no sustained periods of deflation in recent memory. However, that is not to say that some companies have not faced periods of decreasing unit prices in the goods they use or produce. Take, for example, the microchip industry, which has seen significant drops in the cost per unit of its products. For these types of business, FIFO would make sense for tax purposes: in cases of declining costs, FIFO would produce the highest cost of goods sold and the lowest net income.

In periods of stable prices, all three cost flow assumptions produce the same values for cost of goods sold and ending inventory. The differences among the assumptions are driven by changes in prices across time. The magnitude of the effect depends on the size of the change in prices and on the size and turnover characteristics of the inventory. Users of financial statements, therefore, need to know more than just the inventory method that is being used. They must also know the type of inventory being sold and how the economy may be affecting the cost of that inventory.

Consider the use of FIFO and the effects of changing prices. The balance sheet reflects the most recent prices. The cost of goods sold reflects older prices. How old can these prices be? The oldest costs in the cost of goods sold figure are those that existed in beginning inventory. Those costs may have been incurred in the last month of the last year or even earlier, depending on how often the company turns over its inventory. Inventory turnover measures the number of times the total inventory is sold during the period.

If the inventory turnover ratio is 12, the inventory turns over on average once a month, and the ending inventory costs come from the purchases made in the last month of the year. If inventory turnover is four, the company turns over its inventory on average once a quarter, and the oldest costs in ending inventory could come from the beginning of the last quarter of the year. Therefore, while these costs are viewed as "old," in reality they are not very old. When prices are not rising very rapidly, the differences between current year prices and those from the end of the last year will be relatively small.

Now, consider LIFO. Cost of goods sold reflects the most recent prices. Inventory, on the other hand, reflects old prices. How old can these old prices be? The oldest prices in ending inventory are associated with the oldest layer of inventory, which could have been acquired in the first year the company was in business. For a 50-year-old company, these unit prices could be from half a century ago. Even with small levels of annual inflation, the cumulative difference in prices for these layers and current prices can be very substantial. The effects of inflation can cause a company's LIFO inventory value to be very different from the inventory's current replacement cost. For this reason, LIFO companies often provide information in the footnotes to their annual reports to inform the reader of the current cost of their inventories.

The choice of cost flow assumption depends on the nature of the inventory, but the same assumption does not have to apply to all inventories held by the company. For example, note the multiple inventory methods used by **Suncor Energy Inc.** in Exhibit 7-12.

EXHIBIT 7-12

SUNCOR ENERGY INC. 2003 ANNUAL REPORT

Excerpted from the Notes to the Statements Summary of significant accounting policies

(g) Inventories

Inventories of crude oil and refined products are valued at the lower of cost (using the LIFO method) and net realizable value.

Materials and supplies are valued at the lower of average cost and net realizable value.

AN INTERNATIONAL PERSPECTIVE

Reports from Other Countries

NAFTA Facts

United States—Inventory accounting is very similar to Canada except that LIFO is more commonly used because it is acceptable for tax purposes, and if it is used for tax purposes, it must also be used for reporting purposes.

Mexico—Inventory is initially recorded at its acquisition or production cost and then restated at the balance sheet date, using either price level adjusted or replacement cost amounts, subject to the constraint that this amount cannot exceed net realizable value. Cost flow methods are essentially the same as in Canada.

INVENTORY ESTIMATION

LEARNING OBJECTIVE 9

Estimate a value for ending inventory using the cost-to-sales ratio method.

There are several circumstances in which a company needs the cost of goods sold or inventory value, but either chooses not to count inventory (too costly to close the business to count inventory) or simply cannot count it (it has been stolen or destroyed). In these cases, the company may attempt to estimate the cost of goods sold amount if it wants to prepare monthly income statements. It may need to estimate the amount and value of inventory for insurance purposes if the inventory is destroyed or stolen. As mentioned earlier, it is difficult to determine inventory shrinkage when using the periodic system. Companies will often estimate the inventory before they start the annual physical inventory count so that they can determine if shrinkage has occurred.

Using the Cost-to-Sales Ratio

One way to estimate the cost of goods sold is to multiply the sales revenue for the period (a figure that is readily determinable) by the normal cost-to-sales ratio. The normal cost-to-sales ratio reflects the normal markup that the company applies to its products. For example, a company that normally marks up its products by 50% prices an item that costs $60 at $90. The cost-to-sales ratio then is 67% ($60/$90). If the sales for a given month are $12,000, the estimated cost of goods sold is $8,000 (67% × $12,000).

This cost-to-sales ratio can be used to estimate ending inventory as well. The company would be able to determine the cost of the goods available for sale by referring to the accounting records and finding the beginning inventory and the purchases for the period. For example, if the beginning inventory is $2,000 and the purchases for the period were $9,000, the goods available for sale would be $11,000.

Beginning inventory	$2,000
Purchases	9,000
Goods available for sale	11,000
Cost of goods sold (above calculation)	8,000
Ending inventory	$3,000

If we use the cost-to-sales ratio and the sales amount from the previous paragraph, we can determine that the cost of goods sold is $8,000 for the period. Because we know that goods available for sale must equal cost of goods sold plus ending inventory, all we need to do is subtract the calculated cost of goods sold ($8,000) from the goods available for sale ($11,000) to find the cost of ending inventory ($3,000). This method is often referred to as the **gross margin estimation method**.

STATEMENT ANALYSIS CONSIDERATIONS

Because of the diversity of cost flow assumptions that can be made by companies and the significant differences that these assumptions can cause in the financial statements, adjustments must be made when inventory ratios are compared across companies. Cross-industry analyses are most affected by cost flow assumptions. Analyses of the same company over time are not affected as much, as long as the inventory method has been consistently applied (the company used FIFO or weighted average all the time). Changes in the cost flow assumption across time make time series analyses difficult. When using the inventory or cost of goods sold amounts in ratio analysis, keep these points in mind as you evaluate your results.

LEARNING OBJECTIVE 10

Calculate the inventory turnover ratio and explain how it can be interpreted by users.

Inventory Turnover

The one ratio that looks exclusively at inventory is the inventory turnover ratio. This ratio tells the user how fast inventory is sold or how long it is held before it is sold. It is calculated as:

$$\text{Inventory turnover} = \frac{\text{Cost of goods sold}}{\text{Average inventory}}$$

The numerator contains the cost of goods sold, which measures the costs assigned to all the items of inventory that were sold. The denominator contains the average inventory. Average inventory is used, where possible, rather than ending inventory because it represents a more appropriate measure of inventory levels if the inventory level has changed over the year. Average inventory is the beginning inventory plus the ending inventory in a year divided by two. Inventory turnover for **Sun-Rype Products Ltd.** for 2003 was:

$$\frac{\$71,925,000}{\dfrac{(\$13,271,000 + \$10,520,000)}{2}} = 6.04$$

If the turnover is 6.04, it takes Sun-Rype Products about 60 days to sell an average-sized batch of inventory. The 60 days is calculated by dividing the number of days in a year (365) by the inventory turnover. This will tell you approximately how many days inventory is held before it is sold. For Sun-Rype Products, the number of days that inventory was held in 2003 was:

$$365 \text{ days}/6.04 = 60 \text{ days}$$

In order to determine if a turnover of 6.04 is reasonable for Sun-Rype Products, you would need to calculate the ratio for previous years so that you could see if it was changing. You should also compare Sun-Rype's ratio with those of other companies in the same industry to see how it compares with its competitors. A look at the 2002 inventory turnover shows that turnover was a little slower in 2002. Inventory was held approximately four days longer.

$$\frac{\$67,528,000}{\dfrac{(\$10,520,000 + \$13,126,000)}{2}} = 5.71$$

$$365 \text{ days}/5.71 = 63.9 \text{ days}$$

One concern about this ratio exists when LIFO is used. The ratio attempts to provide information about how fast the physical inventory turns over. Ideally, the ratio would put the number of units sold in the numerator and the number of units in ending inventory in the denominator. Because information about the number of units sold or in ending inventory is not provided in the financial statements, we use the cost figures provided in the statements and divide cost of goods sold by the average cost of inventory. With FIFO and weighted average, we can use values in the numerator and denominator without risk of distortion since both values were determined in similar time frames. Because LIFO assigns the most recent costs to the cost of goods sold, the units in the numerator are stated at current prices. The units in the denominator, however, may be stated at very old unit prices because of the layers that exist with LIFO. Because of this, during periods of rising prices the ratio is likely to overstate the turnover since higher-priced units are in the numerator and lower-priced units are in the denominator. Because very few companies in Canada use LIFO, this will not pose a problem for most of the analyses that you do.

HELPFUL HINT:

It is sometimes difficult to calculate the inventory turnover ratio for some companies because of the disclosure of cost of goods sold on the income statement. Sun-Rype Products has a line on its income statement called Cost of sales. Le Château Inc., on the other hand, has an item on its income statement called Cost of sales, buying and occupancy. This means that it has included additional costs with the cost of sales (selling costs and rent, etc.). If we try to calculate the inventory turnover for Le Château using the cost of sales, buying and occupancy amount, the resulting turnover number will be larger because the numerator is larger as a result of the additional costs included in it. Inventory will appear to turn over faster than it does in reality.

Other Ratios

Other ratios are affected by the use of LIFO vs. FIFO if they contain inventory figures or the cost of goods sold. The most dramatic effects are in those ratios that use balance sheet information. The ratio that is probably most affected is the current ratio, which compares current assets with current liabilities (current assets/current liabilities). If costs are rising, the choice of LIFO can cause this ratio to be significantly lower than it would be with FIFO. Also, remember that the current ratio is used in many debt agreements. If a company using LIFO is in danger of violating the requirement for this ratio, a switch to FIFO might solve the problem.

On the income statement, the gross profit percentage (gross profit/sales) is also affected by the choice of FIFO vs. LIFO. In Exhibit 7-10, the gross profit for Rhoda's Appliances varied from $6,875 under FIFO to $6,690 under LIFO. The difference is only $185, but remember that we are dealing with the sale of only 26 units of a single type of inventory. The gross margin percentage is 36.0% under FIFO and 35.0% under LIFO. With a greater fluctuation in unit costs and more years of application of the individual methods, the difference between the two would be more dramatic.

SUMMARY

This chapter discussed inventory, a current asset that is vital to a company's health, and its related expense, cost of goods sold. Because of the many kinds of inventory, managing all aspects of inventory is a very complex task. Managers need to order the right kind and amount of inventory, price it competitively (but high enough to ensure that the company makes a profit), and safeguard it so that it cannot be stolen. Over time, accountants have developed two major systems for accounting for inventory: the perpetual system, which keeps a continuous record of the inventory on hand, and the periodic system, which records the purchase of inventory but does not cost the amount that has been sold until the end of an accounting period. Within these two systems, four methods have been developed for assigning costs to inventory: specific identification, FIFO, LIFO, and weighted average. When unit costs are changing, each of these methods results in a different cost for ending inventory and cost of goods sold. Users need to be aware of how these methods are used so that they can factor their effect into any ratio analysis that they perform. Because counting inventory to determine the amount on hand is a costly endeavour, accountants have developed methods for estimating inventory. Estimates are used for interim reports, for determining inventory values when it has been stolen or destroyed, and for establishing a pre-count value against which management is able to compare the actual physical count of inventory. In this chapter, we described the cost-to-sales ratio method for estimating inventory. We finished the chapter by discussing the inventory turnover ratio, a ratio that helps users evaluate the management of inventory.

At this point, all the major current asset accounts have been covered, and attention turns next to the noncurrent assets, which have longer lives than current assets. The benefits of these assets are received over much longer periods of time than those of current assets. The next chapter considers the most common noncurrent asset accounts, capital assets, with an emphasis on property, plant, and equipment.

SUMMARY PROBLEM

The statements of financial position (balance sheets), income statements, and Note 3 from the 2003 annual report of **IPSCO Inc.** are shown in Exhibit 7-13. IPSCO is a Canadian company that manufactures steel products. Note 2 of the report states that inventories are valued at the lowest of average cost, replacement cost, and net realizable value.

Additional Demonstration Problems

1. In 2003, IPSCO's net income declined from $20,279 thousand in 2002 to $12,362 thousand. Based solely on the sale of inventory, can you suggest reasons why the net income declined in 2003?

2. Calculate the inventory turnover for IPSCO for 2003. Provide a brief discussion of what this ratio means.

3. Calculate the current ratio for IPSCO for 2003 and 2002. How important is the inventory value in this ratio?

EXHIBIT 7-13
PART A

IPSCO INC. 2003 ANNUAL REPORT

IPSCO Inc. Consolidated Statements of Financial Position

As at December 31 (thousands of United States dollars)

	2003	2002
Current Assets		
Cash and cash equivalents	$ 131,567	$ 22,859
Accounts receivable		
Trade, less allowances	168,956	135,421
Other, including current portion of mortgages receivable	45,722	18,331
Inventories (Note 3)	286,159	255,410
Prepaid expenses	2,833	2,847
Future income taxes (Note 4)	22,976	41,402
	658,213	476,270
Non-Current Assets		
Capital assets (Note 5)	1,109,418	1,129,716
Mortgages receivable (Note 6)	10,882	5,403
Deferred financing costs, less amortization	8,107	2,785
Deferred pension asset (Note 7)	3,964	3,911
Future income taxes (Note 4)	149,430	121,586
	1,281,801	1,263,401
Total Assets	$1,940,014	$1,739,671
Current Liabilities		
Accounts payable and accrued charges (Note 9)	$ 162,812	$ 101,514
Accrued payroll and related liabilities	15,624	13,775
Current portion of long-term debt (Note 8)	34,286	35,386
Other current liabilities	10,515	16,142
	223,237	166,817
Long-Term Liabilities		
Long-term debt (Note 8)	401,244	342,202
Future income taxes (Note 4)	181,643	143,229
	582,887	485,431
Shareholders' Equity		
Preferred shares (Note 10)	98,695	98,553
Common shares (Note 11)	354,095	351,311
Subordinated notes (Note 12)	104,250	104,250
Retained earnings (Note 13)	487,924	494,599
Cumulative translation adjustment	88,926	38,710
	1,133,890	1,087,423
Total Liabilities and Shareholders' Equity	$1,940,014	$1,739,671

Commitments and contingencies (Notes 18 & 21)

The accompanying notes are an integral part of the consolidated financial statements.

On behalf of the Board

Burton Joyce, Director

David Sutherland, Director

IPSCO INC. 2003 ANNUAL REPORT

IPSCO Inc. Consolidated Statements of Income

Years ended December 31 (thousands of United States dollars except per share data)

	2003	2002	2001
Sales	**$1,294,566**	$1,081,709	$ 903,743
Cost of sales			
Manufacturing and raw material	**1,130,886**	929,140	772,516
Amortization of capital assets	**61,138**	51,049	37,107
	1,192,024	980,189	809,623
Gross income	**102,542**	101,520	94,120
Selling, research and administration	**54,683**	51,358	55,799
Operating income	**47,859**	50,162	38,321
Other expenses (income)			
Interest on long-term debt (Note 8)	**30,583**	23,821	6,634
Other interest (income) expense, net	**(1,625)**	174	(928)
Foreign exchange (gain) loss	**(5,170)**	938	882
Other	**(720)**	–	–
Gain on sale of assets held for sale (Note 6)	**–**	(6,464)	–
Litigation settlement (Note 21)	**–**	–	(39,000)
Provision for loss on assets held for sale (Note 5)	**–**	–	10,000
Income before income taxes	**24,791**	31,693	60,733
Income taxes (Note 4)	**12,429**	11,414	21,865
Net Income	**12,362**	20,279	38,868
Dividends on preferred shares, including part VI.I tax (Note 10)	**6,304**	5,608	5,692
Interest on subordinated notes, net of income tax (Note 12)	**5,771**	5,771	5,771
Net Income Available to Common Shareholders	**$ 287**	$ 8,900	$ 27,405
Earnings Per Common Share			
Basic (Note 14)	**$ 0.01**	$ 0.19	$ 0.67
Diluted (Note 14)	**$ 0.01**	$ 0.19	$ 0.66

The accompanying notes are an integral part of the consolidated financial statements.

3. Inventories

	2003	2002
Finished goods	**$106,310**	$ 99,489
Work-in-process	**85,790**	70,492
Raw materials	**35,780**	31,831
Supplies	**58,279**	53,598
	$286,159	$255,410

SUGGESTED SOLUTION TO SUMMARY PROBLEM

All figures in the solution are in thousands.

1. In 2001, the gross margin on revenues of $903,743 was $131,227, or 14.5%. In 2002, the gross margin on $1,081,709 of revenues was $152,569, or 14.1%. Note that the revenue increased but the gross margin percentage decreased. In 2003, the revenues increased further to $1,294,566. The gross margin also increased in dollar terms to $163,680, but the gross margin percentage decreased further to 12.6%. In other words, revenues increased but the cost of sales increased more proportionately, which caused the gross margin percentage to decrease. The decrease in the margin from 14.5% to 12.6% makes it more difficult for IPSCO to cover all of its other costs. IPSCO manufactures steel products and is, therefore, subject to international steel markets. Over the last number of years, world steelmaking capacity has exceeded demand, which has caused a decline in prices. When prices decline, it is important for companies to reduce their production costs so that they remain competitive. IPSCO has been trying to counter the decline in prices by becoming more efficient in the production process. In its 2003 annual report, IPSCO says that over the last three years, it has tripled its output of steel and improved its productivity. The decline in the gross margin percentage is an indication that more production efficiencies may have to be implemented.

2.
$$\frac{\$1,130,886}{\dfrac{(\$286,159\ 1\ \$255,410}{2}} = 4.18)$$

$$365/4.18 = 87 \text{ days}$$

ISPCO's inventory turnover is 4.18. It takes about 87 days for it to manufacture and sell its inventory. IPSCO is an international supplier of steel products. It is probable that because of the nature of its product, it will hold inventory for several months without selling it. Without additional information about IPSCO's activities in previous years or about its competitors, it is not possible to comment further on this ratio.

3.
$$\text{Current ratio (2003)} = \frac{\$658,213}{\$223,237} = 2.94$$

$$\text{Current ratio (2002)} = \frac{\$476,270}{\$166,817} = 2.86$$

The current ratio has improved from 2002 to 2003. Inventory represents approximately 43% of the current assets in 2003 and approximately 54% in 2002. This means that it has a significant impact on this ratio. Without the inventory, the ratio in both years would be close to one. The company would have difficulty meeting its current liabilities without selling inventory.

APPENDIX

COST FLOW ASSUMPTIONS UNDER THE PERPETUAL INVENTORY SYSTEM

Under the perpetual inventory system, all four methods of costing inventory (specific identification, FIFO, LIFO, and weighted average) can be used. Specific identification is determined in the same way under both the periodic and the perpetual system. Because the cost of goods sold amount is determined each time inventory items are sold and the inventory account is adjusted for the sold inventory, the calculation of cost of goods sold and ending inventory is determined differently under the two methods but the end result is the same.

To illustrate FIFO, LIFO, and weighted average (called moving average under the perpetual system), we are going to use the same example of Rhoda's Appliances that we used to illustrate the costing assumptions for the periodic system earlier in the chapter. It is repeated here so that we can refer to it easily.

RHONDA'S APPLIANCES, INC.

EXHIBIT 7-14

Inventory of Refrigerators

Date		Units	Unit cost	Total
January 1	Beginning inventory	6	$450	$ 2,700
January 10	Purchase #1	15	475	7,125
January 20	Purchase #2	12	480	5,760
Goods available for sale		33		$15,585

Sale record

		Units	Unit price	Total
January 15	Sale #1	16	$725	$11,600
January 25	Sale #2	10	750	7,500
		26		$19,100

First-In, First-Out (FIFO)

Each time inventory is sold, we need to determine the cost of the inventory sold and reduce the inventory account by that amount. Using the Rhoda's Appliances data (Exhibit 7-14) and the FIFO assumption, we can assign a cost to the cost of goods sold and ending inventory as follows.

First Sale January 15
Cost of goods sold (16 units)

6	units @ $450 (beginning inventory)	$2,700
+10	units @ $475 (first purchase)	4,750
16	units	$7,450

Ending inventory (5 units)

5	units @ $475 (second purchase)	$2,375

Second Sale January 25
Cost of goods sold (10 units)

5	units @ $475 (left over from first sale)	$2,375
+ 5	units @ $480 (second purchase)	2,400
10	units	$4,775

Ending inventory (5 units)

7	units @ $480 (second purchase)	$3,360

Total cost of goods sold for the period = $7,450 + $4,775 = $12,225
Ending inventory at the end of the period = $3,360

Note that the sum of the units in cost of goods sold and ending inventory (16 + 10 + 7) equals the 33 units in goods available for sale. The sum of the dollar amounts ($12,225 + $3,360) equals the dollar amount of the goods available for sale, $15,585. As inventory is sold, the cost of goods sold is calculated using the earliest inventory purchases. As those items are used to determine a cost for the inventory sold, we move forward to the next inventory that has been purchased. You will notice that the cost of goods sold amount, $12,225, and the ending inventory amount, $3,360, are the same as they were under the periodic system. This will always be the case. This should make sense to you because we are assigning costs using the oldest costs and flowing forward through the inventory amounts. Remember the items flowing through the pipe in Exhibit 7-7? Although the end value for cost of goods sold and ending inventory are the same under both methods, the way we determined those amounts was different under the two methods.

Last-In, First-Out (LIFO)

The **last-in, first-out** or **LIFO** method is more complicated to calculate. Recall that in Exhibit 7-8, we used the illustration of new inventory being put on top of older inventory and then assigning the costs from the most recent purchases. Under the periodic system we waited until the end of the period and then determined those costs. Under the perpetual system we are going to assign a cost to the inventory sold each time there is a sale.

Using Rhoda's Appliances (Exhibit 7-14) and the LIFO assumption, let us now assign a cost to the cost of goods sold and ending inventory for each sale.

First Sale January 15
Cost of goods sold (16 units)

15	units @ $475 (first purchase)	$7,125
+ 1	units @ $450 (beginning inventory)	450
16	units	$7,575

The most recent purchase was for 15 refrigerators so the initial cost of the 16 sold on January 15 is taken from that purchase. The remaining 1 refrigerator cost is taken from the beginning inventory.

Ending inventory (5 units)

5	units @ $450 (beinning inventory)	$2,250

Second Sale January 25
Cost of goods sold (10 units)

10	units @ $480 (second purchase)	$4,800

Ending inventory (7 units)

2	units @ $480 (second purchase)	$ 960
+ 5	units @ $450 (beginning inventory)	2,250
7	units	$3,210

Total cost of goods sold for the period = $7,575 + $4,800 = $12,375
Ending inventory at the end of the period = $3,210

Note again how the sum of the units in cost of goods sold and ending inventory (16 + 10 + 7) equals the 33 units in goods available for sale. The sum of the dollar amounts ($12,375 + $3,210) equals the dollar amount of the goods available for sale, $15,585. As inventory is sold, the cost of goods sold is calculated using the most recent inventory purchases. As those items are used to determine a cost for the inventory sold, we add the next inventory purchased to the pile and use it for the next sale. You will notice that the cost of goods sold amount, $12,375, and the ending inventory amount, $3,210, are not the same as they were under the periodic system. This is usually the case. Each sale takes its cost from the most recent purchases and the inventory that was left over from the last sale. It may be possible to get all of the cost of a sale from a recent purchase. In other cases, you may have to go as far back as beginning inventory to find enough units and costs.

Note also that the dollar amount of ending inventory is lower than it is under FIFO and that, therefore, the dollar amount of the cost of goods sold is higher. The unit cost of inventory has been rising through January, and because the cost of goods sold is assigned costs from the most recent purchases, it receives higher unit costs than under FIFO.

LIFO and FIFO represent the two extremes of the cost assumptions. LIFO will produce the highest cost of goods sold and, therefore, the lowest net income when unit costs are rising. This might be of interest to a manager who wants to discourage shareholders from requesting cash dividends. FIFO, on the other hand, will produce the lowest cost of goods sold and, therefore, the highest net income under the same conditions. This might be of interest to a manager who wants to attract new investors. Because these two assumptions produce dramatically different financial results during times of changing prices, it is important for users of financial statements to know which method is being used and to understand the managerial objectives that might underlie the selection of that method.

LIFO is used the least often in Canada for several reasons. First, it produces the lowest net income when costs are rising. Second, the value of inventory on the balance sheet quickly becomes unrealistic. Third, the Canada Revenue Agency does not accept it as a method for determining inventory costs for tax purposes, probably because it produces the lowest net income and would therefore produce the lowest taxable income. We now turn our attention to the last potential cost flow assumption: the moving average method.

Moving Average

The name of this cost assumption has changed to the moving average method because each time we purchase new inventory we are going to calculate a new average cost that we will assign to the inventory that is sold. Recall in Exhibit 7-9 how new inventory was added to original inventory and mixed together. Inventory that is sold is therefore a mixture of beginning inventory and recent purchases.

In the moving average method, the average cost is calculated by taking the total cost of the goods available for sale after each purchase and dividing it by the number of units available for sale at that time to produce an average cost per unit. This unit cost is then assigned to all the units sold. Using Rhoda's Appliances (Exhibit 7-14) and the moving average assumption, let's work through the assignment of costs for each sale.

Calculation of first average cost after the first purchase:

Jan. 10	6	units @ $450 (beginning inventory) =	$2,700
+ 15		units @ $475 (first purchase) =	7,125
21		units	$9,825

First average cost = $9,825 / 21 = $467.857

First sale Jan. 15 (16 units)
Cost of goods sold = 16 × $467.857 = $7,485.71
Remaining inventory (5 units) = $9,825 − $7,485.71 = $2,339.29

Calculation of second average cost after the second purchase:

Jan. 20	5	units (left over from first sale) =	$ 2,339.29
+ 12		units @ $480 (second purchase) =	5,760.00
17		units	$ 8,099.29

Second average cost = $8,099.29 / 17 = $476.429

Second sale Jan. 25 (10 units)
Cost of goods sold = 10 × $476.429 = $4,764.29
Remaining inventory (7 units) = $8,099.29 − $4,764.29 = $3,335

Total cost of goods sold for the period = $7,485.71 + $4,764.29 = $12,250.00
Ending inventory at the end of the period = $3,335.00

Note that the weighted average method produces results on the income statement and balance sheet that lie somewhere between those of LIFO and FIFO. Because it produces a lower pre-tax income than FIFO when prices are rising, many companies in Canada choose it for tax purposes. They like the higher net income produced by FIFO for reporting purposes and so will maintain two sets of inventory records. This is acceptable practice. The recent increase in the use of the weighted average method for reporting purposes indicates that companies are choosing to maintain only one set of inventory records.

Financial Statement Results

All three cost flow assumptions we have discussed are in accordance with GAAP. How different are the results under the periodic and perpetual cost assumptions? Examine Exhibit 7-15 to see the different financial statement effects of each of the three assumptions under each method.

EXHIBIT 7-15 **FINANCIAL STATEMENT RESULTS**

Periodic System

| | | Cost flow assumption | |
	FIFO	Weighted Average	LIFO
Sales revenue	$19,100	$19,100	$19,100
Cost of goods sold	12,225	12,279	12,410
Gross profit	$ 6,875	$ 6,821	$ 6,690
Balance sheet			
Inventory	$ 3,360	$ 3,306	$ 3,175

Perpetual System

| | | Cost flow assumption | |
	FIFO	Moving Average	LIFO
Sales revenue	$19,100	$19,100	$19,100
Cost of goods sold	12,225	12,250	12,375
Gross profit	$ 6,875	$ 6,850	$ 6,725
Balance sheet			
Inventory	$ 3,360	$ 3,335	$ 3,210

The FIFO costing assumption produces the same results under the periodic and perpetual systems. The weighted (moving) average and LIFO cost assumptions produce slightly different amounts but maintain the same relationship relative to the other methods. Moving average remained in the middle between FIFO and LIFO. LIFO continued to produce the lowest gross profit, highest cost of goods sold, and lowest ending inventory number. Using the costing systems through the perpetual system provides more precise amounts (calculated each time there is a sale) and more current information that management can use for decision-making and better inventory control.

ABBREVIATIONS USED

EDI	Electronic data interchange	LCM	Lower of cost and market
FIFO	First-in, first-out	LIFO	Last-in, first-out
FISH	First-in, still-here	LISH	Last-in, still-here
IASB	International Accounting Standards Board	NRV	Net realizable value

SYNONYMS

Entry market/Input market/Wholesale market
Exit market/Output market/Retail market
Entry price/Input price/Replacement cost
Exit price/Output price/Net realizable value
Freight in/Transportation in

GLOSSARY

Cost flow assumption An assumption made as to how the costs of inventory should be assigned to individual units when it is impossible or impractical to assign costs specifically to units.

Current gross margin The difference between the current selling price of a unit of inventory and its current replacement cost.

Electronic data interchange The linkage of two companies with computers such that inventory is ordered directly over the computer connection.

Entry market The market from which goods or materials enter the company; sometimes also referred to as the wholesale market.

Exit market The market in which goods exit the company; sometimes also referred to as the retail market.

First-in, first-out (FIFO) The cost flow assumption that assigns the cost of the first unit into the company to the first unit sold.

First-in, still-here (FISH) The ending inventory units with the LIFO cost flow assumption.

Freight in The transportation cost paid when inventory is acquired.

Going-concern assumption An assumption made in GAAP that the company for which the financial statements are being prepared will continue to exist into the foreseeable future.

Goods available for sale The units of inventory available to be sold during the period. These units include those available from the beginning inventory plus those produced or purchased during the current period.

Input market Another name for entry market.

Inventory shrinkage The losses of inventory due to spoilage, damage, thefts, etc.

Laid-down cost The inventory costs including invoice cost plus customs, tariff, and excise duties, and transportation. Although transportation in should be included in the laid-down cost, it is often treated as a period cost because it is impractical to allocate it to inventory items. In a manufacturing company, the laid-down cost comprises direct materials, direct labour, and overhead.

Last-in, first-out (LIFO) The cost flow assumption that assigns the cost of the last unit purchased by the company to the first unit sold.

Last-in, still here (LISH) The ending inventory units using the FIFO cost flow assumption.

Market Net realizable value, net realizable value less a profit margin, or replacement cost.

Moving average A method of assigning costs to units of inventory in which a new average cost is calculated each time new inventory is purchased. That average cost is assigned to sales that occur after the purchase but before the next purchase. It is used under the perpetual inventory system.

Net realizable value (NRV) A selling price of a unit of inventory less any costs necessary to complete and sell the unit.

Output market Another name for exit market.

Periodic inventory system An inventory system in which cost of goods sold is determined by counting ending inventory, assigning costs to these units, and then subtracting the ending inventory value from the sum of the beginning inventory plus purchases for the period.

Perpetual inventory system An inventory system in which the cost of goods sold is determined at the time a unit is sold.

Realized holding gain A gain that results from the sale of a unit of inventory that had been held during a period of time in which prices increased. The profits that result from the change in price are the portion referred to as a holding gain.

Replacement cost The current price at which a unit of inventory can be replaced by the company.

Retail market Another term for exit market.

Specific identification method A method of assigning costs to units of inventory in which the cost of a unit can be specifically identified from company records.

Stockout A situation arising when a company sells all of a specific item of inventory and has no more in stock.

Transportation in A synonym for freight in.

Weighted average A method of assigning costs to units of inventory in which each unit is assigned the average cost of the units available for sale during the period. This method is used under the periodic inventory system.

Wholesale market Another term for entry market.

ASSIGNMENT MATERIAL

Assessing Your Recall

Self-Assessment Quiz

7-1 Describe the inventory valuation methods allowed under GAAP.

7-2 Describe how the lower of cost and market rule is applied to inventory under GAAP.

7-3 Define replacement cost and net realizable value, and explain the difference between them.

7-4 Describe the basic differences between the periodic and perpetual inventory systems.

7-5 Discuss the advantages and disadvantages of the periodic inventory system compared with the perpetual inventory system.

7-6 What is inventory shrinkage and how and when is it measured?

7-7 Describe the three major cost flow assumptions that are most commonly used for determining the value of ending inventory and cost of goods sold.

7-8 Discuss a company's incentives for choosing one cost flow assumption over another. Be sure to include a discussion of the choice from both a reporting and a tax perspective.

7-9 How important is the choice of cost flow assumption for a company that turns over its inventory rapidly? Explain.

7-10 Explain the term "holding gain" and discuss how it might arise with various cost flow assumptions.

7-11 Under what circumstances would a company want or need to estimate the cost of goods sold or ending inventory?

7-12 Describe the effects the choice of LIFO or FIFO may have on the ratios related to inventory. Discuss specifically the inventory turnover ratio and the current ratio in times of rising prices.

Applying Your Knowledge

7-13 (Calculation of ending inventory and cost of goods sold)

Burke Ltd. had 4,500 units, at a cost of $12.00 each, in its inventory at the beginning of February. The company's purchases during February were as follows.

February 6	3,500	units	@	$12.00
14	2,000	units	@	$11.80
23	8,200	units	@	$11.65
28	3,600	units	@	$11.40
	17,300	units		

Burke uses a periodic inventory system. At the end of February, the company had 6,600 units of inventory on hand.

> **Required:**
> a. Calculate the cost of goods sold for February using the weighted average cost flow assumption.
>
> b. Calculate the cost of goods sold for February using the first-in, first-out cost flow assumption.
>
> c. Calculate the cost of goods sold for February using the last-in, first-out cost flow assumption.
>
> d. Which inventory cost flow assumption results in the greatest net income for February? Which results in the smallest? (Note that prices decreased during the period.)
>
> e. Which inventory cost flow assumption results in the largest inventory balance at the end of February? Which results in the smallest?
>
> f. Compare your answers in parts d) and e) above and comment on the relationship between these items.

7-14 (Calculation of ending inventory and cost of goods sold)

Exquisite Jewellers purchases chiming clocks from around the world for sale in Canada. According to its records, Exquisite Jewellers had the following purchases and sales of clocks in the current year.

Clock No.	Date Purchased	Amount Paid	Date Sold	Sale Price
423	Jan. 5	$2,150	Mar. 8	$3,800
424	Mar. 15	4,500		
425	May 27	4,400	June 16	6,200
426	July 14	2,400	Aug. 9	3,350
427	Oct. 24	3,720		
428	Dec. 5	1,930	Dec. 24	2,640

Exquisite Jewellers has used the average cost method in calculating its cost of goods sold and inventory balances, but is thinking of changing to specific identification.

> **Required:**
> a. Compare the dollar amounts that would be reported as cost of goods sold and ending inventory under the average cost and specific identification methods.
>
> b. Is average cost an appropriate method to use in a situation such as this? Explain.
>
> c. What conditions generally must exist for specific identification to be used? Explain.

d. Which of the two methods best represents the operating results for Exquisite Jewellers? Explain.

7-15   (Calculation of cost of goods sold and gross profit)

Black Company, which uses a periodic inventory system, recorded the following inventory transactions during 2006.

	Unit Number of Units	Unit Purchase Price	Sale Price
Inventory balance,			
January 1, 2006	45	$8	
January 25	150	$9	
March 6	65	$10	
Sale #1	120		$16
August 7	50	$12	
Sale #2	130		$17

Required:

a. Calculate the cost of goods sold and gross profit for Black Company for 2006 if it uses each of the following cost flow assumptions.

   1. First-in, first-out

   2. Last-in, first-out

   3. Weighted average

b. On the balance sheet, which of the three assumptions provides the most conservative estimate of the carrying value of inventory? Which provides the best estimate of the current cost of replacing the inventory? Explain your answers.

c. Which method provides the most conservative estimate of reported income? Under what circumstances would the opposite be true?

7-16   (Calculation of ending inventory and cost of goods sold)

If your instructor has assigned the Appendix to this chapter, then redo Problem 7-15 assuming that the company uses a perpetual inventory system.

7-17   (Calculation of ending inventory and cost of goods sold)

The following information relates to the merchandise inventory of Aspen Company for the month of October.

				Cost
October	1	Beginning inventory	3,500 units	$70,000
October	3	Purchased	4,200 units	$88,200
October	7	Sold	2,600 units	
October	15	Sold	1,900 units	
October	23	Purchased	2,050 units	$45,100
October	29	Sold	3,300 units	
October	31	Purchased	1,750 units	$35,875

Required:

Calculate the cost of goods sold and ending inventory as at October 31 using a periodic inventory system and the following cost flow assumptions.

a. FIFO

b. LIFO

c. Weighted average

7-18 **(Calculation of ending inventory and cost of goods sold)**
If your instructor has assigned the Appendix to this chapter, then redo Problem 7-17 assuming that the company uses a perpetual inventory system.

7-19 **(Gross margin and the lower of cost and market)**
The Corral Saddle Company's information about merchandise inventories is as follows.

Year	Purchases	Sales	Ending Inventory Cost	Market Value
1	$140,000	$115,000	$75,000	$70,000
2	100,000	175,000	80,000	67,000
3	155,000	253,000	72,000	80,000
4	104,000	225,000	31,000	31,000

There was no beginning balance in inventories prior to Year 1.

> *Required:*
> a. Calculate the gross margin for each year, valuing the ending inventory at acquisition cost. (Hint: Use the relationship: Beginning inventory + Purchases – Ending inventory = Cost of goods sold.)
>
> b. Calculate the gross margin for each year, valuing the ending inventory at the lower of cost and market value.
>
> c. Compare the gross margin for each year using the two methods, and explain the reason(s) for any differences you observe.
>
> d. Compare the total results (gross margins) over the entire four-year period, using the two methods of valuation, and explain what you see.

7-20 **(Lower of cost and market)**
Canadian Paper Company (CPC) produces newsprint in its paper mills. At the end of 2006, the chief financial officer of CPC noted that the international market price of newsprint had been dropping appreciably. Tonnes of newsprint produced in 2006 at an average cost of $520 per metric tonne could only be sold at the end of December 2006 for $505 per metric tonne. CPC has also been working to reduce its production costs, hoping that they can be reduced to $495 per metric tonne in 2007.

> *Required:*
> a. Why is the decline in the market price for newsprint relevant in this type of situation?
>
> b. If CPC has 1,250 metric tonnes of newsprint on hand at December 31, 2006, at what dollar amount should inventory be reported?
>
> c. What other information would be relevant in determining the year-end reporting amount?
>
> d. Which accounting concepts are relevant in deciding the dollar amount of inventory to be reported? Explain why these concepts are important.

7-21 **(LIFO, FIFO, and the lower of cost and market)**
The following presentation relates to the inventory valuations of Aurora Inc. using different inventory methods (the company started operations in 2004).

Date	LIFO	FIFO	Lower of FIFO Cost and Market
December 31, 2004	$ 65,000	$ 60,000	$ 55,000
December 31, 2005	135,000	125,000	120,000
December 31, 2006	150,000	143,000	130,000
December 31, 2007	110,000	125,000	125,000

There was no beginning balance of inventory in 2004. The market referred to in the third column is the net realizable value.

> ***Required:***
> a. For 2004, state whether the prices for purchasing inventory went up or down.
>
> b. For 2007, state whether the prices went up or down.
>
> c. State which of the three inventory methods would show the highest income in each year. (Hint: you will need to calculate cost of goods sold expense in each year. You can do this by assuming a constant amount of purchases in each of the four years under each method. Use the relationship: Beginning inventory + Purchases − Ending inventory = Cost of goods sold expense.)
>
> d. Which method would show the lowest income for the four years combined? (Hint: you can answer this question much more quickly than part c). You start at January 1, 2004, with no beginning inventory: what do you end with?)

7-22 (LIFO and the production of additional inventory)

In mid-September, Waterford Incorporated needed to decide how many units should be produced for the balance of the accounting year, which ends on December 31. The company began its operations in the current year with an inventory of 20,000 units at a unit cost of $15. Thus far during the year, it has produced 85,000 units at a unit cost of $18. The annual production capacity of the plant is 200,000 units. It is estimated that the unit cost of producing additional units (for the remaining part of the year) will be $20. The company, after doing time-series and cross-industry analyses, expects annual sales to be 125,000 units at a selling price of $30 per unit. The company uses a periodic LIFO inventory system.

> ***Required:***
> a. Assume the company produces just enough units to cover the 125,000 units it sells (that is, it will end the year with no inventory). Determine the cost of goods sold and the gross profit at this level of production.
>
> b. Assume the company produces the maximum this year that the plant can produce, but still sells only 125,000 units. Determine the cost of goods sold, the gross profit, and the value of the ending inventory at this level of production.
>
> c. If the company sold the same number of units under assumptions a) and b), why is there a difference in the value of cost of goods sold and gross profit?
>
> d. What conclusion can you draw from this regarding the LIFO method?

7-23 (Inventory estimation)

On March 31, 2005, Cellular Building Supplies had a major fire in its main lumberyard. All the inventory in that yard was destroyed. In order to complete the insurance claim, the accountant needed an estimate of the inventory that had been in the lumberyard at the time of the fire. A search through the accounting records (which, luckily, had been kept in another building that was not destroyed by the fire) produced the following information.

2004 cost-to-sales ratio of 72%	
Purchases for the year up to March 31	$485,000
Sales for the year up to March 31	$712,700
Inventory on hand on January 1, 2005	$128,400

> ***Required:***
> a. Assuming the 2004 cost-to-sales ratio is appropriate for 2005, calculate how much inventory should have been on hand at March 31, 2005.
>
> b. Assuming the 2005 cost-to-sales ratio was closer to 70%, calculate how much inventory should have been on hand at March 31, 2005.
>
> c. What factors could make the estimate of ending inventory inaccurate?

7-24 **(FIFO, LIFO, and holding gains)**

At the beginning of the year, the Seattle Company had merchandise inventory consisting of 1,200 units at a cost of $300 per unit. During the year, the company produced 4,000 units at an average cost of $350. The company sold 3,500 units for $500 each. Production costs continued to rise during the year, and the replacement cost for units on December 31 was $380 per unit.

Required:

a. Calculate the cost of goods sold and gross margin using both the FIFO and LIFO cost flow assumptions.

b. Separate the gross margin on sales into operating gross margin and realized holding gains, using both FIFO and LIFO.

c. Calculate the unrealized holding gains and the total gains (operating margin + realized gain + unrealized gain) using both FIFO and LIFO.

d. Compare the total gains and explain the result.

7-25 **(Inventory turnover and gross margin calculations)**

Stream Ltd. reported total inventory at January 1 and December 31, 2006, of $180,000 and $150,000, respectively. Cost of goods sold for 2006 was $1,240,000. Stream's nearest competitor reported inventories of $410,000 and $460,000 at January 1 and December 31, 2006, respectively, and reported cost of goods sold of $2,270,000 for 2006. Total 2006 sales revenues for Stream Ltd. and its competitor were $1,610,000 and $3,365,000, respectively.

Required:

a. Calculate the inventory turnover ratios for the two companies for 2006.

b. Calculate the gross margin percentage (gross margin divided by sales) for the two companies for 2006.

c. On the basis of inventory turnover, which company is superior?

d. On the basis of gross margin percentage, which company is superior?

e. Which company would you recommend as being better managed? Indicate why.

7-26 **(Evaluation of the inventory turnover ratio)**

The inventory turnover ratios of Silver Nugget Mining Company, Best Cellar Books Limited, and Ken's Fresh Fruits Incorporated are 3.8, 8.1, and 21.4, respectively.

Required:

a. How is the inventory turnover ratio calculated? What information is provided by this ratio?

b. Is the company with the highest turnover ratio being run the most efficiently? Explain.

c. Evaluate the turnover ratios for the three companies. Are the differences in ratios consistent with what you would expect? Explain.

d. What other ratios would you examine in assessing the companies' operating efficiency?

User Perspective Problems

7-27 **(Measurement issues related to ending inventory)**

As an auditor, what concerns might you have about the measurement of inventories at year end? If inventory is misstated, what other amounts on the financial statements will be incorrect?

7-28 **(Use of ratio analysis during audit procedures)**

Auditors typically conduct a preliminary review of a company's financial statements using analytical procedures that include ratio analysis. As an auditor, what ratio(s) would you find useful in auditing amounts related to inventory? Would you be equally concerned if the ratios(s) were unexpectedly high or unexpectedly low? Explain.

7-29 **(Ratio analysis and foreign currencies)**

Suppose that you are analyzing two competitors, one a Canadian company and the other a company in Japan whose statements are expressed in yen. Discuss whether it is necessary to convert the statements of the Japanese company into Canadian dollars before calculating inventory ratios. Other than the currency used, would you have any other concerns with the ratio analysis of inventories for these two competitors?

7-30 **(Effects of changing inventory costing method)**

Suppose that a company has used LIFO since it began operations, and that prices have generally risen from that point to the present. In one of the company's debt agreements, there is a restrictive covenant stating that the company must maintain a current ratio greater than 2, or it would violate the debt agreement and the debt immediately becomes due. If you represent the lender, what reaction would you have if the company wanted to change its inventory method from LIFO to FIFO? How would your answer change if the debt covenant required the company to maintain a quick ratio greater than 1?

7-31 **(Decision-making with respect to inventory valuation)**

Your company manufactures a line of processed snack foods using a soybean base with a low fat content. The line was very popular until some negative publicity emphasized that the product is very high in salt and contains numerous chemical preservatives. The manufacturing division is undertaking the development of a new product that will have a lower salt content and fewer preservatives. However, right now you have inventory on hand that will be hard to sell. The inventory originally cost $3.5 million. Its wholesale selling price prior to the publicity had been $7 million. The sales division has presented the following alternative proposals to the executive committee, of which you are a member.

Proposal 1: Offer the product at deep discounts to regular customers. If the discounts are large enough, all of the inventory will probably sell. The selling price for the total inventory under these conditions is estimated to be $3 million.

Proposal 2: Recall all of the products from the market with the explanation that the company is developing a new product that will be better tasting and better nutritionally. None of the original cost will be recovered. Marketing costs will probably be $1 million, but there is the expectation that the company's recall action will create a positive reaction from the market that will result in more sales when the new product goes to market.

> *Required:*
> a. Do any accounting entries need to be made at this time? Or does it depend on the proposal chosen? Explain.
>
> b. Which proposal would you favour? Would you suggest any other alternatives?
>
> c. What type of financial disclosure would you expect your company to make if financial statements were prepared prior to the selection of an alternative for disposing of the inventory?

7-32 **(Decision-making with respect to inventory estimation)**

Slick Surf Boards Company reported sales of $595,000 in the first quarter of 2006. Because the company does not keep a running tally of the cost of inventory sold, the controller does not know how much inventory is actually on hand at the end of the quarter. The company, for the first time, is going to prepare quarterly financial reports to issue to its shareholders, but counting the inventory at the end of each quarter is too costly. Therefore, the controller decides to estimate how much inventory is on hand. By looking at the last annual balance sheet, the controller is able to determine that inventory on hand on January 1, 2006, was $88,200, and he knows that an additional $420,000 of inventory was purchased during the first quarter. The company normally earns a 36% gross profit on sales. Based on this information, and using the cost-to-sales method, the controller arrives at what he thinks is a reasonable estimate of the cost of inventory on hand at the end of the first quarter of 2006.

> **Required:**
> a. What would you estimate as the cost of Slick Surf Board's inventory on hand at the end of the first quarter of 2006? Explain how you arrived at your estimate.
>
> b. If the controller believes that the gross profit on sales is likely to be closer to 34% in 2006, estimate the cost of Slick Surf Board's inventory on hand at the end of the first quarter of 2006. Comment on the sensitivity of your estimate of the inventory on hand to changes in the gross profit on sales percentage.
>
> c. What other factors might reduce the reliability of using this method to estimate inventory?
>
> d. If the gross margin estimation method works reasonably well for interim estimates of inventory on hand, why not use it at year end as well and avoid altogether the cost of an annual inventory count?
>
> e. Based on your original estimate of Slick Surf Board's inventory at the end of the first quarter, what is your assessment of the company's inventory position? Does the amount seem reasonable? Why might inventory levels change from one quarter to the next?

7-33   (Just-in-time inventory; minimal inventory levels)

Suppose that your company has always used LIFO and that prices have been rising over the years. In order to increase efficiency you have recommended that the company change its manufacturing process and adopt a just-in-time process, in which the raw materials are purchased just in time for production and goods are produced just in time for sale. The new system will either eliminate or significantly reduce inventory levels.

> **Required:**
> a. As you reduce inventory levels during the change to the new policy, what effect will this have on your financial statements?
>
> b. What might be the financial tradeoffs that you should consider in changing your manufacturing process to a just-in-time basis?
>
> c. For a company with just-in-time inventory, what is the impact of the choice among a FIFO, LIFO, or weighted average cost flow assumption?

Reading and Interpreting
Published Financial Statements

7-34   (The nature of inventory and inventory valuation)

Finning International Inc.'s 2003 consolidated balance sheets, statements of income and retained earnings, and Note 1(e) on inventory from the summary of significant accounting policies are presented in Exhibit 7-16. Finning International Inc. is a Canadian company that sells, rents, finances, and provides customer support services (supplies parts and performs maintenance services) for Caterpillar equipment and engines. Caterpillar equipment is used in industries such as mining and forestry, and in large infrastructure projects such as the construction of a new terminal at London's Heathrow airport. All amounts are in thousands of dollars.

Financial Statement Analysis Assignments

EXHIBIT 7-16
PART A

FINNING INTERNATIONAL INC. 2003 ANNUAL REPORT

CONSOLIDATED FINANCIAL STATEMENTS

CONSOLIDATED BALANCE SHEETS AS AT DECEMBER 31

(C$ thousands)

	2003	2002
ASSETS		
Current assets		
Cash and short-term investments	$ 66,385	$ 34,626
Accounts receivable	481,397	465,601
Inventories		
On-hand equipment	438,715	402,316
Parts and supplies	270,984	248,093
Other assets	98,379	107,352
Future income taxes (Note 2)	35,133	15,698
Current portion of instalment notes receivable	25,944	13,926
Total current assets	1,416,937	1,287,612
Finance assets		
Instalment notes receivable	7,145	13,410
Equipment leased to customers (Note 3)	97,925	197,115
Total finance assets	105,070	210,525
Rental equipment (Note 4)	1,046,130	897,891
Land, buildings and equipment (Note 5)	287,778	257,200
Future income taxes (Note 2)	39,344	35,863
Goodwill (Note 7)	393,109	379,866
Intangible assets (Note 7)	9,692	2,300
Other assets (Note 11)	130,550	91,290
	$ 3,428,610	$ 3,162,547
LIABILITIES		
Current liabilities		
Short-term debt (Note 9)	$ 104,910	$ 258,140
Accounts payable and accruals	848,888	868,069
Income tax payable	8,884	39,068
Future income taxes (Note 2)	5,711	8,186
Current portion of long-term debt (Note 9)	235,243	42,324
Total current liabilities	1,203,636	1,215,787
Long-term debt (Note 9)	748,181	514,051
Future income taxes (Note 2)	93,212	77,349
Total liabilities	2,045,029	1,807,187
Commitments and Contingencies (Notes 21 and 22)		
NON-CONTROLLING INTERESTS (Note 10)	425,000	425,000
SHAREHOLDERS' EQUITY		
Share capital (Note 12)	248,939	233,450
Retained earnings	775,113	699,741
Cumulative currency translation adjustments (Note 13)	(65,471)	(2,831)
Total shareholders' equity	958,581	930,360
	$ 3,428,610	$ 3,162,547

Approved by the Directors:

D.W.G. Whitehead, Director   C.A. Pinette, Director

FINNING INTERNATIONAL INC. 2003 ANNUAL REPORT

EXHIBIT 7-16
PART B

CONSOLIDATED FINANCIAL STATEMENTS

CONSOLIDATED STATEMENTS OF INCOME AND RETAINED EARNINGS FOR THE YEARS ENDED DECEMBER 31

(C$ thousands except per share amounts)

	2003	2002
Revenue		
New mobile equipment	$ 966,042	$ 825,301
New power & energy systems	262,352	192,036
Used equipment	363,549	329,661
Equipment rental	821,315	744,506
Operating leases	65,925	87,610
Customer support services	1,109,571	1,019,184
Finance and other	4,541	9,188
Total revenue	3,593,295	3,207,486
Cost of sales	2,555,682	2,247,760
Gross profit	1,037,613	959,726
Selling, general and administrative expenses	778,138	687,523
Other expenses (income) (Note 14)	4,307	(5,580)
Earnings before interest, income taxes and non-controlling interests	255,168	277,783
Finance cost and interest on other indebtedness (Notes 9 and 17)	76,868	79,828
Income before provision for income taxes and non-controlling interests	178,300	197,955
Provision for income taxes (Note 2)	26,648	47,730
Non-controlling interests (Note 10)	19,701	17,972
Net income	$ 131,951	$ 132,253
Retained earnings, beginning of year	$ 699,741	$ 590,588
Net income	131,951	132,253
Dividends on common shares	(27,816)	(23,100)
Premium on common share repurchase (Note 12)	(28,763)	–
Retained earnings, end of year	$ 775,113	$ 699,741
Earnings per share (Note 15)		
Basic	$ 1.71	$ 1.72
Diluted	$ 1.68	$ 1.68
Weighted average number of shares outstanding	77,326,253	76,954,609

FINNING INTERNATIONAL INC. 2003 ANNUAL REPORT

EXHIBIT 7-16
PART C

NOTES TO CONSOLIDATED FINANCIAL STATEMENTS

(e) Inventories

Inventories are stated at the lower of cost and net realizable value. Cost is determined on a specific item basis for on-hand equipment. For approximately two-thirds of parts and supplies, cost is determined on a first-in, first-out basis. An average cost basis is used for the remainder.

Required:

Using the information in these statements, answer the following questions.

a. Calculate the inventory turnover ratios for Finning International Inc. for 2003 and 2002, and comment on any changes.

b. The balance sheet breaks down inventories into two categories: on-hand equipment and parts and supplies. While the revenue on the income statement is broken down into many categories, cost of sales on the income statement is shown as one amount. Explain how this impacts the analysis done in part a). What other information would you like to be able to obtain from the income statement? How would this help in your analysis of the company's inventory management?

c. Note 1(e) indicates that Finning uses the specific item basis for on-hand equipment. Explain why this is possible and appropriate.

d. Note 1(e) indicates that Finning uses either first-in, first-out or the average cost basis for the parts and supplies inventory. Why would the specific item basis not be appropriate for this category of inventory? Suggest a reason why the company uses two different methods for the parts and supplies inventory. What might the company be trying to achieve?

7-35 **(Inventory turnover and valuation)**

The 2003 consolidated statement of earnings, Note 3, and an excerpt from Note 1 accompanying the financial statements of **Falconbridge Limited** are presented in Exhibit 7-17. Falconbridge is a Canadian company with operations around the world, which mines, mills, and smelts minerals, primarily nickel and copper. All statement amounts are in thousands of U.S. dollars. Note 3 is in millions of U.S. dollars.

EXHIBIT 7-17
PART A

FALCONBRIDGE LIMITED 2003 ANNUAL REPORT

Consolidated Statements of

IN THOUSANDS OF UNITED STATES DOLLARS
YEARS ENDED DECEMBER 31,

	2003	2002 Note 2
Revenues	$ 2,083,480	$ 1,524,672
Operating expenses		
Costs of sales		
Costs of metal and other product sales	1,414,829	1,103,925
Depreciation of plant and equipment (note 2)	174,758	171,022
Amortization of development and preproduction expenditures (note 2)	69,950	59,316
	1,659,537	1,334,263
Selling, general and administrative	85,968	86,779
Exploration	22,875	21,513
Research and process development	13,042	8,241
Other income (note 16)	(2,916)	(4,209)
	1,778,506	1,446,587
Operating income	304,974	78,085
Interest (notes 2, 11)	42,873	50,586
Earnings before taxes and non-controlling interest	262,101	27,499
Income and mining taxes (note 7)	63,137	(22,464)
Non-controlling interest in earnings (loss) of subsidiaries	4,540	(21)
Earnings for the year	$ 194,424	$ 49,984
Dividends on preferred shares	8,606	7,964
Earnings attributable to common shares	$ 185,818	$ 42,020
Basic earnings per common share (note 10(c))	$ 1.05	$ 0.24
Diluted earnings per common share (note 10(c))	$ 1.04	$ 0.24

See accompanying Notes to Consolidated Financial Statements.

FALCONBRIDGE LIMITED 2003 ANNUAL REPORT

EXHIBIT 7-17
PART B & C

VALUATION OF INVENTORIES

Metals inventories are valued at the lower of cost, determined on a "first-in, first-out" basis, and net realizable value. Supplies inventories are valued at the lower of average cost of acquisition, less appropriate allowances for obsolescence, and replacement cost. Effective January 1, 2003, the Corporation retroactively changed its accounting policy for inventory costing. Under the previous policy, depreciation and amortization of property, plant and equipment was treated as a period cost. Under the new policy depreciation and amortization is treated as a product cost and expensed when the inventory is sold.

3. Inventories

Inventories of $441.7 million (2002 – $330.2 million) includes, in-process – $217.8 million (2002 – $148.5 million); finished metals – $122.6 million (2002 – $99.8 million); supplies – $85.0 million (2002 – $81.9 million); and raw materials – $16.3 million (2002 – nil).

Required:

Using the information in these statements, answer the following questions.

a. Note 3 breaks down Falconbridge's inventory into four categories: raw materials, in-process, supplies, and finished metals are the products mined that are processed and then sold. Only the finished metals are currently in a state ready for sale. Assume the supplies refer to items that Falconbridge will use in its operations, and will not be re-sold. Which categories of inventory do you believe should be used in determining the inventory turnover ratio? Why?

b. In your own words, describe Falconbridge's inventory valuation policies.

c. The excerpt from Note 1 refers to a change in accounting policy for inventory. This change has been incorporated into both the 2002 and 2003 results. Amortization on equipment used to mine and process the minerals is now included as part of the cost of inventory on the balance sheet. Do you believe this is appropriate? Does it follow the matching principle? Explain.

d. Calculate the inventory turnover ratios for 2003 and 2002 and then convert them into days. Explain the amounts you selected from the financial statements to use in your calculation, and why.

7-36 **(Inventory turnover)**

The Forzani Group Ltd. is Canada's largest sporting goods retailer. It operates more than 200 stores across Canada under the names Sport Chek, Sport Mart, and Coast Mountain Sports. The company also franchises stores. Note 2(b) is included in Exhibit 7-18. The company reported the following amounts for inventory and cost of sales in its February 1, 2004, and February 2, 2003, financial statements.

Inventory:
2004 $267,221 thousand
2003 $268,519 thousand

Cost of sales:
2004 $635,059 thousand
2003 $603,326 thousand

Required:

a. Calculate the inventory turnover (by ratio and by days) for The Forzani Group Ltd. for 2004 and 2003, using the inventory value at each year end instead of the average inventory amount. Comment on the results.

b. What do you think is meant by freight and distribution costs in Note 2(b)? Is it appropriate that these costs be included in inventory cost? Explain.

c. If the company purchases a large shipment of sports shoes from a manufacturer and is given a 10% volume discount on the manufacturer's usual selling price, how and when does Forzani record the discount? Explain whether you believe this is appropriate.

EXHIBIT 7-18

FORZANI GROUP LTD. 2003 ANNUAL REPORT

(b) Inventory

Inventory is valued at the lower of laid-down cost and net realizable value. Laid-down cost is determined using the weighted average cost method and includes invoice cost, duties, freight, and distribution costs. Net realizable value is defined as the expected selling price.

Volume rebates and other supplier discounts are included in income when earned. For volume and advertising rebates, "earned" is when the Company receives the related product. For all other rebates and discounts, "earned" is when the related expense is incurred.

7-37 (Inventory cost)

Glamis Gold Ltd. is a Canadian company that explores, develops, and extracts precious metals (primarily gold) in North and Central America. Note 2(d) in Exhibit 7-19 contains the company's accounting policy related to inventory.

EXHIBIT 7-19

GLAMIS GOLD LTD. 2003 ANNUAL REPORT

(d) Inventory:

(i) Finished goods inventory is metals available for sale and is stated at the lower of cost and net realizable value.

(ii) Work-in-progress inventory, which consists of ore on leach pads, is valued at the lower of average production cost and net realizable value. Production costs relate to the cost of placing the ore on the leach pad and include direct mining, crushing, agglomerating and conveying costs, as applicable, for the different mine operations. These costs are charged to operations and included in cost of sales on the basis of ounces of gold recovered. Based upon actual gold recoveries and operating plans, the Company continuously evaluates and refines estimates used in determining the costs charged to operations and the carrying value of costs associated with the ore on the leach pads.

(iii) Supplies and spare parts inventory is stated at the lower of average cost and replacement cost.

Required:

a. Explain in your own words the company's policy for valuing work-in-process inventory and comment on whether you think this is appropriate.

b. The following information was included in the company's 2003 Annual Report.

Mine site	Location	Gold production (oz.)	Avg. cost of production (oz.)
San Martin	Honduras	101,835 oz.	$269 per oz.
Marigold	Nevada	94,796 oz.	$243 per oz.
Rand	California	33,663 oz.	$298 per oz.
Total		230,294 oz.	
Company average			$262 per oz.

All the 230,294 oz. of gold produced in 2003 were sold in 2003 at an average selling price of $368 per oz.

1. Calculate the company's 2003 revenues and 2003 cost of goods sold. Determine the average gross margin percentage.

2. Why do you think it is particularly important for a company in this industry to provide the analysis above? (Hint: what factors influence its revenues? Will all three mines continue to produce at the same levels in the future?)

c. The annual report explains that the average cost of production includes mining, processing costs, and an estimate of costs for "site closure and reclamation accruals."

When the company closes a mine it is required under law to perform an environmental cleanup, which may include revegetation of the area and re-sculpting rock
stockpiles to improve water runoff. Why would these costs be accrued and included
in the cost of inventory production while the mine is still in operation?

7-38 (Inventory turnover)

Magna International Inc. is a Canadian company operating internationally, supplying
technologically advanced automotive components, systems, and modules. Because it is a
manufacturing company, its inventory is composed of raw materials, work in process, and
finished goods. Note 12 Inventories is included in Exhibit 7-20.

The cost of sales was $12,805 million and $10,273 million for 2003 and 2002, respectively.

MAGNA INTERNATIONAL INC. 2003 ANNUAL REPORT

EXHIBIT 7-20

12. INVENTORIES

Inventories consist of:

	2003	2002
Raw materials and supplies	$ 435	$ 306
Work-in-process	146	118
Finished goods	177	138
Tooling and engineering	358	354
	$ 1,116	$ 916

Tooling and engineering inventory represents costs incurred on separately priced tooling and engineering services contracts in excess of billed
and unbilled amounts included in accounts receivable.

Required:

a. The tooling and engineering inventory is created when Magna does work for a
   customer, but the customer has not yet been invoiced by Magna. Why is it appropriate to include these costs as inventory? Explain.

b. Calculate the inventory turnover for Magna in 2003 and 2002 using the following
   directions. Use the inventory value for the given year rather than the average
   inventory.

   1. Cost of sales divided by total inventory

   2. Cost of sales divided by finished goods inventory

   3. Cost of sales divided by finished goods plus tooling and engineering inventory

c. Which of the ratios calculated in part b) do you think is more useful? Why?

7-39 (Impact of inventory on current ratio; gross profit impact of changing sales levels)

Chai-Na-Ta Corp. is the largest producer of ginseng in the world. It grows ginseng on farms
in Canada and then sells its product primarily in Hong Kong and China. Ginseng reaches
maturity and can be harvested in three years, but Chai-Na-Ta sometimes allows the crops
to mature longer to allow for higher yields and additional seed harvests. The balance sheet
and statement of operations for 2003 are presented in Exhibit 7-21.

Required:

a. Calculate the current ratio (CA/CL) for both 2003 and 2002. Comment on the
   impact that inventory has on this ratio in each year.

b. Included with the current assets and long-term assets is an asset called Ginseng
   crops. This account collects all of the cost of growing the ginseng. The portion in
   the current asset section includes the accumulated costs associated with the ginseng that is expected to be sold in the following year. Is it appropriate to classify
   this as an inventory item? Explain.

consolidated
BALANCE SHEETS

(STATED IN CANADIAN DOLLARS)

AS AT DECEMBER 31	2003	2002
ASSETS		
Current assets		
Cash and cash equivalents	$ 505,876	$ 2,757,553
Accounts receivable and other receivables	2,907,439	136,796
Inventory	9,040,873	8,082,946
Ginseng crops (Note 3)	4,915,618	7,577,892
Prepaid expenses and other assets	67,161	85,696
	17,436,967	18,640,883
Ginseng crops (Note 3)	11,732,216	10,922,182
Property, plant and equipment (Note 4)	6,949,577	6,648,832
	$ 36,118,760	$ 36,211,897
LIABILITIES		
Current liabilities		
Bank indebtedness (Note 5)	$ 1,790,000	$ -
Short-term borrowings (Note 6)	-	3,632,145
Accounts payable and accrued liabilities	457,571	771,310
Customer deposits (Note 7)	388,356	1,993,971
Current portion of long-term debt (Note 8)	39,742	126,197
	2,675,669	6,523,623
Long-term debt (Note 8)	86,364	26,256
Future income taxes (Note 12)	2,185,000	1,130,000
	$ 4,947,033	$ 7,679,879
SHAREHOLDERS' EQUITY		
Share capital (Note 10)	38,200,398	38,200,398
Cumulative translation adjustments	17,227	(70,986)
Deficit	(7,045,898)	(9,597,394)
	31,171,727	28,532,018
	$ 36,118,760	$ 36,211,897

Commitments (Note 14)

APPROVED BY THE BOARD

William Zen, *Chairman and Chief Executive Officer*

Steven T.M. Hsieh, *Director*

CHAI-NA-TA CORP. 2003 ANNUAL REPORT

EXHIBIT 7-21
PART B

ANNUAL REPORT 2003

consolidated
STATEMENTS OF OPERATIONS

(STATED IN CANADIAN DOLLARS)

YEARS ENDED DECEMBER 31	2003	2002	2001
Revenue	$ 16,581,614	$ 16,017,375	$ 13,885,635
Cost of goods sold	10,213,121	14,343,472	11,680,559
	6,368,493	1,673,903	2,205,076
Selling, general and administrative expenses	1,651,566	1,696,202	2,883,611
Interest on short-term debt	18,385	8,446	151,854
Write-down of inventory and crop costs (Notes 1(e) and (f))	1,000,000	-	1,573,466
	2,669,951	1,704,648	4,608,931
Operating profit (loss)	3,698,542	(30,745)	(2,403,855)
Other income (loss) (Note 13)	(92,046)	32,823	246,585
Income (loss) before income taxes	3,606,496	2,078	(2,157,270)
Provision for (recovery of) income taxes (Note 12)	1,055,000	(332,000)	-
NET EARNINGS (LOSS)	$ 2,551,496	$ 334,078	$ (2,157,270)
Basic earnings (loss) per share (Note 1(l))	$ 0.17	$ 0.02	$ (0.15)
Weighted average number of shares used to calculate basic earnings (loss) per share	15,113,823	14,264,508	14,264,508
Diluted earnings (loss) per share (Note 1(l))	$ 0.07	$ 0.01	$ (0.15)
Weighted average number of shares used to calculate diluted earnings (loss) per share	34,663,657	34,663,657	14,264,508

c. Calculate the gross profit percentage for 2003, 2002, and 2001. Revenues increased significantly in 2002, and then by a lesser amount in 2003. Have the changes in cost of goods sold mirrored the changes in revenue? What effect has this had on the gross profit?

d. Provide two reasons that may have led to the writedowns of inventory and crop costs that appeared on the 2001 and 2003 statements of operations. Provide the journal entry that would have been recorded in each year. Why is this company particularly susceptible to inventory writedowns?

Beyond the Book

7-40 (Examination of a company's financial statements)

Choose a Canadian company as directed by your instructor and answer the following questions.

a. What kind of inventory does your company carry?

b. Calculate the inventory turnover for each of the last two years, using the inventory of the year instead of the average inventory. Report any difficulties that you had in finding the appropriate numbers to make this calculation.

c. Describe any significant change that occurred in the inventory balance and try to determine what caused it.

d. Calculate a current ratio for each of the last two years. Describe the significance that inventory has on this ratio in each year.

Cases

7-41   Bema Gold Corporation

Case Primer

Bema Gold Corporation is a Canadian company headquartered in Vancouver, British Columbia. It explores and develops gold properties in South America. Rani, a Business Administration student, has recently inherited some money from a grandparent. She intends to create a diversified portfolio of share investments. Although they can be risky, she has heard that investing in gold properties can be quite profitable. Rani is contemplating investing in Bema Gold Corporation. She has the annual report, which includes the financial statements (see Exhibit 7-22). She is concerned because the company has not shown a profit for the last three years, yet issued new common shares in each of the last three years. 196,632,000 shares have been issued between January 1, 2001, and December 31, 2003, and share capital has increased from $258,191,000 (U.S.) to $441,309,000 (U.S.) in that period. If other investors are willing to buy so many new shares, they obviously have confidence in this company.

Required:
a. Knowing that Bema explores and develops gold properties, explain the significance of gold inventory on its balance sheet by calculating a current ratio for each year and explaining the impact that inventory has on this ratio.

b. Review the financial statements and draw up a list of questions you would like to ask an investment advisor about this company.

7-42   Flick's Electronics

Jeff Stevenson was recently hired as a new manager for Flick's Electronics. His compensation is composed of a base salary and a bonus based on gross profit. The bonuses are to be paid monthly as determined by the gross profit for the preceding month.

Flick's Electronics currently uses a periodic inventory system but Jeff would like to see the company move to a perpetual system. The company's owners are willing to consider the change, provided that Jeff prepares a written analysis outlining the two methods and detailing the benefits and costs of switching to the perpetual system.

Required:
Prepare a report that Jeff could present to the owners of Flick's Electronics to support his request to change to a perpetual inventory system.

7-43   Park Avenue Tire Company

Park Avenue Tire Company has been operating in Winnipeg for over 30 years and has a very loyal customer base. The company sells and installs tires and the owners pride themselves on the excellent business relationships they have developed with both their customers and suppliers. The company often sells tires on credit, allowing customers to pay their balances

BEMA GOLD CORPORATION 2003 ANNUAL REPORT

CONSOLIDATED BALANCE SHEETS

as at December 31
(in thousands of United States dollars)

	2003	2002
ASSETS		
Current		
Cash and cash equivalents	$ 30,773	$ 16,658
Accounts receivable	5,754	2,278
Marketable securities *(Note 11)*	3,567	3,272
Inventories *(Note 3)*	14,932	9,519
Other	4,845	892
	59,871	32,619
Investments *(Note 5)*	2,706	12,664
Property, plant and equipment *(Note 6)*	290,822	148,906
Goodwill *(Note 4)*	27,344	–
Unrealized fair value of derivatives *(Notes 2, 10 and 11)*	20,792	–
Deferred losses *(Note 2)*	3,965	–
Other assets *(Note 7)*	14,206	11,787
	$419,706	$205,976
LIABILITIES		
Current		
Accounts payable	$ 23,292	$ 3,979
Current portion of long-term debt *(Note 8)*	45,864	11,167
	69,156	15,146
Unrealized fair value of derivatives *(Notes 2, 10 and 11)*	48,382	–
Long-term debt *(Note 8)*	7,084	18,250
Future income tax liabilities *(Note 13)*	2,098	–
Asset retirement obligations *(Note 2)*	15,380	3,676
Other liabilities	3,465	2,754
Non-controlling interest	830	892
	146,395	40,718
SHAREHOLDERS' EQUITY		
Capital stock *(Note 9)*		
Authorized		
Unlimited number of common shares with no par value		
Issued		
355,688,190 common shares (2002 – 255,997,194)	441,309	317,494
Share purchase warrants and stock options *(Note 4)*	14,814	–
Deficit	(182,812)	(152,236)
	273,311	165,258
	$419,706	$205,976

Commitments *(Notes 6 and 10)*
Subsequent events *(Note 18)*

Approved by the Board

_____ Director   _____ Director

BEMA GOLD CORPORATION 2003 ANNUAL REPORT

CONSOLIDATED STATEMENTS OF OPERATIONS

for the years ended December 31
(in thousands of United States dollars, except shares and per share amounts)

	2003	2002	2001
Gold revenue	$86,817	$36,286	$21,209
Expenses			
Operating costs	69,110	18,519	16,639
Depreciation and depletion	17,909	12,476	5,840
Write-down of inventory	342	–	2,248
Other	2,381	367	269
	89,742	31,362	24,996
Arbitration settlement *(Note 6)*	–	(4,169)	–
	89,742	27,193	24,996
Operating (loss) earnings	(2,925)	9,093	(3,787)
Other expenses (Income)			
General and administrative	7,125	3,821	2,844
Interest on long-term debt	4,298	4,089	1,200
Amortization of deferred financing costs	1,707	2,836	2,231
General exploration	340	284	304
Stock-based compensation	3,147	–	–
Foreign exchange (gains) losses	(1,747)	780	168
Other	524	1,512	1,109
	15,394	13,322	7,856
Loss before taxes and other items	18,319	4,229	11,643
Realized derivative gains	(2,362)	–	–
Unrealized derivative losses	7,481	–	–
Equity in losses of associated companies	94	424	129
Investment losses (gains) *(Note 5)*	45	(1,957)	(554)
Write-off of mineral property *(Note 6)*	720	–	–
Loss before income taxes	24,297	2,696	11,218
Current income tax	5,024	561	–
Future income tax	1,255	–	–
Loss for the year	$30,576	$ 3,257	$11,218
Loss per common share – basic and diluted	$ 0.09	$ 0.02	$ 0.07
Weighted average number of common shares outstanding (in thousands)	323,475	220,384	166,750

BEMA GOLD CORPORATION 2003 ANNUAL REPORT

CONSOLIDATED STATEMENTS OF DEFICIT

for the years ended December 31
(in thousands of United States dollars)

	2003	2002	2001
Deficit, beginning of year, as previously reported	$152,557	$149,145	$137,188
Change in accounting policy *(Note 2)*	(321)	(454)	(334)
Restated balance, beginning of year	152,236	148,691	136,854
Loss for the year	30,576	3,257	11,218
Charges related to convertible debt	–	288	619
Deficit, end of year	$182,812	$152,236	$148,691

within 30 days. Collection of accounts receivable has never been a problem, with most people paying their balances within 60 days.

Park Avenue purchases tires from most of the large national brands and, due to the nature of the business, generally maintains a fairly large inventory. It is essential that the company have the necessary tires on hand to meet customer needs due to increased competition from large retailers such as Canadian Tire and Wal-Mart.

The company has always had sufficient cash to pay its suppliers immediately and take advantage of cash discounts. However, this month, for the first time ever, Park Avenue does not have sufficient cash in the bank to meet its supplier payments. Chris Park, son of the original owner Ernest Park, is currently operating the business and is very concerned about the company's inability to maintain what he feels are adequate levels of cash.

Your firm has been the accountants for Park Avenue Tire Company for the past 20 years. Chris has approached the firm expressing his concerns and asking for advice as to how the cash flow problems can be solved. As part of your analysis, you review the company's financial statements for the past three years. Excerpts from the financial statements are presented below.

	Dec. 31 2006	Dec. 31 2005	Dec. 31 2004
Current assets			
Cash	$ 10,000	$ 35,000	$ 31,500
Accounts receivable	15,000	12,000	9,000
Inventory	169,000	122,000	116,000
Prepaid expenses	6,000	8,000	6,500
Total current assets	$ 200,000	$177,000	$ 163,000
Current liabilities			
Accounts payable	$ 62,000	$ 47,000	$ 33,000
Salaries payable	4,200	5,850	3,775
Income tax payable	1,200	1,150	1,950
Total current liabilities	$ 67,400	$ 54,000	$ 38,725

EXHIBIT 7-22
PART D

BEMA GOLD CORPORATION 2003 ANNUAL REPORT

CONSOLIDATED STATEMENTS OF CASH FLOWS

for the years ended December 31
(in thousands of United States dollars)

	2003	2002	2001
Operating activities			
Loss for the year	$(30,576)	$(3,257)	$(11,218)
Non-cash charges (credits)			
Depreciation and depletion	17,909	12,476	5,905
Amortization of deferred financing costs	1,707	2,836	2,231
Equity in losses of associated companies	94	424	100
Derivative instruments	10,565	942	(1,696)
Investment losses (gains)	45	(1,957)	(554)
Write-off of mineral property	720	–	–
Write-down of inventory	342	–	2,248
Foreign exchange	548	96	(1)
Stock-based compensation	3,147	–	–
Future income tax expense	1,255	–	–
Other	743	1,529	459
Changes in non-cash working capital *(Note 15)*	1,629	(2,760)	2,388
	8,128	10,329	(138)
Financing activities			
Common shares issued, net of issue costs *(Note 9)*	58,714	35,872	4,609
Subsidiary shares issued *(Note 5)*	–	1,540	–
Julietta project loans and overrun facility	–	–	21,200
Julietta project loan repayments	(11,167)	(5,583)	–
Petrex project loan repayments	(8,000)	–	–
Refugio loans repayments	–	(6,000)	(8,000)
Deferred financing costs	–	–	(1,840)
Other	(450)	(1,345)	(303)
	39,097	24,484	15,666
Investing activities			
Petrex Mines	(7,593)	–	–
Julietta Mine	(3,813)	(2,519)	–
Refugio exploration and development	(2,981)	(446)	(111)
Julietta development and construction	–	(2,435)	(20,064)
Kupol exploration and development	(35,920)	(8,684)	–
Acquisition, exploration and development	(6,275)	(2,145)	(1,082)
Arbitration settlement *(Note 6)*	–	5,512	–
Acquisition of EAGC, net cash acquired *(Note 4)*	6,742	–	–
Sale/ (purchase) of EAGC special warrants *(Note 4)*	16,935	(10,000)	–
Proceeds from the sale of notes receivable	–	–	3,300
Other	(977)	(1,475)	3,336
	(33,882)	(22,192)	(14,621)
Effect of exchange rate changes on cash and cash equivalents	772	(96)	1
Increase in cash and cash equivalents	14,115	12,525	908
Cash and cash equivalents, beginning of year	16,658	4,133	3,225
Cash and cash equivalents, end of year	$30,773	$16,658	$4,133

Supplementary cash flow information *(Note 15)*

During 2006, credit sales and cost of goods sold were $160,000 and $97,000, respectively. The 2005 and 2004 credit sales were $175,000 and $177,000 and cost of goods sold for the same periods were $93,000 and $95,000. The accounts receivable and inventory balances at the end of 2003 were $8,000 and $99,000, respectively.

Required:
Provide a report to Chris Park detailing options that he can take to alleviate the company's cash problems. Remember that you are to present options, not recommendations. As a basis for the report, you should calculate and comment on the following ratios.

1. Current ratio

2. Quick ratio

3. Receivables turnover ratio and Average collection period

4. Inventory turnover ratio and Days in inventory

7-44 North End Television Services

North End Television Services sells and services a variety of high-end home entertainment products. An inventory count is prepared at each year end to verify the information contained in the company's periodic inventory system. Once counted, the inventory is valued for purposes of preparing the financial statements. The following inventory items represent a cross-section of North End's inventory for the year ended June 30, 2006. Because computerized records are maintained and a specific identification method of inventory is applied, the historical cost of each inventory item can be easily determined.

In addition to the historical cost, the store management has also included information detailing net realizable value for each item.

Item	Quantity on hand June 30, 2006	Historical cost (per unit)	Net realizable value (per unit)
Sony DVD Player	4	$400	$325
RCA High Definition 52-inch Television	2	$2,100	$1,999
Sony High 8 Camcorder	3	$600	$200
JVC Surround Sound System	6	$700	$900
Nikon Digital Camera	4	$600	$750

Tim Cappelino, the manager of North End, is confused as to why there is a difference between historical cost and net realizable value. Tim is not an accountant and is unfamiliar with these terms. He is also wondering which number should be used to value the company's inventory at June 30, 2006.

Required:
For the purposes of this case, assume that the above items represent the total inventory of North End Television Services at June 30, 2006.

a. Define for Tim the meaning of historical cost and net realizable value in the context of inventory valuation.

b. Based on Canadian practice, determine for Tim the value of North End's ending inventory at June 30, 2006.

7-45 **(Cost flow assumptions)**

Jim Wong has been a public accountant for the past 20 years and is now a partner in a prominent accounting firm based in Truro, Nova Scotia. Recently, he was approached by the local chamber of commerce to be a guest speaker at its monthly meeting. Since many members of the chamber are small to mid-sized retailers, Jim decided to prepare a talk on determining inventory values and cost flow assumptions.

It is now Friday afternoon and Jim has just returned to his office following the presentation to the chamber. He is surprised to see messages from two clients who were at the meeting. The first message is from Bryan Cartel, who owns and operates the local Ford dealership. In addition to selling cars, the dealership also has a large service department and maintains an extensive inventory of parts and accessories.

The second caller is Jenny Mead, who manages her family's grocery store. Jim returns the calls and discovers that both business people want further advice as to the best cost flow assumption they should be using in their respective inventory systems.

In particular, Jenny would like to know why her family is using the weighted average approach instead of LIFO. From Jim's chamber presentation, she learned that LIFO results in lower net income in times of rising prices, and since lower net income means less taxes, she is wondering why Jim has not previously recommended switching to LIFO.

Required:

a. Determine which inventory cost flow assumption would best suit the needs of each client. Be prepared to support your recommendation.

b. Writing as Jim, draft a response to Jenny regarding her concerns about the use of LIFO in her business. Do you think that the business should change to this method? Why or why not?

7-46 **Armstrong Hardware**

Armstrong Hardware lost most of its inventory in an electrical fire that destroyed the company's warehouse and retail store. Fortunately, the accounting records were backed up on the owner's computer in her home office and could therefore be recovered.

However, Armstrong uses a periodic inventory system, so without being able to perform a physical count, the company could not determine the amount of inventory lost in the fire. In order to process the insurance claim, the insurance company requires Armstrong to prepare a reasonable estimate of the lost inventory.

As Armstrong's accountant, you have been able to gather the following information.

1. Ending inventory, from the accounting records of last year, was $85,800.

2. In the current year, purchases up to the time of the fire totalled $486,500.

3. According to last year's financial statements, sales and the cost of goods sold were $964,000 and $578,400, respectively.

4. According to this year's accounting records, sales in the current year were $678,000.

Required:

a. Prepare an estimate of the amount of inventory lost in the fire. To ensure the reasonableness of the amount claimed, write a brief memo to the insurance company outlining your approach for determining the amount of inventory destroyed. You should also specify any assumptions used in preparing your estimate.

b. How would this process have differed if Armstrong had used a perpetual instead of a periodic inventory system?

Critical Thinking Questions

7-47 **(Inventory decision-making with respect to buying and selling)**
You and two of your friends have decided to apply some of the knowledge that you are learning in your business classes. You plan to start a wholesale business, buying goods in the Czech Republic and selling them to small specialty stores. One of your friends has an uncle in the Czech Republic who has some contacts that will enable you to buy the merchandise you want. Another friend has an aunt who owns a trucking company that transports merchandise all over Europe. You hope to use the trucking company to transport your merchandise from the Czech Republic to Rotterdam for shipment to Canada.

You are going to have a meeting to discuss the necessary details surrounding the buying and selling of the inventory. In preparation for the meeting, write a short report outlining the items that you think should be discussed. To make this more realistic and to make your task easier, decide on what types of inventory you are going to buy. The type of inventory you import will affect some of the decisions you need to make.

7-48 **(Impact of various definitions of Market value under LCM)**
The management of Handy Hardware has collected the following information related to the lower of cost and market (LCM) valuation of a particular item of inventory at the end of 2006.

400 units on hand
Acquisition cost, $100 per unit
Replacement cost, $80 per unit
Expected selling price, $170 per unit
Expected selling expense, $37 per unit
Normal profit margin, 40% of the selling price

Required:
a. Determine the amount of the inventory writedown (if any) that would be recorded in 2006, using each of the following definitions of market value.

1. Replacement cost

2. Net realizable value

3. Net realizable value less a normal profit margin

b. Assume that all these units are sold in the next accounting period, at the expected selling price and expected selling expense. Determine the amount of profit that would be recognized in 2007, after taking into consideration the writedown in part a), under each of the three definitions of market value.

c. In your opinion, which of these definitions of market value resulted in the best financial reporting outcome, in terms of the profit or loss that was reported in 2006 and 2007? Explain.

How Do You Amortize a Hippopotamus?

When developing accounting policies and procedures for recording its capital assets, the Calgary Zoological Society considers three things: generally accepted accounting principles (GAAP), ongoing and possibly transferable benefit or value, and a way to match the capital asset's useful life with the length of time it provides a tangible benefit, says Warren Perzel, Manager of Financial Services.

Although the Calgary Zoo's animals would appear to be very tangible assets with ongoing benefits in terms of generating future income, it is difficult to develop depreciation schedules according to GAAP for everything from a polar bear to a hippopotamus, explains Mr. Perzel. Instead, the Zoo expenses the acquisition costs of obtaining a new animal and records any animal sales as revenues.

The Zoo funds the development of assets such as buildings and animal exhibits through its operations or fundraising; however, once they are complete, it transfers the title of these assets to the City of Calgary, since the City owns the land. "This creates an even greater accounting complexity in that we now have both a tangible and intangible asset at our disposal," Mr. Perzel points out. It is tangible because it has value and a measurable cost; it will have future benefit and will deteriorate over time, thus requiring a depreciation schedule; and it is carried on the balance sheet as an asset. However, it is also intangible in some respects, since the Zoo can't mortgage it, sell it, or take the asset with it if it moved.

A good example of such an asset is the Destination Africa exhibit, which opened in 2003. The construction costs of the complex, which includes a large open area where giraffes, monkeys, and other African species can roam freely, were in excess of $33 million, with funding from three levels of government, numerous private donations, and Society operating surpluses. Although the Zoo manages the complex, pays for all the utility and maintenance costs, and expects to offset those expenses with visitor revenues, the City actually owns the title to the asset. "You

Discover Life on Earth

could say we have beneficial ownership, but not legal ownership," Mr. Perzel says.

Examples of other capital expenditures planned for the future are the restoration of 25- to 40-year-old buildings, such as the Australasia/Nocturnal building, the Conservatory (containing exotic plants and birds), and the Tropical Asia building. The Zoo is replacing its Northern Forest Lodge, which is used primarily by its education department, with a themed log structure. It is also conducting a long-range feasibility study for an Arctic Shores exhibit, featuring both land and aquatic animal displays. Mr. Perzel expects these projects to cost more than $75 million, the accounting for which will be handled in the same way as Destination Africa.

"In the accounting profession, you cannot simply say 'An asset is an asset is an asset,'" Mr. Perzel says. "Things we do not own are on our balance sheet, and things we do own are not there."

Capital Assets– Tangible and Intangible

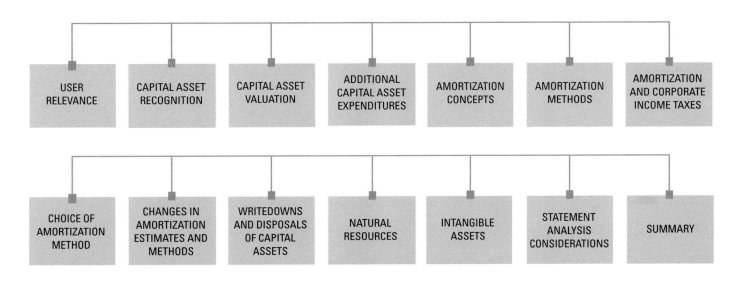

After studying this chapter, you should be able to:

1. Describe the valuation methods used for capital assets.

2. Identify the acquisition costs that are usually added to capital asset accounts at acquisition.

3. Describe the purpose of amortization and implement the most common methods of amortization, including capital cost allowance.

4. Identify the factors that influence the choice of amortization method.

5. Describe and implement changes in amortization estimates and methods.

6. Account for the disposal and writedown of capital assets.

7. Describe and implement the amortization method used most frequently for natural resources.

8. Explain the accounting difficulties associated with intangible assets.

9. Amortize intangible assets, where appropriate.

10. Calculate the return on assets ratio and discuss the potential implications of the results.

Our opening story describes some difficulties associated with recording and reporting capital assets at the Calgary Zoological Society. The Zoo faces some unique problems because of the nature of the assets it has and its relationship with the City of Calgary. The Calgary Zoological Society is a not-for-profit entity, similar to the Wellness Institute at Winnipeg's Seven Oaks General Hospital, described at the beginning of Chapter 5. Because it is a not-for-profit entity, it has some unique ways of accounting for things. Let's look at some of the capital asset issues that it faces.

First, although the Calgary Zoological Society raises funds for capital expenditures such as buildings and exhibits, the actual assets become the property of the City of Calgary as soon as they are complete. This type of arrangement is not uncommon for a public organization like a zoo. Because the assets are transferred to the city, you would expect to find them on the City of Calgary's financial statements. Prior to December 2000, that is where they were. Now, however, you will find them on the Zoo's balance sheet. Although the City of Calgary has legal title, the Zoo manages, maintains, and repairs them and has, therefore, decided to include them on its financial statements—even though it doesn't own them. (This is an example of the application of the concept of "substance over form," which says that an item's economic substance should take precedence over its legal form.)

The Zoo's animals represent a whole different problem. Should we record them as assets, and amortize them over their lives? You know from your accounting studies so far that we do not record employees as assets in the accounting system although they, like the animals, may be essential to the organization's operations. A complicating factor is that there are some animals that the Zoo actually buys, but there are many other animals that the Zoo receives by trading with other zoos or that are born in the Calgary Zoo. How would we value those animals? This is a problem that accountants have not solved yet. Until they do, zoos like Calgary's will continue to expense the cost of animals when they are purchased, instead of recording them in the accounting system as capital assets.

This chapter will discuss the measurement, recording, and reporting issues related to capital assets. In the previous two chapters, current assets whose value would be realized within one year (or operating cycle) were studied. In this chapter, assets with lives longer than a year (or operating cycle) are discussed. We are going to focus on **capital assets**, those which management intends to use in the company's operations to generate revenue. Long-term investments that also have lives longer than a year are discussed briefly in Appendix B at the end of the text. You will study these assets if you take courses in intermediate financial accounting.

Of the capital assets that we are going to study, property, plant, and equipment are the most recognizable. These are a type of noncurrent asset called **tangible assets**, which are usually defined as those assets with some physical form (tangible comes from the Latin word meaning to touch). In other words, you can usually see them and touch them. **Intangible assets**, on the other hand, are noncurrent assets that are associated with certain legal rights or privileges of the company, such as patents, trademarks, leases, and goodwill.

In the sections that follow, the recognition and valuation issues for capital assets are discussed, much as they were for current assets. Because of the long-term nature of these assets, the issue of how, over time, to show the income statement effects (expensing of the cost) of these assets must be addressed. The expense that is recorded is referred to as **amortization** or **depreciation**.

USER RELEVANCE

Capital assets provide the underlying infrastructure of many companies. They include the real estate, buildings, equipment, vehicles, computers, patents, etc., that companies need to carry out their day-to-day operations. They often require a substantial outlay of funds to acquire, which means that companies will often secure long-term mortgages or other forms of debt to finance them. Another common way to acquire long-lived assets is to lease them. You may find some assets on a balance sheet labelled as assets under capital leases.

Because of their importance to the operations of the business, their high cost, and their long lives, it is essential that users understand the role capital assets play in a company's success. Users need to monitor the assets' lives so that they can anticipate the future outflows of cash to replace them. They need to know what methods a company is using to amortize its assets, and what impact those methods have on the income statement. They need to understand that the value that is being carried on the balance sheet for capital assets represents a future benefit that the company expects to earn from using the assets. If the company did not expect to earn that much, it would be required to reduce (or "write down") the assets' carrying value. In most instances, companies expect to earn amounts that are significantly in excess of the carrying value of their capital assets.

This chapter will provide you, the user, with the background information about capital assets that will help you better understand the impact of these assets on financial statements.

CAPITAL ASSET RECOGNITION

Assets must have probable future value for the company. The company must have the right to use them and must have acquired that right through a past transaction. When a company buys a capital asset, it has the right to use it, and the transaction has occurred. Therefore, the only asset criterion that merits further discussion is the probable future value, which takes at least two forms. Capital assets are used, first and foremost, to generate revenues, usually by facilitating sales, producing products, or providing services. Therefore, the future value is represented by the cash that will eventually be received from the sales of products and services in the future. This type of value is sometimes referred to as **value in use**. Because of the long-term nature of capital assets, these cash flows will be received over several future periods.

The second source of value for capital assets is their ultimate disposal value. Many capital assets are used until the company decides to replace them with a new asset. For example, a business may use a truck for three or four years and then trade it in for a new one. This type of value is called **residual value** (or **resale value**) and can be very important, depending on the type of asset.

Value in use is normally the most appropriate concept for capital assets because companies usually invest in them to use them, not to sell them. Residual value cannot, however, be totally ignored because it affects the asset's value at the end of the time during which the company uses it. In Chapter 2, you saw how we use residual value to determine the amount of amortization that should be recorded.

The difficulty with the *value in use* concept for capital assets is the inherent uncertainty with regard to future revenue (and, ultimately, income) that will be generated by the use of the asset. The company does not know to what extent the demand for its products or services will continue into the future. It also does not know what prices it will be able to command for its products or services. Other uncertainties relate to technology. Equipment can become obsolete as a result of technological change. New technology can give competitors a significant advantage in producing and pricing products. Technological change can also reduce or eliminate the need for the company's product. Consider the manufacturer of cassette tapes when CDs came on the market, or the typewriter manufacturer with the advent of the personal computer.

The problem of uncertainty regarding the ultimate residual value is similar to that of the value in use, because the ultimate residual value depends on whether the asset has any value in use to the ultimate buyer. There may also be a question of whether a buyer can even be found. Equipment that is made to the original buyer's specifications may not have much of a residual market, because it may not meet the needs of other potential users.

HOW ARE CAPITAL ASSETS VALUED?

LEARNING OBJECTIVE 1

Describe the valuation methods used for capital assets.

In the sections that follow, the discussion is limited to valuation issues regarding property, plant, and equipment, which are similar to those relating to other noncurrent capital assets. At the end of the chapter, specific concerns and issues with regard to natural resources and intangible assets are discussed.

In Canada, property, plant, and equipment are usually valued at historical cost, with no recognition of any other value unless the asset's value becomes "impaired" (i.e., the value of the estimated future cash flows is less than the current carrying value). Some countries allow the recognition of changes in the market values of property, plant, and equipment, and there have been instances of companies disclosing supplementary information about the market values of these assets. Before Canadian practice is discussed in detail, several possible valuation methods will be considered.

Historical Cost

In a historical cost value system, the asset's original cost is recorded at the time of acquisition. Changes in the asset's market value are ignored in this system. During the period in which the asset is used, its cost is expensed (amortized) using an appropriate amortization method (discussed later). Market values are recognized only when the asset is sold. The company then recognizes a gain or loss on the sale, which is determined by the difference between the proceeds from the sale and the net book value (**carrying value**) of the asset at the time of sale. The net book value or carrying value is the original cost less the portion that has been charged to expense, in the form of amortization. This net **book value** is sometimes called the asset's **amortized cost** of the asset.

Market Value

Another possible valuation method records capital assets at their market value. There are at least two types of market value: replacement cost and net realizable value.

Replacement Cost

In this version of a market valuation system, the asset is carried at its replacement cost. By **replacement cost**, accountants mean the amount that would be needed to acquire an equivalent asset. At acquisition, the historical cost is recorded because this is the replacement cost at the time of purchase. As the asset is used, its carrying value is adjusted upward or downward to reflect changes in the replacement cost. Unrealized gains and losses are recognized for these changes. The periodic expensing of the asset, in the form of amortization, has to be adjusted to reflect the changes in the replacement cost. For example, if the asset's replacement cost goes up, the amortization expense will also have to go up, to reflect the higher replacement cost. A realized gain or loss is recognized upon disposal of the asset. The amount of the gain or loss is determined by the difference between the proceeds from the sale and the amortized replacement cost at the time of sale.

The Accounting Standards Board at one time recommended that companies report supplementary information on the replacement cost of their property, plant, and equipment. At that time, inflation in Canada exceeded 10% and users were expressing concern over the historical cost carrying values of capital assets. However, the level of inflation declined and users' interest in replacement cost declined along with it. The Accounting Standards Board subsequently removed the recommendation from the *CICA Handbook*. In countries experiencing extreme rates of inflation, capital assets may be recorded at their replacement values to provide a better measure of the results for the period. For example, in Mexico, replacement cost valuation of property, plant, and equipment is required for companies whose shares trade on stock exchanges.

Net Realizable Value

With a **net realizable value** system, assets are recorded at the amount that could be received by converting them to cash in the normal course of business; in other words, selling them. During the periods in which assets are being used, gains and losses are recognized as the net realizable value changes over time. Amortization in this type of system is based on the net realizable value and is adjusted every year for the change in this value. At the time of sale, there should be no further recognition of gain or loss, as the asset should be carried at its resale value at that date. This system is not consistent with the notion of value in use, which assumes that the company has no intention of selling the asset. Therefore, this method is generally not used in Canada, even in times of high inflation.

The word "market" must be used with some care. The preceding discussions assume that both the replacement market and the selling market are the markets in which the company normally trades. There are, however, special markets if a company must liquidate its assets quickly. The values in these markets can be significantly different from those in normal markets. As long as the company is a going concern, these specialty markets are not appropriate for establishing values for its assets. On the other hand, if the company is bankrupt or going out of business, these specialty markets may be the most appropriate places to obtain estimates of market values of its assets.

AN INTERNATIONAL PERSPECTIVE

Reports from Other Countries

While most countries value property, plant, and equipment at historical cost, a few (such as France, Holland, Switzerland, and the United Kingdom,) allow for revalutations of these assets based on current replacement costs.

In France, these revaluations are seldom made, because they would be taxable. In the United Kingdom, on the other hand, such revaluations are quite common. The increase in the value of the assets that occurs under the replacement cost valuation is not usually considered part of net income, but is recorded directly in the shareholder's equity section of the balance sheet, in an account called a *revaluation reserve*.

What Is Canadian Practice?

Capital assets are normally valued at their historical cost (their original acquisition cost). During the period of use, the asset's cost is expensed using an amortization method that is rational, systematic, and appropriate to the asset. Changes in market values of assets are generally not recognized. If it is ever determined that an asset's net recoverable amount is less than its net carrying value, the difference is recognized as an impairment loss and the asset's carrying value must be written down. The **net recoverable amount** is the total of all future cash flows, without discounting them to present values. Unlike temporary investments and inventory, once a capital asset has been written down, it is not written back up if the net recoverable amount subsequently increases.

ethics in accounting

Ethics in Accounting

The ability to control the timing of a writedown of property, plant, and equipment provides management with an opportunity to manage or manipulate earnings. The issue of **earnings management** has been studied by many researchers, in an attempt to demonstrate its existence and to estimate its effects. In one study, Bruns and Merchant[1] surveyed 649 managers using a questionnaire that described 13 earnings-management situations and asked respondents to describe each as ethical, questionable, or unethical. To quote the authors directly:

> We found striking disagreements among managers in all groups. Furthermore, the liberal definitions revealed in many responses of what is moral or ethical should raise profound questions about the quality of financial information that is used for decision-making purposes by parties both inside and outside a company. It seems many managers are convinced that if a practice is not explicitly prohibited or is only a slight deviation from the rules, it is an ethical practice regardless of who might be affected either by the practice or the information that flows from it. This means that anyone who uses information on short-term earnings is vulnerable to misinterpretation, manipulation, or deliberate deception.

The write-off of property, plant, and equipment is but one way that management may attempt to manipulate earnings. The reader of financial statements must be aware of this possibility.

Capitalizable Costs

At the date of acquisition, the company must decide which costs associated with the purchase of the asset should be included as a part of the asset's cost, or *capitalized*. The general guideline is that any cost that is necessary to acquire the asset and get it ready for use is a **capitalizable cost**. The following is a partial list of costs that would be considered capitalizable costs.

LEARNING OBJECTIVE 2

Identify the acquisition costs that are usually added to capital asset accounts at acquisition.

CAPITALIZABLE COSTS

Purchase price (less any discounts)
Direct taxes
Interest cost (on self-constructed assets)
Legal costs
Transportation costs
Installation costs

The determination of which costs appropriately belong in an asset account is not always easy. For example, the cost associated with the salaries of the employees who plan for and order the new asset are normally not included in the acquisition cost itself. This is true even though the time spent by these employees is necessary to acquire the asset. On the other hand, if employees' time is required to install a new piece of equipment, these employees' wages usually are included. The costs associated with clearing land in preparation for constructing a new building are usually added to the land account. The cost of digging the hole for the building foundation, on the other hand, is usually added to the building account.

Land is a unique capital asset. Even after it has been used by a company for several years, it will still be there. Therefore, unlike other capital assets, its original

---

[1] Bruns, W.J., and Merchant, K.A., "The Dangerous Morality of Managing Earnings," *Management Accounting*, August 1990, pp. 22–25.

cost is not amortized. Consequently, assigning costs to land means that those costs will not appear on the income statement in the future, as amortization expense.

Deciding which costs to capitalize is also influenced by the rules used for tax purposes. For tax purposes, the company would like to expense as many costs as possible, in order to reduce taxable income and save on taxes. Capitalizing a cost, on the other hand, means that the company will have to wait until the asset is amortized before its cost can be deducted for tax purposes. There is, therefore, an incentive to expense rather than to capitalize costs that are only indirectly related to the assets' acquisition, and a company may decide to expense a cost for financial reporting purposes to bolster its argument that the cost is an expense for tax purposes.

The materiality criterion also plays a part in which costs are capitalized. Small expenditures related to the purchase of an asset may be expensed rather than capitalized, because it is easier to expense them, and adding the amount to the asset account would not change it significantly.

Basket Purchases

Sometimes a company acquires several assets in one transaction. This is called a **basket purchase**. For example, when a forest products company acquires timberland, it is buying both land and timber; so the price paid for the timberland must be divided between the land and the timber. In Canada, the price paid for these two assets must be divided between them on the basis of their relative fair values at the time of acquisitions, for three reasons. First, full disclosure requires that each important type of asset should be shown separately. Second, assets that have different rates of amortization should be separated in the accounts. Third, some assets, such as land, are not amortized at all. Suppose that the timberland's purchase price was $1 million and the relative fair values of the land and timber were assessed at $300,000 and $900,000 respectively. In this case, 25% [$300,000 ÷ ($300,000 + $900,000)] of the cost, or $250,000, should be assigned to the land and the remaining 75%, or $750,000, should be assigned to the timber. In the case of timberland, splitting the cost has significant implications for the company because the cost of land will not be amortized but the cost of timber will be expensed as the timber is harvested.

Another example of a basket purchase could be the purchase of a building. Part of the real estate cost must be allocated to the land on which the building is sitting and the remainder to the building. If the building includes various pieces of equipment or furniture, part of the purchase cost will have to be allocated to these items as well. Management's bias in favour of high profits would lead them to allocate more of the cost to the land and less to the building. However, their conflicting interest in paying less tax would lead them to allocate more of the cost to the building.

Interest Capitalization

The issue of **interest capitalization** deserves special consideration. Companies often borrow money to finance a capital asset. The interest paid on the borrowed money is sometimes capitalized, by including it in the capital asset account rather than expensing it. This is an issue for companies that construct some of their own capital assets. For example, some utility companies construct their own plant and equipment assets. In addition to the costs incurred in the assets' actual construction, such as raw materials, labour, and overhead, the company may also incur interest costs if it has to borrow money to pay for the materials, labour, and overhead. In Canada, companies can capitalize interest costs for capital assets that are constructed or acquired over time, if the costs are directly attributable to the acquisition. The interest costs can only be capitalized until the capital asset is substantially complete and ready for use. For assets that are purchased rather than constructed, interest costs are usually not capitalized. The time between acquisition and use is usually too short to make interest capitalization meaningful.

AN INTERNATIONAL PERSPECTIVE

Reports from Other Countries

NAFTA Facts

United States   The accounting for property, plant, and equipment is essentially the same as in Canada.

Mexico   Property, plant, and equipment are initially recorded at acquisition costs and then restated to current values at balance sheet dates, using either price indices or replacement costs.

AMORTIZATION CONCEPTS

Amortization or depreciation is a systematic and rational method of allocating the cost of capital assets to the periods in which the benefits from the assets are received. This matches, in a systematic way, the asset's expense to the revenues earned from its use, and therefore satisfies the matching principle described in Chapter 4.

> **LEARNING OBJECTIVE 3**
>
> *Describe the purpose of amortization and implement the most common methods of amortization, including capital cost allowance.*

Ammortization Tutorial

The allocation of any cost across multiple periods will always be somewhat arbitrary. In Canada, the amortization method used must be a rational and systematic method appropriate to the nature of the capital asset with a limited life and to its use by the enterprise. In addition, the method of amortization and estimates of the useful life should be reviewed on a regular basis.

Amortization, as used in accounting, does not refer to valuation. Rather, it is a process of cost allocation. While it is true that a company's capital assets generally decrease in value over time, amortization does not attempt to measure this change in value each period.

Matching some portion of a capital asset's cost to the company's revenues, along with its other expenses, results in a net profit or loss during the period. The company does not show the capital asset's entire cost as an expense in the period of acquisition, because the asset is expected to help generate revenues over multiple future periods.

To allocate the expense systematically to the appropriate number of periods, the company must estimate the asset's useful life; that is, the periods over which the company will use the asset to generate revenues. The company must also estimate the asset's ultimate residual value at the end of its useful life.

Once the asset's useful life and residual value have been estimated, the amortizable cost (cost minus the residual value) must then be allocated in a systematic and rational way to the years of useful life. Even though in Canada we do not specify which amortization methods may be used, most Canadian companies use one of the methods that are discussed in the next section.

AMORTIZATION METHODS

As GAAP developed in the twentieth century, rational and systematic methods of amortizing capital assets were created. The simplest and most commonly used method (used by more than 50% of Canadian companies) is the straight-line method (illustrated in Chapter 2), which allocates the asset's amortizable cost evenly over its useful life. Many accountants have argued in favour of this method for two reasons. First, it is a very simple method to apply. Second, they argue that it properly matches expenses to revenues for assets that generate revenues evenly throughout their lives. It might also be argued that, if an asset physically deteriorates evenly throughout its life, then straight-line amortization would capture this physical decline.

A second type of amortization recognizes that the usefulness or benefits derived from some capital assets can be measured fairly specifically. These methods are called production or units-of-activity methods. Their use requires that the output or usefulness that will be derived from the asset be measurable as a specific quantity. For example, a new truck might be expected to be used for a specific number of kilometres. If so, the amortization cost per kilometre can be calculated and used to determine each period's amortization expense, based on the number of kilometres driven in the accounting period.

For certain assets, decline in revenue-generating capabilities (and physical deterioration) do not occur evenly over time. In fact, many assets are of most benefit to the company during the early years of their useful lives. In later years, when an asset is wearing out and requires more maintenance and perhaps produces inferior products, the value to the company declines significantly. This scenario argues for a more rapid amortization in the early years of the asset's life when a larger amortization expense is matched to the larger revenues produced. Methods that match this pattern are known as accelerated or declining-balance amortization methods.

A fourth, but rarely used, amortization method argues that, for some assets, the greatest change in usefulness and/or physical deterioration takes place in the last years of the asset's life, rather than in the first few years. A method that captures this pattern is called decelerated amortization. Although this type of amortization method is not used much in practice, it is conceptually consistent with a present-value method of asset valuation. Present-value amortization methods, sometimes also called compound interest methods, are of this type.

Exhibit 8-1 illustrates the pattern of decline in an asset's carrying value under three basic methods: straight-line, accelerated, and decelerated (these methods are discussed in detail later). Exhibit 8-2 illustrates the pattern of amortization expense recognition with the same methods. The graphs are based on a 40-year useful life, a zero residual value, and a $10,000 original cost. Note that Exhibits 8-1 and 8-2 do not show production methods because there is usually no consistent or predictable pattern with those methods. The amount of amortization expense depends on the actual usage each year.

In Exhibit 8-1, note that using the straight-line method produces an even (or straight-line) decline in the asset's carrying value. The accelerated method produces a more rapid decline in the carrying value during the early years of the asset's life, and the decelerated method shows a less rapid decline (until later in the asset's life). Note that all methods start and end at the same value.

ASSET CARRYING VALUE

EXHIBIT 8-1

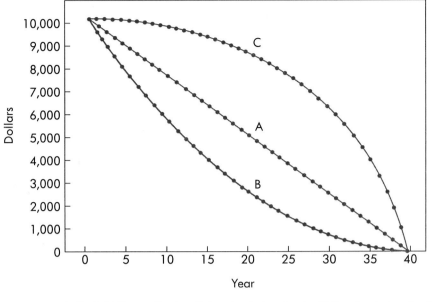

A Straight-Line method   B Accelerated method   C Decelerated method

ANNUAL AMORTIZATION EXPENSE

EXHIBIT 8-2

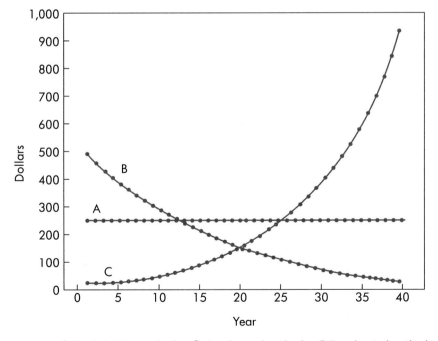

A Straight-Line method   B Accelerated method   C Decelerated method

In Exhibit 8-2, you can see with the straight-line method that the amortization expense for each period is the same. With the accelerated method, the amortization expenses are higher in the earlier years of the asset's life, corresponding to the more rapid decline in carrying value as seen in Exhibit 8-1. The decelerated method, on the other hand, shows a slower decline in the asset's carrying value and hence small amounts of amortization expense in the earlier years compared with the later years. Although the pattern of recognition is different, the total amount of the expense taken over the asset's life will be the same for all methods.

Straight-Line Method

The most common method used for financial reporting is the **straight-line method**. It assumes that the asset's cost should be allocated evenly over its life. Estimates must be made of the useful life and residual value. To illustrate the straight-line calculation and the calculation of amortization using other methods, the following simple example is used. A company buys an asset for $10,000; the asset has an estimated useful life of five years and an estimated residual value of $1,000. Straight-line amortization would be calculated as shown in Exhibit 8-3.

EXHIBIT 8-3   **STRAIGHT-LINE METHOD**

Original Cost	$10,000
Estimated Residual Value	$ 1,000
Estimated Useful Life	5 years

$$\text{Straight-Line Amortization Expense} = \frac{\text{Original Cost} - \text{Estimated Residual Value}}{\text{Estimated Useful Life}}$$

$$= \frac{\$10,000 - \$1,000}{5 \text{ years}}$$

$$= \$1,800 \text{ per year}$$

Amortization Schedule:

Year	Beginning Book Value	Amortization Expense	Ending Book Value
1	$10,000	$1,800	$8,200
2	8,200	1,800	6,400
3	6,400	1,800	4,600
4	4,600	1,800	2,800
5	2,800	1,800	1,000
		$9,000	

$1,800 of amortization expense is recorded each year for five years, so that by the end of the asset's useful life, the entire amortizable cost ($9,000 = $10,000 − 1,000) will have been expensed and the residual value of $1,000 will remain on the company's books.

Even though the straight-line method can be described by the estimated useful life and estimated residual value, it is sometimes characterized by a rate of amortization. The **rate of amortization** with the straight-line method is determined by taking the inverse of the number of years, 1/N, where N is the number of years of estimated useful life. In the case of the asset in the example, amortizing it over five years means a rate of 1/5, or 20% per year. This will be referred to as the **straight-line rate**. Note that 20% of the amortizable cost, $9,000, is $1,800 per year.

Production Methods

Another method used to calculate amortization is based on the assumption that benefits derived from a capital asset are related to the output or use of that asset. Note that the straight-line and accelerated methods of amortization assume that benefits derived from capital assets are related to time, disregarding how much the assets are actually used during the period. **Production** or **units-of-activity methods** relate benefits to actual usage, which means that they best satisfy the matching principle.

The use of production methods requires that the assets' useful lives are known or can be estimated and expressed as units of output or activity. For example, trucks can be amortized using a production method if their expected useful lives can be expressed in kilometres driven or hours used. Machinery used in manufacturing products may have an expected useful life based on the total number of units of output. Amortization expense is determined by calculating the amortization cost per unit, then multiplying this cost per unit by the actual number of units produced for the period. The formula for calculating amortization expense per unit for the production or units-of-activity method is as follows.

$$\text{Amortization expense per unit} = \frac{(\text{cost} - \text{residual value})}{\text{estimated total units of output}}$$

To calculate the amortization expense for the period, simply multiply this per-unit cost by the total number of units produced during the period. Exhibit 8-4 illustrates this method using our previous example.

PRODUCTION METHOD

EXHIBIT 8-4

Original Cost	$10,000	
Estimated Residual Value	$ 1,000	
Estimated Usage	Year 1	5,000 units
	Year 2	4,500 units
	Year 3	5,500 units
	Year 4	3,000 units
	Year 5	2,000 units
		20,000 units

$$\text{Amortization Expense per Unit} = \frac{(\text{Cost} - \text{Residual Value})}{\text{Estimated Total Units of Output}}$$

$$= \frac{(\$10,000 - \$1,000)}{20,000 \text{ units}}$$

$$= \$0.45 \text{ per unit}$$

Amortization Schedule:

Year	Cost per Unit	×	Units Produced		Amortization Expense
1	$0.45	×	5,000	=	$2,250
2	$0.45	×	4,500	=	2,025
3	$0.45	×	5,500	=	2,475
4	$0.45	×	3,000	=	1,350
5	$0.45	×	2,000	=	900
					$9,000

Accelerated Methods

The use of an accelerated method assumes that most of the benefits from the asset's use are realized in the early years. Most accelerated methods are calculated by multiplying the asset's carrying value by a fixed percentage. Because the carrying value (cost less accumulated amortization) decreases each year (since the accumulated amortization increases each year by the amount of the amortization expense recorded), the amount of amortization expense decreases each year.

The formula for calculating accelerated or *declining-balance* amortization is as follows.

HELPFUL HINT:

Notice that the asset's residual value does not enter into this formula.

$$(\text{Cost} - \text{Accumulated Amortization at beginning of period}) \times \text{Amortization \%} = \text{Amortization Expense}$$

The percentage used in these calculations is selected by management based on their judgement of how quickly the asset's usefulness will decline. The faster the decline, the higher the percentage selected. Different types of capital assets will be assigned different percentages. A capital asset with a relatively long expected useful life (such as a building) would have a fairly small percentage (such as 5% or 10%), while a capital asset with a relatively short expected useful life (such as equipment) would have a larger percentage (such as 20% or 30%).

One method of establishing the percentage rates to be used is called the **double-declining-balance method**. With this method, the percentage selected is double the straight-line rate. Thus, using the example shown in Exhibit 8-3, the cost of an asset with a five-year expected useful life would be amortized over five years on a straight-line basis (that is, 1/5 per year, or 20%), but would be amortized at 40% using a double-declining-balance method. However, even though this method appears to be based on fairly concrete numbers, it must be remembered that the 40% rate is very questionable (since the 20% is an estimate, and doubling it is arbitrary).

Double-declining-balance amortization is calculated for our example asset in Exhibit 8-5. Note that, under this method, the asset's residual value does not directly enter into the calculation of the amortization expense. Instead, the estimated residual value serves as a constraint; the net book value cannot drop below the residual value. In the example in Exhibit 8-5, this means that in year 5 the company would not take the full amortization expense determined by the calculation because this would reduce the asset's carrying value below the estimated residual value. In other cases, the residual value may not be reached prior to the end of the useful life, so that additional amortization must be taken in the year of disposal of the asset. (Alternatively, a loss on disposal could be recognized.) In the example in Exhibit 8-5, suppose that the residual value was only $500. The amortization schedule would be the same as in Exhibit 8-5 except that in year 5 the company would have to recognize $796 in amortization expense so the asset's final carrying value would be $500, which is the amount of the residual value.

| EXHIBIT 8-5 | **DOUBLE-DECLINING-BALANCE METHOD** |

Original Cost	$10,000
Estimated Residual Value	$ 1,000
Estimated Useful Life	5 years
Double-Declining-Balance Method	

Double-Declining-Balance rate = 2 × Straight-Line rate

$$= 2 \times 1/\text{years of life}$$
$$= 2 \times 1/5$$
$$= 40\%$$

Amortization Schedule:

Year	Balance in PP&E	Beginning Accumulated Amortization	Beginning Net Book Value	Calculation of Expense	Amortization Expense	Ending Net Book Value
1	$10,000	$ 0	$10,000	40% × 10,000 =	$4,000	$6,000
2	10,000	4,000	6,000	40% × 6,000 =	2,400	3,600
3	10,000	6,400	3,600	40% × 3,600 =	1,440	2,160
4	10,000	7,840	2,160	40% × 2,160 =	864	1,296
5	10,000	8,704	1,296	40% × 1,296 =	296*	1,000
					$9,000	

*The calculation of amortization expense in year 5 results in a calculated amortization expense of $518, which would reduce the book value below the residual value. Therefore, only the amount of expense necessary to make the book value equal to the residual value ($1,000) is recorded.

Recording Amortization Expense

Regardless of the amortization method, the recording of the expense is the same. Amortization expense is debited and accumulated amortization is credited. The credit side of the entry is made to an accumulated amortization account and not to the asset account. The accumulated amortization account is a contra asset account that is used to accumulate the total amount of amortization expense that has been recorded for the capital asset over its lifetime. The asset account shows the asset's original historical cost, and the accumulated amortization account shows how much of the cost has already been expensed. We use the accumulated amortization account instead of reducing the asset directly so that users have more information. If they can see what the original cost was, they may be able to estimate how much the company will have to pay to replace the assets. When the accumulated amortization is offset against the asset, users can determine how much of the asset has been amortized and can make a judgement about how soon the assets will need to be replaced.

In financial statements, companies normally show the total original costs of all tangible capital assets separately by category (such as land, buildings, and equipment) with accumulated amortization for each category. Some companies show only one total for accumulated amortization for all the various asset categories. Many companies show only the total net book value (cost less accumulated amortization) in the balance sheet, with the details provided in a note to the financial statements.

An example of detailed disclosures regarding property, plant, and equipment (sometimes called fixed assets) and related accumulated amortization (sometimes called depreciation) is shown in Exhibit 8-6. The information provided by **Garneau Inc.** related to its property, plant, and equipment in its 2003 annual report is fairly typical of the type of supporting detail that is usually provided in notes accompanying the financial statements.

EXHIBIT 8-6

GARNEAU INC. 2003 ANNUAL REPORT

Notes to the Consolidated Financial Statements
For the Years Ended December 31, 2003 and 2002

3. PROPERTY, PLANT AND EQUIPMENT

2003

(In thousands)	Cost		Accumulated amortization		Net book value	
Land and land improvements	$	4,288	$	1,384	$	2,904
Buildings and extrusion plant		5,534		1,219		4,315
Machinery and equipment		21,457		9,366		12,091
Leasehold improvements		264		255		9
Rental equipment		832		577		255
		32,375		12,801		19,574
Equipment under capital lease		1,932		612		1,320
	$	34,307	$	13,413	$	20,894

2002

(In thousands)	Cost		Accumulated amortization		Net book value	
Land and land improvements	$	3,398	$	1,229	$	2,169
Buildings and extrusion plant		5,875		983		4,892
Machinery and equipment		19,329		7,825		11,504
Leasehold improvements		264		249		15
Rental equipment		794		513		281
		29,660		10,799		18,861
Equipment under capital lease		1,883		422		1,461
	$	31,543	$	11,221	$	20,322

In addition to recording regular amortization expense, companies must periodically compare their assets' carrying values with the future benefits they expect to derive from their use. If the future amount recoverable from an asset is less than its net book value (or carrying value), it must be written down and a loss recorded to reflect the *impairment* in the asset's value.

CORPORATE INCOME TAXES

The Canada Revenue Agency (CRA) does not allow companies to deduct amortization expense when calculating taxable income. However, it does allow a similar type of deduction, called **capital cost allowance (CCA)**. CCA is calculated in a manner similar to accelerated amortization, with several exceptions.

Since the amortization expense for accounting income and CCA for taxable income are calculated differently, the asset's net carrying value in each case is different. When there is a difference in the net capital asset amounts because accounting guidelines and tax rules are different, a future income tax asset or liability results that accounts for the difference.

While it is not the purpose of this text to teach you about income taxes, which are subject to very complex rules, you should understand the basics of how capital cost allowance works. For tax purposes, capital assets are grouped into classes as defined by the *Income Tax Act*. For example, most vehicles are grouped into Class 10 and most equipment into Class 8. Each class has a prescribed rate used to calculate the maximum amount that may be deducted. For example, Class 10 has a maximum rate of 30% and Class 8 has a 20% rate. Companies may deduct any amount of the undepreciated capital cost (UCC) in the class up to the stated maximum in a year, except for assets acquired in the current year. In the year of acquisition, the maximum CCA that may be deducted for new assets is restricted to 50% of the normal amount.

As an example, assume that Central Corp. purchases new equipment (Class 8) in year 1 with a total cost of $20,000. For tax purposes, it may deduct a maximum of the following.

CCA Year 1	50% × 20% × $20,000 = $2,000
CCA Year 2	20% × ($20,000 − $2,000) = $3,600
CCA Year 3	20% × ($20,000 − $2,000 − $3,600) = $2,880

Note that the UCC is the net book value for tax purposes, and declines each year by the amount of CCA claimed.[2]

For accounting purposes, Central Corp. uses straight-line amortization and estimates that the equipment will have a useful life of eight years and no residual value. The annual amortization expense is therefore $20,000 − 8 = $2,500.

The differences between tax and financial statement amounts can produce significant differences between the asset's carrying value measured in accordance with accounting guidelines and the UCC measured in accordance with tax regulations. For example, Exhibit 8-7 presents some additional data for Central Corp. and the calculation of income taxes for the first year of the asset's life. The income tax rate is 40%

FUTURE TAX CALCULATIONS

EXHIBIT 8-7

Income Statement

	For Accounting Purposes	For Income Tax Purposes
Revenues	$ 90,000	$90,000
Expenses (except amortization or CCA)	50,000	50,000
Income before amortization CCA	40,000	40,000
Amortization/CCA	2,500	2,000
Income before taxes	$ 37,500	$38,000
Tax expense (40%)	$ 15,000	
Taxes payable (40%)		$15,200
Carrying value of the asset	$ 17,500	$18,000

Future tax asset = 40% × ($17,500 − $18,000) = $200

As shown above, the company will owe the CRA 40% of $38,000 = $15,200 in taxes, based on the taxable income reported on its tax return. However, it seems logical that the tax expense should be calculated based on the accounting income times the tax rate.[3] In this case, the tax expense would be 40% of $37,500 = $15,000.

---

[2] The cost of new capital assets is added to the class to increase the UCC. When capital assets are sold, the lesser of the original cost or the proceeds from the sale is deducted from the UCC.

[3] More precisely, the tax expense reported in the income statement should be based on the difference between the income taxes payable and the future tax asset.

The entry that would be recorded for Central Corp. would therefore be:

Tax expense (SE)	15,000	
Future tax asset (A)	200	
Income taxes payable (L)		15,200

As you can see in the preceding entry, the debit to tax expense is less than the credit to the taxes payable account. As shown at the bottom of Exhibit 8-7, the difference between these two entries, the **future tax asset**, represents the difference between the asset's carrying values for accounting purposes (NBV = $20,000 − $2,500 = $17,500) and tax purposes (UCC = $20,000 − 4872,000 = $18,000), multiplied by the tax rate. If the future tax amount has a debit balance, it means that the asset's carrying value for tax is larger than the carrying value for accounting and, therefore, less tax will be paid in the future because the larger tax asset remaining will result in larger tax deductions in the future.

If the future tax amount has a credit balance (a **future tax liability**), it means that the asset's carrying value for tax is smaller than the carrying value for accounting and, therefore, more tax will be paid in the future (because the smaller tax carrying amount represents a smaller tax deduction in the future). These taxes will have to be paid by the company later in the asset's life, when the CCA deduction for tax purposes is less than the amortization for accounting purposes.

In summary, these future income tax balances arise from differences between an asset's carrying value for tax purposes (i.e., its **undepreciated capital cost**) compared with its carrying value for financial accounting purposes (i.e., its net book value). The discussion of income taxes is continued in more detail in Chapter 9.

CHOICE OF AMORTIZATION METHOD

Identify the factors that influence the choice of amortization method.

Companies are free to choose from the amortization methods that have been discussed, or other systematic and rational methods that suit their circumstances. The majority of companies use the straight-line method, probably because of its simplicity.

For practical reasons, because CCA is required for tax purposes, many smaller companies choose to use it for their accounting amortization calculation as well. By doing so, they only have to do one calculation, and their record keeping and tax reporting are simplified.

CHANGES IN AMORTIZATION ESTIMATES AND METHODS

Describe and implement changes in amortization estimates and methods.

Because the amounts used for useful life and residual value are estimates, the assumptions used in their estimation may change over time. Companies must periodically revisit these estimates to ensure that they are still valid. For example, after an asset has been in service for several years, the company may change its estimate about the asset's remaining useful life. The asset may last longer or deteriorate faster than originally anticipated. Changes in the estimates used to calculate amortization expense are *accounting estimate changes*. Accounting estimate changes are handled prospectively (in current and future periods). Note that there is no restatement of prior periods with a change of estimate.

To illustrate a prospective change in amortization assumptions, the amortization example in Exhibit 8-3 will be used. Assume that during year 4 the company decides that the asset has three more years of useful life left (i.e., it should have had an original life of six rather than five years), and that the residual value at the end of the sixth year will be $400. The company recalculates the amortization for years 4, 5, and 6 based on these new assumptions. The new calculation is based on the remaining book value at the end of year 3 of $4,600 [$10,000 − (3 × $1,800)]. The entire schedule of amortization, then, is as shown in Exhibit 8-8.

CHANGES IN ESTIMATES OF USEFUL LIFE AND RESIDUAL VALUE

EXHIBIT 8-8

Original cost	$10,000
Estimated residual value	$ 1,000
Estimated useful life	5 years
Straight-line method of amortization	

Change during Year 4:

Remaining estimated useful life	3 years
Estimated residual value	$ 400

Calculation of remaining amortization (years 4–6):
Straight-line method

$$\text{Amortization Expense} = \frac{\text{Remaining Book Value} - \text{Estimated Residual Value}}{\text{Estimated Useful Life}}$$

$$= \frac{\$4,600 - \$400}{3 \text{ years}}$$

$$= \$1,400 \text{ per year for years 4, 5 and 6}$$

Amortization Schedule:

Year	Book Value Beginning	Amortization Expense	Ending Book Value
1	$10,000	$1,800	$8,200
2	8,200	1,800	6,400
3	6,400	1,800	4,600
4	4,600	1,400	3,200
5	3,200	1,400	1,800
6	1,800	1,400	400
		$9,600	

The disclosure of changes in estimates in financial statements usually describes the nature of the change and the effects on the current year. Companies are not required to make this type of disclosure, but voluntary disclosure improves the usefulness of the financial information.

Amortization amounts can also change as new costs are added to the asset account, for major repairs and improvements. These generally will require new estimates of the asset's useful life and/or residual value, and are handled as changes in accounting estimates.

A company may also decide, during an asset's life, that a different amortization method more appropriately matches the amortization expense with the benefits received from the asset. If the decision to change to a different amortization method is made as a result of changed circumstances, experience, or new information, the change is treated in the same way as changes in estimates are treated. The new amortization method is applied to the asset's carrying value at the time that the change is made, and the company uses the new method over the asset's remaining useful life.

ADDITIONAL EXPENDITURES ON CAPITAL ASSETS DURING THEIR LIVES

LEARNING OBJECTIVE 6

Account for the disposal and writedown of capital assets.

It was mentioned above that new costs may be added to an asset account, during its life, for things such as major repairs and improvements. Typically, there will also be expenditures for maintenance and minor repairs, etc. throughout an asset's life. We must therefore consider how we should account for these costs. Should they be capitalized, as part of the asset's cost, or charged directly to expense? If such costs are capitalized, they will be charged to expense over several periods, in the form of amortization. On the other hand, if they are expensed they go directly onto the current period's income statement.

The general guideline to be followed here is that non-routine costs (such as those for major repairs and improvements) are usually capitalized, while the costs of routine items (such as maintenance and minor repairs) are expensed. The former are likely to increase the future benefits to be received from the asset, (by extending its useful life, lowering its operating costs, or increasing its productivity). Therefore, it makes sense to capitalize these expenditures initially and then amortize the costs over the periods that benefit from them.

WRITEDOWNS AND DISPOSALS OF PROPERTY, PLANT, AND EQUIPMENT

Sometimes the future recoverable amount of a capital asset (reflecting its ability to generate revenue in the future) declines below its carrying value. Some of the reasons for this decline could be technological change, damage to the asset, or a change in the company's market. When the recoverable amount declines, the company must write down the asset's carrying value to its new lower value. This is accomplished by recognizing a loss on the income statement and increasing the accumulated amortization account by the amount of the loss. Increasing the accumulated amortization decreases the asset's net book value. For example, suppose that at the end of the third year, when the book value of the asset in Exhibit 8-3 is $4,600, the company determines that, as a result of some damage, the asset's future recoverable amount has declined to $3,600. The following entry would be made to record this change.

Loss due to damage to equipment (SE)	1,000	
Accumulated amortization (XA)		1,000

In all likelihood, subsequent to this decline in value the company would review the asset's estimated residual value and the useful life, so that changes could be made to the amortization in future periods if they were necessary.

At the end of an asset's useful life, the company usually disposes of it and replaces it with another asset, especially if the line of business is growing and prospering. In lines of business that are on a decline or discontinued, old assets are not replaced and assets may be sold or written off before they reach the end of their useful lives.

Normally, at the end of an asset's life, it is sold. If the company has accurately projected the residual value, there is no gain or loss on the transaction. However, if the residual value was not estimated accurately, either a gain or a loss results from this transaction. For example, suppose that the asset in Exhibit 8-3 is sold at the end of its useful life for $1,200. (Recall that its original cost was $10,000 and that its residual value was $1,000.) The following entry would be made to record the transaction.

Cash (A)	1,200	
Accumulated amortization (XA)	9,000	
Property, plant, and equipment (A)		10,000
Gain on sale of property, plant, and equipment (SE)		200

In this entry, the amortization recorded during the asset's life is removed from the accumulated amortization account, as well as the original cost being removed from the equipment account. Note that the net of these two amounts is the asset's carrying value at the point of sale, $1,000 ($10,000 − 9,000). This amount is also known as the book value or the net book value at the time of sale. Note also that you cannot credit the equipment account for the book value amount of $1,000, as that would leave $9,000 in the asset account and $9,000 in the accumulated amortization account, even though the asset is no longer owned by the company.

If the asset had been worthless at the end of its useful life, the asset's disposal would be recorded as above, except that no cash is received. If we assume that no cash is received, then the write-off of the asset in our example results in the following entry.

Accumulated amortization (XA)	9,000	
Loss on disposal of property, plant, and equipment (SE)	1,000	
Property, plant, and equipment (A)		10,000

Note that the remaining book value of $1,000 is recorded as a loss on disposal and not as an adjustment to the amortization that has been recorded.

NATURAL RESOURCES

Companies that deal with natural resources face some unique problems not associated with investments in property, plant, and equipment. For example, consider the situation of an oil exploration company. The company incurs large costs to find oil. Some explorations are successful in finding oil and others are not. Should the costs of unsuccessful exploration be capitalized on the balance sheet as assets, or should

LEARNING OBJECTIVE 7

Describe and implement the amortization method used most frequently for natural resources.

they be written off directly as expenses? If these costs are capitalized as assets, that implies that they have future value. But do they? On successful explorations, if the costs are capitalized, how should they be expensed? That is, what is the useful life of the asset created, and what is a reasonable pattern of expense allocation over the useful life?

In Canada, oil exploration companies have a choice of two methods to account for exploration costs: the full costing method and the successful efforts method. The **full costing method** capitalizes the costs of all explorations, both successful and unsuccessful, as long as the expected revenues from all the explorations are estimated to exceed the total costs. The **successful efforts method**, on the other hand, capitalizes only the cost of successful explorations and expenses unsuccessful exploration costs. Sufficient time is allowed to determine whether an effort is or is not successful.

Generally, smaller oil companies use the full costing method, because using the successful efforts method would make their income appear to be very uneven from year to year, depending on the results of the wells they drilled during the year. Larger oil companies drill more wells every year, so they tend to use the successful efforts method as it is simpler to apply and its use over a large base does not produce uneven results from year to year.

Exhibit 8-9 includes examples from two companies.

EXHIBIT 8-9

EXAMPLES OF FULL COSTING AND SUCCESSFUL EFFORTS METHODS

Excerpts from the Notes to the Financial Statements

Purcell Energy Ltd. (2003)

Summary of Significant Accounting Policies

(d) Property, plant and equipment

The Company accounts for crude oil and natural gas properties in accordance with the Canadian Institute of Chartered Accountants' guideline on full cost accounting in the oil and gas industry. Under this method, all costs associated with the acquisition of, exploration for and the development of, natural gas and crude oil reserves, including asset retirement costs, are capitalized. Costs accumulated within each cost centre are depreciated, depleted and amortized using the units-of-production method based on the estimated gross proved reserves.....

Suncor Energy Inc. (2003)

Summary of Significant Accounting Policies

(d) Property, Plant and Equipment, and Intangible Assets

The company follows the successful efforts method of accounting for its conventional and in-situ oil sands crude oil and natural gas operations. Under the successful efforts method, acquisition costs of proved and unproved properties are capitalized. Costs of unproved properties are transferred to proved properties when proved reserves are confirmed. Exploration costs, including geological and geophysical costs, are expensed as incurred. Exploratory drilling costs are initially capitalized. If it is determined that the well does not contain proved reserves, the capitalized exploratory drilling costs are charged to expense, as dry hole costs, at that time.

Note that Suncor Energy uses the successful efforts method for its acquisition costs and exploratory drilling costs. Other exploration costs, however, are expensed as they are incurred.

Under the full costing method, all exploration costs are capitalized and then expensed, through amortization, over the life of the producing wells. Under the successful efforts method, only the costs associated with successful sites are capitalized and then amortized over the period of production.

The amortization of natural resources is often referred to as **depletion**. The amortization method most commonly used is the units-of-production method. With this method, the total number of barrels of oil (in the case of an oil field) that exist in the field is estimated. The amortization expense is then calculated by dividing the capitalized costs by the estimated total number of barrels to be produced from the field, to get an amortization rate per barrel. This is then multiplied by the number of barrels extracted during the period. For example, assume that a company estimates a field to have 2 million barrels of oil. In a given period, 500,000 barrels are extracted. If the capitalized costs are $6 million, then the amortization expense during the period would be $1.5 million ($6,000,000 ÷ 2,000,000 barrels = $3 per barrel; $3 per barrel × 500,000 barrels = $1,500,000).

INTANGIBLE ASSETS

As discussed earlier in the chapter, some assets can have probable future value to the company but not have any physical form. The knowledge gained from research and development, or the customer loyalty and awareness spawned by a well-run advertising campaign, are examples of intangible assets. The company certainly hopes that it benefits from having spent money on these things. However, the difficulty in trying to quantify the benefits and assess the costs of producing intangible assets, such as research and development or advertising, is what makes intangible assets a troublesome area for accountants. Although accountants would generally agree that these might constitute assets, the inability to provide reliable data concerning their costs and future benefits makes it hard to record these items objectively in the company's accounting system.

The capitalization guideline for intangible assets is that if an intangible asset is developed internally by the company, the costs of developing it are expensed as incurred. If the intangible asset is purchased from an independent third party, however, it can be capitalized at its acquisition cost.

An exception to this general guideline occurs with the **development costs** for a product or process. If certain conditions are met, these development costs may be capitalized and amortized over the product's useful life. However, the basic **research costs** that occurred prior to any decision to develop the product or process are still expensed. The conditions stipulate that the product or process be clearly definable, that technical feasibility be established, that management intend to market the product in a defined market, and that the company have the resources needed to complete the project. These requirements are intended to ensure that development costs will be capitalized only if the product or process is actually marketable and will therefore produce future benefits, in the form of revenues. In the United States, both research and development costs are expensed. This can result in very large income differences between a Canadian company and an American one.

Amortizing the cost of an intangible asset is similar to amortizing other capital assets. The company must estimate the asset's useful life and residual value (if any). Because of the estimation problems associated with intangible assets, this is sometimes very difficult to do. Typically, the method used to amortize intangibles is the straight-line method, with an estimated residual value of zero. The useful life depends on the type of intangible. The one aspect of amortization that is different

LEARNING OBJECTIVE 8

Explain the accounting difficulties associated with intangible assets.

LEARNING OBJECTIVE 9

Amortize intangible assets, where appropriate.

for intangibles is that the accumulated amortization account is rarely used. Most often the company reduces the intangible asset directly. Because of the uncertain valuation of intangibles and the fact that the asset normally cannot be replaced, it is not as important for users to know what the original cost was. For example, the journal entry to record the amortization of a patent would probably be:

Amortization expense (SE)	xxx	
Patents (A)		xxx

When estimating the useful life of an intangible asset, both economic life and legal life should be considered. Many intangible assets (such as patents and copyrights) have very well-defined legal lives, but may have less well-defined and shorter economic lives. Intangible assets that have definite lives have to be amortized over the asset's useful life or legal life, whichever is shorter.

It should be noted, however, that some intangible assets (such as trademarks and goodwill) have indefinite lives. Intangible assets with indefinite lives should not be amortized in the usual manner. Instead, each such asset must be evaluated each year to determine whether there has been any impairment in the asset value. If there has, the asset should immediately be written down. If there has not, the asset will remain at its current carrying amount until the following year when it is evaluated again. Note the following example.

accounting in the news

INTANGIBLES IN BIOTECH COMPANIES

Small biotech companies are often founded on the strength of intangible assets in the form of scientific patents that hold potential for drug discoveries. The costs associated with developing a drug, however, are very high, and pharmaceutical companies can spend a lot of money with no guarantee of their drug's ever reaching the marketplace.

In 1997, Novopharm Biotech Inc., a drug development company in Toronto, acquired Genesys Pharma of Winnipeg, largely because of the potential of an anticancer drug being developed by the smaller company. Two years later, Novopharm stopped development following reports of side effects during Phase 1 clinical trials. Novopharm planned to account for the costs associated with GP1-2A's development by taking a $19.6-million writedown.

Source: "Novopharm Biotech suspends drug," by John Greenwood, *National Post*, *Financial Post*, February 11, 1999, p. C9.

Several types of intangible assets involve special problems. They are discussed in the following sections.

Advertising

Companies spend enormous amounts of money advertising their products to increase current and future sales. Does the incurrence of advertising costs create an asset for the company? If the advertising is successful, then the answer is probably yes. But how will the company know if the advertising is successful, and what time periods will receive the benefits from advertisements during the current period? If a customer buys a product, did he/she buy it because of the advertisement, because he/she happened to be in the store and saw it on the shelf, or because his/her neighbour has one? These questions are very difficult to address. The intent of advertising is clearly to create an asset, but measuring its value can be extremely difficult. These measurement uncertainties are so severe that accountants generally expense all advertising costs in the period in which the advertising occurs. If a company does capitalize this cost, it has to provide very strong evidence to support the creation of an asset.

Many companies spent advertising dollars for the 2002 Winter Olympics in Salt Lake City. The spending began in 2001 and continued into 2002. For many companies, the money was not just spent on advertisements during the games but also on pre-game financial support to the athletes, who then wore clothing with the sponsor's logo on it. As you can probably imagine, it's very difficult to know what future benefits will be received from these expenditures, and over what period of time.

accounting in the news

THE GAMES

Corporate sponsorship helps make going to the Olympics a reality for many amateur athletes. But what do corporations receive in return for their promotional dollars? For Visa Canada, sponsoring the Canadian bobsleigh teams at the Salt Lake City games was a chance to be connected with Olympians, who embody leadership and world-wide acceptance.

Promoting the sponsorship carried a $1.9-million price tag, but several factors helped justify the cost. First was the fact that the Olympics is a 17-day event followed around the world, drawing an audience of all ages and from all walks of life.

Then the company compared the volume of impressions of Visa that viewers would receive from television coverage of the bobsleigh teams with the volume of impressions from paid television advertising. Including the cost of a PR firm to promote the teams, the return in value was twice the cost, one Visa official said. Focus groups and telephone surveys also found that people who knew about the sponsorships reacted differently from those who didn't—another sign that the promotion was scoring.

Finally, the sponsorship fit into a larger marketing strategy. A sweepstakes contest in malls, featuring cutouts of a bobsleigh in Visa's colours, offered a winning trip to the Winter Olympics. Visa also sponsored World Cup events in Calgary. And track-level footage to highlight the speed and risks that make the sport exciting was included in prime-time television commercials.

Source: "The Final Push," by Michael Grange, *The Globe and Mail, Report on Business Magazine*, January 25, 2002, p. 59.

Patents, Trademarks, and Copyrights

Patents, trademarks, and copyrights are legal entitlements that give the owner rights to use protected information. If the protected information is valuable, then the agreements are considered assets. Of course, determining whether they have value or not is a difficult task, as is estimating the period over which the rights will continue to have value. Each entitlement may have a legal life associated with it, which may differ from its economic life. For example, a patent has a legal life of 20 years, but this does not mean that it will have an economic life of 20 years. The patent on a computer chip, for example, may have a useful economic life of only a year or two, as a result of technological innovation. On the other hand, trademarks like **Coca-Cola** may have an indefinite life. Copyrights have a legal term of the life of the creator plus 50 years. Legal life serves as a maximum in the determination of the asset's useful life for accounting purposes.

A company records these types of intangible assets only when it buys them from a third party. The costs of most internally developed patents, trademarks, and copyrights are expensed. Some minor costs, such as registration and the legal costs of filing a patent, trademark, or copyright can be capitalized. The costs are then usually amortized on a straight-line basis over the asset's estimated useful life.

It is sometimes difficult to establish and defend patents, trademarks, and copyrights. Any costs related to successfully defending these rights can be capitalized. Note the following example.

accounting in the news

PROTECTING PATENTS

During the anthrax scare in Canada and the United States in 2001, then federal Health Minister Allan Rock ignored Bayer Inc.'s patent on the anti-anthrax antibiotic Cipro when he agreed to buy a cheaper generic version. He changed his mind following a high profile protest over patent rights.

Patent protection can be a key factor in drug manufacturers' commitment to drug discovery. In Canada, drug companies are reaping the benefits of patent protection laws that give them exclusivity for 20 years before generic drug manufacturers can bring cheaper versions to market. This exclusivity can be traced to 1987, the result of federal patent law changes designed to increase drug R&D in Canada.

In exchange for longer exclusivity, drug companies agreed that by 1996 their R&D budgets would almost double, to 10% of sales. They kept the bargain. Federal figures show that total R&D spending grew 277% between 1988 and 1995, when spending for drug discovery represented 11.7% of sales.

Drug companies have reaped even better rewards—revenue growth from increased exclusivity has outpaced R&D spending. In 2000, while sales for the 79 patent holders reporting to the federal government rose 12%, R&D spending increased by only 5.6%, representing 10.1% of sales.

Source: "Swallow this: Drug R&D spending is waning," by Zena Olijnyk, *Canadian Business*, December 10, 2001.

Goodwill

The intangible asset called **Goodwill** represents the above-average profits that a company can earn as a result of a number of factors. For example, above-average management expertise, a desirable location, and excellent employee or customer relations could give one company an advantage over another company in the same industry.

Companies incur costs to create these types of goodwill. Advertising campaigns, public service programs, charitable gifts, and employee training programs all require outlays that to some extent develop goodwill. This type of goodwill is sometimes referred to as internally developed goodwill.

As with other intangible assets, the costs of internally developed goodwill are expensed as they are incurred. In practice, goodwill is recorded as an asset only when it is part of the purchase price paid to acquire another company. Goodwill is not an easily identifiable asset, but is represented by the dollar figure paid by the acquiring company for various valuable but intangible characteristics of the acquired company (such as good location, good management, etc.). These characteristics, in effect, give the acquired company more value than its identifiable assets (its buildings, inventory, etc.).

The measurement and recognition of goodwill are discussed in more detail in Appendix B at the end of the book. As mentioned in an earlier section, as an intangible asset with an indefinite life, goodwill is not amortized. Instead, management is required to periodically review the goodwill's carrying value to determine whether the amount plus the fair value of the acquired net assets is still greater than the investment's carrying value. If it is not, an impairment in goodwill has occurred and the goodwill should be written down and an impairment loss recognized.

During the period 2001 to 2003, many companies reviewed their acquisitions and recognized impairment losses.

HELPFUL HINT

Recorded goodwill arises only when it is externally purchased, and this happens only in situations in which one company buys another company. When the purchase price exceeds the fair value of the identifiable net assets acquired, then the company has purchased goodwill.

accounting in the news

GOODWILL WRITEDOWNS IN GOOD COMPANY

In 2002, when AOL Time Warner Inc. (now Time Warner Inc.) set a record by writing off up to $60 billion (U.S.) in goodwill, analysts predicted other major companies would soon follow suit. Some estimated that goodwill writedowns could total more than $1 trillion by the end of the year.

Massive writedowns are a legacy of the late 1990s, as companies concede that acquisitions they paid dearly for during the high-tech go-go years will not deliver the returns they expected. Nortel Networks Corp., for instance, bought 20 companies in two years at the height of the market. It has since written off billions for its buying spree.

The incidence of writedowns is tied to changes in accounting rules. Goodwill is the amount a company pays that is higher than the value of the assets of a company it is acquiring. While companies used to be able to write off goodwill over several years, changes in American and Canadian standards now demand an assessment every year. If the company does not foresee recovering its investment (in other words, if it paid too much), it must acknowledge this by writing down "impaired assets."

Source: "Goodwill writedowns to hit $1 trillion," by Steve Maich, *National Post, Financial Post,* January 10, 2002, p. FP2.

Examples of the disclosure of goodwill and other intangible assets are shown in Exhibit 8-10 for **Sierra Wireless, Inc.** (As of December 31, 2003, Sierra's goodwill and other intangible assets constituted 11.2% and 8.3% of its assets, respectively, or almost 20% of the company's total asset value. This is not uncommon, especially in high-technology industries.)

EXHIBIT 8-10

SIERRA WIRELESS, INC. 2003 ANNUAL REPORT

8. Goodwill and intangible assets

Goodwill was acquired in 2003 as a result of the acquisition of AirPrime (note 3). An annual impairment test has been performed which resulted in no impairment loss. We assessed the realizability of goodwill related to our reporting unit during the fourth quarter and determined that its fair value did not have to be re-computed because the components of the reporting unit had not changed since the fair value computation completed at August 12, 2003, the date of acquisition, the previous fair value amount exceeded the carrying amount of the reporting unit by a substantial margin, and no evidence exists to indicate that the current fair value of the reporting unit would be less than its current carrying amount.

The components of intangible assets at December 31, 2003 and 2002 are as follows:

	Cost	2003 Accumulated Amortization & Writedown	Net Book Value
Patents and trademarks	$ 2,604	$ 241	$ 2,363
License fees	15,156	7,404	7,752
Intellectual property	4,214	718	3,496
Customer relationships	940	70	870
Databases	150	11	139
	$ 23,064	$ 8,444	$ 14,620

	Cost	2002 Accumulated Amortization & Writedown	Net Book Value
Patents and trademarks	$ 1,569	$ 137	$ 1,432
License fees	11,744	6,269	5,475
Intellectual property	1,434	1,434	—
	$ 14,747	$ 7,840	$ 6,907

The estimated aggregate amortization expense for each of the next five years is expected to be $2,924 per year.

Due to the large number of policy issues associated with accounting for capital assets, companies usually have extensive disclosures related to them in their notes. Exhibit 8-11 shows excerpts from **Imperial Oil Limited's** summary of significant accounting policies related to *property, plant, and equipment* and *goodwill and other intangible assets,* accompanying its 2003 financial statements. Notice that it includes references to the successful-efforts method of accounting for its exploration and development activities; its treatment of the costs of maintenance, repairs, and improvements; its depreciation and depletion policies; and its policy of periodically reviewing its properties to check for impairment of their values.

IMPERIAL OIL LIMITED 2003 ANNUAL REPORT

EXHIBIT 8-11

Summary of significant accounting policies

Property, plant and equipment

Property, plant and equipment are recorded at cost.

Investment tax credits and other similar grants are treated as a reduction of the capitalized cost of the asset to which they apply.

The company follows the successful-efforts method of accounting for its exploration and development activities. Under this method, costs of exploration acreage are capitalized and amortized over the period of exploration or until a discovery is made. Costs of exploration wells are capitalized until their success can be determined.

If the well is successful, the costs remain capitalized; otherwise they are expensed. Capitalized exploration costs are re-evaluated annually. All other exploration costs are expensed as incurred. Development costs, including the cost of natural gas and natural gas liquids used as injectants in enhanced (tertiary) oil-recovery projects, are capitalized.

Imperial selected the successful-efforts method over the alternative full-cost method of accounting because it provides a more timely accounting of the success or failure of exploration and production activities.

Maintenance and repair costs, including planned major maintenance, are expensed as incurred. Improvements that increase or prolong the service life or capacity of an asset are capitalized.

Production costs are expensed as incurred. Production involves lifting the oil and gas to the surface and gathering, treating, field processing and field storage of the oil and gas. The production function normally terminates at the outlet valve on the lease or field production storage tank. Production costs are those incurred to operate and maintain the company's wells and related equipment and facilities. They become part of the cost of oil and gas produced.

Depreciation and depletion for assets associated with producing properties begin at the time when production commences on a regular basis. Depreciation for other assets begins when the asset is in place and ready for its intended use. Assets under construction are not depreciated or depleted. Depreciation and depletion are calculated using the unit-of-production method for producing properties, including capitalized exploratory drilling and development costs. Depreciation of other plant and equipment is calculated using the straight-line method, based on the estimated service life of the asset. In general, refineries are depreciated over 25 years; other major assets, including chemical plants and service stations, are depreciated over 20 years.

Proved oil and gas properties held and used by the company are reviewed for impairment whenever events or changes in circumstances indicate that the carrying amounts may not be recoverable. Assets are grouped at the lowest level for which there are identifiable cash flows that are largely independent of the cash flows of other groups of assets.

The company estimates the future undiscounted cash flows of the affected properties to judge the recoverability of carrying amounts. Cash flows used in impairment evaluations are developed using annually updated corporate plan investment evaluation assumptions for crude oil commodity prices and foreign-currency exchange rates.

Annual volumes are based on individual field production profiles, which are also updated annually. Prices for natural gas and other products sold under contract are based on corporate plan assumptions developed annually by major contracts and also for investment evaluation purposes.

Gains or losses on assets sold are included in "investment and other income" in the consolidated statement of earnings.

Goodwill and other intangible assets

Goodwill and intangible assets with indefinite lives are not subject to amortization. These assets are tested for impairment annually or more frequently if events or circumstances indicate the assets might be impaired. Impairment losses are recognized in current period earnings. The evaluation for impairment of goodwill is based on a comparison of the carrying values of goodwill and associated operating assets with the estimated present value of net cash flows from those operating assets.

Intangible assets with determinable useful lives are amortized over the estimated service lives of the assets. Computer software development costs are amortized over a maximum of 15 years and customer lists are amortized over a maximum of 10 years. The amortization is included in "depreciation and depletion" in the consolidated statement of earnings.

STATEMENT ANALYSIS CONSIDERATIONS

The use of different amortization methods for capital assets can produce significantly different results in the financial statements of two otherwise similar companies. For the first few years, a company using the straight-line method will show higher carrying values for its capital assets than a similar company using an accelerated amortization method. This affects the balance sheet value as well as the amortization expense that is reported in the income statement. Unfortunately, there is no easy way for the user to convert from one method to another to make the statements more comparable.

Probably the biggest concerns in the analysis of capital assets are understanding which assets have been left out (i.e., those that were developed internally and therefore not recorded), and what market values can be assigned to the assets listed. The historical cost figures for property, plant, and equipment may be very old. Even though the company is not holding these assets for resale, it will have to replace them at some point and, therefore, the replacement cost may be relevant. In Canada, companies are not required to disclose replacement cost information. If a company reports property, plant, and equipment as a single amount, the user is not able to determine how much is invested in each component. This information could be important to users as they attempt to anticipate future outflows of cash for the replacement of some of these assets. Even if a company assigns three separate amounts for property, plant, and equipment, the user is still missing some important pieces of information that could be useful in evaluating the company. For example, if a single amount for buildings is disclosed, the user still does not know (1) how many buildings are included, (2) where the buildings are located, or (3) when the buildings were acquired. Without this information, the user does not have any way of determining market value or replacement cost.

Another problem is that many intangible assets that have been developed internally do not appear on the company's financial statements because their costs have been expensed as they were developed. It is possible for a company to have the rights to a patent that it has developed that will generate revenues for several years. This valuable economic resource is often not listed as an asset at all. The large dollar amounts that companies are willing to pay for goodwill when taking control of other companies testify to the substantial value of these unrecorded assets. A failure to consider these assets can lead different analysts to draw significantly different conclusions about a company's value.

One final general concern with regard to financial statement analysis is whether the capital assets listed on the company's balance sheet are really worth the amounts recorded. For example, the conditions that gave rise to goodwill at the date of acquisition may have changed since acquisition. Suppose the goodwill was due to the technical expertise of a key employee of the business that was acquired. If the employee dies or leaves the company after acquisition, then the goodwill could be worth much less. Although this decline in value may result in an impairment loss being recorded, due to the way the annual impairment test is conducted, it might not. For this reason, analysts generally have a healthy scepticism about the value of goodwill and other intangibles.

Using the Return on Assets (ROA) Ratio

Despite the unknowns associated with the capital asset values, a ratio using assets has been developed. This ratio, called the return on assets ratio, or ROA, is used to calculate how well management has managed the company assets. This ratio simply expresses the total return (income) earned as a percentage of total assets.

LEARNING OBJECTIVE 10

Calculate the return on assets ratio and discuss the potential implications of the results.

The return on the investment in assets should be calculated prior to any payments or returns to the debtholders or shareholders. Net income has interest expense already deducted, but not dividends. Therefore, the net income, if it is to be used as a measure of return on assets, must be adjusted for the effects of interest expense, so that the treatment of interest is similar to the treatment of dividends.

A complicating factor exists because interest is a deductible expense in the calculation of income tax expense. Therefore, when the net income figure is adjusted for the interest expense we must also adjust the amount of income tax expense that would result. In other words, the effect of the tax saving (i.e., the reduction in income tax expense) associated with the interest deduction must also be removed from the income. The ROA ratio is thus calculated as the ratio of the return (income before interest) divided by the investment in total assets, as follows.

$$\text{ROA} = \frac{\text{Income Without Interest}}{\text{Average Total Assets}}$$

$$= \frac{\text{Net Income} + [\text{Interest Expense} - \text{Tax Saving from Interest Expense}]}{\text{Average Total Assets}}$$

$$= \frac{\text{Net Income} + [\text{Interest Expense} - (\text{Tax Rate} \times \text{Interest Expense})]}{\text{Average Total Assets}}$$

$$= \frac{\text{Net Income} + [\text{Interest Expense} \times (1 - \text{Tax Rate})]}{\text{Average Total Assets}}$$

For **Le Château Inc.**, the calculation of ROA for the year ended January 31, 2004, is as follows:

$$\text{ROA} = \frac{\text{Net Income} + [\text{Interest Expense} \times (1 - \text{Tax Rate})]}{\text{Average Total Assets}}$$

$$= \frac{\$10,648 + [\$339 \times (1 - 0.378)]}{(\$94,546 + \$80,519) \div 2}$$

$$= \frac{\$10,648 + \$211}{\$87,533}$$

$$= 0.124 \text{ or } 12.4\%$$

Note: The amounts presented in Le Château's financial statement are in thousands of dollars.

As with many ratios, the ROA alone is not as meaningful as a comparison over time or among companies. However, before using ROA to compare different companies, you should be sure their amortization policies are comparable, as different amortization policies will affect the total assets figure. You should also determine whether the companies you are comparing have recently invested in new assets. New assets will significantly increase the total asset amount and thus may decrease the ROA.

SUMMARY

In this chapter, we described the initial acquisition of capital assets—both tangible and intangible—paying attention to the costs that are included in the asset account. Capital assets include land, buildings, vehicles, equipment, natural resources, intangibles, and many other assets that have a useful life of more than one year. We explored several systematic, rational methods of amortizing capital assets. Amortization of capital assets is an estimate of the expense that relates to the use of the assets each year. As an estimate, it is up to management to determine appropriate amortization rates, incorporating useful lives and residual values. We took a brief look at what happens with respect to the CRA and amortization. Because the CRA has restricted the amortization method to CCA, there is often a difference between the income tax recorded on the accounting income statement and the income tax that is actually owed to the CRA. This difference is referred to as a future tax asset or liability.

Because amortization methods are estimates, it is important to periodically review the useful life and residual value assumptions to determine if they are still appropriate. If new values are established, the asset's book value is amortized over its remaining useful life using the new values. Also, if the company decides to change amortization methods because a new method now seems more appropriate, it will amortize the asset over its remaining useful life using the new method.

We completed the chapter with a discussion of the calculation of ROA and its limitations.

SUMMARY PROBLEM

Additional Demonstration Problems

Pete's Trucking Company has a fleet of large trucks that cost a total of $1,410,000. The trucks have an estimated useful life of 10 years and an estimated residual value of 10%. For tax purposes, their capital cost allowance (CCA) rate is 30%. The trucks are expected to be driven a total of one million kilometres.

Required:

1. Calculate the annual straight-line amortization that would be recorded over the lives of these trucks.

2. Prepare a schedule showing amortization on a production or units-of-activity basis, if the following usage was expected.

Year 1	125,000 km
Year 2	120,000 km
Year 3	120,000 km
Year 4	110,000 km
Year 5	110,000 km
Year 6	100,000 km
Year 7	90,000 km

Year 8   85,000 km
Year 9   75,000 km
Year 10   65,000 km

3. Prepare a schedule showing the amortization that would result if Pete's had used the double-declining-balance method. (Alternatively, if you want to check your comprehension without having to do a lot of repetitive calculations, just calculate the amortization expense for years 1, 2, 3 and 10. For the year 10 calculation, assume that the net book value of the trucks at the end of year 9 is $189,300.)

4. Prepare a schedule showing the capital cost allowance that could be deducted each year for income tax purposes. (Alternatively, if you wan to check your comprehension without having to do a lot of repetitive calculations, just calculate the capital cost allowance for years 1, 2, 3 and 10. For the year 10 calculation, assume that the undepreciated capital cost of the trucks at the end of year 9 is $69,100.)

5. At the end of the ninth year, the trucks were sold for a total of $95,000. Prepare journal entries to record the disposal of the trucks, assuming:

    a. Pete's used straight-line amortization

    b. Pete's used the units-of-activity method of amortization

    c. Pete's used double-declining-balance amortization

6. Briefly explain why there is a loss on disposal of the trucks in these circumstances.

SUGGESTED SOLUTION TO SUMMARY PROBLEM

1. The equipment's residual value would be $141,000 (10% of $1,410,000). The straight-line amortization would be:

$$\text{Amortization Expense} = \frac{\text{Original Cost} - \text{Estimated Residual Value}}{\text{Estimated Useful life}}$$

$$= (\$1,410,000 - \$141,000) \div 10 \text{ years}$$

$$= \$126,900 \text{ year}$$

2. Cost per kilometre: ($1,410,000 − $141,000) ÷ 1,000,000 kilometres
   = $1.269 per kilometre

   Amortization in year 1: $1.269 × 125,000 = $158,625
   Amortization in year 2: $1.269 × 120,000 = $152,280
   Amortization in year 3: $1.269 × 120,000 = $152,280
   Amortization in year 4: $1.269 × 110,000 = $139,590
   Amortization in year 5: $1.269 × 110,000 = $139,590
   Amortization in year 6: $1.269 × 100,000 = $126,900
   Amortization in year 7: $1.269 × 90,000 = $114,210
   Amortization in year 8: $1.269 × 85,000 = $107,865
   Amortization in year 9: $1.269 × 75,000 = $ 95,175
   Amortization in year 10: $1.269 × 65,000 = $ 82,485

3. Double-declining-balance method:

   Declining balance rate = 200% × straight-line rate
                           = 200% × 1/10 = 20%

   The amortization schedule for the double-declining-balance method (in thousands) is:

Year	Net Book Value (beginning)	Calculation	Amortization Expense
1	1,410.0	20% × 1,410.0	$282.0
2	(1,410.0 − 282.0) = 1,128.0	20% × 1,128.0	225.6
3	(1,128.0 − 225.6) = 902.4	20% × 902.4	180.5
4	(902.4 − 180.5) = 721.9	20% × 721.9	144.4
5	(721.9 − 144.4) = 577.5	20% × 577.5	115.5
6	(577.5 − 115.5) = 462.0	20% × 462.0	92.4
7	(462.0 − 92.4) = 369.6	20% × 369.6	73.9
8	(369.6 − 73.9) = 295.7	20% × 295.7	59.1
9	(295.7 − 59.1) = 236.6	20% × 236.6	47.3
10	(236.6 − 47.3) = 189.3		48.3

4. The capital cost allowance schedule (in thousands, rounded to one decimal place) is:

Year	Undepreciated Capital Cost	Calculation	Capital Cost Allowance
1	1,410.0	50% × 30% × 1,410.0	$211.5
2	(1,410.0 − 211.5) = 1,198.5	30% × 1,198.5	359.6
3	(1,198.5 − 359.6) = 839.0	30% × 839.0	251.7
4	(839.0 − 251.7) = 587.3	30% × 587.3	176.2
5	(587.3 − 176.2) = 411.1	30% × 411.1	123.3
6	(411.1 − 123.3) = 287.8	30% × 287.8	86.3
7	(287.8 − 86.3) = 201.4	30% × 201.4	60.4
8	(201.4 − 60.4) = 141.0	30% × 141.0	42.3
9	(141.0 − 42.3) = 98.7	30% × 98.7	29.6
10	(98.7 − 29.6) = 69.1	30% × 69.1	20.7

5. a. Straight-line method:

Cash (A)	95,000	
Accumulated amortization (XA)	1,142,100	
Loss on disposal of trucks (SE)	172,900	
Trucks (A)		1,410,000

b. Units-of-activity method:

Cash (A)	95,000	
Accumulated amortization (XA)	1,186,515	
Loss on disposal of trucks (SE)	128,485	
Trucks (A)		1,410,000

c. Double-declining-balance method:

Cash (A)	95,000	
Accumulated amortization (XA)	1,220,700	
Loss on disposal of trucks (SE)	94,300	
Trucks (A)		1,410,000

6. The actual life of the trucks was only 9 years, rather than the expected 10 years; therefore, less of the cost was written off through amortization. In addition, the trucks' residual value was only $95,000 rather than the $141,000 that was expected.

    Notice that in each case above—(part a)., b)., and c.)—, the amount of the loss is equal to the amortization expense that would have been charged in year 10 plus the shortfall in the residual value (i.e., $141,000 – $95,000 = $46,000).

ABBREVIATIONS USED

AcSB   Accounting Standards Board
CCA   Capital cost allowance
CRA   Canada Revenue Agency
DB   Declining-balance
UCC   Undepreciated capital cost

SYNONYMS

Amortization/depreciation
Amortized cost/net book value/carrying value
Compound-interest amortization/present-value amortization
Units-of-activity/units-of-production

GLOSSARY

Accelerated amortization   A method of amortization that allocates higher expenses to the earlier years of an asset's life and lower amounts to the later years.

Amortizable cost   The amount of an asset that can be amortized over its useful life. It is calculated as the original cost less the residual value.

Amortization   The allocation of the cost of capital assets to expense over their useful lives.

Amortized cost   The amount of an asset's cost that remains after it has been amortized. It is another term for net book value or carrying value.

Basket purchase   A purchase of assets in which more than one asset is acquired for a single purchase price.

Book value   The value of an asset or liability carried on a company's books. For capital assets, this value is the asset's acquisition cost less the accumulated amortization.

Capital assets   Assets with expected useful lives of more than one year (or normal operating cycle, if longer) that are used in the business and are not intended for resale.

Capital cost allowance   The deduction permitted by the CRA for tax purposes in place of amortization.

Capitalizable cost   A cost that can be recorded as an asset on the financial statements rather than being expensed immediately.

Carrying value   The acquisition cost of a capital asset minus its accumulated amortization. Synonym for book value.

Compound interest amortization   An amortization method that calculates the amortization expense for a period by the change in the asset's present value.

Decelerated amortization   A method of amortization that allocates lower expenses to the earlier years of an asset's life than to the later years.

Declining-balance amortization   Amortization methods that calculate the amortization each period by multiplying the rate of amortization by the asset's carrying value.

Depletion   A term sometimes used to describe amortization of the cost of natural resources to expense over the lives of the resources.

Depreciation   A term sometimes used for amortization, especially for tangible assets that are not natural resources.

Development costs   Costs incurred to get a product or service ready for commercial production, after the initial stages of exploration or research (to discover the product or service) have been completed.

Double-declining-balance method   A particular type of declining-balance amortization method that is calculated by using a percentage rate that is double the rate that would be used for straight-line amortization.

Full costing method   A method of accounting for the exploration and drilling costs of oil exploration companies in which all costs of exploration are capitalized and amortized, without regard to the success or failure of individual wells. Commonly used in smaller oil and gas companies.

Future tax asset or liability An asset or liability account that arises when there is a difference between the revenues or expenses used for tax purposes and book purposes. With respect to capital assets, it represents the tax effect of the temporary differences between their net carrying values for accounting purposes and their carrying values for tax purposes.

Goodwill An intangible asset that represents a company's above-average earning capacity as a result of reputation, advantageous location, superior sales staff, expertise of employees, etc. It is only recorded when a company acquires another company and pays more for it than the fair market value of its identifiable net assets.

Intangible asset A non-physical capital asset that usually involves a legal right.

Interest capitalization The recording of interest as a part of the construction cost of a capital asset.

Net book value An asset's carrying value on the company books.

Net realizable value An asset's selling price less any costs to complete and sell it.

Net recoverable amount The estimated future net cash flow from the use of a capital asset, together with its residual value.

Present-value amortization An amortization method that calculates the amortization expense for a period by the change in an asset's present value.

Production method A method of amortization that allocates an asset's amortizable cost to the years of its useful life as a function of the volume of production or usage during each period. Often called the units-of-output or units-of-activity method.

Rate of amortization A percentage that describes the amount of amortization to be taken during a given period. For straight-line amortization, the rate is the reciprocal of the number of years of useful life .

Replacement cost An asset's market value, determined from the market in which the company can purchase the asset, or the cost to reproduce the asset based on current prices of the inputs.

Resale value An asset's market value as determined in the market in which it can be sold.

Research costs Costs incurred to discover a new product or service. Subsequent costs to get the product or service ready for commercial production are classified separately, as "development" costs.

Residual value A capital asset's estimated net realizable value at the end of its useful life to the company.

Straight-line amortization A method of amortization that allocates an asset's amortizable cost evenly over its useful life.

Straight-line rate The rate of amortization for the straight-line method. Calculated as the reciprocal of the number of years of useful life .

Successful efforts method A method of accounting for the exploration and drilling costs of oil exploration companies in which the costs of exploration are capitalized and amortized only for successful wells. (The costs of unsuccessful efforts are charged to expense.) Commonly used in larger oil and gas companies.

Tangible asset An asset that has physical substance.

Undepreciated capital cost An asset's carrying value for tax purposes. The portion of the original cost that has not yet been deducted as capital cost allowance.

Units-of-activity method A method of amortization that allocates an asset's amortizable cost to the years of its useful life as a function of the amount of its usage or production each period. Also called the units-of-output or production method.

Useful life An estimate of the period of time over which an asset will have economic value to the company.

Value in use The value of an asset expected to result from using it in the business. Relevant if the intent is to use the asset rather than to sell it.

ASSIGNMENT MATERIAL

Assessing Your Recall

8-1 Describe what is meant by "value in use" vs. "resale value" as applied to capital assets.

8-2 Discuss the types of costs that should be capitalized for a piece of equipment.

8-3 Describe the procedure used in Canada to allocate the cost of a basket purchase of assets to the individual assets.

Self-Assessment Quiz

8-4 Explain why interest can be capitalized as part of an asset's construction costs.

8-5 Discuss the purpose of amortization expense and the possible patterns of amortization for a company.

8-6 Discuss the motivations that a company might have for choosing one amortization method over another.

8-7 Describe how residual value and useful life are used in the calculation of amortization under the following methods: straight-line, production, and declining-balance.

8-8 Explain what is done when a company changes its estimate of an asset's useful life and/or residual value partway through the asset's life.

8-9 Describe the differences between capital cost allowance and accelerated amortization.

8-10 Discuss the nature of future income taxes in the context of differences between amortization and CCA.

8-11 Describe the conditions under which intangible assets can be recorded on a company's books and the guidelines under which their value can then be expensed over the assets' lives. Specifically, discuss goodwill, research and development costs, and patents.

8-12 Discuss the conditions under which a company is required to write down the value of its capital assets.

Applying Your Knowledge

8-13 **(Acquisition cost and interest capitalization)**

Cedar Homes Ltd. decided to upgrade some of its log preparation equipment and to expand its facilities. The following events occurred during the year.

Jan.	4	Equipment with an invoice price of $105,000 was received.
	9	Construction of a new addition to the main building was started, with an estimated cost of $300,000.
	24	A bill in the amount of $2,400 was received for transporting the equipment (received Jan. 4) to Cedar Homes.
	27	Architect's fees of $7,500 were paid for the preliminary design of the building addition.
Feb.	3	Payment was made for the equipment and transportation.
May	9	Payment was made to the construction company in the amount of $290,000 following completion of the building addition.
	14	Work crews installed the equipment and were paid $2,000.

15   A special ad was run in the local paper at a cost of $250 informing residents that the company would begin interviewing for new employees in two weeks.

24   A party costing $850 was held to celebrate the completion of the new building.

June   7   Testing of the new equipment was completed and it was placed in service.

Total testing costs were $1,000.

Required:

a. Determine the costs that should be capitalized as assets by Cedar Homes in the buildings and equipment accounts. (These must be accounted for separately, as they will be subject to different amortization rates.)

b. What should be done with any costs that are not capitalized?

c. If Cedar Homes had borrowed money to finance the expansion, what two options would it have had with respect to the interest cost?

8-14   (Valuation of capital assets)

Lundon Company purchased a tract of land for $150,000 roughly 20 years ago and has now divided the land into two parcels. The company intends to sell one parcel and keep the other. Lundon estimates it can sell the one parcel for $240,000. It already has an offer of $180,000 from a local business, and it has a tentative offer from the brother of the president of Lundon Company for $270,000.

Required:

a. What accounting concepts and objectives might the accountant use in support of recognizing the parcel's value at $240,000?

b. What accounting concepts and objectives might be used to argue against recognizing either offer in the accounting records?

c. Would it be appropriate to revalue one parcel and not the other?

d. At what amount should the parcel in question be valued?

8-15   (Valuation of capital assets)

Four years ago, Litho Printers Ltd. purchased a large, four-colour printing press for $440,000 with the intent of using it for 10 years. Recently, the production manager learned that replacing the press with a comparable new one would cost $600,000. On the other hand, the production manager estimates that if the company were to sell the current machine it would receive $300,000. The manager also estimates that the company could make $950,000 from selling materials produced on the press over the next six years.

Required:

a. What value should be assigned to the press in Litho Printers' financial statements?

b. Under what conditions should the press be valued at $950,000?

c. Under what conditions should the press be valued at $600,000?

d. Under what conditions should the press be valued at $300,000?

8-16   (Amortization calculations and journal entries)

Polar Company purchased a building with an expected useful life of 30 years for $660,000 on January 1, 2006. The building is expected to have a residual value of $60,000.

Required:

a. Give the journal entries that would be made by Polar to record the building purchase in 2006 and the amortization expense for 2006 and 2007, assuming straight-line amortization is used.

b. Give the journal entries that would be made by Polar to record the amortization expense for 2006 and 2007, assuming the double-declining-balance method is used.

8-17 (Calculation of amortization)

A machine is purchased on January 1, 2006, for $100,000. It is expected to have a useful life of six years and a residual value of $10,000. The machine is expected to produce a total of 200,000 components during its life, distributed as follows: 20,000 in 2006; 30,000 in 2007; 35,000 in 2008; 45,000 in 2009; 40,000 in 2010; and 30,000 components in 2011. The company closes its books on December 31.

Required:

a. Calculate the amount of amortization to be charged each year, using each of the following methods.

   1. Straight-line method

   2. Production method

   3. Double-declining-balance method

b. Which method results in the highest amortization expense:

   1. During the first three years?

   2. Over all six years?

8-18 (Amortization [including CCA] and income calculation)

On January 1, 2003, Johnson Company invested $500,000 in equipment with an expected useful life of 20 years and an anticipated residual value of $50,000. For tax purposes, this is a Class 8 asset with a CCA rate of 20%. In 2006, Johnson reported sales of $1,100,000 and operating expenses other than amortization of $800,000. At December 31, 2006, Johnson held $750,000 of assets in addition to its equipment. Johnson's tax rate is 30%.

Required:

a. Assuming Johnson uses straight-line amortization, what amount of net income will it report for 2006? What will be the return on assets, using the total assets reported at December 31, 2006, and assuming there is no interest expense on the income statement?

b. What is the maximum amount of CCA that Johnson would be able to claim for tax purposes in 2006? Assuming the company used straight-line amortization for accounting purposes, give the journal entry to record the company's income taxes for 2006.

c. Assuming Johnson uses double-declining-balance amortization, what amount of net income will it report for 2006? What will be the return on assets, using total assets reported at December 31, 2006?

d. For what type of asset would it be appropriate to use double-declining-balance amortization?

8-19 (Change in estimates)

On October 31, 2002, Steelman Company acquired a new machine for $135,000. The company estimated the useful life to be 10 years and expected a residual value of $5,000. During 2005, the company decided that the machine would be used for another 10 years (including all of 2005), and estimated that the residual value would be $3,000. On June 30, 2007, the machine was sold for $85,000. The company uses the straight-line method of amortization and closes its books on December 31.

Required:

Give the necessary journal entries related to the acquisition, amortization, and disposal of this asset for the years 2002, 2005, and 2007.

8-20   (Straight-line amortization with disposal)

On June 4, 2004, Sherman Bros. Corp. purchased a new machine for $30,000. A useful life of 10 years and a residual value of $1,000 were estimated. On November 25, 2004, another machine was acquired for $80,000. Its useful life was estimated to be 12 years and its residual value $8,000. On April 24, 2006, the first machine was sold for $20,000. Sherman Bros. closes its books on December 31 each year, uses the straight-line method of amortization, and calculates amortization to the nearest month.

Required:

Give the necessary journal entries for the years 2004 through 2006 for both machines.

8-21   (Disposal of capital assets)

On March 31, 2006, Hammer & Holding Inc. purchased new machinery. The company acquired the new machinery by trading in its old machine, paying $20,375 in cash and issuing a 10% note payable for $6,000. The old machinery was acquired on June 30, 2003, for $25,000. At that time, its estimated useful life was 10 years, with a $1,000 residual value. The old asset's market value at the date of the trade-in was approximately the same as its book value. The new machinery's estimated life is six years, with a residual value of $3,000. The company uses the straight-line method of amortization and closes its books on December 31.

Required:

a. Give the necessary journal entry to record the amortization of the old asset up to the date of the trade-in, in 2006. Assume that the amortization was correctly recorded for 2003, 2004, and 2005. Give the necessary journal entry to record the trade-in of the old asset and the acquisition of the new one. (Hint: The cost of the new asset includes the value of the old asset plus the cash and note given in payment for the new asset.)

b. Assume that on March 31, 2012, the machinery acquired in 2006 could not be sold and the company decided to write it off. Give the necessary journal entries for 2012.

8-22   (Intangibles and amortization)

Pinetree Manufacturing Company reports both equipment and patents in its balance sheet.

Required:

a. Explain how the dollar amount for each type of asset is determined.

b. If both types of assets were purchased three years ago for $40,000 each and had estimated useful lives of 10 years, what amount would be reported in the balance sheet at the end of the current period? Explain.

c. Financial analysts sometimes ignore intangible assets in analyzing financial statements. Do you think this is appropriate? Explain.

8-23 (Intangibles and amortization)

Vinay Company purchases several intangible assets, as follows.

Asset	Cost
Patent	$80,000
Copyright	200,000
Licence	320,000

In addition to the purchase cost of each asset, legal fees associated with the licence acquisition are $24,000. While the patent has a legal life of 20 years, technological changes are expected to render it worthless after about five years. The copyright is good for another 30 years, but nearly all the related sales are expected to occur during the next eight years. The licence is good in perpetuity, and sales under the licence are expected to continue at the same level for many decades.

Required:

a. Calculate the annual amortization, if any, for each of Vinay's intangible assets.

b. Show the balance sheet presentation of the Intangible Assets section of Vinay's balance sheet four years after acquisition of the intangible assets, assuming that there has been no evidence that their values have been impaired.

User Perspective Problems

8-24 (Valuation of assets in discontinued business)

Suppose that a company decides to discontinue a line of business and sell the related assets. Describe what you think would be the most appropriate valuation basis for the property, plant, and equipment for the discontinued operations. As an investor in the company, discuss what disclosure might be most useful to you in these circumstances.

8-25 (Capital assets as collateral for a loan)

As a lender, discuss how much comfort you might get from the existence of long-term assets, specifically plant and goodwill, in making a long-term loan to a company.

8-26 (Auditing and valuation of capital assets)

As an auditor, discuss how you might evaluate a company's property, plant, and equipment to decide whether it should write down the value of these assets.

8-27 (Goodwill's effect on financial statements)

In some countries (such as the United Kingdom), companies can write off goodwill at the date of acquisition by directly reducing shareholders' equity; that is, the write-off does not pass through net income. Suppose that a Canadian company and a UK company agreed to purchase the same company for the same amount of money. As a stock analyst, describe how the balance sheets and income statements would differ for the two companies after the acquisition. Discuss whether this provides any advantage for either company.

8-28 (Impact of writedowns on remuneration)

Suppose that you are the accounting manager of a division of a large company and your remuneration is partly based on meeting an income target. In the current year, it seems unlikely that your division will meet its target. You have some property, plant, and equipment that has been idle for a while but has not yet been written off. What incentives do you have to write off its value during the current year? If you do write it off, how will it affect your future ability to meet the income targets for your division?

8-29 **(Basket purchase)**

Companies that buy real estate often face a basket purchase situation. The purchase of real estate usually involves both the land that is purchased and the building that is on the land. If you are the accounting manager, how would you attempt to allocate the real estate's purchase price between the land and the building? Why must you allocate the cost between the two assets? What incentives might you have to allocate a disproportionate amount to either the land or the building?

8-30 **(Analysis of an R&D company)**

As a stock analyst, discuss any difficulties or inadequacies that you might find with the financial statements of a company that is predominately a research and development firm.

8-31 **(Capital assets and company valuation)**

Suppose that you have been asked to analyze a potential acquisition by your company. Which long-term assets on its financial statements are the most likely to be misstated by their book values, and why? Are there long-term assets of the potential acquiree that might not be represented on the financial statements at all?

8-32 **(Accounting for idle assets)**

Conservative Company purchased a warehouse on January 1, 2001, for $800,000. At the time of purchase, Conservative anticipated that the warehouse would be used to facilitate its expanded product line. The warehouse is being amortized over 20 years and is expected to have a residual value of $100,000. On January 1, 2006, Conservative concluded that the warehouse would no longer be used and should be sold for its book value. At the end of 2006, the warehouse still had not been sold and its net realizable value was estimated to be only $450,000.

Required:

a. Calculate the warehouse's book value on January 1, 2006.

b. Prepare all journal entries that Conservative would make during 2006 related to the warehouse.

c. If, during 2007, Conservative sells the warehouse for $400,000, what entry would be made for the sale?

d. During 2006, the financial vice-president expressed concern that if Conservative put the building up for sale, the company might have to report a loss, and he didn't want to reduce 2006 earnings; he wanted to continue treating the warehouse as an operating asset. How would the 2006 and 2007 financial statements be different if the warehouse were still treated as an operating asset during 2006? From a shareholder's perspective, do you think the treatment makes any difference? Explain.

8-33 **(Analysis of a company with goodwill)**

The 2006 annual report of Fedders Company contained the following financial statement information.

	2006	2005
Inventory	$19,270,000	$40,939,000
Net property, plant, and equipment	31,637,000	78,399,000
Other assets	8,125,000	35,236,000
Total assets	81,285,000	169,249,000
Net loss	1,775,000	24,931,000

The notes further indicate that the figures of $8,125,000 and $35,236,000 for other assets reported for 2006 and 2005, respectively, included goodwill of $5,823,000 and $17,670,000.

Fedders' sales are concentrated in room air conditioners. Sales are made directly to dealers and through private-label arrangements with major retailers and distributors.

> ***Required:***
>
> a. What factor or factors are most likely to have led to the $46,762,000 reduction in net property, plant, and equipment?
>
> b. According to the information in the annual report, a significant portion of the reduction in inventory was not directly related to the reduction in property, plant, and equipment. What factors might have led to such a large reduction in inventory?
>
> c. As noted, more than half of other assets was goodwill. Given that the company reported a net loss in both 2005 and 2006, is it appropriate to continue to report goodwill in the balance sheet? Explain.
>
> d. In light of the net loss for the year, ratios such as return on equity may not be meaningful. What ratios might be useful in evaluating Fedders' performance over the 2006 fiscal year?
>
> e. What is your conclusion about Fedders' activities during 2006? What additional information would you like to have for analysis?

Reading and Interpreting Published Financial Statements

8-34 **(Reconstruction of capital asset transactions)**

Garneau Inc. is primarily in the business of applying high-performance protective coatings and linings for oil and gas pipeline protection, plus designing and fabricating oilfield equipment for both the Canadian and international markets. Its consolidated balance sheets, statements of operations and deficit, and statements of cash flows are presented in Exhibit 8-12. (In addition, Garneau's note regarding its property, plant, and equipment was presented earlier in this chapter, in Exhibit 8-6.)

Financial Statement Analysis Assignments

> ***Required:***
>
> Prepare summary journal entries to reconstruct the transactions that affected Garneau's property, plant, and equipment during the 2003 fiscal year (i.e., acquisitions, disposals, and amortization expense). Deal with the total property, plant, and equipment, rather than with the individual components. (Hint: You may find the use of T accounts helpful in reconstructing the events that affected the property, plant, and equipment and accumulated amortization accounts during the year.)

8-35 **(Research and development costs)**

The 2003 and 2002 consolidated statements of operations and deficit for **MOSAID Technologies Incorporated** are shown in Exhibit 8-13. In addition, a portion of its note on Accounting Policies, outlining the company's policies regarding accounting for research and development costs, is also shown in the exhibit.

As one would expect for a company in the semiconductor business, MOSAID incurs substantial costs related to research and development. However, it has expensed all these costs in the years in which they were incurred.

EXHIBIT 8-12
PART A

GARNEAU INC. 2003 ANNUAL REPORT

CONSOLIDATED BALANCE SHEETS

(In thousands)	at December 31, 2003	at December 31, 2002
Assets		
Current Assets:		
Cash	$ 1,414	$ ---
Accounts receivable	11,376	3,682
Inventory	3,336	2,625
Prepaid expenses and deposits	101	91
	16,227	6,398
Property, plant and equipment (note 3)	20,894	20,322
	$ 37,121	$ 26,720
Liabilities and Shareholders' Equity		
Current Liabilities:		
Operating Loan (note 2)	$ 6,726	$ 1,379
Accounts payable and accrued liabilities	4,746	2,263
Loans payable (note 4(a))	6,598	5,217
Current portion of capital lease obligations	362	315
	18,432	9,174
Capital lease obligations (note 4(b))	712	981
	19,144	10,155
Shareholders' Equity:		
Share capital (note 5)	20,727	20,718
Deficit	(2,750)	(4,153)
	17,977	16,565
Commitments (note 6)		
	$ 37,121	$ 26,720

The accompanying notes are an integral part of these consolidated financial statements.

On behalf of the Board:

Dan Motyka
Director

Michael Lang
Director

GARNEAU INC. 2003 ANNUAL REPORT

EXHIBIT 8-12
PART B

CONSOLIDATED STATEMENTS OF OPERATIONS AND DEFICIT

(In thousands except per share data)	Year Ended December 31, 2003	Year Ended December 31, 2002
Revenue	$ 44,955	$ 17,187
Operating costs	36,404	14,121
	8,551	3,066
Other operating expenses (income):		
Selling, general and administrative	3,665	3,187
Amortization	2,324	2,283
Research and development	207	226
Bad debts	3	28
Gain on disposal of property, plant and equipment	(6)	(106)
	6,193	5,618
Operating income (loss)	2,358	(2,552)
Financing:		
Interest on loans payable	387	274
Interest on operating loans	232	27
Other	---	(32)
Foreign exchange losses	376	---
Other income	(80)	(88)
Earnings (loss) before income taxes	1,443	(2,733)
Income taxes (note 7):		
Current	40	20
	40	20
Net earnings (loss)	1,403	(2,753)
Deficit, beginning of year	(4,153)	(1,400)
Deficit, end of year	$ (2,750)	$ (4,153)
Earnings (loss) per share (note 5):		
Basic	$ 0.12	$ (0.24)
Diluted	$ 0.12	$ (0.24)

The accompanying notes are an integral part of these consolidated financial statements.

EXHIBIT 8-12
PART C

GARNEAU INC. 2003 ANNUAL REPORT

CONSOLIDATED STATEMENTS OF CASH FLOWS

(In thousands)	Year ended December 31, 2003	Year ended December 31, 2002
Cash provided by (used in):		
Operations (note 10):		
Net earnings (loss)	$ 1,403	$ (2,753)
Items not involving cash:		
Amortization	2,324	2,283
Gain on disposal of property, plant and equipment	(6)	(106)
	3,721	(576)
Changes in non-cash operating working capital	(5,932)	841
	(2,211)	265
Financing:		
Proceeds from exercise of share purchase options	9	---
Repayment of loans payable and capital leases	(7,381)	(2,793)
Increase (decrease) in Operating Loan	5,347	1,379
Advances under term loan	8,540	1,600
Proceeds from sale and lease-back of assets	104	610
	6,619	796
Investments:		
Proceeds from disposal of property, plant and equipment	269	115
Additions to property, plant and equipment	(3,263)	(1,297)
	(2,994)	(1,182)
Increase (decrease) in cash	1,414	(121)
Cash, beginning of year	---	121
Cash, end of year	$ 1,414	$ ---

The accompanying notes are an integral part of these consolidated financial statements.

Required:

a. Calculate what MOSAID's earnings (losses) from operations would have been for 2003 and 2002 if it had capitalized its research and development costs and then amortized them on a straight-line basis over a six-year period. Note: In order to do this with the data available, you will have to assume that 2002 was the company's first year of operations.

b. Compare your results in part a. to the losses from operations shown in Exhibit 8-13. Are the differences significant?

c. Explain why MOSAID does not capitalize its research and development costs.

MOSAID TECHNOLOGIES INCORPORATED 2003 ANNUAL REPORT

EXHIBIT 8-13
PART A

Consolidated Statements of Operations and Deficit

(in thousands, except per share amounts)

Year ended	April 25, 2003	April 26, 2002
Revenues		
Operations	$ 37,067	$ 50,153
Interest	1,108	1,708
	38,175	51,861
Expenses		
Labour and materials	7,827	9,734
Research and development (Note 9)	23,987	28,139
Selling and marketing	10,685	13,811
General and administration	6,918	8,590
Bad debt	(165)	88
Restructuring (Note 10)	6,519	11,005
	55,771	71,367
Loss from operations	(17,596)	(19,506)
Write-down of long-term investment (Note 5)	(518)	(700)
Loss on disposal of long-term investment (Note 5)	(426)	-
Loss before income taxes	(18,540)	(20,206)
Income tax expense (Note 11)	1,357	4,480
Net loss	(19,897)	(24,686)
(Deficit) retained earnings, beginning of year	(462)	24,552
Premium on redemption of common shares	-	(328)
Deficit, end of year	$ (20,359)	$ (462)
Loss per share (Note 12)		
Basic	$ (1.94)	$ (2.45)
Diluted	$ (1.94)	$ (2.45)
Weighted average number of shares		
Basic	10,238,808	10,086,543
Diluted	10,238,808	10,086,543

See accompanying Notes to the Consolidated Financial Statements.

EXHIBIT 8-13
PART B   **MOSAID TECHNOLOGIES INCORPORATED 2003 ANNUAL REPORT**

Research and development

Research costs are expensed as incurred. Development costs are deferred once technical feasibility has been established and all criteria for deferral under generally accepted accounting principles are met. Such costs are amortized commencing when the product is released, over the expected life of the product. To date, no development costs have met the criteria for deferral.

8-36 (Accounting for oil and gas properties)

Imperial Oil Limited is an integrated producer, refiner, and marketer of petroleum and petrochemical products. The portion of its *summary of significant accounting policies* dealing with property, plant, and equipment was presented earlier in this chapter, in Exhibit 8-11.

> *Required:*
>
> a. What method does Imperial Oil Limited use to account for its costs related to exploration and development activities? Explain in your own words how these costs are handled under this method.
>
> b. What reason does Imperial Oil give for choosing this method of accounting for costs related to its exploration and development activities? Explain in your own words what you think this means.
>
> c. Is the method that Imperial Oil uses to account for exploration and development costs the method that you would expect a large oil and gas company to use? Explain why or why not.
>
> d. Assume that a smaller company has been in operation for two years, during which it explored 10 sites each year at a cost of $2 million per site. Only one of the sites each year proved to be economically viable; the remaining wells were dry. The reserves in each successful well are estimated to be 900,000 barrels, extracted evenly over a six-year period commencing in the year of discovery.
>
> Demonstrate your understanding of the full cost method of accounting for these expenditures by indicating what the company would report as:
>
>> 1. The asset's value on the balance sheet at the end of each of the two years
>>
>> 2. The amount of expense on the income statement for each of the two years

8-37 (Accounting for oil and gas properties)

Arrow Energy Ltd. is an Alberta-based "junior" oil and gas company. Note 2 accompanying its 2003 financial statements outlines its significant accounting policies; a portion of this note, related to exploration and development costs, is reproduced in Exhibit 8-14.

> *Required:*
>
> a. What method does Arrow Energy use to account for its exploration and development costs? Explain in your own words how these costs are handled under this method.
>
> b. Is the method that Arrow uses to account for exploration and development costs the method that you would expect smaller oil and gas companies to use? Explain.
>
> c. Assume that a large company has been in operation for two years, during which it explored 20 sites each year at a cost of $4 million per site. Only three of the sites each year proved to be economically viable; the remaining wells were dry. The

reserves in each of the successful wells are estimated to be 1.2 million barrels, extracted evenly over an eight-year period commencing in the year of discovery.

Demonstrate your understanding of the successful efforts method of accounting for these costs by indicating what the company would report as:

1. The asset's value on the balance sheet at the end of each of the two years

2. The amount of expense on the income statement for each of the two years

ARROW ENERGY LTD. 2003 ANNUAL REPORT

EXHIBIT 8-14

ARROW ENERGY LTD.

Notes to the Financial Statements
Years Ended December 31, 2003 and 2002

---

2.   SIGNIFICANT ACCOUNTING POLICIES

Exploration and development costs

The Company follows the full-cost method of accounting for petroleum and natural gas properties whereby all costs relating to the acquisition, exploration and development of petroleum and natural gas reserves are capitalized in one Canadian cost centre and charged against income, as set out below. Such costs may include lease and land acquisition costs, geological and geophysical expenses, lease rentals and other costs on non-producing properties, costs of drilling and completing both productive and non-productive wells, production equipment and corporate expenses directly related to acquisition, exploration and development activities. These costs along with estimated future capital costs in the current reserve report related to the development of proved reserves, net of salvage values are included in the depletion calculation. Costs of acquiring and evaluating unproved properties may be excluded from the depletion base until it is determined whether proved reserves are attributable to the properties or impairment has occurred.

Depletion of petroleum and natural gas properties and depreciation of production equipment is provided on the unit-of-production basis using estimated gross (before royalties) proved oil and natural gas reserves as determined by independent reservoir engineers. Natural gas reserves and production are converted, at a ratio of six thousand cubic feet of natural gas to one barrel of oil, for depletion and depreciation purposes.

8-38   (Deferred exploration expenditures)

Atikokan Resources Inc. is a junior mining company based in Ontario. In the assets section of its December 31, 2003, balance sheet, Atikokan reported "mineral properties and deferred exploration expenditures" of $1,566,476. Note 6 accompanying its financial statements provided extensive details related to this item, and revealed that $1,355,589 of the total amount was attributable to deferred exploration expenditures. The relevant portion of this note is reproduced in Exhibit 8-15.

EXHIBIT 8-15

ATIKOKAN RESOURCES INC. 2003 ANNUAL REPORT

ATIKOKAN RESOURCES INC.
Notes to the Financial Statements
December 31, 2003 and 2002

6. MNERAL PROPERTIES AND DEFERRED EXPLORATION EXPENDITURES
(a) Amounts expended from inception to date are summarized as follows:

	2003	2002
Mineral property costs		
Claims and staking	$ 205,209	$ 186,075
Mining recorder	5,678	5,678
Total mineral property costs	210,887	191,753
Deferred exploration expenditures		
Magnometer surveys	23,020	23,020
Diamond drilling	175,020	175,020
Assays	21,882	21,446
Stripping and surface blasting	82,956	82,956
Line cutting	74,214	74,214
Contract geologists	480,376	480,376
Down hole geophysics	17,496	17,496
Mapping	58,174	58,174
IP surveys	49,660	49,660
Deep gradient surveys	40,524	40,524
Magnetic surveys	13,185	13,185
Geological supplies	1,699	1,699
Soil geochemistry	32,326	32,326
Bulk sampling	76,963	15,452
Equipment rentals	11,268	11,268
Field camp and supplies	11,145	10,857
Truck expenses	91,921	79,968
Field labour	28,868	28,868
Travel	19,703	16,325
Field office expenses	55,189	42,247
Option fee recovery (b)	(10,000)	(10,000)
Total deferred exploration expenditures	1,355,589	1,265,081
Total mineral properties and deferred exploration expenditures	$ 1,566,476	$ 1,456,834

(b) In May 2001, Atikokan signed an option agreement with Inco Limited ("Inco") on 160 units of the Company's 100% owned Lumby Lake property in Northern Ontario. In order to earn a 55% interest in the property, Inco was required to spend $1.5 million on exploration on the property and pay Atikokan $200,000 over a five year period.

Atikokan received an initial payment of $10,000 on the signing of the option agreement which was recorded as a reduction in mineral property and deferred exploration expenditures. However, in April 2002, Inco terminated the option agreement.

Required:

Examine the items listed under *Deferred exploration expenditures* in Exhibit 8-15, and notice that they include costs such as truck expenses, travel, and field office expenses. Explain the conditions under which it would be appropriate for a company to defer (capitalize) costs such as these. What accounting principles could be cited to support deferral or capitalization of these costs?

8-39 **(Accounting policies related to capital assets)**

Notes dealing with significant accounting policies for *property and equipment* and *goodwill* and intangible assets accompanying the 2003 financial statements of **Fairmont Hotels and Resorts Inc.** are shown in Exhibit 8-16.

FAIRMONT HOTELS AND RESORTS 2003 ANNUAL REPORT

EXHIBIT 8-16

Notes to the Consolidated Financial Statements...

Property and equipment

Property and equipment are recorded at cost. The Company's policy is to capitalize major renewals and replacements and interest incurred during the construction period on new facilities and during the renovation period of major renovations to existing facilities. Interest is capitalized, based on the borrowing rate of debt related to the project or if no specific financing is obtained, the Company's average cost of borrowing. Maintenance, repairs and minor renewals and replacements are charged against income when incurred.

Computer system development costs for internal use software are capitalized to the extent the project is expected to be of continuing benefit to the Company.

Amortization is provided at rates designed to amortize the assets over their estimated economic lives, except for buildings on leased land, which are amortized over the lesser of the term of the lease, including options, and the economic life of the building. The annual rates of amortization are as follows:

Buildings	40 years straight-line
Building equipment	17 – 25 years straight-line
Furniture, fixtures and equipment	5 – 17 years straight-line
Computer software	2 – 7 years straight-line
Vehicles	3 – 5 years straight-line
Leasehold improvements	over the term of the leases

Goodwill and intangible assets

Goodwill represents the excess of purchase price over the fair value of identifiable assets acquired in a purchase business combination. Intangible assets with indefinite useful lives represent costs that have been allocated to brand names and trademarks. Intangible assets with definite useful lives are costs that have been allocated to management contracts acquired in the acquisitions of Delta and Fairmont, as well as amounts paid to acquire individual management contracts.

Goodwill and intangibles with indefinite useful lives

Goodwill and intangible assets with indefinite useful lives are not amortized but are subject to impairment tests on at least an annual basis. The Company performs such impairment tests on at least an annual basis and additionally, whenever events and changes in circumstances suggest that the carrying amount may not be recoverable. Impairment of goodwill is tested at the reporting unit level by comparing the reporting unit's carrying amount, including goodwill, to the fair value of the reporting unit. The fair values of the reporting units are estimated using a combination of the income or discounted cash flows approach and the market approach, which utilizes comparable companies' data. If the carrying amount of the reporting unit exceeds its fair value, then a second step is performed to measure the amount of impairment loss, if any. Any impairment loss would be expensed in the consolidated statements of income. The impairment test for intangibles with indefinite useful lives consists of a comparison of the fair value of the intangible asset with its carrying amount. When the carrying amount of the intangible asset exceeds its fair value, an impairment loss is recognized for the difference.

Intangibles with definite useful lives

Management contracts acquired in a business combination are recorded at values that represent the estimated present value of net cash flows that, on acquisition, were expected to be received over the estimated lives of the contracts. They are amortized on a straight-line basis, reflecting the weighted average of the fixed, non-cancellable terms and certain renewal periods of the underlying contracts. Management contracts acquired in other than business combinations are recorded at cost and are amortized on a straight-line basis over the term of the contracts, including renewal terms where applicable.

Required:

Examine the company's accounting policies with respect to property and equipment, and goodwill and intangible assets, and answer the following questions.

a. Hotel and resort operators such as Fairmont have significant amounts invested in property and equipment, which must be regularly maintained or repaired, and periodically renewed or replaced. How does Fairmont account for the costs of major renewals and replacements? How does it account for the costs of maintenance, repairs, and minor renewals and replacements?

b. Does Fairmont Hotels and Resorts capitalize interest costs, or charge them directly to expense?

c. How does Fairmont account for computer system development costs for software to be used internally?

d. Over what period of time does Fairmont amortize its buildings? Furniture, fixtures, and equipment? Vehicles?

e. What general term does Fairmont use to refer to brand names and trademarks? Are these assets amortized?

Beyond the Book

8-40 (Financial statement disclosures)

Choose a company as directed by your instructor and answer the following.

a. Use the balance sheet and the notes to the financial statements to prepare an analysis of the capital assets, by listing the beginning and ending amounts in the various asset and accumulated amortization amounts and calculating the net change, in both dollar and percentage terms, for the most recent year.

b. If any of the amounts in part a) have changed more than 10%, provide an explanation for this change.

c. What percentage of the company's total assets is invested in property, plant, and equipment? Has this percentage changed significantly over the last year?

d. What amortization method(s) does the company use?

e. Use the following formulae to examine the property, plant, and equipment for the company.

Average Useful Life of PP&E = Total Gross PP&E / Annual Amort. Exp.

Average Age of PP&E = Total Accum. Amort. / Annual Amort. Expense

Note: Remember that amortization (depreciation) expense may not be disclosed in the income statement but will usually appear in the cash flow statement.

Compare your results with any information disclosed in the notes. Do these results make sense?

f. Does the company have any significant intangible assets? If so, describe each of them.

Cases

8-41   Onta and KewBee Sales Companies

Case Primer

Summary balance sheet and income statement information for Onta Sales Company and KewBee Sales Company, for the first year of operations for both, are shown below. The operations of the two businesses are similar. Upon investigation, you find that Onta is financed mainly by shareholders' equity and KewBee mainly by long-term debt. Onta amortizes all equipment at 10% straight-line and buildings at 5% straight-line, while KewBee amortizes equipment at 20% declining-balance and buildings at 10% declining-balance. Both have effective corporate income tax rates of 25%.

	Onta	KewBee
Balance Sheet Information		
Total current assets	$ 75,000	$ 80,000
Capital assets		
Land	140,000	125,000
Equipment	200,000	200,000
Accumulated amortization	(20,000)	(40,000)
Buildings	500,000	500,000
Accumulated amortization	(25,000)	(50,000)
Total assets	$ 870,000	$ 815,000
Total liabilities	$ 300,000	$ 700,000
Total shareholders' equity	570,000	115,000
Total liabilities and equity	$ 870,000	$ 815,000
Income Statement Information		
Revenues	$1,000,000	$1,000,000
Expenses		
Amortization	45,000	90,000
Interest	30,000	70,000
Other	770,000	770,000
Income taxes	38,750	17,500
Net income	$ 116,250	$ 52,500

Required:

a. Which company has the higher return on assets without adjusting for differences in amortization policy?

b. Using numbers from this example, explain why the ROA formula adjusts for interest after taxes in the numerator.

c. Which company has the higher return on assets after adjusting for differences in amortization policy? (Determine this using two different calculations: Onta's amortization method for KewBee, and KewBee's amortization method for Onta.)

d. Using numbers from this example, explain why you should adjust for differences in amortization policy when comparing different companies.

8-42   Rolling Fields Nursing Home

Rolling Fields Nursing Home purchased land to use for a planned assisted-living community. As a condition of the sale, a title search had to be performed and a survey completed. Rolling Fields incurred both these costs. In order to prepare the land for new construction, a small barn that was on the land when it was purchased had to be torn down. Finally, a series of streets and roads through the planned community had to be constructed and paved.

The year after the land was purchased, construction of new homes began. The homes are to be owned by Rolling Fields and will be rented on a long-term basis to elderly residents who no longer feel they can live completely on their own but do not yet need nursing home care. Rolling Fields will be responsible for all maintenance and repair costs associated with the properties. By the end of the year, Phase 1 was complete and 30 homes had been constructed and were occupied. The average cost of each home was $90,000.

In the first year, repair and maintenance costs averaged $600 per property. The company also borrowed $1,450,000 to finance thehome construction of the homes. Interest on the loan for the year was $108,000.

Required:

a. Determine which of the above expenditures should be capitalized. For those expenditures that are capitalized, identify the appropriate account to which the costs should be charged.

b. How should each asset class be amortized?

8-43 Hugh White

Hugh White is a real estate developer with several properties located throughout St. John's, Newfoundland. Although Mr. White sells most properties upon completion, in some instances he arranges to purchase the property either by himself or in a consortium with other investors.

During the current year, Mr. White was involved in two properties. The first property, a large residential rental complex that generates revenue of more than $1 million per year, was purchased solely by Mr. White. Because it is operated as a proprietorship, he pays personal income taxes on any profits earned by this property. Consequently, Mr. White has a strong incentive to maximize expenses in order to minimize net income and his tax liability.

The second property is owned by a group of professionals living in St. John's and is very similar in nature to the property owned by Mr. White. They have purchased the property as an investment opportunity and hired Mr. White to be the property manager. The group is very concerned with earning a reasonable return on the investment and Mr. White's compensation is based upon the property's profitability.

During the year, both properties required a new parking lot to be constructed. The new parking lots replace existing dirt lots but are significantly improved in that they are now paved and lighted, with a security system installed.

Required:

a. In discussions with Mr. White, you discover that he would like to capitalize the costs of the parking lot for which he is the property manager and expense the parking lot for his own building. What is his rationale for wanting this accounting treatment?

b. What is the appropriate accounting treatment for the costs of both parking lots?

8-44 Rock Maple Development Co.

Rock Maple Development Co. recently purchased a property for use as a manufacturing facility. The company paid $850,000 for a building, warehouse, and four hectares of land. When recording the purchase, the company accountant allocated $750,000 to the building, $50,000 to the warehouse, and $50,000 to the land. The warehouse is very old and after an independent appraisal, was deemed to have a value of only $35,000. The same appraisal valued the building at $650,000. The property is located near a major new highway and provides excellent access for shipping. Similar properties in the area have been selling for $75,000 per hectare.

Rock Maple is a very successful company and has traditionally reported very high net income. Last year, the company paid more than $200,000 in income taxes.

Required:

a. Determine the appropriate allocation between buildings and land for this basket purchase.

b. Why would the company accountant have wanted to allocate most of the costs to the building and warehouse, rather than the land?

8-45 Peterson Manufacturing

Peterson Manufacturing is a division of Wentworth Enterprises, a large multinational computer manufacturer. Peterson was acquired by Wentworth for its ability to manufacture high-quality, low-cost microchips. Wentworth has developed a compensation package whereby all division vice-presidents are compensated with a base salary and a bonus based on divisional performance as measured by the division's return on assets. If return on assets for the division exceeds the previous year's, the vice-president receives a $100,000 bonus. Wentworth allows its vice-presidents complete autonomy in running their divisions, with the guideline that the company considers any project with a projected ROA greater than 10% (after taxes) to be an excellent investment opportunity. Excerpts from the divisional financial statements for Peterson Manufacturing for the past three years are presented below.

The vice-president of Peterson Manufacturing, Haley Straub, is considering a new investment in equipment that will lead to higher quality chips that are able to process information much faster. The technology is very innovative and would revolutionize the industry. The cost of the related equipment will cause average total assets to increase by $8,500,000 and it is expected that net income before interest will increase by $975,000. The cost of financing the new project will cause interest expense to increase by $330,000.

PETERSON MANUFACTURING
Selected Financial Information
For the year ended July 31

	2006	2005	2004
Net Income	$ 1,150,000	$ 985,000	$ 947,000
Interest Expense	$ 337,500	$ 326,800	$ 322,500
Total Assets	$ 8,675,000	$ 8,425,000	$ 8,524,000

The company has a tax rate of 30%. Total assets in 2003 were $8,346,000.

> **Required:**
>
> a. Calculate Peterson Manufacturing's return on assets for the past three years.
>
> b. Calculate the return on assets of the new microchip project.
>
> c. From a personal perspective, what do you think Haley Straub's decision will be regarding the new project? Is this decision good for the company as a whole?

8-46 Preakness Consulting and Bellevue Services

Preakness Consulting and Bellevue Services are two petroleum engineering firms located in Calgary, Alberta. Both companies are very successful and are looking to attract additional investors to provide them with an infusion of capital to expand. In the past year, both companies had consulting revenue of $1.5 million. Expenses for both businesses are detailed below. Both companies have a tax rate of 25%.

On January 1, 2006, both companies purchased new computer systems. Currently, the only other asset owned by the companies is office equipment, which is fully amortized. The computer systems, related hardware, and installation cost each company $860,000 and the systems have an expected life of five years. The residual value at the end of the five-year period is expected to be $40,000 in each case.

Preakness has chosen to amortize the computer equipment using the straight-line method, while Bellevue has taken a more aggressive approach and is amortizing the system using the double-declining-balance method. Both companies have a December 31, 2006, year end.

Expense Information:

	Preakness	Bellevue
Salaries and wages	$650,250	$647,500
Rent	24,800	26,400
Office supplies	8,542	9,267
Other operating expenses	110,675	109,790

Required:

    a. For each company, prepare an amortization schedule showing the amount of amortization to be charged each year for the computer system.

    b. Prepare an income statement for the current year for both companies.

    c. How might an unsophisticated investor interpret the financial results? Is one company really more profitable than the other?

Critical Thinking Questions

8-47 (Classification of assets and liabilities)

O&Y Properties Corporation is a leading Canadian office property owner, manager, and developer. Its consolidated balance sheets for December 31, 2003 and 2002 are presented in Exhibit 8-17.

Required:

Notice that O&Y Properties does not present its balance sheets in a classified format (that is, the company does not subdivide its assets and liabilities into current and long-term sections). Do you think companies such as O&Y Properties should be required to present classified balance sheets? Why or why not?

8-48 (Capitalization of labour costs)

In the notes accompanying its 2002 financial statements, **Big Rock Brewery Ltd.** included the following statement.

    During the year ended March 31, 2002, the Company capitalized labour costs of $60,854 (2001 – $41,002; 2000 – $34,296) relating to certain enhancements at its brewing facilities.

Required:

    a. Under what conditions do you think it would be acceptable accounting practice for a company to capitalize labour costs?

    b. How would the company's balance sheets and income statements have been different if these labour costs had not been capitalized?

O&Y PROPERTIES CORPORATION 2003 ANNUAL REPORT

EXHIBIT 8-17

CONSOLIDATED BALANCE SHEETS

(in thousands of dollars)	NOTES	DECEMBER 31, 2003	DECEMBER 31, 2002
ASSETS			
Rental properties	3	$ 1,187,022	$ 1,060,722
Development properties	4	130,381	119,088
Goodwill and intangible assets	5	18,276	19,246
Deferred costs	6	46,902	29,285
Other assets	7	35,871	37,499
Cash and cash equivalents	8	32,057	22,708
		$ 1,450,509	$ 1,288,548
LIABILITIES			
Mortgages payable	9	$ 590,360	$ 494,137
Construction financing	10	65,418	51,027
Bank and other indebtedness	11	9,921	32,889
Accounts payable and other liabilities	12	68,312	72,207
Future income taxes	13	73,788	54,123
Debentures, notes and preferred shares, liability component	14	6,849	10,486
		814,648	714,869
Interest of others in O&Y REIT		230,745	164,916
Shareholders' equity		405,116	408,763
		$ 1,450,509	$ 1,288,548

See accompanying notes to consolidated financial statements.

On behalf of the Board:

Tibor Donath,
Director

Maureen Sabia,
Director

Good Payroll Systems Contribute to Good Employee Relations

Mountain Equipment Co-op, which sells outdoor clothing and gear in stores across Canada as well as through its catalogue and website world-wide, has a reputation among its members for its helpful, knowledgeable staff. Founded in 1971, the retailer now has more than 950 employees working at stores in Vancouver, Calgary, Edmonton, Winnipeg, Toronto, Ottawa, Montreal, Quebec City, and Halifax.

As a consumer co-operative, to which customers pay $5 for a lifetime membership, MEC depends on the dedication of its staff. Sales staff, who are all active outdoor enthusiasts themselves, do not receive commissions. This is why Treasury Manager Jennifer Henrey considers payroll to be the most important aspect of its accounting for liabilities. "Payroll is a huge area," she explains. "In fact, it is our biggest expense. It's also an area where there is little margin for error—pay reflects how valued employees feel, and they are understandably sensitive about it. So we endeavour to have accurate payroll, and we do."

Four full-time staff members, plus a part-time clerk, at MEC's Vancouver head office handle all payroll functions for the stores across Canada, which have salaried and hourly full- and part-time employees. While inventory, general accounting, and warehouse operations are managed by one software program, MEC uses a separate system for payroll. The actual calculation of pay, deductions (for the Canada Pension Plan, employment insurance), and benefits (both statutory benefits and disability and premium health-care plans) is straightforward with today's computerized accounting systems. However, exceptions, such as people leaving, provincial variations in rules for statutory holiday pay, or hours that need to be keyed in, require human intervention or additional calculations, Ms. Henrey explains.

Employees at each store report on how much of their time is spent on different functions: working the floor area, the cash area, the stock room, and so forth. The head office tracks and collates this information, so store managers can see how their resources are allocated.

Up to now, hourly employees have manually filled in time sheets; the payroll clerks then manually entered that data. But MEC plans to implement an automated time-tracking system. Hourly workers, which are the majority of MEC's staff, will swipe a card as they arrive and leave, and the number of hours they work will be automatically entered into the system, explains Controller Laura Colwill. "Once the system's up and running, it should be more efficient than the manual work," Ms. Colwill says. "Plus, it should be more accurate because, no matter how good your data-entry people are, there's always room for error."

With this automated system, MEC will still be able to monitor the amount of work done in specific areas. "The automated time and attendance system allows us to track time in the same manner," says Payroll Manager Shannon Beatty. "For example, employees could swipe every time they work in a different area, or they could be scheduled to work in different areas, and the time and attendance system can pay to that schedule. Essentially, MEC can configure the system to track time in many ways."

Short-Term Liabilities

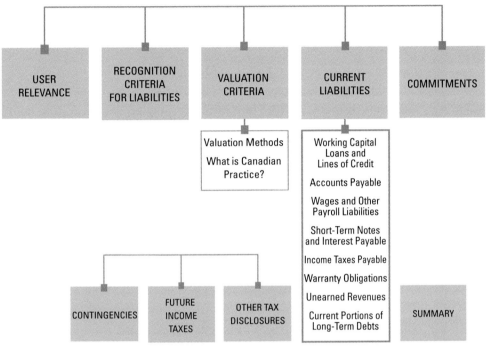

After studying this chapter, you should be able to:

1. Describe the valuation methods used for liabilities in Canada.

2. Explain why companies use working capital loans and lines of credit.

3. Explain why accounts payable are sometimes thought of as "free debt."

4. Prepare journal entries to record a company's payroll.

5. Calculate the amount of interest that is owed on a short-term note payable.

6. Describe how warranty obligations differ from current liabilities such as accounts payable.

7. Describe situations where unearned revenues must be recorded.

8. Explain why the portion of long-term debt that is due in the next year is recorded as a current liability.

9. Explain what a commitment is and how it is recognized by a company.

10. Explain contingencies and the criteria governing their accounting treatment.

11. Describe why future income taxes exist.

12. Calculate future income taxes in amortization and warranty situations.

People like Jennifer Henrey of Mountain Equipment Co-op would agree that good employee relations are important to a successful business. One way that MEC fosters good relations is through strict attention to detail with respect to payroll. Errors in payroll can affect morale. MEC used to use an outside contractor to manage its payroll function. Smaller businesses and even some medium-sized and large companies may find it more cost-effective to use an outside group with expertise in a particular accounting area (such as payroll) rather than to hire people as full-time employees. MEC has now grown to the point where it wants more information from its payroll data and it has found it easier to customize its information flow by making the payroll function an internal one.

Successful businesses also pay attention to obligations owed to people outside the company. A good reputation for paying debts on time enables a company to use credit to operate effectively and to take on new initiatives. A poor credit rating, on the other hand, means a curtailment of options for outside financing.

In this and the next two chapters, our attention turns to the credit side of the balance sheet and the accounting for liabilities and shareholders' equity. Both liabilities and shareholders' equity can be viewed as sources of assets. Liability holders contribute assets in return for a promise of repayment at some future date, usually with interest. Shareholders contribute assets to the company in return for an ownership interest and the right to share in company profits.

The general nature of liabilities is discussed first, followed by current liabilities, contingent liabilities, and future income taxes. Chapter 10 covers major noncurrent liabilities, such as bonds, leases, and pensions. In Chapter 11, shareholders' equity transactions are discussed.

USER RELEVANCE

Current liabilities represent obligations that the company must settle within the next year. Most of these obligations—accounts payable, income taxes payable, wages payable, notes payable, etc.—will require an outflow of cash. Users can examine the current liabilities to determine how much cash will be required and to estimate when that cash will need to be paid in one week, one month, three months, etc. Examining the current assets, especially cash, accounts receivable, and temporary investments, will provide the user with information about the availability of cash. We have already talked about determining how quickly accounts receivable are collected and inventory is sold. These turnover ratios help users estimate whether enough cash is going to be available when the various liabilities come due. If there is not enough cash available, the company will have to go to outside sources—short-term debt, long-term debt, issuing more shares—in order to raise additional cash. Understanding a company's short-term cash needs is essential to determining its financial health and its long-term viability.

RECOGNITION CRITERIA FOR LIABILITIES

Liabilities represent obligations agreed to by the company through some past transaction. To be classified as a liability, an item must have three characteristics. First, it requires that the company settle the obligation through the transfer of assets, the performance of services, or the conferring of some other benefit specified in the transaction. There is usually a specific time when the settlement must occur. Second, companies usually have little or no discretion with respect to liabilities. If they do not satisfy the obligation, the creditor usually has the right to pursue legal action. Third, the transaction or event that gave rise to the obligation must have already occurred.

The transfer of assets or services criterion is similar to the probable future value criterion for assets. The uncertainty associated with liabilities concerns the dollar value of the assets to be given up, and when that sacrifice will be made.

To avoid uncertainty about the amount and timing of the settlement, some liabilities have fixed payments and fixed due dates. Most loans and accounts payable are of this type. The interest and principal payments are specified in the loan agreement, as are the dates on which those payments will be made. Other liabilities, such as warranty obligations, may have neither fixed payments nor fixed dates. The settlement of a warranty obligation will depend on when the customer detects a warranty problem and the cost the company incurs to fix it. Liabilities, therefore, differ in the amount of uncertainty that is associated with them.

If the uncertainty associated with either the amount or the timing of the future transfer is sufficiently high, the liability will probably not be recognized in the financial statements. Suppose, for example, that the company is under investigation by the government for an alleged chemical spill into a river. Does the company have an obligation to transfer assets in the future? If the company is found negligent, there could be a significant liability if a fine is imposed and/or if the company is required to clean up the spill. The company may have a difficult time, however, predicting whether it will be found negligent and, if so, how much it will cost to satisfy the obligation. In this case, it is likely that no liability will be recorded in the accounts. However, because assets may have to be transferred in the future, the company could disclose information about the investigation in the notes to the financial statements. Such an item would be referred to as a **contingent liability**, in that the future obligation is dependent or contingent upon certain events occurring.

The ownership criterion that is used for assets does not strictly apply to liabilities, but a similar notion is present. Companies should record only those obligations that they will be required to satisfy. For example, if a customer falls on the company's sidewalk, sues the company for medical costs, and wins, the company may not be obliged to make the payment. If the company is insured against such claims, the insurance company will pay the claim. The company, therefore, would not record the obligation to settle the customer's claim as a liability on its books, because it is the insurance company's obligation. (However, if the insurance does not cover all the obligation, the company would record any excess as a liability.)

The third characteristic of a liability—proving that the event that gave rise to the obligation has already occurred—is sometimes difficult to evaluate. For example, in the case of the lawsuit mentioned in the preceding paragraph, what is the event that gave rise to the obligation? Is it the customer falling on the sidewalk, the filing of a lawsuit, or the court decision? In this case, the obligation's certainty increases as each subsequent event occurs. However, the event that gives rise to the ultimate obligation is debatable.

Another difficulty that can make evaluation difficult arises when the company signs a binding contract. Suppose, for example, the company signs a contract to purchase 1,000 units of inventory at $30 per unit, to be delivered 30 days from now. Is the signing of the contract the event that gives rise to the obligation to pay for the inventory, or is it the delivery of the inventory? The company's obligation is contingent upon the seller performing its part of the contract, by delivering the goods on time. If the goods are not delivered, then the company is not obliged to pay. The contract signing creates what is known as a **mutually unexecuted contract** because, at the time of signing, neither the buyer nor the seller has performed its part of the contract. The seller has not delivered any inventory, and the buyer has not paid any cash. Such contracts are normally not recorded in the accounting system, although the company may include information about the contract in the notes to its financial statements.

A **partially executed contract** is one in which one party has performed all or part of its obligation. In the example just given, the contract would be viewed as partially executed if the buyer had made a $3,000 deposit. A partial transaction would then be recorded. In this case, the seller would show an inflow of cash of $3,000 and create a liability account to represent its obligation to deliver inventory valued at $3,000. The liability account would probably be called "unearned revenue." Once inventory valued at $3,000 was delivered to the customer, the obligation would be satisfied and the revenue would be earned. The buyer would show an outflow of cash of $3,000, and create an asset account for the right to receive the inventory valued at $3,000. The account would be called "deposits on purchase commitments" (or something similar). Note that only the amount of the deposit is recorded at this time, not the full amount of the contract ($30,000 = 1,000 units $\times$ $30 per unit).

VALUATION CRITERIA

LEARNING OBJECTIVE 1

Describe the valuation methods used for liabilities in Canada.

Just as there are different methods for valuing assets, there are different methods for valuing liabilities. Theoretically, liabilities are valued at their **net present value** on the date they are incurred. There are, however, several possible valuation methods to be considered before discussing Canadian practice in depth.

Valuation Methods

One way to value a liability is to record it at the gross amount of the obligation; that is, the total of the payments to be made. For example, if an obligation requires the company to pay $1,000 each month for the next three years, the gross obligation would be $36,000. While this amount accurately measures the total payments to be made, it may not accurately measure the company's obligation as at the date it is recorded on the balance sheet. For example, suppose the obligation is a rental agreement for a piece of machinery. If the company can cancel the rental agreement at any time, it is obliged to pay only $1,000 each month. The remaining payments are an obligation only if it decides to keep using the asset. If the contract was non-cancellable, valuing the full $36,000 would make more sense.

Another reason why the gross obligation may not adequately measure the liability's value is that it ignores the time value of money. Suppose that, in the example, the $1,000 a month is to repay a loan. The total payments of $36,000 include both the repayment of principal and the payment of interest. Interest accrues as an obligation only as the company uses the money over time. If the company has the option to pay off the loan early, it merely has to pay off the principal balance and any accumulated interest. It does not have to pay the full amount. Suppose, for example, that the loan principal is $31,000. The difference ($5,000) between this amount and the gross amount is the interest that accrues over time. The company could settle the obligation today with a payment of $31,000. Therefore, recording the liability at $36,000 would overstate the company's obligation at the present time.

To recognize the time value of money, a company may record its obligations at their net present value. Both the future payments on the principal and the interest payments are discounted back to the current period, using an appropriate interest rate. Chapter 10 will go into more detail about present value calculations. Under this valuation system, the company records the obligation at the net present value, rather than the gross amount of the payments to be made. As payments are made, the obligation is reduced and interest expense is recorded to represent the cost of the loan over time. It is important to remember that interest is only recorded as time passes.

What Is Canadian Practice?

In Canada, liabilities should be recorded at the present value of the future payments. The interest rate used depends on the type of liability and the company's creditworthiness. It should be the appropriate interest rate for an arm's-length transaction of the type that gives rise to the obligation. However, accountants do not use present-value calculations for short-term liabilities such as accounts payable because the time to maturity is so short that the difference would not be material. Instead, current liabilities such as accounts payable and wages payable are recorded at the gross amount that is owed. (In most cases, interest is not charged on these types of liabilities.) Short-term notes payable that have an interest component are recorded at the total principal amount, and the interest is recorded as it accrues over time.

Once a liability is recorded, the carrying value is not usually adjusted except when the liability is paid. One exception occurs when a company is in financial trouble and restructures its debt in negotiations with its creditors. Based on the concessions that the company may obtain from the lenders, it may be able to reduce the amount owed on the obligations, to reduce the interest rates used to calculate interest expense on the existing balances, or to extend the periods over which the debts are to be paid. This is called **troubled debt restructuring**.

CURRENT LIABILITIES

Current liabilities are those obligations that require the transfer of assets or services within one year, or one operating cycle of the company. As just discussed, most of them are carried on the books at their gross amount. In order for a company to stay solvent (able to pay its debts as they fall due), it must have sufficient current assets and/or assets generated by operations to pay the current liabilities. Creditors, such as bankers, will often use total current liabilities to assess the company's ability to remain viable. The most frequently encountered current liabilities are discussed in the following subsections.

Working Capital Loans and Lines of Credit

As mentioned in the preceding paragraph, companies need to have sufficient current assets or inflows of cash from operations to pay debts as they fall due. However, some of those current assets may not be converted into cash fast enough to meet current debt obligation deadlines. To manage this shortfall, companies have a few options. For example, they can arrange a **working capital loan** with a bank. This short-term loan is often secured by customer balances in accounts receivable, by inventory, or both. As money is received from accounts receivable or as the inventory is sold, the amounts received are used to pay off the loan.

Another way that companies can deal with cash shortages is to arrange a **line of credit** with a bank. In this case, the bank assesses the company's ability to repay short-term debts and establishes a short-term debt balance that it feels is reasonable. This provides the company with more flexibility and freedom to take advantage of business opportunities and/or to settle debts. If cheques written by the company exceed the current cash balance in the bank, the bank covers the excess by immediately activating the line of credit and establishing a short-term loan. Subsequent cash deposits by the company are used by the bank to repay the loan.

A company that is using a working capital loan or a line of credit might have a negative cash balance, which must be shown with the current liabilities. This negative cash balance would be obvious to users on the cash flow statement because the ending cash balance would also be negative. For example, at the end of 2003 **Sleeman Breweries Ltd.** had an "authorized working capital facility" (or operating line of credit) from a syndicate of lenders with a limit of $20,000,000. Of this amount, the company had used only $555,000 at the end of 2003; this was reported as bank indebtedness, in the current liabilities section of Sleeman's balance sheet. A year earlier, the company had a line of credit with a limit of $22,000,000, against which it had borrowed $10,461,000. Sleeman's use of this credit facility therefore declined dramatically during 2003. The interest rate applicable to this line of credit was the prime lending rate (i.e., the rate that is offered to the banks' very best customers), which at the time was 4.5%.

Accounts Payable

Accounts payable occur when a company buys goods or services on credit. These are sometimes referred to as *trade accounts payable*. (For an example, see the liability section of the balance sheet for **Metro Inc.** in Exhibit 9-1.) Payment is generally deferred for a relatively short period of time, such as 30 to 60 days. These accounts generally do not carry explicit interest charges and are sometimes thought of as "free debt." However, there is sometimes a provision for either a penalty for late payment or a discount for early payment. The penalty and the difference between the discounted payment and the full payment can both be viewed as interest charges for delayed payments on these liabilities.

METRO INC. 2003 ANNUAL REPORT

EXHIBIT 9-1

Liabilities

Current

Bank loans *(note 10)*	$ 79.6	$ 53.1
Accounts payable	536.6	511.5
Income taxes payable	20.8	2.9
Future income taxes *(note 5)*	37.8	—
Current portion of long-term debt *(note 11)*	3.9	3.6
	678.7	571.1
Long-term debt *(note 11)*	8.8	25.0
Future income taxes *(note 5)*	67.7	91.8
	755.2	687.9

Wages and Other Payroll Liabilities

LEARNING OBJECTIVE 4

Prepare journal entries to record a company's payroll.

Wages owed to employees can be another significant current liability. Its magnitude depends somewhat on how often the company pays its employees, because the balance in the account reflects the accrual of wages since the last pay period. In addition to the wages themselves, the company may provide fringe benefits for employees that must be quantified. These accruals for health care, pensions, vacation pay, and other benefits must also be recognized in the periods in which they occur. Because these may be paid in periods other than those in which they are earned by the employees, liabilities have to be recorded.

Additionally, the company acts as a government agent (federal and provincial) in collecting certain taxes. For example, income taxes must be withheld from employees' wages and remitted to the government. While this is not an expense to the company, the company must nevertheless keep track of the amounts deducted from employees' earnings and show the liability to pay these amounts to the government. The liability to pay the employees is reduced by the amount withheld.

Other items, such as Canada Pension Plan (CPP) or Quebec Pension Plan (QPP) and employment insurance (EI), are also deducted from employees' total wages and remitted to the government. This further reduces the amount paid to employees. Beyond the amount deducted from employees' wages, companies must make their own payments to the government for CPP or QPP, EI, workers' compensation, and in some provinces, public health care premiums. These amounts are shown as an expense to the employer and are recorded as liabilities until they are remitted to the government.

For 2004, CPP was deducted from employees' earnings at the rate of 4.95%, while the rate for EI deductions was 1.98%. Employers were required to contribute an amount equal to the employees' deductions for CPP, and 1.4 times the amount deducted from their employees for EI. However, these rates are subject to change from year to year. Therefore, for simplicity, we will use rates of 5% for CPP and 2% for EI in our calculations for the examples and assignment materials.

As an example, assume that Angelique's Autobody Shop has a two-week payroll of $7,500 for its seven employees. Income tax totalling $1,900 is deducted from the employees' cheques, as well as 5% for CPP and 2% for EI. The employer has to submit an additional 5% for CPP and 2.8% (1.4 times the amount deducted from the employees) for EI as the company's contribution. The journal entries to record the payroll would be as follows.

DEDUCTIONS FROM EMPLOYEES' EARNINGS

Wages expense (SE) [given]	7,500	
Employee income taxes payable (L) [given]		1,900
CPP contributions payable (L) [5% of 7,500]		375
EI premiums payable (L) [2% of 7,500]		150
Cash (A)		5,075
ADDITIONAL AMOUNTS TO BE PAID BY THE EMPLOYER:		
Wages expense (SE)	585	
CPP contributions payable (L) [5% of 7,500]		375
EI premiums payable (L) [2.8% of 7,500]		210

The amounts in the three liability accounts are remitted periodically to the government, according to its regulations. The following journal entry illustrates the remittance.

Employee income taxes payable (L) [from above]	1,900	
CPP contributions payable (L) [375 + 375]	750	
EI premiums payable (L) [150 + 210]	360	
Cash (A)		3,010

Note that the total amount recorded by the employer as an expense ($8,085) exceeds the amount it has agreed to pay the employees ($7,500). Because of these extra amounts that the government requires companies to pay, businesses are concerned each time the government makes changes to the Canada Pension Plan or employment insurance scheme (unless of course, the government reduces the rates). The additional amounts must always be taken into account by an employer, because they increase the costs of hiring employees.

Short-Term Notes and Interest Payable

LEARNING OBJECTIVE 5

Calculate the amount of interest that is owed on a short-term note payable.

Short-term notes payable represent company borrowings that require repayment in the next year or operating cycle. They either carry explicit interest rates or are structured such that the difference between the original amount borrowed and the amount repaid represents implicit interest. Interest expense and interest payable should be recognized over the life of these loan agreements.

Assume that the Checkerboard Taxi Company borrowed $10,000 at 9% from the local bank. The loan was to be repaid in monthly instalments of $1,710.70 over six months. The monthly instalments included reductions of the principal ($10,000) as well as interest at 9% per annum. The interest is calculated on the decreasing amount of principal. The following amortization table illustrates the interest component and the reductions of the principal.

Month	Payment	Interest	Principal Reduction	Principal Balance
				$10,000.00
1	$1,710.70	$75.00[a]	$1,635.70	$ 8,364.30
2	$1,710.70	$62.73[b]	$1,647.97	$ 6,716.33
3	$1,710.70	$50.37	$1,660.33	$ 5,056.00
4	$1,710.70	$37.92	$1,672.78	$ 3,383.22
5	$1,710.70	$25.37	$1,685.33	$ 1,697.89
6	$1,710.70	$12.81[c]	$1,697.89	-0-

[a] $10,000 × .09 × 1/12 = $75.00
[b] $8,364.30 × .09 × 1/12 = $62.73
[c] rounding of $0.08

The journal entry to record the first payment, at the end of the first month, would be:

Interest expense (SE)	75.00	
Short-term note payable (L)	1,635.70	
Cash (A)		1,710.70

Try to reconstruct the journal entries for the remaining months. The short-term note payable would initially have been recorded at the principal amount of $10,000, then gradually reduced as monthly payments were made; it should have a balance of zero after the final payment is made.

Income Taxes Payable

Companies are subject to both federal and provincial corporate income taxes. Multinational companies may also be subject to taxation in the other countries in which they operate. As mentioned earlier in the book, the rules governing the calculation of income for tax purposes differ from the accounting guidelines in many respects. The discussion in Chapter 8 concerning future income taxes highlighted this difference (future income taxes are discussed in greater detail later in this chapter). The taxes that become payable under the rules of the taxing authorities must be recorded as a liability.

The payment of taxes does not always coincide with the incurrence of the taxes. In Canada, companies are required to make monthly tax payments, usually based on taxes paid the previous year, so that the government has a steady flow of cash during the year on which to operate. The deadline for filing the yearly tax return is six months after the corporate year end, but the balance of taxes owed for a year must be paid within two months of the year end. Penalties are imposed if the company significantly underestimates the amount of tax payable.

Warranty Obligations

LEARNING OBJECTIVE 6

Describe how warranty obligations differ from current liabilities such as accounts payable.

When a company sells goods or services, there are either explicit or implicit guarantees to the buyers. If the product or service fails to satisfy the customer, the seller may have to provide warranty service. Although at the time of sale, the company will not know how much service it will have to provide, it should estimate the cost in order to match the expense from the warranty to the revenue from the sale. Therefore, to satisfy the matching principle, at the time of sale a warranty expense and a warranty liability are recognized, based on an estimate of the future warranty costs for that sale. If the company has been in business for a reasonable length of time, this estimate can be made fairly easily, based on the history of product defects. For new products and new companies, this may be much more difficult. Later, as warranty service is provided (paid for by cash or other resources), the estimated liability amount is reduced.

As an example of a warranty situation, let us consider Hubble Appliance Company, which sells large appliances such as stoves and refrigerators. During December 2005, it sold eight refrigerators, each of which carried a three-year warranty against mechanical defects. If the refrigerators sold for an average price of $1,150, Hubble would record revenues of $9,200 ($1,150 × 8). Although Hubble buys quality merchandise from its supplier, it is possible that within three years of sale, one or more of these refrigerators may break down. In reviewing its record of mechanical breakdowns, Hubble estimates that, over the long term, it costs approximately 5% of the sales revenue to fix all the units that ultimately require repair work under the warranty. Over the next three years, Hubble therefore expects to spend about $460 ($9,200 × .05) to fix one or more of the eight refrigerators just sold. Of course, this is just an estimate, based upon averages; it may spend more or less than $460. Experience and knowledge of the merchandise usually allow companies to make reasonably accurate estimates of what the warranty costs will be.

To record the estimated warranty obligation in the year of the sale, Hubble would make the following journal entry.

Warranty expense (SE)	460	
Estimated warranty obligation (L)		460

If Hubble needed to spend $126 in 2006 to replace a leaking seal on a refrigerator, it would record the warranty repair work by reducing the liability account as follows.

Estimated warranty obligation (L)	126	
Cash (A)		126

As you can see, an expense is not recorded when actual repair costs are incurred. By estimating its potential future obligation at the same time that it recorded revenue from the sale, Hubble was able to record the warranty expense in the same period that it recorded the revenue. In this way, users get a clearer picture of the profitability of each period's operations. If Hubble had delayed recognizing an expense until it actually incurred some warranty costs, that expense could easily have appeared in a period other than the one in which the revenue was recognized, and the matching principle would have been violated. The profit reported for the sale would then have been overstated. (This was illustrated in the foregoing example, in which the sale occurred and the warranty cost was estimated in 2005, and the

---

HELPFUL HINT:

Warranties provide another illustration of the importance of the matching principle in measuring income. Whenever revenues are recorded, it is important to record all the related expenses in the same period (even if the costs will not actually be incurred until later), so that the income statement shows a complete picture of the results of operations during that period.

Of course, it is also important to ensure that the balance sheet shows the company's true financial position at the end of the period. By recording a warranty liability, accountants recognize that when goods are sold with a warranty the company incurs an obligation to honour the claims that will arise under it.

warranty work was performed in 2006.) For this reason, companies are required to estimate the potential future warranty obligation and to record it at the time of sale, if the amount of warranty costs is material.

accounting in the news

FREQUENT FLYER POINTS

Frequent flyer programs, which allow people to accumulate points they later trade in for free air travel, are a good example of a future liability. Airlines need to account for them because people eventually redeem their points. By one estimate, two trillion points were outstanding in 1997—enough to fill 440,000 300-seat planes and send airlines into bankruptcy!

However, major airlines only rate the liability at 25 cents per $1,000 of outstanding cashable miles. Why? They don't expect to pay for every mile outstanding. Many people never claim their free flights: some people forget, and some never fly enough to reach minimum award levels.

Source: "Frequent travellers: How a frequent flyer can make a point," Advertising Special Report, *Globe and Mail*, April 25, 1997, p. C11.

In the airline industry, frequent flyer programs are treated in much the same manner as warranties. As customers accumulate travel miles, the company records an expense (to represent the cost of providing free flights) and a liability (to represent the company's future obligation to honour the credits earned by customers). But some customers never collect enough points to earn a free flight. Others may not redeem their points even though they have enough for a free flight. Should the companies accrue a liability for all the potential free flights, or would it be more appropriate to estimate future redemptions of points and accrue a liability to represent that estimate? The article summary above should provide some insight into this problem.

Unearned Revenues

In many businesses, customers are required to pay deposits or make down payments prior to receiving goods or services. This creates partially executed contracts between buyers and sellers. Because the sellers have not fulfilled their part of the contract, it would be inappropriate for them to recognize revenue at this point. Therefore, sellers must defer the recognition of revenue from deposits or down payments. These deferrals create liabilities that are known as **unearned revenues** or **deferred revenues**.

Businesses that require prepayments show unearned revenues in the liability section of the balance sheet, because by accepting the money in advance they incur an obligation to provide the related goods or services (or, failing that, to return the money). Magazine and newspaper publishers and airline companies are among these types of businesses. For example, the current liability section of Air Canada's balance sheet as of December 31, 2003, included $529 million for Advance Ticket Sales. The note on air transportation revenue stated that "Airline passenger and cargo sales are recognized as operating revenues when the transportation is provided. The value of unused transportation is included in current liabilities."

HELPFUL HINT:

Remember that a key concept in revenue recognition is that revenues cannot be recorded until they have been earned. Consequently, unearned (or deferred) revenues are reported as liabilities on the balance sheet, rather than as revenues on the income statement. Once the related goods have been delivered or services performed, these amounts will be considered earned and an adjusting entry will be made to transfer them out of the liability account and into a revenue account.

LEARNING OBJECTIVE 7

Describe situations where unearned revenues must be recorded.

Current Portions of Long-Term Debts

LEARNING OBJECTIVE 8

Explain why the portion of long-term debt that is due in the next year is recorded as a current liability.

When long-term debts (discussed in Chapter 10) come within a year of being due, they must be reclassified as current liabilities. This reclassification enables users to estimate more accurately the outflow of cash expected during the following year. Therefore, this liability category, generally known as **current portion of long-term debt**, is used for all the debt that was originally long-term but is now within one year, or one operating cycle, of being paid off or retired. In the case of long-term mortgages or other debt obligations requiring monthly or annual payments, the current maturity part that is shown with the current liabilities represents the amount of principal that will be paid off in the next year. Remember that the interest on debt is only recorded as it accrues or is paid. Note in Exhibit 9-1 that in 2003, approximately 31% of Metro's long-term debt ($3.9 ÷ [3.9 + 8.8]) was due to be paid within the next year.

COMMITMENTS

LEARNING OBJECTIVE 9

Explain what a commitment is and how it is recognized by a company.

In the course of business, many companies sign agreements committing them to certain transactions. A common type of commitment transaction is a **purchase commitment**, which is an agreement to purchase items in the future for a pre-negotiated price. As discussed earlier, this is an example of a mutually unexecuted contract and is therefore not recorded as a liability. The company would, however, discuss it in a note to the financial statements if it thought that the commitment would have a material effect on future operations. An example of this type of disclosure can be seen in Exhibit 9-2.

EXHIBIT 9-2   **AT PLASTICS INC. 2003 ANNUAL REPORT**

16. COMMITMENTS AND CONTINGENCIES

(a) Operating leases

Under the terms of operating leases, the Company is committed to rental payments until expiry of leases as follows:

2003	$	3,907
2004		3,483
2005		3,335
2006		3,147
2007		2,684
Thereafter		8,915

(b) Purchases

The Company has entered into a 15-year ethylene supply contract that commenced in 1999 for approximately 125,000 tonnes per year under a limited take-or-pay arrangement.

The Company has entered into a 10-year electrical energy supply contract that commenced in 2000 for a minimum of 1.57 billion kilowatts per year at a fixed rate per kilowatt.

AT Plastics disclosed the information about the leases because the company is committed to the given outflows of cash as a result of the lease contracts. It disclosed the information about the ethylene supply contract because of the type of contract involved, and because it is committed for several years. A **take-or-pay contract** means that the company must pay for the 125,000 tonnes of ethylene whether it actually takes that much from the supplier or not. No monetary amounts are discussed, but the fact that the take-or-pay contract is limited may mean that the amount that must be paid each year has an upper limit. The electrical supply contract states the minimum number of kilowatts that must be purchased each year.

This disclosure of information about the two supply **commitments** is useful to users in two ways. First, it lets them know of a possible future cost to the company whether the item is purchased or not. Second, and probably more importantly, it lets users know that the company is planning ahead and attempting to get long-term commitments at fixed prices for items that it knows it is going to need in its manufacturing process. Such commitments would be of concern to users if the price of these items started to fall in the marketplace, leaving the company committed to paying prices higher than would have been paid if no contract was in place. If this happens, the company will incur a loss as a result of having made the purchase commitment.

accounting in the news

Technology equipment manufacturers, major casualties of the high-tech crash in 2001, have been left vulnerable by commitments they made to suppliers when the sector was at its peak.

One study estimates that manufacturers, especially those in the telecom industry, would have to write off billions. The 2002 study by Booz Allen & Hamilton, a management consultancy firm, noted that seven companies in the technology equipment sector tallied up a $5.4-billion (U.S.) inventory write-off for 2001.

Responding to a supply squeeze in 1999 and 2000, equipment manufacturers entered into contracts to buy a certain share of a supplier's production for a specified period. But demand collapsed, and these companies were locked into commitments that would result in mounting inventory, which can quickly become obsolete.

Renegotiating the terms of the commitments could mean cash penalties for companies. A co-author of the study said these companies could put the lure of future contracts, as well as the possibility of withdrawing their business, on the renegotiating table with suppliers.

The analysis included Canadian companies Nortel Networks Inc., Celestica Inc., and JDS Uniphase Corp., though it did not identify which companies had the most exposure.

Source: "Huge writeoffs predicted to hit tech firms," by Patrick Brethour, *The Globe and Mail*, January 29, 2002, p. B4.

When a company's financial statements are analyzed, undisclosed purchase commitments are a significant risk to be considered. The problem this can pose for the reader of financial statements is illustrated by an international example from **Westinghouse Company** in the United States in the mid-1970s. Westinghouse was in the business of building nuclear power plants for utility companies. To secure the construction business, Westinghouse offered utility companies fixed-price contracts to supply them with uranium after the plants were completed and running. The average prices stated in these contracts were approximately $8 to $10 (U.S.) per pound of uranium. By the mid-1970s, Westinghouse was committed to providing a total of approximately 70 million pounds over a 20-year period. Since these were mutually unexecuted contracts, they were not recorded or disclosed in the financial statements.

When market price of uranium was close to the price fixed in the contracts, these mutually unexecuted contracts were a break-even proposition for Westinghouse (i.e., no gain or loss would occur when the contracts were satisfied), and no disclosure was required. The problem began when a cartel formed in the uranium supply market and drove up the price of the fuel. When the price reached $26 (U.S.) per pound in September 1975, Westinghouse informed the utility companies that it had to be excused from performing on its contracts because of a legal doctrine called commercial impracticability. The utility companies then brought lawsuits against Westinghouse, alleging breach of contract. By 1978, the price of uranium had risen to $45 (U.S.) per pound.

Because the price escalated so significantly above the contract price of $8–$10 (U.S.) per pound, Westinghouse had to disclose the loss on these commitment contracts. In 1975, the estimated cost to Westinghouse of settling the contracts approached $2 billion, which was about 75% of its total equity at the time. The first lawsuit was settled in 1977, for $20.5 million. The audit opinion on Westinghouse was qualified by the auditors until 1979, when the company accrued an additional loss of $405 million (net of taxes) to cover the estimated costs of settling the remaining suits. Remember that auditors qualify their opinion about a company's financial statements if the company does not follow GAAP. Failing to accrue the expected liability for the lawsuits would have led to such a qualification.

LEARNING OBJECTIVE 10

Explain contingencies and the criteria governing their accounting treatment.

CONTINGENCIES

Contingent liabilities (also referred to as **contingent losses**) arise when the incurrence of the liability depends upon some future event. The settlement of a lawsuit, for example, the company may or may not incur a liability, depending upon the judgement in the case. Exhibit 9-3 provides an example of how such **contingencies** can be disclosed.

EXHIBIT 9-3

ALCAN INC. 2003 ANNUAL REPORT

Alcan, in the course of its operations, is subject to environmental and other claims, lawsuits and contingencies. The Company has environmental contingencies relating to approximately 111 existing and former Alcan sites and third-party sites. Accruals have been made in specific instances where it is probable that liabilities will be incurred and where such liabilities can be reasonably estimated. Environmental provisions were recorded in 2002 and 2001 for treatment costs relating to spent potlining in Canada and for remediation costs relating to red mud disposal at other sites in Canada and the U.K.

Although there is a possibility that liabilities may arise in other instances for which no accruals have been made, the Company does not believe that it is reasonably possible that losses in excess of accrued amounts are sufficient to significantly impair its operations, have a material adverse effect on its financial position or liquidity, or materially and adversely affect its results of operations for any particular reporting period, absent unusual circumstances, will occur.

In Canada, a contingent loss should be recognized as a loss on the income statement and a liability on the balance sheet if it meets the following criteria.

1. It is likely that some future event will result in the company incurring an obligation that will require the use of assets or the performance of a service.

2. The amount of the loss and the resulting liability can be reasonably estimated.

If either of these criteria is not met, but the potential for loss is significant, the company should provide users with information about the potential loss in a note disclosure similar to the two examples that follow.

Another kind of contingency is the guarantee of one company's loan by another company. This happens many times when a subsidiary company takes out a loan and the parent company (the company that owns most of the subsidiary's shares) guarantees repayment of the loan. The liability to repay the loan is a contingent liability to the parent company, because it depends on the default of the subsidiary; if the subsidiary company repays the loan according to its terms, the parent will have no liability. Such a contingency is illustrated in another excerpt from the 2003 annual report for **Alcan Inc.**, shown in Exhibit 9-4.

ALCAN INC. 2003 ANNUAL REPORT

EXHIBIT 9-4

"The Company has guaranteed the repayment of approximately $187 (million U.S. dollars) of indebtedness of third parties. Alcan believes that none of these guarantees is likely to be invoked."

As a third and final example, the selling of accounts receivable with recourse creates a contingent liability for the selling company, because it may be required to buy back the receivables under the recourse provision if the customers default on their payments. (A further discussion of the sale of receivables is presented in Chapter 6.) As shown in Exhibit 9-5, **Canada Bread Company Limited** disclosed in its 2003 annual report that it had sold trade accounts receivable to financial institutions, and as a result had contingent liabilities in the form of limited recourse obligations for delinquent receivables.

CANADA BREAD COMPANY, LIMITED 2003 ANNUAL REPORT

EXHIBIT 9-5

3. ACCOUNTS RECEIVABLE

Under a revolving securitization program, the Company has sold, with limited recourse, certain of its trade accounts receivable to financial institutions. The Company retains servicing responsibilities and assumes limited recourse obligations for delinquent receivables. At December 31, 2003, trade accounts receivable amounting to $50 million (2002 – $50 million) had been sold under these programs.

FUTURE INCOME TAXES

LEARNING OBJECTIVE 11

Describe why future income taxes exist.

Future income taxes arise because, although companies use accounting revenues and expenses to determine income tax expense on their income statements, they use Canada Revenue Agency (CRA) calculations of revenues and expenses to determine their income tax payable (that is, the amount that must actually be paid to the government). In other words, companies prepare their financial statements according to the requirements of generally accepted accounting principles, but they prepare their income tax returns (which determine the amount of tax they have to pay each year) according to the requirements of the *Income Tax Act* and regulations. Differences between these two sets of calculations result in future income tax assets and liabilities.

For example, in Chapter 8, we mentioned future income taxes because companies must use capital cost allowance (CCA) for tax purposes, while they can use any one of several amortization methods to prepare their financial statements. The use of different methods for tax purposes vs. accounting purposes results in an accounting asset balance that is different from the tax asset balance. The different asset balances will result in different future tax effects.

Other areas that create differences between what is currently taxed by the government and what is reported in the accounting system include the warranty costs we mentioned earlier in this chapter. The warranty liability on the balance sheet is an estimate of future warranty costs, based on revenue that was recognized in the current period. For tax purposes, however, the warranty liability and the related accounting expense are not recognized. Rather, the actual amount that the company paid to repair items under warranty in the current period is used as a tax deduction.

Amortization expense vs. CCA deductions and warranty expense vs. warranty payment deductions are just two examples of how accounting procedures for determining revenues, expenses, assets, and liabilities can have future tax impacts that are different from those as measured by the CRA. There are many other differences between GAAP and the tax regulations that give rise to future income taxes.

The method used in Canada to measure future taxes is called the **liability method**. This method focuses on the balance sheet, and attempts to measure the liability to pay taxes in the future due to (or the future tax benefit to be derived from) the imbalance between accounting and tax carrying amounts. Once the **future tax liability** or benefit is calculated and the amount currently owed to the CRA is established, the tax expense to be reported on the income statement is equal to the taxes currently owed plus or minus the future tax amount.

AN INTERNATIONAL PERSPECTIVE

NAFTA Facts

The liability method is used in both Mexico and the United States.

To illustrate the liability method, we will use the data in Exhibit 9-6. The data represent a company that sells equipment that carries a three-year warranty. The company estimates the probable future costs associated with the sale and records a liability (Obligations under warranties) and a warranty expense in the year of the sale. The CRA allows a tax deduction for the actual costs the company incurs each year to repair equipment under warranty. Assume that the warranty is the only difference between the company's accounting and tax methods.

EXHIBIT 9-6 **INCOME TAX DATA**

Income before tax and warranty expense (same in year 1, year 2, and year 3) $10,000

Estimated warranty expense (for accounting purposes):
Year 1: $500
Actual warranty costs incurred:
Year 1: $125
Year 2: $175
Year 3: $200
Tax rate (same in year 1, year 2, and year 3):   40%

the following year. For longer
to reverse, and therefore the
income taxes that result from
current, because it takes sev
notice that Metro Inc. has th
sheet: one portion is shown
liabilities, and yet another is

One more issue regardi
between the methods used
differences. One example is
investment in another Canad
purposes; for tax purposes, l
the company that paid the d
of the dividend would, in eff
Exhibit 9-6. In that example
costs. Assume that in year 1
an investment in another C
accounting tax expense wou

INCOME TAX CALCULATIO

a. Calculation of income tax currently
  Income before warranty costs and
  Less: tax-exempt income (permane

  Actual warranty costs incurred
  Taxable income
  Taxes payable (taxable income ×

b. Calculation of future income taxes
  Beginning warranty obligation
  Actual warranty costs incurred
  Ending warranty obligation
  Tax rate
  Future tax asset (ending obligatio
  Increase/(decrease) in future tax a

c. Calculation of income tax expens
  Credit to income taxes payable (f
  Debit/(credit) to future tax asset
  Debit to income tax expense

  Note that because th
from income tax, they are
taxes payable in year 1 are
ence (i.e., this dividend in
affected.

The liability method requires the company to do a *pro forma* ("as if") calculation of the amounts of income tax that will be payable in the future, based on the **temporary differences** that exist in the current period. The pro forma calculations require that the company prepare a schedule showing the differences that exist and how they will reverse in future periods. In the case of warranties, the company accrues a warranty liability in the current period that will become a tax deduction in the current and future periods, as actual costs are incurred. This creates a **future tax asset**, because fewer taxes will be paid in the future as these deductions are claimed. Exhibit 9-7 illustrates how this occurs.

INCOME TAX CALCULATIONS

	Year 1	Year 2	Year 3
a. Calculation of income tax currently payable:			
Income before warranty costs and income tax	$ 10,000	$ 10,000	$ 10,000
Actual warranty costs incurred	125	175	200
Taxable income	9,875	9,825	9,800
Taxes payable (taxable income × tax rate)	3,950	3,930	3,920
b. Calculation of future income taxes:			
Beginning warranty obligation	$ 500	$ 375	$ 200
Actual warranty costs incurred	125	175	200
Ending warranty obligation	$ 375	$ 200	$ 0
Tax rate	40%	40%	40%
Future tax asset (ending obligation × tax rate)	$ 150	$ 80	$ 0
Increase/(decrease) in future tax asset	$ 150	($ 70)	($ 80)
c. Calculation of income tax expense:			
Credit to income taxes payable (from a.)	(3,950)	(3,930)	(3,920)
Debit/(credit) to future tax asset (from b.)	150	(70)	(80)
Debit to income tax expense	$ 3,800	$ 4,000	$ 4,000

Notice how the original $375 difference (between the $500 warranty expense deducted for accounting purposes and the $125 warranty payments deducted for tax purposes) creates a future tax asset of $150, which reverses in years 2 and 3 as actual warranty costs in those years are incurred. Because the actual warranty costs are deductible for tax purposes, the amount of taxes payable to the government will be reduced in years 2 and 3 (by $70 and $80, respectively). This expected future benefit, in the form of a reduction in the taxes that will be payable in the future, allows us to create the future tax asset of $150 in year 1.

Note that in this example the original estimate in year 1 was completely accurate (that is, the total actual warranty costs incurred over the three years were exactly equal to the estimated amount). Under the liability method, the company must review its estimates periodically, to ensure that the future tax asset still exists and that the amount estimated is still valid. Also note that in this example the tax rate remained the same for all three years. If there is a planned change in rates for years 2 and 3, the new rates for these years must be used. In other words, the company must use the tax rate that is expected to be in effect in future years, when calculating the future tax asset. The purpose of these two provisions is to ensure that the amount represented on the balance sheet for the future tax asset or liability is as accurate as possible, in terms of the value of the tax benefits that will be received or the amount of additional taxes that will be paid in the future.

LEARNING OBJECTIVE 12

Calculate future income taxes in amortization and warranty situations.

EXHIBIT 9-7

HELPFUL HINT:

Notice that there is no attempt to calculate tax expense directly, using the income tax rates and accounting income. Rather, the changes in the future taxes and the incomes taxes currently payable to the CRA are calculated; then the tax expense is simply the balancing figure.

Required:

a. In your own words, briefly summarize the key information contained in CN's notes regarding contingencies and environmental matters. Specify whether the company has (1) recorded liabilities related to these in its accounts, (2) not recorded liabilities related to contingencies and environmental matters in its accounts but disclosed information about them in its notes, or (3) both recognized liabilities in the financial statements and provided additional disclosure in the footnotes accompanying them.

b. Under GAAP, contingent liabilities must be recorded in the accounts if they are considered likely to occur and can be reasonably estimated. Discuss the extent to which CN focuses on each of these criteria (i.e., considered likely to occur and can be reasonably estimated) in its discussion of environmental matters.

c. If you were a CN shareholder or investment analyst, how would the information presented in these notes affect your assessment of the company's contingencies and environmental matters?

9-35 (Guarantees and commitments)

In the 2001 annual report of Alcan Inc., the following note was included under Commitments and Contingencies. (Amounts are in millions of U.S. dollars.)

The Company has guaranteed the repayment of approximately $17 of indebtedness by third parties. Alcan believes that none of these guarantees is likely to be invoked. Commitments with third parties and certain related companies for supplies of goods and services are estimated at $175 in 2002, $94 in 2003, $103 in 2004, $86 in 2005, $86 in 2006, and $884 thereafter. Total payments to these entities, excluding $218 in relation to the smelter at Alma, were $36 in 2001, $106 in 2000 and $18 in 1999.

In 1997, as part of the claim settlement arrangements related to the British Columbia Government's cancellation of the Kemano Completion Project, Alcan received the right to transfer a portion of a power supply contract with BC Hydro to a third party. Alcan sold the right to supply this portion to Enron Power Marketing Inc. (EPMI), a subsidiary of Enron Corporation (Enron) for cash consideration. In order to obtain the consent of BC Hydro to this sale, Alcan was required to retain residual liability for EPMI's obligations arising from the supply contract, including in the event that EPMI became unable to perform. This contingent liability is subject to a maximum aggregate amount of $100, with mitigation and subrogation rights. On December 2, 2001, EPMI and Enron filed for protection under Chapter 11 of the U.S. Bankruptcy Code. The Company is unable to estimate reasonably the amount of the contingent loss, if any, after mitigation, which might arise in respect of this matter.

Required:

a. What is meant by guaranteeing the indebtedness of third parties?

b. With respect to the guarantees, why was it important for Alcan to include a note about them with the financial statements?

c. With respect to the commitments for the supplies of goods and services, has Alcan recorded these transactions in its accounting records? If not, why not?

d. The note's second paragraph relates to a transaction involving Alcan and a subsidiary of **Enron Corporation**, which became the centre of a huge accounting scandal and the largest bankruptcy (to date) in American history. The note discloses that Alcan's liability could be as high as $100 million (U.S.), but concludes with the statement that Alcan was not able to reasonably estimate the amount of the contingent loss (if any) that might ultimately arise from these events.

Check Alcan's 2002 financial statements on the SEDAR website (www.sedar.com) for additional information regarding this contingency. Has the matter been resolved? What additional action, if any, has Alcan taken on this issue?

Beyond the Book

9-36 **(Comparative treatment of contingent liabilities and losses)**

During 2000, **Bridgestone Corporation** and **Ford Motor Company** were confronted with a large public liability issue regarding Firestone AT, ATX, and ATX II radial tires that were used on Ford Explorers. Many sudden failures of these tires had occurred with Explorer vehicles, some of which resulted in serious accidents. Millions of tires and thousands of vehicles were involved in the ensuing controversy and litigation alleging defective product design and/or manufacture.

> *Required:*
>
> Determine how Bridgestone Corporation and Ford Motor Company handled this liability question. Outline how each company dealt with this issue in its annual reports for 2000 and subsequent years. Be sure to specify, for each company, whether it recognized a loss and recorded a liability in the financial statements and/or disclosed a contingent loss and liability in the notes accompanying its statements.

9-37 **(Financial statement disclosures)**

Choose a company as directed by your instructor and do the following exercises.

a. Prepare a quick analysis of the current liability accounts by listing the beginning and ending amounts in these accounts and calculating the net change, in both dollar and percentage terms, for the most recent year. If the company you have selected does not prepare a classified balance sheet, you will need to determine which liabilities are current.

b. If any account changed by more than 10%, try to give an explanation for this change.

c. What percentage of the company's total assets is funded by current liabilities? Has this percentage changed significantly in the last year?

d. Does the company have any significant (greater than 3% of total liabilities) accrued liabilities, such as warranties? If so, read any notes discussing these items and summarize the nature of these liabilities.

e. Does the company have unearned revenues? If so, explain the nature of these liabilities.

f. Read the note on income taxes and answer the following questions.

   1. What is the company's effective tax rate? What are the major items that cause it to be different from the statutory rate?

   2. What are the major items that result in future (or deferred) tax assets and liabilities for the company?

   3. Try to reconcile the total net future tax assets (liabilities) presented in the note with what is reported in the financial statements. Note: To do this, you will need to consolidate all the future tax accounts from the balance sheet into a single, net amount.

g. Does the company have any significant commitments or contingencies? Read any related notes and then write a short paragraph summarizing each significant item. For the contingencies, are you aware of anything that has happened related to these contingencies since the financial statements were issued? If so, give a brief description.

Cases

Case Primer

9-38 Greenway Medical Equipment Corporation

At a recent meeting of the board of directors of Greenway Medical Equipment Corporation, Chief Financial Officer Robert Ables presented to the board a draft set of financial statements for the year. It is Greenway's corporate policy that all directors be given an opportunity to review the financial statements before they are finalized.

Yesterday, Ables received a memo from Dr. Clarise Locklier posing some questions with regard to the draft financial statements. Dr. Locklier is a relatively new member to the board and is not familiar with some accounting terms and concepts used in the statements. She has several questions she would like Ables to answer before approving the financial statements at the next board meeting.

Memorandum

To: Robert Ables, CFO, Greenway Medical Equipment Corporation

From: Dr. Clarise Locklier, Director, Greenway Medical Equipment Corporation

Re: Draft financial statements

I have carefully reviewed the financial statements that you presented to the board last week. As a physician, I do not have a lot of experience reading accounting information and I am confused about several items presented in the financial statements.

1. I have always been under the impression that revenues are reported on the income statement, which is why I was confused to see unearned revenues presented as a liability on the balance sheet. As well, if the revenues are unearned, shouldn't they be presented in the period when earned and not in the current year?

2. I notice that under current liabilities you have reported a current portion of long-term debt. How can debt be current and long-term at the same time? Are we overstating our liabilities if we report this?

3. In note 4 to the financial statements, you state that the liability for warranty costs is based on an estimate, not actual warranty repair costs. If we know what our actual costs are for the year, why do we need this estimated liability?

I would appreciate a response to these questions prior to our next board meeting, so that I can feel more comfortable approving the financial statements.

Thank you for your time in addressing these matters.

> *Required:*
>
> As Robert Ables, prepare a memo to Dr. Locklier addressing her concerns.

9-39 Altabet Company

Altabet Company is completing its financial statements for the year ended April 30, 2006. Janet Kramer, Altabet's controller, is reviewing the company's legal correspondence and trying to decide which, if any, of the potential contingencies facing the company need to be accrued in the financial statements. As part of her review, Kramer has identified three contingencies.

1. In May 2005, the company was sued for breach of contract concerning a sale of equipment to a local manufacturer. The manufacturer claims that because Altabet was unable to deliver the equipment in the period specified in the contract, the manufacturer lost profits of $100,000. Correspondence with Altabet's lawyer indicated that there was no breach of contract because the manufacturer failed to make all the required payments and therefore Altabet was under no obligation to deliver the equipment. The lawyer feels this is a nuisance suit and believes there is little possibility of the manufacturer being successful. Kramer does not consider the potential loss to be significant.

2. In January 2006, Terry Chambers fell on some ice in Altabet's parking lot. As a result of the fall, Chambers suffered a concussion and a broken arm that required a two-day hospital stay. She is suing Altabet for $1,000,000 to cover her medical bills, loss of wages, and personal suffering. Altabet's lawyer feels that Altabet will probably lose the suit and has strongly advised it to settle out of court. On April 25, 2006, Altabet instructed its lawyer to offer Chambers a settlement of $750,000. The lawyer believes this is reasonable and that Chambers will probably accept the offer.

3. Jeff Altabet, the company owner's son, needed to borrow $500,000. The loan is a five-year, 10% term loan requiring monthly payments of principal and interest. Because Jeff had just graduated from college and had no credit history, the company guaranteed the note, stating that if Jeff failed to make three consecutive payments Altabet Company would repay the loan in full. Jeff has invested the money in a business venture that is turning out to be very profitable. He has made every required payment on the note thus far, and expects to be able to repay the remaining balance of $350,000 within the next six months. As of April 30, 2006, Kramer still considers the balance of the loan to be significant.

Required:

How should each of the above contingencies be accounted for in the April 30, 2006, financial statements of Altabet Company?

9-40   Slip-n-Slide Water Park

It is now July 31 and Slip-n-Slide Water Park has just completed its first three months of operations. The company's owners, Kelly and Derek Neil, are very pleased with the results of operations and are trying to prepare the company's first set of financial statements. You have been controller for a local manufacturing firm for several years and are good friends with Kelly and Derek. The couple approaches you one afternoon with some questions concerning how certain items should be recorded in their financial statements.

Derek: "I can figure out how to record most revenues and expenses, but I don't know how to treat the revenues associated with the 300 season passes we sold in May and June. The season passes sold for $50 each and are good for June, July, and August. Holders of season passes have unlimited access to the park for these three months."

Kelly: "The other problem we have is that we have just taken out a $60,000 bank loan. The loan agreement requires us to repay the loan at $500 per month plus interest over the next 10 years. The interest rate on the loan is 7% annually. Since some of the loan has to be repaid in the next year, I want to record the $60,000 as a current liability, but Derek thinks that the entire amount should be recorded as a long-term liability since it does not have to be fully repaid for 10 years."

Required:

Provide the Neils with some advice on how the above transactions should be recorded in the July 31 financial statements. Be sure to explain to them why they should record the transactions in the manner you recommend.

9-41 Hanson's Consulting

Jenny Shea is in the process of renegotiating her annual employment contract with her employer, Hanson's Consulting. Jenny knows that it is important that she negotiate a good contract because the amount of her raise will become a benchmark for the raises to be received by the rest of Hanson's 15 consultants. Currently, Jenny and the other consultants are receiving a payroll transfer into their personal bank accounts of $3,000 per month.

Under her existing contract, Jenny is allowed to review Hanson's annual financial statements. She is aware that each consultant receives the same monthly payments, which total $540,000 per year, and is therefore confused to see that Hanson is reporting over $650,000 in consulting wages on its annual income statement. Jenny approaches you, the company controller, to see why the consulting wages on the income statement are higher than the amounts paid to the employees. She is concerned that the company may be posting other expenses to the consulting salaries account in order to improve its bargaining position in contract negotiations.

Required:

Explain to Jenny why payroll costs as per the company's accounting records are higher than the net amounts being received by the employees.

Critical Thinking Questions

9-42 (Revenue recognition/expense accrual and income measurement)

Software Solutions produces inventory-tracking and supply-chain management software, which it sells to large commercial clients. Its main software packages sell for approximately $100,000 each and require the company to customize the programs to each buyer's operations and organizations. There is no additional charge for this customization service; it is included in the initial selling price. This work is done by a special team of employees, usually takes several months to complete, and involves significant costs (averaging approximately $20,000 per sale) for Software Solutions. Aside from the customization work, the company's costs per software package sold average $50,000.

Required:

a. Discuss appropriate accounting treatments for handling the income measurement issues that arise in this type of situation. You should be able to describe at least two alternative approaches that could be taken within GAAP.

b. Indicate an approach that would be appropriate if:

   1. the company wants to treat the software customization unit as a "cost centre" (i.e., the customization team is expected to cover its costs, but not to generate a profit).

   2. the company wants to treat the software customization unit as a "profit centre" (i.e., the customization work is viewed as a profit-generating line of business, separate from the software sales unit).

9-43 (Recognition and disclosure of contingent liabilities)

An issue discussed in this chapter is financial statement recognition and disclosure of contingent liabilities, such as the potential claims associated with litigation and environmental obligations. Loss and liability recognition is a function of whether it is likely that an asset has been impaired or a liability has been incurred, and the degree to which a loss can reasonably be estimated. Evaluating whether these conditions exist is often a matter of judgement by management and auditors, perhaps more so than with any other issue of recognition or disclosure. Research has shown that reliance on judgement leads to differences among companies regarding whether and how contingencies are disclosed.

Required:

a. As discussed in this chapter (and Chapter 10), some long-term liabilities are measured using present values. Discuss the appropriateness of using present values for long-term liabilities, and whether liabilities that are recorded for lawsuits are, or should be, subject to present value measurement.

b. In today's environmentally conscious world, regulatory bodies are making more demands on resource companies to be environmentally responsible. For example, companies involved in mineral exploration are often required to plan for the cleanup and restoration of resource sites. A review of the annual reports of several resource companies reveals that some companies create liabilities on their balance sheets in anticipation of these future events, some companies disclose a contingent liability in the notes to the financial statements, and some companies do or say nothing about it. In a brief essay, discuss the criteria that a company should use when deciding on the kind of disclosure necessary to account for future cleanup and restoration costs.

Using Debt Wisely

As part of its 2003 financing plan, Bell Canada needed to raise $600 million to meet its operational and refinancing requirements. So the Montreal-based telecommunications company did what it frequently does—it raised the funds by selling debt, specifically medium-term notes (MTNs). The issue, directed at retail investors, was carried out in February of that year and consisted of $600 million in seven-year MTNs. "Given the uncertainty in the equity markets at the time, investors were looking for products that offered more confident returns, and the issue subsequently sold out within hours," says Paul Stinis, vice-president and assistant treasurer at Bell's parent company BCE Inc.

Bell Canada used the proceeds to cover capital expenditures (such as new high-speed digital telephone lines and switching equipment), general corporate expenses, and debt repayments. On average, Bell spends about $3 billion a year on capital outlays. After this issue, at the end of first quarter of 2003, Bell had a total of $12 billion in outstanding net debt.

Issued through a consortium of nine dealers led by Scotia Capital Inc., Bell's offering was one of the largest retail directed issues of its kind ever carried out in Canada. The bonds sold at a unit price of $99.678 and had a coupon rate of 5.5%; with interest compounding semi-annually, the effective yield will be slightly higher. Standard and Poor's assigned the issue its A senior unsecured debt rating, based on a number of factors, including the company's competitive position, increasing geographic diversity, and conservative financial policies.

But why raise funds through debt rather than issuing shares? Mr. Stinis explains: "Common shares create dilution, which in turn could adversely impact share price. They are also a very expensive form of capital. With this latest issue of debentures, although there's a coupon rate of 5.5%, after tax, it works out to around

3.6%, so that's very cheap money." Corporations cannot simply issue debt ad infinitum, however, since rating agencies and debt investors look closely at a company's financial ratios, he adds.

While most of Bell's debt usually goes to institutional investors—big mutual funds, life insurance companies, and the like—the company occasionally borrows from the general public. "By issuing to retail investors from time to time, the investor base is diversified," Mr. Stinis says. "Maintaining sufficient demand with institutional investors is essential for successful debt issues. Demand for Bell Canada's debt ensures fair pricing. Also, by giving retail investors the opportunity to buy our paper at least once a year, Bell ensures that these investors can get a hold of it at a decent price. This helps us and it helps them."

chapter 10

Long-Term Liabilities

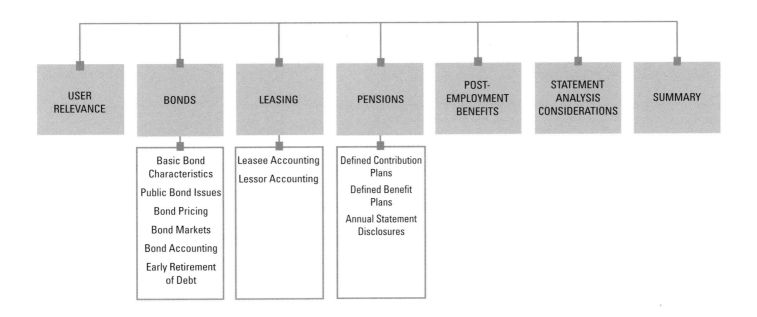

LEARNING OBJECTIVES

After studying this chapter, you should be able to:

1. Describe the basic characteristics of a bond.

2. Explain how bonds are issued and how the pricing of bonds is affected by risk.

3. Calculate a bond's issue price and prepare journal entries for the issuance of the bond and interest payments subsequent to the issuance for bonds issued at par, below par, and above par.

4. Discuss the advantages and disadvantages of leasing.

5. Distinguish between an operating lease and a capital lease and prepare journal entries for a lessee under both conditions.

6. Explain the distinguishing features of a defined contribution pension plan and a defined benefit plan.

7. Describe other employment benefits and explain how they are treated in Canada.

8. Calculate the debt/equity ratio and the times-interest-earned ratio and write a statement describing a company's financial health using the information from these ratios.

Companies like Bell Canada frequently use long-term debt or the issuance of new shares as a means of raising outside capital that they then use to finance growth. They use the new cash to buy long-term assets or invest in other companies in order to expand their operations or enter new markets. Long-term debt is often preferable to short-term debt because the benefits from their expansion efforts will be long-term. They can use the cash generated from the growth to repay the debt. Bell Canada used some of its new long-term debt to buy some equipment, pay for some corporate expenses, and repay some of its debt. When new debt is used to pay off old debt, it is referred to as the rollover of debt. When short-term debt is repaid with the proceeds from long-term debt, a company is able to spread out its debt payments over a longer period of time, which means that there is less pressure on short-term cash needs.

USER RELEVANCE

Users of financial statement information need to pay particular attention to the type and extent of debt within a company. All debt must be paid back at some time. In addition to the principal amount, there is often a requirement to make periodic interest payments. As Bell Canada has done, many companies will sell new debt to settle either short- or long-term debt as it reaches maturity. In the **Bell Canada** vignette, Mr. Stinis stated that issuing debt is cheaper than issuing shares and it does not dilute the current shareholders' interests. However, a company cannot rely too extensively on debt for financing because investors and lenders become concerned if the proportion of debt to equity gets too high.

As a user, you should pay attention to the following items with respect to debt.

First, what are the maturity dates and interest rates on the debt? Knowing this will enable you to determine the amount and timing of the future cash flows that will be necessary to meet the debt conditions.

Second, are there any special conditions attached to the debt? For example, is the company required to maintain a certain debt/equity ratio or level of retained earnings? Failure to meet debt conditions (called covenants) could make the debt come due immediately, which could have a detrimental effect on the business operations.

Third, what is the proportion of debt to equity? The higher the amount of debt to equity, the greater the risk that the company may have difficulty meeting the debt requirements as they fall due. Financial lenders will be watching this ratio as well. A high proportion of debt to equity may result in higher interest rates being charged to the company. It could also make lenders reluctant to extend further debt to the company, which could affect its future financial viability. As you will see later in this chapter, it is possible for a company to borrow at a rate lower than the return it can earn by employing the money in revenue-generating activities. We call this leverage. This return increases shareholder wealth. Bell Canada plans to gain leverage by borrowing at the after-tax rate of 3.6%. If it can earn an after-tax return greater than 3.6%, the return to shareholders grows. As a user, you will want to examine the company's financial statements to see if leverage is being used effectively.

In this chapter, we are going to illustrate some of the more common liabilities that will be repaid over a period of time longer than a year. The three major long-term debts discussed are bonds payable, lease liabilities, and pension and other employment benefit liabilities. The general nature of liabilities was discussed in Chapter 9, along with the recognition and valuation criteria for liabilities. You might want to refresh your memory before moving on.

BONDS

When a public company wants to raise long-term funds to support its operations, it has two basic alternatives: the equity (stock) market or the debt market. Issuing shares in the equity market is discussed in Chapter 11. Issuing debt in the debt market is the subject of this section. Within the debt market, there are various long-term sources of funds. The company may borrow money from a commercial bank, much as individuals borrow money from the bank to buy a new home or car. These borrowings are often listed on a company's financial statements as **notes** payable. The note's term can be short or long, and it may carry a fixed or floating interest rate. Another source of funds is what is known as the **commercial paper** market. Commercial paper is an unsecured promissory note that is generally sold to other businesses by a company that has a fairly high credit rating. In effect, one company borrows from another. The term "unsecured" means that there is not a specific asset that is used as collateral against default of the debt.

Another market in which the company may borrow money is the **bond market**. Generally, **bonds** are sold initially to institutional and individual investors through an **investment banker** (who gets a commission for handling the transaction). The investment banker, or a group of investment bankers (sometimes known as a **syndicate**), works with the company to decide which bond terms will be most attractive to investors. In our opening vignette, you learned that Bell Canada used nine dealers led by Scotia Capital Inc. when it issued its bonds. Once all the bonds have been sold by the investment bankers, they can be freely traded between investors in a bond market much as shares are traded on the stock market. The most widely known bond market is the New York Bond Market, which is a **public bond market**. Sometimes bonds are sold to investors through what is referred to as a **private placement**. These types of bonds do not trade in public markets. Private placements are usually made to institutional investors such as trustees in charge of pension funds.

A full understanding of how the various debt markets differ is beyond the scope of this book. Various markets are mentioned so that you can gain some appreciation of the disclosures you will typically find as you read annual reports. Publicly traded bonds in Canada are used to illustrate the accounting issues surrounding long-term debt. There are some complex issues related to **foreign-denominated debt** that we will mention briefly, but in-depth coverage falls outside the parameters of this book.

accounting in the news
NO DEBT, NO BONDS

As an organization's financial health improves, the need to issue bonds may diminish. Retail investors in Alberta found it difficult to purchase Alberta provincial bonds after the province's 2004 budget anticipated the elimination of its debt by the following year. Alberta bonds are the only provincial debt with an AAA rating; they are seen as very secure, both in coupon payments and the repayment of the initial investment. Also, because a government can raise taxes to repay debt, government bonds are viewed as less risky than corporate bonds or equities. The most recent significant sale of Alberta bonds was in 1999, when the province sold $350 billion in five-year bonds. In 2004, these bonds yielded 3.54%, compared with a yield of 3.39% on a similar five-year Canadian bond. If the province does become debt-free by 2005, there may not be a need to issue bonds at all. However, a spokesperson for Alberta's treasury management finance unit said there will occasionally be new Alberta debt issues, mostly for the Agricultural Financial Services Corp., a Crown cor-

poration set up to assist farmers. The corporation received $30 million in debt financing issued by the province in March 2004.

Source: "Alberta bonds in short supply," by Roma Luciw, *The Globe and Mail*, March 30, 2004.

Basic Bond Characteristics

LEARNING OBJECTIVE 1

Describe the basic charac-teristics of a bond.

A bond is a formal agreement between a borrower (the company) and a lender (the investor) that specifies how the borrower is to pay back the lender and any conditions that the borrower must meet during the loan period. The loan conditions are stated in a document called the indenture agreement. The indenture agreement may specify certain restrictions on the company that are known as bond covenants. These covenants may limit the company's ability to borrow additional amounts, to sell or acquire assets, or to pay dividends. The restrictions placed in the bond covenants are intended to protect the investor against a company defaulting on the loan.

Bonds that are traded in public markets are fairly standardized. The indenture agreement will state a face value for the bonds, which, in almost all cases, is $1,000 per bond. The Bell Canada bonds had a face value of $100 per bond. Unless stated otherwise, you should assume that a bond's face value is $1,000. The face value specifies the cash payment the borrower will make to the lender at the bond's maturity date (which is also specified in the indenture agreement). In addition to the cash payment at maturity, most bonds make semi-annual interest payments to the lender. The amount of these payments is determined by multiplying the bond interest rate times the face value and dividing by two (because they are semi-annual). The bond interest rate is stated as an annual percentage and is not an effective or true interest rate, but simply a rate that determines the periodic amount of the interest payments. The Bell Canada bonds will pay $2.75 per bond every six months ($100 × .055 × 1/2).

One other important item described in the indenture agreement is the collateral the company pledges to the lenders. If collateral is pledged, it means that if the company defaults on the interest or maturity payment, the bondholders can demand that the pledged assets be sold in order to settle the debt. Some bonds specify particular assets as collateral. A bond known as a mortgage bond has some type of real property as collateral. A collateral trust bond provides shares and bonds of other companies as collateral. A bond that carries no specific collateral but is backed by the company's general creditworthiness is known as a debenture bond. Bell Canada refers to its bonds as debentures. General debenture bonds can be either senior debenture bonds or subordinated debenture bonds. The distinction between senior and subordinated is the order in which creditors are paid in the event of bankruptcy: senior creditors are paid first.

Some indenture agreements specify special provisions that are designed to make the bonds more attractive to investors. Convertible bonds, for example, are convertible to a specified number of common shares in the company issuing the bond. In the 1970s and 1980s, investors became concerned about the effects of inflation on the fixed payments, particularly the large final payment that characterizes bond agreements. Remember from earlier chapters that in a period of inflation, fixed payments decline in terms of their purchasing power. Therefore, the payment the investor receives at the maturity date may be worth considerably less (in terms of purchasing power) than the dollars lent to the company initially. To protect investors from the effects of inflation, some companies have issued bonds that index the final payment to a commodity.

Sunshine Mining Corporation issued one of the first of these bonds in 1980. It indexed the maturity payment to be the greater of $1,000 (the normal maturity payment of a bond) or the market value of 50 ounces of silver. If inflation was significant, the market value of silver would rise, and the investor would get that value at maturity. Since that time, other bonds have indexed maturity values to oil and other commodities.

Public Bond Issues

LEARNING OBJECTIVE 2

Explain how bonds are issued and how the pricing of bonds is affected by risk.

When a company decides to issue bonds in the public bond market, it contacts an investment banker who will assist the company in issuing the securities. The investment banker will consult with the company about its objectives, and will help design an issue that will both meet the company's objectives and attract investors. All the bond's basic features that have been discussed in the previous section will be considered when structuring the offering.

The investment banker will not only help design the bond issue, but will also be responsible for the initial sale of the issue to its investor clients. Because most issues involve larger amounts than one investment banker can easily sell, the investment banker usually forms a syndicate with other investment bankers, who will be jointly responsible for selling the issue. The syndicate members are sometimes known as the **underwriters** of the issue.

The syndicate will agree on a price for the bond issue and will attempt to sell all the bonds to its clients. The bonds' price is fixed at this point and will not change until the syndicate has sold all its bonds. If events occur that make the price unattractive to the investment bankers' clients, then it is likely that the syndicate will not sell the entire issue. In some cases, the syndicate agrees to sell the issue on what is known as a **best efforts basis**. If the syndicate cannot sell all the securities, it simply returns them to the company, which means that the company will not be able to raise the amount of money it had hoped. For financially strong companies, however, the syndicate guarantees to sell the entire issue, thereby accepting the risk that it will not be able to sell all the issue to its clients. Bell Canada's issue sold out within hours of the initial offering.

Once all the bonds have been sold to syndicate clients, they are thrown on the open market. This means that bondholders are free to trade them with any other investors. Prices of the bonds can then fluctuate with changes in economic conditions.

accounting in the news
BALANCING ACT ON THE BOND MARKET

Outside influences, such as politics, can have an effect on the bond market, and some may try to anticipate the market's reaction to significant world events. In 1995, before the Quebec referendum on sovereignty, the provincial government set aside $17 billion to buy up Quebec bonds that it thought nervous investors might dump in the event of a referendum victory. The plan included potential contributions from several of the province's major financial institutions and pension funds. The government planned to allow the bonds to drop to a certain value, then it would have bought the funds at the lower price, selling them later. The expectation was that the bonds would have returned to their original value soon after the vote, so the government would have reaped a tidy profit.

Source: "Parizeau set aside $17-billion to bolster separation," by Rhéal Séguin, *The Globe and Mail*, March 29, 2004.

Bond Pricing

Bond prices are established in the marketplace by negotiations between buyers and sellers. At the initial bond issuance, the buyers are institutional and individual investors, and the seller is the company issuing the bonds. The buyers determine what the cash flow is going to be for the bond (both in the return of the principal amount and the interest) and the rate of return they want to earn based on the risk of potential default by the company. They then use these amounts to calculate the present value of the cash flows they will receive from the bond so that they can decide the amount they are willing to pay for it. The process of calculating the bond's present value involves discounting (at the desired earning rate) the future cash flows (repayment of principal and periodic interest) from the bond. The seller does a similar calculation to decide what it is willing to accept for the bond. The buyer weighs the yield (desired) interest rate against the interest rate that could be earned from the next best alternative investment, and also against the risk involved with the particular bond issue. The higher the risk, the higher the yield rate should be. In other words, if buyers are going to accept a higher risk of default, they want to be compensated for that risk with a higher return. In addition to calculating the present value, the buyer also has to factor in any special features of the bond such as convertibility into shares or any indexing of the maturity value to a commodity. To keep things as simple as possible in the rest of this section, these special features are ignored as we discuss bond pricing.

The starting point in determining a bond's value is to calculate the cash flows that will be received by the buyer (and paid by the seller). To illustrate the calculation of interest payments, assume a company issues bonds on January 1, 2001, with a total face value of $100,000 and a bond interest rate of 10%. The company issues 100 bonds, each with a face value of $1,000 and a maturity date of December 31, 2007. The company must make a $100,000 payment to the lenders on December 31, 2007, and must make interest payments every six months of $5,000 each. The $5,000 amount is calculated as follows.

$$\text{Interest Payment} = \text{Face Value} \times \text{Bond Interest Rate} \times 1/2$$
$$= \$100,000 \times 10\% \times 1/2 = \$5,000$$

There will be a total of 14 interest payments because there are seven years to maturity and two interest payments per year. The interest payments on a bond are typically structured to come at the end of each six-month period. In other words, the stream of interest payments is an annuity in arrears, meaning the payments are made at the end of the period.

To illustrate the pricing of a bond, we will use a very simple example. Suppose that Baum Company Ltd. wishes to issue a $1,000 bond (a single bond will be used to make it simple) with two years to maturity. The bond is to have an interest rate of 10% and pay interest semi-annually. Suppose that Baum expects the investor to demand a return of 8% compounded semi-annually from an investment in its bonds. What price can Baum expect to get from this offering?

The cash flows that Baum will pay must be discounted using the yield rate of 8%. The yield rate is sometimes referred to as the discount rate or the market rate. Exhibit 10-1 shows the timeline and the cash flows that would result from this bond.

Note that the interest payments (the four payments of $50 each) are an annuity in arrears and that the maturity payment ($1,000) is a lump sum cash flow at the end of the fourth period. There are four periods because interest payments are made at the end of each six-month period. The bond's total net present value, based on a 4% desired or yield rate, is calculated as follows.

BAUM COMPANY LTD.

EXHIBIT 10-1

Assumptions:

Face value	$1,000
Bond interest rate	10%
Time to maturity	2 years
Yield rate	8%

Calculation:

Number of periods	= Time to maturity × 2
	= 2 years × 2 = 4
Yield rate per period	= Yield rate ÷ 2
	= 8% ÷ 2 = 4%
Interest payments	= Face amount × bond interest rate × 1/2
	= $1,000 × 10% × 1/2 = $50

					$1,000
Cash flows		$50	$50	$50	$50
End of period (semi-annual periods)	0	1	2	3	4

To calculate the net present value, we will use the Time Value of Money tables[1] found in the Appendix at the end of this chapter.

We need to calculate the present value of each of the future cash flows.

				$1,000
	$50	$50	$50	$50
1	4%			
2		4%		
3			4%	
4				4%

For illustrative purposes we will use Table 2, Present value of $1, found on pages 639 and 640.

($50 × 0.96154) + ($50 × 0.92456) + ($50 × 0.88900) + ($50 × 0.85480) + ($1,000 = 0.85480)

48.08 + 46.23 + 44.45 + 42.74 + 854.80 = $1,036.30

The result of this calculation is that Baum should expect buyers to pay up to $1,036.30 for this bond. If buyers pay exactly this amount, they will earn an 8% return (compounded semi-annually). If they pay more for this bond, they will earn less than 8% and, if they pay less than this amount, they will earn more than 8%. Note that because the payments to be made by Baum are fixed by the terms of the bonds, the only way buyers of the bonds can change the return is by changing the amount they invest initially (i.e., the price they pay). If Baum thinks that 8% is too high an interest rate to pay, it should not offer these bonds at the price calculated here. It should offer them at a higher price (which will lower the interest rate). Recognize, however, that buyers may not be willing to buy the bonds at that higher price.

An easier way to arrive at the above amount of $1,036.30 is to treat the interest payments of $50 as an annuity (calculate the present value by using Table 4 from the Appendix, Present Value of an Annuity in Arrears) and add to this calculation the present value of the payment at maturity ($1,000). The calculation would be as follows.

---

[1] There are four Time Value of Money Tables in the Appendix. We will be using Table 2, Present value of $1, and Table 4, Present value of an annuity in arrears. These tables contain pre-calculated factors for given interest rates and time periods. When the factors are multiplied times the cash flow amount, the present value of that cash flow is determined.

$50 × 3.62990 (present value for 4 periods at 4%) + ($1,000 × 0.85480)
$181.50 + $854.80 = $1,036.30

This is the method we will use for subsequent calculations of the present value of a bond issue. These calculations can also be made using a financial calculator that has present value and future value functions.

How does a different desired or yield rate affect the bond's value? Suppose that, instead of 8%, buyers demand a 12% return from this type of investment. The only thing that would change in the calculation would be the factors that enter the present value calculation. The calculation would then be:

Present value of the Baum Company Ltd. bond at 12%:
PV of bond = PV of interest payments + PV of maturity payment
= PV of the annuity of $50 for 4 periods at 6% (Table 4) + PV of the $1,000 for 4
  periods at 6% (Table 2)
= ($50 × 3.46511) + ($1,000 × 0.79209)
= $965.35

Consistent with the preceding explanation, if buyers pay less for the bond (in this case, $965.35), they earn a higher return (12%). Baum Company Ltd., in this case, receives a lower initial amount from this borrowing and effectively pays a higher interest rate (12%).

According to the terminology used to describe bond pricing, when the bond is issued (or sells) at a price higher than its face value (i.e., greater than $1,000), it is issued (sells) at a **premium**. When the bond is issued for less than its face value, it is issued at a **discount**. If it is issued for exactly its face value, it is said to be issued at **par**. You should avoid placing any connotations on the words "premium" and "discount." They do not mean either that buyers paid too much or that they got a good deal. The price they pay, whether it is par, premium, or discount, is the appropriate value for the bond, given the desired or yield rate used. Bell Canada issued its bonds at $99.678, which is below the par value of $100. This means that the bonds were issued at a discount of $.322.

A question that might be asked is: what rate would have to be used to present value or discount the cash flows in the example for the bonds to be issued at par? The answer is 10%. Whenever a bond's yield rate is exactly equal to its interest rate, the bond will sell at par. Consequently, if the yield rate is higher than the bond interest rate, the bond sells at a discount and, when the yield rate is lower than the bond interest rate, it sells at a premium. This relationship is represented in Exhibit 10-2, which shows the price of the bond in the example for various combinations of bond interest rates and yield rates.

EXHIBIT 10-2 | **RELATIONSHIP OF BOND PRICE TO BOND INTEREST AND YIELD RATES**

		Yield Rates			
		6%	8%	10%	12%
Bond Interest Rates	6%	$1,000.00	$963.70	$929.08	$896.05
	8%	$1,037.17	$1,000.00	$964.54	$930.70
	10%	$1,074.34	$1,036.30	$1,000.00	$965.35
	12%	$1,111.51	$1,072.60	$1,035.46	$1,000.00

Note that, in Exhibit 10-2, all the prices on the diagonal, which represent situations in which the bond interest rate equals the yield rate, are equal to the bond's face value (it would sell at par). Prices below the diagonal represent premium price situations, where the yield rate is below the bond interest rate, and the area above the diagonal represents discount prices.

Another question might be: why would a company agree to issue (sell) a bond at other than its par value? Remember the earlier discussion about how the company gets advice from investment bankers when it is initially deciding on the terms of a new bond issue? The investment bankers will provide information to the company about how the market is assessing its risk. The company takes this information into consideration, but it also assesses its ability to pay the interest and the length of time over which it needs the money. The interest rate set for the bond may or may not be close to the market's interest rate demands. The company considers this when it is trying to determine how much capital it will be able to raise by issuing the bonds. The other aspect of the issue price that must be considered is the time factor. When a company decides to issue bonds as a way of raising capital, it must get financial advice as to what interest rate it can afford and legal advice as to aspects of the indenture agreement. Once all those decisions are made, it takes time to have the bond certificates printed and ready for issue. By the time the bonds are actually issued to investors, the market's risk assessment of the company may have changed, which will cause the issue price to change.

Bond Markets

All financial newspapers and several local newspapers provide information about bond prices to interested investors. Bond prices are quoted in the *Financial Post* in a section entitled Bonds. An excerpt from this section on July 31, 2004, is shown in Exhibit 10-3. You will notice that it lists Federal, Provincial, Corporate, and International bonds. Look for a moment at the Corporate section. The first column of the listing shows who is issuing each bond. An abbreviation of the company name is given, followed by a set of numbers, a date, and then numbers in the next two columns. These columns identify the bond interest rate of the issue (Coupon), the maturity date (Mat. date), then in the last two columns, the current selling price (Bid $) and the yield rate (Yld %) at that selling price. For instance, locate the line Loblaw 6.000 June 02/08 105.92 4.30. This is a bond from **Loblaws** that carries a 6.00% interest rate and that matures on June 02, 2008. Prices in the market are quoted as a percentage of the face value. The bond is currently selling at 105.92, which means that investors are paying $1,059.20 for a $1,000 bond. In other words, the bond is selling at 105.92% of its face value: it is selling at a premium. When investors buy this bond at a premium, they will earn a return of 4.3%. The yield is lower than the actual interest on the bond because the bond sold for more than the face or principal value. Investors are satisfied with this return because they can invest their money elsewhere at the same risk and earn a similar return.

Bond Accounting

The accounting for bonds will be illustrated using the simple example developed earlier for a bond issued at par, at a discount, and at a premium. For each bond, the entries made at issuance, to recognize the interest accrual and payments, and to record the final payment of the face amount at maturity will be illustrated.

BONDS ISSUED AT PAR

Consider the issuance of the Baum Company Ltd. bond (see data in Exhibit 10-1) when bond interest rates were 10%. To record the bond issued at par, the cash proceeds must be recorded in the cash account and the bond's present value in the liability account. When bonds are issued at par, they are said to be issued at 100. Because the cash proceeds equal the present value at issuance, the following entry is made (any commissions that are paid to the underwriters are ignored to keep the entries simple).

 EXHIBIT 10-2

BONDS 07.30.04

Excerpted from the *Financial Post*, Saturday, July 31, 2004, Page IN12.

Data provided by RBC Capital Markets Inc. Reprinted with permission.

	Coupon	Mat. date	Bid$	Yld%
FEDERAL				
Canada	6.000	Sep 01/05	103.44	2.73
Canada	12.250	Sep 01/05	109.99	2.76
Canada	8.750	Dec 01/05	107.57	2.88
Canada	12.500	Mar 01/06	114.27	3.14
Canada	5.750	Sep 01/06	104.91	3.28
Canada	14.000	Oct 01/06	122.05	3.32
Canada	7.000	Dec 01/06	108.01	3.39
Canada	7.250	Jun 01/07	109.72	3.60
Canada	4.500	Sep 01/07	102.34	3.69
Canada	13.000	Oct 01/07	127.35	3.73
Canada	12.750	Mar 01/08	129.47	3.84
Canada	6.000	Jun 01/08	107.27	3.93
Canada	10.000	Jun 01/08	121.41	3.91
Canada	5.500	Jun 01/09	105.70	4.18
Canada	11.000	Jun 01/09	129.75	4.13
Canada	10.750	Oct 01/09	130.18	4.18
Canada	9.750	Mar 01/10	126.55	4.34
Canada	5.500	Jun 01/10	105.67	4.39
Canada	9.500	Jun 01/10	126.26	4.35
Canada	8.750	Oct 01/10	123.19	4.41
Canada	9.000	Mar 01/11	125.43	4.49
Canada	6.000	Jun 01/11	108.39	4.55
Canada	8.500	Jun 01/11	123.16	4.52
Canada	5.250	Jun 01/12	103.75	4.67
Canada	5.250	Jun 01/13	103.53	4.75
Canada	10.250	Mar 15/14	142.24	4.73
Canada	5.000	Jun 01/14	101.38	4.82
Canada	11.250	Jun 01/15	154.51	4.75
Canada	10.500	Mar 15/21	161.23	5.02
Canada	9.750	Jun 01/21	152.65	5.06
Canada	9.250	Jun 01/22	148.53	5.08
Canada	8.000	Jun 01/23	133.23	5.21
Canada	9.000	Jun 01/25	146.75	5.27
Canada	8.000	Jun 01/27	135.75	5.28
Canada	5.750	Jun 01/29	106.48	5.28
Canada	5.750	Jun 01/33	107.50	5.24
CHT	5.527	Jun 15/06	104.13	3.22
CHT	4.750	Mar 15/07	102.86	3.59
CHT	4.400	Mar 15/08	101.40	3.98
CMHC	5.750	Dec 01/04	101.17	2.09
CMHC	6.250	Dec 01/05	104.32	2.90
CMHC	5.250	Dec 01/06	103.98	3.45
CMHC	5.300	Dec 03/07	104.39	3.88
CMHC	5.500	Jun 01/12	104.17	4.85
EDC	5.000	May 04/06	103.10	3.16
EDC	5.000	Feb 09/09	103.08	4.24
PROVINCIAL				
Alberta	7.500	Dec 01/05	105.89	2.92
Alberta	5.650	Oct 01/07	104.93	3.97
Alberta	5.000	Dec 16/08	103.08	4.22
Alberta	5.930	Sep 16/16	105.68	5.29
B C	8.000	Aug 23/05	105.41	2.73
B C	5.250	Dec 01/06	103.96	3.46
B C	6.000	Jun 09/08	106.78	4.08
B C	4.300	Dec 18/08	100.11	4.27
B C	5.700	Jun 01/09	105.73	4.37
B C	6.250	Dec 01/09	108.23	4.49
B C	6.375	Aug 23/10	108.95	4.66
B C	5.750	Jan 09/12	105.31	4.89
B C	9.500	Jan 09/12	128.71	4.85
B C	8.500	Aug 23/13	124.97	5.03
B C	7.500	Jun 09/14	118.15	5.13
B C	5.300	Jun 18/14	101.15	5.15
B C	5.300	Jun 17/19	99.40	5.36
B C	9.950	May 15/21	148.77	5.47
B C	8.000	Sep 08/23	128.14	5.58
B C	6.150	Nov 19/27	106.21	5.67
B C	5.700	Jun 18/29	100.34	5.67
B C	6.350	Jun 18/31	109.25	5.67
B C	5.400	Jun 18/35	96.03	5.67
B C	5.250	Jun 18/43	93.83	5.64
B C MF	7.750	Dec 01/05	106.18	2.94
B C MF	5.500	Mar 24/08	104.79	4.07
B C MF	5.900	Jun 01/11	106.02	4.85
HydQue	8.500	Aug 15/05	105.80	2.74
HydQue	7.000	Feb 15/07	108.25	3.56
HydQue	6.000	Jul 15/09	106.94	4.42
HydQue	6.500	Feb 15/11	109.34	4.82
HydQue	10.000	Sep 26/11	130.55	4.88
HydQue	10.250	Jul 16/12	133.89	5.02
HydQue	5.500	Aug 15/18	101.03	5.39
HydQue	11.000	Aug 15/20	156.16	5.63
HydQue	10.500	Oct 15/21	152.84	5.65
HydQue	9.625	Jul 15/22	144.12	5.67
HydQue	6.000	Aug 15/31	102.27	5.83
HydQue	6.500	Feb 15/35	109.33	5.84
HydQue	6.000	Feb 15/40	103.27	5.78
Manit	7.750	Jun 05/06	107.94	3.25
Manit	5.100	Dec 01/06	103.53	3.50
Manit	6.625	May 16/07	107.64	3.71
Manit	5.750	Jun 02/08	105.88	4.07
Manit	4.450	Dec 01/08	100.82	4.24
Manit	5.250	Mar 02/09	103.87	4.31
Manit	3.325	May 10/09	98.71	3.62
Manit	6.250	Sep 01/09	108.17	4.43
Manit	5.850	Jan 25/11	106.09	4.75
Manit	5.250	Dec 03/12	101.57	5.02
Manit	8.500	Jul 22/13	124.70	5.04
Manit	5.050	Dec 03/13	99.64	5.10
Manit	5.200	Dec 03/15	99.92	5.21
Manit	6.500	Sep 22/17	111.15	5.31
Manit	5.500	Nov 15/18	101.55	5.34
Manit	7.750	Dec 22/25	125.95	5.64
Manit	10.500	Mar 05/31	165.48	5.69
NewBr	7.500	Dec 15/05	105.97	2.99
NewBr	7.750	Jun 19/06	108.07	3.27
NewBr	7.100	Oct 16/06	107.68	3.44
NewBr	5.700	Jun 02/08	105.59	4.10
NewBr	4.250	Dec 02/08	99.96	4.26
NewBr	5.250	Jun 02/09	103.66	4.40
NewBr	4.500	Dec 02/09	99.97	4.51
NewBr	6.375	Jun 15/10	108.71	4.66
NewBr	5.800	Jul 12/11	105.47	4.86
NewBr	10.125	Oct 31/11	131.43	4.91
NewBr	5.850	Dec 01/11	105.63	4.92
NewBr	5.875	Dec 06/12	105.55	5.05
NewBr	9.250	Jan 18/13	128.44	5.07
NewBr	8.500	Jun 28/13	123.91	5.12
NewBr	8.750	May 12/15	128.63	5.24
NewBr	6.750	Jun 27/17	113.05	5.34
NewBr	6.000	Dec 27/17	106.04	5.36
NewBr	5.650	Dec 27/28	98.57	5.76
NewBr	5.500	Jan 27/34	96.29	5.76
Newfld	5.700	Oct 07/08	105.43	4.26
Newfld	6.700	Nov 03/09	109.89	4.56
Newfld	6.400	Jul 25/11	108.64	4.92
Newfld	5.250	Jun 04/14	99.54	5.31
Newfld	10.950	Apr 15/21	157.30	5.61
Newfld	6.150	Apr 17/28	103.31	5.89
Newfld	6.500	Oct 17/29	107.84	5.90
Newfld	6.550	Oct 17/30	108.63	5.90
Newfld	5.600	Oct 17/33	95.86	5.90
NovaSc	5.500	Mar 15/06	103.69	3.13
NovaSc	7.250	Oct 11/06	107.96	3.43
NovaSc	5.400	Jun 01/09	104.27	4.41
NovaSc	6.400	Sep 01/10	108.80	4.72
NovaSc	6.250	Jun 01/11	107.91	4.87
NovaSc	9.600	Jan 30/22	143.46	5.65
NovaSc	6.600	Jun 01/27	110.50	5.77
NovaSc	6.600	Dec 01/31	110.98	5.79
NovaSc	5.800	Jun 01/33	99.95	5.80
Ontario	9.000	Sep 15/04	100.74	1.99
Ontario	8.250	Dec 01/05	106.81	2.95
Ontario	7.500	Jan 19/06	106.30	3.04
Ontario	5.900	Mar 08/06	104.28	3.12
Ontario	7.750	Jul 24/06	108.37	3.32
Ontario	3.500	Sep 08/06	100.21	3.39
Ontario	5.200	Mar 08/07	103.83	3.64
Ontario	6.125	Sep 12/07	106.58	3.85
Ontario	4.400	Nov 19/08	100.61	4.24
Ontario	5.700	Dec 01/08	105.63	4.26
Ontario	4.000	May 19/09	98.37	4.38
Ontario	3.210	Aug 13/09	97.03	3.87
Ontario	6.200	Nov 19/09	107.87	4.51
Ontario	6.100	Nov 19/10	107.34	4.74
Ontario	6.100	Dec 02/11	107.28	4.90
Ontario	5.375	Dec 02/12	102.28	5.04
Ontario	4.750	Jun 02/13	97.58	5.09
Ontario	5.000	Mar 08/14	98.73	5.17
Ontario	9.500	Jul 13/22	144.01	5.58
Ontario	8.100	Sep 08/23	128.54	5.64
Ontario	7.500	Feb 07/24	121.58	5.66
Ontario	8.500	Dec 02/25	134.61	5.68
Ontario	8.000	Jun 02/26	128.67	5.69
Ontario	7.600	Jun 02/27	123.84	5.72
Ontario	6.500	Mar 08/29	109.88	5.74
Ontario	6.200	Jun 02/31	106.26	5.74
Ontario	5.850	Mar 08/33	101.35	5.75
OntHyd	7.750	Nov 03/05	105.90	2.88
OntHyd	5.600	Jun 02/08	105.24	4.10
OntHyd	10.500	Jan 15/10	103.61	2.25
OntHyd	10.000	Oct 17/14	138.20	5.14
OntHyd	10.125	Oct 15/21	150.20	5.55
OntHyd	8.900	Aug 18/22	137.03	5.61
OntHyd	8.500	May 26/25	134.47	5.66
OntHyd	8.250	Jun 22/26	131.58	5.70
Quebec	6.500	Dec 01/05	104.58	2.94
Quebec	7.750	Mar 30/06	107.34	3.15
Quebec	6.500	Oct 01/07	107.74	3.87
Quebec	11.000	Apr 01/09	127.91	4.32
Quebec	5.500	Jun 01/09	104.68	4.41
Quebec	3.149	Aug 17/09	96.83	3.85
Quebec	10.000	Jun 28/10	127.19	4.67
Quebec	6.250	Dec 01/10	107.93	4.78
Quebec	9.500	Sep 02/11	127.36	4.88
Quebec	9.000	Feb 10/12	124.99	4.97
Quebec	6.000	Oct 01/12	105.95	5.10
Quebec	5.250	Oct 01/13	100.25	5.21
Quebec	9.375	Jan 16/23	141.56	5.70
Quebec	8.500	Apr 01/26	133.31	5.78
Quebec	6.000	Oct 01/29	102.19	5.83
Quebec	6.250	Jun 01/32	105.59	5.84
Quebec	5.750	Dec 01/36	98.62	5.85
Saskat	7.500	Dec 19/05	106.04	2.97

	Coupon	Mat. date	Bid$	Yld%
Saskat	6.000	Jun 01/06	104.84	3.24
Saskat	4.750	Dec 01/06	102.76	3.50
Saskat	6.250	Mar 09/07	106.44	3.63
Saskat	5.000	Sep 06/07	103.33	3.85
Saskat	5.500	Jun 02/08	105.00	4.07
Saskat	6.500	Nov 12/09	109.34	4.49
Saskat	6.150	Sep 01/10	107.82	4.66
Saskat	5.250	Dec 03/12	101.51	5.03
Saskat	4.900	Dec 03/13	98.39	5.12
Saskat	10.250	Apr 10/14	138.74	5.12
Saskat	5.250	Jun 03/14	100.76	5.15
Saskat	9.600	Feb 04/22	144.48	5.58
Saskat	8.750	May 30/25	137.51	5.66
Saskat	5.750	Mar 05/29	100.47	5.71
Saskat	6.400	Sep 05/31	109.31	5.72
Saskat	5.800	Sep 05/33	101.22	5.71
Toronto	6.100	Aug 15/07	106.31	3.87
Toronto	6.100	Dec 12/17	106.01	5.46
CORPORATE				
407ETR	4.000	Feb 21/06	100.64	3.57
407ETR	0.000	Oct 18/06	106.01	3.68
407ETR	9.000	Aug 15/07	113.00	4.37
407ETR	6.900	Dec 17/07	108.40	4.20
407ETR	6.050	Jul 27/09	106.24	4.63
407ETR	6.470	Jul 27/29	102.40	6.28
407ETR	6.750	Jul 27/39	101.70	6.62
ADM	6.950	Apr 16/32	107.14	6.40
AGT Lt	8.800	Sep 22/25	122.13	6.81
Alianc	7.230	Jun 30/15	110.32	5.93
Alianc	7.181	Jun 30/23	111.29	6.16
Alianc	5.546	Dec 31/23	99.13	5.62
Alianc	7.217	Dec 31/25	110.68	6.30
Alianc	6.765	Dec 31/25	106.63	6.20
ALTA	5.430	Jun 05/13	100.52	5.35
BCCT	3.848	Mar 17/09	97.58	4.43
BCCT	4.804	Mar 17/14	96.22	5.31
BCE	6.750	Oct 30/07	107.36	4.29
BCE	7.350	Oct 30/09	111.28	4.88
BCFerry	5.740	May 27/14	101.55	5.53
Bell	6.700	Jun 28/07	107.32	4.00
Bell	6.150	Jun 15/09	106.58	4.62
Bell	6.900	Dec 15/11	110.13	5.22
Bell	6.250	Apr 12/12	105.91	5.30
Bell	6.550	May 01/29	99.65	6.58
Bell	7.850	Apr 02/31	115.88	6.58
Bell	7.300	Feb 23/32	109.12	6.58
Bell	6.100	Mar 16/35	93.73	6.58
BMO	8.800	Sep 13/05	106.31	2.95
BMO	8.150	May 09/06	108.11	3.36
BMO	4.660	Mar 31/09	100.78	4.47
BMO	7.000	Jan 28/10	111.30	4.64
BMO	6.903	Jun 30/10	109.37	5.05
BMO	6.647	Dec 31/10	107.87	5.19
BMO	4.690	Jan 31/11	99.09	4.86
BMO	6.685	Dec 31/11	107.98	5.36
BMO	4.780	Apr 30/14	95.92	5.32
BNS	7.400	Feb 08/06	106.09	3.23
BNS	6.250	Jul 16/07	106.20	4.00
BNS	5.650	Jul 22/08	104.75	4.33
BNS	4.295	Aug 22/08	100.16	4.25
BNS	4.515	Nov 19/08	100.66	4.34
BNS	5.750	May 12/09	104.95	4.58
BNS	3.318	Aug 18/09	97.40	3.89
BNS	7.310	Dec 31/10	111.50	5.18
Boreal	6.270	May 03/11	105.99	5.20
Cad Sch	4.900	Dec 01/08	99.79	4.95
Caisse	4.470	Nov 10/08	100.06	4.45
CanLif	8.000	Sep 19/06	108.82	3.64
CardTr	5.630	Dec 21/05	103.39	3.09
CAT	4.500	Aug 07/08	100.43	4.38
CDI	5.552	Jun 01/07	104.13	3.99
CDI	3.887	Mar 17/09	97.13	4.58
CDI	6.322	Jun 01/12	106.32	5.32
CDP	4.200	Oct 14/08	99.76	4.26
CGFCan	4.050	Jan 30/06	101.28	3.16
CGFCan	5.750	Aug 17/06	104.31	3.53
CGFCan	5.030	Sep 17/07	103.02	3.99
CGFCan	4.300	Aug 05/08	99.92	4.32
CGFCan	4.780	Jun 15/09	100.99	4.55
CIBC	7.400	Jan 31/06	106.04	3.20
CIBC	8.150	Apr 25/06	107.99	3.33
CIBC	7.000	Oct 23/06	107.12	3.62
CIBC	4.750	Jan 21/08	101.89	4.16

	Coupon	Mat. date	Bid$	Yld%
CIBC	4.400	Aug 26/08	100.47	4.27
CIBC	4.250	Jun 01/09	98.62	4.57
CIBC	4.950	Sep 02/10	100.86	4.79
CIBC	4.950	Jan 23/14	97.39	5.30
CnCrTr	4.806	Jan 24/08	102.15	4.13
CnTrRT	6.163	Jul 21/06	105.03	3.48
CnTrRT	4.820	Dec 20/07	102.44	4.04
ConsWHT	4.700	Jan 28/08	101.97	4.09
CPRR	4.900	Jun 15/10	99.57	4.99
CRAFT	5.188	Dec 15/06	103.45	3.65
CRAFT	4.645	Feb 15/08	101.62	4.15
CU Inc	6.800	Aug 13/19	109.89	5.80
DlmrCCF	4.650	Aug 11/05	101.44	3.20
DlmrCCF	5.000	May 29/06	101.81	3.95
DlmrCCF	5.200	Nov 07/06	102.05	4.24
DlmrCCF	4.600	May 22/07	100.29	4.49
Domtar	10.000	Apr 15/11	122.37	5.90
Enbrdg	5.450	Apr 12/06	103.49	3.30
ERAC	7.125	Mar 01/06	105.53	3.48
Ford C	7.100	Sep 01/05	103.78	3.48
Ford C	5.800	Sep 26/06	102.65	4.48
Ford C	4.600	Feb 20/07	99.56	4.79
GE CAP	4.350	Feb 06/06	101.73	3.16
GE CAP	5.300	Jul 24/07	103.84	3.92
GE CAP	5.000	Apr 23/08	102.64	4.22
GE CAP	6.250	Jul 24/12	107.04	5.16
GE CAP	5.150	Jun 06/13	99.12	5.27
Genss	6.462	Nov 15/05	104.23	3.05
GLAC	4.444	Nov 20/08	100.31	4.36
GldCrd	5.700	Aug 15/06	104.42	3.42
GldCrd	4.159	Oct 15/08	99.45	4.30
GlouCrd	6.578	Jul 15/05	103.46	2.83
GlouCrd	5.693	Mar 15/06	103.78	3.26
GlouCrd	5.590	Jun 15/07	104.62	3.87
GlouCrd	4.716	May 15/08	101.77	4.20
GlouCrd	4.274	Oct 15/08	99.74	4.34
GlouCrd	5.376	May 15/14	100.26	5.34
GrTAA	5.950	Dec 03/07	105.10	4.29
GrTAA	5.170	Jun 02/08	102.56	4.43
GrTAA	6.700	Jul 19/10	108.20	5.09
GrTAA	6.250	Jan 30/12	104.84	5.45
GrTAA	6.250	Dec 13/12	104.48	5.57
GrTAA	6.450	Dec 03/27	97.66	6.65
GrTAA	6.450	Jul 30/29	101.14	6.36
GrTAA	7.050	Jun 12/30	104.92	6.65
GrTAA	7.100	Jun 04/31	105.61	6.65
GrTAA	6.980	Oct 15/32	104.19	6.65
GrTAA	6.470	Feb 02/34	97.71	6.65
GTC Tr	6.200	Jun 01/07	103.52	4.85
Gulf C	6.450	Oct 01/07	106.75	4.39
GWLife	6.750	Aug 10/10	109.45	4.92
GWLife	5.995	Dec 31/12	103.28	5.50
GWLife	6.140	Mar 21/18	102.49	5.87
GWLife	6.740	Nov 24/31	104.64	6.38
GWLife	6.670	Mar 21/33	103.81	6.38
HolRec	5.672	Apr 26/06	103.96	3.29
HouseF	6.440	Jun 01/07	106.51	3.98
HouseF	4.500	Jul 02/08	100.65	4.32
HouseF	4.200	Apr 13/09	98.32	4.60
HSBC	7.780	Dec 31/10	113.68	5.24
HydOne	4.000	Oct 31/05	101.22	2.98
HydOne	4.150	Apr 21/06	101.43	3.28
HydOne	4.450	May 04/07	101.69	3.80
HydOne	4.000	Jun 23/08	99.17	4.23
HydOne	3.950	Feb 24/09	98.03	4.43
HydOne	7.150	Jun 03/10	112.06	4.76
HydOne	6.400	Dec 01/11	108.02	5.07
HydOne	5.770	Nov 15/12	103.71	5.21
HydOne	7.350	Jun 03/30	115.02	6.18
HydOne	6.930	Jun 01/32	109.92	6.18
HydOne	6.350	Jan 31/34	102.32	6.18
IntrAm	5.625	Jun 29/09	105.52	4.36
Invest	6.750	May 09/11	108.71	5.20
IPL	8.200	Feb 15/24	122.36	6.21
Jdeere	6.750	Apr 03/07	107.19	3.88
LauBnk	6.000	Oct 02/06	104.34	3.88
Loblaw	6.000	Jun 02/08	105.92	4.30
Loblaw	7.100	May 11/10	111.43	4.81
Loblaw	6.500	Jan 19/11	108.33	4.98
Loblaw	7.100	Jun 01/16	112.27	5.66
Loblaw	6.650	Nov 08/27	102.52	6.44
Marit	6.900	Nov 30/19	108.62	6.03
Merril	5.350	Nov 19/07	103.90	4.07

	Coupon	Mat. date	Bid$	Yld%
Merril	4.700	Sep 12/08	101.29	4.35
MilitA	5.750	Jun 30/19	103.70	5.38
MLI	5.700	Feb 16/06	103.70	3.20
MLI	6.240	Feb 16/11	106.64	5.03
MLI	6.700	Jun 30/12	107.86	5.46
MstrCr	6.060	Jun 21/07	105.91	3.87
NatBnk	6.250	Oct 31/07	106.33	4.14
NatBnk	5.700	Apr 16/09	104.25	4.68
NatBnk	4.660	Sep 10/09	99.86	4.69
NavCda	4.250	Feb 13/06	101.62	3.15
NavCda	6.600	Dec 01/06	106.61	3.61
NavCda	6.500	Jun 01/09	108.21	4.58
NavCda	7.560	Mar 01/27	116.45	6.20
NavCda	7.400	Jun 01/27	115.70	6.11
Nexen	6.300	Jun 02/08	106.14	4.53
OMER	4.690	Jun 02/08	101.70	4.20
OMER	5.480	Dec 31/12	102.42	5.12
Ontrea	5.700	Oct 31/11	104.42	4.96
Ontrea	5.570	Apr 09/13	103.01	5.13
PanPet	5.300	Dec 03/07	103.29	4.23
Power	6.900	Mar 11/33	106.54	6.40
Renais	6.850	Feb 06/07	106.93	3.92
Rogers	10.500	Jun 01/06	109.25	5.11
RoyBnk	6.400	Aug 15/05	103.62	2.80
RoyBnk	6.500	Sep 12/06	105.98	3.52
RoyBnk	6.750	Jun 04/07	107.54	3.91
RoyBnk	6.100	Jan 22/08	106.17	4.17
RoyBnk	5.600	Apr 22/08	104.82	4.18
RoyBnk	3.960	Jan 27/09	97.90	4.48
RoyBnk	4.180	Jun 01/09	98.24	4.59
RoyBnk	7.100	Jan 25/10	111.15	4.76
RoyBnk	7.288	Jun 30/10	111.26	5.06
RoyBnk	6.300	Apr 12/11	106.93	5.06
RoyBnk	7.183	Jun 30/11	110.74	5.30
RoyBnk	5.450	Nov 04/13	100.10	5.43
RoyBnk	5.000	Jan 20/14	97.83	5.29
ScoreTr	5.035	Nov 15/06	103.09	3.61
ScoreTr	4.949	Feb 20/14	97.07	5.34
SDM	4.970	Oct 24/08	101.31	4.62
SNCLav	7.700	Sep 20/10	112.21	5.34
StrtCr	6.170	Sep 15/31	92.35	6.79
Suncor	6.800	Mar 05/07	107.12	3.88
Suncor	6.700	Aug 22/11	108.73	5.20
SunLife	5.800	May 15/08	105.20	4.29
SunLife	6.650	Oct 12/10	109.04	4.94
SunLife	6.865	Dec 31/11	108.88	5.39
SunLife	6.150	Jun 30/12	104.76	5.40
Talism	5.800	Jan 30/07	104.63	3.83
TD Bnk	6.000	Jul 26/06	104.80	3.46
TD Bnk	6.550	Jul 31/07	107.22	3.96
TD Bnk	5.200	Sep 04/07	103.48	3.99
TD Bnk	4.540	Sep 05/08	100.69	4.35
TD Bnk	7.600	Dec 31/09	112.72	4.89
TD Bnk	5.690	Jun 03/13	101.98	5.40
TEL	7.500	Jun 01/06	106.31	3.87
Ternet	6.480	Sep 08/09	108.30	4.63
Ternet	5.737	Mar 31/17	101.67	5.55
Thomso	7.950	Nov 15/05	106.13	3.01
Thomso	6.200	Jan 30/06	104.31	3.20
Thomso	7.150	Oct 23/06	107.50	3.59
Thomso	6.500	Jul 09/07	106.85	4.00
Thomso	6.550	Jul 17/07	107.09	3.98
Thomso	6.900	Jun 04/08	109.04	4.31
Thomso	4.500	Jun 01/09	99.56	4.60
Thomso	6.850	Jun 01/11	110.19	5.06
TorHsp	5.640	Dec 08/22	101.32	5.52
TorHyd	6.110	May 07/13	105.07	5.37
Trizec	7.950	Jun 01/07	111.15	5.36
TrnAlC	6.050	Jan 16/06	103.02	3.38
TrnCan	6.050	Feb 15/07	105.36	3.81
TrnCan	5.840	Jun 27/08	105.34	4.33
TrnCan	5.650	Jan 15/14	101.20	5.48
TrnCan	6.500	Dec 09/30	100.26	6.48
UniGas	6.650	May 04/11	108.25	5.18
UniGas	8.650	Nov 10/25	124.38	6.51
Weston	5.900	Feb 05/09	105.22	4.60
Weston	6.450	Oct 24/11	107.23	5.23
Wstcoa	6.750	Dec 15/27	100.76	6.68
YPG	4.570	Apr 21/09	98.20	5.00
YPG	5.710	Apr 21/14	97.72	6.02
YrkRec	3.568	Jul 21/06	100.29	3.41
YrkRec	4.272	Jul 21/08	100.00	4.27

BAUM COMPANY LTD. BOND ISSUED AT PAR—ISSUANCE ENTRY

Cash (A)	1,000	
Bond Payable (L)		1,000

No interest is recognized on the date of issuance because interest accrues as time passes. The recognition of interest requires two entries. The first is to accrue the interest expense for the period and the amount payable to the bondholders. The second is to record the cash payment made. The recognition of expense should be based on a time value of money calculation using the yield rate (10% for the Baum Company Ltd. bond sold at par) and the bond's carrying value ($1,000 when sold at par). The amount payable to the bondholders is dictated by the bond interest rate. The following calculations and entries would be made at the end of the first interest payment period (six months).

BAUM COMPANY LTD. BOND ISSUED AT PAR—INTEREST ENTRIES
(AT END OF FIRST INTEREST PERIOD)

Interest Expense[a] (SE)	50	
Interest Payable[b] (L)		50
Interest Payable (L)	50	
Cash (A)		50

[a]Interest expense = Carrying Value × Yield Rate × Time
= $1,000 × 10% × 6/12 = $50
[b]Interest payable = Face Amount × Bond Interest Rate × Time
= $1,000 × 10% × 6/12 = $50

The calculation of the interest expense (the interest incurred during the period) and interest payable (the cash amount owed based on the bond contract) results in the same number for a bond sold at par. This is not the case for bonds issued at a premium or a discount.

The calculation of the interest payable amount will be the same in all four interest periods over the life of the bond because neither the bond's face amount nor interest rate change over that time. The calculation of interest expense in each period will depend on the bond's carrying value at the beginning of each period. The carrying value will equal the bond's face value less the discount, or the face value plus the premium. The carrying value (book value) at the end of each period can be calculated using the following formula.

Carrying Value (ending) = Carrying Value (beginning) + Interest Expense − Interest Payments

In the first period:

Carrying Value (ending) = $1,000 + 50 − 50 = $1,000

Because the expense and the cash payment are the same in every period, a bond sold at par will have a carrying value of $1,000 at the end of every period. The entries for interest recognition, therefore, would be exactly the same at the end of each of the four interest periods.

At the end of the fourth period, the company will make the final interest payment plus the additional payment of return of the face value to the bondholder. The entry will be:

BAUM COMPANY LTD. BOND ISSUED AT PAR—MATURITY PAYMENT ENTRY (AT MATURITY DATE)		
Bond Payable (L)	1,000	
Cash (A)		1,000

The bond's carrying value over time can be shown graphically as in Exhibit 10-4. Note that the carrying value remains constant over the four six-month periods. The balance in the liability account at the end of the four interest periods is $1,000. This is the balance prior to the maturity payment and, therefore, should be exactly $1,000.

CARRYING VALUE OF A BOND ISSUED AT PAR

EXHIBIT 10-4

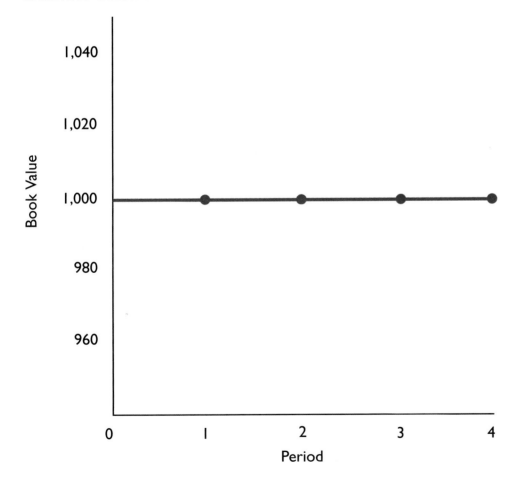

Sometimes, a bond's change in value over its life is also summarized in what is known as an amortization table. Exhibit 10-5 shows a typical amortization table for the bond issued at par.

EXHIBIT 10-5 **AMORTIZATION TABLE—BOND ISSUED AT PAR**

Period	Beginning Carrying Value	Interest	Payment	Ending Carrying Value
1	$1,000.00	$50.00	$50.00	$1,000.00
2	$1,000.00	$50.00	$50.00	$1,000.00
3	$1,000.00	$50.00	$50.00	$1,000.00
4	$1,000.00	$50.00	$1,050.00	$0.00

BONDS ISSUED AT A DISCOUNT

Now assume that investors demanded a 12% return for the bond issued by Baum. As calculated earlier in the chapter, the bond would be issued at a price of $965.35 under these conditions. Another way of expressing the issue price would be to say that the bond sold at 96.535 (96.535% of its face value). The following entry would then be made by Baum Company Ltd. at issuance.

BAUM COMPANY LTD. BOND ISSUED AT A DISCOUNT—ISSUANCE ENTRY

Cash (A)	965.35	
Discount on Bond Payable (XL)	34.65	
Bond Payable (L)		1,000

In this case, the liability's present value is $965.35, and this is the amount that should be recorded on Baum's books. This amount could be credited directly to the bond payable account. However, in Canada, we normally credit the bond payable account with the bond's face value and then reduce the amount by creating a contra liability account called *discount on bond payable*. The contra account (note that the XL notation in the journal entry represents a contra liability account) is most commonly reported directly with the bond payable account.[2] The net of these two amounts is the present value; that is, $1,000 − $34.65 = $965.35. Note that this presentation allows for the disclosure of both the bonds' face amount and net present value at the date of issuance. Over the life of the bond, we will gradually reduce the discount on bond payable account such that at maturity, the discount will be zero.

The interest entries for the bond issued at a discount are shown in the following box. Notice that the interest expense is now different from the amount payable. The reason for this is that the yield rate and the carrying value are now different from the bond interest rate and the face amount. The difference between the expense and the interest payable is credited to the discount account, which decreases the balance in the account. This is known as the **amortization of the discount**. This method of calculating interest expense is known as the **effective interest method**. The yield rate times the debt's carrying value determines the interest expense for the period.

BAUM COMPANY LTD. BOND ISSUED AT A DISCOUNT—INTEREST ENTRIES (AT END OF FIRST INTEREST PERIOD)

Interest Expense[a] (SE)	57.92	
Discount on Bond Payable (XL)		7.92
Interest Payable[b] (L)		50.00
Interest Payable (L)	50.00	
Cash (A)		50.00

---

[a]Interest expense = Carrying Value × Yield Rate × Time
= $965.35 × 12% × 6/12 = $57.92

[b]Interest payable = Face Amount × Bond Interest Rate × Time
= $1,000 × 10% × 6/12 = $50

Because the discount is being amortized each period, the bond's net carrying value changes from period to period. The discount can be amortized in a straight-line fashion; that is, the same amount each period, as long as the effect on the financial statements is not materially different from applying the effective interest method, which is illustrated in this section. Under the straight-line method, the total discount ($34.65) would be divided by the number of periods to maturity (4). In the case of Baum, the discount amortization would be $8.66 ($34.65 ÷ 4) each period. You will notice that there is a difference between the first period discount amortization under the effective interest method vs. the straight-line method. That difference appears to be small but remember that we are only dealing with one $1,000 bond in our example.[3]

Under the effective interest method, the carrying value at the end of the period would be calculated as before.

Carrying Value (ending) = Carrying Value (beginning) + Interest Expense − Payments

In the first period:

Carrying Value (ending) = $965.35 + 57.92 − 50.00 = $973.27

Notice that the carrying value increases a little by the end of the first period. This new carrying value balance is used to calculate the interest expense in the second period. Therefore, the interest expense will increase slightly each period to reflect the increase in the carrying value. The ending carrying value could also be calculated by subtracting the balance in the discount account from the face amount of the bond in the bond payable account. The discount account will have a balance of $26.73 ($34.65 − $7.92) at the end of the first period. The face amount minus this discount will give a carrying value of $973.27, the same amount as calculated in the preceding equation.

---

[2] The bond discount can also be reported under Other Assets in the long-term asset section of the balance sheet.

[3] Because Canadian GAAP requires the use of the effective method, we will continue with the remaining illustrations using that method. Your instructor may allow you to use the straight-line method to keep the accounting simple.

Exhibit 10-6 shows graphically how the bond's carrying value changes over time. Notice that because this bond is issued at a discount, the beginning carrying value is below $1,000. As time passes, the discount is amortized (decreases) and the carrying value increases, eventually reaching $1,000 by the maturity date, when the final payment of $1,000 is made.

EXHIBIT 10-6 **CARRYING VALUE OF A BOND ISSUED AT A DISCOUNT**

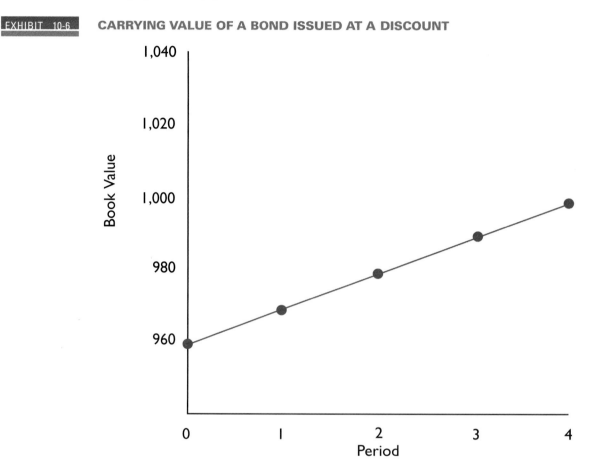

At the maturity date, the final maturity payment is made with the same entry as that made in the par case because the final carrying value is the same ($1,000). Recognize that the payments made at the interest dates are not sufficient to pay for the interest that has accrued during the period. Because the investors initially paid less than the face value for the bond but are being paid interest based on the face value and will receive the face value at maturity, the company is, in effect, paying a higher rate of interest than is reflected in the bond interest rate. This higher rate of interest needs to be reflected on the income statement. The excess of the interest expense over the payment decreases the discount, creating the rising carrying value shown in the graph. Exhibit 10-7 shows the amortization table for the bond issued at a discount.

AMORTIZATION TABLE—BOND ISSUED AT A DISCOUNT

EXHIBIT 10-7

Period	Beginning Carrying Value	Interest	Payment	Ending Carrying Value	Beginning Discount
1	$965.35	$57.92	$50.00	$973.27	($34.65)
2	$973.27	$58.40	$50.00	$981.67	($26.73)
3	$981.67	$58.90	$50.00	$990.57	($18.33)
4	$990.57	$59.43	$1,050.00	$0.00	($9.43)

BONDS ISSUED AT A PREMIUM

If the interest rate demanded by investors is 8%, then the Baum Company Ltd. bond would be issued at a premium. The issue price in this scenario was calculated earlier in the chapter as $1,036.30. Another way of expressing the issue price would be to say that the bond sold at 103.63 (103.63% of its face value). The following entry would be made at issuance by Baum Company Ltd.

BAUM COMPANY LTD. BOND ISSUED AT A PREMIUM—ISSUANCE ENTRY

Cash (A)	1,036.30	
Premium on Bond Payable (L)		36.30
Bond Payable (L)		1,000.00

AN INTERNATIONAL PERSPECTIVE

Reports from Other Countries

In Canada and the United States, the amortization of the discount (or premium) on a bond is calculated using effective interest methods, as described earlier. In some countries (Australia and Denmark, for example), the discount is typically amortized in a straight-line fashion, in much the same way as straight-line amortization of a capital asset. Straight-line amortization of the discount (or premium) is acceptable in Canada and the United States as long as the results of doing so are not materially different from the use of the effective interest method.

In some countries, the discount amount is written off in the year of issuance rather than being amortized to income over the life of the bond.

As in the case of the bond issued at a discount, the $1,000 face value is credited to the bond payable account. The excess of the proceeds over the face amount is credited to an account called *premium on bond payable*. This account is a liability account, but is also known as an **adjunct account**. The balance in this account is reported directly with the bond liability account; that is, the accounts are linked together. Adjunct accounts are used to contain balances that add to a related account in the same way that contra accounts subtract from related accounts. The sum of the two accounts creates a liability that is measured at its net present value. The interest entries for the bond issued at a premium would be:

BAUM COMPANY LTD. BOND ISSUED AT A PREMIUM—INTEREST ENTRIES (AT END OF FIRST INTEREST PERIOD)

Interest Expense[a] (SE)	41.45	
Premium on Bond Payable (L)	8.55	
Interest Payable[b] (L)		50.00
Interest Payable (L)	50.00	
Cash (A)		50.00

[a]Interest expense = Carrying Value × Yield Rate × Time
= $1,036.30 × 8% × 6/12 = $41.45
[b]Interest payable = Face Amount × Bond Interest Rate × Time
= $1,000 × 10% × 6/12 = $50

The premium on the bond payable is amortized in much the same way as a discount. As the premium is amortized, the premium account is reduced and, consequently, the bond's carrying value is reduced from period to period. This should make sense because the cash payments made each period are more than enough to pay for the interest expense. The excess of the payments over the expense (i.e., the **amortization of the premium**) reduces the debt's carrying value. The carrying value at the end of the period would be calculated as before.

Carrying Value (ending) = Carrying Value (beginning) + Interest Expense − Payments

In the first period:

Carrying Value (ending) = $1,036.30 + 41.45 − 50.00 = $1,027.75

Exhibit 10-8 shows graphically how the liability's carrying value changes over time. Notice that, because this bond is issued at a premium, the beginning carrying value is above $1,000. As time passes, the premium is amortized (decreases), and the carrying value decreases, eventually reaching $1,000 by the maturity date. The payments made at the interest dates are higher than the interest expense that has accrued during the period. Because the investors initially paid more than the face value for the bond but are being paid interest based on the face value and will receive the face value at maturity, the company is, in effect, paying a lower rate of interest than is reflected by the bond interest rate. This lower rate of interest needs to be reflected on the income statement.

The excess of the interest payment over the interest expense decreases the premium, creating the falling carrying value shown in the graph.

At the maturity date, the final maturity payment is made with the same entry as that made in the par case in that the final carrying value is the same ($1,000). Exhibit 10-9 shows the amortization table for the bond issued at a premium.

CARRYING VALUE OF A BOND ISSUED AT A PREMIUM

EXHIBIT 10-8

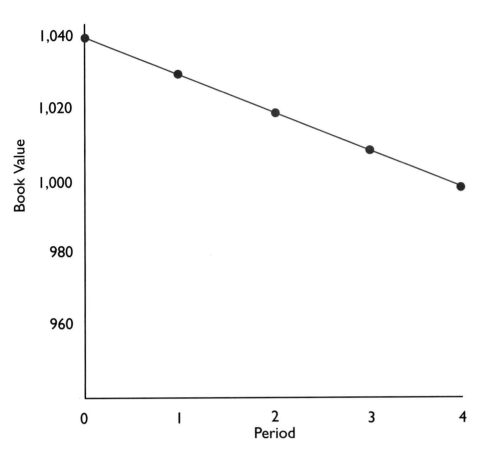

AMORTIZATION TABLE—BOND ISSUED AT A PREMIUM

EXHIBIT 10-9

Period	Beginning Carrying Value	Interest	Payment	Ending Carrying Value	Beginning Premium
1	$1,036.30	$41.45	$50.00	$1,027.75	$36.30
2	$1,027.75	$41.11	$50.00	$1,018.86	$27.75
3	$1,018.86	$40.75	$50.00	$1,009.62	$18.86
4	$1,009.62	$40.38	$1,050.00	$0.00	$9.62

Early Retirement of Debt

Although a company does not have to pay off its debts until maturity, there are times when it makes sense for it to pay the debt earlier. This transaction is known as **early retirement**, or **early extinguishment**, of debt. Bonds can be retired by buying them in the bond market or by **calling the bonds**. The bonds may have a call feature that allows the company to buy them back from the investors at a predetermined price. If the intention is to buy them in the bond market, it is likely that interest rates in the economy have changed between the issuance date and the date at which the company wants to buy back the debt. Because the interest rate used to account for the bond is fixed at the issuance date, it is likely that the bond's carrying value will be different from its market value. A gain or loss will, consequently, result from this transaction. The gains and losses from the early retirement of debt are shown on the income statement.

To demonstrate the accounting for an early retirement, suppose the Baum Company Ltd. bond we discussed in the last section was issued when interest rates were 8%. Further, suppose that after one year Baum wishes to retire the bond. Interest rates in the economy have increased to 12% by this time. The carrying value at the end of year 1 would be $1,018.86, as shown in Exhibit 10-9.

The bond's market value based on the 12% interest would be determined by discounting the remaining two coupon (interest) payments and the maturity value at 12%. This value would be the same as the value from the amortization table shown in Exhibit 10-7 for the bond, as if it were originally issued at 12%. Therefore, the market value would be $981.67 or, for clarification, the market value calculation would be as follows: $50 × 1.83339 (PV for 2 periods at 6%) × $1,000 × 0.8900 (PV for 2 periods at 6%) = $91.67 + $890.00 = $981.67. If Baum buys back the bond at this price, it will be satisfying an obligation on its books at $1,018.86 with a cash payment of $981.67. A gain will, therefore, result from this transaction. The entry to record this transaction would be:

EARLY RETIREMENT ENTRY

Bond Payable (L)	1,000.00	
Premium on Bond Payable (L)	18.86	
Cash (A)		981.67
Gain on Early Retirement of Bond (SE)		37.19

The example with Baum Company Ltd. illustrates one reason why a company may decide to retire its debt early: the bond's market value is lower than the maturity value. The company can pay off its debt with less money than would be required at maturity. The downside of this, however, is that if the company needs to raise more capital through the use of debt, it is probable that it will have to pay a higher interest rate. The short-term gain on the debt retirement could be replaced by higher interest costs over the long term. Under these circumstances, is the company better off (as reflected by the gain) for having retired its old debt?

In Note 15 of its 2003 financial statements Bell Canada disclosed the following:

"On March 1, 2004, Bell Canada redeemed its $125 million Series DU debentures at 101% of the principal amount. The original maturity date of these debentures was March 1, 2011. They had an interest rate of 9.45%."

This is an example of a company retiring debt early because interest rates have declined. You will notice that Bell Canada had to pay a premium (101%) to redeem them. In the opening story, Bell Canada had recently issued bonds at 5.5%, which is significantly below the 9.45% on the bonds that were redeemed.

LEASING

When a company needs to use an asset such as a piece of machinery, it can obtain the use of the asset in two ways. One is to purchase the asset outright. A second is to enter into a **lease agreement** in which another company (the **lessor**) buys the asset and the company that wants to use the asset (the **lessee**) makes periodic payments to the lessor in exchange for the use of the asset over the length of the lease agreement (**lease term**).

LEARNING OBJECTIVE 4

Discuss the advantages and disadvantages of leasing.

There are benefits and costs to both alternatives. One benefit of ownership is that the company can amortize the asset for tax purposes and, in some cases, obtain an investment tax credit for the purchase. Investment tax credits are incentives provided by the Canada Revenue Agency to encourage investment in certain types of assets. These credits usually take the form of a direct reduction in the company's tax bill based on a fixed percentage of the asset's acquisition cost.

Profit from appreciation in the asset's value is another benefit of ownership. The downside is loss from the asset's amortization, which could be dramatic if the asset becomes technologically obsolete or loses its market popularity. If the company has to borrow to buy the asset, the company's debt/equity and interest coverage ratios will change, which could affect its future borrowing capabilities. (These ratios are discussed later in this chapter as well as in Chapter 12.) This also ties up capital that might be used for other projects.

To the lessee, the benefits of leasing are several. The lessee does not have to put up its own capital to buy the asset. It also does not have to borrow to buy the asset, which means that its debt/equity and interest coverage ratios will not be affected. If the company is in a tax situation in which little taxable income is generated, the tax advantages of amortizing the asset or claiming an investment tax credit would be of limited value to the lessee. If the lessor can take advantage of the capital cost allowance deduction, then the lease payments that the lessee makes will be reduced as a result of the decrease in the lessor's costs. Because the lessee does not own the asset, the risk of loss from obsolescence falls on the lessor. Another advantage, along these same lines, is that the lessee may not want to use the asset for its full useful life. If the company wants to use the asset for only a short time, there is significant risk associated with the resale value if the company decides to buy the asset rather than to lease it.

Lessee Accounting

The accounting issues for a lessee can be illustrated using two extreme examples. At one extreme, suppose that the lease contract is signed for a relatively short period of time, say two years, whereas the leased asset's useful life is eight years. In this case, it is clear that the lessee is not buying the asset, but is instead renting it for only a short period. The lease contract may be viewed as a mutually unexecuted contract, and the cash payments required by the lease are recorded by the lessee as rent expense and an outflow of cash. This type of lease is known as an **operating lease**.

LEARNING OBJECTIVE 5

Distinguish between an operating lease and a capital lease and prepare journal entries for a lessee under both conditions.

Suppose at the other extreme that the lease contract was signed for the asset's entire useful life and that the title to the asset passes to the lessee at the end of the lease term (not an uncommon event). In this case, the substance of the transaction is that the lessee has bought an asset and has agreed to pay for it in instalments. There is essentially no difference between this arrangement and one in which the lessee borrows the money and buys the asset for cash. The lender, in this case, is the lessor. It seems appropriate for the lessee to account for this as a borrowing and as a purchase of an asset. The asset is therefore recorded at its cost (in this case, the present value of the lease payments), and is amortized over time in the same way that a purchased capital asset would be. The asset account name often includes the lease aspect (i.e., equipment under capital leases). The obligation to the lessor is recorded as a liability, and interest expense is recognized over time. This type of lease is known as a **capital lease**.

Although the appropriate accounting procedures for these extreme situations seem fairly clear, the question arises: what does the company do when the lease is somewhere in between these extremes? Suppose, for example, that the lease term is for 70% of the asset's useful life and the company has an option to buy the asset at the end of the lease term. Should this qualify as a capital lease? In terms of the financial statement effects, a company would generally prefer to treat the lease as an operating lease. This would keep the lease obligation off the books, and there would be no effect on the debt/equity and interest coverage ratios. To address this issue, criteria have been developed to distinguish capital leases from operating leases. From the lessee's point of view, the lease qualifies as a capital lease if one of the following criteria is met.[4]

CAPITAL LEASE CRITERIA

1. The title to the asset passes to the lessee at the end of the lease term.
2. The lease term is equal to or greater than 75% of the asset's useful life.
3. The present value of the minimum lease payments is greater than 90% of the leased asset's fair value.

If the transaction does not meet any of the three criteria, the lease is an operating lease.

Criterion 1 indicates that the company will own the asset by the end of the lease term and, hence, is buying an asset. Many leases provide an option for the lessee to buy the asset at the end of the lease term. If the price to buy the asset is considered a bargain (i.e., the price is considered below the expected value at the end of the lease term, and therefore, it is likely that the company will exercise its option and buy the asset), then Criterion 1 would be met. If, on the other hand, the asset price is the market value at the end of the lease term, Criterion 1 has not been met because there is no certainty that the lessee will buy the asset. Criterion 2 means that the company will have the use of the asset during most of its useful life, even though it may not retain title to it at the end of the lease term. Criterion 3 means that if the price the lessee pays to lease the asset is close to the price it would pay to buy the asset, it should account for the transaction as a purchase.

To illustrate the differences in accounting under a capital lease and an operating lease, let's consider the following simple situation. Suppose that an asset is leased for five years and requires quarterly lease payments of $2,000 each, payable

---

[4] *CICA Handbook*, Section 3065.06.

in advance. The title does not pass at the end of the lease term, and there is no purchase option. The interest rate that is appropriate for this lease is 12%.

If the lease qualifies as an operating lease, the only entry to be made would be to record the payments as rent expense each quarter. The following entry would be made each quarter.

OPERATING LEASE ENTRY

Rent expense (Lease expense) (SE)	2,000	
Cash (A)		2,000

If the lease qualifies as a capital lease, the transaction must be recorded as the purchase of an asset and a related obligation. Both the asset and the obligation would be recorded at the present value of the lease payments. Because there are quarterly payments and the lease term is five years, there would be a total of 20 payments. This transaction is structured as an annuity in advance (the first payment is made immediately and then there are 19 more payments). The interest rate per period for use in discounting would be 3% (the quarterly rate is determined from the 12% annual rate). Using Table 4 from the Appendix at the end of the chapter for the present value of an annuity, the following would be the calculation of the present value.

$$
\begin{aligned}
\text{PV of lease payments} &= \text{First payment} + \text{PV of 19 payments at 3\%} \\
&= \$2,000 + (\$2,000 \times 14.32380) \\
&= \$2,000 + \$28,647.60 \\
&= \$30,647.60
\end{aligned}
$$

The entry to record the purchase of the asset and the related obligation at the time of contract signing would be:

CAPITAL LEASE ENTRY
(AT DATE OF SIGNING)

Asset under capital lease (A)	30,647.60	
Obligation under capital lease (L)		30,647.60

The lease obligation would result in the recognition of interest expense similar to that generated by a bond. In the first quarter, two things happen. The first is that a payment is made at the beginning of the quarter (the first payment). This entire payment reduces the principal of the obligation because no time has passed and no interest has accrued. The principal at the beginning of the quarter is, therefore, $28,647.60 ($30,647.60 − $2,000). Interest is then calculated on this principal in the amount of $859.43 ($28,647.60 $\times$ 12% $\times$ 3/12). The entries to record these transactions in the first quarter are:

CAPITAL LEASE PAYMENT ENTRY
(ON THE FIRST DAY OF EACH QUARTER)

Obligation under capital lease (L)	2,000	
Cash (A)		2,000

CAPITAL LEASE EXPENSE ENTRY
(ON THE LAST DAY OF THE QUARTER)

Interest expense (SE)	859.43	
Obligation under capital lease (L)		859.43

An amortization table of the lease obligation, similar to those constructed earlier for bonds, could be prepared. By the end of the lease term, the lease obligation would be zero. Note that in the case of a lease, the interest is added directly to the lease obligation account and the cash payments directly reduce the obligation balance.

In addition, subsequent to acquisition, the asset would be amortized over its useful life (in this case, the lease term, since the title does not pass at the end of the lease term). Assuming the company uses straight-line amortization, the amortization for the first quarter would be $1,532.38 ($30,647.60 ÷ 20 quarters). Note that the residual value is zero in this calculation because the lessee does not retain title to the asset at the end of the lease term and, therefore, it is necessary to amortize the whole amount of the leased asset. The entry to record amortization would be:

CAPITAL LEASE EXPENSE ENTRY
(ON THE LAST DAY OF THE QUARTER)

Amortization expense (SE)	1,532.38	
Accumulated amortization (XA)		1,532.38
(on leased assets)		

These transactions have certain effects on the financial statements. If the asset qualifies as a capital lease, the company's assets and liabilities would be $30,647.60 higher than under an operating lease. On the income statement, the company would report both amortization expense and interest expense with the capital lease, whereas, with the operating lease, the company would report only rent expense. In the first quarter, the amortization plus interest would be $2,391.81 ($1,532.38 + $859.43). The expense under the operating lease would be $2,000. Therefore, in the first quarter, the capital lease results in higher expenses (they would be even higher if the company used an accelerated method of amortization). The total expenses reported over the life of the lease would be the same, however, regardless of which method is used to record the transaction. With the operating lease, the total expenses would be $40,000: $2,000 × 20 payments. The total capital lease expenses would also be $40,000: $30,647.60 in amortization and $9,352.40 in interest (total payments minus principal = $40,000 − $30,647.60). The difference, then, is in the pattern of expense recognition over the life of the lease, with operating leases showing a level amount of expense and capital leases showing larger expenses in the early years (when amortization and interest are high) and smaller expenses in later years.

Exhibit 10-10 graphs the pattern of expense recognition over the life of the lease, treating the lease as an operating lease vs. a capital lease.

PATTERNS OF EXPENSE RECOGNITION FOR LEASES

EXHIBIT 10-10

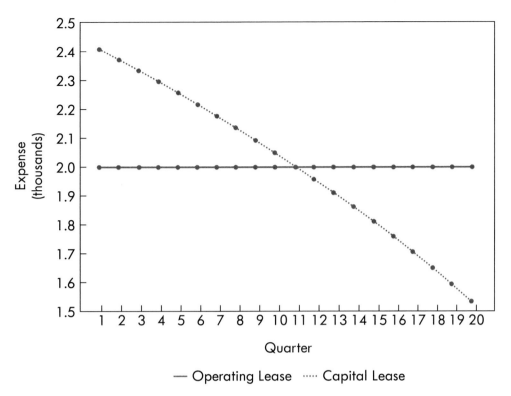

— Operating Lease ····· Capital Lease

accounting in the news

WHEN LEASE CONTRACTS GO WRONG

The City of Toronto has been locked in a legal battle with MFP Financial Services Ltd. from which it leased computer equipment. Late in 2001, the city's auditor determined that the city had leased more equipment from MFP than the amount that city council thought it had authorized. The city stopped making its lease payments and sued MFP early in 2002. MFP countersued.

By mid 2004, the legal battle had still not been resolved. The city wanted to replace its leased computer equipment with purchased equipment but did not have a solution to what to do with the leased computers. The original lease agreements were about to run out, but because the contract was in dispute, it was not clear if the leased equipment could be returned to MFP.

City council needed to decide if it wanted to negotiate a settlement with MFP or pursue the legal battle to the end.

Source: "Mayor suggests settling lease deal with MFP," by James Rusk, *Globe and Mail.Com*, July 16, 2004.

Because no asset or liability is recorded under operating leases in Canada, companies that have significant operating leases have to disclose their commitments to pay for these leases. Companies are required to disclose the future lease payments to be made in total and for each of the next five years. Capital leases also require similar disclosure. The obligations associated with leases would typically be shown in a footnote that relates either to long-term debt or to commitments or contingencies. In the financial statements for CHC Helicopter Corporation, these disclosures can be found in Note 22 (Exhibit 10-11).

EXHIBIT 10-11 **CHC HELICOPTER CORPORATION, 2003 ANNUAL REPORT**

Excerpted from the Notes to the Statements

The Company has commitments with respect to operating leases for aircraft, buildings and equipment. Total rentals paid in fiscal 2003 was $53.0 million (2002 – $50.6 million). The minimum lease rentals required under such leases were $218.1 million as at April 30, 2003 and are payable as follows:

	Aircraft operating leases	*Building and equipment operating leases*	*Total operating leases*
2004	$ 42,352	$ 5,966	$ 48,318
2005	35,721	5,399	41,120
2006	30,542	4,883	35,425
2007	22,264	4,104	26,368
2008	16,528	4,096	20,624
and thereafter	25,214	21,054	46,268
	$ 172,621	$ 45,502	$ 218,123

Assets under capital leases are sometimes also segregated in the property, plant, and equipment section of the balance sheet. Note the example in Exhibit 10-12 from WestJet Airlines Ltd. WestJet leases some of its aircraft using capital leases.

EXHIBIT 10-12 **WESTJET AIRLINES LTD., 2003 ANNUAL REPORT**

Excerpted from the Notes to the Financial Statements

2. Property and equipment:

2003	Cost	Accumulated depreciation	Net book value
Aircraft – 700 series	$ 758,135	$ 17,265	$ 740,870
Aircraft – 200 series	152,487	70,424	82,063
Ground property and equipment	93,636	22,524	71,112
Buildings	39,474	1,852	37,622
Spare engines and parts – 700 series	36,754	2,518	34,236
Aircraft under capital lease	31,135	17,221	13,914
Spare engines and parts – 200 series	26,376	11,634	14,742
Leasehold improvements	5,055	2,377	2,678
	1,143,052	145,815	997,237
Deposits on aircraft	141,640	-	141,640
Assets under construction	1,349	-	1,349
	$ 1,286,041	$ 145,815	$ 1,140,226

Reports from Other Countries

Most developed countries have criteria for the capitalization of leased assets that are similar to Canada's. International accounting standards recommend capitalization for situations where substantially all the risks and benefits of ownership are transferred to the lessee. Some countries (such as Spain and Sweden) require that the lease contain a bargain purchase option before capitalization is used.

Lessor Accounting

Lessor accounting is designed to be a mirror image of the accounting by the lessee. If the lessee qualifies for capital lease treatment, then the lessor should be viewed as having provided an asset to the lessee (the lessor will replace the capital asset with a receivable asset). If the lessee must treat the lease as an operating lease, then the lessor should retain the asset on its books as the owner and record lease revenue from the lease payments. In both of these situations, the lessor does not have a long-term liability (the subject of this chapter) on its books. An intermediate financial accounting course will discuss lease accounting in more detail.

PENSIONS

Pensions are agreements between employers and employees that provide the latter with specified benefits (income) upon retirement. To the extent that the company is obliged to make payments under these agreements, some recognition should be given to their cost in the years when the company receives the benefits from the work of its employees. Because the payments to retired employees occur many years in the future, pensions represent an estimated future obligation. Two kinds of pension plans are commonly used by employers: defined contribution plans and defined benefit plans.

Defined Contribution Plans

In a **defined contribution plan**, the employer agrees to make a set (defined) contribution to a retirement fund for the employees (e.g., 10% of gross salary). The amount is usually set as a percentage of the employees' salary. Employees sometimes make their own contributions to the same fund to add to the amounts invested. The benefits to the employees at retirement depend on how well the investments in the retirement fund perform. The employer satisfies its obligation to the employees by payment into the fund. The fund is usually managed by a trustee (someone outside the company's employ and control), and the assets are legally separated from the company's other assets, which means they are not reported with the other assets on the company's balance sheet. The accounting for defined contribution funds is relatively straightforward.

Explain the distinguishing features of a defined contribution pension plan and a defined benefit plan.

The company accrues the amount of its obligation to the pension fund, and then records a payment. Because the liability is settled, no other recognition is necessary in the financial statements. The entry to recognize pension expense and the related payment is:

Pension expense (SE)	XXX	
Pension obligation (L)		XXX
Pension obligation (L)	XXX	
Cash (A)		XXX

Companies generally make cash payments that coincide with the accruals because they cannot deduct the cost for tax purposes if no cash payment is made. Therefore, no net obligation usually remains with a defined contribution plan.

Defined Benefit Plans

A **defined benefit plan** is more complex. It guarantees to pay an employee a certain amount of money during each year of retirement. The formula used to calculate how much is paid usually takes into consideration the amount of time an employee has worked for the company as well as the highest salary (or an average of the highest salaries) that the employee earned while working for the company. For example, a plan might guarantee that the employee will receive 2% of the average of the highest three years of salaries multiplied by the number of years that the employee works for the company. If the employee worked for the company for 30 years and had an average salary of $40,000 for the highest three years, the pension benefit would be $24,000 per year [($40,000 × 2%) × 30 years].

Each year, as employees provide service to the company, they earn pension benefits that oblige the company to make cash payments at some point in the future. In estimating the cost of the obligation today (the liability's present value), several projections must be included. These include: the length of time the employee will work for the company, the age at which the employee will retire, the employee's average salary during the highest salary years, the number of years the employee will live after retiring, and whether the employee will work for the company until retirement. All these factors will affect the amount and timing of the cash flows. In addition, the company must choose an appropriate interest rate at which to calculate the net present value.

A given employee may leave the company at some point prior to retirement. If the pension benefits belong to employees only as long as they work there, then there may be no obligation on the company's part to pay out pension benefits. In most plans, however, there is a provision for **vesting** the benefits. Benefits that are vested belong to employees, even if they leave the company. In addition, while one employee may leave, many others will stay. Thus, even without vesting, it is likely that some fraction of the employees will continue to work for the company until retirement. The total obligation of the pension plan may, therefore, have to be estimated based on the characteristics of the average employee rather than on particular employees.

Calculating the present value of the future pension obligation generally requires the services of an **actuary**. The actuary is trained in the use of statistical procedures to make the types of estimates required for the pension calculation.

The accounting entries for defined benefit pension plans are essentially the same as the preceding entry for defined contribution plans. The company must make an accrual of the expense and the related obligation to provide pension benefits. The amounts are much more difficult to estimate in the case of defined benefit plans, but the concept is the same as for defined contribution plans. The entry made to recognize the pension expense is called the **accrual entry**. Setting aside cash to pay for these future benefits is done by making a cash entry. This is sometimes called the **funding entry**. Many employee pension plan agreements have clauses that require the company to fund the pension obligation. Because of the uncertainties associated with the liability amounts, some companies have been somewhat reluctant to fully fund their pension obligations. There is no accounting requirement that the amount expensed be the same as the amount funded. Therefore, a net pension obligation may result if more is expensed than funded, or a net pension asset may exist if funding is larger than the amount expensed. The actual calculation of the pension expense incorporates many factors and is beyond the scope of this book.

Pension funds are described as **overfunded** if the assets exceed the present value of future pension obligations. In **underfunded** pension plans, the present value of future obligations exceeds fund assets. Funds in which the assets actually equal the present value of the future obligations are called **fully funded** plans. The pension fund itself is usually handled by a trustee, and contributions to the fund cannot be returned to the employer except under extraordinary circumstances. To provide sufficient funds to pay benefits, the trustee invests the assets contributed to the fund. Benefits are then paid out of these fund assets to retired employees.

accounting in the news
PENSION WOES

The balance sheets of Canada's workplace pension funds fell by as much as $180 billion in the three years up to 2002, says a C.D. Howe Institute report published in February 2004. Anemic returns on equity investments and higher liabilities for future pension payouts caused the losses. The report said there had been a 30% decline in the financial position of plans; the median net return on investment was 1%, while liabilities grew by 10% a year as declining interest rates increased the cost of providing future benefits. The report's author, Ken Ambachtsheer, said the notion that the employer bears all the risk and employees are guaranteed a pre-defined pension on retirement is a fiction. The employer may go broke or terminate the plan. The financial problems of some large pension plans have been well documented in recent years. For example, the under-funding of its pension plan played a large role in Air Canada's 2003 bankruptcy protection and the ensuing negotiations with its employees.

Source: "Pensions at risk from poor oversight: report," by Ian Jack, *National Post*, February 13, 2004.

Annual Statement Disclosures

In Canada, for a defined contribution plan, contribution amounts for the period are disclosed. For a defined benefit plan, the required disclosure is very extensive. Rather than list all the requirements, look at the disclosure provided by **Petro-Canada** in Exhibit 10-13. Petro-Canada has both defined benefit and defined contribution pension plans, as well as some health care and life insurance benefits that it offers to its retired employees.

EXHIBIT 10-13
PART A

PETRO-CANADA 2003 ANNUAL REPORT
Excerpted from the Notes to the Financial Statements

Note 19 **EMPLOYEE FUTURE BENEFITS**

The Company maintains pension plans with defined benefit and defined contribution provisions, and provides certain health care and life insurance benefits to its qualifying retirees. The actuarially determined cost of these benefits is accrued over the estimated service life of employees. The defined benefit provisions are generally based upon years of service and average salary during the final years of employment. Certain defined benefit options require employee contributions and the balance of the funding for the registered plans is provided by the Company, based upon the advice of an independent actuary. The defined contribution option provides for an annual contribution of 5% to 8% of each participating employee's pensionable earnings. Substantially all of the pension assets are invested in equity, fixed income and other marketable securities.

Benefit Plan Expense	Pension Plans			Other Post-Retirement Plans		
	2003	2002	2001	**2003**	2002	2001
(a) Defined benefit plans						
Employer current service cost	$ **27**	$ 25	$ 22	$ **4**	$ 3	$ 2
Interest cost	**78**	74	70	**12**	11	11
Expected return on plan assets	**(65)**	(83)	(88)	**–**	–	–
Amortization of transitional (asset) obligation	**(5)**	(5)	(5)	**2**	2	2
Amortization of net actuarial losses	**26**	7	–	**–**	–	–
	61	18	(1)	**18**	16	15
(b) Defined contribution plans	**11**	10	7			
Total expense	$ **72**	$ 28	$ 6	$ **18**	$ 16	$ 15
Benefit Plan Funding	$ **86**	$ 22	$ 9	$ **8**	$ 7	$ 7

Financial Status of Defined Benefit Plans	Pension Plans		Other Post-Retirement Plans	
	2003	2002	**2003**	2002
Fair value of plan assets	$ **1 052**	$ 927	$ **–**	$ –
Accrued benefit obligation	**1 344**	1 206	**211**	186
Funded status – plan deficit [1]	**(292)**	(279)	**(211)**	(186)
Unamortized transitional (asset) obligation	**(34)**	(39)	**19**	21
Unamortized net actuarial losses	**375**	352	**39**	22
Accrued benefit asset (liability)	$ **49**	$ 34	$ **(153)**	$ (143)
Reconciliation of Plan Assets				
Fair value of plan assets at beginning of year	$ **927**	$ 1 039	$ **–**	$ –
Acquisition	**–**	26	**–**	–
Contributions	**86**	22	**8**	7
Benefits paid	**(63)**	(61)	**(8)**	(7)
Actual gain (loss) on plan assets	**115**	(91)	**–**	–
Other	**(13)**	(8)	**–**	–
Fair value of plan assets at end of year	$ **1 052**	$ 927	$ **–**	$ –
Reconciliation of Accrued Benefit Obligation				
Accrued benefit obligation at beginning of year	$ **1 206**	$ 1 119	$ **186**	$ 172
Acquisition	**–**	33	**–**	–
Current service cost	**27**	25	**4**	3
Interest cost	**78**	74	**12**	11
Benefits paid	**(63)**	(61)	**(8)**	(7)
Actuarial losses	**99**	12	**17**	7
Other	**(3)**	4	**–**	–
Accrued benefit obligation at end of year	$ **1 344**	$ 1 206	$ **211**	$ 186

1 The pension and other post-retirement plans included in the financial status information are not fully funded.

PETRO-CANADA 2003 ANNUAL REPORT
Excerpted from the Notes to the Financial Statements

EXHIBIT 10-13
PART B

Note 19 **EMPLOYEE FUTURE BENEFITS** *continued*

Defined Benefit Plan Assumptions	2003
Year-end obligation discount rate	**6.0%**
Long-term rate of return on plan assets	**7.5%**
Rate of compensation increase, excluding merit increases	**3.0%**
Annual increase in the per capita cost of:	
Medical benefits	**7.5%** [1]
Dental benefits	**3.5%**

1 4.5% in 2009 and thereafter.

POST-EMPLOYMENT BENEFITS

As you just saw with Petro-Canada, employers sometimes offer other types of **post-employment benefits** in addition to pensions. Health care benefits and life insurance are two of the most commonly offered benefits. In the past, the obligation to provide these benefits has, for the most part, been ignored in the financial statements of companies in Canada. The benefits used to be recorded on a pay-as-you-go basis; that is, the costs were expensed as the cash was paid out to insurance companies that cover the benefit costs. To date, corporate exposure in Canada has been limited because of publicly funded health care. This may not be true in the future. In Canada, as of January 1, 2000, companies are required to account for these items in much the same way as pensions.

LEARNING OBJECTIVE 7

Describe other employment benefits and explain how they are treated in Canada.

AN INTERNATIONAL PERSPECTIVE

Reports from Other Countries

While a significant number of countries require accrual of pension costs, many other countries require only that the costs of pension plans be recognized as benefits are paid: the pay-as-you-go method. Countries with this type of accounting include Belgium, India, Norway, and Spain.

NAFTA Facts

The accounting for pension benefits in the United States and Mexico is essentially the same as in Canada. However, both Canada and the United States have additional requirements with respect to accruing of post-employment benefits.

STATEMENT ANALYSIS CONSIDERATIONS

LEARNING OBJECTIVE 8

Calculate the debt/equity ratio and the times-interest-earned ratio and write a statement describing a company's the financial health using the information from the ratios.

Two ratios that are commonly used to evaluate a company's ability to repay its obligations are the debt/equity ratio and the times-interest-earned ratio. Using the balance sheet and statement of earnings (Exhibit 10-14) of **METRO INC.**, a Montreal-based company that is a leader in the food distribution industry in Quebec, we will demonstrate how these two ratios can provide insights into the riskiness of a company.

EXHIBIT 10-14
PART A

METRO INC. 2003 ANNUAL REPORT

Consolidated Statements of Earnings

	2003	2002
Sales	$ 5,567.3	$ 5,146.8
Cost of sales and operating expenses	5,252.9	4,864.7
Depreciation and amortization *(note 4)*	64.9	57.6
	5,317.8	4,922.3
Operating income	249.5	224.5
Interest		
Short-term	2.2	1.5
Long-term	0.6	1.5
	2.8	3.0
Earnings before income taxes	246.7	221.5
Income taxes *(note 5)*	80.4	77.8
Net earnings	$ 166.3	$ 143.7
Earnings per share *(note 6)*		
Basic	$ 1.68	$ 1.44
Fully diluted	$ 1.67	$ 1.41

See accompanying notes

The formula for the debt/equity ratio is:

$$\frac{\text{Total liabilities}}{\text{Total liabilities} + \text{Shareholders' equity}}$$

The 2003 and 2002 debt/equity ratios of METRO INC. are:

$$\frac{\$755.2}{\$755.2 + \$751.9} \qquad \frac{\$687.9}{\$687.9 + \$644.2}$$
$$= 50.1\% \qquad\qquad = 51.6\%$$

These calculations demonstrate that in 2002, 51.6% of METRO INC.'s assets were financed through debt. The ratio dropped a little in 2003 to 50.1%. From the

METRO INC. 2003 ANNUAL REPORT
Consolidated Balance Sheets

EXHIBIT 10-14
PART B

	2003	2002
Assets		
Current		
Accounts receivable	$ 352.4	$ 272.9
Inventories	284.8	270.4
Prepaid expenses	2.4	3.0
Future income taxes *(note 5)*	8.2	10.3
	647.8	556.6
Investments and other assets *(note 7)*	43.9	35.7
Fixed assets *(note 8)*	474.9	400.7
Intangible assets *(note 9)*	159.2	160.8
Goodwill *(note 3)*	181.3	178.3
	$ 1,507.1	$ 1,332.1
Liabilities		
Current		
Bank loans *(note 10)*	$ 79.6	$ 53.1
Accounts payable	536.6	511.5
Income taxes payable	20.8	2.9
Future income taxes *(note 5)*	37.8	—
Current portion of long-term debt *(note 11)*	3.9	3.6
	678.7	571.1
Long-term debt *(note 11)*	8.8	25.0
Future income taxes *(note 5)*	67.7	91.8
	755.2	687.9
Shareholders' equity		
Capital stock *(note 12)*	159.9	161.7
Retained earnings	592.0	482.5
	751.9	644.2
	$ 1,507.1	$ 1,332.1

Commitments and contingencies *(notes 14 and 15)*

See accompanying notes

On behalf of the Board:

Pierre H. Lessard, FCA
Director

Pierre Brunet, FCA
Director

balance sheet, we can see that, over the two years, METRO INC. increased its short-term liabilities by approximately $26.5 million, decreased its long-term liabilities by approximately $16.2 million, and increased its shareholders' equity by approximately $107.7 million, practically all of which was from earnings. The increase in the short-term liabilities puts increased demands on the company's cash flows in the short run. It would be important to continue to follow this ratio before drawing too many conclusions about any major shifts in financing strategy by the company.

The times-interest-earned ratio provides a measure of the company's ability to make interest payments out of earnings. It is calculated by the following formula.

$$\frac{\text{Income before interest and taxes}}{\text{Interest}} = \frac{\text{Net income} + \text{Taxes} + \text{Interest}}{\text{Interest}}$$

The calculation of the times-interest-earned ratio for METRO INC. for 2003 and 2002 would be:

$$2003 \quad \frac{\$166.3 + \$80.4 + \$2.8}{\$2.8} = 89.1 \text{ times}$$

$$2002 \quad \frac{\$143.7 + \$77.8 + \$3.0}{\$3.0} = 74.8 \text{ times}$$

In 2002, METRO INC. could pay its interest obligation almost 75 times out of earnings. This is a very comfortable position. The risk of nonpayment of interest is very low. By the end of 2003, interest costs had declined such that METRO could now pay its interest obligations 89 times out of earnings. Any creditor would likely be very confident about lending funds to METRO. The increase in the times-interest-earned ratio, coupled with the decrease in the debt/equity ratio, demonstrates to creditors that the risk of nonpayment of interest or principal of the debt has declined over the two years.

The biggest concern for analysts regarding liabilities is the possibility of unrecorded liabilities. As we saw in the last chapter, commitments and contingent liabilities can have significant effects on a company's health. In this chapter, a company's obligations under operating leases are an example of liabilities that are not reported on the financial statements. Unrecorded liabilities will cause the debt/equity ratio to be understated and the times-interest-earned ratio to be overstated. Certain disclosures give the analyst some help in understanding the effects of these unrecorded liabilities. For example, the disclosure of the next five years of lease payments for operating leases allows an analyst to approximate the present value of these lease payments for inclusion in ratio analysis. The effects of other commitments and other off-balance-sheet liabilities may be more difficult to estimate, but the analyst should have a good understanding of the company and the type of contracts it enters into with suppliers, customers, and employees so that these liabilities do not come as surprises.

Another concern is whether liabilities' book values reflect their current market values. Because liabilities are recorded at the interest rates that were in effect when the debt was issued, changes in market rates can cause changes in the value of these liabilities that are not reflected on the company's books. This does not mean that the company will be paying more or less interest as a result of the market changes, but it does mean that the company may be paying more or less than it would have if it had taken out new debt today. Knowledge of this change in interest rates is particularly important when one company is trying to buy another. Book value can be adjusted either by looking at the debt's market value (for publicly traded debt) or by recalculating the debt's present value based on current market interest rates. This, of course, requires some detailed information about the terms of the outstanding debt. Another reason why it is important for users to know about changes in interest rates is that companies are often refinancing their debt. Users need to know what the potential costs are to the company the next time it uses debt financing to increase its cash flow.

Another risk that the analyst should consider is the one posed by debt that is denominated in a foreign currency. As you can imagine, if the company is required to repay a debt in a foreign currency, fluctuations in the exchange rate for that currency can cause increases or decreases in the liability as expressed in dollars. When financial statements are prepared, any debt that is denominated in a foreign currency will be restated in Canadian dollars using the current exchange rate. This provides the user with some knowledge about future costs.

Another risk is that the company may enter into debt agreements in which the interest rate is not fixed but floats with interest rates in the economy (sometimes called variable-rate debt). If interest rates go up, the company can find itself making significantly higher interest payments. Both these risks can be managed through the use of sophisticated hedging techniques involving financial instruments such as interest rate and foreign currency options, and swaps. To help readers of financial statements understand these complex transactions and the risks posed to the company, companies in Canada are required to disclose these types of transactions and to provide some details concerning the risks the company faces because of them. Many of these risks are associated with amounts that are off-balance-sheet. As an example, consider the disclosure made by **Intrawest Corporation** in its 2003 annual report (Exhibit 10-15).

INTRAWEST CORPORATION 2003 ANNUAL REPORT

EXHIBIT 10-15
PART A

Notes to Consolidated Financial Statements

9 BANK AND OTHER INDEBTEDNESS:

The Company has obtained financing for its ski and resort operations and properties from various financial institutions by pledging individual assets as security for such financing. Security for general corporate debt is provided by general security which includes a floating charge on the Company's assets and undertakings, fixed charges on real estate properties, and assignment of mortgages and notes receivable. The following table summarizes the primary security provided by the Company, where appropriate, and indicates the applicable type of financing, maturity dates and the weighted average interest rate at June 30, 2003:

	MATURITY DATES	WEIGHTED AVERAGE INTEREST RATE(%)	2003	2002
SKI AND RESORT OPERATIONS:				
Mortgages and bank loans	Demand – 2017	3.68	$ 62,432	$ 124,578
Obligations under capital leases	2004 – 2052	9.09	45,070	3,869
			107,502	128,447
PROPERTIES:				
Interim financing on properties under development and held for sale	2004 – 2017	5.71	264,032	141,337
Resort club notes receivable credit facilities	2006	5.21	28,121	27,436
Mortgages on revenue-producing properties	2004 – 2011	nil	—	12,485
			292,153	181,258
General corporate debt	2004 – 2005	5.63	240,243	184,000
Unsecured debentures	2004 – 2010	10.20	621,021	562,214
		7.91	1,260,919	1,055,919
Current portion			287,176	282,047
			$ 973,743	$ 773,872

EXHIBIT 10-15
PART B

INTRAWEST CORPORATION 2003 ANNUAL REPORT

Principal repayments and the components related to either floating or fixed interest rate indebtedness are as follows:

YEAR ENDING JUNE 30,	INTEREST RATES FLOATING	FIXED	TOTAL REPAYMENTS
2004	$ 252,630	$ 34,546	$ 287,176
2005	267,620	10,680	278,300
2006	19,257	12,836	32,093
2007	80	2,942	3,022
2008	1,278	653	1,931
Subsequent to 2008	5,231	653,166	658,397
	$ 546,096	$ 714,823	$1,260,919

The Company has entered into a swap agreement to fix the interest rate on a portion of its floating rate debt. The Company had $14,126,000 (2002 – $16,000,000) of bank loans swapped against debt with a fixed interest rate ranging from 4.70% to 5.58% (2002 – 4.70% to 5.58%) per annum.

Bank and other indebtedness includes indebtedness in the amount of $306,458,000 (2002 – $263,691,000) which is repayable in Canadian dollars of $412,952,000 (2002 – $399,808,000).

The Company is subject to certain covenants in respect of some of the bank and other indebtedness which require the Company to maintain certain financial ratios. The Company is in compliance with these covenants at June 30, 2003.

SUMMARY

This chapter completes the discussion of liabilities. The risks associated with long-term liabilities are more extensive than those associated with the short-term liabilities discussed in the previous chapter because of the longer time frame, the larger amounts being borrowed, and the uncertainty of the future. Large companies use bonds as a way of raising additional funds for financing growth. The issuance of bonds is a complex procedure involving the use of financial experts and investment bankers. Depending on the market's perception of the company's riskiness, the bonds will be issued at par, above par, or below par. The chapter described the accounting for the bonds once they are issued.

The other two items described in the chapter are leases and pensions. Leasing is used extensively across Canada. When a company needs to buy or replace a capital asset, it will determine whether it is more advantageous to buy the asset or to lease it. The details of the leasing contract will determine whether the company must account for the lease as an operating lease or a capital lease.

Many large companies have pension plans for their employees. The two basic types of plans are defined contribution plans and defined benefit plans. We did not go into extensive detail about the accounting for either leases or pensions, but rather tried to give you an understanding of what these items are and how they are reported on the financial statements. Because these two items can have significant effects on the financial statements, knowledge of them is essential to any evaluation of an organization's future profitability.

The two ratios that are important in this chapter are the debt/equity ratio and the times-interest-earned ratio. These ratios will provide users with an analysis of some risks associated with debt financing. The discussion of balance sheet accounts concludes in the next chapter with a discussion of shareholders' equity. Following that, we provide a complete review of the ratio analysis used in this book.

SUMMARY PROBLEMS

Additional Demonstration Problems

1. The Higgins Company Ltd. issued $100,000 face value bonds with a bond interest rate of 8% on January 1, 2006. The bonds mature on December 31, 2015, (i.e., there are 10 years to maturity) and pay interest semi-annually on June 30 and December 31. The issue price set for these bonds reflected an assumption that investors would need a 10% return (yield rate) in order to be convinced to buy the bonds.

    a. What issue price was set for these bonds under the assumptions set forth above? (Ignore commissions to the underwriters in your answer.)

    b. If the bonds were issued at the price calculated in part a), what entries would the Higgins Company make during 2006 to account for these bonds?

    c. If, prior to the issuance of the bonds, interest rates increase in the economy such that investors demand a 12% return from investments such as Higgins bonds, what price would they be willing to pay on January 1, 2006, for these bonds?

2. The Acme Company Ltd. enters into a lease for the use of a computer system. The lessor paid $35,000 for the computer system and will lease the computer system to Acme for five years. At the end of the lease term, the computer will be returned to the lessor, who estimates that the computer will have a zero residual value. The lease contract will call for monthly payments of $778.56 to be made at the end of each month. These payments provide the lessor with a 12% return on the contract.

    a. Based on the above facts, how should Acme account for this lease?

    b. Construct the entries that Acme should make during the first two months of the lease, assuming that the lease is signed on January 1, 2006, and that payments are made on the last day of each month.

    c. Give some reasons why Acme would choose to lease the computer system rather than buy it.

3. Exhibit 10-16 shows the pension footnote for **Teck Cominco Ltd.** (an integrated natural resource corporation involved in mineral exploration, mining, smelting, and refining).

    a. What kind of pension plan does Teck Cominco Ltd. have?

    b. How is Teck Cominco accounting for its non-pension retirement benefits?

    c. On its income statement, Teck Cominco does not disclose the total pension expense for 2003. On the balance sheet, it lists Other liabilities of $408 million. In the note with this amount it states that the accrued pension liability is $39 million for the defined benefit pension plan and $130 million for other post-retirement benefits. This is up from the 2002 balances of $21 million and $127 million respectively. By listing this as an accrued liability, what information is Teck Cominco giving users about its employee future benefits?

TECK COMINCO LTD. 2003 ANNUAL REPORT

EXHIBIT 10-16

Excerpted from the Notes to the 2003 Statements

1. Nature of Operation and Significant Accounting Policies

PENSION AND OTHER EMPLOYEE FUTURE BENEFITS

Pension and other employee future benefit expenses and liabilities are based on actuarial determinations. Certain actuarial assumptions used in the determination of future benefits and defined benefit pension plan liabilities are based upon management's best estimates, including expected plan performance, salary escalation, and retirement dates of employees. The discount rate used to determine the accrued benefit obligation is determined by reference to market interest rates at the measurement date of high quality debt instruments. Differences between the actuarial liabilities and the amounts recorded in financial statements will arise from changes in plan assumptions, changes in benefits, or through experience as results differ from actuarial assumptions. Differences which are greater than 10% of their fair value of the plan's assets or the accrued benefit obligation are taken into the determination of income over the average remaining service life of the related employees. The cost of providing benefits through defined contribution plans is charged to earnings as the obligation to contribute is incurred.

Non-pension post-retirement benefits are accrued and are funded by the company as they become due.

SUGGESTED SOLUTIONS TO SUMMARY PROBLEMS

1. a. Present Value of the Higgins Company Bond at 10%:

PV of Bond = PV of Interest Payments + PV of Maturity Payment

$$= (\$4,000 \times 12.46221 \text{ (Table 4)}) + (\$100,000 \times 0.37689 \text{ (Table 2)})$$
$$= \$87,537.84$$

b.

HIGGINS COMPANY BOND — ISSUANCE ENTRY
(AT DATE OF ISSUANCE)

Cash (A)	87,537.84	
Discount on Bond Payable (XL)	12,462.16	
Bond Payable (L)		100,000.00

HIGGINS COMPANY BOND — INTEREST ENTRIES
(AT THE END OF THE FIRST INTEREST PERIOD)

Interest Expense[a] (SE)	4,376.89	
Discount on Bond Payable (XL)		376.89
Interest Payable[b] (L)		4,000.00
Interest Payable (L)	4,000.00	
Cash (A)		4,000.00

[a]Interest Expense = Carrying Value $\times$ Yield Rate $\times$ Time
= $\$87,537.84 \times 10\% \times 6/12 = \$4,376.89$

[b]Interest Payable = Face Amount $\times$ Bond Interest Rate $\times$ Time
= $\$100,000 \times 8\% \times 6/12 = \$4,000.00$

Ending Carrying Value = Beginning Carrying Value + Interest − Payment
= $\$87,537.84 + 4,376.89 - 4,000 = \$87,914.73$

HIGGINS COMPANY BOND—INTEREST ENTRIES
(AT THE END OF THE SECOND INTEREST PERIOD)

Interest Expense[a] (SE)	4,395.74	
Discount on Bond Payable (XL)		395.74
Interest Payable[b] (L)		4,000.00
Interest Payable (L)	4,000.00	
Cash (A)		4,000.00

[a]Interest Expense	= Carrying Value × Yield Rate × Time	
	= $87,914.73 × 10% × 6/12 = $4,395.74	
[b]Interest Payable	= Face Amount × Bond Interest Rate × Time	
	= $100,000 + 8% × 6/12 = $4,000.00	
Ending Carrying Value	= Beginning Carrying Value + Interest − Payment	
	= $87,914.73 + 4,395.74 − 4,000 = $88,310.47	

c. Present Value of the Higgins Company Bond at 12%:

$$\text{PV Bond} = \text{PV Interest of Payments} + \text{PV of Maturity Payment}$$
$$= (\$4,000.00 × 11.46994 \text{ (Table 4)}) + (\$100,000 × 0.31180 \text{ (Table 2)})$$
$$= \$77,059.68$$

2. a. Because the lease covers more than 75% of the asset's useful life, Acme should account for it as a capital asset. You can assume that the computer system's useful life is the full term of the lease because the residual value at the end of that time is zero.

b. The following entries should be made in the first two months.

The present value of the lease payments at 12% per year over 60 months is equal to $778.56 × 44.95504 (Table 4 (60 periods at 1%)) = $35,000.

CAPITAL LEASE ENTRY
(AT JANUARY 1, 2006)

Asset under Capital Lease (A)	35,000	
Lease Obligation (L)		35,000

The amortization of the obligation and the paying of the first lease payment must be recorded in the first month. Because this is an annuity in arrears, the first payment reduces the principal of the obligation at the end of the month. The following entries would be made.

CAPITAL LEASE EXPENSE ENTRY
(ON JANUARY 31, 2006)

Lease Obligation (L)	778.56	
Cash (A)		778.56
Interest Expense[a] (SE)	350.00	
Lease Obligation (L)		350.00

[a]Interest Expense	= Carrying Value × Interest Rate × Time
	= $35,000 × 12% × 1/12
	= $350.00

Assuming that the corporation amortizes its leased assets straight-line over the lease term, the following entry would be made at the end of the first month.

CAPITAL LEASE EXPENSE ENTRY (ON JANUARY 31, 2006)

Amortization Expense[a] (SE)	583.33	
Accumulated Amortization (XA)		583.33
(on leased assets)		

[a]Straight-Line Amortization = \$35,000/60 months = \$583.33 per month

CAPITAL LEASE EXPENSE ENTRY (ON FEBRUARY 28, 2006)

Lease Obligation (L)	778.56	
Cash (A)		778.56
Interest Expense[a] (SE)	345.71	
Lease Obligation (L)		345.71

[a]Interest Expense = Carrying Value × Interest Rate × Time
$$= (\$35,000 - \$778.56 + \$350.00) \times 12\% \times 1/12$$
$$= \$34,571.44 \times 12\% \times 1/12$$
$$= \$345.71$$

CAPITAL LEASE EXPENSE ENTRY (ON FEBRUARY 28, 2006)

Amortization Expense[a] (SE)	583.33	
Accumulated Amortization (XA)		583.33
(on leased assets)		

[a]Straight-Line Amortization = \$35,000/60 months = \$583.33 per month

c. There are several reasons why Acme might choose to lease the computer system.

1. Acme may or not have \$35,000 available to buy the system. Rather than borrow the \$35,000 from the bank, it may choose to lease the asset and make monthly payments. The interest rate charged on the lease may be less than what the bank would charge.

2. Because Acme does not own the computer system, if something goes wrong with the system, the lessor is responsible for fixing it. It is likely that in the lease agreement there are clauses that outline the types of problems that the lessor agrees to fix and the types that are Acme's responsibility.

3. At the end of the five years, Acme is required to return the system to the lessor. This means that it will have to replace it. The end of the lease term forces Acme to stay technologically current (if you assume that five years is not too long to keep a computer system without replacing it). There may be clauses in the lease agreement about annual upgrades to the system and who is responsible for the upgrades. If the lessor is responsible, it is to Acme's advantage to lease the system.

3. a. Teck Cominco Ltd. appears to have a defined benefit pension plan. It mentions actuarial assumptions and the basis of those assumptions. If it had a defined contribution pension plan, it would need to disclose how much of the employee salaries is being contributed to the pension plan. There would be no need for information about actuarial assumptions.

   b. Teck Cominco Ltd. is accounting for its post-employment benefits by accruing them as the employees are working but paying for them as they are incurred.

   c. Teck Cominco Ltd. is telling users that its pension plan and other post-retirement benefits are not fully funded. The amount Teck Cominco has expensed for these items is greater than the amount that it has deposited in a pension fund to pay for those future benefits.

SYNONYMS

Bond interest rate/coupon rate/stated rate
Early retirement of debt/early extinguishments of debt
Market rate of interest/yield rate/effective rate/discount rate

GLOSSARY

Accrual entry In the context of pension accounting, this is the entry to accrue pension cost and create the pension obligation.

Actuary A professional trained in statistical methods who can make reasonable estimates of pension costs.

Adjunct account An account that adds to a related account; it has the same type of balance as the related account. In this chapter, an example of this type of account is the premium on bond payable account.

Amortization of the discount The systematic reduction of the discount account balance over the life of a bond. The reduction of the discount account each period adds to the interest expense recorded during the period.

Amortization of the premium The systematic reduction of the premium account balance over the life of a bond. The reduction of the premium account each period reduces the interest expense recorded during this period.

Best efforts basis The basis on which underwriters sometimes sell bonds for companies. The underwriters make their best effort to sell the bonds but, if they cannot sell them, the bonds are returned to the company.

Bond A corporation's long-term borrowing that is evidenced by a bond certificate. The borrowing is characterized by a face value, interest rate, and maturity date.

Bond covenants Restrictions placed on a company that issues bonds. The restrictions usually apply to the company's ability to pay dividends or require that the company maintain certain minimum ratios.

Bond interest rate An interest rate specified in a bond used to determine the interest payments that are made on the bond.

Bond market A market in which company bonds are actively traded.

Calling the bonds A situation in which, prior to maturity, a corporation buys back the bonds from investors at a pre-determined price.

Capital lease A lease that the lessee must record as an asset and a related borrowing as if the transaction represented the asset purchase.

Collateral trust bond A bond that provides marketable securities as collateral in the event of default by the company.

Commercial paper A short-term borrowing in which the lender is another company rather than a financial institution.

Convertible bond A bond that is convertible, under certain conditions, into common shares.

Debenture bond   A bond that is issued with no specific collateral.

Defined benefit plan   A pension plan that specifies the benefits that employees will receive upon retirement. The benefits are usually determined based on the number of years of service and the highest salary earned by the employee.

Defined contribution plan   A pension plan that specifies how much the company will contribute to its employees' pension fund. No guarantee is made of the amount that will be available upon retirement.

Discount   A term used to indicate that a bond that is sold or issued at a value below its face value.

Early extinguishment of debt   The settlement of debt (by paying the obligation) prior to its scheduled maturity date.

Early retirement of debt   Synonym for early extinguishment of debt.

Effective interest method   A method of calculating interest expense in which the interest is determined by multiplying the debt's carrying value by the yield rate.

Face value   A value specified in a bond that determines the cash payment that will be made on the bond's maturity date. The face value is also used to determine the periodic interest payments made on the bond.

Foreign-denominated debt   Borrowings of a company that must be repaid in a foreign currency.

Fully funded   A pension plan in which the plan assets equal the projected benefit obligation.

Funding entry   The entry made to show the cash payment made to a pension plan to fund the obligation.

Indenture agreement   An agreement that accompanies the issuance of a bond specifying all the borrowing terms and restrictions.

Interest payment   The periodic interest payments made on a bond. The payments are typically made semi-annually. The amount is calculated by multiplying the bond's face value by its interest rate.

Investment banker   The intermediary who arranges the issuance of a bond in the public debt market on a company's behalf. The investment banker sells the bonds to its clients before the bond is traded in the open market.

Lease agreement   An agreement between a lessee and a lessor for the rental or purchase of an asset, or both.

Lease term   The period or term over which a lessee makes payments to a lessor in a lease.

Lessee   The party or entity that is renting or purchasing the asset in a lease.

Lessor   The owner of an asset that is rented to a lessee under a lease agreement.

Maturity date   A date specified in a bond that determines the final payment date of the bond.

Mortgage bond   A bond that provides some type of real asset as collateral in the event of a default by the company.

Note   A long- or short-term borrowing.

Operating lease   A lease in which the lessee does not record an asset and related obligation but treats the lease as a mutually unexecuted contract. Lease expense is then recognized as payments are made per the lease contract.

Overfunded   A pension plan in which the plan assets exceed the projected benefit obligation.

Par   A term used to indicate that a bond is sold or issued at its face value.

Pension   A plan that provides benefits to employees upon retirement.

Post-employment benefit   Benefits provided to retirees other than pensions. These benefits are typically health care or life insurance benefits.

Premium   A term used to indicate that a bond is sold or issued at a value above its face value.

Private placement   A borrowing arranged privately between two companies or entities.

Public bond market   A market in which bonds are publicly traded.

Senior debenture   A general borrowing of the company that has priority over other types of long-term borrowing in the event of bankruptcy.

Subordinated debenture   A general borrowing of the company that has a lower priority than senior debentures in the event of bankruptcy.

Syndicate   A group of underwriters that collectively help a company sell its bonds.

Underfunded   A pension plan in which the plan assets are less than the projected benefit obligation.

Underwriter   An investment bank that arranges and agrees to sell the initial issuance of a company's bonds.

Vesting   An event by which employees are granted pension benefits even if they leave the company's employ.

ASSIGNMENT MATERIAL

Assessing Your Recall

10-1   Describe the following terms relating to a bond: indenture agreement, bond covenants, face value, maturity date, bond interest rate, interest payments, and collateral.

10-2   Explain what is meant by the yield rate of interest with respect to bond issues.

10-3   Distinguish between the stated or nominal rate of interest on a bond and the effective or real rate.

10-4   Will the bond interest rate and the yield rate of interest each remain constant between issue date and maturity? If either interest rate may change over time, provide examples of factors that could lead to a change.

10-5   Describe what the term "best efforts basis" means in the issuance of bonds and why it is important to a company.

10-6   Discuss how bonds are priced and how the price is affected by changes in market interest rates.

10-7   Describe the following terms as they relate to the issuance and sale of bonds: par, premium, and discount.

10-8   Explain why a bond is issued at a discount. What happens to the bond discount account over time?

10-9   Describe the procedure for retiring debt before maturity. Why would a company retire debt early?

10-10   Discuss the benefits of leasing from the point of view of both the lessee and the lessor.

10-11   List and discuss the criteria used to distinguish capital leases from operating leases for lessees.

10-12   Differentiate between defined contribution pension plans and defined benefit plans.

10-13   Explain why vesting and full funding would be important to an employee.

10-14   Explain the difficulties in accounting for a defined benefit pension plan.

10-15   Explain what the following ratios tell you about a company's financial health: debt/equity ratio and times-interest-earned ratio.

Applying Your Knowledge

10-16   (Entries for bond transactions)

The Standard Mills Corporation issues 100 bonds, each with a face value of $1,000, that mature in 15 years. The bonds carry a 6% interest rate and are sold to yield 4%. They pay interest semi-annually.

> *Required:*
>
> a. Calculate the issuing price of the bonds, and show the journal entry to record the issuance of the bonds.
>
> b. Explain why the issue price is not exactly $1,000.
>
> c. Calculate interest expense for the first year, and show the journal entries to record this expense and the corresponding interest payments.

10-17   (Entries for bond transactions)

Spring Water Company Ltd. needed to raise $5 million of additional capital to finance the expansion of its bottled water company. After consulting an investment banker and the company's VP Finance, it decided to issue bonds. The bonds had a maturity value of $5 million and an annual interest rate of 7.5%, paid interest semi-annually, on June 30 and December 31, and matured on December 31, 2014. The bonds were issued on January 1, 2005, for $4,830,137, which represented a yield of 8%.

> ***Required:***
>
> a. Show the journal entry to record the issuance of the bonds.
>
> b. Calculate the interest expense for the first year and show the journal entries to record the interest expense and the corresponding interest payments.
>
> c. Spring Water Company wanted to raise $5 million but succeeded in raising only $4,830,137. Explain why the investors may not have been willing to pay $5 million for the bonds.

10-18   (Issuance of bonds)

The Alphabet Toy Company has plans for a plant expansion and needs to raise additional capital to pay for the construction. The company is considering issuing seven-year, 6% first mortgage bonds with a par value of $800,000. The bonds will pay interest semi-annually.

> ***Required:***
>
> a. Calculate the amount of cash the company will receive if the bonds are sold at a yield rate of:
>
> 1. 6%
> 2. 8%
> 3. 4%
>
> b. Prepare the journal entry Alphabet Toy would record at the time of the issuance under each of the alternative yields. Also prepare the journal entries to record the interest expense for the first two periods under each alternative.
>
> c. What is a mortgage bond? Explain how the fact that this is a mortgage bond would affect the interest rate dictated by the market (the yield rate).

10-19   (Interest calculation on a bond)

Birch Company Ltd. issued bonds twice in recent years. The first issue has a $500,000 par value, a 5% bond interest rate, and a seven-year maturity; it sold on January 1, 2005, to yield 6%. The second issue has a $1 million par value, a 6.5% bond interest rate, and a five-year maturity; it sold on January 1, 2006, to yield 6%. Both issues pay interest on July 1 and January 1.

> ***Required:***
>
> a. What amount of interest payments will Birch Company make related to the year 2006?
>
> b. What amount of interest expense will Birch report for the year 2006?
>
> c. Prepare journal entries to record Birch's interest expense and payments in 2006.
>
> d. Explain why it is reasonable that both bonds sold to yield 6%.

10-20   (Interest accrual with bond discount)

On January 1, 2006, Rupert Company Ltd. issued $500,000 of eight-year, 7.5% debentures. The effective yield on the bonds at the time of issue was 8%. Interest is paid semi-annually.

Required:

a. What amount of interest will Rupert pay every six months?

b. Calculate the bonds' issue price and prepare the journal entry for the issuance.

c. Prepare the journal entries for June 30, 2006, and December 31, 2006, to record the accrual of interest expense and the payment of the interest owed.

d. Give the balance sheet presentation of the bond liability at December 31, 2006.

10-21 **(Calculation of bond issuance and redemption amounts)**

Fraser Equipment Company Inc. issues 400 $1,000, 9% bonds maturing in six years. The bonds pay interest semi-annually and are issued to yield 8%.

Required:

a. Calculate the bonds' issue price and the interest expense for the first year and give the journal entry to record the issuance.

b. Calculate the bonds' book value two years after issuance; that is, at the beginning of the third year.

c. Calculate the bonds' market value two years after issuance, if the market yield has increased to 10%.

d. Compare the book value (calculated in part b) and the market value (calculated in part c) at the end of two years. Explain why a difference exists.

e. Assume the company redeems the bonds at the beginning of the third year by purchasing them in the open market; give the journal entry to record this.

10-22 **(Lease)**

Dash Corporation leases automobiles from Speedy Leasing for use by its sales personnel. The leased vehicles are used for two years and then returned to Speedy Leasing. All maintenance and repair is done by Speedy. Dash makes a deposit of $6,000 at the beginning of the lease on each car and makes monthly payments of $450 per car. The deposit is refunded when the car is returned in reasonable condition. Dash currently has 25 cars under lease from Speedy.

Required:

a. Is the lease an operating lease or a capital lease? Explain.

b. What amount of expense related to the lease will Dash record for the current year?

c. How should the $6,000 deposit per car be recorded by Dash? Where is it reported in Dash's financial statements?

10-23 **(Capital lease)**

On July 1, 2006, ABC Manufacturing Corporation leased one of its machines to Start Mechanical Corporation. The machine had cost ABC $480,000 to manufacture, and would normally have sold for $600,000. The 10-year lease was classified as a capital lease for accounting purposes. The lease agreement required equal semi-annual payments of $44,936 payable on December 31 and June 30 each year, which reflected an interest rate of 10%. Start Mechanical closes its books annually on December 31.

Required:

a. Show the necessary journal entries relating to the lease in the books of Start Mechanical Corporation during 2006 and 2007. Assume that the machine has a useful life of 10 years and zero residual value, and that the company uses straight-line amortization.

b. For any information in the question that you did not use in your answer, explain why the information was not relevant.

10-24 (Lease)

Transprovincial Buslines experienced a major increase in people using the buses in the last three months of 2005. On January 1, 2006, Transprovincial entered into an agreement to lease four new buses from NewBus Leasing Ltd. The 10-year lease agreement on each bus requires Transprovincial to pay $1,200 per month at the end of each month starting January 31, 2006. At the end of the lease term, title to the buses transfers to Transprovincial. The lease is structured with a 9% interest rate. The buses have a useful life of 15 years and are amortized on a straight-line basis with no anticipated residual value.

Required:

a. Is the agreement a capital or an operating lease? Explain.

b. Assuming Transprovincial records the leases on the four buses as capital leases, calculate the present value of the lease payments.

c. Should Transprovincial amortize these buses over 10 years or over 15 years? Explain.

d. Present the amounts related to the lease that would appear on the income statements and balance sheets of Transprovincial Buslines at the end of January 2006 and February 2006.

10-25 (Operating or capital lease)

The *Provincial Star* newspaper has decided to lease a truck to deliver its newspapers. The company signs an agreement on January 1, 2006, to lease a truck for $800 per month for the next four years. The title to the truck reverts to the lessor at the end of the lease term. The lease calls for payments on the last day of the month starting on January 31, 2006. The Provincial Star closes its books monthly and believes that 6% is an appropriate yield rate for the lease.

Required:

a. Assuming that the truck's fair market value is $50,000 and its expected useful life is 10 years, how should the Provincial Star account for this lease?

b. Assuming that the truck's market value is $36,000 and that the lessor believes its useful life is eight years, how should the Provincial Star account for this lease?

c. Show the appropriate accounting entries for the first two months of 2006 for the lease under both the operating lease method and the capital lease method. Assume that the Provincial Star amortizes its assets using the straight-line method.

User Perspective Problems

10-26 (Bond covenants)

Why would bond investors like to see bond covenants included in a bond indenture agreement? Give two examples of possible covenants, and explain why each would be effective.

10-27 (Seniority of bond investments)

In assessing the riskiness of investing in a particular bond, discuss the importance of the seniority of various company liabilities.

10-28 **(Collateral for long-term debt)**

As a potential lender considering making a long-term loan to a company, discuss how much comfort you might get from knowing about the existence of the company's long-term assets, specifically (1) property, plant, and equipment and (2) goodwill. As well as the existence of these assets, what else would you like to know?

10-29 **(Operating leases)**

Suppose that you are a stock analyst and you are evaluating a company that has a significant number of operating leases.

> *Required:*
>
> a. Discuss the potential misstatement of the financial statements that may occur because of this treatment. Specifically, address the impact of this type of accounting on the debt/equity ratio and return on assets ratio.
>
> b. Using disclosures provided in the notes to the financial statements, explain how you would adjust the statements to address the issues discussed in part a).

10-30 **(Capital lease criteria)**

"If two separate companies were each to lease identical capital assets under identical lease terms, the capital lease criteria used under Canadian generally accepted accounting principles (GAAP) will guarantee that each company report the asset in the same way." As a financial statement analyst, would you agree or disagree with this statement? Explain.

10-31 **(Impact of lease treatment on net income)**

Suppose that you are a manager whose remuneration is partially tied to meeting a particular income target for your company. Your company leases an asset. How is your ability to meet the income target affected by the decision to record the transaction as either an operating lease or a capital lease? Which accounting treatment would you prefer? Does your answer depend on whether you are in the early years of the lease vs. the later years?

10-32 **(Lease or buy)**

Starburst Brewery Ltd. must replace some of its old equipment with new stainless steel equipment. The controller is unsure whether to purchase the equipment with borrowed money or to lease the equipment. If purchased, the equipment will cost $800,000 and have an estimated useful life of 16 years and no residual value. The Sussex Bank is willing to provide the $800,000 to Starburst. The loan terms are that the 10-year note would bear interest at 8%. Starburst would be required to pay the interest annually at the end of each year. The principal amount would be due at the end of the 10 years. A local rental company is willing to lease the equipment to Starburst for 12 years at an interest rate of 7%. At the end of each year, Starburst would be required to pay the leasing company $96,000. At the end of the lease period, title to the equipment would remain with the lessor.

> *Required:*
>
> a. Calculate the present value of the future cash flows under both arrangements.
>
> b. State what amounts would appear in Starburst's income statement and balance sheet for the first year, under both alternatives. Assume the new equipment arrives on January 1.
>
> c. Which of the two financing alternatives would you recommend to the controller? Why? What factors, other than cash payments directly related to financing, might be important to the decision?

10-33 (Pension plans)

Describe the two main types of pension plans. As a manager, which plan would you recommend to the company's senior executives? Explain. As an employee, which plan would you prefer? Explain.

10-34 (Post-employment benefits)

In Canada, accountants now have to record the future obligation for post-employment benefits. In the past, the cost of these benefits was recorded as it was incurred (pay-as-you-go). As a manager, explain why you would prefer to continue to use the pay-as-you-go method. What accounting concepts support the change in accounting method from pay-as-you-go to recording the future obligation before the employees retire?

10-35 (Liabilities not recorded)

In assessing the risk of investing in a company, stock analysts are often concerned that there may be liabilities that do not appear on the company's financial statements. Discuss the major types of these liabilities. Describe the information that may be included in the notes to the financial statements concerning these liabilities.

10-36 (Risks associated with liabilities)

Notes to the financial statements regarding liabilities may include details of any foreign currency repayment requirements and the interest terms on all loans. Why are such disclosures important to a financial statement analyst?

10-37 (Valuation of liabilities)

Does the concept of market value apply to liabilities? Is the market value the same as the balance sheet value? Explain. Which would be more relevant to an investor?

Reading and Interpreting Published Financial Statements

Financial Statement Analysis Assignments

10-38 (Long-term debt and bank indebtedness)

Note 9 to the 2003 financial statements of West Fraser Timber Co. Ltd. (Exhibit 10-17) describes the long-term debt and bank indebtedness currently held by the company. All amounts are in thousands of Canadian dollars.

EXHIBIT 10-17   **WEST FRASER TIMBER CO. LTD. 2003 ANNUAL REPORT**

9. LONG-TERM DEBT AND BANK INDEBTEDNESS

Long-term debt

	2003	2002
US $125,000 term notes due 2005; interest at 7.50%	$ 162,063	$ 197,082
Cdn $125,000 term notes due 2007; interest at 6.80%	124,911	124,887
US $10,000 (2002 – US $22,500) notes due 2004; interest at 8.44%	12,965	35,496
	299,939	357,465
Less: Current portion	12,965	19,720
	$ 286,974	$ 337,745

Principal repayments required are as follows:

2004	$ 12,965
2005	162,063
2006	—
2007	124,911
	$ 299,939

Bank indebtedness

The company has approximately $275,000 (2002 – $385,000) in demand or revolving lines of credit available, none of which was utilized as at December 31, 2003.

All long-term debt and bank lines of credit are unsecured.

Required:

a. What are demand or revolving lines of credit?

b. How much is the liability in West Fraser's balance sheet at December 31, 2003, related to the revolving lines of credit? Why is this information included in Note 9?

c. Suggest reasons why the company may have borrowed in U.S. dollars. How does this affect the risk of investing in West Fraser?

d. What does it mean that the long-term debt and bank lines of credit are unsecured?

10-39   (Long-term debt)

Note 7 to the financial statements of **The Spectra Group of Great Restaurants Inc.** (Exhibit 10-18) describes the company's long-term debt at March 31, 2004.

THE SPECTRA GROUP OF GREAT RESTAURANTS INC. 2003 ANNUAL REPORT   EXHIBIT   10-18

7.   *Long-term debt:*

	March 28, 2004	March 30, 2003
Secured demand instalment loan, bearing interest at prime rate plus 2% per annum (2003 - 1.5%), payable monthly		
Principal payments to be made quarterly	$ 1,783	$ 1,000
First mortgage payable, bearing interest at 5% per annum, interest payable monthly, maturing September 1, 2008	972	–
	2,755	1,000
Current portion	2,755	1,000
	$ –	$ –

At March 28, 2004, the demand loans were drawn under a $2,250,000 (2003 - $1,000,000) credit facility which is secured by a floating charge debenture over the Company's business assets, a general security agreement and an assignment of fire and other perils insurance. The terms of the demand loan requires that the Company maintain a minimum equity and a minimum debt service ratio. At March 28, 2004, the Company did not meet these tests. Failure to meet such tests causes the mortgage payable to be due on demand and, as such, it has been classified in these financial statements as a current liability. The lender has agreed to carry the account provided there is no further deterioration.

Notwithstanding the loans are currently repayable on demand should the Company's lenders require the loans to be settled, the scheduled future principal repayments required on the long-term debt are as follows:

2005	$	1,502
2006		422
2007		75
2008		78
2009		678
	$	2,755

a. Under what conditions were the secured demand loans borrowed? Have these conditions been met?

b. How has the situation with the secured demand loans affected the mortgage payable? Is the mortgage payable a current or non-current liability?

10-40 **(Long-term notes)**

Note 10 (b) to the 2003 financial statements of CHC Helicopter Corporation (Exhibit 10-19) describe the senior subordinated notes currently held by the company.

EXHIBIT 10-19 **CHC HELICOPTER CORPORATION 2003 ANNUAL REPORT**

(b) Senior subordinated notes

The Company's $151.1 million (€94.3 million) (2002 – $204.7 million (€145.0 million)) senior subordinated notes bear interest at 11.75% per annum, payable semi-annually on January 15 and July 15, and are due July 2007.

The senior subordinated notes and the guarantees of this debt by certain of the Company's subsidiaries are senior subordinated indebtedness and rank behind all of the Company's existing and future senior indebtedness including borrowings under the senior credit facilities (Note 10(a)). The senior subordinated notes rank equally with other senior subordinated indebtedness and rank senior to other subordinated indebtedness. The guarantees of the senior subordinated notes rank behind all existing and future guarantor senior indebtedness of the guarantor subsidiaries, including guarantees of borrowings under the senior credit facilities.

The Company may redeem the senior subordinated notes in whole or in part at any time on or after July 15, 2004 at a redemption price ranging from 105.875% to 100% of the principal amount of the senior subordinated notes being redeemed. In addition, at any time prior to July 15, 2003, the Company could redeem up to 35% of the original principal amount of the senior subordinated notes, within 90 days of one or more public equity offerings, with the net proceeds of such offerings at a redemption price equal to 111.75% of the principal amount provided that immediately after giving effect to such redemption at least 65% of the original principal amount of the senior subordinated notes remained outstanding. In May 2002, with partial proceeds from its equity offering in April 2002, the Company repaid €50.8 million ($71.9 million) of its 11.75% senior subordinated notes at an 11.75% premium or €6.0 million ($8.4 million). This repayment represented 35% of the original principal amount of the senior subordinated notes.

Required:

a. What are senior subordinated notes?

b. The senior subordinated notes pay interest each January 15 and July 15. CHC Helicopter Corporation's year end is April 30. Assume interest was paid on January 15, 2003, as required. Prepare the journal entry to accrue the interest to April 30, 2003, and then prepare the journal entry on July 15, 2003, to pay the second instalment of interest.

c. Note 10 (b) states that the company may redeem [buy back from the investors] the notes at a redemption price ranging from 105.875% to 100% of the principal amount of the notes being redeemed. Why is the redemption feature a valuable option for the company? How does it affect the investor?

d. Why did the company use the redemption feature in May 2002? Hint: The interest rate on a significant portion of the company's other long-term debt in 2003 was UK LIBOR + 1.125%. At April 30, 2003, UK LIBOR was 3.62%. UK LIBOR is the London Interbank Offered Rate, which is the interest rate European banks pay one another on interbank deposits.

ALIANT INC. 2003 ANNUAL REPORT

EXHIBIT 10-20

10 LONG-TERM DEBT

As at December 31

(thousands of dollars)	Interest rate	Maturity	2003	2002
Telecommunications				
Notes				
Aliant Telecom Inc.				
Series 1	6.46%	2004	**100,000**	100,000
Series 2	6.65%	2009	**100,000**	100,000
Series 3	6.70%	2005	**150,000**	150,000
Series 4	6.80%	2011	**150,000**	150,000
Series 5	5.35%	2007	**100,000**	100,000
			600,000	600,000
Bonds				
Maritime Tel & Tel Limited				
AD	10.45%	2013	**50,000**	50,000
Island Telecom Inc.				
S	11.45%	2008	**—**	7,500
T	10.60%	2009	**3,500**	3,500
U	11.15%	2010	**6,500**	6,500
V	9.77%	2018	**5,000**	5,000
W	8.76%	2019	**5,000**	5,000
NewTel Communications Inc.				
T	10.75%	2014	**75,000**	75,000
V	11.40%	2010	**40,000**	40,000
			185,000	192,500
Debentures				
Maritime Tel & Tel Limited				
Series 2	8.30%	2019	**50,000**	50,000
Series 4	9.70%	2019	**50,000**	50,000
Series 5	9.05%	2025	**60,000**	60,000
NBTel Inc.				
AI	6.40%	2003	**—**	65,000
AA	11.13%	2013	**40,000**	40,000
			200,000	265,000
Other			**—**	2,000
Present value of obligations				
under capital leases			**4,746**	3,526
Total – Telecommunications			**989,746**	1,063,026
Information Technology				
Mortgages and other		2004	**313**	917
Present value of obligations				
under capital leases			**—**	429
Total – Information Technology			**313**	1,346
Total long-term debt			**990,059**	1,064,372
Less: Portion due within one year			**101,535**	68,724
			888,524	995,648

Telecommunications:

On June 16, 2003, a $65.0 million 6.40 per cent debenture NBTel series AI matured.

On July 28, 2003, a $7.5 million 11.45 per cent first mortgage bond was repaid.

All bonds are issued in series and are redeemable at the option of the Company prior to maturity at the prices, times and conditions specified in each series. The bonds are secured by deeds of trust and mortgage and by supplemental deeds. These instruments contain a first fixed and specific mortgage, a pledge and charge upon certain real and immovable property and equipment of Aliant Telecom Inc., and a floating charge on certain other property of Aliant Telecom Inc., both present and future.

All debentures and notes are issued in series and certain series are redeemable at the option of the Company prior to maturity at the prices, times and conditions specified in each series. The debentures and notes are issued under trust indentures and are unsecured.

All mortgages are secured by a fixed charge against specific assets of the Company.

The aggregate amount of payments required in each of the next five years to meet principal repayments and maturities of the Company's long-term debt and the future minimum lease payments under capital leases presently outstanding is as follows: 2004 – $101.5 million; 2005 – $151.7 million; 2006 – $1.8 million; 2007 – $100.0 million; 2008 – $nil million; and thereafter $635.0 million.

10-41 **(Long-term debt)**

Accompanying its 2003 financial statements, **Aliant Inc.** presented Note 10 describing its long-term debt. This is reproduced in Exhibit 10-20. Aliant Inc. provides telecommunications services in Atlantic Canada. All amounts are in thousands of dollars.

> ***Required:***
>
> a. Aliant Inc. has seven bond issues outstanding at the end of 2003. Were these bonds issued at par, below par, or above par? How do you know?
>
> b. Calculate the amount of bond interest that would be paid out by Aliant Inc. in 2004, assuming that no new bonds were issued and that none of the bonds were retired early.
>
> c. The notes are all issued by Aliant Telecom Inc., a company controlled by Aliant Inc. Although the notes have maturity dates several years apart, the interest rate being paid on each issue is very similar. Provide some reasons why the interest rates would be similar.
>
> d. The note also provides information on the aggregate amount of payments required in each of the next five years. Why is such information disclosed? Why is it useful to readers of the financial statements?
>
> e. The payment required in 2004 is $101.535 million. Prepare a schedule showing what components of long-term debt make up this payment. Hint: You will have to estimate the principal to be paid on the capital lease obligations in 2004.

10-42 **(Long-term debt)**

Exhibit 10-21 provides excerpts from Note 14 (a) and (c) to the 2003 financial statements of **Placer Dome Inc.**, which describes the company's long-term debt and capital leases. Placer Dome Inc. is one of the world's largest gold mining companies. Amounts are stated in millions of U.S. dollars.

EXHIBIT 10-21
PART A

PLACER DOME INC. 2003 ANNUAL REPORT

Notes to the Consolidated Financial Statements

14. Long-term Debt and Capital Leases

(a) Consolidated long-term debt and capital leases comprise the following:was 1.1588% (three-month term).

December 31	2003	2002
Placer Dome Inc.		
Bonds, unsecured		
May 15, 2003 at 7.125% per annum [i]	$ —	$ 200
June 15, 2007 at 7.125% per annum	100	100
June 15, 2015 at 7.75% per annum	100	100
March 3, 2033 at 6.375% per annum [ii]	200	—
October 15, 2035 at 6.45% per annum [iii]	300	—
Preferred securities, unsecured [iv]		
Series A, December 31, 2045 at 8.625% per annum [i]	$ —	$ 185
Series B, December 31, 2045 at 8.5% per annum	77	77
Medium-term notes, unsecured [iv]	140	140
Senior convertible debentures, unsecured, October 15, 2023 at 2.75% [iii]	$ 230	$ —
AurionGold Limited, unsecures [i]	—	137
East African Gold, non-recourse [note 3(b)] [vi]	36	—
Capital leases [vii]	6	8
	1,189	947
Current portion	[10]	[340]
	$ 1,179	$ 607

(iii) On October 10, 2003, Placer Dome completed two private debenture offerings totaling $530 million in aggregate principal amount. Of the aggregate principal amounts, $300 million was raised as unsecured 32-year senior debentures with interest payable at a rate of 6.45% per year. An additional $230 million was raised as unsecured 20-year senior convertible debentures with interest payable at 2.75% per year. Upon occurrence of certain prescribed conditions, holders of the convertible debentures will have the right to convert each $1,000 principal amount into 47.7897 common shares of Placer Dome, representing a conversion price of $20.925 per common share. As at December 31, 2003, none of these prescribed conditions had occurred.

The holders of the debentures and, in the case of the convertible debentures, the underlying shares are entitled to the benefits of registration rights granted pursuant to registration rights agreements dated October 10, 2003 (the "Registration Rights Agreements"). The Registration Rights Agreements require, among other things, that the Corporation prepare and file registration documentation that will permit the debentures and, in the case of the convertible debentures, the underlying shares to be resold to the public. The registration documentation for both debentures must be filed within 180 days of the private placement and be effective within 210 days of the private placement. If either date is missed, or if the Corporation fails to comply with certain other continuing obligations thereafter, there is an interest penalty payable until the Corporation complies with its obligations. The interest penalty payable in connection with the non-convertible debentures is 0.25%, and in connection with the convertible debentures is 0.25% for the first 90 days following a registration default and 0.50% thereafter.

(iv) Series B Preferred Securities are redeemable by the Corporation, in whole or in part, on or after December 17, 2001 and December 17, 2006, respectively, at the principal amount plus accrued and unpaid interest to the date of redemption (hereafter referred to as the "Maturity Amount"). The Corporation may, at its option, pay the Maturity Amount by delivering common shares, in which event the holder of the securities shall be entitled to receive a cash payment equal to the Maturity Amount from proceeds of the sale of the common shares on behalf of the holder. Holders of the securities will not be entitled to receive any common shares in satisfaction of the obligation to pay the Maturity Amount.

(c) At December 31, 2003, Placer Dome had unused bank lines of credit of $781 million comprised of A$40 million, CAD$18 million and credit facilities of $686 million with an international consortium of banks of which $400 million is fully committed until 2005 and $285 million is extendable on an annual basis. The funds are available for general corporate purposes. The Majority of these facilities are long-term at interest rates determined with reference to LIBOR which at December 31, 2003 was 1.1588% [three-month term.]

EXHIBIT 10-21
PART B

Required:

a. The bonds are all unsecured and mature at different dates, spanning more than 32 years. However, the bond interest rates are fairly similar. Provide some reasons why the interest rates would be similar.

b. The Series B preferred security is also unsecured. Can you suggest a reason why the interest rate of 8.5% is higher than the bond interest rates?

c. The senior convertible debenture issued in 2003 is also unsecured. Can you suggest a reason why the interest rate on this debt is only 2.75%?

d. Explain the importance to a reader of the financial statements of Note 14 (c). How do the dollar amounts quoted there affect the total balance sheet liabilities?

10-43 **(Pension plans)**

Winpak Ltd. produces packaging for perishable foods and pharmaceuticals. Note 11 to its 2003 financial statements deals with its pension plans and other employee benefit obligations. Note 11 is presented in Exhibit 10-22. All amounts are in thousands of dollars.

Required:

a. What types of pension plans and other post-employment benefit plans does Winpak Ltd. have?

b. At the end of 2003, were Winpak's pension and other post-employment benefit plans underfunded or overfunded? By how much?

c. Why do you think there is so much less information provided on the defined contribution pension plans than on the other plans? Can we tell whether the defined contribution pension plans are underfunded or overfunded?

10-44 **(Employee benefits)**

Note 16 from the 2003 financial statements of **Talisman Energy Inc.**, dealing with employee benefits, is presented in Exhibit 10-23. Dollar amounts are in millions of Canadian dollars.

Required:

a. Are Talisman's pension plans underfunded or overfunded, and by what amount? What dollar amounts will appear in the Talisman financial statements related to the pension plans?

b. If you were a Talisman employee, what question would you like to ask about your pension plan?

c. Note 16 includes a table of significant actuarial assumptions used to determine the periodic pension expense and the accrued benefit obligation. Why would a reader of the financial statements be interested in these assumptions?

d. Review the information disclosed in Note 16 regarding significant actuarial assumptions made by Talisman, and answer the following questions.

1. What is the expected rate that the company estimates will be earned on the pension plan assets?

2. By what average rate does the company estimate its salaries will rise?

3. What does the discount rate represent, and why is it needed?

4. How would a shareholder evaluate the reasonableness of the expected long-term rate of return on plan assets and rate of compensation increase?

WINPAK LTD. 2003 ANNUAL REPORT

NOTES TO CONSOLIDATED FINANCIAL STATEMENTS

11. Employee benefit plans:

The following presents the financial position of the Company's defined benefit pension plans and other postretirement benefits, including the supplementary income plan:

	Defined Benefit Pension Plans		Other Postretirement Benefits	
	2003	2002	**2003**	2002
Change in benefit obligation				
Benefit obligation, beginning of year	**33,088**	28,921	**5,374**	4,845
Current service cost	**1,670**	1,543	**225**	165
Interest cost	**2,071**	1,994	**393**	331
Actuarial loss	**446**	1,549	**465**	155
Plan amendment - prior service	**-**	-	**(491)**	-
Benefits paid	**(963)**	(856)	**(89)**	(110)
Foreign exchange	**(2,684)**	(63)	**(393)**	(12)
Benefit obligation, end of year	**33,628**	33,088	**5,484**	5,374
Change in plan assets				
Fair value of plan assets, beginning of year	**28,512**	32,335	**-**	-
Actual return on plan assets	**4,082**	(3,129)	**-**	-
Employer contributions	**929**	242	**1,643**	110
Asset transfer	**(577)**	-	**577**	-
Benefits paid	**(963)**	(856)	**(89)**	(110)
Foreign exchange	**(1,779)**	(80)	**-**	-
Fair value of plan assets, end of year	**30,204**	28,512	**2,131**	-
Funded status				
Plan assets less than benefit obligation	**(4,367)**	(5,644)	**(3,353)**	(5,374)
Plan assets greater than benefit obligation	**943**	1,068	**-**	-
Net plan assets less than benefit obligation	**(3,424)**	(4,576)	**(3,353)**	(5,374)
Unrecognized net transition amount	**(2,110)**	(2,625)	**-**	-
Unrecognized prior service cost	**85**	121	**1,528**	1,662
Unamortized actuarial loss	**8,437**	11,296	**663**	360
Accrued pension asset (postretirement benefits liability)	**2,988**	4,216	**(1,162)**	(3,352)
Amounts recognized in the consolidated balance sheet				
Accrued pension asset	**4,399**	5,455	**-**	-
Less: Accrued benefit liability	**(1,411)**	(1,239)	**(1,162)**	(3,352)
Accrued pension asset (postretirement benefits liability)	**2,988**	4,216	**(1,162)**	(3,352)
Benefit plans with fair value of plan assets less than benefit obligation				
Fair value of plan assets	**12,888**	12,417	**2,131**	-
Benefit obligation	**(17,255)**	(18,061)	**(5,484)**	(5,374)
Plan assets less than benefit obligation, end of year	**(4,367)**	(5,644)	**(3,353)**	(5,374)

WINPAK LTD. 2003 ANNUAL REPORT

NOTES TO CONSOLIDATED FINANCIAL STATEMENTS

The following presents the pension expense of the Company's defined benefit pension plans and other postretirement benefits, including the supplementary income plan:

	Defined Benefit Pension Plans		Other Postretirement Benefits	
	2003	2002	**2003**	2002
Net benefit plan expense (income)				
Current service cost	**1,670**	1,543	**225**	165
Interest cost	**2,071**	1,994	**393**	331
Expected return on plan assets	**(2,136)**	(2,498)	**-**	-
Amortization of:				
Net transition amount	**(263)**	(266)	**-**	-
Prior service cost	**15**	17	**(319)**	606
Actuarial loss	**441**	206	**47**	-
Net benefit plan expense	**1,798**	996	**346**	1,102

The following significant weighted average actuarial assumptions were used in calculating the pension expense and funded status of the benefit plans:

	2003	2002	**2003**	2002
Discount rate	**6.4%**	6.5%	**6.4%**	6.5%
Expected return on plan assets	**7.8%**	8.2%	**-**	-
Rate of compensation increases	**4.2%**	4.2%	**-**	-

Defined Contribution Pension Plans
In the United States, the Company maintains two savings retirement plans (401(k) Plans) for certain employees. In Canada, the Company maintains four defined contribution plans for certain employees. The Company has recorded an expense of $2,101 (2002 – $1,553) for these plans.

TALISMAN ENERGY INC. 2003 ANNUAL REPORT
Notes to the Consolidated Financial Statements

EXHIBIT 10-23
PART A

16. Employee Benefits

The Company sponsors both defined benefit and defined contribution pension arrangements covering substantially all employees. The Company uses actuarial reports prepared by independent actuaries for funding and accounting purposes. The Company uses a December 31 measurement date for the majority of its defined benefit pension plans. The following significant actuarial assumptions were employed to determine the periodic pension expense and the accrued benefit obligations:

	2003	2002	2001
Expected long-term rate of return on plan assets (%)	**7.5**	7.5	7.5
Discount rate (%)	**6.4**	6.5	6.5
Rate of compensation increase (%)	**4.5**	4.5	4.5

The Company's net benefit plan expense (credit) is as follows:

	2003	2002	2001
Current service cost — defined benefit	**7**	5	2
Current service cost — defined contribution	**7**	6	5
Interest cost	**8**	7	5
Expected return on plan assets	**(9)**	(11)	(10)
Amortization of net transitional asset	**(1)**	(1)	(1)
Amortization of actuarial losses	**2**	—	—
Net benefit plan expense	**14**	6	1

Information about the Company's defined benefit pension plan is as follows:

	2003		2002	
	Pension plans grouped by funded status		Pension plans grouped by funded status	
	Surplus	**Deficit** [1]	Surplus	Deficit [1]
Accrued benefit obligation				
Accrued benefit obligation, beginning of year	**54**	**63**	53	42
Current service cost	**1**	**6**	1	4
Interest cost	**4**	**4**	3	3
Actuarial losses	**7**	**8**	1	14
Plan participants' contributions	**–**	**1**	–	1
Benefits paid	**(4)**	**(4)**	(4)	(1)
Accrued benefit obligation, end of year	**62**	**78**	54	63
Plan assets				
Fair value of plan assets, beginning of year	**114**	**21**	128	21
Actual gain (loss) on plan assets	**14**	**3**	(4)	(5)
Employer contributions	**–**	**8**	–	5
Plan participants' contributions	**–**	**1**	–	1
Surplus applied to defined contribution plan	**(7)**	**–**	(6)	–
Benefits paid	**(4)**	**(4)**	(4)	(1)
Fair value of plan assets, end of year	**117**	**29**	114	21
Funded status — surplus (deficit)	**55**	**(49)**	60	(42)
Unamortized net actuarial loss	**19**	**26**	18	21
Unamortized net transitional (asset) obligation	**(11)**	**3**	(11)	2
Net accrued benefit asset (liability)	**63**	**(20)**	67	(19)

TALISMAN ENERGY INC. 2003 ANNUAL REPORT

Notes to the Consolidated Financial Statements

1 The net accrued benefit liability for pension plans with a deficit funding status is included in deferred credits on the Consolidated Balance Sheet.

At December 31, 2003 the actuarial net present value of the accrued benefit obligation for other post-retirement benefit plans was $8 million (2002 – $7 million).

The net benefit plan expense of $14 million for the year ended December 31, 2003 (2002— $6 million; 2001 — $1 million) is determined by using actuarial assumptions including expected return on plan assets and includes the amortization of net actuarial losses and net transitional assets and obligations as described in note 1(j). Had the net benefit expense for the year been calculated without deferring and amortizing net actuarial losses and net transitional assets and obligations, the net benefit expense for 2003 would have been $12 million (2002 – $37 million; 2001 – $23 million).

At December 31, 2003, the composition of plan assets as a percentage of fair value was 70% equities and 30% bonds. The approximate target allocation percentage is 70% equities, 30% bonds and expected return on assets is 8.5% equities and 5.3% bonds.

10-45 (Pension and retirement plans)

Exhibit 10-24 is Note 15 from the 2003 financial statements of **MacDonald Dettwiler and Associates Ltd.** MacDonald Dettwiler is an information company that provides its customers with either information systems, or the information necessary for critical decision-making. All amounts are in thousands of dollars.

Required:

a. Are the pension plans of MacDonald Dettwiler underfunded or overfunded, and by what amount? What dollar amounts will appear in the MacDonald Dettwiler financial statements related to the pension plans?

b. Why are there no plan assets listed for the post-retirement benefits plans?

c. By what amount does MacDonald Dettwiler expect the average cost of health benefits, dental care, and life insurance to increase each year?

d. Compare and contrast MacDonald Dettwiler's approach to accounting for pension plans vs. post-retirement plans in terms of conservatism and the matching principle.

10-46 (Debt/equity ratios)

The consolidated balance sheet and income statement from the 2003 annual report of the **Canadian Pacific Railway** are included in Exhibit 10-25.

Required:

a. Calculate the debt/equity ratios and the times-interest-earned ratios for 2003 and 2002.

b. Write a short report evaluating the ratios you calculated in part a).

MACDONALD DETTWILER AND ASSOCIATES LTD. 2003 ANNUAL REPORT
Notes to Consolidated Financial Statements

EXHIBIT 10-24
PART A

15. **PENSION AND RETIREMENT PLANS:**

The Company maintains contributory and non-contributory, defined benefit pension plans covering a portion of its employees. The defined benefit plans provide pension benefits based on various factors including earnings and length of service. The present value of accumulated pension benefits based on earnings and length of service is provided for in the financial statements. The Company also provides for post-retirement benefits for these employees, comprised of extended health benefits, dental care and life insurance. The cost of these benefits is funded annually out of general revenues.

The plan assets are invested primarily in publicly traded equity and fixed income securities.

The total pension expense for the Company's defined contribution pension plans for the year ended December 31, 2003 was $1,831,000 (2002 - $1,147,000).

The status of the Company's defined benefit pension plans and post-retirement plans as of December 31, 2003 and 2002 is as follows:

	2003		2002	
	Pension plans	Post-retirement plans	Pension plans	Post-retirement plans
Pension and post-retirement expense:				
Current service cost	$ 601	231	578	179
Interest cost	973	359	880	464
Expected return on plan assets	(1,397)	-	(1,408)	-
Amortization of past service costs	63	-	63	-
Amortization of losses (gains)	-	(529)	(81)	(89)
Net benefit plan expense	$ 240	61	32	554

10-47 (Debt/equity ratios)

The 2003 consolidated balance sheet and statement of operations for **La Senza Corporation**, a lingerie retailer, are included in Exhibit 10-26. All amounts are in thousands of dollars. The company's 2003 fiscal year ends on January 31, 2004.

Required:

a. Calculate the debt/equity ratios and the times-interest-earned ratios for the years ending January 31, 2004 and February 1, 2003. In calculating the times-interest-earned ratio, use the company's operating income rather than net loss.

b. Write a short report evaluating the ratios you calculated in part a). What are the major factors contributing to the change in the debt/equity ratio?

MACDONALD DETTWILER AND ASSOCIATES LTD. 2003 ANNUAL REPORT
Notes to Consolidated Financial Statements

MACDONALD, DETTWILER AND ASSOCIATES LTD.
Notes to Consolidated Financial Statements
(tabular amounts in thousands of dollars)
Years ended December 31, 2003 and 2002

15. PENSION AND RETIREMENT PLANS (CONTINUED):

	2003		2002	
	Pension plans	Post-retirement plans	Pension plans	Post-retirement plans
Accrued benefit obligation:				
Projected benefit obligations, beginning of year	$ 15,045	7,004	14,876	6,450
Service cost	742	231	713	179
Interest cost	973	359	880	464
Benefits paid	(150)	-	(150)	-
Actuarial (gains) losses	225	(1,460)	(1,274)	(89)
Projected benefit obligations, end of year	$ 16,835	6,134	15,045	7,004
Plan assets:				
Fair value of plan assets, beginning of year	$ 19,786	-	19,866	-
Actual return on plan assets	900	-	(65)	-
Employer contributions	285	-	-	-
Employee contributions	141	-	135	-
Benefits paid	(150)	-	(150)	-
Fair value of plan assets, end of year	$ 20,962	-	19,786	-
Funded status of the plan, end of year:				
Funded status – surplus (unfunded)	$ 4,127	(6,134)	4,741	(7,004)
Unamortized past service costs	417	-	480	-
Unamortized net actuarial (gains) losses	(133)	(931)	(855)	-
Net accrued benefit asset (liability)	$ 4,411	(7,065)	4,366	(7,004)

The significant actuarial assumptions adopted in measuring the Company's accrued benefit obligations are as follows:

	2003		2002	
	Pension plans	Post-retirement plans	Pension plans	Post-retirement plans
Discount rate, beginning of year	6.5%	6.5%	6.5%	7.0%
Discount rate, end of year	6.0%	6.3%	6.5%	6.5%
Expected rate of return on plan assets	7.0%	n/a	7.0%	n/a
Rate of compensation increase	4.5%	n/a	4.5%	n/a
Rate of increase in medical inflation	n/a	9.0% reducing by 0.5% per annum to 5.0% ultimate rate	n/a	9.5% reducing by 0.5% per annum to 5.0% ultimate rate

CANADIAN PACIFIC RAILWAY 2003 ANNUAL REPORT

EXHIBIT 10-25
PART A

consolidated balance sheet

Year ended December 31 (in millions)	2003	2002
Assets		
Current assets		
Cash and short-term investments	$ 134.7	$ 284.9
Accounts receivable (Note 9)	395.7	443.0
Materials and supplies	106.4	108.9
Future income taxes (Note 7)	87.4	72.5
	724.2	909.3
Investments (Note 11)	105.6	92.2
Net properties (Note 12)	8,220.0	8,149.3
Other assets and deferred charges (Note 13)	907.3	510.0
Total assets	$9,957.1	$ 9,660.8
Liabilities and shareholders' equity		
Current liabilities		
Accounts payable and accrued liabilities	$ 907.0	$ 984.2
Income and other taxes payable	13.5	92.6
Dividends payable on Common Shares	20.2	20.2
Long-term debt maturing within one year (Note 14)	13.9	400.8
	954.6	1,497.8
Deferred liabilities (Note 16)	671.2	654.4
Long-term debt (Note 14)	3,348.9	2,922.1
Future income taxes (Note 7)	1,307.2	1,200.1
Shareholders' equity (Note 18)		
Share capital	1,118.1	1,116.1
Contributed surplus	294.6	291.1
Foreign currency translation adjustments	87.7	122.3
Retained income	2,174.8	1,856.9
	3,675.2	3,386.4
Total liabilities and shareholders' equity	$9,957.1	$ 9,660.8

Approved on behalf of the Board: J.E. Newall, Director   R. Phillips, Director

EXHIBIT 10-25 PART B **CANADIAN PACIFIC RAILWAY 2003 ANNUAL REPORT**

statement of consolidated income

Year ended December 31 (in millions, except per share data)	2003	2002	2001
Revenues			
Freight	$ 3,479.3	$3,471.9	$ 3,496.7
Other	181.4	193.7	201.9
	3,660.7	3,665.6	3,698.6
Operating expenses			
Compensation and benefits	1,152.6	1,131.1	1,122.1
Fuel	393.3	357.5	403.0
Materials	176.8	165.7	180.9
Equipment rents	238.2	255.0	272.1
Depreciation and amortization	381.5	348.4	334.4
Purchases services and other	577.7	551.4	545.1
	2,9201	2,809.1	2,857.6
Operating income, before the following:	740.6	856.5	841.0
Labour restructuring and asset impairment (Note 4)	228.5	–	–
Loss on transfer of assets to outsourcing firm (Note 4)	28.9	–	–
Incentive compensation and unusual charges (Note 18)	–	–	24.5
Operating income	483.2	856.5	816.5
Other charges (Note 5)	33.5	21.8	26.4
Foreign exchange (gain) loss on long-term debt	(209.5)	(13.4)	58.2
Bridge financing fees related to spin-off (Note 18)	–	–	17.2
Interest expense (Note 6)	218.7	242.2	209.6
Income tax expense (Note 7)	41.8	109.9	132.6
Net income	$ 398.7	$ 496.0	$ 372.5
Basic earnings per share (Note 8)	$ 2.51	$ 3.13	$ 2.35
Diluted earnings per share (Note 8)	$ 2.51	$ 3.11	$ 2.34

LA SENZA CORPORATION 2003 ANNUAL REPORT

EXHIBIT 10-26
PART A

CONSOLIDATED BALANCE SHEETS
(thousands of dollars)

	As at January 31, 2004	As at February 1, 2003
ASSETS		
Current		
Cash	$ **9,960**	$ 20,361
Short-term investments (note 3)	**7,951**	27,482
Marketable securities (note 3)	**17,360**	5,133
Accounts and sundry receivables	**9,267**	6,730
Income taxes recoverable	**2,358**	452
Inventory	**50,032**	33,764
Prepaid expenses	**2,341**	3,022
Assets of discontinued operations (note 4)	**369**	13,312
Future income taxes (note 13)	**8,161**	-
	107,799	110,256
Fixed Assets (note 5)	**85,905**	78,288
Trademarks	**1,113**	897
Assets of Discontinued Operations (note 4)	**1,581**	3,512
Future Income Taxes (note 13)	**813**	8,843
Investment in Significantly Influenced Company (note 6)	**26,926**	32,813
	224,137	234,609
Liabilities		
Current		
Accounts payable and accrued liabilities (note 8)	**38,239**	25,985
Current maturity of obligations under capital leases	**9,658**	7,867
Current maturity of long-term debt	**1,096**	1,878
Liabilities of discontinued operations (note 4)	**6,286**	25,441
	55,279	61,171
Obligations Under Capital Leases (note 9)	**24,157**	17,401
Long-Term Debt (note 10)	**6,463**	2,902
Liabilities of Discontinued Operations (note 4)	**-**	462
Deferred Lease Inducements	**7,021**	6,619
Future Income Taxes (note 13)	**1,179**	1,698
	94,099	90,253
Commitments and Contingencies (note 11)		
Shareholders' Equity		
Capital Stock (note 12)	**31,606**	30,921
Contributed Surplus	**7,852**	7,852
Retained Earnings	**90,580**	105,583
	130,038	144,356
	$ **224,137**	234,609

EXHIBIT 10-26
PART B

LA SENZA CORPORATION 2003 ANNUAL REPORT

CONSOLIDATED STATEMENTS OF OPERATIONS
(thousands of dollars except for per share amounts)

	Fiscal Year Ended	
	January 31, 2004	February 1, 2003
Sales	**$336,523**	$292,640
Cost, Expenses and Other		
Cost of sales and store, warehouse, general, administrative and sales support expenses	**304,921**	255,625
Amortization	**16,472**	14,399
Interest on obligations under capital leases	**1,422**	1,399
Interest on long-term debt	**307**	446
Other interest	**592**	159
Interest income	**(56)**	(62)
Foreign exchange loss	**586**	133
	324,244	272,099
Operating Income		
Equity in net earnings (loss) of a significantly influenced company	**12,279** **(6,247)**	20,541 1,140
Interest income on short-term investments	**788**	1,167
Other income	**636**	243
Foreign exchange loss on investment activities	**(2,380)**	(623)
Gain on dilution of investment in significantly influenced company	**360**	550
Earnings From Continuing Operations Before Income Taxes	**5,436**	23,018
Income taxes (note 13)		
Current	**3,094**	7,374
Future	**4,000**	(880)
	7,094	6,494
Earnings (Loss) From Continuing Operations	**(1,658)**	16,524
Discontinued operations, net of income taxes (note 4)	**(11,213)**	(20,299)
Net Loss	**$ (12,871)**	$ (3,775)
Basic Earnings (Loss) Per Share – Continuing Operations (note 14)	**(0.12)**	1.26
Diluted Earnings (Loss) Per Share – Continuing Operations (note 14)	**(0.12)**	1.24
Basic Loss Per Share (note 14)	**(0.97)**	(0.29)
Diluted Loss Per Share (note 14)	**(0.97)**	(0.28)

See accompanying notes

Beyond the Book

10-48 (Analysis of a company's liabilities)

Choose a company as directed by your instructor and do the following exercises.

   a. Prepare a quick analysis of the noncurrent liability accounts by listing the beginning and ending amounts in these accounts and calculating the net change, in both dollar and percentage terms, for the most recent year.

   b. If any of the accounts changed by more than 10%, try to give an explanation for this change.

c. What percentage of the company's total liabilities comes from long-term bank loans? Long-term bonds? Has this percentage changed significantly over the last year?

d. Does the company have any other long-term liabilities? If so, describe each of them.

e. What interest rates is the company paying on its long-term debt? (You will likely need to look in the notes to the financial statements to find the answer to this question.)

f. Calculate the company's debt/equity ratio and the times-interest-earned ratio. Comment on the company's financial health.

Cases

10-49   Wasselec's Moving and Storage Corporation

Wasselec's Moving and Storage Corporation is a small company based in the Halifax area. It operates in both the residential and commercial markets. To serve its various clients, Wasselec's owns two large moving trucks (tractor and trailer units), six medium-sized cartage trucks, two large vans, and two cars. Because its business relies on its vehicles, it has always been the corporation's policy to purchase new vehicles on a regular rotation basis. Its accountant and vehicle service manager have established guidelines that trigger when a new vehicle should be purchased. For example, the large vans are replaced every 200,000 km, the tractors every nine years, and the trailers every 15 years. The president of the corporation recently read an article about the increasing trend toward leasing. She wonders if Wasselec should start leasing its vehicles instead of buying them, and has asked the accountant for some guidance in this matter. The accountant has asked you, a recent addition to the accounting department, for a summary of the advantages and disadvantages of ownership vs. leasing.

Case Primer

Required:

Draft a memo to the accountant summarizing the advantages and disadvantages of ownership vs. leasing with reference to the types of assets currently owned by Wasselec. Remember as well that the accountant is very busy. Therefore, your memo should be concise.

10-50   Grant's Homemade Ice Cream Shop

Jack and Gillian Grant, owners of Grant's Homemade Ice Cream Shop, have recently expanded their business by moving into a second location in a nearby town. To open the second location, the company had to obtain three large ice-cream machines. To buy the machines would have cost over $15,000, so Jack and Gillian instead decided to lease them.

The lease term is for five years and the machines are expected to have a useful life of 8 to 10 years. According to the lease contract, the present value of the lease payments over the lease term is $8,000 and the Grants can purchase the leased machines for $500 at the end of the five-year lease term. The leased assets' market value is expected to be approximately $4,000 at the end of the lease.

Jack Grant is thrilled with the arrangement. "Not only do we get the machines we need, but we don't have to record any liabilities on the balance sheet since I can just report the annual lease payments as rental expense on the income statement."

Required:

Is Jack correct in assuming that the lease payments will be recorded as an expense and that no debt will have to be reported on Grant's balance sheet as a result of this transaction? Fully explain your answer using the three criteria for capital lease recognition presented in the text.

10-51 **Regal Cars**

Regal Cars has been manufacturing exotic automobiles for more than 50 years. It has always prided itself on quality products and high customer satisfaction. All Regal Cars are hand-built to owner specifications. In the past year, the popularity of Regal Cars has increased dramatically following an advertising campaign whereby Regal provided complimentary cars to star members of the local NHL team. To meet this increasing demand, Mark Quaid, owner of Regal Cars, is considering partially automating the production line.

To finance the conversion of the manual line to a robotic system, Quaid will have to raise more than $800,000 in capital. The company has been in the Quaid family for more than 50 years and Mark is unwilling to sell shares and risk diluting his family's equity in the business. He has identified three potential sources of debt financing and has asked you, the company's accountant, to explain how each option would affect the company's financial statements.

Option 1 Bank Loan

A national bank has offered to lend Regal the necessary funds in the form of a 10-year, 12% bank loan. Annual payments of $80,000 plus interest will be required. Because of the loan's size, the bank requires that Mark Quaid personally guarantee the loan with a mortgage on the family estate.

Option 2 Bond Issue

Regal can issue a 10-year, 10% bond for the amount required. Currently, similar bonds in the market are providing a return of 8%.

Option 3 Lease

Regal can lease the equipment. The lease terms state that annual lease payments of $137,000 must be made over a 10-year lease period. The present value of these payments, assuming an annual interest rate of 14%, would be $662,000. The equipment has a useful life of 12 years and is expected to be worth $100,000 at the end of the 10 years.

> *Required:*
>
> Prepare a memo to Mark Quaid discussing how each of these options would be reported in Regal Cars' financial statements. You should also include in your memo any other pertinent observations that could influence the financing decision.

10-52 **Peterson Corporation**

As part of recent contract negotiations, Peterson Corporation has presented two pension plan options to its employees. The employees are to vote on which plan they would like the company to implement. Peterson Corporation owns and operates a chain of grocery stores throughout western Canada and employs more than 3,000 people. Most employees have little education and limited accounting knowledge. Your cousin, Karen Cooper, is a cashier at a Peterson store located in Kamloops, British Columbia, and she has approached you asking for help in determining which pension option to select. She is confused over the terminology used in the proposal and would like you to explain both options in layman's terms so that she can make an informed decision.

Option 1

The company will establish a defined contribution pension plan. The company will contribute 10% of the employee's gross wages to the pension plan each pay period. Vesting will occur immediately and the funds will be placed with an independent trustee to be invested. Employees will have the option of contributing additional funds to the plan.

Option 2

The company will establish a defined benefit plan. The plan guarantees that the employees will receive 2% of the average of the highest five years of salary multiplied by the number of years the employee works for the company. The plan is fully employer funded and vests after five years of continuous service.

Required:

Briefly explain to Karen the difference between the two plan options. You should remember that Karen is unfamiliar with pension terminology and you may have to explain some terms used in the plan descriptions.

10-53 Jonah Fitzpatrick

Jonah Fitzpatrick would like to start investing and is considering purchasing some of the bonds being issued by Jennings Financial. Details of the bond issue were outlined in a recent article in *Financial Times Magazine*. The following is an excerpt from the article.

> "Jennings Financial is planning to issue a series of bonds to help finance the acquisition of a large manufacturing facility. In consultation with its investment bankers, the company has decided to issue $25 million of 8%, five-year bonds. Each bond will be denominated at $1,000. The bonds will be classified as senior debenture bonds and will be sold to yield a return of 10%. Because this is such a large issue, the investment banker is required to underwrite the issue. However, given the company's historical performance and financial strength, a syndicate is willing to guarantee the entire issue."

Jonah is unfamiliar with bond issues and approaches Mike Jacobs, his stockbroker, with some basic questions.

Jonah: "I have always invested in equity securities, but would like to consider investing in the bonds of Jennings Financial this time; however, since I know very little about bond trading, I have a few questions that need answering."

Mike: "Sure, Jonah, why don't you e-mail me a list of questions and I'll get back to you later in the day."

Required:

Jonah has just sent Mike the following e-mail. Draft an appropriate response.

Mike, here is a list of my questions. I look forward to hearing from you.

1. The advertisement for the bonds issue states that the bonds will be 8% bonds but will yield 10%. Why are there two interest rates presented? Which interest rate should I use when determining my expected return on the bonds?

2. What is a debenture bond? Will I have any security if the company defaults on the bond?

3. What is the purpose of the investment banker? What does it mean to use a syndicate?

4. What if I need my money back before the five-year period? Does the five-year term mean I am locked into this investment for five years?

10-54 Fiche Limited

It is now January 1, 2006, and Fiche Limited is considering a $10 million share issue. The company would like to improve its debt/equity ratio before proceeding with the issue. Fiche's Chief Financial Officer has suggested to the board of directors that the company could retire its $5 million of 9%, 10-year bonds. Currently, interest rates have risen, and therefore the bonds could be retired at 99. The board is willing to consider the proposal but would like to see the effect of the transaction on the company's debt/equity ratio.

The bonds were originally sold for 102 and pay interest semi-annually on June 30 and December 31. They will mature on June 30, 2007. The company has always maintained a bond sinking fund (a cash fund set aside specifically to repay the bonds at maturity) so it already has most of the cash needed to retire the bonds. Fiche Limited's accounting policy is to amortize any bond premium or discount using the straight-line method.

Debt and equity information for the company for the past three years is as follows.

FICHE LIMITED
Partial Balance Sheet
December 31

	2005	2004	2003
Current Liabilities	$ 2,650,555	$ 2,695,400	$ 2,873,650
Long-Term Debt			
Bank Loans	8,555,000	7,950,000	7,667,200
Bond Issue	5,015,000	5,025,000	5,035,000
Total Liabilities	$ 16,220,555	$ 15,670,400	$ 15,575,850
Total Equity	$ 13,520,000	$ 13,125,000	$ 12,998,000

Required:

a. Prepare the journal entry to record the retirement of the bond issue.

b. Calculate the effect of retiring the bonds on Fiche's debt/equity ratio.

Critical Thinking Question

10-55 **(Pension plans)**

For defined benefit pension plans, a formula has been devised for use in calculating the pension expense for each accounting period. When the calculated pension expense is compared with the amount of cash transferred to a trustee to invest in managing the pension plan's future obligations, there could be a difference between the two amounts. If the amount of cash transferred is less than the pension expense, a liability for the difference results. If the amount of cash transferred is greater, an asset results. The difference between the two amounts is a reflection of either an overfunded or underfunded pension plan. However, these amounts are insignificant compared with the corporation's total liability with respect to the pension plan.

Required:

Describe the current disclosure requirements for pensions in Canada. Should a company be required to include a liability on the balance sheet that reflects its future obligation with respect to its pension plan? What impact would such a requirement have on the debt/equity ratio? Are users being given enough information about pension plans to allow them to make informed decisions?

APPENDIX : TIME VALUE OF MONEY TABLES

TABLE 1
Future Value of $1.00

Periods	0.50%	0.75%	1.00%	1.50%	2.00%	3.00%	4.00%	5.00%	6.00%	7.00%	8.00%
1	1.00500	1.00750	1.01000	1.01500	1.02000	1.03000	1.04000	1.05000	1.06000	1.07000	1.08000
2	1.01003	1.01506	1.02010	1.03023	1.04040	1.06090	1.08160	1.10250	1.12360	1.14490	1.16640
3	1.01508	1.02267	1.03030	1.04568	1.06121	1.09273	1.12486	1.15763	1.19102	1.22504	1.25971
4	1.02015	1.03034	1.04060	1.06136	1.08243	1.12551	1.16986	1.21551	1.26248	1.31080	1.36049
5	1.02525	1.03807	1.05101	1.07728	1.10408	1.15927	1.21665	1.27628	1.33823	1.40255	1.46933
6	1.03038	1.04585	1.06152	1.09344	1.12616	1.19405	1.26532	1.34010	1.41852	1.50073	1.58687
7	1.03553	1.05370	1.07214	1.10984	1.14869	1.22987	1.31593	1.40710	1.50363	1.60578	1.71382
8	1.04071	1.06160	1.08286	1.12649	1.17166	1.26677	1.36857	1.47746	1.59385	1.71819	1.85093
9	1.04591	1.06956	1.09369	1.14339	1.19509	1.30477	1.42331	1.55133	1.68948	1.83846	1.99900
10	1.05114	1.07758	1.10462	1.16054	1.21899	1.34392	1.48024	1.62889	1.79085	1.96715	2.15892
11	1.05640	1.08566	1.11567	1.17795	1.24337	1.38423	1.53945	1.71034	1.89830	2.10485	2.33164
12	1.06168	1.09381	1.12683	1.19562	1.26824	1.42576	1.60103	1.79586	2.01220	2.25219	2.51817
13	1.06699	1.10201	1.13809	1.21355	1.29361	1.46853	1.66507	1.88565	2.13293	2.40985	2.71962
14	1.07232	1.11028	1.14947	1.23176	1.31948	1.51259	1.73168	1.97993	2.26090	2.57853	2.93719
15	1.07768	1.11860	1.16097	1.25023	1.34587	1.55797	1.80094	2.07893	2.39656	2.75903	3.17217
16	1.08307	1.12699	1.17258	1.26899	1.37279	1.60471	1.87298	2.18287	2.54035	2.95216	3.42594
17	1.08849	1.13544	1.18430	1.28802	1.40024	1.65285	1.94790	2.29202	2.69277	3.15882	3.70002
18	1.09393	1.14396	1.19615	1.30734	1.42825	1.70243	2.02582	2.40662	2.85434	3.37993	3.99602
19	1.09940	1.15254	1.20811	1.32695	1.45681	1.75351	2.10685	2.52695	3.02560	3.61653	4.31570
20	1.10490	1.16118	1.22019	1.34686	1.48595	1.80611	2.19112	2.65330	3.20714	3.86968	4.66096
24	1.12716	1.19641	1.26973	1.42950	1.60844	2.03279	2.56330	3.22510	4.04893	5.07237	6.34118
36	1.19668	1.30865	1.43077	1.70914	2.03989	2.89828	4.10393	5.79182	8.14725	11.42394	15.96817
48	1.27049	1.43141	1.61223	2.04348	2.58707	4.13225	6.57053	10.40127	16.39387	25.72891	40.21057
60	1.34885	1.56568	1.81670	2.44322	3.28103	5.89160	10.51963	18.67919	32.98769	57.94643	101.2571
120	1.81940	2.45136	3.30039	5.96932	10.76516	34.71099	110.6626	348.9120	1088.188	3357.788	10252.99
240	3.31020	6.00915	10.89255	35.63282	115.8887	1204.853	12246.20	1.22E+05	1.18E+06	1.13E+07	1.05E+08
360	6.02258	14.73058	35.94964	212.7038	1247.561	41821.62	1.36E+06	4.25E+07	1.29E+09	3.79+10	1.08E+12

(continued)

TABLE 1(continued)
Future Value of $1.00

Periods	9.00%	10.00%	11.00%	12.00%	13.00%	14.00%	15.00%	16.00%	18.00%	20.00%	25.00%
1	1.09000	1.10000	1.11000	1.12000	1.13000	1.14000	1.15000	1.16000	1.18000	1.20000	1.25000
2	1.18810	1.21000	1.23210	1.25440	1.27690	1.29960	1.32250	1.34560	1.39240	1.44000	1.56250
3	1.29503	1.33100	1.36763	1.40493	1.44290	1.48154	1.52088	1.56090	1.64303	1.72800	1.95313
4	1.41158	1.46410	1.51807	1.57352	1.63047	1.68896	1.74901	1.81064	1.93878	2.07360	2.44141
5	1.53862	1.61051	1.68506	1.76234	1.84244	1.92541	2.01136	2.10034	2.28776	2.48832	3.05176
6	1.67710	1.77156	1.87041	1.97382	2.08195	2.19497	2.31306	2.43640	2.69955	2.98598	3.81470
7	1.82804	1.94872	2.07616	2.21068	2.35261	2.50227	2.66002	2.82622	3.18547	3.58318	4.76837
8	1.99256	2.14359	2.30454	2.47596	2.65844	2.85259	3.05902	3.27841	3.75886	4.29982	5.96046
9	2.17189	2.35795	2.55804	2.77308	3.00404	3.25195	3.51788	3.80296	4.43545	5.15978	7.45058
10	2.36736	2.59374	2.83942	3.10585	3.39457	3.70722	4.04556	4.41144	5.23384	6.19174	9.31323
11	2.58043	2.85312	3.15176	3.47855	3.83586	4.22623	4.65239	5.11726	6.17593	7.43008	11.64153
12	2.81266	3.13843	3.49845	3.89598	4.33452	4.81790	5.35025	5.93603	7.28759	8.91610	14.55192
13	3.06580	3.45227	3.88328	4.36349	4.89801	5.49241	6.15279	6.88579	8.59936	10.69932	18.18989
14	3.34173	3.79750	4.31044	4.88711	5.53475	6.26135	7.07571	7.98752	10.14724	12.83918	22.73737
15	3.64248	4.17725	4.78459	5.47357	6.25427	7.13794	8.13706	9.26552	11.97375	15.40702	28.42171
16	3.97031	4.59497	5.31089	6.13039	7.06733	8.13725	9.35762	10.74800	14.12902	18.48843	35.52714
17	4.32763	5.05447	5.89509	6.86604	7.98608	9.27646	10.76126	12.46768	16.67225	22.18611	44.40892
18	4.71712	5.55992	6.54355	7.68997	9.02427	10.57517	12.37545	14.46251	19.67325	26.62333	55.51115
19	5.14166	6.11591	7.26334	8.61276	10.19742	12.05569	14.23177	16.77652	23.21444	31.94800	69.38894
20	5.60441	6.72750	8.06231	9.64629	11.52309	13.74349	16.36654	19.46076	27.39303	38.33760	86.73617
24	7.91108	9.84973	12.23916	15.17863	18.78809	23.21221	28.62518	35.23642	53.10901	79.49685	211.7582
36	22.25123	30.91268	42.81808	59.13557	81.43741	111.8342	153.1519	209.1643	387.0368	708.8019	3081.488
48	62.58524	97.10723	149.7970	230.3908	352.9923	538.8065	819.4007	1241.605	2820.567	6319.749	44841.55
60	176.0313	304.4816	524.0572	897.5969	1530.053	2595.919	4383.999	7370.201	20555.14	56347.51	652530.4
120	30987.02	92709.07	274636.0	805680.3	2.34E+06	6.74E+06	1.92E+07	5.43E+07	4.23E+08	3.18E+09	4.26E+11
240	9.60E+08	8.59E+09	7.54E+10	6.49E+11	5.48E+12	4.54E+13	3.69E+14	2.95E+15	1.79E+17	1.01E+19	1.81E+23
360	2.98E+13	7.97E+14	2.07E+16	5.23E+17	1.28E+19	3.06E+20	7.10E+21	1.60E+23	7.54E+25	3.20E+28	7.72E+34

TABLE 2
Present Value of $1.00

Periods	0.50%	0.75%	1.00%	1.50%	2.00%	3.00%	4.00%	5.00%	6.00%	7.00%	8.00%
1	0.99502	0.99256	0.99010	0.98522	0.98039	0.97087	0.96154	0.95238	0.94340	0.93458	0.92593
2	0.99007	0.98517	0.98030	0.97066	0.96117	0.94260	0.92456	0.90703	0.89000	0.87344	0.85734
3	0.98515	0.97783	0.97059	0.95632	0.94232	0.91514	0.88900	0.86384	0.83962	0.81630	0.79383
4	0.98025	0.97055	0.96098	0.94218	0.92385	0.88849	0.85480	0.82270	0.79209	0.76290	0.73503
5	0.97537	0.96333	0.95147	0.92826	0.90573	0.86261	0.82193	0.78353	0.74726	0.71299	0.68058
6	0.97052	0.95616	0.94205	0.91454	0.88797	0.83748	0.79031	0.74622	0.70496	0.66634	0.63107
7	0.96569	0.94904	0.93272	0.90103	0.87056	0.81309	0.75992	0.71068	0.66506	0.62275	0.58349
8	0.96089	0.94198	0.92348	0.88771	0.85349	0.78941	0.73069	0.67684	0.62741	0.58201	0.54027
9	0.95610	0.93496	0.91434	0.87459	0.83676	0.76642	0.70259	0.64461	0.59190	0.54393	0.50025
10	0.95135	0.92800	0.90529	0.86167	0.82035	0.74409	0.67556	0.61391	0.55839	0.50835	0.46319
11	0.94661	0.92109	0.89632	0.84893	0.80426	0.72242	0.64958	0.58468	0.52679	0.47509	0.42888
12	0.94191	0.91424	0.88745	0.83639	0.78849	0.70138	0.62460	0.55684	0.49697	0.44401	0.39711
13	0.93722	0.90743	0.87866	0.82403	0.77303	0.68095	0.60057	0.53032	0.46884	0.41496	0.36770
14	0.93256	0.90068	0.86996	0.81185	0.75788	0.66112	0.57748	0.50507	0.44230	0.38782	0.34046
15	0.92792	0.89397	0.86135	0.79985	0.74301	0.64186	0.55526	0.48102	0.41727	0.36245	0.31524
16	0.92330	0.88732	0.85282	0.78803	0.72845	0.62317	0.53391	0.45811	0.39365	0.33873	0.29189
17	0.91871	0.88071	0.84438	0.77639	0.71416	0.60502	0.51337	0.43630	0.37136	0.31657	0.27027
18	0.91414	0.87416	0.83602	0.76491	0.70016	0.58739	0.49363	0.41552	0.35034	0.29586	0.25025
19	0.90959	0.86765	0.82774	0.75361	0.68643	0.57029	0.47464	0.39573	0.33051	0.27651	0.23171
20	0.90506	0.86119	0.81954	0.74247	0.67297	0.55368	0.45639	0.37689	0.31180	0.25842	0.21455
24	0.88719	0.83583	0.78757	0.69954	0.62172	0.49193	0.39012	0.31007	0.24698	0.19715	0.15770
36	0.83564	0.76415	0.69892	0.58509	0.49022	0.34503	0.24367	0.17266	0.12274	0.08754	0.06262
48	0.78710	0.69861	0.62026	0.48936	0.38654	0.24200	0.15219	0.09614	0.06100	0.03887	0.02487
60	0.74137	0.63870	0.55045	0.40930	0.30478	0.16973	0.09506	0.05354	0.03031	0.01726	0.00988
120	0.54963	0.40794	0.30299	0.16752	0.09289	0.02881	0.00904	0.00287	0.00092	0.00030	0.00010
240	0.30210	0.16641	0.09181	0.02806	0.00863	0.00083	0.00008	0.00001	8.4E-07	8.9E-08	9.5E-09
360	0.16604	0.06789	0.02782	0.00470	0.00080	0.00002	7.4E-07	2.4E-08	7.8E-10	2.6E-11	9.3E-13

(continued)

TABLE 2 (continued)

Present Value of $1.00

Periods	9.00%	10.00%	11.00%	12.00%	13.00%	14.00%	15.00%	16.00%	18.00%	20.00%	25.00%
1	0.91743	0.90909	0.90090	0.89286	0.88496	0.87719	0.86957	0.86207	0.84746	0.83333	0.80000
2	0.84168	0.82645	0.81162	0.79719	0.78315	0.76947	0.75614	0.74316	0.71818	0.69444	0.64000
3	0.77218	0.75131	0.73119	0.71178	0.69305	0.67497	0.65752	0.64066	0.60863	0.57870	0.51200
4	0.70843	0.68301	0.65873	0.63552	0.61332	0.59208	0.57175	0.55229	0.51579	0.48225	0.40960
5	0.64993	0.62092	0.59345	0.56743	0.54276	0.51937	0.49718	0.47611	0.43711	0.40188	0.32768
6	0.59627	0.56447	0.53464	0.50663	0.48032	0.45559	0.43233	0.41044	0.37043	0.33490	0.26214
7	0.54703	0.51316	0.48166	0.45235	0.42506	0.39964	0.37594	0.35383	0.31393	0.27908	0.20972
8	0.50187	0.46651	0.43393	0.40388	0.37616	0.35056	0.32690	0.30503	0.26604	0.23257	0.16777
9	0.46043	0.42410	0.39092	0.36061	0.33288	0.30751	0.28426	0.26295	0.22546	0.19381	0.13422
10	0.42241	0.38554	0.35218	0.32197	0.29459	0.26974	0.24718	0.22668	0.19106	0.16151	0.10737
11	0.38753	0.35049	0.31728	0.28748	0.26070	0.23662	0.21494	0.19542	0.16192	0.13459	0.08590
12	0.35553	0.31863	0.28584	0.25668	0.23071	0.20756	0.18691	0.16846	0.13722	0.11216	0.06872
13	0.32618	0.28966	0.25751	0.22917	0.20416	0.18207	0.16253	0.14523	0.11629	0.09346	0.05498
14	0.29925	0.26333	0.23199	0.20462	0.18068	0.15971	0.14133	0.12520	0.09855	0.07789	0.04398
15	0.27454	0.23939	0.20900	0.18270	0.15989	0.14010	0.12289	0.10793	0.08352	0.06491	0.03518
16	0.25187	0.21763	0.18829	0.16312	0.14150	0.12289	0.10686	0.09304	0.07078	0.05409	0.02815
17	0.23107	0.19784	0.16963	0.14564	0.12522	0.10780	0.09293	0.08021	0.05998	0.04507	0.02252
18	0.21199	0.17986	0.15282	0.13004	0.11081	0.09456	0.08081	0.06914	0.05083	0.03756	0.01801
19	0.19449	0.16351	0.13768	0.11611	0.09806	0.08295	0.07027	0.05961	0.04308	0.03130	0.01441
20	0.17843	0.14864	0.12403	0.10367	0.08678	0.07276	0.06110	0.05139	0.03651	0.02608	0.01153
24	0.12640	0.10153	0.08170	0.06588	0.05323	0.04308	0.03493	0.02838	0.01883	0.01258	0.00472
36	0.04494	0.03235	0.02335	0.01691	0.01228	0.00894	0.00653	0.00478	0.00258	0.00141	0.00032
48	0.01598	0.01031	0.00668	0.00434	0.00283	0.00186	0.00122	0.00081	0.00035	0.00016	0.00002
60	0.00568	0.00328	0.00191	0.00111	0.00065	0.00039	0.00023	0.00014	0.00005	0.00002	1.5E-06
120	0.00003	0.00001	3.6E-06	1.2E-06	4.3E-07	1.5E-07	5.2E-08	1.8E-08	2.4E-09	3.1E-10	2.3E-12
240	1.0E-09	1.2E-10	1.3E-11	1.5E-12	1.8E-13	2.2E-14	2.7E-15	3.4E-16	5.6E-18	9.9E-20	5.5E-24
360	3.4E-14	1.3E-15	4.8E-17	1.9E-18	7.8E-13	3.3E-21	1.4E-22	6.2E-24	1.3E-26	3.1E-29	1.3E-35

TABLE 3
Future Value of an Annuity in Arrears

Periods	0.50%	0.75%	1.00%	1.50%	2.00%	3.00%	4.00%	5.00%	6.00%	7.00%	8.00%
1	1.00000	1.00000	1.00000	1.00000	1.00000	1.00000	1.00000	1.00000	1.00000	1.00000	1.00000
2	2.00500	2.00750	2.01000	2.01500	2.02000	2.03000	2.04000	2.05000	2.06000	2.07000	2.08000
3	3.01502	3.02256	3.03010	3.04522	3.06040	3.09090	3.12160	3.15250	3.18360	3.21490	3.24640
4	4.03010	4.04523	4.06040	4.09090	4.12161	4.18363	4.24646	4.31013	4.37462	4.43994	4.50611
5	5.05025	5.07556	5.10101	5.15227	5.20404	5.30914	5.41632	5.52563	5.63709	5.75074	5.86660
6	6.07550	6.11363	6.15202	6.22955	6.30812	6.46841	6.63298	6.80191	6.97532	7.15329	7.33593
7	7.10588	7.15948	7.21354	7.32299	7.43428	7.66246	7.89829	8.14201	8.39384	8.65402	8.92280
8	8.14141	8.21318	8.28567	8.43284	8.58297	8.89234	9.21423	9.54911	9.89747	10.25980	10.63663
9	9.18212	9.27478	9.36853	9.55933	9.75463	10.15911	10.58280	11.02656	11.49132	11.97799	12.48756
10	10.22803	10.34434	10.46221	10.70272	10.94972	11.46388	12.00611	12.57789	13.18079	13.81645	14.48656
11	11.27917	11.42192	11.56683	11.86326	12.16872	12.80780	13.48635	14.20679	14.97164	15.78360	16.64549
12	12.33556	12.50759	12.68250	13.04121	13.41209	14.19203	15.02581	15.91713	16.86994	17.88845	18.97713
13	13.39724	13.60139	13.80933	14.23683	14.68033	15.61779	16.62684	17.71298	18.88214	20.14064	21.49530
14	14.46423	14.70340	14.94742	15.45038	15.97394	17.08632	18.29191	19.59863	21.01507	22.55049	24.21492
15	15.53655	15.81368	16.09690	16.68214	17.29342	18.59891	20.02359	21.57856	23.27597	25.12902	27.15211
16	16.61423	16.93228	17.25786	17.93237	18.63929	20.15688	21.82453	23.65749	25.67253	27.88805	30.32428
17	17.69730	18.05927	18.43044	19.20136	20.01207	21.76159	23.69751	25.84037	28.21288	30.84022	33.75023
18	18.78579	19.19472	19.61475	20.48938	21.41231	23.41444	25.64541	28.13238	30.90565	33.99903	37.45024
19	19.87972	20.33868	20.81090	21.79672	22.84056	25.11687	27.67123	30.53900	33.75999	37.37896	41.44626
20	20.97912	21.49122	22.01900	23.12367	24.29737	26.87037	29.77808	33.06595	36.78559	40.99549	45.76196
24	25.43196	26.18847	26.97346	28.63352	30.42186	34.42647	39.08260	44.50200	50.81558	58.17667	66.76476
36	39.33610	41.15272	43.07688	47.27597	51.99437	63.27594	77.59831	95.83632	119.1209	148.9135	187.1021
48	54.09783	57.52071	61.22261	69.56522	79.35352	104.4084	139.2632	188.0254	256.5645	353.2701	490.1322
60	69.77003	75.42414	81.66967	96.21465	114.0515	163.0534	237.9907	353.5837	533.1282	813.5204	1253.213
120	163.8793	193.5143	230.0387	331.2882	488.2582	1123.700	2741.564	6958.240	18119.80	47954.12	128149.9
240	462.0409	667.8869	989.2554	2308.854	5744.437	40128.42	306130.1	2.43E+06	1.97E+07	1.61E+08	1.31E+09
360	1004.515	1830.743	3494.964	14113.59	62328.06	1.39E+06	3.39E+07	8.50E+08	2.15E+10	5.41E+11	1.35E+13

(continued)

TABLE 3 (continued)

Future Value of an Annuity in Arrears

Periods	9.00%	10.00%	11.00%	12.00%	13.00%	14.00%	15.00%	16.00%	18.00%	20.00%	25.00%
1	1.00000	1.00000	1.00000	1.00000	1.00000	1.00000	1.00000	1.00000	1.00000	1.00000	1.00000
2	2.09000	2.10000	2.11000	2.12000	2.13000	2.14000	2.15000	2.16000	2.18000	2.20000	2.25000
3	3.27810	3.31000	3.34210	3.37440	3.40690	3.43960	3.47250	3.50560	3.57240	3.64000	3.81250
4	4.57313	4.64100	4.70973	4.77933	4.84980	4.92114	4.99338	5.06650	5.21543	5.36800	5.76563
5	5.98471	6.10510	6.22780	6.35285	6.48027	6.61010	6.74238	6.87714	7.15421	7.44160	8.20703
6	7.52333	7.71561	7.91286	8.11519	8.32271	8.53552	8.75374	8.97748	9.44197	9.92992	11.25879
7	9.20043	9.48717	9.78327	10.08901	10.40466	10.73049	11.06680	11.41387	12.14152	12.91590	15.07349
8	11.02847	11.43589	11.85943	12.29969	12.75726	13.23276	13.72682	14.24009	15.32700	16.49908	19.84186
9	13.02104	13.57948	14.16397	14.77566	15.41571	16.08535	16.78584	17.51851	19.08585	20.79890	25.80232
10	15.19293	15.93742	16.72201	17.54874	18.41975	19.33730	20.30372	21.32147	23.52131	25.95868	33.25290
11	17.56029	18.53117	19.56143	20.65458	21.81432	23.04452	24.34928	25.73290	28.75514	32.15042	42.56613
12	20.14072	21.38428	22.71319	24.13313	25.65018	27.27075	29.00167	30.85017	34.93107	39.58050	54.20766
13	22.95338	24.52271	26.21164	28.02911	29.98470	32.08865	34.35192	36.78620	42.21866	48.49660	68.75958
14	26.01919	27.97498	30.09492	32.39260	34.88271	37.58107	40.50471	43.67199	50.81802	59.19592	86.94947
15	29.36092	31.77248	34.40536	37.27971	40.41746	43.84241	47.58041	51.65951	60.96527	72.03511	109.6868
16	33.00340	35.94973	39.18995	42.75328	46.67173	50.98035	55.71747	60.92503	72.93901	87.44213	138.1085
17	36.97370	40.54470	44.50084	48.88367	53.73906	59.11760	65.07509	71.67303	87.06804	105.9306	173.6357
18	41.30134	45.59917	50.39594	55.74971	61.72514	68.39407	75.83636	84.14072	103.7403	128.1167	218.0446
19	46.01846	51.15909	56.93949	63.43968	70.74941	78.96923	88.21181	98.60323	123.4135	154.7400	273.5558
20	51.16012	57.27500	64.20283	72.05244	80.94683	91.02493	102.4436	115.3797	146.6280	186.6880	342.9447
24	76.78981	88.49733	102.1742	118.1552	136.8315	158.6586	184.1678	213.9776	289.4945	392.4842	843.0329
36	236.1247	299.1268	380.1644	484.4631	618.7493	791.6729	1014.346	1301.027	2144.649	3539.009	12321.95
48	684.2804	960.1723	1352.700	1911.590	2707.633	3841.475	5456.005	7753.782	15664.26	31593.74	179362.2
60	1944.792	3034.816	4755.066	7471.641	11761.95	18535.13	29219.99	46057.51	114189.7	281732.6	2.61E+06
120	344289.1	927080.7	2.50E+06	6.71E+06	1.80E+07	4.81E+07	1.28E+08	3.39E+08	2.35E+09	1.59E+10	1.70E+12
240	1.07E+10	8.59E+10	6.86E+11	5.41E+12	4.22E+13	3.24E+14	2.46E+15	1.84E+16	9.92E+17	5.04E+19	7.25E+23
360	3.31E+14	7.97E+15	1.88E+17	4.36E+18	9.87E+19	2.19E+21	4.73E+22	1.00E+24	4.19E+26	1.60E+29	3.09E+35

TABLE 4

Present Value of an Annuity in Arrears

Periods	0.50%	0.75%	1.00%	1.50%	2.00%	3.00%	4.00%	5.00%	6.00%	7.00%	8.00%
1	0.99502	0.99256	0.99010	0.98522	0.98039	0.97087	0.96154	0.95238	0.94340	0.93458	0.92593
2	1.98510	1.97772	1.97040	1.95588	1.94156	1.91347	1.88609	1.85941	1.83339	1.80802	1.78326
3	2.97025	2.95556	2.94099	2.91220	2.88388	2.82861	2.77509	2.72325	2.67301	2.62432	2.57710
4	3.95050	3.92611	3.90197	3.85438	3.80773	3.71710	3.62990	3.54595	3.46511	3.38721	3.31213
5	4.92587	4.88944	4.85343	4.78264	4.71346	4.57971	4.45182	4.32948	4.21236	4.10020	3.99271
6	5.89638	5.84560	5.79548	5.69719	5.60143	5.41719	5.24214	5.07569	4.91732	4.76654	4.62288
7	6.86207	6.79464	6.72819	6.59821	6.47199	6.23028	6.00205	5.78637	5.58238	5.38929	5.20637
8	7.82296	7.73661	7.65168	7.48593	7.32548	7.01969	6.73274	6.46321	6.20979	5.97130	5.74664
9	8.77906	8.67158	8.56602	8.36052	8.16224	7.78611	7.43533	7.10782	6.80169	6.51523	6.24689
10	9.73041	9.59958	9.47130	9.22218	8.98259	8.53020	8.11090	7.72173	7.36009	7.02358	6.71008
11	10.67703	10.52067	10.36763	10.07112	9.78685	9.25262	8.76048	8.30641	7.88687	7.49867	7.13896
12	11.61893	11.43491	11.25508	10.90751	10.57534	9.95400	9.38507	8.86325	8.38384	7.94269	7.53608
13	12.55615	12.34235	12.13374	11.73153	11.34837	10.63496	9.98565	9.39357	8.85268	8.35765	7.90378
14	13.48871	13.24302	13.00370	12.54338	12.10625	11.29607	10.56312	9.89864	9.29498	8.74547	8.24424
15	14.41662	14.13699	13.86505	13.34323	12.84926	11.93794	11.11839	10.37966	9.71225	9.10791	8.55948
16	15.33993	15.02431	14.71787	14.13126	13.57771	12.56110	11.65230	10.83777	10.10590	9.44665	8.85137
17	16.25863	15.90502	15.56225	14.90765	14.29187	13.16612	12.16567	11.27407	10.47726	9.76322	9.12164
18	17.17277	16.77918	16.39827	15.67256	14.99203	13.75351	12.65930	11.68959	10.82760	10.05909	9.37189
19	18.08236	17.64683	17.22601	16.42617	15.67846	14.32380	13.13394	12.08532	11.15812	10.33560	9.60360
20	18.98742	18.50802	18.04555	17.16864	16.35143	14.87747	13.59033	12.46221	11.46992	10.59401	9.81815
24	22.56287	21.88915	21.24339	20.03041	18.91393	16.93554	15.24696	13.79864	12.55036	11.46933	10.52876
36	32.87102	31.44681	30.10751	27.66068	25.48884	21.83225	18.90828	16.54685	14.62099	13.03521	11.71719
48	42.58032	40.18478	37.97396	34.04255	30.67312	25.26671	21.19513	18.07716	15.65003	13.73047	12.18914
60	51.72556	48.17337	44.95504	39.38027	34.76089	27.67556	22.62349	18.92929	16.16143	14.03918	12.37655
120	90.07345	78.94169	69.70052	55.49845	45.35539	32.37302	24.77409	19.94268	16.65135	14.28146	12.49878
240	139.58077	111.14495	90.81942	64.79573	49.56855	33.30567	24.99796	19.99984	16.66665	14.28571	12.50000
360	166.79161	124.28187	97.21833	66.35324	49.95992	33.33254	24.99998	20.00000	16.66667	14.28571	12.50000

(continued)

TABLE 4 (continued)

Present Value of an Annuity in Arrears

Periods	9.00%	10.00%	11.00%	12.00%	13.00%	14.00%	15.00%	16.00%	18.00%	20.00%	25.00%
1	0.91743	0.90909	0.90090	0.89286	0.88496	0.87719	0.86957	0.86207	0.84746	0.83333	0.80000
2	1.75911	1.73554	1.71252	1.69005	1.66810	1.64666	1.62571	1.60523	1.56564	1.52778	1.44000
3	2.53129	2.48685	2.44371	2.40183	2.36115	2.32163	2.28323	2.24589	2.17427	2.10648	1.95200
4	3.23972	3.16987	3.10245	3.03735	2.97447	2.91371	2.85498	2.79818	2.69006	2.58873	2.36160
5	3.88965	3.79079	3.69590	3.60478	3.51723	3.43308	3.35216	3.27429	3.12717	2.99061	2.68928
6	4.48592	4.35526	4.23054	4.11141	3.99755	3.88867	3.78448	3.68474	3.49760	3.32551	2.95142
7	5.03295	4.86842	4.71220	4.56376	4.42261	4.28830	4.16042	4.03857	3.81153	3.60459	3.16114
8	5.53482	5.33493	5.14612	4.96764	4.79877	4.63886	4.48732	4.34359	4.07757	3.83716	3.32891
9	5.99525	5.75902	5.53705	5.32825	5.13166	4.94637	4.77158	4.60654	4.30302	4.03097	3.46313
10	6.41766	6.14457	5.88923	5.65022	5.42624	5.21612	5.01877	4.83323	4.49409	4.19247	3.57050
11	6.80519	6.49506	6.20652	5.93770	5.68694	5.45273	5.23371	5.02864	4.65601	4.32706	3.65640
12	7.16073	6.81369	6.49236	6.19437	5.91765	5.66029	5.42062	5.19711	4.79322	4.43922	3.72512
13	7.48690	7.10336	6.74987	6.42355	6.12181	5.84236	5.58315	5.34233	4.90951	4.53268	3.78010
14	7.78615	7.36669	6.98187	6.62817	6.30249	6.00207	5.72448	5.46753	5.00806	4.61057	3.82408
15	8.06069	7.60608	7.19087	6.81086	6.46238	6.14217	5.84737	5.57546	5.09158	4.67547	3.85926
16	8.31256	7.82371	7.37916	6.97399	6.60388	6.26506	5.95423	5.66850	5.16235	4.72956	3.88741
17	8.54363	8.02155	7.54879	7.11963	6.72909	6.37286	6.04716	5.74870	5.22233	4.77463	3.90993
18	8.75563	8.20141	7.70162	7.24967	6.83991	6.46742	6.12797	5.81785	5.27316	4.81219	3.92794
19	8.95011	8.36492	7.83929	7.36578	6.93797	6.55037	6.19823	5.87746	5.31624	4.84350	3.94235
20	9.12855	8.51356	7.96333	7.46944	7.02475	6.62313	6.25933	5.92884	5.35275	4.86958	3.95388
24	9.70661	8.98474	8.34814	7.78432	7.28288	6.83514	6.43377	6.07263	5.45095	4.93710	3.98111
36	10.61176	9.67651	8.87859	8.19241	7.59785	7.07899	6.62314	6.22012	5.54120	4.99295	3.99870
48	10.93358	9.89693	9.03022	8.29716	7.67052	7.12960	6.65853	6.24497	5.55359	4.99921	3.99991
60	11.04799	9.96716	9.07356	8.32405	7.68728	7.14011	6.66515	6.24915	5.55529	4.99991	3.99999
120	11.11075	9.99989	9.09088	8.33332	7.69230	7.14286	6.66667	6.25000	5.55556	5.00000	4.00000
240	11.11111	10.00000	9.09091	8.33333	7.69231	7.14286	6.66667	6.25000	5.55556	5.00000	4.00000
360	11.11111	10.00000	909091	8.33333	7.69231	7.14286	6.66667	6.25000	5.55556	5.00000	4.00000

Taking Care of Business

Since its founding in 1962, Shoppers Drug Mart (Pharmaprix in Quebec) has grown from a small family-run pharmacy on Toronto's Danforth Avenue to a nationwide network of more than 900 retail outlets with 35,000 employees. The success of the company, Canada's largest drugstore chain, is built on a franchising concept that combines a pharmacist–owner with the benefits of a corporate infrastructure.

In November 2001, Shoppers went public, issuing 30 million common shares at a price of $18 per share. Underwritten by a consortium of dealers led by CIBC World Markets, the initial public offering (IPO) raised $540 million, making it Canada's largest IPO in 2001. Proceeds were used to help pay back $591 million of the company's long-term debt, much of which was incurred in a leveraged buyout by a group of institutional investors the year before. As a result, Shoppers improved its debt/equity ratio to 0.78:1 from 1.88:1. At the end of 2001, its balance of long-term debt was $1.1 billion.

The shares made their debut on the Toronto Stock Exchange on November 21, under the symbol SC. Criticized by some analysts as being too pricey, they initially fell in the first few weeks of trading but recovered by year end. Since then, they have been climbing steadily. In December 2003, SC was trading at more than $28.

"Going public has given us more than just an opportunity to raise capital through a different market," says Arthur Konviser, Senior Vice President, Corporate Affairs. "It also gives us greater exposure through wider shareholding. Obviously the more Canadians who own Shoppers Drug Mart shares, the better it is—in as much as they're consumers as well as shareholders, it gives them an affinity towards the company."

Since it went public, Shoppers has continued to show earnings. In the first three quarters of 2003, net earnings increased 28.3% to $188 million or 88 cents per share (diluted) from $147 million or 69 cents per share (diluted) the previous year.

And the next few years look just as promising. Canada's $23-billion-a-year retail drugstore market is expected to grow in the coming decades. "It's a buoyant market," Mr. Konviser says. "People are aging, and there's a greater need for health and beauty aid services. So we are in the market to provide those services to the consumer."

Shoppers' plans for 2004 included adding 50 more stores and continuing with its renovation policy, which will see average store sizes increase from 7,500 square feet to approximately 14,000 square feet. "The larger stores offer a wider range of products for the health, beauty, and convenience needs of our patients and customers," Mr. Konviser says.

chapter 11

Shareholder's Equity

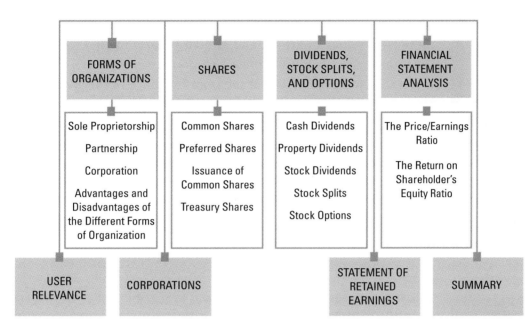

After studying this chapter, you should be able to:

1. Distinguish among different types of organizations and explain the advantages and disadvantages of each form.

2. Describe the different types of shares and explain why corporations choose to issue a variety of share types.

3. Prepare journal entries for share transactions, including the issuance and payment of dividends.

4. Describe the different types of dividends and explain why companies might opt to issue one type of dividend rather than another.

5. Explain the purpose of the statement of retained earnings.

6. Calculate and interpret the price/earnings ratio and the return on shareholders' equity ratio, which are often used in decision-making.

The opening story describes how an established company, Shoppers Drug Mart, moved from being a private corporation to a public corporation. A private corporation has shareholders, but those shareholders are a controlled, usually relatively small group (compared with a publicly traded company). Because of the limited number of shareholders, it is more difficult to buy and/or sell an ownership interest. Once it went public, Shoppers Drug Mart increased its access to funds, increased its number of shareholders, and lost some control over who its shareholders are. Shoppers' financial statements are public information now and the company must produce quarterly and annual reports for the stock exchange and its shareholders. When it was a private corporation, it produced financial information for its shareholders but not for the stock exchange or the general public. Shoppers saw the issuance of the IPO as an opportunity to expand not only its capital base, but also its ownership base. It views new shareholders as probable new customers.

A company can also go from being a public company to a private one. Note the following article summary.

accounting in the news
GOING PRIVATE

For many companies, the ultimate goal is to go public, giving them access to a lot of money through the stock market. But some companies choose to go private, as Cara Operations Ltd., the Toronto-based owner of several restaurant chains, including Swiss Chalet, Harvey's, and Second Cup coffee shops, did in early 2004. Cara Holdings Ltd. offered $8 per share to take the business private. The privatization bid had to be revised twice in the previous six months during a public battle among members of the company's founding Phelan family. The original bid was for $7.50 per share, representing an aggregate value of $324 million. In commenting on the proposal, Gail Regan, president of Cara Holdings, said, "At a time when a number of divisions of Cara are experiencing challenging operating conditions, this proposal will provide liquidity to Cara's minority shareholders for their investment at a substantial premium." An independent valuation indicated that the fair market value of Cara shares was in the range of $7.25 to $8.50 per share. The $8 bid represented a premium of approximately 17.7% and 45.5% above the closing market prices of the common shares (at $6.80) and class A non-voting shares (at $5.50) on August 28, 2003, the last trading day before the original privatization bid. However, in February 2004, just before all shareholders approved the revised offer, common shares were trading at $7.95, and class A non-voting shares reached $7.94.

Source: "Cara shareholders vote to take the company private," by Richard Bloom, *The Globe and Mail*, February 25, 2004; "Cara deal likely to go through," by Wojtek Dabrowski, *National Post*, February 7, 2004; "Jarislowsky backs new Cara bid," by Richard Bloom, *The Globe and Mail*, February 7, 2004.

In this chapter, we are going to delve more deeply into the components of shareholders' equity. Remember that shareholders' equity represents the residual amount (assets minus liabilities) and it measures the investment made by owners in the company. Before getting into a detailed discussion of the components of shareholders' equity in a corporation, we want to take a short detour in which we will briefly discuss why knowing more about shareholders' equity is important to users and also to look at alternative forms of business organization. Although many companies in Canada are established as corporations, they could have been established as proprietorships or partnerships.

USER RELEVANCE

The chances are relatively high that in the future you will invest in one or more companies, either directly by buying shares, or indirectly by buying mutual funds. As a future shareholder, you need to understand how your ownership interest is measured and disclosed in the financial statements. So far in the book, we have only talked about a common share. In reality, there are several different kinds of share (ownership interest). With the help of financial experts, companies design and create financial instruments that have a variety of features that provide investors with different levels of risk and return. These instruments also have varying rights and privileges. You should know what some of those features are so that you can assess the value of your ownership interest. When a company raises additional capital by issuing shares, you will need to be aware of how that new issuance affects your current holdings.

Sometimes investors buy shares to receive a periodic dividend payment. More frequently, however, shares are purchased in anticipation of the share value increasing so that the shares can be sold in the future for a profit. Buying and selling shares today is much easier than it was in the past, but investors still need to do their homework. The information that you have gained by studying accounting should provide you with a reasonable level of knowledge so that you can assess a company's current and future financial health.

Let's take a brief look at some of the different forms of organization.

FORMS OF ORGANIZATION

Sole Proprietorship

As discussed briefly in Chapter 1, the simplest form of business is the **sole proprietorship**. The sole proprietorship is a single-owner business. All profits and losses belong to the owner, and all decisions are made either by the owner or under the owner's direction. It is probably this aspect of control that keeps the proprietorship form of business alive. Most owners like to be the ones making decisions and to be active in the day-to-day operations. Proprietorships can be small, single-unit operations, or they can be larger operations with units in several places.

Proprietors must assume all the risk if the business runs into trouble. They have **unlimited liability**. Unlimited liability means that the sole proprietor is 100% liable for all debts of the business. Should a claim be made by a stakeholder against the company, both the business assets and the owner's personal property (if necessary) may be used to fulfill the obligation and satisfy the claim. It is this aspect of unlimited liability that makes many single owners consider establishing the business as a corporation rather than a proprietorship.

Because the sole proprietor does not have to report to shareholders, there is less concern about preparing reports according to Canadian standards. The sole proprietor might want to follow Canadian standards if the business is trying to obtain a bank loan, since loan officers could insist on financial statements prepared according to GAAP. GAAP statements might also be required if the sole proprietorship is regulated. The owner might want to deviate from Canadian standards if using a different method would produce information that was more useful in making the decisions needed to run the business.

The Canada Revenue Agency (CRA) also wants information about the financial results of a sole proprietorship. Sole proprietors are required to combine the profits or losses from their businesses with their personal income for tax purposes. There is no separate taxation for sole proprietorships as there is for corporations. The rules for reporting income to the CRA are, therefore, a motivator for producing financial statements. The accounting methods used by the sole proprietor are more likely to follow those used for tax purposes than those set forth under GAAP.

With regard to owners' equity accounts, there is little reason for the owner to distinguish the initial investment from the income retained in the business. For this reason, the owner's equity section of a sole proprietorship typically has only one account, which is sometimes called **owner's capital**. This account is used when the owner puts new capital into the business, when the business earns income (revenues and expenses are closed to this account), and when the owner withdraws cash from the business. Cash withdrawn from the business for personal use is usually referred to as a withdrawal by the owner. These withdrawals are the equivalent of dividends in a corporation. Because the owner is taxed on the combined basis of personal income and business income, these withdrawals are not taxed in the same manner as corporate dividends.

Partnership

LEARNING OBJECTIVE 1

Distinguish among different types of organizations and explain the advantages and disadvantages of each form.

A second form of business that is very similar to a sole proprietorship is a **partnership**. In a partnership, two or more individuals agree to conduct business under one name. The partners' involvement in the partnership can vary greatly. The partners' rights and responsibilities are generally specified in a document called a **partnership agreement**. This document is very important because it specifies how the partners will make decisions about the business, including how they will share in profits and losses, as well as how the assets will be distributed if the partnership dissolves. In the absence of a partnership agreement, the distribution of assets and profits is assumed to be equal for all partners. If the partners intend to share profits in some other proportion, this must be stated in a partnership agreement. For tax purposes, partnerships are not taxable entities; the income earned by the partners is passed through to them and must be reported on their personal tax returns, similar to the treatment of sole proprietorship income.

Partners can assume different responsibilities and risk in a partnership. **General partners** normally make day-to-day decisions about the business, share in profits and losses, and have unlimited liability. If the partnership defaults on its debts, creditors can sue one, more than one, or all of the general partners, taking both business assets and personal ones. **Limited partners**, on the other hand, have limited involvement in the partnership. Normally, they invest in the partnership but do not make day-to-day decisions about its operations. They share in profits and losses but creditors cannot normally sue them if the partnership runs into financial difficulty.

One of the major accounting problems in a partnership is distinguishing the roles that partners play as owners, creditors, and employees. For example, should the compensation paid to a partner who works as an employee of the partnership be treated as an expense of the partnership? That is, should all partners share in this expense, or should it be treated as a part of the partner's share of the profits from the business? As another example, suppose a partner lends money to the partnership. Should this be viewed as a liability of the partnership, or as part of the equity contributed by this partner? If the partnership liquidates, should this partner get paid first as a creditor and then share in whatever is left, or should the loan be considered part of the partner's equity? There is no single right answer to these questions, which is why these issues should be addressed in the partnership agreement.

The accounting for the owners' equity section of a partnership requires that the partnership keep a separate account for each partner, usually called the partner's **capital account**. Each period, the profits or losses of the partnership must be distributed among the partners' capital accounts. This is usually a relatively complex process that takes into consideration the issues discussed in the preceding paragraph. Sometimes there is also an account for each partner called a **drawing account**. This is an account that keeps track of the amounts withdrawn by the partner during the period. It is similar to a dividends declared account in a corporation, in that it collects payments made to owners. In the case of the drawings account, at the end of each accounting period it is closed into the capital account of the specific partner. As with sole proprietorships, such withdrawals are not taxable.

Detailed accounting rules for partnerships are sometimes covered in advanced accounting texts and will not be discussed here. The accounting for the transactions of a partnership other than owners' equity is essentially the same as that discussed in this book for corporations.

Corporation

The third major form of business organization is the **corporation**, which has been the focus of most of this book. It differs from sole proprietorships and partnerships in at least three significant ways. The first is that the corporation is legally separate from the shareholders. While the owners of sole proprietorships and partnerships can be held liable for the debts of their businesses, corporate shareholders have **limited liability** for the debts of the companies they own. Corporate shareholders cannot be made to pay for the company's debts out of their personal assets. Sole proprietors and partners do not enjoy this limited liability.

The second significant way in which corporations differ from proprietorships is the manner in which they are taxed. Because the corporation is viewed as a separate legal entity, the CRA and provincial governments impose a corporate tax on the income it earns. This corporate tax is in addition to the personal income tax that shareholders pay on their personal income when they receive dividends or when they sell their shares and experience a gain or loss. The basics of accounting for shareholders' equity in a company have been covered in preceding chapters of this book. Later in this chapter, details will be provided concerning more complex transactions that involve shareholders' equity.

The third way in which corporations differ is that they are a separate legal entity. There is usually a distinct separation between the owners and the business in a corporation. The corporation has a board of directors who are the ultimate decision-makers in the business. They are elected by the shareholders and select (hire and fire) the management team that runs the day-to-day business operations. Since the bankruptcy of **Enron** and other major companies in the United States, regulators have been developing stronger rules around who can be a member of a board and what their responsibilities should be. The *Sarbanes-Oxley Act* was passed by the United States Congress in 2002. It stipulates that a board must have five financially literate members who are appointed for five years. Two of those five must be professional accountants and the other three cannot be professional accountants. The board is ultimately responsible for the financial information that is prepared by management and examined by auditors. Because many companies in Canada are either subsidiaries of U.S. companies or have U.S. subsidiaries, they are implementing the *Sarbanes-Oxley Act* in Canada.

accounting in the news

A NEW KIND OF COMPANY

Since 2001, there has been a rapid growth in a new kind of company, an income trust. Many companies in Canada, such as Big Rock Brewery, were corporations and are now income trusts. An income trust is structured with investment units instead of shares. Each unit represents an ownership part of the income trust. Whereas a corporation will sometimes pay out some of its after-tax earnings to shareholders in the form of a dividend, an income trust pays out almost all of its income-generated cash flows to the unit holders as untaxed income. The amount becomes taxable in the hands of the unit holder rather than the tax being paid for by the income trust. It is referred to as a tax flow-through. Many unit holders have their investment inside a retirement savings plan (RSP) and, therefore, the tax effect of the tax flow-through is delayed until money is withdrawn from the RSP.

The corporate structure of an income trust is different from a corporation. There are usually two companies: an income trust company and an operating company. The board of directors is replaced by a trustee (or board of trustees) who supervises the operating company, oversees the distribution of cash to the unit holders, and acts on behalf of the unit holders.

Source: "Income trusts—Understanding the issues," Bank of Canada Working Paper 2003-25 by Michael R. King, Financial Markets Department, Bank of Canada.

Advantages and Disadvantages of the Different Forms of Organization

While there are many differences among sole proprietorships, partnerships, and corporations, two of the primary differences just mentioned—legal liability and taxes—are sufficiently important to warrant detailed discussion here. With regard to legal liability, the owners of a sole proprietorship or partnership are fully liable for the business debts. If the business does not have sufficient assets to pay its debts, creditors have the right to try to collect from the owners' personal assets. This feature is sometimes referred to as unlimited liability. The shareholders of corporations, on the other hand, enjoy limited liability unless required to give personal guarantees. The most a shareholder can lose is the amount of the investment in the shares. Creditors cannot seek satisfaction of their claims from the personal assets of corporate shareholders.

Limited liability is obviously an advantage of the corporate form of organization. There are some forms of partnerships, called **limited partnerships**, that share some of this advantage. In limited partnerships, there are general partners and limited partners. General partners have unlimited liability, whereas limited partners have limited liability. The downside for the limited partners is that they also have a limited say in making decisions within the partnership.

Where taxes are concerned, the income of partnerships and sole proprietorships is not taxed at the business level because it flows through to the individuals. Personal tax is then assessed according to the individual owner's tax bracket. Corporations, on the other hand, are subject to corporate taxation. An incorporated small business can obtain a tax advantage through tax deferral when profits are retained in the business. This occurs because the corporate tax rate is approximately 22% for a small business. The tax to be paid by the individual shareholders on dividends or capital gains (if they sell their shares) is deferred until dividends are received or the shares are sold. It is then taxed at the individual level. Corporate income is, therefore, subject to double taxation: once when the corporation pays taxes on corporate income and again when the shareholder pays taxes on a dividend distributed by the corporation. The income tax rules include methods intended to reduce the impact of this double taxation. This does not necessarily mean that the corporate form results in more tax being paid. The sum of the corporate tax and individual tax for a small business is approximately equal to the individual tax on business income. For larger corporations that cannot take advantage of the small business tax rate, the tax effect could be a disadvantage of the corporate form.

There are other advantages and disadvantages to each form of business. For example, incorporation requires a significant amount of paperwork and regulation, which makes a corporation more difficult to form than a sole proprietorship or partnership. (Although partnerships can be formed without any written agreement, a written partnership agreement prepared with legal assistance is advisable in order to avoid possible disagreements among the partners.) Once established, corporations can raise additional capital much more easily than partnerships: they can issue more shares or bonds. Partnerships and sole proprietorships are limited by the assets contributed by the owners and those earned by the business and not withdrawn. It is much easier to change your ownership interest if you are a shareholder than if you are a partner or a sole proprietor. You simply sell your shares on the stock market. If you no longer want to own a proprietorship, you must sell the whole business. If you are a partner and want to withdraw from the partnership, you must convince the other partners to buy you out or find another partner to buy your ownership interest. When establishing a new business, it is important to weigh all the issues before deciding on the organizational form that will work best.

In Canada, corporations own the vast majority of business assets and almost all large businesses are organized as corporations. That is why we focus on accounting for corporations in this text.

CORPORATIONS

Let's look at corporations in more detail. Shareholders of corporations require certain types of legal protection, especially because the owners of most corporations are absentee shareholders; that is, they are not intimately involved in the day-to-day business. This protection is provided by the laws of the jurisdiction under which the company is incorporated. In Canada, companies may be incorporated under the federal *Canada Business Corporations Act*, or under similar provincial acts that have been established in all 10 provinces. When investors decide to establish a business in the form of a corporation, they must first decide under which act they want to be incorporated. Normally, most companies in Canada are incorporated under the laws of the province in which the business, or at least the company head office, is to be located. Companies that intend to carry on business interprovincially or internationally may decide that being incorporated under federal legislation will provide them with more options. After deciding on where to be incorporated, the founding investors prepare a document called the **articles of incorporation**. The articles of incorporation include information about what type of business the company will conduct, how the board of directors will be organized, who the management will be, what kinds of shares will be issued, and other information. The exact content of the articles will depend on the decisions of the incorporating shareholders. Once the company has been incorporated, the articles of incorporation can generally be amended only by a shareholder vote.

SHARES

For accounting purposes, the most important section of the articles of incorporation is the description of the shares that will be issued. The maximum number of shares that the company can issue is specified in the articles. These are referred to as the **authorized shares**. In the past, companies would establish a fixed number of shares that they assumed would carry them for many years. When a company is first starting up, it is difficult to anticipate that it will ever issue the number of shares that it set as its authorized limit. (Remember our opening story? **Shoppers Drug Mart** issued 30 million shares in its first public offering.) However, companies found that issuing all the authorized shares was not very hard to do. To increase the number of authorized shares, however, requires a change in the articles of incorporation, which requires a vote by the shareholders. To give you some perspective on numbers of shares, **Sun-Rype Products**, a medium-sized company, had 10,796,900 shares issued by the end of December 2003. **Domtar Inc.**, one of the largest companies in Canada, had 227,937,812 common shares issued at the end of December 2003. In the United States, **Microsoft** had issued 10,766,000,000 shares by the end of June 2003. The magnitude of these numbers is difficult to conceive when starting a company. To overcome the problem of reaching the authorized limit set in the articles of incorporation, many companies today establish an unlimited number of authorized shares. This allows them the greatest freedom to use the issuance of shares as a means for raising capital.

In the past, the articles could also specify a dollar amount that was attached to each share. This dollar amount was known as the **par value**. Under most jurisdictions in Canada, par value shares are no longer permitted. Instead, most companies issue **no par value** shares. The original purpose of the par value was to protect the company's creditors by setting a limit on the dividends the company could pay. In most jurisdictions, a company was able to declare dividends only up to the value of the retained earnings. It could not pay dividends out of the balance in the par value shares account. If a company were allowed to declare a dividend equal to the total of retained earnings and the balance in the other equity accounts, the shareholders might then pay themselves a dividend of this amount (sometimes called a **liquidating dividend** because it liquidated the shareholders' investment). This might have left creditors with insufficient assets to satisfy their claims. Companies were able to avoid this constraint by setting very low par values and selling the shares at prices above the par value. Only the total of the par values was credited to the share account; the excess was credited to an account called paid-in capital, or premium on shares. Dividends paid out of this second account were permitted in some jurisdictions and were in fact liquidating dividends since they reduced the company's paid-in equity.

While this is still theoretically true about par values today, the practical value of a par value is almost nonexistent. The par value of most shares is so small compared with the level of other shareholders' equity accounts and the level of liabilities that it provides very little protection to creditors. For this reason, when the *Canada Business Corporations Act* was changed in 1976, par value shares were no longer allowed. Instead, shares had to be no par value. When no par value shares are issued, the total amount received for the shares is put into one account, the share account. This larger amount is referred to as the **legal capital** and must be kept intact. Except under specific circumstances, it cannot be paid out as dividends. This provides more protection for creditors. Once the *Canada Business Corporations Act* changed, most of the provincial acts were changed as well.

The articles of incorporation also specify the classes or types of shares that can be issued by the company if more than one class of shares is to be issued. **Le Château Inc.** has two classes of common shares and three classes of preferred shares (which can be issued in series). In 2003, there were no preferred shares issued. There were 2,226,041 Class A voting shares and 3,020,000 Class B voting shares issued. In many companies, more than one class is authorized so that the company has more flexibility in attracting different kinds of investors. For example, some investors want the assurance of regular dividends to provide a steady income; others prefer no regular dividends but hope for increasing share values so that they can earn capital gains when they eventually sell their shares.

The different classes of shares differ in the rights that accrue to their holders. Two major classes of shares, common shares and preferred shares, are discussed in the following subsections. Different classes of shares can be authorized within each of these two major types. As noted in Le Château, some companies have multiple classes of common shares and multiple classes (sometimes these are called issues) of preferred shares. Le Château's Class A shares carry one vote per share, whereas the Class B shares carry 10 votes per share.

accounting in the news

FASHIONABLE GOVERNANCE

T-shirt maker Gildan Activewear announced plans to abandon its dual-class share structure in February 2003, with founders and controlling shareholders, Greg and Glen Chamandy, converting their voting class B shares into subordinate voting shares. The Chamandys owned slightly more than 90% of the company's 6.1 million class B shares and another 53,000 class A shares, which amounted to 0.2% of that class. But, because the B shares carried eight votes each compared with one vote for the A shares, the brothers controlled 61% of the votes. With the conversion, they will have the same amount of votes as equity, or 18.8%. Gildan adopted the dual-class share structure when it went public in the late 1990s. These structures are particularly widespread among major Canadian companies. However, firms controlled by families with more votes than equity have received criticism that "minority" shareholders are relegated to second-class status. Several companies have dumped their two-class structure in response. While recognizing this as progress, the Canadian Coalition for Good Governance (CCGG) wants the Toronto Stock Exchange to clearly identify firms with two share classes by changing their stock symbols. The CCGG hopes with would discourage new companies from going public with dual-class shares.

Source: "Gildan in fashionable governance," by Sean Silcoff, *National Post*, February 4, 2004; "Multiple voting shares targeted," by Janet McFarland and Andy Hoffman, *The Globe and Mail*, February 13, 2004.

Common Shares

LEARNING OBJECTIVE 2

Describe the different types of shares and explain why corporations choose to issue a variety of share types.

Every corporation must have one class of shares that represents the basic voting ownership rights of the company. These shares are normally referred to as **common shares**. Corporations generally issue common shares through a firm of investment bankers, known as underwriters, in much the same way that bonds are issued (see Chapter 10 for a discussion of this process). When common or preferred shares are issued, the details and features of the shares being issued are discussed in a legal document called a **prospectus**, which is distributed to potential investors when shares (or a bond) are initially issued (sold).

Common shares carry a basic set of rights that allow the owner to share proportionately (based on the number of shares held) in:

1. Profits and losses

2. The selection of corporate management

3. Assets upon liquidation

4. Subsequent issues of shares (although not all jurisdictions in Canada provide for this basic right)

Rather than establishing complex income-sharing rules similar to a partnership, a corporation retains control over the distribution of its profits. It is sometimes useful to think of a corporation's profits or losses as being allocated to its shares, even if these earnings or losses are not actually paid out. The resulting per-share figure is useful in determining whether the corporation's profits are increasing or decreasing on an individual share basis. This earnings per share figure that corporations calculate provides a measure of performance that all shareholders can use. Recall from Chapter 3 that this is a calculation that consists of dividing the corporation's net income by the average number of common shares outstanding during the year. A weighted average is used if the number of common shares outstanding changed during the year. Different classes of shares are entitled to different portions of the earnings. Normally, preferred shares are restricted to the amounts of their dividends and no more. Common shares normally have no restrictions on their rights to share in earnings once the claims of the creditors and the preferred shareholders have been satisfied. If a corporation opts to pay dividends (it is not obliged to do so), owners of the same class of shares receive a proportionate share of earnings in the form of dividends. Corporations, in addition to reporting earnings per share, often report dividends per share. As will be seen shortly, the right to share in dividend distribution may be amended for different classes of shares, especially for preferred shares.

Common shareholders also have the right to vote on the selection of management for the corporation. The standard rule for voting is one share equals one vote. The more shares an individual owns, the greater the influence that individual has in the company. One of the shareholders' most important tasks is to elect members of the board of directors. The board of directors then represents the shareholders, and most decisions are made by a vote of the board of directors rather than by a vote of all shareholders. The board of directors hires (and fires) the company's top-level management and also declares the dividends that are paid to shareholders.

The third right of common shareholders is to share in assets upon liquidation. If a company goes bankrupt or otherwise liquidates, there is an established order in which creditors and shareholders are paid. Common shareholders come last on that list; whatever is left after creditors are paid is then divided proportionately among them based on their relative number of shares. This means that common shareholders bear the highest risk, since there may be nothing left over for them. They could, of course, reap the largest benefit if there is a substantial sum left over.

The fourth right of common shares is to share proportionately in any new issuance of shares. This is called the **preemptive right**. Preemptive rights are not automatic. They must be explicitly stated in the articles of incorporation. This right allows current shareholders to retain their proportionate interest in the company when new shares are issued. For example, a shareholder owning 20% of a company's shares has the preemptive right to purchase 20% of any new shares of that class that may be issued. Without this right, an investor that had a **controlling interest** in a company (i.e., more than 50% of the outstanding shares) could lose that controlling interest if the new shares were issued to another investor. Of course, this scenario is unlikely as controlling interest includes the right to vote for the company's directors so that directors who support the majority owner can be elected. The greatest protection is for shareholders who own a **minority** or **noncontrolling interest** in a company. Preemptive rights prevent their ownership interests from being diluted.

When more than one class of common shares is issued, each class is distinguished by some amendment to the fundamental rights just described. For example, a second class of non-voting common shares might be issued that may be entitled to conversion to voting common shares under certain conditions. This obviously affects the control that holders of the voting common shares have over the company's operations. There might also be differences in the rights to share in the assets' liquidation values. As mentioned earlier, Le Château Inc. has two classes of common shares. The various features of those two classes are as shown in Exhibit 11-1.

EXHIBIT 11-1   **LE CHÂTEAU, INC. 2004 ANNUAL REPORT**

Note 8 Capital Stock

8. CAPITAL STOCK

Authorized

An unlimited number of non-voting First, Second and Third Preferred Shares issuable in series

An unlimited number of Class A Subordinate Voting Shares

An unlimited number of Class B Voting Shares

Issued	**January 31 2004** $	January 25 2003 $
2,226,041 Class A Shares [2003 - 2,001,481]	**13,710**	12,616
3,020,000 Class B Shares	**1,064**	1,064
	14,774	13,680

During the year ended January 31, 2004, the Company issued 224,560 [2003 - 78,940] Class A Shares under the stock option plan for $1,094,000 [2003 - $235,000].

Principal features

[a] With respect to the payment of dividends and the return of capital, the shares rank as follows:

First Preferred
Second Preferred
Third Preferred
Class A and Class B

[b] Subject to the rights of the Preferred shareholders, the Class A shareholders are entitled to a non-cumulative preferential dividend of $0.05 per share, after which the Class B shareholders are entitled to a non-cumulative dividend of $0.05 per share; any further dividends declared in a fiscal year must be declared and paid in equal amounts per share on all the Class A and Class B Shares then outstanding without preference or distinction.

[c] Subject to the foregoing, the Class A and Class B Shares rank equally, share for share, in earnings.

[d] The Class A Shares carry one vote per share and the Class B Shares carry 10 votes per share.

[e] The Class A Shares are convertible into Class B Shares on a share-for-share basis if the parent company ceases to control the Company, or if an offer is accepted to sell more than 20% of the then outstanding Class B Shares at a price in excess of 115% of their market price. The Class B Shares are convertible into Class A Shares at any time on a share-for-share basis.

Dividends paid to different classes of common shares may also be paid on a different basis, although each outstanding share of any class of shares will be paid the same amount.

Preferred Shares

Preferred shares are shares that have preference over common shares with regard to dividends. This does not mean that preferred shareholders are guaranteed a dividend, but if dividends are declared, they will receive them before common shareholders.

Many times, in addition to the preference for dividends, there is also some preference with regard to assets in the event of liquidation.

The preferred dividend amount is usually stated as a dollar amount per share, such as a $2 preferred share issue. Such an issue would pay a dividend of $2 per share per year. For example, in 2003, **BCE Inc.** reported that it had $1.5435 Series Q, $1.3298 Series Z, $1.3625 series AA, and $1.385 Series AC preferred shares.

Besides the difference in priority for dividends, another difference between common and preferred shares is that preferred shares are usually non-voting. One of the troubling issues in accounting is how to deal with securities such as preferred shares that have characteristics that make them look more like debt than common shares. Non-voting preferred shares with a fixed dividend amount are not much different from debt (which is also non-voting) that has a fixed interest payment. The only real difference is that the company is not obliged to pay the preferred dividend, whereas the debt interest on the debt is a true obligation and a legal liability. Also, most preferred shares do not have a maturity date. Preferred shareholders often only receive the initial investment back when the company liquidates.

There are other features of preferred shares with which you should be familiar. Preferred dividends may be **cumulative**. Cumulative means that if a dividend is not declared on the preferred shares in one year, it carries over into the next year. In the second year, both the prior year's preferred dividend and the current year's preferred dividend must be declared before any common dividends can be declared. Dividends from prior years that have not been declared are called **dividends in arrears**. In the case of BCE, all the series of preferred shares are cumulative. In fact, most preferred shares are cumulative.

Convertible preferred shares are convertible, at the shareholder's option, into common shares (or other preferred shares) based on a ratio stated in the articles of incorporation. **CCL Industries Ltd.** has an interesting share capital arrangement. It has Class A shares that are voting and are convertible into Class B shares on a one-for-one basis. The Class B shares are non-voting but in all other respects rank equal to the Class A shares. Currently, the dividend on Class A shares has been set at 5 cents less than that for the Class B shares. As a result, some Class A shareholders have converted to Class B shares. All of BCE's preferred share series are convertible into another series of preferred shares at the holder's option.

Redeemable preferred shares can be bought back by the company (retired) at a price and time specified in the articles of incorporation, at the issuing company's option. **Bombardier Inc.** has three preferred share issues, all of which are redeemable. The Series 2 shares are redeemable at $25.00 per share on August 1, 2002, or at $25.50 thereafter. The Series 3 shares are redeemable at $25.00 per share on August 1, 2007, and on August 1 of every fifth year thereafter. The Series 4 shares are redeemable at $26.00 per share at any time on or after March 31, 2007, if redeemed prior to March 31, 2008, $25.75 if redeemed on or after March 31, 2008, but prior to March 31, 2009, $25.50 if redeemed on or after March 31, 2009, but prior to March 31, 2010, $25.25 if redeemed on or after March 31, 2010, but prior to March 31, 2011, and $25.00 if redeemed on or after March 31, 2011. As a potential investor in Bombardier's preferred shares, you would need to read very carefully in order to understand the special features of the redemption aspect of these shares. **Retractable preferred shares** are similar to redeemable shares in that they can be sold back to the company (retired) at the shareholder's option. The price that must be paid for them and the periods of time when they can be sold are specified in the articles of incorporation.

The last feature we are going to discuss is participation. **Participating preferred shares** are preferred shares that not only have a preference with regard to dividends but, if dividends are declared to common shareholders beyond the level declared to the preferred shareholders, the preferred shareholders share in the excess dividends. At one time, BCE had preferred shares that were participating. However, none of its current series of preferred shares has this feature. Most preferred shares are non-participating. Le Château has the participating feature on its Class A and Class B common shares.

While the features of various classes of shares differ, the accounting issues relating to all of them are basically the same. Therefore, in the sections that follow, we limit the discussion to common shares.

Issuance of Common Shares

When common shares are issued for cash, the company accounts for these proceeds by debiting the cash account. The credit entry is then to a common shares account. This common shares account is sometimes referred to as **paid-in capital** or **legal capital**.

To illustrate the issuance entry, suppose that Rosman Company issues 1,000 common shares for $20 a share. The following entry would be made.

SHARE ISSUANCE ENTRY		
Cash (A)	20,000	
Common shares (SE)		20,000

Historically, companies were permitted to issue shares that had a stated or par value. With stated or par value shares, only the total of the stated or par value was credited to the common shares account, and any remaining amount was credited to another equity account. Although few jurisdictions now allow par value shares, you may still encounter them.

To illustrate the issuance entry for par value shares, suppose that Green Company issued 1,000 common shares for $15 a share that had a par value of $10 per share. The following entry would have been made.

SHARE ISSUANCE ENTRY		
Cash (A)	15,000	
Common shares (SE)		10,000
Contributed capital (SE)		5,000

Note that the additional $5 per share (the amount in excess of par) is recorded in an account called Contributed capital. This account is sometimes called *contributed surplus in excess of par* or *additional paid-in capital*.

Treasury Shares

Subsequent to issuance, the company may decide to buy back some of its own shares. It might do this because it wants to reduce the number of shares outstanding, or because it wants to use those shares to satisfy its stock option plans rather than issue new shares. Shares that have been repurchased by the issuing company are called **treasury shares**. In most jurisdictions in Canada, treasury shares are cancelled immediately upon purchase. In a few jurisdictions, they are not cancelled immediately and are considered issued but not outstanding.

Three terms are used to refer to the number of company shares: **authorized shares, issued shares**, and **outstanding shares**. The maximum number of shares that can be issued by the company according to the articles of incorporation are the authorized shares. As mentioned earlier, many companies avoid the possible limitations that might result from an authorized limit by stating that they have the right to issue an unlimited number of shares. Those that have been sold (issued) by the company are considered issued shares. As long as the shares remain in the possession of shareholders outside the company, they are considered outstanding. If, however, the company purchases some of its own shares from the market, the shares remain issued but are no longer outstanding. If the company subsequently cancels the shares, they will cease to be issued and will revert to the status of only being authorized. If the company does not have to cancel the shares but instead holds them as treasury shares, the issued shares minus those held as treasury shares are the outstanding shares. Examples of the use of these terms can be found in Note 9 of the financial statements of **METRO Inc.** shown in Exhibit 11-2. METRO has an unlimited number of First Preferred Shares, Class A Subordinate Shares, and Class B Shares. No preferred shares have been issued. The Class A shares have one voting right per share, are participating, and are convertible into Class B shares in case of a takeover bid. The Class B shares have 16 votes per share, are participating, and are convertible into Class A shares.

When a company repurchases its own shares and cancels them, a credit is made to cash for the cost of the shares. The debit entry then has to reduce shareholders' equity since the shares are no longer issued or outstanding. A problem arises if the cost of the shares repurchased is different from the amount received when the shares were originally issued. Shares that were issued in the past were issued perhaps at different times and for different amounts. If this is the case, then the average issue price must be determined by dividing the total amount in the shares account by the total number of shares outstanding before the repurchase.

As an example, suppose that Lee Industries Ltd. had 150,000 common shares outstanding and a balance of $1.5 million in its Common Shares account. The average issue price is $10 ($1,500,000 ÷ 150,000). If Lee repurchases 1,000 shares for $9 each, then it is paying $1 less than the average issue price. This $1 per share is not considered to be a profit or gain, and therefore does not appear on the income statement. The reason for this is that the $1 does not result from an activity that is part of the normal company operations. The company was not incorporated to earn money by trading in its own shares. As a general rule, companies never earn revenues or incur losses from

METRO INC. 2003 ANNUAL REPORT

12. Capital stock

Authorized

Unlimited number of First Preferred Shares, non-voting, without par value, issuable in series.

Unlimited number of Class A Subordinate Shares, bearing one voting right per share, participating, convertible into Class B Shares in the event of a takeover bid involving Class B Shares, without par value.

Unlimited number of Class B Shares, bearing 16 voting rights per share, participating, convertible in the event of disqualification into an equal number of Class A Subordinate Shares on the basis of one Class A Subordinate Share for each Class B Share held, without par value.

EXHIBIT 11-2
PART B

METRO INC. 2003 ANNUAL REPORT

12. Capital stock (cont'd)

Issued

	Class A Subordinate Shares		Class B Shares		Total
	Number		Number		
	(Thousands)		*(Thousands)*		
Balance as at September 29, 2001	98,929	$ 159.8	1,236	$ 2.5	$ 162.3
Share issue for cash	51	0.6	—	—	0.6
Share redemption for cash, excluding premium of $12.4	(730)	(1.2)	—	—	(1.2)
Conversion of Class B Shares into Class A Subordinate Shares	162	0.3	(162)	(0.3)	—
Balance as at September 28, 2002	98,412	159.5	1,074	2.2	161.7
Share issue for cash	86	1.0	—	—	1.0
Share redemption for cash, excluding premium of $30.6	(1,760)	(2.8)	—	—	(2.8)
Conversion of Class B Shares into Class A Subordinate Shares	65	0.1	(65)	(0.1)	—
Balance as at September 27, 2003	**96,803**	**$ 157.8**	**1,009**	**$ 2.1**	**$ 159.9**

During the year ended September 28, 2002, the Company split all its Class A Subordinate Shares and all its Class B Shares on a 2-for-1 basis. All information about the shares and data per share have been restated to take the split into account.

transactions involving their own equities. Rather, the $1 is still part of shareholders' equity and is credited to a separate account called "Contributed Surplus." The entry to record this repurchase would be as follows.

Common shares (SE)	10,000	
Cash (A)		9,000
Contributed surplus (SE)		1,000

If Lee had paid $12 per share, it would have paid $2 more than the average issue price per share of $10. In this case, the $2 extra per share would reduce shareholders' equity. Normally, the $2 is debited to Retained Earnings as follows.

Common shares (SE)	10,000	
Retained earnings (SE)	2,000	
Cash (A)		12,000

If there had been a previous repurchase and cancellation of treasury shares that created a contributed surplus account (similar to the first part of this example), the contributed surplus account could have been debited instead of retained earnings. Further details on the accounting for treasury share transactions can be found in more advanced accounting texts.

DIVIDENDS, STOCK SPLITS, AND OPTIONS

Cash Dividends

Dividends are payments to shareholders from the total net income retained in a company in the Retained Earnings account. Dividends are a payment in return for the company's use of the shareholders' money. They are paid to shareholders only if the board of directors has voted to declare a dividend. The declaration of a cash dividend makes the dividend a legal liability of the company. Dividends are not paid on treasury shares because these are held internally by the company, and companies cannot pay dividends to themselves. They are paid only on outstanding shares.

Here is an example of a dividend notice. On July 27, 2004, **Sears Canada** announced that it was paying a quarterly dividend on its common shares of $0.06 a share. The dividend was payable on September 15, 2004, to shareholders of record on August 16, 2004. This announcement was made as a press release and was reported in several financial newspapers in Canada so that investors would know that a dividend was forthcoming.

Three dates are important in the **dividend declaration** process. The first is the **date of declaration**. This is the date on which the board of directors votes to declare a dividend. For Sears Canada, that date is July 27, 2004. On the date of declaration, the company records its obligation to pay the dividend by creating a dividends payable account and a dividends declared account. Suppose that Sears Canada had 106,800,000 common shares outstanding on July 27, 2004. The entry to record the declaration would be:

> **LEARNING OBJECTIVE 4**
>
> *Describe the different types of dividends and explain why companies might opt to issue one type of dividend rather than another.*

DIVIDEND DECLARATION ENTRY

Dividends declared (SE)	6,408,000	
Dividends payable (L)		6,408,000

The debit is usually to a Dividends declared account, which is a temporary account that is closed to Retained Earnings at the end of the accounting period. Companies typically declare dividends quarterly. Therefore, the Dividends declared account accumulates all four quarterly dividends by the end of the fiscal year. Not all companies use a Dividends declared account. Some debit dividends directly to Retained Earnings.

In declaring the dividend, the board of directors specifies that the dividend is payable to shareholders of record on the **date of record**. This second important date is the date on which a shareholder must own the shares in order to receive the dividend. For Sears Canada, that date is the close of business on August 16, 2004. The date of record is typically two weeks after the declaration date. This delay is needed because most public companies' shares are traded every day, so the company has no up-to-date record of the owners of its shares. The delay also allows new owners time to inform the company that they are owners of the shares. If a shareholder sells shares before the date of record, the new owner of the shares will then be entitled to receive the dividend.

In the shares market, traders talk about the **ex-dividend day**. The ex-dividend day is the day on which shares are sold without the right to receive the dividend.

> **HELPFUL HINT:**
>
> Dividends declared does not appear on the income statement. It is not an expense of doing business; it is a return to shareholders on their investment.

Purchasing the shares on the ex-dividend day means that the buyer will not receive the dividend; it belongs to the seller. As you might expect, the share price decreases on the ex-dividend day to reflect the loss of this dividend.

A few weeks after the date of record, the company pays the dividend. This third important date is called the date of payment. Sears Canada's date of payment is September 15, 2004. Again, a delay is needed so the company can update its list of shareholders and calculate the total amount of dividends owed to each. This total amount is calculated as dividends per share times the number of shares owned.

At the date of record, no entry is made. The company is simply trying to find out who owns the shares on this date to determine who is entitled to receive a dividend cheque. On the payment date, the company sends out the cheques to the shareholders and must make an entry to record the reduction in cash and the payment of the liability. Sears Canada would make the following entry for the payment of the dividend declared.

DIVIDEND PAYMENT ENTRY		
Dividends payable (L)	6,408,000	
Cash (A)		6,408,000

Property Dividends

It is also possible for a company to declare a dividend that will be settled with some resource other than cash. Dividends of this type are called property dividends or dividends in kind. These dividends are rare, because the assets other than cash that can be paid out are necessarily limited to assets that can be divided into small, equal parts. A story is told of a liquor company that was short on cash but long on excess inventory and declared a dividend of one bottle per share. Whether this actually happened or not is not as important as the concept it illustrates. If a company issues a property dividend, it must be able to give the same amount per share to each shareholder. In May 2000, BCE owned approximately 37% of Nortel Networks. It decided to distribute 35% of its 37% investment to its shareholders in the form of a dividend. BCE shareholders received 1.57 Nortel shares for every BCE common share held. This was a property dividend.

The major accounting question for property dividends is how to value the dividend. Should the property be valued at its fair market value, or at its cost? In Canada, property dividends are valued at their fair market value because this represents the value the company is giving up to pay the dividend. This means that if the property is currently being carried at cost, a gain or loss must be recognized to bring the property to its fair market value. Suppose that a company declares a property dividend that it will make by transferring inventory with a fair market value of $12,000 to its shareholders. The inventory is recorded at $9,000, which is the original cost to the company. The following entries would be made.

PROPERTY DIVIDEND ENTRIES		
Declaration of dividend (at fair market value)		
Property dividend declared (SE)	12,000	
Dividend payable (L)		12,000

Recognition of fair market value on declaration date and payment of dividend on payment date:

Dividend payable (L)	12,000	
Inventory (A)		9,000
Gain on inventory (SE)		3,000

Stock Dividends

Stock dividends are dividends that are satisfied by issuing additional company shares to shareholders instead of cash or property. Stock dividends can be used to issue dividends when the company does not want to, or is not in a position to, use any of its assets for dividends. Shareholders who receive stock dividends have the option of keeping the new shares received or selling them for cash.

Whereas issuing a cash or property dividend reduces a company's overall value (because cash or other assets have been removed), issuing a stock dividend does not. For example, assume that a company has 100 shares outstanding. These shares are held by 10 different people, each with 10 shares. In other words, each owns 10% of the company. If the company issues a 10% stock dividend, it will issue 10 additional shares (100 shares × 10%), one for every 10 shares held. Each shareholder will now have 11 shares and the company will have 110 shares outstanding. Where before the company's value was divided among 100 shares, now the same value is divided among 110 shares. The company's overall value has not changed, nor has the percentage ownership of each of the shareholders—they still own 10% each—but the value attached to each share is a little less.

If shareholders are no better off after a stock dividend than they were before, why would a company issue such a dividend? There are a couple of good reasons. First, it is possible that the shareholders are better off. Going back to our example, if the shares' market value prior to the stock dividend was $10 a share, the market would have valued the company at $1,000 ($10 × 100 shares). After the stock dividend, there are 110 shares so their market value should drop to $9.09 ($1,000 ÷ 110 shares). If the market price drops to $9.09, each shareholder is no better off. However, often the market price does not fully compensate for the increase in the number of shares. If the market price only drops to $9.15, the shareholders are better off. The market value of a 10% interest would now be $100.65 ($9.15 × 11 shares) where before it was $100 ($10 × 10).

The second reason for issuing a stock dividend is that it provides an opportunity for the company to capitalize its retained earnings. When cash or property dividends were declared and subsequently issued, a temporary account called dividends declared was used. At the end of the accounting period, this account is closed into retained earnings, causing it to decrease. When stock dividends are issued, the same procedure will be followed, and retained earnings will decrease. However, at the same time that retained earnings decreases, the share capital account will increase because more shares were issued. Because the amount in the share capital account represents stated or legal capital (meaning that it cannot be reduced to issue dividends), the company has taken an amount from an account from which dividends can be issued and put it in an account from which they cannot, thus capitalizing it. Companies that have a substantial accumulation of retained earnings but do not have cash available for a dividend will sometimes issue a stock dividend to reduce the retained earnings amount.

As with property dividends, the question that underlies stock dividends is: what value should be attached to the shares that are issued? Should the shares' fair market value be used, or should some other value be selected?

To answer this question, consider the following extreme situations. When a stock dividend is declared, it is stated as a percentage of the outstanding shares. Suppose a company declares a 100% stock dividend. This means that each shareholder will receive one additional share for each one that is currently held. No cash changes hands in this transaction. What would you expect to happen to the shares' market value? It is likely that a share's value would be cut in half. There is no change in the value of the company's assets or liabilities, only a doubling of the number of shares that represent ownership. If there is no change in the company's value, then the price per share should adjust for the number of new shares that have been issued. This suggests that the value of the new shares issued is zero.

At the other extreme, suppose the company issues one additional share as a stock dividend. The recipient of the share can probably sell it for the fair market value of the existing shares on that date. Assuming that there are large numbers of shares already on the market, it is unlikely that the price per share would adjust for the issuance of this one additional share. In this case, then, the fair market value of the share issued would seem to measure adequately the dividend value. In theory, the market price should adjust for the issuance of new shares in a stock dividend regardless of the number of shares issued. As a practical matter, however, it is unlikely that the market will fully adjust for very small stock dividends, which makes the shares' fair market value a reasonable measure of the value given up by the company.

How, then, does the company value the shares that are issued in a stock dividend? Since most stock dividends are for relatively small percentages of the shares issued (similar to the second extreme example), most companies account for them by using the shares' fair market value as at the date of declaration.

The market price that is used to record the issuance of a small stock dividend should be the market price on the date the dividend is declared. Unlike a cash or property dividend, the board of directors has the power to revoke the stock dividend at any time prior to its actual issuance. This means that the dividend does not represent a legal liability to the company on the date of declaration. For this reason, some companies do not record an entry on the date of declaration. If an entry is recorded, the credit part of the entry is made to a shareholders' equity account called Stock Dividends Issuable and not to a Dividends Payable account. Upon issuance, the credit is made to the shares account and the Stock Dividends Issuable account is removed.

To illustrate, let's suppose that a company decides to issue a 15% stock dividend when 100,000 shares are outstanding and a share's market price is $30. The following entries would be made for the declaration and issuance.

HELPFUL HINT:

When a stock dividend is declared, a liability account is not credited. Liability accounts signal that an asset or another liability will be used to satisfy the original liability. In the case of a stock dividend, no assets will be used, nor will another liability be created. It is, therefore, appropriate to credit a shareholders' equity account rather than a liability.

SMALL STOCK DIVIDEND ENTRIES

Declaration		
Dividends declared (SE)	450,000	
Stock dividend issuable (SE)		450,000
Issuance		
Stock dividend issuable (SE)	450,000	
Common shares (SE)		450,000

Stock Splits

Another transaction that is very similar to a stock dividend is a stock split. A stock split is usually stated as a ratio. A two-for-one stock split is one in which each share currently held by shareholders is exchanged for two new shares. When this is done, the numbers of shares authorized and outstanding are adjusted to compensate for the increase in the number of shares. In a two-for-one split, the number of shares outstanding is doubled. Splits typically involve large numbers of shares, and the arguments discussed earlier with regard to large stock dividends apply here as well. The additional shares mean no increase or decrease in the company's value, so the shares' market price simply adjusts to compensate for the split. Note the following information from WestJet Ltd.

WESTJET LTD., 2004

EXHIBIT 11-3

WestJet stock has been split three times since it went public on July 13, 1999. The first three-for-two split took place on May 10, 2000, as approved by WestJet shareholders on May 4, 2000. The second three-for-two split occurred on May 1, 2002, as approved by shareholders on April 25, 2002. The third three-for-two split occurred on May 5, 2004 as approved by shareholders on April 28, 2004.

Source: www.westjet.ca.

In accounting for a stock split, there is no change in the dollar amounts of any of the shareholders' equity accounts. No journal entry is made in the accounting system. The only change is that the number of shares issued and outstanding changes. This change can be accomplished with an informal or memorandum entry in the accounting system.

Why would a company want to double or triple the number of shares outstanding? The main reason is that a stock split improves the marketability of a company's shares. As a company grows, the market value of its shares generally rises. The share price can get quite high. As the price rises, fewer investors have the necessary funds to buy the shares. To lower the price so that it is within reach of more investors, the company may split its shares, which will cut the market price per share. IBM, for example, has split its shares numerous times since its incorporation as its price per share escalated.

Stock Options

A stock option on common shares is an agreement between two parties to either buy or sell shares at a fixed price at some future date. One type of option is granted by a company to its employees, which allows them to purchase the company's shares at a fixed price. This type of option is generally used as a form of compensation and as an incentive to employees. If employees are also shareholders, they may work harder for the company because they are owners as well. If the company grows because of their efforts, they can share in that growth by having shares that are increasing in value. For example, it was reported in many newspapers in 1996 that an executive with the Potash Company of Saskatchewan earned almost $3 million by cashing in stock options, buying 12,900 shares from the company at $17.50 and selling them the same day at $102.50 and then buying 22,500 shares at $25.50 and selling them at $104.125. You might wonder why the price the executive paid was so low. The stock option plans were probably created several years before the executive exercised the options. At the time the plans were created, those prices of $17.50 and $22.50 may not have been so different from the market price at the time. It is not uncommon for large corporations to compensate their senior executives with stock option plans. It is also not uncommon for the exercise price on those plans to be significantly below the market value. If, through effective management, the executive can increase the company's value, which will translate into an increase in the market value of the company's shares, both the executive and the company benefit.

Stock option plans offered to employees who are not top executives often have exercise prices closer to the market price at the time the plan was created. The idea behind these plans is similar to the rationale behind the executive plans. The plan provides an incentive for the employees to work hard to improve the company's performance so that the shares' market price exceeds the exercise price. When the time comes for employees to exercise their options, they pay the exercise price, obtain the shares, and can either sell them for the current market price and realize a profit, or continue to hold the shares in hopes that the price will go up even further. Obviously, if the share price never exceeds the exercise price, the employees will not exercise their options.

Companies normally disclose details regarding their stock option plans. Exhibit 11-4 shows the stock option plan outstanding for **Sleeman Breweries Ltd.** on December 27, 2003.

Note that the plan is for company employees. The exercise price varies from a low of $5.00 to a high of $11.35 and the stock options generally have a term of 5 to 10 years after the date of grant. The market price on December 31, 2003, was just under $10.00. At that time, there were stock options that were exercisable at an average price of $5.00 per share. The probability of these options being exercised is high.

EXHIBIT 11-4
PART A

SLEEMAN BREWERIES LTD. 2003 ANNUAL REPORT

13. STOCK OPTION PLAN

The Company maintains two discretionary employee stock option plans. Under the terms of the plans, the Board of Directors determines stock option allocations to employees. Stock options generally have a term of five to ten years and each grant typically vests one-third per year over the following three years.

A summary of the status of the Company's stock option plans as of December 27, 2003 and December 28, 2002 and changes during the years then ended are as follows:

	2003 Units	2003 Weighted Average Exercise Price	2002 Units	2002 Weighted Average Exercise Price
Outstanding, at beginning of year	1,341,195	$ 7.57	1,620,544	$ 7.46
Granted	150,000	9.94	48,862	10.15
Exercised	(177,895)	7.46	(309,911)	7.38
Forfeited	(41,945)	10.05	(18,300)	7.80
Outstanding, at end of year	1,271,355	$ 7.85	1,341,195	$ 7.57

SLEEMAN BREWERIES LTD. 2003 ANNUAL REPORT

EXHIBIT 11-4
PART B

A summary of the options issued and exercisable as at December 27, 2003 is as follows:

Exercise prices	Options outstanding			Options Exercisable	
	Number outstanding	Weighted average remaining term	Weighted average exercise price	Number exercisable	Weighted average exercise price
$5.00	65,000	1.52 years	$5.00	65,000	$5.00
$7.00	318,025	2.68 years	$7.00	318,025	$7.00
$7.75	416,500	4.13 years	$7.75	416,500	$7.75
$7.80	252,968	1.51 years	$7.80	212,890	$7.80
$9.76	35,000	4.70 years	$9.76	–	$9.76
$10.00	115,000	4.96 years	$10.00	–	$10.00
$10.15	38,862	3.21 years	$10.15	12,954	$10.15
$11.35	30,000	2.70 years	$11.35	20,000	$11.35
	1,271,355			1,045,369	

Options granted in 2003

The fair value of each option grant is estimated on the date of grant using the Black-Scholes option pricing model with the following weighted average assumptions used for grants during the period: dividend yield of 0%; expected volatility of 25%; risk-free interest rate of 3.5%; and an expected life of 4 years. The compensation cost that has been charged against income for the two plans for grants in the current year is $28 (2002 – nil).

Options granted in 2002

If the Company had determined compensation cost related to its stock option plan based on the fair value at the grant dates for awards granted during the period beginning December 30, 2001 through to December 28, 2002, the Company's net earnings per share would have been reduced to the pro forma amounts indicated below:

	Year ended December 27, 2003	Year ended, December 28, 2002
Net earnings as reported	$ 12,253	$ 12,321
Net earnings - pro forma	$ 12,221	$ 12,280
Net earnings per share as reported	$ 0.77	$ 0.79
Net earnings per share - pro forma	$ 0.77	$ 0.79
Diluted earnings per share as reported	$ 0.76	$ 0.77
Diluted earnings per share - pro forma	$ 0.75	$ 0.77

The fair value of each option grant was estimated on the date of grant using the Black-Scholes option pricing model with the following weighted average assumptions used for grants during the period: dividend yield of 0%; expected volatility of 27%; risk-free interest rate of 5%; and an expected life of 4 years.

During 2003, 150,000 new options were granted, 177,895 were exercised, and 41,945 were cancelled or expired (forfeited).

With respect to stock option plans, one major question for accounting purposes is whether to record compensation expense for this type of incentive-based plan. When options are granted, most of them are not immediately worth anything since the exercise price may be close to, or even above, the current share price. In addition, some stock option plans allow employees to exercise them only after a certain period of time, and only if they are still employed by the company. So, even if the option appears to be worth something, an employee may not be able to benefit immediately from the granting of the option.

If an option is priced at or above the current market price, does that mean it is worthless? The answer is a qualified no. Employees may not be able to, nor do they have to, exercise the options immediately. There is generally an extended period of time over which the employees can exercise the option. There may, however, be an **expiration date** specified, after which the option can no longer be exercised. The option will be of some value (in present-value terms) if there is some probability that the share price will exceed the exercise price before the expiration date. The more likely this is, the higher the value of the option.

Regardless of whether the stock option plans appear to have value or not, they generally cannot be traded because they are restricted to the employees to whom they are issued. Therefore, the value of employee stock options is difficult to establish. Because they do not trade, the value of employee stock options can only be estimated. Financing methods have been developed that enable accountants to determine a value for the option. You can see in the Sleeman Breweries example in Exhibit 11-4 that the company used the Black-Scholes option pricing model to determine a fair value of the option grants issued in 2003. The difference between the calculated value and the exercise price is recorded as compensation expense by the company over the period between the date of the grant and the date when the options are exercisable.

When the employee exercises the option (buys the shares from the company at the stated price), the company normally recognizes the receipt of the proceeds from the employee and the issuance of common shares. The shares are valued at the amount of cash received by the company plus an amount equal to the amount that was recorded as compensation expense. Thus, in the accounting system, the shares are recorded at or close to their fair value.

AN INTERNATIONAL PERSPECTIVE

Reports from Other Countries

The accounting for the issuance and retirement of common shares is fairly standard across different countries. The biggest difference between Canada and some other countries is the establishment of reserves. Reserves in other countries can be used to set aside retained earnings in separate accounts so that they are unavailable to pay dividends. The part set aside is termed "appropriated retained earnings" and the amount remaining is called "unappropriated retained earnings." Another way reserves can be used is to record changes in the value of assets or liabilities that do not pass through the income statement. In Canada, these reserves do not affect earnings for the period and are only allowed under very specific circumstances. In the United Kingdom, property, plant, and equipment can be revalued based on market values. The increase (or decrease) in value does not pass through the income statement, but is instead recorded in a separate account in shareholders' equity. In Japan, several types of reserves are permitted in the shareholders' equity section. A portion of the balance sheet and a footnote for **Nippon Steel Corporation** are shown in Exhibit 11-5. These disclosures illustrate the use of shareholders' equity reserves. The "reserve for revaluation of land" arose when the company revalued its land according to Japan's Law concerning the Revaluation of Land. The company determined that the land's market value was higher than its current carrying value and, therefore, increased it on the balance sheet and recorded the reserve.

In Canada, use of the word "reserve" is generally discouraged because users of financial statements may believe it refers to cash that has been set aside, which is erroneous. In Canada, its use is limited to references to appropriations of retained earnings.

NIPPON STEEL CORPORATION 2003 ANNUAL REPORT

EXHIBIT 11-5
PART A

SHAREHOLDERS'EQUITY
Common stock:

Authorized - 9,917,077,000 shares			
Issued and outstanding - 6,806,980,977 shares as of March 31, 2003 and 2002	419,524	419,524	*3,490,224*
Additional paid-in capital	105,518	105,518	*877,857*
Retained earnings (Note 11)	278,315	338,565	*2,315,434*
Unrealized gains on revaluation of land(Note 6)	6,621	7,488	*55,090*
Unrealized gains on available-for-sale securities(Note 15)	21,243	54,898	*176,738*
Foreign currency translation adjustments	(20,958)	(18,822)	*(174,364)*
Less: Treasury stock, at cost (159,415,679 shares at March 31, 2003)	(20,822)	(21)	*(173,230)*
Total shareholders'equity	789,443	907,150	*6,567,749*
Total liabilities and shareholders'equity	¥ 3,757,175	¥ 4,030,596	*$ 31,257,702*

6. Revaluation of Land

(Year ended March 31, 2003)
Revaluation of land used for business purpose was carried out in accordance with the "Law concerning Revaluation of Land" and relating amendments for certain of Nippon Steel Corporation's consolidated subsidiaries and affiliates to which the equity method is applied.

Revaluation differences computed by consolidated subsidiaries, net of tax and minority interest, which were charged to "Deffered tax assets and liabilities on revaluation of land" and "Minority interest in consolidated subsidiaries", respectively, were recorded as a separate component of shareholders' equity as of "Unrealized gains on revaluation of land".

Additionally, revaluation differences accounted for by affiliates were recorded as a separate component of shareholders' equity as of "Unrealized gains on revaluation of land" in proportion to the equity rate.

• Method of revaluation
Calculations were made in accordance with the Law concerning Revaluation of Land

(Revaluation made on March 31, 2000)
• Excess of carrying amounts of the revalued land over fair value at the end of March 31, 2003: ¥14,181 million *($117,981 thousand)*

(Revaluation made on March 31, 2002)
• Excess of carrying amounts of the revalued land over fair value at the end of March 31, 2003: ¥274 million *($2,283 thousand)*

(Year ended March 31, 2002)
Revaluation of land used for business purpose was carried out in accordance with the "Law concerning Revaluation of Land"and relating amendments for certain of Nippon Steel Corporation's consolidated subsidiaries and affiliates to which the equity method is applied.

Revaluation differences computed by consolidated subsidiaries, net of tax and minority interest, which were charged to "Deffered tax assets and liabilities on revaluation of land" and "Minority interest in consolidated subsidiaries", respectively, were recorded as a separate component of share-

EXHIBIT 11-5
PART B **NIPPON STEEL CORPORATION 2003 ANNUAL REPORT**

holders' equity as of "Unrealized gains on revaluation of land".

Additionally, revaluation differences accounted for by affiliates were recorded as a separate component of shareholders' equity as of "Unrealized gains on revaluation of land" in proportion to the equity rate.
• Method of revaluation
  Calculations were made in accordance with the Law concerning Revaluation of Land

(Revaluation made on March 31, 2000)
• Excess of carrying amounts of the revalued land over fair value at the end of March 31, 2002: ¥10,936 million

(Revaluation made on March 31, 2002)
• Book-value of the land for business before the revaluation thereof: ¥2,199 million
• Book-value of the land for business after the revaluation thereof: ¥5,675 million

STATEMENT OF RETAINED EARNINGS

LEARNING OBJECTIVE 5

Explain the purpose of the statement of retained earnings.

In the preceding discussions of shares and dividends, we made several references to the use of the retained earnings account. Many companies summarize the changes in their retained earnings in a separate statement, the Statement of Retained Earnings. The format of this statement is very simple. It starts with the opening balance of the retained earnings at the beginning of the year. Then it shows the net income or loss for the year, which comes directly from the income statement. This is followed by the dividends declared in the year. Next appear any other items that affect retained earnings. Finally, the balance of the retained earnings at the end of the year appears. The end balance is the one that appears on the current balance sheet.

An example is shown in Exhibit 11-6 for **High Liner Foods Incorporated.** Note that the balance of the retained earnings at the beginning of the 2003 fiscal year was $37,080 thousand, net income for the year was $46,119 thousand, and dividends of $7,940 thousand were declared. Note that High Liner Foods paid dividends on four different classes of shares: common, second preference shares on which there were dividends in arrears, and Class C and D preference shares. The end balance of $75,259 thousand is the amount that appears for retained earnings on the December 31, 2003, balance sheet.

EXHIBIT 11-6 **HIGH LINER FOODS INC. 2003 ANNUAL REPORT**

CONSOLIDATED STATEMENTS OF RETAINED EARNINGS
For the fifty-three weeks ended January 3, 2004
(wth comparative figures for the fifty-two weeks ended December 28, 2002)

(in thousands of Canadian dollars)	Fiscal 2003 $	Fiscal 2002 $
Balance, beginning of period	**37,080**	29,289
Net income for the period	**46,119**	10,242
Dividends		
Common Shares	**(537)**	-
Second Preference Shares		
Current	**(1,078)**	(1,017)
Arrears	**(6,260)**	(1,362)
Class C and D Preference Share	**(65)**	(72)
Balance, end of period	**75,259**	37,080

See accompanying notes to the financial statements.

FINANCIAL STATEMENT ANALYSIS

The Price/Earnings Ratio

LEARNING OBJECTIVE 6

Calculate and interpret the price/earnings ratio and the return on shareholders' equity ratio, which are often used in decision-making.

A key ratio that involves shareholders' equity is earnings per share. We introduced this ratio in Chapter 3, and are returning to it now. Earnings per share provides a measure of the earnings relative to the number of common shares outstanding. It is useful for tracking the return per share earned by the company over time. This ratio can also be related to the current market price per share by calculating the multiple or price/earnings ratio. This is calculated as:

$$\frac{\text{Market price per share}}{\text{Earnings per share}}$$

The ratio relates the accounting earnings to the market price at which the shares trade. If two companies in the same industry had the same earnings per share of $5, and Company A's shares were selling for $25 and Company B's shares were selling for $50, the price/earnings ratios would be different. Company A's price/earnings ratio would be 5 ($25/$5) and Company B's would be 10 ($50/$5). The market is placing a higher value on Company B's shares. There are probably many reasons for the higher valuation, such as an assessment of higher earning potential in the future, a lower risk with respect to debt repayment, or an assessment of future market share. The price/earnings ratio for Le Château for 2004 and 2003 for the basic earnings per share was:

2004 $10.50 / 2.07 = 5.07
2003 $10.00 / 1.52 = 6.58

The price/earnings ratio did drop in 2004 although the shares' market price did not change very much.

When evaluating a company's price/earnings ratio, it is important to compare it with those of other companies in the same industry. This comparison gives the user information about how the market is valuing the company in relation to others.

The Return on Shareholders' Equity Ratio

Another useful indicator of return is return on shareholders' equity (ROE). This is a more general measure than earnings per share because it relates the net income available to common shares to the total of the common shareholders' equity. It is calculated as follows.

$$\text{ROE} = \frac{\text{Net income} - \text{Preferred dividends}}{\text{Average common shareholders' equity}}$$

Preferred dividends need to be subtracted from the net income because preferred shareholders have a prior claim on the income. Preferred dividends must be declared before dividends on common shares. We want this ratio to determine a measure of return to the common shares only. Common shareholders' equity is the shareholders' equity less any amounts that represent owners other than common shareholders. This means that the amount in the preferred shares account would need to be subtracted from the total shareholders' equity to arrive at common shareholders' equity.

This ratio tells you the return the common shareholder is earning on each dollar of income. For Le Château in 2004 and 2003, that return is $0.19 ($10,648 ÷ ($61,162 + $51,492) ÷ 2) and $0.16 ($7,562 ÷ ($51,492 + $45,694) ÷ 2), respectively. Le Château has no preferred shares issued so all the net income accrues to the common shareholders. The return to common shareholders increased in 2004 because earnings increased that year. Another way to think about this return is as a percentage. The common shareholders earned a 19% return on their investment in Le Château in 2004 based on the earnings of that year.

A more detailed discussion of other analyses that involve shareholders' equity can be found in Chapter 12.

SUMMARY

This chapter discussed the most common forms of business organization: sole proprietorships, partnerships, and corporations. Advantages and disadvantages for each form were discussed. Because the predominant business structure is the corporation, this form was discussed in more detail. Particular attention was paid to shares. Corporations authorize different types or classes of shares with the intention of attracting capital investment. These shares come with different rights and privileges, which were also outlined in the chapter.

Shareholders can be given a return from the company in the form of dividends. Dividends can come in various forms: cash, property, or stock. This section of the chapter concluded with a brief discussion about stock splits and employee stock option plans.

Because the chapter concerns shareholders' equity, we discussed the fourth financial statement, the statement of retained earnings. An example from High Liner Foods Corporation was included as an illustration.

The chapter concluded with two ratios: the price/earnings ratio and the return on shareholders' equity ratio. These two ratios help investors evaluate the current return to common shareholders.

This concludes the discussion of the primary accounts on the balance sheet. In the final chapter of the book, financial statement analysis is summarized. You have already been introduced to most of the ratios discussed in Chapter 12. There is a further discussion of complex companies in Appendix B to help you understand some issues behind consolidated financial statements.

SUMMARY PROBLEM

Additional Demonstration Problems

The Balukas Company had the following shareholders' equity section balances at December 31, 2005.

Common shares	$4,700,000
(Unlimited number of common shares authorized, 240,000 shares issued)	
Retained earnings	4,000,000
Total shareholders' equity	$8,700,000

During 2006, the following transactions occurred.

    a. On January 2, 2006, Balukas repurchased 5,000 of its own common shares at $35 per share and immediately cancelled them.

    b. On March 15, 2006, Balukas issued 10,000 new shares and received proceeds of $40 per share.

    c. On June 29, 2006, Balukas declared and paid a 10% stock dividend. The market price of Balukas' shares on June 29, 2006, was $45 per share.

    d. On June 30, 2006, Balukas declared a cash dividend of $3.00 per share to shareholders of record on July 15, 2006, payable on July 31, 2006.

    e. On September 1, 2006, Balukas issued 100,000 new shares at $50 per share.

    f. On December 31, 2006, Balukas declared a four-for-one stock split.

Required:

    1. Construct journal entries for each of the transactions as they occurred during 2006.

    2. Explain why no journal entry was recorded for transaction f).

SUGGESTED SOLUTION TO SUMMARY PROBLEM

1. a. Repurchase of Common Shares and Cancellation Entry

Common shares (SE)	97,917[a]	
Retained earnings (SE)	77,083	
Cash (A)		175,000

[a]($4,700,000 \div 240,000 \times 5,000) = \$97,917$

  b. Common Share Issuance Entry:

Cash (A)	400,000	
Common Shares (SE)		400,000

  c. Small Stock Dividend Entries:

Declaration

Dividend issuable (SE)	1,102,500[b]	
Stock dividend issuable (SE)		1,102,500

Issuance

Stock dividend issuable (SE)	1,102,500	
Common shares (SE)		1,102,500

[b]Number of shares = 240,000 − 5,000 + 10,000 = 245,000 shares

245,000 shares × 10% × $45 per share = $1,102,500

  d. On June 30, 2002:

Dividends declared (SE)	808,500[c]	
Dividends payable (L)		808,500

On July 31,2002:

Dividends payable (L)	808,500	
Cash (A)		808,500

[c](245,000 shares + 24,500 shares) = 269,500 shares

269,500 shares × $3.00 per share = $808,500

e. Issue of New Shares:

Cash (A)	5,000,000	
Common Shares (SE)		5,000,000

f. No entry is needed. However, a memorandum entry could be made to indicate that the number of shares outstanding has changed from 369,500 to 1,478,000.

2. During a stock split or a large stock dividend, the number of shares increases but the company's value does not change. The purpose of the stock split is to lower the current market price of the company's shares. In the four-for-one split that was used in the sample problem, the market price would immediately drop to one quarter of the price before the split. The lower price would make the shares accessible to more investors.

SYNONYMS

Exercise price/Strike price/Option price
Property dividends/Dividends in kind

GLOSSARY

Articles of incorporation A document filed with federal or provincial regulatory authorities when a business incorporates under that jurisdiction. The articles include, among other items, the authorized number of shares and dividend preferences for each class of shares that is to be issued.

Authorized shares The maximum number of shares that a company is authorized to issue under its articles of incorporation.

Capital account An account used in a partnership or proprietorship to record the investment and accumulated earnings of each owner.

Common shares Certificates that represent portions of ownership in a corporation. These shares usually carry a right to vote.

Controlling interest The holding of enough common shares (usually greater than 50%) such that the investor is able to set the strategic, operating, investing, and financing policies for the company.

Convertible preferred shares Preferred shares that are exchangeable or convertible into a specified number of common shares.

Corporation A form of business in which the shareholders have limited liability and the business entity is taxed directly. Shareholders receive distributions from the entity in the form of dividends.

Cumulative preferred shares Preferred shares that accumulate dividends that are not declared from one period to the next. These accumulated dividends, called dividends in arrears, must be paid before a dividend can be declared for common shareholders.

Date of declaration The date the board of directors votes to declare a dividend. On this date, the dividend becomes legally payable to shareholders.

Date of payment The date on which a dividend is paid to shareholders.

Date of record The date on which a shareholder must own the shares in order to receive the dividend from a share.

Dividend declaration An action by a corporation's board of directors that legally obliges the corporation to pay a dividend.

Dividends Payments to shareholders from the total net income retained by a company in the Retained Earnings account.

Dividends in arrears Dividends on cumulative preferred shares that have not yet been declared from a prior year.

Dividends in kind Synonym for property dividend.

Drawing account An account used in a partnership or proprietorship to record the cash withdrawals by owners.

Ex-dividend day A date specified in the shares market on which the shares are sold without the most recently declared dividend.

Exercise price The price per share that is required to be paid by the holder of a stock option upon exercise.

Expiration date The date on which a stock option holder must either exercise the option or lose it.

General partners The partners who have unlimited liability in a limited partnership.

Issued shares The shares of a corporation that have been issued.

Legal capital The amount that is recorded in the common share account when the shares are first issued.

Limited liability A feature of share ownership that restricts the liability of shareholders to the amount they have invested in the corporation.

Limited partners The partners in a limited partnership that have limited liability.

Limited partnership A partnership that allows some partners to have limited liability (limited partners) and others to have unlimited liability (general partners).

Liquidating dividend A dividend paid to shareholders that exceeds the amount held in the retained earnings account.

Memorandum entry An entry made to record a stock split. No amounts are affected; only the record of the number of shares issued is affected.

Minority interest Synonym of noncontrolling interest.

Noncontrolling interest A block of shares owed by an investor that represents less that 50% of the outstanding shares.

No par value shares Shares that have no par value associated with them.

Outstanding shares The number of shares that are held by individuals or entities outside the corporation (which does not include treasury shares).

Paid-in capital The amount paid by an investor to purchase shares in a corporation when they are first issued.

Par value A value per share of common shares set in the articles of incorporation.

Participating preferred shares Preferred shares that can also participate in dividends declared beyond the level specified by the preferred shares; that is, beyond the fixed dividend payout specified in the preferred shares contract.

Partnership A form of business in which the owners have unlimited legal liability and the business entity is not taxed directly; the income from the entity passes through to the partners' individual tax returns.

Partnership agreement An agreement between the partners in a partnership that specifies how they will share in the risks and rewards of ownership.

Preemptive right The right of shareholders to share proportionately in new issuances of shares.

Preferred shares An ownership right in which the shareholder has some preference as to dividends; that is, if dividends are declared, the preferred shareholders receive them first. Other rights that are normally held by common shareholders may also be changed in preferred shares; for example, many issues of preferred shares are non-voting.

Property dividend A dividend that is satisfied with the transfer of some type of property other than cash.

Prospectus A document filed with a securities commission by a corporation when it wants to issue public debt or shares.

Redeemable preferred shares Preferred shares that can be bought back (redeemed) by the corporation under certain conditions and at a price stated in the articles of incorporation.

Retractable preferred shares Shares that can be sold back to the company (retired) at the shareholder's option. The price that must be paid for them and the periods of time within which they can be sold are specified in the articles of incorporation.

Sole proprietorship A form of business in which there is a single owner (sole proprietor). This form is characterized by unlimited liability to the owner and exemption from corporate taxation.

Stock dividend A distribution of additional common shares to shareholders. Existing shareholders receive shares in proportion to the number of shares they already own.

Stock option An option granted to an employee to buy shares at a fixed price, usually as part of an incentive compensation plan.

Stock split A distribution of new shares to shareholders. The new shares take the place of existing shares, and existing shareholders receive new shares in proportion to the number of old shares they already own.

Treasury shares Shares that are repurchased by a corporation and held internally. Repurchased shares are normally cancelled immediately upon purchase.

Unlimited liability A characteristic of sole proprietorships and partnerships where the owners are personally responsible for the liabilities incurred by the business entity.

ASSIGNMENT MATERIAL

Assessing Your Recall

Self-Assessment Quiz

11-1 Characterize the following forms of business in terms of the owners' legal liability and their tax status: corporations, sole proprietorships, partnerships, and limited partnerships.

11-2 Discuss the purpose and importance of a partnership agreement.

11-3 Describe what is contained in a company's articles of incorporation and what significance they have for the accounting system.

11-4 List and briefly describe the four rights that common shareholders typically have in a corporation.

11-5 Discuss how preferred shares differ from common shares.

11-6 Briefly describe what each of the following features means in a preferred share issue: participating, cumulative, convertible, and redeemable.

11-7 Briefly describe each of the following terms: authorized shares, issued shares, and outstanding shares.

11-8 Describe the process of declaring and paying a cash dividend, including information about the declaration date, date of record, and payment date.

11-9 Explain what property dividends are and why they are not used very often by companies.

11-10 Discuss the nature of a stock dividend and why a distinction is made between small and large stock dividends.

11-11 Compare and contrast a 100% stock dividend with a two-for-one stock split.

11-12 Explain why companies might declare a stock dividend rather than a cash dividend.

11-13 Discuss why companies issue employee stock options and what immediate and potential effects these options have on a company's financial results.

11-14 Explain why a company's shareholders might want an expense to be recognized related to the company's employee stock option plans.

11-15 Describe what the price/earnings ratio is intended to tell users about a company.

11-16 Explain why the return on shareholders' equity provides information on the rate of return to common shareholders only.

Applying Your Knowledge

11-17 **(Selecting a business entity)**

Indicate whether each of the following business entities is more likely to be established as a sole proprietorship (SP), a partnership (P), or a corporation (C). Provide reasons for your choice.

    a. A small legal practice set up by two recent law school graduates

    b. A restaurant with six locations in southern Alberta

    c. A second-hand outdoor equipment store owned by Rose Johnston

    d. A mining company operating in Quebec

    e. A family-owned farm in Saskatchewan

    f. A salmon fish farm off the coast of British Columbia

11-18   **(Selecting a business entity)**

Indicate whether each of the following business entities is more likely to be established as a sole proprietorship (SP), a partnership (P), or a corporation (C). Provide reasons for your choice.

    a. A spa opened by massage therapists Jo and Robin

    b. A local investment firm consisting of 25 financial advisors

    c. A national chain of hotels

    d. A security firm that supplies and trains guards for office towers and shopping malls

    e. One of the big four accounting firms

    f. An auto body shop owned by a mother and daughter

11-19   **(Business formation)**

Albert Wong just graduated from university and is planning to start his own software development company. He is trying to decide on the best form of business organization and is debating between setting up practice as a sole proprietor or establishing a corporate entity and serving as its president.

Required:

    a. What advantages would there be to operating as a sole proprietorship?

    b. What advantages would there be to operating as a corporation?

    c. Which form of business organization would his customers likely prefer? Why?

    d. Which form of business organization would his creditors likely prefer? Why?

    e. Which form of business would be most advantageous to Albert Wong if he anticipated that the business would grow rapidly? Why?

11-20   **(Business formation)**

Janice Allen just inherited a large amount of money from her grandfather. She intends to start her own architectural company and plans within a few years to expand the operation by bringing in other architects.

Required:

    a. What advantages would there be to operating as a sole proprietorship?

    b. What advantages would there be to beginning operations as a sole proprietorship and then switching to a partnership when she expands?

    c. What advantages would there be to operating as a corporation?

    d. Which form of business organization would her customers likely prefer? Why?

    e. Which form of business would be most advantageous to Janice Allen if she wanted to maintain control as the business expanded? Why?

11-21   (Equity transactions)

Southern Exposure Ltd. begins operations on January 2, 2006. During the year, the following transactions affect shareholders' equity.

1. Southern Exposure authorizes the issuance of 1 million common shares and 100,000 preferred shares, which pay a dividend of $2 per share.

2. 240,000 common shares are issued for $5 a share.

3. 15,000 preferred shares are issued for $14 per share.

4. The full annual dividend on the preferred shares is declared and paid.

5. A dividend of $0.10 per share is declared on the common shares but is not yet paid.

6. The company earns income of $120,000 for the year. (Can assume revenues of $720,000 and total expenses of $600,000.)

7. The dividends on the common shares are paid.

8. A 5% stock dividend is declared on the common shares and distributed. On the date of declaration, the shares' market price was $5.50.

Required:

a. Prepare journal entries to record the above transactions.

b. Prepare the shareholders' equity section of the balance sheet as at December 31, 2006.

c. Why would an investor choose to purchase the common shares rather than the preferred shares? Or vice versa?

11-22   (Equity transactions)

Four firefighters set up a corporation and plan to do small renovation and construction jobs between shifts at their regular job. During the first year, the following transactions occurred.

1. 20,000 common shares were issued to the four owners (5,000 shares each) at $4 per share. The company was authorized to issue up to 100,000 common shares.

2. 5,000 non-voting preferred shares were issued to people other than the owners at $10 per share. The company was authorized to issue 25,000 non-voting preferred shares.

3. A dividend of $1 per share was declared for the preferred shareholders.

4. The preferred dividend was paid.

5. The company purchased 2,500 of its own common shares from one of its owners, at an agreed price of $5 per share, and immediately cancelled them.

6. During the first year of operations the company earned income of $60,000. (Can assume revenues of $300,000 and total expenses of $240,000.)

Required:

a. Prepare journal entries to record the above transactions.

b. Prepare the shareholders' equity section of the balance sheet at the end of the first year.

c. Why would the owners have designated the preferred shares as non-voting?

11-23   (Equity transactions)

Green Grocers Ltd. had been operating for several years. At December 31, 2005, it had an unlimited number of common shares authorized and 300,000 shares issued at $25 per share. As well, there were 500,000 preferred shares authorized, 25,000 issued at $20 per share, and the balance in retained earnings was $2,610,000. The preferred shares paid an annual dividend of $2.00 per share. During 2006, the following transactions affecting shareholders' equity occurred.

1. 20,000 common shares were issued at $32 per share.

2. The preferred dividend for the year was declared and paid.

3. A 10% common stock dividend was declared when the shares' market price was $35. The shares were distributed one month after the declaration.

4. In early December 2006, a dividend of $1.50 per share was declared on the common shares. The date of record was December 15, 2006. The dividend would be paid in the following year.

5. The company earned income of $1,420,000. (Can assume revenues of $8.6 million and total expenses of $7.18 million.)

6. On December 31, 2006, the company declared a two-for-one stock split on common shares.

Required:

a. Prepare journal entries to record the above transactions.

b. Prepare the shareholders' equity section of the balance sheet as at the end of 2006.

11-24   (Share issuance, repurchase, and cancellation)

On December 31, 2005, the shareholders' equity section of Piccadilly Ltd.'s balance sheet appears as follows.

Preferred shares, no par, non-voting,	
$8, redeemable at 103%,	
100,000 shares authorized, 30,000 shares issued	$ 3,000,000
Common shares, no par, unlimited number authorized,	
500,000 shares issued	4,780,000
Retained earnings	2,120,000
Total shareholders' equity	$ 9,900,000

During 2006, the following events occurred.

1. Piccadilly issued 120,000 additional common shares for $15 per share.

2. The company declared and paid the dividend on the preferred shares for the first half of the year.

3. Immediately after paying the preferred dividend for the first half of the year, the company repurchased and cancelled all the preferred shares at the redemption price of $103 per share.

4. The company repurchased 50,000 common shares at the market price of $12 per share and immediately cancelled the shares.

5. The company earned income of $750,000 for 2006. (Can assume revenues of $2,500,000 and total expenses of $1,750,000.)

Required:

a. Prepare journal entries to record the above transactions.

b. Prepare the shareholders' equity section of the balance sheet as at December 31, 2006.

c. Give possible reasons why Piccadilly might change its equity financing by eliminating the preferred shares and issuing more common shares.

d. Give possible reasons why Piccadilly might buy back and cancel some of its outstanding common shares.

e. If you owned 50,000 common shares on January 1, 2006, and did not buy or sell any shares during the year, how has your ability to influence the management of the company changed over the year? Did you need to consider the existence of preferred shares at January 1, 2006? Explain.

11-25   (Stock dividends)

Sealand Company has 60,000 common shares outstanding. Because it wants to use its cash flow for other purposes, the company has decided to issue stock dividends to its shareholders. The market price of each Sealand Company share is $24. Give the journal entries recording the issuance of the stock dividend if:

a. The company decides to issue a 10% stock dividend.

b. The company decides to issue a 100% stock dividend.

c. What should happen to the market price of the company's shares in either situation?

11-26   (Change in shareholders' equity)

The shareholders' equity of Deer Ltd. at the end of 2006 and 2005 appears as follows.

	2006	2005
Preferred shares, no par, $2 cumulative, 2,000,000 shares authorized, 25,000 shares issued	$200,000	$200,000
Common shares, no par, 5,000,000 shares authorized, 1,200,000 shares issued (2005 − 1,000,000 shares)	5,000,000	4,000,000
Retained earnings	3,920,000	3,160,000
Total shareholders' equity	$9,120,000	$7,360,000

During 2006, Deer paid a total of $125,000 in cash dividends.

Required:

a. Assuming the preferred shares were not in arrears, how was the $125,000 in cash dividends distributed between the two classes of shares?

b. Assuming the preferred share dividends were in arrears for one year, how was the $125,000 in cash dividends distributed between the two classes of shares?

c. Both the common shares and the retained earnings changed during the year. Provide journal entries that would account for the changes.

11-27   (Equity transactions)

The following information relates to the shareholders' equity section of McLaren Ltd. (in thousands).

	Dec. 31, 2006	Dec. 31, 2005
Preferred shares (15,000 shares issued and outstanding)	$4,500	$ 4,500
Common shares (250,000 shares issued and outstanding at end of 2005)	?	6,250
Retained earnings	6,400	3,750
Total shareholders' equity	?	$14,500

Early in 2006, 30,000 common shares were issued at a price of $28 per share. Mid way through the year, cash dividends of $210,000 and $300,000 were paid to common shareholders and preferred shareholders, respectively. Just before year end, the company acquired 15,000 treasury shares at $30 per share and cancelled them. Immediately thereafter, the company issued 5,000 common shares under employee stock option plans at $25 per share.

Required:

a. Calculate the ending balance in common shares at the end of 2006.

b. Determine the number of common shares issued and the number outstanding at the end of 2006.

c. Calculate the amount of net income reported in 2006.

11-28 (Equity transactions)

Give the journal entries for the following shareholders' equity transactions of Green Sleeves Apparel Company.

a. On January 10, 2005, the articles of incorporation are filed with the provincial secretary. The company is authorized to issue 5 million common shares and 1 million cumulative preferred shares, which carry a dividend of $8.00 per share.

b. On January 12, 2005, the company issues 125,000 common shares at $15 each.

c. On January 20, 2005, 25,000 of the preferred shares are issued at $80 per share.

d. On January 25, 2005, the assets of Tritex Knits Ltd. are acquired in exchange for 20,000 common shares and 10,000 preferred shares. The market value of the common shares was $16 and that of the preferred shares $85 on this date. The assets acquired and their relative fair market values are: land, $250,000; building, $325,000; equipment, $410,000; and inventory, $185,000.

e. No dividends are paid in 2005 on either the preferred or common shares.

f. Net income in each of 2005 and 2006 is $1 million. (Can assume revenues of $5 million and total expenses of $4 million each year.)

g. In 2006, a $2 per share dividend is declared on the common shares, to be paid in early 2007. A cash dividend is paid to the preferred shareholders such that there are no dividends in arrears at December 31, 2006.

11-29 (Income statement and statement of retained earnings)

The following are selected account balances from Kimberley Ltd.'s trial balance on December 31, 2006.

	Debits	Credits
Assets	$14,330,000	
Liabilities		$4,545,000
Amortization expense	65,000	
Common dividends declared	150,000	
Common shares		4,500,000
Contributed surplus		90,000
Cost of goods sold	740,000	
Interest expense	60,000	
Miscellaneous expense	230,000	
Preferred dividends declared	60,000	
Preferred shares		2,500,000
Retained earnings		2,640,000
Revenues		1,620,000
Wage expense	260,000	
	$15,895,000	$15,895,000

Required:

a. Prepare the 2006 income statement and retained earnings statement, in good form, for Kimberley Ltd. (Hint: At what date is the retained earnings balance of $2,640,000 measured? How can you tell?)

b. Based on this information, does it appear likely that Kimberley will be able to continue the common and preferred dividends at similar levels in the future? Explain.

c. Why might viewing Kimberley Ltd.'s income statements for the previous few years help you in answering b)? What other information would you find helpful in reaching a conclusion?

User Perspective Problems

11-30 (New share issuance)

You are a loan officer at a bank. You helped Cedar Ltd. arrange a $1.5-million, 20-year mortgage with your bank just six months ago. Cedar Ltd. has just announced an issuance of new shares from which it intends to raise $5 million. How do you think this new issuance will affect the bank's outstanding loan? Identify some positive outcomes and some negative ones.

11-31 (Price/earnings ratio)

As a stock analyst, explain the importance and limitations of the price/earnings ratio.

11-32 (Capital stock disclosures)

As a shareholder, list the information you would expect to find in the financial statements regarding the company's different classes of shares issued, and why you would find this information valuable.

11-33 (Cash dividends)

You have been considering buying some common shares of Sherlock Ltd. Sherlock has 1.5 million common shares outstanding. The company has been through difficult times but is now doing better. Your main concern is whether you will receive cash dividends. In addition to the common shares, the company has 50,000 shares of $8, no par, Class A preferred outstanding that are non-cumulative and non-participating. The company also has 10,000 shares of $7.50, no par, Class B preferred outstanding. These shares are non-participating but are cumulative. The normal dividend was paid on both classes of preferred shares until last year, when no dividends were paid. This year, however, Sherlock is doing well and is expecting net income of $2.1 million. The company has not yet declared its annual dividends but has indicated that it plans to pay total dividends equal to 35% of net income. If you immediately buy 100 shares of Sherlock Ltd. on the stock market:

a. What amount of common dividend would you expect to receive?

b. What amount of common dividend would you expect to receive if the Class B preferred shares were non-cumulative?

11-34 (Stock dividends and splits)

The shareholders' equity section of Bonanza Ltd.'s balance sheet appears as follows on December 31, 2005.

Common shares, 5,000,000 authorized,	
400,000 issued and outstanding	$2,400,000
Retained earnings	3,165,000
Total shareholders' equity	$5,565,000

Near the beginning of 2006, Bonanza declared and distributed a 5% stock dividend. At the date of declaration, the common shares were selling for $65 per share. By the end of October, the share price had risen to $90 per share. Bonanza's board of directors decided to split the shares five-for-one. Late in December, the board declared a cash dividend on the common shares of $1.50 per share, payable in early January 2007. (In past years, the dividend had generally been about $6 per share.) During 2006, Bonanza Ltd. earned net income of $3,110,000.

Required:

a. What effect did each dividend (i.e., the stock dividend and the cash dividend) have on Bonanza's financial statements?

b. Prepare the shareholders' equity section of Bonanza's balance sheet at December 31, 2006.

c. What reasons might the company have for declaring a stock dividend? What is your assessment of these reasons?

d. What reasons might the company have for splitting its shares? What is your assessment of these reasons?

e. If you were one of Bonanza's common shareholders, would you be happy or unhappy with the stock dividend and split? Why? What do you think about the reduction in the cash dividend from $6 to $1.50? Explain.

11-35 (Retained earnings and dividends)

You have recently been considering investing in some of Stanley Ltd.'s common shares. The company has been relatively profitable over the years and prospects for the future look good. However, it has recently had to make heavy expenditures for new capital assets. The company's summarized balance sheet at the end of 2005 is as follows.

Cash	$ 37,500
Other current assets	740,500
Capital assets (net)	4,702,000
Total	$5,480,000
Current liabilities	$ 414,000
Long-term debt	2,000,000
Common shares	1,000,000
Retained earnings	2,066,000
Total	$5,480,000

The company has 150,000 common shares outstanding and its earnings per share has increased by at least 10% in each of the last 10 years. In several recent years, earnings per share increased by more than 14%. Given the company's earnings and the amount of retained earnings, you judge that it could easily pay cash dividends of $3 or $4 per share, resulting in hardly a dent in retained earnings.

Required:

a. Discuss whether it is likely that you would receive a cash dividend from Stanley during the next year if you were to purchase its shares.

b. Discuss whether it is likely that you would receive a cash dividend from Stanley during the next five years if you were to purchase its shares.

c. In making an investment decision, would it help you to know whether Stanley has paid dividends in the past? Explain.

d. Suppose Stanley borrowed $2 million cash on a five-year bank loan to provide working capital and additional operating flexibility. While no collateral would be required, the loan would stipulate that no dividends be paid in any year in which the ratio of long-term debt to equity was greater than 60%.

   1. If Stanley were to enter into the loan agreement, would you be likely to receive a dividend next year?

   2. Would you be likely to receive a dividend at some point in the next five years? (Hint: What would you expect to happen to the balance sheet values for long-term debt and for equity?)

11-36 (Return on investment)

Oscar Corporation's balance sheet at December 31, 2006, appears as follows.

Cash	$ 46,000
Other current assets	820,000
Capital assets (net)	5,280,000
Total	$6,146,000
Current liabilities	$ 410,000
Long-term debt	1,000,000
Preferred shares	500,000
Common shares	1,500,000
Retained earnings	2,736,000
Total	$6,146,000

For the year just ended, Oscar reported net income of $440,000. During the year, the company declared preferred dividends of $40,000 and common dividends of $220,000.

Required:

a. Calculate the following ratios for Oscar.

   1. Return on assets

   2. Return on long-term capital (long-term debt + shareholders' equity)

   3. Return on common shareholders' equity

b. Assume the company had issued $1 million worth of common shares at the beginning of last year, and paid off the long-term debt. The company's interest expense last year related to its long-term debt was $50,000 for the year, after taxes.

   1. What would the return on common shareholders' equity have been?

2. Would shareholders have been better or worse off?

3. Would switching from debt to equity financing always have this effect on the return on common shareholders' equity? Explain.

c. Suppose the long-term debt remains as shown on the balance sheet, but last year the company had issued an additional $500,000 worth of common shares and used the proceeds to redeem and cancel the preferred shares.

1. What would the return on common shareholders' equity have been?

2. Would shareholders have been better or worse off?

3. Would switching from preferred equity financing to common equity financing always have this effect on the return on common shareholders' equity? Explain.

Reading and Interpreting
Published Financial Statements

11-37 (Capital stock)

Note 8 to the 2004 financial statements of **Le Château, Inc.** is shown in Exhibit 11-1. All dollar amounts are in thousands.

Financial Statement Analysis Assignments

Required:

a. Describe the differences between the Class A Subordinate Voting Shares and Class B Voting Shares with respect to:

1. Their ability to influence the selection of management and company decision-making.

2. The amount and priority of expected dividends.

b. If you own 100,000 Class A Subordinate Voting Shares, what proportion of total votes do you control? If you own 100,000 Class B Voting Shares, what proportion of total votes do you control?

c. Why would investors choose to purchase the Class A rather than the Class B shares? Or vice versa?

d. Why might Class B shareholders choose to convert their shareholdings into Class A shares, as described in principal feature [e]?

11-38 (Share transactions)

An excerpt from Note 13 to the consolidated financial statements for **CHC Helicopter Corporation** is shown in Exhibit 11-7. All amounts are in thousands, except for per share amounts.

Required:

a. Reconstruct all the journal entries that affected CHC's Class A subordinate voting shares and the Class B multiple voting shares during the year ended April 30, 2003.

b. Explain the purpose of the table entitled "Class A subordinate voting shares that would be issued upon conversion of the following." Why is such information useful to investors?

c. Has CHC purchased any treasury shares during the year ended April 30, 2003? Does it plan to next year? Explain.

EXHIBIT 11-7
PART A

CHC HELICOPTER CORPORATION 2003 ANNUAL REPORT

NOTES TO THE CONSOLIDATED FINANCIAL STATEMENTS

April 30, 2003 and 2002 (Tabular amounts in thousands unless otherwise noted, except per share amounts)

13. Capital stock and contributed surplus

Capital stock

Authorized:

Unlimited number of each of the following:
    First preferred shares, issuable in series
    Second preferred shares, issuable in series
    Class A subordinate voting shares
    Class B multiple voting shares
    Ordinary shares

Issued:	Number of shares		Consideration	
	2003	2002	2003	2002
Class A subordinate voting shares	17,918	17,689	$ 218,147	$ 216,978
Class B multiple voting shares	2,955	2,978	18,815	19,029
Ordinary shares	11,000	11,000	33,000	33,000
Share loan	–	–	(33,000)	(33,000)
			$ 236,962	$ 236,007
Contributed surplus			$ 3,291	$ 3,291

Class A subordinate voting shares that would be issued upon conversion of the following:

	2003	2002
Class B multiple voting shares	2,955	2,978
Stock options	1,996	1,427
Convertible debt	690	795

Capital stock transactions	Class A subordinate voting shares	Class B multiple voting shares	Ordinary shares
Number of shares			
Balance, April 30, 2001	13,400	2,975	11,000
Shares issued for cash	4,200		
Shares issued to employees for cash			
Share option plan	66	13	
Share purchase plan	13		
Share conversions	10	(10)	
Balance, April 30, 2002	17,689	2,978	11,000
Shares issued to employees for cash			
Share option plan	91		
Share purchase plan	10		
Share conversions	23	(23)	
Conversion of 5.75% convertible promissory note *(Note 10)*	105		
Balance, April 30, 2003	17,918	2,955	11,000

CHC HELICOPTER CORPORATION 2003 ANNUAL REPORT

EXHIBIT 11-7
PART B

NOTES TO THE CONSOLIDATED FINANCIAL STATEMENTS

April 30, 2003 and 2002 (Tabular amounts in thousands unless otherwise noted, except per share amounts)

13. Capital stock and contributed surplus *(continued)*

	Class A subordinate voting shares	Class B multiple voting shares	Contributed surplus
Stated value			
Balance, April 30, 2001	$ 100,464	$ 19,029	$ 3,291
Shares issued for cash, net of share issue costs	115,899		
Shares issued to employees for cash			
Share option plan	400		
Share purchase plan	215		
Balance, April 30, 2002	216,978	19,029	3,291
Equity offering costs	(130)		
Shares issued to employees for cash			
Share option plan	449		
Share purchase plan	246		
Share conversions	214	(214)	
Conversion of 5.75% convertible promissory note *(Note 10)*	390		
Balance, April 30, 2003	$ 218,147	$ 18,815	$ 3,291

During the year a normal course issuer bid was filed by the Company allowing it to purchase up to a maximum of 1,299,458 of its Class A subordinate voting shares (representing 10% of the public float of such shares as of February 28, 2003). Any purchases under the normal course issuer bid are made in the open market through the facilities of the TSX and all shares repurchased by the Company are cancelled. Under the normal course issuer bid the Company had not purchased any Class A subordinate voting shares as at April 30, 2003. The normal course issuer bid remains in effect until March 11, 2004, or such earlier date as of when the Company has purchased the maximum number of shares.

In January 2003, the Company's 5.75% demand, convertible, promissory note with a Canadian chartered bank in the principal amount of U.S. $250,000 ($389,875) was fully converted into 105,000 Class A subordinate voting shares (Note 10).

11-39 **(Share transactions and return on shareholders' equity)**

The consolidated balance sheets and statements of income and retained earnings for **Aliant Inc.**, together with an excerpt from Note 12 in its 2003 annual report, are presented in Exhibit 11-8. The company provides telecommunications services in Atlantic Canada. All amounts are in thousands.

> *Required:*
>
> a. Reconstruct all the journal entries that affected Aliant's capital stock, contributed surplus, and retained earnings accounts for 2003.
>
> b. Calculate Aliant's return on common shareholders' equity in 2003 and 2002. Comment on the results.
>
> c. Prove the total dollar amount of preferred dividends declared in 2003 from information in Note 12.
>
> d. In July 2002, Aliant announced plans to repurchase 1.6 million common shares, and in July 2003 announced plans to repurchase another 6,925,000 common shares. How many shares were repurchased in 2003, and what would be the maximum number of common shares that could be repurchased in 2004?

EXHIBIT 11-8
PART A

ALIANT INC. 2003 ANNUAL REPORT

Statements

CONSOLIDATED BALANCE SHEETS

As at December 31

(thousands of dollars)	2003	2002
		(note 2)
Assets		
Current assets		
Cash and short-term investments	365,330	178,212
Accounts receivable (notes 3 and 19)	315,903	306,349
Inventory	21,177	17,092
Prepayments	25,871	17,229
Income tax receivable (note 4)	23,423	55,536
Current assets of discontinued operations (note 2)	—	211,270
	751,704	785,688
Capital investments (note 5)	2,013,522	2,076,470
Other assets		
Long-term investments	—	11,506
Deferred charges	92,932	91,864
Future income tax asset (note 4)	12,891	16,811
Accrued benefit asset (note 6)	163,440	74,674
Goodwill (note 7)	31,804	31,804
Non-current assets of discontinued operations (note 2)	—	652,905
	301,067	879,564
Total assets	**3,066,293**	**3,741,722**
Liabilities and shareholders' equity		
Current liabilities		
Notes payable and bank advances (note 8)	17,827	46,591
Payables and accruals (notes 9 and 19)	238,332	139,150
Income tax payable (note 4)	18,806	12,655
Future income tax liability (note 4)	3,797	6,953
Long-term debt due within one year (note 10)	101,535	68,724
Current liabilities of discontinued operations (note 2)	—	187,622
	380,297	461,695
Long-term debt (note 10)	888,524	995,648
Accrued benefit liability (note 6)	159,156	148,547
Deferred credits	10,337	10,919
Non-current liabilities of discontinued operations (note 2)	—	451,064
	1,438,314	2,067,873
Non-controlling interest (note 11)	4,051	3,274
Shareholders' equity		
Capital stock (note 12)	1,208,062	1,242,815
Contributed surplus (note 12)	—	64,155
Retained earnings	415,866	354,080
Cumulative translation adjustment	—	9,525
	1,623,928	1,670,575
Total liabilities and shareholders' equity	**3,066,293**	**3,741,722**

See accompanying notes to the consolidated financial statements

Signed on behalf of the board of directors

Charles White
Chairman

Edward Reevey
Director

CONSOLIDATED FINANCIAL STATEMENTS

ALIANT INC. 2003 ANNUAL REPORT

EXHIBIT 11-8
PART B

CONSOLIDATED STATEMENTS OF INCOME

For the years ended December 31

(thousands of dollars except per share amounts)	2003	2002
		(note 2)
Operating revenues (note 13)	2,069,389	2,046,474
Expenses		
Cost of operating revenues	310,718	361,487
Operating expenses	929,320	849,099
Depreciation and amortization	390,597	385,604
Restructuring charge (note 9)	14,550	—
	1,645,185	1,596,190
Operating income	424,204	450,284
Other income (expenses) (note 14)		
Writedown of goodwill	—	(50,000)
Other income (expenses)	(8,203)	159
	(8,203)	(49,841)
Interest charges		
Interest on long-term debt	81,038	87,991
Other interest expense	2,067	2,302
	83,105	90,293
Income before underlisted items	332,896	310,150
Income taxes (note 4)	137,574	157,250
Income before non-controlling interest	195,322	152,900
Non-controlling interest	453	1,203
Net income from continuing operations	194,869	151,697
Net income from discontinued operations (note 2)	111,342	25,879
Net income	306,211	177,576
Earnings per common share (note 15)		
Basic from continuing operations	1.35	1.02
Basic from discontinued operations	0.81	0.19
Basic	2.16	1.21
Diluted from continuing operations	1.35	1.02
Diluted from discontinued operations	0.81	0.19
Diluted	2.16	1.21

See accompanying notes to the consolidated financial statements

CONSOLIDATED STATEMENTS OF RETAINED EARNINGS

For the years ended December 31

(thousands of dollars)	2003	2002
Retained earnings, beginning of year	354,080	317,988
Net income	306,211	177,576
Preferred share dividends	(9,538)	(9,538)
Common share dividends	(147,509)	(131,946)
Excess of repurchase of common shares over stated value (note 12)	(87,378)	—
Retained earnings, end of year	415,866	354,080

See accompanying notes to the consolidated financial statements

EXHIBIT 11-8
PART C

ALIANT INC. 2003 ANNUAL REPORT

12 CAPITAL STOCK

Authorized

Unlimited number of preference shares, cumulative redeemable at the price of $25.00 per share and with a fixed annual dividend rate of $1.3625 per share. These shares are non-voting, except under certain conditions, and are redeemable at the Company's option on June 30, 2006 or on June 30 of each fifth year thereafter. Preference shareholders (series 2) may convert series 2 preference shares to series 3 shares on June 30, 2006 or on June 30 each fifth year thereafter, provided that the Company has not delivered a notice of redemption.

Unlimited number of common shares, without par value.

Issued

	2003		2002	
As at December 31	Number		Number	
(thousands of dollars)	of shares	Value	of shares	Value
Preference shares, series 2	7,000,000	172,264	7,000,000	172,264
Common shares	133,616,920	1,035,798	139,513,639	1,070,551
		1,208,062		1,242,815

The following table provides the details of the change in the issued common shares of the Company:

	2003		2002	
As at December 31	Number		Number	
(thousands of dollars)	of shares	Value	of shares	Value
Common shares, beginning of year	139,513,639	1,070,551	137,526,147	1,014,416
Stock option plan (note 16)	434,132	8,629	437,018	7,369
Common shareholder dividend reinvestment and stock purchase plan	197,719	5,927	1,373,235	38,335
Employees' stock savings plan (note 16)	—	—	441,539	12,452
Shares purchased for cancellation	(6,528,570)	(49,309)	(264,300)	(2,021)
Common shares, end of year	133,616,920	1,035,798	139,513,639	1,070,551

ALIANT INC. 2003 ANNUAL REPORT

EXHIBIT 11-8
PART D

On July 18, 2002, Aliant Inc. announced acceptance by the Toronto Stock Exchange of Notice of intention to purchase from time to time up to 1,600,000 of its outstanding common shares on the Toronto Stock Exchange, representing approximately 1.1 per cent of the issued and outstanding common shares of Aliant Inc. as of that date, being 139,567,382 common shares. Under the bid, the Company would acquire, from time to time, its common shares at the market price with cash through the facilities of the Toronto Stock Exchange. Purchases of common shares could be made during the 12-month period commencing July 22, 2002 and ending on July 21, 2003. Aliant Inc. purchased and cancelled all of the 1,600,000 shares as of June 2003, of which 1,335,700 shares were in 2003.

On July 30, 2003, Aliant Inc. announced acceptance by the Toronto Stock Exchange of Notice of intention to purchase from time to time up to 6,925,000 of its outstanding common shares on the Toronto Stock Exchange, representing approximately 5.0 per cent of the issued and outstanding

common shares of Aliant Inc. as of that date, being 138,517,283 common shares. Under the bid, the Company would acquire, from time to time, its common shares at the market price with cash through the facilities of the Toronto Stock Exchange. Bell Canada, Aliant's majority shareholder, will sell shares into the normal course issuer bid on a pro-rata basis and the Toronto Stock Exchange has granted an exemption to permit Aliant to make purchases from Bell Canada on that basis. Purchases of common shares may be made during the 12-month period commencing August 6, 2003 and ending on August 5, 2004. As of December 31, 2003, 5,192,870 shares were purchased for cancellation.

For the year ended, December 31, 2003, the Company purchased for cancellation 6,528,570 shares (2002 – 264,300) for an aggregate price of $200.9 million (2002 – $7.2 million) which reduced capital stock by $49.3 million (2002 – $2.0 million), contributed surplus by $64.2 million (2002 – $5.2 million) and retained earnings by $87.4 million (2002 – $nil million).

e. Assume the company had increased its long-term debt at January 1, 2003, and used the cash borrowed to redeem the preference shares (series 2). The interest paid on the long-term debt was 7%. Calculate Aliant's 2003 return on common shareholders' equity if this had occurred and explain the result.

11-40 **(Share options)**

In Exhibit 11-9 you will find the consolidated balance sheets, statements of earnings and retained earnings, and an excerpt from Note 11 to the 2003 financial statements of West Fraser Timber Co. Ltd. All amounts are in thousands.

Required:

a. West Fraser has a share option plan for its directors, officers, and employees.

1. What is a share option plan and why would the company issue options to these groups?

2. Explain the change to the share option plan in July 2003. Do you think this amendment changes the share option plan's effectiveness?

3. West Fraser had declared a 10% stock dividend in each of 2002 and 2003. How do you think this has affected the number of share options outstanding? Why is it important for the company to consider the 10% stock dividends in its granting of share options?

EXHIBIT 11-9
PART A

WEST FRASER TIMBER CO. LTD. 2003 ANNUAL REPORT

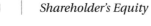 Consolidated Balance Sheets

As at December 31 (in thousands of Canadian dollars)	2003	2002
ASSETS		
Current assets		
Cash and short-term investments	$ 265,860	$ 192,916
Accounts receivable	158,055	173,983
Inventories (note 5)	324,236	319,443
Prepaid expenses	9,166	7,009
	757,317	693,351
Other assets (note 6)	64,318	84,003
Property, plant and equipment (note 7)	1,244,794	1,316,889
Deferred charges (note 8)	21,301	20,217
	$ 2,087,730	$ 2,114,460
LIABILITIES AND SHAREHOLDERS' EQUITY		
Current liabilities		
Accounts payable and accrued liabilities	$ 186,193	$ 163,041
Current portion of reforestation obligation	30,769	29,464
Current portion of long-term debt (note 9)	12,965	19,720
	229,927	212,225
Long-term debt (note 9)	286,974	337,745
Other liabilities (note 10)	70,198	72,214
Future income taxes (note 17)	186,485	201,725
	773,584	823,909
Shareholders' equity (note 11)	1,314,146	1,290,551
	$ 2,087,730	$ 2,114,460

Commitments (note 12)

Contingencies (note 20)

Approved by the Board of Directors

William P. Ketcham

Director

J. Duncan Gibson

Director

WEST FRASER TIMBER CO. LTD. 2003 ANNUAL REPORT

EXHIBIT 11-9
PART B

West Fraser Consolidated Statements of Earnings and Retained Earnings

For the years ended December 31 (in thousands of Canadian dollars)	2003	2002
EARNINGS		
Net sales *(note 20)*	$ 1,508,147	$ 1,632,239
Costs and expenses		
Cost of products sold	1,287,743	1,243,765
Amortization of property, plant and equipment	142,284	135,434
Selling, general and administrative *(note 11)*	69,102	69,181
Recovery of prior year export duties *(note 20)*	—	(25,010)
	1,499,129	1,423,370
Operating earnings	9,018	208,869
Other		
Interest expense – net *(note 15)*	(16,895)	(32,559)
Exchange gain on long-term debt	40,825	5,495
Other income *(note 16)*	3,295	3,442
Earnings from continuing operations before income taxes	36,243	185,247
Provision for (recovery of) income taxes *(note 17)*		
Current	8,362	60,852
Future	(15,240)	(4,644)
	(6,878)	56,208
Earnings from continuing operations	43,121	129,039
Earnings from discontinued operations *(note 2)*	—	8,521
Earnings	$ 43,121	$ 137,560
Earnings per share *(note 18)*		
From continuing operations — Basic	$ 1.17	$ 3.50
— Diluted	$ 1.16	$ 3.47
After discontinued operations — Basic	$ 1.17	$ 3.74
— Diluted	$ 1.16	$ 3.70

For the years ended December 31 (in thousands of Canadian dollars)	2003	2002
RETAINED EARNINGS		
Balance — beginning of year	$ 964,238	$ 845,626
Earnings	43,121	137,560
	1,007,359	983,186
Common share dividends	(20,639)	(18,742)
Preferred share payment *(note 12(b))*	—	(206)
Balance — end of year	$ 986,720	$ 964,238

EXHIBIT 11-11
PART B
SIERRA WIRELESS, INC. 2003 ANNUAL REPORT
Notes to Consolidated Financial Statements

The following table summarizes the stock options outstanding at December 31, 2003:

Range of Exercise Prices	Options Outstanding					Options Exercisable		
	Number of Shares	Weighted Average Remaining Contractual Life	Weighted Avg. Exercise Price		Number Exercisable	Weighted Avg. Exercise Price	
		In years	Cdn.$	U.S.$		Cdn.$	U.S.$
$0.70 - $1.16 (Cdn$0.90 - Cdn$1.50)	55,288	3.6	$ 1.14	$ 0.88	55,288	$ 1.14	$ 0.88
$1.17 - $2.71 (Cdn$1.51 - Cdn$3.50)	476,473	3.7	3.35	2.59	193,782	3.28	2.54
$2.72 - $9.30 (Cdn$3.51 - Cdn$12.00)	306,209	4.6	9.61	7.45	13,636	5.17	4.00
$9.31 - $15.50 (Cdn$12.01 - Cdn$20.00)	371,691	1.3	15.09	11.70	296,448	15.14	11.73
$15.51 - $23.26 (Cdn$20.01 - Cdn$30.00)	440,640	4.2	21.30	16.51	86,719	22.96	17.80
$23.27 - $136.47 (Cdn$30.01 - Cdn$176.05)	76,059	1.4	81.53	63.20	68,472	81.76	63.38
	1,726,360	3.4	11.58	7.25	714,345	17.98	13.94

The options outstanding at December 31, 2003 expire between March 29, 2004 and December 31, 2008.

c. For each type of share authorized by the company, list the nature of the issue, the number of shares (authorized, issued, and outstanding), par value or no par value, market price at the end of the year, and any special features of the issue.

d. What was the company's market value at the end of the most recent year? (Multiply the number of shares outstanding by the market price.) Compare this with the company's book value and discuss the reasons why these amounts are different. Be as specific as possible.

e. Did the company pay dividends in the most recent year? If so, what was the dividend per share and has this amount changed over the past three years?

f. Did the company declare any stock dividends or have a stock split during the most recent year? If so, describe the nature of the event and the effects on the shareholders' equity section.

Cases

Case Primer

11-44 Manonta Sales Company

Manonta Sales Company's summary balance sheet and income statement as at December 31, 2005, are shown below.

Balance Sheet (in thousands)

Current assets	$178,000
Investments	1,000
Net property, plant, and equipment	56,000
Total assets	$235,000
Current liabilities	$105,000
Long-term debt	93,000
Shareholders' equity	37,000
Total liabilities and shareholders' equity	$235,000

Income Statement (in thousands)

Sales	$560,000
Cost of goods sold, operating and other expenses	525,000
Earnings before income taxes	35,000
Income taxes	15,000
Net income	$ 20,000
Earnings per share	$1.25

The long-term debt has an interest rate of 8% and is convertible into 9.3 million common shares. After carefully analyzing all available information about Manonta, you decide the following events are likely to happen. First, Manonta will increase its earnings before income taxes by 10% next year because of increased sales. Second, the effective tax rate will stay the same. Third, the holders of long-term debt will convert it into shares on January 1, 2006. Fourth, the current multiple of earnings per share to market price of 20 will increase to 24 if the debt is converted, because of the reduced risk.

You own 100 common shares of Manonta and are trying to decide whether you should keep or sell them. You decide you will sell the shares if you think their market price is not likely to increase by at least 10% next year. Based on the information available, should you keep the shares or sell them? Support your answer with a detailed analysis.

11-45   Tribec Wireless Inc.

Tribec Wireless Inc. had the following shareholders' equity section as at December 31, 2005.

Common Shares, authorized: an unlimited number of no par value common shares; issued and outstanding:

2,000,000 shares	$4,000,000
Retained earnings	1,958,476
Total shareholders' equity	$5,958,476

In 2002 and 2003, Tribec paid a cash dividend of $.75 per share. In 2004, the company expanded operations significantly and the board of directors decided to retain earnings in the business rather than pay them out as a cash dividend. In lieu of the cash dividend, the board voted to distribute a 10% stock dividend. In December 2005, the company returned to its previous dividend policy and again paid a $0.75 cash dividend.

In 2002 you inherited 5,000 shares of Tribec Wireless. At that time, the shares were trading at $5.00 per share. Given the tremendous growth in the wireless market by 2004 when the stock dividend was distributed, the company's shares were trading at $80 per share. After the stock dividend, the share price dropped slightly but has since risen again, and as at December 31, 2005, they were trading at $82 per share.

Required:

a. From Tribec's perspective, how would the accounting for the stock dividend distributed in 2004 differ from that used for the cash dividends paid in the other years?

b. Immediately after the stock dividend, the price of the Tribec shares dropped slightly. Does this mean the value of the company (and your investment) decreased due to the payment of the stock dividend?

c. Prepare a schedule illustrating the total amount of cash dividends you have received since inheriting the Tribec shares. What is the value of your investment at December 31, 2005?

11-46   Blooming Valley Custom Landscaping

Blooming Valley Custom Landscaping provides landscaping services to a variety of clients in southern Ontario. The company's services include planting lawns and shrubs and installing outdoor lighting and irrigation systems as well as constructing decks and gazebos. The company also remains very busy in the winter by using its trucks for snow clearing. Blooming Valley would like to extend its operations into the northern United States, but Jack Langer, the owner, feels that the company would require at least $2 million in new capital before such a venture could be successful. Langer is excited about the prospects of expanding because his projections indicate that the company could earn an additional $750,000 in income before interest and taxes.

Currently, Blooming Valley has no long-term debt and the company is owned entirely by the Langer family. There are 300,000 common shares outstanding and the company currently has net income before tax of $900,000. The company's tax rate is 25% and is not expected to change as a result of the planned expansion. The family does not have sufficient financial resources to undertake the expansion, and therefore, it is essential to obtain outside financing. Mr. Langer is considering three financing options.

Option 1

The first option is to borrow, using a conventional bank loan. Interest on the loan would be 9% annually with monthly payments of principal and interest required.

Option 2

The second possibility is to issue 100,000 common shares to a local venture capitalist. As part of the plan, the venture capitalist would be given a seat on the board of directors and would also have a say in the day-to-day running of the company.

Option 3

The final option is to sell 100,000 of the non-voting cumulative preferred shares. The preferred shares would have an annual dividend of $2.85. A number of investors have expressed interest in purchasing these shares.

Required:

a. Calculate the effect of each financing option on the company's earnings per share. Which option will result in the highest earnings per share?

b. Recommend an option to Mr. Langer. Be sure to consider both quantitative and qualitative factors as part of your analysis.

11-47   Thai restaurant

Sam Able, Abby Moss, and Kendra McDonald have just graduated from the Toronto Culinary Institute and are excited about opening their own restaurant. The three want to open a trendy Thai restaurant in Toronto and have been busy looking for the perfect location. Sam, who completed several business management courses as part of his degree, has estimated that the three will require $400,000 at a minimum to start the business. This would provide cash for rent, equipment, supplies, and advertising as well as small salaries for the three graduates until such time as the restaurant is up and running.

Having recently graduated, none of the three has significant assets to invest in the venture. Sam's parents are willing to loan them $50,000, but they want to see a solid business plan before committing to the loan. Sam and Abby are willing to work full-time in the business, but Kendra has a small child and feels that initially she may not be able to work full-time. Instead, she would be willing to work nights and weekends when her husband is home to take care of the baby.

The three friends recently had a meeting to discuss matters and to try to decide on how to form the business. Sam has proposed that they incorporate, but the others are concerned about the additional cost of incorporation and wonder if it would not be better to operate as a partnership. They feel that they need additional information before making this decision and decide to ask you, an independent business consultant, for advice.

Required:

a. Prepare a report for the three friends outlining how operating as a partnership differs from incorporating. Be sure to include the advantages and disadvantages of each form of organization.

b. Based on the information given above, make a preliminary recommendation as to which form of organization would best suit your clients' needs.

11-48   Teed's Manufacturing Corporation

Teed's Manufacturing Corporation has the following shareholders' equity at December 1, 2005.

Shareholders' Equity

Share capital

$4 preferred shares, no par value, cumulative,	
10,000 shares authorized, 8,000 shares issued	360,000
Common shares, no par value, unlimited	
number of shares authorized, 60,000 shares issued	600,000
Total share capital	960,000
Retained earnings	687,500
Total shareholders' equity	$1,647,500

The company was formed in January 2003 and there has been no change in share capital since that time. It is now December 1, 2005, and after a very strong year the company has just declared a $150,000 cash dividend to shareholders of record as at February 10, 2006. The dividend payment date is February 28, 2006. Teed's has always used business earnings for further expansion and has never paid a dividend before.

Jan Kielly owns 500 shares of Teed's Manufacturing common stock and is curious how much of a dividend she will receive. She is confused as to the difference between preferred and common stock and wonders why the preferred shareholders would purchase shares in a company without having the right to vote. Finally, she is confused about the differences among the declaration date, date of record, and payment date. She wants to know when she will actually receive her dividend.

Required:

a. Determine how much of the dividend will be paid to the preferred shareholders and the common shareholders.

b. Prepare a memo addressing Jan's questions.

Critical Thinking Question

11-49   (Stock options)

Corporate executives are normally remunerated with a package that consists of a combination of one or more of the following:

a. Salary

b. Perks such as company cars, expense accounts, nice offices, and club memberships

c. Bonuses based on net income

d. Bonuses based on gross sales

e. Stock option plans

Required:

Discuss the impact of each of the above items on the actions of executives. What would each item encourage the executive to achieve? Which of these actions might be beneficial to the company? Which might be harmful? If you were designing a remuneration package for executives running a company you owned, what would you include? Explain why you included the items that you did.

Dr. David Stanley, a food science professor at the University of Guelph, took early retirement and received a lump sum payment from the university as part of the package. He could have asked a financial advisor to invest the money for him. Instead, he chose to read and learn the basics of financial analysis and investing so that he could make his own investment decisions. He became knowledgeable enough that he could successfully manage his own funds and began providing advice to other investors. He employed strategies that you have been learning throughout this book. You have a head start on what Dr. Stanley learned on his own. After studying this text, you know something about accounting, you can read and understand most of the items on financial statements, you are aware of the various methods that can be used to measure and report transactions, and you understand some of the limitations affecting the numbers on the statements. As we move through the various methods and ratios of financial analysis, we are going to refer to some of the lessons that Dr. Stanley learned about measuring companies' health.

In the first 11 chapters of this book, we described the basic components of the financial reporting system and how accounting numbers are accumulated and recorded. In most of these chapters we identified ratios that use the material that was being discussed. In this chapter, we pull all those ratios together and summarize how financial information can be analyzed. Here you will see how the various components of the reporting system work together.

USER RELEVANCE

As a user, you need to analyze financial information effectively so that you can make knowledgeable decisions. This involves more than a basic understanding of what each individual statement means. You need to understand the relationships among the three major financial statements and the methods that produce the numbers. You also need to compare and contrast these relationships over time and among different companies. This discussion was left until near the end of the book because proper analysis requires a good understanding of all financial statement components.

As we worked through the material in the book, we introduced the ratios that pertained to the topics under discussion. This has given you some tools, but they are not organized cohesively. Now you need to think about analysis as a structured activity. You need to know what information would help you make informed decisions and then identify the tools (ratios) that will give you that information. The ratios in this chapter have been organized according to decision-making needs so that you can now pull together the tools you have acquired.

This chapter provides an overview of financial statement analysis and a discussion of the basic ratios used. However, because financial statement analysis is very complex, it can serve only as an introduction. Remember two things as you work through this chapter. First, there is no definitive set of rules or procedures that dictate how to analyze financial statements. Second, every analysis should be tailored to suit the underlying reason for making the analysis. These two features make comprehensive analysis quite complex. A more detailed discussion of financial statement analysis is left to more advanced texts.

The leasing business is very different from the manufacturing business and exposes the company to different types of risk. You must take this new information into consideration when evaluating the company.

A reading of the financial statements is not complete unless the notes to the financial statements are read carefully. Because the major financial statements provide summary information only, there is not much room on the statements to provide all the details necessary for a full understanding of the company's transactions. Therefore, the notes provide a place for more details and discussion about many items on the financial statements. Also pay attention in the notes to the summary of the company's significant accounting policies. Remember that GAAP allows considerable flexibility in choosing accounting methods and different choices result in different amounts on the financial statements, so you should be aware of the choices that were made by management. These will generally be listed in the first note to the financial statements.

Once you have an overall understanding of the business and the financial statements, you can begin a detailed analysis of the financial results.

Retrospective vs. Prospective Analysis

LEARNING OBJECTIVE 2

Describe the various ways of analyzing a company's financial statements.

As discussed earlier, most analysis is done with a particular objective in mind. Most objectives involve making decisions that have future consequences. Therefore, almost every analysis of a set of financial statements is, in one way or another, concerned with the future. Because of this, you should make a **prospective** (forward-looking) **analysis** of the company to try to determine what the future will bring. For example, commercial loans officers in banks try to forecast companies' future cash flows to ensure that loans will be repaid.

The problem with prospective analysis is that the world is an uncertain place; no one can predict the future with complete accuracy. Analysts, however, are expected to make recommendations based on their predictions of what the future outcomes will be for specified companies. In trying to predict the future, one of the most reliable sources of data you have is the result of a company's past operations as summarized in the financial statements. To the extent that the future follows past trends, you can do a **retrospective analysis** to assist in predicting the future. You must also understand the economics of a company well enough to know when something fundamental has changed in the economic environment to make it unlikely that the company's past results will predict the future. In such a situation, you cannot rely on the retrospective data.

If you believe that retrospective data may be useful in predicting the future, a complete analysis of those data is in order. Two major types of analysis of retrospective data are time-series and cross-sectional analyses.

Time-Series vs. Cross-Sectional Analysis

In a **time-series analysis**, the analyst examines information from different time periods for the same company to look for any pattern in the data over time. For example, you may look at the sales data over a five-year period to determine whether sales are increasing, decreasing, or remaining stable. This would have important implications for the company's future sales. The assumption underlying a time-series analysis is that there is some predictability in the time series; that is, past data can be used to predict the future. Without this assumption, there is no reason to do a time-series analysis.

Many companies recognize the importance of time-series information and provide five- or 10-year summaries to assist in making this analysis. An example is shown in Exhibit 12-2 from the High Liner Food Incorporated 2003 annual report. The financial highlights report selected pieces of financial data across five years. In High Liner's information, it is interesting to note that it sold its Nova Scotia-based fishing assets at an after-tax gain, which was partly offset by a writedown of other fishing assets, debt settlement, and potential acquisition costs. It considered all these items non-operating items, which means that they result from normal activities but are not part of normal operations. The summary includes an earnings per share amount excluding non-operating items so that users understand what its earnings are from operations before these items. You need to read the information carefully so that you do not make the wrong assumptions in your analysis. The amount given for earnings per share in this summary ($0.78) is not the same as the earnings per share number given on the income statement ($4.52).

A **cross-sectional analysis** compares the data from one company with the data from another company for the same time period. Usually, the comparison is with another company in the same industry (a competitor perhaps), or with an average of the other companies in the industry. For example, you might look at the growth in sales for **General Motors of Canada** compared with the growth in sales for **Ford of Canada** or **DaimlerChrysler Canada**. Other cross-sectional analyses might compare companies across different industries (General Motors of Canada compared with BCE), different countries (General Motors of Canada compared with Nissan of Japan), and so forth. However, any such cross-sectional comparisons must consider that different industries may have slightly different accounting principles (for example, accounting principles for banks and insurance companies are slightly different from those for most other industries). Comparing across countries is much more difficult because of different accounting methods and sets of standards used in different countries. However, using as wide a range of investments as possible, investment analysts want to recommend the best investment strategy to their clients. To make the best recommendation, they must consider the return vs. risk trade-off across many companies. They must, therefore, directly compare companies in different industries and different countries.

The choice of which type of analysis to conduct is driven, in part, by the type of decision that motivated the analysis. In a lending situation, for example, the commercial loans officer will use a time-series analysis of the company in conjunction with a cross-company comparison. The time-series analysis is important because it will help the lender determine the company's ability to repay any money loaned. As part of the decision-making process, the lender must also be aware of industry trends in the analysis of a particular company so as to get an overall assessment of how well this company performs relative to its competitors. This information will help ascertain its future viability.

Data to Be Used

The type of data used in a time-series or cross-sectional analysis will vary depending on the purpose of the analysis. Three general types of frequently used data are raw financial data, common size data, and ratio data.

HIGH LINER FOODS INCORPORATED 2003 ANNUAL REPORT

2003 Highlights

Sales

$315.9M

$400 (millions)
320 — 272.0
240 — 282.0 — 299.2 — 324.5 — 315.9
160
80
0 — '99 '00 '01 '02 '03

Following seven consecutive years of growth, total sales for fiscal 2003 declined from the previous year, the result of the sale of the Company's Nova Scotia-based fishing assets, which reduced sales by $26.0 million, and the stronger Canadian dollar, which reduced the value of reported sales in 2003 by approximately $20.0 million. Sales for our core Packaged Foods business, however, increased by $16 million or 6% to $282.7 million, despite the impact of the stronger Canadian dollar, which had the effect of reducing reported Packaged Foods sales by $16.0 million. Growth in Packaged Foods sales was driven by successful execution of our strategy, including new product introductions, expansion of distribution channels, and migrating successful products to new markets.

Net Income

$46.1M

$50 (millions)
40 — 46.1
30
20
10 — (4.1) — 6.4 — 6.2 — 10.2
0
(10) — '99 '00 '01 '02 '03

The increase in net income for 2003 reflects a one-time after-tax gain of $43.7 million realized on the sale of our Nova Scotia-based fishing assets, which was partly offset by an after-tax write down of $6.5 million relating to other fishing assets, debt settlement and potential acquisition costs. While the strengthening Canadian dollar has the immediate effect of reducing the Canadian dollar value of U.S. dollar denominated sales, we manage foreign currency risk with appropriate hedging strategies and, due to the magnitude of U.S. dollar denominated raw materials purchases, a strengthening Canadian dollar has a positive effect on our earnings. In the fourth quarter of fiscal 2003, we began to experience this positive effect on earnings, which we expect to continue in 2004.

Earnings per Share
(Excluding Non-Operating Items)

$0.78

$0.80 — 0.78
0.60 — 0.62 — 0.55 — 0.71
0.40
0.20 — (0.38)
0.00
(0.20)
(0.40) — '99 '00 '01 '02 '03

In 2003, we achieved our goal of growing earnings per share excluding non-operating items by 10% compared with 2002. Non-operating items for 2003 included the one-time after-tax gain of $4.39 per share realized on the sale of our Nova Scotia-based fishing assets, partly offset by an after-tax write down of $0.65 per share relating to other fishing assets, debt settlement and potential acquisition costs. Non-operating items for 2002 included a $0.22 per share gain resulting from the closure of our primary processing operations in Lunenburg and a gain from the release of escrow funds held for several years after the disposal of a foreign subsidiary several years ago.

Interest-Bearing Debt

$11.4M

$140 (millions)
112 — 114.0 — 93.3 — 98.9
84 — 62.0% — 55.3% — 54.7% — 71.3
56 — 44.5%
28 — 11.4
0 — 8.6% — '99 '00 '01 '02 '03

● Debt as a proportion of capitalization

During 2003, High Liner significantly strengthened its balance sheet, paying off most of its long-term debt using the proceeds from the sale of the Company's Nova Scotia-based fishing assets. Interest-bearing debt at the end of the fiscal year was $11.4 million, down almost $60 million from $71.3 million at the end of 2002. Debt as a proportion of capitalization was reduced to 8.6% from 44.5%. Over the last five years, the Company has reduced its interest-bearing debt levels by 90%. The proceeds of the sale of the fishing assets also allowed the Company to pay all dividends in arrears on our Second Preference Shares and redeem our Class C and Class D Preference Shares.

Ten-Year Operating Statistics

Tonnage (Metric Tonnes)[1]	2003	2002	2001	2000	1999	1998	1997	1996	1995	1994
Groundfish fleet landings[2]	2,343	6,572	7,454	8,680	7,834	10,110	6,413	8,945	7,477	11,794
Scallop fleet landings[2]	490	1,355	1,440	1,419	852	865	825	663	767	1,168
Raw uncooked product processing – finished weight[3]	7,539	10,585	10,167	9,971	11,083	13,666	11,770	10,816	10,128	10,925
Prepared foods processing – finished weight	42,296	36,543	38,285	33,882	33,671	35,472	35,423	33,158	29,334	29,529
Total production	49,835	47,128	48,452	43,853	44,754	49,138	47,193	43,974	39,462	40,454
Prepared foods processing as a % of total production	84.9%	77.5%	79.0%	77.3%	75.2%	72.2%	75.1%	75.4%	74.3%	73.0%
Number of employees	1,061	1,274	1,359	1,435	1,435	1,425	1,492	1,400	1,375	1,570
Gross capital expenditures ($000s)	7,239	4,869	6,480	5,112	5,107	7,084	6,273	2,237	4,799	5,478

[1] One metric tonne = 2204.6 lbs.   [2] The fleet was sold on May 21, 2003, except for one vessel.   [3] Lunenburg primary processing plant closed December 2002.

RAW FINANCIAL DATA

Raw financial data are the data that appear directly in the financial statements. An example of a time-series analysis of this type of data might be the time-series data from income statements, as shown for High Liner Foods in Exhibit 12-2, or the time-series of total net debt for the past five years. Cross-sectional analysis can also be used with this type of data. For example, you might compare total revenues across companies in the same industry for the past three years.

Time-series data are almost always available directly from financial statements, since they usually show data for a two-year period. In addition to the main financial statements, many annual reports contain additional time-series data in the form of a five- or 10-year summary such as that shown in Exhibit 12-2. Note that this summary does not include all items that appear on the income statement. Annual reports may also contain data other than strictly financial data, such as numbers of employees or sales volumes expressed in physical units rather than dollars (see Exhibit 12-2).

In the remainder of the chapter, data from a set of financial statements will be used to illustrate various types of analyses. For purposes of illustration, we are going to continue to use the financial statement data of High Liner Foods Incorporated for the 2003 fiscal year. High Liner Foods, with headquarters in Lunenburg, Nova Scotia, is a processor and marketer of seafood and frozen pasta under the brand names High Liner®, Fisher Boy®, Gina Italian Village®, and Floresta®. The raw financial statement data for High Liner Foods appear in Exhibit 12-3, which includes the balance sheets, statements of income and retained earnings, and statements of cash flows.

COMMON SIZE DATA

Although a company's raw data can reveal much about its performance, certain relationships are more easily understood when some elements of the raw data are compared with other elements. For example, in the statement of income for High Liner Foods in Exhibit 12-3, you can see that sales decreased from $324,458 thousand in 2002 to $315,879 thousand in 2003. Cost of sales has also decreased over this same period from $254,461 thousand to $251,372 thousand. What happened to profit margins on a relative basis? This is a question of the relationship of the costs to the revenues. One way to address this question is to compare the cost of goods sold expressed as a proportion of the sales revenue. Often, this is done by preparing a set of financial statements called common size statements.

In a common size statement of earnings, all line items are expressed as percentages of net revenues (sales). In the case of High Liner Foods, a common size income statement is shown in Exhibit 12-4 with every item calculated as a percentage of gross revenue.

HIGH LINER FOODS INCORPORATED 2003 ANNUAL REPORT

EXHIBIT 12-3
PART A

CONSOLIDATED BALANCE SHEETS

(000s)	January 3, 2004 $	December 28, 2002 $
ASSETS		
Current:		
Cash	926	1,088
Accounts receivable *(note 2)*	31,840	35,001
Inventories *(note 2)*	49,870	50,053
Prepaid expenses	1,502	1,600
Future income taxes *(note 9)*	7,525	6,991
Total current assets	91,663	94,733
Property, plant and equipment *(note 3)*	27,492	44,303
Other:		
Goodwill	45,781	55,661
Deferred charges	8	931
Future income taxes *(note 9)*	7,282	5,037
Other receivables and sundry investments *(note 15)*	5,513	6,702
	58,584	68,331
	177,739	207,367
LIABILITIES AND SHAREHOLDERS' EQUITY		
Current:		
Bank loans *(note 4)*	10,252	5,960
Accounts payable and accrued liabilities *(note 4)*	37,424	42,490
Current portion of long-term liabilities *(note 5)*	328	15,919
Total current liabilities	48,004	64,369
Long-term liabilities *(note 5)*	845	49,395
Employee future benefits *(note 12)*	1,143	571
Future income taxes *(note 9)*	6,351	4,004
Shareholders' Equity:		
Preference Shares *(note 6)*	20,000	21,246
Common Shares *(note 6)*	34,030	28,361
Retained earnings	75,259	37,080
Foreign currency translation account *(note 7)*	(7,893)	2,341
	121,396	89,028
	177,739	207,367

See accompanying notes to the financial statements.

On behalf of the Board

Henry E. Demone
Director

David J. Hennigar
Director

EXHIBIT 12-3
PART B
HIGH LINER FOODS INCORPORATED 2003 ANNUAL REPORT

CONSOLIDATED STATEMENTS OF INCOME
For the fifty-three weeks ended January 3, 2004
(with comparative figures for the fifty-two weeks ended December 28, 2002)

(000s except per share amounts)	Fiscal 2003 $	Fiscal 2002 $
Sales	**315,879**	324,458
Cost of sales	**251,372**	254,461
Gross Profit	**64,507**	69,997
Selling, general and administrative expenses	**44,330**	41,606
Earnings before interest, taxes, depreciation, amortization and the undernoted (Operating EBITDA)	**20,177**	28,391
Litigation costs	**(42)**	(2,655)
Depreciation	**(3,911)**	(5,643)
Interest expense:		
Short-term	**(53)**	(252)
Long-term	**(2,320)**	(6,334)
Foreign exchange gains	**58**	32
Other income	**122**	199
Non-operating transactions *(note 8)*	**31,968**	157
Income before income taxes	**45,999**	13,895
Income taxes *(note 9)*		
Current	**(110)**	(287)
Future	**230**	(3,366)
Total income taxes	**120**	(3,653)
Net income for the period	**46,119**	10,242
PER SHARE INFORMATION		
Earnings per Common Share *(note 10)*		
Basic	**4.52**	0.93
Diluted	**4.13**	0.87
Average Common Shares Outstanding *(note 10)*		
Basic	**9,945,101**	9,822,044
Diluted	**10,940,861**	10,769,929

See accompanying notes to the financial statements.

CONSOLIDATED STATEMENTS OF RETAINED EARNINGS
For the fifty-three weeks ended January 3, 2004
(wth comparative figures for the fifty-two weeks ended December 28, 2002)

(in thousands of Canadian dollars)	Fiscal 2003 $	Fiscal 2002 $
Balance, beginning of period	**37,080**	29,289
Net income for the period	**46,119**	10,242
Dividends		
Common Shares	**(537)**	-
Second Preference Shares		
Current	**(1,078)**	(1,017)
Arrears	**(6,260)**	(1,362)
Class C and D Preference Share	**(65)**	(72)
Balance, end of period	**75,259**	37,080

See accompanying notes to the financial statements.

HIGH LINER FOODS INCORPORATED 2003 ANNUAL REPORT

EXHIBIT 12-3
PART C

CONSOLIDATED STATEMENTS OF CASH FLOWS

For the fifty-three weeks ended January 3, 2004

(wth comparative figures for the fifty-two weeks ended December 28, 2002)

(000s)	Fiscal 2003 $	Fiscal 2002 $
Cash provided by (used in) operations:		
Net income for the period	46,119	10,242
Charges (credits) to income not involving cash from operations:		
Depreciation and amortization	3,992	5,850
Gain on asset disposals	(39,699)	(3,569)
Non-cash severance and other costs	7,609	3,272
Future income taxes	(230)	3,366
Cash flow from operations before changes in non-cash working capital	17,791	19,161
Net change in non-cash working capital balances	(9,441)	10,033
	8,350	29,194
Cash provided by (used in) financing activities:		
Change in current bank loans	4,291	(11,224)
Long-term debt proceeds	379	268
Repayments of long-term debt	(54,416)	(15,841)
Funding of employee future benefits less than expense	656	19
Dividends paid		
Preferred	(7,403)	(2,451)
Common	(537)	-
Debt settlement cost	(2,706)	-
Foreign exchange translation	(399)	(51)
Redemption of C and D Preference Shares	(1,246)	-
Issue of equity shares	794	179
	(60,587)	(29,101)
Cash provided by (used in) investing activities:		
Purchase of property, plant and equipment	(7,239)	(4,869)
Proceeds on disposal of non-current assets	60,105	4,631
Decrease (increase) in other assets	(791)	645
	52,075	407
Increase (decrease) in cash during the period	(162)	500
Cash, beginning of period	1,088	588
Cash, end of period	926	1,088

See accompanying notes to the financial statements.

EXHIBIT 12-4

HIGH LINER FOODS INCORPORATED

Common Size Statements of Income

	2003	2002
Sales	100.0%	100.0%
Cost of sales	79.5%	78.4%
Gross profit	20.5%	21.6%
Selling, general and administrative expenses	14.0%	12.8%
Earnings before interest, taxes, depreciation,		
amortization and the undernoted (Operating EBITDA)	6.5%	8.8%
Litigation costs	(.01%)	(0.8%)
Depreciation	(1.2%)	(1.7%)
Interest expense		
Short-term	(.02%)	(0.1%)
Long-term	(0.7%)	(2.0%)
Foreign exchange gain	0.02%	0.01%
Other income	0.04%	0.06%
Non-operating transactions	10.1%	0.05%
Income before income taxes	15.03%	4.32%
Income taxes		
Current	(.03%)	(.09%)
Future	.07%	(1.04%)
Total income taxes	.04%	(1.13%)
Net income for the period	15.07%	3.19%

This common size statement of earnings shows that High Liner Foods' operations have been very stable. Sales have fallen, but the cost of those sales has fallen proportionately slightly less than the sales. This has caused the gross profit to fall slightly from 21.6% to 20.5%. This is a good sign because it means that High Liner Foods is controlling its major costs. Because the cost of sales has fallen slightly less than the sales, an analyst would monitor this change next year to see if the proportionate change worsens. An analyst will examine a company's financial statements carefully when sales are rising or falling. If they are rising and the cost of those sales rises proportionately more than the sales themselves, the new sales are costing the company more and management should be looking for ways to control the costs. Most items on the statement of earnings are proportionately slightly less than the previous year, although the non-operating transactions are higher. From Exhibit 12-3, you know that High Liner Foods sold its Nova Scotia fishing assets at a gain in 2003. A review of the balance sheet shows that the property, plant, and equipment has fallen $16.8 thousand. Much of the increase in earnings in 2003 was a result of the gain on the sale of these assets. In Note 3 to the financial statements, the carrying value of the vessels has dropped from $33,391 thousand in 2002 to $3,891 thousand in 2003. The remaining vessels are fully depreciated at the end of 2003.

Common size statements could also be prepared for the balance sheet and the cash flow statement. The common size data can then be used in a time-series analysis, as they were earlier, or they could be used in a cross-sectional analysis of different companies. In fact, in cross-sectional analysis, common size statements allow one to compare companies of different sizes.

RATIO DATA

Common size data are useful for making comparisons of data items within a given financial statement. They are not useful for making comparisons across the various financial statements. Ratios compare a data element from one statement with an element from another statement, or with an element within the same statement. These ratios can then be used in a time-series or cross-sectional analysis. Ratio data are potentially the most useful because they reveal information about relationships between the financial statements. To further illustrate this, the remainder of the chapter is devoted to discussing various ratios, their calculation, and interpretation. Most of them have already been introduced in previous chapters, but a discussion of the ratios as they relate to one another should help you understand the usefulness of ratio analysis.

Before you begin that analysis, it is important to remember that financial statements are based on GAAP. This means that they contain assumptions and estimates. As well, many of the assets and liabilities are reported at historical cost values rather than market values. Consequently, the limitations inherent in the financial statements are carried over into the ratios that are used to evaluate them.

RATIOS

Ratios explain relationships among data in the financial statements. The relationships differ across companies, if for no other reason than that the companies underlying transactions are different. For example, a manufacturing company is very concerned about the management of inventory and focuses on various ratios related to inventory. A bank, on the other hand, has no inventory and would not be able to calculate such ratios. It might, however, be very concerned about the loans that it makes, whereas the manufacturer might not have any items comparable to loans receivable.

LEARNING OBJECTIVE 3

Describe the types of ratios that are best suited to providing insight into specific decisions.

Because of the differences across companies, it is impossible for us to address all the ratio issues related to all types of industries. The main focus of our discussion will, therefore, be restricted to High Liner Foods. Most of our discussion also applies to companies in other industries, such as manufacturing or retailing. At the end of the chapter, we include a brief discussion of ratio analysis for non-retailing/manufacturing companies in areas where there may be differences in interpretation.

The ratios that will be discussed are divided into three general categories, but you will see that they are all related. The categories are performance, short-term liquidity, and long-term liquidity. Most of these ratios apply to any company regardless of the nature of its business, but some (such as inventory ratios) apply only to certain types of businesses.

Before the calculations of the various ratios are presented, one general caveat should be made. There are often several ways to calculate a given ratio. Therefore, it makes sense to understand the basis of a calculation before you attempt to interpret it. The use of ratios in this book will be consistent with the definitions given. However, if you use similar ratios from other sources, you should check the definition used in that source to make sure that it is consistent with your understanding of the ratio.

accounting in the news
STOCK BARGAIN HUNTING

Bargain hunting for the right stocks can pay off. Just look at the success of Irwin Michael, president of the ABC Group of Funds in Toronto. "I poke around for stocks that have been mispriced by other investors who do not see the values that I do," Mr. Michael says. "I look for managers who can make risk-reward ratios work for their shareholders. I may find cash on the balance sheet that others have not seen. On income statements, I look for anything that can add value to the portfolio." His strategy has worked. The $50-million ABC American-Value Fund returned 51.6% for the 12 months ended February 29, 2004, compared with the 35.3% average gain of U.S. Equity Funds. For the previous five years, the fund produced a 17.2% average annual compound return, compared with the 3.9% average annual gain of peers.

Source: "Manager's bargain hunting pays off," by Andrew Allentuck, *GlobeinvestorGold.com*, March 19, 2004.

Performance Ratios

Calculate specific ratios and explain how the ratios can be interpreted.

Net income and cash flow as measures of performance have already been discussed in Chapters 4 and 5. Although much can be learned from studying the income and cash flow statements, both in their raw data and common size forms, the ratios discussed in this section complement that understanding and also draw out some of the relationships between these statements and the balance sheet.

For example, in Chapter 4, a performance ratio called the return on investment (ROI) was briefly discussed. In that chapter, ROI was discussed in generic terms as a measure of an investment's performance. The generic form of the ROI calculation can be used to formulate several different ratios depending on the perspective taken in measuring performance. For example, one perspective is that of the shareholders who make an investment in the company and want to measure the performance of their investment. A form of the ROI measure that captures the return to shareholders is referred to as the return on equity (ROE).

A second perspective is that of the debtholders who make an investment in the company by lending money to it. The return they receive is the interest paid by the company. The interest rate paid to them is a measure of their ROI. This type of ROI calculation is not explicitly discussed in this chapter.

The third perspective is that of management. Management obtains resources from both shareholders and debtholders. Those resources are then invested in assets. The return generated by the investment in assets is then used to repay the debtholders and the shareholders. The performance of the investment in assets is, therefore, very important. This type of ROI is captured in a ratio referred to as the **return on assets** (ROA).

In this chapter, both ROE and ROA are considered. In addition to these two overall measures of performance, three additional ratios, referred to as turnover ratios, are discussed. The turnover ratios provide additional insight into the major decisions management makes regarding accounts receivable, inventory, and accounts payable policies.

RETURN ON ASSETS (ROA)

Company management must make two fundamental business decisions. The first is the type of assets in which the company should invest (sometimes referred to as the investment decision), and the second is whether to seek more financing to increase the amount the company can invest in assets (referred to as the financing decision). The ROA ratio, in this book, separates the investment decision from the financing decision. Regardless of the mix of debt and shareholder financing, this ratio asks: what type of return is earned on the investment in assets? From this perspective, the return on the investment in assets should be calculated prior to any payments or returns to the debtholders or shareholders. Net income is a measure of return on assets that is calculated prior to any returns to shareholders, but after the deduction of interest to the debtholders. Therefore, the net income, if it is to be used as a measure of return on assets, must be adjusted for the effects of interest expense so it is treated similarly to dividends.

A complicating factor exists because interest is deductible in the calculation of income tax expense. Therefore, if interest expense is to be removed from the net income figure, we must also adjust the amount of income tax expense that would result. In other words, the tax savings (i.e., the reduction in income tax expense) associated with this interest deduction must also be removed. The ROA ratio is then calculated as the ratio of the return (income before interest) divided by the investment in total assets, as follows.

$$ROA = \frac{\text{Income before interest}}{\text{Average total assets}}$$

$$= \frac{\text{Net income + Interest expense − Tax saving of interest expense}}{\text{Average total assets}}$$

$$= \frac{\text{Net income + Interest expense − (Tax rate × Interest expense)}}{\text{Average total assets}}$$

$$ROA = \frac{\text{Net income + [Interest expense × (1 − Tax rate)]}}{\text{Average total assets}}$$

Based on the data for High Liner Foods in 2003, the calculation of the ROA for 2003 and 2002 has the following results. The income tax rate of 36.9% for 2003 and 40.5% for 2002 is found in a note to the financial statements.

ROA — HIGH LINER FOODS INCORPORATED, 2003

$$ROA = \frac{\text{Net income + [Interest expense × (1 − Tax rate)]}}{\text{Average total assets}}$$

$$= \frac{\$46,119 + [\$2,373 \times (1 − 36.9\%)]}{\dfrac{\$177,739 + \$207,367}{2}}$$

$$= 24.7\%$$

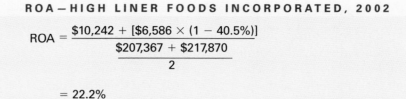

ROA—HIGH LINER FOODS INCORPORATED, 2002

$$ROA = \frac{\$10{,}242 + [\$6{,}586 \times (1 - 40.5\%)]}{\dfrac{\$207{,}367 + \$217{,}870}{2}}$$

$$= 22.2\%$$

This 24.7% ROA in 2003 indicates that High Liner Foods earned 24.7% on the average total assets before making any payments to the suppliers of capital. This 24.7% should be compared with the 22.2% ROA earned by High Liner Foods in 2002. As well, it should be compared with the ROA of other companies.

Calculating the appropriate tax rate to use in the ROA formula is somewhat problematic. The rate that should be used is the company's marginal tax rate. The marginal rate is the rate of tax the company would pay on an additional dollar of income before taxes. This marginal rate would be a combination of the federal and provincial corporate income tax rates. Many analysts use the effective tax rate, which is calculated by dividing the tax expense by the income before taxes. Many companies, including High Liner Foods, show the effective tax rate in a note to the financial statements. In 2003, High Liner Foods sold its fishing assets. For tax purposes, the gain on this sale is treated as a capital gain and only 50% of it is taxable. The 36.9% effective tax rate used in the previous calculation does not take into account the capital gain tax effect. Because the net income used on the calculation includes the gain on the sale, the ROA is unusually high. It is probable that the 22.2% ROA earned in 2002 is closer to the normal return.

The ROA is useful to measure the overall performance of the investment in the company assets. However, comparisons of ROAs across industries must be made with care. The level of ROA reflects, to some extent, the risk inherent in the type of assets in which the company invests. Investors trade off the risk for the return. The more risk investors take, the higher the return they demand. If the company invested its assets in a bank account (a very low-risk investment), it would expect a lower return than if it invested in oil exploration equipment (a high-risk business). Although this factor cannot explain all the variations in ROA between companies, it must be kept in mind. It may be more appropriate either to do a time-series analysis of this ratio, or to compare it cross-sectionally with a direct competitor in the same business. Data obtained from a source of industry ratios such as Dun and Bradstreet can provide you with median measures of ROA that can be used for comparison purposes to determine if the calculated ROA is reasonable or not.

In addition, there is another useful breakdown of the ROA ratio that can provide insight into the cause of a change in this ratio. The most common breakdown of this ratio is as follows.

$$ROA = \frac{\text{Net income} + [\text{Interest expense} \times (1 - \text{Tax rate})]}{\text{Average total assets}}$$

$$= \frac{\text{Net income} + [\text{Interest expense} \times (1 - \text{Tax rate})]}{\text{Sales revenue}}$$

$$\times \frac{\text{Sales revenue}}{\text{Average total assets}}$$

$$= \text{Profit margin ratio} \times \text{Total asset turnover}$$

This breakdown of the ratio into a **profit margin ratio** and a total asset turnover allows the analyst to assess some of the reasons why a company's ROA has gone up or down. The profit margin ratio is, of course, affected by the level of the company's costs relative to its revenues. Changes in this ratio would indicate a change in the product's profitability and may indicate changes in the cost structure or pricing policy. The **total asset turnover ratio** is the ratio of sales to total assets, or the dollars of sales generated per dollar of investment in assets. Changes in this ratio could reflect an increase or decrease in sales volume or major changes in the level of investment in company assets.

The breakdown for High Liner Foods in 2003 would be as follows.

ROA (BREAKDOWN)—HIGH LINER FOODS INCORPORATED, 2003

$$\text{ROA} = \frac{\text{Net income} + [\text{Interest expense} \times (1 - \text{Tax rate})]}{\text{Sales revenue}}$$

$$\times \frac{\text{Sales revenue}}{\text{Average total assets}}$$

$$\text{ROA} = \frac{\$46{,}119 + [\$2{,}373 \times (1 - 36.9\%)]}{\$315{,}879} \times \frac{\$315{,}879}{\dfrac{\$177{,}739 + \$207{,}367}{2}}$$

$$= 15.07\% \times 1.64 = 24.7\%$$

These calculations indicate that High Liner Foods earned the 24.7% ROA by achieving a profit margin ratio of 15.07% and a total asset turnover of 1.64. Note that the 24.7% could be increased by increasing either the profit margin ratio or the total asset turnover, or both.

Note that the same ROA could be achieved by companies in the same industry with different strategies. For example, a discount retailer operates on smaller profit margins and hopes to make that up by a larger volume of sales relative to investment in assets. Discounters generally have less invested in their retail stores. Other full-price retailers have a much larger investment in assets relative to their sales volume and, therefore, must charge higher prices to achieve a comparable ROA. Both businesses face the same general sets of risks and should earn comparable ROAs.

RETURN ON EQUITY (ROE)

Return on equity (ROE), discussed earlier in this section, is the return the shareholders are earning on their investment in the company. There is one additional quirk that must be understood in calculating this ratio. If there is more than one class of shares (generally the second class would be preferred shares), the ROE calculation should be done from the point of view of the common shareholders. This means that any payments to the other classes of shares (preferred dividends, for example) should be deducted from net income in the numerator of this ratio because these amounts are not available to common shareholders. The denominator in such cases should include only the shareholders' equity accounts that belong to common shareholders. This usually means that the preferred shares equity account is subtracted from the total shareholders' equity to arrive at the common shareholders' equity.

The calculation of a company's ROE is as follows.

$$ROE = \frac{\text{Net income} - \text{Preferred dividends}}{\text{Average common shareholders' equity}}$$

High Liner Foods has preference shares as well as common shares. In 2003, it paid $1,078 thousand in dividends for the current year and $6,260 for dividends in arrears. When removing the preferred dividends for this calculation, you need to remove the dividends that were owed in the current year for preferred shares that are cumulative. If the current year's owed dividends are removed each year, it is not necessary to remove the dividends in arrears that were paid in a given year because prior years had already included them in an ROE calculation. For High Liner Foods, the calculation of ROE is as follows.

ROE — HIGH LINER FOODS INCORPORATED, 2003

$$ROE = \frac{\text{Net income} - \text{Preferred dividends}}{\text{Average common shareholders' equity}}$$

$$= \frac{\$46,119 - 1,078}{\dfrac{\$101,396 + \$67,782}{2}}$$

$$= \frac{45,041}{84,589} = 53.3\%$$

This calculation shows that High Liner Foods earned 53.3% ROE, indicating that it earned an average of 53.3% on the average shareholders' equity balances. This is up substantially from the previous year's ROE of 14.4% (the net earnings were over four times higher in 2003). Just as with the ROA, this 53.3% could be compared with other similar companies, or with the results of High Liner Foods itself over time. Cross-sectional comparisons of ROE (among different companies) are also difficult for the same reason that ROA is difficult. Differences in the risks involved should result in differences in returns. Differences in the risks cannot, however, always explain large differences in return as there are many factors that affect ROE.

accounting in the news

STOCK LIQUIDITY MORE IMPORTANT THAN PROFITS

Good financial returns don't necessarily guarantee good reviews from the most stringent financial analysts, like those at the Standard & Poor's/TSX index. Big box retailer Leon's was kicked out of the composite index because it no longer met its set criteria. Leon's earned a record $38.8 million in 2003 and has a market capitalization of about $560 million. Its return on equity averaged 18% in the five years before 2004, with shareholders enjoying 14% compounded annual returns over the same period; management was careful with investors' money, and the company used extra cash to buy back stock and increase dividends. But the seven-person S&P/TSX

index committee looks for liquidity—the size of the public float and trading volumes—more than profits. Leon's founding family still owns 60% of the company, so the float is small and the trading thin. On an average day in 2003, investors traded 13,000 of Leon's shares; on some days the volume was in the hundreds, which was not enough volatility for the index.

Source: "Individual shareholders pay price for S&P/TSX indexing criteria," by Derek DeCloet, *The Globe and Mail*, March 25, 2004.

LEVERAGE

Comparing the ROE calculated for High Liner Foods with the associated ROA shows that the company, while earning only a 24.7% return on assets, showed a return of 53.3% on the shareholders' equity. This higher return on equity results from the company successfully applying financial leverage. Financial **leverage** simply means that some of the funds obtained to invest in assets came from debtholders rather than from shareholders. A company that has a larger proportion of debt to shareholders' equity is said to be highly leveraged. In the case of a totally shareholder-financed company—that is, a company with no debt—the ROE (assuming only one class of shares) would equal the ROA. There would be no interest expense and, therefore, the numerators of both ratios would be the same. The denominators would be the same because the accounting equation (Assets = Liabilities – Shareholders' Equity) is adjusted for the assumed absence of any liabilities (Assets = Shareholders' Equity).

To understand the effects of leverage, consider first the data in Exhibit 12-5 for a 100% equity-financed company, Baker Company (a fictitious company). To keep the illustration simple, all liabilities are considered interest-bearing for Baker Company. Note that in this example, Baker generates a 16.67% return on its assets before taxes (income before interest and taxes/assets = $166.67/$1,000). After the 40% corporate income taxes, this translates into a 10% after-tax return (ROA). Note also that the ROE is the same as the after-tax ROA because there is no debt.

BAKER COMPANY (100% EQUITY-FINANCED)   EXHIBIT 12-5

Balance Sheet

Assets	Liabilities
$1,000	$ 0
	Shareholders' equity
	$1,000

Income Statement

Income before interest and taxes	$ 166.67
Interest	0.00
Income before taxes	166.67
Income taxes (40%)	66.67
Net income	$ 100.00

ROA = $100/$1,000 = 10%
ROE = $100/$1,000 = 10%

Now consider the data in Exhibit 12-6 for Baker Company, which now assumes that the company is only 90% shareholder-financed.

EXHIBIT 12-6

BAKER COMPANY (90% EQUITY-FINANCED)

Balance Sheet

Assets	Liabilities
$1,000	$ 100
	Shareholders' equity
	$ 900

Income Statement (assuming an interest rate of 16.67%)

Income before interest and taxes	$ 166.67
Interest	16.67
Income before taxes	150.00
Income taxes (40%)	60.00
Net income	$ 90.00

ROA = [$90 + {16.67 × (1 − .4)}]/$1,000 = $100/$1,000 = 10%
ROE = $90/$900 = 10%

In Exhibit 12-6, several things should be noted. The first is that the ROA is the same as in Exhibit 12-5, because the mix of assets has not changed; only the amount of debt in the balance sheet has changed. The assets should be earning exactly what they would have earned in a 100% shareholder-financed company. Second, note that the ROE is again the same as the ROA. This will be the case only if the after-tax borrowing rate is the same as the after-tax ROA.

Note that the before-tax borrowing rate is 16.67%. To adjust the rate to an after-tax rate, multiply it by 1 minus the tax rate, or 16.67% × (1 – 40%) = 10%. This means that the company borrowed $100 at a net cost of 10% (the after-tax borrowing rate) and invested the $100 in assets that return 10% after taxes (ROA). Therefore, the company breaks even on the money it borrowed. The shareholders' return of 10% is the income after taxes ($90) divided by their investment ($900).

Next, consider Exhibit 12-7, in which a lower interest rate is assumed (12%). Note that the ROE is greater than the ROA. This occurs because the company was able to borrow at a rate that was less than the rate it could earn by investing in assets. The after-tax cost of borrowing is 7.2% [12% × (1 – 40%)], whereas the after-tax return on the assets is 10% (ROA). Therefore, when the company borrowed $100, it cost the company $7.20 in interest, but it was able to generate $10 in income. The difference is $2.80, which goes to the shareholders as an incremental return. Therefore, the shareholders earn a 10% (or $90) return on their investment of $900, plus they get the excess return of $2.80 that is earned on the money that was borrowed, for a total ROE of 10.3%. This improves their percentage return (ROE) over what they could have earned as a 100% equity-financed company without any further investment on their part.

BAKER COMPANY (90% EQUITY-FINANCED)
(12% INTEREST RATE)

EXHIBIT 12-7

Balance Sheet

Assets	Liabilities
$1,000	$ 100
	Shareholders' equity
	$ 900

Income Statement (assuming an interest rate of 12%)

Income before interest and taxes	$ 166.67
Interest	12.00
Income before taxes	154.67
Income taxes (40%)	61.87
Net income	$ 92.80

ROA = [$92.80 + {12.00 $\times$ (1 − .4)}]/$1,000 = $100/$1,000 = 10%
ROE = $92.80/$900 = 10.3%

This, then, is the advantage of leverage. The shareholders can improve their return (ROE) if the company can borrow funds at an after-tax borrowing rate that is less than the after-tax ROA. This is a big "if." The company that leverages itself is committed to making fixed interest payments to debtholders prior to earning a return on its assets. It is betting that the return on assets will be higher than the after-tax cost of its borrowing. If it is wrong, the return to the shareholders (ROE) could fall below what they could have earned with no debt at all. Consider, for example, the results of Baker Company in Exhibit 12-8, where the company commits to paying lenders 20% (before taxes). Return on equity in this case falls below the ROA to 9.8%. This is the risk of leveraging a company.

BAKER COMPANY (90% EQUITY-FINANCED)
(20% INTEREST RATE)

EXHIBIT 12-8

Balance Sheet

Assets	Liabilities
$1,000	$ 100
	Shareholders' equity
	$ 900

Income Statement (assuming an interest rate of 20%)

Income before interest and taxes	$ 166.67
Interest	20.00
Income before taxes	146.67
Income taxes (40%)	58.67
Net income	$ 88.00

ROA = [$88 + {20 $\times$ (1 − .4)}]/$1,000 = $100/$1,000 = 10%
ROE = $88/$900 = 9.8%

If leveraging the company a little is potentially a good thing, as Exhibit 12-7 illustrated, why not leverage it a lot? In other words, why not borrow funds to buy most of the company's assets? In Exhibit 12-7, why not have 90% debt and 10% equity in the company? Exhibit 12-9 illustrates the kind of return the company could expect given 90% debt and the same interest rate as in Exhibit 12-7. A return of 35.2% is certainly very attractive compared with the ROE of 10% that could be achieved with a 100% equity-financed company. The problem with this financing strategy is that lenders will find the riskiness of their investment much higher in Exhibit 12-9 than they would in Exhibit 12-6. As the company adds more and more debt to its capital structure, it is committing itself to higher and higher fixed-interest payments. Therefore, lenders will start demanding higher and higher returns from their investments as the risk increases. The interest rates will rise, and Baker Company will no longer be able to borrow at the 12% that was assumed in Exhibit 12-7. When the company's average borrowing costs start to equal or exceed its ROA, it will become unattractive to borrow any further funds.

| EXHIBIT 12-9 | **BAKER COMPANY (10% EQUITY FINANCED)** |
| | **(12% INTEREST RATE)** |

Balance Sheet

Assets	Liabilities
$1,000	$ 900
	Shareholders' equity
	$ 100

Income Statement (assuming an interest rate of 12%)

Income before interest and taxes	$ 166.67
Interest	108.00
Income before taxes	58.67
Income taxes (40%)	23.47
Net income	$ 35.20

ROA = [$35.20 + {108.00 × (1 − .4)}]/$1,000 = $100/$1,000 = 10%
ROE = $35.20/$100 = 35.2%

In theory, the increase in the borrowing rate would be an increasing function of the amount of leverage the company employs. Return on equity would improve over that of a 100% equity-financed company up to some point. Exhibit 12-10 graphs the change (at least in theory) in ROE for various levels of leverage. Based on this graph, you can see that there is a point (at the top of the curve) at which ROE would be maximized. The amount of leverage that corresponds to this point has sometimes been called the company's **optimal capital structure**. For the hypothetical company illustrated in the graph, the optimal capital structure would be approximately 40% debt and the rest equity. This point exists in theory, but is more difficult to determine in the real world. It is true, however, that as you look across industries, different industries have different average levels of leverage. This would indicate that, based on the risk characteristics of those industries, the companies in those industries borrow to the point they think is profitable, and no further.

LEVERAGE AND OPTIMAL CAPITAL STRUCTURE

EXHIBIT 12-10

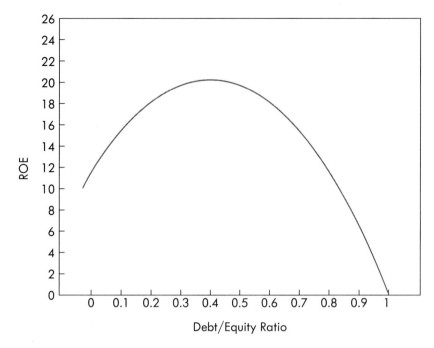

High Liner Foods' interest rate on its debt varied from 2.46% to 8.67% before taxes. Its tax rate was approximately 37%, which means the after-tax interest rate ranged from 1.55% to 5.46%. If its ROA was 24.7%, it was earning a substantially higher return on its assets than it paid to borrow money. Its ROE of 53.3% illustrates how the increase in ROA translated into an increase in its return to shareholders.
A company's use of leverage can be judged, to some extent, by the difference in its ROE vs. the ROA, as illustrated in the hypothetical example and by High Liner Foods. In addition, several other ratios are used to measure the amount of leverage the company employs, as well as how well it uses that leverage. These ratios include the debt/equity ratio and the times-interest-earned ratio, which are discussed in a later section on liquidity.

Turnover Ratios

In addition to the overall measures of performance, ROA and ROE, there are other measures that are helpful in understanding more specific items that make up the company's overall performance. Three turnover measures are discussed in this book. They relate to the three policy decisions that were discussed in Chapter 5 with regard to the company's cash flow performance. They are the accounts receivable, inventory, and accounts payable turnovers. These ratios provide some quantitative measures of the lead/lag relationships that exist between the revenue and expense recognition and the cash flows related to these three items.

ACCOUNTS RECEIVABLE TURNOVER

The **accounts receivable turnover** ratio attempts to provide information about the company's accounts receivable policy. This ratio measures how many times during a year the accounts receivable balance turns over; that is, how many times old receivables are collected and replaced by new receivables. It is calculated as follows.

$$\text{Accounts receivable turnover} = \frac{\text{Sales on account}}{\text{Average accounts receivable}}$$

When data from financial statements are used, the assumption is usually made that all sales were on account because there is usually no information in the financial statements about the percentage of sales on account vs. cash sales. If the turnover ratio was being prepared for internal use by management, this type of information would be available and would be used when calculating this ratio.

When the data from High Liner Foods are used, the ratio for 2003 is:

ACCOUNTS RECEIVABLE TURNOVER — HIGH LINER FOODS INCORPORATED, 2003

$$\text{Accounts receivable turnover} = \frac{\text{Sales on account}}{\text{Average accounts receivable}}$$

$$= \frac{\$315,879}{\dfrac{\$31,840 + \$35,001}{2}}$$

$$= 9.45 \text{ times}$$

The level of turnover of accounts receivable depends on several factors, especially the normal credit terms granted by the company. If the company normally allows 30 days for the customers to pay, and if customers pay in 30 days, the resulting accounts receivable turnover would be 12 because there would be 30 days of sales always outstanding in accounts receivable. If the normal credit term is 60 days, the resulting accounts receivable turnover would be 6. With an accounts receivable turnover of 9.45, it appears that many of High Liner Foods' receivables have between 30-day and 60-day credit terms. It is also probable that most of High Liner Foods' sales are credit sales in that it sells its products to retail outlets such as grocery store chains.

The turnover number can also be converted into a measure of the days necessary to collect the average receivable by dividing the numbers of days in one year by the turnover ratio. Users may find that the average days to collect is easier to interpret than accounts receivable turnover numbers, although they measure the same thing. To simplify calculations, the number of days in a year is sometimes assumed to be 360 rather than 365. The average days to collect for High Liner Foods are:

**DAYS TO COLLECT ACCOUNTS RECEIVABLE—
HIGH LINER FOODS INCORPORATED, 2003**

$$\text{Days to collect} = \frac{365}{\text{Accounts receivable turnover}}$$

$$= \frac{365}{9.45}$$

$$= 38.6 \text{ days}$$

You cannot simply look at the 38.6 days and decide whether it is bad or good. You need to know what the normal credit terms are, if the average monthly sales are fairly equal, since large sales in the last month of the fiscal year would result in an apparently lower turnover and higher number of days sales in the year-end balance. You also need to know the proportion of total sales that are made on credit. To analyze this ratio more fully, we should also consider a time-series analysis (the trend compared with previous years) and a cross-sectional analysis (a comparison with the competitors of High Liner Foods).

INVENTORY TURNOVER

The **inventory turnover** ratio gives the analyst some idea of how fast inventory is sold or, alternatively, how long the inventory is held prior to sale. The calculation of the turnover is similar to that of the accounts receivable turnover, with a measure of the flow of inventory in the numerator (top number), and a measure of the balance in inventory in the denominator (bottom number). It is calculated as follows.

$$\text{Inventory turnover} = \frac{\text{Cost of goods sold}}{\text{Average inventory}}$$

Note that the numerator contains the cost of goods sold, not the sales value of the goods sold (revenues). Total sales revenue, while it does measure the flow of goods sold to customers, would be inappropriate in the numerator, because it is based on the inventory's selling price while the denominator is measured at cost. Cost of goods sold is measured at cost and is therefore more appropriate.

The number of days for which inventory is held can be calculated from the turnover ratio in the same way as was the accounts receivable turnover ratio.

INVENTORY TURNOVER—HIGH LINER FOODS INCORPORATED, 2003

$$\text{Inventory turnover} = \frac{\$251{,}372}{\dfrac{\$49{,}870 + \$50{,}053}{2}}$$

$$= 5.03 \text{ times}$$

$$\text{Days inventory held} = \frac{365}{\text{Inventory turnover}}$$

$$= \frac{365}{5.03}$$

$$= 72.6 \text{ days}$$

The average number of days that inventory is held depends on the type of inventory produced, used, or sold. In the ratio just calculated, the inventories of High Liner Foods were used. Remember that High Liner Foods' major operations involve the sale of frozen food products to retail grocery outlets. The 72.6 days, therefore, refers to the average length of time that costs remain in inventory from original processing to sale of the products to the grocery outlets. Because the product is frozen, this length of time could be reasonable. Before making this assumption, however, you would want to review this turnover over time and against the inventory turnover ratio of other companies that sell frozen food products.

There is one limitation that must be considered when interpreting the inventory turnover ratio for some companies. Several companies do not disclose the cost of goods sold amount on the statement of earnings. They will sometimes skip from the revenue amount directly to earnings before other operating expenses. You will need to find the cost of goods sold by subtracting earnings before other operating expenses from gross revenue. Another problem with determining this ratio is that companies do not always disclose the cost of goods sold as a separate item on the income statement. Instead, the cost of goods sold is combined with other operating expenses. The resulting figure is, therefore, larger than the cost of goods sold figure and the resulting inventory turnover would be larger as well. Under these circumstances, it is important to treat this ratio with some scepticism.

High Liner Foods is a manufacturing company. The inventory turnover ratio that we calculated used all the inventory: finished goods, raw and semi-finished products and supplies, and repair parts. A more appropriate inventory turnover measure could be to use only the finished goods amounts. If we recalculated the turnover ratio with only the finished goods inventory amount, the ratio would be:

FINISHED GOODS INVENTORY TURNOVER — HIGH LINER FOODS INCORPORATED, 2003

$$\text{Inventory turnover} = \frac{\$251,372}{\dfrac{\$24,143 + \$24,240}{2}}$$

$$= 10.4 \text{ times}$$

$$\text{Days inventory held} = \frac{365}{\text{Inventory turnover}}$$

$$= \frac{365}{10.4}$$

$$= 35.1 \text{ days}$$

Based on this recalculated ratio, it is obvious that the finished goods are not held very long before they are sold (approximately 35 days). As with the accounts receivable turnover ratio, deciding whether this ratio is good or bad would require either a time-series or a cross-sectional analysis, as well as some detailed knowledge of the industry.

ACCOUNTS PAYABLE TURNOVER

The **accounts payable turnover** ratio is similar to the accounts receivable ratio, but provides information about the company's accounts payable policy. In its ideal form, it would be calculated as follows.

$$\text{Accounts payable turnover} = \frac{\text{Credit purchases}}{\text{Average accounts payable}}$$

The problem with the preceding calculation is that a company's credit purchases do not appear directly in the financial statements. It may be possible to approximate the credit purchases by finding the cash payments made to suppliers in the cash flow statement, assuming that the balance in accounts payable did not change drastically during the period. However, this requires that the company prepare its cash flow statement using the direct approach. As mentioned in Chapter 5, almost all companies use the indirect approach to the cash flow statement, and cash payments to suppliers do not appear directly in that statement.

Another alternative is to use the cost of goods sold figure in place of purchases on credit because cost of goods sold appears in the income statement. To the extent that the purchase of goods is the main item that affects cost of goods sold, this would be appropriate. In a retailing company, this would probably be a good approximation, again assuming that the level of inventories did not change dramatically during the period. For a manufacturing company, however, many items other than credit purchases affect the cost of goods sold. For example, a manufacturing company such as High Liner Foods will probably include the amortization of its production equipment in the cost assigned to the inventory it produces.

When this ratio is calculated, most analysts would use the cost of goods sold in the numerator. It would therefore be calculated as:

$$\text{Accounts payable turnover} = \frac{\text{Cost of goods sold}}{\text{Average accounts payable}}$$

For High Liner Foods in 2003, this ratio is:

ACCOUNTS PAYABLE TURNOVER —
HIGH LINER FOODS INCORPORATED, 2003

$$\text{Accounts payable turnover} = \frac{\$251,372}{\dfrac{\$37,424 + \$42,490}{2}}$$

$$= 6.3 \text{ times}$$

$$\text{Days to pay} = \frac{365}{\text{Accounts payable turnover}}$$

$$= \frac{365}{6.3}$$

$$= 58 \text{ days}$$

For High Liner Foods, the calculation of this ratio and the average days to pay appears to be high if the normal credit terms received by High Liner Foods are 30 days. In this case, it may not be appropriate to use the cost of goods sold as an approximation of purchases on credit in that High Liner Foods is a manufacturing company. The cost of sales amount we used probably includes some expenses that are not part of credit purchases (e.g., amortization of equipment). Also, you will notice that we used the accounts payable and accrued liabilities amount from the balance sheet because accounts payable were not listed separately. It is probable that the accrued charges include amounts such as interest payable, which are not included in the cost of goods sold. However, we cannot really understand these numbers without knowing more details of the operations and the amounts that are included in the cost of goods sold and accrued liabilities. Again, cross-sectional and time-series analyses should be undertaken.

Short-Term Liquidity Ratios

As discussed in Chapter 1, liquidity refers to a company's ability to convert assets into cash to pay liabilities. A basic understanding of the company's short-term liquidity position should result from a consideration of the financial statements, particularly the cash flow statement, as well as the turnover ratios discussed in the performance section. Understanding the liquidity position requires knowledge of the leads and lags in the company's cash-to-cash cycle. Additionally, there are at least three ratios that provide quantitative measures of short-term liquidity: the current and quick ratios and the operating cash flow to short-term debt ratio.

CURRENT RATIO

The **current ratio** is calculated by comparing the total current assets with the total current liabilities. It is calculated as follows.

$$\text{Current ratio} = \frac{\text{Current assets}}{\text{Current liabilities}}$$

Remember that current assets are those that are going to be converted into cash in the next year (or company operating cycle if it is longer than one year), and that current liabilities are going to require the use of cash or other assets in the next year. As such, this ratio should be greater than 1; otherwise, it is difficult to see how the company will remain solvent in the next year. The rule of thumb for this ratio for most industries is that it should be 1 or more, but, to be conservative, approximately 2 or more. However, the size of this ratio depends on the type of business and the types of assets and liabilities that are considered current.

One caveat: the current ratio is subject to manipulation by a company at year end. This ratio may not, therefore, be a very reliable measure of liquidity. For example, consider a company that has $100 in current assets and $50 in current liabilities at the end of a given year. Its current ratio would be 2 ($100/$50). Suppose that $25 of the $100 is in cash and the rest is in inventory. Suppose further that the company uses up all of its $25 in cash to pay $25 of current liabilities at year end. The current ratio becomes 3 ($75/$25); now the company looks more liquid. Notice, however, that it is actually less liquid; in fact, it is virtually illiquid in the short term because it has no cash and must sell its inventory and wait until it collects on the sale of that inventory before it will have any cash to pay its bills. In this case, the current ratio is deceptive.

The current ratios for High Liner Foods in 2003 and 2002 are:

CURRENT RATIO—HIGH LINER FOODS INCORPORATED, 2003 AND 2002

2003

$$\text{Current ratio} = \frac{\$91{,}663}{\$48{,}004} = 1.91$$

2002

$$\text{Current ratio} = \frac{\$94{,}733}{\$64{,}369} = 1.47$$

This current ratio of 1.91 in 2003 is an improvement over the 1.47 of the previous year. High Liner Foods can more comfortably handle the short-term obligations. The biggest change from last year to this year is that the long-term liabilities have been significantly reduced in 2003. As a result, the current portion of long-term debt is down to $328 thousand from $15,919 thousand.

QUICK RATIO

One problem with the current ratio is that some assets in the current section are less liquid than others. For example, inventory is usually less liquid than accounts receivable, which are less liquid than cash. In some industries, inventory is very illiquid because of the long period of time that it may have to be held before sale. Consider, for example, the holding period in the manufacture of 12-year-old Scotch whisky. The current ratio in such cases will not adequately measure the company's short-term liquidity because the inventory will not be converted into cash for a long time. In this case, the **quick ratio** is a better measure of short-term liquidity. It differs from the current ratio in that only the most liquid current assets (cash, accounts receivable, and marketable securities) are included in the numerator. Prepaid expenses do not convert into cash. Instead they used cash in the past and the company will be saving cash because amounts have been paid in advance. The ratio is calculated as:

$$\text{Quick ratio} = \frac{\text{Cash} + \text{Accounts receivable} + \text{Short-term investments (held for trading)}}{\text{Current liabilities}}$$

The rule of thumb for this ratio is that it should be approximately 1 or more. A quick ratio of 1 means that the very short-term current assets are equal to the total current liabilities. Again, the actual value depends on the type of industry. For High Liner Foods, the calculation results in:

QUICK RATIO—HIGH LINER FOODS INCORPORATED, 2003 AND 2002

2003

$$\text{Quick ratio} = \frac{\$926 + \$31{,}840}{\$48{,}004} = 0.68$$

2002

$$\text{Quick ratio} = \frac{\$1{,}088 + \$35{,}001}{\$64{,}369} = 0.56$$

Just as with the current ratio, the quick ratio of 0.68 in 2003 is higher than the quick ratio of 0.56 in 2001. The quick ratio in 2003 is still below the 1.0 rule of thumb amount. Taken together, the current ratio and quick ratio indicate that High Liner Foods' liquidity position has improved in the last year. Just reviewing these two years illustrates the importance of time-series analyses in understanding a ratio. Going back further than the two years would enable you to see whether the quick ratio of 0.68 is normal or if the 0.56 is more common. Cross-sectional analyses should also be undertaken with other companies in the food industry.

OPERATING CASH FLOW TO SHORT-TERM DEBT RATIO

In Chapter 5 we discussed the importance of the information on the cash flow statement, how it was prepared and how it should be interpreted. Refer to Chapter 5 to refresh your understanding of the interpretation of the information on the cash flow statement. The cash flow statement details the inflows and outflows of cash from operating, financing, and investing activities. The **operating cash flow to short-term debt ratio** is another measure of the company's ability to meet its short-term debt. The ratio is calculated as:

$$\frac{\text{Operating cash flow}}{\text{Current short-term debt and current maturities of long-term debt}}$$

Like the current ratio and the quick ratio, the higher this ratio is, the better the company can meet its short-term debt obligations. For High Liner Foods, the ratio results for 2003 and 2002 are:

OPERATING CASH FLOW TO SHORT-TERM DEBT RATIO — HIGH LINER FOODS INCORPORATED, 2003 AND 2002

2003

$$\text{Operating cash flow to} = \frac{\$8,350}{\$10,580} = 0.79$$

2002

$$\text{Current ratio} = \frac{\$29,194}{\$21,879} = 1.34$$

The operating cash flow to short-term debt ratio of 0.8 in 2003 has dropped from the 1.34 of the previous year. The decline indicates that High Liner Foods can less comfortably handle the short-term debt obligations. Although most of the long-term debt has been paid off, the short-term bank loan has almost doubled in size and the cash from operations is about a third of the 2002 amount. The decline in the cash from operations is a concern that an analyst would want to follow.

Long-Term Liquidity Ratios

Long-term liquidity refers to the company's ability to pay its obligations in the long term (meaning more than one year in the future). This means its ability to pay its long-term debt. A time-series analysis of the cash flow statement and the patterns of cash flow over time should provide much of the insight you need to assess a company's abilities in this regard. There are at least three ratios that are generally used in the assessment of long-term liquidity: the debt/equity ratio, the times-interest-earned ratio, and the operating cash flow to total debt ratio.

DEBT/EQUITY RATIO

The **debt/equity ratio** is really a set of ratios that are used to assess the extent to which the company is leveraged. From our earlier discussion about leverage, you know that the more leverage a company has, the riskier its situation and the more fixed are its commitments to pay interest. Comparing the amount of debt with the amount of equity in a company is important in assessing its ability to pay off these debts in the long term.

Of the many different definitions of the debt/equity ratios that could be used here, we will show you three. They will be referred to as D/E(I), D/E(II), and D/E(III). D/E(I) expresses the company's total debt as a percentage of total liabilities plus shareholders' equity (the same as total assets). The total liabilities are assumed to include all company liabilities, and the shareholders' equity to include all shareholders' equity accounts. This ratio is calculated as:

$$D/E(I) = \frac{\text{Total liabilities}}{\text{Total liabilities} + \text{Shareholders' equity}}$$

$$\text{Or} \quad \frac{\text{Total liabilities}}{\text{Total assets}}$$

For High Liner Foods in 2003 and 2002, this ratio is:

D/E(I) — HIGH LINER FOODS INCORPORATED, 2003 AND 2002

2003
$$D/E(I) = \frac{\$56,343}{\$177,739}$$
$$= 0.32$$

2002
$$D/E(I) = \frac{\$118,339}{\$207,367}$$
$$= 0.57$$

This first debt/equity ratio tells you that High Liner Food's debt made up just over half of total liabilities and shareholders' equity in 2002. In other words, High Liner Foods used equity and debt almost equally to finance its investment in assets. However, in 2003 the company paid off most of its long-term debt. This action dropped the debt/equity ratio to 0.32. Now less than one third of the financing of assets occurs through debt.

The second debt/equity ratio provides the same information, but in a slightly different form. It is calculated as the ratio of the total liabilities to the total shareholders' equity, as follows.

$$D/E(II) = \frac{\text{Total liabilities}}{\text{Total shareholders' equity}}$$

For High Liner Foods in 2003 and 2002, this ratio is:

D/E(II) — HIGH LINER FOODS INCORPORATED, 2003 AND 2002

2003

$$D/E(II) = \frac{\$56,343}{\$121,396}$$

$$= 0.46$$

2002

$$D/E(II) = \frac{\$118,339}{\$89,028}$$

$$= 1.33$$

This ratio tells you, in a different way, that in 2003, the debt is about half of the equity amount. In other words, High Liner Foods uses equity more often to finance its assets. In 2002, the debt and equity were closer to the same amount, with the debt being slightly larger than the equity. The reduction of the debt in 2003 changed the company's financing structure.

The third debt/equity ratio focuses on the company's long-term debt relative to its equity. It is calculated as the ratio of the total long-term liabilities to the sum of the total long-term liabilities plus the shareholders' equity, as follows.

$$D/E(III) = \frac{\text{Total long-term liabilities}}{\text{Total long-term liabilities + Shareholders' equity}}$$

For High Liner Foods in 2003 and 2002, this ratio is:

D/E(III) — HIGH LINER FOODS INCORPORATED, 2003 AND 2002

2003

$$D/E(III) = \frac{\$8,339}{\$8,339 + \$121,396}$$

$$= 0.06$$

2002

$$D/E(III) = \frac{\$53,970}{\$53,970 + \$89,028}$$

$$= 0.38$$

This ratio dramatically shows you the impact on the company's financial structure of paying off most of the long-term debt. In 2002, 38% of the long-term debt and shareholders' equity was long-term debt. In 2003, that amount dropped to 6%.

The three debt/equity ratios have portrayed similar messages to the user using different ratios. Because of the variety of ways that this information can be determined, you need to know what formula was used so that you can appropriately interpret the results. Is the level of debt represented in these ratios appropriate for High

Liner Foods? Again, a cross-sectional analysis could reveal whether the company has excessive debt compared with other companies. A time-series analysis could reveal the trend over time. As a general guide, however, the average of corporate debt on the books of nonfinancial companies is somewhere between 45% and 50%. High Liner Foods, with a ratio of 57% in 2002, appeared to be very close to that average. In 2003, however, the drop to 32% put it below the average of corporate debt.

TIMES-INTEREST-EARNED RATIO

The second ratio in the long-term liquidity section is the **times-interest-earned** (TIE) ratio. It compares the amount of earnings available to pay interest with the level of interest expense. Because interest is tax-deductible, the earnings available to pay interest would be the earnings prior to the payment of interest or taxes. The easiest way to find the income before interest and taxes is to start with the net income amount and add the income taxes and interest expense to it. One complication in the calculation of this ratio is that some companies capitalize interest when they construct long-term assets. This means that instead of expensing interest, a company can record the interest in an asset account. This generally happens only when a company is constructing an asset and incurs interest on money borrowed to finance the construction. The adjustment to the ratio is that the amount of interest capitalized should be added to the denominator. (Note: when we first introduced this ratio in Chapter 10, we did not bring capitalized interest into the calculation.) The numerator does not require adjustment if the amount of interest expensed is added back to net income. The ratio is therefore calculated as:

$$\text{Times interest earned} = \frac{\text{Income before interest and taxes}}{\text{Interest (including capitalized interest)}}$$

High Liner Foods does not say anything in the notes to the financial statements about capitalizing interest on assets constructed over time. We, therefore, do not need to adjust the denominator. The ratio is therefore calculated as:

TIMES INTEREST EARNED — HIGH LINER FOODS INCORPORATED, 2003 AND 2002

2003

$$\text{TIE} = \frac{\$46,119 + (\$120) + \$2,373}{\$2,373}$$

$$= 20.4$$

2002

$$\text{TIE} = \frac{\$10,242 + \$3,653 + \$6,586}{\$6,586}$$

$$= 3.2$$

In 2002, prior to the payment of most of the long-term debt, the company could pay the interest expense the equivalent of three times out of earnings. This is not a very comfortable cushion. As a lender, a low times-interest-earned ratio should concern you. In 2003, the company's ability to pay interest expense jumped to 20 times out of earnings. This is a very comfortable margin. The earnings would have to drop to 1/20 of the current level before the company would have trouble paying the interest. Lenders would see this as a positive sign with respect to High Liner Foods' ability to repay debt.

OPERATING CASH FLOW TO TOTAL DEBT RATIO

The final ratio in the long-term liquidity section is the **operating cash flow to total debt ratio**. This ratio measures the company's ability to cover its total debt with the annual operating cash flow. Like the current ratio, the higher this ratio, the stronger the indication of the company's ability to generate cash and pay for its obligations. This ratio is broader than the previous operating cash flow ratio. Because not all of the debt will need to be paid at once, this ratio can be less than one. From the ratio you should be able to estimate how many years of operating cash flow would be necessary to pay for the total debt. The ratio is calculated as:

$$\text{Operating cash flow to total debt} = \frac{\text{Operating cash flow}}{\text{Total debt}}$$

For High Liner Foods in 2003 and 2002, the ratio is:

OPERATING CASH FLOW TO TOTAL DEBT — HIGH LINER FOODS INCORPORATED, 2003 AND 2002

2003

$$\text{Operating cash flow to total debt} = \frac{\$8,350}{\$56,343} = 0.15$$

2002

$$\text{Operating cash flow to total debt} = \frac{\$29,194}{\$118,339} = 0.25$$

Because of the decline in the cash from operations in 2003, the operating cash flow to total debt declined from 0.25 in 2002 to 0.15 in 2003 despite the fact that a large portion of the long-term debt had been paid off. Another way of looking at this ratio is to determine how many years of operating cash flow at the current level would be required to pay off the total debt. In 2003, the ratio of 0.15 could be converted into 6.7 years by inverting the ratio ($56,343/$8,350). In other words, with the current level of operating cash flow ($8,350), it would take the company 6.7 years to generate enough cash to pay off all the debt in 2003. Remember that some of the debt must be paid off in the following year and the rest over several years depending on the maturity dates associated with the debt. You would need to read the notes associated with the long-term debt to determine if the current level of operating cash flow will be sufficient for the company's future cash needs.

Earnings Per Share Ratios

The **earnings per share ratio** is one that is quoted quite often in the financial press and one in which shareholders are very interested. In its simplest form, it is the company's earnings divided by the weighted average number of common shares outstanding. Although this ratio may be of some help in analyzing a company's results, its usefulness is limited. The major problem with using it as a measure of performance is that it ignores the level of investment. Companies with the same earnings per share might have very different profitabilities, depending on their investment in net assets. The other limitation is that the shares of different companies are not equivalent, and companies with the same overall profitability may have different earnings per share figures because they have a different number of shares outstanding that represent ownership. The best use of the earnings per share figure is in a time-series analysis rather than in a cross-sectional analysis.

The earnings per share calculation represents the earnings per common share. Therefore, if the company also issues preferred shares, the effects of the preferred shares must be removed in calculating the ratio. With preferred shares outstanding, this means that any dividends that are paid to preferred shareholders should be deducted from net income because that amount of income is not available to common shareholders. The number of preferred shares outstanding should also be left out of the denominator. The calculation of basic earnings per share then becomes:

$$\text{Basic earnings per share} = \frac{\text{Net income} - \text{Preferred dividends}}{\text{Weighted average number of common shares outstanding}}$$

The preferred dividends that should be deducted are the cumulative preferred dividends, whether they are declared in the year or not, and any noncumulative preferred dividends that have been declared in the year. Recall from Chapter 11 that cumulative means that if a dividend is not declared on the preferred shares in one year, the dividends then carry over into the next year. In the second year, both the prior year's preferred dividends and the current year's preferred dividends must be declared before any common dividends can be declared. In addition to preferred shares, another complicating factor in the calculation of earnings per share arises when the company issues any securities that are convertible into common shares. Examples of these types of securities are convertible debt, convertible preferred shares, and stock option plans. The key feature of these securities is that they are all convertible into common shares under certain conditions. If additional common shares are issued upon their conversion, the earnings per share number could decrease because of the larger number of shares that would be outstanding. This is called the potential dilution of earnings per share.

At the end of a given accounting period, the presence of convertible securities creates some uncertainty about how to report the earnings per share number. Should the company report earnings per share without considering the potentially dilutive effects of the convertible securities, or should it disclose some information that would allow readers of the financial statements to understand these effects? To provide the best information for users of financial statements, we should disclose information about the dilutive effects of convertible securities.

Thus, financial statements may include several earnings per share figures, the main ones being the basic earnings per share and the fully diluted earnings per share.

BASIC EARNINGS PER SHARE

Basic earnings per share is usually a very simple number that considers only the net income, preferred dividends, and weighted average number of common shares outstanding. Every published financial statement shows this figure. Note in Exhibit

12-3 on the statement of income for High Liner Foods that there is a basic earnings per share of $4.52. If High Liner Foods had any extraordinary items or had discontinued some of its operations during the year, there would have been earnings per share amounts on the income statement balances both before the extraordinary items or discontinued operations and after. The reason for multiple amounts is that the company would have backed these amounts out of the normal continuing operations and shown them separately. When users review the financial statements, it is usually with two objectives in mind: first, to see how the company did during the last year, and second, to assess how it might do in the future. Because of this future focus, it is important for companies to take extraordinary items and discontinued operations that will not affect the future and isolate them from continuing operations that may be a good measure of future operations. To help users in their evaluation, whenever there are non-future items such as discontinued items or extraordinary items, multiple basic earnings per share figures are disclosed: one for continuing operations and one for net income. The basic earnings per share from continuing operations is probably more useful.

FULLY DILUTED EARNINGS PER SHARE

Fully diluted earnings per share is calculated under the worst-case scenario set of assumptions. The company identifies all the dilutive securities that will have a negative effect on the earnings per share amount if they are converted. For example, if convertible preferred shares are converted to common shares, the number of common shares outstanding will increase. At the same time, the numerator will also increase because, if the preferred shares are now common shares, there will no longer be any preferred dividends and all the net income will be available to the common shareholders. Because both the numerator and the denominator increase, the effect of a conversion on earnings per share is not always negative. Under the worst-case scenario for determining fully diluted earnings per share, the calculation includes only those conversions that will have a negative effect on earnings per share. The calculation of fully diluted earnings per share is a heads-up calculation for users. It attempts to tell them how much the earnings per share could decline in the future if all the dilutive convertible securities were converted to common shares.

High Liner Foods has convertible subordinated debentures and stock options. As a result of these items, in 2003 it reported a fully diluted earnings per share amount of $4.13 (compared with the basic earnings per share of $4.52). If the company had extraordinary items or discontinued operations, it would have disclosed a fully diluted earnings per share from continuing operations and from net earnings. Like the disclosure for basic earnings per share, it is important to distinguish between the amounts that reflect possible future earnings and those that represent net earnings. For High Liner Foods, convertible debentures and stock options have caused the fully diluted earnings per share amounts to be lower than the basic earnings per share amounts. The decline from $4.52 to $4.13 is a fairly significant drop (approximately an 8.5% decline). Shareholders should pay attention to the future conversion of the debentures and stock options to common shares because they will have a negative effect on common earnings per share.

Price/Earnings Ratio

The **price/earnings ratio**, or **multiple**, compares the price per share on the stock market with the company's earnings per share. Many analysts think of this ratio as the price investors are willing to pay for a dollar's worth of earnings. The interpretation of this ratio is somewhat difficult because stock market price levels are not well understood. It might help to think of the multiple in terms of its inverse. If a company is earning $1 per common share and the shares are selling for $20 on the stock market, this indicates that the current multiple is 20. The inverse of this multiple is 1/20, or 5%. This indicates that the shares are returning 5% in the form of earnings per share when compared with the market price. Many factors affect the level of stock market prices, including the prevailing interest rates and the company's future prospects. It is sometimes useful to think that the market price reflects the present value of all future expected earnings of the company. Companies with a high growth potential tend to have a higher price/earnings ratio. Companies with a low growth potential have a lower price/earnings ratio. The earnings per share figure serves as an important link between the accounting numbers produced in the financial statements and the stock market price of the company's shares.

NON-MANUFACTURING OR NON-RETAIL COMPANY ANALYSIS

Although the above discussion applies to most companies in most industries, some differences for non-manufacturing or non-retail companies should be noted. As an example of a non-manufacturing or non-retail company, consider the analysis of a financial services company such as a bank, an insurance company, or a finance company. These types of companies invest in very different kinds of assets than manufacturers or retailers, and they obtain their financing from different sources. The assets of financial services companies consist of almost no inventories and relatively little property, plant, and equipment. The majority of their assets consist of loans that they made to their customers or other investments. The assets of most non-financial companies consist mainly of property, plant, and equipment, inventories, and receivables.

The liability sections of financial services companies' balance sheets are also very different from those of manufacturers or retailers. The first major difference is the debt/equity ratio. Financial services companies tend to have considerably higher debt/equity ratios than manufacturers or retailers because of the large amounts of cash received from depositors. In the insurance industry, the high ratio results from amounts owed to policyholders. Second, liabilities of financial services companies such as banks tend to be predominantly short-term in nature because of the deposits received from customers, which are normally payable upon demand. Many customers, however, leave amounts with these companies for long periods of time. This means that, although they are technically short-term because the customer can withdraw the funds at any time, in reality they are often long-term in nature.

The higher leverage employed by financial services companies reflects, in part, the lower risk of the types of assets in which these companies invest. In addition to employing financial leverage, manufacturers also employ something called operating leverage. Operating leverage involves investing in large amounts of property, plant, and equipment (capital assets with fixed amortization costs). The property, plant, and equipment allow manufacturers to make their own inventory rather than buying it from an outside supplier (variable costs). The risk is that the manufacturers must operate at a sufficient volume to allow their profit from the sale of goods to cover their fixed costs. At large volumes, this makes manufacturing companies very profitable, but at low volumes, they generate large losses because the fixed costs must be paid from the lower sales volumes. Partially because of the amount of operating leverage, lenders generally do not lend to manufacturers as much as they lend to financial services companies.

A complete analysis of financial services companies is beyond the scope of this book. It is hoped that this brief discussion of some of the differences between these companies and manufacturers and retailers will provide some insights into how an analysis of these companies may differ.

SUMMARY

At this point in the book, we have discussed all the major financial statements and specific accounting methods and principles that apply to each category within the asset, liability, and shareholders' equity sections of the balance sheet. We have devoted this final chapter to methods you can use to gain some insight into how to interpret the information that you find reported on the financial statements. By comparing amounts on one financial statement with related amounts on another financial statement, we are able to assess the impact of various items on a company's health and future prospects. We restricted the discussion to fairly simple companies to make it easier for you to learn the basics.

In Appendix B at the back of the book, you will find additional information about complex organizations. These are companies (usually called parent companies) that buy an interest in other companies (called subsidiaries) to obtain control of the subsidiary's resources. The majority of the real companies reported in this book are parent companies that have one or more subsidiaries. You can tell if a company is a parent company if it prepares consolidated financial statements. If you flip back through the examples of financial statements that we showed you in the book, you will see that most of them are consolidated. Complex issues face the accountant, such as how to represent the resources controlled by the shareholders of the parent company.

Ratio Summary

Exhibit 12-11 summarizes the ratios that were developed in the chapter.

EXHIBIT 12-11 **RATIO SUMMARY**

$$ROA = \text{Profit Margin Ratio} \times \text{Total Asset Turnover}$$

$$= \frac{\text{Net income} + [\text{Interest expense} \times (1 - \text{Tax rate})]}{\text{Sales revenue}} \times \frac{\text{Sales revenue}}{\text{Average total assets}}$$

$$ROE = \frac{\text{Net income} - \text{Preferred dividends}}{\text{Average shareholders' equity}}$$

$$\text{Accounts Receivable Turnover} = \frac{\text{Sale on account}}{\text{Average accounts receivable}}$$

$$\text{Inventory Turnover} = \frac{\text{Cost of goods sold}}{\text{Average inventory}}$$

$$\text{Accounts Payable Turnover} = \frac{\text{Cost of goods sold}}{\text{Average accounts payable}}$$

$$\text{Current Ratio} = \frac{\text{Current assets}}{\text{Current liabilities}}$$

$$\text{Quick Ratio} = \frac{\text{Cash} + \text{Accounts receivable} + \text{Marketable securities}}{\text{Current liabilities}}$$

$$\text{Operating Cash Flow to Short-term Debt Ratio} = \frac{\text{Operating cash flow}}{\text{Current short-term debt and current maturities of long-term debt}}$$

$$\text{D/E(I)} = \frac{\text{Total liabilities}}{\text{Total liabilities} + \text{Shareholders' equity}}$$

$$\text{D/E(II)} = \frac{\text{Total liabilities}}{\text{Shareholders' equity}}$$

$$\text{D/E(III)} = \frac{\text{Total long-term liabilities}}{\text{Total long-term liabilities} + \text{Shareholders' equity}}$$

$$\text{Times Interest Earned (TIE)} = \frac{\text{Net income} + \text{Taxes} + \text{Interest}}{\text{Interest}}$$

$$\text{Operating Cash Flow to Total Debt Ratio} = \frac{\text{Operating cash flow}}{\text{Total Debt}}$$

$$\text{Price/Earnings Ratio} = \frac{\text{Stock market price}}{\text{Earnings per share}}$$

SUMMARY PROBLEM

The statements of earnings, balance sheets, and cash flow statements of **Canadian Tire Corporation, Limited** are shown in Exhibit 12-12. Calculate the following ratios for 2003 based on the data in the financial statements. Comment on what the ratios tell us about the financial position of Canadian Tire and what further analyses you should undertake.

LEARNING OBJECTIVE 5

Assess a company's financial health through the use of ratios.

Performance Ratios:

1. ROA (Break down into profit margin ratio and total asset turnover; use 36% for the tax rate)

2. ROE

3. Accounts receivable turnover

4. Inventory turnover

5. Accounts payable turnover

Additional Demonstration Problems

EXHIBIT 12-12 PART A **CANADIAN TIRE CORPORATION, LIMITED 2003 ANNUAL REPORT**
Consolidated Statements of Earnings and Retained Earnings

Consolidated Statements of Earnings and Retained Earnings

For the years ended (Dollars in millions except per share amounts)	January 3, **2004** **(53 weeks)**	December 28, 2002 (52 weeks)
Gross operating revenue	**$ 6,552.8**	$ 5,944.5
Operating expenses		
Cost of merchandise sold and all other operating expenses except for the undernoted items	**5,916.3**	5,369.5
Interest		
Long-term debt	**82.4**	80.3
Short-term debt	**2.6**	2.7
Depreciation and amortization	**154.0**	158.5
Employee profit sharing plan (Note 9)	**23.7**	19.9
Total operating expenses	**6,179.0**	5,630.9
Earnings before income taxes and minority interest	**373.8**	313.6
Income taxes (Note 10)		
Current	**107.5**	96.6
Future	**11.0**	7.2
Total income taxes	**118.5**	103.8
Net earnings before minority interest	**255.3**	209.8
Minority interest (Note 16)	**8.7**	7.4
Net earnings	**$ 246.6**	$ 202.4
Basic earnings per share	**$ 3.06**	$ 2.56
Diluted earnings per share (Note 8)	**$ 3.02**	$ 2.53
Weighted average number of Common and Class A Non-Voting Shares outstanding	**80,605,607**	79,055,846
Retained earnings, beginning of year	**$1,138.0**	$ 973.1
Net earnings	**246.6**	202.4
Dividends	**(32.5)**	(31.6)
Repurchase of Class A Non-Voting Shares (Note 8)	**(17.9)**	(5.9)
Retained earnings, end of year	**$ 1,334.2**	$ 1,138.0

CANADIAN TIRE CORPORATION, LIMITED 2003 ANNUAL REPORT
Consolidated Balance Sheets

Consolidated Balance Sheets

As at (Dollars in millions)	January 3, 2004	December 28, 2002
ASSETS		
Current assets		
Cash and cash equivalents (Note 11)	$ **726.6**	$ 628.2
Accounts receivable (Note 11)	**489.4**	584.1
Credit charge receivables (Note 2)	**562.8**	579.8
Merchandise inventories	**493.9**	503.0
Prepaid expenses and deposits	**27.9**	19.1
Total current assets	**2,300.6**	2,314.2
Long-term receivables and other assets (Note 3)	**64.1**	126.7
Goodwill (Note 4)	**40.6**	32.8
Intangible assets (Note 4)	**52.0**	52.0
Property and equipment (Note 5)	**2,443.4**	2,349.7
Total assets	**$ 4,900.7**	$ 4,875.4
LIABILITIES		
Current liabilities		
Accounts payable and other	**$1,266.6**	$1,294.7
Income taxes payable	**96.5**	80.7
Current portion of long-term debt (Note 6)	**244.5**	208.2
Total current liabilities	**1,607.6**	1,583.6
Long-term debt (Note 6)	**886.2**	1,125.2
Employee future benefits (Note 7)	**34.2**	31.3
Future income taxes (Note 10)	**39.4**	28.4
Total liabilities	**2,567.4**	2,768.5
Minority interest (Note 16)	**300.0**	300.0
SHAREHOLDERS' EQUITY		
Share capital (Note 8)	**700.5**	661.0
Contributed surplus	**0.7**	—
Accumulated foreign currency translation adjustment	**(2.1)**	7.9
Retained earnings	**1,334.2**	1,138.0
Total shareholders' equity	**2,033.3**	1,806.9
Total liabilities, minority interest and shareholders' equity	**4,900.7**	$ 4,875.4

EXHIBIT 12-12
PART C

CANADIAN TIRE CORPORATION, LIMITED 2003 ANNUAL REPORT
Consolidated Statements of Cash Flows

Consolidated Statements of Cash Flows

For the years ended (Dollars in millions)	January 3, 2004 (52 weeks)	December 28, 2002 (52 weeks)
Cash generated from (used for):		
Operating activities		
Net earnings	$ 246.6	$ 202.4
Items not affecting cash		
Depreciation and amortization of property and equipment	149.6	146.1
Net provision for credit charge receivables	147.9	107.8
Future income taxes	11.0	7.2
Amortization of other assets	4.4	12.4
Employee future benefits (Note 7)	2.9	3.0
Stock-based compensation expense	0.7	—
Gain on sales of credit charge receivables (Note 2)	(16.8)	(12.2)
Gain on disposals of property and equipment	(4.3)	(4.4)
Cash generated from operations	542.0	462.3
Changes in other working capital components (Note 11)	(23.4)	(18.0)
Cash generated from operating activities	518.6	444.3
Investing activities		
Investment in credit charge receivables	(646.3)	(596.7)
Additions to property and equipment	(278.7)	(249.7)
Purchases of franchise stores (Note 18)	(11.2)	(10.4)
Long-term receivables and other assets	58.2	(12.8)
Proceeds on disposition of property and equipment	40.2	31.2
Purchase of subsidiary (note 17)	—	(112.7)
Cash used for investing activities	(837.8)	(951.1)
Financing activities		
Securitization of credit charge receivables	532.2	446.6
Sale of Associate Dealer receivables (Note 11)	98.7	150.9
Class A Non-Voting Share transactions (Note 8)	21.6	33.0
Issuance of long-term debt	5.8	—
Repayment of long-term debt	(208.5)	(42.7)
Dividends	(32.2)	(31.6)
Cash generated from financing activities	417.6	556.2
Cash generated in the year	98.4	49.4
Cash and cash equivalents, beginning of year	628.2	578.8
Cash and cash equivalents, end of year(Note 11)	$726.6	628.2

Short-Term Liquidity Ratios:

6. Current ratio

7. Quick ratio

8. Operating cash flow to short-term debt ratio

Long-Term Liquidity Ratios:

9. Debt/equity ratios

10. Times-interest-earned ratio

11. Operating cash flow to total debt ratio

SUGGESTED SOLUTION TO SUMMARY PROBLEM

ROA:

ROA (BREAKDOWN)—CANADIAN TIRE CORPORATION, LIMITED, 2003

ROA = Profit Margin Ratio $\times$ Total Asset Turnover

$$= \frac{\text{Net income} + [\text{Interest expense} \times (1 - \text{Tax rate})]}{\text{Sales revenue}} \times \frac{\text{Sales revenue}}{\text{Average total assets}}$$

$$= \frac{\$246,600 + [\$85,000^* \times (1 - .36)]}{\$6,552,800} \times \frac{\$6,552,800}{\dfrac{\$4,900,700 + \$4,875,400}{2}}$$

$$= 4.6\% \times 1.34 = 6.16\%$$

*The interest expense is the sum of the short-term and long-term interest.

ROE:

ROE—CANADIAN TIRE CORPORATION, LIMITED, 2003

$$\text{ROE} = \frac{\text{Net income} - \text{Preferred dividends}}{\text{Average shareholders' equity}}$$

$$= \frac{\$246,600 - 0^*}{\dfrac{\$2,033,300 + \$1,806,900}{2}}$$

$$= 12.8\%$$

*Although the company had Class A Non-voting shares, it has always treated them as equivalent to common shares because they are fully participating. The earnings per share is calculated using both the Class A Non-voting shares and the Common shares.

Accounts Receivable Turnover:

A/R TURNOVER—CANADIAN TIRE CORPORATION, LIMITED, 2003

$$\text{Accounts Receivable Turnover} = \frac{\text{Credit sales}}{\text{Average accounts receivable}}$$

$$= \frac{\$6,552,800^*}{\dfrac{\$1,052,200 + \$1,163,900}{2}}$$

$$= 5.9 \text{ times}$$

$$\text{Days to collect} = \frac{365 \text{ days}}{\text{Receivable turnover}}$$

$$= \frac{365 \text{ days}}{5.9}$$

$$= 61.9 \text{ days}$$

*Total sales was used because no amount for credit sales was given. Because the total amount does include some cash sales, the accounts receivable turnover will be inflated. It will actually take longer to collect the accounts receivable than is indicated by this ratio. Average accounts receivable includes both accounts receivable and credit charge receivables. Because CanadianTire has its own credit card, customers will be able to pay over a period of longer than 30 days.

Inventory Turnover:

INVENTORY TURNOVER — CANADIAN TIRE CORPORATION, LIMITED, 2003

$$\text{Inventory Turnover} = \frac{\text{Cost of goods sold}}{\text{Average inventory}}$$

$$= \frac{\$5,916,300^*}{\dfrac{\$493,900 + \$503,000}{2}}$$

$$= 11.87 \text{ times}$$

$$\text{Days Inventory Held} = \frac{365 \text{ days}}{\text{Inventory turnover}}$$

$$= \frac{365 \text{ days}}{11.87}$$

$$= 30.7 \text{ days}$$

*Cost of merchandise sold and all other operating expenses was used because the company did not disclose cost of goods sold separately. Because other operating expenses were included in the numerator, the inventory turnover will be inflated. It will actually take longer to sell the inventory than is indicated by this ratio.

Accounts Payable Turnover:

A/P TURNOVER — CANADIAN TIRE CORPORATION, LIMITED, 2003

$$\text{Accounts Payable Turnover} = \frac{\text{Cost of goods sold}}{\text{Average accounts payable}}$$

$$= \frac{\$5,916,300^*}{\dfrac{\$1,266,600 + \$1,294,700}{2}}$$

$$= 4.62$$

$$\text{Days to Pay} = \frac{365 \text{ days}}{\text{Payable turnover}}$$

$$= \frac{365 \text{ days}}{4.74}$$

$$= 79 \text{ days}$$

*The company does not disclose accounts payable as a separate item. It provides instead the sum of accounts payable and other (current liabilities). This means that the average accounts payable amount used in the ratio is larger than accounts payable, and the number of days to pay is therefore much higher than would be the reality for the company. Because the cost of goods sold amount also includes additional expenses, it becomes even more difficult to interpret this ratio.

Current Ratio:

CURRENT RATIO — CANADIAN TIRE CORPORATION, LIMITED, 2003

$$\text{Current Ratio} = \frac{\text{Current assets}}{\text{Current liabilities}}$$

$$= \frac{\$2,300,600}{\$1,607,600}$$

$$= 1.4$$

Quick Ratio:

QUICK RATIO — CANADIAN TIRE CORPORATION, LIMITED, 2003

$$\text{Quick ratio} = \frac{\text{Cash and cash equivalents} + \text{Accounts receivable} + \text{Credit charge receivables}}{\text{Current liabilities}}$$

$$= \frac{\$726,600 + \$489,400 + \$562,800}{\$1,607,600}$$

$$= 1.11$$

Operating Cash Flow to Short-Term Debt Ratio:

OPERATING CASH FLOW TO SHORT-TERM DEBT RATIO — CANADIAN TIRE CORPORATION, LIMITED, 2003

$$\frac{\text{Operating cash flow to}}{\text{Short-term debt}} = \frac{\text{Operating cash flow}}{\text{Current short-term debt and current maturities of long-term debt}}$$

$$= \frac{\$518,600}{\$244,500^*}$$

$$= 2.12$$

*The company does not have any short-term debt (no bank loans), therefore only the current maturities of long-term debt was used.

D/E(I):

D/E(I) — CANADIAN TIRE CORPORATION, LIMITED, 2003

$$\text{D/E(I)} = \frac{\text{Total liabilities}}{\text{Total liabilities} + \text{Shareholders' equity}}$$

$$= \frac{\$2,767,462^*}{\$2,767,462 + \$1,603,694}$$

$$= 63.3\%$$

*Includes Minority Interest (the same as noncontrolling interest)

D/E(II):

D/E(II) — CANADIAN TIRE CORPORATION, LIMITED, 2003

$$\text{D/E(II)} = \frac{\text{Total liabilities}}{\text{Shareholders' equity}}$$

$$= \frac{\$2,767,462}{\$1,603,694}$$

$$= 1.73$$

D/E(III):

D/E(III) — CANADIAN TIRE CORPORATION, LIMITED, 2003

$$\text{D/E(III)} = \frac{\text{Total long-term liabilities}}{\text{Total long-term liabilities} + \text{Shareholders' equity}}$$

$$= \frac{\$1,259,800}{\$1,259,800 + \$2,033,300}$$

$$= 0.38$$

Times Interest Earned:

TIE — CANADIAN TIRE CORPORATION, LIMITED, 2003

$$\text{TIE} = \frac{\text{Net income} + \text{Taxes} + \text{Interest}}{\text{Interest}}$$

$$= \frac{\$246,600 + \$118,500 + \$82,400 + \$2,600}{\$82,400 + \$2,600}$$

$$= 5.3 \text{ times}$$

Operating Cash Flow to Total Debt:

OPERATING CASH FLOW TO TOTAL DEBT — CANADIAN TIRE CORPORATION, LIMITED, 2003

$$\text{Operating cash flow to total debt} = \frac{\text{Operating cash flow}}{\text{Total debt}}$$

$$= \frac{\$518,600}{\$2,867,400}$$

$$= .18$$

Performance Ratios

In analyzing the performance of any company, first consider the net income and its trend. For Canadian Tire, the net income is positive. It is up about 10% from 2002. This indicates that Canadian Tire is growing. It sells automotive and household goods, which do not change as much as clothing does. In 2002, Canadian Tire acquired **Mark's Work Wearhouse Limited**. This may cause some fluctuation in its earnings in the future. The earnings per share has been growing, reflecting the growth in earnings. Next, consider the ROA and ROE ratios. ROA is 6.16% and the ROE is 12.8%. The ROA of 6.16% indicates that Canadian Tire is earning a modest return on assets, although it is somewhat larger than could be earned if the assets were invested in bank deposits. From the breakdown in the ROA calculation, the performance by Canadian Tire is seen in its profit margin (4.6%) and not its asset turnover (1.34%). Canadian Tire has a reasonable markup on its automotive and household merchandise but it is much lower than many clothing or furniture stores. The ROE of 12.8% is significantly larger than the ROA and indicates the company is making use of leverage.

The turnover figures are interesting and some may be distorted. The calculation of the accounts receivable turnover of 5.9 times indicates there are 61.9 days sales in accounts receivable. This is not within the normal credit term of 30 days. Because Canadian Tire has its own credit card, customers can probably take longer than 30 days to pay off the amount owed. However, in calculating the ratio we were not able to use credit sales because that amount was not disclosed. Canadian Tire accepts credit cards but also makes a large number of cash sales. Using the total sales amount to calculate this ratio has obviously inflated the turnover rate; by how much, we cannot determine. The inventory turnover of 11.87 times indicates that there are 30.7 days sales of inventory on hand. This indicates that the company is carrying just over a month of inventory. Considering that much of Canadian Tire's merchandise is not time sensitive, this seems to be a very quick turnover.

The accounts payable turnover of 4.62 times indicates that the company pays its suppliers an average of 79 days after incurring the obligation. This ratio is obviously distorted by the inclusion of accrued liabilities in the denominator and the cost of merchandise sold and all other operating expenses in the numerator. There are more items included besides the amounts owed to suppliers of inventory, which makes this ratio impossible to interpret.

Further analyses would include common size financial statements to determine the trends in the cost of goods sold and other expenses (shown in Exhibit 12-13), and trend analyses of the ROA and ROE.

CANADIAN TIRE CORPORATION, LIMITED

EXHIBIT 12-13

Common Size Income Statement

	2003	2002
Gross operating revenue	100.0%	100.0%
Operating expenses		
Cost of merchandise sold and all other operating expenses except for the undernoted items	90.29%	90.33%
Interest		
Long-term debt	1.26%	1.35%
Short-term debt	.04%	.05%
Depreciation and amortization	2.35%	2.67%
Employee profit sharing plans	.36%	.33%
Total operating expenses	94.30%	94.73%
Earnings before income taxes	5.70%	5.27%
Income taxes		
Current	1.64%	1.63%
Future	.17%	.12%
Total income taxes	1.81%	1.75%
Net earnings before minority interest	3.89%	3.52%
Minority interest	.13%	.12%
Net earnings	3.76%	3.40%

These common size statements show that net earnings improved slightly in 2003. Sales have increased and supporting expenses, including cost of goods sold, have declined slightly, which enables the company to improve its net earnings. There are a few fluctuations in the other expenses, but where one has risen, another has fallen so that overall the total expenses are relatively constant.

Short-Term Liquidity Ratios

The current ratio is reasonable at 1.4. The quick ratio at 1.11 shows that the company has a number of liquid assets that will enable it to pay its liabilities as they come due. Because of this company's large cash sales, the cash inflow from inventory will probably improve the payment of liabilities even more. The cash flow from operations on the cash flow statement is positive and more than twice the size of the net income amount. This provides evidence that the company does not have a cash flow problem. The cash flow from operations is, as well, much higher than it was last year, which is another positive signal. The operating cash flow to short-term debt ratio at 2.12 shows that the company generates more than twice the amount of cash from operations needed to settle short-term debt.

Long-Term Liquidity

Canadian Tire Corporation is financed 58.5% by debt and 41.5% by equity. Approximately 40% of the total liabilities are in long-term debt with 22% of the debt coming due in 2004. The moderately high debt/equity ratios result in an increment for leverage. The ROE of 12.8% is quite a bit higher than the ROA at 6.16%. This means that the company is able to make good use of leverage. High debt/equity ratios require a stable market for the products sold. The automotive and household products market is relatively stable. Canadian Tire must monitor its use of debt because it requires repayment.

Interesting information can be found in the cash flow statement. In 2003, the cash inflow from operating activities was positive, as it should be. The income was higher than the previous year and the cash generated from operations was higher than 2003. In both 2003 and 2002, the working capital components (noncash current assets and liabilities) resulted in a negative amount ($23,400 thousand and $18,000 thousand respectively). There have been small changes in the various current assets and liabilities. All of these generated a negative working capital adjustment. With the increase in sales, you would expect to see an increase in the inventory and accounts receivable levels. However, both inventory and accounts receivable are lower than in 2002. Income tax payable has increased, which is probably a function of the increase in earnings.

Cash is being used to invest in property and equipment, credit charge receivables, and the purchase of franchise stores, which is also a good sign. This new investment is being financed with securitization of credit card receivables, the sale of associate dealer receivables, and the issuance of new shares. Long-term debt has been reduced. The company's times-interest-earned ratio indicates that it can cover the interest payment at least five times from earnings. The operating cash flow to total debt at .18 indicates that five years of operating cash flows would be sufficient to cover all the debt. Canadian Tire consistently pays dividends every year. As an investor, if you were looking for an investment that would pay you periodically in the form of dividends, this may be what you are looking for.

ABBREVIATION USED

P/E ratio	Price/earnings ratio
ROA	Return on assets
ROE	Return on equity
TIE	Times interest earned

GLOSSARY

Accounts payable turnover   The number of times that accounts payable are replaced during the accounting period. It is usually calculated as the cost of goods sold divided by the average accounts payable.

Accounts receivable turnover   The number of times that accounts receivable are replaced during the accounting period. It is calculated as the credit sales divided by the average accounts receivable.

Basic Earnings per share ratio   A measure of a company's performance, calculated by dividing the earnings for the period available to common shares by the weighted average number of common shares that were outstanding during the period.

Common size data Data that are prepared from the financial statements (usually the income statement and balance sheet) in which each element of the financial statement is expressed as a percentage of some denominator value. On the income statement, the denominator value is usually the net sales revenues for the period and, on the balance sheet, the denominator is the total assets as at the year end.

Cross-sectional analysis A type of financial statement analysis in which one company is compared with other companies, either within the same industry or across industries, for the same time period.

Current ratio A measure of a company's short-term liquidity. It is measured as the ratio of the company's current assets divided by the current liabilities.

Debt/equity ratios Measure a company's leverage. There are numerous definitions of these ratios, but all of them attempt to compare the amount of debt in the company with the amount of equity.

Fully diluted earnings per share A type of earnings per share calculation that provides the lowest possible earnings per share figure under the assumption that all the company's convertible securities and options are converted into common shares. It measures the maximum potential dilution in earnings per share that would occur under these assumed conversions.

Inventory turnover The number of times that inventory is replaced during the accounting period. It is calculated as the cost of goods sold divided by the average inventory.

Leverage A company's use of debt to improve the return to shareholders.

Multiple Synonym of Price/earnings ratio.

Operating cash flow to short-term debt ratio A short-term liquidity ratio that measures a company's ability to cover its short-term debt with the cash flow generated from operations.

Operating cash flow to total debt ratio A long-term liquidity ratio that measures a company's ability to cover all its debt with the cash flow generated from operations.

Operating leverage The replacement of variable costs with fixed costs in the operation of the company. If a sufficient volume of sales is achieved, the investment in fixed costs can be very profitable.

Optimal capital structure A theoretical point at which the company's leverage maximizes the return to the shareholders (ROE).

Price/earnings ratio (P/E ratio) A performance ratio that compares the market price per share with the earnings per share.

Profit margin ratio A performance measure that compares a company's after-tax but before-interest income with its revenues.

Prospective analysis A financial statement analysis of a company that attempts to look forward in time to predict future results.

Quick ratio A measure of a company's short-term liquidity calculated by dividing the current assets less inventories and, in most cases, prepaid items by the current liabilities.

Raw financial data The data that appear directly in the financial statements.

Retrospective analysis A financial statement analysis of a company that looks only at historical data.

Return on assets (ROA) A measure of performance that measures the return on the investment in company assets. It is calculated by dividing the income after tax but before interest by the average total company assets during the accounting period. The ratio can be split into the profit margin ratio and the total asset turnover ratio.

Return on equity (ROE A measure of performance that measures the return on the investment made by common shareholders. It is calculated by dividing the net income less dividends for preferred shares by the average common shareholders' equity during the accounting period.

Time-series analysis A financial statement analysis in which data are analyzed over time.

Times-interest-earned (TIE) ratio A measure of a company's long-term liquidity. It measures the company's ability to make its interest payments. It is calculated by dividing the income before interest and taxes by the interest expense.

Total asset turnover A measure of company performance that shows the number of dollars of sales that is generated per dollar of investment in total assets. It is calculated by dividing the sales revenue by the average total assets for the accounting period.

ASSIGNMENT MATERIAL

Assessing Your Recall

Self-Assessment Quiz

12-1 Explain the difference between a retrospective analysis and a prospective analysis of a company.

12-2 Would an investor find retrospective analysis or prospective analysis more useful in making investment decisions? Why is the other technique used?

12-3 Compare and contrast time-series analysis and cross-sectional analysis.

12-4 For each of the following ratios, reproduce the formula for their calculation.

  a. ROA (Break down into profit margin percentage and total asset turnover rate)

  b. ROE

  c. Accounts receivable turnover

  d. Inventory turnover

  e. Accounts payable turnover

  f. Current ratio

  g. Quick ratio

  h. Operating cash flow to short-term debt ratio

  i. D/E(I)

  j. D/E(II)

  k. D/E(III)

  l. Times-interest-earned ratio

  m. Operating cash flow to total debt ratio

12-5 Explain how the turnover ratios relate to the cash produced from a company's operations.

12-6 Why are ratios using cash flows useful under accrual-based accounting?

12-7 Describe leverage, and explain how it is evidenced in the ROA and ROE ratios.

12-8 Explain, using the profit margin and total asset turnover ratios, how two companies in the same business (use retail clothing stores as an example) can earn the same ROA, yet have very different operating strategies.

12-9 What is the advantage of preparing common size statements in financial statement analysis?

12-10 Explain why the current ratio is subject to manipulation as a measure of liquidity.

12-11 Discuss the problems associated with calculating an accounts payable turnover ratio that make it difficult to interpret.

12-12 Describe how earnings per share is calculated, and discuss the purpose of producing basic and fully diluted earnings per share for a company.

Applying Your Knowledge

12-13 (Common size analysis and differences in profitability)

Comparative financial statement data for First Company and Foremost Company, two competitors, appear below.

	First Company 2006	First Company 2005	Foremost Company 2006	Foremost Company 2005
Net sales	$225,000		$1,300,000	
Cost of goods sold	135,000		728,000	
Operating expenses	45,500		312,000	
Interest expense	2,250		25,200	
Income tax expense	11,600		47,000	
Current assets	110,000	$ 95,000	680,000	$ 520,000
Capital assets (net)	280,000	245,000	1,020,000	950,000
Current liabilities	35,000	28,500	150,000	160,000
Long-term liabilities	45,000	63,500	420,000	360,000
Common stock	230,000	180,000	800,000	750,000
Retained earnings	80,000	68,000	330,000	200,000

Required:

a. Prepare a common size analysis of the 2006 income statement data for First Company and Foremost Company.

b. Calculate the return on assets and the return on shareholders' equity for both companies.

c. Comment on the relative profitability of these companies.

d. Identify two main reasons for the difference in profitability.

12-14 (Liquidity ratios)

The financial data for Alouette Resources are as follows (amounts in thousands).

	Year 1	Year 2	Year 3	Year 4
Current assets				
Cash	$ 120	$ 80	$ 140	$ 160
Accounts receivable	400	520	480	430
Inventories	650	920	1,240	1,810
Other current assets	100	100	150	100
	$1,270	$1,620	$2,010	$2,500
Current liabilities				
Accounts payable	$ 600	$ 660	$ 780	$ 820
Accrued salaries	70	100	120	150
Other current liabilities	100	150	160	300
	$ 770	$ 910	$1,060	$1,270

Required:

a. Calculate the current and quick ratios for years 1 through 4.

b. Comment on the short-term liquidity position of Alouette Resources.

c. Which ratio do you think is the better measure of short-term liquidity for Alouette Resources? Can you tell? Explain. What would your answer depend on?

12-15   (Accounts receivable turnover)

The financial data for McLaren Pharmaceuticals Company Inc. and Johnston Pharmaceuticals Ltd. for the current year are as follows (amounts in thousands).

	Annual sales	Accounts receivable, Jan. 1	Accounts receivable, Dec. 31
McLaren Pharmaceuticals	$20,212	$2,098	$2,740
Johnston Pharmaceuticals	8,043	914	806

> **Required:**
>
> a. Calculate the accounts receivable turnover for each company.
>
> b. Calculate the average number of days required by each company to collect the receivables.
>
> c. Which company appears to be more efficient in terms of handling its accounts receivable?
>
> d. What additional information would be helpful in evaluating management's handling of the collection of accounts receivable?

12-16   (Accounts receivable turnover)

The Super Gym Company Limited sells fitness equipment to retail outlets and fitness centres. The majority of these sales are on credit. The financial data related to accounts receivable over the last three years are as follows.

	2005	2006	2007
Accounts receivable	$ 181,200	$ 192,400	$ 186,000
Sales	1,634,200	1,788,600	1,947,500

> **Required:**
>
> a. Calculate the accounts receivable turnover for each year. In 2005, use the accounts receivable in 2005. For the other two years, use the average accounts receivable.
>
> b. Calculate the average number of days required to collect the receivables in each year.
>
> c. As a user of this information, describe what trends you see. What additional information would you like to know to help you understand the trends?

12-17   (Inventory turnover)

Information regarding the activities of Novel-T Toy Company is as follows.

	Year 1	Year 2	Year 3	Year 4	Year 5
Cost of goods sold	$893,100	$1,002,700	$1,174,500	$1,326,300	$1,391,780
Average inventory	128,450	157,100	206,310	323,420	442,990

> **Required:**
>
> a. Do a time-series analysis of the inventory turnover for each year. Also, calculate the average number of days that inventories are held for the respective years.
>
> b. Is Novel-T Toy Company managing its inventories efficiently? Do you have enough information to answer this question? If not, what else do you need to know?

c. Provide an example of a situation where management may deliberately reduce inventory turnover, but still be operating in the company's best long-term interests.

12-18 (Inventory turnover)

The financial data for Ken's Fresh Fruits Incorporated and Al's Supermarket Corporation for the current year are as follows.

	Annual cost of goods sold	Inventory Jan. 1	Inventory Dec. 31
Ken's Fresh Fruit	$ 6,582,400	$463,100	$423,900
Al's Supermarket	35,924,400	3,184,500	3,691,900

Required:

a. Calculate the inventory turnover for each company.

b. Calculate the average number of days the inventory is held by each company.

c. Knowing the type of inventory these companies sell, comment on the reasonableness of the inventory turnover. Which company manages its inventory more efficiently?

d. Which company would be a more profitable investment? Can we tell? Explain.

e. What are the potential problems associated with fast inventory turnovers? Would these be a concern for Ken's Fresh Fruits?

12-19 (Analysis using selected ratios)

The following ratios and other information are based on a company's comparative financial statements for a two-year period.

	Year 1	Year 2
Current ratio	1.84	2.20
Quick ratio	1.07	.89
D/E(I) ratio	.43	.58
D/E(II) ratio	.75	1.38
Earnings per share	.24	.15
Gross profit percentage	42.3%	45.6%
Total assets	$2,143,702	$3,574,825
Current assets	$ 965,118	$1,462,763

Required:

a. What is the amount of current liabilities at the end of year 2?

b. What is the amount of total debt at the end of year 2?

c. What is the total shareholders' equity at the end of year 2?

d. Do you think this company is a retail company, a financial institution, or a service organization? Explain.

e. If the company has 1,650,200 common shares outstanding for most of year 2 and has issued no other shares, what is its net income for year 2?

f. Based on the information available, what is your assessment of the company's liquidity? Explain.

g. Given the limited information, what is your assessment of the company's overall financial position? Explain.

h. What changes do you see between year 1 and year 2 that appear particularly significant? What explanations might there be for these changes?

12-20 (ROE and ROA)

The following financial information relates to Stanton Publishing Inc. (amounts in thousands).

	Year 1	Year 2	Year 3	Year 4
Sales	$31,860	$38,220	$43,180	$55,410
Average total assets	41,345	53,950	68,426	135,829
Average shareholders' equity	13,110	18,425	28,550	49,135
Net income	420	990	2,360	6,112
Interest expense	95	120	180	165
Tax rate	40%	40%	40%	30%

Required:

For each year, calculate:

a. Return on shareholders' equity (ROE)

b. ROA, broken down into:

    1. Profit margin percentage

    2. Total asset turnover rate

c. Comment on the profitability of Stanton Publishing Inc.

d. How has the company changed in year 4, and how has this affected the ratios?

12-21 (ROE and ROA)

The following financial information relates to Smooth Suds Brewery Ltd. (amounts in thousands).

	Year 1	Year 2	Year 3
Sales	$18,360	$25,840	$36,120
Average total assets	23,715	31,965	47,340
Average shareholders' equity	24,664	32,415	51,515
Net income	715	1,845	3,580
Interest expense	120	150	210
Tax rate	25%	30%	30%

Required:

For each year, calculate:

a. Return on shareholders' equity (ROE)

b. ROA

    1. Profit margin percentage

    2. Total asset turnover rate

c. Comment on the profitability of Smooth Suds Brewery Ltd.

12-22 (ROE and ROA)

Canadian Import Company's summarized balance sheet is as follows.

Total assets	$500,000	Liabilities	$200,000
		Shareholders' equity	300,000
	$500,000		$500,000

The interest rate on the liabilities is 6% and the income tax rate is 40%.

Required:

a. If the ROE is equal to the ROA, calculate the net income.

b. Calculate the ROE, using the net income determined in part a). Check this by calculating the ROA and confirming that it is equal to the ROE.

c. Explain what causes the ROE to be equal to the ROA.

d. Calculate the income before interest and taxes for the net income derived in part a).

e. Assume that the interest rate is now 8% and that the income tax rate remains at 40%. What is the net income if the ROA is the same as that calculated in part b)? What is the ROE?

f. Compare the ROE in both situations, and explain why there is a difference.

12-23 (D/E(I), D/E(II), D/E(III), and times interest earned)

Artscan Enterprises' financial data are as follows.

	Year 1	Year 2	Year 3
Income before interest and taxes	$1,100	$ 1,750	$2,200
Interest	105	225	290
Current liabilities	425	525	750
Non-current liabilities	1,320	2,750	3,200
Shareholders' equity	2,845	3,950	4,850

Required:

a. Calculate the debt/equity ratios (I, II, and III) and times-interest-earned ratio.

b. Comment on the long-term liquidity position of Artscan Enterprises.

12-24 (D/E(I), D/E(II), D/E(III), and times interest earned)

Waverly Company's financial data are as follows.

	Year 1	Year 2	Year 3
Income before interest and taxes	$2,100	$2,850	$3,410
Interest	230	255	280
Current liabilities	750	880	1,010
Noncurrent liabilities	1,300	2,380	2,670
Shareholders' equity	3,050	3,525	3,920

Required:

a. Calculate the debt/equity ratios (I, II, and III) and times-interest-earned ratio.

b. Comment on the long-term liquidity position of Waverly Company.

12-25 (Transaction effects on ratios)

State the immediate effect (increase, decrease, no effect) of the following transactions on the selected ratios. You may want to format your answer in a table with the ratios down the left, and the transactions across the top.

a. Current ratio

b. Quick ratio

c. Accounts receivable turnover

d. Inventory turnover

e. Debt/equity ratio (D/E(I))

f. ROA

g. ROE

Transactions:

1. Goods costing $200,000 are sold to customers on credit for $380,000.

2. Accounts receivable of $140,000 are collected.

3. Inventory costing $110,000 is purchased from suppliers.

4. A long-term bank loan for $500,000 is arranged with the bank, and the company receives the cash at the beginning of the year.

5. The bank loan carries an interest rate of 18% and the interest payment is made at the end of the year.

6. The company uses $40,000 to buy temporary investments.

7. New common shares are issued for $250,000.

12-26   (Earnings per share)

Zipper Ltd. has 150,000 common shares and 40,000 preferred shares outstanding. The preferred shares pay a dividend of $5.00 per share and are convertible into 80,000 common shares. During the year, Zipper earned net income of $1,220,000.

Required:

a. Calculate the basic earnings per share that should be reported in the financial statements.

b. Why is it important that the notes to the financial statements describe the preferred shares as convertible?

c. If the preferred shares had been converted to common shares half-way through the year, and a dividend of $2.50 per share was declared and paid immediately before the conversion, calculate Zipper's earnings per share for the year.

d. Assume, however, that the preferred shares were not converted to common shares this year. Calculate Zipper's fully diluted earnings per share. Why is this disclosed in Zipper's financial statements?

12-27   (Earnings per share)

In 2006, Signal Communications Ltd. reported earnings per share of $0.34. Signal had 28.1 million common shares outstanding during 2006 and 2007, and no preferred shares. In 2007, Signal reported net income of $10,926,000.

Required:

a. What was the net income for 2006?

b. Calculate the earnings per share for 2007.

c. Will Signal also disclose a fully diluted earnings per share amount? Explain.

d. Assume that in December 2007 Signal decided to split its common shares three for one. What effect will this have on the earnings per share amount calculated in b)? Will the year 2006 earnings per share amount be affected as well? Explain.

12-28   (Analysis of assets)

You have inherited money from your grandparents and a friend suggests that you consider buying shares in Galena Ski Products. Because you may need to sell the shares within the next two years to finance your university education, you start your analysis of the company data by calculating (1) working capital, (2) the current ratio, and (3) the quick ratio. Galena's balance sheet is as follows.

Current assets

Cash	$154,000
Inventory	185,000
Other current assets	21,000

Noncurrent assets

Land	50,000
Building and equipment	145,000
Other	15,000
Total	$570,000

Current liabilities	$165,000
Long-term debt	190,000
Common shares	80,000
Retained earnings	135,000
Total	$570,000

Required:

a. What amount of working capital is currently maintained? Comment on the adequacy of the working capital.

b. Your preference is to have a quick ratio of at least 0.80 and a current ratio of at least 2.00. How do the existing ratios compare with your criteria? Using these two ratios, how would you evaluate the company's current asset position?

c. The company sells only on a cash basis currently and has sales of $900,000 this past year. How would you expect a change from cash to credit sales to affect the current and quick ratios?

d. Galena's balance sheet is presented just before the start of shipments for its fall and winter season. How would your evaluation change if these balances existed in late February, following completion of its primary business for the skiing season?

e. How would Galena's situation as either a public company or private company affect your decision to invest?

12-29 **(Ratio analysis of two companies)**

You have obtained the financial statements of A-Tec and Bi-Sci, new companies in the high-tech industry. Both companies have just completed their second year of operations. You have acquired the following information for an analysis of the companies. All dollar amounts are stated in thousands.

	A-Tec		Bi-Sci	
	2006	2005	2006	2005
Cash	$ 3	$ 2	$ 1	$ 1
Accounts receivable	30	15	20	20
Inventory	40	20	30	30
Other current assets	5	1	3	1
Capital assets (net)	260	170	115	104
Current liabilities	67	40	24	24
Long-term debt	210	130	0	0
Common shares	28	18	72	72
Retained earnings	33	20	73	60
Sales (all credit sales)	950	675	610	600
Cost of goods sold	625	450	455	450
Net income	95	80	60	55

Required:

a. Calculate the following ratios for the two companies for the two years.

1. Current ratio

2. Working capital (dollar amount)

3. Accounts receivable turnover

4. Inventory turnover

5. Asset turnover

6. D/E(I)

7. Shareholders' equity to total assets

8. Gross margin ratio

9. Return on sales

10. ROA

11. ROE

b. Write a brief analysis of the two companies based on the information given and the ratios calculated. Be sure to discuss issues of liquidity, leverage, and profitability. Which company appears to be the better investment for the shareholder? Explain. Which company appears to be the better credit risk for the lender? Explain.

12-30 (Comparative ratios and comments on results)

Selected financial data for two intense competitors in a recent year are presented below, in millions of dollars.

	X Corporation	Y Company
Income Statement data:		
Net sales	$ 3,350	$ 6,810
Cost of goods sold	2,980	5,740
Selling and administrative expenses	95	410
Interest expense	130	175
Other expenses	8	0
Income taxes	62	110
Net income	$ 75	$ 375
Cash Flows Statement data:		
Net cash inflow from operating activities	$ 125	$ 260
Net increase in cash during the year	10	37
End-of-Year Balance Sheet data:		
Current assets	$ 1,020	$ 1,620
Property, plant, and equipment (net)	1,865	2,940
Other assets	720	1,020
Total assets	$ 3,605	$ 5,580
Current liabilities	575	830
Long-term debt	2,220	3,130
Total shareholders' equity	810	1,620
Total liabilities and shareholders' equity	$ 3,605	$ 5,580
Beginning-of-Year Balances:		
Total assets	$ 3,250	$ 5,160
Total shareholders' equity	750	1,245
Other Data:		
Average net receivables	$ 350	$ 790
Average inventory	290	575

Required:

a. For each company, calculate the following ratios.

  1. Average collection period (in days) for receivables

  2. Average holding period (in days) for inventory

  3. Current ratio

  4. Total debt to total assets

  5. Times interest earned

  6. Return on assets

  7. Return on equity

b. Compare the financial position and performance of the two companies, and comment on their relative strengths and weaknesses.

User Perspective Problems

12-31   (Use of ratios in debt restrictions)

Contracts with lenders typically place restrictions on a company's activities in an attempt to ensure that the company will be able to repay both the interest and the principal on the debt covered by the restrictions. These restrictions are frequently stated in terms of ratios. For instance, a restriction could be that the debt/equity ratio (D/E(II)) cannot exceed 2.0. If it does exceed 2.0, the debt covered by the restrictions falls due immediately. Two commonly used ratios are the current ratio and the debt/equity ratio. Explain why these might appear as restrictions. How do they protect the lender?

12-32   (Cross-sectional analysis)

In using cross-sectional analysis to evaluate performance, what factors should an investor match in choosing companies for comparison? Why are these factors important?

12-33   (Use of ratios for performance measurement)

A company's business strategy often leads to better performance on some financial statement ratios than on others. For example, management of a high volume retailer may deliberately keep prices low, reducing the gross margin percentage, in order to achieve a high inventory turnover. Give an example of another conflict between financial statement ratios, where management's attempt to improve one ratio may result in decreased performance on the other ratio.

12-34   (Use of ROA in performance measurement)

Management compensation plans typically specify performance criteria in terms of financial statement ratios. For instance, a plan might specify that management must achieve a certain level of return on investment, for example, ROA. If managers were trying to maximize their compensation, how could they manipulate the ROA ratio to achieve this goal?

12-35   (Use of ratios for investing decisions)

You are considering investing in the stock market. As a potential investor, choose four ratios that you think would be most helpful to you in making your investment decision. Explain your choices.

12-36   (Use of cash flow ratios)

There is judgement involved in preparing financial statements. For example, management must often estimate warranty expense and bad debts expense. Management may also need to select an accounting policy if generally accepted accounting principles allow a choice. As a result, there is judgement involved in determining net income. Do you believe financial statement ratios using cash flows are more reliable than measures of performance that use net income? Discuss.

12-37 (Ratio analysis and auditors)

Auditors review the financial statements to determine whether the information reported has been collected, summarized, and reported according to generally accepted accounting principles. Although auditors are not expected to identify fraud, they do perform tests to see if there are any apparent abnormalities. If an auditor wanted to ensure that a company's sales revenues were not overstated, how might an auditor use ratio analysis to detect a possible overstatement?

12-38 (Using ratios to evaluate creditworthiness)

You are the sales manager in a company that sells automotive supplies to service stations and car dealerships. You have been contacted by a large car dealership that wants you to supply its service department with automotive parts. The dealership would like to purchase on credit, with 30 days to pay from the date of invoice. You have access to the dealership's financial statements for last year. Which ratios could be useful to you in making the decision about whether to sell on credit? Explain your choices.

12-39 (Use of ratios in decision-making)

Managers, investors, and creditors usually have a specific focus when making decisions about a business.

> *Required:*
>
> For each of the following cases, identify the ratio or ratios that would help the user in making a decision or in identifying areas for further analysis.
>
> a. A company's net income has declined. Is the decrease in net income from:
>
> > 1. A decrease in sales or an increase in cost of goods sold?
> >
> > 2. An increase in total operating expenses?
> >
> > 3. An increase in a specific expense, such as tax expense?
>
> b. Does a company generate sufficient cash to pay the debts that come due without having to borrow additional money?
>
> c. Does a company rely more heavily on long-term debt financing than other companies in the same industry?
>
> d. In a comparison of two companies, how would you decide which company uses its assets most effectively?
>
> e. In a comparison of two companies, how would you decide which company has been more profitable in relation to invested capital?
>
> f. Has the decline in the economy affected a company's ability to collect its accounts receivable?
>
> g. Has a company been successful in reducing its investment in inventories as a result of installing a new ordering system?

Reading and Interpreting
Published Financial Statements

12-40 (Ratio analysis for CHUM Limited)

The 2003 consolidated financial statements for **CHUM Limited** are shown in Exhibit 12-14. CHUM Limited is a leading Canadian communications and media broadcasting company, which owns and operates radio and television stations. All amounts are in thousands of dollars.

Financial Statement Analysis Assignments

Required:

Based on these financial statements, answer each of the following questions.

a. Calculate the following ratios for each of 2003 and 2002, and comment on the changes. For the 2002 ratios, use the year-end balance sheet amounts, rather than an average for the year.

   1. ROA (split into profit margin percentage and total asset turnover rate)

   2. ROE (Assume the Class B shares are not preferred shares)

   3. Accounts receivable turnover

   4. Operating cash flow to short-term debt

b. Comment on the use of leverage by CHUM Limited, using appropriate ratios to support your analysis.

c. The balance sheet of CHUM includes intangible assets such as program rights, broadcast licences, and goodwill. How significant is the impact of these assets on the ROA calculated above? As a potential investor would you have any particular concerns about the extent of intangible assets? Explain.

d. "Program rights" are described in the notes to the financial statements. This asset represents the amount paid for the licence agreements that CHUM has to broadcast movies and syndicated television programs. The licence agreements give CHUM the rights to broadcast the material either a stated number of times, or over a stated period of usage. Do you think the asset program rights should be amortized? Explain. If so, what amortization method would you suggest? Why does the asset have both a current and non-current portion?

12-41 (Ratio analysis for Maple Leaf Foods Inc.)

The 2003 consolidated financial statements of **Maple Leaf Foods Inc.** are shown in Exhibit 12-15. The company is a food processor with three major lines of business: meat products, agricultural feed, and bakery products. All amounts are in thousands of dollars.

Required:

Based on these financial statements, answer each of the following questions.

a. Calculate the following ratios for each of 2003 and 2002, and comment on the company's profitability and use of leverage. For the 2002 ratios, use the year-end balance sheet amounts, rather than an average for the year.

   1. ROA (broken down into profit margin percentage and total asset turnover rate)

   2. ROE (There are no preferred shares)

EXHIBIT 12-14
PART A

CHUM LIMITED 2003 ANNUAL REPORT

CONSOLIDATED BALANCE SHEETS

AS AT AUGUST 31 (in thousands of dollars)	2003	2002
ASSETS		
CURRENT ASSETS		
Cash and short-term investments	$ 21,452	$ 7,472
Accounts receivable	101,377	98,426
Income taxes recoverable	-	2,301
Program rights	70,457	56,836
Prepaid expenses and other assets	11,052	15,875
	204,338	180,910
Program rights	94,086	91,249
Investments and other assets	3,317	3,978
Fixed assets (note 2)	185,092	189,088
Broadcast licences	87,109	86,119
Goodwill (note 4)	138,858	138,858
	712,800	690,202
LIABILITIES		
CURRENT LIABILITIES		
Accounts payable and accrued liabilities	54,902	55,577
Income taxes payable	14,513	-
Current portion of long-term debt (note 5)	192	175
Program rights payable	65,893	57,618
	135,500	113,370
Program rights payable	26,441	26,780
Long-term debt (note 5)	125,963	247,678
Future income taxes (note 9)	33,581	36,958
Minority interest	2,075	1,608
	323,560	426,394
SHAREHOLDERS' EQUITY		
Capital stock (note 7)	124,242	21,343
Retained earnings	264,998	242,465
	389,240	263,808
	712,800	690,202

Approved by the Board of Directors

DIRECTOR

DIRECTOR

CHUM LIMITED 2003 ANNUAL REPORT

EXHIBIT 12-14
PART B

CONSOLIDATED STATEMENTS OF EARNINGS

FOR THE YEARS ENDED AUGUST 31 (in thousands of dollars, except per share amounts)	2003	2002
REVENUE – less agency commissions	$ 540,509	$ 479,939
EXPENSES		
Operations	460,596	428,518
Depreciation	24,705	23,008
Interest	11,826	12,200
Interest and other income	(780)	(988)
	496,347	462,738
Operating income	44,162	17,201
Gain on exchange of assets (note 3(c))	-	9,737
	44,162	26,938
Provision for income taxes (note 9)	17,963	12,336
Earnings before minority interest in earnings of subsidiaries	26,199	14,602
Minority interest in earnings of subsidiaries	770	472
Net earnings for the year	25,429	14,130
Net earnings per Class B share and per common share (note 7(b))	2.13	1.21

CONSOLIDATED STATEMENTS OF RETAINED EARNINGS

FOR THE YEARS ENDED AUGUST 31 (in thousands of dollars)	2003	2002
Retained earnings – Beginning of year	$ 242,465	$ 230,894
Net earnings for the year	25,429	14,130
	267,894	245,024
Deduct		
Dividends paid ($0.08 per share, regular and $0.14 per share, special)		
Class B shares	2,154	1,817
Common shares	742	742
	2,896	2,559
Retained earnings – End of year	264,998	242,465

CHUM LIMITED 2003 ANNUAL REPORT

CONSOLIDATED STATEMENTS OF CASH FLOWS

FOR THE YEARS ENDED AUGUST 31 (in thousands of dollars)	2003	2002
CASH PROVIDED BY (USED IN)		
OPERATING ACTIVITIES		
Net earnings for the year	$ 25,429	$ 14,130
Items not affecting cash		
Depreciation	24,705	23,008
Minority interest in earnings of subsidiaries	770	472
Future income taxes	(1,826)	4,464
Amortization of other assets	662	-
Gain on exchange of assets	-	(9,737)
	49,740	32,337
Changes in non-cash balances related to operations		
Increase in accounts receivable	(3,101)	(7,750)
Decrease (increase) in income taxes recoverable	2,301	(2,916)
Increase in program rights	(16,458)	(2,986)
Decrease (increase) in prepaid expenses and other assets	4,823	(3,981)
Increase (decrease) in accounts payable and accrued liabilities	(675)	3
Increase (decrease) in income taxes payable	14,513	(7,351)
Increase (decrease) in program rights payable	7,936	(609)
	9,339	(25,590)
	59,079	6,747
INVESTING ACTIVITIES		
Additions to fixed assets - net	(20,300)	(35,515)
Acquisitions - net of cash acquired	(1,600)	(129,882)
Decrease (increase) in investments and other assets	136	(142)
Proceeds on exchange of assets	-	8,000
	(21,764)	(157,539)
FINANCING ACTIVITIES		
Decrease in bank indebtedness	-	(52,511)
Dividends paid	(2,896)	(2,559)
Financing costs	(90)	(1,345)
Long-term debt repayments	(134,925)	(5,160)
Increase in long-term debt	13,227	219,839
Net proceeds from issuance of non-voting, Class B shares	101,349	-
	(23,335)	158,264
Change in cash and short-term investments during the year	13,980	7,472
Cash and short-term investments - Beginning of year	7,472	-
Cash and short-term investments - End of year	21,452	7,472
SUPPLEMENTARY INFORMATION		
Income taxes paid	2,975	13,840
Interest paid	11,557	9,825

MAPLE LEAF FOODS INC. 2003 ANNUAL REPORT

EXHIBIT 12-15
PART A

Consolidated Balance Sheets

As at December 31

(in thousands of Canadian dollars)	2003	2002
ASSETS		
Current assets		
Cash and cash equivalents	$ 38,908	$ 156,866
Accounts receivable (Note 3)	242,306	243,121
Inventories (Note 4)	259,758	266,889
Future tax asset – current (Note 16)	4,854	5,847
Prepaid expenses and other assets	9,355	8,959
	555,181	681,682
Investments in associated companies	58,189	59,497
Property and equipment (Note 5)	802,332	785,425
Other long-term assets (Note 6)	171,262	159,910
Future tax asset – non-current (Note 16)	29,906	21,733
Goodwill and other intangibles	531,851	481,000
	$ 2,148,721	$ 2,189,247
LIABILITIES AND SHAREHOLDERS' EQUITY		
Current liabilities		
Accounts payable and accrued charges	$ 501,997	$ 532,132
Income and other taxes payable	12,212	42,283
Current portion of long-term debt (Note 7)	4,959	22,588
	519,168	597,003
Long-term debt (Note 7)	730,627	713,689
Future tax liability (Note 16)	50,397	46,453
Other long-term liabilities	35,274	6,981
Minority interest	70,068	93,220
Shareholders' equity (Note 10)	743,187	731,901
	$ 2,148,721	$ 2,189,247

Contingencies and commitments (Note 20 and Note 22)

See accompanying Notes to the Consolidated Financial Statements.

On behalf of the Board:

Michael H. McCain
Director

Robert W. Hiller
Director

EXHIBIT 12-15
PART B

MAPLE LEAF FOODS INC. 2003 ANNUAL REPORT

Consolidated Statements of Earnings

Years ended December 31

(in thousands of Canadian dollars, except share amounts)	2003	2002
Sales	$ 5,041,896	$ 5,075,879
Earnings from operations before restructuring costs	$ 152,428	$ 203,550
Restructuring costs (Note 9)	(17,732)	—
Earnings from operations	134,696	203,550
Other income (expense) (Note 14)	(1,377)	5,355
Earnings before interest and income taxes	133,319	208,905
Interest expense (Note 15)	68,369	56,289
Earnings before income taxes	64,950	152,616
Income taxes (Note 16)	22,879	54,947
Earnings before minority interest	42,071	97,669
Minority interest	7,003	12,983
Net earnings	$ 35,068	$ 84,686
Basic and diluted earnings per share (Note 13)	$ 0.27	$ 0.71
Weighted average number of shares (millions)	113.1	112.5

See accompanying Notes to the Consolidated Financial Statements.

Consolidated Statements of Retained Earnings

Years ended December 31

(in thousands of Canadian dollars)	2003	2002
Retained earnings, beginning of year	$ 63,758	$ 1,817
Net earnings	35,068	84,686
Dividends declared ($0.16 per share; 2002: $0.16 per share)	(18,094)	(18,035)
Premium on repurchase of share capital (Note 10)	(899)	—
Convertible debenture charge (Note 11)	(4,851)	(4,710)
Retained earnings, end of year	$ 74,982	$ 63,758

See accompanying Notes to the Consolidated Financial Statements.

MAPLE LEAF FOODS INC. 2003 ANNUAL REPORT

EXHIBIT 12-15
PART C

Consolidated Statements of Cash Flows

Years ended December 31

(in thousands of Canadian dollars)	2003	2002
CASH PROVIDED BY (USED IN)		
Operating activities		
Net earnings	$ 35,068	$ 84,686
Add (deduct) items not affecting cash		
Depreciation	100,868	96,212
Stock-based compensation (Note 12)	849	—
Minority interest	7,003	12,983
Future income taxes	580	(8,215)
Increase in pension asset	(29,501)	(18,910)
Undistributed losses of associated companies	1,483	1,453
Loss (gain) on sale of property and equipment	142	(14)
Gain on sale of investments	(362)	(1,340)
Other	(8,943)	10,390
Change in other long-term receivables	(3,856)	17,560
Proceeds from pension plan wind-up	27,251	—
Change in non-cash operating working capital	(55,637)	1,014
	74,945	195,819
Financing activities		
Dividends paid	(18,094)	(18,035)
Dividends paid to minority interest	(1,663)	(2,770)
Decrease in long-term debt	(20,332)	(229,572)
Increase in long-term debt	69,338	312,563
Convertible debenture interest paid	(5,478)	(5,478)
Increase in share capital	3,118	8,079
Shares repurchased for cancellation (Note 10)	(1,829)	—
Other	1,858	819
	26,918	65,606
Investing activities		
Additions to property and equipment	(132,607)	(92,160)
Proceeds from sale of property and equipment	1,933	5,306
Purchase of Canada Bread shares (Note 18)	(74,831)	—
Purchase of net assets of businesses, net of cash acquired (Note 19)	(7,002)	(66,967)
Change in investments, net	(6,196)	(1,307)
Other	(1,118)	(2,042)
	(219,821)	(157,170)
Increase (decrease) in cash and cash equivalents	(117,958)	104,255
Cash and cash equivalents, beginning of year	156,866	52,611
Cash and cash equivalents, end of year	$ 38,908	$ 156,866
Supplemental cash flow information:		
Net interest paid	$ 66,611	$ 55,540
Net income taxes paid	53,566	54,567

See accompanying Notes to the Consolidated Financial Statements.

b. Calculate the following operating ratios for both 2003 and 2002 and comment on the results.

   1. Current ratio

   2. Quick ratio

   3. Accounts receivable turnover

   4. Operating cash flow to short-term debt

c. Can you calculate an inventory turnover ratio for this company? Explain. Do you think this has a significant impact on your ability to evaluate the company's performance? Explain.

d. Examine Maple Leaf's consolidated statements of cash flows and comment on any significant differences in the company's cash-related activities during 2003 and 2002.

e. The statement of earnings includes a $17,732,000 "restructuring cost" in 2003. Management discussion and analysis in the annual report describes this as the cost of shutting down various plants in Eastern Canada, and moving the production capacity to other plants. The cost is also described as "not representative of ongoing underlying operations." By describing the cost thus, and showing it as a separate item on the statement of earnings, how is management hoping that investors will interpret this cost? How significant is the cost to the 2003 operating results?

12-42   **(Ratio analysis for Sierra Wireless, Inc.)**

The 2003 consolidated financial statements of **Sierra Wireless, Inc.**, which sells products involved in wireless communications, are shown in Exhibit 12-16. After a number of years of reporting losses, resulting in a deficit in retained earnings on the balance sheet, the company reported net earnings in 2003. Note that the 2003 (most recent) financial results are in the right hand column of the statements. All amounts are in thousands of U.S. dollars.

Required:

Based on these financial statements, answer each of the following questions.

a. Prepare a common sized income statement for each of 2001, 2002, and 2003 and comment on any significant changes.

b. Analyze liquidity by commenting on the changes from 2002 to 2003 in the following ratios.

   1. Current ratio

   2. Cash flow from operations to total debt

c. Review the company's statements of cash flows and explain how the company has maintained a positive cash position over the last three years, despite net losses in 2001 and 2002.

d. Despite the net losses in 2001 and 2002, what evidence do you see that investors are optimistic about the company's future prospects?

e. Assume you are thinking of investing in Sierra Wireless. Comment on its financial health, highlighting any areas about which you might be concerned. Use not only the ratios calculated above, but any other information you believe relevant from the financial statements.

f. How useful is retrospective analysis in making an investment decision for a company such as Sierra Wireless, Inc.?

SIERRA WIRELESS, INC. 2003 ANNUAL REPORT

EXHIBIT 12-16
PART A

SIERRA WIRELESS, INC.

Consolidated Balance Sheets

(Expressed in thousands of United States dollars)
(Prepared in accordance with Canadian GAAP)

December 31,	2002	2003
Assets		
Current assets:		
Cash and cash equivalents	$ 34,841	$ 70,358
Short-term investments	—	14,760
Accounts receivable, net of allowance for doubtful accounts of $2,230 (2002 — $3,068)	13,865	21,566
Inventories (note 6)	6,673	1,511
Prepaid expenses	864	2,223
	56,243	110,418
Long-term investments	—	24,639
Capital assets (note 7)	7,198	5,985
Intangible assets (note 8)	6,907	14,620
Goodwill (note 8)	—	19,706
Future income taxes (note 13)	500	500
Other	241	—
	$ 71,089	$ 175,868
Liabilities and Shareholders' Equity		
Current liabilities:		
Accounts payable	$ 3,017	$ 5,966
Accrued liabilities	12,431	22,221
Deferred revenue and credits	297	399
Current portion of long-term liabilities (note 9)	2,803	1,328
Current portion of obligations under capital lease (note 10)	831	141
	19,379	30,055
Long-term liabilities (note 9)	2,896	2,266
Obligations under capital lease (note 10)	60	—
Shareholders' equity:		
Share capital (note 11)		
Authorized		
Unlimited number of common and preference shares with no par value		
Common shares, 24,822,071 (2002 – 16,345,396) issued and outstanding	121,824	212,824
Warrants	—	1,538
Deficit	(72,586)	(70,331)
Cumulative translation adjustments	(484)	(484)
	48,754	143,547
	$ 71,089	$ 175,868

Commitments and contingencies (note 16)

See accompanying notes to consolidated financial statements.

EXHIBIT 12-16
PART B **SIERRA WIRELESS, INC. 2003 ANNUAL REPORT**

SIERRA WIRELESS, INC.

Consolidated Statements of Operations and Deficit

(Expressed in thousands of United States dollars, except per share amounts)
(Prepared in accordance with Canadian generally accepted accounting principles (GAAP))

Years ended December 31,		2001		2002		2003
Revenue	$	62,348	$	77,259	$	101,709
Cost of goods sold		47,035		69,261		60,551
Gross margin		15,313		7,998		41,158
Expenses:						
Sales and marketing		12,726		11,564		11,585
Research and development, net (note 14)		17,402		15,146		15,994
Administration		10,647		4,785		6,597
Restructuring and other charges (note 4)		—		12,869		1,220
Integration costs (note 5)		—		—		1,947
Amortization		2,084		2,331		2,327
		42,859		46,695		39,670
Earnings (loss) from operations		(27,546)		(38,697)		1,488
Other income		2,504		247		965
Earnings (loss) before income taxes		(25,042)		(38,450)		2,453
Income tax expense (recovery) (note 13)		(273)		3,463		198
Net earnings (loss)		(24,769)		(41,913)		2,255
Deficit, beginning of year		(5,904)		(30,673)		(72,586)
Deficit, end of year	$	(30,673)	$	(72,586)	$	(70,331)
Earnings (loss) per share (note 15):						
Basic	$	(1.54)	$	(2.57)	$	0.12
Diluted	$	(1.54)	$	(2.57)	$	0.12

See accompanying notes to consolidated financial statements.

18 Consolidated Financial Statements

SIERRA WIRELESS, INC. 2003 ANNUAL REPORT

SIERRA WIRELESS, INC.

Consolidated Statements of Cash Flows

(Expressed in thousands of United States dollars)
(Prepared in accordance with Canadian GAAP)

Years ended December 31,	2001	2002	2003
Cash flows from operating activities:			
Net earnings (loss)	$ (24,769)	$ (41,913)	$ 2,255
Adjustments to reconcile net earnings (loss) to net cash provided by operating activities			
Amortization	7,161	7,038	5,669
Non-cash restructuring and other charges	—	28,593	895
Loss on disposal	—	597	2
Deferred income taxes	(15)	3,754	—
Accrued warrants	671	481	386
Changes in operating assets and liabilities			
Accounts receivable	12,084	(3,361)	(5,360)
Inventories	(13,031)	2,517	5,878
Prepaid expenses	59	159	(1,087)
Accounts payable	(6,945)	(1,339)	225
Accrued liabilities	3,420	(463)	5,296
Deferred revenue and credits	300	(753)	101
Net cash provided by (used in) operating activities	(21,065)	(4,690)	14,260
Cash flows from investing activities:			
Business acquisitions (note 3)	—	—	33
Proceeds on disposal	—	338	4
Purchase of fixed assets	(10,523)	(2,219)	(1,972)
Increase in intangible assets	(3,328)	(1,431)	(4,077)
Increase in other assets	(143)	—	—
Purchase of long-term investments	—	—	(24,639)
Purchase of short-term investments	(69,411)	(14,662)	(25,103)
Proceeds on maturity of short-term investments	109,676	46,541	10,492
Net cash provided by (used in) investing activities	26,271	28,567	(45,262)
Cash flows from financing activities:			
Issue of common shares, net of share issue costs	499	374	68,623
Increase in long-term liabilities	255	—	—
Repayment of long-term liabilities	(766)	(1,495)	(2,104)
Net cash provided by (used in) financing activities	(12)	(1,121)	66,519
Net increase in cash and cash equivalents	5,194	22,756	35,517
Cash and cash equivalents, beginning of year	6,891	12,085	34,841
Cash and cash equivalents, end of year	$ 12,085	$ 34,841	$ 70,358

See supplementary cash flow information (note 17)

See accompanying notes to consolidated financial statements.

20 Consolidated Financial Statements

12-43 **(Ratio analysis for Methanex)**

The 2003 consolidated financial statements for **Methanex** are shown in Exhibit 12-17. This Canadian company is a global leader in methanol production and marketing. Methanol is produced from natural gas and is a chemical building block used in the manufacture of many products. All amounts are in thousands of U.S. dollars.

> ***Required:***
>
> Based on these financial statements, answer each of the following questions.
>
> a. Calculate the following ratios for 2003 and 2002 and comment on the trends and the company's use of leverage.
>
> > 1. ROE (There are no preferred shares)
> >
> > 2. ROA (The company operates in many tax jurisdictions and has a very complicated tax structure. Consider only the current income taxes in estimating the company's tax rate.)
>
> b. Prepare a common size or vertical analysis of Methanex's income statements down to the Income before income taxes line, for 2002 and 2003, and comment on any significant differences that you observe.
>
> c. Methanex's statements of income for 2003 includes asset restructuring charges related to the downsizing of plants in New Zealand and Medicine Hat, Alberta, and a write-off of plant and equipment related to a Western Australian plant that is being abandoned. (The 2002 asset restructuring charge was related to the shutdown of a plant in Louisiana.) How important are each of these items in evaluating 2003 performance? Explain.
>
> d. During the year, the company repurchased and cancelled some outstanding common shares and also issued some common shares under stock options. From information in the financial statements prepare an analysis of the balance sheet change in Capital stock.
>
> e. Calculate the following ratios for 2003 and 2002 and comment on the trends.
>
> > 1. D/E (I)
> >
> > 2. Times interest earned (Do you think you should consider the interest expense net of the interest and other income on the statements of income?)
>
> f. Compare the amount of dividends paid in 2003 with the 2003 net income. As an investor, how would you interpret this?

Beyond the Book

12-44 **(Ratio analysis of a company)**

Choose a company as directed by your instructor and answer the following questions.

> a. Using the ratios given in the text, prepare an analysis of the company for the past two years with respect to performance, short-term liquidity, long-term liquidity, and earnings per share ratios.
>
> b. Even though the ratios do not span a long period of time, discuss the company's financial health. Would you invest in it? Why or why not?

METHANEX 2003 ANNUAL REPORT

EXHIBIT 12-17
PART A

Consolidated Balance Sheets

(thousands of US dollars, except number of shares)

AS AT DECEMBER 31	2003	2002
ASSETS		
Current assets:		
Cash and cash equivalents	$ **287,863**	$ 421,387
Receivables (note 3)	**220,871**	201,037
Inventories	**126,729**	119,125
Prepaid expenses	**14,852**	12,079
	650,315	753,628
Property, plant and equipment (note 4)	**1,320,227**	979,935
Other assets (note 6)	**111,258**	85,748
	$ **2,081,800**	$ 1,819,311
LIABILITIES AND SHAREHOLDERS' EQUITY		
Current liabilities:		
Accounts payable and accrued liabilities	$ **178,420**	$ 136,035
Current maturities on long-term debt and other long-term liabilities	**33,026**	6,079
	211,446	142,114
Long-term debt (note 7)	**756,185**	547,224
Other long-term liabilities (note 8)	**69,377**	52,980
Future income taxes (note 14)	**261,218**	172,915
Shareholders' equity:		
Capital stock (note 9)	**499,258**	517,210
Issued and outstanding common shares at December 31, 2003 was 120,007,767 (2002 – 125,651,639)		
Retained earnings	**284,316**	386,868
	783,574	904,078
	$ **2,081,800**	$ 1,819,311

See accompanying notes to consolidated financial statements.

Approved by the Board:

Brian D. Gregson
Director

Pierre Choquette
Director

EXHIBIT 12-17
PART B **METHANEX 2003 ANNUAL REPORT**

Consolidated Statements of Income and Retained Earnings

(thousands of U.S. dollars, except number of common shares and per share amounts)

FOR THE YEARS ENDED DECEMBER 31	2003	2002
Revenue	$ 1,394,450	$ 1,008,792
Cost of sales and operating expenses	1,002,853	739,156
Depreciation and amortization	95,107	111,289
Operating income before undernoted items	296,490	158,347
Interest expense (note 11)	(38,815)	(28,972)
Interest and other income	13,843	10,365
Asset restructuring charges (note 12)	(139,352)	(115,387)
Write-off of plant and equipment under development (note 4)	(39,833)	—
Site restoration adjustment (note 8)	—	26,972
Income before income taxes	92,333	51,325
Income taxes (note 14):		
Current	39,586	16,465
Future	45,239	8,446
	84,825	24,911
Net income	7,508	26,414
Retained earnings, beginning of year	386,868	397,310
Excess of repurchase price over assigned value of common shares (note 9)	(51,523)	(24,349)
Dividend payments	(58,537)	(12,507)
Retained earnings, end of year	$ 284,316	$ 386,868
Weighted average number of common shares outstanding	122,961,809	126,610,754
Basic and diluted net income per share	$ 0.06	$ 0.21

See accompanying notes to consolidated financial statements.

METHANEX 2003 ANNUAL REPORT

Consolidated Statements of Cash Flows

(thousands of US dollars)

FOR THE YEARS ENDED DECEMBER 31	2003	2002
CASH FLOWS FROM OPERATING ACTIVITIES:		
Net income	$ 7,508	$ 26,414
Add (deduct) non-cash items:		
Depreciation and amortization	95,107	111,289
Future income taxes	45,239	8,446
Asset restructuring charges (note 12)	129,565	115,387
Write-off of plant and equipment under development	39,833	—
Site restoration adjustment	—	(26,972)
Other	13,158	10,030
Cash flows from operating activities before undernoted changes	330,410	244,594
Changes in non-cash working capital (note 15)	28,405	(56,519)
Utilization of prepaid natural gas	2,149	2,034
	360,964	190,109
CASH FLOWS FROM FINANCING ACTIVITIES:		
Proceeds on issue of limited recourse long-term debt	46,547	97,578
Proceeds on issue of unsecured notes	—	200,000
Repayment of long-term debt	(40,731)	(150,000)
Proceeds on issue of shares on exercise of stock options	19,173	10,684
Dividend payments	(58,537)	(12,507)
Payment for shares repurchased	(88,648)	(55,974)
Repayment of other long-term liabilities	(10,335)	(8,352)
Other	(6,135)	(11,772)
	(138,666)	69,657
CASH FLOWS FROM INVESTING ACTIVITIES:		
Acquisition of Titan Methanol Company, net of cash acquired (note 2)	(74,130)	—
Plant and equipment under construction or development	(206,968)	(142,245)
Property, plant and equipment	(35,982)	(17,913)
Accounts payable and accrued liabilities related to capital expenditures	1,522	(6,542)
Other assets	(40,264)	(3,808)
	(355,822)	(170,508)
Increase (decrease) in cash and cash equivalents	(133,524)	89,258
Cash and cash equivalents, beginning of year	421,387	332,129
Cash and cash equivalents, end of year	$ 287,863	$ 421,387

Cases

Case Primer

12-45 Wineland Appliance Sales and Service Limited

Wineland Appliance Sales and Service Limited owns several retail and service centres in northern British Columbia. Financial ratios for the company for the years ended December 31, 2006 and 2005 are provided below. For comparative purposes, industry averages have also been provided.

Ratio	2006	2005	Industry average
Current ratio	1.6:1	1.7:1	2:1
Quick ratio	0.75:1	0.80:1	1:1
Accounts receivable turnover	8 times	7.75 times	12 times
Inventory turnover	4 times	3.8 times	7 times

The company is in the process of opening two new retail outlets and will need to obtain a line of credit to finance receivables and inventory. To receive a competitive interest rate on its line of credit, it needs to ensure that its liquidity ratios are close to the average for the industry. In particular, the company would like to see the current ratio at 2:1. The company has hired you, an independent consultant, to suggest how it might improve its liquidity ratios.

In preparing your report, you have gathered the following additional information.

1. The company's credit terms to its customers are net 45 days; no discounts are provided for early payment.

2. The company policy is to pay accounts payable every 45 days regardless of the credit terms. Many supplier invoices offer discounts for payments within 30 days.

3. Wineland's policy is to keep high amounts of inventory on hand to ensure that customers will have maximum selection.

Required:

Propose several steps that Wineland Appliance Sales and Service Ltd. might take to improve its liquidity. All suggestions must be ethical.

12-46 Wildings Furniture and Guild Custom Furniture

Kelly Connors is considering investing in one of two furniture manufacturing companies. The first company, Wildings Furniture, is a national manufacturer that has been in business for 25 years. It manufactures reasonably priced, comfortable furniture with a price range that is attractive to the general public. Retailers sell its furniture nationwide, including large department stores. After a slow start, Wildings has enjoyed considerable success over the past five years. The company is publicly traded and its shares are currently selling for $12.

The second company, Guild Custom Furniture, also manufactures furniture, but has traditionally catered to the more discriminating buyer who is willing to pay a high price for custom designs. Recently, however, the company has started to manufacture a variety of retail lines, but it is still very selective as to the retailers with whom it will deal. Retailers must meet high quality standards before they are able to carry the Guild brand. Guild has been in business for more than 100 years. The company went public five years ago, which coincided with the decision to carry the retail lines of furniture. The movement to retail sales has been very successful for Guild Custom Furniture and the company's share price is now $32.

To make an informed investment decision, Kelly has obtained the most recent annual reports for both companies. She has summarized the following financial information for use in her analysis.

	Wildings Furniture (in thousands)	Guild Custom Furniture (in thousands)
Sales	$45,600	$6,798
Net Income	$3,200	$876
Average Inventory	$12,500	$1,542
Average Accounts Receivable	$4,700	$575
Average Current Assets	$29,450	$3,967
Average Total Assets	$36,475	$5,285
Average Current Liabilities	$13,658	$726
Average Total Liabilities	$16,266	$836
Average Common Shareholders' Equity	$20,209	$4,449

In addition to the above financial information, Karen learns that both companies make all their sales on account and that the cost of sales is about 30% for Wildings and 40% for Guild. Both companies have a corporate tax rate of 30%. The most recent annual reports available to the public show that Wildings has 4 million common shares outstanding while Guild has 500,000 common shares outstanding.

Through her research, Kelly has also obtained the following industry averages for furniture manufacturers.

Ratio	Industry Average
Current Ratio	4:1
Accounts Receivable Turnover	30 days
Inventory Turnover	180 days
Debt/Equity Ratio	25%
Return on Equity	22%
Earnings Per Share	$1.25
Price/Earnings Ratio	16 times

Required:

a. Based on raw data such as net income and sales, which company appears to be the better investment?

b. Prepare a ratio analysis of the two companies. Does your answer from part a) differ after studying the financial ratios?

c. Explain any difference between your answers in parts a) and b). Which approach offers the better analysis of these two companies? Why would the two analyses produce such different results?

12-47 Albert Long

Albert Long has just been awarded a large academic scholarship. Luckily, he had saved enough from his summer job to pay for his current year's expenses. Consequently, he has decided to invest the scholarship to maximize the funds he will have available for the next school year. Because he will need the money in about a year, Albert wants to invest in a fairly stable company and has decided that RBC Financial seems to be a very profitable investment.

Albert has obtained the company's annual report and has completed a very thorough ratio analysis. However, he has relied heavily on financial statements to perform the ratio analysis and only skimmed the other components of the annual report. You are a good friend of Albert's and explain to him that, although ratio analysis will provide a good indication as to a company's financial strength, there is much more information available that an informed investor should consider before making any investment decisions.

Required:

Albert has asked you to help him investigate the Royal Bank further. Other than ratio analysis, give him four examples of information that an investor might want to examine in order to fully understand a business. Where might such information be available?

12-48 Hencky Corporation

The management of Hencky Corporation is developing a loan proposal to present to a local investor. The company is looking for a $1 million loan to finance the research and development costs of producing a revolutionary new handheld computer. Most of the loan proceeds will be spent on intangible costs, such as salaries, and this will therefore be a very risky investment. Because of the risk associated with the project, the investor is requiring some assurance that the company is currently solvent and operating as a going concern.

As the accountant for Hencky Corporation, you have used the most recent financial statements to calculate the following ratios.

	2006	2005
Current Ratio	1.8:1	1.7:1
Quick Ratio	1.10:1	1.08:1
Receivable Turnover	10 times	11 times
Inventory Turnover	6 times	5 times
Debt/Equity Ratio	25.2%	35.8%

Required:

Provide an explanation of how each of the above ratios should be interpreted and any indication they provide as to the company's solvency and ability to continue as a going concern.

Critical Thinking Questions

12-49 (Discussion of the value of comparability)

One qualitative characteristic underlying financial accounting is comparability. As you will recall, comparability refers to similarities of financial information between different companies, and consistency of the financial information produced by a company over time. Two of the many ways of achieving comparability are by limiting the number of different ways transactions may be recorded, and by specifying how assets, liabilities, equities, revenues, and expenses will be disclosed in the financial statements.

One argument against comparability is that it limits companies' ability to choose among accounting methods, and thus may result in disclosures that may not be agreeable to management or best suited to the particular circumstances.

Required:

Discuss the pros and cons of comparability, with reference to the analysis of financial statements.

12-50 **(Use of subsidiaries to manage debt financing)**

A major reason that companies such as General Motors form finance subsidiaries (separate companies that they control) is the potential to increase leverage as they seek ways to finance the manufacture and sale of their products. Such subsidiaries are referred to as "captive" finance subsidiaries.

Required:

Explain why a company that finances its operations through a subsidiary has greater debt capacity than a similar company that finances its operations internally.

Appendix A

le château 2003 ANNUAL REPORT

le château 2003 ANNUAL REPORT

CORPORATE PROFILE

Le Château is a leading Canadian specialty retailer offering fashion-forward apparel, accessories and footwear to style-conscious women and men. Our brand's success is built on quick identification of and response to fashion trends through our design, product development and vertically integrated operations.

Le Château brand name clothing is sold exclusively through our 165 retail locations – which average 3,500 square feet in size. All stores are in Canada, except for four locations in the New York City area.

Le Château, committed to research, design and product development, manufactures approximately 45% of the Company's goods in its own Canadian production facilities.

LE CHÂTEAU STORES
and Square Footage

	January 31, 2004		January 25, 2003	
	Stores	**Square Footage**	Stores	Square Footage
Ontario	**54**	**203,983**	55	206,844
Quebec	**46**	**217,707**	43	173,542
Alberta	**20**	**75,293**	18	65,297
British Columbia	**20**	**67,798**	20	63,563
Manitoba	**6**	**24,050**	6	27,951
Nova Scotia	**6**	**12,669**	6	12,669
Saskatchewan	**4**	**13,209**	4	13,209
New Brunswick	**4**	**12,467**	4	12,454
Newfoundland	**1**	**2,500**	1	2,500
Total Canada	**161**	**629,676**	157	578,029
Total United States	**4**	**22,506**	4	22,606
Total Le Château Stores	**165**	**652,182**	161	600,635

SALES [in '000]

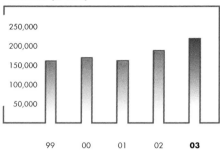

250,000
200,000
150,000
100,000
50,000

99   00   01   02   **03**

NET EARNINGS (LOSS) [in '000]

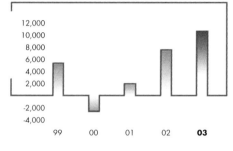

12,000
10,000
8,000
6,000
4,000
2,000
-2,000
-4,000

99   00   01   02   **03**

SHAREHOLDERS' EQUITY [in '000]

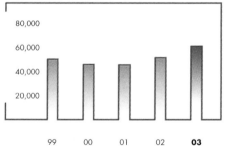

80,000
60,000
40,000
20,000

99   00   01   02   **03**

CASH FLOW FROM OPERATIONS
[in '000]

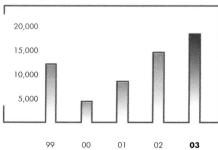

20,000
15,000
10,000
5,000

99   00   01   02   **03**

FINANCIAL HIGHLIGHTS

(in thousands of dollars except per share data and ratios)

Fiscal years ended	January 31 2004 (53 weeks)	January 25 2003	January 26 2002	January 27 2001	January 29 2000
Results					
Sales	226,766	217,660	187,540	161,120	168,666
Earnings (loss) before income taxes	17,123	12,375	4,010	(4,346)	9,019
Net earnings (loss)	10,648	7,562	1,852	(2,607)	5,269
• Per share	2.07	1.52	0.38	(0.53)	1.07
Dividends per share	0.40	0.40	0.40	0.40	0.40
Average number of shares outstanding (000)	5,134	4,980	4,936	4,935	4,925
Financial Position					
Working capital	24,987	18,443	14,621	13,804	19,585
Shareholders' equity	61,162	51,492	45,694	45,800	50,380
Total assets	94,546	80,519	69,915	68,189	68,624
Financial Ratios					
Current ratio	1.99:1	1.79:1	1.80:1	1.89:1	2.41:1
Quick ratio	0.96:1	0.70:1	0.63:1	0.46:1	0.94:1
Long-term debt to equity [1]	0.11:1	0.08:1	0.10:1	0.13:1	0.08:1
Other Statistics (units as specified)					
Cash flow from operations (in '000)	18,311	14,503	8,544	4,394	12,048
Capital expenditures (in '000)	14,438	9,019	5,025	10,379	10,628
Number of stores at year-end	165	161	160	161	159
Square footage	652,182	600,635	592,898	598,983	585,860
Sales per square foot [2]	386	391	338	292	322

SHAREHOLDERS' INFORMATION

Ticker symbol: **CTU.A**

Listing: **TSX**

Number of participating shares outstanding
(as of May 28, 2004):

2,286,451 Class A Subordinate Voting Shares
3,020,000 Class B Voting Shares

Float: [3]

1,910,521 Class A Shares held by the public

As of May 28, 2004:
High/low of Class A Shares
(12 months ended May 28, 2004):

	$ 16.00 / $ 9.17
Recent price:	**$15.21**
Dividend yield:	**3.9 %**
Price/earnings ratio:	**7.35 X**
Price/book value ratio:	**1.30 X**

Earnings per share: [4]	**$ 2.07**
Book value per share: [5]	**$ 11.66**

[1] Including capital leases and current portion of debt. Excluding deferred lease inducements.

[2] Excluding Le Château outlet stores.

[3] Excluding shares held by officers of the Company.

[4] For the year ended January 31, 2004.

[5] As at January 31, 2004.

le château

MESSAGE TO SHAREHOLDERS

We have just completed a record-breaking year. Le Château has maintained and enhanced its appeal to our vibrant and ever-growing demographic. The style and value of our merchandise, the quality of our customer service, and above all, the trust associated with our brand, has brought the Company to an unprecedented level of success.

In 2003, Le Château achieved the highest sales and profitability in its history. The upward trend is firm and ongoing in 2004. The first four months of the current year yielded an encouraging same store sales increase of 5.2%. Notably, we have posted a total sales increase of 10.5%.

We are proud to report that our pre-tax earnings reached $17 million in 2003, up from $12 million the previous year. Total sales were a best-ever $226.8 million, up from $217.7 million in 2002. Although same store sales increased a modest 0.6%, it indicates how company wide resolve and employee teamwork achieved results in a period of uncertain economic conditions.

Net profit after tax was $10.6 million or $2.07 per share in 2003, compared to $7.6 million or $1.52 per share last year.

Dividends paid in 2003 totaled $0.40 per share. Le Château has paid dividends for forty-one consecutive quarters. Moreover, on April 30, 2004, the Board of Directors approved a 50% increase in the quarterly dividend from $0.10 to $0.15 per share.

In 2003, our strategy was to further differentiate ourselves through ongoing improvements in the quality and design of our products. We also made advancements in our planning, buying and production processes to reduce lead times and increase speed to market. All this enabled our energetic sales team to deliver the right fashion in a more timely way.

In 2004, our objective to further improve profitability has intensified. We will maintain our emphasis on efficient management, product differentiation, and superb customer service. In our 45th Anniversary year, we will continue to fine-tune every aspect of our business, to remain entrepreneurial leaders in our industry and to reach internationally recognized levels of performance.

In addition to the fundamentals of good fashion value and unstinting service, Le Château constantly pursues a third core strategy. It is to provide a dynamic shopping experience, and to do so with a flair and friendliness that will attract customers back into our stores time and again. This approach, contributing to and benefiting from the well-entrenched personality of our brand, has always sent a distinctive message to the marketplace.

We wish to take this opportunity to thank our shareholders for their support, trust and confidence in our leadership. In 2004, Le Château's management remains dedicated to maximizing the return to shareholders.

No expression of gratitude could possibly be sufficient to recognize the profound talent, creativity, loyalty and spirit of our employees. To an overwhelming degree, their commitment to the Company aligns their careers with the long-term goals of Le Château. May their passion and devotion, once again, be the driving force in this year's success.

HERSCHEL H. SEGAL
Chairman of the Board and
Chief Executive Officer

JANE SILVERSTONE, B.A.LLL
Vice-Chairman
of the Board

le château

MANAGEMENT'S DISCUSSION AND ANALYSIS

May 3, 2004

The 2003 year refers, in all cases, to the 53 week period ended January 31, 2004, and comparatively, the 2002 year refers to the 52 week period ended January 25, 2003. Management's Discussion and Analysis should be read in conjunction with the audited consolidated financial statements and notes to the consolidated financial statements for the 2003 fiscal year.

SELECTED ANNUAL INFORMATION

[In thousands of dollars except per share amounts]

	2003 $	2002 $	2001 $
Sales	226,766	217,660	187,540
Earnings before income taxes	17,123	12,375	4,010
Net earnings	10,648	7,562	1,852
Net earnings per share			
Basic	2.07	1.52	0.38
Diluted	1.98	1.45	0.37
Total assets	94,546	80,519	69,915
Long-term debt [1]	4,580	1,978	1,958
Dividends per share	0.40	0.40	0.40
Cash flow from operations	18,311	14,503	8,544
Comparable store sales increase %	0.6%	18.4%	14.2%
Square footage of gross store space at year-end	652,182	600,635	592,898
Sales per average square foot, excluding fashion outlet stores (in dollars)	386	391	338

[1] Including capital lease obligations. Excluding current portion of debt and deferred lease inducements.

SALES

Sales increased 4.2% in 2003 to reach a record level of $226.8 million, compared to $217.7 million the previous year. Comparable store sales increased 0.6% in the year. Sales per average square foot of retail space - excluding fashion outlets – decreased to $386 from $391 in 2002.

Profit optimization became a key component of our business strategies in a year adversely affected by external conditions and events. We remained focused on broadening our customer base and brand differentiation by offering the most innovative blend of quality fashion and value on a timely and continuous basis.

We continued with the rollout of our new 2002 Store Concept, a remodeling program implemented in approximately one-third of our stores to date. This store design concept reflects our efforts to elevate the quality of our brand and broaden our customer base through a cleanly designed and clearly merchandised store environment that allows each division to become a distinct destination with greater visibility and impact.

TOTAL SALES BY DIVISION
[In thousands of dollars]

	2003 $	2002 $	2001 $	% change 2003-2002	2002-2001
Ladies' Clothing	138,047	134,848	121,904	2.4 %	10.6 %
Men's Clothing	26,707	24,721	18,033	8.0 %	37.1 %
JUNIOR GIRL Clothing	17,363	19,731	18,303	(12.0)%	7.8 %
Footwear	16,700	14,623	14,078	14.2 %	3.9 %
Accessories	27,949	23,737	15,222	17.7 %	55.9 %
	226,766	217,660	187,540	4.2 %	16.1 %

The Ladies' clothing division recorded a sales increase of 2.4% in 2003 and continues to be the main revenue driver among the Company's divisions, accounting for 60.9% of total sales. We continue to further upgrade the design and fabrications of our products and focus on expanding our customer base.

The highest sales increase in 2003 came from the Accessories and Footwear divisions with increases of 17.7% and 14.2%, respectively. Both these divisions represent significant growth potential in 2004 and beyond.

Revenues in the Men's division increased 8.0% in 2003. During the year, 5 existing stores were expanded into adjacent premises and we are in the process of expanding an additional 6 stores in the first quarter of 2004, as we continue to build on this market segment.

Sales in the JUNIOR GIRL clothing division, serving pre-teens aged 8-12, decreased 12.0% in 2003. The entire pre-teen market experienced stagnating sales and struggled through a very difficult and challenging year. In response, we re-aligned our existing real estate space to maximize profitability, shifting selling space to more profitable divisions, when and where required.

TOTAL SALES BY REGION
[In thousands of dollars]

	2003 $	2002 $	2001 $	% change 2003-2002	2002-2001
Ontario	78,991	76,242	64,793	3.6 %	17.7 %
Quebec	63,556	59,199	47,576	7.4 %	24.4 %
Prairies	39,322	36,591	31,598	7.5 %	15.8 %
British Columbia	27,530	26,865	23,869	2.5 %	12.6 %
Atlantic	9,776	9,523	8,350	2.7 %	14.0 %
United States	7,591	9,240	11,354	(17.8)%	(18.6)%
	226,766	217,660	187,540	4.2 %	16.1 %

The strongest growth in total sales came from the Prairies and Quebec with sales increases of 7.5% and 7.4% respectively. Same store sales increased 2.2% in the Prairies while they were flat in Quebec. Ontario and the Maritimes also had increases in same store sales of 2.5% and 1.3%, respectively.

Comparable store sales (in US$) for the Company's four U.S. stores, all located in the New York City area, decreased by 8.3% in 2003, compared to the same period a year ago. We are working diligently to contain costs in these operations and will be reconfiguring our real estate portfolio to ensure profitability. For the first quarter ended May 1, 2004, comparable store sales have increased 22.5% (in US$).

During the year, Le Château opened 6 new stores and renovated 18 existing stores. As at January 31, 2004, the Company operated 165 stores (including 11 fashion outlet stores) compared to 161 (including 8 fashion outlets) at the end of the previous year. Total floor space at the end of the year was 652,000 square feet compared to 601,000 square feet at the end of the preceding year, an increase of over 8%.

EXPENSES

Cost of sales, buying and occupancy, as a percentage of sales, decreased to 62.0% from 64.6% in 2002. This decrease is due to the continued improvement of inventory management, resulting in increased merchandise margins.

Selling, general and administrative expenses were $60.5 million in 2003, compared to $57.0 million in 2002. As a percentage of sales, selling, general and administrative expenses increased to 26.7% in 2003 from 26.2% in 2002.

Interest expense decreased to $339,000 in 2003 from $350,000 in 2002, due to the repayment of $2.8 million of long-term debt during the year and to lower interest rates in 2003.

Depreciation and amortization increased to $7.7 million from $6.9 million in 2002, due to the additional investments in fixed assets.

The $6.5 million provision for income taxes in 2003 represents an effective income tax rate of 37.8%, compared to 38.9% the previous year. The reduction in the effective tax rate is the result of a decrease in the Federal income tax rate.

EARNINGS

Net earnings reached a record level of $10.6 million or $2.07 per share (basic) in 2003 compared to $7.6 million or $1.52 per share in 2002.

Net earnings attributable to Canadian operations amounted to $11.9 million or $2.32 per share (basic), while the U.S. recorded a net loss of $1.3 million Cdn or $(0.25) Cdn per share.

LIQUIDITY AND CAPITAL RESOURCES

The Company has a high level of liquidity, more than sufficient to cover its operating requirements, as well as a strong financial position. The Company's liquidity follows a seasonal pattern based on the timing of inventory purchases and capital expenditures, with liquidity being at its highest level at year-end and the lowest at the end of the second quarter.

The Company's net cash position increased to $22.1 million or $4.21 per share in 2003 from $15.0 million or $3.00 per share in 2002. Cash flow from operations increased to $18.3 million in 2003, compared to $14.5 million the previous year, mainly as a result of higher net earnings. Cash provided by operating activities (including net changes in non-cash working capital items) increased to $19.2 million from $16.0 million in 2002.

Cash provided by operating and financing activities was used in the following financing and investing activities:

• Capital expenditures of $14.4 million, consisting of:

CAPITAL EXPENDITURES
[In thousands of dollars]

	2003 **$**	2002 $	2001 $
New Stores (6 stores; 2002 - 1 store; 2001 - 2 stores)	**1,434**	298	341
Renovated Stores (18 stores; 2002 - 16 stores; 2001 - 11 stores)	**7,336**	5,681	3,341
Information Technology	**4,447**	1,033	721
Other	**1,221**	2,007	622
	14,438	9,019	5,025

Of the $14.4 million in total capital expenditures, $14.3 million was attributed to Canadian operations, and $0.1 million to the U.S. Included in the investments in information technology was $3.5 million for the new point of sale equipment which is being launched in the first half of 2004. Total amount budgeted for the project is approximately $4.5 million.

• Dividend payments of $2.1 million

• Capital lease and long-term debt repayments of $2.8 million

CONTRACTUAL OBLIGATIONS

[In thousands of dollars]

	Total $	Less than 1 year $	1-3 years $	4-5 years $	After 5 years $
Long-term debt	1,766	914	852	—	—
Capital Lease Obligations	5,253	1,525	2,888	840	—
Operating leases [1]	111,914	21,599	36,806	27,509	26,000
	118,933	24,038	40,546	28,349	26,000

[1] Minimum rentals payable under long-term operating leases excluding percentage rentals.

For fiscal 2004, projected capital expenditures approximate $17 million, of which $15.5 million will be used for the opening of 6 to 10 stores and the renovation of 20 to 25 existing stores, with the balance of $1.5 million for investments in information technology. In an effort to offer our brand to all parts of Canada, we are continually searching for new opportunities in key markets.

Management expects to be able to continue financing the Company's activities and most of its capital expenditures through cash flow from operations. If necessary, it can also draw upon its financial resources, which include cash and cash equivalents of $22.1 million at year-end, as well as a revolving line of credit of $16.0 million with its bank.

The Company has a $4.5 million facility to finance the new point of sale system available until July 31, 2004. Draw downs under the facility are repayable over 60 months, and will bear interest at a fixed rate of the three year Government of Canada bond interest rate plus 2.26%. The facility is collateralized by the equipment financed. Subsequent to January 31, 2004, $3.2 million was drawn under this facility.

In addition, the Company has a $6 million facility to finance renovations available until August 31, 2004. Draw downs under the facility are repayable over 48 months, and will bear interest at a fixed rate of the three year Government of Canada bond interest rate plus 2.35%. The facility is collateralized by the store fixtures and equipment financed. As at May 1, 2004, no amounts had been drawn under this facility.

The Company does not have any off-balance sheet financing arrangements.

FINANCIAL POSITION

Working capital stood at $25.0 million at the end of the fiscal year, compared to $18.4 million at the end of 2002.

Inventories increased to $26.1 million from $25.5 million a year earlier, due primarily to earlier receipts of our Spring line and the fact that the current fiscal year closed a week later as compared to the previous year.

Shareholders' equity increased to $61.2 million at year-end, after the payment of $2.1 million in dividends. Book value per share increased to $11.66 at year-end, compared to $10.25 as at January 25, 2003, and included $4.21 in cash and cash equivalents.

Long-term debt and capital lease obligations, including the current portions, increased to $7.0 million from $4.2 million in 2002, after the additional long-term debt financing of $5.6 million and the repayment of $2.8 million during the year. The long-term debt to equity ratio remained conservative at 0.11:1, compared to 0.08:1 the previous year.

DIVIDENDS

In 2003, Le Château continued – for the tenth consecutive year – its policy of paying quarterly dividends on the Class A Subordinate Voting and Class B Voting Shares. Total dividends per Class A and Class B share amounted to $0.10 per quarter or $0.40 in 2003.

On April 30, 2004, the Board of Directors approved a 50% increase in the quarterly dividend, from $0.10 to $0.15 per share, payable on June 7, 2004 to shareholders of record at the close of business on May 21, 2004. The dividend yield, based on the April 30, 2004 closing price of $15.25 per share, was 3.9%.

As at May 1, 2004, there were 2,229,841 Class A Subordinate Voting and 3,020,000 Class B Voting Shares outstanding. Further, there were 425,250 options outstanding with exercise prices ranging from $2.33 to $7.25, of which 193,950 were exercisable.

ACCOUNTING STANDARDS IMPLEMENTED IN 2003

Stock-based Compensation

Effective January 27, 2002, the Company adopted, on a prospective basis, the Canadian Institute of Chartered Accountants' ("CICA") recommendations on Stock-based Compensation and Other Stock-based Payments. These recommendations require that compensation for all awards made to non-employees and certain awards made to employees, including stock appreciation rights, direct awards of stock and awards that call for settlement in cash or other assets, be measured and recorded in the financial statements at fair value. These recommendations were later revised and require that compensation cost be recorded in the statement of earnings.

In accordance with the CICA's recommendations described above, any consideration paid by employees on the exercise of stock options granted is credited to capital stock. The pro forma disclosures of the related compensation cost required under the fair value method are included in note 8 of the "Notes to Consolidated Financial Statements". For stock options granted before January 27, 2002, there are no requirements to disclose or to record the related compensation cost and comparative figures have not been restated.

The compensation cost related to stock options granted to employees after January 25, 2003 will be recorded in the consolidated statement of earnings. For the year ended January 31, 2004, there was no impact on the Company's results as there were no options granted during the year.

RECENTLY ISSUED ACCOUNTING STANDARDS

Hedging Relationships

During 2003, the CICA issued Accounting Guideline 13 "Hedging Relationships", which deals with identification, documentation, designation and effectiveness of hedges and also the discontinuance of hedge accounting, but it does not specify hedge accounting methods. This guidance is applicable to hedge relationships in effect in fiscal years beginning on or after July 1, 2003.

Impairment of Long-lived Assets

On February 1, 2004, the company will prospectively adopt the CICA's section 3063, Impairment of Long-lived Assets, under which an impairment loss is recognized when the carrying amount of a long-lived asset held for use is not recoverable and exceeds its fair value.

The Company is evaluating the impact of adopting these new standards and guidance, and therefore has not yet assessed the effect, if any, on future Consolidated Financial Statements.

CRITICAL ACCOUNTING ESTIMATES

The preparation of financial statements requires the Company to estimate the effect of various matters that are inherently uncertain as of the date of the financial statements. Each of these required estimates varies in regard to the level of judgement involved and its potential impact on the Company's reported financial results. Estimates are deemed critical when a different estimate could have reasonable been used or where changes in the estimates are reasonably likely to occur from period to period, and would materially impact the Company's financial condition, changes in financial condition or results of operations. The Company's significant accounting policies are discussed in note 1 of the "Notes to Consolidated Financial Statements"; critical estimates inherent in these accounting policies are discussed in the following paragraphs.

Inventory Valuation

The Company records a provision to reflect management's best estimate of the net realizable value, including a normal profit margin of its inventory. In addition, a provision for shrinkage and obsolescence is calculated based on historical experience. Management continually reviews the entire provision, to assess whether, based on economic conditions and an assessment of past sales trends, it is adequate.

Fixed Asset Impairment

Management evaluates the ongoing value of assets associated with retail stores. When undiscounted cash flows estimated to be generated by those assets are less than the carrying value of those assets, impairment losses would be recorded.

RISKS AND UNCERTAINTIES

Competitive and Economic Environment

Fashion is a highly competitive global business that is subject to rapidly changing consumer demands. In addition, there are several external factors which affect the economic climate and consumer confidence over which the Company has no influence.

This environment intensifies the importance of in-store differentiation, quality of service and continually exceeding customer expectations, thereby delivering a total customer experience.

With this view, Le Château believes that its distinctive edge on fashion, its innovative store design and merchandising, its strong financial position and its winning team of vibrant employees dedicated to providing the best whole store experience will facilitate continued success.

Leases

All of the Company's stores are held under long-term leases, most of which include favorable lease terms. Any increase in retail rental rates would adversely impact the Company.

Foreign Exchange

The Company's foreign exchange risk is limited to currency fluctuations between the Canadian and U.S. dollar. The Company uses forward contracts to fix the exchange rate of its expected requirements for U.S. dollars.

The Company is party to foreign exchange contracts used to manage currency rate risks. Realized gains and losses on foreign exchange contracts entered into to hedge future transactions are included in the measurement of the related foreign currency transaction.

The Company enters into foreign exchange forward contracts that oblige it to purchase specific amounts of foreign currencies at set future dates at forward predetermined exchange rates. The contracts are matched with anticipated foreign currency purchases in the United States. The Company enters into the foreign exchange forward contracts to hedge itself from the risk of losses should the value of the Canadian dollar decline compared to the foreign currency. The Company only enters into foreign exchange contracts with Canadian Chartered Banks to minimize risk.

QUARTERLY RESULTS

[In thousands of dollars except per share amount]

	First Quarter		Second Quarter		Third Quarter		Fourth Quarter		Total	
	2003 $	2002 $	2003 $	2002 $	2003 $	2002 $	2003 $	2002 $	2003 $	2002 $
Sales	45,270	42,960	54,180	51,597	57,763	60,434	69,553	62,669	226,766	217,660
Earnings before income taxes	826	667	4,153	3,888	6,120	4,946	6,024	2,874	17,123	12,375
Net earnings	381	343	2,543	2,422	3,810	3,009	3,914	1,788	10,648	7,562
Net earnings per share										
Basic	0.08	0.07	0.50	0.49	0.74	0.60	0.75	0.36	2.07	1.52
Diluted	0.07	0.07	0.48	0.47	0.71	0.57	0.72	0.34	1.98	1.45

The Company's business follows a seasonal pattern, with retail sales traditionally being higher in the third and fourth quarters due to the back-to-school period and the Christmas season, respectively.

Fourth Quarter Results

The Company recorded a sales increase of 11.0% to reach $69.6 million for the 14 week period ended January 31, 2004, compared with sales of $62.7 million for the 13 week period ended January 25, 2003 last year. Comparable sales increased by 3.4% in the fourth quarter compared to the same period a year ago.

Net earnings for the fourth quarter rose 119% to $3,914,000 or $0.75 per share, compared to $1,788,000 or $0.36 per share for the same period the previous year.

OUTLOOK

Le Château expects stable growth in sales and earnings through 2004. For the first quarter ended May 1, 2004, total retail sales increased 11.9% and comparable store sales increased 5.3%. The Company will continue to remain focused on the customer by elevating our service standards and by focusing on product innovation. We will remain centered on improving all aspects of our business through ongoing brand-building efforts, better inventory management, tighter cost controls and continued investments in research, design and development, renovations and new technologies.

FORWARD-LOOKING STATEMENTS

This "Management's Discussion and Analysis" along with the Annual Report may contain forward-looking statements relating to the Company and/or the environment in which it operates that are based on the Company's expectations, estimates and forecasts. These statements are not guarantees of future performance and involve risks and uncertainties that are difficult to predict and/or are beyond the Company's control. A number of factors may cause actual outcomes and results to differ materially from those expressed. These factors include those set forth in other public filings of the Company. Therefore, readers should not place undue reliance on these forward-looking statements. In addition, these forward-looking statements speak only as of the date made and the Company disavows any intention or obligation to update or revise any such statements as a result of any event, circumstance or otherwise.

Factors which could cause actual results or events to differ materially from current expectations include, among other things: the ability of the Company to successfully implement its strategic initiatives and whether such strategic initiatives will yield the expected benefits; competitive conditions in the businesses in which the Company participates; changes in consumer spending; general economic conditions and normal business uncertainty; customer preferences towards product offerings; seasonal weather patterns; fluctuations in foreign currency exchange rates; changes in the Company's relationship with its suppliers; interest rate fluctuations and other changes in borrowing costs; and changes in laws, rules and regulations applicable to the Company.

Carrefour Laval - Quebec, Canada

le château

CONSOLIDATED FINANCIAL STATEMENTS

MANAGEMENT'S RESPONSIBILITY
For Financial Information

The accompanying consolidated financial statements of Le Château Inc. and all the information in this annual report are the responsibility of management.

The financial statements have been prepared by management in accordance with Canadian generally accepted accounting principles. When alternative accounting methods exist, management has chosen those it deems most appropriate in the circumstances. Financial statements are not precise since they include certain amounts based on estimates and judgement. Management has determined such amounts on a reasonable basis in order to ensure that the financial statements are presented fairly, in all material respects. Management has prepared the financial information presented elsewhere in the Annual Report and has ensured that it is consistent with that in the financial statements.

The Company maintains systems of internal accounting and administrative controls of high quality, consistent with reasonable cost. Such systems are designed to provide reasonable assurance that the financial information is relevant, reliable and accurate and the Company's assets are appropriately accounted for and adequately safeguarded.

The Board of Directors is responsible for ensuring that management fulfills its responsibilities for financial reporting and is ultimately responsible for reviewing and approving the financial statements. The Board carries out this responsibility principally through the Audit Committee which consists of three outside directors appointed by the Board. The Committee meets quarterly with management as well as with the independent external auditors to discuss internal controls over the financial reporting process, auditing matters and financial reporting issues. The Committee reviews the consolidated financial statements and the external auditors' report thereon and reports its findings to the Board for consideration when the Board approves the financial statements for issuance to the Company's share-holders. The Committee also considers, for review by the Board and approval by the shareholders, the engagement or re-appointment of the external auditors. The external auditors have full and free access to the Audit Committee.

On behalf of the shareholders, the financial statements have been audited by Ernst & Young LLP, the external auditors, in accordance with Canadian generally accepted auditing standards.

Herschel H. Segal
Chairman of the Board and
Chief Executive Officer

Emilia Di Raddo, CA
President and Secretary

AUDITORS' REPORT
To the Shareholders of Le Château Inc.

We have audited the consolidated balance sheets of Le Château Inc., as at January 31, 2004 and January 25, 2003 and the consolidated statements of retained earnings, earnings and cash flows for the years then ended. These financial statements are the responsibility of the Company's management. Our responsibility is to express an opinion on these financial statements based on our audits.

We conducted our audits in accordance with Canadian generally accepted auditing standards. Those standards require that we plan and perform an audit to obtain reasonable assurance whether the financial statements are free of material misstatement. An audit includes examining, on a test basis, evidence supporting the amounts and disclosures in the financial statements. An audit also includes assessing the accounting principles used and significant estimates made by management, as well as evaluating the overall financial statement presentation.

In our opinion, these consolidated financial statements present fairly, in all material respects, the financial position of the Company as at January 31, 2004 and January 25, 2003 and the results of its operations and its cash flows for the years then ended in accordance with Canadian generally accepted accounting principles.

Ernst & Young LLP

Montreal, Canada
March 25, 2004

Chartered Accountants

CONSOLIDATED BALANCE SHEETS
As at January 31, 2004
[With comparative figures as at January 25, 2003]
[In thousands of dollars]

	2004 $	2003 $
ASSETS [note 2]		
Current		
Cash and cash equivalents [note 15]	22,067	15,040
Accounts receivable and prepaid expenses	1,394	1,169
Inventories [note 3]	26,075	25,482
Loan to director [note 4]	566	—
Total current assets	50,102	41,691
Loan to director [note 4]	—	566
Fixed assets [note 5]	44,444	38,262
	94,546	80,519
LIABILITIES AND SHAREHOLDERS' EQUITY		
Current		
Accounts payable and accrued liabilities [note 11]	20,148	17,609
Dividend payable	525	503
Income taxes payable	2,003	2,877
Current portion of capital lease obligations [note 6]	1,525	776
Current portion of long-term debt [note 7]	914	1,483
Total current liabilities	25,115	23,248
Capital lease obligations [note 6]	3,728	212
Long-term debt [note 7]	852	1,766
Future income taxes [note 9]	1,758	1,888
Deferred lease inducements	1,931	1,913
Total liabilities	33,384	29,027
Shareholders' equity		
Capital stock [note 8]	14,774	13,680
Retained earnings	46,388	37,812
Total shareholders' equity	61,162	51,492
	94,546	80,519

Commitments [note 11]

See accompanying notes

On behalf of the Board:

Herschel H. Segal
Director

Jane Silverstone, B.A.LLL
Director

14

CONSOLIDATED STATEMENTS OF RETAINED EARNINGS

Year ended January 31, 2004

[With comparative figures for the year ended January 25, 2003]
[In thousands of dollars]

	2004 $	2003 $
Balance, beginning of year	37,812	32,249
Net earnings	10,648	7,562
	48,460	39,811
Dividends	2,072	1,999
Balance, end of year	46,388	37,812

See accompanying notes

CONSOLIDATED STATEMENTS OF EARNINGS

Year ended January 31, 2004

[With comparative figures for the year ended January 25, 2003]
[In thousands of dollars, except share data]

	2004 $	2003 $
Sales	226,766	217,660
Cost of sales and expenses		
Cost of sales, buying and occupancy	140,537	140,705
Selling, general and administrative	60,511	57,012
Interest on long-term debt	339	350
Depreciation and amortization	7,745	6,937
Write-off of fixed assets	511	281
	209,643	205,285
Earnings before income taxes	17,123	12,375
Provision for income taxes [note 9]	6,475	4,813
Net earnings	10,648	7,562
Net earnings per share [note 10]		
Basic	2.07	1.52
Diluted	1.98	1.45
Weighted average number of shares outstanding	5,133,949	4,979,581

See accompanying notes

15

CONSOLIDATED STATEMENTS OF CASH FLOWS

Year ended January 31, 2004
[With comparative figures for the year ended January 25, 2003]
[In thousands of dollars]

	2004 $	2003 $
OPERATING ACTIVITIES		
Net earnings	**10,648**	7,562
Adjustments to determine net cash from operating activities		
Depreciation and amortization	**7,745**	6,937
Write-off of fixed assets	**511**	281
Amortization of deferred lease inducements	**(463)**	(393)
Future income taxes	**(130)**	116
	18,311	14,503
Net change in non-cash working capital items related to operations [note 13]	**847**	1,526
Cash flows from operating activities	**19,158**	16,029
FINANCING ACTIVITIES		
Repayment of loan to director	**—**	120
Proceeds of capital leases	**5,620**	—
Repayment of capital lease obligations	**(1,355)**	(1,537)
Proceeds of long-term debt	**—**	2,500
Repayment of long-term debt	**(1,483)**	(1,210)
Deferred lease inducements	**481**	82
Issue of capital stock	**1,094**	235
Dividends paid	**(2,050)**	(1,990)
Cash flows from financing activities	**2,307**	(1,800)
INVESTING ACTIVITIES		
Additions to fixed assets	**(14,438)**	(9,019)
Cash flows from investing activities	**(14,438)**	(9,019)
Increase in cash and cash equivalents	**7,027**	5,210
Cash and cash equivalents, beginning of year	**15,040**	9,830
Cash and cash equivalents, end of year	**22,067**	15,040
Supplementary information:		
Interest paid during the year	**339**	350
Income taxes paid during the year, net	**7,473**	3,555

See accompanying notes

NOTES
TO CONSOLIDATED FINANCIAL STATEMENTS
January 31, 2004 and January 25, 2003

[Tabular amounts in thousands of dollars except per share amounts and where otherwise indicated]

1. ACCOUNTING POLICIES

Use of estimates

The consolidated financial statements of the Company have been prepared by management in accordance with accounting principles generally accepted in Canada. The preparation of financial statements in conformity with generally accepted accounting principles requires Management to make estimates and assumptions that affect the amounts reported in the financial statements and accompanying notes. Actual results could differ from those estimates. The financial statements have, in Management's opinion, been properly prepared within reasonable limits of materiality and within the framework of the accounting policies summarized below.

Principles of consolidation

The consolidated financial statements include the accounts of Le Château Inc. and its wholly owned subsidiary.

Foreign currency translation

Transactions denominated in foreign currencies and an integrated foreign operation use the temporal method. Monetary assets and liabilities are translated into Canadian dollars at the rates in effect at the balance sheet date. Other assets and liabilities are translated at the rates prevailing at the transaction dates. Revenues and expenses are translated at the average exchange rates prevailing during the year, except for the cost of inventory used and depreciation and amortization, which are translated at exchange rates prevailing when the related assets were acquired. Gains and losses arising from the fluctuations in exchange rates are reflected in earnings.

Cash and cash equivalents

Cash consists of cash on hand and balances with banks. Cash equivalents are restricted to investments that are readily convertible into a known amount of cash, that are subject to minimal risk of changes in value and which have a maturity of three months or less at acquisition.

Inventories

Raw materials and work-in-process are valued at the lower of specific cost and net realizable value. Finished goods are valued, using the retail inventory method, at the lower of cost and net realizable value less normal profit margin.

Fixed assets, depreciation and amortization

Fixed assets are recorded at cost. Depreciation and amortization are charged to income on the following bases:

Building	10% diminishing balance
Furniture and equipment	5 to 10 years straight-line
Automobiles	30% diminishing balance

Leasehold rights and improvements are amortized on the straight-line basis over the initial term of the leases, plus one renewal period, not to exceed 10 years.

On February 1, 2004, the company will prospectively adopt the Canadian Institute of Chartered Accountants' ("CICA") Section 3063, Impairment of Long-lived Assets, under which an impairment loss is recognized when the carrying amount of a long-lived asset held for use is not recoverable and exceeds its fair value. The Company has not yet assessed the impact of the new standard.

Deferred lease inducements

Deferred lease inducements are amortized on the straight-line basis over the initial term of the leases, plus one renewal period, not to exceed 10 years.

1. ACCOUNTING POLICIES [Continued]

Stock-based Compensation

Effective January 27, 2002, the Company adopted, on a prospective basis, the Canadian Institute of Chartered Accountants' ("CICA") recommendations on Stock-based Compensation and Other Stock-based Payments. These recommendations require that compensation for all awards made to non-employees and certain awards made to employees, including stock appreciation rights, direct awards of stock and awards that call for settlement in cash or other assets, be measured and recorded in the financial statements at fair value. These recommendations were later revised and require that compensation cost be recorded in the statement of earnings.

In accordance with the CICA's recommendations described above, any consideration paid by employees on the exercise of stock options granted is credited to capital stock. The pro forma disclosures of the related compensation cost required under the fair value method are included in note 8. For stock options granted before January 27, 2002, there are no requirements to disclose or to record the related compensation cost and comparative figures have not been restated.

The compensation cost related to stock options granted to employees after January 25, 2003 will be recorded in the consolidated statement of earnings. For the year ended January 31, 2004, there was no impact on the Company's results as there were no options granted during the year.

Store opening costs

Store opening costs are expensed as incurred.

Income taxes

The Company uses the liability method of accounting for income taxes, which requires the establishment of future tax assets and liabilities, as measured by enacted or substantially enacted tax rates, for all temporary differences caused when the tax bases of assets and liabilities differ from those reported in the financial statements.

Earnings per share

The diluted earnings per share are calculated using the treasury stock method. Under the treasury stock method, the diluted weighted average number of shares outstanding is calculated as if all dilutive options had been exercised at the later of the beginning of the reporting period or date of issuance, and the proceeds from the exercise of such dilutive options are used to repurchase common shares at the average market price for the period.

Derivative financial instruments

The Company is party to foreign exchange contracts used to manage currency rate risks. Realized gains and losses on foreign exchange contracts entered into to hedge future transactions are included in the measurement of the related foreign currency transaction.

Year End

The Company's fiscal year ends on the last Saturday in January. The year ended January 31, 2004 covers a 53-week fiscal period, whereas the year ended January 25, 2003 covers a 52-week period.

2. CREDIT FACILITIES

The Company has operating lines of credit totaling $11 million, which is increased to $16 million during the period April 15 to September 15. These operating lines of credit are collateralized by the Company's accounts receivable, inventories, the issued shares of a subsidiary company and a moveable hypothec providing a charge on the Company's assets. This credit agreement is renewable annually. Amounts drawn under these lines of credit are payable on demand and bear interest at rates based on the prime bank rate for loans in Canadian dollars, U.S. base rate for loans in U.S. dollars and banker's acceptance plus 1.25% for banker's acceptances in Canadian dollars. Furthermore, the terms of the banking agreement require the Company to maintain certain financial and non-financial ratios.

The Company has a $4.5 million facility to finance the new point of sale system available until April 30, 2004. Draw downs under the facility are repayable over 60 months, and will bear interest at a fixed rate of the three year Government of Canada bond interest rate plus 2.26%. The facility is collateralized by the equipment financed. Subsequent to January 31, 2004, $3.2 million was drawn under this facility.

In addition, the Company has a $6 million facility to finance renovations available until August 31, 2004. Draw downs under the facility are repayable over 48 months, and will bear interest at a fixed rate of the three year Government of Canada bond interest rate plus 2.35%. The facility is collateralized by the store fixtures and equipment financed. As at March 25, 2004, no amounts had been drawn under this facility.

3. INVENTORIES

	January 31 2004 $	January 25 2003 $
Raw materials	**4,246**	4,800
Work-in-process	**1,119**	1,234
Finished goods	**20,710**	19,448
	26,075	25,482

4. LOAN TO DIRECTOR

The loan is non-interest bearing and was issued under the stock purchase plan.

As at January 31, 2004, the shares held by the Company as security for the loan have a market value of $625,000 [2003 – $503,000]. The loan was repaid on February 27, 2004.

5. FIXED ASSETS

	Cost $	Accumulated depreciation & amortization $	Net book value $
January 31, 2004			
Land and building	**989**	**519**	**470**
Leasehold rights and improvements	**26,847**	**11,951**	**14,896**
Point-of-sale cash registers and computer equipment	**8,339**	**3,933**	**4,406**
Other furniture and fixtures	**36,567**	**15,386**	**21,181**
Automobiles	**130**	**94**	**36**
Point-of-sale equipment not yet in use	**3,455**	**—**	**3,455**
	76,327	**31,883**	**44,444**
January 25, 2003			
Land and building	989	474	515
Leasehold rights and improvements	24,867	10,887	13,980
Point-of-sale cash registers and computer equipment	8,311	3,507	4,804
Other furniture and fixtures	32,040	13,111	18,929
Automobiles	131	97	34
	66,338	28,076	38,262

An amount of $6,290,000 [2003 – $2,645,000] of the fixed assets is held under capital leases. Accumulated depreciation relating to these fixed assets amounts to $553,000 [2003 – $691,000].

19

6. CAPITAL LEASE OBLIGATIONS

The future minimum lease payments required under the capital lease agreements are as follows:

	$
2005	1,812
2006	1,594
2007	1,594
2008	858
Total minimum lease payments	5,858
Amount representing interest at rates varying between 5.5% and 6.4%	605
	5,253
Less: current portion	1,525
	3,728

The fair value of fixed rate capital leases is based on estimated future cash flows discounted using the current market rate for debt of the same remaining maturities. The fair value of these capital leases approximates the carrying value.

7. LONG-TERM DEBT

	January 31 2004 $	January 25 2003 $
Loan repaid in the year	–	446
6.97% Specific Security Agreement II, maturing July 15, 2004	178	524
6.35% Specific Security Agreement III, maturing February 27, 2006	1,588	2,279
	1,766	3,249
Less: current portion	914	1,483
	852	1,766

The loan agreements are collateralized by all of the fixed assets acquired with the long-term debt proceeds.

Principal repayments are due in the following fiscal years:

	$
2005	914
2006	784
2007	68
	1,766

The fair values of the loans described above approximate their carrying value.

8. CAPITAL STOCK

Authorized

An unlimited number of non-voting First, Second and Third Preferred Shares issuable in series

An unlimited number of Class A Subordinate Voting Shares

An unlimited number of Class B Voting Shares

Issued

	January 31 2004 $	January 25 2003 $
2,226,041 Class A Shares [2003 - 2,001,481]	**13,710**	12,616
3,020,000 Class B Shares	**1,064**	1,064
	14,774	13,680

During the year ended January 31, 2004, the Company issued 224,560 [2003 - 78,940] Class A Shares under the stock option plan for $1,094,000 [2003 - $235,000].

Principal features

[a] With respect to the payment of dividends and the return of capital, the shares rank as follows:

First Preferred
Second Preferred
Third Preferred
Class A and Class B

[b] Subject to the rights of the Preferred shareholders, the Class A shareholders are entitled to a non-cumulative preferential dividend of $0.05 per share, after which the Class B shareholders are entitled to a non-cumulative dividend of $0.05 per share; any further dividends declared in a fiscal year must be declared and paid in equal amounts per share on all the Class A and Class B Shares then outstanding without preference or distinction.

[c] Subject to the foregoing, the Class A and Class B Shares rank equally, share for share, in earnings.

[d] The Class A Shares carry one vote per share and the Class B Shares carry 10 votes per share.

[e] The Class A Shares are convertible into Class B Shares on a share-for-share basis if the parent company ceases to control the Company, or if an offer is accepted to sell more than 20% of the then outstanding Class B Shares at a price in excess of 115% of their market price. The Class B Shares are convertible into Class A Shares at any time on a share-for-share basis.

8. CAPITAL STOCK [Continued]

Stock option plan

Under the provisions of the stock option plan, the Company may grant options to key employees and directors to purchase Class A Shares. The plan, which was amended on May 28, 1997, on April 7, 2000, on April 20, 2001 and on April 25, 2003, provides that the maximum number of shares which may be issued thereunder is 1,500,000 Class A Shares. The option price may not be less than the simple average of the high and low board lot trading prices for the Class A Shares on the Toronto Stock Exchange on the last business day before the date on which the option is granted. The stock options may be exercised by the holder progressively over a period of 2 to 5 years from the date of granting. 891,690 options have been exercised since inception.

A summary of the status of the Company's stock option plan as of January 31, 2004 and January 25, 2003, and changes during the years ending on these dates is presented below:

| | January 31, 2004 | | January 25, 2003 | |
	Shares	Weighted average exercise price $	Shares	Weighted average exercise price $
Outstanding at beginning of year	734,210	5.81	620,950	5.05
Granted	–	–	284,960	6.84
Exercised	224,560	4.87	78,940	2.98
Cancelled / Expired	80,500	9.78	92,760	6.31
Outstanding at end of year	429,150	5.55	734,210	5.81
Options exercisable at end of year	127,570	4.77	282,370	5.49

The following table summarizes information about the stock options outstanding at January 31, 2004.

Range of exercise prices $	Number outstanding at Jan. 31 2004	Weighted average remaining life	Weighted average exercise price $	Number of options exercisable at Jan. 31 2004	Weighted average exercise price $
2.33 – 2.99	17,000	2 years	2.33	17,000	2.33
3.00 – 5.99	160,300	2.5 years	3.76	60,400	3.75
6.00 – 6.99	52,750	3 years	6.05	15,070	6.06
7.00 – 7.25	199,100	3 years	7.14	35,100	7.15
2.33 – 7.25	429,150	3 years	5.55	127,570	4.77

The weighted average grant date fair value of options granted during the year ended January 25, 2003 amounted to $1.54 per option. The fair value of each option grant was established on the date of the grant using the Black Scholes option pricing model with the following weighted average assumptions used for options granted in the period. On a pro-forma basis, if the Company had used the fair market value method of accounting for its option plan, the Company's net earnings for the year would have been $10,568,000 ($2.06 basic and $1.97 diluted earnings per share). No compensation was recorded for these stock options.

8. CAPITAL STOCK [Continued]

	Assumptions
Expected dividends	$0.40
Expected volatility	46%
Risk free interest rate	4.40%
Expected life	3.1 years

During the year ended January 31, 2004, no stock options were granted. Accordingly, no compensation for the year was recorded.

Stock purchase plan

Under the provisions of the stock purchase plan, the Company may grant the right to key employees to subscribe for Class A Shares. The plan, which was amended on May 28, 1997, provides that the maximum number of shares that may be issued thereunder from and after May 28, 1997 is 10,000 Class A Shares. The subscription price may not be less than the closing price for the Class A Shares on the Toronto Stock Exchange on the last business day before the date on which the right to subscribe is granted. Since May 28, 1997, there have been no shares issued under the stock purchase plan.

9. INCOME TAXES

As at January 31, 2004, a U.S. subsidiary has accumulated losses amounting to C$11.7 million [US$8.8M million] which expire during the years 2005 to 2019. A full valuation allowance has been taken against the related future income tax asset and accordingly, the tax benefits pertaining to these loss carry-forwards have not been recognized in the financial statements.

The U.S. tax losses expire in the following years:

	$
2005	1,421
2006	1,837
2007	2,727
2008	509
2009	100
2010 – 2019	5,113
	11,707

A reconciliation of average statutory income tax rate to the actual effective tax rate is as follows:

	2004 %	2003 %
Average statutory tax rate	35.1	37.5
Increase (decrease) in income tax rate resulting from:		
Non-deductible U.S. tax losses	2.9	2.8
Non-deductible items and large corporations tax	(0.2)	(1.4)
Effective tax rate	**37.8**	38.9

9. INCOME TAXES [Continued]

The details of the provision for income taxes is as follows:

	2004 $	2003 $
Current income taxes	6,605	4,697
Future income taxes	(130)	116
Provision for income taxes	6,475	4,813

The tax effects of temporary differences and net operating losses that give rise to future income tax assets and liabilities are as follows:

	2004 $	2003 $
Future income tax liabilities		
Carrying values of capital assets in excess of tax bases	4,099	2,732
Total future income tax liabilities	4,099	2,732
Future income tax assets		
Operating leases	1,706	193
Deferred lease inducements	635	651
U.S. tax losses	5,139	4,328
Valuation allowance	(5,139)	(4,328)
Total future income tax assets	2,341	844
Net future income taxes	1,758	1,888

10. EARNINGS PER SHARE

Basic earnings per share are calculated using the weighted average number of shares outstanding for the year.

Diluted earnings per share reflect the dilutive effect of the exercise of the stock options outstanding at the end of the year or those options exercised during the year, as if they had been exercised at the beginning of the year or the date granted, if later. The following is a reconciliation of the numerators and the denominators used for the computation of the basic and diluted earnings per share:

	2004 $	2003 $
Net earnings (numerator)	**10,648**	7,562
Weighted average number of shares outstanding (denominator)		
Weighted average number of shares outstanding – basic	**5,134**	4,980
Dilutive effect of stock options	**238**	232
Weighted average number of shares outstanding – diluted	**5,372**	5,212

11. COMMITMENTS

The Company has letters of credit available in the amount of $4,727,000 of which $1,388,000 has been accepted at year-end. The letters of credit represent guarantees for payment of purchases from foreign suppliers and the fair value approximates their carrying value. The available letters of credit reduce the available operating lines of credit disclosed in note 2.

The minimum rentals payable under long-term operating leases are as follows:

	$
2005	21,599
2006	19,662
2007	17,144
2008	15,263
2009	12,246
Thereafter	26,000
	111,914

Certain of the operating leases provide for additional annual rentals based on store sales and for annual increases in operating charges of the landlord.

12. SEGMENTED INFORMATION

The Company's only operating segment is the retail of apparel, accessories and footwear aimed at young-spirited, fashion-conscious men, women and children.

Segmented information is attributed to geographic areas based on the locations of the Company's stores. The following is a summary of the Company's operations and assets by geographic area:

	January 31 2004 $	January 25 2003 $
Sales to customers		
Canada	219,175	208,420
United States	7,591	9,240
	226,766	217,660
Depreciation and amortization		
Canada	7,297	6,489
United States	448	448
	7,745	6,937
Net earnings (loss)		
Canada	11,929	8,507
United States	(1,281)	(945)
	10,648	7,562
Net earnings (loss) per share (basic)		
Canada	2.32	1.71
United States	(0.25)	(0.19)
	2.07	1.52
Identifiable assets		
Canada	90,590	76,025
United States	3,956	4,494
	94,546	80,519
Additions to fixed assets		
Canada	14,377	8,960
United States	61	59
	14,438	9,019
Fixed assets		
Canada	41,483	34,911
United States	2,961	3,351
	44,444	38,262

13. CHANGES IN NON-CASH WORKING CAPITAL

The cash generated from non-cash working capital is made up of changes related to operations in the following accounts.

	2004 $	2003 $
Accounts receivable and prepaid expenses	(225)	416
Inventories	(593)	(4,129)
Accounts payable and accrued liabilities	2,539	4,287
Income taxes payable	(874)	952
Cash generated from working capital	**847**	1,526

14. FINANCIAL INSTRUMENTS

Fair values

The estimated fair values of financial instruments as at January 31, 2004 and January 25, 2003 are based on the relevant market prices and information available at the time. The fair value estimates are not indicative of the amounts that the Company might receive or pay in actual market transactions.

Current financial assets and liabilities

The carrying amounts of current financial assets and liabilities are reasonable estimates of their fair values due to the current nature of these instruments. Current financial assets consist of cash and cash equivalents, accounts receivable and loan to director, while current financial liabilities consist of accounts payable and accrued liabilities, dividend payable, income taxes payable and current portion of capital lease obligations and long-term debt.

Foreign exchange forward contracts

The Company enters into foreign exchange forward contracts that oblige it to purchase specific amounts of foreign currencies at set future dates at forward predetermined exchange rates. The contracts are matched with anticipated foreign currency purchases in the United States. The Company enters into the foreign exchange forward contracts to hedge itself from the risk of losses should the value of the Canadian dollar decline compared to the foreign currency.

The amount of anticipated future purchases in foreign currencies are projected in light of current conditions in the Company's markets and its past experience in similar circumstances.

Some foreign exchange forward contracts that qualify as hedges have become favorable to the Company since their inception and accordingly, constitute financial assets. Other contracts have become unfavorable and accordingly constitute financial liabilities. These outstanding contracts are to be settled during the next fiscal period. Their nominal values and contract values are as follows:

	Average contractual exchange rate	Nominal foreign currency value [000's]	Contract value [000's] $
Purchase contracts:			
U.S. dollar	1.3162	8,300	10,924

The range of maturity of these contracts is from February 2, 2004 to April 30, 2004. As at January 31, 2004, the unrealized foreign exchange gain was $84.

15. CASH AND CASH EQUIVALENTS

Included in cash and cash equivalents are two corporate loans guaranteed by a Canadian chartered bank, amounting to $10 million and $5 million, respectively. The loans bears interest at 2.61% and 2.48%, respectively and were repaid on February 10, 2004 and February 23, 2004, respectively.

27

CORPORATE INFORMATION

5695 Ferrier Street, Town of Mount Royal, Quebec H4P 1N1 TEL.: 514.738.7000
www.lechateau.com

BOARD OF DIRECTORS

Herschel H. Segal
Chairman of the Board and Chief
Executive Officer of the Company

Jane Silverstone, B.A.LLL
Vice-Chairman of the board

Emilia Di Raddo, CA
President and Secretary

A.H.A Osborn
Chief Executive Officer
Alexon Group plc

Herbert E. Siblin, CM, FCA*
President
Siblin and Associates Ltd.

William Cleman*
Management Consultant

David Martz*
Management Consultant

*Member of the Audit Committee

OFFICERS

Herschel H. Segal
Chairman of the Board and
Chief Executive Officer

Jane Silverstone, B.A.LLL
Vice-Chairman of the Board

Emilia Di Raddo, CA
President and Secretary

Betty Berliner
Senior Vice-President
Buying and Merchandising

Franco Rocchi
Vice-President
Sales and Operations

Auditors
Ernst and Young LLP
Chartered Accountants

Registrar and Transfer Agent
Computershare
Trust Company of Canada

Corporate Counsel
Davies Ward Phillips & Vineberg LLP

Bankers
Royal Bank of Canada

Annual Meeting of Shareholders
Wednesday, July 7, 2004
at 10:00 am at our head office

Produced By Maison Brison Inc.

le château

Appendix B
Complex Organizations

Throughout this text we have shown you excerpts from financial statements from various Canadian and international companies. Without exception, all of those financial statements were consolidated financial statements. Consolidated financial statements become necessary when one company buys a controlling ownership interest in another company, thus creating a complex organization. Before we end this text, we want to provide you with a broad understanding of how financial statements become consolidated, and the implications of using consolidated statements for decision-making. Because an investment in a company's common shares carries with it a right to vote, one company can influence and, under the right circumstances, control the activities of another company. In this section, we also consider accounting issues related to organizations that are considered complex due to intercompany investments. We start with briefly discussing the purpose of such intercompany investments, and then turn to their accounting and analysis aspects.

PURPOSE OF INTERCOMPANY INVESTMENTS

A company may have many reasons for acquiring an ownership interest in another company. Buying the shares of another company may be viewed as a good short-term or long-term investment. The equity securities that a company carries in its current asset account, called temporary (short-term) investments or "held for trading" financial instruments, are examples of this type of investment. If the shares are bought for this reason, the number of shares purchased is usually small compared with the number of outstanding shares in the purchased company. Consequently, the acquiring company has little influence or control over the affairs of the company in which it has invested. Such investments are sometimes called **passive investments** or **portfolio investments** because the acquiring company cannot exercise any control over the decisions of the acquired company. Some passive investments can also be long term if management's intention is to hold the security for long-term returns.

A second major reason for obtaining ownership of the shares of another company is to influence or control the decisions made by that other company. Common targets for this kind of purchase are competitors, suppliers, and customers. Acquiring a block of shares in a supplier or customer allows the acquiring company to exercise some influence over the production, buying, and selling decisions of the acquired company, which may benefit the acquiring company. If the block of shares purchased is large enough, the acquiring company could have a controlling interest in a competitor, which would allow it to increase its market share by increasing its productive capacity, its geographic market, or both. Buying a controlling interest in a supplier or customer allows the company to ensure a market in which to buy its raw materials (in the case of a supplier), or to sell and distribute its product (in the case of a customer). Buying a supplier or customer is sometimes referred to as **vertical integration**. **Weyerhaeuser Company Limited** is an example of a company that is vertically integrated. Together with the various companies that it controls, it is involved in growing and harvesting trees, producing and selling forest products, collecting and recycling paper products, and building homes and developing land. Combining with a competitor is sometimes referred to as **horizontal integration**. Horizontal integration may also offer other benefits that come from economies of scale. The company may be able to reduce its workforce or use a single distribution system to avoid duplication of effort.

Another reason for buying and controlling another company is **diversification**. If a company is in a cyclical business, it can protect itself from cyclical declines in one business by investing in another business that is counter-cyclical. **Cyclical businesses** are those that have significant peaks and valleys of activity. A greeting card company is an example of a cyclical business. Some cards, such as birthday cards, are purchased relatively evenly throughout the year. Other cards, such as Christmas cards and Valentine cards, cause peaks in revenue generation. Such a company may wish to diversify by buying into an automobile dealership business. The peak times for the dealership are likely to be the late summer when the new cars are introduced and early spring when people are anticipating travelling over the summer. The greeting card business and the automobile dealership would have peak activities at different times, which would help to even out the revenue flows for the whole business.

Algoma Central Company is an example of a diversified Canadian business. Its main focus of operation is marine transportation. It operates several ships, organizes the transportation of goods, provides for the repair and maintenance of ships, and provides marine-engineering services. This business depends not only upon the type of goods shipped, but also upon the economic environment of the countries to and from which goods are transported. Algoma has countered some of the shipping industry's cyclical nature by investing in commercial real estate. It owns and manages various commercial properties in Ontario. This business is also subject to the economic environment, but is much more localized and would be unlikely to experience the same peaks and valleys as marine transportation.

METHODS OF OBTAINING INFLUENCE AND CONTROL

Perhaps the simplest way to obtain control of the assets of another company is to purchase the assets directly from that company. This is called an **asset purchase**. The accounting for asset purchases is discussed in Chapter 8. If several assets are acquired at one time, such as in the acquisition of an entire division or plant, a single price may be negotiated. As discussed in Chapter 8, this type of purchase is called a basket purchase. The purchased assets' total cost must be allocated to the individual assets acquired on the basis of their relative fair market values. Even if one company buys all the assets of another company, it is not able to either influence or control the second company: it controls only the assets it has purchased. The company from which it has purchased the assets can continue to operate, but now it has different assets that it must use to generate revenue. An asset purchase does not require consolidated financial statements. Once the new assets are recorded in the accounting system of the buying company, there are no further accounting complications.

The only way to obtain influence or control over another company is to buy common shares in a **share acquisition**. For the sake of this discussion, we will refer to the acquiring company as the **investor**, and to the company whose shares are acquired as the **investee**.

One way the shares can be obtained is for the investor to pay cash to the shareholders of the investee (i.e., the shares are bought on the stock market). Another way is to exchange the investor's shares for shares of the investee. This form of investment is called a **stock swap**. A variation of this is an exchange of the investor's debt (bonds) for shares of the investee in a transaction that may be called a **debt for equity swap**. In fact, some investments involve the exchange of all three (cash, shares, and debt) for the investee's shares.

In a share acquisition, the investor can obtain a large degree of influence or control over the investee by buying (or swapping) more shares. That influence or control is obtained by exercising the voting rights that the investor obtains when buying the shares. Ultimate control over the investee's assets and liabilities will occur when the percentage ownership of the voting rights is greater than 50%. This is called a **controlling interest**. An investor can sometimes effectively control an investee even though it owns less than 50% of the shares. This can occur in situations where the remainder of the shares are owned by a large number of investors, none of whom has a very large percentage ownership in the investee (the shares are said to be **widely held** in such situations). Therefore, if an investor owns 30% to 50% of an investee and the rest of the shares are widely held, the investor may be able to effectively control the investee's assets and liabilities. Because it is possible to control with less than 50%, GAAP defines control as occurring when one company can make "strategic operating, investing, and financing policies without the co-operation of others."[1] If a company owns 40% of the shares of another company, it may be able to elect a majority of people to the board of directors. It has, however, elected

---

[1] *CICA Handbook*, para. 1590.03(B).

them with the co-operation of the other shareholders. If those shareholders became dissatisfied with the way the board manages the company, they could get together and outvote the 40% shareholder. For this reason, a company with a 40% interest in another company would probably not prepare consolidated financial statements, but a company that owned 51% probably would.

In a share acquisition, the investee remains a legal entity separate from the investor. The investor company is like any other owner in that it has limited liability with regard to the investee's debts. The investor's liability is limited to the amount invested in the shares. The separation of the legal status of the two companies is one reason this form of acquisition is appealing. The tax status of each company is also separate. Each company must file its own return. For accounting purposes, the separate legal status also means that the investor and the investee each keeps its own set of accounting records, even if the investor has acquired 100% of the investee's shares. This presents an accounting problem if the investor controls the investee because they are, in substance, one accounting entity.

VALUATION ISSUES AT DATE OF ACQUISITION

In any type of acquisition, whether the purchase of a single asset or of an entire company, the fundamental accounting valuation method is historical cost. The new asset or the investment in the investee is recorded at its cost. If the asset is acquired with a payment of cash, the amount of cash serves as the proper measure of the cost. If debt is exchanged for the asset or company, the debt's value should be used as the measure of cost. Under GAAP, debt is usually measured at its net present value. The debt's net present value at the date of issuance is used to measure the cost of an acquisition in which debt is exchanged.

When shares are issued in the acquisition, their fair market value should be used as the measure of cost at the date of acquisition. A problem exists in valuing shares when the issue is large because the number of shares outstanding increases significantly and the value of the investment acquired is not exact. How the market will adjust the existing share price to reflect this acquisition is not known at the date of the transaction. In these situations, instead of using the value of the shares to measure the acquisition, accountants sometimes turn to the fair market value of the assets acquired to measure the value of the shares given up. If the shares are used to swap for the shares of another company, the value of the other company's shares may not be estimated easily. Stock swaps involving 100% of the shares of another company present the most difficulty in measuring the transaction's value.

Share Acquisition

In a share acquisition, the investor records the acquisition cost in an investment account. There is no breakdown of this cost into individual assets and liabilities because the assets and liabilities do not technically belong to the investor; they remain the investee's legal property or legal obligation. An investor that owns a large enough percentage of the investee's shares may control the assets economically through its voting rights, but it does not hold the title to the assets, nor is it legally obliged to settle the liabilities. Under GAAP, we currently use the purchase method to account for an acquisition of a controlling interest.

Purchase Method

The **purchase method** assumes that after the shares are purchased or exchanged, one company can be identified as an acquirer. This method is used when the investor pays cash or issues debt in exchange for the investee's shares. When shares are swapped for the shares of the investee, this method is used when the original shareholders of the investor company control more shares than the new shareholders from the investee company. For example, assume that Company A has 500,000 common shares currently issued. It is interested in purchasing all the shares of Company B, which has 100,000 common shares currently issued.

COMPANY A	COMPANY B
500,000 shares issued	100,000 shares issued
Company A issues 100,000 new shares and exchanges them with the shareholders of Company B on a 1-for-1 basis	
After the exchange	
600,000 shares issued	100,000 shares issued, now owned
(500,000 shares held by the original shareholders of Company A; 100,000 held by the old shareholders of Company B)	by Company A

Result: The original shareholders of Company A still hold most of the shares of Company A and therefore still control Company A, which now controls Company B.

The purpose of most share exchanges in Canada is to gain control of another company. When this is achieved, the acquiring company is called the **parent** and the acquired company is called the **subsidiary**. The subsidiary is an integral part of the parent company's total operations and, therefore, users need to know how it is performing. Both parent and subsidiary are separate legal entities that keep separate books, prepare separate financial statements, and pay separate taxes. To provide users with information about the whole entity (parent and subsidiaries), accountants prepare **consolidated financial statements**, which add the components of the various financial statements of the parent and the subsidiaries together. Users see the entity's total cash it controls, the total inventory it owns, the total revenues it earns, and so forth. Complications in this addition arise if there have been transactions between the parent and the subsidiaries. Because such transactions occur within the total accounting entity (parent and subsidiaries), they are deemed not to have occurred and they must be eliminated. More will be said about this later.

As well as providing information about the total entity, consolidated financial statements hide information about the individual companies in the group. Because users are often not given information about these individual companies, they have difficulty determining the risks and rewards contributed by each. If a company, through its activities, is involved in various industries or geographic locations, it is required to disclose segmented information in the notes to its financial statements. The segmented information provides some breakdown of accounts in the different segments so that users can evaluate the segments' potential future impact on the total entity.

As mentioned earlier, when the parent purchases a controlling number of shares in a subsidiary company, it has an investment on its books that it has recorded at the cost of the purchase. Because another company is being controlled and therefore consolidated financial statements are going to be prepared, the transaction is viewed like a basket purchase. The cost to acquire the subsidiary needs to be allocated to the subsidiary's individual assets and liabilities based on their relative fair market values at the date of acquisition, just as with any other basket purchase. This allocation is not recorded on the actual books of either the parent or the subsidiary, but instead is determined during the work sheet preparation of the financial statements. When the subsidiary's assets and liabilities are added to those of the parent so that consolidated financial statements can be prepared, it is the fair values of the subsidiary's assets and liabilities that are added to the historical cost assets and liabilities of the parent.

When allocating the purchase price, all the assets and liabilities in the subsidiary are first measured at their fair market values. Some assets that did not exist on the subsidiary's books may be found and included in this measurement process. For example, if the subsidiary developed a patent or a trademark internally, the costs of such an item would have been expensed (see Chapter 8 for a discussion of whether to capitalize or expense the costs of these types of assets). The parent would need to identify all assets that the subsidiary owned or had the right to use, and establish values for those items using current items similar to them in the market, estimations of future benefits, or appraisals as a guide. By buying the shares, the parent is now also controlling these assets, and part of the acquisition cost should be allocated to them if they have a measurable market value. All of these assets and liabilities, those on the books and those that have value but are not on the books, are known as the subsidiary's **identifiable net assets**. In the year that a parent buys a subsidiary, the components of the assets and liabilities that were purchased will be disclosed in the notes to the consolidated financial statements. Exhibit B-1 includes an example of this disclosure from the financial statements of **Suncor Energy Inc.**

You should note from Suncor's description that values have been assigned to three asset groups and one liability group. By far the most valuable asset acquired was property, plant, and equipment, and intangible assets. The identifiable net assets' fair value was $272 million. Suncor's acquisition did not result in goodwill since the purchase price was negotiated at the fair value of the net assets.

However, if the purchase price is more than the fair market value of the identifiable net assets (often referred to as **excess fair market value**), another asset called **goodwill** must be reported (refer to Chapter 8). It represents all the intangible reasons that motivated the investor to pay more for the investee than the sum of the fair market values of its individual assets and liabilities. Perhaps the acquirer expects to earn extra future cash flows, or perhaps the business is located in a high traffic area and so has a greater chance at higher revenues than businesses located elsewhere. Perhaps the sales personnel in the business have created a loyal customer following that leads to consistent revenues, or previous advertising cam-

SUNCOR ENERGY INC., 2003 ANNUAL REPORT
Notes to the Consolidated Financial Statements

2. ACQUISITION OF REFINERY AND RELATED ASSETS

On August 1, 2003, the company acquired a Denver refinery, 43 retail stations and associated storage, pipeline and distribution facilities, and inventory from ConocoPhillips for cash consideration of $272 million. The purchase price was determined through a competitive bid process. The results of operations for these assets have been included in the consolidated financial statements from the date of acquisition.

The acquisition was accounted for by the purchase method of accounting. The allocation of fair value to the assets acquired and liabilities assumed was:

($ millions)	
Property, plant and equipment, and intangible assets	242
Inventory	88
Other assets	9
Total assets acquired	339
Liabilities assumed	(67)
Net assets acquired	272

Suncor recorded an environmental liability of $9 million at the acquisition date for the estimated costs of environmental clean-up work currently under way. A $9 million receivable was also recorded as ConocoPhillips agreed to indemnify Suncor for these costs. The recorded liability is part of an agreement between Suncor and ConocoPhillips whereby Suncor will be indemnified for any reclamation work identified prior to closing for a period up to 10 years from acquisition date, and up to $30 million. Additional costs ordered by a governmental agency are subject to indemnification from ConocoPhillips on a rolling 10-year limitation period from the date the contamination is discovered by Suncor. There is no time or dollar limit for any third party claims against Suncor for which ConocoPhillips is liable.

Additionally, a $39 million liability was recorded at acquisition for environmental work required pursuant to a consent decree between ConocoPhillips, the Colorado Department of Public Health and the Environment and the United States Environmental Protection Agency.

For segmented reporting purposes, the results of the new Denver-based operations since the date of acquisition are reported in a new operating segment (Refining and Marketing – U.S.A.) in the accompanying Schedules of Segmented Data.

paigns may have made this a well-known business. If, on the other hand, the purchase price is less than the fair value of the identifiable net assets, negative goodwill is created. This negative goodwill must be allocated proportionately to the fair values of the noncurrent, nonmonetary assets. This is a topic for an advanced accounting course.

INCOME RECOGNITION ISSUES SUBSEQUENT TO ACQUISITION

Income recognition issues subsequent to acquisition are a consequence of the valuation decisions made at the date of acquisition. In the following subsections, these issues are discussed for asset acquisitions and share acquisitions.

Asset Purchases

Subsequent to purchase, asset acquisitions are accounted for in the same way as any other acquisition of assets. If the asset acquired is property, plant, or equipment, it is amortized like any other such asset. If the asset purchased is inventory, it ultimately affects cost of goods sold when it is sold.

Share Acquisitions

The accounting treatment of income subsequent to a share acquisition depends on the level of control the investor exerts over the investee. As examples of the conceptual differences, consider two extreme cases. The first case is one in which the investor owns only a few shares in the investee, and the second is one in which the investor buys 100% of the investee's shares.

CASE 1

If the investor buys only a few shares of the investee, it has virtually no control or influence over the investee. The investor may not dictate the dividend policy or any other strategic policy to the investee. As indicated earlier, this is a passive investment. The shareholders of the investor company in such a situation are unlikely to be interested in the full details of the investee's operating performance. They are probably more interested in the cash flows that have come in from their investment (dividends) and in its current market value. Therefore, income recognition should probably show dividend revenue.

CASE 2

In this case, where the investor owns 100% of the investee's shares, the investor's shareholders will likely want to know the operating details of the investee's performance, because they economically control all of its the assets and liabilities. For example, if the investee purchased was a competitor, the results of sales of the company's product are the combined results of the investor and the investee. To show only the details for the investor would be misleading in terms of the resources controlled by the shareholders. The investor's shareholders would probably find information about the two companies' combined assets and liabilities more useful than simply a listing of the investor's assets and liabilities. A set of statements that conveys this information is a set of consolidated financial statements. Consolidated financial statements are prepared as if the investor and investee were one legal company. Under GAAP, the two companies represent one economic accounting entity. In this situation, the investor is typically referred to as the parent company and the investee as the subsidiary.

What Is Canadian Practice?

This section of the appendix will describe the guidelines that have been established under Canadian GAAP for the acquisition of various blocks of shares. It is important to understand these guidelines because companies will describe their various acquisitions and tell you how they are accounting for them. You will need to know the various methods used so that you can understand each one's effects on the financial statements.

Under Canadian GAAP, control is determined by the investor's ability to determine the investee's strategic operating, investing, and financing activities without seeking the permission of any others. This usually means that the investor owns more than 50% of the investee's voting shares.

Because control is evidenced by the ability to determine certain activities in another company, GAAP provides guidelines for recommended cutoffs for the percentage ownership (in voting shares) that require different accounting treatment. Exhibit B-2 outlines these cutoffs. For small investments (less than 20%), GAAP specifies the cost method. Small investments are also subdivided into those that are current, which we usually label "temporary investments," and those that are noncurrent, which are generally labelled "investments." Larger investments (greater than 50%) require consolidation; that is, consolidated financial statements must be prepared. For investments that fall between these two extremes, the acquirer is considered to have significant influence over activities in the investee. Significant influence is evidenced by being able to elect a person to the board of directors, having significant transactions between the two companies, or having an exchange of technology or managerial personnel. When significant influence exists, another method, called the equity method, is required. Each of these methods is discussed in detail in the following pages.

ACCOUNTING METHODS FOR INVESTMENTS

EXHIBIT B-2

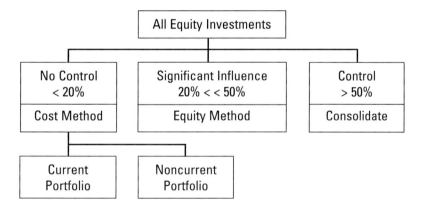

The percentage cutoffs identified in Exhibit B-2 are only a guide. If a company can demonstrate that it possesses either more or less control than the percentage ownership indicates, it can apply a different method. For example, if a wholly owned subsidiary (100% ownership) goes into receivership, control often passes from the parent company to a trustee. The investment in the subsidiary should then be carried using the cost method. Also, an investor that owns less than 50% of an investee's voting shares, but also owns convertible rights on other securities that, if converted, would increase its ownership beyond 50%, would be required to prepare consolidated financial statements. Each method carries its own set of implications for the company, as discussed in the following subsections.

COST METHOD The cost method was discussed in Chapter 6. To refresh your memory, the investment is carried in the investment account at its cost. During the period in which the investment is held, dividend revenue is recognized. If the investment is in marketable securities (short-term), at the end of each period the portfolio of securities is valued at market value. The unrealized losses (or recoveries) are shown in the income statement. If the investment is long-term, the portfolio is compared to market, but written down only if the decline is a permanent one. Once a long-term investment is written down, it is not written back up. To review the details of these accounting procedures, see Chapter 6. Note that no recognition is made of the investee's net income results during the period except to the extent that these results are captured by its willingness to pay dividends.

CONSOLIDATION METHOD **Consolidation** is required when an investor (parent company) controls the activities of an investee (subsidiary). For instructional purposes here, we will assume that the investor owns more than 50% of an investee's outstanding shares. Because the subsidiary is still a legally separate company, the parent company records its investment in the subsidiary company in an investment account in its accounting system. However, because the parent company, through its ownership of the majority of shares, controls the subsidiary's assets and liabilities, it is probably more useful to the parent company's shareholders to report the full details of the assets, liabilities, and income statement items rather than a single amount in the investment account and a single amount of income from the subsidiary on the income statement. The purpose of consolidating, therefore, is to replace the investment account with the subsidiary's individual assets and liabilities. On the consolidated financial statements, it then looks as though the two companies are legally one; that is, as if they had merged. You must recognize, however, that this is simply an "as if" representation of the combined company. The accounting systems are not merged. In fact, the consolidated statements are prepared on "working papers;" no actual entries are made to either company's accounting system.

Because a consolidation tries to make it look as though the two companies were merged, the consolidated statements are prepared using the fair market value of the assets and liabilities acquired as well as any goodwill. These amounts are combined with the book values of the parent's assets and liabilities.

EQUITY METHOD Between the two extremes of no control and complete control lies the situation in which the investor can significantly influence the investee but not completely control its decisions. The accounting method used, the **equity method**, tries to strike some middle ground between showing the results of all the assets, liabilities, and income items in the financial statements (consolidation) and showing only the dividend revenue from the investment (cost method). The equity method requires that the investor show the effects of its share of the investee's financial results; that is, as if it consolidated its share of the assets, liabilities, and income statement items. The difference is that its share of the net assets (assets minus liabilities) is reported as a single line item, "Investment in shares," on the investor's balance sheet. Its share of the net income is also reported as a single revenue item, "Equity in earnings of investment" or simply "Income from investment," on the income statement. Because of the netting of assets and liabilities as well as revenues and expenses, this method is sometimes referred to as a **one-line consolidation**.

To illustrate the entries made in a simple case using the cost method and the equity method, let us assume the following facts. Assume that the investor bought 30% of an investee's outstanding shares for $10,000. During the first year of the investment, the investee's earnings were $3,000 and dividends of $1,500 were declared. We will assume that in Case A, the 30% does not give the investor significant influence (cost method required), and in Case B significant influence is present (equity method required). The entries the investor makes to account for the investment in the first year are as follows.

CASE A (COST METHOD)		CASE B (EQUITY METHOD)	
Investor's entry for acquisition:			
Investment in Shares (A) 10,000		Investment in Shares (A) 10,000	
Cash (A)	10,000	Cash (A)	10,000
Investor's entry to record earnings from investee:			
No entry		Investment in Shares (A) 900	
		Equity in Earnings of Investment (SE)	900[a]
Investor's entry to record dividends from investee:			
Cash (A) 450[b]		Cash (A) 450	
Dividend Revenue (SE)	450	Investment in Shares (A)	450

[a]Investor's percentage ownership $\times$ Earnings of investee = 30% $\times$ $3,000
[b]Investor's percentage ownership $\times$ Dividends of investee = 30% $\times$ $1,500

Under the equity method, the entry to record the earnings shows that the investment account increases by the investor's share of the investee's earnings. The investment account represents the investor's investment in the investee and, as the investee earns income and increases its shareholders' equity, the investor's investment also increases in value. The credit part of this entry is to the income statement in a revenue line item called "**Equity in earnings of investment**." We will subsequently abbreviate this as EEI.

The entry to record the investee's dividends causes a decrease in the investor's investment account. This should make sense because, on the investee's books, the declaration of dividends causes a decrease in the shareholders' equity of the company. Because the investor's investment account measures its share of that equity, the investment account should decrease with the declaration of dividends. Another way to think about this is to imagine that the investment represents a deposit in a savings account. The interest on the savings account would be equivalent to the subsidiary's earnings. Withdrawals from the savings account would be the equivalent of the dividends declared. Withdrawals decrease the balance in the savings account in the same way that dividends reduce the investment account.

CONSOLIDATION PROCEDURES AND ISSUES

Numerous procedures and issues are important to understanding consolidated statements, but they are complex enough that an advanced accounting course is usually necessary to thoroughly understand them. To give you a general idea of the procedures necessary for consolidation, we will show you the consolidation of a 100%-owned subsidiary. This will be followed by a discussion of the issues surrounding the handling of intercompany transactions.

Consolidation Procedures—100% Acquisition

To illustrate the concepts behind the preparation of a consolidated set of financial statements, let's consider a share acquisition in which the parent acquires a 100% interest in the subsidiary. To make the example as concrete as possible, let's assume that the balance sheet of the parent (referred to as Parent Company) and the subsidiary (referred to as Sub Company) just prior to the acquisition are as shown in Exhibit B-3.

EXHIBIT B-3 **PARENT AND SUBSIDIARY BALANCE SHEETS**

Balance Sheets

	Parent Company	Sub Company
Assets other than PP&E	$2,200	$2,500
Property, plant, and equipment	$1,800	$1,500
Total assets	$4,000	$4,000
Total liabilities	$2,000	$3,000
Shareholders' equity	$2,000	$1,000
Total liabilities and shareholders' equity	$4,000	$4,000

Assume that, at acquisition, Parent Company pays $1,400 in cash for all the outstanding shares of Sub Company. Because the book value of Sub Company's equity (net assets) is $1,000 at the date of acquisition, Parent Company has paid $400 more than the book value for Sub Company's assets and liabilities. Assume further that $250 of this $400 relates to the additional fair market value of Sub's property, plant, and equipment. It will be assumed that the fair market value of Sub's other assets and liabilities are equal to their book values. This means that the remainder of the $400, or $150, is due to goodwill. Exhibit B-4 represents these assumptions.

REPRESENTATION OF THE PURCHASE PRICE COMPOSITION

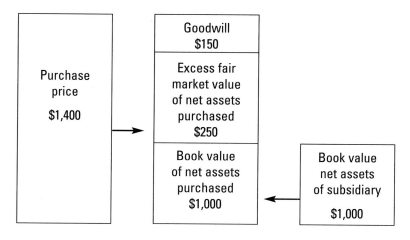

Parent Company records its investment in an account called Investment in Sub Company. Because Parent Company owns more than 50% of the shares of Sub Company, it controls Sub Company and will have to prepare consolidated financial statements. Because Sub Company remains a separate legal entity, it will continue to record its transactions in its own accounting system. Parent Company will also continue to keep track of its own transactions on what are known as the **parent-only books**. At the end of each accounting period, the two entities' separate financial statements will be combined on a work sheet to produce the consolidated financial statements, as if the two companies were one legal entity. One question that arises is how Parent Company should account for its Investment in Sub Company on its parent-only books. Because the Investment in Sub Company account will be replaced in the consolidation process by the individual assets and liabilities of Sub Company, it does not really matter, from a consolidated point of view, how Parent accounts for its investment on the parent-only statements. However, it will make a difference in the parent-only financial statements. GAAP is somewhat silent on this issue, and there is some diversity in practice. Some companies use the equity method to account for the investment, and some use the cost method. It will be assumed that Parent Company uses the equity method. The investment entry would be:

INVESTMENT ENTRY

Investment in Sub Company (A)	1,400	
Cash (A)		1,400

The above entry would be the same if the company was intending to use the cost method. After recording the investment, the balance sheets of Parent Company and Sub Company will appear as in Exhibit B-5.

PARENT AND SUBSIDIARY BALANCE SHEETS AT DATE OF ACQUISITION

Balance Sheets

	Parent Company	Sub Company
Assets other than PP&E	$ 800	$2,500
Property, plant, and equipment	1,800	1,500
Investment in Sub Company	1,400	–
	$4,000	$4,000
Total liabilities	$2,000	$3,000
Shareholders' equity	2,000	1,000
Total liabilities and shareholders' equity	$4,000	$4,000

To prepare a consolidated balance sheet for Parent Company at the date of acquisition, the Investment in Sub Company account must be replaced by the individual assets and liabilities of Sub Company. This would normally be done on a set of **consolidating working papers**, and no entries would be made directly in either the parent company's or the subsidiary company's accounting system. The consolidating entries that are discussed next are made on the consolidating working papers. The accountant starts the working papers by placing the financial statements as prepared by the parent company and the subsidiary side by side as shown in Exhibit B-6. The working papers will then have columns for the consolidating entries and for the consolidated totals. Note that the exhibit shows debit and credit columns for all four items.

CONSOLIDATING WORKING PAPERS

Account	Parent Company Debit	Parent Company Credit	Sub Company Debit	Sub Company Credit	Consolidating Entries Debit	Consolidating Entries Credit	Consolidated Totals Debit	Consolidated Totals Credit
Assets other than PP&E	800		2,500					
Property, plant, and equipment	1,800		1,500					
Investment in Sub Company	1,400							
Liabilities		2,000		3,000				
Shareholders' equity		2,000		1,000				
Totals	4,000	4,000	4,000	4,000				

On the consolidating working papers, each row will be added across to obtain the consolidated totals. If no adjustments are made to the balances as stated in Exhibit B-6, several items will be double-counted. In the first place, the subsidiary's net assets will be counted twice: once in the individual accounts of Sub and again as the net amount in Parent's investment account. One or the other of these two must be eliminated. Because the idea of consolidated statements is to show the subsidiary's individual assets and liabilities in the consolidated totals, the best option is to eliminate the parent's investment account. The second item that will be counted twice is the shareholders' equity section. The only outside shareholders of the consolidated company are the parent company's shareholders. The shareholders' equity represented by the subsidiary's balances is held by the parent company. The shareholders' equity section of the subsidiary must, therefore, be eliminated. Both of these are eliminated in a working paper entry called the **elimination entry**. The elimination entry in the example would be:

WORKING PAPER ELIMINATION ENTRY

Shareholders' Equity (Sub Company) (SE)	1,000	
???	400	
Investment in Sub Company (A)		1,400

In the preceding entry you can see that, in order to balance the entry, a debit of $400 has been made. What does this represent? It represents the excess amount that Parent Company paid for its interest in Sub Company over the net assets' book value. Remember the assumption that this excess is broken down into $250 for excess fair market value of property, plant, and equipment over its book value and $150 for goodwill. Therefore, the complete entry would be:

WORKING PAPER ELIMINATION ENTRY (ENTRY 1)

Shareholders' Equity (Sub Company) (SE)	1,000	
Property, plant, and equipment (A)	250	
Goodwill (A)	150	
Investment in Sub Company (A)		1,400

As a result of the elimination entry, the consolidating working papers would appear as in Exhibit B-7. The working paper entries are numbered so that you can follow them from the journal entry form to the working paper form.

CONSOLIDATING WORKING PAPERS (BALANCE SHEET ONLY)   EXHIBIT B-7

Account	Parent Company Debit	Parent Company Credit	Sub Company Debit	Sub Company Credit	Consolidating Entries Debit	Consolidating Entries Credit	Consolidated Totals Debit	Consolidated Totals Credit
Assets other than PP&E	800		2,500				3,300	
Property, plant, and equipment	1,800		1,500		(1) 250		3,550	
Goodwill	–		–		(1) 150		150	
Investment in Sub Company	1,400					1,400 (1)	–	
Liabilities		2,000		3,000				5,000
Shareholders' equity		2,000		1,000	(1) 1,000			2,000
Totals	4,000	4,000	4,000	4,000	1,400	1,400	7,000	7,000

Note that shareholders' equity on a consolidated basis is the same as on the parent company's books. This is true because all that consolidation has really done is replace the net assets represented in the investment account with the individual assets and liabilities that make up the subsidiary's net assets. In this sense, the statements of the parent company (which are referred to as the parent-only statements) portray the same net results to the shareholders as a consolidation. However, the consolidated statements present somewhat different information to the shareholders in that ratios, such as the debt/equity ratio, can be quite different from those found in parent-only statements. For example, from Exhibit B-7 you can calculate the debt/equity ratio for the parent-only statements as 1.0 ($2,000/$2,000) whereas, in the consolidated statements, it is 2.5 ($5,000/$2,000). This occurs because Parent Company has acquired a subsidiary that is more highly leveraged than it is (note that the debt/equity ratio for Sub Company is 3.0 [$3,000/$1,000]). Consolidating the two companies produces a leverage ratio that is a weighted average of the two ratios. Although the debt/equity ratio appears to be less favourable on the consolidated statements, users must remember that Sub Company is a separate legal entity and is responsible for its own debts. Parent Company has limited liability. For this reason, creditors such as banks prefer to see parent-only financial statements when they assess a company's ability to repay debt.

Now consider what the financial statements of Parent Company and Sub Company might look like one year after acquisition. The two companies' accounts are shown in Exhibit B-8 (remember that EEI stands for equity in earnings of the investment).

EXHIBIT B-8 **PARENT AND SUBSIDIARY BALANCE SHEETS AND INCOME STATEMENTS**
One Year Subsequent to Acquisition

Balance Sheet

	Parent Company	Sub Company
Assets other than PP&E	$ 1,440	$ 3,000
Property, plant, and equipment	1,850	1,600
Investment in Sub Company	1,500	–
Total assets	$ 4,790	$ 4,600
Total liabilities	$ 2,420	$ 3,450
Shareholders' equity	2,370	1,150
Total liabilities and shareholders' equity	$ 4,790	$ 4,600

Income Statement

	Parent Company	Sub Company
Revenues	$ 1,500	$ 2,000
Expenses	(1,010)	(1,475)
Amortization	(250)	(225)
EEI	250	–
Net income	$ 490	$ 300
Dividends declared	$ 120	$ 150

Using the equity method, Parent Company would make the following entries during the year to account for its investment.

**ENTRIES USING THE EQUITY METHOD
(ON PARENT COMPANY'S BOOKS)**

Parent's share of Sub's income:		
Investment in Sub Company (A)	300	
EEI (SE)		300
Parent's share of Sub's dividends:		
Cash (A)	150	
Investment in Sub Company (A)		150

After these entries, the ending balance in the investment account would be $1,550 ($1,400 + $300 − $150). You will note in the statements in Exhibit B-8 that the investment account has a balance of $1,500. The difference in these amounts is due to the fact that Parent Company paid more than the book value for the net assets of Sub Company. As we assumed earlier, Parent Company paid $400 more than the book value ($1,000). The $400 is due to the extra fair market value of property, plant, and equipment ($250) and goodwill ($150). Subsequent to acquisition, the property, plant, and equipment must be amortized and the amortization is shown as part of the EEI. Companies will establish amortization periods based on the expected useful life of the assets acquired. Assume that the property, plant, and equipment have a remaining useful life of five years, have a residual value of zero, and are amortized using the straight-line method. Therefore, Parent Company must take an additional $50 ($250/5 years) in amortization expense over that shown on the books of Sub Company. The $150 of goodwill is not amortized. Instead, it is checked each year to determine if its value is impaired. To keep our example simple, we are going to assume that the goodwill is still worth $150. The amortization of the property, plant, and equipment means that Parent Company has to report an additional $50 in expenses during the year subsequent to acquisition. Using the equity method, Parent Company shows these additional expenses as a part of the EEI. The following entry is made (in addition to those shown earlier).

AMORTIZATION ENTRY UNDER EQUITY METHOD (ON PARENT COMPANY'S BOOKS)

EEI (SE)	50	
Investment in Sub Company (A)		50

With this additional entry, the balance in the Investment in Sub Company account is $1,500, exactly the balance shown in Exhibit B-8.

The consolidated working papers at the end of the first year are presented in Exhibit B-9. You should note that they are shown in the **trial balance phase**. In the trial balance phase, the temporary income statement and dividends declared accounts still have balances that have not been closed to retained earnings. (Refer to Chapter 3 if you need to refresh your memory concerning the meaning of the trial balance phase.) Note that shareholders' equity has the same balance as at the beginning of the year. This is how the accounts must be listed in order to correctly prepare the consolidated financial statements.

In the year subsequent to acquisition, three basic consolidating working paper entries are made if the parent company is using the equity method to account for the investment on the parent-only financial statements. In addition to eliminating the investment account and the shareholders' equity accounts discussed earlier, the EEI must be eliminated, as must the subsidiary's dividends declared account. Otherwise, the subsidiary's income would be counted twice, once as EEI and a second time as the individual revenue and expense items. Dividends declared by the subsidiary are intercompany transfers of cash from a consolidated point of view. They are not dividends to outside shareholders and, as such, they should be eliminated in the consolidation process. The entry to eliminate EEI and dividends will be called the reversal of current year entries because the entry is, in effect, removing income and dividends recognized during the period. Once these two entries have been made, the third set of entries recognizes the extra amortization expense discussed earlier. The consolidating working paper entries are as follows.

EXHIBIT B-9

CONSOLIDATING WORKING PAPERS (YEAR SUBSEQUENT TO ACQUISITION)

Account	Parent Company Debit	Parent Company Credit	Sub Company Debit	Sub Company Credit	Consolidating Entries Debit	Consolidating Entries Credit	Consolidated Totals Debit	Consolidated Totals Credit
Assets other than PP&E	1,440		3,000					
Property, plant, and equipment	1,850		1,600					
Goodwill								
Investment in Sub Company	1,500							
Liabilities		2,420		3,450				
Shareholders' equity		2,000[a]		1,000[a]				
Revenues		1,500		2,000				
Expenses	1,010		1,475					
Amortization expense	250		225					
Amortization expense—goodwill								
EEI		250						
Dividends declared	120		150					
Totals	6,170	6,170	6,450	6,450				

[a]Beginning of period balances (trial balance phase).

CONSOLIDATING WORKING PAPER ENTRIES

Reversal of current year entries (Entry 1):

EEI (SE)	250	
Dividends Declared (SE)		150
Investment in Sub Company (A)		100

Investment elimination entry (Entry 2):

Shareholders' Equity (SE)	1,000	
Property, Plant, and Equipment (A)	250	
Goodwill (A)	150	
Investment in Sub Company (A)		1,400

Amortization of PP&E (Entry 3):

Amortization Expense (SE)	50	
Property, Plant, and Equipment (A)		50
(or Accumulated Amortization (XA))		

The preceding entries are added to the consolidating working papers as shown in Exhibit B-10. Note that a separate accumulated amortization account has not been provided and that the amount of extra amortization for the period has simply been credited to the property, plant, and equipment account. You can think of property, plant, and equipment as a net account; that is, net of accumulated amortization.

CONSOLIDATING WORKING PAPERS (YEAR SUBSEQUENT TO ACQUISITION)

EXHIBIT B-10

Account	Parent Company Debit	Parent Company Credit	Sub Company Debit	Sub Company Credit	Consolidating Entries Debit	Consolidating Entries Credit	Consolidated Totals Debit	Consolidated Totals Credit
Assets other than PP&E	1,440		3,000				4,440	
Property, plant, and equipment	1,850		1,600		(2) 250	50 (3)	3,650	
Goodwill					(2) 150		150	
Investment in Sub Company	1,500					100 (1)	–	
						1,400 (2)		
Liabilities		2,420		3,450				5,870
Shareholders' equity		2,000a		1,000a	(2) 1,000			2,000
Revenues		1,500		2,000				3,500
Expenses	1,010		1,475				2,485	
Amortization expense	250		225		(3) 50		525	
EEI		250			(1) 250			–
Dividends declared	120		150			150 (1)	120	
Totals	6,170	6,170	6,450	6,450	1,700	1,700	11,370	11,370

aBeginning of period balances (trial balance phase).

Income, on a consolidated basis, is as follows.

PARENT COMPANY — CONSOLIDATED NET INCOME

Revenues	$3,500
Expenses	(2,485)
Amortization expense	(525)
Net Income	$ 490

Note that this is exactly the same as the net income that was reported by Parent Company using the equity method as shown in Exhibit B-8. This will always be the case with the parent company uses the equity method to account for its investment in a subsidiary. As mentioned earlier, the equity method is sometimes referred to as a one-line consolidation. It is a one-line consolidation because the balance sheet effects of consolidation are captured in the one-line item called the investment account. The income statement effects of consolidation are captured in the one-line item called EEI. The only difference, then, between the equity method and a full consolidation is that the one-line items are replaced with the full detail of the subsidiary's assets and liabilities on the balance sheet and the full detail of the subsidiary's revenues and expenses on the income statement.

BELL CANADA 2003 ANNUAL REPORT

CONSOLIDATED BALANCE SHEETS

At December 31 (in $ millions)	Notes	2003	2002
ASSETS			
Current assets			
Cash and cash equivalents		398	1,013
Notes receivable from related parties		450	270
Accounts receivable	9	1,711	1,961
Other current assets		499	432
Current assets of discontinued operations	8	–	212
Total current assets		3,058	3,888
Capital assets	10	19,270	18,648
Other long-term assets	11	3,526	3,565
Indefinite-life intangible assets	12	796	772
Goodwill	13	1,586	1,543
Non-current assets of discontinued operations	8	–	639
Total assets		28,236	29,055
LIABILITIES			
Current liabilities			
Accounts payable and accrued liabilities		3,211	3,160
Note payable to parent company	14	–	975
Debt due within one year	14	1,165	1,837
Current liabilities of discontinued operations	8	–	178
Total current liabilities		4,376	6,150
Long-term debt	15	10,024	10,223
Other long-term liabilities	16	2,682	2,115
Non-current liabilities of discontinued operations	8	–	280
Total liabilities		17,082	18,768
Non-controlling interest		1,627	1,917
Commitments and contingencies	22		
SHAREHOLDERS' EQUITY			
Preferred shares	18	1,100	1,100
Equity-settled notes	18	–	2,068
Common shareholders' equity			
Common shares	18	7,602	4,264
Contributed surplus	18	512	815
Retained earnings		313	118
Currency translation adjustment		–	5
Total common shareholders' equity		8,427	5,202
Total shareholders' equity		9,527	8,370
Total liabilities and shareholders' equity		28,236	29,055

On behalf of the board of directors:

Tom C. O'Neill

Director

Director

When a parent owns less than 100% of a subsidiary, the accounting can become quite complex. The discussion of these aspects will be left to more advanced texts. It is enough that you understand what the NCI account represents.

Consolidations—Intercompany Transactions

One final complication that deserves mentioning is the impact that intercompany transactions have on the consolidated financial statements. When a parent company buys a controlling interest in a supplier or a customer, it is likely that there are many transactions between the two companies. Prior to the acquisition, these transactions are viewed as taking place between two independent parties but, after the acquisition, they are viewed as intercompany transactions.

Sales of goods and services between a parent and a subsidiary cannot be viewed as completed transactions unless there has been a sale of the goods or services outside the consolidated entity. Therefore, any profits (revenues and expenses) from those transactions that are not completed by a sale outside the consolidated entity must be eliminated. If there are remaining balances in accounts receivable and accounts payable that relate to intercompany transactions, these, too, must be removed.

To show you briefly this elimination process, let us consider the following example. Company A owns 100% of Company B. During 2006, Company A sells a parcel of land to Company B for $60,000. This land had originally cost Company A $45,000. Company A records the transaction on its books in the following manner.

Cash (A)	60,000	
Land (A)		45,000
Gain on sale of land (SE)		15,000

Company B records the acquisition of the land as follows.

Land (A)	60,000	
Cash (A)		60,000

Note that Cash went out of one entity and into the other entity. The consolidated entity still has the same amount of cash. Land went from $45,000 on one entity's balance sheet to $60,000 on the other entity's balance sheet. To the consolidated entity, this is the same parcel of land that was on last year's consolidated balance sheet at its historical cost of $45,000. If it is not reduced back to $45,000 on the consolidated balance sheet, it will be overstated. If we allowed the sale price of items sold intercompany to appear at the sale price on the consolidated financial statements, the two entities could sell items back and forth merely to increase asset value and to record revenue when, in reality, no external transactions with independent third parties took place. The last item, the Gain on the sale of land, must also be removed from the consolidated income statement. No gain can be recognized by the consolidated entity because the land has not been sold to an outside party. The journal entry to eliminate this unrealized gain on the consolidating working papers would be:

Gain on sale of land (SE)	15,000	
Land (A)		15,000

An entry similar to this would have to be repeated each year on the consolidating working papers when the consolidated financial statements are prepared. The entry in subsequent years would have a debit to Retained earnings rather than Gain on sale of land because in future years the income statement does not have the gain reported. The gain caused the retained earnings of Company A to increase in the year that the land was sold to Company B. Entries similar to these are prepared for all the intercompany transactions that occur between the two entities.

STATEMENT ANALYSIS CONSIDERATIONS

The consolidation of a subsidiary considerably changes the appearance of both the income statement and the balance sheet from the parent-only financial statements under equity. The income statement is different only in its detail; the net income for the period is the same regardless of whether or not the subsidiary is consolidated. Also, because the balances in the shareholders' equity accounts are the same with either method, ratios such as return on equity are unaffected by the consolidation policy.

Other ratios that involve other balance sheet figures can be dramatically affected. Earlier in the appendix, the effect that consolidation has on the debt/equity ratio was described using the information provided in Exhibit B-7. The debt/equity for Parent Company was 1.0, whereas the debt/equity for the consolidated entity was 2.5. Users who need information about an entity's ability to repay debt should not rely solely on consolidated financial statements. These statements contain the liabilities of all the companies in the consolidated entity, but each of those companies is responsible for only its own debt. A parent and its subsidiaries may guarantee each other's debt. This would reduce the risk of nonpayment and could result in lending institutions charging lower interest rates or loaning larger amounts. When the debt is guaranteed, the consolidated entity's debt/equity ratio is useful. All the assets are available to service the debt.

Other ratios will also be affected. The ROA ratio, for example, divides the net income before interest by the average total assets. The numerator changes to the extent that the subsidiary's interest expense is included on the consolidated income statement and is, therefore, added back to the net income. The denominator (average total assets) also changes because the investment account is replaced by the subsidiary's individual assets and liabilities. In the example in Exhibit B-8, the parent's total assets prior to consolidation were $4,790. After consolidation, the total assets were $8,240 (Exhibit B-10). This dramatic increase would certainly affect the ROA. The ROA prior to consolidation would have been 10.2% ($490/$4,790). After consolidation, the ROA was 6.0% ($490/$8,240).

The current ratio will also be affected. The current assets and liabilities that are embedded in the investment account are shown in full detail when they are consolidated. The subsidiary's current assets and liabilities would be added to the parent's when they are consolidated. Because our example in Exhibit B-7 does not distinguish current liabilities from long-term liabilities, it is not possible to demonstrate the change that would occur. Obviously, the quick ratio will also be affected by consolidation for the same reason as the current ratio.

Shareholders, potential investors, and most other outside users may not be able to determine the impact that various subsidiaries have on the consolidated financial statements. If a parent owns 100% of a subsidiary, the subsidiary will often not publish financial statements for external users other than the Canada Revenue Agency. A lender would be able to request individual financial statements for any company that wanted to borrow funds, but most other external users would not have this luxury. This means that users should have some understanding of which ratios are affected by the consolidation process. If the parent owns less than 100% of the shares, the subsidiary must publish publicly available financial statements if it is traded on the stock market. Users then have the opportunity to get more information about the components of the consolidated entity. A 100%-owned subsidiary does not trade on the stock exchange and does not need to make its financial statements public. Parent companies often have many subsidiaries. Evaluating each subsidiary individually is usually not necessary. Rather, users determine the ratios but keep in mind that each company is responsible for its own debt and taxes.

SUMMARY

In this appendix, we provided more background to improve your understanding of consolidated financial statements. You learned about the different levels of investments in other companies, from portfolio investments to significant influence investments to controlled subsidiaries. Through simple examples, we demonstrated the acquisition of a 100%-owned subsidiary. We expanded your knowledge through a discussion of non-wholly owned subsidiaries and of intercompany transactions. We concluded the appendix with a brief discussion of the impact of the consolidation process on ratio analysis.

The environment of corporate financial reporting is one of constant change and growing complexity. This book has introduced you to most of the fundamental concepts and principles that guide standard-setting bodies, such as the Accounting Standards Board, as they consider new business situations and issues. You should think of the completion of this appendix as the end of the beginning of your understanding of corporate financial reporting. As accounting standard-setting bodies and regulators adjust and change the methods and guidelines used to prepare financial statements, you must constantly educate yourself so that you understand the impacts of these changes on the financial statements of your company or of other companies you need to understand.

AN INTERNATIONAL PERSPECTIVE

Reports from Other Countries

In 1991, the FASB in the United States issued a discussion memorandum entitled "International Accounting Research Project: Consolidations/Equity Accounting" that concerned consolidation issues. Conducted by Price Waterhouse, the study surveyed practices in Australia, Canada, France, Germany, Italy, Japan, the Netherlands, the United Kingdom, and the United States as of November 1990. In its findings, Price Waterhouse concluded that, in virtually all the countries surveyed, consolidated financial statements were required for companies that were publicly traded on securities exchanges. In some countries, however, the consolidated statements are not considered the primary financial statements. In Japan, for instance, consolidated statements are provided as supplementary information. In many of the countries surveyed, non-publicly traded companies did not prepare consolidated financial statements.

The survey also found widespread use of a criterion of control rather than ownership in deciding whether to consolidate an entity. France, for instance, explicitly allows subsidiaries in which the parent owns more than 40% to be consolidated if no other group of shareholders has a greater share. Finance subsidiaries were generally not consolidated in countries other than the United States, but within seven months after the survey had been completed, Canada, New Zealand, and the United Kingdom had revised their standards to require consolidation of these subsidiaries. The revised international standard, IAS 22, on business combinations requires the use of the purchase method with the criterion of control and the consolidation of all subsidiaries.

In 2001, standard setters in Canada and the United States introduced new consolidation standards that resulted in greater similarities between the two countries in the guidelines for consolidation. As a result of the changes, both countries now require the exclusive use of purchase accounting for acquisitions. Prior to the change, both countries allowed a second method called pooling, but that method is no longer used. The second change was the treatment of goodwill. Prior to the change, goodwill was amortized within a maximum period of 40 years. With the 2001 changes, goodwill is no longer amortized. Instead, it is checked periodically for impairment.

SUMMARY PROBLEM

Additional Demonstration Problems

Peck Company (parent) bought 100% of the shares of Spruce Company (subsidiary) on January 1, 2006, for $600,000. On January 1, 2006, the shareholders' equity section of Spruce Company was as follows.

Common shares	$125,000
Retained earnings	75,000
Total shareholders' equity	$200,000

The amount paid by Peck for Spruce was larger than the book value of the assets acquired. This excess amount was attributed partially to land ($50,000) and equipment ($250,000). The equipment had a remaining useful life of 10 years and an assumed residual value of zero. Peck amortizes its assets using the straight-line method.

The following represents the trial balance of Peck and Spruce as at December 31, 2006, (the end of the fiscal year).

Trial Balance, December 31, 2006

Account	Peck Company Debit	Peck Company Credit	Spruce Company Debit	Spruce Company Credit
Cash	$ 780,000		$ 240,000	
Accounts receivable	400,000		200,000	
Inventory	525,000		350,000	
Investment in Spruce	695,000		–	
PP&E	800,000		600,000	
Accumulated amortization		$ 300,000		$ 200,000
Accounts payable		425,000		290,000
Long-term debt		900,000		580,000
Common shares		700,000		125,000
Retained earnings (1/1)		400,000		75,000
Revenues		5,000,000		2,000,000
Expenses (other than amort'n)	4,200,000		1,700,000	
Amortization	100,000		100,000	
Equity in Spruce earnings		175,000		–
Dividends declared	400,000		80,000	
Totals	$ 7,900,000	$ 7,900,000	$ 3,270,000	$ 3,270,000

Required:

a. Reconstruct the entries that Peck made during 2006 to account for its investment in Spruce using the equity method.

b. Prepare a set of consolidating working papers for Peck and Spruce for 2006. Separately, show the consolidating entries in journal entry form.

c. Calculate the following ratios for Peck Company using its parent-only financial statement information and the consolidated entity information.

  1. Debt/equity

  2. Return on equity

  3. Return on assets

  4. Current ratio

SUGGESTED SOLUTION TO SUMMARY PROBLEM

a. Using the equity method, the following entries would be made.

At acquisition:

Investment in Spruce (A)	600,000	
Cash (A)		600,000

At year end:

To recognize income: Spruce's net income is calculated as follows.

Revenues	$2,000,000
Expenses	1,700,000
Amortization	100,000
Net income	$ 200,000

Since Peck's share of Spruce's income is 100%, the following entry would be made.

Investment in Spruce (A)	200,000	
Equity in Spruce Earnings (SE)		200,000

To recognize dividends: Spruce declared $80,000 in dividends and Peck's share is 100%; therefore, the following entry would be made.

Cash (A)	80,000	
Investment in Spruce (A)		80,000

To recognize amortization of the fair value increment on the equipment: At the date of acquisition, Peck paid $400,000 more for the shares of Spruce than the book value ($200,000) of the net assets. This excess amount would be attributable to the following balance sheet items.

Land	$ 50,000
Equipment	250,000
Goodwill	100,000
Total	$400,000

The land is not amortized, but the excess amount due to the equipment must be amortized. Since Peck uses straight-line amortization, the extra amortization expense would be $25,000 per year ($250,000/10 years). The goodwill is not amortized. Using the equity method, the extra expenses would be recognized with the following entry.

Equity in Spruce Earnings (SE)	25,000	
Investment in Spruce (A)		25,000

Based on these entries, the investment account balance would be $695,000 and the equity in Spruce earnings would be $175,000, as shown in the trial balance.

b. The consolidating working papers are shown in Exhibit B-13.

EXHIBIT B-13 **CONSOLIDATING WORKING PAPERS, PECK COMPANY AND SPRUCE COMPANY, 2001— 100% ACQUISITION**

Account	Peck Company Debit	Peck Company Credit	Spruce Company Debit	Spruce Company Credit	Consolidating Entries Debit	Consolidating Entries Credit	Consolidated Totals Debit	Consolidated Totals Credit
Cash	780,000		240,000				1,020,000	
Accounts receivable	400,000		200,000				600,000	
Inventory	525,000		350,000				875,000	
Property, plant, & equipment	800,000		600,000		(2) 300,000		1,700,000	
Accumulated amortization		300,000		200,000		25,000 (3)		525,000
Goodwill					(2) 100,000		100,000	
Investment in Spruce	695,000					95,000 (1) 600,000 (2)	—	
Accounts payable		425,000		290,000				715,000
Long-term debt		900,000		580,000				1,480,000
Common shares		700,000		125,000	(2) 125,000			700,000
Retained earnings		400,000ᵃ		75,000ᵃ	(2) 75,000			400,000
Revenues		5,000,000		2,000,000				7,000,000
Expenses	4,200,000		1,700,000				5,900,000	
Amortization expense	100,000		100,000		(3) 25,000		225,000	
EEI		175,000			(1) 175,000			—
Dividends declared	400,000		80,000			80,000 (1)	400,000	
Totals	7,900,000	7,900,000	3,270,000	3,270,000	800,000	800,000	10,820,000	10,820,000

ᵃBeginning of period balances (trial balance phase).

The consolidating working paper entries are as follows.

1. To reverse current income and dividends:

Equity in Spruce Earnings (SE)	175,000	
Dividends Declared (SE)		80,000
Investment in Spruce (A)		95,000

2. To eliminate the investment account and shareholders' equity and to create extra fair market value and goodwill:

Common Shares (SE)	125,000	
Retained Earnings (SE)	75,000	
Land (PP&E) (A)	50,000	
Equipment (PP&E) (A)	250,000	
Goodwill (A)	100,000	
Investment in Spruce (A)		600,000

3. To amortize the extra fair market value of the equipment:

Amortization Expense (SE)	25,000	
Accumulated Amortization (XA)		25,000

c. Parent-only   Consolidated entity

1. Debt/equity

$\$1,325,000/1,575,000^a = 0.84$ $\$2,195,000/1,575,000^b = 1.39$

[a] $\$700,000 + 400,000 + 5,000,000 - 4,200,000 - 100,000 + 175,000 - 400,000 = \$1,575,000$
[b] $\$700,000 + 400,000 + 7,000,000 - 5,900,000 - 225,000 - 400,000 = \$1,575,000$

2. Return on equity

$\$875,000^a/1,575,000 = 0.56$ $\$875,000^b/1,575,000 = 0.56$

[a] $\$5,000,000 - 4,200,000 - 100,000 + 175,000 = \$875,000$
[b] $\$7,000,000 - 5,900,000 - 225,000 = \$875,000$

3. Return on assets

$\$875,000/2,900,000^a = 0.30$ $\$875,000/3,770,000^b = 0.23$

[a] $\$780,000 + 400,000 + 525,000 + 800,000 - 300,000 + 695,000 = \$2,900,000$
[b] $\$1,020,000 + 600,000 + 875,000 + 1,700,000 - 525,000 + 100,000 = \$3,770,000$

4. Current ratio

$\$1,705,000^a/425,000 = 4.0$ $\$2,495,000^b/715,000 = 3.5$

[a] $\$780,000 + 400,000 + 525,000 = \$1,705,000$
[b] $\$1,020,000 + 600,000 + 875,000 = \$2,495,000$

ABBREVIATIONS USED

EEI   Equity in earnings of investment
NCI   Noncontrolling interest
PP&E   Property, plant, and equipment

GLOSSARY

Asset purchase   An acquisition of assets from another company in which the acquiring company purchases the assets directly rather than buying a controlling interest in the shares of the other company. Title to the assets passes to the acquiring company.

Consolidated financial statements   Financial statements that represent the total financial results of a parent company and its various subsidiaries as if they were one company, even though they are separate legal entities.

Consolidating working papers   A work sheet that adjusts the financial statements of a parent and its subsidiaries so that the statements can be combined to show the consolidated financial statements.

Consolidation   An accounting method that companies are required to use to represent their ownership in other companies when they have control over the activities in other companies. The method requires the preparation of consolidated financial statements.

Controlling interest   The amount of ownership of a subsidiary that a parent company must have in order to control the subsidiary's strategic operating, financing, and investing activities. An ownership interest of greater than 50% usually meets this criterion.

Cyclical business   A business that is subject to significant swings in the level of its activity, such as the greeting card business.

Debt for equity swap   A transaction in which debt securities are exchanged for equity securities.

Diversification   A reason for acquiring ownership in another company. Diversification typically implies that the new company acquired is in a business very different from the company's current business. The idea is to find a business that is counter-cyclical to the company's current business.

Elimination entry   A working paper consolidating entry that eliminates the balance in the investment in subsidiary account against the shareholders' equity accounts of the subsidiary. At the same time, if the price paid by the parent company exceeds the book value of the subsidiary's shareholders' equity section, the excess fair market value of the net assets acquired and goodwill are recognized as part of the entry.

Equity in earnings of investment (EEI)   An account used in a parent company's books to record its share of the subsidiary's net income for the period using the equity method.

Equity method   An accounting method that companies use to represent their ownership in companies in which they have significant influence. This is usually true when the percentage of ownership is between 20% and 50%. In addition, this method is often used in parent-only statements to account for the investment in a subsidiary. In the latter case, the account will be eliminated on the consolidating working papers at the end of the year when consolidated financial statements are prepared.

Excess fair market value   The difference between the fair market value and book value of the net assets of a subsidiary company whose shares are acquired by a parent company. The difference is measured at the date of acquisition.

Goodwill   An intangible asset that arises when a parent company acquires ownership in a subsidiary company and pays more for the shares than the fair market value of the underlying net identifiable assets at the date of acquisition. The difference between the price paid and these net assets' fair market value is the value of the goodwill. It can represent expected excess earnings that result from, for example, the subsidiary's reputation, its exceptional sales staff, or an advantageous location.

Horizontal integration   A type of acquisition in which a parent company buys a competitor company in order to gain a larger market share or to expand its markets geographically.

Identifiable net assets   The assets and liabilities that can be specifically identified at the date of a merger or acquisition. Some of the identifiable assets may not have been recorded on the subsidiary's books, such as patents and trademarks.

Investee   A company whose shares are being acquired by another company.

Investor   A company that acquires shares of another company as an investment.

Minority interest   A synonym for noncontrolling interest.

Noncontrolling interest (NCI)   The portion of a less-than-100%-owned subsidiary that is owned by other shareholders.

One-line consolidation   The equity method is referred to as a one-line consolidation method because it produces the same net results as the full consolidation method except that the subsidiary's results are shown in a single line on the balance sheet (the investment account) and a single line on the income statement (the equity in earnings of investment).

Parent company   A company that acquires control (usually can elect a majority of the board of directors) of another company. The acquired company is referred to as a subsidiary.

Parent-only books   The accounting records of a parent company that have not been combined with its subsidiary's records in consolidated financial statements.

Passive investment   An investment by one company in another company in which the acquiring company has no capability of controlling or influencing the decisions of the acquired company.

Portfolio investment   Synonym for passive investment.

Purchase method   An accounting method used to record the acquisition of another company. The acquisition is treated as a purchase, and the assets and liabilities acquired are measured at their fair market value. Because this is typically a basket purchase, the cost is allocated to the individual assets and liabilities on the basis of their relative fair market values.

Share acquisition   An acquisition of another company that is accomplished through the acquisition of its shares. The acquired company continues as a separate legal entity.

Stock swap   An acquisition in which an acquiring company exchanges its shares for the shares of the acquired company.

Subsidiary   A company controlled by another company (the parent), which usually owns more than 50% of its outstanding shares and controls its strategic operating, financing, and investing decisions.

Trial balance phase   A phase in the preparation of financial statements in which the temporary accounts still contain income statement and dividend information from the period and have not been closed out to retained earnings.

Vertical integration   A type of merger or acquisition in which a parent company buys a supplier or customer company in order to ensure a supply of raw materials or a market for its end product.

Widely held shares   Shares of a company that are held by a large number of individuals or institutions such that no one shareholder has significant influence on the company's decisions.

ASSIGNMENT MATERIAL

Assessing Your Recall

B-1   Identify and briefly explain the major reasons why a company might want to buy shares in another company.

B-2   Compare and contrast a share acquisition and an asset acquisition in terms of their effects on the financial statements.

Self-Assessment Quiz

B-3   Explain the financial statement implications of accounting for an acquisition using the purchase method:

    a. At the date of acquisition

    b. Subsequent to the date of acquisition

B-4   Briefly describe the GAAP guidelines for accounting for long-term acquisitions in the shares of other companies. In your description, identify the criteria used to distinguish the various accounting methods.

B-5   Explain the nature of goodwill and how it arises in the context of an acquisition.

B-6   The equity method is sometimes referred to as a one-line consolidation. Explain.

B-7   Discuss what a consolidation is trying to accomplish.

B-8   The consolidating working paper entries are needed to eliminate double accounting for certain items on the parent's and subsidiary's books. Explain which items would be accounted for twice if the subsidiary company's books were added directly to the parent's books.

B-9 The consolidated balances in the asset and liability accounts do not exist in either the parent company's or the subsidiary company's accounting systems. Explain why you agree or disagree with this statement.

Applying Your Knowledge

B-10   (Acquisition of 100%-owned subsidiaries)

Down Company purchased 100% ownership of Topp Company for $80,000 and 100% of Steady Company for $240,000 on January 1, 2006. Immediately after the purchases the companies reported the following amounts.

Company	Total Assets	Total Liabilities	Total Shareholders' Equity
Down Company	$950,000	$250,000	$700,000
Topp Company	120,000	40,000	80,000
Steady Company	370,000	130,000	240,000

Required:

If a consolidated balance sheet is prepared immediately after the purchase of the two companies:

a. What amount of total assets will be reported?

b. What amount of total liabilities will be reported?

c. What amount of total shareholders' equity will be reported?

d. Why is it necessary to eliminate the balance in Down's investment accounts for each of the two subsidiaries when a consolidated balance sheet is prepared?

B-11   (Investments ranging from 10% to 100%)

On April 1, the Red Tin Company acquired some common shares of the Timber Steel Company. The book value of the Timber Steel Company's net assets on April 1 was $10 million, and the market value of the net assets was $12.5 million. During the year, the Timber Steel Company had net earnings of $1 million and declared dividends of $600,000.

Required:

For each of the following assumptions, give the amount of income recognized by the Red Tin Company from its investment in Timber Steel Company and show the beginning and ending balances for the investment account on Red Tin's books. Both companies close their books annually on December 31. Assume that any excess fair market value is to be amortized straight-line over five years. Goodwill, if any, is not amortized. Assume in each case that the shares' market value on December 31 is the same as the acquisition price.

a. The acquisition price is $1,250,000 for 10% of the common shares of Timber Steel.

b. The acquisition price is $1,500,000 for 15% of the common shares of Timber Steel.

c. The acquisition price is $3,125,000 for 25% of the common shares of Timber Steel.

d. The acquisition price is $6,000,000 for 45% of the common shares of Timber Steel.

e. The acquisition price is $13,000,000 for 100% of the common shares of Timber Steel.

B-12 **(Acquisition alternatives for a 100% purchase)**

Hartney Limited decided to acquire 100% of the Southern Company for $450,000. To pay for the acquisition, Hartney's management concluded it could (1) sell temporary investments it holds and pay cash, (2) issue new bonds and use the cash receipts, or (3) issue common shares with a market value of $450,000 in exchange for the shares of Southern.

Required:

Answer each of the following questions and explain why your answer is appropriate.

a. Under which of the alternatives will total liabilities in the consolidated balance sheet be greater than the amount reported by Hartney prior to the purchase of Southern's shares?

b. Under which of the alternatives will total assets in the consolidated balance sheet be greater than the amount reported by Hartney prior to the purchase of Southern's shares?

c. Under which of the alternatives will total shareholders' equity in the consolidated balance sheet be greater than the amount reported by Hartney prior to the purchase of Southern's shares?

d. Which of the alternatives would appear to increase the risk of investing in Hartney Company?

e. Which of the alternatives would appear to reduce the risk of investing in Hartney Company?

B-13 **(Portfolio investment and significant influence investment)**

On January 1, Waxton Company acquired portions of the common shares of two companies, Toss Company and Ball Company. The data relating to the acquisition and the first year of operations are as follows.

Company	Common Shares Acquired	Book Value of Net Assets as of 1/1	Market Value of Net Assets as of 1/1	Acquisition Price	Net Income for the Year	Dividends Declared for the Year
Toss Company	14%	$3,200,000	$4,800,000	$ 800,000	$ 950,000	$ 200,000
Ball Company	40%	$6,000,000	$7,500,000	$3,200,000	$2,500,000	$1,000,000

All the companies close their books annually on December 31. Goodwill, if any, is not amortized. Property, plant, and equipment acquired have a remaining useful life of six years, have a residual value of zero, and are amortized using the straight-line method. Any excess fair market value in the transaction relates to property, plant, and equipment. The market values of the Toss Company and the Ball Company shares held on December 31 were $750,000 and $4 million, respectively.

Required:

Show the journal entries (including the acquisition) to account for these two investments during the year.

B-14 **(Consolidation of a 100%-owned subsidiary)**

Large Company owns all the common shares of Small Company. Income statements for the companies for 2006 contained the following amounts.

	Large Co.	Small Co.
Sales revenue	$600,000	$300,000
Cost of goods sold	400,000	160,000
Gross profit	200,000	140,000
Dividend income from subsidiary	90,000	
Operating expenses	(130,000)	(50,000)
Net income	$160,000	$ 90,000

During 2006, Small Company purchased inventory for $10,000 and immediately sold it to Large at cost. Large has not sold this inventory yet.

Required:

In the consolidated income statement for 2006:

a. What amount will be reported as sales revenue?

b. What amount will be reported as cost of goods sold?

c. What amount will be reported as dividend income from subsidiary?

d. What amount will be reported as operating expenses?

e. Why are some amounts reported in the consolidated income statement not equal to the sum of the amounts from the statements of the parent and subsidiary?

B-15 **(Consolidation of a 100%-owned subsidiary)**

On January 1, Lid Company acquired 100% of the common shares of Ant Company at a price of $1.5 million. The book value of Ant Company's net assets on January 1 was $1,250,000. The net assets' book value approximates the fair value at the date of acquisition. During the year, Ant earned $340,000 and declared dividends of $290,000. At the end of the year, the dividends receivable of Lid Company included an amount of $290,000 that was due from Ant Company. (Hint: Lid's balance sheet would have a dividend receivable and Ant's would have a dividend payable. The consolidated entity cannot owe money to itself. Therefore, both of these accounts must be removed on the working papers before consolidated financial statements are prepared.) Goodwill, if any, will not be amortized.

Required:

a. Show the journal entries for the acquisition of the common shares and other entries during the year, assuming that Lid uses the equity method on its own books.

b. Prepare the consolidating working paper entries.

B-16 **(Consolidation of a 100%-owned subsidiary)**

Jennie's Plumbing and Heating recently purchased 100% of the shares of Ron's Repair Service. The balance sheets for the two companies immediately after the purchase of Ron's shares were:

	Jennie's Plumbing	Ron's Repair
Cash	$ 20,000	$ 8,000
Accounts receivable	50,000	30,000
Inventory	80,000	72,000
Investment in Ron's Repair	150,000	
Buildings and equipment	300,000	240,000
Less: accumulated amortization	(110,000)	(80,000)
Total assets	$490,000	$270,000

Accounts payable	$ 60,000	$ 75,000
Taxes payable	70,000	45,000
Common shares	200,000	100,000
Retained earnings	160,000	50,000
Total liabilities and equity	$490,000	$270,000

At the balance sheet date, Ron's Repair owes Jennie's Plumbing $15,000 on accounts payable.

Required:

a. Prepare a consolidated balance sheet for Jennie's Plumbing and its subsidiary.

b. Why are the shareholders' equity balances of Ron's Repair not included in the consolidated balance sheet?

c. Monona Wholesale Supply has extended credit of $10,000 to Jennie's Plumbing, and Winona Supply Company has extended credit of $10,000 to Ron's Repair. Which supplier has the stronger claim on the consolidated cash balance? Explain.

d. Jennie's Plumbing has applied to the Sussex Bank for a $75,000 short-term loan to open a showroom for bathroom and kitchen fixtures. Accounts receivable will be used as collateral and Jennie's Plumbing has provided the bank with its consolidated balance sheet prepared immediately after the acquisition of Ron's Repair. From the bank's perspective, how would you rate the sufficiency of the collateral? Explain.

e. If Jennie's Plumbing had purchased only 80% of the shares of Ron's Repair, an item labelled Noncontrolling Interest would have been reported on the balance sheet. What does the amount assigned to the noncontrolling interest represent?

B-17 **(Consolidation of a 100%-owned subsidiary)**

The balance sheets as of December 31 for Porter and Associates and Rachel Excavation are provided below.

	Porter	Rachel
Assets		
Cash	$196,000	$10,000
Accounts receivable	150,000	40,000
Inventory	300,000	40,000
Capital assets	400,000	130,000
Total assets	$1,046,000	$220,000
Liabilities and Shareholders' Equity		
Accounts payable	$ 80,000	$20,000
Long-term liabilities	300,000	50,000
Common shares	540,000	100,000
Retained earnings	126,000	50,000
Total liabilities and shareholders' equity	$1,046,000	$220,000

As of December 31, the market values of Rachel's inventories and capital assets were $70,000 and $120,000 respectively. Liabilities are at fair market value on the balance sheet.

On December 31, Porter and Associates purchased Rachel Excavation for $180,000 cash. The preceding balance sheets were prepared immediately prior to the acquisition.

Required:

a. Prepare the journal entry recorded by Porter to recognize the acquisition.

b. Prepare a consolidating working paper and a consolidated balance sheet.

B-18 **(Consolidation of a 100%-owned subsidiary)**

The following are the balance sheets and income statements for Jungle Company and Forest Company as at December 31, 2006.

Balance Sheet as at December 31, 2006

	Jungle Company	Forest Company
Assets		
Cash	$ 29,000	$ 15,000
Accounts Receivable	35,000	45,500
Investment in Forest Company	130,000	–
Other Assets	61,000	74,500
Total Assets	$255,000	$135,000
Liabilities and Shareholders' Equity		
Accounts Payable	$ 39,500	$ 20,000
Other Current Liabilities	10,500	10,000
Common Shares	150,000	80,000
Retained Earnings	55,000	25,000
Total Liabilities and Shareholders' Equity	$255,000	$135,000

Income Statement for the Year Ended December 31, 2006

	Jungle Company	Forest Company
Sales Revenue	$100,000	$ 60,000
Cost of Goods Sold	(55,000)	(35,000)
Amortization	(25,000)	(5,000)
EEI	20,000	–
Net Income	$ 40,000	$ 20,000
Dividends Declared	$ 25,000	$ 15,000

On January 1, 2006, Jungle had acquired 100% of the common shares of Forest Company. The acquisition price was $125,000. The shareholders' equity section of Forest Company on January 5 was as follows.

Forest Company

Common Shares	$ 80,000
Retained Earnings	20,000
Total	$100,000

The fair market value of Forest's net assets equalled their book values at the date of acquisition. Goodwill, if any, will not be amortized.

> *Required:*
>
> a. Prepare the consolidating working papers supported by the necessary working paper journal entries.
>
> b. Prepare the consolidated balance sheet and income statement.

B-19 **(Accounting for a subsidiary)**

Varwood Company Ltd. is a subsidiary of Tabor Company Ltd. The balance sheets for Varwood Company and for the consolidated entity at December 31, 2006, contained the following balances.

	Varwood Company	Consolidated Amounts for Tabor Co. and Subsidiary
Cash and receivables	$ 80,000	$120,000
Inventory	150,000	260,000
Land	70,000	200,000
Building and equipment	150,000	450,000
Less: accumulated amortization	(70,000)	(210,000)
Total assets	$380,000	$820,000
Accounts payable	$ 40,000	$ 70,000
Notes payable	90,000	290,000
Noncontrolling interest		100,000
Common shares	80,000	180,000
Retained earnings	170,000	180,000
Total liabilities and equity	$380,000	$820,000

Required:

a. Does Tabor own 100% or less than 100% of Varwood's common shares? How do you know?

b. What percentage of Varwood's assets and liabilities is included in the consolidated balance sheet? Explain.

c. What is the amount of cash and accounts receivable reported by Tabor at December 31, 2006, if (1) there are no intercompany receivables and payables, and (2) Tabor's accounts receivable include a $20,000 receivable from Varwood?

d. Must Tabor share a portion of Varwood's net income with others? Explain. What portion of the income from Tabor's separate operations must be shared with the other shareholders of Varwood?

e. Which of parts a) through d) could be answered only if the consolidated financial statements were available?

B-20 **(Consolidation of a 100%-owned subsidiary)**

On December 31, 2005, Multi Corp. acquired 100% of the outstanding shares of Littleton Company Ltd. The acquisition price was $64,000. The market value of Littleton's assets and liabilities on that date were:

Cash	$6,000
Accounts receivable	9,000
Inventory	15,000
Capital assets	40,000
Accounts payable	(14,000)
Long-term notes payable	(16,000)

The balance sheets prior to acquisition were as follows.

Balance Sheets, December 31, 2005

Account	Multi Corp Debit	Multi Corp Credit	Littleton Co. Debit	Littleton Co. Credit
Cash	$ 65,000		$ 6,000	
Accounts receivable	70,000		9,000	
Notes receivable	35,000			
Inventory	120,000		10,000	
Capital assets	230,000		35,000	
Accounts payable		$ 90,000		$14,000
Long-term notes payable		130,000		16,000
Common shares		200,000		22,000
Retained earnings		100,000		8,000
Totals	$520,000	$ 520,000	$ 60,000	$60,000

Required:

a. Prepare the consolidating working papers in preparation for preparing the consolidated balance sheet.

b. Prepare the consolidated balance sheet.

B-21 (Consolidation of a 100%-owned subsidiary)

On January 1, 2006, Neptune Company Ltd. acquired 100% of the outstanding shares of Baker Company Ltd. The acquisition price was $250,000, which included $20,000 related to the excess fair market value of the capital assets acquired. The shareholders' equity as at January 1, 2006, was as follows.

	Neptune Co.	Baker Co.
Common shares	$500,000	$150,000
Retained earnings	10,000	50,000
Total	$510,000	$200,000

During the year, Neptune Company lent $50,000 to Baker Company, which was to be repaid by December 31, 2006; however, $20,000 was still due from Baker at year end. The trial balances of Neptune and Baker on December 31, 2006, were as follows.

Trial Balance, December 31, 2006

Account	Neptune Co. Debit	Neptune Co. Credit	Baker Co. Debit	Baker Co. Credit
Current assets	$ 150,000		$ 90,000	
Capital assets	350,000		200,000	
Investment in Baker	251,000		–	
Cost of goods sold	200,000		75,000	
Other expenses	25,000		10,000	
Dividends declared	50,000		30,000	
Current liabilities		$ 85,000		$ 35,000
Noncurrent liabilities		100,000		50,000
Common shares		500,000		150,000
Retained earnings		10,000		50,000
Sales revenue		300,000		120,000
EEI		31,000		
Totals	$1,026,000	$1,026,000	$405,000	$405,000

The capital assets' entire fair market value is to be amortized using the straight-line method. The remaining useful life is five years, and the residual value is zero. Goodwill, if any, will not be amortized.

Required:

a. Prepare the consolidating working papers supported by the necessary working paper journal entries.

b. Prepare the consolidated balance sheet.

B-22   (Equity method and consolidation of a 100%-owned subsidiary)

On January 1, 2006, Casey Incorporated acquired 100% of the outstanding common shares of Smith Company Ltd. and List Company Ltd. The details of the acquisitions and the earnings of both companies are as follows.

	Smith Co.	List Co.
Book value of net assets as of 1/1/06	$140,000	$175,000
Acquisition price	150,000	200,000
Earnings (loss) for 2006	(20,000)	15,000
Dividends declared for 2006	–	10,000

Goodwill, if any, will not be amortized. Assume that the net assets' fair market value on 1/1/06 is adequately measured by the book values.

Required:

a. Construct the journal entries that Casey will make in 2006 to account for these investments on its own books assuming it uses the equity method.

b. Prepare the consolidating working paper entries for the consolidation of these investments as of 12/31/06 assuming the entries in part a) have been recorded.

B-23   (Acquisition of a subsidiary)

A summary of the January 1, 2006, balance sheet of Alsop, Ltd., prior to any acquisition, follows.

Assets	$180,000	Liabilities	$ 90,000
		Shareholders' equity	90,000
Total	$180,000	Total	$180,000

On January 1, 2006, Alsop acquired 100% of the outstanding common shares of Martin Monthly for $62,000 cash. At the time of the acquisition, the fair market values of Martin's assets and liabilities were $86,000 and $64,000, respectively. During 2006, Martin operated as a subsidiary of Alsop; it recognized $15,000 of net income and paid a $10,000 dividend.

Required:

a. Account for the acquisition as a purchase. Provide the journal entry to record the acquisition, and prepare Alsop's consolidated balance sheet as of January 1, 2006.

b. Account for the acquisition using the equity method. Provide the journal entry to record the acquisition, and prepare Alsop's balance sheet as of January 1, 2006.

c. Calculate the debt/equity ratios produced by the two methods of accounting for this investment. Explain why Alsop's management might wish to use the equity method instead of preparing consolidated financial statements.

d. Provide the journal entries that would be made by Alsop to record the income earned and the dividends paid by Martin during 2006 assuming that Alsop used the equity method.

B-24 **(Acquisition of a subsidiary)**

The following are the balance sheets for Trident Inc. and Gum Company Ltd. as at December 31, 2006, (prior to any acquisition).

Balance Sheet as at December 31, 2006

	Trident Inc.	Gum Co.
Assets		
Current Assets	$175,000	$ 65,000
Noncurrent Assets	500,000	130,000
Total Assets	$675,000	$195,000
Liabilities and Shareholders' Equity		
Current Liabilities	$ 85,000	$ 28,000
Noncurrent Liabilities	190,000	57,000
Common Shares	350,000	100,000
Retained Earnings	50,000	10,000
Total Liabilities and Shareholders' Equity	$675,000	$195,000

On December 31, 2006, Trident Inc. issued 5,000 shares having a market value of $300,000 in exchange for all 7,500 shares of Gum. The value of the shares exchanged over the book value of Gum includes $100,000 of excess fair market value of the noncurrent assets. All other assets and liabilities of Gum were properly valued on its books.

Required:

a. Construct the entry that Trident would make on its books to account for its investment in Gum.

b. Prepare a consolidated balance sheet as at December 31, 2006.

B-25 **(Calculation of consolidated net income)**

Refer to the data in Problem B-24. For 2006, the details of the net income and dividends reported by the two companies were as follows.

	Trident Inc.	Gum Co.
Net Income for 2006	$250,000	$75,000
Dividends Declared for 2006	$225,000	$65,000

Required:

What is the net income of Trident Inc. on a consolidated basis?

B-26 **(Preparation of a consolidated income statement)**

Refer to the data in Problem B-24 and assume that the net income and dividends declared for 2007 are as follows.

	Trident Inc.	Gum Co.
Revenues	$700,000	$280,000
Cost of Goods Sold	400,000	160,000
Other Expenses	95,000	30,000
Net Income	$205,000	$ 90,000
Dividends Declared	$150,000	$ 75,000

Trident's net income excludes the income from its investment in Gum. Goodwill is not amortized, and any excess fair market value of noncurrent assets is to be amortized using the straight-line method over a 10-year useful life with a zero residual value.

Required:

Prepare a consolidated income statement for 2007.

Reading and Interpreting
Published Financial Statements

B-27　(Business acquisitions)

In its 2003 annual report, Maple Leaf Foods Ltd. described its acquisition of Canada Bread and Canada Bread's acquisition of a waffle manufacturer, Ben's Limited, along with Olafson's Baking Company Inc. and Grace Baking Company. The details are described in Notes 18 and 19 in Exhibit B-14.

**Financial Statement
Analysis Assignments**

MAPLE LEAF FOODS LTD. 2003 ANNUAL REPORT

EXHIBIT B-14

Notes to the Consolidated Financial Statements

18. INVESTMENT IN CANADA BREAD

2003

On January 28, 2003, the Company purchased four million shares from Canada Bread treasury at $26.50 per share in a private placement transaction. Proceeds from the financing of $106.0 million were used to pay down debt owing by Canada Bread to Maple Leaf Foods.

During the year, the Company purchased 2,068,400 common shares of Canada Bread on the market at an average cost of $25.65 per share and a further 819,400 shares for $26.50 pursuant to several private agreements.

These share purchases, aggregating $180.8 million, increased Maple Leaf Foods' ownership of Canada Bread from 68.3% to 84.7%. The preliminary allocation of the purchase cost has created $43.8 million in goodwill.

2002

In December 2002, Canada Bread purchased all of Maple Leaf Foods' U.S. and U.K. bakery operations, including Grace Baking Company, for approximately $262.3 million, inclusive of debt assumption of $10.7 million. This transaction has been accounted for at book value, however, transaction costs of $1.8 million (2002: $3.4 million) have been expensed and included in other income (expense).

19. ACQUISITIONS AND DIVESTITURES

On July 4, 2003, Canada Bread purchased the assets of a waffle manufacturer located in Richmond Hill, Ontario, for $6.2 million. The allocation of the purchase cost to the assets and liabilities is preliminary.

In April 2002, Canada Bread acquired the remaining 40% of the shares of Ben's Limited in Atlantic Canada to hold 100%.

In July 2002, Canada Bread acquired all of the outstanding shares of Olafson's Baking Company Inc. of Delta, British Columbia. The initial purchase price was $11.5 million with additional consideration of up to $10.2 million payable until February 28, 2004, depending on the attainment of certain financial targets. In 2003, the Company paid a further $3.2 million in respect of these amounts. As at December 31, 2003, a maximum remaining amount of $7.0 million may be payable which would result in additional goodwill.

In October 2002, the Company acquired Grace Baking Company of San Francisco, California. Grace Baking Company is a leading U.S. producer of premium fresh and frozen artisan bread products.

Details of net assets acquired and purchase adjustments made in 2003 and 2002 are as follows:

	2003	2002
Cash	$ —	$ 988
Net working capital (deficit)	(9,915)	(2,415)
Other long-term assets	56	(1,715)
Property and equipment	(2,524)	4,674
Goodwill and other intangibles	17,162	78,055
Long-term debt and debt due to parent company	—	(10,347)
Future income taxes	2,985	5,924
Minority interest	(762)	4,406
Total purchase cost	$ 7,002	$ 79,570
Consideration:		
Cash	$ 7,002	$ 67,955
Accounts payable, accrued charges and long-term debt	—	11,615
	$ 7,002	$ 79,570

Required:

a. What accounting method is Maple Leaf Foods most likely to use to account for its investment in Canada Bread? What items in the note led you to that conclusion?

b. Part of Maple Leaf's acquisition of Canada Bread involved Maple Leaf purchasing some of the treasury shares of Canada Bread (Canada Bread's own shares that it had purchased on the market and not cancelled). Canada Bread then used the money that it received from Maple Leaf to repay a loan that was owed by Canada Bread to Maple Leaf. Describe in your own words the essence of this transaction.

c. For each of the four acquisitions made by Canada Bread, describe the accounting treatment that Canada Bread will most likely use to account for these investments.

B-28   (Business acquisitions)

Finning International Inc. acquired three **Caterpillar** dealership operations and a materials handling business in 2003. The details of the acquisitions are described in the notes to its 2003 annual report. The information in the notes is reproduced in Exhibit B-15. All amounts are expressed in thousands of dollars or pounds.

EXHIBIT B-15

FINNING INTERNATIONAL INC. 2003 ANNUAL REPORT
Notes to the Consolidated Financial Statements

6. ACQUISITIONS

During 2003, the Company acquired the Caterpillar dealership operations in Argentina, Uruguay, and Bolivia and a materials handling business in the U.K. The purchases of these operations are accounted for under the purchase method of accounting. The allocation of the purchase price to the materials handling business in the U.K. is preliminary and may be adjusted when additional information on asset and liability valuations becomes available.

	Argentina and Uruguay (a)	Bolivia (b)	UK Operations: Lex Harvey (c)	Combined
Total assets	$ 91,915	$ 18,043	$ 190,871	$ 300,829
Total liabilities	(37,981)	(5,842)	(21,274)	(65,097)
Goodwill (Note 7)	953	2,123	38,236	41,312
Intangible assets (Note 7)	2,935	–	4,826	7,761
Net assets acquired	57,822	14,324	212,659	284,805
Less: assumed debt	(14,497)	(5,416)	–	(19,913)
Total purchase price	$ 43,325	$ 8,908	$ 212,659	$ 264,892

(a) In January 2003, the Company completed its acquisition of 100% of the voting shares of Macrosa Del Plata S.A. and Servicios Mineros S.A., the Caterpillar dealerships in Argentina and General Machinery Co S.A., the Caterpillar dealership in Uruguay. The purchase price of $43,325 (US$27,951) was financed through debt. The sellers are also entitled to additional future consideration, to a maximum of US$20,000, based on realization of certain performance criteria over a six-year period ending December 31, 2008 for these operations. This other consideration will be accrued as a cost of the acquisition if and when the performance criterion is achieved.

(b) In April 2003, the acquisition of 100% of the voting shares of Matreq S.A., the Bolivian Caterpillar dealership was completed. The purchase price of $8,908 (US$6,000) was financed through debt. In addition, other consideration of $5,938 (US$4,000) was advanced to the seller and is contingent upon certain future performance criteria of this operation extending to the end of 2010. This other consideration is recorded in other assets.

(c) In June 2003, the Company, through its UK operation, acquired the materials handling business and majority of the assets of Lex Harvey Limited and its associated company (Lex Harvey) from RAC plc, a publicly listed company in the U.K. The results from Lex Harvey have been integrated and reported within the UK operation results. The aggregate purchase price of $212,659 (£94,616) was funded through debt.

Required:

a. The purchase of the Caterpillar operations in Argentina and Uruguay was financed through debt. What do you think this means? There are also certain contingencies associated with these acquisitions. How do you think the company should account for them?

b. A large portion of the purchase price for the materials handling business in the UK was allocated to goodwill. What are some of the potential reasons why Finning may have been willing to pay this additional amount?

c. Two of the acquisitions list intangible assets as part of the assets that were purchased. These usually represent the value of customer contracts. Do you think these items should be amortized? Explain.

B-29   (Acquisition of a subsidiary)

In its 2003 annual report, CHC Helicopter Corporation described its long-term investments in other companies. These investments are described in Note 7 of its annual report. That note has been reproduced in Exhibit B-16.

CHC HELICOPTER CORPORATION 2003 ANNUAL REPORT

EXHIBIT B-16

NOTES TO THE CONSOLIDATED FINANCIAL STATEMENTS

April 30, 2003 and 2002 (Tabular amounts in thousands unless otherwise noted, except per share amounts)

7. Investments

	2003	2002
Long-term investments, at equity		
Canadian Helicopters Limited (2003 – 43.5%, 2002 – 44.5%)	$ 5,759	$ 3,420
Long-term investments, at cost		
Canadian Helicopters Limited, preferred shares	15,000	15,000
Other	284	297
	$ 21,043	$ 18,717

Required:

a. CHC Helicopter accounts for its investment in Canadian Helicopters Limited using equity. Explain why that would likely be appropriate. As a result of the use of equity, what would you expect to see on the income statement that relates to this investment?

b. CHC Helicopter's investment in Canadian Helicopters Limited declined slightly during 2003. What could have caused this decline?

c. CHC Helicopter accounts for its investment in the preferred shares of Canadian Helicopters Limited using cost. The company has not given the percentage of its ownership interest. Why is that disclosure not necessary? Explain why it would account for some of its investment in Canadian Helicopters using equity and another part using cost.

B-30 (Business acquisitions)

In its 2003 annual report, **Brampton Brick Limited** describes investments that it made in two companies, **Oaks Concrete Products Ltd.** and **Da Vinci Stone Craft Ltd.** (Exhibit B-17). Brampton Brick's core business is the manufacture and sale of clay bricks. It has subsidiaries in concrete products, Medical Waste Management and Roxy Construction, a trucking company.

EXHIBIT B-17   **BRAMPTON BRICK LIMITED 2003 ANNUAL REPORT**
Notes to Consolidated Financial Statements

2. Business acquisition

Da Vinci Stone Craft

On September 12, 2003, Oaks Concrete Products Ltd. acquired the assets of a fireplace surrounds and wall tiles manufacturing business carried on in the province of Ontario. The assets were acquired for cash of $325. The new business is now operated under a newly incorporated subsidiary, Da Vinci Stone Craft Ltd., which is 75% owned by Oaks Concrete Products Ltd. and 25% owned by non-controlling interests. The acquisition has been accounted for by the purchase method. The financial statements include the results of Da Vinci Stone Craft from the date of acquisition.

Oaks Concrete Products

On May 13, 2002, the Company acquired the assets of a concrete paving stone and retaining wall business carried on in the Province of Ontario and the State of Michigan. The assets acquired include three manufacturing plants, accounts receivable, inventories and goodwill. The new business is now operated under the name Oaks Concrete Products.

The acquisition was completed through newly incorporated subsidiaries, which are 63% owned by the Company and 37% owned by non-controlling interests. Financing for the acquisition was provided as follows:

	$
Term bank loans	38,500
Equity investment by non-controlling interests	18,500
Bank operating advances	7,190
Cash	2,800
Due to vendor	1,132
Other current liabilities	367
	68,489

The acquisition has been accounted for by the purchase method and, accordingly, the financial statements include the results of operations of Oaks Concrete Products from the date of acquisition.

The assets acquired and the consideration given are summarized below:

Assets acquired	$
Accounts receivable	1,649
Inventories	6,330
Property, plant and equipment	30,457
Goodwill	30,053
	68,489
Consideration given	**$**
Cash	66,990
Due to vendor	1,132
Other current liabilities	367
	68,489

The purchase price has been allocated to the fair value of the assets acquired based on management's best estimate of fair values. The goodwill amount that is expected to be deductible for income tax purposes is $26,457.

Required:

a. In 2002, Brampton Brick purchased the assets of a concrete paving stone and retaining wall business that it operates under the name Oaks Concrete Products. Does Brampton own all of Oaks Concrete Products? Does it need to consolidate Oaks Concrete Products when it produces its financial statements? Explain.

b. In 2003, Oaks Concrete Products acquired the assets of a fireplace surrounds and wall tiles manufacturing business and renamed the company Da Vinci Stone Craft Ltd. Is Da Vinci Stone Craft a subsidiary of Oaks Concrete Products? Explain.

c. Is Da Vinci Stone Craft a subsidiary of Brampton Brick? Explain.

B-31   (Business acquisition)

METRO Inc. is a leading food retailer and distributor in eastern Canada. In July 2002, it acquired the assets of **Grossiste Sue Shang Inc.**, a grocery distributor in Quebec. In 2003, it acquired the shares of **Alexandre Gaudet Ltée.**, a grocery distributor serving small stores. The acquisitions are described in Exhibit B-18.

METRO INC. 2003 ANNUAL REPORT

Notes to Consolidated Financial Statements

3. Business acquisitions

On May 31, 2003, the Company acquired the shares of Alexandre Gaudet Ltée, a grocery distributor serving small surface stores, for a cash consideration of $6.7. Following this acquisition, goodwill in the amount of $3 has been recorded.

On July 3, 2002, the Company acquired the assets, made up primarily of short-term assets, of Grossiste Sue Shang Inc., a grocery distributor serving independent convenience stores in Québec, for a cash consideration of $16.7. Stores were also acquired by the Company in 2002. Following these acquisitions, goodwill in the amount of $7 was recorded.

Required:

a. Both of these acquisitions were of grocery distributors. Do they represent vertical or horizontal integration? Explain.

b. The 2002 acquisition is described as an acquisition of assets. What accounting would be required with respect to this acquisition?

c. The 2003 acquisition is described as an acquisition of shares. What accounting would be required with respect to this acquisition?

d. In both of these acquisitions there is reference to the acquisition of goodwill. What accounting will be required for the goodwill in future years?

B-32   (Business acquisition)

Enerflex Systems Ltd. acquired **EnSource Energy Services Inc.** in 2002. The acquisition is described in Exhibit B-19.

ENERFLEX SYSTEMS LTD. 2003 ANNUAL REPORT

EXHIBIT B-19
PART A

Note 2. 2002 ACQUISITION

On July 18, 2002, the Company acquired 92.4% of the issued and outstanding common shares of EnSource Energy Services Inc. ("EnSource"). On July 23, 2002, Enerflex mailed a Notice of Compulsory Acquisition to the holders of the remaining EnSource common shares which were not tendered to the offer, pursuant to Enerflex's right of compulsory acquisition under the Business Corporations Act (Alberta). EnSource became a wholly-owned subsidiary of Enerflex.

ENERFLEX SYSTEMS LTD. 2003 ANNUAL REPORT

The acquisition was accounted for using the purchase method, and the results of operations of EnSource have been included with those of the Company from July 19, 2002. The final cost of the acquisition was $144,645,000. At December 31, 2002, certain items were reclassified in the purchase price equation to conform with Enerflex's financial statement presentation.

The final purchase price was allocated as follows:

December 31	2002
Shares issued	$ 141,040
Transaction costs	3,408
Fair value of options issued	197
	$ 144,645
Non-cash working capital	$ 38,631
Future income taxes	2,522
Property, plant and equipment	29,145
Rental assets	24,054
Assets held for sale	4,591
Other long-term assets	431
Goodwill	104,924
Bank indebtedness	(37,612)
Long-term debt	(22,041)
	$ 144,645

Required:

a. Enerflex purchased 92.4% of the shares of EnSource and then issued a Notice of Compulsory Acquisition to the shareholders of the remaining 7.4%. Those shareholders would need to sell their shares to Enerflex. Express an opinion on the advantages and disadvantages of having such an action available to companies. As a shareholder, what is your opinion of this action?

b. Did Enerflex pay more than the market value of EnSource's net assets? How do you know?

c. Enerflex lists the amount that it paid to facilitate the acquisition as transaction costs. It added this amount to the purchase price. Adding it to the shares' value increases the purchase price and capitalizes this expenditure. Comment on the appropriateness of adding it to the purchase price as opposed to expensing it in the year in which it occurred.

Critical Thinking Question

B-33 (Strategic planning of future growth)

As explained at the beginning of this appendix, companies buy all or parts of other companies for many reasons. You might assume that this type of activity is undertaken only by large corporations, but that is not the case. Many owners of small businesses will establish or buy subsidiaries as they start to expand. Often these small subsidiaries will represent a specific niche in the owner's business. This enables the owner to undertake various activities without exposing the whole organization to the risk of failure.

Assume that you are the owner of a small business. Your initial business is installing carpets. You have a crew of three people who do the installation for you. Your ultimate goal is to do finishing contract work on residential and commercial construction. You hope eventually to control a multimillion-dollar operation. Think about the path that could be taken so that you can expand your business from carpet installation to your eventual goal. Draft an expansion plan that would take you gradually from one to the other. Include in your plan the purchase or establishment of subsidiaries.

Photo Credits

Chapter 1:   Opener: Courtesy of Clear-Green Environmental Inc. Page 6: PhotoDisc, Inc. Page 13: Paul Sakuma/Canadian Press. Page 15: John Mahoney/Canadian Press. Page 35: Steve Young/Canadian Press.

Chapter 2:   Opener: Courtesy of Krave's Candy Co. Page 75: Corbis Digital Stock.

Chapter 3:   Opener: Courtesy of Fulton's Pancake House and Sugar Bush. Page 157: Lampo Communications Inc./Canadian Collection vol.1.0.

Chapter 4:   Opener: Courtesy of *Outpost* magazine. Page 231: Joe Cavaretta/Canadian Press. Page 235: Michael Wallrath/Canadian Press. Page 241: PhotoDisc, Inc.

Chapter 5:   Opener: Courtesy of Wellness Institute at Seven Oaks General Hospital. Page 280: Paul Chiasson/Canadian Press. Page 284: PhotoDisc/Getty Images.

Chapter 6:   Opener: Courtesy of Santa's Village & Sportsland. Page 350: Steve White/Canadian Press. Page 353: Ryan Remiroz/Canadian Press. Page 366: Doug Ives/Canadian Press.

Chapter 7:   Opener: Courtesy of Veseys Seeds. Page 412: PhotoDisc, Inc. Page 422: PhotoDisc, Inc.

Chapter 8:   Opener: Courtesy of The Calgary Zoo. Page 492: Corbis Digital Stock. Page 493: Mike Ridewood/Canadian Press. Page 494: Kevin Frayer/Canadian Press. Page 495: Frank Gunn/Canadian Press.

Chapter 9:   Opener: Courtesy of Mountain Equipment Co-op. Page 537: Corbis Digital Stock. Page 539: Corbis Digital Stock.

Chapter 10:   Opener: Courtesy of Bell Canada. Page 571: Jeff McIntosh/Canadian Press. Page 573: Paul Chiasson/Canadian Press. Page 593: Copyright 2005 © Gail Brown. Page 597: Dick Loek/Canadian Press.

Chapter 11:   Opener: Courtesy of Shoppers Drug Mart. Page 648: Adrian Wyld/Canadian Press. Page 652: Courtesy of Big Rock Brewery. Page 656: Francois Roy/Canadian Press.

Chapter 12:   Opener: Photodisc. Page 722: Corbis Digital Stock. Page 726: Steve White/Canadian Press.

Company Index

Subject Index